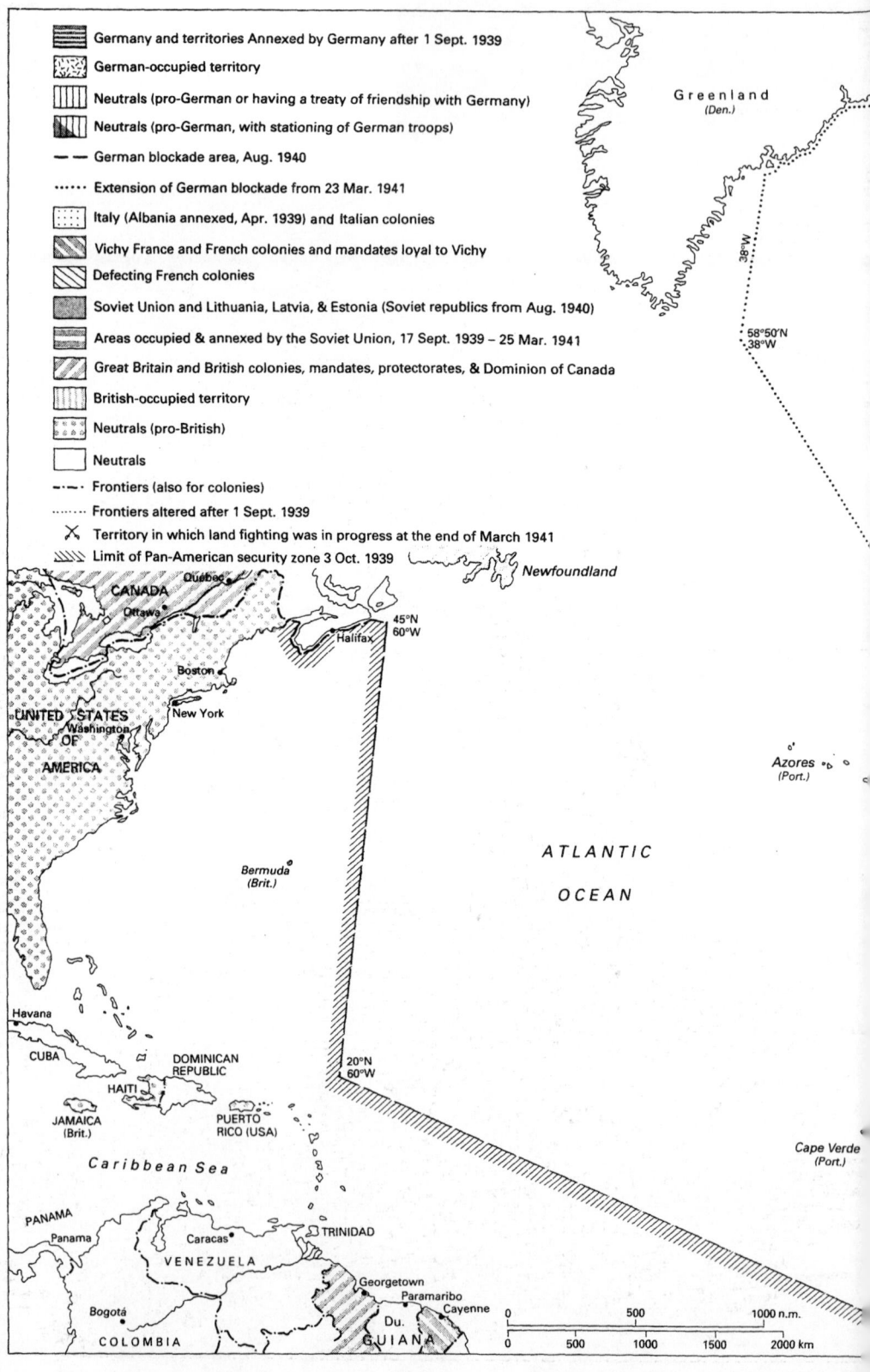

GERMANY AND THE SECOND WORLD WAR

III

The Mediterranean, South-East Europe, and North Africa
1939–1941

Germany and the Second World War

Edited by the
Militärgeschichtliches
Forschungsamt (Research
Institute for Military History),
Freiburg im Breisgau, Germany

VOLUME III
The Mediterranean,
South-East Europe, and
North Africa
1939–1941

From Italy's declaration of
non-belligerence to the
entry of the United States into the war

GERHARD SCHREIBER
BERND STEGEMANN
DETLEF VOGEL

Translated by
DEAN S. McMURRY
EWALD OSERS
LOUISE WILLMOT

Translation editor
P. S. FALLA

CLARENDON PRESS · OXFORD

OXFORD
UNIVERSITY PRESS

Great Clarendon Street, Oxford, OX2 6DP,
United Kingdom

Oxford University Press is a department of the University of Oxford.
It furthers the University's objective of excellence in research, scholarship,
and education by publishing worldwide. Oxford is a registered trade mark of
Oxford University Press in the UK and in certain other countries

© Deutsche Verlags-Anstalt GmbH, Stuttgart, 1995 Inc.

The moral rights of the author have been asserted

First published 1995
First published in paperback 2015

All rights reserved. No part of this publication may be reproduced, stored in
a retrieval system, or transmitted, in any form or by any means, without the
prior permission in writing of Oxford University Press, or as expressly permitted
by law, by licence or under terms agreed with the appropriate reprographics
rights organization. Enquiries concerning reproduction outside the scope of the
above should be sent to the Rights Department, Oxford University Press, at the
address above

You must not circulate this work in any other form
and you must impose this same condition on any acquirer

Published in the United States of America by Oxford University Press
198 Madison Avenue, New York, NY 10016, United States of America

British Library Cataloguing in Publication Data
Data available

Library of Congress Cataloging in Publication Data
Data available

ISBN 978–0–19–822884–4 (Hbk.)
ISBN 978–0–19–873832–9 (Pbk.)

Links to third party websites are provided by Oxford in good faith and
for information only. Oxford disclaims any responsibility for the materials
contained in any third party website referenced in this work.

Contents

LIST OF ILLUSTRATIONS	xi
NOTES ON THE AUTHORS	xiii
NOTE ON THE TRANSLATION	xv
ABBREVIATIONS	xvi
GLOSSARY OF GERMAN TERMS	xviii
INTRODUCTION	1

PART I

Political and Military Developments in the Mediterranean Area, 1939–1940

BY GERHARD SCHREIBER — 5

Preliminary Note — 7

I. MUSSOLINI'S 'NON-BELLIGERENCE'	8
1. The Alliance Policy in General from the German Point of View	8
2. Italy as a Coalition Partner	12
(*a*) Political Aspects	13
(*b*) Economic Aspects	25
(*c*) Military Aspects	39
3. Strategic Considerations up to June 1940	50
4. The Italian Fighting Forces	62
(*a*) Equipment and Organization	62
(*b*) The Problem of Top-level Organization	92
II. ITALY'S ENTRY INTO THE WAR	99
1. Events and Reactions: Mussolini's Decision in 1940	99
2. Causes and Objectives: 'Imperial Design' or 'Unplanned Opportunism'?	110
3. Consequences: The Reorientation of British Strategy in the Summer of 1940	126
4. The Axis Powers after the Victory in the West	137
(*a*) Ideas of Peace	137

(b) War Gains: The French Example	138
(c) Hopes: Hitler, Franco, and the Anglo-Saxons	145
(d) Zones of Conflict: The Near and Middle East	153
(i) Turkey	153
(ii) Afghanistan	162
(iii) The Arab world	165
III. THE STRATEGIC DILEMMA OF THE SUMMER AND AUTUMN OF 1940: AN ALTERNATIVE OR INTERIM STRATEGY?	180
1. Hitler and the Mediterranean Area	181
(a) Personal Factors	181
(b) Power-political Aspects	183
2. Ideas as to the Continuation of the War	197
(a) The Jodl Memorandum	198
(b) Gibraltar, Egypt, and the Atlantic Islands	200
3. Italy's Conduct of the War between the Armistice with France and the Attack on Greece	246
(a) Initial Situation, Intentions, and First Results of Naval and Air Warfare	246
(b) The War in Italian East Africa	259
(c) The Offensive against Sidi Barrani	266
IV. IDEAS OF GERMAN RULING CIRCLES CONCERNING A COLONIAL EMPIRE	278

PART II

Germany, Italy, and South-east Europe: From Political and Economic Hegemony to Military Aggression

BY GERHARD SCHREIBER	303
Preliminary Note	305
I. UNEQUAL HEIRS OF THE FIRST WORLD WAR	308
1. Albania	310
2. Yugoslavia	316
3. Bulgaria	326
4. Greece	332

II. GERMAN AND ITALIAN POLICY TOWARDS THE STATES OF SOUTH-EAST EUROPE — 341

1. Political and Economic Development in the Interwar Period — 342
   - (*a*) Bulgaria — 356
   - (*b*) Yugoslavia — 362
   - (*c*) Greece — 372
   - (*d*) Albania — 376
2. Moves towards a New Policy after the Outbreak of War: The 'Balkan Bloc' Project — 380
3. 'Quiet in the Balkans'? — 386

III. MUSSOLINI'S INVASION OF GREECE: THE BEGINNING OF THE END OF ITALY'S GREAT-POWER STATUS — 401

1. The Political Decision — 401
2. Italy's Plan of Operations — 418
3. Greek Countermeasures — 424
4. Military Developments between October 1940 and March 1941 — 429

PART III

German Intervention in the Balkans

BY DETLEF VOGEL — 449

I. GERMANY'S BALKAN POLICY IN THE AUTUMN OF 1940 AND THE SPRING OF 1941 — 451

1. The General Aims of German Policy in South-east Europe — 451
2. German Political and Military Preparations for the Invasion of Greece — 454

II. FROM THE COUP IN YUGOSLAVIA TO THE OUTBREAK OF WAR ON 6 APRIL 1941 — 479

1. The Coup in Yugoslavia — 479
2. The German Deployment against Greece and Yugoslavia — 485
3. The Military Reactions of Yugoslavia, Greece, and Britain to the Events of 27 March 1941 — 493

III. THE GERMAN ATTACK ON YUGOSLAVIA AND GREECE — 497

1. The Attack of Twelfth Army on Greece and Southern Yugoslavia — 499
2. The Conquest of the Rest of Yugoslavia — 516

IV. THE CAPTURE OF CRETE 527
1. The Place of Crete in German and British Military Planning, 1940–1941 527
2. Preparations for Operation Merkur and British Defence Measures 534
3. The Battle for Crete 543

PART IV

Politics and Warfare in 1941
BY GERHARD SCHREIBER 557

Preliminary Note 559

I. THE ANGLO-AMERICAN ASSOCIATION AND ITS CONSEQUENCES FOR BRITISH STRATEGY 560

II. HITLER'S STRATEGIC DELIBERATIONS IN CONNECTION WITH THE ATTACK ON THE SOVIET UNION 573
1. Attempts to Create a Forefield in the West 574
2. Chances and Dangers for German Strategy in the Middle East 589
3. Planning for the Period after Barbarossa 624

PART V

The Italo-German Conduct of the War in the Mediterranean and North Africa
BY BERND STEGEMANN 641

I. THE BRITISH TAKE THE OFFENSIVE IN NORTH AND EAST AFRICA 643

II. GERMAN INTERVENTION AND ITS EFFECTS ON THE NAVAL AND AIR WAR IN THE MEDITERRANEAN 654

III. THE RECONQUEST OF CYRENAICA AND THE FAILURE OF THE ATTACKS ON TOBRUK 673

IV. THE FIGHTING ON THE SOLLUM FRONT 695

Contents

V. THE NAVAL AND AIR WAR IN THE MEDITERRANEAN AND SUPPLIES FOR THE NORTH AFRICAN THEATRE 708

VI. OPERATION CRUSADER 725

CONCLUSION 755

BIBLIOGRAPHY 769

INDEX OF PERSONS 817

List of Illustrations

DIAGRAMS

I.I.1. Combat-readiness of Italian divisions, June 1940	69
I.I.2. Establishment and authorized allowance of equipment of Italian divisions, 1940	70

MAPS

Europe and the Atlantic and Mediterranean Areas, 1 September 1939–25 March 1941	*front endpapers*
I.II.1. Occupied France, 1940–1941	140
I.III.1. The British–Italian War in East Africa, 1940–1941	260
I.III.2. The Italian Conquest of British Somaliland, August 1940	265
I.III.3. Italian Plans of Attack, August–September 1940	272
I.III.4. The Italian Offensive against Sidi Barrani, 13–16 September 1940	275
I.IV.1. German Ideas of a Colonial Empire in Africa, 1940–1941	279
II.I.1. Yugoslavia and Bulgaria, 1918 to March 1941	319
II.III.1. The Italo-Greek War: Plan of Operations and Disposition of Italian Forces at End of October 1940	421
II.III.2. The Italo-Greek War: Defensive Lines and Disposition of Greek Forces on 27 October 1940	427
II.III.3. The Italo-Greek War: Lines of Communication Albania–Northern Greece, October 1940	431
II.III.4. The Italo-Greek War: Changes in the Front, October 1940 to March 1941	434
III.III.1. Operations in Southern Yugoslavia and Greece, 6–30 April 1941	500
III.III.2. Operations in Yugoslavia, 6–17 April 1941	517
III.III.3. The Partition of Yugoslavia and Greece after the Balkan Campaign, 1941	523
III.IV.1. The Battle of Crete, 20 May–1 June 1941	544
III.IV.2. The Fighting in the West of Crete	545
IV.II.1. The Fighting in Iraq, 2–31 May 1941	602
IV.II.2. The War in Syria, 8 June–14 July 1941	614
V.I.1. The Battle of Sidi Barrani, 9–11 December 1940	647
V.I.2. The British Advance to Al Uqaylah, 12 December 1940–8 February 1941	649
V.II.1. The Mediterranean: General Map Showing Main Events, 1940–1941	660
V.II.2. The Battle of Cape Matapan, 28 March 1941	666
V.III.1. Tobruk: The Attacks of 11–18 April 1941	682
V.III.2. Tobruk: The Night Attack on Ras al Mudawwarah, 30 April–1 May 1941	690
V.III.3. Tobruk: The Course of the Attack on 1 May 1941	691

V.IV.1.	Operation Battleaxe, 15 June 1941 (Morning)–16 June 1941 (Afternoon)	698
V.IV.2.	Operation Battleaxe, 16 June 1941 (Afternoon)–17 June 1941 (Evening)	698
V.V.1.	The First Battle of Sirte	721
V.VI.1.	Operation Crusader: Deployment, 18 November 1941	732
V.VI.2.	Operation Crusader, 19 November 1941	734
V.VI.3.	Operation Crusader, 20 November 1941	734
V.VI.4.	Operation Crusader, 21 November 1941	736
V.VI.5.	The Battle of Commemoration Sunday: Afternoon, 23 November 1941	736
V.VI.6.	Operation Crusader, 24–6 November 1941	740
V.VI.7.	Operation Crusader, 27–8 November 1941	740
V.VI.8.	Operation Crusader, 30 November–2 December 1941	745
V.VI.9.	The Italo-German Retreat from Cyrenaica, 8 December 1941–10 January 1942	748
East Africa, the Middle East, and India, 1 September 1939–25 March 1941		*back endpapers*

The diagrams and maps are taken from originals by Ulf Balke, Hans Gaenshirt, Vera Kluge, and Rolf Schindler of the Cartographic Section, Research Institute for Military History.

Notes on the Authors

Dr GERHARD SCHREIBER (b. 1940). Publications: *Revisionismus und Weltmachtstreben: Marineführung und deutsch-italienische Beziehungen 1919 bis 1944* (Stuttgart, 1978); *Die Zerstörung Europas im Zweiten Weltkrieg* (Tübingen, 1983); *Hitler-Interpretationen 1923–1983: Ergebnisse, Methoden und Probleme der Forschung*, 2nd, enlarged edn. (Darmstadt, 1988); *Die italienischen Militärinternierten im deutschen Machtbereich 1943–1945: Verraten, verachtet, vergessen* (Munich, 1990); 'Die Rolle Frankreichs im strategischen und operativen Denken der deutschen Marine', in *Deutschland und Frankreich 1936–1939*, ed. Klaus Hildebrand and Karl Ferdinand Werner (Munich, 1981), 167–213; 'Problemi generali dell'alleanza italo-tedesca 1933–1941', in *Gli italiani sul fronte russo*, ed. Istituto Storico della Resistenza in Cuneo e Provincia (Bari, 1982), 63–117; 'The Mediterranean in Hitler's Strategy in 1940: "Programme" and Military Planning', in *The German Military in the Age of Total War*, ed. Wilhelm Deist (Leamington Spa, 1985), 240–81; 'La Linea Gotica tedesca: Obiettivi politici e compiti militari', in *Linea Gotica 1944: Eserciti, populazioni, partigiani*, ed. Giorgio Rochat [et al.] (Milan, 1986), 25–67; 'Lo sgombero delle truppe tedesche dalla Corsica', in *Le operazioni delle unità italiane in Corsica nel settembre–ottobre 1943*, ed. Paolo Battistini e Guido Tuccinardi (Lucca, 1987), 121–42; 'Der Zweite Weltkrieg in der internationalen Forschung: Konzeptionen, Thesen und Kontroversen', in *Der Zweite Weltkrieg: Analysen, Grundzüge, Forschungsbilanz*, ed. Wolfgang Michalka, 2nd edn. (Munich and Zurich, 1990), 3–24.

Dr BERND STEGEMANN (b. 1938). Publications: *Die deutsche Marinepolitik 1916–1918* (Berlin, 1970); 'Hitlers "Stufenplan" und die Marine', in *Festschrift für Richard Dietrich* (Frankfurt am Main, 1975), 301–16; 'Hitlers Ziele im ersten Kriegsjahr 1939/40: Ein Beitrag zur Quellenkritik', *MGM* 27 (1980), 93–105; 'Der Entschluß zum Unternehmen "Barbarossa": Strategie oder Ideologie?', *Geschichte in Wissenschaft und Unterricht*, 33 (1982), 205–13; 'Die italienisch-deutsche Kriegführung im Mittelmeer und in Afrika', in *Der Mittelmeerraum und Südosteuropa*, ed. Gerhard Schreiber, Bernd Stegemann, and Detlef Vogel (Das Deutsche Reich und der Zweite Weltkrieg, 3; Stuttgart, 1984), 591–682; 'Geschichte und Politik: Zur Diskussion über den deutschen Angriff auf die Sowjetunion 1941', *Beiträge zur Konfliktforschung*, 17/1 (1987), 73–97; articles on naval history and naval warfare.

Dr DETLEV VOGEL (b. 1942). Publications: *Der Stellenwert des Militärischen in Bayern (1849–1975): Eine Analyse des militär-zivilen Verhältnisses am Beispiel des Militäretats, der Heeresstärken und des Militärjustizwesens* (Boppard, 1981); 'Die militärischen Aspekte bei den Verhandlungen der Verfassungskommission von 1814/15 in Bayern', *MGM* 39 (1986), 9–35; 'Die Belagerungen Freiburgs i.Br. während des 17. und 18. Jahrhunderts', in *Stadt und Festung Freiburg*, ii. *Aufsätze zur Geschichte der Stadtbefestigung*, ed. Hans Schadek and Ulrich Ecker (Freiburg 1988), 41–73; 'Probleme sanitätsdienstlicher Versorgung in der Endphase deutscher Blitzkriege (Balkanfeldzug und Eroberung von Kreta', *MGM* 45 (1989), 93–109; 'Deutschland und Südosteuropa: Von politisch-wirtschaftlicher Einflußnahme zur offenen Gewaltanwendung und Unterdrückung', in *Der Zweite Weltkrieg: Analysen, Grundzüge, Forschungsbilanz*, ed. Wolfgang Michalka, 2nd edn. (Munich and Zurich, 1990).

Note on the Translation

PART I was translated by Ewald Osers, Part II by Louise Willmot, Parts III–V, as well as the Introduction and Conclusion, by Dean S. McMurry. The translation as a whole was revised and edited by P. S. Falla.

In the Bibliography information has been added concerning English translations of German and other foreign-language works. These translations are cited in the footnotes and have been used whenever possible for quotations occurring in the text.

Geographical names in the text and maps, except for those for which established English names exist (e.g. Warsaw, Moscow, Athens), have been given in the form laid down by *Official Standard Names Approved by the US Board of Geographic Names* (US Department of the Interior, Office of Geography), but with the omission of accents and diacriticals in transliterating from non-roman alphabets. In most instances these forms do not differ substantially from the popular spellings used during the war (El Mechili = Zawiyat al Mukhayla), but a few which would not be readily identifiable are listed below.

Arco dei Fileni	Al Qaws
Berta	Al Qubbah
Msus	Zawiyat Masus

Abbreviations

AA	anti-aircraft
Abw.	Abwehr: foreign intelligence
ADAP	*Akten zur deutschen auswärtigen Politik*: Documents on German Foreign Policy (cf. *DGFP*)
AK	Armeekorps: army corps
AOK	Armeeoberkommando: army headquarters staff
BA-MA	Bundesarchiv-Militärarchiv (Federal German military archives), Freiburg im Breisgau
BdE	Befehlshaber des Ersatzheeres: Director-General of Training
Chefs.	Chefsache: to be seen by senior officer only
COS	Chiefs of Staff
DAK	Deutsches Afrika-Korps: German Africa Corps (cf. GAC)
DDI	*I documenti diplomatici Italiani*
DGFP	*Documents on German Foreign Policy* (see the Bibliography)
DHM	Deutsche Militärmission: German military mission
FRUS	*Foreign Relations of the United States* (see the Bibliography)
GAC	German Africa Corps
GenStdH	Generalstab des Heeres: Army General Staff
g.Kdos./g.K.	geheime Kommandosache: top secret (military)
GS	Generalstab (general staff)
GWU	*Geschichte in Wissenschaft und Unterricht*
IMT	International Military Tribunal (see *Trial of Major War Criminals* in the Bibliography)
KTB	Kriegstagebuch: war diary
KTB OKW	*Kriegstagebuch des Oberkommandos der Wehrmacht* (q.v. in Bibliography)
LIK	Chief of the naval section in the Home Defence Department of OKW
LIL	Chief of the air-force section in the Home Defence Department of OKW
M.G.Doc.	Montanari, *Grecia* (documents in vol. ii)
MGM	*Militärgeschichtliche Mitteilungen*
MR	*Marinerundschau*
NPL	*Neue politische Literatur*
NSDAP	Nationalsozialistische Deutsche Arbeiterpartei: National Socialist German Workers' Party (Nazis)
ObdH	Oberbefehlshaber des Heeres: commander-in-chief of the army
ObdL	Oberbefehlshaber der Luftwaffe: commander-in-chief of the air force
ObdM	Oberbefehlshaber der Kriegsmarine: commander-in-chief of the navy
OKH	Oberkommando des Heeres: army high command
OKL	Oberkommando der Luftwaffe: air force high command
OKM	Oberkommando der Kriegsmarine: navy high command
OKW	Oberkommando der Wehrmacht: high command of the armed forces

Abbreviations

OQu	Oberquartiermeister: deputy chief of the general staff
PA	Politisches Archiv des Auswärtigen Amtes (political archives of the foreign ministry), Bonn
PWT	*Principal War Telegrams* (see *Great Britain, Cabinet Office* in the Bibliography)
RAM	Reichsaußenminister: Reich foreign minister
RdL	Reichsminister der Luftfahrt: Reich minister of aviation
SKL/Skl.	Seekriegsleitung: naval war staff
St.S.	Staatssekretär: state secretary
SS	Schutzstaffel: political police and military organization
VfZG	*Vierteljahreshefte für Zeitgeschichte*
WFA	Wehrmachtführungsamt: armed forces operations department
WFSt	Wehrmachtführungsstab: armed forces operations staff
WStK	Waffenstillstandskommission: armistice commission
WWR	*Wehrwissenschaftliche Rundschau*

Glossary of German Terms

Anschluss	The union of Austria with Germany, 1938
Außenpolitisches Amt	Foreign affairs office of the Nazi Party
Geschwader (pl. same)	Air force unit consisting of 3–4 Gruppen (q.v.)
Gruppe (pl. *-n*)	Unit of 27 aircraft, plus 9 in reserve
Lebensraum	'Living-space' for Germany, with connotation of conquest in the east
Luftwaffe	German air force
Staffel (pl. *-n*)	Unit of 9 aircraft, plus 3 in reserve
Wehrmacht	German armed forces
Wilhelmstrasse, the	Term denoting the German ministry of foreign affairs (from its address in Berlin)

Introduction

WHILE German expansion to the east, north, and west was described in earlier volumes of the work, the present volume is concerned with German and Italian policies and conduct of the war in the Mediterranean area. It thus concludes the account of the part of the war in which the initiative was clearly in German hands.

The spectacular military events of this period, especially the battles in the Libyan desert, attracted from the very beginning the strong interest of the general public on both sides and thus also the early interest of historians. The authors of this volume therefore had at their disposal a secondary literature so vast and varied as to be difficult for even the professional scholar to master. In many cases they were able to base their accounts on the sound insights it provided. But it again became clear that scholars usually tend to concentrate on the analysis and interpretation of individual aspects of developments. In the present volume, by contrast, the attempt is also made, within the context indicated by the title of the whole work, to place in perspective and weigh the ideological, political, military, and war-economy problems reflected in the events and developments described. This intention is also in accord with the conception presented in the introduction to Volume I, which takes as its point of orientation a modern approach to military history.

German policy and the conduct of the war in the Mediterranean were largely determined by the attitude of the German leadership, especially Hitler, towards Mussolini's Italy. The constant, not to say extraordinary, loyalty which Hitler demonstrated towards the Duce made Italy Germany's most important ally. A conscious effort has been made to give this fact due prominence in the present volume, in contrast to a certain tradition in German historical writing on the two world wars in which Germany's allies receive relatively little attention, and aspects essential to understanding developments as a whole are in consequence neglected. To correct this shortcoming an attempt has been made to place the evaluation of the quality of the alliance and its military effectiveness on a broader basis by offering a comprehensive interpretation of the conflicting political aims of the two Axis partners in the Mediterranean, as well as a thorough study of Italian economic and military realities. Together with the sections of Volume IV concerning the part played by Finland, Slovakia, Hungary, and Romania as Germany's allies, this account is intended to provide a clearer and more differentiated picture of the alliance policy of the Third Reich and thus, at the same time, of a specific aspect of its system of rule and domination.

Within this general framework, familiar relationships and problems appear in a different perspective. This may be seen in a few examples. The circumstances of Italy's entry into the war in June 1940 made obvious what diplomatic manœuvres of previous years had already indicated: neither Italy nor Germany had the will or intention to convert their loose, tactically very useful alliance into a war coalition in the full sense, which would have required an agreed, common strategy. It is necessary to examine the motives which prevented even a serious attempt to co-ordinate the ambitious aims of the two Axis partners—a state of affairs which naturally had its effect on the quality of the alliance. On the one hand, in German planning for the period 'after Barbarossa'—i.e. after the expected victory over the Soviet Union—Italy was considered an unimportant political and military factor; on the other Italy herself was throughout actuated by mistrust of the ambitions of her northern neighbour. This attitude found its clearest expression at the outset in Mussolini's phrase about the 'parallel war', which Italy conducted at Germany's side but for her own purposes. Even these few points underline the necessity of explaining in detail the political, economic, and military conditions of the Italo-German alliance, without which an adequate interpretation of the policies and conduct of the war by the Axis in the Mediterranean is hardly possible.

Mussolini waged his 'parallel wars' in North and East Africa, and after September 1940 especially in the Balkans against Greece. This war on several fronts, without any overall strategic plan, exceeded the capabilities of the Italian armed forces and led to a military crisis in the autumn and winter of 1940. To understand and explain the political dimension of this crisis it appears necessary to present the diverging interests of the alliance partners in the Balkans. This in turn requires an explanation of the political and economic factors determining German and Italian policy in the Balkans between the wars. Against this background the question arises of the importance of the alliance for German policy and strategy. Did not especially the German intervention in North Africa and the Balkans show the continuing importance of the alliance as a factor which on the one hand forced Germany to prevent the defeat of its partner and at the same time offered it the chance to bind Italy to its own strategy? From this point of view the interpretation of the joint operations in the North African theatre acquires a special interest: for they did not at all reflect the strategic plan that Hitler and the German military developed after July 1940 to secure the southern flank of the areas under German domination against the sea powers, Great Britain and the United States.

As part of the war against Britain after the victory in the west, German policy aimed at harnessing not only Italy but also Vichy France, with its politically and economically valuable North African possessions, and the Franco regime in Spain to serve German interests. The individual phases of this policy, connected as it was with military planning, are shown in their sequence and complexity in the present volume. In this regard an important conclusion is that German political aims in the Mediterranean were subordinate to Hitler's programmatic policy in the east. But Hitler's failure to achieve significant successes during his visits to Montoire, Hendaye, and Florence in October 1940 shows with surprising clarity the limits of his power a few months after his triumph over France. Franco, despite his indebtedness to the Axis powers, as well as Pétain, the representative of humiliated France, and Hitler's ally Mussolini, all resisted his political wishes. The necessity and value of the broad interpretational framework of the present volume will, it is hoped, be demonstrated by the comprehensive analysis of these well-known events in the total context of the war.

Another aspect of the present account of German policy and the conduct of the war in south-east Europe and the Mediterranean should be underlined here. The thorough treatment of developments on the south-east flank—influenced by the imminent, in German eyes decisive, attack on the Soviet Union—as well as in the south-west of the German-dominated area, brings into clearer focus the later global expansion of the European war. During the preparations for the attack on the Soviet Union and the first weeks of victories over the Red Army, in German military planning the United States came to be considered increasingly as a potential threat to the south-west flank, but also as a possible target for future military operations. This development points to the future volumes of this series, in which the global aspects of political and military developments will become the most typical feature of the war.

These remarks can only indicate briefly the diversity of problems and developments dealt with in the present volume. Especially because this volume treats subjects previously examined in a more cursory manner or only in their more spectacular aspects, and seldom in the context of large questions about the war, its composition presented particular difficulties. Not only the political, military, and economic situation of the Axis powers, but also the situation of their adversaries had to be analysed, described, and placed in perspective within the volume as a whole. The authors are aware that the solution they have devised cannot fulfil all expectations. It would, for example, have been desirable to establish uniform criteria for the accounts of military operations, which are necessarily not the central topic of discussion in this volume. However, the natural conditions of the various theatres—East Africa, Libya, Albania, Yugoslavia, mainland Greece, and Crete—the differences in the size of the military forces employed, the special forms of warfare, and finally concentration on the effects of the operations required consideration of military structures and units at greatly differing levels, a circumstance reflected in the maps accompanying the different chapters. This disadvantage nevertheless has its positive aspects, as the method chosen shows the entire range of forms of military operations.

It is in the nature of the work as a whole that the subjects of the individual volumes inevitably overlap in some areas. For example, the present volume treats of topics—such as the problems connected with the armistice with

France, or German policy in the Balkans—which have been dealt with from other points of view in the volumes already published. But this variation of perspective in the individual volumes should enhance the scholarly value of the work as a whole. It must, however, be pointed out that the war-economy problems in the Italo-German relationship after Italy's entry into the war, as well as the broad subject of the occupation policy of the Axis powers in the Balkans, have been left out of the present volume. Both subjects will be treated in the subsequent volumes, especially in Volume V, *The Structure of Axis Rule in Europe (1939–1941)*.

Working as a team was not without its problems for the authors of the present volume; but their own contributions have benefited from the advantages this method offers, such as the opportunity to discuss different views with colleagues. We should also like to thank the archives that provided the sources listed in the bibliography, as well as Dr Lucio Ceva (Milan), Professors Paul G. Halpern (Tallahassee, USA) and MacGregor Knox (Rochester, USA), and General Fabijan Trgo (Belgrade), for their readiness to provide information and materials. Mr Georg Evangelou (Freiburg) furnished assistance by translating relevant Greek publications. Finally, we owe special thanks to Professor Raimondo Luraghi (Genoa) and Dr Wolfgang Michalka (Darmstadt) for their critical reading of the manuscripts.

The reaction to the earlier volumes has been very friendly and encouraging. Although some comments have clearly been influenced by group interests, the critical voices of historians and others have stimulated discussion and thinking among the authors about future volumes. It would, no doubt, be overoptimistic to expect all the authors' conclusions to find a similar degree of acceptance, but they hope that their continued work will give fresh impulses in that direction.

WILHELM DEIST

PART I

Political and Military Developments in the Mediterranean Area, 1939–1940

GERHARD SCHREIBER

PRELIMINARY NOTE

ANY attempt at interpreting German–Italian policy and military operations in the Mediterranean area within the framework of the strategies pursued by Hitler from 1939 to 1941 must take as its basis not only the general political developments during the period of Italian non-belligerence from September 1939 to June 1940, but also the specific material and ideological conditions within the German–Italian alliance. These determined both the military concepts and the operations[1] of the Axis powers in a variety of ways. It is, in addition, necessary to take into account Hitler's long-term, programmatic aims.[2] The interpretation of these aims must underlie any analysis or examination of German strategy in the Second World War, over and above a purely descriptive account.[3] It is only when the objectives defined by Hitler as far back as the 1920s[4]—the realization of which he had been pursuing since 1933, not rigidly but nevertheless consistently—are borne in mind that points of reference can be found for the appropriate categorization of historical events. This applies equally to the interpretation of German strategy from 1939 to 1945 under the conceptual aspect of the 'epoch of world wars' as it does to that of partial aspects in the context of the Second World War. In brief, the present approach, within an examination of German and Italian policies and military operations in the Mediterranean area, aims at establishing the specific importance of this area in relation to the concept and the practical implementation of Hitler's strategy—the latter being always viewed in its strained relationship with the intentions of the 'Duce'.

[1] On Italian military operations up to the armistice with France cf. vol. ii of the present work, VI.v.4 (Umbreit); Bernotti, *Guerra nel Mediterraneo*, 45–50; also Rossi, *Mussolini*, and Gallinari, *Operazioni*.

[2] See Hildebrand, *Third Reich*, 141–51, on the present state of research; an excellent survey of the debate on the origins of the Second World War in Hillgruber, *Entstehung*; on Italy ibid. 38 ff.

[3] 'Strategy' here is intended to mean the deliberately mobilized and employed sum total of a country's moral and material potential which its political leadership can use for the attainment of its war aims. The term 'warfare' denotes the purely military dimension of the overall strategic picture.

[4] Cf. vol. i of the present work, IV.I.I (Messerschmidt).

I. Mussolini's 'Non-belligerence'[1]

1. THE ALLIANCE POLICY IN GENERAL FROM THE GERMAN POINT OF VIEW

UNTIL just before the outbreak of the war in 1939 Hitler had shown great interest in military support by the Italian armed forces.[2] This was by no means a matter of course, as relations between Germany and Italy—despite the existence since 1936 of the 'Berlin–Rome Axis'—could certainly not be described as particularly harmonious during the first six months of 1939.[3] As is well known, quite acute, though short-lived, tensions arose between the Axis powers in March as the direct consequence of German aggression against Czechoslovakia.[4] The Italians accordingly gave Berlin no notice of their invasion of Albania on 7 April 1939.[5] Undoubtedly this operation, in the situation prevailing at the time, was an immediate reaction—for domestic as well as foreign-policy reasons—to the German strike at Prague, but more than this it was in line with the long-term strategic objectives of a policy inspired in particular by business circles close to the foreign minister, Count Galeazzo Ciano.[6]

Although Hitler contemptuously described the operation as an 'aping' of his own political moves in the recent past,[7] he actually regarded Mussolini's step as dangerous because it was apt to affect adversely the political situation of the Axis partners. His remarks also indicated that he was not unaware of the rivalry existing between Italy and Germany.[8]

---

[1] Some characteristics of the German–Italian alliance were described in vols. i and ii of the present work. For the period 1939–40 cf. vol. ii, VI.v.4 (Umbreit). A very informative article, addressing the essential aspects of Italian non-belligerence, in *Dictionnaire*, ii. 972–3.

[2] Schreiber, *Revisionismus*, 186–91; Irving, *War Path*, 246.

[3] Anchieri, 'Mißverständnis'; Collotti, 'La politica dell'Italia', 5–11; Hassell, *Tagebücher*, 56–7 (30 May 1939); Pastorelli, 'La politica estera fascista', 112 ff.; Siebert, *Italiens Weg*, 108–28.

[4] Vol. i of the present work, IV.v.7(c) (Messerschmidt).

[5] Siebert, *Italiens Weg*, 130. Not until the evening of 6 Apr. did the Italian ambassador in Berlin inform the foreign ministry that Italy was going to occupy Albania the following day.

[6] Anfuso, *Roma, Berlino*, 112 ff.; Smith, *Roman Empire*, 149–58; Tasso, *Italia e Croazia*, i. 182–9. It should, however, be noted that Italy's economic interest in Albania had already influenced Italian foreign policy in the 19th cent. Thus the 'Italia irredenta' movement, originally nationally motivated and championed by the Italo-Albanians, was harnessed by the Rome government towards the end of the 19th cent. to an imperialist policy pursuing economic and military objectives. On this cf. primarily Schinner, *Der österreichisch-italienische Gegensatz*, 165–8, and Wernicke, *Theodor Anton Ippen*, 56; specifically on the military operations of the occupation: Montanari, *Albania*, 254–78.

[7] Engel, *Heeresadjutant*, 45 (8 Apr. 39).

[8] This rivalry emerged very early. Cf. Catalano, 'Les ambitions', 16 ff.; Poulain, 'Deutschlands Drang nach Südosten'. On the anti-German aspect of the occupation of Albania see esp. Collotti, 'La politica dell'Italia', 6; Wiskemann, *Axis*, 135–6. A survey of the peculiarities of German–

1. German View of Alliance Policy

German–Italian relations in 1939 cannot of course be interpreted apart from the international situation, especially relations between the Axis powers and Japan.[9] Suffice it at this point to record that Hitler, not least out of consideration for the difficulties between Berlin and Rome—which were evident even before the annexation of Albania[10]—eventually agreed to discussions between the German and Italian armed forces commands,[11] which had been talked about since 1938. The main reason why they had not taken place earlier was that Germany declared itself ready for them only following the conclusion of a formal alliance, whereas Italy favoured the opposite course. What eventually brought about the holding of the talks was no doubt the fact that the events of March and April 1939 had persuaded the Italian and the German leadership of the need to keep a check on each other and to prevent, as far as possible, any independent adventures—though these could never be entirely ruled out.

It is not surprising, therefore, that in analysing what German and Italian military chiefs were discussing between April and June 1939 one discovers more mistrust than trust, or that an interpretation of the talks between the Axis partners suggests a need for political protection against each other rather than for joint military action. It is in this light that the 'Pact of Steel'—the pact of friendship and alliance concluded by the Axis partners on 22 May 1939—has to be viewed.[12] Originally, Japan was also to join the alliance, but as it was not immediately possible to balance interests within the triangle Berlin–Rome–Tokyo, the intended three-power pact had to be postponed for a time.[13]

The different motivation for the alliance,[14] as well as its markedly divergent interpretation by the German and Italian sides, clearly demonstrated the existence of totally dissimilar ideas on the significance and function of the Pact of Steel.[15] As regards Germany, at least, it may be assumed that she was practising a deliberate deception of her ally.[16] Whereas Mussolini was confident that the pact had ensured several years of peace in Europe,[17] Hitler by

---

Italian relations is provided, by, *inter alios*, Deakin, *Brutal Friendship*; Funke, *Sanktionen*; Palumbo, 'Uncertain Friendship'; Petersen, *Hitler—Mussolini*; Siebert, *Italiens Weg*; Schreiber, *Revisionismus*.

[9] Ferretti, 'La politica estera'; cf. also the compact account in Herde, *Pearl Harbor*, 4–41; id., *Italien*, 8–29; Sommer, *Deutschland und Japan*; and esp. Krebs, *Japans Deutschlandpolitik*.

[10] The annexation was completed *de facto* by 3 June 1939, even though the Italian government tried to mask this state of affairs by a formal regulation of relations—union of the two Crowns and an Italian governor; cf. Siebert, *Italiens Weg*, 131–2.

[11] Ceva, 'Altre notizie'; Schreiber, *Revisionismus*, 154–88; Toscano, 'Le conversazioni'.

[12] *DGFP* D vi, No. 426, pp. 561 ff.; cf. Siebert, 'Stahlpakt'; Toscano, *Origins*; Wiskemann, *Axis*, 130–50.

[13] An informative survey, with special reference to Hitler's calculations in his plans for such alliances, is given by Hillgruber, 'Hitler-Koalition', 470 ff. Extensively on German–Japanese relations: Sommer, *Deutschland und Japan*, 165–239.

[14] Herde, *Pearl Harbor*, 9–10; Perticone, *La politica*, 376–83.

[15] Schütt, 'Stahlpakt', 498–9.

[16] Watt, 'Rome–Berlin', 537.

[17] Anchieri, 'Mißverständnis', 511–12; Collotti, 'L'alleanza', 3; Hughes, *Fall and Rise*, 195–6; Lill, 'Italiens Außenpolitik', 106 ff.

May 1939 no longer had any intention of giving up his war against Poland.[18] Initially, however, each of the dictators after 22 May believed that he had firmly tied down the other into his own national plan. In August, when the Duce's mistake and the deception by the Führer became equally patent, the Italians displayed surprise. Their gullibility concerning verbal assurances from Germany was now seen to have been a mistake; in view of past experience of Hitler they should have made sure that the stipulated period of peace was laid down more clearly in the treaty. As a direct reaction to Germany's behaviour Count Ciano, the Italian foreign minister, attempted to get an anti-German line adopted in Italian foreign policy. In this Ciano was acting as a pragmatist, an Italian nationalist, but he was certainly no pacifist, even though he became the centre of a clique whose objectives, directed against Hitler's warmongering, were soon no secret.[19] Besides Ciano, the most prominent representatives of this peace party were Dino Grandi, the Italian ambassador in London until the spring of 1939 and appointed minister of justice that same year, and the treasury minister Raffaello Riccardi. The Church and—with certain reservations—the royal family were among its sympathizers, as were such leading business figures as Giovanni Agnelli, Count Giuseppe Volpi, and Alberto Pirelli. The 'hawks', on the other hand, were led, among others, by Roberto Farinacci, member of the Fascist grand council, and Achille Starace, the secretary of the Fascist Party.[20]

Berlin was aware of the displeasure caused in Rome, but Hitler, disregarding it, continued to believe in the automatic functioning of the Pact of Steel. He evidently thought, in August 1939, that he could not do without open support from Italy, even though his arrangements with the USSR were entirely in line with the maxims he had formulated in *Mein Kampf*. According to the programme, war against Britain could only be risked if Germany's rear was covered by the Soviet Union, and this cover Hitlerite Germany achieved beyond any doubt with the non-aggression pact signed on 24 August.[21] Poland, unassisted by the Red Army, was a negligible quantity. Naturally, as an immediate consequence of the arrangement with Stalin, military assistance from Mussolini had become less urgent, since, after a rapid victory over Poland—which Hitler anticipated—if indeed not before, there would no longer be any military threat from the east. Among these reflections, however, it should not be forgotten that in August Hitler was primarily interested in stopping Britain and France from directly intervening in the war, or preventing them from launching an offensive in the west at a time when German

---

[18] Fest, *Hitler* (trans.), 871–2; vol. i of the present work, IV.VI.2 (Messerschmidt).
[19] 'Betrachtungen über die politische Situation Italiens 1935–1941' (undated), PA Dienststelle Ribbentrop 35/i. Cf. also Anchieri, 'Bündnisverrat'; and Anfuso, *Roma, Berlino*, 132 ff., whose statements, however, should be treated with caution.
[20] Bocca, *Storia*, 60; Knox, *Mussolini*, 47.
[21] Allard, *Stalin*, 148–65; Hillgruber, *Sowjetische Außenpolitik*, 26–35; vol. i of the present work, IV.VI.4 (Messerschmidt); Hillgruber, 'Hitler-Stalin-Pakt'; Hildebrand, 'Hitler-Stalin-Pakt'.

troops were fighting in Poland.[22] This objective, it seemed, could best be achieved by the creation of a power-structure as disadvantageous as possible to Paris and London. Within this plan—designed ultimately to achieve political cover for German expansion—Italy, since 1937, had occupied a firm place.[23]

There was great disappointment in Berlin, therefore, when it became clear that Rome would keep out of the conflict. Hitler tried everything to bring about a last-minute change of mind by Mussolini, but without success. This was the context of the tragicomedy staged by Italy shortly before the announcement of her definitive decision not to enter the war—the so-called 'molybdenum list' addressed to Germany with its unrealizable demands for war material.[24] A closer look behind the scenes of Italian policy in August 1939 reveals Mussolini's behaviour as camouflage in many respects. At any rate, there was no clear indication of what he really intended to do in the long run, or what his attitude was to the war as such. In connection with these questions mention should be made of a letter from Mussolini received by Admiral of the Fleet Domenico Cavagnari, the commander-in-chief of the Italian navy, on 27 May, immediately after the conclusion of the Pact of Steel. In it the Duce once more emphasized his determination to join in a major war.[25] It is also a fact that, following the agreement between Stalin and Hitler, he was strongly inclined—at least for a while—to intervene in the impending conflict.[26] All this again tends to show that it was not the war itself that was an open question between the Axis partners after 22 May 1939, but solely the moment when it could, or should, commence.

Hitler, when he learnt of the Italian demands for material, decided to do without Mussolini's direct participation in the war. Berlin now merely asked for such propaganda support as might confuse Paris and London about Italian intentions and therefore tie down French troops in the south. Italian industrial workers and farm labourers were, moreover, welcome in Germany. The Italians were ready to comply in all these respects.[27] Simultaneously, however —encouraged by the British and French governments—they attempted once more, on 2 September, to restore peace. However, a second Munich was bound to remain an illusion of Mussolini's, since Hitler was bent on achieving total victory over Poland.[28]

---

[22] Vol. i of the present work, IV.VI.4 (Messerschmidt).
[23] Martin, *Friedensinitiativen*, 34–5; Schreiber, *Revisionismus*, 107–34; also Funke, 'Hitler', 349–69.
[24] Anchieri, 'Italiens Ausweichen'; Bocca, *Storia*, 62 ff.; Irving, *War Path*, 250–1; Siebert, *Italiens Weg*, 304 ff. There is nothing in the sources to justify the assumption, made by Lukacs, *Last European War*, 48, that Mussolini's attitude did not surprise Hitler.
[25] *La marina italiana*, i. 348 ff.
[26] Schreiber, *Revisionismus*, 248–61; Siebert, *Italiens Weg*, 265.
[27] Anchieri, 'Italiens Ausweichen', 657–8.
[28] Martin, *Friedensinitiativen*, 38–46. On Mussolini's attitude to the war between Germany and Poland cf. Borejsza, 'Italiens Haltung'; on last-minute efforts to save the peace cf. also Dahlerus, *Last Attempt*, 116–34.

In order to assess Mussolini's attitude it must first be remembered that the war began at what was in fact the worst possible moment for Italy. The country—as will be shown—was in no position to enter into a major military conflict. Italian reaction was determined not by what Mussolini wanted to do but by what he was able to do. Practical constraints, resulting from the inadequate armament of the Italian forces, simply could not be disregarded—at least not in a phase when the end of the conflict was not yet in view. The Duce simply had to bow to them. For this reason alone it seems unlikely that Italy would have entered the war in September 1939 if Britain had adopted an emphatically anti-Italian policy.[29] And there is plenty of room for argument on whether developments in the Mediterranean area in such an event would have improved the British position: such questions cannot be answered solely by reference to Italy's military weakness. What is certain is that Mussolini, judging the situation correctly, avoided being embroiled in the conflict and did not find himself able even to give Hitler the promised propaganda support. Italy's position appeared so precarious that when, on 31 August, the British retorted to Italy's sabre-rattling propaganda by cutting off telecommunications, Rome immediately assured London that Italy would not intervene in events.[30] Consistent in his approach to the situation, Mussolini urged Hitler as late as 1 September to release him from his obligations as an ally,[31] and in view of the situation Hitler had no choice but to comply.[32] Refusal would have changed nothing in Italy's attitude but might have dangerously strained relations between the Axis powers. Hitler and Mussolini saved face, declaring that all decisions had been made in complete agreement,[33] but otherwise for the time being each went his own way. What then was the real position as regards the Italian partner?

2. ITALY AS A COALITION PARTNER

The world was notified of Italy's decision in favour of non-belligerence on 1 September.[34] The Italian people would certainly have preferred Mussolini to

---

[29] Thus Murray, 'Role of Italy', 48, who regards Chamberlain's policy of appeasement towards Mussolini as a mistake, since Italy's immediate involvement in the war would—under certain conditions—have been of decisive advantage to Britain. This line of argument essentially reflects the mood of certain Allied circles that favoured confrontation with Italy: cf. Bonnet, *Défense*, ii. 381. For a very good account of the attitude of Italy's political leadership, aimed as it was at neutrality up to the moment when the outcome of the war became foreseeable, see Borejsza, 'Italiens Haltung', 172–84.

[30] Schreiber, *Revisionismus*, 187; Ciano, *Diary 1939–1943*, 140–1 (31 Aug. 1939).

[31] Siebert, *Italiens Weg*, 350.

[32] *DGFP* D vii, No. 500, p. 483 (1 Sept. 1939). A good overall view, within a comprehensive discussion of published Italian documents, in Schmitt, 'Italian Diplomacy', 165 ff.; on Italy's actual situation on the basis of structural conditions cf. Schreiber, 'Les structures'.

[33] Siebert, *Italiens Weg*, 352.

[34] Bocca, *Storia*, 64; Faldella, *L'Italia*, 52–3; a well-informed survey of the period of Italian non-belligerence in Knox, *Mussolini*, 44–86; Michaelis, *Mussolini*, 276–90. The latter discusses, in

2. Italy as a Coalition Partner

declare unreserved neutrality, in which case the future would have been more calculable, but on the whole there was relief that, for the time being, the country remained at peace.[35] To Mussolini this applied only with fundamental reservations: to him non-belligerence seemed an acceptable solution only so long as, on the one hand, there remained the hope of European peace being mediated by Rome and, on the other, the uncertainty of a decisive victory by Germany. To the extent that hopes of peace were stultified by political developments, and as a direct reaction to the successes of German military operations, Mussolini visibly moved away from the stance he had adopted in September. It is also clear that his non-participation in the war was soon causing him severe psychological stress. This was reflected, for instance, in desperate efforts to allay any doubts as to the factual justification of Italian non-belligerence.[36] The Duce was suffering from the idea that he might be suspected of wishing to repeat the story of 1915 by switching to the side of the Western allies.[37] Complexes of this kind, to be seen moreover against the background of Mussolini's constant fear of being condemned to a shadowy existence by Hitler's side in the realm of power politics, were apt to flare suddenly into aggressive moods.[38] Although these placed a certain burden on the Axis partnership, they reflected no change in Mussolini's basic attitude at this period. That attitude might be reduced to this simplified formula: either Italy could mediate a peace, which undoubtedly would mean a considerable enhancement of her status as a political power, or else she would enter the war at a suitable moment, i.e. when a German victory over the Western powers was beginning to take shape.

(a) Political Aspects

Apart from the psychological tensions mentioned above, there were unmistakable strains on German–Italian relations for reasons of international politics, especially such questions as the South Tyrolean problem and competing national interests in south-east Europe,[39] as well as the divergent attitudes of the two Axis partners to the war between Finland and the Soviet Union.

On the issue of South Tyrol (Alto Adige) it should be pointed out that the magnanimous gesture with which Hitler on his visit to Rome in May 1938

---

particular, the fate of the Jews in Italy, an issue that cannot be gone into here. It should, however, be pointed out that Italy's more or less anti-Semitic policy was undoubtedly introduced by Mussolini, even though there was no extermination of Jews prior to the fall of the Fascist regime in 1943. During the German occupation after September 1943, German special squads had Italian Jews transported to German concentration camps; see the basic study in De Felice, *Ebrei italiani*.

[35] Badoglio, *Italy*, 10; Villari, *Italian Foreign Policy*, 242, though often very unreliable and tendentious.

[36] On Mussolini's various attempts to bring about a negotiated peace cf. the detailed examination by Viault, 'Mussolini'; Schreiber, *Revisionismus*, 248.

[37] Anfuso, *Roma, Berlino*, 134; André, 'La politica estera', 117, justifiably rejects as untenable the thesis that Mussolini was prepared to enter the war against Germany.

[38] *DGFP* D viii, No. 68, pp. 64 ff. (14 Sept. 1939).

[39] Cf. the present volume, II.1–III.

confirmed the finality of the Brenner frontier and Italy's possession of the territory of South Tyrol was scarcely followed up by any deeds.[40] The difficulties stemmed primarily from different ideas concerning the modalities of the resettlement of ethnically German South Tyroleans. Although Berlin and Rome had agreed as early as June on a plan to be implemented in three phases, the whole matter was still in the air at the outbreak of war. German dilatoriness in tackling the issue, admittedly largely due to economic and financial problems, on which neither partner in the negotiations was able to offer universally satisfying proposals, gave rise to the suspicion, initially on Ciano's part, that Berlin was trying to go back on the agreements.[41] Mussolini too reacted with indignation, and the Italian ambassador in Berlin, Bernardo Attolico, had to intervene at the German foreign ministry in order to urge the Germans to fulfil their obligations.[42] The resettlement issue was therefore reactivated as both Hitler and Heinrich Himmler, who was in charge of such matters, showed themselves amenable to the Italian claims. This relaxation of attitudes was probably due primarily to the realization that any change in the mood of the South Tyrolean Germans as a result of stagnation in the negotiations might place a dangerous strain on relations between Berlin and Rome. The South Tyroleans were clearly hoping—as neither German nor Italian observers failed to notice—that the resettlement programme would fail because the Italians would once again desert Germany in the war, in which case Hitler would be released from the obligations he had undertaken in May 1938. South Tyrolean circles therefore expected that secret orders would shortly be given to them to stay put.[43]

Mussolini, continuing to reflect towards the end of September that a great nation could not in the long run keep aloof from the war, and that Italy would have to intervene unless she wished to downgrade herself as a great power,[44] was certainly pleased and relieved at Germany's compliant attitude. In contrast to Ciano, who was then pursuing the decisively anti-German line[45] foreshadowed in his speech of 1 September,[46] the Duce continued to incline towards joining the conflict on the German side at the appropriate time. For

---

[40] A fundamental account of the South Tyrol problem between 1933 and 1939 in Steurer, *Südtirol*, here 320 ff.; cf. also Latour, *Südtirol*, 26–42.

[41] Ciano, *Diary 1939–1943*, 150–1 (12 Sept. 1939); extensively on the resettlement negotiations in the summer of 1939: Steurer, *Südtirol*, 342–61. The intention, according to the agreements of 23 June, was in a first phase to resettle the approximately 10,000 Reich citizens living in South Tyrol, for which a period of 4 weeks was envisaged. During the second phase those ethnic German South Tyroleans who were not tied to their land were to be evacuated; in the third phase it was planned to resettle the ethnic German South Tyroleans who were tied to their land. Cf. Steurer, *Südtirol*, 346–54, especially on the financial problems of the resettlement operation.

[42] *DDI*, 9th ser., i, No. 267, p. 168 (17 Sept. 1939).

[43] Ibid., No. 336, p. 206 (20 Sept. 1939); No. 467, p. 280 (27 Sept. 1939); cf. Steurer, *Südtirol*, 354–5.

[44] Ciano, *Diary 1939–1943*, 157 (24 Sept. 1939).

[45] Anfuso, *Roma, Berlino*, 138.

[46] Ciano, *Diary 1939–1943*, 142–3 (1 Sept. 1939).

the moment he believed he had enough latitude to bide his time and reach an independent decision;[47] in the end it was the unpredictable and rapid German successes which forced his hand.

From the Italian point of view the meeting between Ciano and Hitler on 1 October 1939 must be assessed against the background of the South Tyrolean situation and within the framework of Mussolini's domestic and foreign-policy plans.[48] Hitler touched relatively briefly on the contentious resettlement issue, though he allowed it to be understood that he was thinking about finding a new home for the South Tyroleans.[49] Such vague ideas, needless to say, did not suggest to Rome that any progress was being made. Italy was interested in precise dates, in a binding regulation of property matters associated with resettlement, and in a decision as between total or partial resettlement. But Hitler provided no precise data[50] on any of these. It would have been entirely possible to suspect deliberate procrastination behind the German attitude; the reason why Ciano did not protest against it was presumably that the Italians expected to arrive at satisfactory arrangements concerning the financial and economic problems of the resettlement programme, in the course of a conference which had been called for the beginning of October.[51]

On 21 October it really looked as if a solution had been found; at any rate, the negotiating parties had come to an agreement on 'directives for the repatriation of Reich citizens and the transfer of ethnic Germans from the Alto Adige into the German Reich'. Simultaneously the agreements regulating the 'economic implementation of the resettlement of ethnic Germans and Reich citizens into the German Reich' were signed. It has rightly been pointed out that German advantages resulting from the financial regulations were 'largely illusory', as Italy certainly possessed the leverage for steering the resettlement operation in the direction of the partial solution desired by Rome. Ultimately, of course, Germany realized that—despite Himmler's support for a 'total solution'—the economic clauses permitted no more than a very limited resettlement. Seen in this light the South Tyrolean issue continued to be 'in practice shelved and subordinated to the further development of German–Italian relations'.[52]

Nothing, therefore, had really been settled. But when the 'directives' were published on 26 October, five days after being agreed, a fierce electoral campaign erupted over the option, to be made by 31 December 1939, of being resettled or staying put. Both sides, after the beginning of November, conducted this campaign in a markedly aggressive manner. The South Tyroleans

---

[47] Ibid. 161–2 (30 Sept. 1939).
[48] *Staatsmänner*, 33–7.
[49] Ibid. 40.
[50] Latour, *Südtirol*, 33.
[51] *DDI*, 9th ser., i, No. 580, pp. 356–7 (3 Oct. 1939); No. 581, p. 367 (3 Oct. 1939); cf. also *DGFP* D viii, No. 231, pp. 253 ff. (10 Oct. 1939); on the negotiations cf. Steurer, *Südtirol*, 355 ff.
[52] Quoted according to Steurer, *Südtirol*, 357, 358. *DDI*, 9th ser., ii. 601–8, with complete text of the agreements; cf. Latour, *Südtirol*, 54–5.

were divided. By mid-November the propaganda for and against resettlement had escalated. A mood of crisis existed between the Axis partners. Ciano spoke of a direct threat to the alliance emanating from the unrest in South Tyrol.

It is doubtful whether Mussolini would have really been prepared to adopt an anti-German course as a consequence of that development. It might be pointed out that, after the outbreak of the war, he had ordered fortification work to be continued on the *vallo alpino*, his northern frontier. In view of the friction between the Axis powers this was predominantly a propaganda move, designed to emphasize his own freedom of action and independence. Ciano, admittedly, was devoutly hoping for a break between Mussolini and Hitler.[53] This was a vain hope, if only because Mussolini continued to believe that his imperialist aims were realizable only at the side of Hitler.

This was his attitude, at the latest, from the moment when Germany believed that she could reorganize the European power-system by force of arms in line with her own ideas. This removed the basis of the Italian political concept of 'holding the balance', a concept which involved the absence of options. Mussolini in 1939 was merely hesitating over a decision which, from his point of view, could only be in favour of Germany. It is necessary to bear in mind the objectives of the Fascist regime in order to see in its relevant historical framework anything that, in a different frame of reference, would have led to a divergent development of German–Italian relations. It is therefore significant in Mussolini's reflections that, following Hitler's speech of 6 October 1939 with its suggestion of a peace offer, he was afraid the war might soon be over and finished without him.[54] We have noted the chagrin which non-belligerence caused him.[55] At no time after September 1939 did he seriously intend remaining neutral in the long run.[56] Typical of his calculations is, among other things, this incident. In October he instructed Ciano to prepare a major speech in which Axis solidarity was to be emphasized. The following day he wanted the burden of the speech to be a massive accusation against Germany.[57] In view of the South Tyrol situation this could reflect an understandable reaction with primarily domestic aims. There was, moreover, the attempt to acquire a sharper foreign-policy profile *vis-à-vis* Hitler. However, his instruction implied no change in Rome's political position. Mussolini was out to regain territory and to ensure that Italy did not become the plaything of German policy. And Ciano himself at that moment emphasized that the Duce intended to continue an unambiguously pro-German line.[58]

This attitude of Mussolini's corresponded entirely to Hitler's judgement of his Axis partner. Despite the numerous difficulties within the German–Italian

---

[53] Schreiber, *Revisionismus*, 200, 242–3; Steurer, *Südtirol*, 373–85.
[54] Ciano, *Diary 1939–1943*, 164 (6 Oct. 1939).
[55] Ibid. 164–5, 167 (7, 9, 16 Oct. 1939).
[56] Ibid. 164 (7 Oct. 1939).
[57] Ibid. 170–1 (25, 26 Oct. 1939).
[58] Ibid. 170–1 (26 Oct. 1939).

alliance, Hitler, for instance on 23 November, once again declared to the commanders-in-chief of the armed services that for Germany a lot depended on Italy. Mussolini alone was the guarantee that the Italians would actually turn into reality their intention of building a Mediterranean empire. However, Hitler at that time—quite correctly—expected that his Axis partner would not intervene until there was a promising start of the German offensive against France.[59]

A little later, but before the South Tyrolean crisis was settled, the Soviet–Finnish war (30 November 1939 to 12 March 1940) brought further friction between Berlin and Rome. This is not the place to examine the real significance of this conflict for European politics or its weight within Hitler's strategy.[60] Only its effects on the Axis partnership need be outlined. Three aspects should be borne in mind in judging Italy's attitude to the Finnish–Soviet 'Winter War'.

First is the ambivalence of Italian foreign policy. This stemmed from the distinctly different attitudes of Ciano and Mussolini to the German–Italian alliance. As for the anti-Soviet aspects of Italy's political actions, her foreign minister must clearly be seen as their guiding spirit, rather than her head of government.

Secondly, there was Mussolini's endeavour to show himself on the international scene as an independent political force alongside Hitler. These endeavours must largely explain his—no doubt mainly tactical—harassing fire against excessive German–Soviet intimacy. To the extent that Berlin and Moscow were intensifying their co-operation, Italy's political freedom of action was bound to diminish. That freedom, for the time being, appeared to be guaranteed by non-belligerence, but in actual fact it had always been limited in view of Mussolini's foreign-policy aims. As Stalin and Hitler were inclining more strongly towards each other, Mussolini found himself forced to take his stand openly, in order—as he saw it—not to become a negligible quantity for the Germans.

Thirdly, it should be remembered that Italian policy towards the Soviet Union was not merely the result of the ideological antagonism between Fascism and Communism, but that, especially with regard to the Balkans, it also stemmed from Mussolini's power-political objectives.

Towards the end of 1939 there was some anxiety in Italy about a division of Scandinavia and the Balkans into German and Soviet spheres of interest. The unreserved support given by the German press to the Soviet attack on Finland, as well as its anti-Scandinavian news-reporting, gave rise to suspicion in Rome

---

[59] 'Besprechung beim Führer, zu der alle Oberbefehlshaber befohlen sind', published in Domarus, *Hitler*, ii. 1421–7; identical with the document in 'Führer Conferences', 60; a divergent record in Groscurth, *Tagebücher*, 414–18; ibid. 234–5 n. 638, further bibliography and references to documents; cf. also Watt, 'Rome–Berlin', 540–1.

[60] See Ueberschär, *Finnland*, 92–165, on the Winter War; for the Marxist-Leninist viewpoint cf. *Deutschland im Zweiten Weltkrieg*, i. 250–5; *Geschichte des Zweiten Weltkrieges*, iii. 58–61, 64.

that Hitler and Stalin might have come to an agreement about Denmark and Norway being ceded to Germany, and Finland to the Soviet Union. As for the Balkans, it was similarly assumed that Greece, Yugoslavia, and Hungary were to be annexed to the German living-space, which would have given the Germans their own Mediterranean coastline, while Bulgaria and Romania were to go to the USSR.[61] The marked chill which descended on Italian–German relations in the autumn of 1939 was certainly not due to primarily ideological reasons.[62] Thus Rome in November felt no inhibitions about inciting certain unnamed figures in Czechoslovakia to resist German rule. They were to proclaim themselves pro-Communist and publish an appropriate manifesto[63]—a suggestion which surely was anti-German rather than anti-Communist. The ultimate aim, of course, was solely to provoke German–Soviet tension.

In line with these attempts was the fact that, at the peak of the crisis between Helsinki and Moscow, Ciano had information passed to the Russians to the effect that the Germans were supplying arms to the Finns—which was not correct,[64] because Hitler had ordered an arms embargo for Finland as early as October. Only a few anti-aircraft guns were sent to Helsinki—prior to the beginning of the Finno-Soviet conflict—on the basis of obligations entered into earlier.[65] After the outbreak of the Winter War there was violent anti-Soviet reaction in the Italian press and among the public, reaction which, on closer scrutiny, could be interpreted as at least equally anti-German. This was confirmed by Ciano's observation that the 'fate of the Finns would be of much less concern to the Italians if the Russians were not from all practical points of view the allies of Germany'.[66] Commenting on the pro-Finnish and anti-Soviet demonstrations which took place in all Italian cities at the beginning of December, he remarked: 'We must not forget that the people say "Death to Russia" and really mean "Death to Germany".'[67] This is in agreement with the information sent back by the German military attaché, who reported anti-German demonstrations outside the German embassy in Rome.[68]

Italy, however, did not intend to confine herself to pro-Finnish propaganda. When the Finnish Ambassador thanked Ciano for the moral support given to his country and, in this connection, asked for arms and the dispatch of specialists,[69] Ciano did not show himself disinclined. In addition to the aircraft already delivered, further machines were to be made available to Finland, provided Germany permitted the traffic. But this was precisely what the

---

[61] Cf. Catalano, *Trionfo dei fascismi*, 282.
[62] Siebert, *Italiens Weg*, 372.
[63] *DDI*, 9th ser., ii, No. 270, pp. 231–2 (20 Nov. 1939).
[64] Ciano, *Diary 1939–1943*, 178 (28 Nov. 1939).
[65] In detail Ueberschär, *Finnland*, 84–91.
[66] Ciano, *Diary 1939–1943*, 180 (3 Dec. 1939).
[67] Ibid. 181 (4 Dec. 1939).
[68] Rintelen, *Mussolini als Bundesgenosse*, 79.
[69] *DDI*, 9th ser., No. 490, p. 377 (6 Dec. 1939), concerning the purchase of Italian arms through Helsinki via Sweden; Ciano, *Diary 1939–1943*, 182 (8 Dec. 1939).

German government—much to the disappointment of the Finns and Italians—was not prepared to do. The Italian war material was detained at the port of Sassnitz and eventually sent back to Italy.[70] By the sea route, which took considerably longer, a total of seventeen Italian aircraft and 150 volunteers—out of an alleged 5,000—eventually reached Finland by the end of February.[71] Although this support proved insignificant with regard to the course of the war between Helsinki and Moscow, it was seen as usefully demonstrating Rome's independence in matters of foreign policy. In point of fact, it must be assumed that Mussolini was not too happy about this development, which was merely a tactical success. Only a change in Berlin's attitude could have genuinely eased his situation. In the long run, however—since Mussolini, because of his own objectives, was neither willing nor able to change his political course in the direction of Ciano's—it was fairly obvious that, in consequence of this unsuccessful attempt to establish an independent profile, Italy's dependence on Germany was bound to appear even more clearly. Against that background, Mussolini's readiness—evidenced as recently as 9 December—to maintain correct relations with the Soviet Union in spite of the Winter War presumably represented a concession to Germany. It was only Moscow's decision, notified on the same day, to respond to the anti-Soviet demonstrations in Italy by recalling the Soviet ambassador even before he was able to present his credentials, as had been planned for 12 December, that led Mussolini to draw back again.[72] Yet this unsuccessful episode in no way touched on the fundamentally pro-German attitude of the Duce, who was just then reviving his intention of demanding Tunisia and Corsica from France—a move which in Ciano's view would inevitably lead to war.[73] Given these premises, the outcome of the meeting of the Fascist grand council on 7 December loses much of the weight often attributed to it, seeing that its justification and confirmation of Italy's decision in favour of non-belligerence in no way called into question the fundamental Italian line of military co-operation with Germany, a line demonstrably present after August 1939[74] and prevalent in 1940.

A few days later, on 16 December, Ciano delivered a speech which had been on the stocks since 26 October and is often interpreted as the culmination of German–Italian tensions in the second half of 1939.[75] This speech, however, originally had nothing to do with the so-called December low point in relations between Berlin and Rome. The situation in December could not have been foreseen in October. Ciano's arguments quite simply reflected the anti-German

---

[70] Schreiber, *Revisionismus*, 241; cf. also Schütt, 'Stahlpakt', 508.
[71] Ueberschär, *Finnland*, 101.
[72] Ciano, *Diary 1939–1943*, 183 (9 Dec. 1939); Italy recalled her ambassador from Moscow on 28 Dec.; ibid. 190.
[73] Ibid. 183 (9 Dec. 1939).
[74] Ibid. 182; cf. Siebert, *Italiens Weg*, 386.
[75] For details: Siebert, *Italiens Weg*, 386–9; Schütt, 'Stahlpakt', 512 ff. On the December crisis cf. also Wiskemann, *Axis*, 186–7.

policy pursued by him at the time, a policy which Mussolini occasionally made use of, within the framework of his tactical calculations, without however identifying with it. What Ciano had intended as a distancing from Hitler Mussolini saw mainly as an attempt to obtain specific information on further German intentions.

Ever since November Mussolini had displayed increasing nervousness with regard to a German offensive in the west, because, if the Wehrmacht were to move within a foreseeable period of time, this would force his hand[76] in a situation when his own military preparations were far from complete. Dr Robert Ley, the leader of the German Labour Front, on a visit to Rome at the beginning of December, confirmed that Germany was preparing to attack Holland. But Ley, who acted as Hitler's mouthpiece—Ciano's comment on his demeanour leaves no doubt on that score—also allowed it to be understood that, regardless of the momentary co-operation between Moscow and Berlin, war against the Soviet Union was still a firm part of the plan.[77] For obvious reasons Ley spoke of long-term perspectives. But even so it must have been clear to his interlocutors that Hitler was continuing to develop his policy towards the USSR according to his programme. Co-operation with the Communists was to him purely a tactical measure. It did not represent any renunciation of that central feature of his programme, both on power-political and on racially ideological grounds, which was the conquest of living-space in the east, the *sine qua non* of a German continental empire.[78] Entirely in this spirit Ley emphasized in Rome that the conflict between Fascism and Communism would be decided by the defeat of the democracies in the western campaign.[79] Hitler had always proceeded from the argument that, in order to cover his rear for his campaign against the Soviet Union, he had to eliminate France as a military opponent in the west. That done, he would seek an arrangement with Britain, in order to conquer German living-space, i.e. European Russia, with British approval. However, from about May 1940 there were indications that Hitler was greatly inclined to attack the Soviet Union immediately after the campaign in the west—if at all possible before the end of 1940—forgoing the originally planned interval of peace.[80] The Italians had

---

[76] Cf. Ciano, *Diary 1939–1943*, 175 (11 Nov. 1939); *DDI*, 9th ser., ii, No. 230, pp. 185–6 (15 Nov. 1939).

[77] Ciano, *Diary 1939–1943*, 181 (5 Dec. 1939); *DGFP* D viii, No. 436, pp. 509 ff. (10 Dec. 1939); immediately before his departure for Rome Ley received instructions from Hitler, the contents of which were unknown to the foreign ministry and to Ribbentrop. Ley certainly, despite the foreign minister's advice to the contrary, informed the Italians of Germany's long-term intentions, though not always accurately; after his return from Rome he made a detailed report to Hitler. On Ley's conversation with Ciano see *DDI*, 9th ser., ii, No. 491, pp. 377–82 (6 Dec. 1939); cf. also ibid., No. 571, pp. 435 ff. (12 Dec. 1939), with an Italian comment on the Berlin echo of Ley's visit.

[78] Cf. the summary by Hillgruber, 'Hitler-Stalin-Pakt', 13–16.

[79] Schütt, 'Stahlpakt', 509.

[80] On developments in the summer of 1940 cf. Schreiber, 'Mittelmeerraum', 69–84; Cecil, *Hitler's Decision*, 68–76; Hillgruber, 'Hitlers Wendung'; generally on German strategy and Hitler's intention to attack the USSR: Leach, *German Strategy*, 38–71 (Oct. 1939–July 1940).

2. Italy as a Coalition Partner

therefore been reliably informed by Ley, at least as regards Hitler's unchanged basic attitude—which casts considerable doubt on the usual belief that Mussolini was genuinely censuring Hitler's co-operation with Moscow as a betrayal of the National Socialist revolution.

The international repercussions of Ciano's speech of 16 December[81] might have suggested that it was a success with regard to his own anti-German policy and also with regard to Mussolini's calculations. Yet the foreign minister sadly deceived himself when he assumed that his remarks had tolled the knell for the 'funeral of the Axis'.[82] Mussolini certainly intended no turn-about in his foreign policy.[83] His conversation with Himmler on 20 December in Rome once more confirmed this. Ciano, disturbed by the satisfaction displayed by Himmler after his two-hour talk, subsequently learnt that Mussolini had assured the totally anti-Soviet Reich leader of the SS that he would never allow a German defeat to take place. To Ciano, this was 'already a lot', but he feared that Mussolini had 'gone even further'.[84]

Himmler's visit to Rome also took the sting out of the South Tyrolean issue. Between the Axis partners an arrangement acceptable to both sides was beginning to take shape. This did not mean that the problem had actually been solved. However, quite apart from the financial problems already mentioned, the mood among South Tyroleans was clearly swinging over in the spring of 1940, and increasingly so after Germany's victory over France. This emerged, among other things, from the line of argument of the Arbeitsgemeinschaft der Optanten für Deutschland (Working Party of Optants for Germany). In the summer of 1940 this body took up the demand—propagated by the Völkischer Kampfring Südtirols (Ethnic Fighting-circle of South Tyrol) during the option period which ran until 31 December 1939—that a united vote for Germany should be accompanied by the decision, also if possible unanimous, to remain in the province. Underlying this change of front on the resettlement question was, on the one hand, the hope that South Tyrol might after all be incorporated into the Reich, as after the French defeat it should be possible to compensate Italy in some other way, and, on the other, a growing belief that Hitler would eventually use military means to settle matters with Mussolini, who had remained neutral too long and who, even after entering the war, had pushed ahead with his fortification work on the *vallo alpino* regardless of cost.[85]

As matters stood in December 1939 it can be said that, to the extent that Himmler had succeeded in dispelling Mussolini's doubts about German

---

[81] Schreiber, *Revisionismus*, 250–1.
[82] Ciano, *Diary 1939–1943*, 185 (19 Dec. 1939).
[83] Schreiber, *Revisionismus*, 248–54.
[84] Ciano, *Diary 1939–1943*, 187 (21 Dec. 1939).
[85] Cf. also the arrangement on South Tyrol negotiated between Himmler and Guido Buffarini-Guidi, under-secretary of state in the Italian foreign ministry, which came as a great relief to Mussolini: *DDI*, 9th ser., ii, No. 681, p. 531 (22 Dec. 1939), and appendix VI, pp. 619–22. On the persisting problems of South Tyrol cf. Steurer, *Südtirol*, 385, 397–401, and esp. Gable, 'Italy'.

policy,[86] Ciano's hopes of a break between Germany and Italy were becoming unrealistic. However, this did not mean that after 21 December Italian mistrust of Germany's power-political objectives had altogether been dispelled. There were certainly numerous occasions for such mistrust. Immediately after Himmler's success with the Duce a speech made by the deputy mayor of Prague, Dr Joseph Pfitzner, at the Deutsches Haus there led to violent diplomatic upheavals between Berlin and Rome. Pfitzner, whose remarks have to be read in close connection with the South Tyrolean issue, called in December 1939 for a 'swift settling of accounts' with the Italians. To him, not only the entire Alpine region but also the north Italian plain were 'German space'. For centuries, he said, Germany had endeavoured to reach the Mediterranean; Trieste, above all, must become German. Against the background of such objectives he interpreted the Anschluss of 1938 as a prelude to the annexation of northern Italy, including the Po plain. He also demanded the consolidation of German positions in the Balkan countries in order to control Italy's communications with her African colonies and reduce her influence on the northern Slav nations, in the Danubian region, and in the Balkans generally.[87] Mussolini's reaction to this speech, according to Ciano, was to say that for the first time he wanted Germany defeated. And as, just at that time, the Italian military attaché reported from Berlin that he had it from a reliable source that the German attack on Belgium and Holland was imminent, the Duce expressed readiness to inform the Belgians and Dutch of this discreetly,[88] which his foreign minister actually did on 30 December.[89]

Nevertheless, it is not the case that such frictions called the Axis alliance between Germany and Italy in doubt. As Ciano observed resignedly, likewise at the end of December, Mussolini continued to be pro-German and was preparing for Italy to enter the war on Germany's side—exactly what Ciano had been trying to prevent ever since August 1939. The foreign minister was still left with the hope that the reality of Italy's armament situation would put the brakes on Mussolini. According to the experts, those war preparations—even assuming unrestricted supplies of raw materials and a doubling of performance in the factories—could not be completed before October 1942. To Ciano, therefore, the war, for the moment, seemed a long way off.[90]

The shadow-boxing between Rome and Berlin entered a decisive phase when, at the beginning of January 1940, Mussolini, who had talked to Ley and Himmler but had had no direct exchange of ideas with Hitler, sent him a letter[91] which the majority of historians regard as an indication that Italian

---

[86] Cf. Latour, *Südtirol*, 65–6.
[87] In detail Schreiber, *Revisionismus*, 68; Wiskemann, *Axis*, 182.
[88] Ciano, *Diary 1939–1943*, 188 (26 Dec. 1939).
[89] Ibid. 191 (30 Dec. 1939).
[90] Ibid. 191–2 (31 Dec. 1939).
[91] The letter is published in *DGFP* D viii, No. 504, pp. 604–9 (3 Jan. 1940); *DDI*, 9th ser., iii, No. 33, pp. 19–22 (5 Jan. 1940); *Hitler e Mussolini*, 33–9. The correct date is 5 Jan.; it is the draft of the letter that dates from 3 Jan.

policy was then endeavouring to free itself from German influence.[92] The letter, it should be remembered, was written at a time when Mussolini was making the most varied remarks about German policy. Read as a whole, however, it leaves no doubt that Mussolini continued to see the Western democracies as the enemy and Germany as his ally.[93] True, the Duce criticized Hitler, and he also backed Ciano's speech of 16 December, which had been sharply criticized in Germany. But an overall assessment of the letter suggests that these emphases were carefully calculated and that they slotted perfectly into Mussolini's attempts to use a little pressure in order to gain information and, at the same time, to make his own stance clearer. He justified his co-operation with France and Britain on the grounds of compelling economic needs. He also made it clear that there would be neither a repetition of 1915 nor any co-operation with the Western allies in the Balkans. Mussolini's suggestion of a new regulation of German–Polish relations, his remarks on Finland, and his warning against an offensive in the west were—as Ciano believed[94]—probably intended only as advice. It is significant that there was no alternative concept for the event that German foreign policy would not change. His observations concerning the Soviet Union were grandiloquent. Basically they were mere bombast and, if one can take such remarks seriously, boiled down to the suggestion that Germany should first of all turn east, in order subsequently, along with Italy, to defeat the democracies. After all this it was only logical that Mussolini should conclude his letter with the assurance that, at all events, he stood unreservedly by Hitler and would implement their brotherhood-in-arms as soon as his material conditions permitted. Admittedly the remark that Italy would hold herself available as Germany's 'reserve' in case of need might also reflect Mussolini's continuing hope of keeping out of the conflict and acting as the decisive political force in a possible compromise peace.[95] This, however, did not rule out his readiness to provide for military assistance in a situation in line with his above-mentioned calculations, and certainly does not imply any distancing from Hitler. Reservations—as suggested above—are justified as regards the strength of the Duce's ideological antagonism to the Soviet Union, emphasized though it was in the letter. For one thing, Mussolini knew from an excellent source that Hitler was keeping to his plan for the conquest of living-space in the east, and, for another, Italy was entirely flexible with regard to her relations with the USSR. This was true regardless of power-political conflicts.[96]

---

[92] Cf. Cliadakis, 'Neutrality and War', 177–8; Siebert, *Italiens Weg*, 394–9; Wiskemann, *Axis*, 187–8; considerable doubt about such an interpretation is expressed by e.g. André, 'La politica estera', 118–19.

[93] Ciano, *Diary 1939–1943*, 191–2 (31 Dec. 1939). Cf. also Anfuso, *Roma, Berlino*, 138; Smith, *Roman Empire*, 197–201: the portrait painted there of a paralysed, totally undecided Mussolini does not seem to correspond to historical truth.

[94] Ciano, *Diary 1939–1943*, 191–2 (31 Dec. 1939).

[95] Thus De Felice, 'Beobachtungen', 326.

[96] Cf. Siebert, *Italiens Weg*, 372–6.

It should be pointed out in this connection that the possibility of a German *rapprochement* with the Soviet Union had been quite specifically discussed in April 1939, when Göring informed Mussolini of his intention to encourage Hitler to take such a step.[97] Some German circles, whose views the field marshal evidently shared, believed that it was worth a try, seeing that Stalin in his address to the Eighteenth Party Congress on 10 March[98]—and again by his ready acceptance of the coup against Prague—seemed to have signalled that he would not let himself be used as 'cannon-fodder' for the democracies. Mussolini at the time had 'welcomed [Göring's] idea most warmly and said that in Italy too they had had similar ideas for some time'. There had in fact been an unmistakable relaxation in Rome's relations with Moscow, which entirely confirmed the German observations as expressed by Göring. As for the ideological differences, so promptly invoked on other occasions, Mussolini noted that 'in their ideological struggle against plutocracy and capitalism the Axis powers had to a certain extent the same objectives as the Russian regime'.[99] In so far as tactical co-operation with the Soviet government was concerned, Italy's political leadership was thus no less adaptable than Germany's.

Mussolini's letter of 5 January had no influence on Hitler's policy. To him it was finally clear that Italy would only enter the war after further major successes by the Wehrmacht.[100] Ciano had expected an offhand reaction by Hitler from the outset,[101] and after an extensive discussion between Attolico and Ribbentrop, the foreign minister, on 10 January, Rome had to assume that Mussolini's foray had failed.[102] The Germans in fact delayed sending a written reply until 10 March, when Ribbentrop went to Rome under changed political circumstances. Mussolini for his part had been more clearly moving towards the German view since early January, and from the end of the month Ciano was convinced that Italy's entry into the war was firmly decided on, even though the date remained open.[103] The realization that his plan to influence German policy by holding back had failed led Mussolini into a 'flight forward' in February 1940. No doubt Italy's position between Germany and the Allies presented Rome with complicated problems, but, seen objectively, there was nobody and nothing to force Mussolini to take a stand against the

---

[97] *DGFP* D vi, No. 211, pp. 258–63 (18 Apr. 1939); cf. Shirer, *Rise and Fall*, 579–80.
[98] *DGFP* D vi, No. 1, pp. 1 ff. (13 Mar. 1939); cf. vol. i of the present work, IV.VI.4 (Messerschmidt).
[99] *DGFP* D vi, No. 211, pp. 258–63 (18 Apr. 1939). Cf. also Mussolini's reflections, which, on the same basis, even envisaged a press campaign in Sept.–Oct. 1939 to explain to the Italians that Bolshevism had turned into 'a kind of Slavic Fascism'; on this see Ciano, *Diary 1939–1943*, 167 (16 Oct. 1939).
[100] 'Führer Conferences', 79 (26 Jan. 1940).
[101] Ciano, *Diary 1939–1943*, 193–4 (5 Jan. 1940).
[102] *DGFP* D viii, No. 518, pp. 636–40 (10 Jan. 1940); *DDI*, 9th ser., iii, No. 78, p. 54 (10 Jan. 1940).
[103] Cf. Schreiber, *Revisionismus*, 254.

Western powers except his own political calculations.[104] After the end of February he seemed to be even more firmly convinced that the Allies would lose the war, and Ciano held that this belief was the basis of Mussolini's policy from the beginning of 1940. There was talk of territorial claims against France and of the inalienable need for free access to the high seas.[105] It is probably in such reflections, rather than in the effects of British economic warfare, that the decisive element of Mussolini's calculations must be seen.[106] British pressure, however, probably accelerated Mussolini's decision.[107] This was in fact taken at the time of the German–Italian and Anglo-Italian economic negotiations of February 1940, to be discussed below. Yet Germany's enormous difficulties in meeting Italy's economic requirements—difficulties which had clearly emerged just at that time—should have warned Mussolini against a course leading to war with the Allies.[108]

(b) Economic Aspects

The difficulties of the Axis powers are most convincingly demonstrated by a few data on Italy's economic situation; these also reveal—at least partially—the two countries' strategic structures, which ran fundamentally counter to a German–Italian military alliance. Not only did Italy not possess a level of industrialization commensurate with a modern war economy,[109] but she was very largely dependent on imports of all kinds of raw materials.[110] Thus the Italian economy, even in peacetime, needed some three to four million tonnes of crude oil annually; its requirements in the event of war were estimated at 8.5m. t. Italian production in 1939 yielded a mere 153,265 t., of which 141,220 came from Albania.[111] In order to improve this decidedly precarious situation

---

[104] De Felice, 'Beobachtungen', 326–7.

[105] Ciano, *Diary 1939–1943*, 212 (25 Feb. 1940).

[106] Cf. Schreiber, *Revisionismus*, 222–8; Siebert, *Italiens Weg*, 403–8, while emphasizing that for Mussolini political considerations had priority over economic ones, does not draw the conclusion that, from the Duce's subjective point of view, there was no alternative for him but to align himself with the German course. The effect of Britain's economic measures would seem to be overestimated in Cliadakis, 'Neutrality and War', 179–80, and Schütt, 'Stahlpakt', 514.

[107] Only in this sense can one agree with the interpretation offered—in line with Faldella, *L'Italia*, 61–2—in Bandini, *Tecnica della sconfitta*, 276–9. On British–Italian economic relations see also Knox, *Mussolini*, 71–5.

[108] Clough, *Economic History*, 209–59, presents a good survey of the economic policy of Fascist Italy; cf. Schreiber, *Revisionismus*, 217–31; Siebert, *Italiens Weg*, 384–5, 403–8.

[109] Bocca, *Storia*, 50 ff.; a good picture is provided in De Grand, *Italian Fascism*, 105–16, who concentrates on the structures of the Italian war economy and the social implications of rearmament. Cf. also 'Die wichtigsten Firmen der italienischen Rüstungsindustrie', ed. Institut für Weltwirtschaft an der Universität Kiel (May 1940), BA-MA RW 19 appendix I/650; *Dictionnaire*, ii. 973.

[110] These facts were also allowed for in the German paper exercises, especially after war preparations against Britain and France had started in 1939. Cf. e.g. OKW/WStb/W Wi VI, No. 5015/39g., 'Vortrag des Kapitän zur See Dose...über "Möglichkeiten der Versorgung Deutschlands/Italiens in einem Krieg mit den Westmächten aus dem voraussichtlich neutralen europäischen Raum"' (20 June 1939), BA-MA Wi/I 339.

[111] On this Bandini, *Tecnica della sconfitta*, 354–88, here 367–71; Bocca, *Storia*, 50, 142–3; different data in Favagrossa, *Perchè perdemmo la guerra*, 81.

in the event of war Italian scientists were experimenting with the production of synthetic fuels, though—unlike their German colleagues—without appreciable success. The only noteworthy improvement was in refining capacity. Whereas in 1934 Italy had imported the relatively insignificant quantity of 143,000 t. of crude oil, the figure for 1938 was 1,474,000 t. This meant a saving of foreign currency urgently needed for other imports, as processed oil was of course substantially more expensive than crude. However, the country remained dependent on imports.[112] As the targets of the Italian government's autarky programme[113] could not even remotely be reached in this field, stockpiling acquired major importance in connection with preparations for war. Precise figures are not provided in available sources, but such data as exist make it possible to calculate reasonably realistic figures. It is known, for instance, that, at the time Italy entered the war, the Italian navy had fuel-oil reserves of between 1.7m. and 2m. t.[114] If Italian naval forces accounted for 676,560 t. during the first seven war months of 1940 and for 1,123,148 t. in 1941, this means—assuming that the navy continued to be dependent on stockpiled fuel—that its reserves were as good as exhausted by the turn of 1941/2.[115] The air force is thought to have had stocks of 130,000 to 142,000 t. of aviation spirit, not counting supplies of units stationed in the Aegean and in Ethiopia. This was sufficient, against pessimistic forecasts, for nearly a year of active operations.[116] Least reliable are the figures for the army. General Carlo Favagrossa, the minister responsible for war production, reported that in June 1940 the ground forces had at their disposal sufficient fuel for about eight months' warfare.[117] Since he proceeded from an estimate based on conventional warfare, one may assume a total amount of 200,000 t. The large-scale war of movement which subsequently developed in North Africa naturally overturned all such calculations.[118] All in all, the army, navy, and air force consumed some 5,312,000 t. of fuel between June 1940 and the armistice in

---

[112] Cf. 'Die Selbstversorgungsmöglichkeiten und die versorgungspolitischen Maßnahmen Italiens auf dem Gebiet der Mineralölwirtschaft', ed. Institut für Weltwirtschaft an der Universität Kiel (May 1940), BA-MA RW 19, appendix I/648; according to Favagrossa, *Perchè perdemmo la guerra*, 81, only 33,000 t. of synthetic fuel was produced in Italy in 1939.

[113] 'Die Selbstversorgungsmöglichkeiten' (previous n.), 3-4. On the autarky programme and its implementation cf. also D'Auria, *L'Italia contemporanea*, 249-54; Catalano, *L'economia italiana*; id., 'L'économie de guerre'; Raspin, 'Aspekte', 204-11.

[114] Bandini, *Tecnica della sconfitta*, 374 ff.; Bernotti, *Guerra nel Mediterraneo*, 27; Bocca, *Storia*, 142-3.

[115] *La marina italiana*, i. 245; ibid. iv. 27.

[116] Bandini, *Tecnica della sconfitta*, 376 ff.; Santoro, *L'aeronautica italiana*, i. 53-4.

[117] Favagrossa, *Perchè perdemmo la guerra*, 27; cf. also DGFP D viii, No. 236, p. 263 (10 Oct. 1939): report by Rome embassy to foreign ministry that Italy had at her disposal reserves of liquid fuel amounting to 930,000 t., excluding naval stocks. In detail: 25,000 t. of aviation spirit, 119,000 t. of motor-fuel, 260,000 t. of heavy oil for diesel engines. These quantities, according to Italian information, would ensure the army's supplies for one month at the most. The problems of supplying the North African theatre of war, which began to emerge early, are discussed in Creveld, *Supplying War*, 180-201; for 1940-2, see Stegemann, Part V below.

[118] Bandini, *Tecnica della sconfitta*, 378; Bocca, *Storia*, 143.

September 1943. Given the above-mentioned stockpiles, to which must be added German deliveries of at least 3,572,000 t. and 860,000 t. from Italian production, it follows that only some 1.3m. t. would have been available for civilian consumption throughout those thirty-nine months. Yet the civilian sector required at least 1.5m. t. annually, assuming rigorous restrictions. This deficit was made good primarily by the 2m. t. supplied by Romania up to July 1943, and by captured stocks from France, Yugoslavia, Greece, and Tunisia. Added to this were the secret reserves held by nearly all civil and military authorities. All this makes it difficult to judge whether the disastrous fuel shortage repeatedly invoked by Italy during the war was really quite as precarious as it was represented. A reliable judgement on this point would require precise statistics on consumption in different spheres and on the simultaneous replenishment of fuel. However, these figures are lacking; all we have is global data.[119]

Thus, if one assumes that Italian military and political personnel correctly assessed their country's inadequate supply situation, then one must be astonished at the refusal over several weeks to allow oil obtained by the German navy to be discharged in Italian ports. The Germans were willing to make far-reaching concessions, and the Italian navy could have greatly benefited from the transaction. But Rome was not even willing to make colonial ports available. Specifically this concerned 200,000 t. of diesel oil waiting at Baytown near Houston for shipment to some south European port. Destinations in northern Europe would have aroused the suspicion of the US control authorities. By the time the Italians eventually decided to approve this basically safe enterprise, with the entire cargo of fuel remaining in the country, it was too late. The Allied surveillance system, whose efficiency had improved in the meantime, apparently no longer authorized the shipment because of its German implications.[120]

If one considers the situation following Italy's entry into the war from the aspect of logistic requirements, it becomes obvious that the seizure of petroleum sources had to be a priority objective of Italian warfare. Once it was realized that the war would be prolonged, the strategists could no longer close their eyes to this truth. This applied even more to the period when, owing to the attack on the Soviet Union, German assistance to Italy was becoming ever more difficult. The military in Rome were faced from the outset with the same kind of problems as their colleagues in Berlin and later in Tokyo. It was not that they underrated the importance of oil in modern warfare or that they did not realize where the wanted raw material was to be found; however, when, after the armistice with France, it turned out that Mussolini had badly mis-

---

[119] Extensively on this problem Bandini, *Tecnica della sconfitta*, 379–88.
[120] See Schreiber, *Revisionismus*, 211–14; on the German navy's efforts to obtain oil from the US and Mexico cf. Compton, *Swastika and Eagle*, 132.

calculated and the war would continue, the Italian armed forces lacked all the prerequisites for reaching the vital oilfields in the Middle East.[121]

Mussolini's fateful mistakes in assessing the military situation in May–June 1940 do not reflect on his concept of the war as such. As far as modern warfare was concerned, he seemed to be well aware of the interdependence between political and military freedom of action on the one hand and economic self-sufficiency on the other.[122] He certainly pressed for national coal production to be stepped up as early as 1935, with a view to cutting back on oil imports, and for metals and synthetic fuels to be produced. He was thus taking account of the most important bulk products alongside oil—coal and steel.

The German side showed a great deal of interest in this development and was in possession of quite good information on progress made. It was known in Berlin that the Italians had been able to increase their relatively modest output of steel from 1,800,000 t. in 1934 to 2,209,117 t. by the end of 1935 and to as much as 2,321,000 t. in 1939.[123] Even so, the Reichsamt für Wirtschaftsausbau (Reich Office for Economic Development) as late as 1939 estimated that roughly 70 to 80 per cent of Italian steel production came from imported scrap.[124] Italian pig-iron production improved from 671,000 t. in 1929 to 1,005,000 t. in 1939.[125] It must be borne in mind, however, that processing of Italian ores was regarded as decidedly expensive. Basically they were not suitable for a peacetime economy at all. From 1937 onward Italy had therefore increasingly resorted to Spanish deliveries. Her involvement in the Spanish civil war facilitated this, and it was now possible to meet increased requirements.[126] On an international scale Italian output continued to be of scarcely more than slight importance. This is shown very clearly by comparison with other countries. Thus Germany in 1939 produced a total of 22,319,000 t. of crude steel, 18,258,000 t. of pig-iron, and 16,210,000 t. of rolling-mill products,[127] while by 1938 the USA produced 28,805,000 t. of

---

[121] See Bandini, *Tecnica della sconfitta*, 365 ff., with harsh criticism of the neglect of this problem in Italy. As regards practical measures, one can agree with Bandini, though it is not correct that the importance of fuel was not realized; cf. Catalano, 'Les ambitions', 17, who argues convincingly that the Fascist regime was correctly assessing the significance of oil supplies for the impending war.

[122] Guarneri, *Autarkie*, 3, 22–3.

[123] D'Auria, *L'Italia contemporanea*, 250; *Statistisches Jahrbuch* (1941–2), p. 75 of 'Internationale Übersichten'. The figures include ingot steel and weld steel. In 1938 production had reached a peak with 2,377,000 t., cf. also Bocca, *Storia*, 51; and for the various metals used in steel improvement esp. Favagrossa, *Perchè perdemmo la guerra*, 87 ff.

[124] Cf. Raspin, 'Aspekte', 208.

[125] *Statistisches Jahrbuch* (1941–2), p. 75 of 'Internationale Übersichten'; D'Auria, *L'Italia contemporanea*, 250, gives production in 1935 as 663,383 t.

[126] Raspin, 'Aspekte', 208; cf. also Broué and Témime, *Révolution*, 436 ff.; Guarneri, *Battaglie economiche*, 134 ff.

[127] *Statistisches Jahrbuch* (1941–2), 197 (without Bohemia and Moravia). Cf. also vol. i of the present work, II.IV.3 (Volkmann), with figures (and survey of developments for 1928–39) which diverge somewhat from those given above.

2. Italy as a Coalition Partner

crude steel, Britain 10,745,000, and France 6,137,000.[128] These figures reveal Italy's industrial backwardness at the outbreak of the war. Not even during the period of non-belligerence, from September 1939 to June 1940, was Italy consistently able to utilize available production capacities for the requirements of the war economy. When the country was eventually at war, its slight stockpiles—covering, on average, the needs for two or three months—did not suffice for a full-capacity operation of the armaments industry.[129]

Italy was also largely dependent on imports for her coal supplies. In 1939 Italian mines produced 2,024,000 t. of hard coal and 1,100,000 t. of lignite (brown coal). Yet the hard-coal requirements of industry in 1938 already amounted to approximately 13,855,000 t., which meant that some 12m. t. had to be imported annually.[130] At no time after June 1940 was it possible to reduce this dependence on imports, even though coal production was one of the few areas in which Italy increased her output during the war. In 1942 she actually produced 5,800,000 t. It should, however, be mentioned, in order to convey a picture of the overall situation, that over the same period agricultural production—taking 1938 as 100 per cent—declined to 84 per cent and industrial production to 89 per cent overall. It should also be remembered, whenever Italy's economic potency is to be assessed, that her peacetime industrial production had accounted for a mere 2.7 per cent of world production. The corresponding figure for Germany was 10.7 per cent and for Japan 3.5 per cent. By way of comparison, the countries of the coalition which subsequently confronted the Axis accounted for a share of about 70 per cent.[131]

These shortages and weaknesses of the war economy were appreciated in Rome. Earlier on, the war in Abyssinia had shown that Britain was able to jeopardize Italy's raw-material base by coal and oil sanctions,[132] whereas the Third Reich was able—in theory—to cope with any bottlenecks in coal supplies. As early as 1929 Germany—mainly as a result of reparation payments—delivered to Italy some 5,500,000 t. of coal, representing 37.9 per cent of total Italian imports. Although Britain at that time was still exporting 7,100,000 t. of coal to Italy and thereby had a share of 48.7 per cent in Italy's imports, this was nevertheless, from the British point of view, a disturbing

---

[128] *Statistisches Jahrbuch* (1942-2), p. 75 of 'Internationale Übersichten'; considerably divergent figures in Bocca, *Storia*, 51.

[129] Schinzinger, 'Wirtschaftsbeziehungen', 177; cf. also Bocca, *Storia*, 52-5; Faldella, *L'Italia*, 106-7, 116 ff.; Favagrossa, *Perchè perdemmo la guerra*, 84-7; Smith, *Roman Empire*, 216; *Survey of International Affairs*, iii. 217 ff., also on Italy's financial position; cf. on this point Catalano, 'L'économie de guerre', 111-16.

[130] *Statistisches Jahrbuch* (1941-2), p. 193 of 'Internationale Übersichten'; on this also 'Die Selbstversorgungsmöglichkeiten und die versorgungspolitischen Maßnahmen Italiens in der Kohlewirtschaft', ed. Institut für Weltwirtschaft an der Universität Kiel (Apr. 1940), BA-MA RW 19 appendix I/655.

[131] Bocca, *Storia*, 51; Raspin, 'Aspekte', 208-9; Schinzinger, 'Wirtschaftsbeziehungen', 176-7.

[132] Petersen, *Hitler—Mussolini*, 442 ff.; on the economic consequences also D'Auria, *L'Italia contemporanea*, 249-50; Raspin, 'Aspekte', 206-7.

trend compared with 87 per cent before the First World War—a trend which London endeavoured to reverse prior to the Abyssinian crisis. Yet it was just that crisis which induced the Italian government to free itself progressively from its ties with Britain. From 31 July 1935 onwards there existed a state import monopoly for coal in Italy, and for strategic reasons the country increasingly reorientated itself towards Germany. The German share of Italian coal imports thereupon increased within a single year from 51.1 per cent in 1935 to 63.9 per cent in 1936. In connection with armament measures for the Abyssinian war, as a consequence of the League of Nations sanctions and the general difficulty of finding a suitable market for Italian exports—the negative balance of payment resulting from marketing problems affected rearmament through the lack of foreign currency for imports—there began a trend which, long before the war, made Italy into what after 1940 could no longer be overlooked: an inferior member of the German large-area economy.[133]

In order to demonstrate the dangerous consequences which the war between Germany and Britain might have for the Italian economy, it is not enough to point to the coal-production volume of these two main suppliers of Italy. In theory either Germany, with a hard-coal output of 187,944,000 t. in 1939, or Britain, then with 236,800,000 t.,[134] could have met the Italian requirement of a little over 12m. t. of hard coal.[135] But Italy's lack of foreign currency ruled out a straightforward switch to British coal[136] if, as the result of German–British economic warfare, Germany found herself under a naval blockade; moreover, the capacity of the rail link between Germany and Italy was too limited to replace the sea route without problems.[137]

At the beginning of the war Germany, with a delivery volume of 6,828,950 t. of hard coal—a volume stepped up in the course of 1940 to 11,003,130 t.—was Italy's most important supplier of coal.[138] German exports therefore exceeded the quotas considered feasible when the German–Italian trade agreement of 13 February 1939 was concluded. By that agreement the Axis powers intended, among other things, to regulate the exchange of raw materials, which seemed for the time being to have reached its limits, so that in the event of war it could be further intensified. However, it was already pointed out at the time that, in the event of a European conflict, some 10m. t. of material which in peacetime was predominantly shipped by sea would have to be taken to Italy by rail and road. Experts assessed the capacity of the Brenner, Tauern, and

---

[133] Quoted according to Milward, *War*, 37; cf. Petersen, *Hitler—Mussolini*, 451–4; Funke, *Sanktionen*, 48–81, extensively on German–Italian economic relations.
[134] *Statistisches Jahrbuch* (1941–2), p. 60 of 'Internationale Übersichten'.
[135] BA-MA RW 19 (n. 130 above), appendix II/655, p. 3. Favagrossa, *Perchè perdemmo la guerra*, 79, speaks of a need for 16 m. t., which resulted in demands on Germany for some 14.4 m. t., though only 11.6 m. was attained.
[136] Schreiber, *Revisionismus*, 255–6; *Survey of International Affairs*, iii. 217 ff.
[137] Cf. BA-MA Wi/I 339 (n. 110 above), pp. 32–5; BA-MA RW 19 (n. 130 above) appendix I/655, pp. 4–5; cf. Schinzinger, 'Wirtschaftsbeziehungen', 174–5.
[138] *Statistisches Jahrbuch* (1941–2), 301.

2. Italy as a Coalition Partner

Semmering rail links at 7,700,000 t. annually, and that of the possibly available St Gotthard railway at 1,920,000 t. The latter therefore played a vital role in the solution to the German–Italian transport problem. Needless to say, the Germans as well as the Italians realized that even the most careful calculations of this kind might at any time be upset by the weather. In point of fact, weather-related difficulties caused a shortfall of 1.5m. t. of coal deliveries in 1938.[139]

In November 1939 the Allies intensified their naval blockade against German coal exports. Allegedly this was a reaction to the use of floating mines by Germany, but it is probably more to the point to see it as a British economic-warfare measure designed to isolate the Reich. Italy's economy, which in September and October had still received 670,000 t. of coal a month from Germany—only an insignificant shortfall from the 750,000 t. agreed in principle in 1939 as a monthly delivery quota—now seemed to be directly threatened in its ability to function. Yet by rail it was only possible to transport a maximum of 277,000 t. in October, and this figure dropped to 175,000 t. in November. During that month some 330,000 t. of hard coal reached Italy via Rotterdam—which was not included in the blockade—and thence by the overland route.[140] This development clearly indicated that alarming bottlenecks in Italy's energy supplies could only be avoided by a substantial expansion of overland transport capacities. Two solutions offered themselves to this problem—and this was true especially for the period following the imposition of the Allied blockade in March 1940, which also halted German coal exports via Rotterdam: an increase in the frequency of deliveries by train, which was of course subject to technical limitations, and the extensive use of the Swiss rail network. During the period of Italian non-belligerence this was no problem: Switzerland was neutral under international law and maintained economic relations with both Germany and Italy. When they imposed their total naval blockade against the Reich, the Allies evidently underestimated the amount of coal which Hitler actually succeeded in delivering to Italy by way of the St Gotthard and the Simplon.[141] But even after Mussolini's entry into the war, which went hand in hand with—though it was not the cause of—a deterioration of German–Swiss relations, the Berne government ultimately had no choice but to yield to the power-political realities brought about by the defeat of France. During June and July 1940 Switzerland was virtually cut off from overseas and from Europe; she was isolated within the German–Italian power-sphere, on which unoccupied

---

[139] *Aufzeichnungen über die deutsch-italienischen Wirtschaftsbeziehungen* (1939), PA Büro St.S., 'Italien', i. 115–18; cf. BA-MA Wi/I 339 (n. 110 above), pp. 32–5.

[140] *Aufzeichnungen über Kohlelieferungen* (8 Jan. 1940), PA Büro St.S., 'Italien', ii. 212; cf. *DGFP* D viii, No. 489, pp. 576–99 (26 Dec. 1939); and *DDI*, 9th ser., ii, No. 543, p. 416 (10 Dec. 1939), according to which 203,000 t. of hard coal arrived in Italy by rail in November.

[141] Bonjour, *Geschichte der schweizerischen Neutralität*, vi. 213; *Survey of International Affairs*, iii. 235; ibid. vii. 14; a survey of the German–Italian rail links is provided by Kreidler, *Eisenbahnen*, 95–6; Schwarz, *The Eye*, 62–6.

France was now also dependent. Only the economic agreements of 9 August 1940, which governed economic relations between Berlin and Berne until the end of 1941, restored normal economic conditions for the Swiss and guaranteed the country access—though admittedly more difficult access—to Italian and French ports. In return Berne had to allow the Axis powers to make use of the Swiss rail network for their transit shipments, with the exception of troop and armament transports. Germany apparently complied with this; at any rate the Swiss customs authorities failed to detect any war-material deliveries until 1945.[142]

From August 1940 onward some 1,800 railway goods wagons a day, loaded with all kinds of cargo, were rolling through Switzerland to Italy. As it was obvious that any closure of the St Gotthard tunnel must result in major supply problems for the Axis powers, the Swiss, despite their generally precarious situation, found that they had a lever for persuading Germany to do mutually advantageous business. Berne demanded of Berlin the right to receive the same goods as were moving through Switzerland to Italy—primarily coal and iron. The Germans, indeed, derived a double advantage from this arrangement, at least after their victory in the west. Previously, although Switzerland had been ready since the outbreak of the war to continue the supply of arms to all belligerent states, Germany had made virtually no use of this offer. The Western powers, anxious to catch up with the German lead in armaments, had therefore been able to utilize Swiss arms-manufacturing capacity to the full until the summer: Switzerland practically became an Allied arms workshop. After the French defeat—the Germans having thought better of their previous attitude—Berne was obliged, in addition to its concessions concerning the Swiss rail network, to deliver to the Third Reich weapons manufactured with German coal and from German steel.[143]

As for an increase in German coal exports towards the end of 1939, this ran into complications at first—primarily because of the already very limited transport space of the German and Italian railways. By October the available wagons no longer sufficed.[144] In November, when deliveries fell short, Rome actually felt itself to be the victim of discrimination, observing that wagon capacity seemed to be lacking for transports to Italy but not to other countries.[145] Of course the Germans tried to refute this accusation and appealed to their Axis partner to mobilize absolutely all reserves. In view

---

[142] Extensively Bonjour, *Geschichte der schweizerischen Neutralität*, vi. 223–7; cf. also C. Howard, 'Switzerland', 211, 216–19; Kimche, *Spying for Peace*, 52 ff., on the domestic situation and military reaction; Zimmermann, 'Die "Nebenfrage Schweiz"'. So far, the best study of Switzerland during the Second World War is Schwarz, *The Eye*; esp. 67–80 on the economic situation.

[143] Cf. the characterization of German–Swiss economic relations in Rings, *Schweiz*, 381–96; Fink, *Schweiz*, 233; Zimmermann, *Schweiz und Großdeutschland*, 420; on trade with Britain cf. Bonjour, 'Wirtschaftliche Beziehungen'.

[144] *DDI*, 9th ser., ii, No. 36, p. 27 (28 Oct. 1939); cf. on this point *DGFP* D viii, No. 192, pp. 207–8 (4 Oct. 1939).

[145] *DDI*, 9th ser., ii, No. 268, p. 230 (20 Nov. 1939).

2. Italy as a Coalition Partner

of the threat to supplies via Rotterdam, consideration was even given to importing coal into Italy from the United States and the USSR.[146] This idea offered itself because by the end of November Germany realized that it would no longer be possible to supply Italy adequately by the overland route. Once the sea route was lost, 44,000 goods wagons would have to be made available —which neither Italy nor Germany was in a position to do. Germany conceded that something had to be done to ensure Italy's coal supplies, but the central problem remained the rail wagons. Its solution was further complicated by the fact that of the German rolling-stock, which was inadequate anyway, 10,000 wagons were not available because the military were keeping them back for a possible offensive by the Wehrmacht.[147] Conversely, the Italians were handing over goods wagons to Hungary and Yugoslavia, who used them to transport merchandise for Britain.[148] Ribbentrop nevertheless instructed the foreign ministry to try to get the military authorities to release their reserved wagons. Simultaneously Berlin urged the Italians to provide a further 7,000 wagons, in addition to the 3,000 already in use.[149] All in all, the coal problem—in line with the hopes of the Italian ambassador in Berlin—was gradually turning from a technical into a political matter which seemed to call for a decision by the Führer.[150] But this was something in which Ciano—who was trying to prevent a political *rapprochement* between Germany and Italy over the coal problem—was not in the least interested.[151]

In December the technical negotiations under preparation for the past few weeks were held in Berlin. Surprisingly, the Italians announced that they did not, as they had demanded until then, require 1m. t. tons of coal by the overland route per month, but only 500,000 t.[152] The Germans—knowing that Italy's coal stocks in November were worse than in August 1939,[153] which was why they were just then considering an intensified utilization of the Swiss railways in order to supply the 12m. t. needed annually by their Axis partner[154]—were completely surprised to hear this, although of course they must have been pleased to know that they only had to make available 10,000 wagons instead of the envisaged 20,000.[155] But very soon, on 28 December, came a denial from Rome. The quota of 500,000 t., they said, had been suggested only because Germany insisted on a provision of wagons in a ratio of 2:1. As Italy for the time being was totally unable to provide more than 5,000

---

[146] Ibid., No. 296, pp. 251–2 (22 Nov. 1939).
[147] Ibid., No. 358, pp. 292 ff. (27 Nov. 1939); cf. also No. 419, p. 335 (2 Dec. 1939).
[148] Ibid., No. 359, pp. 294–5 (27 Nov. 1939).
[149] Ibid., No. 444, pp. 351–2 (4 Dec. 1939), and No. 445, p. 352 (4 Dec. 1939).
[150] Ibid., No. 419, p. 335 (2 Dec. 1939).
[151] Ibid., No. 448, p. 353 (4 Dec. 1939).
[152] Ibid., No. 593, pp. 453–6 (14 Dec. 1939); and 'Aufzeichnung über italienische Kohleforderungen' (16 Dec. 1939), PA Büro St.S., 'Italien', ii. 105.
[153] 'Aufzeichnung über deutsche Liefermöglichkeiten' (27 Nov. 1939), PA Büro St.S., 'Italien', ii. 136.
[154] Ibid. (9 Dec. 1939), p. 85.
[155] Ibid. (16 Dec. 1939), p. 105; (26 Dec. 1939), p. 169.

wagons, and Germany would therefore provide only 10,000, this had inevitably resulted in a halving of the maximum amount envisaged. This correction was evidently made after intervention by Mussolini. It is interesting that there was no longer any objection to the request that Italy's coal supplies be treated as a political problem within the context of Italy's war preparations. Rome was concerned with attaining the maximum possible freedom of action *vis-à-vis* Britain in order to rule out a 'repetition of the "tragic moment" of last August'. Italy's ambassador, Attolico, explained the so-called misunderstanding to Ribbentrop, who promised to use his influence to ensure that Germany made 20,000 goods wagons available under all circumstances, even if Italy provided only 5,000.[156] Weather conditions in December—when only 189,000 t. of coal crossed the Alps into Italy[157]—later demonstrated the danger of operating with minimum demands. With the best will on the German side, which no longer made the provision of wagons dependent on any ratios, nothing could change the fact that by the end of January the Reichsbahn was scarcely able to provide more than 10,000 wagons.[158] The foreign ministry was concerned that only 377,000 t. were delivered by rail in January and insisted that the amount be stepped up in February to at least 500,000 t. An attempt was to be made, once the cold period was over, to transport to Italy 750,000 t. of coal per month. Given the provision of additional wagons, this seemed entirely feasible. But the Germans themselves by that time no longer believed in the possibility of supplying 1m. t. per month. Following conversations between representatives of the foreign ministry, the ministries of economics and transport, the Reich commissioner for coal, and the Wehrmacht high command, it even emerged that Berlin could not promise more than 500,000 t. a month even for the frost-free part of the year. The representatives of the different departments were merely prepared to do everything possible to increase the amount of 500,000 t. a month as soon as conditions within Germany permitted.[159]

Government quarters in Berlin nevertheless kept promising to deliver the commodities needed by Italy's economy, even after her entry into the war. They did so despite the fact that it had become obvious even during Italy's non-belligerence that this would be impossible. Although in May 1940 Germany did in fact export 1,050,000 t. of coal to Italy, i.e. 50,000 t. more than the agreed amount,[160] after 10 June 1940 the Italian economy received, each year, amounts considerably below the promised quantities—although it certainly is not correct to say that over a period of twelve months only the quantity

---

[156] Ibid. (28 Dec. 1939), pp. 181 ff. Göring had once before authorized the 20,000 wagons following an intervention by Ribbentrop: ibid. (26 Dec. 1939), p. 169.
[157] Ibid. (8 Jan. 1940), p. 212.
[158] Ibid. (28 Jan. 1940), p. 271.
[159] Ibid. (1 Feb. 1940), pp. 282 ff.
[160] *DGFP* D ix, No. 480, pp. 611 ff. (18 June 1940).

2. Italy as a Coalition Partner

promised for two and a half months was delivered.[161] The Germans tried everything to avoid bottlenecks, and even managed, after Italy's entry into the war, to transport by rail considerably more than had previously been thought possible—but the shortfalls proved unavoidable. Ultimately the deliveries of 12m. t. annually, laid down in the German–Italian economic agreement of 24 February 1940, remained an ideal target that could not be attained. Admittedly the parties had proceeded from the assumption that even a shipment of 500,000 t. a month by the overland route could be guaranteed only if Italy made 5,000 coal wagons available at all times. Germany for her part undertook to make these deliveries in any event, save only where *force majeure* intervened. Otherwise these transports were to enjoy express priority, even if the Reichsbahn had to cope with bottlenecks in domestic traffic.[162] The foreign ministry thus essentially endorsed the views of the departments concerned with the shipments.

In view of transport-related misgivings about Italy's supply situation, Germany's efforts to bring Mussolini into the war must be regarded as somewhat frivolous—the more so as the German ministries were well acquainted with the war-economy position of their Axis partner. The Wehrmacht high command departments concerned with these questions were also, of course, well aware (for example) that Italy was able to cover only 15 per cent of her petroleum, coal, copper, and tin requirements from her own production. Manganese called for 50 per cent imports, and nickel, tungsten, and molybdenum for a full 100 per cent. The high command entertained some hopes with regard to Albania, provided the technical potential for an optimum utilization of the country's mineral resources was created—which meant more mines and improved communications. Given these, the Germans counted on Italy's requirements of iron ore, chromium ore, haematite, and bitumen being met in full. This was decidedly optimistic, however. In actual fact Italy had appreciable quantities only of pyrites, bauxite, sulphur, zinc, lead, magnesium, and mercury. Unhampered mutual support between the Axis partners was possible only to the extent that Germany supplied coal and potassium while Italy supplied, in particular, sulphur, mercury, silk, and hemp.[163] The decisive consideration for the subsequent assessment of Italy's entry into the war

---

[161] This in correction of Schinzinger, 'Wirtschaftsbeziehungen', 176. As regards the German deliveries, which not only failed to reach the 1.2m. t. per month required by Italy, but with an average of 900,000 fell short even of the promised amount of 1m. t., see Schreiber, 'Problemi generali', 84 ff.; cf. also Giannini, 'L'accordo'; Milward, *War*, 88, with a table of imports from Germany for 1937–43.

[162] *DDI* 9th ser., iii, appendix II, pp. 640 ff.; *DGFP* D viii, No. 634, pp. 809 ff. (24 Feb. 1940); but cf. also *KTB OKW* i. 107 (1 Oct. 1940), according to which, by the provision of 2,000 wagons (per day) deliveries of 1m. t. of hard coal were—at least temporarily—implemented.

[163] 'Die Selbstversorgungsmöglichkeiten und die versorgungspolitischen Maßnahmen Italiens auf dem Gebiet der NE-Metalle und sonstigen Mineralien', ed. Institut für Weltwirtschaft an der Universität Kiel (May 1940), BA-MA RW 19 appendix I/656; on the Italian situation generally cf. also D'Auria, *L'Italia contemporanea*, 249–54; details on the economic situation in Favagrossa, *Perchè perdemmo la guerra*, 87–90. Specifically on Albania and its economic potential cf. Pernack,

should have been the realization that her expected military strength and value as an ally depended, as an indispensable condition, on an adequate cover of her coal and crude-oil requirements. Only if Germany and Romania were able to guarantee appropriate deliveries was Mussolini's entry into the war justifiable. With an assessment of this type the Wehrmacht high command ignored for the time being the question of the fighting qualities of the Italian formations. As to the advantages afforded by a neutral Italy, the German view was that, in the field of raw materials, one could expect supplies of sulphur, zinc, roasted pyrites, and mercury, as well as hemp linen, cotton, and silk, also foodstuffs such as rice, vegetables, and fruit, and possibly also some utilization of underused Italian industrial capacities, provided the Reich supplied the necessary raw materials. As for 'transit passage', however, the high command believed that Italy could help only 'to a very modest extent'.[164] In this situation Berlin must have been well content to see Mussolini trying to use his non-belligerence for intensified rearmament and stockpiling—especially as Germany continued to believe that Italy would sooner or later enter the war. Rome meanwhile swiftly established contact with the only potential suppliers of raw materials—the Allies. As London and Paris, for their part, were anxious to prise Italy out of the Axis alliance, Rome found itself in the entirely advantageous position of being able to obtain extensive economic accommodations from Britain and France at the cost of modest concessions.

There was certainly far-reaching agreement among Allied political and military leaders that every effort should be made to keep Mussolini from entering the war on Hitler's side. If only for that reason, Italy was, as a matter of principle, benevolently treated after the outbreak of war in 1939, in spite of fears that she might use the time left to her for pushing ahead with rearmament against the democracies.[165] Paris and London regarded Italy's non-belligerence as a noteworthy success of their diplomacy, even though it was realized that Mussolini had not yet reached a final decision. The Allies, after all, had Ciano's very clear warning: there was no doubt in his mind that Italy would march only on the victorious side. In his opinion, not propaganda but victories alone could induce Mussolini to join the Allied side. If, however, the Germans were victorious, then he would choose confrontation with the Western powers. To prevent this, on 10 September 1939 the French foreign minister, Georges Bonnet, instructed his ambassador in Rome, André François-Poncet, to do all he could to convert Italy's attitude, whose 'provisional character' was obvious, into a 'more unambiguous and more reliable neutrality'; this would amount to a significant 'moral victory' for the Allies.[166]

Probleme, 10–23; according to Pernack the country in 1938 produced 108,000 t. of crude oil, 4,000 t. of coal, and 7,000 t. of chromium ores (p. 173); the principal foreign trade partners were Italy (36.1% of imports and 67% of exports), the US, and Greece (p. 170).

[164] Wi IIIa, 'betr. Italien, Beurteilung der Lage' (14 Dec. 1939), BA-MA Wi/I B 1.64.
[165] Paul-Boncour, *Entre deux guerres*, 162–8.
[166] Bonnet, *Défense*, ii. 384.

2. Italy as a Coalition Partner

Intensification of economic relations between London, Paris, and Rome seemed a suitable way of achieving that end. There was no overlooking the fact that Italy needed economic support in order to act as—from the Allied point of view—a stabilizing force in the Mediterranean and south-east Europe. Orders for merchandise placed with Italian firms served as an incentive.[167] At the beginning of September France offered bilateral trade negotiations, and Rome, after Ciano had persuaded a hesitant Mussolini, accepted.[168] By the middle of the month Franco-Italian talks were held at San Remo, and, at the express wish of the Italian foreign minister, they were kept from the Germans.[169] The result was a secret agreement according to which Italy would supply to France aluminium, pumice, Duralumin, aircraft engines, hemp, lorries, tanker lorries, sulphur, pyrites, silk, and tankers.[170] No doubt all this was material important to the war: however, contrary to British and French statements,[171] the Italians did not sell the bombers asked for or the arms needed by the Allies,[172] but essentially confined themselves to civilian and semi-military merchandise.[173] These exports, together with her deliveries of foodstuffs,[174] as well as her economic co-operation under the Anglo-Italian agreement of October 1939, earned Italy valuable foreign currency,[175] which she tried to use for stockpiling raw materials.[176]

Italian non-belligerence was advantageous to Italy in that it enabled her to crank up her own economy, penetrate into markets previously dominated by Germany, Britain, and France, and boost her share in international transport. At the same time it brought certain benefits not only to the Allies but to Germany, enabling her for a time to slip under the Anglo-French blockade. Needless to say, in so far as the transit of goods destined for Germany was concerned, the Italians, for fear of Allied countermeasures, practised extreme caution. Rome justified its caution by arguing that it did not wish to be drawn

---

[167] *Survey of International Affairs*, iii. 234.

[168] Cf. Ciano, *Diary 1939–1943*, 145–6 (5 Sept. 1939); Bonnet, *Défense*, ii. 382, gives the date as 6 Sept.

[169] Bonnet, *Défense*, ii. 382; Siebert, *Italiens Weg*, 367–8; *Survey of International Affairs*, iii. 234.

[170] Giannini, 'Convegno italo-francese'; cf. *DDI*, 9th ser., i, No. 5, p. 2 (4 Sept. 1939); No. 36, p. 22 (5 Sept. 1939).

[171] Bonnet, *Défense*, ii. 383: 'Italy undertook to make deliveries to France which primarily concerned our national defence and amounted to several billion francs . . . Italy even delivered to us gunpowder, explosives, anti-tank mines and indeed aircraft'; *Survey of International Affairs*, iii. 234.

[172] *DDI*, 9th ser., i, No. 211, pp. 133–4 (15 Sept. 1939); No. 240, pp. 148–9 (16 Sept. 1939).

[173] Ibid., No. 328, p. 201 (19 Sept. 1939); cf. also *DGFP* D viii, No. 231, pp. 253 ff. (10 Oct. 1939). Ciano informed the Germans that 'England and France had tried at first to place large orders in Italy for war equipment, including guns, tanks, and more than 1,000 aeroplanes. Italy had naturally refused.' On this also: 'Betrachtungen über die politische Situation Italiens 1935–1941' (undated), p. 42, PA Dienststelle Ribbentrop 35/i.

[174] Schreiber, *Revisionismus*, 216.

[175] *Survey of International Affairs*, iii. 234. On the British–Italian economic talks from 12 Oct. 1939 to 29 Dec. 1939 generally *DDI*, 9th ser., iii, appendix I, pp. 631–9.

[176] *Survey of International Affairs*, iii. 217–18; Bocca, *Storia*, 69–70.

prematurely into conflict with the Western powers. It also explained its exports to France by the need—in order to avoid a repetition of August 1939—to export finished articles as otherwise the finance for obtaining urgently required raw materials would be lacking.[177]

There was little to object to in this from the German point of view, and even the (time-limited) Anglo-Italian agreement on the blockade issue at the end of 1939 could only meet with consent.[178] But Berlin was worried by the Anglo-Italian negotiations, in progress since November, concerning the purchase by London of Italian aircraft, guns, and other military equipment. At the beginning of February Britain offered generous accommodation in economic matters provided the Italians supplied the war material.[179] The Germans were aware of this development from at least 4 January.[180] They protested, but Italy stood firm. Rome pointed to its shortage of raw materials and once more emphasized the inevitability of exporting. The British meanwhile again gave notice of a total blockade against the Reich, which to Mussolini meant the loss of his coal shipments by sea. London was clearly seeking to squeeze Italy out of the Axis alliance. It even offered to replace German supplies, but Rome, because of its shortage of foreign currency, was unable to provide finance readily. An exchange for arms was ruled out by Italy's own rearmament plans: Mussolini closed his mind on this issue.[181]

London meanwhile continued to seek an agreement, the British having no doubt noticed that there was no unanimity in the Italian cabinet on whether or not war material should be supplied.[182] Lord Halifax, the foreign secretary, announced new proposals, which the ambassador in Rome, Sir Percy Loraine, presented on 13 February 1940.[183] But following Mussolini's renewed rejection of the British ideas the economic talks finally foundered against Italy's own rearmament plans.[184] Immediately afterwards London announced that, as of 1 March, German coal shipments via Rotterdam would also come under the contraband regulations.[185]

Parallel to the Anglo-Italian trade talks ran the economic negotiations between Germany and Italy, already mentioned, but these did not make any real progress until Mussolini intervened personally.[186] Italy thereupon made

---

[177] Schreiber, *Revisionismus*, 215 ff.; Corbino, *Vita economica*, 459–60.
[178] Schreiber, *Revisionismus*, 217–24; *Survey of International Affairs*, vii. 12 ff.; iii. 235–6.
[179] *DDI*, 9th ser., iii, No. 254, pp. 216–19 (3 Feb. 1940).
[180] *DGFP* D viii, No. 509, pp. 617 ff. (4 Jan. 1940).
[181] Schreiber, *Revisionismus*, 226–7.
[182] See Ciano, *Diary 1939–1943*, 206–8 (9–15 Feb. 1940).
[183] *DDI*, 9th ser., iii, No. 300, 254–63 (13 Feb. 1940).
[184] Ciano, *Diary 1939–1943*, 208 (15 Feb. 1940); cf. *Cadogan Diaries*, 254 (11 Feb. 1940); Woodward, *British Foreign Policy*, i. 148. Villari, *Italian Foreign Policy*, is quite wrong in maintaining that Mussolini refused because Italy feared a German invasion and needed the weapons herself in view of the uncertain situation.
[185] Ciano, *Diary 1939–1943*, 209–10 (18 Feb. 1940); cf. Schreiber, *Revisionismus*, 227 ff.; *Survey of International Affairs*, iii. 235.
[186] Ciano, *Diary 1939–1943*, 211 (21 Feb. 1940); cf. Schreiber, *Revisionismus*, 230.

considerable concessions over the surrender of various raw materials which she was herself basically short of, so that even the Germans spoke of Italy making a 'sacrifice'.[187] The new course of Italian foreign policy, even though—as shown by Mussolini's reserve on the transit issue—it represented neither a direct nor the shortest route into the war, was registered in Berlin with satisfaction.[188] Thanks to the Duce's attitude it was no longer difficult to proceed to the signature of the German–Italian economic agreement of 24 February 1940.[189] Germany undertook to deliver 12m. t. of coal, 10,000 t. of crude benzene, 1,500 t. of pure toluene, 2,500 t. of naphthalene, 300 t. of acetone, and 200 t. of magnesium. In return Italy was to supply Germany with 25,000 t. of hemp, 1,500 t. of raw cork, 1,000 t. of tanning materials, 100,000 t. of bauxite, 35,000 t. of zinc ore, 50,000 t. of pyrites, 50,000 t. of roasted pyrites, 70,000 t. of sulphur, 40,000 t. of mercury, 300 t. of boric acid, 2,500 t. of raw tartrates, 105 t. of citrus fruit, 5,000 t. of chestnut-wood extract, 300 t. of sumac extract, and 1,350 t. of various kinds of silk. Added to these were large quantities of tobacco goods, cheese, and rice.

Against the background of the two decisive events of February 1940—the trade arrangements between Rome and Berlin on the one hand, and Mussolini's rejection of the British attempt to bring Italy into the Allied camp by means of economic pressure on the other, with London simultaneously striving to impair Italian rearmament—Ciano and his fellow rebels found themselves in political limbo.[190] In this situation the economic agreement, even though formally it did no more than extend earlier accords of this nature between the Axis powers since 1937, represented an important milestone along the road of Mussolini's preparations for entry into the war.

(c) Military Aspects

On a par with political and economic relations between Berlin and Rome, military collaboration between the Axis partners is a further indicator of the nature of the alliance and its development during the period of Italian non-belligerence. After all, the Pact of Steel was a military alliance which implied no more and no less than an all-out coalition in the event of war. After May 1939, therefore, it would have been reasonable to expect political, economic, and military contacts far in excess of the scope of German–Italian co-operation hitherto.

However, as is well known, the Axis alliance remained a decidedly unproductive partnership, a fact strikingly proved by the events of August 1939.

---

[187] *DGFP* D viii, No. 627, pp. 800–1 (22 Feb. 1940); Italy delivered, among other things, 1,500 t. of hemp and 3,500 t. of copper.

[188] *DDI*, 9th ser., iii, No. 514, pp. 445–6 (10 Mar. 1940).

[189] See n. 160 above: this was the fourth secret protocol. The first had been signed on 14 May 1937, the second on 18 Dec. 1937, and the third on 13 Feb. 1939.

[190] Cf. 'Betrachtungen über die politische Situation Italiens 1935–1941' (undated), pp. 31–42, esp. 32–3: PA Dienststelle Ribbentrop 35/i.

On the other hand, given the general structural conditions of the two countries, the alliance could not possibly, during the three months after the signing of the Pact, have been developed into an effective coalition even if the attempt had been made. However, as both Hitler and Mussolini continued after September 1939 to work for Italy's entry into the war, and moreover made this clear, the question has to be asked—apart from the political and economic problems raised by Italy's participation—to what extent the conditions described above had an influence on German–Italian military relations between the beginning of the war and June 1940. In this way further light can be thrown on the nature of the Rome–Berlin Axis.

In mid-August 1939 German military circles were aware that Italy—as had been recognized at the conclusion of the Pact of Steel—would need a few more years to adapt the state of her armaments to the requirements of a major war. Italy lacked raw materials, the equipment of her forces was thought to be inadequate, and her long coastline had virtually no fortifications. In North Africa the state of the Italian troops did not suggest the ability to launch offensive operations, and so far the Italians had not been able to derive the advantages expected from the occupation of Albania. Any new enterprises in the Balkans appeared to be ruled out, at least for the moment. The fighting value of the Italian forces compared with the French was assessed very low, at no more than a ratio of $1:5$.[191]

Despite all these drawbacks, Italy continued to be counted on as an ally in German military planning.[192] It is therefore misleading to say that the generals 'urgently warned' Hitler against the military burdens of the alliance with Rome;[193] such warnings dated from long before the summer of 1939.[194] It was only when it became known that Italian politicians and military men had deliberately overpitched their demands for material, as contained in the 'molybdenum list', in order to make them unacceptable to Germany and thus have an excuse to keep out of the war, that the army commander-in-chief, Colonel-General von Brauchitsch, together with Göring, minister for aviation and commander-in-chief of the Luftwaffe, once again temporarily advised against strengthening Italy in the military sphere.[195]

Following the outbreak of war the military contacts between the Axis powers, which had intensified during the first half of 1939, declined to a minimum. They rarely went above attaché level. Naturally a number of material problems remained under discussion, such as deliveries of anti-aircraft guns to Italy.[196] A partial exception, no doubt, was the matter of naval

---

[191] Halder, *Diaries*, i. 12 (14 Aug. 1939); on the political background cf. Schreiber, *Revisionismus*, 185–6; Siebert, *Italiens Weg*, 238–49.
[192] Halder, *Diaries*, i. 17 (18 Aug. 1939).
[193] Halder, *Hitler als Feldherr*, 33.
[194] Rintelen, *Mussolini als Bundesgenosse*, 55–6; cf. Schreiber, *Revisionismus*, 122–91.
[195] Halder, *Diaries* i. 28 (26 Aug. 1939); 32 ff.
[196] Schreiber, *Revisionismus*, 242–7, esp. 244 n. 451.

relations,¹⁹⁷ the initiative coming from the German side. The German army staff, on the other hand, adopted a waiting attitude from September onwards, which was essentially in line with that of the foreign ministry.

Nor was this changed by the fact that, on the question of whether Mussolini should take on the leadership of the bloc of neutral states, which became the subject of discussion around the middle of September, the commander-in-chief of the army showed a much more favourable attitude than some German diplomats.¹⁹⁸ Brauchitsch at that time was concerned lest Italy might after all decide to enter the war on the Allied side¹⁹⁹—but in this he overrated the capriciousness of Italian policy, and his judgement was not shared by Hitler. By the end of September, in discussing with his military chiefs the conduct of the war against France, Hitler was convinced that Mussolini would intervene in the war on the German side as soon as the Germans 'abandoned the Westwall' (i.e. went on the offensive), which might be the case within three weeks.²⁰⁰ Nothing substantial had therefore changed in Hitler's assessment: regardless of Mussolini's disappointing reaction in August, and despite his inadequate armament (which was known only too well in Berlin), Hitler considered Mussolini's entry into the war to be basically possible.

This exaggeration of Italy's military potential was presumably not just the result of Hitler's wishful thinking. Typically, two aspects combined in his argument that an offensive against France was the only way to sweep Mussolini finally into the war: for one thing, he was applying his old diversionary tactics, and, for another, by suggesting that Italy's entry would tie down French forces he hoped to win over his generals more easily in favour of an attack in the west. To support his thesis he urged that there was no reason to assume that Mussolini's highly encouraging remarks to Mackensen, the German ambassador in Rome, had not been meant sincerely.²⁰¹ While it was probably true that every further day of Italian non-belligerence was a gain to that country, there could still be no hope of any considerable strengthening of Italy after 1 September.²⁰² On 10 October Hitler repeated his established assertion: 'As long as we are sitting idly behind the Westwall, Italy will not enter the war.'²⁰³ When, on 23 November, he spoke again to the commanders-in-chief about his intentions, there had been no change in this respect.²⁰⁴

After Ley's visit to Rome the chief of the army general staff, Colonel-General Franz Halder, recorded, as a piece of information from the Reich

---

¹⁹⁷ Ibid. 202–39.
¹⁹⁸ Halder, *Diaries*, i. 78 (12 Sept. 1939); on the bloc problem see II. II. 2 below.
¹⁹⁹ Rintelen, *Mussolini als Bundesgenosse*, 76.
²⁰⁰ Halder, *Diaries*, i. 91–2 (27 Sept. 1939); on the war against France cf. vol. ii of the present work, Part VI (Umbreit).
²⁰¹ Halder, *Diaries*, i. 102–3 (10 Oct. 1939); Hitler mistakenly supposed Italy had 165,000 men stationed in Libya: see next n. 206.
²⁰² DGFP D viii, No. 205, pp. 226–30 (6 Oct. 1939).
²⁰³ See n. 201 above.
²⁰⁴ DGFP D viii, No. 384, pp. 439–46 (23 Dec. 1939); Domarus, *Hitler*, ii. 1421–7.

chancellery, that Mussolini was keen to strike soon and was 'mortified' by the delay in getting his country ready for war.[205] When at the beginning of January the Duce indicated that he would make certain proposals to Hitler at the middle of the month, the general staff learnt that Hitler was thinking of assigning to the Italians independent operations in the west. The Italian army was to operate against 'southern France, through Savoy, to the south-west'.[206] Following Mussolini's letter of 5 January the German military were rather more reserved about Italy joining the war. Italy would no doubt join 'only at the very last moment'. That was in accordance with the text of the letter.[207] Even earlier Colonel-General (retd.) Ludwig Beck, in a memorandum dated 2 January, had concluded that there was now little likelihood of Rome joining the war on the side of a 'Soviet-allied' Germany.[208] Beck is likely to have formed his view after Ciano's speech in December 1939 and the divergent positions adopted by Hitler and Mussolini towards the Soviet–Finnish war. In the foreign ministry it was then believed that—as the general staff were informed by the ministry's liaison officer with the army high command, Legation Counsellor Hasso von Etzdorf—Italy was increasingly succumbing to Allied propaganda.[209]

By the beginning of February the armed services were back to believing that Mussolini—as Hitler himself had never seriously doubted—would after all join the war on the German side. The only question was when,[210] as the Italians wanted first of all to be adequately rearmed. Hitler was therefore entirely correct in not expecting military action on the part of his ally until 'great German successes' were taking shape.[211] The Wehrmacht high command had meanwhile come to the conclusion that Italy's participation in the war—mainly because of the great demands for material that were to be expected—would yield no substantial advantages. As Hitler seemed for the moment to share this view, the Wehrmacht operations staff saw no reason to plan a joint German–Italian strategy and no specific assumption on which to do so.[212]

This indifference on the part of the Wehrmacht high command is rather surprising, however, seeing that, in connection with the economic agreement of 24 February, comprehensive contacts had been established between General Mario Roatta, representing the Italian general staff, and the German military attaché in Rome, Enno von Rintelen. This Italian initiative at the end of February 1940 should have made the Germans more receptive: evidently the

---

[205] Halder, *Diaries*, i. 158 (14 Dec. 1939).
[206] Ibid. 167 (1 Jan. 1940); cf. Jacobsen, *Fall Gelb*, 120 ff.
[207] Halder, *Diaries*, i. 172 (10 Jan. 1940); cf. ibid. 174 (11 Jan. 1940).
[208] Groscurth, *Tagebücher*, No. 69, pp. 493–7 (2 Jan. 1940), here 494.
[209] Halder, *Diaries*, i. 183 (19 Jan. 1940).
[210] Ibid. 225 (12 Feb. 1940).
[211] 'Führer Conferences', 79 (26 Jan. 1940).
[212] Warlimont, *Inside Hitler's HQ*, 63.

2. Italy as a Coalition Partner

general staff in Rome was anxious to lend new impulses to the stagnating military relations between the Axis powers.

Roatta and Rintelen—emphasizing the 'private character' of their conversation—for the first time frankly discussed the problems which had accumulated since September 1939. At the Italian war ministry, it appeared, there was still annoyance that Berlin had not so far definitively responded to the request for the 'supply of anti-aircraft batteries'. According to Roatta, Rome suspected that the reason was a basic mistrust on the Germans' part and, more especially, the fear that Italy might 'change sides as she did in 1915'. That was fairly close to the mark: such considerations did indeed play an important part in the dilatory treatment of the Italian request, not least with Göring, who was responsible for this matter. The affair was exceedingly annoying to Italy, who, immediately before the beginning of the war in 1939, had asked for 150 antiaircraft guns. Although the issue continued to be under discussion during the next few months—Rintelen in particular strongly advocated the delivery of the AA guns—it was not until 19 March 1940, i.e. a day after the Brenner meeting between Hitler and Mussolini, that Göring ordered modern 8.8-cm. antiaircraft guns to be handed over to Italy.

Regardless of such friction, in February Rome suggested that, with a view to military co-operation between the Axis powers, matters should not be left to improvisation. Roatta was especially keen on the harmonization of technical and logistical problems, vital for any effective conduct of operations. Discussion of operational problems could and should follow. On 27 March Rintelen reported that the Italian general staff was even ready to discuss the joint employment of German and Italian troops in a German or an Italian theatre of war, or else their employment in separate theatres of war.[213] The possibility cannot be ruled out that such offers were a direct reply to Hitler's remarks on 18 March, when he proposed to Mussolini the participation of Italian troops on the upper Rhine within the framework of the German offensive in the west.[214] The ideas of the Italian general staff could have been based on the (temporary) realization that the structural prerequisites of the Axis powers in the industrial and economic sphere practically precluded the 'parallel war' intended by Mussolini.

Be that as it may, Mussolini, regardless of his readiness for general-staff talks, wanted a parallel war for a variety of reasons, and therefore did not show himself very responsive to Hitler's proposal.[215] Nevertheless, the German general staff, even before any firm reply was received from Rome, began to include thirty to thirty-five Italian divisions in its plan for the Vosges oper-

---

[213] On this and the sources see Schreiber, *Revisionismus*, 243–7; also *IMT* xxviii, No. 1809, p. 416 (28 Mar. 1940) (Jodl's diary).

[214] Cf. also vol. ii of the present work, VI.v.4 (Umbreit). On the Brenner meeting, e.g. Knox, *Mussolini*, 87–8; Wiskemann, *Axis*, 200 ff.

[215] Schreiber, *Revisionismus*, 257 ff.

ations envisaged for the French campaign.[216] This can probably be explained as the result of the confidence radiated by Hitler: after his conversation with Mussolini he was evidently convinced that the Duce was aiming at an early entry into the war.[217] It seems, moreover—as is suggested by the OKW's preliminary thoughts on the deployment of forces for the offensive on the upper Rhine—that, at least in the Wehrmacht high command, the combative effectiveness of the Italian divisions was rated as equal to that of the German ones.[218] To begin with, however, the general staff counted on no more than twelve Italian divisions, which, moreover, would scarcely be available before July. If greater numbers of Italian formations were to be employed, an even longer assembly-time would have to be expected. Yet Halder, while he did not at that time reject the use of Italian troops, pointed to the great material strain which would result from the expected Italian demands: he also questioned the value of an operation through Savoy, considering that the Italians lacked anti-aircraft guns, heavy artillery, and bridging-units.[219] On 27 March, at lunch with Hitler, he learnt how the Führer pictured the intervention of his Axis partner. Some twenty Italian divisions should be allowed for in the plans for Operation Brown—the name for the upper Rhine operation—which could be mobilized within fourteen days, i.e. during the two weeks following the German attack, during which it would become clear whether or not there were 'any prospects of a major success'. Only in the affirmative case did Hitler expect Mussolini to march. The general staff accordingly proceeded with the necessary theoretical and practical preparations. These assumed that the German–Italian attack on the upper Rhine would start six weeks after X-day, the opening of the campaign against France.[220] In view of these developments it was considered necessary for German and Italian officers to make contact in order, at long last, to discuss the prerequisites and nature of a possible joint operation. Needless to say, this readiness in principle did not in the least mean that German scepticism *vis-à-vis* Italy had been dropped. Mistrustful reserve hung over the envisaged talks. It was in this spirit that Major-General Alfred Jodl, the head of the Wehrmacht operations staff, suggested to Hitler on 22 March that the contacts should be made through the military attaché in Rome, who should first of all establish how the Italian general staff envisaged alleviating Germany's burden in the war. Only after that should the possibility of an Italian operation on the upper Rhine be examined. General-staff discussions, however, should only be held once Germany's own cards were on the table,[221] i.e. at the last moment.

[216] Halder, *Diaries*, i. 281 (22 Mar. 1940); ibid. 281 (23 Mar. 1940).
[217] Warlimont, *Inside Hitler's HQ*, 64; Knox, *Mussolini*, 88–91.
[218] Halder, *Diaries*, i. 280 ff. (21 Mar. 1940).
[219] Ibid. 282 (26 Mar. 1940); ön the state of equipment of the Italian forces cf. I.1.4 (*a*) below.
[220] Halder, *Diaries*, i. 285 (27 Mar. 1940); ibid. 287 (28 Mar. 1940), 290–1 (31 Mar. 1940); cf. also Halder, *Hitler als Feldherr*, 33. In detail Vetsch, *Aufmarsch*, 32–41.
[221] Warlimont, *Inside Hitler's HQ*, 64–5; *IMT* xxviii, No. 1809, p. 415 (22 Mar. 1940) (Jodl's diary), and p. 416 (27 Mar. 1940).

2. Italy as a Coalition Partner

Hitler's directive of 4 April, according to which the German–Italian military conversations interrupted by the war were to be resumed in order to examine all the questions which Italy's belligerence would raise, essentially followed Jodl's suggestions. The Wehrmacht high command took the chairmanship of the discussions, which first of all sought to clarify the strategic-operational objectives of German–Italian warfare. Two hypotheses were to be examined: first, that Italy wished to participate in a joint operation in the German theatre of war, and, second, that she did not wish to do so.[222]

More specifically, the German side proceeded from the following considerations: firstly, the war would be decided in the west European theatre of war, which was why all Italy's efforts must be directed to the defeat of the Allied troops in France; this, however, in no way corresponded to Mussolini's intentions.[223] The Wehrmacht high command's ideas differed from those of the Italian generals on the use of the Italian formations, which, as the difficulties of the terrain on the Alpine front would merely allow them to hold down part of the French forces, were to be offensively employed on the German southern wing. As for the difficulties arising from the fact that there did not exist even a theoretical preparation by the German and Italian operations staffs for a coalition war, it was hoped to avoid these by assigning to the Italians an independent task. The erroneous assessment of the Italian forces by the Wehrmacht high command emerges clearly from its assignment of tasks to the army, air force, and navy. The Italian army was to attack with at least twenty divisions on the upper Rhine front through the south Vosges–Burgundy gap, simultaneously pinning down French forces on the Alpine front. The Italian air force was to support the ground operations with massive sorties, tying down French air-defence forces by conducting attacks from northern Italy; Italian air defences were to be strengthened in that area, for which the Germans promised support. The navy was not only to disrupt Allied east–west communications in the Mediterranean, which was thought to present no problem, but also to eliminate British sea power in the eastern Mediterranean, with the object of keeping the British and French away from the Balkans and the Black Sea. In the western Mediterranean the Italian navy was to attack French communications with North Africa. Should the Balkans, against expectation, be drawn into the conflict, then the Italians were to prevent the British or French from establishing themselves in Greece, Yugoslavia, or the Straits, while Germany was to take over the military safeguarding of Romania. Bulgaria was to be supported by both German and Italian forces. In addition Berlin even considered blocking the Suez Canal. The Luftwaffe

---

[222] The following account according to *DGFP* D ix, No. 46, pp. 76 ff. (4 Apr. 1940).
[223] Cf. on this point *DDI*, 9th ser., iii, No. 669, pp. 576–9 (31 Mar. 1940), memorandum from Mussolini on the political and military situation, addressed to the king and the foreign minister as well as to Badoglio (chief of the general staff), Graziani (chief of the army general staff), Cavagnari (chief of the navy staff), and Pricolo (chief of the air force general staff). The following account according to the source in the preceding n.

would take part in the operations envisaged in the Mediterranean area, and Italy's overseas bases would be available to German ships engaged in economic warfare.

In the event that Mussolini did not wish any joint operations in a German theatre of war, the directive envisaged an attack by the Italian army on the Alpine front—although, paradoxically, this was described as unpromising—and an operation against Corsica. The Italian air force would then—in close collaboration with the Luftwaffe—take part in the air war against France. At the same time, German pilots were to co-operate in the aerial defence of Italy and in the war in the Mediterranean area.

As regards immediate contacts, it was laid down that the separate services could only embark on their own operational talks once the above-mentioned questions were clarified by the Wehrmacht high command. Regardless of this, however, the army high command was permitted to open talks with the Italians on the basis of the Roatta–Rintelen conversations. The navy and the Luftwaffe for their part could resume the negotiations of 1939. It was, however, forbidden to mention, in any form whatsoever, 'Case Yellow', the intended German offensive in the west with its attack through Belgium, Luxemburg, and The Netherlands, or Operation Weserübung, the strike at Denmark and Norway,[224] prior to the start of these operations. Discussion of a joint command was to be excluded on principle. In this respect the attitude adopted in the Spanish civil war was maintained.[225]

As a start, on 5 and 6 April the German military attaché in Rome, charged with setting up the talks between representatives of the Wehrmacht and the Italian general staff,[226] was briefed on the Wehrmacht's intentions.[227] On 10 April he reported to Graziani and Roatta, who in turn promised to obtain a decision by Mussolini.[228] The following day Mussolini received the comments of the army general staff, signed by Graziani. The latter did not inform Badoglio until 13 April of the German proposal for twenty to thirty Italian divisions to be deployed against France from southern Germany, or instead to take the offensive in North Africa and to support the Germans on the Alpine front. At the same time, on 13 April Roatta submitted to Badoglio the army general staff's adverse views on the German proposals. Two days later, on 15 April, Badoglio handed Mussolini his own negative assessment, in which—contrary to an immediately preceding entry in the war diary of his department—he no longer regarded as useful an exchange of ideas, proposed by the Germans for 16 April, between Colonel-General Wilhelm Keitel, the

---

[224] On this point see vol. ii of the present work, V.I (Maier) and V.III (Stegemann).
[225] Cf. Schreiber, *Revisionismus*, 102 n. 238.
[226] Halder, *Diaries*, i. 301 (6 Apr. 1940), 302–3 (8 Apr. 1940).
[227] Ibid. 301 (6 Apr. 1940). On 6 Apr. a discussion took place between Jodl, Warlimont, Canaris, Rintelen, and the Italian military attaché, Gen. Efisio Marras; cf. *IMT* xxviii, No. 1809, p. 418 (6 Apr. 1940) (Jodl's diary).
[228] Memorandum of 10 Apr 1940, in *Africa settentrionale, La preparazione*, 166 ff.; Rintelen, *Mussolini als Bundesgenosse*, 82.

2. Italy as a Coalition Partner

chief of the Wehrmacht high command, and Roatta. The Duce endorsed this evaluation.[229] For him there was, at that time, only one acceptable form of military action: parallel war. Seen in this light, it is not surprising that Rintelen, whose statement was confirmed by the reports sent from Berlin by the Italian military attaché, never received an official reply. The decision to reject the German proposals was presumably taken in the course of a meeting between Mussolini, Badoglio, and the three chiefs of staff on 15 April. Although Mussolini sent word to Rintelen by way of General Ubaldo Soddu, the under-secretary of state in the war ministry, that he would write an explanatory letter to Hitler prior to the start of the talks between Roatta and the German representatives, that letter—as noted above—was never drafted. It is true, of course, that after 10 April the Wehrmacht was no longer greatly concerned about this matter, so that the first and only attempt to discuss joint operations before Italy's entry into the war just petered out.[230]

Military support from Rome, however, continued for the time being to be part and parcel of Berlin's theoretical preparations for the offensive in the west,[231] even though Germany soon realized the dilatoriness shown by her Axis partner in the handling of the decisions involved.[232] The euphoria which followed the meeting of the two dictators on the Brenner, on 18 March 1940, proved short-lived. As before, there took place merely a rather general exchange of ideas at attaché level. On the German side the realization was gaining ground that little had changed since the summer of 1939 as regards the inadequate equipment of the Italian forces, and that Mussolini's main interest was in the Balkans. Only there, if anywhere, were Italian military operations to be expected.[233] It was now quite realistically assumed on all sides that Mussolini would enter the war only after some spectacular German successes in the west;[234] and, given this state of affairs, Hitler refused to let Italy have any arms beyond the agreed amount.[235]

The German attack on the western front was launched on 10 May.[236] Loose contacts continued for the time being with the Italians, whose entry into the war was not expected by the Germans, but neither was it opposed.[237] As it became increasingly clear that the offensive on the upper Rhine, envisaged no earlier than the middle of June, could equally well be launched without Italian assistance, the generals displayed a good deal of indifference concerning Italy's

---

[229] Cf. *Africa settentrionale, La preparazione*, 168–72; Faldella, *L'Italia*, 155 ff.; Schreiber, *Revisionismus*, 258, 264–5.
[230] Rintelen, *Mussolini als Bundesgenosse*, 82; Knox, *Mussolini*, 94–5.
[231] Halder, *Diaries*, i. 314 (13 Apr. 1940).
[232] Ibid. 323 (19 Apr. 1940), 335 (29 Apr. 1940), 343 (6 May 1940).
[233] Ibid. 340 (3 May 1940), 341 (4 May 1940), 348 (9 May 1940); cf. also Jacobsen, *Fall Gelb*, 129–30.
[234] Halder, *Diaries*, i. 343 (6 May 1940).
[235] Ibid. 347 (8 May 1940).
[236] In detail vol. ii of the present work, VI.II (Umbreit).
[237] Halder, *Diaries*, i. 409 (19 May 1940).

entry into the war.²³⁸ A contributory factor may have been that this was essentially a secondary operation. Another probable cause was the fact that Mussolini and Hitler in their conduct of the war pursued rather divergent objectives. Whereas the Duce saw London as the main enemy,²³⁹ the Führer was already thinking of an arrangement with Britain, in order, following the expected victory over France and the expulsion of the British from the Continent, to devote himself to his programmatic goal: the racially and ideologically motivated war of annihilation against the Soviet Union.²⁴⁰

In early June, surprised by the rapidity of the German advance, Mussolini conveyed his intention of intervening soon in the conflict. But in order not to compromise the secrecy of Operation Red, the 'battle of France', Berlin now requested that this step should not be taken before 5 June.²⁴¹ In this connection Hitler offered to make a mountain division available to Italy.²⁴² This readiness, however, suggests a realization of the Italian army's low efficiency rather than the wish to improve military co-operation to any marked degree. This is confirmed by the fact that only a few days before, on 24 May, the Italians had—unsuccessfully—urged the holding of talks with the Wehrmacht.²⁴³ All this goes to show the insignificance that Italy had at that time for German military planning. Generally speaking, it may be said that, while Italian and German generals and politicians more or less confidently expected a joint war, co-operation had in no way improved compared with the pre-war period—and in this respect the Axis proved an inadequate alliance. Even in June 1940, when, on the occasion of the Hitler–Mussolini meeting, talks also took place between Keitel and Roatta, military relations were not a topic of conversation.²⁴⁴ Only the realization that Britain's determination to resist was not broken by the defeat in the west—which was beyond doubt from early July—eventually led the Germans to try to make a joint conduct of the war possible after all.²⁴⁵

Naval relations occupied a somewhat special position within this general development, but will be touched upon here only marginally. The most determined advocates of German–Italian collaboration undoubtedly sat in the navy high command in Berlin. This was due, on the one hand, to historical reasons and, on the other, to the material situation of the German naval forces.²⁴⁶ The bulk of the officers on the Tirpitz-Ufer, the seat of naval headquarters, were by no means Italophile, but, as a result of a global concept of the war and of a specific way of thinking, conclusions and demands were

---

[238] Ibid. 413 (21 May 1940).
[239] Ibid. 413 (21 May 1940).
[240] Schreiber, 'Mittelmeerraum'.
[241] Halder, *Diaries*, i. 435 (1 June 1940).
[242] Ibid. 439 (4 June 1940).
[243] Minute by state secretary von Weizsäcker, 24 May 1940, PA Büro St.S., 'Italien', iii, 17.
[244] *Staatsmänner*, 142.
[245] Cf. I.III below.
[246] Schreiber, *Revisionismus*, passim.

arrived at which went far beyond the objective pursued by Hitler at that time. As early as October 1939, for instance, Grand Admiral Erich Raeder, the commander-in-chief of the navy, was prepared to accept a world war if that should be the outcome of the intensified naval warfare against Britain.[247] And within the pattern of operations against Britain the Italian navy acquired significance. Raeder counted on Italian operations having a diversionary strategic effect by compelling the enemy to fragment his forces. Even at the beginning of November 1939 Raeder was still convinced that he would be able to dispatch his armoured cruisers—then operating in Atlantic waters—to wage worldwide economic war only if Italy had by then actively joined the conflict. Only thus would the British Mediterranean fleet, which until then—thanks to Italian non-belligerence—had operated on all the seas without hindrance, remain tied down within its proper area of operations.[248]

For the moment, however, such expectations remained unfulfilled. Nevertheless, the naval war staff, which had at first noted Mussolini's decision of September 1939 without comment,[249] continued until January 1940 to cling to the hope that Italy would soon enter the war. The German navy was, at the very least, counting on generous support for its own operations from its Axis partner. However, disillusionment soon gained ground on this very point. The Italians, in fact, were no more willing than were the Spaniards arbitrarily to interpret in Germany's favour the international regulations concerning neutral states. On grounds of *raison d'état* they thought it wiser to annoy the Germans than the Allies.[250]

Among the questions the naval war staff was anxious to see clarified as soon as possible, the top place was held by German–Italian co-operation on the deployment of German U-boats in the Mediterranean. Almost equally urgent was the purchase of Atlantic-going submarines in Italy. Rome had been aware of these German wishes since mid-September. A little later the Italians also learnt about German intentions to convert some freighters in Italian ports into minelayers and submarine supply-ships.

The Italian admirals viewed the German demands with disfavour from the start. There was a lot of friction, and this no doubt contributed to making collaboration between the two navies troublesome, even after Italy's entry into the war. One direct consequence of the growing irritation in Berlin was, moreover, the absence of any exchange of information on modern weapons or new developments in this field. Thus the German naval high command was not prepared, in the circumstances, to pass on to the Italian navy any electrical torpedoes or submarine fire-control systems, let alone details of the German torpedo-firing pistol. True, the Italians offered netting-booms, front tor-

---

[247] Memorandum by the naval staff on intensified naval operations against Britain, 15 Oct. 1939, published in Salewski, *Seekriegsleitung*, iii. 70–104; 'Führer Conferences', 46 (10 Oct. 1939).
[248] 'Führer Conferences', 54–5 (1 Nov. 1939).
[249] 1. Skl., KTB, Teil A, p. 27 (1 Sept. 1939), BA-MA, RM 7/4.
[250] Ibid. 63–4 (13 Sept. 1939), 82 (15 Sept. 1939).

pedoes, and anti-submarine mines, but this was not enough for Raeder. He wanted concessions on essential German demands before complying with Italian requests. When, in the course of this acrimonious tug of war, Italy eventually agreed to sell midget submarines, Berlin rejected the offer on the ground that the types offered were virtually useless for German naval operations.[251] In March 1940, as a result of the political developments outlined above, a *rapprochement* eventually took place between the two navies. By then the Mediterranean had, at least temporarily, lost its importance to the German navy, as Weserübung was fully engaging maritime operational planning. The occupation of Denmark and Norway was followed by the campaign in the west, which, with the seizure of the French Atlantic coast, placed German naval operations on a new basis. By that time Italy's entry into the war had been taking on ever clearer shape, so that the dispatch of German U-boats into the Mediterranean began to look unnecessary anyway.

In summary it may be stated that Italy's non-belligerence failed to yield any direct advantages for Germany's conduct of the war.[252] Nor did it produce any good reason for activating the German–Italian military alliance, which existed on paper but remained dormant until 10 June 1940. On economic, military, and psychological grounds the Axis revealed itself as a highly unprofitable alliance. When Mussolini at last entered the war, it was, as we shall see, primarily on account of his own political objectives. In this connection he overrated the German position in the summer of 1940 and underrated Hitler's power-political ambitions. Simplifying a little, one might say that it was basically the imperialist greed of the two dictators which—within the pattern of a very complex process—helped them to overcome the barriers of an ideologically motivated rivalry and to wage war in concert. Strategic constraints after 10 June 1940—not surprisingly in the light of the experience acquired during non-belligerence—then brought it about that, on the one hand, there was a rapidly progressing erosion of the Axis alliance, while, on the other, Germany and Italy were ever more deeply entangled in an enforced association to which there appeared to be no alternative.

3. STRATEGIC CONSIDERATIONS UP TO JUNE 1940

As regards the Italian armed forces' preparedness in terms of war material, Mussolini's generals at the time of Italy's entry into the war expressed the opinion that the 'state of effectiveness of the armed forces' revealed some 'slight, but in no way sufficient, improvement' as against the situation in 1939.[253]

---

[251] Schreiber, *Revisionismus*, 207–17, 231–9.
[252] This should be emphasized in contrast to the interpretation of isolated remarks by Mussolini and Hitler—not examined as to their propaganda content—by Araldi, *Non belligeranza*, 63.
[253] German Naval HQ Italy, 'Denkschrift aus militärischen Akten Rom, betr. die "Wirkungsfähigkeit der italienischen Streitkräfte 1939 und zu Beginn des Kriegseintritts Juni

3. Strategic Considerations to June 1940

We shall return to the details which gave rise to this resigned admission of the ineffectiveness of Italian rearmament policy and planning. For the moment we are concerned to enquire in what way Fascist military policy reacted to the general development of European politics from 1939, and what attitude was taken by Italy's top military men as Mussolini's involvement in a major war became increasingly probable.

As for relations between the Italian military and Fascism, it may generally be stated that there is no doubt about the sympathy with which the bulk of the officer corps greeted Mussolini's seizure of power.[254] Like the reaction of the German generals in 1933, that of the Italian generals in 1922 can, generally speaking, be explained by the fact that they saw in the new regime an excellent champion of their own military, political, and social interests. At the same time, the monarch played an important part in relations between the Italian armed forces and the political leadership, since, even after 1922, his person carried great weight in the officers' understanding of their own role. Yet the Fascisticization of the army was prevented, not so much by the opposition of the king or of the top military leaders as by that of Mussolini. Attempts by party bosses such as Cesare Maria De Vecchi, Roberto Farinacci, and Italo Balbo proved unsuccessful because Mussolini did not wish for a party army. Instead he endeavoured, bypassing the party, to establish his influence on the forces as a personal monopoly. The fact that from 1925 to 1929, and again from 1933 to 1943, he was minister for the army, air force, and navy as well as head of government proves that he succeeded in his intention. It is scarcely surprising that, parallel to this development, the Fascist militias declined in political importance.[255]

As the war in Ethiopia, the Spanish civil war, and the Second World War showed, Mussolini in fact occupied a predominant position in the military sphere. By systematically making changes in the top posts of the military hierarchy he moreover made sure that no dangerous opponent could arise. The military leaders saw through these tactics but accepted them. With the complacency of experts they assessed Mussolini's behaviour as an expression of his lack of assurance in professional matters.

After the Second World War, at all events, they emphatically pointed to the Duce's incompetence in military policy and strategy.[256] However, criticism from within their own ranks did not spare the military leaders themselves even

---

1940"' (undated), BA-MA III M 2001/1. A good survey of the part played by *matériel* in determining Italy's military policy 1935–43 in Minniti, 'Il problema'; cf. also Mazzetti, *La politica, passim*.

[254] Cf. the fundamental study by Rochat, *L'esercito italiano*; also in this context Caviglia, *Diario, passim*, who, as Marshal of Italy, kept his distance from the Fascist regime.

[255] Rochat and Massobrio, *Storia dell'esercito*, 208 ff.; Mussolini was war minister in 1925–9 and 1933–43, navy minister in 1933–43, and air minister in 1925–9; cf. Kramer, 'Die italienische Luftwaffe', 264.

[256] Corselli, *Cinque anni*, 38 ff.

during the Fascist era.[257] Yet at no time did the legend arise in Italy that Mussolini's failures had prevented the generals from winning the war,[258] even though the generals and admirals after 1945 tried to saddle him with all the blame for the war itself.[259] In point of fact Italy's totally inadequate preparation for war was due, besides the economic and industrial factors already mentioned, as much to Mussolini's political mistakes as to the inability of Marshal Badoglio and other senior officers to carry out the necessary reforms within the forces.[260] But to conclude from all this that Mussolini had no wish whatever to go to war carries scant conviction.

It has nevertheless been argued that the opposite conclusion may justifiably be drawn from Italy's operations in Ethiopia, Spain, and Albania, not to mention her declaration of war on France, Britain, Greece, the Soviet Union, and the United States.[261] After the conclusion of the Pact of Steel, if not before then, the military leaders must have increasingly realized that they would have to prepare for a major war, especially when, a few days later, on 27 May 1939, the under-secretaries of state in the army, the air force, and the navy ministries received a memorandum from Mussolini informing them of his ideas on future developments. Mussolini proceeded from the assumption that war between what were called the plutocratic Western democracies and the populous 'have-nots' was inevitable. Italy, in consequence, was to make appropriate preparations, but he did not expect his country to be ready for war before 1943 at the earliest. In the meantime the requisite military infrastructures were to be created in Libya and Albania. Ethiopia was to be pacified by then; indeed, Mussolini expected to be able to draw on half a million African troops from that colony. The navy would have at its disposal the six battleships which were under construction or reconstruction. By 1943, moreover, the army's entire medium and heavy artillery would be renewed. More particularly, autarky plans were to be implemented as far as possible to enable Italy to withstand an Allied blockade.

The exhibition envisaged in the Italian capital for the twentieth anniversary of the March on Rome (October 1942) should also be seen within this context. It was to provide hard currency for rearmament. Mussolini moreover wanted a further transfer of armament industries from northern to southern Italy, where they would be less at risk.

As for military operations, Mussolini expected positional warfare on the

---

[257] Zanussi, *Guerra*, i. 36–41.
[258] On Mussolini as a military leader cf. mainly Rochat, 'Mussolini, chef de guerre', and id., 'Mussolini et les forces armées'. For a very readable biography see De Luna, *Mussolini*; for the period of the war, pp. 123–36.
[259] Cf. esp. Canevari, *Guerra italiana*, *passim*; Rochat and Massobrio, *Storia dell'esercito*, 208, 263 ff.
[260] Whittam, 'Italian General Staff', 95; on Badoglio's role cf. the sharp criticism of Ceva, *La condotta*, 23, and Smith, *Roman Empire*, 184–5, as well as the detailed appraisal of the marshal's enigmatic personality in Pieri and Rochat, *Badoglio*, 737–70.
[261] Smith, *Roman Empire*, 183.

3. Strategic Considerations to June 1940

Rhine, in the Alps, and in Libya, while offensives were to be mounted from Ethiopia against the neighbouring British and French colonies. Generally speaking, an air and naval war was to be anticipated in the west; only towards the east and south-west would dynamic operations unfold. It might well be possible to paralyse Poland before Western or Soviet support could become effective. Mussolini assumed that in the event of a conflict the Western powers would opt for a war of attrition, which would be unfavourable to the Axis powers. In order to limit the dangers which might result he demanded that, immediately upon the outbreak of war, the Danube basin and the Balkans should be occupied. Declarations of neutrality from the states concerned would be of no significance. Only from Hungary and Bulgaria could Italy expect support. Mussolini communicated these ideas to the Germans in order that, if they agreed, corresponding directives might be issued for the military planning of the general staffs.[262] These intentions, as is well known, were overtaken by political events after May 1939.

A further reminder about the necessary stepping-up of strategic planning was received by the Italian operational staffs in mid-August 1939, when Marshal Badoglio was informed that the Duce did not share Hitler's optimism about a limitation of the German–Polish war, but instead expected the conflict to spread throughout Europe. Italy in that case would adopt a neutral attitude, though Mussolini did not think one could rule out the possibility of the democracies mounting an attack on their part. He might, in this context, have referred to the Pact of Steel, to the ideological front against the Western powers, and to political rivalry in the Mediterranean. But the Duce operated primarily with defensive arguments: above all, he wanted to know that the frontiers of the mother country and of the colonies would be defended if his fears turned into reality. It did not seem unusual, however—in view of the long-term plans discussed above—that he should instruct his generals to prepare for an offensive against Greece, with Salonika as the objective, in the event of Britain and her allies attacking. Mention was also made of Croatia, though any appropriate Italian action would need to be preceded by massive internal upheavals in Yugoslavia.

Badoglio's objections were not of a fundamental character but stemmed from departmental considerations. They were determined in particular by the time factor. The forces were in the midst of a re-equipment phase, and the situation in Libya was decidedly precarious. Yet it was precisely there that an extension of the war must be expected. A war would be untimely if it occurred now, which was why it should be avoided. Mussolini seemed to be understanding and promised to remedy matters as far as the forces were concerned,

---

[262] *La marina italiana, il 10 giugno 1940*, No. 3, pp. 6–9; cf. also Badoglio, *Italy*, 1 ff.; Bagnasco, *Le armi*, especially on the navy, from a weapons-engineering point of view; also Andò and Bagnasco, *Navi e marinai*.

but in the end he ordered plans for a possible offensive against Greece and Yugoslavia to be prepared with the utmost urgency.[263]

The studies ordered in the separate staffs proceeded with astonishing expedition, yet their results presumably did not match up to Mussolini's hopes. Badoglio, at any rate, reported on 31 August that Italy's extremely weak forces called for concentration on defence against the expected enemy offensive. An attack on Greece could be considered only when it was obvious that the fronts in North Africa—and wherever else the enemy attacked—were holding. Also, a benevolent attitude on the part of Bulgaria and Hungary would be a prerequisite of any operation in the Balkans. The general staff agreed with the Duce that an operation against Yugoslavia could only be recommended if that country was already in a state of dissolution.[264]

Such prospects did not seem too promising, and it appears that the Balkan states were, for the time being, mentioned no more. Instead deliberations after the end of August were concerned with possible operations in East Africa. Plans for an offensive against Jibuti were to be brought up to date, and attention was to be given to simultaneous or subsequent operations against British Somaliland.[265] On this point too the generals arrived at a realistic, and accordingly pessimistic, assessment of the situation. They addressed fundamental demands to the political leadership, culminating in the requirement—in view of the special conditions of overseas operations and their dependence on constantly threatened supplies—of stocks sufficient for twelve months. Other demands were for fortifications, improved unloading capacity in the African ports, and the enhancement of air defences, especially in the coastal areas. A lot of important points and some indispensable ones had clearly been considered—yet practical consequences failed to materialize.[266]

Thus, when on 3 September France and Britain declared war on Germany, when Hitler's frivolous optimism turned to deception and Mussolini's pessimism turned into reality, Italy, by declaring her non-belligerence, avoided finding herself between the jaws of the Allies' strategic pincers from Egypt and Tunisia. With his hopeless overestimation of the military effectiveness of the Italian armed forces, Hitler seems to have regarded even that situation as in no way dangerous, especially as Mussolini's entry into the war, which he hoped to see, would have provoked that very situation anyway. The western front would undoubtedly have been relieved as a result, but the simultaneous move by the British and French in North Africa would just as surely have meant the loss of Italy's possessions there. This was very clearly realized in Rome, which

---

[263] Faldella, *L'Italia*, 132–3.
[264] Ibid. 134.
[265] 'Direttive di carattere operativo per le Terre Italiane d'Oltremare in dipendenza dell'attuale situazione internazionale, Capo di Stato Maggiore Generale Badoglio, 29. 8. 1939, N. 4691', in *Africa settentrionale, La preparazione*, 157–8.
[266] 'Direttive per la preparazione bellica delle Terre Italiane d'Oltremare, Capo di Stato Maggiore Generale Badoglio, 27. 8. 1939, N. 4672', ibid. 155–6.

3. Strategic Considerations to June 1940

was why on 2 September explicit instructions were issued, focusing military efforts on the defence of Libya. An Italian counter-offensive was suggested only as a very vague possibility.[267]

These new directives did not go unopposed. Air Marshal Balbo in particular, the commander-in-chief in Libya, called for offensive action against the British position at Suez in the event of military confrontation with Britain. His proposal not only betrayed ambition but was also skilfully argued, with an eye to Mussolini's imperialist propaganda. Balbo, alluding to the strategic maxims of the Fascist regime, which called for autarky, emphasized the enormous economic advantages Italy would derive from the conquest of Egypt. Even though Mussolini and Badoglio rejected Balbo's plan, it was still being discussed in 1940. This may be seen as an indication of his powerful position within the Fascist Party. But the fact that discussion continued does mean that his ideas were, after all, in line with the military capabilities of the Italian armed forces. No doubt the general staff realized this, so that one may justifiably speak of purely formal concessions[268] when Rome, after much argument back and forth, eventually granted the air marshal permission for his offensive, provided it could be mounted under extremely favourable conditions; however, in any case new plans were to be worked out first.[269]

It must be admitted that from a military point of view, and on the assumption that Mussolini was not merely planning a purely formal entry into the war, as part of his political calculations, Balbo's plan was the only one which would have matched up to the well-known intentions of the Fascist regime. Yet in an evaluation of realistic military options the pitiful state of Italy's armaments[270] was bound to be decisive, rather than objectives which were unattainable by the existing defensive army. If one examines Mussolini's attitude after the outbreak of war in 1939, there is at least some evidence that, with a realistic assessment of Italian military strength, he was from the outset envisaging a participation in the war which aimed not at military victory but merely at earning the right to participate in peace negotiations. That was when Italy's demands on France and Britain might—as it were peacefully—be asserted.

Yet it was reckless on the part of the Italian military leaders to rely entirely on Mussolini's judgement, i.e. to rule out the possibility that Italy would find herself, before 1943, involved in a war that required an all-out military effort. The effect of this mistake was that responses to almost certain eventualities were not prepared for even within the bounds of what would have been possible. The result was later strikingly demonstrated by the march of the Italian infantry through Libya's sands with nothing even approaching suitable

---

[267] Ibid. 62–3.
[268] Faldella, *L'Italia*, 136.
[269] *Africa settentrionale, La preparazione*, 63–6; Santoro, *L'aeronautica italiana*, i. 75–83.
[270] On the state of the equipment of the Italian armed forces on 1 Nov. 1939 cf. *Africa settentrionale, La preparazione*, 158 ff.

equipment for desert warfare.[271] To those men it was scant consolation that in February 1940 Badoglio still seems to have honestly believed that the Duce would stick to his timetable as communicated in May 1939.[272]

On 31 March 1940 Mussolini issued a further memorandum on Italy's situation depending on the further development of Germany's war with the Western powers.[273] He proceeded from the assumption that even a moderately reliable evaluation of the strategic situation was no longer possible, and that therefore the date for Italy's entry into the war could not be fixed even approximately. However, even in the event of a protracted war, which then seemed most probable, he could not in the long run remain neutral because that would disqualify Italy from becoming a great power. Only in the event of peace negotiations at an unexpectedly early date could he still hope to achieve the essential objectives of his policy at the conference table despite having observed non-belligerence until then. Such a possibility would be excluded if the conflict were to continue and Italy remained aloof for an indefinite period. What mattered basically was for Italy to intervene at the right moment: that moment should have been chosen objectively on the grounds of the state of the Italian armed forces, whereas in fact it was determined solely by the Duce's political judgement.

Apart from this interrelation between the development of the war and decision-making in the Palazzo Venezia, Mussolini also revealed his so-called war plan. In this he once more ruled out the possibility of Italy entering the war at any time on the Anglo-French side. In very general terms he outlined the strategic framework into which the speediest possible planning of army, air force, and navy was to fit. Mussolini proceeded from the view that the army would essentially remain on the defensive on all fronts. Even on the Alpine frontier an offensive against France was to be launched only if the German attack—against all expectation—were to result in the total collapse of the French army. He further considered the occupation of Corsica. Of course it would be necessary to assess carefully the advantages and risks of such an operation; basically he believed it sufficient to eliminate the French air-bases on the island. This was another indication that Mussolini wanted to play with only a small stake.

As for Yugoslavia, Italy should for the time being confine herself to a heightened state of alert of the forces, seeing that—as had been assumed as early as 1939—offensive action would be possible only if there were signs of an imminent collapse of the Yugoslav state in consequence of secession by the

---

[271] Faldella, *L'Italia*, 138–44; *Africa settentrionale, La preparazione*, 66–7, a presentation confined to logistic considerations.

[272] Faldella, *L'Italia*, 44; Badoglio, *Italy*, 12–13.

[273] *DDI*, 9th ser., iii, No. 669, pp. 576–9 (31 Mar. 1940); Knox, *Mussolini*, 183, points out that Mussolini's hesitation was due not only to the inadequate equipment of the armed forces, but also to his conviction that fortifications were virtually impregnable. This thesis certainly has some attraction in view of the importance Mussolini attached to the *vallo alpino*.

3. Strategic Considerations to June 1940

Croats. Such reflections naturally concerned the troops in Albania as well, who, Yugoslavia apart, were also to be kept in readiness for operations against Greece. Mussolini intended to take his final decision as to whom and where to attack according to the development of the situation in the west.

For the divisions in Libya he ordered a defensive attitude both on the Egyptian and on the Tunisian frontier. In this context he was able to rule out Balbo's plan for an offensive against the Suez Canal, without any loss of face either for the air marshal or for himself, by means of an adroit reference to the French Armée de l'Orient under General Maxime Weygand. At the same time he ordered an absolutely defensive stance for the entire Aegean area.

Only in Ethiopia was an offensive envisaged. This was hardly a surprise, considering that the plan—as we have seen—had been under discussion ever since 1939. The Italian forces were to move against the Anglo-Egyptian Sudan and French Somaliland, with the ultimate aim of making Eritrea safe. Mussolini did not rule out an offensive against Kenya at a later date.

All this primarily concerned the army. Air-force orders stated rather generally that missions were essentially to be integrated into the operations of the ground troops and the navy. From this, as well as from the necessary response to enemy measures, the character of air-force actions was to emerge on its own. By contrast, Mussolini wanted to employ his naval forces in an unrestrictedly offensive manner.

On 6 April the commanders-in-chief of the different services were informed of these ideas, and Badoglio gave his first comment on them. He told Mussolini that planning in line with his instructions had been going on for some time, but he drew his attention to the serious shortages which existed in the very areas where offensive action was envisaged. The only possible offensive action was by air and by sea, and that by no means in an unrestricted manner.[274] Despite these remarks it may well be that Mussolini registered the marshal's agreement in principle with his concept. Badoglio's formulations were too reserved, they looked too undecided. It seems that many Italian military leaders were inhibited from practising consistent critique by their opportunistic alignment with the government and by personal or departmental rivalries,[275] though such a statement cannot be unreservedly generalized.

Only three days later the commanders-in-chief of the army, the air force, and the navy left Badoglio in no doubt about the totally inadequate state of equipment of their forces. They warned against illusions; indeed Admiral Cavagnari regarded the initial situation as less favourable than in September 1939.[276] Although Badoglio also considered the situation 'extremely delicate',

---

[274] *DDI*, 9th ser., iii, No. 716, p. 618 (6 Apr. 1940); Fioravanzo, 'Italian Strategy', 65.

[275] For a characterization of the Italian military cf. Whittam, 'Italian General Staff', 77–95; Smith, *Roman Empire*, 169–89.

[276] The protocol of 9 Apr. 1940 is published in Faldella, *L'Italia*, 728–34. Cf. also *La marina italiana*, xxi. 308–9; Bandini, *Tecnica della sconfitta*, 567 ff.; Bocca, *Storia*, 155–8, judges the attitude of the military very critically.

his practical conclusions were confined to an appeal for a sense of duty. It is the more astonishing—considering subsequent relations between Rome and Berlin—that any commitment to co-operation with Germany was ruled out. Exchange of information, certainly—but no request was to be made for material support, because Mussolini wished to preserve his freedom of political action. Badoglio's account of the conference appears to have been attuned to the expectations of the head of government rather than those of the service chiefs, who were entitled to expect that he would try once more to warn Mussolini.[277] It was not that the marshal wished Italy to enter the war; but he was in thrall to hierarchical modes of thinking, fearing even to be suspected of insubordination. Hence the reservations which he unquestionably formulated were almost invariably weakened by the qualification that everyone had full confidence in Mussolini's decisions.[278] Badoglio evidently lacked the resoluteness which Cavagnari displayed on 14 April when he drew attention to the dangerous consequences of the incipient gamble. To him the intended operations were an academic exercise, as Italy was basically in no position to achieve strategic objectives. Nevertheless, even Cavagnari did not oppose the war as such, but merely the decision to wage it at that particular moment. He warned that, if things came to the worst, Mussolini would have to take his seat at the negotiating table without any territorial pledges, without a navy, and possibly without an air force.[279] Yet it was precisely these services that lent weight to Italy in the Mediterranean arena. Cavagnari made it clear that he considered it unwarrantable for Italy to join the war. On 22 April he pointed out to the army general staff that transports to Libya would have to be effected prior to general mobilization, as the navy would not be able to guarantee adequate escorts for all convoys once hostilities had begun. The shipments of material, at least, should be completed before Italy entered the war, in order to have fast ships available for troop transports.[280]

Mussolini now intervened, and on 6 May there was a conference between Badoglio, the commanders-in-chief of the three services, and the undersecretary of state in the war ministry, General Ubaldo Soddu, on Italy's means of increasing her military strength in Libya. Badoglio pointed out that 130,000 Italian troops were stationed there, while the French and the British in Morocco, Algeria, Tunisia, Egypt, and Syria had several times as many soldiers ready for action.[281] It is noteworthy that this meeting, which followed

---

[277] The letter of 11 Apr. 1940 is published in Faldella, *L'Italia*, 150–1.

[278] This is true also of the surprisingly vigorous letter written to Mussolini by Badoglio on 13 Apr., following a disillusioning conversation with the Duke of Aosta: published in Faldella, *L'Italia*, 152–3.

[279] Published in *La marina italiana*, xxi. 351–2; cf. Bernotti, *Guerra nel Mediterraneo*, 33–8; Iachino, *Tramonto*, 313–14; Bragadin, *Che ha fatto la marina?*, 8; Baum and Weichold, *Krieg der 'Achsenmächte'*, 35–6; Schreiber, *Revisionismus*, 265 ff.

[280] Faldella, *L'Italia*, 157–8.

[281] *Africa settentrionale, La preparazione*, 72 ff.; the record of the meeting also in *Verbali*, i. 43–7.

3. Strategic Considerations to June 1940

Badoglio's exposé and went on for many hours, concerned itself almost exclusively with reinforcement of personnel, when it must have been obvious that increasing the troop strength to 220,000 was a pointless exercise so long as the lack of motor-vehicles, light armour, and modern equipment persisted. On 11 May Balbo—then governor-general of Libya—drew Mussolini's attention in no uncertain terms to the lack of realism displayed by the commanders-in-chief at the conference.[282] He listed the serious shortages of equipment: an out-dated, and in any case insufficient, artillery, and the lack of anti-tank and anti-aircraft guns. Another serious consideration was that the fortified locations had been denuded of weapons. A few days after the discussion between the commanders-in-chief Balbo emphasized that there was no point in sending thousands of soldiers to Libya if weapons, vehicles, ammunition, and motor-fuel were not also dispatched as quickly as possible.[283] However—and this was soon made clear by Soddu and Favagrossa—definite limitations in this field were imposed by Italy's economic[284] and industrial circumstances.[285]

Soon thereafter the campaign against France opened with the German attack of 10 May and, as a result of the German advance—as is clear from the letters exchanged between Mussolini and Hitler—the Duce's determination to intervene in events was growing apace. His very last doubts, however, seem to have been dispelled only after Hitler's announcements of victory on 25 May. On 26 May he notified Badoglio and Balbo that he had indicated to Hitler that, from 5 June onward, he could expect Italy to enter the war any day.[286] Also on 26 May he indicated to Mackensen that he could wait no longer. Three days later the commanders-in-chief of the three services were informed of his decision.[287]

Although Mussolini expressed his conviction as to the absolute superiority of the Wehrmacht over the Allies, he nevertheless spoke of the possibility that Italy—whose army in his and Graziani's view was in a satisfactory, if by no means ideal, condition—might have the power to bring about the real decision in the war. There are, of course, a good many indications that this was merely wishful thinking, a not too convincing variant of the political calculation which had determined Fascist foreign policy since the early 1930s. In the situation of May 1940 Italy certainly—in contrast to earlier on—no longer had the option

---

[282] Faldella, *L'Italia*, 159; on 6 May Gen. Guidi, C.-in-C. Tenth Army, drew the attention of Marshal Graziani, chief of the army general staff, to the shortages of equipment of the Italian troops in Africa and the dangers resulting therefrom: *Africa settentrionale, La preparazione*, 74–5.
[283] *Africa settentrionale, La preparazione*, 75, 172 ff.
[284] Favagrossa, *Perchè perdemmo la guerra*, 126 ff., 263–6.
[285] *Africa settentrionale, La preparazione*, 75–6, 174 ff., Promemoria per il Duce, 13 May 1940, from Gen. Soddu; also 176–80, Promemoria per il Capo del Governo, 13 May 1940, from Gen. Favagrossa.
[286] Badoglio, *Italy*, 14; Bocca, *Storia*, 161–2; the letter is dated 30 May, cf. *DGFP* D ix, No. 356, p. 396.
[287] *DDI*, 9th ser., iv, No. 642, pp. 495 ff. (29 May 1940); Rossi, *Mussolini*, 165 ff.; Badoglio, *Italy*, 16; *Hitler e Mussolini*, 43–7; Bernotti, *Guerra nel Mediterraneo*, 39 ff.; Faldella, *L'Italia*, 159–60; *Africa settentrionale, La preparazione*, 77 ff., 185 ff.; Knox, *Mussolini*, 121 ff.

of playing a waiting-game. Mussolini, as he fully realized, was constrained by the time factor. In view of the imminent decision in the western campaign, any reservations based on the insufficient readiness of the Italian forces had lost all weight. The remaining time-span of at most four weeks did not seem to permit of any appreciable improvement in that respect.[288] In any case, what had questions of *matériel* to do with deliberations which were based on the belief that victory in the west would mean the end of the war, and which, as the direct consequence of that belief, were constantly haunted by the fear of coming too late? 'Our opponents now', Mussolini remarked in a very intimate circle, 'are the Germans, who want to take Paris and, if possible, decide the war before we join in.'[289] With regard to the operational measures to be taken by Italy, he referred to the political and strategic directives of his memorandum of 31 March. He continued to regard the launch of any spectacular action on the ground as out of the question; the Italian army therefore had to remain on the defensive. True, to the eastward 'something might be considered: for instance Yugoslavia'. Basically, however, there would be the naval and air war he had spoken of on 26 May: one of its objectives must be an attack on British bases in the Mediterranean.[290]

The decision had thus been taken. When on 30 May Badoglio discussed the situation with Cavagnari, Graziani, Pricolo (the air-force chief of staff), and Soddu, they would all have wished for a less hectic period of preparation, but they also realized that 5 June was now a binding date on which they would have to base their immediate plans and practical steps. However, they ruled out the idea of an air attack on France, as well as operations against British bases, which were in any case impracticable. In this respect Mussolini proved amenable to the arguments of the generals. On the whole—with the exception of the navy—the discussions on 30 May concentrated on achieving the most effective possible defence capacity on all fronts. Cavagnari, whose submarines were to guard the Mediterranean, a task which included offensive actions, urged in this context that Italy's entry into the war should be delayed, if only because it was impossible by 5 June to bring back from outside the Mediterranean all of the 225 merchant ships, which included important tankers. From a strategic point of view the basic rule for the navy was: 'defence against right and left; control of the Straits of Messina.'[291]

On 1 June Badoglio submitted to Mussolini another estimate of the situation, in which he again argued that Italy was in no way under compulsion to move, as—in the opinion of various Italian generals—a German victory in the west was not to be expected for a few weeks yet. Hence Italy could avoid any

---

[288] *DDI*, 9th ser., iv, No. 642, p. 496 (29 May 1940); *Africa settentrionale, La preparazione*, 186.
[289] Anfuso, *Roma, Berlino*, 152, also 147–56.
[290] *DDI*, 9th ser., iv, No. 642, p. 496; Faldella, *L'Italia*, 160, points to the unreal nature of even these intentions.
[291] The minutes of the conference on 30 May 1940 are published in Faldella, *L'Italia*, 739–42; cf. *Africa settentrionale, La preparazione*, 79–80.

3. Strategic Considerations to June 1940

precipitate entry into the war. Thus the supplying of Libya, which would take the whole month of June, could first be completed, which was of great importance for the colony's defence.[292]

The marshal met with unexpected support, for on the same day Mussolini received Hitler's reply in which, while not definitively opposing the date of 5 June, he urged that Italy's entry be delayed by three days so as not to jeopardize forthcoming German operations.[293] Remembering the measures still needed to establish Italian defensive capacity in Libya, Mussolini with evident relief decided that hostilities should not begin until 11 June.[294] He maintained this decision,[295] even though the German side changed their minds on 2 June, granting Italy an entirely free hand in choosing her date, including 5 June.[296] The reason was that the full-scale raids of the Luftwaffe on Paris and on French air-force bases began—sooner than originally planned—on 3 June. This was realized by the Italians in good time,[297] but their own plans now remained unchanged. The elderly King Victor Emmanuel likewise agreed with 11 June: for him entry into the war was a kind of birthday present. That it would prove to be a dubious gift he did not then suspect, although he was probably tormented by a good many doubts.[298] On 1 June he consented to transfer to Mussolini 'supreme command of operating fighting forces':[299] on the first day of war Mussolini accepted this dignity with appropriate full powers from his monarch.

Rintelen, the German military attaché in Rome, was officially informed by Badoglio on 5 June that not too much should be expected of the Italian armed forces, as neither the army nor the air force were fully equipped; besides, Italy had to protect her long frontier. Basically, therefore, one had to hope for an early conclusion to the war.[300] That same day a further conference was held between Badoglio and the commanders-in-chief of the three services, which discussed the countless tactical and material problems of the Italian forces but from which it is clear that Mussolini and Badoglio only intended to conduct a 'war of immobility' (*Sitzkrieg*) against France.[301]

---

[292] *DDI*, 9th ser., iv, No. 694, pp. 536–7 (1 June 1940); cf. Araldi, *Non belligeranza*, 137 ff., who believes that Badoglio may not have demanded much, but invariably did so too late; on this in detail Knox, *Mussolini*, 241–2.

[293] *DGFP* D ix, No. 357, pp. 484 ff. (31 May 1940).

[294] Ciano, *Diary 1939–1943*, 258–9 (1 June 1940).

[295] Ibid. 259–60 (2 June 1940); *DGFP* D ix, No. 372, p. 504 (2 June 1940): 'declaration of war 10 June; opening of hostilities 11 June.'

[296] *DGFP* D ix, No. 370, pp. 502–3 (2 June 1940).

[297] Ciano, *Diary 1939–1943*, 260 (3 June 1940); cf. Halder, *Diaries*, i. 435–6 (2 June 1940).

[298] Ciano, *Diary 1939–1943*, 260 (3 June 1940); on the reservations of the king, who was disturbed by the possibility of America entering the war, cf. ibid. 251 (16 May 1940), 258 (1 June 1940).

[299] Badoglio, *Italy*, 19; on the king's opposition to the transfer of supreme command to Mussolini cf. Ciano, *Diary 1939–1943*, 254–5 (26 May 1940), 261 (6 June 1940).

[300] *DGFP* D ix, No. 387, pp. 518–19 (5 June 1940); cf. Rintelen, *Mussolini als Bundesgenosse*, 87.

[301] Cf. minutes of meeting of 5 June 1940, published in Faldella, *L'Italia*, 743–6.

Another topic which came under discussion on 5 June was the island of Malta, the capture of which had been regarded ever since the end of 1938, especially by the Italian admiralty, as an indispensable prerequisite for successful operations in North Africa.[302] The problem of Malta was now for the first time discussed among the commanders-in-chief. Surprisingly enough, it was Cavagnari who opposed the idea of a landing, whereas Soddu and Graziani—the latter had broached the subject—thought it entirely feasible. No decision was taken, but Badoglio gave instructions for the project to be further examined.[303] This was done, and on 18 June the navy submitted a study whose negative findings had in part been known since 5 June. The sceptical attitude shown by Cavagnari at that time presumably stemmed from his knowledge of this paper. It advised against such an exceedingly difficult operation, which moreover was held to be unnecessary as Malta would in any case fall into Italy's lap at the end of the war. It would therefore be sufficient, for the time being, to hold Malta down by means of aerial attacks.[304] Appropriate preparations—along with plans for strikes against Alexandria—had already been ordered on 5 June.[305]

A few days before the opening of hostilities Mussolini is reported to have described his plan with the words: 'This time I'll declare war, but I won't wage it.' The directives of the general staffs of the three services, dated 7 June, were in line with the Duce's intentions. Against France an absolutely defensive stance was to be observed both on the ground and in the air. This applied to the Alpine front, Corsica, Tunisia, and Somaliland. At sea, French warships sailing in company with British units were to be considered 'hostile' and to be attacked. Against individual vessels, however, or against purely French formations fire was to be opened only if the Italian ships would be in jeopardy through waiting. In other words, Mussolini wanted to declare war on France, while at the same time forbidding any shooting.[306]

4. The Italian Fighting Forces

(a) Equipment and Organization

During the years preceding the outbreak of the Second World War Hitler and Mussolini—for obvious reasons—endeavoured to deceive one another about the real efficiency of their armies. They indulged in a kind of military braggadocio, as illustrated in the impressive staging of the Duce's visit to Berlin in 1937 and the Führer's return visit to Italy in 1938. Armed strength has always been part of the 'image' of dictators, and Mussolini was no exception to that

---

[302] Fioravanzo, 'Kriegführung', 19; detailed examination of Italian plans up to the beginning of the war in Gabriele, *Operazione C 3*, 3–46.
[303] Faldella, *L'Italia*, 162.
[304] Gabriele, *Operazione C 3*, 56–9; complete text of the document ibid. 305–10.
[305] Santoro, *L'aeronautica italiana*, i. 78.
[306] On this Faldella, *L'Italia*, 165 ff.

rule. As early as 1934 he boasted that he could effortlessly mobilize six million soldiers; in 1936 he considered it opportune to bluff the world with a figure of eight million; and his escalating propaganda even raised the figure to twelve million in 1939. In actual fact no more than three million could eventually be called up.[307] Even in retrospect it seems grotesque that in 1940 the Fascist regime, whose leaders regarded war and aggression as instruments of policy, had to send to the front an army worse equipped than the Italian troops had been in the First World War.[308]

Generally speaking, if one compares the great-power claims of Italian Fascism with its military preparations, one is struck by the discrepancy between proclaimed intentions and military reality, which was of a different order of magnitude from similar shortcomings on the part of the other two aggressors, Japan and Germany. This applies at least up to the conclusion of the war in Abyssinia, but essentially also until 1938–9. Researchers have so far only begun to examine this phenomenon, seeking its explanation mainly in the low efficiency of the political system and in the failure of individual decision-makers. On the whole, historiography continues to follow this line of interpretation. More recently, however, it has also been argued that the Italian armed forces' inadequate preparation for a major war can be explained by the political priorities set by the system itself. From the latter it appears, according to this view, that Fascist military policy was guided primarily by domestic and propaganda objectives, rather than pursuing any power politics based on long-term plans. Although Mussolini had claimed to have such plans, Fascism—according to the champions of this new thesis—had been quite unable to implement them. If one accepts this view, then any preparation for a world war may safely be deleted from the list of tasks facing the Italian generals.[309] Nevertheless, the rearmament efforts of the Fascist regime are not altogether disputed. Indeed they are credited with a measure of success. But this is qualified by the observation that, basically, they followed traditional lines. Such rearmament as was taking place could not suffice for the realization of the imperialist goals proclaimed by Mussolini.

Researches into this subject are based primarily on the example of the war in Ethiopia. As a working hypothesis the results arrived at in this context have undoubtedly provided new impulses to research—they seem especially attractive in connection with the controversy over the primacy of domestic policy.[310] On the other hand, the Abyssinian war has been, and still is, quoted as an illustration of the consistent imperial policy of the Mussolini government.[311] Yet as far as the developments beginning to take shape in 1938–9 are

---

[307] Smith, *Roman Empire*, 169–70.
[308] Bocca, *Storia*, 123.
[309] Rochat and Massobrio, *Storia dell'esercito*, 208–13; Rochat, 'Il ruolo delle forze armate'; id., 'Mussolini et les forces armées', 42–3; cf. also Petersen, 'Außenpolitik', 445 ff.
[310] Rochat, *Militari, passim*.
[311] e.g. Baer, *Test Case*.

concerned, the above interpretation—in the sense of an alternative claiming exclusivity—is not entirely convincing in determining the seriousness to be attributed to the political objectives proclaimed by Fascism. No doubt these were accompanied by propaganda exaggeration, but when comparing propaganda and reality we cannot conclude that, just because the regime was unable to pursue its goals, it was also unwilling to do so.

In the military sphere, more than anywhere else, numerous indications exist for the period 1935–40 to suggest that it was the inefficiency of the system that prevented practical lessons from being converted into appropriate measures to prepare for a major war. In this context it should again be emphasized that the development inaugurated by the conclusion of the Pact of Steel in May 1939, and scheduled for completion by 1943, was interrupted by the war.[312] Yet even for the period preceding the Pact it cannot simply be asserted that the lessons of the Spanish civil war[313] were being ignored by the Italian military leaders.[314] Indeed the generals realized very soon that mobile warfare, seeking a swift decision, was in fact the operational concept appropriate to Italy's strategic structures. After the war in Ethiopia, the course of which confirmed the theory of blitzkrieg,[315] they quite logically demanded modern weapons for the army and a higher degree of motorization.[316] Nevertheless, in Italy, generally speaking, there was only the myth of blitzkrieg, and not a blitzkrieg doctrine guiding military planning and producing practical results. In contrast to Germany,[317] blitzkrieg in Italy remained essentially an argument of Fascist propaganda, and the army's modernization efforts after 1937–8 did little to change this situation.[318]

The reasons for this state of affairs and the low efficiency of Fascist military policy are various. There were, as mentioned earlier, the difficulties encountered by the Italian economy in adjusting, and later converting, to effective armament production.[319] Added to these were inherent organizational inadequacies, as well as the problem of allocation of resources.[320] Moreover, the

---

[312] The inefficiency of the system is confirmed by e.g. De Luna, *Mussolini*, 112–22; Minitti, 'Aspetti'; Kogan, *Politics*, 30–1, where it is analysed in terms of Italy's armaments policy since 1876. The same thesis is supported by Maione, *L'imperialismo straccione*, 215–16, 227–40, who examines the links between the financial policy and the armament efforts of the Fascist regime: here too is seen the inability of Fascism to master in practice a problem which has been correctly identified in theory.

[313] On this in detail Coverdale, *Italian Intervention*; id., 'Guadalajara'.

[314] A different interpretation is offered in Whittam, 'Italian General Staff', 93.

[315] Rochat and Massobrio, *Storia dell'esercito*, 221 ff. A comprehensive presentation of the development of Italian military doctrine in Botti and Ilari, *Il pensiero militare*, 35–336, for the period 1919–41. On the Italian army's blitzkrieg concept, which goes back to Gen. Federico Baistrocchi, cf. Knox, *Mussolini*, 25–30; also Rutherford, *Blitzkrieg, passim*.

[316] Smith, *Roman Empire*, 170–1; *L'esercito italiano dal 1° tricolore*, 230; Sweet, *Iron Arm*, 109–77.

[317] Bradley, *Generaloberst Heinz Guderian*, 193–218.

[318] Rochat and Massobrio, *Storia dell'esercito*, 223.

[319] Basic information as always in Favagrossa, *Perchè perdemmo la guerra*, 44–102.

[320] Faldella, *L'Italia*, 105 ff.; Rochat and Massobrio, *Storia dell'esercito*, 216 ff.

4. The Italian Fighting Forces

wars in Ethiopia and Spain, protracted beyond expectation, had drawn huge quantities of material and weapons from the army's stores. For this reason alone the country, for years ahead, would be in no condition to participate in a European war.[321] The operational fitness of the forces, more especially the army,[322] was greatly impaired by these developments. Admittedly, most of what had been handed over or lost had been outdated material, but even an ancient rifle is better than none at all. It was largely for this reason, because of the state of the armed forces, that Mussolini in the agreements connected with the Pact of Steel so emphatically insisted on an interval of peace. Italy in 1939 lacked almost everything that was necessary for waging a modern war. Moreover, at the outbreak of hostilities in September the army and air force were in the midst of a reorganization and re-equipment phase, which, if Italy were to enter the war then, was bound to lead to a crisis. Needless to say, the theoretical concepts accompanying these measures inevitably affected rearmament, as this is governed not only by the volume of industrial output but also quite decisively by military planning. It was likewise in the nature of things that prolonged trial periods had to precede any decisions on armament.

Since 1937, for instance, the Italian army command had been endeavouring to assess the experience of the past as well as more recent theoretical findings by holding manœuvres, in order to arrive at up-to-date conclusions with regard to modern warfare. One of the results was a restructuring of what had been 'triangular' divisions into two-part divisions—that is, the *divisione ternaria*, which, in addition to other units, comprised three infantry regiments, became the *divisione binaria* with only two regiments. This move was intended, first of all, to adapt the infantry divisions to the conditions of mobile warfare. The formations were to become more manœuvrable, faster, and easier to command. The risks of personnel reduction, which was bound to affect fighting strength detrimentally, were to be offset by the provision of modern weapons. In parallel to the infantry divisions, the introduction of two-part mobile divisions, motorized divisions, and armoured divisions was being examined.[323]

The project was not without controversy from the outset. The opponents of reform pointed out that a restructuring of the divisions—since 1937–8 these had been pared down from three to two regiments of infantry, plus one regiment of artillery of three battalions, with three batteries each and with sappers, which admittedly was not enough—would weaken both the combative effectiveness and the morale of the units. Increased mobility, it was claimed, was no adequate compensation for that disadvantage. The champions

---

[321] Bocca, *Storia*, 116; Rochat and Massobrio, *Storia dell'esercito*, 221.

[322] *L'esercito italiano dal 1° tricolore*, 231; Bocca, *Storia*, 116, states that in the Spanish civil war alone 730 aircraft, 7,688 machine-guns, 11,305 motor-vehicles, and 1,930 guns were forfeited through cession and losses. On the occasion of the signing of the Tripartite Pact on 27 Sept. 1940 Ciano gave the Italian losses in Spain as 1,000 aircraft, 6,000 killed, and 14,000m. lire: data according to *Staatsmänner*, 224 (28 Sept. 1940). On 4 Oct. 1940 Mussolini spoke to Hitler of 800 aircraft lost, ibid. 236; cf. also Bandini, *Tecnica della sconfitta*, 404–5.

[323] *L'esercito italiano tra la 1ª e la 2ª guerra*, 124 ff.

of the new organization maintained the opposite, however. What appears to have been overlooked was that the troops could in fact acquire greater mobility only if the level of motorization of the army were decisively increased. So long as that was not done, any diminution of the personnel strength of the divisions was bound to lower their combative effectiveness. In replaying the arguments of those days one cannot avoid the suspicion that Italy's military leaders did not conduct the controversy either openly or with reference to factual arguments. Decisions seem largely to have been based on wishful thinking rather than an appreciation of the industrial and economic realities of the country in the early 1930s. A question that has to be asked in this connection, even though it cannot be answered, is to what extent political opportunism, or the thinking in terms of establishment sizes so dear to military hierarchies, or indeed a general conformism, were determining attitudes.[324] The new army structure, at any rate, resulted in more divisions, more armies, and more army corps, which meant the creation of a whole string of well-endowed posts; this must have made it easier for many an officer to approve of it. Admittedly the reform was, first of all, triggered by the experience of the First World War and the war in Ethiopia,[325] so that the motivation for it was not only negative: but there can be little doubt today that the restructuring of the divisions was one of the most grievous mistakes of Fascist military policy. Outwardly the impression was created that Italy was purposefully adapting herself to the war of the future. Propaganda emphasized only the larger number of divisions, creating the illusion of increased strength, and eventually this was probably believed—except by a handful of initiates and a few sceptical opponents. In reality, the whole business, so long as there was no technical modernization of the army, was nothing more nor less than deception and bluff as part of the Fascist striving for great-power status.[326] And no amount of subjective good intentions can change this fact.

At any rate, the Italian army in September 1939 was in a very precarious state. The controversial restructuring of the formations had by then only been completed in 16 divisions. These alone were regarded as up to establishment in terms of weapons and equipment. Altogether there were 67 divisions: 43 infantry, 3 armoured, 2 motorized, 3 mobile, 5 Alpini, and 11 others for special duties. This does not include the major formations in Ethiopia. The armament of the troops was, as a rule, totally outdated. But even if one regarded this material as operational equipment, there was no question of

---

[324] Bocca, *Storia*, 114–15; Favagrossa, *Perchè perdemmo la guerra*, 13; Fuduli, 'La fanteria', 43 ff.; Smith, *Roman Empire*, 170.

[325] *L'esercito italiano tra la 1ª e la 2ª guerra*, 128–33.

[326] Rochat and Massobrio, *Storia dell'esercito*, 223–4; Faldella, *L'Italia*, 106; a more positive assessment of the reform of the army in Bandini, *Tecnica della sconfitta*, 405–6. As Knox, *Mussolini*, 27–8, points out, Pariani, the real initiator of the transformation of the 'divisione ternaria' into the 'divisione binaria', was well aware that the new formations represented mixed brigades rather than divisions, but for propaganda reasons they were invariably referred to as divisions.

adequate stocks. It was generally agreed that the equipment envisaged for the refurbishing or upgrading of the army would not be available in sufficient quantities within a foreseeable period. It was moreover known that the Italian divisions, because they were short of artillery, tanks, and anti-aircraft and anti-tank guns, had only very limited fire-power. Almost equally serious was the lack of transport capacity.[327]

The situation of the navy was substantially more favourable, even though it also suffered from shortages of equipment. Above all, it lacked anti-aircraft guns both afloat and at its shore-bases. Stocks of ammunition appeared to be reasonably good; less so were its stocks of fuel, especially when, following Italy's entry into the war, nearly all its overseas supplies ceased. Stocks of high-quality foodstuffs and clothing were considerably more satisfactory in the navy than in the army.[328]

The material situation of the air force in the autumn of 1939 was just as unsatisfactory as that of the army. The service suffered from a proliferation of types. It is significant—and was ultimately a consequence of insufficient standardization—that in September 1939 only 1,190 out of 2,586 bomber aircraft were reported operational. There were, moreover, serious shortages in the armament of Italian aircraft. Organization of supplies also fell short of requirements. Crews were inadequately trained. The production capacity of the aircraft industry, which over the period 1939–40 produced a mere 150–270 aircraft per month,[329] was much too low.

Bearing in mind the industrial and economic prerequisites, no substantial improvement in the equipment of the Italian forces could be expected in less than a matter of years. It is not therefore surprising that, even though certain improvements had unquestionably been achieved, the situation in June 1940 had still to be described as highly unsatisfactory. Most of the divisions still lacked the envisaged level of equipment. They were short of weapons, ammunition, fuel, transport capacity, and qualified staff. As it was not too difficult—in view of Italy's raw-material supplies, her production volume, and her mobilization system—to make long-term predictions of all these bottlenecks, General Favagrossa, the minister for war production, had convinced Mussolini as early as December 1939 that it was not desirable to inflate the army to 126 divisions. It would be more realistic to restrict it to 73 new-style divisions. Favagrossa's arguments, based as they were on economic facts, were irrefutable. The originally planned rearmament programmes were therefore

---

[327] Favagrossa, *Perchè perdemmo la guerra*, 13–14; *L'esercito italiano tra la 1ª e la 2ª guerra*, 128–33; Rochat and Massobrio, *Storia dell'esercito*, 224–5; on the mechanization of the Italian army between 1930 and 1940 cf. Sweet, *Iron Arm*, 78–177. An excellent analysis of the Italian army's state of equipment in 1939–40, of Italy's strategic situation, and of organizational problems is provided by Montanari, *L'esercito italiano*; numerous documents in the appendix.

[328] Favagrossa, *Perchè perdemmo la guerra*, 20–1; Smith, *Roman Empire*, 178–9.

[329] Favagrossa, *Perchè perdemmo la guerra*, 22–5; production figures according to Gentile, *Storia delle operazioni*, 41.

cut back for the air force and navy as well.[330] All these measures, admittedly, were based on the assumption that Italy would not enter the war in the foreseeable future. When she did so in June 1940 it was obvious that even a modified rearmament plan, as put in hand by Favagrossa, was unable to bring about any appreciable changes in the military conditions described. This was also largely due to the fact that Italy, even if she were able to rearm on an adequate scale, could only do so slowly, as the urgently required foreign currency had first to be earned by the export of manufactured goods—which in turn had to be at the expense of armament production for her own fighting forces. Paradoxically, therefore, Italy's rearmament was, on the one hand, made possible by her export of merchandise and, on the other, curtailed by it. The German model[331] would not have been applicable even in the past, in view of the structure of the Italian armaments industry; after the outbreak of war in 1939 Italy was in even less of a position to copy it.

As for the reduction in the number of divisions in the Italian army, it was at least hoped that, within the given framework, this would make it possible to field a fully equipped army. By 10 June 1940, however, as indicated in Diagram I.I.1, there was no question of that. The army then comprised 1,687,950 men, shared out among 51 divisions in the mother country, 14 in Libya, 5 in Albania, and 1 in the Aegean. It was subdivided into Army Group Commands West, East, and South, into 10 Army and 30 Army Corps Commands, into 43 classical infantry divisions, 5 divisions of Alpini, and 3 armoured divisions, 3 mobile divisions, 12 partly motorized divisions and 2 motorized divisions, 2 Libyan divisions, and 3 divisions of militia. Additionally there were 2 native divisions and 23 colonial brigades in Italian East Africa.[332] Although, taken as a whole, the actual situation came nowhere near the famous 'eight million bayonets' of Fascist propaganda, the figures nevertheless looked quite respectable on paper. In reality, however, the Italian army was inferior to that sent to the front line in 1915, absolutely in terms of numbers and relatively in terms of quality. In the First World War the Italian army had available to it weapons and equipment which could essentially be described as on a par with the military hardware of the other nations. Nothing of the kind could be claimed in the summer of 1940, with regard either to the French or—then a potential adversary—the Yugoslav forces.[333] Moreover, only 19 divisions were regarded as fully equipped, i.e. with 100 per cent of their establishment of servicemen, of their necessary equipment, and of their weapons, as well as of draught animals and motor-vehicles, which could

---

[330] Favagrossa, Perchè perdemmo la guerra, 115.
[331] Fully described in vol. i of the present work, III.II (Deist).
[332] L'esercito italiano tra la 1ª e la 2ª guerra, appendix 77; Bocca, Storia, 122–3; Cruccu, 'La presenza italiana', 44; according to Ceva, La condotta, 63, there were in fact only 3 partially motorized (vehicle-transportable) divisions, so that the number of infantry divisions must have been 52. It is on this figure that the following argument above is based. Faldella, L'Italia, 107–8.
[333] Faldella, L'Italia, 108; Africa settentrionale, La preparazione, 182; Favagrossa, Perchè perdemmo la guerra, 26–7.

4. The Italian Fighting Forces

DIAGRAM I.1.1. Combat-readiness of Italian divisions, June 1940
Source: *L'esercito italiano tra la 1ª e la 2ª guerra*.

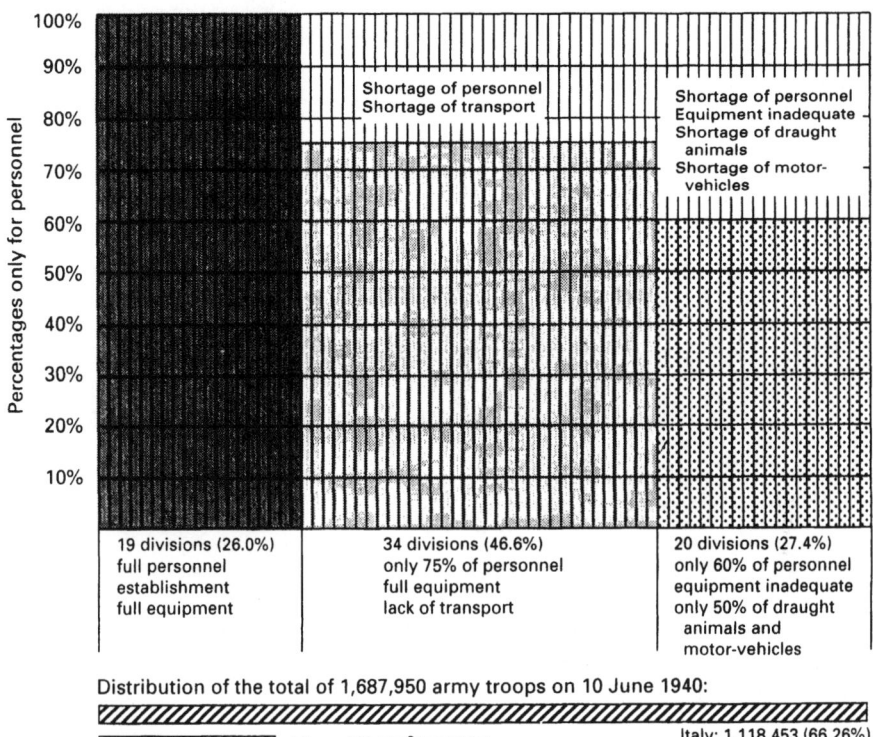

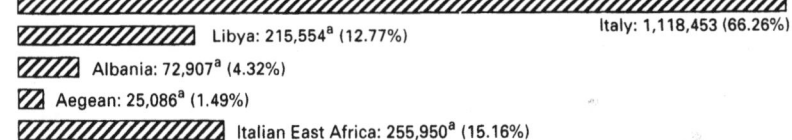

Chart shows, with y-axis "Percentages only for personnel" from 10% to 100%:
- 19 divisions (26.0%) full personnel establishment, full equipment
- 34 divisions (46.6%) only 75% of personnel, full equipment, lack of transport (Shortage of personnel, Shortage of transport)
- 20 divisions (27.4%) only 60% of personnel, equipment inadequate, only 50% of draught animals and motor-vehicles (Shortage of personnel, Equipment inadequate, Shortage of draught animals, Shortage of motor-vehicles)

Distribution of the total of 1,687,950 army troops on 10 June 1940:
- Italy: 1,118,453 (66.26%)
- Libya: 215,554[a] (12.77%)
- Albania: 72,907[a] (4.32%)
- Aegean: 25,086[a] (1.49%)
- Italian East Africa: 255,950[a] (15.16%)

[a] Total, i.e. fighting forces plus staffs, supplies, administration, etc.

moreover easily be replenished by requisitioning. Another 34 divisions could be regarded as operational, though they did not by any means possess their full equipment. While having the scheduled level of weapons and equipment, their personnel was 25 per cent below establishment. They also suffered from a shortage of transport capacity. The remaining 20 divisions were classified as only conditionally operational. They possessed only 60 per cent of their personnel and 50 per cent of their draught animals and motor-vehicles, as well as suffering from a lack of weapons and shortages of equipment.[334]

Diagram I.1.2 represents the establishment strength and the actual condition

---
[334] *Africa settentrionale, La preparazione*, 150–1; Favagrossa, *Perchè perdemmo la guerra*, 27; *Esercito italiano: Immagini*, p. xi–xii.

Infantry division
12,979 men

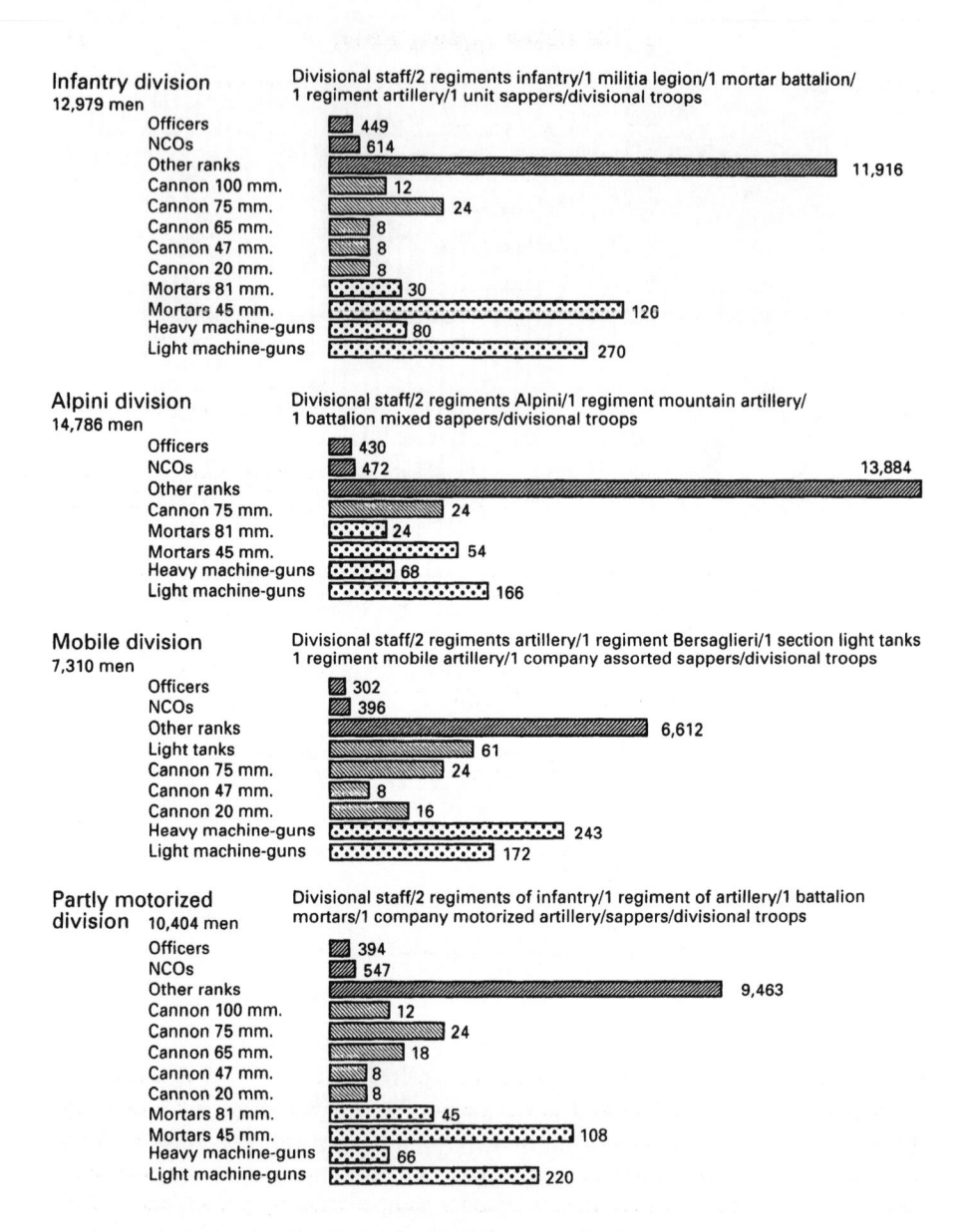

Divisional staff/2 regiments infantry/1 militia legion/1 mortar battalion/ 1 regiment artillery/1 unit sappers/divisional troops

- Officers: 449
- NCOs: 614
- Other ranks: 11,916
- Cannon 100 mm.: 12
- Cannon 75 mm.: 24
- Cannon 65 mm.: 8
- Cannon 47 mm.: 8
- Cannon 20 mm.: 8
- Mortars 81 mm.: 30
- Mortars 45 mm.: 126
- Heavy machine-guns: 80
- Light machine-guns: 270

Alpini division
14,786 men

Divisional staff/2 regiments Alpini/1 regiment mountain artillery/ 1 battalion mixed sappers/divisional troops

- Officers: 430
- NCOs: 472
- Other ranks: 13,884
- Cannon 75 mm.: 24
- Mortars 81 mm.: 24
- Mortars 45 mm.: 54
- Heavy machine-guns: 68
- Light machine-guns: 166

Mobile division
7,310 men

Divisional staff/2 regiments artillery/1 regiment Bersaglieri/1 section light tanks 1 regiment mobile artillery/1 company assorted sappers/divisional troops

- Officers: 302
- NCOs: 396
- Other ranks: 6,612
- Light tanks: 61
- Cannon 75 mm.: 24
- Cannon 47 mm.: 8
- Cannon 20 mm.: 16
- Heavy machine-guns: 243
- Light machine-guns: 172

Partly motorized division
10,404 men

Divisional staff/2 regiments of infantry/1 regiment of artillery/1 battalion mortars/1 company motorized artillery/sappers/divisional troops

- Officers: 394
- NCOs: 547
- Other ranks: 9,463
- Cannon 100 mm.: 12
- Cannon 75 mm.: 24
- Cannon 65 mm.: 18
- Cannon 47 mm.: 8
- Cannon 20 mm.: 8
- Mortars 81 mm.: 45
- Mortars 45 mm.: 108
- Heavy machine-guns: 66
- Light machine-guns: 220

DIAGRAM I.I.2. Establishment and authorized allowance of equipment of Italian divisions, 1940

Source: *Africa settentrionale, La preparazione*.

of the Italian divisions in 1940,[335] though it should be pointed out that this structure changed a great deal during the war; in addition, new divisions were set up in response to general developments. Personnel strength, in particular,

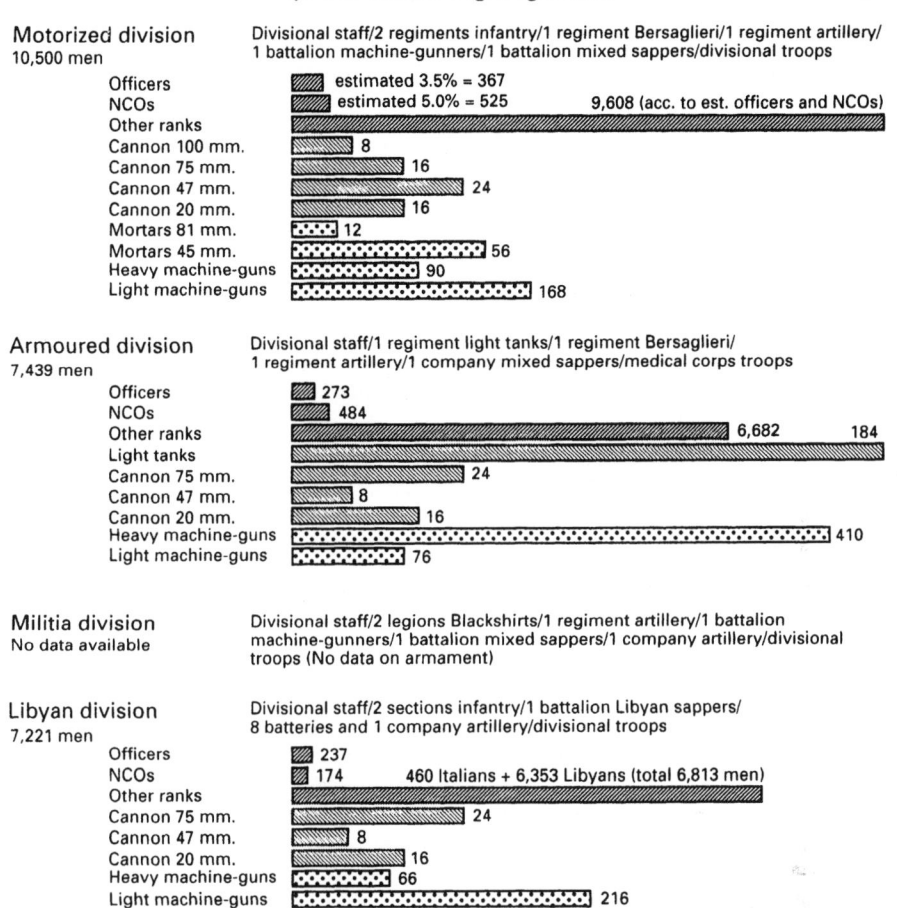

4. The Italian Fighting Forces

Motorized division
10,500 men

Divisional staff/2 regiments infantry/1 regiment Bersaglieri/1 regiment artillery/
1 battalion machine-gunners/1 battalion mixed sappers/divisional troops

Officers	estimated 3.5% = 367
NCOs	estimated 5.0% = 525
Other ranks	9,608 (acc. to est. officers and NCOs)
Cannon 100 mm.	8
Cannon 75 mm.	16
Cannon 47 mm.	24
Cannon 20 mm.	16
Mortars 81 mm.	12
Mortars 45 mm.	56
Heavy machine-guns	90
Light machine-guns	168

Armoured division
7,439 men

Divisional staff/1 regiment light tanks/1 regiment Bersaglieri/
1 regiment artillery/1 company mixed sappers/medical corps troops

Officers	273
NCOs	484
Other ranks	6,682
Light tanks	184
Cannon 75 mm.	24
Cannon 47 mm.	8
Cannon 20 mm.	16
Heavy machine-guns	410
Light machine-guns	76

Militia division
No data available

Divisional staff/2 legions Blackshirts/1 regiment artillery/1 battalion
machine-gunners/1 battalion mixed sappers/1 company artillery/divisional
troops (No data on armament)

Libyan division
7,221 men

Divisional staff/2 sections infantry/1 battalion Libyan sappers/
8 batteries and 1 company artillery/divisional troops

Officers	237
NCOs	174
Other ranks	460 Italians + 6,353 Libyans (total 6,813 men)
Cannon 75 mm.	24
Cannon 47 mm.	8
Cannon 20 mm.	16
Heavy machine-guns	66
Light machine-guns	216

DIAGRAM I.1.2 (cont.)

changed all the time: target figures and actual figures hardly ever agreed.

Of the 73 divisions mobilized at the beginning of the war, 52 were infantry divisions, which, as it were, represented the backbone of the Italian army. This circumstance of course affected the character of combat operations, and resulted in a situation where all other units were essentially perceived, and in fact employed, as supporting the infantry. This was renewed evidence of how

---

[335] Figures according to *Africa settentrionale, La preparazione*, 307–15. As to the divisions described here as 'partially motorized', it should be noted, on the grounds of information provided by Sig. Lucio Ceva, that these were slightly reduced infantry divisions, less the small legion of militia soldiers; they had a considerably reduced number of animals—913 instead of 3,424—and had one regiment of motorized artillery. It had originally been planned to move them by motor-vehicles, but this proved impossible because of the lack of transport. The divisions of this type employed in Libya had no animals.

little Italy's military leaders had learnt from international developments[336]—a conclusion confirmed also by the low level of motorization of the Italian army.

At the end of 1939 the army had 23,000 motor-vehicles, 8,700 special vehicles, 4,400 staff cars, and 12,500 motor-cycles.[337] When Italy entered the war the total number of motor-vehicles, including some 1,600 tanks and 17,000 requisitioned motor-cars, was approximately 55,000—excluding two-wheeled transport. This meant, even with the exhaustion of all available reserves, that the shortfall in the motorization of the ground forces was something like 50 per cent.[338]

In view of these circumstances, as well as the outdated operational principles of Italian land-warfare doctrine and the low fire-power of the Italian divisions—among the infantry this was a quarter of comparable French and a ninth of comparable German formations—it is not difficult to see that this army could not be expected to conduct a blitzkrieg. This assessment of its actual potential in no way diminishes the performance of the Italian soldier, who had no need to fear international comparison.[339] Quite apart from any psychological considerations, it is obvious that Italy's forces, whose equipment and weapons at the time should not be sweepingly described as bad, were in principle better suited to positional than to mobile warfare. This is suggested not only by their lack of transport capacity, but also by a relatively heavy rifle, an over-large field-pack, poor-quality footwear, and a most unpractical battle-dress.[340]

The state of the Italian army even called into question its defensive capability. Although in the First World War Italy had manufactured some 19,000 guns, she had allowed her artillery to become outdated between 1920 and 1930. Since 1928-9 the generals, impressed by international developments, had been drawing attention to this state of affairs and demanded 15,371 new guns from an industry which was then manufacturing 65 per month. Mussolini at first agreed, but the ministry of finance time and again insisted on a postponement in the allocation of the necessary billions.[341] There ensued a bureaucratic tug of war which clearly revealed Italy's difficulties in maintaining a modern armaments industry.[342] There was a lack of raw materials, of currency for obtaining them, and of a sufficient industrial capacity. Between 1932 and 1935 a start, at least, was made on the development of new prototypes, and in 1938 a production programme was launched, with a provisional

---

[336] Bocca, *Storia*, 116; a comprehensive account of the history of Italian infantry in Scala, *Storia delle fanterie italiane*; for employment in the Second World War, pp. 229–542; for developments between 1936 and 1940, pp. 35–48.
[337] Bocca, *Storia*, 121.
[338] Favagrossa, *Perchè perdemmo la guerra*, 27; *Africa settentrionale, La preparazione*, 182–3.
[339] Extensively on this point Pallotta, *L'esercito italiano*, 9–23.
[340] Bocca, *Storia*, 117; Cruccu, 'La presenza italiano', 44.
[341] Bandini, *Tecnica della sconfitta*, 398 ff.; Bocca, *Storia*, 118–19; Faldella, *L'Italia*, 95–9; Raspin, 'Aspekte', 212.
[342] Bandini, *Tecnica della sconfitta*, 419–20.

4. The Italian Fighting Forces

completion-date in 1943–4. The target was the production of over 2,000 cannon of different calibres:[343] in particular the 75/32 and the 149/19 guns, as well as the 90/53 anti-aircraft gun, which in quality equalled the famous German 8.8-cm. gun, raised the hope that the forces would now be supplied with good equipment.[344] Soon, however, it turned out that the authorized quantities would not meet the requirements of the fighting forces. Supplementary programmes with further orders proved inevitable. New plant had to be set up, which resulted in budgetary problems. Added to these were technical difficulties. Besides, ordnance production was more labour-intensive than in the past. In the First World War a gun of 149/35 calibre required, on average, 1,286 man-hours; in 1940 the Italian armament industry needed 12,475 hours to produce a gun of 149/40 calibre. Only by making allowance for such developments is it possible to avoid misjudgements about the armament efforts of the Fascist regime, efforts which could be observed after 1939—always of course within limits which, in absolute terms, were on too small a scale by international comparison to qualify Italy as an equal among the great powers. Thus Italy, between 1939 and 1943, manufactured altogether 12,500 guns—2,500 fewer than during the First World War. It would be quite wrong, however, to conclude that the armaments industry was stagnating under Fascism: in point of fact its production capacity was sufficient, had it built cannon of the kind employed during 1914–18, to deliver 75,000 guns during the same period of time. This represents a fivefold increase in the output volume of ordnance production compared with 1915–18.[345] As the manufacture of heavy guns was virtually suspended from 1918 to 1932, owing to the atmosphere of reassurance prevailing after the First World War,[346] comparison of these figures shows that Italy's rearmament failed not only in the face of organizational difficulties but also because increased qualitative and quantitative demands by the military had brought it up to the limits of what was possible for the country.

In 1939 Italy was still producing only about 70 guns a month. From 1941 onward an annual production of 3,000 to 3,600 was expected. In setting this target the planners assumed that there would be no bottlenecks in raw-material supplies, but even in 1939 this proved unrealistic. Yet even under ideal conditions—allowing for the requirements of the forces and the performance of the armament industry—it would have taken something like ten years to equip Italy's armed forces with ordnance sufficient for twelve months of warfare.[347] As late as in May 1940, immediately before Italy's entry into the war, the general staff proceeded from the assumption that a few modern artillery battalions equipped with 75/18, 149/40, and 210/22 calibres could be

---

[343] Faldella, *L'Italia*, 100; Raspin, 'Aspekte', 212.
[344] Faldella, *L'Italia*, 98.
[345] Bandini, *Tecnica della sconfitta*, 395.
[346] Raspin, 'Aspekte', 212.
[347] Favagrossa, *Perchè perdemmo la guerra*, 48–9; Bandini, *Tecnica della sconfitta*, 407–8.

allocated to the army by the end of the year, at the earliest. The army's operational formations in the mother country possessed only 15 more or less modern batteries of 75/46 calibre.[348] The remainder of the 225 batteries were considered outdated, which was why Mussolini now demanded a minimum of 1,000 batteries—but this again took no account of Italy's industrial realities in 1940. The bottlenecks in armament production could simply not be liquidated in the short run. In the event of an early entry into the war, the Italian army would therefore inevitably have to operate with outdated artillery and without any appreciable anti-aircraft defences.[349] An aggravating circumstance was that ammunition supplies to the units were likewise giving cause for anxiety.[350]

Another weakness of the army was the fact that Italy's armour, twenty years after the First World War, was still in its infancy, even though the tank had, between the wars[351]—after 1935 especially in Germany[352]—increasingly gained in importance. Reflections on new combat tactics dominated discussion among military experts, a circumstance of which Italy's officers were, of course, aware.

As a direct consequence of this development, between 1936 and 1938 the Italian army began to concentrate its tanks into armoured brigades or divisions. The tank, therefore, was no longer viewed only as a weapon to support the infantry.[353] Italian military leaders, in fact, were far from underrating the tank—this emerged indirectly also from the vast exaggerations of Fascist propaganda.[354] The fact that Italy's generals gave preference to a light type does not contradict what has just been said, but was due to their thinking primarily of warfare in mountainous terrain, on the Alpine front.[355]

The possibility of a conflict with France lent a good deal of support to that concept. Yet Italy could just as easily be involved in conflict in North Africa, where the terrain offered ideal conditions for tank warfare. But although Mussolini attended major German tank manœuvres in Mecklenburg, where he and his entourage were not only able to form an idea of this new kind of warfare but also had a demonstration of the importance of co-operation between air force and armour, this does not seem to have greatly influenced the development of Italian armour or even advanced it.[356]

---

[348] *Africa settentrionale, La preparazione*, 182.
[349] Bocca, *Storia*, 119; Raspin, 'Aspekte', 213; Rochat and Massobrio, *Storia dell'esercito*, 225.
[350] Favagrossa, *Perchè perdemmo la guerra*, 50 ff.; Bandini, *Tecnica della sconfitta*, 408–13, who views the ammunition situation of the Italian forces less pessimistically than Favagrossa, and believes that even during the war there never was a crisis in ammunition supplies.
[351] Deighton, *Blitzkrieg*, 140–3; Messenger, *Blitzkrieg*, 79–124; Bradley, *Generaloberst Heinz Guderian*, 147–89; on the development of Italian armour between the wars: *Fronte terra*, passim.
[352] Bradley, *Generaloberst Heinz Guderian*, 193–215; Deighton, *Blitzkrieg*, 143–8.
[353] Faldella, *L'Italia*, 101–2; extensively on the armoured formations: Scala, *Storia delle fanterie*, 70–139.
[354] Smith, *Roman Empire*, 171–2.
[355] Faldella, *L'Italia*, 101.
[356] Bocca, *Storia*, 120.

4. The Italian Fighting Forces

The three armoured divisions existing in June 1940 had nothing except their name in common with genuine large-scale formations of this type.[357] The fact that, when Italy entered the war on 10 June, not one of the so-called armoured divisions was stationed in Libya would seem to suggest an as yet insufficient acceptance of the new weapon in the strategic and operational thinking of Italy's military leaders. The general staff obviously underestimated the possibilities of tank warfare there. Admittedly, 24 medium tanks of the M 11/39 type, weighing 11 t., capable of 38 km./h., carrying 30-mm. armour, and equipped with two 8-mm. machine-guns as well as a 37/40 gun, were transferred to Italian East Africa in April 1940; but not until early July did 74 armoured fighting vehicles of this type reach Libya, where until then Balbo had available to him only 332 light tanks.

At that time the M 13/40 tank, weighing 13.5 t., fitted with 20-mm. armour, capable of 32 km./h., and carrying four machine-guns—one for anti-aircraft defence—as well as a 47/32 gun, was already in production. It was introduced to the troops in November 1940.[358] Unlike these types, which in many ways were equal to the British armoured fighting vehicles, the approximately 1,200 light L 3/35 tanks of 3.5 t., which were the principal equipment of the Ariete, Littorio, and Centauro armoured divisions, did not constitute offensive weapons. Only the Ariete, which, along with the Littorio, was stationed in the Po plain—after Italy's entry into the war it was moved to the Alpine front—and which was part of the Corpo d'Armata Corazzato (armoured corps), had shortly before 10 June 1940 been supplied with 70 medium tanks of the M 11/39 type. The Centauro was by then deployed in Albania, on the Greek frontier. The armour of these 42 km./h. tanks could withstand only simple rifle fire. The weapons it carried—two 8-mm. machine-guns or one machine-gun and a flame-thrower—likewise indicate that this was principally a support weapon.[359] Although by the summer of 1940 a successor to this type became available, the 6-t. L 6/40, this could hardly be described as a major improvement. Altogether the Italian army, at the time of Italy's entry into the war, possessed the above-mentioned armoured corps, which, in addition to the Ariete and the Littorio, comprised two motorized infantry divisions. Additionally there were some independent formations or units, assigned according to need: the Centauro, three tank regiments (each of five battalions), two tank battalions in Libya, and three tank battalions attached to the mobile divisions.[360]

---

[357] Faldella, *L'Italia*, 102; a strongly critical examination of attempts to explain the inefficiency of Italy's conduct of the war by the material inferiority of the Italian army in Bandini, *Tecnica della sconfitta*, 576–82. Bandini points out that overestimation of the enemy was having a paralysing effect on Italian military leaders.

[358] Pirrone, 'La brigata corazzata', 105–6.

[359] Bocca, *Storia*, 120.

[360] Fuduli, 'La fanteria', 46 ff.: in 1943 the Type M 15/42, equipped with the 47/40-calibre gun, was supplied to the forces; cf. also Zanussi, *Guerra*, i. 56–7.

I.I. Mussolini's 'Non-belligerence'

The state of equipment of the Italian fighting forces becomes clear if one examines the output of the war industry in relation to the raw materials available at the end of 1939. Although the reduction of the army, decreed on 12 December, and the cancellation of rearmament projects for the air force and the navy theoretically resulted in improved allocations of various materials, nevertheless the fact was that, according to Italian estimates, the requirements of one year of warfare could be met only to the percentages shown in the following list.[361]

Ordnance (total)	6
Ammunition, small calibre	25
Ammunition, medium calibre	7
Ammunition, heavy calibre	10
Rifles (1891 model)	35
Machine-guns	10
Machine-guns, 20-mm.	25
Anti-tank guns 37 and 47	25
Mortars, 45 calibre	40
Mortars, 81 calibre	70
Cartridges up to 8 calibre	25
Cartridges, calibre 8 to 13.2	10
Cartridges, calibre 20, 37, 47	10
Shells, calibre 81	10
Shells, calibre 45	26
Propellants	46
Explosives	23
Armoured fighting vehicles	*insignificant*
Motor-cars and tractors	50
Aircraft	42
Engines	40
Aerial bombs, various calibres but all under 1,000 kg.	40

Not everything, of course, can be explained by figures; yet a single glance at Italian raw-material statistics should have convinced all of the responsible political and military leaders that Italy—allied as she was to Germany, who was likewise dependent on imports to an extreme degree—should not risk confrontation with a US-supported France and Britain. The German victories in Poland, Denmark, Norway, Belgium, Holland, and eventually France represented, from a strategic point of view, no more than initial successes, even though from a tactical point of view they looked impressive. The belief that they would induce a world power like Britain to make peace with Hitler's Germany suggests—and not only with hindsight—a certain irresponsibility in

---

[361] Data according to Favagrossa, *Perchè perdemmo la guerra*, 69.

the assessment of the overall situation. To say the least, such optimism was tantamount to gambling. And yet, given the anticipated prolonged conflict, there existed objective criteria for predicting with a high degree of probability the course of such a war as was taking shape in the summer of 1940. The actual ratio of strength is best illustrated by the industrial capacities and the raw-material bases of all states involved in the conflict.

On this basis it is evident that the Allies, given their material circumstances, were in a position to catch up fairly quickly on any qualitative or quantitative lead; much the same applied to the different level of training observed, at least initially, with regard to the German Wehrmacht. On the other hand, the geo-strategic and industrial factors on the side of the Axis powers, allowing for a conflict—expected since July 1939—with Britain, the Soviet Union, and the United States, were not susceptible to change beyond a definite, insufficient measure.

From such a long-term perspective—one chosen also by many contemporary observers—it must have seemed rather irrelevant that Allied generals and admirals were likewise anxious about the state of their forces in North Africa and in the Middle East.[362] Moreover, any gaps on the British or the French side did not offset the shortages of the Italian forces.

As for the forces confronting the Italian army in the African–Arabian region prior to 10 June, the French troops in the Tunisian area, consisting of seven infantry divisions and one light cavalry division, were suitable, according to statements by General Noguès, only for local operations with limited objectives.[363] In all they numbered no more than 100,000 men, of whom 50,000—with no air force and no tanks—stood on the Libyan frontier.[364] Three further French divisions were in Syria; however, this 'Weygand army', which the Italians vastly overrated,[365] could not be described unreservedly as an effective combat force. The degree of training of its men, and the quality of their equipment, varied a great deal. Added to these forces there were approximately 40,000 men, earmarked for guarding the frontier and for policing tasks.[366] According to a report, dated 10 December 1940, by General Sir Archibald Wavell, the British commander-in-chief Middle East, in June 1940 Britain had some 36,000 troops available in Egypt, of whom, however, only some 25,500 had as yet been organized into fighting units. They lacked equipment of every kind: ammunition, motor transport, artillery, and armour. In the Sudan there were 9,000 servicemen from Britain and the Common-

---

[362] Conditions in the European theatre of war are not taken into account here; cf. vol. ii of the present work, VI.v.1–4 (Umbreit).
[363] Playfair, *Mediterranean*, i. 92–3; cf. *Africa settentrionale, La preparazione*, 89, where the French divisions are credited with the ability to launch an offensive into Libya. On this point Bandini *Tecnica della sconfitta*, 461 ff., with sharp criticism of Italian reconnaissance, whose figures are often still accepted as correct in the literature.
[364] Bandini, *Tecnica della sconfitta*, 462.
[365] Ibid. 463–77.
[366] Playfair, *Mediterranean*, i. 93.

wealth, in Kenya 8,500, in Somalia 1,475, in Palestine 27,500, in Aden 2,500, and in Cyprus 800. The backbone of the British war effort in North Africa was the 7th Armoured Division, stationed in Egypt; after its first clashes with the Italians it went down in the history of the North African theatre of war under the nickname 'desert rats'. Far below establishment strength, in June 1940 it comprised a mere 4,000 men as well as 24 field-guns, 12 anti-tank guns, 38 armoured scout cars, and fewer than 70 tanks.[367] These were a type of light armoured fighting vehicle for reconnaissance tasks, weighing 4 t., scantily armoured and fitted with one machine-gun, but very fast and therefore comparable to the Italian L 3. In addition there was the medium A 9 tank, weighing 13 t. and equipped with a gun and machine-guns. This had a stronger armour and was capable of about 37 km./h. Its opposite numbers, generally speaking, were the 'I' armoured fighting vehicles, which had even stronger armour but, in consequence, weighed a tonne more and had a top speed of only 30 km./h.[368]

Quite apart from these circumstances, an explanation of the strategic measures taken by the Italian generals following Italy's entry into the war should also take into consideration their subjective estimate of the situation. Obviously there was an extraordinary overestimation of British and French strength, and this, in view of their own decidedly inadequate readiness, was bound to act as an additional impediment to Italy's conduct of the war. At the beginning of June Italian reconnaissance reported the following dispositions:[369] Tunisia, Algeria, and Morocco, 314,000 men;[370] Egypt, 100,000 to 105,000; Syria (Weygand's army), 200,000; Sudan, 30,000; Kenya, 50,000; Somalia, 10,000. In Palestine the Italian high command suspected 'considerable forces'; for Aden and Cyprus no data were available. If one compares these figures with the actual ones reported above, it becomes obvious that Italian assumptions had virtually nothing in common with reality in North Africa and the Middle East. However, the misjudgement of the forces opposing her explains, at most, only the beginning and not the further course of Italy's conduct of operations.

As for the three services of the Italian armed forces, the air force was widely regarded as a creation of the Fascist regime, its origins being closely linked with the name of Italo Balbo. It is quite correct that it became a separate service independent of the army and navy only on 28 March 1923, i.e. under Mussolini's government.[371] Less accurate is the role usually assigned to Balbo

---

[367] These figures are based on the very detailed examination in Bandini, *Tecnica della sconfitta*, 493–511; cf. also Liddell Hart, *History of the Second World War*, 93 ff.; Playfair, *Mediterranean*, i. 93; the figures in *Africa settentrionale, La preparazione*, 89–90, are incorrect.

[368] Pirrone, 'La brigata corazzata', 106–7, though the overall assessment of the British 7th Armoured Division (p. 105) underrates its real state in June 1940; on this point cf. Deighton, *Blitzkrieg*, 196; Playfair, *Mediterranean*, i. 104–5.

[369] Figures according to Bandini, *Tecnica della sconfitta*, 574.

[370] The actual figure was 150,000, of which 50,000 alone were in Algeria.

[371] D'Avanzo, *Ali e poltrone*, 846–50, for the relevant decree.

4. The Italian Fighting Forces

in this connection. Most accounts here follow the myth created by Fascist propaganda. The fact is that Balbo, when he became head of Italian aviation in November 1926, inherited from his predecessor anything but a bankrupt estate in the military field. He was able to build on fairly sound foundations—which is not to belittle his undoubted merits in ensuring the exceptionally rapid and successful further development of the Italian air force.[372]

Under Balbo, who remained aviation minister until 1933, the air force soon gained a privileged position, at least formally and superficially. However, while such an impression was in line with the pronouncements of Fascist propaganda, it did not reflect the reality of the military budget. In all budgetary allocations the air force invariably came after the army and the navy.[373] Regardless of this it was considered, probably rightly, the most Fascist of the armed services, also styled 'the wings of Fascism'. The aviational successes of Italian pilots and the technical brilliance of Italian constructors—time and again exploited by the regime for its own stabilization—largely resulted, as a kind of feedback effect, in an intensive Fascisticization of the air force. Added to this was the fact that the officer corps of the Regia Aeronautica, unlike the army and navy, did not have behind it a prolonged tradition of loyalty to the throne,[374] but was still in search of its own identity—which was bound to facilitate the penetration of Fascist ideas. It is significant that members of the Fascist leadership stratum were found with particular frequency in the ranks of the Italian air force.[375]

As far as the war doctrine of the air force is concerned, reference should be made above all to various studies by the air-war theoretician, General Giulio Douhet. The ideas developed by him in the 1920s must be seen in a wider context. It should, however, be remembered that they were presented both by Mussolini and by Balbo as a kind of official (though not compulsory) guideline for the understanding and the concept of modern aerial warfare. However, there never was any open discussion of Douhet's theses. Even within the specialized departments concerned there does not appear to have been any internal examination of the general's views, though they were published in the Party newspaper, *Popolo d'Italia*.[376]

Generally speaking, the origins of the modern air arm have to be viewed against the background of the 1914–18 war. But the war theories developed after that war, including Douhet's, go back, in a sense, to the nineteenth century. What was formulated and discussed after 1919 expressed the im-

---

[372] Extensively on this: Rochat, *Italo Balbo*, 25–45, 57–81; on the ideas concerning aerial rearmament developed in the 1920s and 1930s cf. Licheri, 'Sul potere aereo', 251–2.
[373] Cf. Rochat, *Italo Balbo*; also for statistics on military expenditure for 1925–34.
[374] A general picture of the Italian air force up to 1930 is given in Gentile, *Storia dell'aeronautica*, 102–58, with reference to developments in other countries. Very concise but informative: Rochat and Massobrio, *Storia dell'esercito*, 230–5.
[375] Bocca, *Storia*, 134.
[376] Extensively on Douhet's role in connection with the Fascist regime: Rochat, *Italo Balbo*, 82–90; cf. also Segrè, 'Douhet in Italy'. Still informative is Gentile, *Storia delle operazioni*, 9–24.

mediate reaction to a new kind of operational strategy. Born as a consequence of the industrial revolution and practised for the first time in the American civil war,[377] this form of industrialized warfare[378] reached a climax in the positional 'war of destruction' of 1914–18. The development had therefore come about which the Polish writer Johann von Bloch (Jan Bloch)—as a result of his studies of the Russo-Turkish conflict of 1877–8—had predicted with astonishing clarity and far-sightedness at the turn of the century in his book *Der Krieg*.[379] In accordance with his predictions, and against the general expectation even of experts, the First World War developed into a long drawn-out conflict. In the debate as to the reasons for this, and in search of alternatives to positional warfare, Douhet belonged to the school of thought which not only accepted industrialized warfare as such but wished to make it even more efficient in the form of 'total war'—a doctrine among whose stoutest champions was Erich Ludendorff.[380] Douhet's theory should therefore be seen in terms of the crisis of mobile warfare in the First World War, the discussion, since the early 1920s, of the tank weapon, and the problems of mechanized warfare generally. This complex of questions was under discussion, especially in connection with new tactics of armoured warfare,[381] by military circles of nearly all the great powers.[382]

In Douhet's view, modern technical developments provided the key to overcoming the kind of bogging-down of operations experienced in the First World War. The air arm—assuming unrestricted offensive operational principles—seemed to him designed to revolutionize the concept of traditional strategy, always provided that control of the air was achieved. Given this condition, it would soon be possible to force one's enemy to his knees with bombing raids, especially by attacking residential areas in order to break the resistance of the population.[383]

Such theories, even though confirmed up to a point by the reality of subsequent strategic bombing, were ultimately based on an overestimation of the strategic and operational potential of aircraft. They offered an ideal solution to the dilemma in which warfare seemed to find itself after 1918, the

---

[377] For an excellent analysis of the American civil war, highlighting its military-historical importance in relation to the First and the Second World Wars, see Luraghi, *Storia*.

[378] On the development of industrial warfare between 1861 and 1945 see Luraghi, 'L'ideologia'. The above reflections closely follow the interpretational framework developed by Luraghi for the problem of industrial warfare.

[379] Bloch, *Der Krieg*, *passim*, but esp. vols. iv–vi; cf. Luraghi, 'L'ideologia', 183 ff., in particular as to Fuller's critique of Bloch, which Luraghi rejects as unjustified.

[380] Luraghi, 'L'ideologia', 186–7.

[381] See the very informative surveys in Bond, *Liddell Hart*, 37–64; Messenger, *Blitzkrieg*, 47–125, which discusses the US, the Soviet Union, and all the West European great powers; Trythall, *Fuller*, 97–119, 145–79. J. F. C. Fuller was, alongside Sir B. Liddell Hart, one of the leading British military theoreticians. Fuller differed from Liddell Hart principally in regarding the infantry merely as an armour-supporting weapon, whereas Liddell Hart conceded its independence as a weapon capable of autonomous offensive operations.

[382] Messenger, *Blitzkrieg*, 40–6; generally on this discussion Borgert, 'Grundzüge', 529–84.

[383] Luraghi, 'L'ideologia', 187.

4. The Italian Fighting Forces

possibility of achieving a strategic decision with this new system of weapons, operating beyond all operational front lines, in the enemy's hinterland. It should, however, be recalled that modern war is at least three-dimensional, to be conducted as a combination of land, air, and naval warfare. Indeed it is probably more correct to describe it as five-dimensional, since economics and propaganda have long ranged themselves as equals alongside the classical categories of warfare. Douhet's teachings, therefore, did not go unchallenged in Italy. In particular, General Amedeo Mecuzzi resolutely opposed the independent conduct of operations by each of the three services, as essentially proposed by Douhet.[384] Yet when Douhet's various articles appeared in book form in the 1930s, as two titles,[385] one of them was graced with a preface by Balbo, indicating beyond doubt that the general continued to be held in esteem as the air-war theoretician of the Fascist government.

The Fascist regime clearly indulged in the illusion that air forces were the appropriate instrument of war especially for poorer countries. As the war was soon to show, no assumption could have been more wrong,[386] for ambitious and up-to-date aerial armament was and remains the preserve of countries rich in raw materials or in hard currency. Fascist propaganda nevertheless cherished such Utopias. The most extravagant remarks by Mussolini are recorded. Doubtless not all of them genuinely reflected his estimate of the situation, but some would seem to have been directly inspired by Douhet. Most of all Mussolini was fascinated by the idea that he might free Italy, by means of the new weapons system, from her geo-strategic and economic constraints. Certain calculations suggested that during the very first week of war 300 aircraft could cause losses of some five million civilians among the enemy population. What their authors had in mind was both bacteriological weapons and the use of gas. Air Marshal Balbo declared himself convinced that Italy, in the event of war, would have undisputed control of the air in the Mediterranean. That sounded reassuring, and the realization of that forecast would have met Douhet's postulates concerning the decisive function of aerial warfare. After Italy entered the war, however, there was no question of her air force exercising any sovereign control of the Mediterranean air-space.[387]

This came as a general surprise, considering that Italy, as indicated above, enjoyed a good reputation in international aviation. Fascist propaganda, moreover, had not omitted to heighten that impression.[388] However, a downturn in the development of the Italian air force came presumably in the mid-thirties. That was when the worldwide armament expansion began, and when

---

[384] Rochat, *Italo Balbo*, 89; extensively on the two principal opponents—Mecozzi and Rougeron—Gentile, *Storia delle operazioni*, 24–34.
[385] *Command* and *Guerra integrale*.
[386] Bocca, *Storia*, 134; Smith, *Roman Empire*, 174.
[387] Smith, *Roman Empire*, 173–6, on the state of equipment of the Italian air force in 1939; cf. also Favagrossa, *Perchè perdemmo la guerra*, 22–5.
[388] Kramer, 'Die italienische Luftwaffe', 265–6; Raspin, 'Aspekte', 213–14.

Italy, lacking raw materials and foreign currency, was no longer able to keep pace. Moreover, the country showed itself incapable of organizing mass production centred on certain prototypes.[389] Just as the army generals' requests for equipment towards the end of the 1930s—when the likelihood of war about the middle of the next decade was increasing—were necessarily described above as impracticable and unrealistic, so the same is true of the demands of their air-force colleagues. Towards the end of 1938 their leaders called for 12,885 aircraft and 22,542 aircraft engines in 1939. Against the background of the capacity of the Italian aviation industry, which was then, at most, manufacturing 2,798 aircraft and 4,425 aircraft engines annually, i.e. about 20 per cent of what was being asked for, there was no hope of meeting this demand even approximately.[390] In fact, in 1939 Italy produced a total of 1,750 aircraft and 4,191 engines. In 1940 this was increased to 3,257 aircraft, or about 45 per cent of the notified requirement. In addition, 5,607 aircraft engines were manufactured.[391] During the subsequent years, in 1941 Italy produced 3,503 aircraft, but in 1942 the figure was down to 2,813, and in January–August 1943 (inclusive) 1,930 aircraft left the production shops of the aviation industry. At no time was it possible to meet the requirements of the fighting forces to any appreciable extent. A comparison with other countries shows that the Italian armament industry, which between 1941 and 1943 produced altogether 8,246 aircraft (between January 1939 and September 1943, when Italy surrendered to the Allies, 13,253 were produced), was relatively insignificant. The British, for instance, produced 92,034, the Germans 72,030, and the Americans 163,049 aircraft.[392] Thus, between 1940 and 1943 Italy achieved an average annual production rate which was only slightly above the monthly production figure of the British aircraft industry in 1943.[393]

Although at the time of entering the war in June 1940 the situation of the Italian air force showed certain improvements over September 1939, its state of equipment was far from satisfactory.[394] Italy, at that point—disregarding

---

[389] Bocca, *Storia*, 136 ff.; Kramer, 'Die italienische Luftwaffe', 266, which, however, seems to be based excessively on Balbo's dismissal as chief of the Italian air force.

[390] Favagrossa, *Perchè perdemmo la guerra*, 60–1.

[391] Santoro, *L'aeronautica italiana*, i. 61.

[392] Figures according to Gentile, *Storia delle operazioni*, 41; Licheri, 'Sul potere aereo', 254. The figures given in Smith, *Roman Empire*, 177–8, are inaccurate.

[393] Overy, *Air War*, 41, though he proceeds from the incorrect assumption that Italy produced 7,183 aircraft during the years of her participation in the war. In fact, some 10,143 aircraft were produced between June 1940 and Sept. 1943, if one calculates from the data given in Gentile, *Storia delle operazioni*, 41; on the production of the Italian aircraft industry cf. Santoro, *L'aeronautica italiana*, ii. 471; Gentile, *Storia dell'aeronautica*, 186–93, with a good survey of the situation in June 1940.

[394] The following figures are taken from Gentile, *Storia delle operazioni*, 51 (non-operational aircraft in brackets). Gentile's data are confirmed in Licheri, *L'arma aerea*, 29–30, with a survey of the overall strength of the Italian air force, which amounted to 5,240 aircraft. Santoro, *L'aeronautica italiana*, i. 88, also confirms Gentile's figures; ibid. 33 ff., data on the state of equipment of the Italian air force in Sept. 1939. The data in Kramer, 'Die italienische Luftwaffe',

4. The Italian Fighting Forces

trainer aircraft—had 1,796 combat-ready military aircraft, plus 554 which were not combat-ready at that time. Of these 783 (281) were bombers, 594 (165) fighters, 268 (69) ground reconnaissance, and 151 (39) sea reconnaissance planes, not taking into account the aircraft stationed in Italian East Africa. Admittedly, only 1,482 of these aircraft could be described as modern; of these no more than 666 bombers and 435 fighters were regarded as strong performers.[395] In spite of the bomber, fighter, and reconnaissance groups specially trained for operations at sea, Italy, like Germany, had no independent naval air arm;[396] and, just as in Germany, there was discussion and controversy among the Italian forces concerning possible solutions to this problem. An assessment of the various arguments strongly suggests that the course of the discussion was governed essentially by departmental jealousies rather than by factual considerations or real strategic needs. No doubt this was partly due to over-optimistic expectations with regard to technical feasibilities as well as to an inaccurate assessment of Italy's geo-strategic situation. Both these factors played a major part—quite apart from the financial side of the problem—in the decision to dispense with the construction of aircraft-carriers.[397]

At the beginning of the war the Italian air force, whose personnel numbered some 84,000 men[398]—including 3,040 pilots of officer rank and 3,300 of NCO rank—was structured, under operational plan PR 12,[399] as follows:[400]

I Air Corps—Milan
II Air Corps—Palermo
III Air Corps—Rome
Air force military district—Bari

266–7, are inaccurate; the figures in Pagliano, *Storia*, 58 ff., are also unreliable, despite many interesting details.
[395] While the literature quoted on the subject of the Italian air force invariably covers the technical data and performance of the Italian aircraft, attention should also be drawn to the following lavishly illustrated publications: Brotzu *et al.*, *Aerotrasporti*; id. *et al.*, *Bombardieri*; id. *et al.*, *Caccia*; as well as Brotzu and Cosolo, *Aerei scuola*. Information on the Italian air force is also contained in Price, *Bomber*.
[396] A highly informative survey of the development of Italian naval aviation is provided by *La marina italiana*, xxi. 197–205.
[397] Specifically on the problem of aircraft-carrier construction, ibid. 52–3; on the questions and conditions discussed above cf. also Baum and Weichold, *Krieg der 'Achsenmächte'*, 28–9; Bernotti, *Guerra nel Mediterraneo*, 60–1; Iachino, *Tramonto*, 95 ff.; Kramer, 'Die italienische Luftwaffe', 267.
[398] Santoro, *L'aeronautica italiana*, i. 89. Licheri, *L'arma aerea*, 28–9, gives the following figures: a total of 105,630 men; of the pilots 900 were reservists, and among pilots serving as career servicemen or long-service personnel a mere 2,000 were available for front-line duty. See also Gentile, *Storia delle operazioni*, 52.
[399] For details of the PR 12 plan cf. Santoro, *L'aeronautica italiana*, i. 76–83.
[400] Ibid. 83–7; special consideration of the war against France is reflected in the deployment survey in Garello, *Regia aeronautica*, 9–32; on developments in the North African theatre of war see Borgiotti and Gori, *La guerra aerea*, 31–40, with extensive information on the British forces also.

Air force Sardinia—Cagliari
Air force Albania—Tirana
Air force Libya—Tripoli
Air force Aegean—Rhodes
Air force units for ground support—Rome (in June 1940 there were, in theory, 37 squadrons available, under the army high command)
Air force units which Supermarina could demand from Superaereo[401] for operations at sea: in all, 237 aircraft were supposed to have been available on 10 June for operations over the Adriatic, Ionian, Tyrrhenian, and Aegean Seas, as well as the sea area around Sardinia and Sicily and off Libya. In actual fact, apart from ship-borne planes, there were only 163 aircraft.[402]

In addition there was the air force in Italian East Africa. At the time of Italy's entry into the war it consisted of 325 aircraft, of which 183 were at the front, 61 were stored at depots, and 81 were undergoing overhaul.[403]

The Italian air force, at the beginning of June 1940, was initially still confronted by the French and British air forces deployed in the Mediterranean area. Italy's military intelligence, the Servizio Informazioni Militari del Regio Esercito (SIM), then estimated that France had 1,117 bombers and other military aircraft stationed in the 'Zone d'Opérations Aériennes Alpes' (ZOAA), i.e. the Alpine front, and 106 in Corsica. This figure was completely incorrect. The Italian intelligence service had clearly ignored the changes which the German attack of May 1940 brought about in the deployment of the French air force. On 10 June there were actually some 70 fighters, 40 bombers, and 20 reconnaissance aircraft in southern France, altogether 130 planes, supplemented by 28 bombers, 38 torpedo-carrying aircraft, and 14 fighters of the naval air arm, as well as 3 fighters and 30 other aircraft types stationed in Corsica.[404] Additionally there were 65 fighters and 85 bombers of the French air force in North Africa, as well as 13 bombers, 26 fighters, and 56 aircraft of other types stationed in Syria.[405]

The commander-in-chief Royal Air Force Middle East, Air Marshal Sir Arthur Longmore, who succeeded Sir William Mitchell in that post on 13

---

[401] For these terms see I.1.4(b) below at n. 454.
[402] *La marina italiana*, xxi. 204.
[403] *La guerra in Africa orientale*, 335.
[404] Garello, *Regia aeronautica*, 31.
[405] More or less reliable figures for the British–French side already in Guedalla, *Middle East*, 71 ff.; cf. now mainly Playfair, *Mediterranean*, i. 95. Santoro, *L'aeronautica italiana*, i. 91–2, gives the figures produced by Italian reconnaissance of enemy strength, though with the reservation that they are not always reliable. According to these there were in southern France, Corsica, Tunisia, Algeria, Morocco, and Syria 900 bombers and 1,160 fighters, i.e. a total of 2,060 aircraft! The British in Egypt, Palestine, Gibraltar, Malta, and Cyprus had altogether 118 bombers, 189 fighters, 51 reconnaissance aircraft, and 262 other types, altogether 620 aircraft. The Italian figures were accepted by Licheri, *L'arma aerea*, 32 ff., who bases his analysis of Italy's position at the time of her entry into the war on these inaccurate data; likewise Faldella, *L'Italia*, 108 ff. Gentile, *Storia delle operazioni*, 201, gives Britain's strength as 626 aircraft.

May, had at his disposal, for operations in the air-space over Egypt, Sudan, Palestine, Transjordan, East Africa, Aden, Somaliland, Iraq and adjacent territories, Cyprus, Malta, Turkey, the Balkans, the Red Sea, and the Persian Gulf, 96 bombers, 75 fighters—including the planes of the Royal Egyptian Air Force—and 24 army co-operation aircraft, as well as 10 flying-boats[406] stationed in Egypt and Palestine. He could not expect any reinforcements in the event of Italy entering the war in the foreseeable future, and the 94 bombers, 30 fighters, and 39 other aircraft available in Aden, Kenya, and Somaliland were hardly able to relieve the situation.[407] Following Mussolini's entry into the war the British in Libya and the Dodecanese found themselves confronted by some 140 Italian bombers, 101 fighters, and 72 other military aircraft.[408]

If the British commander-in-chief lacked modern fighters and long-range bombers, and if there was a shortage of spares and other equipment, the Italians, whose intelligence service suspected the presence in Egypt alone of 100 bombers, 140 fighters, and 270 other military aircraft,[409] were faring no better. They lacked appropriate logistical support, especially repair facilities. Besides, the equipment of their flying formations was still far below establishment level.[410] On the other hand, it must have been easy enough for the Italians to replenish or increase their forces—including those in East Africa—by transfers from the mother country. The fact that the British, despite their numerical inferiority, fancied their chances in a clash with Italy's air force was due primarily to their realization of the shortages on the Italian side. The Italian air force, as far as was known, had fuel reserves for no more than two months, and neither its pilots nor its ground crews were, on average, up to British standards of training.[411] Yet apart from the question of whether or not such optimism was justified, the RAF, with its relatively weak forces in the Mediterranean area, had numerous and comprehensive tasks to tackle, which could soon bring it to the limit of its capabilities.[412] It had to neutralize the Italian forces in Cyrenaica (a task which, after France's dropping out of the war, had to be performed by the British on their own); to attack supply-lines and supply-ports; and to support naval and ground operations, as well as protecting such important bases as Alexandria, Cairo, Port Said, and Suez. Above all else the RAF had to defend Egypt against the expected Italian offensive and keep open the sea route through the Suez Canal and the Red Sea. In addition Longmore realized that, given certain conditions, it might also become necessary to support Turkey in Thrace.

---

[406] Playfair, *Mediterranean*, i. 94–5.
[407] Overy, *Air War*, 41; Playfair, *Mediterranean*, i. 95.
[408] Borgiotti and Gori, *La guerra aerea*, 24; Playfair, *Mediterranean*, i. 95.
[409] Borgiotti and Gori, *La guerra aerea*, 35.
[410] Ibid. 24.
[411] Playfair, *Mediterranean*, i. 96–7; Borgiotti and Gori, *La guerra aerea*, 24.
[412] Overy, *Air War*, 41; Playfair, *Mediterranean*, i. 95.

I.I. Mussolini's 'Non-belligerence'

Any triphibious warfare, of the kind that a theatre like the Mediterranean area positively called for, meant that, alongside the ground forces and the air force, exceptional importance attached to the third component, the navy. This was due not only to the transport pattern of the region, but also to the length of Italy's coastlines, to the fact that communications had to be maintained with her possessions in North Africa, East Africa, and the Aegean, as well as to the necessity—once Italy had joined the war—of being able to conduct operations in overseas regions.

In the judgement of international experts Italy's navy, which enjoyed the most favourable assessment,[413] seemed to be in a better position than the other services to fulfil the expectations placed in it. Mussolini's strong submarine fleet, in particular, was a cause of anxiety to the British Admiralty,[414] but in other respects too Italian naval power looked quite impressive numerically. An attempted 'fleet disposition plan' for June 1940 shows the following distribution of naval forces:[415]

I Squadron (Taranto), flagship Giulio Cesare, *comprising*:

    5th Division with the battleships *Giulio Cesare* and *Conte di Cavour*; attached to it were the 7th and 8th destroyer flotillas, with 4 units each;

    9th Division with the battleships *Littorio* and *Vittorio Veneto*; to it belonged the 14th and 15th destroyer flotillas, with a total of 8 units;

    1st Division with the heavy cruisers *Zara, Gorizia*, and *Fiume*; available to it was the 9th destroyer flotilla with 4 units;

    4th Division with the light cruisers *Alberico da Barbiano, Alberto di Giussano, Luigi Cadorna*, and *Armando Diaz*;

    8th Division with the light cruisers *Duca degli Abruzzi, Giuseppe Garibaldi*, and the 16th destroyer flotilla with 4 units.

II Squadron (La Spezia), flagship Pola, *comprising*:

    6th Division with the heavy cruiser *Pola* and the 4 units of the 12th destroyer flotilla;

    3rd Division with the heavy cruisers *Trento, Bolzano*, and *Trieste*, as well as the 4 units of the 11th destroyer flotilla;

    7th Division with the light cruisers *Eugenio di Savoia, Duca d'Aosta, Muzio Attendolo, Raimondo Montecuccoli*, and the 4 units of the 13th destroyer flotilla;

---

[413] Kramer, 'Über den Seekrieg Italiens', 257.

[414] Cunningham, *Odyssey*, 210–11; Pack, *Sea Power*, 179; Macintyre, *The Battle*, 17 ff., also on the initial British assumption of Italian air superiority, which was regarded as especially dangerous, and only gradually revealed as a bogy.

[415] *Weyers Taschenbuch der Kriegsflotten*, 34 (1940), 396, does not—because of unreliable information—contain any fleet deployment plans for 1940; for 1939 cf. ibid. 33 (1939), 400–1, on Italy. The data above are taken from Andò and Bagnasco, *Navi e marinai*, 13–19; *La marina italiana*, xxi. 338–45.

4. The Italian Fighting Forces 87

2nd Division with the light cruisers *Bande Nere* and *Colleoni*, as well as the 4 units of the 10th destroyer flotilla.

Submarine squadrons, comprising the 1st (La Spezia), 2nd (Naples), 3rd (Messina), 4th (Taranto), and 7th (Cagliari) groups. These groups, consisting of a total of 26 flotillas with 87 units, came directly under the commander of submarines in Rome. On the other hand, the 5th (Rhodes) and 6th (Tobruk) groups, with a total of 4 flotillas and 18 units, came under the admiral commanding the various stationing zones; added to these were 2 flotillas with 8 units stationed in East Africa.

At her entry into the war, Italy therefore possessed four battleships, even though only two of them were operational on 10 June. However, the equipment phase of the two others was nearing completion.[416] The Allies had one British and two French battleships, as well as two modern French battle cruisers (listed in Table I.1.1 below as battleships), stationed in the western Mediterranean. In the eastern Mediterranean they had at their disposal four British battleships and one French battleship. Added to these was the aircraft-carrier *Eagle*, to which Italy had nothing equivalent to oppose.[417] While the British regarded the Italian position as highly favourable, whereas their own appeared precarious,[418] the exact opposite was true for an Italian observer;[419] both approaches have found their way into the post-war literature. There was in fact some hesitation among the British admirals when, in June 1940, they had to define their own commitments. They even considered abandoning the eastern Mediterranean and concentrating their forces at Gibraltar.[420] But Churchill immediately rejected this; and in Admiral Cunningham, the commander-in-chief of the Royal Navy in the Mediterranean, the Allied fleets had a commander who was clearly determined to maintain the successful policy pursued by the Navy since, at least, the eighteenth century:[421] 'seeking out and destroying the enemy fleet.'[422] For Britain this may seem an appropriate operational concept. Admittedly, Cunningham had only a limited number of ships in the Mediterranean. In particular, he was short of destroyers, which had to serve the bulk of the fleet, with countless other tasks for which no special destroyer flotillas were available. But ultimately he always had a chance of offsetting any losses from the many replacement facilities of

---

[416] Maugeri, *Ricordi*, 29.
[417] Auphan and Mordal, *La Marine française*, 160–1; Playfair, *Mediterranean*, i. 91; Belot, *La Guerre*, 19.
[418] Cunningham, *Odyssey*, 233–4; Pack, *Sea Power*, 17; Playfair, *Mediterranean*, i. 90 ff.
[419] Bernotti, *Guerra nel Mediterraneo*, 35–6; even more clearly id., *La guerra, 1939–1941*, 171–6, esp. 173; a good general view of Italy's equipment situation, with particular attention to the separate types of vessels, in Iachino, *Tramonto*, 47–66. Iachino sees the greatest disadvantage of the Italian navy in its lack of an aircraft-carrier and its shortage of spare parts—cf. also Andò and Gay, *Gli incrociatori*; and Bargoni et al., *Le corazzate*.
[420] Ruge, *Seekrieg*, 109.
[421] Cf. the excellent work by Kennedy, *Rise and Fall*, 97–298.
[422] Quoted from Macintyre, *The Battle*, 17.

the British Empire. Added to this was the link with the United States and the assurance of shipyard capacities beyond the reach of the Axis powers.

Italy, enclosed as she was within the Mediterranean and suffering from a shortage of raw materials, was in a completely different position. Her admirals were well advised, from the very outset, to avoid seeking battle at any price, a battle associated with incalculable risks.[423] Sudden major losses could not be replaced speedily but would mean eating into the capital of Italian naval power. In retrospect it is clear that this caution was more than justified: on 1 July 1940 Italy had 4 combat-ready battleships, 18 combat-ready cruisers, 46 combat-ready destroyers, and 63 combat-ready submarines. On 1 July 1943 the position was as follows: of her battleships 2 were combat-ready, of her cruisers 6, and of her destroyers and submarines 30 each. It must, moreover, be pointed out that at no time during the war did the Italian navy again reach the number of combat-ready destroyers and submarines it had on 1 July 1940. In 1941 began the great, inexorable blood-letting of the Italian fleet,[424] which from the start also affected the cruisers; of the battleships, however—except for the period 1 January to 1 May 1941, as well as March 1942 and July 1943—there were always between 4 and 6 combat-ready.

Events in the Mediterranean demonstrated once again that a comparison of the strength of opposing navies should not confine itself to counting their battleships.[425] In the given circumstances the concept of the 'fleet in being' therefore represented the correct policy for Italy's navy. The fact that it did not lead to success was due primarily to the above-mentioned structural conditions of Italy's conduct of the war, rather than to occasional operational inadequacy.

If one extends the numerical comparison of the Italian with the Anglo-French fleet to all naval units, then any interpretation must bear in mind that mere figures—and this applies equally to the army and the air force—carry only limited evidential value with regard to actual conditions. A complete picture would involve comparing, as between the parties, not only technical data on weapons systems but also their respective state of training, infrastructure, geo-strategic position, and the area denoted by the modern concept of 'internal leadership' or morale. As it is intended to make this comparison in the account of military operations, it can be omitted at this point. Instead we shall merely outline the numerical ratios at the moment when Italy joined the war. Table I.I.1 shows the situation for the Mediterranean area on 10 June 1940.[426]

---

[423] Cf. Bernotti, *Guerra nel Mediterraneo*, 36.
[424] *La marina italiana*, i. 25.
[425] Typical of an interpretation focused on battleships is Ruge, *Seekrieg*, 105; a more appropriate assessment in Iachino, *Tramonto*, 51.
[426] The figures in the table are based on a comparison of those in Playfair, *Mediterranean*, i. 91, and *La marina italiana*, i. 21. The latter work lists 115 submarines. In fact Italy possessed only 113, as shown by the breakdown above (text to n. 414). This figure is confirmed also by the new edition of *La marina italiana*, xiii. 23. Playfair mentions 108 submarines, which is incorrect even if

4. The Italian Fighting Forces

TABLE I.I.I. *Naval Strength of Italy, Britain, and France in the Mediterranean, 10 June 1940*

Type	Italy		Britain		France	
	No.	Tonnage	No.	Tonnage	No.	Tonnage
Battleships	4	117,240	5	148,450	5	116,165
Aircraft-carriers	—	—	1	22,600	—	—
Heavy cruisers	7	70,000	—	—	7	70,000
Light cruisers	12	74,630	9	51,000	7	51,724
Destroyers and torpedo-boats	125	120,335	35	48,200	57	67,250
Submarines	113	88,000	12	13,000	46	49,000

It should be noted that at the time of entering the war Italy could boast of having the largest submarine fleet in the world, after the Soviet Union. This had been systematically built up since 1923; its equipment was thought to be modern, and only 32 submarines dated from before 1932.[427] For the surface ships it may be said that, while they had their specific technical difficulties, this is true of all navies the world over. All in all, the Italian units were certainly up to international standards. What they lacked most of all was effective air support. More particularly, an aircraft-carrier would have been needed for a balanced fleet structure in modern terms. The inadequate range of land-based aircraft, moreover, had an adverse effect on the operational employment of Italian vessels, as sailing without air cover was regarded as too dangerous. It is true that, even where it should have been possible, naval–air co-operation frequently did not function because the organizational basis was faulty. Apart from such inadequacies, there were problems with the heavy guns, due primarily to the material of guns and ammunition, but partly also to insufficient practical training. In order to spare the guns, whose overhaul cost a lot of money, firing practice in the past had been cut down to a minimum. Disturbing also was the relatively high frequency of engine breakdowns under prolonged stress. Finally, the navy lacked anti-aircraft artillery and barrage balloons to protect ships in port against air attack.[428]

it is meant to refer only to those stationed in the Mediterranean. Otherwise the table follows the British literature in the case of conflicting data for the Royal Navy (and the French navy), and the Italian literature for the Regia Marina. Tonnage figures are in some cases approximate. The latest work on the naval war in the Mediterranean, Santoni and Mattesini, *La partecipazione tedesca*, 14, accepts the figures in the Italian literature, which, according to British accounts, are incorrect.

[427] The best introduction to the Italian submarine arm is provided by *La marina italiana*, xiii, esp. 5–36; on the implementation of the five-phase (1923–40) construction programme: *La marina italiana*, xxi. 76–82. Critically: Bocca, *Storia*, 133, and Smith, *Roman Empire*, 179–80.

[428] Important literature on the problems here addressed: Baum and Weichold, *Krieg der 'Achsenmächte'*, 29 ff.; Bernotti, *Guerra nel Mediterraneo*, 35–6; id., *La guerra, 1939–1941*, 184–5; Bocca, *Storia*, 130 ff.; Bragadin, *Che ha fatto la marina?*, 2 ff.; id., *The Italian Navy*, 3 ff.; in this

A discussion of the various inadequacies in the Italian navy cannot omit a few remarks on the development of radar. It is well known that the lack of such equipment caused heavy losses to the Italian fleet at Matapan in March 1941. It is also a fact that the Germans practised the greatest reserve on all issues of sharing armament technology;[429] the desired German detection-instruments, of whose existence the Italians were eventually informed after the Matapan disaster, were not supplied to their ships until 1942.[430] Admittedly, Italy, like all major industrial nations, had been working on the development of these new locating devices since the first half of the 1930s.[431] Initial experiments were encouraging, so that the navy ministry involved itself directly in further research. A prototype was to be completed as soon as possible. And although the work suffered from the universal shortage of money, by 1940 there were several types of instrument in existence, though not yet ready for serial production. But it was a start. It was probably mainly the fault of the insuperable organizational, financial, and demarcation problems of the Italian administration that the order for a series of 60 instruments was not placed until 1941.[432] The first practicable instruments of the Gufu type, manufactured in Italy, were installed in Italian ships after the war was over.[433]

The literature on the subject usually states that Italy's premature entry into the war resulted in the loss of some 35 per cent of her merchant fleet. This was indicated in early post-war publications,[434] just as it is in the latest studies of the fate of Italian ships which were outside the Mediterranean on 10 June 1940.[435] Merchant navies do in fact represent an integral factor of modern warfare. For Italy, which in May 1940 first issued directives on the measures to be taken by ships at sea on the outbreak of war,[436] the exceptional importance of her merchantmen arose primarily from the circumstance that she had to supply an overseas theatre of war. Moreover, the country's transport structure relied, even in peacetime, on an intensive use of coastal shipping,

---

American translation of his book Bragadin takes account, here and there, of new findings by historians. Iachino, *Tramonto* (see 47–86), despite its early publication date, is still an exceedingly informative book, written from the angle and with the experience of a senior naval officer. In connection with the accounts by Bernotti and Iachino cf. the positive assessment by Polastro, 'La marina', 110, who sums up the findings of both these authors on shortages and inadequacies in the Italian navy. Polastro altogether deals critically with the literature of Italian naval memoirs. Cf. also *La marina italiana*, xxi, on technical and personnel issues concerning the navy, with a survey of developments between the wars. Judged by the standard of research attained by Italian military historiography by the end of the seventies, the most interesting work is Rochat and Massobrio, *Storia dell'esercito*, 226–30.

[429] Schreiber, *Revisionismus*, passim.
[430] Iachino, *Tramonto*, 76.
[431] *La marina italiana*, xxi. 163–4, 168–9.
[432] Bocca, *Storia*, 132–3; Smith, *Roman Empire*, 188–9.
[433] Iachino, *Tramonto*, 76; *La marina italiana*, iv. 26–7.
[434] Di Giamberardino, *La marina*, 149–50.
[435] Dupuis, *Forzate il blocco!*
[436] *DDI*, 9th ser., iv, No. 568, p. 445 (25 May 1940).

especially small vessels, in order to safeguard a satisfactory flow of merchandise. For the period following Italy's entry into the war all this meant that, with the loss of the ships which were no longer able to return to Mediterranean ports, bottlenecks had to be expected in civilian and military supplies. This was true even supposing that the troops in North Africa were adequately supplied and fully equipped, which was not the case. In actual fact, the situation became badly strained from the moment when supplies for North Africa, owing to enemy action, had to be switched to small and medium-sized ships.[437]

In 1940 the Italian merchant navy numbered 786 ships of over 500 GRT, with a total tonnage of 3,318,129 GRT. Of these merchant ships, 532 (with 1,947,307 GRT) were in the Mediterranean when Italy entered the war, while 254 (with 1,370,822 GRT) were either in foreign ports or had already been seized or sunk by the enemy. Axis shipping in the Mediterranean was supplemented by 54 German freighters which had run to Italian ports at the outbreak of war. Germany's and Italy's total tonnage usable in the Mediterranean area thus amounted to 2,135,651 GRT.[438]

Before describing the organization of the high command of the Italian naval forces, a few data should first be given—as was done for the army and air force—concerning the naval commands existing on 10 June 1940 (the list includes only those which had units afloat under their command). Such commands existed for the northern Tyrrhenian Sea at La Spezia (Marina-La Spezia); for the southern Tyrrhenian Sea in Naples (Marina-Napoli); for the sea area around Sardinia at La Maddalena (the Marina-La Maddalena command was later renamed Marisardegna); for the waters around Sicily in Messina (Marina-Messina, subsequently renamed Marisicilia); for the Ionian and southern Adriatic Seas at Taranto (Marina-Taranto); for the northern Adriatic in Venice (Marina-Venezia); for the Albanian coast at Durazzo (Durres) (Marialbania-Durazzo); for the Aegean at Rhodes (Marina-Rodi, subsequently renamed Mariegeo); for Libya at Tripoli (Marilibia-Tripoli); and for the waters off Italian East Africa at Massawa (Marisupao-Massaua).[439] These commands had of course numerous sectional commands subordinated to them.[440]

---

[437] Discussed in detail in Schreiber, *Revisionismus*, 367–78.

[438] Data according to *La marina italiana*, i. 30–1; Dupuis, *Forzate il blocco!*, 186, speaks of 220 ships totalling 1,225,923 GRT outside the Mediterranean.

[439] *La marina italiana*, xxi. 336–7.

[440] In the sector of the northern Tyrrhenian Sea: Marina-Genova, Marina-Imperia, Marina-Savona, Marina-Livorno, Marina-Portoferraio, Mariser, later Maricomar-Portoferraio. For the southern Tyrrhenian Sea: Marina-Gaeta, Marina-Civitavecchia, Mariser, later Maricomar-Napoli, Marina-Castellammare Stabia. For Sardinia: Marina-Porto Torres, Marina-Olbia, Marina-Cagliari, Marina-S. Antioco. For Sicily: Mariser-Messina, Marina-Augusta, Marina-Catania, Marina-Trapani, Marina-Palermo, Marina-Porto Empedocle, Marina-Pantelleria. For the Ionian Sea and the southern Adriatic: Marina-Crotone, Marina-Gallipoli, Marina-Brindisi, Marina-Bari, Marina-Otranto, Marina-Lagosta. For the northern Adriatic: Marina-Ancona, Marina-Pola, Marina-Zara, Marina-Trieste, Marina-Lussino, Marina-Fiume. For Albania: Marina-Durazzo, Marina-Valona,

(b) The Problem of Top-level Organization

Turning from this brief examination of the Italian forces' armament-technological and organizational problems to that of top-level organization, the first thing to point out is that relations between the Capo di Stato Maggiore Generale (SMG: chief of the general staff) and the head of government were defined in a highly unsatisfactory manner by royal decree No. 68 of February 1927. This left the chief of the general staff with only advisory functions and prevented his intervening responsibly in the affairs of the armed forces. The decree likewise strengthened Mussolini's influence, which he further enhanced by a skilful personnel policy, so that ultimately he exercised sole control over the armed forces. More important still than this weakening of the role of the chief of the general staff was the fact that, parallel with it, an upgrading of the commanders-in-chief of the separate services, envisaged since 1925, had taken place. Each of them was now able to approach Mussolini directly, so that the Duce represented the central pivot of all Fascist military policy. The chief of the general staff, on the other hand, could deal with the commanders-in-chief of the army, navy, and air force only through the official channels, by way of the separate ministries. Basically this meant the paralysis of his authority. A comparison with decree No. 69, which on the same day regulated the role of the Capo di Stato Maggiore dell'Esercito (SME: chief of staff of the army), shows that the latter virtually took over the former sphere of activity and responsibility of the chief of the general staff, at least as far as the army was concerned. He was moreover authorized to deal directly—bypassing official channels—with all ministries and state institutions whenever his duties required it. The contrast between the treatment of the Capo di SMG and the Capo di SME was striking. The shortcomings of this system were patent, and Mussolini's tactics in pursuing his specific interests were equally obvious. Presumably a certain measure of opportunism was to blame for the fact that this manipulation of the Capo di SMG, initiated by the head of government, was accepted without protest.[441] One of the fateful consequences of that system was that there was no harmonization between foreign policy and war preparations. This was reflected, among other things, in the fact that there was no war plan, or rather no operational plan worthy of the name, in existence in June 1940. It is difficult to decide how much responsibility for this omission attaches to whom. But it probably has to be seen as a historic failure on the part of Marshal Badoglio, chief of the general staff, that for a long time he acted as though the primacy of politics—which was a feature of Mussolini's dictatorship—had relieved the military leaders of their specific responsibilities.

Marina-Porto Edda, Marina-S. Giovanni di Medua. In the Aegean: Marina-Lero, Marina-Stampalia, Marina-Rodi. In Libya: Marina-Tripoli, Marina-Bengasi, Marina-Tobruk. In East Africa: Marina-Massaua, Marina-Assab, Marina-Chisimaio. All data from *La marina italiana*, xxi.1. 336–7.

[441] Ceva, *La condotta*, 17–23; for the army a different view in Faldella, *L'Italia*, 126.

4. The Italian Fighting Forces

Without going into previous history, it should be pointed out that Badoglio did not make any serious attempt to reform the top-level organization of the armed forces until February 1940.[442] This attempt began not only late, but quite certainly too late.[443] What the marshal was aiming at was a strengthening of his own position. Directly linked to this was his demand to have the commanders-in-chief of the army, air force, and navy more closely bound to the chief of the general staff, to enable him to exert overall influence. Developments over the preceding few years had shown that, as a result of the decisions of 1927, the services were increasingly inclined to make themselves independent. A typical instance is, as mentioned earlier, Graziani's contact with the Germans in April 1940. The issue then was Italian participation in the campaign in the west. Yet Badoglio, who was formally the senior officer, was initially bypassed.[444] Such incidents were nothing unusual. They had virtually been institutionalized, since the commanders-in-chief of the three services held the rank of under-secretaries of state and thus enjoyed direct access to the head of government.

Any acceptance of Badoglio's proposals, submitted in April and May 1940, would inevitably have meant a diminution of Mussolini's powers within the military hierarchy. The marshal for his part obviously suspected that the Duce was aiming at a position such as Hitler occupied in Germany. Accordingly he argued that the top-level organization of the German armed forces could not serve as a model for Italy. In the event of the head of government deciding in favour of such a model he, Badoglio, would resign: he was not prepared to play the part of an Italian Keitel.[445]

Mussolini, who was just then endeavouring to persuade the king to appoint him supreme commander of the armed forces, reacted calmly. He assured Badoglio that he intended to confine himself to issuing general strategic guidelines, which was in any case the business of the head of government. Badoglio, on the other hand, was to retain unrestricted responsibility for operations. The marshal agreed to this. The question is whether he had no alternative or whether, for whatever reason, he fell for Mussolini's subterfuge. At any rate, the two agreed on the organization of the supreme command, which granted Badoglio exceedingly ill-defined duties as Mussolini's chief of staff, and has been described as typical of the intellectual confusion of Italian armed-forces organization.[446]

In the letter on the new organization of the top echelons, published by Badoglio on 4 June 1940, Mussolini already appeared as supreme commander

---

[442] Pieri and Rochat, *Badoglio*, 746–7.
[443] On this Ceva, *La condotta*, esp. 24–5.
[444] Iachino, *Tramonto*, 107.
[445] According to Badoglio's letter to Mussolini of 3 May 1940, published in Pieri and Rochat, *Badoglio*, 749.
[446] Ceva, *La condotta*, 23–4; Pieri and Rochat, *Badoglio*, 749–50.

of all 'operating forces',[447] which in fact he was to become only on 11 June, by royal patent. Italy had her 'Comandante Supremo' in the Duce; one spoke of the 'Comando Supremo', a kind of Wehrmacht high command (OKW), though as an official institution Mussolini's staff continued to bear the title of Stato Maggiore Generale, 'Stamage' for short, with the Capo di Stato Maggiore Generale at its head. Badoglio retained this description even after the SMG was renamed 'Comando Supremo' on 20 May 1941.[448] On the basis of this new organization Badoglio in theory discharged all the functions which belonged to the chief of staff of the political and military leader, with regard to the co-ordination and supervision of planning and operations. However, as we have seen, he lacked all practical means of performing these tasks, and this, paradoxically enough, relieved him of his responsibilities—a situation in which he was pleased to acquiesce. In practice 'Stamage' was not much more than a modest staff of assistants to the marshal; it did not even succeed in becoming a link between Mussolini and the commanders-in-chief of the three services,[449] as had originally been envisaged.

Regardless of the structures as they appeared on paper without ever having been legislatively enacted, at least seven commanders-in-chief remained directly dependent on Mussolini. They were: Soddu, under-secretary of state in the war ministry and subchief of the general staff, although as Badoglio's deputy (from 13 June 1940) he held no real powers; Rotta, subchief of the SME, who, after Balbo's fatal accident on 28 June 1940, in practice performed the duties of chief of the army general staff when Graziani, the real Capo di SME, became commander-in-chief in Libya; Cavagnari, under-secretary of state and Capo di SM della Marina (commander-in-chief of the navy); Pricolo, under-secretary of state and Capo di SM dell'Aeronautica (commander-in-chief of the air force); Graziani in his function of Comandante Superiore in North Africa; the Duke of Aosta, Viceroy of Ethiopia; and De Vecchi, Capo delle Forze in Egeo (commander-in-chief of the forces in the Aegean).[450]

Not surprisingly, such an organization did not work. It merely made it easier for Mussolini to exercise his chaotic method of command, which of course should not be regarded as exonerating the military. The Duce's habit, accepted by the generals and admirals, of reserving to himself, more or less at random, both major and some decidedly minor decisions, was marked by inconsistencies and by his ceaseless interference in all spheres. If one bears in mind that—apart from Badoglio, effectively shunted to a dead end, and his ineffectual SMG—Mussolini had no qualified expert advisers and was there-

---

[447] On what follows see *Africa settentrionale, La preparazione*, 77 ff., 188 ff.; Iachino, *Tramonto*, 107 ff.; Pieri and Rochat, *Badoglio*, 750 ff.; the latter also point out (n. 1) that Badoglio's letter, containing the grounds for setting up the Comando Supremo, did not accord with the facts, as on 11 June the king had granted Mussolini not supreme command over 'all' but only over the 'operating' forces.

[448] Santoro, *L'aeronautica italiana*, i. 66.

[449] Ceva, *La condotta*, 23–4; Rochat, 'Mussolini et les forces armées', 56–9.

[450] Pieri and Rochat, *Badoglio*, 751–2.

fore exercising supreme command as a military amateur and without any restraints, it will readily be understood why such extraordinary decisions were arrived at as, for instance, demobilization immediately prior to the attack on Greece. Other instances of Mussolini's incompetence in organizational matters are not far to seek. On 9 November 1940 Soddu was appointed commander-in-chief in Albania, but retained his former duties for some little time. On 29 November he was relieved by Graziani, both as under-secretary of state in the war ministry and as subchief of the SMG. On 6 December Cavallero succeeded Badoglio as Capo di SMG, but was immediately sent off to Albania.[451]

The list could be continued, but these instances should suffice to demonstrate that there was method in the disorganization of the Italian armed-forces command. Although, under the given conditions, the Capo di SMG received Mussolini's guidelines and orders, he was unable not only to issue the necessary directions but also to see them carried out, since it was impossible for him to supervise the operations, intervene when necessary, or ensure the timely and co-ordinated employment of the fighting forces. Mussolini thus exercised his command not, as laid down on 4 June 1940, through the chief of the general staff but by bypassing him.[452] The commanders-in-chief of the separate services do not seem to have taken this amiss. Admittedly they recognized the need for establishing a central, effectively functioning post for the co-ordination of the conduct of the war, but they did not see why the Capo di SMG should always have to be an army general—departmental jealousies came into play, of the kind familiar also in Germany. That was why the Italian services originally supported the creation of a command group operating as colleagues, on the British model, and rejected Mussolini's idea of an imitation of the German OKW.[453]

Parallel to the establishment of the Comando Supremo, commands were set up in the three services, subordinated to the Capo di Stato Maggiore of each and roughly representing operations branches for the army, navy, and air force. It was their duty to translate the head of government's strategic directives into operational orders and to pass these on to the various subordinate commanders. These new posts were called 'Superesercito' for the army, 'Supermarina' for the navy, and 'Superaereo' for the air force, or alternatively the 'Alto Comando' of the service in question,[454] a term which only in name meant army, navy, or air force high command. If one tried to compare the German and Italian posts—which on close inspection is almost impossible in

---

[451] Ceva, *La condotta*, 26.

[452] Cf. the extensive catalogue of tasks and the hierarchical structure which Badoglio's announcement of 4 June 1940 envisaged for 'Stamage' or the 'Comando Supremo'; published in e.g. *Africa settentrionale, La preparazione*, 188 ff.

[453] Iachino, *Tramonto*, 108 ff.; on relations between Mussolini and the individual supreme commanders see esp. Rochat, 'Mussolini et les forces armées', 48–53.

[454] Cf. Bernotti, *La guerra, 1939–1941*, 187–8; Bragadin, *Che ha fatto la marina?*, 13–18; Iachino, *Tramonto*, 111–15; *La marina italiana*, iv. 18–24; ibid. xxi. 57–61; Santoro, *L'aeronautica italiana*, i. 73.

view of the differences in detail—then the Stato Maggiore Generale would correspond to the Wehrmacht high command (OKW), the Stato Maggiore della Marina to the German navy high command (OKM), the Stato Maggiore dell'Esercito to the army high command (OKH), the Stato Maggiore dell'Aeronautica to the Luftwaffe high command (OKL), Superesercito to the army general staff, Supermarina to the naval war staff, and Superaereo to the Luftwaffe general staff.

In this context it seems appropriate—beyond the brief references made above to British commands in the Mediterranean area—to deal with a number of British and American institutions which will come up repeatedly in succeeding chapters, and a description of which will permit comparison with the command structures on the German and Italian side.

The first to be mentioned are the US Joint Chiefs of Staff (JCS). This closest body of advisers to the American president was composed of the Chief of Staff of the US Army, the Commanding General of the US Army Air Force, and the Commander in Chief US Fleet and Chief of Naval Operations; if required, the Commandant US Marine Corps took part in its discussions. Subsequently the president's special chief of staff became the fourth regular member.

The Joint Chiefs of Staff at the same time functioned as the United States representatives in the Anglo-American body known as the Combined Chiefs of Staff (CCS), set up in December 1941. This was designed to ensure harmonization of the British and American conduct of the war and simultaneously to act as a Washington-based body for top-level discussions, as well as formulating recommendations for the 'grand strategy' of the two Western Allies. The British chiefs of staff were normally represented by deputies. This advisory body to the US president and the British prime minister met 199 times between January 1942 and July 1945. On the Axis side there was no even approximately comparable institution. Britain's representatives on the CCS were the Chief of Naval Staff, the Chief of the Imperial General Staff, and the Chief of Air Staff. These were the officers who, from 1923, had been responsible, as the Chiefs of Staff Committee (usually called simply Chiefs of Staff), for Britain's entire planning and strategy, acting as advisers to the prime minister, who, in addition, had a Principal Staff Officer sitting on the committee. Mention must also be made of the war cabinet, which, under Chamberlain, consisted of nine members, including the First Lord of the Admiralty, the Secretary of State for War, and the Secretary of State for Air. Under Churchill, who as Minister of Defence was also the direct superior of the Chiefs of Staff, the war cabinet was reduced to five members: the First Sea Lord and the two secretaries of state were no longer part of it.

At the end of this first chapter, which has been devoted to Italian *non belligeranza*, it may be useful to recall a few aspects of Axis policy which proved to have lasting effects on the further development of the war in the Mediterranean area.

During the first six months of 1939 Germany and Italy had strained their mutual relations by independent acts of foreign policy which might, on the surface, make the conclusion of the so-called Pact of Steel in May 1939 seem surprising. On closer inspection, however, it emerges that this pact, constituting as it did a war alliance couched in very general terms, should be interpreted as an attempt by each of the two dictators to bind the other to his own intentions. To Hitler this step also represented a tactical move by which, his eyes firmly on his decision to attack Poland, he hoped to threaten London and Paris by way of Rome, and so deter Britain and France from giving military support to Warsaw.

The outbreak of the war proved that this calculation, first made by Hitler in 1937, was based on a false premiss. Mussolini was in no position to intervene in the conflict, as Italy was neither militarily nor economically ready for a major war.

Our account of the measures embarked on by Italy after September 1939 has shown that the country's inadequate state of armament in the summer of that year did not mean that the Fascist regime maintained a disinterested, let alone a fundamentally opposed, attitude to the war.

It became obvious during the period of non-belligerence that the inefficiency of Italy's political and economic system, its faults of omission in the past, the raw material shortages, and the structure of the economy ruled out any possibility that she might come anywhere near eradicating her shortfalls in supplies and armaments by June 1940.

Moreover, it became obvious that, in view of Italy's economic and industrial situation, a German–Italian coalition must, in a prolonged war, become a misalliance. This was the more true as in the political sphere a rivalry soon began to appear which revealed the Axis as an alliance of a fundamentally negative character, held together by no more than a common rejection of the power-political conditions in Europe at the time.

Nevertheless, from September 1939 onwards Mussolini was increasingly inclined to enter the war—which Hitler wanted him to do, even just before the opening of the campaign in the west, when he wished to send Italian troops into action against France from southern Germany.

Mussolini's rejection of this plan, a rejection he never communicated officially, reveals a central feature of his political calculations. What mattered to the Duce was a place in the concert of European great powers—which was why, from the moment that mediation by Italy was seen to be illusory, his entry into the war was virtually inevitable. On the other hand, Mussolini was trying hard to preserve his own weight and Italy's (relative) independence of Germany. Hence the frontier fortifications in the north, the avoidance of a common theatre of war, and his preference for a short parallel war. Specifically, Mussolini was pursuing the realization of his empire—which, of course, can also be interpreted as part of his design to build up a counter-position to Germany's hegemonistic strivings and claims.

Altogether, as we have shown, in the summer of 1940 Mussolini was about to enter a conflict for success in which Italy's armed forces and her economy were inadequate from military, material, organizational, and domestic points of view. He was doing so, moreover, as a member of a coalition which, on economic and geo-strategic grounds, was bound to become over-stressed by any joint conduct of the war, as in the long run the strategic gap between an increased demand—to offset consumption and losses—and inadequate armament facilities must, with a probability bordering on certainty, grow ever wider.

II. Italy's Entry into the War

MUSSOLINI's attitude during the first quarter of 1940, especially before the conclusion of the Italo-German trade agreement, was marked by extraordinary uncertainty. Outwardly at least the Duce gave the impression of still being capable of the most contradictory decisions.[1] While his New Year's message[2] has to be interpreted as falling into line with Hitler,[3] other statements expressed a claim to the leading position in the Axis alliance.[4] These, of course, were wishful thinking. They may have been typical of Mussolini's self-assurance, but they bore scant relation to the reality of the alliance. Eventually, in 1940, Mussolini—correctly assessing the power-balance between Berlin and Rome, and having maintained his same basic foreign-policy line since 1936—unambiguously aligned himself against the democracies.[5]

This did not, however, prevent him from ordering the fortification work on Italy's northern frontier—including that with Germany—to be continued. Mussolini was fascinated by the notion of establishing a modern European *limes*, and the idea of a nation behind walls developed within him into something like a defensive concept. He therefore made large quantities of iron, aluminium, etc. available for these frontier fortifications even during difficult phases of Italian rearmament. Yet by the summer of 1940 the successes of the German offensive along the Maginot Line began, throughout the world, to call into question the faith placed in such structures—structures which to Mussolini seem to have been prerequisites of the parallel war intended by him.[6]

1. EVENTS AND REACTIONS: MUSSOLINI'S DECISION IN 1940

For many weeks, ever since early March 1940, Mussolini had considered only two options of Italian warfare: the employment of his forces by the side of

---

[1] Bocca, *Storia*, 76 ff.; Grimaldi and Bozzetti, *Dieci giugno*, 344–54; Schreiber, *Revisionismus*, 252–5.
[2] Ciano, *Diary 1939–1943*, 192 (1 Jan. 1940); on the background also Quartararo, *Roma*, 572–3; Canzio, *La dittatura*, 556 ff.
[3] *DDI*, 9th ser., iii, No. 1, p. 1 (1 Jan. 1940).
[4] Ciano, *Diary 1939–1943*, 198–19 (17 Jan. 1940).
[5] Ibid. 201 (22 Jan. 1940).
[6] Cf. the revealing notes in Bottai, *Vent'anni*, 156–9 (20, 23 Jan. 1940, 14 Feb. 1940); the edition of Bottai, *Diario* (Milan, 1982), lacks the passages confirming the connection (indicated in the text above) between 'parallel war' and extension of frontier fortifications—cf. Bottai, *Diario*, 177–8 (1 Mar. 1940). Mussolini first used the term 'parallel war', without defining it, in the ministerial council on 23 Jan. 1940—cf. Bottai, *Diario*, 174–5 (23 Jan. 1940); on the defence-policy consequences drawn in Switzerland from the French defeat cf. Bonjour, *Geschichte der schweizerischen Neutralität*, ix. 379–92, relating to the 'Redoubt Plan'.

Germany, or—his preference—largely independent operations of his own.[7] Initially, however, there was no clear understanding, even within his intimate circle, of what precisely Mussolini understood, in strategic terms, by 'parallel war',[8] and more particularly how he intended to wage it and what his objectives were.[9] It was only during Ribbentrop's visit to Rome in March 1940,[10] in the course of his meeting with Hitler on the Brenner a few days later,[11] and in his above-mentioned memorandum of 31 March[12] that the Duce's ideas took on clearer shape for those around him. It was evident that Mussolini was primarily concerned not only with Nice, Corsica, Jibuti, and Tunis,[13] but also with free access to the high seas—all of which was to be achieved by a pattern of operations not influenced by the Germans.

In this connection it should be pointed out that, by the time Hitler and Mussolini met on the Brenner, the mission of Sumner Welles, the American under-secretary of state, undertaken on President Roosevelt's instructions in the spring of 1940, had to be seen as a failure. This was due, not solely but very largely, to Hitler's intransigence. Sumner Welles's peace efforts foundered on 'Hitler's intransigence' as well as on 'Roosevelt's deliberate reserve'. The decisive aspect was that Hitler had long abandoned any readiness for compromise. According to the pattern of his policy of expansion and aggression it was now the turn of France. Roosevelt for his part was disinclined to jeopardize his own re-election, which in the spring of 1940 was by no means a certainty, by any decisive commitment, which would have had to hint convincingly at a readiness for military intervention. The president was well aware of the isolationist trends in American public opinion, and the half-hearted nature of the peace mission was certainly in line with such considerations.[14]

France and Britain, who did not gain from Roosevelt's policy even the temporary respite which Hitler's involvement in peace talks might have provided, were at first alarmed by Mussolini's course towards war, which had been becoming increasingly clear since April. Further developments, however,

---

[7] Bottai, *Vent'anni*, 159 (1 Mar. 1940); agreeing not literally but largely in content Bottai, *Diario*, 177–8 (1 Mar. 1940). Mussolini first used the term 'parallel war', without defining it, in the ministerial council on 23 Jan. 1940—cf. Bottai, *Diario*, 174–5 (23 Jan. 1940); see also Grimaldi and Bozzetti, *Dieci giugno*, 346 ff.

[8] Bottai, *Vent'anni*, 160–1 (2 Mar. 1940); divergent as regards Bottai's own attitude *Diario*, 178 (2 Mar. 1940).

[9] Rintelen, 'Mussolinis Parallelkrieg', 17–18.

[10] DGFP D viii, No. 665, pp. 882–93 (10 Mar. 1940); No. 667, pp. 894 ff. (11 Mar. 1940); No. 669, pp. 898–909 (11 Mar. 1940); cf. Canzio, *La dittatura*, 558–9; Grimaldi and Bozzetti, *Dieci giugno*, 364–72; Siebert, *Italiens Weg*, 413–18; Wiskemann, *Axis*, 197 ff. A discussion of the importance of the visit in getting Mussolini to come to a decision about entering the war in André, 'La politica estera', 119–20.

[11] DGFP D ix, No. 1, pp. 1–16 (18 Mar. 1940); Salvatorelli and Mira, *Storia d'Italia*, 1037; Schreiber, *Revisionismus*, 257 ff.

[12] See I.1.2 (c) above; extensively dealt with also in Grimaldi and Bozzetti, *Dieci giugno*, 392–5.

[13] On the Tunisian issue in the 19th and 20th cents.: Rainero, *La rivendicazione*; for the period of Fascism until Italy's entry into the war, ibid. 85–334.

[14] Martin, *Friedensinitiativen*, 207–33, quotations 231.

showed that the final decision to enter the war was not taken until the very last moment.

From the Allied point of view, April 1940 was certainly a month of uncertainty as far as Italy's attitude was concerned. In retrospect it is clear that Franco-British conciliatory moves—especially after the Wehrmacht's successes in Norway—no longer carried any weight with Mussolini.[15] However, hope had not been abandoned in the spring of 1940, either in London or in Paris, that an arrangement might be reached with Rome. Thus Paul Reynaud, the French premier, launched a firm initiative at the end of April with a view to avoiding war between the Allies and Italy.[16] The move was supported by French deputies and diplomats.[17] There were clear hints that London and Paris would be loath to open a new front.[18] Mussolini moreover knew from Raffaele Guariglia, the Italian ambassador in Paris, that Reynaud had signalled a readiness to make concessions.[19] He also understood correctly that the British government was likewise ready to make far-reaching concessions, especially in the economic field.[20] On 26 April, however, the Duce informed the French premier in a very curt reply that, as Germany's ally, he was of course hoping for Hitler's victory and that he was not interested in the meeting envisaged by Reynaud. 'It will not be difficult for you, Mr President, to understand the reason.'[21] It was by then no use for the Italian community in France to address itself to the Rome government, urging it to sever its ties with Germany and to join the democracies.[22] At that point the Fascist regime was no longer interested in promoting Italophile tendencies in France.[23]

Georges Mandel, then French minister for the colonies,[24] therefore presented an entirely correct analysis of Italo-French relations when in a lengthy conversation with Guariglia—after enlarging upon his belief in a victory of the Allied forces—he observed that, while he too regarded a policy of arrangement with Italy as necessary, the die had been cast on the Italian side long before 1939, regardless of all present diplomatic finessing and manœuvring. Italy was ostensibly concerned with free access to the Mediterranean, and the internationalization of such access was then on the tapis. Yet all concerned realized that such ideas were an illusion. What was called free access would in fact

---

[15] Extensively on Apr. 1940: Knox, *Mussolini*, 91–8.

[16] *DDI*, 9th ser., iv, No. 165, pp. 134–5 (22 Apr. 1940); No. 166, pp. 135–6 (22 Apr. 1940); also published in *DGFP* D ix, No. 167, p. 237, and ibid., No. 172, p. 246 (text of letter).

[17] *DDI*, 9th ser., iv, No. 191, pp. 160–1 (24 Apr. 1940); No. 192, pp. 161–2 (24 Apr. 1940); No. 193, p. 162 (25 Apr. 1940); No. 201, pp. 168–9 (25 Apr. 1940).

[18] Ibid., No. 205, p. 171 (26 Apr. 1940).

[19] Ibid., No. 206, pp. 171–2 (26 Apr. 1940).

[20] Ibid., No. 213, p. 176 (26 Apr. 1940); No. 215, p. 177 (26 Apr. 1940); No. 217, pp. 180 ff. (26 Apr. 1940).

[21] *DGFP* D ix, No. 173, p. 248 (27 Apr. 1940); original text in *DDI*, 9th ser., iv, No. 219, p. 184 (26 Apr. 1940).

[22] *DDI*, 9th ser., iv, No. 225, p. 187 (27 Apr. 1940).

[23] Ibid., No. 227, p. 189 (27 Apr. 1940).

[24] From 18 May 1940 Mandel was minister of the interior.

always depend on the ratio of strength between Italy, France, and Britain. This, Mandel observed, was realized also in Rome, which was why Mussolini was in truth concerned only with extending his sphere of power at the expense of France—not by treaties but by territorial conquest—in order to achieve a balance of power favourable to himself. This was what lay behind Italy's demand for *libertà mediterranea*. This intention, however, was not realizable without a Franco-Italian war. The conflict, therefore, seemed to have been predetermined by fate. Mandel similarly thought it a mistake to grant Rome a free hand in the Balkans in order to avoid war with Italy. Such concessions would only result in a temporary respite. The Allies, therefore, would be paying an extremely high price merely to gain time. Besides, basically such an arrangement could not eliminate the rivalries in the Mediterranean. This was especially true of the French–Italian antagonism.[25]

Towards the end of April, alarmed by events in Scandinavia and fearing an extension of the conflict to the Mediterranean area, the American president directly involved himself in the efforts to preserve Italy's neutrality. Roosevelt expressed the opinion that it was thanks to Mussolini that the Mediterranean countries, inhabited by some 200 million people, had so far avoided being drawn into the war. Urging the Duce to continue working for the preservation of peace, he pointed to the great influence which Washington and Rome would enjoy in negotiations concerning the conclusion of the conflict.[26] William Phillips, the American ambassador in Rome, put Roosevelt's ideas to Mussolini on 1 May in the presence of Ciano.[27] These remarks about Italy, regardless of the president's attacks on Hitler, are to be interpreted as an attempt to continue a policy of appeasement *vis-à-vis* Mussolini. Washington had no interest whatever in provoking Rome. Italy, however, assured her Axis partner on the very same day that Mussolini's answer to Roosevelt would be clear and to the point.[28]

Accordingly the reply that Prince Ascanio Colonna, the Italian ambassador in Washington, conveyed to Roosevelt at Ciano's behest[29] on 2 May, in the presence of Sumner Welles, left nothing to be desired on the score of plain speaking.[30] It was not Germany's fault that the war had spread to Scandinavia, but that of the Allies, whose behaviour had provoked the German invasion. It was indeed appropriate to attribute to Italy the merit of preserving peace in the Mediterranean area, but mention should be made of the 'gratitude' of France and Britain, which consisted of grievous damage to Italy's seaborne trade. As for an extension of the conflict, Mussolini knew only that this was not desired

---

[25] *DDI*, 9th ser., iv, No. 216, pp. 178 ff. (26 Apr. 1940).
[26] *FRUS* (1940), ii. 691–2 (29 Apr. 1940).
[27] Ibid. 693 ff. (1 May 1940); *DDI*, 9th ser., iv, No. 262, pp. 212–13 (1 May 1940).
[28] *DGFP* D ix, No. 185, pp. 261–2.
[29] *DDI*, 9th ser., iv, No. 263, p. 213 (1 May 1940).
[30] *FRUS* (1940), ii. 695–8 (2 May 1940), including the summary of the conversation prepared by Sumner Welles; in *DDI*, 9th ser., iv, No. 271, pp. 219 ff. (2 May 1940), the notes made for Ciano by the Italian ambassador.

either by Germany or by Italy, whereas the attitude of the Allies was still unclear. In any case he advised the United States to keep out of European affairs, just as Italy had always done, and intended to do, with regard to the American continent.

Mussolini finally pointed out that, in all discussions of the conflict and its settlement, it had to be borne in mind that Britain herself ruled a large part of the world. London alone had a monopoly of numerous raw materials. Rome was prepared to play a part in achieving a better world order. But she would do so only if present conditions were accepted, i.e. the political changes brought about in Europe, and if account was taken of Italy's special problems linked with Britain's position as a world power. In reply Roosevelt displayed understanding on all these points, while avoiding a definite stance. Evidently it was enough for him for the time being that Mussolini was offering his cooperation in achieving a new system of international relations, assuming the impression conveyed by Prince Colonna was correct.

To Hitler, Mussolini explained the 'somewhat drastic tone' of his reply to Roosevelt by the 'obviously threatening character' of the latter's message. At the same time he stated that the suspension of British shipping in the Mediterranean, which had meanwhile taken place, did not greatly alarm him. The measure merely proved that this area was 'not absolutely essential to Great Britain'.[31] In the light of subsequent discussions on the decisive nature of Axis operations this is a significant remark and one which accurately described the British point of view. For Germany, on the other hand, the suspension of navigation in the Mediterranean was of considerable importance inasmuch as it directly affected U-boat warfare.[32] Otherwise Hitler's reactions generally indicated that he was content with the new line of Italian policy; at the same time his crudely disparaging remarks about the French premier dispelled any doubt about France being the next adversary to be eliminated.[33]

The German offensive in the west brought considerable movement into the international power-constellation, even though this was not immediately noticeable. On 7 May, only a few days previously, Paris, regardless of British military and trade measures in anticipation of Italy's entry into the war, which could no longer be ruled out,[34] had again informed Rome that the Allies had no intention of seizing the initiative in the Mediterranean or the Balkans.[35] But contacts continued even after 10 May, especially in connection with the blockade issue, which was being increasingly emphasized by Italy.[36] The British showed themselves ready for extraordinary alleviations in connection

---

[31] *DGFP* D ix, No. 190, pp. 271–2 (2 May 1940).
[32] *DDI*, 9th ser., vi, No. 274, p. 222 (2 May 1940).
[33] Ibid., No. 272, p. 221 (2 May 1940); No. 273, pp. 221–2 (2 May 1940).
[34] Ibid., No. 278, pp. 224–5 (2 May 1940); *FRUS* (1940), ii. 699–700 (2 May 1940).
[35] *DDI*, 9th ser., iv, No. 314, p. 252 (7 May 1940).
[36] Ibid., No. 389, pp. 315–26 (11 May 1940); No. 421, pp. 353–4 (15 May 1940); No. 432, pp. 359–60 (15 May 1940).

with the control of Italian ships at sea,[37] and the French aligned themselves with that attitude.[38]

Comparison of the various documents[39] on this issue—up to the suspension of Italy's readiness to negotiate, announced by circular of 26 May[40]—shows that both the British and the French were ready to discuss openly all relevant problems in order to find a solution acceptable to Italy. Britain, naturally, was reluctant—although this did not initially interfere with the progress of negotiations—to renounce surveillance of Mediterranean shipping entirely. France, on the other hand, fearing Italy's entry into the war rather more than did her ally, favoured unlimited negotiations with the Italians, and suggested a renewed intervention by Roosevelt with Mussolini. Churchill, though rather sceptical about its outcome, agreed with the plan primarily so as not to give France a pretext for a separate peace.[41] Such a separate peace could no longer be ruled out as, after mid-May, the prospect of a French military defeat was emerging ever more menacingly.[42]

In parallel with the negotiations on blockade matters, both the Allies and the Americans now became active at the highest political level in order to stop Mussolini entering the war. Urged on by Paris and London,[43] Roosevelt once more approached the Duce despite his rudeness at the end of April. Churchill's letter to the president, asking for massive help with material, clearly reveals the problem which the opening of a new theatre of war in the Mediterranean would present from the Allied point of view. London was worried mainly about the threat which the powerful Italian submarine fleet would pose to supplies for Great Britain[44] if the Italians were to operate outside the Mediterranean. Roosevelt wrote to Mussolini on 14 May, shortly after the start of the German offensive, when it was already becoming clear that the Allies could not win the battle for France. 'We are defeated; we have lost the battle,' Reynaud informed Churchill on the morning of 15 May.[45] The president's message to the Duce was a highly emotional appeal, an urgent attempt to preserve the peace in the Mediterranean area. But Roosevelt did not hesitate to point to the threat of

---

[37] Ibid., No. 434, pp. 360–1 (16 May 1940).
[38] Ibid., No. 458, p. 373 (17 May 1940).
[39] Ibid., No. 451, p. 369 (17 May 1940); No. 474, pp. 382–3 (18 May 1940); No. 475, p. 383 (18 May 1940); No. 498, p. 398 (19 May 1940); No. 589, pp. 462–3 (26 May 1940); No. 616, p. 479 (28 May 1940).
[40] *DGFP* D ix, No. 342, pp. 463–4 (29 May 1940); for the surprise caused by Italy's step in London cf. also *DDI*, 9th ser., iv, No. 674, pp. 513–14 (31 May 1940); No. 696, pp. 537–8 (1 June 1940).
[41] See Knox, *Mussolini*, 112–16; according to information from the Italian ambassador in Paris, Weygand recommended such a separate peace in the ministerial council towards the end of May: *DDI*, 9th ser., iv, No. 615, p. 479 (28 May 1940).
[42] Extensively on this and on the British–French discussions on developments since 10 May: Woodward, *British Foreign Policy*, i. 195–205.
[43] Dallek, *Franklin D. Roosevelt*, 220–1; *FRUS* (1940), ii. 703–4.
[44] *Roosevelt and Churchill*, No. 8, pp. 94–5.
[45] Churchill, *Second World War*, ii. 39.

another world war in the event of any extension of the conflict.[46] However, by then the American ambassador Phillips was not even permitted to make his approach to Mussolini direct, but had to content himself with seeing Ciano. Ciano, convinced of his father-in-law's determination to enter the war,[47] described Roosevelt's message, whose text[48] he handed over to the German ambassador in Rome, as 'an opus consisting of sentimental Christian observations'. The only thing that by then mattered in Rome was success on the battlefield. The Duce, as if mesmerized, followed the advance of the German armies, clearly unable to believe that victory in the west—to use a familiar, phrase—would mean the end of just a battle and not of the war.

In consequence the prospects of Churchill's direct approach to Mussolini were bound to be minimal, even though the prime minister voiced quite clearly what the Duce dared not consider: 'whatever may happen on the Continent, England will go on to the end, even quite alone... with some assurance that we shall be aided in increasing measure by the United States, and, indeed, by all the Americas.'[49] In Rome it was merely noted with interest that Churchill was allowing for the possibility of a defeat on the Continent; his simultaneously voiced determination to hold out to the end seems to have been regarded as unconvincing rhetoric uttered for transparent reasons.[50] Against this background it was of little consequence that Reynaud caused Mussolini to be informed that Italy, even if she remained non-belligerent, would be able to participate in peace negotiations at which all outstanding questions could be settled.[51] An attempt by the French government to keep Italy out of the war through the mediation of the Spanish dictator Franco seemed equally unpromising.[52]

The replies which Roosevelt and Churchill received from Rome had one advantage—they were unambiguous. The president now realized that Mussolini did not intend to keep aloof from events,[53] and Churchill no longer doubted that Italy would irrevocably enter the war at the most favourable moment.[54]

However, as things were going very badly for the British–French side, and since talks were continuing with the Italians, the Allies made one more attempt. At Reynaud's urging[55] they approached Roosevelt on 25 May,[56]

---

[46] *FRUS* (1940), ii. 704–5; Roosevelt's message is published in English and Italian in *DDI*, 9th ser., iv, No. 415, pp. 348–9 (14 May 1940).
[47] Ciano, *Diary 1939–1943*, 249–50 (13 May 1940).
[48] *DGFP* D ix, No. 255, pp. 354–5 (16 May 1940).
[49] Churchill, *Second World War*, ii. 107; *DDI*, 9th ser., iv, No. 445, pp. 365–6 (16 May 1940).
[50] *DGFP* D ix, No. 266, pp. 366–7 (18 May 1940).
[51] *DDI*, 9th ser., iv, No. 471, p. 381 (18 May 1940).
[52] Ibid., No. 481, pp. 385–6 (18 May 1940).
[53] *FRUS* (1940), ii. 706 (18 May 1940); *DDI*, 9th ser., iv, No. 486, p. 389 (18 May 1940).
[54] Churchill, *Second World War*, ii. 108; *DDI*, 9th ser., iv, No. 487, p. 389 (18 May 1940); Mussolini had informed the press of this decision a month earlier: Catalano, *Trionfo dei fascismi*, 286.
[55] Churchill, *Second World War*, ii. 108–10.
[56] *FRUS* (1940), ii. 709.

authorizing him to inform Italy of their readiness for far-reaching negotiations which would also include Rome's territorial demands. In addition, they again emphasized that in the peace negotiations Italy would be on an absolutely equal footing with the belligerent powers.[57] Roosevelt acted on these lines, his instructions to the American ambassador being couched in exceedingly committed terms.[58] Although Phillips was again denied access to Mussolini, Ciano informed him that he could definitively assure him of Italy's entry into the war: the Duce's irrevocable decision left only the date still open. A few hours later, in a brief note to Phillips, Mussolini himself ruled out all doubt on that score.[59] Roosevelt's reaction was very plain: he informed Mussolini that he would do everything to enable the Allies to wage war successfully.[60] Rome reacted arrogantly and rejected any further pressure.[61] The Fascist regime had long made up its mind. Continued French attempts to change Mussolini's mind were in vain.[62] In this connection the British remained unyielding on the issue of talks on Gibraltar, which Reynaud regarded as possible.[63] But even any British flexibility in this matter would not have improved the prospects of success; matters had reached a point where, as Ciano put it to François-Poncet, the French ambassador: 'Even if Mussolini were served up Tunis, Algiers, Corsica, and Nice on a platter, he could only say no, because there was only one thing for Italy now and that was war.'[64]

Washington therefore assessed the development entirely correctly when it declined an offer by Getulio Vargas, the Brazilian president, to try to keep Mussolini out of the war on the ground that it was now too late, as Mussolini had evidently made up his mind.[65] This view was confirmed a little later by William Christian Bullitt, the US ambassador in Paris, when he reported on the comprehensive French offers of negotiations with Italy and the lack of interest displayed in Rome.[66]

Reference has been made to the contacts between Berlin and Rome immediately preceding Italy's entry into the war.[67] A few days before 10 June 1940 the Germans began an intensive propaganda prelude to this step.[68] Until the

---

[57] Ibid. 709–10 (26 May 1940).
[58] Ibid. 710–11 (26 May 1940).
[59] Ibid. 712–13 (27 May 1940). On Ciano's reproduction of the conversation see *DDI*, 9th ser., iv, No. 609, pp. 475–6 (27 May 1940); and *DGFP* D ix, No. 339, pp. 460–1 (29 May 1940).
[60] *FRUS* (1940), ii. 713–14 (30 May 1940).
[61] Ibid. 715 (1 June 1940); *DGFP* D ix, No. 363, p. 492 (1 June 1940).
[62] Cf. *DDI*, 9th ser., iv, No. 644, pp. 498–9 (30 May 1940); No. 652, p. 503 (30 May 1940); No. 657, p. 505 (30 May 1940); No. 659, pp. 506–7 (30 May 1940); No. 661, pp. 507–8 (30 May 1940); No. 664, p. 509 (31 May 1940); No. 665, p. 510 (31 May 1940); No. 722, pp. 549–50 (3 June 1940); No. 748, p. 573 (5 June 1940); No. 812, pp. 605–6 (8 June 1940).
[63] Churchill, *Second World War*, ii. 109.
[64] *DGFP* D ix, No. 340, pp. 462–3 (28 May 1940); on Ciano's switch to Mussolini's course towards war: Mourin, *Ciano*, 24.
[65] *FRUS* (1940), ii. 715 (1 June 1940); 716 (1 June 1940).
[66] Ibid. 716 (3 June 1940).
[67] See I.1.2(c) above.
[68] *DDI*, 9th ser., iv, No. 830, p. 623 (9 June 1940).

end of May this issue had been treated with great caution in the propaganda ministry, and German statements had merely been echoes of Italian comment.[69]

The moment came on 10 June. Rome informed its embassies in London and Paris that war would be declared on Britain and France at 16.30 hours.[70] All other foreign missions were told of the new situation towards midnight,[71] once Ciano had notified the ambassadors of Britain and France. Unlike François-Poncet, Sir Percy Loraine received the news 'without batting an eyelid or changing colour'.[72] As for the Germans, who—if one accepts State Secretary von Weizsäcker's account[73]—would have preferred to have all the booty for themselves, Mussolini informed them that he felt splendidly armed. He even suggested that his 'Army of the Po' might be employed against England if Hitler wished to do so. At the same time, admittedly, he made some requests for materials.[74] These were more modest than those of the summer of 1939, but Hitler, while hailing the decision of 10 June as an event of historic importance,[75] which indeed it was to become, reacted with reserve. He had not yet forgiven Mussolini for keeping out of the war in 1939, and reserved to himself any decision regarding promises to be made to Italy.[76] Specifically, the Duce then asked for 8.8-cm. anti-aircraft guns.[77] With a view to a new regulation of economic relations between the Axis partners following Italy's entry into the war a 'fifth secret protocol' was concluded at a conference of experts meeting in Rome from 15 to 18 June; this essentially increased the raw-material deliveries agreed in February 1940. Germany, in particular, undertook to export more steel (a total of 5,000 t. per month) and cast iron (a total of 35,000 t. per month). As regards Italian exports to the Reich, to ensure that the promised amounts were delivered. Rome demanded that German supplies of coal must, averaged over the year, actually reach 1m. t. per month. This meant that larger amounts had to be imported by Italy during the summer in order to offset inevitable winter shortfalls.[78]

Mussolini, at any rate, now had his war. Bombast displacing reality, he again slipped into the role of the warlord. He himself seemed joyfully excited, while his people appeared more anxious. Though normally as much a virtuoso of mass mesmerization as Hitler, he conspicuously failed, from the Palazzo Venezia balcony that evening, to reach and sweep along with him those who would have to endure what lay ahead.[79] Aside from the professional Fascist

---

[69] *Kriegspropaganda*, 372.
[70] DDI, 9th ser., iv, No. 833, p. 624 (10 June 1940).
[71] Ibid., No. 842, 627 (10 June 1940).
[72] Ciano, *Diary 1939–1943*, 263 (10 June 1940).
[73] *Weizsäcker-Papiere*, 206–7 (5 June 1940).
[74] *DGFP* D ix, No. 408, pp. 540 ff. (10 June 1940).
[75] Ibid., No. 410, pp. 542–3 (10 June 1940).
[76] Ibid., No. 420, pp. 556–7 (12 June 1940).
[77] Ibid., No. 421, pp. 557–8 (13 June 1940).
[78] Ibid., No. 480, pp. 611 ff. (18 June 1940).
[79] Bocca, *Storia*, 166 ff.; Schreiber, *Revisionismus*, 262 n. 8. For an assessment of Mussolini's speech see Montanelli and Cervi, *L'Italia*, 440–1. A good picture of the public mood in Calvino,

cheer-leaders, Italy's 'warriors on land, on the sea, and in the air, the Black Shirts of the Revolution and the Legions, the men and women of Italy, of the Empire, and of the Kingdom of Albania' seemed to realize that it was not so much the 'hour destined by fate' that was sounding for them as one decreed by their head of government.[80] The dictator proclaimed war against plutocracy and reaction in the Western democracies, he pointed to the humiliations suffered by Italy in the past, and impressively called for the liquidation of Anglo-French hegemony in the Mediterranean. He spoke of a conflict of the 'young and fertile nations' with 'infertile nations doomed to decline', of clashing 'centuries' and 'ideologies', and finally also of victory, of German–Italian unity, and of the historic importance of what was taking place. The last, at least, proved true.

As for the German people's reaction to Italy's entry into the war, the best guides are probably the reports on popular feeling compiled by the propaganda ministry. These present a very varied picture. There was spontaneous joy, probably mingled with a kind of relief at no longer standing alone. If so, this was the precise opposite of a widespread British reaction to the German armistice with France. Some at least of the British people, including their king, felt freer after the fall of France: 'Now we know where we are—no more bloody allies', a skipper on the Thames is reported to have pithily remarked, and he was certainly not alone in this view.[81] In addition the German propaganda experts recorded a certain lukewarm satisfaction, and finally there was also surprise, as many Germans had no longer believed that Mussolini would take this step; indeed, up to the last minute they had expected a rerun of 1915, albeit in modified form.[82] Alongside these reactions there was admittedly also a clearly negative view which represented the Axis partner as a circus clown rolling up the carpet after the acrobat's performance and claiming the applause for himself.[83] Generally speaking, there was no quesion of a basically pro-Italian attitude,[84] even though, at least until the failure of the Alpine offensive against France, the impression persisted that Italian soldiers under the Fascist regime would be better fighters than in the First World War. At any rate, wide

---

L'entrata, esp. 5 ff., also generally on the beginning of the war. In great detail: Araldi, *Non belligeranza*, 162–79; on the Fascist leadership and its uncritical acceptance of Mussolini's course towards war, an attitude which can be explained from the structure of the regime, see Smith, *Roman Empire*, 209–10; differently Collier, *Duce*, 178–9.

[80] Mussolini's address: Jacobsen, *Der Zweite Weltkrieg*, 84–5; Smith, *Roman Empire*, 211–12, exaggerates the swing in public opinion produced by the German successes from the time of the invasion of Denmark and Norway; see Schreiber, *Revisionismus*, 262–3, and Nenni, *Vent'anni*, 255. A broadly based analysis of public opinion in Grimaldi and Bozzetti, *Dieci giugno*, 43–55, although these authors disregard the period May–June. Goebbels appeared to be greatly impressed by Mussolini's speech: cf. Goebbels, *Tagebücher*, iv. 198–9 (11 June 1940).

[81] Quoted from Balfour, *Propaganda*, 211.
[82] Steinert, *Hitlers Krieg*, 130–1.
[83] *Weizsäcker-Papiere*, 206 (5 June 1940).
[84] Balfour, *Propaganda*, 211.

1. Mussolini's Decision in 1940

circles of the German public were convinced by June 1940 that the victory of the Wehrmacht was assured even without Italian help.

This state of affairs prompted Goebbels to take action, even though, as late as 11 June, he had pursued a delicate policy of detachment from Italy. Thus a minute of a conference at his ministry noted that, in the area of news policy, a limit had to be set to the Italian alliance 'where the psychological and publicity warfare appropriate to the Italian people does not agree with our character or our ideas of psychological warfare. It would be a mistake to be excessively influenced in this respect by the Italians; in psychological warfare we should, just as hitherto, march along separately.'[85] Now, however, as a derogatory attitude was increasingly gaining ground in Germany owing to the Axis partner's continued non-belligerence—Italy did not attack immediately in the Alps even after 10 June—the propaganda minister decreed.[86] 'It is necessary to prevent a false picture of the Italian war effort taking root among the German people, as this would offend and discourage the Italians. By means of skilfully launched rumours—since one can neither write nor speak about these things —the belief should be anchored among the public that Italy quite simply was not mounting an attack as yet because an attack at this moment was undesirable, and the conviction should be encouraged that Italy would certainly attack as soon as the situation was ripe.' Goebbels also asked that poking fun at Italy should be stopped; the ally was to be treated with consideration and sympathy.

None of these instructions had any success. The Italians continued to be viewed with mistrust. Goebbels thereupon directed the press to set bounds to the 'incipient feelings of anger and hatred for Italy'. German propaganda was to point out that the latter's inactivity during the winter of 1939–40 had been exceedingly advantageous to Germany. As for the military aspect, this had best be ignored altogether.[87] Such directives, however, carried little conviction in the face of a reality that was fairly obvious, and they were generally seen as tactical excuses. From a psychological point of view, too, the joint conduct of the war by the Axis partners got off to a bad start: it lacked the support of a conflict which, when all was said and done, only began after victory in the west. Similarly, it is certain that the Italians for their part felt anything but sympathy for the Germans. Among the people, in the officers' corps, on the part of the king, and indeed even on Mussolini's part there was mistrust of the alliance[88] for factual, emotional, historical, and power-political reasons.

---

[85] *Kriegspropaganda*, 385.
[86] Ibid. 392 (16 June 1940); cf. *Weizsäcker-Papiere*, 212 (10 July 1940).
[87] Steinert, *Hitlers Krieg*, 131.
[88] See De Felice, *Faschismus*, 82–3; Maugeri, *From the Ashes*, 8–9; cf. also Collier, *Duce*, 176–7, whose account, however, is not free from contradictions.

2. Causes and Objectives: 'Imperial Design' or 'Unplanned Opportunism'?

After what has been said about political developments during the first six months of 1940 it may be stated in summary that Mussolini's entry into the war ran counter to the nation's interests. Such a statement, however, does not contribute much to the historical appraisal of a decision whose interpretation is marked by very conflicting criteria. The spectrum ranges from the assumption of an 'imperial design' to the suggestion of 'unplanned opportunism' as the motivation of Fascist policy. It is true, of course, that the historiography of Italy under Fascism generally, and not just that of 10 June 1940, is characterized by divergent and often conflicting approaches. An attempt will therefore be made here to arrive, first of all, at a general typology of Fascist policy by comparing the central theses formulated in a number of important studies on Italy in the era of Fascism. Next, the specific interpretations put forward in connection with the Italian–Ethiopian war will be summed up in order to arrive at some generally valid statements on the fundamental significance which this first major aggression holds in the framework of Mussolini's foreign policy; and finally the decision of 10 June 1940 will be interpreted against the background of these political structures.

The judgement of contemporaries, in particular those who opposed Fascism, will carry a good deal of weight. These circles viewed Mussolini's action as confirmation of the long-held belief that Fascism and war were no more than two sides of the same coin, and were full of contempt for the circumstances under which Italy entered the conflict. Thus the socialist politician Pietro Nenni, a refugee from the Fascists and living in exile in France, recorded in connection with Italy's declaration of war on France that he had always expected it, and that this was a war

without sense, without possible justification, and without honour. Without sense, because no real Italian interests whatever were at stake. Without possible justification, because a German victory would impose on Italy, as on the rest of Europe, the intolerable and brutal hegemony of Hitler. Without honour, finally, because Mussolini is attacking a France already occupied and in deadly agony, thereby assigning to Italy the role of a jackal.[89]

This description was endorsed not only by numerous contemporaries but also by many historians.[90] Yet Nenni's notes on the evening of 10 June accurately reflected only the outward aspect of Italy's entry into the war. They tell us nothing about the objective causes of Mussolini's decision. To investigate its decisive and causative motives means investigating the character of the foreign policy of the Fascist regime. The basic question is whether Italy's entry into the war represented the culmination of a long-term development beginning with the March on Rome; whether it should be seen as a wrong

---

[89] Nenni, *Vent'anni*, 255.   [90] Petersen, 'Gesellschaftssystem', 462 ff.

2. Design or Opportunism?

decision by 'one man and one man alone', an interpretation based directly on the words of Churchill to the Italian people,[91] or whether Italy's participation in the war on the German side was the result of objective constraints.[92]

Discussion of this issue among historians inclined for a long time to the view that Mussolini was an unprincipled opportunist who had nothing in common with a statesman of genius—though he was fond of being portrayed as such—but a lot with a political cheat chasing after propaganda effects. Mussolini's actions, it was argued, were purposeful in outward appearance only. In reality they were merely an attempt to exploit favourable opportunities in a kind of permanent improvisation. Generally speaking, it was argued, Fascist foreign policy had primarily served the stabilization of the regime at home. This thesis proclaimed the primacy of domestic politics.[93]

Numerous important studies of Fascist Italy have been, or still are, indebted to this interpretation. It is pointed out that, despite frequent vacillations, Mussolini's policy, unpredictable and arbitrary as it often seemed, generally followed the principle of seizing booty at any suitable opportunity. To this end the Fascists proved their willingness to employ military means as well. Although Mussolini was not himself fond of taking political or military risks, because his policy lacked a guiding concept he was pushed into the role of a political adventurer[94] moving ever closer to war.

An intriguing question in this context—perhaps the crucial one, and one which continues to be answered in a variety of ways—is whether involvement in a military conflict by a basically unwarlike regime was the result of a public attitude of expectation, heightened continually by Fascist propaganda, which in turn acted as a compulsion upon Mussolini, or whether his readiness for aggression was not actually a reflection of foreign-policy objectives which he hoped to attain by means of a generally consistent and purposeful policy.

Since 1945 the belief that Fascist foreign policy was lacking both in direction and in concept has been criticized with increasing frequency. The results of these studies, though not universally accepted, pointed to a continuity of imperialist and programmatic features in Mussolini's policy after 1922.[95] German and other historians pointed out that Mussolini's foreign policy had

---

[91] Araldi, *Non belligeranza*, 5; cf. Churchill, *Second World War*, ii. 130–1, reproducing a letter from Ciano to Churchill (23 Dec. 1943), in which the former emphasizes that 'the misfortune of Italy was not the fault of the people, but due to the shameful behaviour of one man'. Ciano thus took his argument directly from Churchill's appeal to the Italian people of 23 Dec. 1940: see Araldi, loc. cit.

[92] Very convincing analysis of the character of Fascist foreign policy in Petersen, 'Außenpolitik' and 'Gesellschaftssystem'. The account above is largely based on Petersen's findings, which are of fundamental importance for an understanding of Italy's entry into the war and, beyond that, for Italy's role in the Second World War.

[93] For an interpretation of the findings of Gaetano Salvemini, reported here, see Petersen, 'Außenpolitik', 417–21.

[94] Salvatorelli and Mira, *Storia d'Italia*, 695–6.

[95] Bibliographical references in Petersen, 'Außenpolitik', 426 ff.

developed far more purposefully than had long been assumed.[96] Finally, various historians, all of them proceeding from Marxist methodology, interpreted the foreign policy of Fascist Italy within the framework of an all-embracing theory of imperialism; these scholars formulated their theses—which confirmed their findings—almost exclusively in terms of Rome's relations with Abyssinia and the Balkan countries.[97] One conclusion arrived at by this school was that the whole of Italian foreign policy between 1922 and 1939 had been specifically in line with a 'long-term programme' of Mussolini's. Indicators adduced for this were his idea (consistently in evidence) that the Mediterranean must become a primarily Italian zone of influence, and his intention of establishing a Rome-dominated Arab–African empire. Such objectives, it was argued, were analogous to the National Socialist programme of living-space in the east, which had been a central and steadfastly pursued goal of Hitler's policy, or the concept of 'Asia for the Asians', which the adherents of Japanese imperialism had championed as a new and progressive order but which was in fact a colonial one.[98]

Such an objectivization of aims, however, scarcely covers all the elements which characterize Fascist foreign policy. It has been contended[99] that Italy's foreign policy under Mussolini can only be understood if viewed in continuous confrontation with socio-economic facts, as the objective preconditions of Italian imperialism. This indeed poses the key question with regard to all attempts at interpretation since the beginnings of Fascism: namely, whether foreign or domestic policy enjoyed primacy under Fascism.[100]

In support of the latter view it has been stated:

From the very first day and from the very first words which Mussolini uttered on foreign-policy topics, he never had any intention other than that of giving priority to the domestic arena. Every gesture... was planned with an eye to the repercussions it might have within the country. For a whole period... Mussolini lacked any clear idea, any considered... plan as to what should be the functions and objectives of Italian foreign policy in Europe after 1922. From this angle Mussolini's actions might seem to have been dictated by improvisation. But if, instead, they are viewed from the aspect of domestic policy, it will be seen that Mussolini had a clear concept of his objectives at an early date. The Palazzo Chigi was in his eyes not so much a foreign ministry as an auxiliary of the propaganda ministry, and one which he made use of in a masterly way.[101]

Such an interpretation rejects the thesis of Mussolini's policy having been improvised and inconsistent, but acknowledges the primacy of domestic policy.

[96] Petersen, *Hitler—Mussolini*.
[97] Carocci, *La politica*; id., 'Contributo'; Collotti, 'La politica dell'Italia'; Sechi, 'Imperialismo'; Zamboni, *Mussolinis Expansionspolitik*.
[98] Santarelli, 'Mussolini'.
[99] Salvadori, *Salvemini*, 233–42; De Caro, *Salvemini*, 364 ff.
[100] Cf. Petersen, 'Außenpolitik', 430–3; on Fascism in Italy cf. also De Grand, *Italian Fascism*.
[101] Quoted from the translation in Ennio Nolfo's study from Petersen, 'Außenpolitik', 447.

2. Design or Opportunism?

Other researches on Fascist foreign policy and on relations between the armed forces and the political leadership tended to support this conclusion,[102] whereby Fascist foreign policy was seen primarily as the result of socio-economic conditions at home. Mussolini used 'foreign policy mainly for propaganda purposes, while in his general plans it played only a subordinate role'.[103] Especially in the period following the March on Rome he viewed foreign policy as entirely subordinated to domestic policy. The magnitude of the problems confronting the regime in domestic, economic, and financial policy makes this interpretation seem reasonable. There was even an impression that Mussolini, at least until 1929, was more concerned with the reaction of Italians to the foreign policy offered by him than with the actual effects of that policy.[104] His paramount aim was to secure a consensus at home, to divert attention from pressing problems, and to provide elements of satisfaction that would make up for the inadequacies of life in Fascist Italy. From this point of view Mussolini's rearmament policy could indeed be an indicator that his plans envisaged only limited colonial conflicts and not a major European war.[105]

Developments at the end of the 1920s and the beginning of the 1930s then caused a break in Fascist foreign policy. This raises the question of whether or not there was a real break with the political line pursued until then. We shall come back to this point later. Meanwhile it need only be stated that Mussolini's regime was just concluding the initial phase of its rule, one primarily serving the stabilization of the regime.

It was at that time that the Rome government developed the foreign-policy concept which assigned to Italy the role of a 'decisive weight' (*peso determinante*). This is elucidated by a number of direct statements. Thus Dino Grandi, then foreign minister, wrote to Mussolini on 31 August 1930 that Italy would 'one day be arbiter on the Rhine'. Until that day she should 'increase her own weight in European policy as comprehensively as possible, employing the means of diplomacy and intrigue, as well as Machiavelli's teachings' on a larger scale. For Italy this meant being 'with all and against all'. The country should 'steadily increase its armaments and its isolation', in order to be able, in the 'great crisis, which is bound to come, to sell itself for a high price'.[106] In a speech on foreign policy on 2 October 1930 Grandi declared that, although Italy was not counted among the European great powers from a political, military, or economic point of view, she was nevertheless already strong enough to 'weigh in the balance' in case of a 'European drama'. What was needed in the future was a policy of open choices and of decision at the last

---

[102] De Felice, 'Beobachtungen', 316 ff.; id., *Mussolini il fascista*, ii. 439–40; id., *Mussolini il duce*, i. 323, but also 323–533 on Fascist foreign policy generally; and Rochat and Massobrio, *Storia dell'esercito*, 265–70.
[103] De Felice, 'Beobachtungen', 315.
[104] Ibid. 316–17.
[105] Ibid. 318; see also D'Auria, *L'Italia*, 223–4.
[106] De Felice, *Mussolini il duce*, i. 378–9.

moment.[107] Grandi reaffirmed this idea on 17 May 1931, when he pointed out that Italy was ever more clearly developing into the 'decisive weight' between France and Germany. This meant the chance of exacting a high price, at the right moment, from either Berlin or Paris. The Italo-French antagonism, he argued, did not rule out a common front against Germany. And a conceivable German–Italian antagonism would, similarly, not rule out opposition to France. Rome's foreign policy must not become a 'slave of the rule of three'.[108]

The concept of the 'decisive weight' is of central importance in the development of Fascist policy during the 1930s. This applies in particular to German–Italian relations, as Germany's growing political importance provided the crucial condition for the smooth working of the whole concept.

An examination of the question of continuity or discontinuity, of consistency or change in Italian policy must moreover ask whether the concept of a scale-tipping weight was also valid for the period after 1936. Answers to this question diverge. Generally speaking, however, it will have to be conceded that utilization of the freedom of action provided by the conflict of interests between the great powers, as advocated by Grandi, became difficult from the moment that Rome's political weight in the international interplay of forces was no longer sufficient to tip the scale. This was the case by 1938, if not before, when Germany—one of the elements in the unstable European balance of power—showed herself willing to risk a major war,[109] so that Italy was increasingly compelled to opt for one side or the other.

It is basically irrelevant what made Mussolini take his decision in the end. It should, however, be pointed out that the policy of the *peso determinante* provided a background which makes it seem unlikely that Italy's entry into the war in June 1940 or any other major decision was governed by 'unplanned opportunism'. Instead, one's interpretation in general has to be related to more or less specific political objectives. The realization of these was, until the early 1930s, subordinated to the requirements of domestic policy; yet it was always part of a long-term diplomatic plan.[110]

Although this does not solve the problem of 'continuity or discontinuity' in Italian foreign policy, it highlights that of a programmatic approach. Was Mussolini, we have to ask in this context, ideologically so rigidly fixed, with regard to the formulation and the pursuit of his objectives, that one may look upon him—in the broadest sense—as a programmatic politician?

Neither the question about continuity nor that about a programmatic stance in Mussolini's foreign policy can be answered by an examination narrowed down to the period of Italy's entry into the war in June 1940. Instead, Italian policy towards Albania and Abyssinia should be chosen as our point of departure. Rome's Albanian policy reveals elements of a foreign-policy concept as early as 1926–7, suggesting that the political, economic, and military infiltration

---

[107] Ibid. 377; on 2 Oct. 1940 generally 370–8.   [108] Ibid. 379.
[109] De Felice, 'Beobachtungen', 326–7.   [110] Cf. ibid. 326.

2. Design or Opportunism?

of that country was intended to encircle Yugoslavia and ultimately to turn the whole of south-east Europe into an Italian zone of influence.[111] There also exists, however, an interpretation to the effect that Mussolini pursued a policy involving a general balancing of interests with Tirana and respect for Albanian sovereignty. Adduced in evidence are the Tirana treaties of 1926 and 1927,[112] which, however, can equally be cited to prove the opposite.[113] As for Rome's policy towards Abyssinia in the 1920s, expansionist and aggressive tendencies have also been identified in it. It is argued, however, that Mussolini was not responsible for these, but was interested solely in a stabilization of the status quo and an extension of trade relations between the two countries.[114] That interpretation has not remained unchallenged, and indeed it seems to be tenable only if one omits to take account of the episodic nature of the friendship treaty of 1928 between Rome and Addis Ababa.[115]

Be that as it may, to place 10 June 1940 in its historical context it is sufficient to look at Italian policy towards Abyssinia in the 1930s. Specifically we should ask whether, at the turn of the decade, there was a fundamental change in Mussolini's policy, which until then had supposedly been directed towards the preservation of peace, or whether something he had always intended, but had been obliged by circumstances to postpone, just then seemed to him to have become realizable. In the latter case, a characterization of Fascist foreign policy based solely on actions—i.e. those that proved feasible in practice—must seem highly questionable.

Answers to the questions posed offer a spectrum of very diverse theses. One view is that the war with Abyssinia sprang from a more or less improvised and impulsive decision by Mussolini, who was disturbed by the 'gap between his doctrine of force and the rather inactive and peaceful foreign policy of the years until then'. Additionally there were considerations of prestige, as well as his intention of adding a 'vast, economically exploitable territory' to Italy's colonial possessions in Libya, Eritrea, and Somalia. These are motivations of a traditional imperialist kind.[116] The Italo-Ethiopian conflict, it is argued, was thus not the 'direct outcome of a long period of . . . unbridgeable conflicts, but a colonial enterprise planned and organized on a short-term basis', which Mussolini decided upon in 1935.[117] Admittedly, there were earlier statements which, at least hypothetically, allowed for the possibility of Italy taking over political control of Abyssinia. But, generally speaking, the endeavours pre-

---

[111] Zamboni, *Mussolinis Expansionspolitik*, pp. lxxvii–lxxviii, lxxxv–lxxxviii; a similar interpretation in D'Auria, *L'Italia*, 225, for Mussolini's policies 1925–7; cf. 280–5.
[112] Pastorelli, *Italia e Albania*.
[113] Cf. II.I.1 below.
[114] Vedovato, *Gli accordi*, 32, also generally; a similar position is adopted by Schieder, 'Italien', 481.
[115] See Petersen, 'Außenpolitik', 448.
[116] Kramer, *Geschichte Italiens*, ii. 95–6.
[117] Schieder, 'Italien', 481; Wiskemann, *Axis*, 43–4, 49; also Watt, 'The Secret Laval–Mussolini Agreement', 227.

dominating in the 1920s aimed at no more than a peaceful economic penetration of the country. Only when it became clear that Addis Ababa would not accept economic hegemony by Rome had Mussolini decided upon war. Economic motives indeed played a certain part. More decisive, however, were considerations of prestige. These, in turn, were not an aim in themselves, but military success was to serve the stabilization of the system by underpinning faith in Fascism as a great, important, and successful political concept.[118]

Whether or not any genuine interest by Mussolini in Abyssinia can be proved prior to 1932, there is certainly agreement that a whole range of motivations existed for the attack in 1935: considerations of prestige, assurance of power, economic reasons, and demographic aspects.[119] All this would be in line with traditional imperialism, though as an Italian variant.[120] This, it is argued, was 'not an imperialism on the British or French model', but an 'imperialism, a colonialism, orientated towards emigration'. It rested on the hope that 'Italians might settle in the new territories in large numbers, in order to work there and find a livelihood which their home country' was no longer able to offer them. It was not so much a matter of 'exploiting the colonies' as of 'the hope of finding land and work'.

Some interpretations of the war in Abyssinia also took into account the effects of the world depression. Economic measures designed to mitigate the hardships suffered had, it was suggested, endangered social consensus in Fascist Italy. Major armament programmes seemed apt in the circumstances to stimulate the economy—but they were bound, almost inevitably, to lead to a policy of war.[121] All this suggests an interpretation of the Abyssinian war as resulting from a pattern of domestic and socio-economic conditions and circumstances.[122] The world depression, internal stability, and aggression in Africa are seen, in that interpretation, as interdependent phenomena. War—in its now almost classical function of an alternative to social reform—naturally also served the glorification of Mussolini. In this way the Fascists endeavoured to manipulate the public when its dissatisfaction with day-to-day conditions threatened to endanger the regime. The method was familiar. Faced with the great depression in Italy between 1932 and 1934, the regime staged prestigious actions in order to arouse nationalist emotions among the public. Simultaneously, investment in armaments was reviving the economy.[123] Nevertheless, aggression became possible only when, as originally contemplated in the *peso determinante* context, a substantial change occurred in the European situation: Germany's return to traditional power politics, which upset the European equilibrium. Only then did Italian imperialism, feeble as it was, gain freedom

---

[118] Smith, *Roman Empire*, 59–65.
[119] De Felice, *Mussolini il duce*, i. 602–6.
[120] De Felice, *Faschismus*, 57.
[121] Catalano, *L'economia italiana*, 3–8; id., *Trionfo dei fascismi*, 151 ff.
[122] Baer, *Italian–Ethiopian War*, 31 ff.
[123] Rochat, *Militari*, 105 ff.; Zamagni, *La distribuzione*, 115.

of action. But whether the war in Abyssinia—leaving aside the constraints mentioned earlier—was or was not, after all, a natural consequence of Fascist foreign policy is still an open question. Certainly it was a case of timely exploitation of a unique situation, but that need not be in conflict with long-term intentions.[124] All the arguments which explain Rome's policy towards Addis Ababa by economic and social conditions can probably be reduced to the formula that Mussolini was trying to distract attention from his failed economic policy, his broken promises, unemployment, and industrial stagnation by providing orders for industry, and hence improving the employment situation, through a militarily enforced territorial expansion.[125] This was possible only through the extension of colonial territory.

In spite of general consensus on these lines, there has been some diversity of emphasis. The Fascist regime, it has been suggested, was in fact successful in reducing the domestic consequences of the depression to a minimum. Moreover, there was no uncontrolled social unrest in Italy, even though the Italian economy had not been able to escape the effects of worldwide depression. Internal stability and order were formally guaranteed by an exceptionally large number of men in uniform and armed. Nevertheless, the trigger for aggression in Africa, it is suggested, was inherent in the regime's difficulties due to the overall situation. Added to this were a particularly favourable political constellation in Europe and the fact that territorial expansion was as much part of the autarky programme of Fascism as it was of the long-standing desire for equality with the traditional colonial powers.[126]

As to the timing of the Italo-Ethiopian war, an aspect somewhat neglected in the past, the view has been, and still is, held by some that without any doubt it had its origins in Mussolini's long-term political objectives, which were simply realized in 1932. If one asks why at that particular point in time, one encounters a whole string of explanations or justifications, such as the above-mentioned economic difficulties, but also certain psychological elements, and of course the foreign-political constellation brought about, among other causes, by the normalization of relations between the Vatican and the Fascist regime.[127] Yet another cause for the *politica periferica*, i.e. the policy of Mediterranean–African expansion and the extension of Italy's zone of influence, was the failure of Mussolini's continental political concept, especially the collapse of the plan for a four-power pact.[128] Mussolini, it is suggested, in order to distract the population from unemployment and to lift it out of its lethargy *vis-à-vis* the regime, needed an overwhelming success in Africa. Finally, the

---

[124] Rochat and Massobrio, *Storia dell'esercito*, 249; for the excessive demands made on Italy's political, economic, and military potential by concentration on two areas of operation see Borejsza, *Il fascismo*, 209–10; ibid. 189–238 extensively on the issue of German–Italian rivalry.

[125] Canzio, *La dittatura*, 328; see also 329–48, especially on the diplomatic background to the conflict.

[126] Nolte, 'Italien', 637.

[127] Robertson, *Mussolini*, 4 ff.; see also Lill, 'Italiens Außenpolitik', 80.

[128] On the pact see vol. i of the present work, IV.II.3 (Messerschmidt).

course of the disarmament conference at Geneva gave rise to the impression in Italy that there would soon be a rearmament race. Swift action in Africa therefore appeared even more urgent, since Rome hoped to pocket its expected gains before the other powers with interests in Africa had rearmed.[129] In this respect, more than in any other, Mussolini's calculations went wrong in the long run. The fact was that he spoilt his political chances in the second half of the 1930s because the Italian forces, contrary to expectation, suffered losses, both through wear and tear and from enemy action, which could not be made good in a hurry.[130]

Other objections to the explanation of Mussolini's step as an inescapable reaction to socio-economic conditions are based on the view that the interdependence of economic crisis, the war in Africa, and the stimulation of industrial production cannot be convincingly demonstrated. The thesis that the conflict with Ethiopia had become necessary in order to distract the Italian public from the country's precarious economic situation has similarly been contested.[131] It appeared rather arbitrary, considering that the depression as such had largely been overcome by 1935, and there was no internal movement of dissent.[132] The Italo-Ethiopian war, therefore—it was maintained—could not be explained by domestic factors. Initially it had even given rise to anxiety among Italians, who expected international complications with Britain and France. Only when it became clear that London and Paris would not make any move while Rome was about to conquer its *impero*, did the conflict give rise to 'noisy consent, culminating in moments of national euphoria'.[133] Thus the decision to go to war at first meant an enormous risk for Mussolini. Therefore, it is argued, the decision in favour of aggression must be understood in terms of a foreign-policy plan.[134]

These diverse interpretations cannot of course be reduced to a common denominator. Nor can this be achieved by an interpretation from the angle of the regime's financial policy. This, indeed, is largely a variant of the socio-economic thesis. Even though it is impossible to establish a convincing causal connection between the world depression and the road to war—it is argued—it would nevertheless be a mistake to present the war as the result of purely political and diplomatic decisions. Regardless of the fact that production figures, especially in armament-related industries, had recovered since 1934, the regime's financial policy, which was relevant to the internal consensus, had, owing to international developments, found itself under such pressure that Mussolini chose a forcible solution of the already evident difficulties.[135]

---

[129] Robertson, *Mussolini*, 93 ff.
[130] Ibid. 112–13.
[131] Chabod, *L'Italia*, 91–2; De Felice, *Mussolini il duce*, i. 613; Hardie, *Abyssinian Crisis*, 31 ff.; Preti, *Impero*, 56.
[132] Further bibliography in Petersen, 'Außenpolitik', 451–2.
[133] De Felice, *Faschismus*, 56–7.
[134] Id., *Mussolini il duce*, i. 614–15.
[135] Maione, *L'imperialismo straccione*, 105–10.

2. Design or Opportunism?

Attempts to find some reconciliation between the conflicting arguments[136] proceeded from the view that, on the one hand, during the second half of the 1920s there was a consensus, based on compromise, between Fascism and the traditional leadership élites in the army, the administration, the economy, and the Church. It had, more particularly, been the arrangement with the Vatican, reached in the Lateran treaties of 1929, that the regime had exploited for its policy of colonial aggression.[137] It was also suggested, on the other hand, that there was a large group of party followers who were disappointed because the expectations aroused by Fascism during its years of struggle had not been satisfied. The regime's unfulfilled promises—there had been no redistribution of power, no substantial changes in conditions of ownership, and the problems of over-population remained unresolved—had created the constraints which, around 1930, induced Mussolini to switch to a policy of expansion. Thereby he hoped to give 'the nation new, integrating objectives'.[138] However, Mussolini, unlike Hitler, had always avoided tying himself down to a programme. His foreign-policy speeches, in terms of content, had not exceeded those aims which Italian nationalists had proclaimed even before 1914. These included the 'restoration of a Roman Mediterranean empire', colonial expansion in Africa, readiness for war, and the slogan of the struggle against the established wealthy powers. Moreover, a central cause of Fascist expansionist policy was to be seen in that 'irrational nationalism' which had developed from Italian history since the last third of the nineteenth century. This, it was argued, was of greater significance than socio-economic factors.

An attempt to sum up at this point would have to proceed from the view that Fascist policy was directed towards war from the outset. Colonial expansion had been Mussolini's dream since the early 1920s, which he merely put aside during the initial and stabilization phases of the system.[139] Mussolini had been considering aggression since 1928; but only after the conclusion of the war in Libya had an escalation of pinpricks against Addis Abeba begun in 1932. Plans for aggression took on clear outlines in 1934. Italy's economy orientated itself towards the prospect of war. By December the conquest of Abyssinia had been decided upon. Mussolini wanted the conflict, he wanted land to cope with Italy's over-population, he wanted the personal prestige he would gain from becoming the avenger of Adowa, he wanted his Fascist empire and Italy's acceptance as a fully fledged great power.[140] The evidence justifies us in regarding Mussolini's war against Abyssinia as part of a long-term plan, in preparation since the mid-1920s, for the creation of a 'north-east African

---

[136] Lill, 'Italiens Außenpolitik', 80–6.
[137] Cf. also Rhodes, *Vatican*, 53–67.
[138] Lill, 'Italiens Außenpolitik', 80.
[139] Grimaldi and Bozzetti, *Dieci giugno*, 129.
[140] Funke, *Sanktionen*, 9 ff.; see also Coffey, *Lion*, 21–4. Adowa: Italian military defeat in the Abyssinian War (1896), renunciation of the plan for an Abyssinian colonial empire.

colonial empire'. Its realization, of course, depended crucially on the 'development of the European power-ratio'.[141]

As to the interpretation of 10 June 1940, many an argument used for an explanation of the war against Abyssinia is encountered again. This applies in particular to the view that Mussolini had become the victim of his own propaganda and was basically out for booty at every suitable opportunity.[142] This interpretation of Italy's entry into the war found support both among contemporaries and among post-war historians.[143]

This approach, which dispenses with more general questions—such as continuity, socio-economic implications, or the ideology in Mussolini's policies—is clearly marked by its ascription of sole responsibility to Mussolini. Although this thesis is convenient in every respect, it is easily refuted against the background of the regime's power-structures.[144] In the debate on the significance of 10 July 1940, the key question of which is the character of Fascist foreign policy, it has been rightly observed that interpretations which blame the 'failure of a system on one single person and on one wrong decision' are based on a total misjudgement of the complex unrolling of historical processes.[145] Any such personalized and voluntaristic interpretation disregards the fact that Mussolini's scope of action in 1939 and—more obviously still—in 1940 was increasingly narrowed down by a number of circumstances, primarily as a result of the development of the war in Europe, and that the Duce in making his decisions, within the constraints of ideology and the interests of Fascist policy, was by then a virtual prisoner of his 'programmatic' promises. As we have repeatedly noted, there was the pressure of expectations which a nationalistically and imperialistically orientated propaganda had aroused among the Fascists and which was now seeking a safety-valve.

Italy's social system, Fascist ideology, and Mussolini's foreign-policy concept formed a tissue of relationships, the components of which interacted with one another. A historical examination of Italy's entry into the war, which sees that step as the result of such interdependences, is bound to do more justice to the objective conditions than either Churchill's 'one man alone' thesis, the theory of opportunism, or the Marxist historians' view that 10 June was the

---

[141] Petersen, 'Außenpolitik', 455; id., *Hitler—Mussolini*, 381–6.

[142] Taylor, *Origins*, 119; in his book *The War Lords* Taylor, in analysing Italy's entry into the war, confines himself to the 'opportunism and booty' thesis and to Churchill's 'one man alone' interpretation. A chronological survey with source-orientated comment on Italy's road to war in Anchieri, 'Die deutsch-italienischen Beziehungen', 77 ff.

[143] Araldi, *Non belligeranza*, 7–8; *Deutschland im Zweiten Weltkrieg*, i. 330; *Geschichte des zweiten Weltkrieges*, iii. 135; Hughes, *Fall and Rise*, 197; H. Michaelis, *Der Zweite Weltkrieg*, 124–8; Schütt, 'Stahlpakt', 520–1; Alfieri, *Dictators Face to Face*, 36–9; Bottai, *Vent'anni*, 85–91; Domarus, *Mussolini*, 313; Smith, *Roman Empire*, 202; the source for this is Ciano, *Diary 1939–1943*, 266–8 (18–19 June 1940).

[144] Perticone, *La politica*, 387–8; in detail also Wiskemann, *Axis*, 208–9. The opposing view is held by Cliadakis, 'Neutrality and War', 181; Petersen, 'Gesellschaftssystem', 463–4; Mieli, 'Voleva la pace', 172.

[145] Petersen, 'Gesellschaftssystem', 464–5; also on what follows.

2. Design or Opportunism? 121

result of a carefully planned German–Italian stratagem.[146] Fascist foreign policy was shaped primarily by the power ideology of the regime and the objective constraints of the system. This is fully confirmed by Mussolini's action in the summer of 1940, which was 'against Italy's interests' but in line with those of the regime.[147]

It is in fact inconceivable that Mussolini could have kept out of the conflict in the long run.[148] It should, moreover, be borne in mind that the government's original intention—due largely to political developments in Europe after the National Socialist seizure of power—of finding new impulses for the Fascist movement and broadening its basis could not be implemented with the tools of domestic policy. Ever since the Italo-Abyssinian war this realization gave foreign policy a central position in political planning and deliberations.[149]

The interaction between Italy's internal and external situation has to be taken into account in any assessment of 10 June 1940—beyond the above-mentioned fact that Fascist foreign policy, as a consequence of the African conflict, enjoyed ever less freedom of movement during the second half of the 1930s. Objective constraints were increasingly impairing Italy's calculated oscillation between the powers. This development provided the background for a situation in which Mussolini at last had to choose. When he made his decision, the character of the regime, as a situation-governed motive, tipped the scale. In spite of mistrust and persisting issues of conflict between Rome and Berlin, Fascist Italy had no other choice but to throw in her lot with Hitler.[150]

In the specific situation of the summer of 1940 Mussolini's long-cherished hope of pulling off a second Munich, albeit in modified form, was definitively dashed. The mood in the inner circle of the Fascist leadership, fired by Germany's military successes, prevented any consideration of the offers made by Britain, France, or America, just as it ruled out any prolonged neutrality.[151] Developments prior to 10 June in fact revealed the objective character of the regime, its ideology and interests. The latter, admittedly, did not conform with those of the Italian nation, but this did not worry Mussolini any longer.[152] It should nevertheless be pointed out that, in spite of an obvious predisposition to a certain course of events, this had nothing in common with strict determinism. On the other hand, there was no unlimited freedom of action either. Mussolini's decision was a mixture of objective and subjective elements.[153] As

---

[146] In the stimulating study by Borejsza, *Il fascismo*, 210, this suggestion is also put forward, albeit less clearly.
[147] Petersen, 'Gesellschaftssystem', 469–70.
[148] De Felice, *Faschismus*, 58.
[149] Ibid. 72–3.
[150] De Felice, 'Beobachtungen', 327.
[151] Mieli, 'Voleva la pace', 171–2.
[152] Petersen, 'Gesellschaftssystem', 467–70.
[153] De Felice, *Faschismus*, 75; the subjective aspects are strongly emphasized in Kramer, *Geschichte Italiens*, ii. 99–100, and Schieder, 'Italien', 488–9.

repeatedly attested by Ciano's diary, he suffered traumatically from Italy's non-participation in the war. No doubt his psychological make-up has to be taken into account; but at the same time he was concerned with preserving Italy's position as a great power. In this connection there was even some fear lest Hitler, after the victory over France and Britain, which seemed to be only a matter of time, might turn against Italy out of irritation and anger over his partner's holding back. This did not necessarily mean military action, but neither could it be ruled out. The more probable result would be a reduction of Italy's standing as a political power. That would probably have been sufficient to entail incalculable consequences for the Fascist regime.

The thesis that Mussolini was ridden with fear of a German hegemony and the resultant revolution in European power-relations is encountered in numerous studies, which represent his fears as a constituent factor of Italy's road to a decision in the first half of 1940.[154] Significantly—so this argument goes—as late as 8–9 June Mussolini followed France's resistance with great satisfaction, expecting it to weaken Germany. For his own objectives the ideal situation would have been a victorious but considerably mauled Germany. Hitler would then have been compelled to treat his Axis partner with restraint. Mussolini was interested primarily in the maintenance of a European balance of power, albeit a newly constituted one. The focus of his decision of 10 June was not therefore the issue of victory or defeat, which had in any case long been decided when Italy entered the war; the Duce simply wished to ensure for himself the right to participate in the peace negotiations, in order thereby to realize his own political objectives.[155]

These factors were pointed out at an early stage in connection with the opportunism thesis. But there was more behind such intentions than an instinct for short-term booty. This is revealed as soon as Mussolini's entry into the war is interpreted within the framework of his concept of foreign policy dating from the early 1930s (outlined above).[156] From that angle Mussolini's calculations in the summer of 1940, which could be and have been mistaken under cursory examination for sheer opportunism, are seen in a new light.[157] Mussolini, who argued entirely imperialistically and who sought to establish a mighty empire on the coasts of the Mediterranean and the Red Sea, basically wanted peace through negotiation and not peace through victory. Only thus could Italy attain her long-term objectives, such as access to the high seas, and escape being degraded into a German province. Mussolini's decision of

---

[154] Cf. Anfuso, *Roma, Berlino*, 152, also 147–56; on these lines also Villari, *Italian Foreign Policy*, 254 ff. Villari's (untenable) thesis that the Western powers, by their intransigence over a revision of the treaty of Versailles, had virtually forced Italy into the war is also found, almost unmodified, in Quartararo, *Roma*. Also Faldella, *L'Italia*, 165; Canzio, *La dittatura*, 590.

[155] Barclay, *Rise and Fall*, 165–6; cf. in this context Knox, 'Fascist Italy', 363 ff., who interprets Mussolini's policy within the framework of a power-political programme pursued since the 1920s.

[156] D'Auria, *L'Italia*, 275.

[157] Quartararo, *Roma*, 624–5.

2. Design or Opportunism?

September 1939 in fact implied such an intention. However, non-belligerence —at least in retrospect—seems to have exposed Italy's political insignificance and initiated her degeneration into a German satellite. Such an interpretation[158] is only seemingly contradicted by the democracies' wooing of Italy in 1939-40. By then—and this applies also to Berlin's attitude to its Axis partner—it was merely a matter of using Italy. From Mussolini's point of view, however, things looked different. He tried to keep his traditional foreign policy alive. This meant that Germany's political preponderance must not be allowed to grow unchecked, that Italian claims in the Mediterranean and in the Balkans had to be safeguarded and the political constellation in Europe reshaped. In this concept, which in many respects was in line with the four-power pact,[159] the balance of power was preferred to the destruction of the democracies. In this context it is irrelevant that Mussolini's decision to enter the war on the side of Germany was always certain to redound to Italy's disadvantage, no matter whether in victory or in defeat,[160] because it simply meant that the regime was, in any case, taking the wrong road. This was so because the point of departure (as outlined above) had been a subjective calculation. Mussolini's imperial objectives, the war as the coping-stone of Fascist self-realization, and German-Italian rivalry—these were the decision-shaping elements.[161] Simplifying a good deal, there was a mixture of imperialism, predatory motives, and rivalry at work.[162] Official Fascist propaganda distorted all this into an anti-imperialist struggle for Italy's natural living-space against the Anglo-French 'intruders'.[163] Perhaps there was a grain of sincerity even in these slogans, because at least since the conclusion of the Pact of Steel Mussolini, as he observed to his intimates, had regarded war with the democracies as unavoidable.[164]

There is certainly no doubt that by June 1940 Mussolini was determined to enter the war. The question whether the fighting forces were ready is, in this context, more or less irrelevant. What mattered, as we have shown, was a political entry into the war.[165] And Mussolini's calculations, it is supposed, certainly included the possibility of avoiding unlimited collaboration with

---

[158] Cf. Nolte, 'Italien', 639; with a different emphasis Cliadakis, 'Neutrality and War', 180 ff.
[159] Schreiber, *Revisionismus*, 69-70.
[160] Salvatorelli and Mira, *Storia d'Italia*, 1039-40.
[161] See Catalano, *Trionfo dei fascismi*, 286-7; an interesting thesis on German-Italian rivalry is put forward by André, 'La politica estera', 121-2, who explains Italy's surprising moderation with regard to the armistice with France not by German pressure—as is generally supposed—but by Mussolini's desire to prepare for Italo-French co-operation in a German-dominated postwar Europe. Cf. also Kirkpatrick, *Mussolini*, 413-14; Smith, *Roman Empire*, 204 ff.; Rintelen, *Mussolini*, 85-6.
[162] Directly on this: Gruchmann, *Der Zweite Weltkrieg*, 69-70; id., 'Die verpaβten strategischen Chancen', 460, with greater emphasis on the opportunism thesis.
[163] Gayda, *Was will Italien?*, 293-4.
[164] Deakin, *Brutal Friendship*, 23 ff.; exhaustively Toscano, *Origins*.
[165] Rochat and Massobrio, *Storia dell'esercito*, 272 ff., who, however, cannot be unreservedly agreed with.

Hitler, which would in all probability result in Italy's subordination to German hegemony. This is borne out also by the general directive issued on 4 April 1940 to the effect that Italy, if she entered the war, should not tie herself too closely to Germany either materially or ideologically.[166] Hence Mussolini's insistence on a 'parallel war', which can be correctly interpreted only from a political point of view. With only slight exaggeration it can be stated that Italy's entry into the war was due not least to anti-German considerations stemming from the interests of the Fascist regime. This appears paradoxical in view of the Axis alliance, but is not really so. In order to curtail the preponderance of the Greater German Reich, Mussolini, according to Badoglio's account, from the outset contemplated an eventual *rapprochement* with France. This interpretation, however, has been vigorously opposed.[167]

At any rate, an examination of Mussolini's decision of 10 June 1940 has to proceed from the view that, for a multiplicity of reasons, the Duce believed that he could not remain aloof from the conflict. This emerges also from his memorandum of 31 March 1940, which listed the pros and cons of entering the war.[168] In that document he expounded the consequences of continuing neutrality and concluded in favour of Italy's entry into the war.[169] In the light of developments in the summer of 1940 alignment with Hitler, seen in the medium term, appeared to provide a guarantee that Italy could achieve her national aims and at the same time preserve her independence.[170] Integrating all the elements which determined Mussolini's concept, and arguing from a 'normative primacy of foreign policy and foreign-trade policy', the following summary has been formulated: 'This normative primacy was transformed, by the challenge of National Socialist foreign policy, into a causative one, which was designed to save the existence of the Italian regime and which thereby once more placed foreign policy under the primacy of domestic policy.'[171] Such an interpretation reduces Mussolini's decision—which has been defined as the result of tensions, of a dynamic interlinking of hypotheses, judgements, emotions, and factual constraints[172]—to a common denominator borrowed from political categories. This describes the character of Fascist policy just as precisely as it does the interpretational framework of Italy's entry into the war.

To come back to what was said at the beginning of these reflections on the nature of Fascist foreign policy and the place held in history by Italy's entry

---

[166] *Africa settentrionale, La preparazione*, 162.
[167] Knox, *Mussolini*, 121 ff.
[168] *DDI*, 9th ser., iii, No. 669, pp. 576–9 (31 Mar. 1940), quotation on p. 578: 'Italy cannot remain neutral for the entire duration of the war without renouncing her mission, without disqualifying herself, without declining to the level of a Switzerland. Ten times the size.'
[169] Pieri and Rochat, *Badoglio*, 738–9.
[170] Funke, 'Deutsch-italienische Beziehungen', 845–6; similarly Siebert, *Italiens Weg*, 444 ff., who is one of the first to discuss the complex structure of the decision of 10 June 1940.
[171] Funke, 'Italien', 84–5.
[172] Bocca, *Storia*, 150.

2. Design or Opportunism?

into the war, some kind of conclusion should be drawn from the various interpretations put forward. It should, however, be premised that there is no such thing as a universally accepted interpretation of the motives behind Mussolini's political actions.

Nevertheless, at the risk of an arbitrary summarization, our decision in favour of the continuity thesis calls for a brief justification. Firstly: a comparison of the different research findings seems to suggest that only by lifting individual phenomena out of the overall context of foreign policy under Mussolini is it possible to deny the existence of an imperial impetus during the 1920s. Secondly: the war against Abyssinia—neither the bulk of the sources documenting it nor the course of its planning leave any doubt on this score—is an illustration of a policy of continuity. Thirdly: Mussolini's tactical manœuvring within the Berlin–London–Paris power-triangle suggests a calculated action which has nothing in common with unplanned opportunism, and even less with the exploitation of a favourable opportunity. Fourthly: the fact that Italian foreign policy in connection with the Abyssinian conflict was in line with the realization of a programmatic imperial intention—although terminological similarities must not be allowed to suggest that this was a concept comparable to Hitler's 'programme'—implies very specific conclusions about the interpretation of Italy's entry into the war in the summer of 1940. And fifthly: there is nothing to suggest that the long-term demands and ambitions of Italian policy with regard to the Balkans and North Africa, or free access to the high seas—aims which could be attained only in opposition to London and Paris—were mere propaganda.

The thesis of a change in Fascist policy in 1929–30 is unconvincing because its supporters cannot point to any new political quality but only to a difference of method. Added to this is the fact that contemporaries—and among them not only the propagandists of the Fascist regime—recognized a deliberate trend in Mussolini's foreign policy, linked to specific objectives. Besides, Mussolini's calculations in connection with the Abyssinian conflict and with his entry into the Second World War prove that his political considerations, which took account of the power-constellation between Germany, Britain, and France, as well as his own position and the time factor, were anything but short-term. There is nothing surprising about the fact that domestic and economic aspects should have played a part within the framework of his concept of a Fascist *impero*, as well as considerations of personal prestige. That said, it is possible to state in summary that Mussolini's important decisions were taken within a foreign policy that was planned in the long term, based on multiple layers of reasoning, and constituted in a complex fashion. The dominant factors in his decision stemmed from the imperial goals of Fascism, from German–Italian rivalry, and from the idea of reshaping the European balance of power.

Only from the point of view of German–Italian relations and with regard to the immediate actual situation in the summer of 1940 does Mussolini's entry into the war appear as a pro-German step or as an act of Axis solidarity. Seen against the background of the long-term objectives of the Fascist regime it emerges as a political decision which may certainly also be interpreted as a preventive step against the Third Reich's claim to European hegemony. At the least it contained elements suggesting that such considerations played their part.

3. CONSEQUENCES: THE REORIENTATION OF BRITISH STRATEGY IN THE SUMMER OF 1940

After the French defeat the question may well have been asked in Britain whether it might not have been better after all to declare war on Italy in 1939 and thereby to bring about the situation on which a number of military planning studies were based in the spring of that year. The officers concerned had proposed a three-phase programme for Anglo-French operations against the Axis powers: first to keep on the defensive, in order to survive the initial German–Italian attacks; next to bring Italy to her knees in North Africa in order to force her to abandon the war—during that phase operations against Germany were to be confined to bombing raids; and finally a direct offensive against the Reich. All this assumed extensive support for Britain and France from the United States.

The chiefs of staff, however, like the war cabinet, backed a policy of endeavouring to keep Italy neutral at any price.[173] This concept, which was essentially designed to prise Mussolini away from Hitler by means of appeasement—which, however, as our examination of Italian non-belligerence has shown, did not rule out certain pressures—had originated with Sir Robert Vansittart, permanent under-secretary in the Foreign Office. As early as April 1933 Vansittart, believing that the Germans would sooner or later unleash a European war, had advised that, within the framework of close co-operation with France and the United States, Italy should, if possible, also be tied to Britain.[174] Among the most outspoken supporters of such a policy were members of the high Tory persuasion. But whereas Italy's declaration of non-belligerence in 1939 initially seemed to confirm Vansittart's view, 10 June 1940 meant the shipwreck of a political concept which Anthony Eden, among others, had long called into question,[175] believing as he did that Italian Fascism and German National Socialism were, by their nature, bound to converge politically. And on 22 June, when General Huntzinger on behalf of France signed the armistice at Compiègne, if indeed not before, British strategy lost

---

[173] Dilks, 'Unnecessary War', 129; Murray, 'Role of Italy', 46 ff.; On the commands cf. I.1.4(b) above.
[174] Colvin, *Vansittart*, 23.
[175] Petersen, *Hitler—Mussolini*, 143–4, 458–9, also 107, 200, 218, 498, 501 in detail on Italy in British political plans during the 1930s.

one of its essential prerequisites, as all plans for the Anglo-French conduct of the war had been based on a global 'division of labour' between London and Paris.[176]

The immediate consequences of these events were the capture by Germany of the coast facing Britain, the interruption of the sea route from Gibraltar to Alexandria, the tying down of strong forces in the Mediterranean area, an inevitable long-term extension of front lines at a time when British troop strength had diminished relative to that of the opponent, and increased difficulties with supplies to the mother country. Britain undoubtedly had her back to the wall, but her situation was by no means as hopeless as German propaganda portrayed it. This was shown, not least, by the fact that the British did not redeploy their forces as at first envisaged, nor evacuate the Mediterranean; on the contrary, they transferred part of the Home Fleet to Gibraltar.[177]

Britain's determination to see the war against Hitler through on her own was also reflected in public opinion, with pacifist tendencies clearly losing support after May 1940.[178] The choice of Churchill as prime minister in Chamberlain's place after the débâcle in Norway[179] no doubt lent further momentum to that trend, even though it was achieved only after difficult behind-the-scenes negotiations, with Lord Halifax as an alternative candidate.[180] In his famous speech of 13 May 1940 Churchill dared not promise the British more than 'blood, toil, tears and sweat', but at the same time he unambiguously proclaimed his own war aim: 'victory, victory at all costs... for without victory there is no survival.'[181] Unlike Chamberlain he drew a rigorous but necessary conclusion from the apocalyptic threat which Hitler's National Socialism represented to life and its moral norms generally: war must be waged until the surrender of the Third Reich.[182] This was not an anticipation of the Casablanca decision of 1943, yet the determination to answer the dictator's aggression with a demand for 'unconditional surrender' seems, in retrospect, to shine through already at that point in the war.

Although the German–French armistice came with remarkable speed, by June 1940 it did not come as a surprise. On 19 May, for instance, the chiefs of staff had already examined the consequences which such a change in the situation might have for London. Naturally, their first conclusions cannot be described as *the* alternative concept to the existing strategy, for what was

---

[176] See Schreiber, 'Die Rolle Frankreichs'; on the immediate military consequences Playfair, *Mediterranean*, i. 125–30; on the political situation R. T. Thomas, *Britain*, 28–37; Woodward, *British Foreign Policy*, i. 289–330.
[177] Hillgruber, *Strategie*, 79–80; Roskill, *Churchill*, 150–1; Pack, *Sea Power*, 179.
[178] Ceadel, *Pacifism*, 296–7.
[179] See vol. ii of the present work, V.IV (Stegemann). On political and military developments extensively Woodward, *British Foreign Policy*, i. 118–31.
[180] Lee, *Churchill*, 31–2.
[181] Quoted from Butler, *Strategy*, ii. 181.
[182] Cf. Churchill's speech in the Commons on 18 June 1940, in Butler, *Strategy*, ii. 206–7.

submitted to the cabinet amounted essentially to points of orientation for a possible contingency—material, in a sense, for war-games. On the other hand, this does not mean that these were purely academic studies. In point of fact they outlined the first preliminary thoughts upon which British strategy was subsequently based. What was impressive, in any case, was the intellectual and psychological homogeneity of the political and military leadership under the new prime minister, which—regardless of differing opinions on specific points—was reflected in the conviction that Britain would come out victorious.[183] This was by no means a self-evident proposition at that time.

In their evaluation the service chiefs assumed that Italy would shortly enter the war, that the whole of French North Africa might become accessible to the Axis, and that Spain, Portugal, and the Balkan countries, apart from Turkey, would come under enemy domination. Britain would thus be isolated in Europe. The military were, of course, aware that even this would not free Germany from the pressure of the blockade, so that Hitler would have to continue his efforts to break British opposition. The assessment of possible German actions concluded that, by unrestricted air attacks designed to break the morale of the population, by starving the country out, and by an invasion of the British Isles, the Wehrmacht could bring about the collapse of the United Kingdom, though not of the empire. In the long term Germany and Italy would also try to destroy the British position in the Middle East and in Egypt, in order to gain access to the Indian Ocean. The enemy undeniably held the initiative for the moment, but the Allies' position would progressively improve so long as they succeeded in preventing a rapid German success. In this context the chiefs of staff, like Churchill, counted on generous support from the United States, whose entry into the war was confidently expected in Britain. And along with the prime minister, who during those weeks was aiming at a grand coalition between London, Moscow, and Washington, the generals likewise speculated that Stalin would distance himself from Hitler, whose enormous increase of power entailed incalculable risks for the Soviet Union.[184]

As for short-term operational developments, the British generals and admirals, while not underestimating the importance of the navy or the army, believed that the principal role in the immediate future would be played by the air force. Indispensable as the navy would be in ensuring supplies and defending the mother country against a possible invasion—especially as the troops available in the British Isles could scarcely hope to throw a German army back into the sea once it had landed—the decision in the 'battle of Britain', it was expected, would come in the air.[185] The British military could assume that the elimination of the Royal Air Force was a *sine qua non* of a German landing, as a

---

[183] Ibid. 209–17 on the account above; more especially Gilbert, *Finest Hour*, 300–18.
[184] In detail Hillgruber, *Strategie*, 82–90.
[185] Butler, *Strategy*, ii. 210–11.

3. British Strategy Change, Summer 1940

seaborne invasion without complete control of the air-space over the area of operations would have been far too risky. The British possibly derived some reassurance from information that the Luftwaffe was not in a position to make its aircraft operational so soon after the campaign in the west. Owing to inadequate supplies of spare parts repairs were progressing slowly,[186] whereas Britain, by the time the battle of Britain began, had made good the losses suffered in France. As aircraft production was stepped up by 43 per cent between July and September, and as crew-training programmes became more efficient, Britain's position at that point was in fact more favourable than before the 'battle for France'.[187]

This relative improvement did not, however, mean that the situation in August 1940 was favourable in every respect. Fighter Command had a total of 700 aircraft available for intercepting the bombers of the German Air Fleets 2, 3, and 5.[188] On the other hand, an advantage the British fighters enjoyed was that the German fighters, because of having to protect the bombers and also because of their long approach-routes, were impaired in their freedom of action.[189] Without going into the details of the battle of Britain, which has already been fully described[190]—British plans and measures come under this heading as well[191]—it is to be noted that British strategy, for the time being, remained defensive. In order to survive—and that was what mattered in the summer of 1940—it was necessary to keep the armament industry intact and to ensure supplies. In this scenario the RAF played the main part. Its vital nerve—this was as well known in Germany as it was in Britain—ran through the workshops of the aviation industry concentrated in the area of Coventry and Birmingham. From that point of view major importance attached to the morale of the workers in the face of German air raids. That was why the chiefs of staff, as early as May 1940, feared that British air defences would be sufficient only against daytime raids but not at night. If the Germans succeeded in utilizing this opportunity, it could not be ruled out that persistent terror raids might bring aircraft production to a halt.[192] The effectiveness of British air defences during the day did in fact compel the Germans to mount night attacks, directed initially against armament factories, i.e. military targets, but developing increasingly—after the abandonment of Operation 'Sea Lion', if not before—into a war of attrition and terrorization.[193]

---

[186] Winterbotham, *The Ultra*, 40–3.
[187] In detail Overy, *Air War*, 32 ff.; vol. ii of the present work, IX.III.1, 2 (Maier); and tables ibid. IX.III.4; also Liddell Hart, *History of the Second World War*, 73–4.
[188] Winterbotham, *The Ultra*, 46; vol. ii of the present work, IX.III.2 (Maier).
[189] Overy, *Air War*, 34.
[190] Vol. ii of the present work, IX.III.3, 4 (Maier); Murray, *Strategy*, 39–55.
[191] The British were trying, by employing their own bombers, to disrupt or prevent German invasion preparations, with a view, eventually, to reversing the entire offensive–defensive pattern, i.e. going over to large-scale strategic air warfare: Overy, *Air War*, 37 ff.
[192] Butler, *Strategy*, ii. 211–12.
[193] On this problem in detail: vol. ii of the present work, IX.III (Maier).

As to developments in the Mediterranean area, the British generals, apart from an Italian offensive in North Africa, expected attacks on Malta and Gibraltar. The latter's fate would largely depend on the attitude of the Spanish head of state. If Franco were to enter the war, the chances of holding Gibraltar were assessed as rather slight. Malta's capacity for defence was thought to be probably sufficient to ward off a resolute attempt at a landing, but after that its strength would be exhausted.[194] In any event, a start was made in May on evacuating women and children.[195] The Admiralty assessed the naval situation in the Mediterranean extremely pessimistically. Although it intended to station an effective force in Alexandria, both to protect Egypt and to hold Italian naval forces in check, it did not rule out the possibility, in the event of a successful Axis offensive in North Africa, of having to transfer its units to Aden and blocking the Suez Canal.[196] By the beginning of July, however, there was no longer any question of that: the Royal Navy would remain in the eastern Mediterranean.[197]

As for their own offensive measures, the chiefs of staff mapped out a kind of concerted action of economic pressure, terror bombing, and resistance activity in German-occupied territories. An unknown quantity in these calculations was the output of the German armament industry. On the one hand, the British proceeded from over-optimistic assumptions by overestimating the actual rate of production reached by Germany at the time and by assuming, in consequence, that there was only slight scope for increasing output further. In actual fact, the volume of aerial armament was still capable of considerable growth. On the other hand, the officers concerned with these estimates underrated the degree of adaptability of which even modern technologies were capable. This mistaken assessment was nothing unusual: even on the German side it was a long time after the outbreak of the war before it was realized what production figures could in fact be achieved, given optimal organization and all-out exploitation of available manpower.[198]

As the feared collapse of France was becoming increasingly probable, Britain tried to persuade her ally to continue the struggle from the French colonies.[199] The British were particularly anxious to gain the French air force and navy for their own operations. It would have been ideal, therefore, if the French had transferred their ships to British ports—a move considered possible in London, though far from likely, as Germany in that case would no doubt dictate especially tough armistice conditions to the French government. On the other hand, it could not be ruled out that the French warships would fall into

---

[194] Butler, *Strategy*, ii. 212.
[195] Cunningham, *Odyssey*, 226.
[196] Playfair, *Mediterranean*, ii. 97–100; Butler, *Strategy*, ii. 212; Roskill, *Churchill*, 150–1; Churchill, *Second World War*, iv. 108.
[197] Roskill, *War at Sea*, i. 297.
[198] Butler, *Strategy*, ii. 213–16; *Deutschlands Rüstung*, 5–25; Speer, *Inside the Third Reich*, 300–20.
[199] R. T. Thomas, *Britain*, 25 ff.; Woodward, *British Foreign Policy*, i. 291–4.

German hands, a nightmare to the Admiralty[200] and a fascinating prospect to the naval staff in Berlin. Entirely confirming British fears, the German admirals expressed the view that the French surrender must not be 'confined to the elimination of France's instruments of power from the present war'; instead its consequences should be utilized 'for continuing the war against Britain'. And such a 'utilization' included, among other things, taking possession of the French navy.[201] To the British, the scuttling of the French warships prior to any agreements between Paris and Berlin also seemed an acceptable solution in the summer of 1940. This confirms that the primary consideration was to deny this instrument of war to the Germans.[202] Another motive for the intransigence shown by London towards Paris in this connection was seen in the interdependence between developments in Europe and President Roosevelt's attitude. A firm stance would help to convince the United States of British determination to hold out, which was a central prerequisite of American readiness for full commitment to the British cause.[203]

The French government did not comply with any of the British proposals, but merely declared its intention of not allowing the fleet to fall into the hands of the Axis powers. This was undoubtedly a sincere intention, but it did not seem to the British a reliable guarantee. Their mistrust, looking to the future, was not affected by the fact that the Germans did not make the French naval vessels a subject of their armistice negotiations. And the efforts, which began shortly afterwards, towards German–French co-operation, designed to bring France into the war on Hitler's side, seem to confirm British scepticism in retrospect. In the summer of 1940 it was only Hitler's political calculations which ensured a relative restraint on the German side. From the autumn onward—after the British and Free French operation against Dakar on 23 September—it was, more especially, the German naval staff which, in parallel with political efforts to create a continental bloc,[204] called for a *rapprochement* with France, implying a French entry into the war. But at the latest after the Allied landing in North Africa in November 1942, when Germany's policy towards France had finally failed, the naval staff returned to their earlier demand for the seizure of the French fleet,[205] which had always remained a possibility in the meantime. The chances of realization of such an action were another matter. But the British for their part had never ruled out such a possibility, and from that point of view the attack on the French warships in July 1940 becomes understandable as a military necessity. Britain admittedly lost nearly all sympathies among the French naval officers' corps, and the

---

[200] Playfair, *Mediterranean*, i. 130–1; R. T. Thomas, *Britain*, 42 ff.
[201] 'Militärische Forderungen der Seekriegsleitung für eine Kapitulation Frankreichs' (undated, without reference No.), Asto II, I c, BA-MA RM 7/255.
[202] Woodward, *British Foreign Policy*, i. 223 ff.; with special reference to the French position Amouroux, *La Grande Histoire*, i. 475–81; ibid. ii. 109 ff.
[203] Hillgruber, *Strategie*, 83–4.
[204] On this subject see I.III.1 (*b*) below.
[205] Contrary to Marder, *Dardanelles*, 285–8; cf. Schreiber, *Revisionismus*, 360–3.

remaining units afloat, except for the ships conceded to the French by Germany for the protection of their colonies, were transferred to Toulon, which rendered a repetition of the British action impossible and made German seizure more feasible than ever. However, London was relieved of the nightmare that the bulk of the French battleships might one day operate on the enemy side.[206] Britain, therefore, had by no means merely won a Pyrrhic victory, especially if the psychological advantage in the United States is considered. In terms of active warfare, however, the British, after the German–French armistice, stood alone against the Axis, and nowhere was the shift in ratios of strength more evident than in the Mediterranean. Three battleships, two battle cruisers, fourteen cruisers, numerous destroyers, submarines, and small craft were lost by France's elimination from the war, and could not readily be replaced. True, the British still had their bases in Malta, Gibraltar, Cyprus, Palestine, and Egypt, but in the western Mediterranean the Italian navy, at least in theory, had an unexpectedly extensive area of action. Admittedly, there was 'H Force', assembled in Gibraltar after 23 June, so that there was no absolute diminution of strength in this naval area, but everything ultimately hinged on Spain. Churchill during those weeks was anxiously posing the question as to how ready Franco was to take risks. The situation in North Africa also gave little cause for optimism. Mussolini's divisions in Libya had their rear covered so long as the French forces in Tunis, Morocco, and Algeria were loyal to the Vichy government. The British, overestimating the fighting strength of the Italians, were expecting an offensive. In that event, could Alexandria be held? Added to this was the fact that Malta and Gibraltar faced a direct threat from the Luftwaffe if bases in French North Africa were available to it. In the eastern Mediterranean the British situation became even more difficult when it became clear that Syria was loyal to Vichy. Turkey, whose participation in the war was desired by Britain, was bound to feel anxiety at becoming increasingly isolated. Romania, moreover, had renounced the Anglo-French guarantee two days after the French armistice. In spite of that, Bucharest was unable to prevent the cession of Bessarabia and northern Bukovina to the Soviet Union—as pressingly advised by Hitler and Mussolini. These developments were scarcely likely to persuade Ankara that it would be advantageous to side actively with Britain. Romania's loss of territories meant that Turkey's 'traditional enemy', the Soviet Union, had moved closer to her European frontier; and German intentions with regard to Bulgaria, which were difficult to assess, might raise the issue of the Straits.[207]

In this situation the British chiefs of staff decided to recommend an essentially defensive style of operations. In the Mediterranean area this was designed, above all, to safeguard British positions in the Middle East. They

---

[206] Butler, *Strategy*, ii. 217–27; Auphan and Mordal, *La Marine française*, 194–220; vol. ii of the present work, IX.1 (Umbreit).
[207] Playfair, *Mediterranean*, i. 125–30.

assumed that it would take about two months before Hitler's future intentions could be judged with some reliability. Until then efforts would be made to supply the forces in the Middle East and Egypt with urgently needed war material, above all with modern fighter aircraft. However, the heavy German air raids expected against Britain at the beginning of July, when these plans were being drawn up, made it necessary to concentrate on home defence, as well as conducting an offensive defence by securing the political or military elimination of the French fleet.[208] In this connection Churchill also turned to President Roosevelt, and on 17 June Cordell Hull, the secretary of state, sent a plain warning to the French government. This made two points clear: first, by a surrender of the French navy to the Germans France would permanently forfeit the friendship and good will of the United States. The French government's reaction to this threat revealed the extent to which it continued to be interested in good relations with the United States. Second, if the French navy were to fall into German hands, American neutrality would be a mere façade.[209] The Americans were firmly convinced that the British would continue the struggle, and there was indeed unanimity on this score between Churchill, the military chiefs, and leading politicians. Would Britain come out victorious? There was always hope. Would Britain consider surrender? The answer was a clear 'no'.[210] At the end of June, when the British had their backs to the wall and a German landing was no longer to be ruled out, Sir Alexander Cadogan, permanent under-secretary of state at the Foreign Office, summed up the basic mood in his diary as follows:[211] 'Certainly everything is as gloomy as can be. Probability is that Hitler will attempt invasion in next fortnight. As far as I can see, we are... completely unprepared. We have simply got to die at our posts—a far better fate than capitulating to Hitler as these Frogs have done. But uncomfortable.'

By September the British had probably overcome the most critical phase of their strategy. In London at that time numerous secret items of information were contributing to the evidence that Hitler would probably attack the Soviet Union in the spring of 1941. That was correct,[212] for Hitler's decision had been taken on 31 July 1940. The British military were entitled to assume that a landing in England, unless it had taken place by mid-September, would be called off. A later date scarcely seemed to leave the Wehrmacht enough time to regroup its divisions for aggression against the USSR.[213]

Since May—to return again to the starting-point for the reorientation of

---

[208] Ibid. 129 ff.
[209] Barclay, *Their Finest Hour*, 4–5; cf. also *FRUS* (1940), ii. 452–3 (26 May 1940); ibid. i. 262 (19 June 1940); also on Hull's very conciliatory telegram of the same date ibid. 262–3; in detail on the development of American–French relations after the armistice Pitz, 'United States'; on economic support 1940–5 esp. Dougherty, *Politics*.
[210] Barclay, *Their Finest Hour*, 5–6.
[211] *Cadogan Diaries*, 308 (29 June 1940).
[212] Schreiber, 'Mittelmeerraum', 69–77.
[213] Winterbotham, *The Ultra*, 42.

British strategy—Churchill had intensified his efforts to get the United States officially to declare their non-belligerence after the Italian fashion. Churchill hoped that in that case Roosevelt would supply the Allies with everything short of sending American troops.[214] The president, however, still reacted with caution. This was true, for instance, in connection with the transfer of destroyers. Not until August did the prospect of a breakthrough on this issue emerge. However, as early as 15 June Joseph Kennedy, the American ambassador in London, had urged that everything should to be done to prevent Hitler gaining possession of the British fleet by political means, which he might then use to threaten the United States. For that reason too it was necessary to support the British government's determination.[215] Roosevelt, however, found himself compelled to proceed cautiously with regard to this and other armament matters.[216] And there could be no question of an official declaration of American 'non-belligerence'. But when the German victory in France was no longer in doubt, Churchill nevertheless urged the president, despite his known difficulties with the public and Congress, to declare the determination of the United States to enter the war if necessary.[217] Churchill did not believe that Washington would dispatch an expeditionary force, but he hoped that the promise of an early entry into the war would prevent France from concluding an armistice, would strengthen morale and resistance in democratic countries throughout the world, and would weaken that of the German and Italian peoples.[218]

The majority of Americans did not yet wish to take such a step in the summer of 1940. But the impending fall of France did change public opinion. This was reflected especially in a now almost unreserved support for a policy of rearmament.[219] Roosevelt took advantage of this to initiate, as a start, the industrial mobilization of the nation.[220] Private support, predominant until

---

[214] *Roosevelt and Churchill*, No. 8, pp. 94–5 (15 May 1940); cf. also Harriman and Abel, *Special Envoy*, 19; Buchanan, *United States*, i. 13.

[215] *Roosevelt and Churchill*, No. 20, pp. 108–9 (13, Aug. 1940), and No. 21, pp. 109–10 (15 Aug. 1940); *FRUS* (1940), iii. 49–50 (16 May 1940); 51 (25 May 1940); 52 (11 June 1940); 53 ff. (15 June 1940); 57–8 (31 July 1940); 58–9 (2 Aug. 1940); 65–6 (13 Aug. 1940); Buchanan, *United States*, i. 14.

[216] *Roosevelt and Churchill*, No. 19, pp. 107–8 (31 July 1940); No. 20, pp. 108–9 (13 Aug. 1940); No. 21, pp. 109–10 (15 Aug. 1940). *Churchill and Roosevelt*, C-20x, pp. 54–8 (5 and 31 July 1940); ibid. R-8x, pp. 58–9 (13 Aug. 1940); C-22x, pp. 63 ff. (22 Aug. 1940); C-23x, pp. 65–6 (25 Aug. 1940); C-24x, pp. 67–8 (27 Aug. 1940); and C-53x, pp. 126–7 (9 Jan. 1941), in which Churchill states that only a few of the 50 destroyers delivered have as yet been deployed because of the necessary overhaul work. Directly on this cf. C-53x/A (draft), p. 119 (25 Dec. 1940). Also R-22x, p. 130 (18 Jan. 1941), where the president replies that the US Navy itself suffers from a shortage of destroyers. This was a negative reaction to Churchill's hint that he could use more destroyers.

[217] Ibid., No. 17, pp. 104 ff. (15 June 1940).

[218] Ibid., No. 18, p. 106 (15 June 1940); Buchanan, *United States*, i. 15.

[219] Small, *Was War Necessary?*, 227; Dallek, *Franklin D. Roosevelt*, 223, dates the change of public opinion from the end of May.

[220] Dallek, *Franklin D. Roosevelt*, 228; Harriman and Abel, *Special Envoy*, 19; Friedländer, *Prelude to Downfall*, 92–3; on the scope of the military measures initiated in May see Marshall et al., *Reports*, 18 ff.

3. British Strategy Change, Summer 1940

then, was beginning to be replaced by state aid, and on 10 June 1940 the president, for the first time, declared openly that 'victory by the gods of force and hate would endanger the institutions of democracy in the Western world', and that America would 'extend its material resources to the opponents of force'.[221]

But beyond such material engagement on Britain's behalf, Roosevelt gave his agreement in mid-June to secret staff talks between the British and American navies—and, if necessary, also their air forces.[222] Towards the end of August officers of the two countries met as a 'Standardization of Arms Committee', the Americans being represented by members of all their services. In these conversations with the chiefs of staff Washington was interested primarily in ascertaining the strength of Britain's determination to resist. Beyond that, however, the generals and admirals discussed basic aspects of a strategy for bringing the Third Reich to its knees. In-depth staff conferences between January and March 1941, whose task it was to work out a common strategy against Germany, Italy, and Japan, further developed the results of August 1940. The British were even then convinced that, although the threat to the United Kingdom was not yet over, time was working against Hitler and Mussolini, who were increasingly under pressure to make a move, and that an invasion need no longer be feared. One result of this was that, to the surprise of the American military, any plans involving the abandonment of the British Isles were no longer even considered by the British. As they explained to the Americans, their entire strategy was based on the assumption that they would stand up to a German attack, and that the whole nation was firmly resolved to do so.[223]

London's strategic directives, as they emerged in August, largely confirmed the ideas put forward in May. It was intended, for the time being, to concentrate on naval and air operations. The enemy's moral powers of resistance must be broken. The focus of offensive warfare was to be in the Mediterranean area, as a defeat of Italy was the precondition of stabilization in the Middle East. Altogether, the British officers envisaged a prolonged war, which would achieve the liberation of Europe in co-operation with the United States and by means of a strategy of attrition. This concept proved correct, not so much in details of timing and operations but in its general assumptions.[224]

In addition to such long-term plans, which constituted the essence of the reorientation of British strategy in the summer of 1940, there were, of course, at a subordinate level, new plans for the continuation of the war; these are to be seen primarily as coming under the heading of tactical actions. They concerned mainly the Atlantic and Mediterranean areas. They were essentially

---

[221] Helbich, *Franklin D. Roosevelt*, 216.
[222] Butler, *Strategy*, ii. 243.
[223] Ibid. 341–5; Hillgruber, *Strategie*, 97–102; Leutze, *Bargaining*, 146–61.
[224] Howard, *Mediterranean Strategy*, is rather critical of British strategic planning, 7–11.

proposed reactions to a threat to the Atlantic islands from the Wehrmacht and to a threat to Gibraltar as a result of German–Spanish action.

One aspect of these developments was the appointment in mid-July of Admiral of the Fleet Lord Keyes of Zeebrugge to be Director of Combined Operations. The new post had its origin in the plans of the chiefs of staff for a kind of guerrilla war. Small assault units were to operate in German-occupied territories. On the initiative of Churchill, who soon enlarged the scope of this activity well beyond what was originally envisaged, the 'Adviser to the Chiefs of Staff on Combined Operations' became a post in its own right; it did not readily lend itself to integration into the command structure of the British forces, and gave rise to a good deal of friction within the military leadership.[225]

As to the Mediterranean area, Keyes planned a number of operations which, though they did not in the end materialize, rounded off the overall picture of British strategy in North Africa.[226] One idea was the occupation of Pantelleria. This action, a seaborne operation code-named 'Workshop', was to be executed by some 2,500 men from Malta.[227] As the strategic usefulness of this operation was highly controversial—Admiral Cunningham, in particular, opposed it[228]—the island was not occupied until 1943. Operation Yorker, a landing at Cagliari in Sicily, similarly failed to win the approval of the British military. Keyes found himself planning in considerable isolation. At the same time, the operations favoured by the Commander-in-Chief Mediterranean under the code-name 'Mandible', envisaging an occupation of the Dodecanese, likewise remained on paper.[229] In this plan, as early as mid-December 1940, Cunningham envisaged the possibility of a German attempt to relieve the Italians by a thrust to the south-east in the spring of 1941, which would endanger Britain's communications with Greece as well as with Turkey.[230] But Churchill—who had been well disposed towards a landing on Pantelleria, which Cunningham regarded as bold and feasible but also as rather unnecessary—rejected a landing in the Dodecanese. If there was any landing at all, in his opinion it should be on one of the large islands. But the 10,000 to 20,000 men necessary were not available. The prime minister also feared that such an action might lead to problems, for which he had no desire, between Ankara, Athens, and London.[231] He therefore favoured 'Workshop', but after mid-January, in view of the strength of the Luftwaffe in Sicily, this plan was finally regarded as unrealizable.[232] In February some smaller operations—originally also proposed by Cunningham—against certain of the Dodecanese islands were carried out, but all the British gained was the conviction that, with regard to such operations, they still had a fair amount to learn; success was denied to them. From March onwards, as a result of developing events in Greece, all landing attempts had to be shelved indefinitely.[233]

[225] *Keyes Papers*, 77–8, 92 ff.   [226] Cf. V.1 below (Stegemann).
[227] *Keyes Papers*, 100–28.   [228] Ibid. 79–80.   [229] Ibid. 125.
[230] Ibid. 126–7.   [231] Playfair, *Mediterranean*, i. 307 ff.
[232] Ibid. 324–5.   [233] Ibid. 325–6.

4. THE AXIS POWERS AFTER THE VICTORY IN THE WEST

While on the British side the summer of 1940 developed into the low point of the war, which, despite London's confidence, brought with it many an unknown factor, the Germans after the French defeat were almost surprised to find that 'Nous sommes les vainqueurs'.[234] In military terms further success seemed assured; all that was needed now was to solve the practical task of the reorganization of Europe.[235] This, of course, was bound to affect the littoral states of the Mediterranean,[236] which were part of the greater European–African sphere that the Axis powers were seeking to dominate. Hitler, moreover, after the conclusion of the armistice at Compiègne on 22 June 1940, was looking for an interval of peace in order, with his rear now safe, to prepare for his real war, his invasion of the USSR.[237]

(a) Ideas of Peace

As for peace-feelers put out even before victory in the west, Hitler, who wished to negotiate from a position of strength, was at first slow to concern himself with them. His calculations seemed to pay off when the impression arose that the collapse of France had caused a cabinet crisis in Britain, which might, at least momentarily, threaten Churchill's position. It was suggested that Conservative politicians did not care much for the prime minister's uncompromising policy of holding out and seeing things through. There was talk of a government reshuffle and of peace plans, but if this was true at all, then it was so only for a short while. At the latest, the British attack on units of the French fleet at Mers el Kebir on 3 July clearly indicated that Churchill's position and policy were safe. Nothing was said officially by the British about any arrangement with Germany, so it was not simply a case of Hitler having missed the right moment when, in his Reichstag speech of 19 July, he appealed to them to 'see reason'—because for Britain there was no question of an arrangement with the Third Reich on its own terms. Semi-official peace efforts, by way of Prince Max Egon zu Hohenlohe-Langenburg, Carl J. Burckhardt (formerly the League of Nations high commissioner in Danzig), Sir David Kelly, the British minister at Berne, and the Vatican, had all failed earlier; and the Germans were too late with their wooing of the Duke of Windsor, who was known to be pro-German. In any case, it is by no means certain that the duke, as the Spanish government hinted, would have allowed himself to be harnessed to Hitler's chariot.

There was under discussion a plan by Albert Plesman, the director-general of the Dutch airline KLM, which he put to Göring on 24 July: in essence this

---

[234] *Weizsäcker-Papiere*, 207–8 (21 May 1940).
[235] Böhme, *Der deutsch-französische Waffenstillstand*, 253–8; Geschke, *Frankreichpolitik*, 50–1; Jäckel, *Frankreich*, 61–2; vol. ii of the present work, VI.v.5 (Umbreit).
[236] Only these are to be considered here; the Balkan states are dealt with at II.II.1–3 below.
[237] Schreiber, 'Mittelmeerraum', 72–7.

amounted to a peaceful agreement among the great powers—the United States, Britain, and Germany—on a share-out of the world into economic and political spheres of interest. For the greater European–African sphere such ideas envisaged a kind of joint rule by Germany and the Soviet Union, without however questioning German hegemony west of the USSR. The United States had the Americas assigned to them, and Britain was to keep her empire. These concepts met with favour mainly, though not exclusively, among German economic experts, who even then feared that the raw-material basis of the Reich was insufficient for a prolonged war. Plesman's project remained on the tapis from 25 July to the end of August, even though Hitler distanced himself from it at a relatively early stage. Presumably he did not like the idea of close ties with the Soviet Union. This fact, as will be shown, clearly influenced Hitler's thinking on the project of a continental bloc in the late summer of 1940. In addition, from the time of Lord Halifax's speech of 22 July he was aware that London would not listen to ideas of a German–British settlement. Very probably the intensification of the military conflict contributed to Plesman's plan remaining an illusion. As, moreover, the battle of Britain revealed more weakness than strength in the German conduct of the war, British determination to resist very soon grew even stronger.

Peace-feelers from German business circles in Washington, on the other hand, failed in the face of President Roosevelt's attitude. Generally speaking, it may be stated that, while there were certain British circles which seemed to favour peace plans, the top leaders gave them a thumbs-down where the fate of the aggressors was concerned. This was unchanged by the fact that, when Pius XII offered to mediate, neither the Germans nor the British rejected his proposal outright. The matter was treated in a dilatory way and was overtaken by political and military developments.[238]

Hitler's hopes that, after his victory over France, he might come to an arrangement with Britain had thus been dashed by the end of July, a fact that was clear to all. The Reich leadership now found itself in an unforeseen situation, the results of which were increasingly leading to a crisis in German strategy and ultimately induced Hitler to run the risk of a war on two fronts. This will be examined below. For the present we have to sketch out the effects of the armistice on relations between Germany and the Mediterranean states, and on the economic situation of the Reich. For the countries of the Near and Middle East, in particular, a review of the period prior to June 1940 is indispensable.

(b) War Gains: The French Example

The German victory in the west meant, among other things, the end of the French Third Republic. In the person of the aged Marshal Pétain, France was

---

[238] On the peace efforts generally: Ansel, *Hitler Confronts England*, 513–17; Barclay, *Their Finest Hour*, 12–19, 22–3; Hillgruber, *Strategie*, 148–55; Martin, 'Das "Dritte Reich"', 534–7.

4. Axis Powers after Victory in the West

endowed with something like an absolute monarch.[239] But this change of regime did not concern the Germans greatly. They exerted no influence on the position of the new head of state. In general, of course, an authoritarian dictatorship, of the kind represented by Hitler's own state, was more attractive than a democratic one—but these, for the time being, were secondary issues. Far more important to Berlin were the military advantages resulting from the occupation of northern France and the French Atlantic coast. After the armistice the Reich had at its disposal not only first-rate bases for its naval and aerial war against Britain, but it had also gained a direct overland link with Spain.

As a result of his new position of power, Hitler immediately initiated measures proclaiming a policy of 'breaking up France' and 'eliminating France as a great power'—in other words, a start was made with the implementation of some programmatic goals of the National Socialist regime. It is not possible to say with absolute certainty which of the occupied territories were intended to become German possessions one day,[240] but there seems to be no doubt that the fate of the 'hereditary enemy' would have been merely that of a supernumerary.[241] Hitler himself repeatedly voiced his intention of incorporating Burgundy, Alsace-Lorraine, and the coal region around Lille—and, of course, also Belgium and The Netherlands—into the Greater German Reich. And the draft of a 'provisional peace programme of the Reichsführer SS' (Himmler) envisaged the future Reich territory as including, along with Poland, Czechoslovakia, Scandinavia, The Netherlands, and Belgium, also north-west France.[242] The German annexation plans took on clear outline immediately after the armistice. A significant move was the establishment of an exclusion zone to which those of the population who had fled before the advancing German armies were not permitted to return because the region was later to be incorporated into the German state. This was the origin of the 'north-east line' in occupied France (see Map I.II.1), which ran as far as the demarcation-line in the south. In practice, however, this rigorous policy could not be enforced because, on the one hand, there was no effective border control and, on the other, there was not enough German manpower fully to utilize the severed territories economically. Nevertheless—and this is instructive with regard to long-term intentions—Berlin in theory always adhered to the institution of the exclusion zone.[243] France, for centuries a centralized state, was thus broken up as an economic and administrative unit. There was a German-occupied and an Italian-occupied part, as well as the unoccupied territory, separated from them

---

[239] In detail Amouroux, *La Grande Histoire*, ii. 55–104; and esp. (from the angle of the Resistance) Michel, *Pétain*.
[240] Böhme, *Der deutsch-französische Waffenstillstand*, 250–3; vol. ii of the present work, VI.v.6 (Umbreit).
[241] Geschke, *Frankreichpolitik*, 33–4, 50–1; Jäckel, *Frankreich*, 46 ff.
[242] Speer, *Sklavenstaat*, 407, and text accompanying the map; also Gruchmann, *Großraumordnung*, 77–80.
[243] Böhme, *Der deutsch-französische Waffenstillstand*, 258–74.

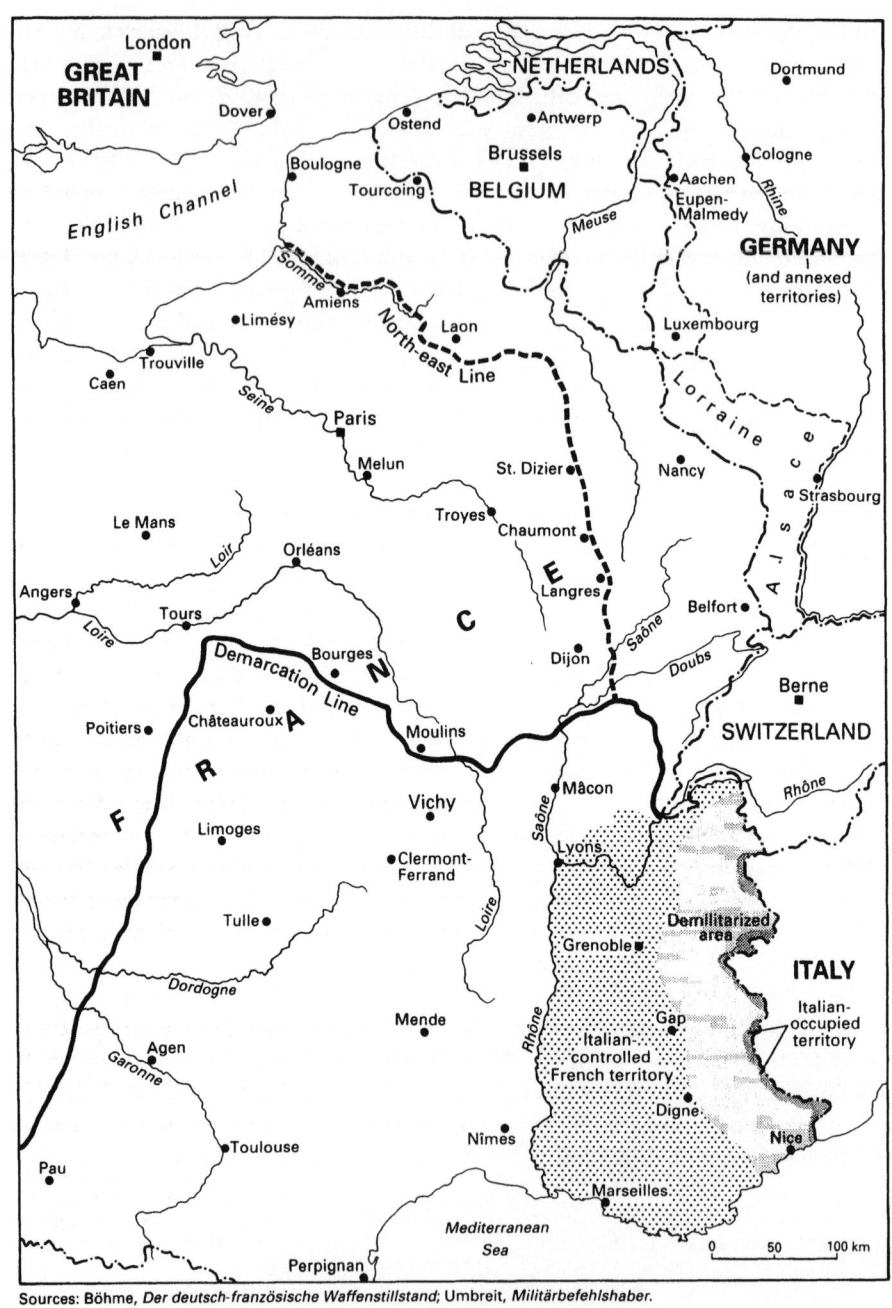

MAP I.II.1. Occupied France, 1940–1941

by the demarcation-line, in which Pétain held sway.[244] This division may have made sense from the military point of view, though it soon became obvious that the strict separation of the occupied country from the unoccupied zone did not entirely favour the German interest in exploiting the economic and industrial potential of France and her colonies. Although the OKW declared on 4 July that the industry of the occupied zones was not to be drawn upon for the production of war material, nor were the economic assets of Vichy France to be employed for the German armament industry,[245] it was not long before the demarcation-line was used to serve the 'alignment of the whole French economy with German interests'. The Germans reserved the right to grant special facilities to traffic crossing the demarcation-line, provided Vichy conceded to them a share in the control of what external frontiers were left to Vichy France.[246] No doubt military and intelligence problems played a part in these demands, but beyond these the Germans were simply aiming at 'total control of French commercial and financial policies'. Moreover, twenty days after the OKW directive Berlin requested the delivery of material vital to the war.[247] The tug of war between the German and the French governments continued until May 1941, when the Germans finally agreed to the free flow of merchandise and money across the demarcation-line after the French had accepted the appointment of a foreign-trade and currency commissioner for the unoccupied zone.[248] The artificial boundary had proved to be anything but watertight even before, so that Germany, by way of the 'free market', participated extensively in French imports from Africa, which London, assuming that their transfer to Reich territory was impossible, had allowed to pass.[249]

What specific military-economic advantages did the Reich derive from the victory in the west? First of all, there were occupation costs. By means of arbitrarily inflated demands Germany not only made France pay for the real cost of maintaining the troops necessary for the occupation, as provided by the Hague convention on land warfare, but also compelled her to finance up to a

---

[244] Ibid. 262–74; Jäckel, *Frankreich*, 78 ff., 89 ff.; on the economic consequences, from a French perspective, Amouroux, *La Grande Histoire*, ii. 124–32. It should be noted that the division of the occupation zone into a German and an Italian one brought temporary relief to Jews living in France: Jews able to flee to the Italian zone, or already resident there, were spared persecution and deportation to concentration camps until Italy's exit from the war: see Cavaglion, *Nella notte*, 15–37.

[245] DGFP D x, No. 106, p. 118 (4 July 1940). This meant that industry in the occupied zone, though not producing war material, was producing 'articles urgently needed' in Germany. From the unoccupied zone material and manufactures relating to armaments could be utilized only 'by way of free exchange'.

[246] Geschke, *Frankreichpolitik*, 51–2; Jäckel, *Frankreich*, 90–1.

[247] Geschke, *Frankreichpolitik*, 53.

[248] Hartmann, 'Frankreich', 52, 55; Jäckel, *Frankreich*, 91; on the establishment of German control authorities in French North-West Africa, negotiations on which proceeded in parallel with the endeavours reported above (but which are not discussed here), cf. Neugebauer, *Militärkontrolle*, 49–68, 120–37.

[249] *Deutschlands Rüstung*, 89.

fifth of the total costs of Germany's war.[250] More important still were those measures which aimed at a 'strengthening of the German war potential' by extensive utilization of the French economy. This was to be achieved by: '(1) support for the formations of the three fighting services deployed in France, to ensure that they remain fully operational . . . (2) removal of raw materials and machinery in so far as these were required in Germany, (3) switching of orders to France, (4) transfer of French manpower to Germany.'[251]

In the realization of such intentions German interests had unlimited precedence over any French wishes. If difficulties arose none the less, these were due not to any consideration for Vichy but to the problem of striking an optimum balance between the utilization of industrial production capacities in France and the volume of raw materials carried off to Germany. The situation was further complicated by the fact that French industry, dependent as it was on imports of coal and fuel, suffered from the removal of means of transport to the Reich. German authorities, on the other hand, often quoted these production problems of the French economy, ultimately brought about by German measures, in order to represent the removal of raw materials as necessary and justified. In spite of various problems, the method practised by Germany paid off from her point of view, as French industry and raw materials, in the opinion of experts, represented an extremely significant contribution to Hitler's war effort.[252]

Table I.II.1, listing the material identified and removed by the end of August 1940, shows the quantity of various materials available to the German economy as a result of the victory over France.

It was largely due to the extensive French stocks of raw materials that the requirements of the German war industry were met in 1940 and the armaments for 1941 produced. But for the resources secured by the campaign in Belgium, Holland, and France, the German armament industry would have faced bottlenecks as early as 1941, which would have necessitated an anticipation of the emergency measures of 1944.[253] Added to the direct gains there was relief for German production in the form of direct or indirect Wehrmacht orders placed in occupied France; these were of the magnitude of RM3,311,463,000.[254] Although the inclusion of French economic potential in German armament production led to some friction, as mentioned earlier, an attempt was made, roughly from September 1940 onwards, to eliminate the initial confusion of competence and the manifest shortcomings in the co-

---

[250] Geschke, *Frankreichpolitik*, 54 ff.; Hartmann, 'Frankreich', 52–3, according to which even the relief granted after May 1941 only reduced the costs of the consequences of German occupation to the overall French budget to 48%; Jäckel, *Frankreich*, 91 ff. These questions will be examined in detail in volume v of the present work.
[251] G. Thomas, *Wehr- und Rüstungswirtschaft*, 222.
[252] Ibid. 223–4.
[253] Ibid. 245.
[254] Ibid. 224, with account of 'France' and 'Northern France'.

TABLE I.II.1. *French Raw-material Stocks, Summer 1940* (t.)

Raw material	Stocks identified	Stocks removed to Germany by end August	Stocks remaining in France
Cast iron	85,952	1,600	84,352
Rolling-mill products	295,133	2,575	292,558
Ferromanganese	3,337	—	3,337
Tungsten	484	355	129
Copper	72,953	33,567	39,386
Brass	18,284	10,454	7,830
Tin	3,412	1,046	2,366
Zinc	36,462	4,040	32,422
Mercury	550	496	54
Aluminium	7,283	—	7,283
Phosphates	42,900	—	42,900
Raw rubber	4,992	1,421	3,571
Pyrites	16,400	—	16,400
Cow-hides	175	105	70
Cotton	14,068	—	14,068

Source: Winkel, 'Ausbeutung', 340.

operation between different German authorities, in order to ensure the systematic economic exploitation of French potential.

This, however, did not affect the continuing practice of removing war materials to Germany and requisitioning railway engines and rolling-stock, as well as all kinds of machinery—a practice which continued in 1941.[255] By 31 December alone, the Germans had removed the following quantities of vital materials in short supply:[256] 213,162 t. of non-ferrous metals, 40,651 t. of non-ferrous waste, 107,841 t. of iron and steel,[257] 19,964 t. of chemical raw materials and rubber, 16,445 t. of industrial oils and fats, 11,043 t. of turpentine, 45,486 t. of rosin, 16,538 t. of hides, skins, and leather, 36,466 t. of textile raw materials, 10,543 t. of stones and earth, and 964,063 t. of scrap. In addition, the following means of production were transferred to Germany by August 1942: more than 17,000 machine-tools, 8,000 motors, and 700 punched-card machines. For the benefit of their war effort the Germans moreover withdrew 'from French industry, on a major scale, iron-structure workshops, cranes, special

---

[255] Ibid. 274; a very critical comment on Germany's economic methods *vis-à-vis* France in Winkel, 'Ausbeutung', 341–6, 352–3, 372 ff.

[256] G. Thomas, *Wehr- und Rüstungswirtschaft*, 274–5, from which the quotation below is also taken.

[257] These figures do not include the amounts of material obtained by Germany through so-called free exchange. Thus, according to French data, in 1941 the Third Reich imported from France a total of 1.255m. t. of ferrous metal. On the exploitative character of these measures cf. Hartmann, *Frankreich*, 52 ff.

machines for ammunition manufacture, assemblies for the mineral-oil programme, powered machines for the construction of U-boat bases, special mining equipment, and other industrial assets'. Almost in parallel, German consumer-goods production was increasingly switched to France, so that German factories could be used even more intensively for armament production. Altogether, Germany after her victory controlled 66 per cent of France's cultivable agricultural soil, which amounted to 62 per cent of grain and 70 per cent of milk production. The principal industrial centres of the country were in the occupied zone, so that the bulk of coal-mining, heavy industry, and textiles, as well as mechanical, electrical, and chemical engineering, was under German control.[258]

The above demonstrates that Germany made her economic interests the principal yardstick for her treatment of France. Under these conditions any kind of economic collaboration amounted essentially to French performance in advance of returns. The range of exploitative measures was extensive; there were enforced economic directives, high occupation costs, an unfavourably fixed rate of exchange creating excessive German purchasing power, and a system of accountancy which unilaterally favoured German firms. The methods were less drastic than those in the eastern territories, but they were highly effective. In 1941, for instance, France's industry had only 44.5 per cent of its normal requirements of iron at its disposal, and during the same year the country was allowed to use only 51 per cent of its usual quantity of coal. People in France altogether lived worse than in Germany. Unoccupied France included 72 per cent of the country's non-cultivated soil; from it came a mere 38 per cent of the grain harvest, 30 per cent of the potato harvest, and 13 per cent of the butter of the whole of France. True, now and again the Germans handed over some foodstuffs—for instance, at the end of 1940 and the beginning of 1941, 450,000 t. of potatoes and 100,000 t. of sugar, which, however, were accounted for in the trade exchanges. By way of rations, in February 1941 the French had only 300 g. of bread per day, as against 340 g. in Germany. The French received 360 g. of meat, 100 g. of fat, and 500 g. of sugar per week; the Germans had 500 g. of meat, 270 g. of fat, and 1,200–500 g. of sugar.[259] It is entirely possible that the exploitation of the country could have been further intensified;[260] but even as it was, the advantages derived by the German war-machine from the armistice have to be described as considerable.

The occupying power, however, was well aware that the dependence of the subjugated countries was not totally one-sided. Berlin, which, in the role of a command centre for the distribution of raw materials in German-occupied

---

[258] Amouroux, *La Grande Histoire*, ii. 142–3; Hartmann, *Frankreich*, 51.

[259] Amouroux, *La Grande Histoire*, ii. 142–3, 179–80; Geschke, *Frankreichpolitik*, 119–20; Hartmann, *Frankreich*, 54–5.

[260] Böhme, 'Deutschland und Frankreich' (B 31), 15.

Europe, decided which enterprises in which countries could maintain production, was also interested in seeing that the industrial capacities available as a result of its conquests were optimally utilized for the German war economy. This was best accomplished by allowing the economic life of those countries to go on as normally as possible. Thus the need of the vanquished to survive and the victor's need to act considerately in his own interest resulted in a kind of symbiosis between exploiters and exploited. Accordingly, Germany granted the Pétain government a certain measure of sovereignty. Negotiations with its representatives therefore took place at the headquarters of the German armistice commission in Wiesbaden. The Germans had good reasons to avoid any brutal diktat. In point of fact they were in an advantageous position not only as victors, but also owing to the behaviour of many a French capitalist. Wherever the Vichy government tried persistently to negotiate some advantage, individual French entrepreneurs would undermine these efforts by collaborating directly with the economic representatives of the Reich—that is, in competition with their own government. No doubt National Socialist Germany derived considerable advantages from these transactions, but the French too were entitled to be satisfied. By the end of April 1941 they secured German orders to the tune of RM1,500m.; in April 1942 transactions already amounted to RM2,300m., and in the autumn of 1942 to over RM4,000m. The French government, under pressure from industrial and financial circles, and given the fact that a million unemployed could find work only if the Germans supplied raw materials, had to be prepared to make almost any concessions. The result of this situation was a positive surplus of economic collaboration. The French supplied, among other things, training aircraft for the Luftwaffe, aircraft engines and spares, as well as finished products for bomber manufacture. Gradually French industry was even producing bomber aircraft for Germany, albeit without on-board armaments.[261]

(c) *Hopes: Hitler, Franco, and the Anglo-Saxons*

Apart from the direct material advantages derived by Germany from her victory in the west, the German–French armistice naturally resulted in a changed political constellation, which could be expected to have favourable consequences in the Mediterranean area and the Middle East. At the centre of German interest in the summer of 1940 were Spain and Turkey, the most important neutrals in the region both from Berlin's and from London's point of view.

Spain in June 1940, against the background of an impending cessation of hostilities between Germany and France, acted as a kind of diplomatic relay station. Any substantial influence on the development of German–French relations was ruled out by the completeness of the French defeat. Yet Franco's

---

[261] Rings, *Leben*, 115–19; on political collaboration, which began in July 1940, see Gordon, *Collaborationism*, 43–63.

caution, appropriate as it was in the circumstances, by no means reflected a lack of interest in the fate of France. On the contrary, the prospect of having the Germans as neighbours across the Pyrenees afforded no pleasure to Madrid. Of course the generalissimo wished for Hitler's victory, but he did not want the dictator to advance right up to his own doorstep. Franco was therefore hoping that a residual France, as intact as possible, would act as a buffer between Spain and the Third Reich.[262]

The cunning game of poker over Spain's entry into the war, which began in June between Berlin and Madrid, will be discussed later on;[263] but in order to judge the attitude of the two sides it is necessary to bear in mind Franco's sceptical reserve towards Hitler, as well as Spain's economic and military situation. Spain's geo-strategic position undoubtedly promised great advantages for military operations by the Axis, the more so if it should prove possible to capture Gibraltar. With Spain as a belligerent, German warships would have unrestricted use of Spanish ports,[264] and the Italian navy would have free access to the Atlantic, while the British navy would be barred from entry into the Mediterranean. The Germans, finally, could easily move into French North Africa, both to ensure order in the French colonies and to dominate the West African Atlantic coast. All these were matters of exceptional importance with regard to the covering of Germany's strategic flank in an attack on the Soviet Union. This will be discussed in detail later.

From a purely military point of view, however, Germany had to expect that she would have to give more assistance to Spain as an ally than she would receive in return. The Spanish army in the summer of 1940 numbered approximately 340,000 men. In the event of conflict a further 160,000 could be enlisted. The army consisted of 27 divisions; 20 of these were stationed in the mother country, 5 in Morocco, and 1 each in the Balearic and Canary Islands. The peacetime strength of a division was 9,000, the wartime strength 12,000 men. The infantry units seemed to be adequately equipped for a conflict. The artillery, on the other hand, was in a pitiful state: too few guns, which were worn out anyway. Moreover, there was a serious shortage of spare parts. The same shortage also affected the armoured units, which consisted of roughly 200 light fighting vehicles. Anti-tank defence, on the other hand, was judged to be quite good. What was disastrous, however, was the overall situation with regard to ammunition. Available stocks were sufficient, at best, for a few days of fighting, with domestic production being in no position at all to ensure the necessary supplies.

The personnel situation, too, was dismal: owing to heavy losses in the civil war many of the scheduled positions were unfilled, and the senior ranks of the officers' corps were considered to be unduly aged. According to information

---

[262] Detwiler, *Hitler*, 20 ff.
[263] See I.III.1, 2s below; cf. also Trevor-Roper, 'Hitler und Franco'; Puzzo, *Spain*, 220 ff.
[264] On such disguised use see Burdick, 'Moro'; *Survey of International Affairs*, vii. 266 ff.

available to the German army high command, 'only the posts of colonels and lieutenant-colonels' were 'filled according to the budget'. Among majors there was a shortage of 50 per cent of budgeted positions, among captains 90 per cent, and among first and second lieutenants almost 100 per cent. In August 1940, therefore, the Spanish army almost exclusively used reserve officers to command platoons. They were, however, to be replaced by regular officers, judged by the Germans as good, within the next eighteen months. Nevertheless, in the opinion of General Martínez Campos, chief of the Spanish general staff, the army would need about eight years to build up a numerically and qualitatively adequate officers' corps. No wonder that German observers regarded Spain's military command as 'sluggish and doctrinaire', although they believed that 'many of the existing deficiencies' were 'compensated for by the fighting spirit of officers and men'. All in all, the Spanish army was regarded as 'conditionally usable in war', but in the event of Spain's entry into the war the country would, in military terms, be a deficiency area for the foreseeable future.[265] Moreover, the general shortage of motor-fuel meant that without German help Spain could wage war for only 30 to 45 days at the most.[266] Here lies the central issue of any discussion about Spain's entry into the war and her value in a war: the country's economic condition. In a discussion of this, sight must not be lost of the various interdependencies in the power-triangle Spain–Axis powers–Allies, the term 'Allies' here exceptionally including by anticipation the United States.

As a consequence of German involvement in the Spanish civil war, Spain held a special position in trade relations with the Reich: since 1936 the Germans had extensively bought into Spanish exports, especially foodstuffs and raw materials. The outbreak of the Second World War at first severed all trade routes between Spain and Germany owing to the British blockade and German–French hostilities. Exports and imports routed through Italy were scarcely worth mentioning. As a result, the Spanish economy, strongly orientated as it was towards trade with Germany, faced considerable problems. For instance, whereas in 1935, even before the intensification of trade relations in the civil war, some 12.7 per cent of all Spanish exports went to Germany, in 1940 these dropped to 5 per cent and imports to 3.7 per cent of the total volume. By 1941, however—an important consequence of the armistice with France, especially for the German war economy after the attack on the USSR put an end to Soviet supplies—Spain was again conducting 28 per cent of her foreign trade with Germany. In terms of gold pesetas this represented a 700

---

[265] GStdH, Abt. Fremde Heere West/IV, No. 606/40 g.Kdos. (10 Aug. 1940): The Spanish Army at Present, *GDFP* D x, No. 326, pp. 461–4. The document carries a marginal gloss by Canaris: 'Foreign ministry: I believe that this presentation will be of interest for the foreign minister.' Halder, *Diaries*, i. 573 (4 Sept. 1940), states: 'Reconstruction of Troop Officer Corps will take 2 to 3 years. Staff officers good. Spain can furnish 350–400,000 men, without equipment. Has 60,000 white soldiers and 20,000 Moors in North Africa.'

[266] *DGFP* D x, No. 313, pp. 442–5 (8 Aug. 1940).

per cent growth compared with 1940. Imports, at 10.3 per cent of the total volume, kept within reasonable bounds.[267] But this very discrepancy shows that the two countries by no means complemented each other economically. While Germany had a great demand for iron ore, tungsten, lead, fluorite, mercury, woollens, leather, and Mediterranean fruit, she was unable to meet Spain's import requests. Only once, in 1942, did Germany export more merchandise to Spain than the latter's principal suppliers: Argentina, the United States, and Britain.[268]

Needless to say, the Allies realized the problems of the Spanish economy, which was still suffering from the disastrous consequences of the civil war. Basically the country depended on Britain's good will, and Madrid was aware of British influence on US deliveries of wheat and oil. These circumstances seemed to make it somewhat easier for London to calculate the risk posed by Franco. But the British government also possessed information that there was an interventionist wing of the Spanish leadership.[269] And when the German successes in France began to take shape, the British felt that, to be on the safe side, they ought to improve their relations with Spain.

On 1 June, therefore, Sir Samuel Hoare arrived in Madrid as a special envoy—certainly an excellent choice. His instructions were clear: British concessions on the blockade issue and in economic matters generally, provided that Spain, in return for bread and economic security, avoided an excessively close alignment with the Axis powers.[270] Hoare thus presented a fair offer; all that Hitler could put up against it were vague statements of intent, associated with countless risks for Spain in view of the still uncertain outcome of the war. German promises, moreover, were bound to become less tempting as Britain's determination to resist was stiffening. With regard to future developments, therefore, two decisive factors emerged in the summer of 1940: time, and US political and economic support—by then assured—for British interests. On this basis London tried to use Spain's dependence on imports of all kinds as a means of tying Madrid into the Anglo-American sphere.[271]

Of course, this British policy was nothing new. As early as 18 March 1940 Britain had concluded various trade agreements which, among other things, granted Spain a credit of £2m. to enable her to purchase goods in the sterling area. Franco did not take up this offer until August, however, which may suggest that the Spanish interventionist party was then losing influence.[272] Before that, on 22 May, the British, of their own accord, had promised further economic aid. They would deliver 100,000 t. of wheat by the end of June, provided the Spanish government affirmed, confidentially, its intention of

---

[267] Ruhl, *Spanien im Zweiten Weltkrieg*, 40 ff.
[268] Ibid.; see also Broué and Témime, *Révolution*, 446–58.
[269] *Survey of International Affairs*, vii. 269–73; Woodward, *British Foreign Policy*, i. 433–4.
[270] Woodward, *British Foreign Policy*, i. 435–9.
[271] For the Spanish viewpoint cf. Serrano Suñer, *Zwischen Hendaye*, 132–3.
[272] Butler, *Strategy*, ii. 238; *Survey of International Affairs*, vii. 28.

4. Axis Powers after Victory in the West 149

remaining neutral. Negotiations on this matter ran simultaneously with the dubious offer made by Franco to Hitler, in which he presented Spain's entry into the war as possible under certain conditions.[273] By 24 July the Anglo-Spanish deal was concluded. At the same time London was anxious to prevent Spain misusing supplies from the Empire and the United States for her war preparations. The British government therefore limited the volume of goods to a scale which seemed to preclude excessive stocking-up by Spain. Stocks amounting to Spanish consumption for two and a half months were considered safe, as it was unlikely that such sparse reserves would be passed on to the Axis powers. How closely the British were in fact watching these supplies subsequently emerged in June, when Spain imported an above-average quantity of oil from the United States. London intervened in Washington, and the US administration, semi-officially, thereupon practised a very effective check on exports.[274]

German plans in June 1940 confirm the justification of Allied caution. When the French collapse provided Germany with the (militarily and economically) invaluable overland link with Spain, Berlin believed the time had come to prepare the most 'comprehensive agreements' possible. Admittedly, all excessive German demands were curtailed from the outset by the fact that the Axis powers were unable to meet from their own catchment areas either Spain's foodstuff and raw-material requirements generally or her demand for wheat in particular.[275] Spain remained dependent on overseas imports and hence on the goodwill of the United States and Britain. This fact remained unchanged even by the German victory in the west.

In connection with Germany's growing interest in Franco's entry into the war[276] the Germans nevertheless carried out a detailed examination of Spanish import requirements and their own potential to meet them. As observed above, Berlin was well aware of Spanish economic and military shortages, but in addition to the difficulty of making the required goods available there was also the transport problem. The only effective lines of communication were the railway line from Bordeaux via Hendaye, Irun, and San Sebastian to Burgos and the road running more or less parallel to it. Both, however, were, along certain sections, under easy surveillance from the sea and hence easily cut.[277] Despite this problem the German foreign ministry, to be prepared for all eventualities, gave instructions that Spain's real requirements should be investigated, but without attracting attention.[278] Initial investigations led to the

---

[273] *DGFP* D IX, No. 488, pp. 620–1 (19 June 1940); see also I.III.1 (*b*) below.
[274] *Survey of International Affairs*, vii. 286 ff.
[275] *DGFP* D ix, No. 476, pp. 605–6 (17 June 1940).
[276] See n. 274 above; *DGFP* D x, No. 3, pp. 2–3 (23 June 1940); No. 16, pp. 15–16 (25 June 1940); No. 274, p. 396 (2 Aug. 1940): Ribbentrop to Ambassador von Stohrer in Madrid: 'Please come to Berlin to report, preferably by the end of the week . . . What we want to achieve now is Spain's early entry into the war.'
[277] *DGFP* D x, No. 313, pp. 442–5 (8 Aug. 1940).
[278] Ibid., No. 329, pp. 466–7 (12 Aug. 1940).

following findings.²⁷⁹ In order to satisfy civilian and military needs even temporarily Spain needed 400,000 t. of motor-fuel annually. With strict rationing 600,000 to 700,000 t. of wheat would be needed until the next harvest. Added to this were 200,000 t. of coal, at least 100,000 t. of diesel oil, 200,000 t. of fuel-oil and other mineral fuels, 40,000 t. of lubricating oil, 20,000 t. of petroleum, 35,000 t. of manganese ore, 100,000 to 150,000 t. of scrap, 100,000 t. of paper pulp, 25,000 t. of raw rubber, 100,000 t. of cotton, 48,000 t. of wood pulp, 55,000 t. of jute and Manila hemp, 30,000 t. of peanut seed, and 625,000 t. of nitrogen fertilizer; data on delivery times or possible minimum quantities are not available.

The OKW thereupon examined the extent to which the Reich could meet such expectations.²⁸⁰ Keitel first turned to Göring, who ruled out any aid to Franco on the suggested scale. Totally impossible, in his opinion, were any supplies of bread-grain, cotton, hemp, and mineral oils. In this respect Göring displayed greater reluctance than the OKW,²⁸¹ which, on the other hand, showed no great inclination to supply military equipment. The officers would have preferred the dispatch of complete German army formations. In the economic sector, however, the OKW discerned certain possibilities of meeting Franco's requests, although they were regarded as excessive. In contrast to the Spanish figures, it was thought that 6,000–7,000 t. of bread-grain, 4,000 t. of motor-fuel, and 25,000 t. of jute and Manila hemp might be made available. All the other commodities could be supplied either immediately or within a period to be decided, though with reservations concerning the amounts requested. Hitler was equally non-committal when, a short time after this report by the armed forces high command, he informed the 'dear Caudillo' that he was prepared 'to provide economic help to the greatest extent possible for Germany herself'.²⁸²

All these, of course, were offers with strings attached: the Germans were not handing out any free gifts. Indeed there was a feeling in Spain that Berlin's economic and military counter-demands were so extensive that they were harmful to Spanish interests. Madrid declared its readiness on principle to comply with the German expectations—even with regard to the use of African territory and the treatment of foreign capital in Spain—but national interests imposed clear limits.²⁸³ All this was discussed by Spanish and German economic

---

²⁷⁹ Ibid., No. 355, pp. 499–500 (16 Aug. 1940); No. 373, p. 521 (21 Aug. 1940).
²⁸⁰ Ibid., No. 404, p. 561 (27 Aug. 1940).
²⁸¹ *DGFP* D xi, No. 62, pp. 81–2 (16 Sept. 1940).
²⁸² Ibid., No. 70, pp. 106–7 (18 Sept. 1940); Hitler's letter was in reply to a message from Franco of 11 Sept. (ibid., No. 48, pp. 62–3) which Serrano Suñer, the minister of the interior, handed to him during his visit to Germany. Directly on this see Serrano Suñer, *Zwischen Hendaye*, 156–180. In his letter Hitler referred mainly to the talks he and Ribbentrop had conducted with Serrano Suñer: *DGFP* D xi, No. 63, pp. 83–91 (16 Sept. 1940), and No. 66, pp. 93–8 (17 Sept. 1940).
²⁸³ *DGFP* D xi, No. 97, pp. 166–74 (26 Sept. 1940), Serrano Suñer's talk with Ribbentrop on 24 Sept., here p. 169. See also Serrano Suñer's conversation with Ambassador von Stohrer on 25

experts in September 1940 on the occasion of Serrano Suñer's visit to Germany. But Hitler's summing up at the end of the month showed what little progress the negotiators had made on this point. Sarcastically he observed to Ciano:[284]

> The Spanish proposals, somewhat crassly expressed, were as follows:
>
> (1) Germany is to deliver for the coming year 400,000–700,000 t. of grain;
> (2) Germany is to deliver all the fuel;
> (3) Germany is to deliver all the equipment which the army lacks;
> (4) Germany is to supply artillery and aeroplanes, as well as special weapons and special troops for the conquest of Gibraltar;
> (5) Germany is to hand over to Spain all of [French] Morocco and, beside that, Oran, and is to help her get a border revision west [*sic: must mean* south] of Rio de Oro;
> (6) Spain is to promise Germany, in return, her friendship.

Although exaggerated, Hitler's characterization of the Spanish and German positions is itself significant of the irritation prevailing in Berlin at the meagre results of the German–Spanish talks.[285] Hitler blamed Serrano Suñer for this disappointing development. Generalissimo Franco, whom he would meet in the foreseeable future, would—so Hitler hoped, misjudging the domestic power situation in Spain—be more obliging.[286]

The manner in which German–Spanish relations were developing after the armistice with France again showed up the principal weakness of the Axis—its dependence on raw-material imports, which, in the long term, proved to be Britain's decisive strategic advantage. The British saw this very clearly and consistently, and exploited their opportunity by conducting a policy of 'conditional assistance'. By means of finely calculated financial and material aid, neutral countries were to be prised or kept away from the influence of the Axis powers.[287]

The situation after the victory in the west, more than anything else, shows that the Second World War—regardless of the periods into which it may be divided—while representing, from an ideological and political point of view, the clash between liberal democratic concepts of order and totalitarian aggressive concepts of domination, was, in terms of everyday practice, also an economic war. The success of German arms in Poland, Denmark, Norway, The Netherlands, Belgium, and France was indeed impressive, but the conflict

---

Sept.: ibid., No. 104, pp. 183–4, and No. 116, pp. 199–200 (27 Sept. 1940). Serrano Suñer's talks in Berlin are extensively reported by Ruiz Holst, *Neutralität*, 93–115.

[284] *DGFP* D xi, No. 124, pp. 211–14 (29 Sept. 1940) conversation between Hitler and Ciano on 28 Sept., quotation p. 211.

[285] Ibid., No. 125, pp. 214 ff. (28 Sept. 1940); No. 126, pp. 216–19 (undated): 'Draft of an Agreement on Economic Questions in the Event of Spain's Entry into the War.'

[286] Detwiler, *Hitler*, 47; Trevor-Roper, 'Hitler und Franco', 625–34.

[287] *Survey of International Affairs*, vii. 64.

had more than just a military dimension. It was the supply of Spain with coal, rubber, cotton, and above all wheat, thanks to British money and British influence, that saved the country from economic collapse in the summer of 1940 and made it possible for Franco to pursue a relatively independent policy towards Hitler after the German–French armistice. This situation remained unchanged during the second half of 1940.[288] Hence Franco's willingness, signalled to Hitler in June 1940 as a return for a rounding-off of his African territory, 'to enter the war after a short period of preparing the public'[289] should not be rated too highly.[290] Although the Caudillo professed that he intended to take this step if Britain continued the war, this would seem to suggest that he did not expect her to do so. In other words, as the war was apparently about to end—and he was not alone in believing this—Franco intended to realize Spain's ambitions without any great risk.[291] The uncertainties of June, however, soon gave way to the realization that the war would go on. And when, in September 1940, the Spanish supply situation reached crisis-point, Anglo-American policy was provided with the scope of action indicated above.[292]

Even at the peak of the war in Europe in 1941, when Franco was acting with increasing self-confidence *vis-à-vis* Washington and London—for a while there seemed to be a danger that Spain would enter the war—the British in particular continued to place their trust in the efficacy of economic pressure. This weapon was handled by them with great skill, and ultimately with success. By the beginning of 1942, if not earlier, once the crises of 1941 had been overcome, it could be considered a certainty that Spain, largely owing to the 'conditional assistance' policy, would stay out of the war.[293]

---

[288] Cf. *DGFP* D xi, No. 198, pp. 329 ff. (19 Oct. 1940): 'Economic Questions Pending with Spain.' The Spanish government refused to stop deliveries of raw materials to Britain, although Berlin had been wanting this since June, because 'supplies vital to Spain—grain and gasoline, for example—depend on the goodwill of the English'. On the persisting efforts to get Spain to enter the war see I.III.1 (*b*), 2 (*a, b*) below. The (unsuccessfully discussed) economic problems to which Franco kept referring in order to justify his intransigence, his detailed demands, and the actual economic situation all emerge from *DGFP* D xi, No. 335, pp. 574 ff. (14 Nov. 1940); all further documents ibid.: No. 340, pp. 581 ff. (15 Nov. 1940); No. 398, pp. 705–6 (25 Nov. 1940); No. 420, pp. 739 ff. (29 Nov. 1940); No. 444, pp. 777–8 (3 Dec. 1940); No. 479, pp. 824–5 (9 Dec. 1940); No. 497, pp. 847–50 (11 Dec. 1940); No. 500, pp. 852–3 (12 Dec. 1940); No. 577, pp. 975–6 (29 Dec.1940); No. 627, pp. 1054–5 (8 Jan. 1941); No. 629, p. 1056 (8 Jan. 1941); No. 677, pp. 1140–3 (20 Jan. 1941); No. 682, pp. 1157–8 (21 Jan. 1941); No. 695, pp. 1173 ff. (23 Jan. 1940); No. 702, pp. 1183–4 (24 Jan. 1941); No. 707, pp. 1188–91 (25 Jan. 1941); No. 718 ff. (27 Jan. 1941); No. 728, pp. 1222–3 (29 Jan. 1941). For the British measures cf. *Churchill and Roosevelt*, C-41x, 86–7 (23 Nov. 1940). Churchill recommends that Roosevelt solve Spain's food-supply problem by American deliveries in order to keep the country out of the war.

[289] *DGFP* D ix, No. 488, pp. 620–1 (19 June 1940).

[290] This impression is created by Abendroth, 'Spanien', 116–17.

[291] *FRUS* (1940), ii. 798 ff. (17 June 1940), showing that the American ambassador, Alexander W. Weddell, correctly assessed Franco's intentions and the situation in Spain.

[292] Ibid. 805–8 (7 Sept. 1940).

[293] In greater detail *Survey of International Affairs*, vii. 288–91; Woodward, *British Foreign Policy*, i. 439–43, 447–52.

4. Axis Powers after Victory in the West

(d) Zones of Conflict: The Near and Middle East

(i) TURKEY

Turkey[294]—situated between the Black Sea and the Mediterranean, bordering on Greece, Bulgaria, the Soviet Union, Iran, Iraq, and Syria, and in possession of the Dardanelles and the Bosporus—was in some respects comparable to Spain. This was true particularly for the time after the Balkan campaign, when, depending on how one looked at it, she represented the last barrier guarding the British position in the Middle East, or the gateway to it. Because of its geo-strategic position and its possession of certain raw materials this weak country, even during the preliminary phase of the Second World War, had been the object of German, British, and French political and economic interest. It was accordingly wooed, and the Turkish government, even before the outbreak of war in 1939, moved closer to the Western powers.[295]

This development had not been foreseen by Germany, since there were strong economic ties between Berlin and Ankara in the pre-war period. Between 1933 and 1939 German imports from Turkey rose from RM37.9m. to RM122.6m. In 1939 Turkey supplied over 60 per cent of German requirements of chromium ore. These are impressive figures, though they do not reveal much about the economic structure of German–Turkish relations. Thus German imports from Turkey and exports to Turkey both amounted to less than 3 per cent of total German imports and exports during that period. However, Germany held top place in Turkish exports and imports: in 1938 some 39.7 per cent of exports went to Germany and 45 per cent of imports came from there. These figures clearly demonstrate Ankara's enormous economic dependence on Berlin. Nevertheless, Turkey's *rapprochement* with the Western powers in 1939 did not, basically, come as a surprise, as it stemmed from predictable objective political and economic circumstances.

There were basically two reasons for the reorientation of Turkish economic policy and the concomitant new course in foreign policy: firstly, it resulted from the realization that excessively German-orientated foreign trade might lay the country open to political blackmail. Economic experts pointed to this danger, and from 1938 onwards, initially only in order to gain greater flexibility in foreign trade, an attempt was made to find new markets. This, however, was a problematical enterprise, as there were scarcely any market gaps for tobacco or Mediterranean fruit. The only possible trading partner was Britain, which was at the time trying to check German influence in the Balkans and beyond, which it saw as a threat to the British position in the Middle East. London might therefore be willing to pay a political price for Turkish merchandise, in order to keep Ankara out of the German 'greater economic

---

[294] Interaction with events in the Balkans will be touched upon here only marginally; these events are more fully discussed at II.1, 11 below.
[295] Onder, *Die türkische Außenpolitik*, 17–35.

sphere'. From the Turkish point of view, however, a *rapprochement* with Britain did not mean a total rejection of Germany. The Turkish government merely used the rivalry between Germany and Britain to gain greater independence for itself.

Secondly—and this is another reason why Ankara so soon abandoned its newly won independence from blocs—the Italian attack on Albania in April 1939, following shortly upon the crushing of rump Czechoslovakia by the Germans, aroused suspicions among the Turks. They assumed that these were the beginnings of a concerted operation by the Axis powers, one that would, in the long run, be continued in the Balkans.[296] A few weeks after these events, on 12 May 1939, Ankara and London made a declaration of mutual assistance, conceived as a preliminary to a treaty; France issued a similar declaration on 23 June.[297]

Turkey was thus steering a pro-British course. Berlin reacted with indignation and disappointment, but could do nothing. Eventually the Germans consoled themselves with the thought that the Turkish decision was primarily directed against Italy. But Mussolini was Hitler's partner, and the Turkish government was well aware that the Duce had no intention of calming the Turks by a show of repentance. Hitler had no influence in this respect, a fact most clearly revealed by his feigned enthusiasm for the Italian intention of 'making Albania a stronghold which will inexorably dominate the Balkans'.[298] Actually, as we have seen, the Italian move did not suit him at all.

Yet despite the British–Turkish *rapprochement* the Reich government remained politically irresolute.[299] It only resorted to economic pressures and sanctions, such as a suspension of deliveries of war material ordered by Turkey. Thereupon İsmet İnönü, the Turkish president, threatened to restrict chrome exports to the Reich. As Germany could not easily find a substitute for Turkish chrome—in 1939 the record quantity of 115,000 t. was imported—Ankara had a very effective means of pressure available. Nevertheless, any fall-off in reciprocal trade was ultimately bound to hurt Turkey more than Germany. For the moment, however, Berlin left matters open. Having in mind the treaty between Turkey and Britain, foreshadowed since May 1939, Berlin hoped thus to exert pressure on Turkey to limit her ties with Britain, in other words to consider possible German reaction. Turkey, on the other hand, had long been planning extensive trade co-operation with the Western powers as a substitute for her German market. Hence Ankara did not renew the German–Turkish

---

[296] Generally on this: Ackermann, 'Türkei', 491–4; Glasneck and Kircheisen, *Türkei und Afghanistan*, 20–34, 36–43; Krecker, *Deutschland*, 22–5; Onder, *Die türkische Außenpolitik*, 101–5.
[297] Krecker, *Deutschland*, 32–40, 49 ff.; ifid. 256, publication of the British–Turkish declaration of mutual assistance in French; Onder, *Die türkische Außenpolitik*, 17–22, though at p. 19 he already, erroneously, refers to an 'assistance pact'; pp. 22–3 on the Turkish–French declaration of 23 June 1939.
[298] Ciano, *Diary 1939–1943*, 90–1 (21 May 1939).
[299] Ackermann, 'Türkei', 495–6.

clearing agreement, which regulated the exchange of chrome and agricultural produce in return for German items of armament, when it expired on 31 August.[300] This did in fact lessen Turkish dependence on Germany; however, in November 1939 Turkey indicated that Germany was again free to purchase chrome, but before an offer could be made to her, Turkey would have to assess its own capacity to increase production. At the end of 1939, therefore, Turkey does not yet seem to have been interested in a complete break with Germany.[301]

For an adequate understanding of Ankara's *rapprochement* with London and Paris we should remember Turkish anxieties about the German–Italian policy of aggression in south-east Europe. After Prague and Tirana the Turks no longer ruled out an attack on their country. And as the convergence of German and Italian policy, which had become increasingly perceptible since the Abyssinian war, took on clear outlines with the Pact of Steel in May 1939, Turkish suspicions naturally grew.[302] The conclusion of the non-aggression treaty between Germany and the Soviet Union on 23 August 1939 increased nervousness in Ankara. Until then, good Turco-Soviet relations had been an important element in the political calculations of the Ankara government. Turkey, moreover, seemed to have assumed in the past that the USSR would give military support to resistance to any German–Italian aggression in the Balkan region. All this was now called into question. From the Turkish point of view, the Soviet Union was resuming its role of Turkey's traditional enemy, anxiously waiting for an opportunity to renew its claim to the Straits.[303]

The Germans, whose relations with Ankara at that time, as our observations on economic contacts have shown, were strained anyway, made the most of the new situation. In his address to the Wehrmacht commanders-in-chief at the Obersalzberg on 22 August 1939, expressing his triumph at the agreements of 21 August, which Ribbentrop was to seal in Moscow on 23 August, Hitler remarked on the situation in the Turkish and Balkan area: 'Since Albania there has been a balance of power in the Balkans. Yugoslavia carries within herself the fatal germ of decay because of her internal conditions. Romania has not grown any stronger. She is threatened by Hungary and Bulgaria. Since Kemal's death Turkey has been ruled by small minds, by rootless weak people.'[304] But despite this derogatory comment, which betrayed a certain lack of interest, Berlin, following suggestions by Franz von Papen, the German ambassador in Ankara, tried to induce the Soviet Union to exert pressure on Turkey. Germany was primarily interested in a complete closure of the Straits

---

[300] Krecker, *Deutschland*, 41–4; Onder, *Die türkische Außenpolitik*, 103 ff.

[301] DGFP D viii, No. 390, pp. 451–2 (27 Nov. 39); the interpretation of this document by Onder, *Die türkische Außenpolitik*, 104–5, is untenable.

[302] Krecker, *Deutschland*, 20–1; Onder, *Die türkische Außenpolitik*, 17; cf. also Catalano, *Trionfo dei fascismi*, 263 ff., on international rivalries in the eastern Mediterranean during the first six months of 1939.

[303] Ackermann, 'Türkei', 496.

[304] Domarus, *Hitler*, ii. 1235.

and in permanent Turkish neutrality. Moscow was thought to have used its influence along these lines,[305] and the Turkish president reportedly showed understanding for the Soviet warning against excessive compliance towards London. In other words, Ankara declared itself willing to avoid any decisions which might offend Moscow.[306]

When, after the German attack on Poland, Turkey declared herself 'outside the war', German hopes that Ankara would after all observe strict neutrality seemed to be fulfilled.[307] To the Turkish statesmen, however—largely as a result of Soviet participation in the occupation of Poland, as well as the German–Soviet frontier and friendship treaty of 28 September 1939, actions which revealed a new dimension of German–Soviet co-operation—it soon became clear that the most effective protection of national interests would be afforded by close ties with the Western Allies. But this did not mean that military intervention in the conflict was intended.[308] On the contrary, to keep out of the war continued to be the declared aim of the Turkish government.

This attitude remained unchanged when, in October, the project of a Turco-Soviet treaty of mutual aid, discussed between Moscow and Ankara, came to nothing, mainly because Turkey did not wish to comply either with the Soviet demand for a reduction of Turkish obligations towards Britain and France or with that for a joint defence of the Straits.[309] But the basic stance of Turkish policy remained unchanged even when Ankara on 19 October, immediately after the breakdown of the negotiations in Moscow, concluded an assistance treaty with the two Western powers. Although, as mentioned above, this was a reaction to what was felt to be a threatening German–Soviet policy, great importance was attached to ensuring that the treaty should not place a strain on Turkish–Soviet relations.

The treaty had a life of fifteen years and was essentially in line with the provisional promises of assistance made in May and June.[310] It provided, among other things, that Turkey would receive assistance in the event of any attack on her by a European power (Article 1) or of her being involved in a war of aggression waged by other states and leading to warlike conflicts in the Mediterranean area (Article 2 (2)). Turkish obligations were more limited. Great Britain and France were entitled to Turkish assistance only in an event analogous to Article 2 (2), as stipulated in Section 1 of the same article, or

---

[305] *DGFP* D viii, No. 6, p. 5 (5 Sept. 1939).
[306] Onder, *Die türkische Außenpolitik*, 28–9.
[307] Ackermann, 'Türkei', 496.
[308] Krecker, *Deutschland*, 57 ff.
[309] Onder, *Die türkische Außenpolitik*, 28 ff.
[310] Text of treaty in Cmd. 6165 (HMSO, 1940). On the close links between the conclusion of a military-aid agreement and the concessions made by London to Ankara see Weber, *Evasive Neutral*, 44–5. Lord Halifax, for instance, feared that the purchasing obligations undertaken vis-à-vis Turkey might render London incapable of paying for the arms supplies negotiated with the US and Canada.

4. Axis Powers after Victory in the West

in the event of their being involved in hostilities while implementing their guarantees to Greece and Romania (Article 3).

Ankara achieved a very substantial limitation of its obligations by the 'Russian clause' in 'Protocol 2', in which the parties declared that Turkey's obligations were not to have the effect, directly or indirectly, of compelling her to go to war with the Soviet Union. This reservation proved subsequently to be of considerable importance. But in the specific situation of the autumn of 1939, Moscow, for whose pacification the Turks had specially included the Russian clause, at first reacted very violently. Molotov spoke of an agreement which sealed Turkey's adherence to the Western powers and was not conducive to peace in the Black Sea region. Relations between the two countries remained tense for several months.[311]

Italy, on the other hand, which should have felt most directly affected by the treaty, reacted calmly. Ciano noted in his diary that he was actually quite pleased about the agreement because it was a score against Germany. This confirms the observation made in connection with Italy's entry into the war, that it was in line with her interests for Germany to suffer some reverses. That was why Rome in October 1939 was satisfied with the assurance from Paris that the treaty was designed solely to maintain the status quo in the Mediterranean and did not represent any anti-Italian action. Although Ciano had his doubts about the sincerity of this statement, he was content with it.[312] At the same time, the Italians were aware of the German disappointment at the Turkish move. Göring, in order to stir up a reaction in Rome, insisted, in conversation with the Italian ambassador in Berlin, on the anti-Italian objectives of the treaty. Attolico's impression was that the Germans were disappointed because Soviet pressure had not produced the desired effect in Ankara.[313] But even after this direct thrust Ciano merely informed Berlin that Rome did not consider that there was any point in an official protest; Italy would show restraint and await developments.[314]

By contrast, Ribbentrop displayed great annoyance at the conclusion of the treaty when Hüsrev R. Gerede, the Turkish ambassador in Berlin, called on him on 11 November to convey his congratulations on the Führer's escape from the assassination attempt in Munich. Ribbentrop warned him that Turkey had 'thereby joined the anti-German front'. Turkish policy was directed against Germany, as could also be seen from the fact that Ankara had wished to conclude an assistance pact with Moscow only if this was also aimed against Germany.[315]

The treaty of October 1939, however, apart from its military and political results, also entailed economic consequences for the Reich. The German–

---

[311] Onder, *Die türkische Außenpolitik*, 33–4.
[312] Ciano, *Diary 1939–1943*, 299 (19 Oct. 1939).
[313] *DDI*, 9th ser, i, No. 832, pp. 531–2 (21 Oct. 1939).
[314] Ibid. ii, No. 7, p. 2 (25 Oct. 1939).
[315] *DGFP* D viii, No. 347, pp. 398–9 (11 Nov. 1939).

Turkish trade and payment agreement had not been renewed, and trade between the two countries had taken place, since 31 August, in conditions not covered by any agreement. Since October, moreover, London had increasingly been urging Ankara to suspend deliveries of chromium ore to Germany. However, friction arose in the Anglo-Turkish trade talks because Turkey had to sell not only ores but also tobacco and fruit, commodities not then in short supply in Britain, and the British, who were at that time trying to catch up on their lag in armaments, had difficulties in supplying Turkey with the finished products she required. Yet despite all problems, by the end of the year Britain displaced Germany, both in exports and in imports, from the leading place among Turkey's trading partners. British credits for Ankara reached a volume of £60m., and a trade agreement of 8 January 1940 assured the Western powers of Turkey's entire chromium-ore production for a period of two years. The Reich had been finally jettisoned. Although at the outbreak of the war Germany had stockpiles of chromium to cover thirteen months' requirements, added to which were the supplies from the Soviet Union, Norway, Greece, and Yugoslavia, the loss of the Turkish exports was nevertheless painful, especially if the war was to be protracted or if—as happened after the attack against the Soviet Union—some of the existing sources of supply were lost.[316] It seemed an obvious step for Germany to vie with Britain for economic arrangements with Turkey in order to prevent the latter from sliding totally into the Allied camp. Although Germany still had some levers of economic pressure available to her, the attempt to have the deliveries of chromium ore resumed[317] was a failure.

Since, following the meeting between Hitler and Mussolini on 18 March 1940, Italy's entry into the war was beginning to seem likely in the near future, the question was being asked in Berlin as to how Turkey would react in that event, since according to the treaty of October 1939 the *casus belli* would then arise. For Germany, which was not anxious to see Ankara enter the war, the 'Russian clause' of the treaty therefore became the focus of consideration. Clearly the best course was to induce Turkey to believe herself sufficiently threatened by the Soviet Union to be entitled, 'if necessary, to invoke this clause'.[318] The Turkish government saw matters very similarly. A few weeks later Turkish diplomats made highly qualified remarks on their country's obligation of assistance. This obligation could not, of course, be

---

[316] Glasneck and Kircheisen, *Türkei und Afghanistan*, 55; Krecker, *Deutschland*, 75–9; *Survey of International Affairs*, vii. 30.

[317] The type of bargain envisaged by both Ankara and Berlin emerges in detail from: *DGFP* D viii, No. 339, pp. 380 ff. (7 Nov. 1939); No. 333, p. 385 (8 Nov. 1939); No. 339, pp. 390–1 (9 Nov. 1939); No. 390, pp. 451–2 (27 Nov. 1939); No. 391, pp. 452–3 (Nov. 39); No. 408, pp. 475–6 (1 Dec. 1939); No. 516, pp. 634–5 (9 Jan. 1940); No. 517, pp. 635–6 (9 Jan. 1940); No. 625, pp. 790–1 (21 Feb. 1940); No. 681, p. 931 (17 Mar. 1940); ibid. ix, No. 30, pp. 55 ff. (30 Mar. 1940).

[318] Ibid. ix, No. 10, pp. 27–8 (24 Mar. 1940); this calculation was more or less vindicated: cf. Barclay, *Their Finest Hour*, 2.

4. Axis Powers after Victory in the West

disputed, but provided Italy attacked neither the Balkans nor Turkish territory, Turkey would refrain from any kind of warlike action, in the hope that in this way the Balkans and the Near East would virtually be spared from the war.[319] Germany, which since 30 May at the latest was aware that Mussolini's military intentions were largely in line with Turkish ideas—the Duce, for the time being, did not wish to extend the conflict in the east and wanted the shortest possible war in the west—therefore viewed future developments calmly,[320] even though Italy, prior to 10 June, refused to make any binding declarations.

After Mussolini's entry into the war the impression arose in Ankara that Italy had no intention of attacking any Balkan countries or Turkey herself.[321] The indications from Rome did not sound implausible. The situation enabled Ankara to delay its own participation in the war, at least until it was proved wrong. In view of Germany's rapid successes in France, Turkey therefore indicated at an early date that she would invoke the Russian clause. Turkish obligingness in her economic discussions with Germany, President İnönü's resolute language when the British pressed him to meet his treaty obligations —he offered to return to them the financial aid granted to Turkey, but not to enter the war—and the content of the lively exchange of information between the Turks and the German ambassador in Ankara all showed that there could be little doubt about Turkey's attitude.[322]

The German victory in the west was a major factor in the struggle for Turkey's neutrality or entry into the war. And the developments of May–June 1940 clearly played the decisive role in a cautious reorientation of Turkish policy towards Berlin. In June a German–Turkish trade agreement was signed, covering the appreciable volume of RM42m. Germany, however, was unable to obtain the chromium ore she desired; on this point the Turks adhered strictly to their agreement with the Western powers. As for supplies of grain,

---

[319] *DGFP* D ix, No. 200, p. 288 (6 May 1940); report of Franz von Papen, the German ambassador in Ankara, to the foreign ministry. The ambassador suggested that the Italian government should issue a statement about the Balkans indicating that it harboured no aggressive intentions against Turkey. There was a lively exchange of ideas on this subject between the foreign ministry, the ambassador in Rome, and Papen, with Ribbentrop eventually (on 31 May) closing the discussion by ruling: 'Joint German–Italian action for the purpose of strengthening Turkey's intention to remain neutral seems to us neither expedient nor necessary in the present situation.' On this issue generally: *DGFP* D ix, No. 244, p. 341 (14 May 1940); No. 245, pp. 341–2 (14 May 1940); No. 265, pp. 364ff. (15 May 1940); No. 324, pp. 443–4 (27 May 1940), quotation from n. 2. On the role of the Soviet Union see Krecker, *Deutschland*, 82–6; on Italian–Turkish relations in detail Weber, *Evasive Neutral*, 46–53.

[320] *DGFP* D ix, No. 356, p. 483 (30 May 1940). Hitler unreservedly supported the intention of keeping the Balkans out of the conflict: ibid., No. 357, pp. 484ff. (31 May 1940).

[321] Krecker, *Deutschland*, 86; on the Turkish plans in June 1940 see also Ackermann, 'Türkei', 497.

[322] Generally on this: *DGFP* D ix, No. 264, p. 363 (17 May 1940); No. 375, pp. 506–7 (3 June 1940); No. 383, pp. 513–14 (4 June 1940); No. 424, p. 560 (13 June 1940); No. 431, p. 566 (14 June 1940); this establishes the connection with the 'Russian clause', though the statement was 'not to be published for the time being'; also No. 464, p. 595 (17 June 1940); cf. Barclay, *Their Finest Hour*, 2.

olive oil, and oil-seed, the commodities most wanted by Germany, only a portion of the German requests were met by the Turks. Also needed were tobacco, hides, mohair, nuts, and raisins. Germany for her part supplied finished industrial products, such as 39 locomotives and 118 railway coaches and freight-cars, although these were in short supply.[323]

Compared with the pre-war arrangements outlined earlier, this agreement was of modest scope. Its economic importance was slight. But when it was signed on 25 July 1940 Berlin was more interested in it as a foreign-policy success. To exploit it to the full, it was made very clear to the Turks that any progress with the bridge-building just begun would greatly depend on whether Ankara would distance itself from London or not. German threats and enticements had yielded a first, if very limited, success in June–July: at least, the British monopoly in trade with Turkey was broken. Hitler could therefore expect, given a favourable development of the military situation, that more might be achieved later.[324] To anticipate, this did in fact happen in October 1941, when Berlin and Ankara signed a new trade agreement.[325]

The Germans resorted to massive political pressure when they published the secret papers of the French general staff, discovered at La Charité in the course of the western campaign. The documents were represented as evidence of Turkish approval of a British–French operation—more strictly, its planning—against the Soviet oilfields at Baku.[326] This is not the place for a detailed account of this affair, in connection with which the Germans did not even shrink from forgery.[327] The documents were published in the so-called Sixth German White Book—one of those concoctions by which National Socialist propaganda, as a rule effectively, attempted to minimize or even justify German acts of aggression—and certainly caused the intended international uproar. The Turkish foreign minister, in particular, found himself in considerable trouble,[328] which was entirely in the German interest, because the Reich chancellery, the foreign ministry, and von Papen, the ambassador

---

[323] *DGFP* D ix, No. 434, pp. 568–72 (14 June 1940); Glasneck and Kircheisen, *Türkei und Afghanistan*, 57–8.
[324] *DGFP* D x, No. 213, p. 279 (23 July 1940).
[325] Krecker, *Deutschland*, 80.
[326] The possibility of an Allied move towards Baku—as well as an offensive in the Balkans (a landing in Romania, an attack through Salonika or from European Turkey)—had been considered by the Germans at an early stage. Within the range of possible German responses mention was even made, among other things, of a joint German–Russian operation, starting from Transcaucasia, against the British position in the Middle East. Such ideas, however, had no direct effect on German policy in that region. See OKW Nr. 494/40 g.Kdos. WFA/Abt. L Ausl/Abw, 21 Mar. 1940, 'Die militärpolitische Lage im Nahen Orient' (12 pages). BA-MA RW 4/v. 35. On the Allies cf. also Lorbeer, *Westmächte*; for plans up to the summer of 1940 ibid. 39–85; Buffotot, 'Le projet'; Richardson, 'French Plans'; generally also Kahle, *Kaukasusprojekt*.
[327] Krecker, *Deutschland*, 93–4; the appropriate changes were made by Deutsches Nachrichtenbüro, the official German news agency. Thus the documents disseminated within Germany stated, among other things, that Turkey was getting used to the idea of an 'offensive war' against the USSR, although the text clearly said 'defensive war'.
[328] *DGFP* D x, No. 148, pp. 183–4 (10 July 1940); No. 179, pp. 230–4 (16 July 1940).

4. Axis Powers after Victory in the West

in Ankara, all hoped for the replacement of Şükrü Saracoğlu, a known Anglophile.[329]

Although Germany did not achieve the desired result with this intrigue, it proved effective against its second target: Turkish–Soviet relations came under a major strain. Conditions for this were favourable anyway at the beginning of July, as relations between Moscow and Ankara had been strained since the end of June 1940.[330] This was precisely the situation Berlin had hoped for,[331] its ultimate aim[332] being to keep the 'situation between Russia and Turkey unstable'. What Germany had to prevent—and what Britain was just then working for[333]—was for Turkey to become a connecting link between Britain and the Soviet Union.[334] Given this pattern of interests, which von Papen does not seem always to have judged correctly, it was hardly surprising that the German foreign ministry was pleased when President İnönü, immediately before concluding the German–Turkish trade agreement, rejected a Soviet demand for the return of the two Caucasian provinces of Kars and Ardahan, which were formerly Russian and were ceded to Turkey after the First World War; he also rejected Moscow's request for the granting of military bases on the Dardanelles. If the Soviet Union insisted on its demands, İnönü informed Moscow, 'the only thing left was war'.[335]

None of this, however, was a reason for Turkey to move away decisively from Britain, and German–Turkish relations did not, in consequence, become any more open. They continued to be marked by mistrust. But Ankara believed that the imponderables of the German–Italian partnership and the special relationship between Berlin and Sofia, with regard to Bulgarian ambitions in Thrace, on the one hand, and the Soviet threat to Turkey on the other, called for a degree of compromise with Berlin at the same time as preservation of British support.[336] The Turks were interested primarily in not tying themselves too closely either to Berlin or to London or Moscow.

German–Turkish relations were affected by the Italian attack on Greece on 28 October 1940, the failure of Molotov's visit to Berlin on 12 and 13 November 1940, and Hitler's decision in favour of military intervention in the Balkans. There was also the German engagement in North Africa. These events will be discussed in detail elsewhere.[337] Relations between the two

---

[329] Krecker, *Deutschland*, 90–5, in detail.
[330] *DGFP* D x, No. 58, pp. 60–1 (29 June 1940).
[331] Ibid., No. 71, pp. 77–8 (1 July 1940).
[332] Hillgruber, *Strategie*, 113–14, 232–3.
[333] *DGFP* D x, No. 202, p. 263 (22 July 1940).
[334] Ibid., No. 272, p. 393 (1 Aug. 1940): Papen to Weizsäcker on the outcome of his talks with Hitler and Ribbentrop. In line with these directives Papen on 16 Aug. called on President İnönü, whose order for the mobilization of the entire Turkish army in Thrace and on the Bosporus, directed primarily against the USSR, he expressly welcomed: ibid., No. 349, pp. 488–9 (16 Aug. 1940).
[335] Ibid., No. 214, pp. 280–1 (23 July 1940).
[336] See Ackermann, 'Türkei', 497; Creveld, *Balkan*, 76; Krecker, *Deutschland*, 95–8.
[337] *Das Deutsche Reich und der Zweite Weltkrieg*, iv. 29 ff. (Förster).

countries acquired a new dimension in March 1941, when Hitler assured İnönü that he had no aggressive intentions towards Turkey. This eased the situation for Ankara very considerably. The account of German–Turkish relations, which were governed meanwhile by events in the Balkans, will be resumed in due course in order to examine developments over the period between the German–Italian victory over Greece and the conclusion of the treaty of friendship between Turkey and the Reich on 18 June 1941.[338]

The question of the consequences which the German–French armistice had for Germany, and of course also for her Italian ally, cannot, however, be fully answered without an examination, both retrospective and topical, of Berlin's relations with the countries of the Middle East and the Arab world.

(ii) AFGHANISTAN

The Außenpolitisches Amt—the foreign-policy department of the National Socialist party—was particularly interested in good German–Afghan relations, believing that imperial Germany had failed to exploit its opportunities in 'Hither Asia' between 1914 and 1918.[339] On its initiative a number of 'fundamental state treaties' were concluded between the Reich and Afghanistan in the military, cultural, and economic spheres in 1936–7. The long-term objective was to make the country less dependent on its neighbours and, more important, to make possible its neutrality in a German–British war; the possibility was even considered of using it, 'if necessary, against British India or Soviet Russia'.[340]

Soon the German colony was the biggest European group in Afghanistan. Officers of the Wehrmacht were in charge of the modernization of the army. Up-to-date war material arrived from Germany. German experts reorganized the police and the secret service. Under the 'Dr Todt agreement' the Reich was responsible for the development of the road system and for all agricultural and industrial planning. In addition, there were agreements on joint exploitation of Afghan mineral deposits, the establishment of German–Afghan construction and transport companies, and the extension and improvement of the production of raw materials of particular interest to Germany. At the end of 1939 Afghanistan and Iran were the Reich's only suppliers of cotton and wool.[341] Kabul maintained its own European import centre in Berlin, and

---

[338] See IV.II.2, 3 below.

[339] Rosenberg, *Tagebuch*, 187 (18 Dec. 1939), 235 (8 July 1941); see also the summary in Fischer, *Griff nach der Weltmacht*, 113–16; basically on German policy in his Middle East during the First World War: Gehrke, *Persien*, passim; on Afghanistan, ibid. 21–8, 53–7, 66–72; Glasneck and Kircheisen, *Türkei und Afghanistan*, 206–10.

[340] See Rosenberg, *Tagebuch*, entry of 18 Dec. 1939 concerning Afghanistan: 'Objectives of the foreign-policy department of the NSDAP' (187–93) and appendix 'Ongoing Co-operation with the Afghan Government' (193–4); directly on this *DGFP* D viii, No. 470, pp. 550–5 (18 Dec. 1939), nn. 1 and 8. The contacts of the foreign-policy department were subject to strictest secrecy: see Hillgruber, *Strategie*, 383–4 n. 34.

[341] On relations between Iran and Germany between 1921 and 1941 see the comprehensive study by Hirschfeld, *Deutschland und Iran*, 196–209, on economic relations during 1938/9; directly on the economic complex also Mahrad, *Wirtschafts- und Handelsbeziehungen*.

from 1939 an economic and credit agreement assured Germany of deliveries of important Afghan raw materials to a value of RM11m. in exchange for German finished goods. This represented a tenfold increase of foreign trade within two years.[342] The National Socialists, moreover, involved themselves intensively in the entire educational and vocational training system of the country.[343]

It should be pointed out that Rosenberg's foreign-policy department and Ribbentrop's foreign ministry held divergent opinions when, immediately before the beginning of the war in 1939, the question of how Afghanistan could best be integrated into the German conduct of the war was discussed. The Party's foreign-policy department consistently supported the government in power in Kabul, thanks to whom Germany had succeeded in gaining a strong position in the country. Rosenberg in particular relied on Abdul Majid Khan, the minister of trade and president of the National Bank, one of the strongest supporters of close relations with Berlin, and regarded as the strong man of the Afghan government. In the summer of 1939, before the attack on Poland, Majid Khan had put forward 'proposals for the event of a German–British conflict', which 'envisaged the closest internal alignment with Germany'. These proposals were to be implemented in several steps, though 'Afghanistan's precarious position *vis-à-vis* the Soviet Union' would have to be taken into account.[344] The German foreign ministry, on the other hand, sought to achieve Germany's aims by the overthrow of the Afghan government and the restoration—if possible, with Soviet support—of King Amanullah, who had been living in exile since 1929.[345] As a result of Rosenberg's intervention Hitler finally turned down this plan; and in July 1941, when the matter gained renewed topicality in connection wih Operation Barbarossa, Berlin officially gave its support to Abdul Majid Khan.[346]

Shortly after the German–French armistice Majid Khan notified Hans Pilger, the German minister in Kabul, in strict confidence, that 'for the purpose of active participation in the German interest Afghanistan was ready to mobilize all opportunities arising from sentimental and religious ties, and especially to induce frontier tribes and the Afghan population in India to take action against the English, in order thereby to prevent the shipping of Indian troops to the Mediterranean both now and in the future'.[347] Although it was by no means certain that the minister was conveying the views of his govern-

---

[342] Glasneck and Kircheisen, *Türkei und Afghanistan*, 188 ff.; on the significance of the 'economic and credit agreement' of the summer of 1939 see Adamec, *Afghanistan*, 238–9.

[343] Glasneck and Kircheisen, *Türkei und Afghanistan*, 178–205, on Germany's growing influence on Afghanistan in the years following the National Socialist seizure of power.

[344] Rosenberg, *Tagebuch*, 235 ff. (8 July 1941), quotation p. 236.

[345] See *DGFP* D viii, No. 60, pp. 56–7 (13 Sept. 1939); No. 369, p. 419 (18 Nov. 1939); No. 449, pp. 527 ff. (12 Dec. 1939); a good summary of the competing ideas in the foreign ministry, the 'Foreign Policy Department', and the 'Abwehr' under Adm. Canaris may be found in Adamec, *Afghanistan*, 240–1.

[346] Glasneck and Kircheisen, *Türkei und Afghanistan*, 216–19; Hillgruber, *Strategie*, 384–5; Rosenberg, *Tagebuch*, 237 (8 July 1941).

[347] *DGFP* D x, No. 30, pp. 29–30 (27 June 1940): conversation between Pilger and Abdul Majid Khan on 26 June 1940; cf. Adamec, *Afghanistan*, 245–6.

ment colleagues,[348] he declared himself convinced of his ability to implement his intentions, provided Germany would ensure, both during the planned advance and fundamentally 'in every respect', that Afghanistan's integrity was guaranteed also by the Soviet Union. Equally indispensable was Berlin's support for 'awarding to Afghanistan an access to the sea',[349] and for Kabul to receive aircraft, tanks, and anti-aircraft guns in the quantities it required. Majid Khan also indicated that the countries united in the Saadabad non-aggression treaty of 8 July 1937—Afghanistan, Iraq, and Iran, as well as Turkey (though he dared not be too sure on this point)—were 'inclined to harmonize their policies with Germany's', in order to 'preclude' any Italian–Soviet 'game of intrigues'.

Kabul was presumably pursuing a double objective with these soundings: to find out what attitude the German government would adopt towards Afghanistan after the conclusion of the war, and meanwhile 'to share in imminent decisions in order to obtain advantages'.[350] As Berlin failed to reply, the Afghan government, through its ambassador Faiz Mohammed Khan, approached von Papen in Ankara in order 'to find out what the aims of the Axis powers really are with regard to the small countries of the world'. Germany should state her position on this point, for the Reich 'had a great many friends, many more than she knew of, but she had to show them the direction which the new order of the world would take'. To the Afghan envoy it must have been highly unsatisfactory that the German ambassador, in response to these urgent questions, merely recommended him to 'study the principles of National Socialism' and to rest assured that 'after achieving victory' the National Socialists would 'proceed accordingly'. For the present, however, 'the issue was whether to decide for or against England'.[351] This was undoubtedly true, but Kabul was far more anxious to know 'whether German aims in Asia coincided with Afghan hopes'. In Afghanistan there was talk of liberating 15 million Afghans 'who were forced to suffer on Indian territory'; the view was held that 'justice would . . . be created only when the country's frontier had been extended to the Indus'.[352] Germany, moreover, should help to secure Afghanistan's northern frontier, at least diplomatically, so that in the south she could thrust forward as far as the Indian Ocean.[353]

---

[348] Glasneck and Kircheisen, *Türkei und Afghanistan*, 219, on the attitude of King Mohammed Zahir Shah.
[349] On British reflections on how their position might be consolidated in Afghanistan cf. Glasneck and Kircheisen, *Türkei und Afghanistan*, 219 ff. Since the autumn of 1939 London had been suggesting a mutual-assistance treaty which would protect Kabul against, among other things, German–Soviet aggression. As a lure the British used economic support and the offer to make available a port on the Arabian Sea, to be linked with Afghanistan by a corridor.
[350] Quotations from *DGFP* D x, No. 30, pp. 29–30 (27 June 1940).
[351] Ibid., No. 179, pp. 230–4 (16 July 1940), here p. 233.
[352] *DGFP* D xi, No. 145, pp. 240–1 (3 Oct. 1940).
[353] Rosenberg, *Tagebuch*, 145 (13 Sept. 1940); Rosenberg's information is in line with a conversation which the Afghan ambassador, just back from Kabul, had with State Secretary von Weizsäcker: cf. Adamec, *Afghanistan*, 246.

4. Axis Powers after Victory in the West

During those weeks of 1940 the concept of a large continental bloc was still under discussion as a kind of interim solution within the realization of Hitler's programme, implying, among other things, the establishment of a greater Soviet sphere. Accordingly, Berlin was unable to adopt any binding position on the offers from Kabul. During Molotov's visit on 12–13 November the 'relation of Russia to Afghanistan and Iran' was originally to have been discussed;[354] Berlin intended, in line with Hitler's political tactics at the time, to make it clear that in those two countries Germany was not pursuing 'any interests opposed to Soviet Russia and would welcome intensified Soviet activity with regard to the two countries, which would be directed against England'.[355] In actual fact neither Hitler nor Ribbentrop touched on Afghanistan in their conversations with Molotov.[356] In Afghanistan, meanwhile, mistrust was spreading that the country was to be sacrificed to a German–Soviet arrangement of interests, although Hitler, especially after Molotov's visit, had no such intention. But that was something Berlin could not communicate to Kabul without endangering its eastern plans.[357] Not until 1941 did the stagnating German–Afghan relations come to life again—but this will be discussed in due course.[358]

(iii) THE ARAB WORLD

Germany's relations with the Arab countries have to be viewed against the two main objectives of German policy, the German–Italian alliance and the desire to achieve a worldwide composition of German and British interests. This dual goal was apt to give rise to complications in the Near and Middle East. It was probably also one of the reasons why German policy was slow to adopt an early and clear attitude towards the Arab world. A further complication arose in October 1936, when, in the context of the Axis partnership, Germany recognized the Mediterranean as a zone of Italian political, but not economic, influence. As economic influence must inevitably entail political consequences,[359] German–Italian friction was to be expected in the future.[360] This did in fact arise. Even more obvious, however, was the difficulty of winning London and Paris over for the idea behind the Berlin–Rome agreement, viz. to enable Mussolini to build up his Mediterranean empire by way of annexations and zones of influence. Any such plan would challenge the Western

---

[354] *DGFP* D xi (i), No. 317, pp. 521–2 (11 Nov. 1940).
[355] Quoted from Hillgruber, *Strategie*, 386; for confirmation see also No. 317 (see previous n.), n. 1.
[356] *DGFP* D xi, No. 325, pp. 533–41 (13 Nov. 1940); No. 326, pp. 541–9 (16 Nov. 1940); No. 328, pp. 550–62 (15 Nov. 1940); No. 329, pp. 562–70 (18 Nov. 1940).
[357] Hillgruber, *Strategie*, 386; Glasneck and Kircheisen, *Türkei und Afghanistan*, 222–3; Adamec, *Afghanistan*, 246–55.
[358] Cf. I.III.2 below.
[359] A detailed account of German economic relations with the countries of the Near and Middle East is provided by Tillmann, *Deutschlands Araberpolitik*, 16–37, esp. for 1935–9.
[360] Hirszowicz, *Third Reich*, 39 ff.

powers' hegemony in the Arab world, and they were bound to react accordingly, especially *vis-à-vis* the Reich. As Hitler, for a long time, remained interested in avoiding a German–British confrontation, German policy in the Arab world only began to take on anti-British features when the European conflict was being accelerated in Berlin and the plan was conceived to limit Britain's scope of action on the Continent by creating political difficulties for her outside Europe. This diversionary strategy of Hitler's, attested earlier in the German–Italian instance, can be documented also by German policy in the Arab world. This is shown specifically in the Palestine issue,[361] which had been one of the subjects of the San Remo conference (9–24 April 1920): there London and Paris reached agreement on the share-out of the estate of the Ottoman empire, which had broken up as a result of the First World War. Under the auspices of the League of Nations, Syria and Lebanon came under French, and Iraq, Transjordan, and Palestine under British mandatory administration, which was intended to prepare these countries for political independence.[362]

Palestine from the beginning occupied a special position among the mandated territories because London had undertaken to implement the Balfour declaration of 2 November 1917, i.e. to facilitate 'the establishment in Palestine of a national home for the Jewish people'. At the time that declaration was made the Allies were in a precarious position in the war, and the undertaking of Zionist leaders to support the Allies anywhere in the world, provided they undertook to promote the Palestine national-home project, was a weighty consideration. Admittedly the Allies 'forgot' to consult the Arabs affected, who, in consequence, insist to this day that Balfour had no right to make such a promise, and that therefore no legal claim could be derived from it. The Jewish view is very different: they argue that the 1917 promise was no more and no less than the restoration of a biblical right. They would of course have preferred London to have undertaken not only to promote but to recognize the Jewish national home in Palestine. The divergent views on whether or not the Balfour declaration made Palestine a Jewish state are at the root of numerous clashes between the Arab and the Jewish populations of Palestine. Declarations made after the First World War, in connection with the Paris peace conference, failed to dispel the risk of conflict on this issue.[363]

Arab circles were alarmed chiefly by the rise of Jewish immigration, especially after the National Socialist seizure of power. Thus, in 1932 a mere 353 German Jews immigrated into Palestine, but in 1933 the total rose to 5,392. By the end of 1937 some 120,000 Jews had emigrated from Germany, of whom about 40,000 sought a new home in Palestine.[364] These shifts in Palestine's population gave rise

---

[361] Ibid. 41–2.
[362] Ibid. 6–7.
[363] Bethell, *Palestine Triangle*, 14–19; cf. also *Die Palästina-Frage*, with various articles on the complex set of problems.
[364] *DGFP* D v, No. 575, pp. 772–7 (7 Dec. 1937).

4. Axis Powers after Victory in the West

to Arab unrest from April 1936 onward, culminating in October that year. Britain as the mandatory power thereupon set up a commission of inquiry under Lord Peel, which in its report, presented in early July 1937, recommended a partition of the country into a Jewish and an Arab Palestine. As might have been expected, neither side agreed with the idea, and each side felt outdone by the other.[365]

This situation was bound to cause concern in Berlin, as the influx of German Jews was threatening to impair Arab sympathy for the Third Reich. On 1 June 1937, therefore, Foreign Minister von Neurath informed the German diplomatic representatives in London, Jerusalem, and Baghdad that the establishment of a 'Jewish state or a Jewish-led political structure' was not in the German interest. Such a state, he argued, would 'not absorb world Jewry, but create an additional position of power under international law for international Jewry'. Berlin had 'an interest in strengthening the Arab world as a counterweight against such a possible increase in power for world Jewry'. Although Neurath did not believe that any direct 'intervention would essentially influence the development of the question', he nevertheless conveyed to the British government Germany's dislike of a Jewish state in Palestine. He also caused non-committal but sympathetic statements to be issued in Baghdad and Jerusalem on the national aspirations of the Arabs.[366] In 1937 Germany was still encouraging the emigration of Jews by all the means at her disposal. Under the so-called Haavara agreement, a transfer agreement concluded between the Reich ministry of economic affairs and the Anglo-Palestine Bank in 1933, she even made foreign-currency sacrifices, as the agreement enabled emigrating Jews 'in order to establish a livelihood, to obtain the release of special amounts in the form of additional German exports to Palestine'. The German government found itself compelled to make these concessions 'by requirements of domestic policy'; but for this very reason it was suspected by the Arabs of promoting the consolidation of Jewry in Palestine. This was indeed the last thing the National Socialists wanted.

Diplomats were therefore instructed in June 1937 to indicate the German interest in 'keeping Jewry dispersed': 'for when no member of the Jewish race is settled on German soil any longer, the Jewish question will still not be solved for Germany. Rather, the developments of recent years have shown that international Jewry will of necessity always be the ideological and therefore political enemy of National Socialist Germany.' The German foreign ministry was Nazified, and it was small wonder therefore that it regarded 'the Jewish question' as 'one of the most important problems of German foreign policy', for which the existence of a Jewish state 'might have fateful consequences'.[367]

At the beginning of July 1937 the Grand Mufti of Jerusalem, one of the leading figures in the Arab nationalist movement—before the year was out he

---

[365] Bethell, *Palestine Triangle*, 30; Dessouki, *Hitler*, 51; a good map of the partition plan in Mejcher and Schölch, *Die Palästina-Frage*, 251; ibid. on the Peel Commission's Report, *passim*.
[366] *DGFP* D v. No. 561, pp. 746–7 (1 June 1937); on the various interests of the Axis powers, especially from the economic viewpoint, cf. Mejcher, 'Palästina'.
[367] *DGFP* D v, No. 564, p. 750 (22 June 1937).

had to flee to Lebanon as an exile[368]—approached Berlin with a request for diplomatic and propaganda support.[369]

There are a number of reasons why German policy after July 1937 practised a tactic of cautious reserve. To begin with, the proposals of the Peel Commission were received in very different ways in the countries of Europe and the Middle East. In Europe the general tendency was merely to take note. Reaction in the Middle East was varied. Sulayman Hikmet, the Iraqi premier, for instance, reacted as violently as the Grand Mufti. Turkey and Egypt showed conspicuous reserve, as did King Ibn Saud of Arabia. Jewish rejection of the plan complicated the situation for London, but was a matter of indifference to Berlin, as the Jews were not opposing a Jewish state as such but only its envisaged form.[370] German–British relations, moreover, played a part in Berlin's reaction. The foreign ministry took the fundamental view that 'the German interest in the promotion of Jewish immigration is offset by the far greater interest in preventing the formation of a Jewish state', because 'the Jewish question as a domestic problem would be replaced by the considerably more dangerous one of an opposition of world Jewry to the Third Reich based on recognition by international law'. In this context it seemed a reasonable conclusion to support the Arab nationalists with money and arms. But this was not done, for fear of straining German–British relations even further. Besides, the 'notorious political unreliability of the Arabs' induced the Germans to proceed with caution.[371] The Arab countries were just as interested in good mutual relations as Germany was, but for both sides, regardless of the Palestine issue, Britain had priority in national political considerations. There were good reasons why the Arabs asked for no more than diplomatic support from the Reich.[372]

What continued to irritate the Arab population, however, was the maintenance of the Haavara agreement. The political and economic departments in the German foreign ministry and other authorities argued among themselves about the continuation or abrogation of the agreement, which operated as follows: it enabled 'Jews emigrating from Germany to transfer a certain portion of their property to Palestine, in that the Jewish emigrant exports a corresponding amount of goods to Palestine. The German exporting firm is paid out of the Jewish emigrant's Reichsmark account; the latter receives in Palestine the proceeds of the sale in foreign exchange.'[373] It was also realized that by the beginning of 1938 the pro-German attitude of the Arabs had markedly changed compared with 1936. Consul-General Döhle in Jerusalem

---

[368] Schechtman, *Mufti*, 51–60; Wiesenthal, *Großmufti*, 13 ff.
[369] *DGFP* D v, No. 566, pp. 755–6 (15 July 1937); cf. also Dessouki, *Hitler*, 51.
[370] *DGFP* D v, No. 569, pp. 758 ff. (29 July 1937); No. 572, pp. 766 ff. (10 Aug. 1937). Generally also Vogel, *Stempel*.
[371] *DGFP* D v, No. 570, pp. 760 ff. (7 Aug. 1937); No. 571, pp. 762–5 (7 Aug. 1937).
[372] Ibid., No. 574, pp. 769–72 (9 Nov. 1937); cf. also Hirszowicz, *Third Reich*, 41–2.
[373] *DGFP* D v, No. 580, pp. 785 ff. (10 Mar. 1938); cf. Boelcke, *Deutsche Wirtschaft*, 121–8.

even feared that the Germans might soon be hated as much as the British.[374] Nevertheless, the Haavara issue remained unresolved for the time being.[375] It must have been welcome to the German government when, following the report of the Woodhead Commission, which had endeavoured since February 1938 to work out a partition plan, London decided in November of that year to drop the whole project.[376]

In connection with the Palestine issue, direct contact was also made between the Reich and Saudi Arabia. As in the case of Afghanistan, there were divergent assessments of the situation between the foreign ministry and the foreign-policy department of the NSDAP. The latter regretted that no German–Saudi relations existed in 1937 either in the political or in the economic or cultural fields. In spite of the department's urgings, the German honorary consulate at Jedda, abandoned in 1932, had remained vacant.[377]

In November 1937 Sheikh Yusuf Yasin, King Ibn Saud's private secretary, informed Fritz Grobba, the German minister in Baghdad, that his country 'would greatly welcome having Germany send diplomatic representatives to Jedda'.[378] In reply Grobba explained the lack of a German diplomat in Saudi Arabia by reasons of economy, and suggested that the king might agree to one of the representatives in a neighbouring country being accredited to Jedda also—a good example of the heavy-handedness occasionally shown by the foreign ministry in its Middle Eastern dealings. Although this German hesitancy was anything but flattering, it seemed that the Saudis would accept such a solution. Admittedly, when Jedda at the beginning of 1938 tried to acquire reasonably priced modern weapons from Germany, the Saudis presented matters as if the issue of mutual diplomatic relations had been a German initiative.[379] Whereas the Außenpolitisches Amt immediately recommended compliance with the Saudi requests,[380] the foreign ministry again reacted with marked reserve. When the Saudi trade minister wished to buy 15,000–20,000 modern carbines and the necessary ammunition for Ibn Saud in the summer of 1938, Legation Counsellor Otto-Werner von Hentig briefly informed him that modern arms were not for sale, if only because Hitler needed them for his own rearmament. Rather typical of the confusion of departmental responsibility at certain levels of National Socialist Germany is the fact that Hentig, by mere chance, learnt that another negotiator from Jedda was being directly put in touch with the Ferrostahl company by the Außenpolitisches Amt, with a view to purchasing modern weapons.[381]

---

[374] *DGFP* D v, No. 577, pp. 780–1 (14 Jan. 1938).
[375] Ibid., No. 587, p. 798 (12 Nov. 1938).
[376] Ibid., No. 581, pp. 787 ff. (5 July 1938).
[377] Rosenberg, *Tagebuch*, 231 (8 July 1941).
[378] *DGFP* D v, No. 574, pp. 769–72 (9 Nov. 1937).
[379] Ibid., No. 578, pp. 781–2 (20 Jan. 1938); cf. Grobba, *Männer und Mächte*, 105 ff.
[380] *DGFP* D v, No. 590, pp. 810–11 (28 Feb. 1939); cf. ibid., No. 583, pp. 791–2 (3 Sept. 1938), n. 3.
[381] Ibid., No. 590, pp. 810–11 (28 Feb. 1939); the account in Grobba, *Männer und Mächte*, 107, does not accord with the statements in the documents.

A little later, in August 1938, Fuad Bey Hamza, the Saudi deputy foreign minister, visited Berlin. He too talked to representatives of the foreign ministry and mentioned the specific situation in which Ibn Saud found himself. The king was bound to London by the economic and political circumstances of his country. Therefore, if it came to the point, one would have to reckon that Ibn Saud might move along with, and not against, London. Nevertheless, the king was interested in good German–Saudi relations in the long term, largely because co-operation with Berlin, which unlike Rome pursued no political aims in the Arab sphere, would not in any way tie him politically and thereby get him into difficulties. Although Fuad Hamza indicated that Jedda also had understanding for Germany's position and expected no immediate favours from German policy, Hentig put him in touch with Admiral Canaris, the head of German counter-intelligence,[382] and eventually Fuad Hamza was negotiating with the OKW about arms deliveries to Saudi Arabia and Palestine. Matters proceeded favourably and terms were on the point of being agreed when the deal suddenly blew up because the Germans had received information that Fuad Hamza 'was in British pay'.[383] Besides, there was still basic mistrust because of the 'unreliability of the Arabs'. There were even fears in Berlin that the arms sent to Ibn Saud might one day be used by him against Germany, on the side of Britain.[384]

Germany, on the other hand, showed interest in an extension of economic relations with Saudi Arabia. In this context Berlin in February 1939 appointed Grobba as the German minister in Jedda.[385] In that capacity he had discussions between 12 and 18 February with Ibn Saud and his political adviser, Sheikh Yusuf Yasin, on Saudi Arabia's relations with Britain, Italy, and Germany.[386] The Saudis were primarily interested in improving political and economic co-operation with the Reich. Grobba's report to the foreign ministry indicates that he was convinced that Ibn Saud was playing a double game vis-à-vis London and was a potential opponent of the British. This conclusion should be accepted rather more sceptically than the statement that Saudi Arabia and Germany had a common enemy in the Jews. Ibn Saud wanted moral support against pressure from London as well as Rome, material assistance in the form of arms supplies, and a friendship and trade agreement between Saudi Arabia and Germany. Jedda was also interested in a general agreement on trade exchanges. Grobba pointed out the military advantages arising from the geography of Saudi Arabia: British sea routes to India could be threatened from there; the Red Sea as well as the Persian Gulf and the

---

[382] *DGFP* D v, No. 582, pp. 789 ff. (27 Aug. 1938).
[383] Ibid., No. 590, pp. 810–11 (28 Feb. 1939).
[384] Ibid., No. 588, pp. 798 ff. (10 Jan. 1939).
[385] Ibid., No. 583, pp. 791–2 (3 Sept. 1938); No. 584, p. 792 (26 Sept. 1938); No. 585, p. 793 (29 Sept. 1938); cf. also Grobba, *Männer und Mächte*, 108 ff.
[386] *DGFP* D v, No. 589, pp. 800–10 (18 Feb. 1939).

4. Axis Powers after Victory in the West 171

Suez Canal could be controlled; the air routes from Palestine to Iraq, and the pipeline from Iraq to the Mediterranean, could likewise be threatened. Politically it was desirable to use the great influence which Ibn Saud exerted on the other Arab countries. Grobba's arguments proceeded from the assumption of war between Germany and the Western powers. Saudi Arabia's attitude could keep Palestine, Transjordan, Iraq, and Syria out of the war. Altogether the country would provide a political base from which all Arab and Muslim countries could be influenced in favour of Germany. Among economic factors Grobba was predominantly interested, whether in peace or in war, in the petroleum and gold deposits which were being opened up at that time. Agreements should be concluded with the greatest discretion but speedily, especially those on arms deliveries.

By the time the reply arrived from Berlin Grobba was already aware that, as far as the arms deal was concerned, a decision against it had been taken at the end of February. He tried to get at least partial deliveries approved, but in April 1939 the foreign ministry was not even prepared to do that. While Germany was interested in friendly relations with Jedda, Ibn Saud's attitude towards Britain seemed so unpredictable that any closer ties through friendship treaties were better avoided. Supplying war material to Saudi Arabia was categorically ruled out. This applied also to the Yemen, especially as the Italians were exceedingly touchy about that country.[387] Grobba realized this, and, although Luigi Sillitti, his Italian colleague, informed him that in the Italian view the interests of the two countries in the Saudi region were complementary—Italy was trying, for her part, to promote Ibn Saud's independence from London and had therefore made him a present of six aircraft, ten guns, and one tank[388]—Grobba did not rule out the possibility that a German engagement in the Arab world could provoke a clash of interests with Italy. After all, Rome's claims to the Saudi Arabian province of Asir and to the Yemen were known. On the other hand, any improvement in relations between Rome and Jedda, which admittedly presupposed Mussolini's renunciation of the two territories, could impair Germany's predominant position in Saudi Arabia as Grobba envisaged it.[389] For all these reasons the foreign ministry proposed to do nothing for the time being and to maintain its existing basic policy on the Middle East.[390]

Grobba, however, did not give up. He believed that there were unique political opportunities for Germany in Saudi Arabia.[391] The foreign ministry should therefore change its attitude. At the end of May 1939 there were in fact signs of such a change. In view of developments in the Arab world the

---

[387] Ibid., No. 592, pp. 813–14 (18 Apr. 1939).
[388] Grobba, *Männer und Mächte*, 109–10.
[389] *DGFP* D v, No. 589, here p. 804 (18 Feb. 1939).
[390] Ibid., No. 592, here p. 814 (18 Apr. 1939).
[391] *DGFP* D vi, No. 313, pp. 403–7 (2 May 1939).

Germans needed a *rapprochement* with the Saudis, as the past few months had shown that:

(1) Egypt has thrown herself completely into the arms of Britain,
(2) resistance in Palestine is visibly weakening,
(3) Syria is not in a position to pursue an independent policy, whilst Iraq has openly ranged herself with Britain,
(4) a threat to the flanks of the British overland route from Turkey has disappeared,
(5) a regular income has accrued to King Ibn Saud during the past year from oil resources on the coast of the Persian Gulf, and
(6) in view of the growing mistrust which Italy is encountering in the Arab world (viz. sending back of the Italian aviation commission by Ibn Saud), according to what Sillitti, the Italian minister in Jedda, says, our co-operation would be extremely welcome to him.[392]

On the strength of this assessment the political department in the German foreign ministry expressed itself in favour of talks by Ribbentrop and Hitler with the king's special envoy Khalid al Hud, as well as an examination of the economic co-operation proposed by Ibn Saud. On 8 June the Saudi special envoy already had a conversation with the Reich foreign minister.[393] Khalid al Hud emphasized that his country was in a state of natural hostility to Britain because she was constricting 'Arab living-space'. However, Ibn Saud had to be cautious so long as Saudi Arabia was not more developed in military respects. He was, first of all, anxious to build up an armed force independent of Britain. For that purpose he intended to acquire in Germany rifles, armoured cars, anti-aircraft guns, and a small munitions factory. Ribbentrop did not hesitate to promise German assistance in principle. This marked a turning-point in German policy towards Jedda. Hitler, to whom Khalid al Hud handed a letter from Ibn Saud on 17 June, likewise promised 'active assistance'. After all, they were 'jointly fighting the Jews'. The German change, of course (needless to say), should be seen against the background of a conflict with Britain, by then scarcely avoidable, and the important diversionary strategic effect which a pro-German Arab state might have. Whether Hitler's assurance that he 'would not rest until the last Jew had left Germany' made the Saudis particularly happy, given conditions in Palestine, is another matter.[394]

Germany and Italy certainly harmonized their arms deliveries to Saudi Arabia. Everything seemed to be running smoothly when the outbreak of the war cut short the transaction.[395] In response to British urgings, in September 1939 Ibn Saud suspended diplomatic relations with the Reich, but he did not break them off as Iraq and Egypt did.[396] Although the arms deal had to be regarded as being off for an unpredictable period, it is questionable whether

---

[392] Ibid., No. 422, pp. 555–6 (22 May 1939).
[393] Ibid., No. 498, pp. 685–6 (20 June 1939).
[394] Ibid., No. 541, pp. 743–4 (20 June 1939); cf. Tillmann, *Deutschlands Araberpolitik*, 72–3.
[395] Grobba, *Männer und Mächte*, 114–15.
[396] Tillmann, *Deutschlands Araberpolitik*, 114 ff.

4. Axis Powers after Victory in the West

the Saudi step necessarily meant the renunciation of all diplomatic contacts. It is possible that the German foreign ministry over-reacted to the somewhat confused situation and withdrew its minister from Jedda too soon. It is worth noting that Italy, even after her entry into the war in June 1940, continued to have a diplomatic representative in Saudi Arabia.[397] It could be argued, in explanation, that the international situation then was different from the summer of 1939. Be that as it may, Grobba in his memoirs clearly interprets the situation to the effect that the foreign ministry's decision to recall him to Berlin, based as it was on a misjudgement of Ibn Saud's personality, meant an unnecessary surrender of the only opportunity for maintaining a diplomatic representative in the Arab world even after the beginning of the war.[398]

The actual break in Germany's ability to exert influence in the Middle East, after 1 September 1939, did not, of course, mean a break in theoretical discussions on how that area could best be utilized for the German conduct of the war. On 13 November the armed forces high command submitted to the foreign ministry, with a request for speedy comment, a study on 'Policy and Warfare in the Near East' by Professor Oskar Ritter von Niedermayer, colonel (for special duties) in the OKW, who had collected relevant information during the First World War. It is not clear whether Niedermayer's study was commissioned by the OKW, but it evidently aroused its interest. The study is fanciful in some respects, and its author was evidently not too familiar with the policy pursued by the foreign ministry. Yet, on the other hand, it revealed certain fundamental ideas on German policy and warfare which, in a modified form, played a part not only in Hitler's plan to divert Stalin towards India, but also in his reflections on operations after his victory over the Soviet Union.[399]

Niedermayer's point of departure was his concern that a direct decision might become impossible on the Continent if, as in the First World War, operations there got bogged down into positional warfare. That was why Britain had to be attacked by way of the Middle East and India if the chance arose.[400] However, as Germany was in no position politically or militarily to mount a decisive operation in that area, at least not for the moment, she could induce Britain only by means of 'feigned and disruptive actions' to conclude an armistice which both sides would use to prepare themselves for the 'decisive struggle'. Niedermayer, like the German naval staff a year later, placed the Mediterranean, the Red Sea, the Persian Gulf, and the Indian Ocean, as

---

[397] Schröder, *Deutschland und der Mittlere Osten*, 40–1.
[398] Grobba, *Männer und Mächte*, 183.
[399] The study is mentioned in a memorandum by the Foreign Policy Department of the NSDAP of 12 Dec. 1939: *DGFP* D viii, No. 449, pp. 527 ff., with the editor's annotation 'not found'. The document is discussed at length by Tillmann, *Deutschlands Araberpolitik*, 102–6. Otherwise Niedermayer's study belongs to the group of ideas, produced for a great variety of reasons and with very disparate motivations during 1939–40, concerning the Near East in the context of the German–British conflict.
[400] The following data on the contents of the Niedermayer study are from Tillmann, *Deutschlands Araberpolitik*, 102–6.

well as British sea communications, at the centre of German warfare. The objectives of the land operations were India, along with her buffer states Afghanistan, Iran, and Turkey, as well as the entire Arab region with its oil deposits. He regarded the Middle East as important for Britain's power of resistance because it was there that India would be strategically defended. Saudi Arabia or the Italian colonial empire might provide jumping-off points for German operations. The ideal base for the German operation against the Middle East, however, was the Caucasus. Niedermayer evidently believed what the OKW did not yet, in March 1940, rule out—that Moscow could be won over for this plan. In 1941 German plans assumed that Germany could conquer that territory. In 1939 a decisive thrust was proposed from the Caucasus across eastern Turkey towards Aleppo and Baghdad in order to control the area around Mosul, which would permit wheeling towards the south-west or the south-east and would open up access to the Arab world just as much as the seizure of the oilfields. Altogether Niedermayer's study had three aspects:

(1) An offensive in the Middle East, in his view, provided the probability of a victorious conclusion of the war, at slight sacrifice on Germany's part.
(2) The Soviet Union might have her expansionist drive turned southwards, and Italy might soon enter the war in order to seize the opportunity of extending her colonial empire in Africa. However, the (nominally independent) Arab countries of the Middle East should come under indirect German influence once the British had been driven out.
(3) Soviet and Anglo-French interests would have to be played off against each other.

This last consideration gained importance in view of political developments in the Near and Middle East, in the sense that the concentration of French troops in Syria, British troops in Egypt, and Turkish troops in Transcaucasia[401] resulted in Soviet troop reinforcements in just that area.[402] With Stalin's permission Hitler exploited these moves in propaganda. On instructions from the foreign ministry, information was published about 'troop reinforcements on the Caucasian front': these attempted to show that it was relatively easy from Transcaucasia to capture the Armenian plateau in Turkey, and thence to occupy Mosul with its oilfields.[403] Berlin was thus systematically pursuing its policy of creating insecurity in the Middle East (a policy mentioned earlier in the German–Turkish context) in order to tie down British and French forces in that region and thus to ease her own position in Europe.

However, propaganda actions were not the only ones under discussion. Following a comprehensive exchange of ideas between Keitel and Ribbentrop

---

[401] *DGFP* D viii, No. 353, p. 404 (14 Nov. 1939).
[402] Ibid., No. 369, p. 419 (18 Nov. 1939).
[403] Ibid., No. 376, pp. 427–30 (20 Nov. 1939).

4. Axis Powers after Victory in the West

at the end of December 1939, on 6 January 1940 Jodl completed a study for the foreign ministry on 'Policy and the War Effort in the East', in which military and political questions of south-east Europe and the Middle East were examined from the point of view of military operations.[404]

To Jodl—and hence to the armed forces high command—the deployment of German forces in the south-east would mean a second front, i.e. a deterioration of the German position. The region, they believed, should remain neutral at least as long as it could serve Germany as a supply-base. It was, moreover, to be feared that military actions in the south-east could lead to an Italian–Soviet clash of interests, which would in turn strain German–Italian relations. On the other hand, needless to say, the German generals were anxious to use every opportunity to tie down the British and French in Syria, in the Arab world, and in India, without having to engage German forces to any marked degree.

Jodl was especially interested in not relieving the French army in Syria, even indirectly. Ways of tying down that force stemmed from its range of tasks: safeguarding communications between the Mediterranean and India, suppression of Arab revolts, counter-actions in the event of a Russian attack, and, if the opportunity offered, establishment of a Balkan front jointly with Turkish forces. In this context Jodl ruled out any Red Army operation against India, because in his view the distances were too great and the terrain too difficult. It would be relatively easy for the Soviet Union to occupy Bessarabia, but this might disturb peace in the Balkans. If Moscow were to aim for the Straits, a clash with Italy would become unavoidable. A Soviet advance into the Middle East, on the other hand, seemed to be viewed favourably by Jodl, as it might cause considerable difficulties to the British and French. However, the Germans lacked data on the strength, disposition, and fighting power of the Soviet formations in Transcaucasia, nor did they know Stalin's operational intentions or plans; but it was considered doubtful that the Red Army would be capable of mounting an attack towards Mosul and Baghdad, welcome though this would be to Germany.

New prospects of German–Arab co-operation emerged after the armistice with France. The loss of the French army in the Middle East—it had once numbered 150,000 men, though at the time of the British and Free French attack against Syria on 8 June 1941 it was down to 45,000[405]—resulted in the summer of 1940 in a marked weakening of Britain, though by the end of September she had fairly well recovered.[406] At any rate, the Arab nationalists saw their chance. Besides, the Allied defeat in the western campaign was interpreted as an opportunity for a readjustment of power-relations in the Middle East. From the Arab point of view alignment with Germany seemed

---

[404] Ibid., No. 514, pp. 631 ff. (8 Jan. 1940).
[405] On the demobilization regulations: Böhme, *Der deutsch-französische Waffenstillstand*, 77–8, 369; figures and implementation in Playfair, *Mediterranean*, ii. 193–4, 200.
[406] Butler, *Strategy*, ii. 308–12; Playfair, *Mediterranean*, i. 190–204.

desirable at that moment, if only because, as previously mentioned, Berlin apparently had no political ambitions in the east, which in Arab eyes distinguished it favourably from Rome. For if Mussolini's troops were to reach the Suez Canal, this would, in the opinion of those affected, mean merely a change of overlord but not independence for the Arab countries.[407]

How justified such anxieties were was proved by Italian ideas in connection with the future peace. In contrast to their restraint at the time of the armistice with France,[408] the Italians gave notice of massive demands for the future. True, these were later changed a few times, nor was there a definitive summary of what would actually have been demanded, but even so it is possible to gain an idea of what Italy had in mind. Thus there were demands for Nice, Corsica, Tunisia, part of Algeria, and Malta. Rome expected an enlargement of Libya as far as Lake Chad in the south, and a broad land-bridge between Libya and Ethiopia. Covetous eyes were also cast on a considerable portion of French Equatorial Africa and the Sudan, remnants of which were to be attached to Egypt; the latter in turn would be closely tied to Italy. Italy was, moreover, considering a land link to the Atlantic coast, to run from Tunisia to south Morocco. In addition, there was the integration of British and French Somaliland into the Italian empire. But Italy's list also included control of the Suez Canal by annexation of the Sinai peninsula, and the acquisition of Aden and the islands of Perim and Socotra in the Arabian Sea. Italy also aspired to extensive influence in the Yemen and Hadramaut. Mussolini intended to conclude bilateral treaties with his future allies in the Arab world—Egypt, Iraq with her oilfields if possible, Palestine, Transjordan, and Syria; these would assure him not only of political and economic influence but also of military bases. He further intended to win Turkey and Saudi Arabia for his plans by ceding Aleppo in northern Syria to the Turks and the port of Aqaba in Transjordan to the Saudis.[409]

Although the Arab nationalists had no more than a vague idea of Italian aspirations, this was sufficient to make them choose the road to Berlin when in the summer of 1940 the military situation changed so strikingly in favour of the Axis powers. On 5 July Naji Shavkat, the Iraqi minister of justice, informed Ambassador von Papen in Ankara that the nationalist group in the government of premier Rashid Ali al Gailani was anxious to achieve independence from Britain, even though, for fear of British reprisals, it had not yet been possible to drop Nuri al-Said, the Anglophile foreign minister and former head of government. Nevertheless, Baghdad's successful resistance to London's demands for a rupture of diplomatic relations with Rome was to be seen as a clearly anti-British action. Shavkat, however, warned against leaving the Middle East, as Papen hinted, at the free disposal of the Italians. Hitler

---

[407] Hillgruber, *Strategie*, 140.
[408] On the debate among scholars about the reasons for this reserve see n. 161 above.
[409] On this Hillgruber, *Strategie*, 130–1; Schreiber, *Revisionismus*, 262.

4. Axis Powers after Victory in the West

should instead prevail on Mussolini to find a solution compatible with the interests of the Arab movement. For just as the Arab movement had 'fought against Anglo-French imperialism, so it would oppose Italian imperialism'. If agreement were reached, however, the Axis powers, as the minister very cautiously hinted, could count on military support from the Iraqi army in the 'final phase of the contest with England'. Before then, if possible, an Arab national government should be installed in Syria to relieve the Arabs' 'anxiety over a possible Italian imperialism'.[410] By way of comment on Papen's report of this conversation and on a paper on 'The Situation in the Mediterranean Area and the Middle East', Under-Secretary of State Dr Ernst Woermann, the head of the political department in the foreign ministry, declared on 21 July that 'any German claim to leadership in the Arabian area, or a division of that claim with Italy', must be ruled out. This 'political *désintéressement*', however, should not be mistaken for indifference in economic matters. Woermann intended to come to an understanding on this issue with the Italians, not with the Arabs, because Germany must not encourage the Arab game of leaning towards Berlin in order to implement anti-Italian designs. This did not mean that the Arab countries need be cold-shouldered. The Arabs, as Secretary of State von Weizsäcker put it, should for the present simply be told what Germany was fighting against, 'namely England', and mention should be made only 'of the "liberation of the Arab world"', without detailed reference to any goals for the future'.[411]

In view of this attitude it was not surprising that the Arab states were forced once more to take the initiative to further their cause. On 6 August Osman Kemal Haddad, the secretary of Muhammad Amin el Huseini, the Grand Mufti of Jerusalem, applied to the German ambassador in Ankara for permission to visit Germany.[412] On that occasion Haddad claimed that Rome had given to 'all Arab countries under mandate or protectorate Italy's positive assurance of their independence'.[413] On that basis the Iraqi government wished to restore relations with Berlin, broken off on 19 September 1939. Baghdad moreover desired to support the Axis powers in their struggle against Britain, 'especially by a new revolt in Palestine', to be organized from Syria. In line with this was the information which Guelfo Zamboni, the Italian embassy counsellor in Berlin, passed on to Under-Secretary of State Woermann on 17 August, viz. that the Iraqi premier Gailani had 'emphatically declared his adherence to the Axis powers' to Luigi Gabbrielli, the Italian minister in Baghdad.[414]

---

[410] *DGFP* D x, No. 58, pp. 60–1 (29 June 1940); on the conversation with Papen ibid., No 125, pp. 141–4 (6 July 1940). On *tentative* Arab approaches to Germany cf. Hillgruber, *Strategi* 140 ff.; El Dessouki, 'Hitler', 54–8; Tillmann, *Deutschlands Araberpolitik*, 126 ff.
[411] *DGFP* D x, No. 200, pp. 261–2 (21 July 1940).
[412] Ibid., No. 209, p. 275 (22 July 1940).
[413] Ibid., No. 289, pp. 415–16 (6 Aug. 1940); on the disputed accuracy of this report s Hillgruber, *Strategie*, 141 n. 64.
[414] *DGFP* D x, No. 359, p. 503 (17 Aug. 1940).

The German foreign ministry, however, in line with the German–Italian agreements on the Mediterranean area, maintained its reserve. A circular of 20 August, addressed to all foreign missions concerned, contained guidance which was essentially in line with Woermann's memorandum of 21 July.[415] Germany pursued no political interests in the Arab world; her interests were in economic matters (participation in the exploitation of the oilfields), communications (especially air transport), and culture (archaeology). In the political reorganization of this area, including the Arabian peninsula, Egypt, Palestine, Transjordan, Syria, Lebanon, and Iraq, Italy would be allowed the unrestricted 'lead'. Needless to say, such directives were not to be made known to the Arabs concerned. They were to be assured of the 'common German and Arab interest in England's defeat' and of Germany's 'full sympathy in their people's fight for liberation'. In general, German diplomats were to observe an interested but non-committal attitude.[416] It soon became obvious that this was exactly what they did.

On 16 August Osman Kemal Haddad, the Grand Mufti's secretary, was in Berlin.[417] He reported on a 'committee for collaboration among Arab countries', which had been set up under the Mufti's chairmanship and was no less interested in friendly co-operation with Berlin and Rome than the Iraqi government. Haddad spoke in detail about the military situation in the Middle East, which he said was decidedly favourable to the Iraqi army, as the British had to concentrate their forces in Egypt. Such remarks sounded like hidden offers, but the Arabs also had requests, for instance for a German–Italian declaration on the reorganization of the Arab world. Haddad moreover reiterated the assertion that the Italian representative in Baghdad had, on Rome's instructions, already made promises in writing.[418] However, Haddad also made some very specific offers on Iraq's behalf: restoration of diplomatic relations between Iraq and Germany; the Baghdad government's willingness to grant Berlin and Rome a position of equal preference in the economic development of the country and the exploitation of its mineral wealth; and the Iraqi government's readiness to exert its 'good offices' to enable Germany and Italy to conclude 'similar treaties with other Arab countries'. Once Baghdad, Berlin, and Rome had agreed on the above points, a secret agreement was to regulate the details of co-operation. The states to be declared independent—Iraq, Palestine, and Transjordan—would declare their 'strict neutrality'. The most important aspect from the German point of view was the plan for a revolt in Palestine and Transjordan. The Arabs would make available 10,000 men and

---

[415] Ibid., No. 200, pp. 261–2 (21 July 1940).
[416] Ibid., No. 370, pp. 515–16 (20 Aug. 1940).
[417] Ibid., No. 403, pp. 556–60 (27 Aug. 1940).
[418] Ibid., No. 289, pp. 415–16 (6 Aug. 1940). According to *DGFP* D xi, No. 57, pp. 74–5 (14 Sept. 1940), Ciano described the idea of such a statement by Rome as 'pure invention', as the Italian government was interested in the very opposite. It seems nevertheless that the Italian minister, possibly owing to a misunderstanding, had made such a statement: see ibid., No. 127, pp. 220–1 (28 Sept. 1940).

4. Axis Powers after Victory in the West 179

the necessary officers for the uprising. Weapons and ammunition were to come from the French army in Syria. These were to be demanded from the French by the Italian commission supervising the army's demobilization, and handed over to the Grand Mufti. Rome and Berlin were to bear a third each of the costs of the revolt, which would tie down 30,000–40,000 British troops in Palestine and prevent the 'transportation of Anglo-Indian troops from India, Bahrain, or Aden to Egypt', thus greatly alleviating the Italian position in the eastern Mediterranean.

The foreign ministry, to begin with, approached Italy to discover her attitude to the Arab proposals.[419] Ciano expressed a good deal of scepticism concerning co-operation with the Grand Mufti.[420] Unlike the Germans, who were beginning to fear a possible 'defection' of Iraq if an answer to Baghdad was delayed any further,[421] the Italians reacted dilatorily. They did not consider any public statement on the future of Arab independence to be 'expedient'. Besides, Rome did not believe that, even with financial support from the Axis powers, Iraq was in a position to organize a revolt. Italy therefore recommended a delay, while naturally not objecting to diplomatic relations between Berlin and Baghdad, non-committal propaganda statements, or limited financial assistance to the Grand Mufti.[422] This, then, was the scope within which further action took place. The Axis powers merely made anodyne declarations of sympathy and intent, and the Arabs were unable to shed their mistrust of the Italians.[423] Reviewing the situation in December 1940, Berlin already feared that it had lost the gamble for the Arab countries. The consideration shown for Italian ambitions was markedly reduced in order to avoid the risk of 'reverses' in the Arab world in the future.[424] A change in fact presented itself once more when the Wehrmacht came to be deployed in North Africa;[425] but the opportunity of 1940 (assuming that one existed, which is by no means undisputed), and certainly valuable time, had by then been wasted.[426]

---

[419] *DGFP* D xi, No. 35, pp. 44–5 (9 Sept. 1940).
[420] Ibid., No. 40, pp. 48–9 (10 Sept. 1940).
[421] Ibid., No. 51, pp. 65–6 (12 Sept. 1940).
[422] Ibid., No. 58, pp. 75–6 (14 Sept. 1940).
[423] Ibid., No. 127, pp. 220–1 (28 Sept. 1940); No. 133, p. 228 (30 Sept. 1940); No. 143, pp. 238–9 (2 Oct. 1940); No. 146, pp. 241 ff. (3 Oct. 1940); No. 160, pp. 268–9 (6 Oct. 1940); No. 190, pp. 320 ff. (18 Oct. 1940); No. 296, p. 481 (6 Nov. 1940); No. 342, pp. 586–7 (15 Nov. 1940).
[424] Ibid., No. 481, pp. 826–9 (9 Dec. 1940).
[425] On German relations with the Arab world after Jan. 1941 cf. IV.II.2 below.
[426] In general also N. Stewart, 'German Relations'.

III. The Strategic Dilemma of the Summer and Autumn of 1940 An Alternative or Interim Strategy?

WHAT has been said above was concerned essentially with the political, economic, and military basis of Germany's and Italy's conduct of the war. The next two chapters, on the other hand, will deal with the plans for a direct or indirect continuation of the war against Britain. Special attention will be given to Italy's military operations and their effect on Germany, even though the second half of 1940 marked a change in the strategic situation brought about predominantly in the political sphere. This was the case, at least, up to the end of October 1940. In order, however, to determine the place of reflections on the summer and autumn of 1940 within the framework of the World War it will be necessary to examine the long-term plans and ideas of the leadership élites for the period after Germany's presumed victory.

Broadly speaking, the top echelons of the Wehrmacht, of the bureaucracy, of politics, and of the economy all took it for granted that the political shape of Europe had to be changed. Independently of Hitler's own approach to this issue, they viewed the Second World War as a vehicle for the realization of the world-power aspirations they had refused to give up after the First World War. Whatever details may have been concealed behind that concept, it certainly implied an attitude involving a claim. From the historiographical point of view it is irrelevant that Germany failed to achieve the prerequisites for the implementation of those aspirations, since the question as to the nature and aims of the Second World War is unambiguously answered by the endeavours and hopes that marked the period from May to December 1940. An examination of military operations or realized political plans cannot even adumbrate the full scope of what was intended, since it can only reveal what was attainable. History, however, is not merely a question of the factual, though this stands in the foreground for contemporaries directly affected.

Nor is the factual aspect to be neglected here. After all, it was at the presumed climax of the war—after the German victory in the west—that it was first seen that the blitzkrieg strategy had failed: Britain was not to be politically induced to come to an arrangement, nor could she be conquered militarily. The Wehrmacht had won an unexpectedly rapid success on the Continent, but had not achieved victory in the war against the Western democracies. Especially in view of the personal and material factors characterizing the German–British balance of forces, as well as in consequence of political developments, it became possible to predict that Germany's partial success would be called in question to the extent that Britain recovered from her defeat in western Europe.

There are additional factors in favour of a detailed examination of events during the period from June to December 1940. Some noteworthy starting-points for a fundamental discussion of strategy date from that time. In addition, a number of individual problems were emerging in the German conduct of the war, which revealed, or at least suggested, its limitations. Generally speaking, the second half of 1940 could be summed up as the equivalent of a lost battle. Although this did not, in a literal sense, take place, the time lost in failing to achieve a decision, as the result of the unfavourable strategic balance (seen in absolute terms), meant that this superficially so successful year concluded with the realization that a long war, and hence a virtually hopeless one from Hitler's point of view, had become inevitable. Added to this was the fact that the Reich had proved more vulnerable through its Italian ally than had been expected, that localized conflicts were no longer able to bring about a final decision—even though Hitler and his generals in the summer of 1940 refused to believe this, any more than they did in the following winter—and that the political reshaping of Europe failed to materialize in the face of British resistance.

1. Hitler and the Mediterranean Area

(a) Personal Factors

Historical research, no doubt correctly on the whole, has found that Mussolini and Hitler ultimately destroyed themselves in 'the struggle for a synthesis of interest and passion, of calculation and dogma'.[1] Although they did not do so reciprocally but each of them for himself, nevertheless, as our remarks on Italy's entry into the war have shown,[2] they did so in a multiple and at times contradictory dependence on each other.[3] Both as a result of his subjective view of events and also because of Italy's situation as it developed between 1940 and 1943, Mussolini, having hitched himself to the German war-chariot on the basis of a genuine political calculation, even though it was based on false premisses, found himself in an increasingly hopeless dependence on Hitler's fate, a dependence that seemed scarcely capable of severance without danger to himself, and which, whatever the outcome, was self-destructive.

Relations between the two dictators certainly changed perceptibly in June 1940 in a way which Mussolini found painful,[4] since from having once been Hitler's mentor he had all too clearly become his vassal. In this connection it should be noted that Hitler's sympathy for Mussolini had probably always been more profound than the other way about. Hitler was not afraid to

---

[1] Funke, 'Deutsch-italienische Beziehungen', 846.
[2] See I.II above.
[3] See also De Felice, *Mussolini il duce*, ii. 798–9; Giurati, *La parabola*, 61–2.
[4] Alfieri, *Dictators*, 37–8.

speculate that 'without the blackshirt . . . the brownshirt would perhaps never have come about'.[5] Admittedly he added the qualification that 'My programme was conceived in 1919; at that time I knew nothing about Mussolini.' Hitler thus attached importance to the fact that the National Socialist movement had its own ideological basis, even though he indicated at the same time that Mussolini's March on Rome in 1922 had been of considerable importance for his own 'seizure of power' in 1933. As a kindred political system with similar reactionary-revolutionary objectives—at least on the surface and from the angle of traditional power politics—Fascist Italy after 1933 gained a place in National Socialist foreign policy as an ally.

This did not come as a surprise. In his 'Secret Book' of 1928, in which he fully formulated the expansionist aims which underlay his programme for Germany's rise to world-power status, Hitler had devoted an entire chapter to German–Italian relations.[6] With no other country, he wrote at the time, did Germany have 'more interests in common' than with Italy.[7] Both states would in future have to 'turn to a territorial policy on a grand scale', to become, almost inevitably, aggressors. In this development 'the shore basins of the Mediterranean Sea constitute, and hence remain, the natural area of Italian expansion'.[8]

This initially (in the given circumstances understandably) vague definition of Italian living-space already contained, between the lines, a limitation which could be significant especially with regard to the Balkan–Near Eastern area of conflict. It has already been pointed out that Mussolini's fear of Pan-Germanism reflected the problems of a delineation of German and Italian spheres of influence. But regardless of these aspects it is interesting that Hitler, at times in conflict with the economic and military élites of National Socialist Germany, continued, well into the war, to respect the Mediterranean area as Italy's autonomous sphere of interest.

Against the background of German claims in Europe and overseas, but also in conjunction with the economic consequences a German victory was bound to have, this attitude represented a paradox: Hitler's consideration for his ally Mussolini simply could not be reconciled with the facts of the position of German hegemony he was aiming at.[9] Moreover, Hitler, whose war policy was initially confined to exerting strategic pressure on Britain and France by way of political tensions in the Mediterranean area and above all by drawing Italy into the war, from the summer of 1940 onward felt increasingly compelled to intervene directly in the Mediterranean area—specifically in south-east Europe, North Africa, and Spain. There can be no doubt that the motivation

---

[5] Picker, *Hitlers Tischgespräche*, 57–8 (21 July 1941).
[6] *Hitler's Secret Book*, 160–206.
[7] Ibid. 160.
[8] Ibid. 162.
[9] Schreiber, *Revisionismus*, 291 ff.; cf. also Groehler, 'Rolle', 412–15.

1. *Hitler and the Mediterranean Area* 183

for this stemmed from the programmatic nature of his strategy.[10] This is not altered by the fact that Hitler abandoned his original intention, whereby that area was to play a purely diversionary part in German war plans.[11] Altogether, the measures associated with this development are a convincing illustration of the fact that the political and military implementation of Hitler's step-by-step plan was not a narrowly designed or rigid process, but was pursued in accordance with a fundamental concept of the objective: flexibly adapted to each new situation, but always in line with the programme.

(b) Power-political Aspects

The changes in the German attitude towards the Mediterranean area took place in view of the new situation following victory in the west. This was also the time of Spain's dubious attempts to move closer to the Axis powers, who in the summer of 1940 cherished the idea that the time had come to throw the British out of Gibraltar.

On 12 June Franco declared his country non-belligerent.[12] Two days later Spanish troops occupied Tangiers.[13] This did not come as a surprise either to the Germans or to the British and French, because London and Paris had long agreed that in the event of Italy's entry into the war they would encourage Madrid to occupy the Tangiers zone.[14] On 16 June General Juan Vigón, the chief of the Spanish 'High General Staff', had a conversation with Hitler and Ribbentrop at the château of Acoz in Belgium,[15] in order, evidently, to discover the attitude the Germans would adopt towards Franco's aspirations in the Mediterranean area. To prepare the ground for the Spanish requests, Vigón emphasized the boundless sympathy the Axis powers enjoyed in his country; however, he also warned of the danger of American intervention if the war continued, and in this context asked for 'material support from Germany'.[16] Hitler for his part spoke of the direct overland link with Spain which, with the possession of northern France and the entire French Atlantic coast, he would have at his disposal. Germany, in the event of 'any attempts by hostile powers to land in Portugal or Morocco', would be able to assist

---

[10] On the interrelation between Hitler's 'programme' and German strategy in 1940 see Schreiber, 'Mittelmeerraum'.

[11] Hillgruber, 'Politik und Strategie Hitlers', 276–7.

[12] *DGFP* D ix, No. 423, p. 560 (13 June 1940).

[13] Cf. ibid., No. 380, p. 511 (4 June 1940); No. 429, p. 565 (14 June 1940); *DDI*, 9th ser., v, No. 17, p. 15 (13 June 1940); No. 40, pp. 32–3 (17 June 1940); cf. also Detwiler, *Hitler*, 18–19.

[14] Woodward, *British Foreign Policy*, i. 435; On the Anglo-Spanish arrangements concerning Tangiers, made towards the end of 1940, see Dankelmann, *Franco*, 140; also *Cadogan Diaries*, 340–1 (14, 16 Dec. 1940), on British anxieties about Spain entering the war—anxieties which, as Cadogan correctly supposed, were unfounded.

[15] *Staatsmänner*, 134–8; extensively in Detwiler, *Hitler*, 22–5. Vigón also brought a letter from Franco, dated 3 June (ibid. 105–6), in which, while emphasizing the close relations between the two countries, he indicated that he was not interested in entering the war precipitately.

[16] Quoted according to *Staatsmänner*, 134–8.

Spain by all the means in her power. Hitler had originally limited German interests in the Mediterranean area to the economic utilization of Morocco, but a change was soon to take place on this point. At the interview of 16 June it appeared that he was prepared, in principle, to engage himself on the southwest European flank as part of his strategic planning. In any case, Madrid had no illusions about Berlin's future political weight in that region. Vigón declared that at the end of the war Spain's interests would be entrusted to Germany. As for Spain's claim to Gibraltar, he could count on Hitler, provided it proved possible to break definitively the British–French position of hegemony throughout the world. With regard to Franco's demands for the whole of Morocco, the Germans were evasive. Although Ribbentrop again emphasized the lack of German interest in the Mediterranean area,[17] he observed that the question of Morocco would best be resolved in a tripartite conference between Franco, Hitler, and Mussolini.[18] From the Spanish point of view all this did not seem an unfavourable result. Franco therefore followed up on 19 June and detailed his ideas.[19] He now demanded 'the territory of Oran, the unification of Morocco under a Spanish protectorate, the extension of Spanish territory in the Sahara to the 20th parallel, and the extension of Spain's coastal territories situated in the area between the mouth of the Niger and Cape Lopez'. If these demands were acknowledged, Madrid would be prepared to enter the war if it continued for some time and provided that Germany was able to meet Spain's extensive requests for foodstuffs and war material. Thus, the point to which Franco had referred in his letter of 3 June, and in the face of which all efforts to make Spain enter the war had failed, was once more brought into play. In mid-June, admittedly, this issue did not greatly concern Hitler, who was still confident that, after his victory in the west, Britain would come to terms.[20] His intention to moderate Mussolini's expectations from the armistice agreement with France is to be interpreted in the same context.[21]

What Hitler was seeking during those weeks was 'an understanding with Britain on the basis of a division of the world'.[22] A certain degree of military

---

[17] Detwiler, *Hitler*, 24.
[18] On the Moroccan issue see *DDI*, 9th ser., v, No. 42, pp. 33–4 (18 June 1940); No. 86, pp. 70–1 (22 June 1940); No. 88, p. 71 (22 June 1940); *DGFP* D x, No. 193, p. 252 (17 July 1940); Schreiber, *Revisionismus*, 262.
[19] *DGFP* D ix, No. 488, pp. 620–1 (19 June 1940); Detwiler, *Hitler*, 25, 148 n. 16.
[20] Hildebrand, *Foreign Policy*, 103; Martin, 'Das "Dritte Reich"', 532–7; Schreiber, 'Mittelmeerraum', 70 ff.; Snell, *Illusion*, 60–1.
[21] *Staatsmänner*, 138–43, Hitler–Mussolini talks on 18 June 1940; *DDI*, 9th ser., v, No. 45, pp. 35–6 (18 June 1940); No. 59, p. 45 (19 June 1940); No. 68, p. 54 (20 June 1940); No. 69, p. 54 (20 June 1940); No. 76, p. 60 (21 June 1940); No. 83, p. 69 (22 June 1940); No. 91, pp. 74–5 (23 June 1940); No. 93, p. 75 (23 June 1940); No. 95, pp. 76–82 (24 June 1940), text of the Italo-French armistice treaty.
[22] Halder, *Diaries*, i. 413 (21 May 1940); for a critical assessment of sources see Schreiber, 'Mittelmeerraum', 70. Cf. also *Weizsäcker-Papiere*, 204 (23 May 1940), 213 (10 July 1940). This interpretation is not shared by Weinberg, 'Hitler and England', 308–9.

pressure in the Mediterranean area, in parallel with the supply-war against the British Isles, might possibly speed up London's readiness to come to terms. In his conversation with Dino Alfieri, the Italian ambassador in Berlin, on 1 July[23] Hitler certainly seemed to think along those lines. His talk with Ciano on 7 July can also be described as a step in the same direction.[24] The possibility of attacking Gibraltar was discussed on that occasion,[25] and Hitler again offered long-range bombers for operations in the eastern Mediterranean. In the western Mediterranean and on the Atlantic coast of Africa he intended to demand 'an airfield east of Spanish Morocco and one to the west of it', allegedly only in order to participate in any continuing conflict that might result from the British attack on the French fleet on 3 July 1940.[26] Specifically the Germans were interested in Casablanca and Oran, which touched on Italian interests, even though Rome pretended to be concerned only about any unfavourable effects which German–French co-operation might have on Italo-French relations. In reality Mussolini was probably more worried about German expansion into the Mediterranean area; and to be on the safe side he reacted by voicing his concern.[27] The Germans very soon afterwards gave up their claim to Oran[28] and demanded from Vichy only 'eight airfields in the region of Casablanca, the surrender of weather stations, the placing at our disposal of the railway from Tunis to Rabat, and French merchant vessels for the transport of supplies across the Mediterranean'.[29]

Several indications seem to suggest that with these demands Hitler made a first attempt to implement a plan, subsequently resumed under changed circumstances, to forestall the defection of French territories from Vichy by a German military presence in North Africa.[30] Moreover, the bases demanded were of exceptional value to German operations in the Atlantic or as bases for air raids on Gibraltar. These demands, however, at least from the French point of view, ran counter to the provisions of the German–French armis-

---

[23] *DDI*, 9th ser., v, No. 161, pp. 147–50 (1 July 1940).
[24] *Staatsmänner*, 150–62; *DDI*, 9th ser., v, No. 200, pp. 186–90 (7 July 1940); *Ciano's Diary 1939–1943*, 275 (7 July 1940).
[25] On the first offer see n. 23 above; also *DDI*, 9th ser., v, No. 180, p. 169 (4 July 1940). On 7 July 1940 Keitel, in the presence of the Italian consul general Renzetti, said that Italy should ask for air-bases in Spain, Spanish Morocco, and on the Balearic Islands in order to attack Gibraltar systematically: *DDI*, 9th ser., v, No. 201, pp. 190 ff. (7 July 1940).
[26] *Staatsmänner*, 152; on the other hand, Ciano in his record of the talks (see n. 24 above) makes no mention of the German plan for bases.
[27] *DDI*, 9th ser., v, No. 215, p. 202 (10 July 1940); *DGFP* D x, No. 151, pp. 186–7 (11 July 1940). Italy first demanded air-bases for herself in Algeria on 5 July. On this and on the genesis of German requests see Böhme, *Der deutsch-französische Waffenstillstand*, 344–5. With regard to Italy's concern about German demands in the Mediterranean see *DGFP* D x, No. 243, pp. 331–2 (27 July 1940).
[28] *DGFP* D x, No. 158, p. 198 (12 July 1940); but cf. ibid. n. 3, according to which Mussolini was said to have been 'in agreement with the proposal for a German base at Oran without any reservation'. On this also Böhme, *Der deutsch-französische Waffenstillstand*, 345.
[29] *DGFP* D x, No. 169, p. 215 (15 July 1940); there was thus no German response to Italy's obligingness (see the preceding n.).
[30] Geschke, *Frankreichpolitik*, 42–5.

tice.³¹ Accordingly Marshal Pétain, in a letter to Hitler, the full text of which seems to have been lost, refused the suggestion to begin with, arguing that the armistice terms did not include any 'restriction of France's rights of sovereignty in her overseas possessions', which was what the German demands, described by him as 'dishonouring', amounted to. Formally this would have been an unambiguous rejection, had not Pétain added a remark which was interpreted, even by contemporaries, as a hint that he remained entirely willing to discuss the issue.³² Basically, the marshal rejected only 'dictation from Germany'; a 'free agreement', on the other hand, would be possible. And his observation that this could 'facilitate a *rapprochement* of the two nations in the future' might tempt one to speak of a diplomatic offensive by Pétain.³³ As a price for compliance the marshal, even at that time, presumably had in mind relaxation of the armistice terms or possibly subsequent binding promises from Germany with regard to peace terms. Be that as it may, Hitler did not react. Evidently he preferred to 'set Spain to attack Gibraltar'.³⁴

All this suggests that, while Hitler's consideration for Mussolini's interests undoubtedly coloured his attitude towards the Mediterranean area, politically calculated factors and subjective psychological elements would occasionally clash when the situation in that region was evaluated from strategic points of view. In February 1945, when Hitler dictated his so-called political testament to Martin Bormann, the head of the Party chancery and secretary to the Führer, he summed up this dichotomy in extensive reflections which, though full of errors of detail and essentially a part of his legend-building, seem psychologically revealing: 'When I pass judgement, objectively and without emotion, on events, I must admit that my unshakable friendship with the Duce and loyalty to the alliance with Italy may well be held to have been an error on my part.'³⁵

Hitler certainly did not 'underrate' the Mediterranean area.³⁶ This is shown not only by his plans for a diversionary strategy, but also by his attitude following the rejection by the British government on 22 July 1940 of his so-

---

³¹ Basically on the armistice: Böhme, *Der deutsch-französische Waffenstillstand*, 15–139; Geschke, *Frankreichpolitik*, 25–32; Jäckel, *Frankreich*, 32–45.
³² *DGFP* D x, No. 208, pp. 274–5 (22 July 1940), here n. 1.
³³ Quoted according to *DGFP*, ibid., pp. 274–5 (22 July 1940). Cf. Böhme, *Der deutsch-französische Waffenstillstand*, 346–50. The present author cannot agree with his conclusions concerning Hilter's reasons for leaving Pétain's letter unanswered. For one thing Böhme disregards the fact that military deliberations about the capture of Gibraltar were being continued, and for another he overlooks the fact that Hitler took up this plan again at a later date under less favourable conditions. On Böhme's account (350–1) see I.III.2 below. Geschke, *Frankreichpolitik*, 42–5, correctly points to the dangers which a forcible attempt to seize the French colonial empire could have triggered and emphasizes that Hitler's overriding intentions, especially his attack on the USSR, played a decisive role here. On the interdependence of the attack on the Soviet Union and German military operations in the summer of 1940 see Schreiber, 'Mittelmeerraum', 70–90.
³⁴ *Weizsäcker-Papiere*, 212–13 (10 July 1940). On the military plans see I.III.2 (*b*) below.
³⁵ *Hitler's Testament*, 69–75, quotation 64.
³⁶ Divergently Loßberg, *Im Wehrmachtführungsstab*, 95.

called final appeal for peace.[37] Hitler at that time made the most varied offers to Italy, Spain, and even France, in an attempt to make safe the Mediterranean area—from whence the continental southern flank of his war against the Soviet Union, decided upon in July 1940, might be threatened—in other words, to bring it under German influence.[38] It became very clear, however, that a penetration into that area was by no means open to Germany so long as Spain and Italy had to be respected as sovereign states. Mussolini's reservations about any German involvement in the Mediterranean area were only too well known to Germany, and Franco's reluctance could scarcely be overlooked, even though Hitler tried to play it down when he subsequently called the generalissimo's government a 'regime of capitalist profiteers, puppets of the clerical gang'.[39] In addition, the mood in the French colonies had to be taken into account. Hitler was primarily interested in France's North African possessions remaining loyal to Vichy. If only for this reason any tensions between Pétain and the Axis powers were to be avoided. This pattern of foreign-policy considerations meant that a Wehrmacht penetration into the Mediterranean area, whether on the European Continent or in North Africa, could only be realized on the basis of political arrangements between Hitler, Franco, and Mussolini, and if possible with Pétain's agreement also. This was the political barrier which Berlin had to surmount.[40]

In a modified form the German intentions, at least as far as the expulsion of Britain from the Mediterranean was concerned, could have been implemented by a proxy war, to be fought by Italy and Spain with very discreet German support. The idea was in fact considered, and in October 1940 Germany even included France in these reflections—but the difficulties involved in all plans of that kind were predictable from the start. And Hitler, who was at that time concerned with the 'worldwide combination' which was to form a Euro-Asian continental bloc[41] from Yokohama to Spain,[42] had by then long realized that 'reconciliation of conflicting French, Italian, and Spanish interests' would be 'possible only by a gigantic fraud'.[43] This realization, as it were, provided the

---

[37] On this Martin, *Friedensinitiativen*, 301–36, on Hitler's peace offer of 19 July 1940 generally.

[38] These intentions of Hitler's governed all military deliberations on German operations in the Mediterranean: see I.III.2 (*b*) below.

[39] *Hitler's Testament*, 47–9 (10 Feb. 1945).

[40] Hillgruber, 'Politik und Strategie Hitlers', 278.

[41] The most comprehensive examination hitherto of the project for an anti-British continental bloc, discussed in greater detail below, is in Michalka, *Ribbentrop*.

[42] *Staatsmänner*, 345, conversation between Hitler and Count Teleki, the Hungarian premier, on 20 Nov. 1940 (344–9).

[43] Quoted according to Halder, *Diaries*, i. 609 (3 Oct. 1940). The 'conflicting interests' are analysed in Detwiler, *Hitler*, 37–50, in connection with an account of the round trip of Serrano Suñer, then Spanish minister of the interior and future foreign minister, in Sept. 1940; directly on this Serrano Suñer, *Zwischen Hendaye*, 156–81. Detwiler was not yet able to use the German version of *DGFP*, and the English version only sporadically. Many of the documents tapped by him in the archives have meanwhile been edited: *DGFP* D xi, No. 30, p. 37 (6 Sept. 1940) and appendix (p. 38); No. 39, p. 48 (10 Sept. 1940); No. 48, pp. 62–3 (11 Sept. 1940); No. 62, pp.

rational background for the second phase of Hitler's endeavours for direct German military engagement in the Mediterranean area, a concept which emerged in the late summer of 1940, in parallel with the isolation of Britain and the neutralization of the United States, as the centre of his short-term political objectives; for Hitler remained anxious to conclude a 'compromise peace' with Britain as a prerequisite of the further realization of his policy of expansion.[44] This was the goal which, from the German point of view, was to be served by the Tripartite Pact concluded between Germany, Italy, and Japan on 27 September 1940.[45]

Although State Secretary von Weizsäcker thought that this treaty might have a deterrent effect on the United States,[46] he was by no means sure of it. From the military point of view the Tripartite Pact could scarcely be regarded as weighty, and it carried the blemish of being a makeshift to cover the operational stagnation of the war.[47] And, as American and British policy in the Far East proved as early as October 1940, the treaty did not result in the expected weakening of the Washington–London coalition of interests.[48] Instead it produced a 'crystallizing effect' on British–American policy.[49] From the German point of view, however, it still seemed possible to bring about the opposite effect if the Soviet Union could be integrated into the treaty system.[50] Sceptics, on the other hand, dared not assume that Moscow would be prepared to join the Tripartite Pact powers: for that, Germany's policy vis-à-vis Britain was too ambivalent. Besides, the Soviet leadership realized that Hitler was still anxious for an arrangement with Britain.[51] Germany could indeed expect that the Russians—who were bound to see the German guarantee to Romania, her policy towards Finland, and the sluggish deliveries of promised goods as provocations—would be greatly irritated by the Tripartite Pact. At the German foreign ministry there seems to have been concern lest the Kremlin might alter its political course. Although an attack by the Red Army was

---

81–2 (16 Sept. 1940); No. 63, pp. 83–91 (17 Sept. 1940); No. 66, pp. 93–8 (17 Sept. 1940); No. 67, pp. 98–102 (17 Sept. 1940); No. 70, pp. 106 ff. (18 Sept. 1940); No. 88, pp. 153 ff. (22 Sept. 1940); No. 97, pp. 166–74 (26 Sept. 1940). The documents contain the records of Serrano Suñer's talks with Hitler and Ribbentrop on 16, 17, and 24 Sept. 1940. His subsequent meeting with Mussolini is treated in *DDI*, 9th ser., v, No. 645, p. 624 (26 Sept. 1940); No. 660, pp. 639–40 (1 Oct. 1940).

[44] *IMT* x. 295, according to Ribbentrop's evidence on 30 Mar. 1946.
[45] Ibid. 294–5; Miyake, 'Japans Beweggrund'.
[46] *Weizsäcker-Papiere*, 218 (15 Sept. 1940).
[47] Ibid. 219 (28 Sept. 1940), on the interpretation of the Tripartite Pact mainly Sommer, *Deutschland und Japan*, 426–49; *Deutschland im zweiten Weltkrieg*, i. 440 ff. For the Japanese interests as regards the pact cf. Krebs, *Japans Deutschlandpolitik*, 466–89. Krebs shows clearly that, at the time of concluding the pact, Japan was taken in by the German propaganda claim that Britain was as good as defeated. This error meant the end of the hope that the alliance might divide the US from Britain and enable Japan, unopposed, to take over the collapsing British Empire.
[48] A summary of political plans in Hillgruber, *Strategie*, 203–6.
[49] Sommer, *Deutschland und Japan*, 455.
[50] Hillgruber, *Strategie*, 206.
[51] *Weizsäcker-Papiere*, 220 (15 Oct. 1940).

1. Hitler and the Mediterranean Area

regarded as entirely out of the question in view of the military weakness the Germans ascribed to it, even a *rapprochement* of Moscow with London might have political consequences no less unpleasant than the economic consequences of a suspension of Soviet grain supplies to the Reich.[52] All these reasons made it desirable once more to associate Stalin more firmly with German political intentions. However, it cannot be sufficiently emphasized that all such German reflections on German–Soviet relations represented only tactical variations of the 'Russian problem', and not a fundamentally different solution from that envisaged in Hitler's programme. What Hitler was planning in the second half of 1940 was no more and no less than an 'interim solution' with regard to the 'inevitably determined "main goal" of his "programme", a campaign of conquest towards the east'.[53] Precisely this was the view of State Secretary von Weizsäcker, who noted in September 1940 that even if Germany succeeded in reaching agreement with London, and if 'America quietly and humbly drew its conclusions therefrom', Hitler's Germany would still not 'leave the Russian problem alone'. One way or another, the state secretary believed, Germany was at 'the beginning and not the end of the struggle'. He was to be proved right.[54]

The diplomatic offensive for the achievement of the political intentions we have outlined was opened by Hitler on 4 October, when he met Mussolini on the Brenner.[55] Hitler wished mainly to discuss the new situation which, from his point of view, had arisen with regard to Spain. Naturally, the two dictators also spoke about Operation 'Sea Lion', and of course they reassured each other that the war had essentially long been won, and that the 'rest' would come about by itself. At issue, therefore, was not victory as such—for Hitler felt sure of that—but solely a speedy conclusion of the war. In this context Hitler advanced his thesis that the British were only holding out in their 'militarily hopeless situation' because of their hopes of the United States and the Soviet Union. However, Hitler professed confidence: after all, Washington had reacted to the Tripartite Pact 'in a very cowardly manner'. The Americans, he suggested, were evidently afraid of becoming involved in a war on two fronts. As for Moscow, he intended to divert it towards 'India or at least the Indian Ocean'. Whether he would succeed in doing this was doubtful, he admitted, but Stalin was at any rate acting quite sensibly, as shown by his first reactions to the conclusion of the Tripartite Pact; in any case, the Soviet Union would

---

[52] Ibid. 219 (27 Sept. 1940); see also *DGFP* D xi, No. 73, pp. 113–23 (20 Sept. 1940), Ribbentrop's conversation with Mussolini on 19 Sept., when Ribbentrop did not see any *rapprochement* between Stalin and the Western powers as an acute issue; No. 87, pp. 150 ff. (22 Sept. 1940), Ribbentrop–Mussolini conversation on 22 Sept., in the course of which Soviet interests figured more prominently than on 19 Sept. Also *DDI*, 9th ser., v, No. 617, pp. 598–601 (19 Sept. 1940).
[53] Hillgruber, *Strategie*, 238–42; concisely summarized by Hildebrand, *Third Reich*, 55.
[54] *Weizsäcker-Papiere*, 218 (13 Sept. 1940).
[55] Quoted from *Staatsmänner*, 229–47; cf. *DDI*, 9th ser., v, No. 677, pp. 655–8 (4 Oct. 1940). On the Spanish question within the framework of the talks see Dankelmann, *Franco*, 141–2; Detwiler, *Hitler*, 54 ff.; on France cf. Geschke, *Frankreichpolitik*, 78–81; Jäckel, *Frankreich*, 110.

not be a serious danger even if the worst came to the worst.[56] These reflections by Hitler in the late summer and autumn of 1940, which were basically concerned with the creation of an anti-British continental bloc by military or political means, again—and this is crucial—represented only a change of method but not of the long-term objectives of National Socialist policy. The timing of the attack on the Soviet Union would have been changed if these political calculations had worked out correctly, but Hitler's determination to conquer living-space in the east would not have been affected as such.

Af for the 'gigantic fraud', Hitler in his talk with Mussolini first examined territorial demands on France. Franco, if he entered the war, would demand Gibraltar and Morocco for Spain. Italy wanted frontier rectifications in Europe, also Corsica and Tunis. Germany insisted on Alsace-Lorraine, bases on the Atlantic coast of Africa, the return of her former colonies, and a 'rounding off of her Central African colonial possessions'. The German demands for bases also affected Spain, but so far Franco was not prepared to make any concessions whatever. This intransigence, Spain's disastrous economic situation, and the realization that the French would not at that moment give up Morocco, let alone Oran, caused Hitler to act as if he did not seek Spain's entry into the war at any cost. In actual fact, he would have been ready to promise almost anything, though not publicly, and without committing himself to dates. He feared that any premature promises to Spain might give rise to a movement for the defection of Morocco—which would mean 'playing into the hands of the British'. Hitler therefore intended to agree to Franco's demands only when a British landing in Africa could be safely ruled out. This would have been the case if England had been defeated, or if the German dive-bombers had bases no more than 350 km. distant from the enemy's potential landing-places.

Ultimately—and here Hitler came to the point—all reflections came down to the question whether it might not be possible to 'bring France and Spain on to a common line, and in this way bring about a continental coalition against Britain'. The French had to expect in any case that after the war they would have to surrender certain territories. And as Hitler saw no difficulties with regard to the German and Italian demands, everything seemed to come down to the question whether France would agree to being compensated for her losses in Morocco by being given parts of British Nigeria. Spain too would have to scale down her demands if such ideas were to have any chance at all. Franco would therefore have to forget about Oran. Needless to say, these reflections and concessions did not mean that Hitler was being honest with Vichy. His true intentions, instead, were reflected in the formulation that France must 'never again become a strong power'. Experience had taught him that the French would seek revenge for the defeat they had suffered. German dominion on the Rhine and Italy's Mediterranean empire would seem

---

[56] On the possibility of a German–Soviet alliance cf. also Fest, *Hitler* (trans.), 880–1, where the temporary nature of Hitler's ideas about joint action with the USSR is clearly demonstrated.

intolerable to France, which was why a British–French *rapprochement* could not be ruled out. In view of such arguments and assumptions Hitler's moderation *vis-à-vis* Vichy must be regarded as strictly limited in time. As mentioned above, he intended to make vague promises only, without entering into binding agreements.[57] From a solely tactical point of view Hitler therefore saw the 'ideal solution' of the problems of the German war effort in the 'creation of a European coalition against Britain, with the inclusion of France and Spain'. But he had his doubts.

When at last it was Mussolini's turn,[58] his observations were essentially an echo of Hitler's exposé. It was too late, he believed, for the United States to acquire any importance in the present war, and he seemed to be no more afraid of the Soviet Union than was Hitler. Mussolini also agreed with Hitler's plan for a continental anti-British coalition, though with certain reservations, his objections being chiefly about the chances of realizing the project. The Duce was concerned that, under the influence of a group around Foreign Minister Juan Beigbeder y Atienza—he was replaced by Ramón Serrano Suñer on 16 October 1940—Spain might even switch over to the British side: great circumspection was therefore needed. Any interpretation of Italy's attitude, however, must allow for the fact that Rome was influenced not only by the presumed uncertainty about Spain, but also by the German–French relationship. The Italian foreign minister was firmly convinced that, regardless of the Brenner talks, a *rapprochement* between Berlin and Vichy would damage Italy's long-term interests. That was why the news that Hitler would meet Franco and Pétain was received in Rome with very mixed feelings.[59]

On 20 October Hitler set out on his round trip, which was to initiate 'Europe's counter-deployment against the Western democracies'.[60] The various conversations had evidently been prepared very differently. Thus, the foreign ministry had been negotiating with Madrid since September about a meeting between the two heads of state,[61] whereas there were virtually no detailed arrangements for Hitler's meeting with Pétain.[62] Basically therefore only Hitler knew what he would say to the French deputy premier, Pierre Laval, when he met him at the railway station of Montoire-sur-le-Loir on 22 October.[63]

---

[57] See *Weizsäcker-Papiere*, 221 (25 Oct. 1940): 'What the Führer is pursuing with the French today by way of a *rapprochement* is a makeshift, and moreover a temporary one.'

[58] On this mainly Ciano, *Diary 1939–1943*, 296 (4 Oct. 1940), who characterizes Mussolini's performance on the Brenner as very successful and describes himself as highly satisfied with the course of the meeting. Significantly Ciano points out that Hitler had spoken in an extremely anti-Bolshevik manner.

[59] Ciano, *Diary 1939–1943*, 472 (20 Oct. 1940).

[60] *Weizsäcker-Papiere*, 222 (26 Oct. 1940).

[61] *DGFP* D xi, No. 88, pp. 153 ff. (22 Sept. 1940); Detwiler, *Hitler*, 37–50.

[62] Geschke, *Frankreichpolitik*, 83; Jäckel, *Frankreich*, 110–14.

[63] *Staatsmänner*, 257–65, 'Conversation between the Führer and Laval, the Vice-President of the French Council of Ministers'. Laval had been deputy premier since 22 June 1940. On the conversation see Geschke, *Frankreichpolitik*, 86–9; Jäckel, *Frankreich*, 115 ff.

The conversation began with all kinds of courtesies from Laval, to turn shortly into a bout of shadow-boxing about the prerequisites and conditions of possible German–French collaboration, with Laval seeking more or less specific guarantees concerning the peace treaty—which Hitler steadfastly refused to provide. A subject of discussion was the war costs which one of the losers had to pay. Hitler did not refrain from speaking very plainly about what he called France's responsibility for the war and its consequences. Although Laval dared not contradict Hitler, he clearly hoped to defend his country's interests as soon as negotiations turned to the details of the proposed collaboration. But Hitler permitted no doubt concerning his own position of strength. He held out the lure of mobilizing, if necessary, 'everything humanly conceivable against England', when France would be given an opportunity to participate in the struggle. And he threatened Laval with the possibility of a compromise peace between Berlin and London, which would be at the expense of Vichy. This was what France would have to expect in the event of unduly delaying her decision on co-operation in order to gain the greatest possible advantages for herself. His message to Pétain, whom he now wished to meet, was at first glance as simple as it was unambiguous: if the French wanted a tolerable peace they would have to earn it. He did not, however, say what exactly he meant by that. From Laval's point of view, anything still seemed possible.[64]

The following day, 23 October, Hitler conferred with Franco.[65] It was the first meeting between them and the preliminaries were correspondingly long-winded.[66] The Caudillo recalled their brotherhood-in-arms in the Spanish civil war, and acted as if he were genuinely sorry not to be able to fight on the German side. The fault lay with the familiar constraints. There was a continuing lack of economic, military, and political preparation—convenient shortages indeed. The Führer was no less eloquent: he made numerous references to the enemies of Spain, who had always been his enemies also; he exulted in the victor's pose, and crowned his performance with an extraordinarily optimistic evaluation of the situation. Ribbentrop subsequently discovered that the generalissimo had understood little of Hitler's rhetoric. The only statement which therefore deserves notice was that there was just one genuine problem at the moment, the need to prevent a movement of defection in France's African colonies. Hitler was evidently haunted by the idea that, as a result of British–Free French co-operation, enemy bases, including American ones, might be set up on the west coast of Africa. This brought him to the real subject of his visit: the continental bloc and its prerequisites. In this

---

[64] Quoted according to *Staatsmänner*, 257–65.

[65] Ibid. 266–71, 'Conversation between the Führer and the Caudillo at Hendaye railway station'. Francisco Franco y Bahamonde had been Spanish head of state since his victory in the civil war in 1939. See also Burdick, *Germany's Military Strategy*, 50–3; Detwiler, *Hitler*, 56–62; Geschke, *Frankreichpolitik*, 89 ff.; *DGFP* D xi, No. 222, p. 380 (23 Oct. 1940).

[66] Quoted according to *Staatsmänner*, 266–71.

matter 'Spanish requests and French hopes' were 'getting in each other's way'. It was therefore necessary to make Franco see reason. Hitler tried to do so by asserting that Spain would derive nothing but advantages from scaling down her demands on France for the time being. The Germans and the Italians too had to show restraint for the present. This did not, of course, rule out the possibility that, regardless of easier peace terms for the French, the victors would carry out further 'corrections'.

What Germany expected from Spain was formulated more precisely in a 'secret protocol', drafted in advance but later variously amended, for which Ribbentrop, after the virtually fruitless conversation between Hitler and Franco,[67] tried to obtain Spanish approval from Serrano Suñer.[68] In accordance with this document Spain was to join the Tripartite Pact and the Pact of Steel, and eventually declare war on Britain.[69] In addition, she was to renounce her demands against France, or at least their clear formulation. Agreement was reached on the principle that 'Spain will receive territories in Africa in the same measure as that in which France may be compensated, by having assigned to her in Africa other territories of equal value, while Germany's and Italy's claims *vis-à-vis* France continue to be maintained.'[70] Serrano Suñer nevertheless expressed surprise that 'evidently a new course was to be followed in the African question and that Germany's attitude towards France had changed'. Madrid believed that its maximal demands were in jeopardy. Serrano Suñer did not trust in the minimizing or soothing German assurances on that point. In his conversation with Ribbentrop he demanded specific promises, a request which the latter tried to dodge by urging him to wait for the peace treaties. There were, as usual, promises without any binding character. Arguments went back and forth until the Spanish foreign minister excused himself on the grounds of fatigue.[71]

The following morning Serrano Suñer declined a further meeting with Ribbentrop. This is another clear indication of the chill which marked the meeting at Hendaye. During the succeeding period there were, first of all, a number of Spanish requests for amendments to formulations in the 'secret protocol'; these, not surprisingly, were followed by corresponding German requests. However, during the first half of November the foreign ministers of Germany, Italy, and Spain, in conditions of great secrecy, at last signed the laboriously produced document.[72] On Spain's entry into the war, point 4 noted:

[67] Franco was merely ready to conclude a treaty: see Detwiler, *Hitler*, 59.
[68] This 'secret protocol' is published in Detwiler, *Hitler*, 118–19, as document VI. On Ribbentrop's conversation with Serrano Suñer on 23 Oct. 1940 see *DGFP* D xi, No. 221, pp. 376–9; also published in Geschke, *Frankreichpolitik*, 145 ff.
[69] Hitler's observations on 10 Feb. 1945 (*Hitler's Testament*, 47–9), when he declared himself to have been uninterested in Spain's entry into the war, therefore blur historical fact.
[70] Quoted according to Point 5 of the final version of the 'secret protocol'.
[71] Quoted according to *DGFP* D xi, No. 221, pp. 376–9 (23 Oct. 1940).
[72] Ibid., No. 294, pp. 478–9 (6 Nov. 1940).

In fulfilment of her obligations as an ally, Spain will intervene in the present war of the Axis powers against Britain, after these have granted her the assistance necessary for her preparations, at a time to be determined by mutual agreement among the three powers, having regard to the military preparations to be decided upon. Germany will grant economic aid to Spain by supplying her with foodstuffs and raw materials in order to meet the needs of the Spanish people and the requirements of the war.

From the Spanish point of view this was a saving solution which left Franco complete freedom of decision.[73]

On 24 October the meeting between Hitler and Pétain took place; this had undoubtedly, as a result of Franco's evasive attitude, become more important than originally intended.[74] The talks were marked by a note of obligingness, and the marshal, briefed by Laval, very soon and without further ado addressed the question of co-operation between Vichy and Berlin, as desired by Hitler. It would have been sensible, he observed, to have started on this even before the war, but 'perhaps there was still time to make up for what had been omitted'. The price demanded by Pétain, however, a guarantee of the continued existence of the French colonial empire, was unacceptable to Hitler. After all, he pointed out, France had started the war against Germany, and now she would have to pay for it 'territorially and materially'. To make his position clear Hitler, for the third time in three days, expatiated on the favourable position of the Axis powers. Nothing except his desire for a quick end to the war was motivating him to 'organize a European, and partly extra-European, community against the British enemy of the Continent'. What he wished to discover at Montoire were the conditions under which France would be prepared to 'join and co-operate with' the European community aspired to by Berlin. This was an unambiguous offer, but Pétain had no intention of committing himself as long as no binding arrangements existed as to the destiny of France. The marshal therefore adopted a dilatory tactic and tried to avoid the German embrace. He did not say no, he was uncertain with regard to possible co-operation in Africa—which from the French point of view was about colonies, and from the German about covering Europe's strategic flank—and justified his reserve by the difficulty of determining the precise limits of German–French collaboration.

All in all, the situation remained open even after Montoire, and any development was still feasible. From Hitler's angle this meeting had certainly not been as frustrating as his encounter with Franco at Hendaye. In summary form it was recorded that:

Marshal Pétain declared himself willing in principle to look towards co-operation with Germany in the sense outlined by the Führer. The modalities of such co-operation

[73] Quoted according to Detwiler, *Hitler*, 118.
[74] Quoted according to *Staatsmänner*, 272–80, 'Conversation between the Führer and Marshal Pétain in the Führer's train at the railway station of Montoire-sur-le-Loir on 24 October 1940'; directly on this Böhme, 'Deutschland und Frankreich' (B 31), 18; Detwiler, *Hitler*, 62–3; Geschke, *Frankreichpolitik*, 91–100; Jäckel, *Frankreich*, 118–23.

1. Hitler and the Mediterranean Area

would be regulated and determined in detail from one instance to another. Marshal Pétain hoped for a more favourable conclusion of the war for France. The Führer expressed himself in agreement.

This assessment of the situation seems to sound a certain note of confidence. In actual fact, however, at least in the foreign ministry, the results of Hitler's tour were viewed much more sceptically. State Secretary von Weizsäcker, for instance, observed that any attentive newspaper-reader could surmise how meagre were the political results of the trip. There was still no date for Spain's entry into the war, and it was scarcely possible to conceal the fact that the French had avoided any excessively close ties with the Reich.[75]

Seen objectively, this was no doubt the true state of affairs, even though things looked different from a British perspective in the autumn of 1940. Hitler's wooing of Franco and Pétain seemed anything but harmless from there. Both in London and in Washington it produced top-level reactions. If one accepts the official British account, there was profound uncertainty among members of the British government as to Vichy's future political course. Reassuring statements from France, reaching London unofficially through various diplomatic channels, did little to change this. Military confrontation between Britain and France moved into the realm of the possible. The British were worried in particular about the French navy and about German and Italian action, by no mean impossible, to secure the French colonial empire.

This uncertain situation persisted approximately until February 1941. Admittedly there were signs of a *détente* in November, but by the beginning of 1941 it was finally clear that neither the hard line which Churchill wished to pursue, nor the near-appeasement policy favoured by Halifax, had succeeded in inducing Vichy to adopt a clear and unambiguous stand. On the contrary, British–French relations, strained by London's measures after the armistice and by Britain's association with De Gaulle, reached a low point at that time.[76]

During those weeks developments in the Mediterranean area could almost be described as a secondary consideration for Hitler. Much later he observed that 'these Latin countries bring us no luck'. For while he was at Montoire, 'buttoning up a futile policy of collaboration with France, and then in Hendaye, where I had to submit to receiving fulsome honours at the hands of a false friend—a third Latin, and one, this time, who really was a friend, took advantage of my preoccupation to set in motion his disastrous campaign in Greece'.[77] Just then, at the end of October, Hitler was on his way to see Mussolini, whose reservations with regard to German–French collaboration and to Spain's entry into the war[78] were well known in Berlin. It was in order to dispel his ally's reservations, and also to restrain the Italian attack against

---

[75] *Weizsäcker-Papiere*, 221 (25 Oct. 1940).
[76] Woodward, *British Foreign Policy*, i. 413–21; R.T. Thomas, *Britain*, 53–87.
[77] *Hitler's Testament*, 79–81 (20 Feb. 1945).
[78] *Weizsäcker-Papiere*, 221 (25 Oct. 1940).

Greece,[79] that, after his conversations with Pétain, Laval, and Franco, Hitler betook himself to Florence.[80]

By the time the German delegation arrived in Florence the attack against Greece could no longer be prevented. Faced with this fact, Hitler did not bother to remonstrate with Mussolini about what he later termed his 'idiotic campaign in Greece'.[81] In fact, in October, in order chiefly to defend Crete against a British occupation, he offered Mussolini a division each of airborne and parachute troops, to operate from North Africa. Most of the time at Florence, however, was devoted to the results which Hitler believed he had achieved on his trip. He vigorously berated Franco and spoke sympathetically about Pétain. It seems unlikely that this would have cleared away Italian suspicions,[82] although Ciano, in his account of the conversation on 28 October, recorded that the Germans had shown undiminished solidarity with Italy.[83] However—now that careful research has proved that Ciano removed his original diary entries for 27 and 28 October, to replace them with a rather unrevealing text—these passages will have to be treated with some caution.[84] The minutes of the talks, at any rate, show that Hitler intended to treat any possible collaboration with France with great circumspection. Primarily he no doubt expected that French adherence to the continental bloc would produce political reactions which would support his policy towards Britain. So as not to alarm Mussolini excessively, he assured him that Germany 'would under no circumstances conclude a peace with France unless Italy's demands were fully satisfied'.

The official balance sheet of his autumnal trip was drawn up by Hitler in his Directive No. 18 of 12 November 1940 (to be discussed in detail later), which set out the directives for 'preparatory measures of the high command for the conduct of the war in the near future'.[85] With regard to the Mediterranean area, it stated that the German position there, as was now officially admitted, had not improved. Though this may not have been instantly obvious, 28 October ultimately represented the opening of a third phase in Hitler's endeavours for German involvement in the Mediterranean area.

In this respect he was progressively losing the initiative, his military planning was getting into the slipstream of Italian actions, and their unfavourable outcome soon had political consequences. The contest for the Mediterranean

---

[79] Ibid. 220–1 (21 Oct. 1940): almost a week before the attack Weizsäcker noted: 'We do not obstruct the Italian intention of shortly striking at Greece. Axis loyalty.' Cf. Domarus, *Hitler*, 320–1, 380–1.
[80] *Staatsmänner*, 280–94; *DDI*, 9th ser., v, No. 807, pp. 771–5 (28 Oct. 1940).
[81] *Hitler's Testament*, 65 (15 Feb. 1945).
[82] Ciano, *Diary 1939–1943*, 299 (20 Oct. 1940).
[83] Ibid. 301 (28 Oct. 1940).
[84] Cf. Palla, 'La fortuna', 32 n. 6.
[85] *Hitler's War Directives*, 81–7.

1. Hitler and the Mediterranean Area

became more complex after the attack on Greece, since, as von Weizsäcker observed, 'politics are straightforward only when weapons have cleared the ground', and in this respect, in particular, Germany's ally proved 'especially troublesome' in this region.[86]

As for the fate of the continental bloc—without going into its history at this point—it should be pointed out that the concept of a bloc limited to southwest Europe failed in December 1940, if not before, as soon as it became obvious that Franco wished to keep out of the war and that France's readiness for collaboration was very severely limited. As for the idea of a large continental bloc including the USSR, Hitler had probably dropped that even earlier, certainly after Molotov's visit to Berlin on 12 and 13 November. By then German efforts for an involvement in the Mediterranean area were already dominated by the campaign in the east.[87]

2. IDEAS AS TO THE CONTINUATION OF THE WAR

Hitler's political vacillation, in the summer and autumn of 1940, about how to continue the war did not result from any lack of objectives, but from the doubtful prospects of success offered by the alternative concepts—an immediate attack on the Soviet Union at the price of a war on two fronts, or the creation of an anti-British alliance, a compromise with Britain, and a subsequent attack on the USSR. This uncertainty about the road to follow, even though its goal—living-space in the east and a German colonial empire— was unquestionable,[88] was reflected also in military thinking. The Wehrmacht leadership was faced with the problem of how to proceed now, after a victory in the west that had yielded only half an armistice.

The British government clearly did not even consider accepting peace on Hitler's terms. How right they were is proved not only by various documents from within the German naval command,[89] implying that anything less than a total defeat of Britain would have been accepted by Germany only in the sense of an interim peace, but also by the Reich's claims to power generally. The breathing-space that German diplomats expected to come from a 'compromise' with London was to be used to soften America's anti-German position, to manœuvre Germany into a better position *vis-à-vis* the Soviet Union, and to prepare the Reich for the task of entering into the 'inheritance of all of Europe and the British Empire'—planned, in Hitler's mind, as the sequel to his victory over the USSR.[90]

---

[86] *Weizsäcker-Papiere*, 221 (25 Oct. 1940).
[87] Hildebrand, *Foreign Policy*, 104 ff.; Hillgruber, *Strategie*, 317–34; cf. also I.II below.
[88] Along with the above account cf. esp. Hildebrand, *Reich*, 673–94; Hillgruber, *Strategie*, 144–277; Michalka, 'Antikominternpakt', 471–92.
[89] Memorandum I m to 1. Skl. of 11 Nov. 1940, here esp. 21–5, BA-MA RM 6/83.
[90] *Weizsäcker-Papiere*, 212–13 (10 July 1940).

(a) The Jodl Memorandum

In view of Britain's uncompromising attitude to political overtures, Germany had to find an operational opening which would enable her to bring the war against Britain to a swift conclusion. Unless London could be got to conclude an armistice or peace in the foreseeable future, Germany would sooner or later be forced on to the defensive. This was suggested equally by the economic circumstances of the Reich and by its geo-strategic position, cut off from overseas. Nevertheless, Hitler's generals and admirals were confident that, after victory in the west, they would be able by resolute action to turn the superficially undecided situation in their favour, in other words to force Britain to come to terms.

Decision-making in this situation was assisted by, among other things, a memorandum from Major-General Alfred Jodl, chief of the Wehrmacht operations staff,[91] submitted on 30 June 1940.[92] It was probably in this study, 'Continuation of the War against Britain', that the Wehrmacht high command first included the Mediterranean area as a theatre of operations in its strategy.[93] For this reason, and also because Jodl's study has to be seen as the precursor of all subsequent ideas concerning an alternative German strategy against Britain in the summer and autumn of 1940, the document will be examined here in some detail.[94] Coming as it did from Hitler's closest military adviser,[95] it reveals the 'basic thinking' on significant 'unknown factors' and on the 'limited nature of the strategic and political thinking of the high command of the Wehrmacht' at that important stage of the war.[96]

By way of introduction it should be pointed out that, although he saw in the Mediterranean area an additional chance of defeating the British, Jodl undoubtedly regarded the sea and air war against British supplies, as well as the invasion of Britain, as having priority.[97] The crucial weaknesses of his estimate of the situation were his disregard of the possibility of direct military intervention by the United States, and the irresponsible way in which wishful ideas about the Soviet Union's attitude were included in his analysis as realistic assumptions. That a change might occur in German–Soviet relations as a

---

[91] From 8 Aug. the 'Wehrmachtführungsamt im Oberkommando der Wehrmacht' (WFA) was officially called the 'Wehrmachtführungsstab' (WFStab) in accordance with 'Amtliche Nachrichten für die Oberkommandos der Wehrmacht 22 (1940)', 153 (9 Aug. 1940).

[92] Published as Document No. 8 in *Dokumente zum Unternehmen 'Seelöwe'*, 298 ff.; see also Ansel, *Middle Sea*, 8–12; Warlimont, *Inside Hitler's Headquarters*, 107.

[93] Raeder's situation report of 20 June 1940 did not cover the Mediterranean area, apart from French naval concerns; see 'Führer Conferences', 110 ff. (20 June 1940). The area was likewise not mentioned in the paper, signed by Raeder, on 'Future Tasks of Naval Warfare', ObdM u. Chef Skl., B.Nr. 1. Skl. I op 987/40 g.Kdos. Chefs., Berlin, 29 June 1940, BA-MA M Box 57, PG 32087 b.

[94] Quoted according to *Dokumente zum Unternehmen 'Seelöwe'*, 298 ff.

[95] On the co-operation between Jodl and Hitler see Hillgruber, *Strategie*, 157 n. 65.

[96] Ibid. 157.

[97] On this Gruchmann, 'Die verpaßten strategischen Chancen', 461; Warlimont, *Inside Hitler's Headquarters*, 107–8.

2. Ideas on the Continuation of the War

result of the very operations proposed by him, which affected the Soviet interest, was not even allowed for in the general's calculations.[98]

The memorandum began with the statement that 'Britain's will to resist must be broken by force' if 'political means fail to achieve their end'. This was to be done

   (a) by operations against the British mother country;
   (b) by an extension of the war along the periphery.

Regarding (a) there are three options:

(1) a 'siege':
    This comprises operations at sea and from the air against all imports and exports, operations against the British air force, and against all military resources of the country.
(2) terror raids on British centres of population;
(3) a landing with the objective of occupying Britain.

'Final German victory over Britain' was only a question of time. As the British were no longer capable of 'large-scale offensive action'. Germany would be able to 'choose a method of operation which would spare her own forces and avoid risks'. In detail, the sequence of operations Jodl had in mind was as follows: elimination of the RAF, destruction of armament factories in southern England, and, if still necessary, a landing, 'to administer the *coup de grâce*' to a Britain economically 'paralysed' by the German air force and navy, 'and scarcely capable of aerial operation any longer'.

On point (b) the memorandum stated:

The struggle against the British empire can be waged only by, or by way of, countries with an interest in the disintegration of the British empire and with hopes of an abundant inheritance. These are primarily Italy, Spain, Russia, and Japan. Activating these countries is a task for politics. Military support for Italy and Spain is possible on a limited scale (e.g. for mining the Suez Canal or for the seizure of Gibraltar).

The Arab countries, moreover, can be given assistance by means of the Abwehr [foreign intelligence]. Most effective would be an Italian offensive operation against the Suez Canal, which, in conjunction with the seizure of Gibraltar, would seal off the Mediterranean.

At the same time, and along with these ideas, Jodl did not reject participation by Italian air-force and naval units in operations against the British mother country. It should be noted that he evidently underrated British determination and that, understandably enough, he had no idea of what character the war had by then acquired in British eyes. Churchill was certainly just as anxious to maintain British possessions as he was to preserve Britain's position in the world. But this was not all the British were fighting for. Even a 'relatively cheap' peace was by then no longer the aim of their war effort. London was instead determined to bring down the aggressors. The British

[98] Hillgruber, *Strategie*, 158–9.

were interested not in the peace which Hitler pretended to offer, but in the nature of the victory they would gain over Fascism in Germany and Italy.

Jodl's strategic ideas proceeded roughly from a political superstructure which, with certain reservations, was close to Ribbentrop's concept of a continental bloc comprising Europe and Asia. However, the political problems—in other words, the scarcely avoidable major concessions to the powers Jodl wished to win for a coalition—and the consequences which his proposals would have for Hitler's 'real war aims in eastern Europe'—specifically, the predictable difficulty of turning back towards these aims once the bloc was formed—caused Hitler, initially, to hesitate until September.[99] Nevertheless, his above-mentioned conversation with the Italian ambassador Alfieri on 1 July showed that his attention had been aroused.[100]

In connection with his proposals to the Duce and his offer to deploy German long-range bombers from Rhodes against Egypt, Hitler emphasized, even at that early date, that it was necessary to attack the Suez Canal and to seize Gibraltar.[101] On the other hand, this offer did not prejudge a decision as to the desirable direction of the next, let alone of the decisive, German operation.

(b) *Gibraltar, Egypt, and the Atlantic Islands*

The Mediterranean question revived again after the Royal Navy's attack on the French fleet.[102] Not much later Hitler told Ciano that the German staffs had 'quite extensively considered' an attack on Gibraltar. The Wehrmacht would participate in the military operations proper with some 'special weapons'; otherwise the seizure of the Rock would have to be performed mainly by Spanish troops.[103] But Hitler also mentioned to the Italian foreign minister the crux of any such plans, namely Franco's consent.

In view of this condition the Wehrmacht high command issued its directive of 12 July, according to which, in a politically absolutely open situation, a 'Gibraltar reconnaissance staff' was to be set up[104] for the preparation of offensive operations or support for a 'Spanish coup'. In point of fact, Madrid did not seem at all enthusiastic about the German idea, and many a Spaniard clearly thought it quite unnecessary to enter the war for the sake of the Rock. After Britain's defeat, which was confidently expected, the base would surely

---

[99] Ibid. 178–9; see also Tippelskirch, 'Hitlers Kriegführung', 145.
[100] *Staatsmänner*, 149.
[101] Ibid. 144–50.
[102] Details on German–French relations during those weeks in Böhme, *Der deutsch-französische Waffenstillstand*, 289–360.
[103] *Staatsmänner*, 150–62, here 154–5; Hitler on this occasion repeated his offer of 1 July 1940 to make German bomber aircraft available for aerial mine-laying operations against the Suez Canal (157).
[104] Burdick, *Germany's Military Strategy*, 18–22, with the deliberations of OKW and OKH/OKM, between 1 and 13 July 1940, on Gibraltar and on a landing in England. The study by Greiner, 'Felix', MGFA C-065h, covers only the deliberations from mid-Aug. 1940 onward (cf. p. 1); 1. Skl., KTB, Teil A, p. 131 (12 July 1940), BA-MA RM 7/14.

2. Ideas on the Continuation of the War

revert to Spain anyway.[105] Hitler, on the other hand, evidently in order to lend emphasis to his peace offer to London, was anxious at that time to 'draw Spain into the game in order to build up a front against Britain from the North Cape to Morocco'.[106] Canaris and several other officers thereupon travelled to Spain between 20 and 23 July in order to examine on the spot the prospects of success of such an operation.[107]

The fact that only five days earlier Hitler's Directive No. 16 was issued on 'Preparations for a Landing Operation against England'[108]—these preparations were to be concluded by mid-August—again demonstrates the confused state of German war-planning after the victory over France. Even if Hitler had been determined to do so, he could not continue the war with any spectacular actions during those weeks. Franco and Mussolini were blocking his road to the Mediterranean, an invasion of the British Isles was considered risky from the outset, quite apart from requiring unrestricted command of the air, and July was too late in the year for turning against the east in 1940; in any case the Wehrmacht, for a variety of reasons, was incapable of such action so soon after the war in the west. The German staffs ran through all operational options. From the end of July it became clear that for Hitler there was ultimately no alternative to the attack on the Soviet Union; at the most he would contemplate intermediate steps which would gain him freedom for his rear. In this light there is nothing contradictory about the fact that on 21 July he brought forward the plan—to be discussed again in October—for 'harnessing everything politically against Britain' if she persisted with the war,[109] while simultaneously giving orders to push ahead with the military solution of the Russian problem, which had been under examination by the army high command since early July. *Vis-à-vis* the Wehrmacht Hitler in this context reiterated defensive considerations in order to justify his intended aggression. As to the generals, they reported already at this time that deployment could be effected in four to six weeks[110]—though this subsequently proved to be incorrect.

As for the possible use of the Wehrmacht in Spain, the reconnoitring trip by Admiral Canaris's party soon produced first results. Although these were

---

[105] Vice-Adm. Kurt Assmann, material for the study 'Die Seekriegsleitung und die Mittelmeerkriegführung', June to Oct. 1940 (undated), BA-MA RM 8/1257; 1. Skl., KTB, Teil A, p. 188 (17 July 1940), BA-MA RM 7/14.
[106] Halder, *Diaries*, i. 505 (13 July 1940).
[107] Brissaud, *Canaris*, 311 ff.; Burdick, *Germany's Military Strategy*, 24-8; Detwiler, *Hitler*, 31; Höhne, *Canaris* (trans.), 423 ff.
[108] *Hitler's War Directives*, No. 16, pp. 74-9 (16 July 1940).
[109] Halder, *Diaries*, i. 515-16 (22 July 1940); see also Seraphim, '"Felix" und "Isabella"', 45 ff.
[110] Halder, *Diaries*, i. 516 (22 July 1940); on the attack against the USSR and the appropriate preparations in 1940 see Hillgruber, *Strategie*, 207-42; Schreiber, 'Mittelmeerraum', 70-7, on the latest state of research. A detailed examination of this problem in *Das Deutsche Reich und der Zweite Weltkrieg*, iv, *passim*.

rather sobering, the officers did consider the capture of the Rock possible in principle. They worked out a plan of attack, listing the military forces necessary, with details about the various phases of the operation, and allowing three days for it.[111] On the strength of the information gathered it had to be expected that the seizure of Gibraltar would entail exceedingly heavy losses. The defenders were in an ideal position, whereas the attackers would not even enjoy the element of surprise. Franco did not turn down the German ideas outright, but he stressed to Canaris the precarious economic situation of his country and, with justification, pointed to likely British retaliatory action against the Canary Islands.[112]

Gibraltar certainly was a very substantial factor in operations along the periphery of Europe, as outlined by Jodl in June. But the Italians also had a number of possible openings for decisive operations against Britain and, in conjunction with this, the engagement of the Wehrmacht in the Mediterranean area.

On 15 July it emerged from a conversation between Rintelen, the German military attaché in Rome, and Marshal Badoglio that preparations of the Italian forces for an offensive from Cyrenaica were in full swing.[113] Hitler's hint about the possible deployment of Luftwaffe units in North Africa should probably be seen in this context.[114] His intention was primarily to support his Axis partner. Although the Germans were aware that the Italians had numerical superiority over the British, they believed that the British forces had greater combative efficiency. Moreover, in the light of past experience and observations there seemed to be some doubt about whether the armed forces command in Rome was in fact capable of a co-ordinated triphibious operation, which was regarded in Berlin as a prerequisite of success. The Italians' obvious supply problems certainly gave rise to concern rather than optimism.[115]

By the end of the month the military attaché confirmed this sceptical view of the combative efficiency of the Italian forces. Although Rintelen assumed that preparations for the offensive against Egypt might indeed be completed by about 6 August, he believed that the Italians would not move off until Operation Sea Lion had been launched. The German army general staff therefore no longer believed that 'anything big can be achieved by the Italians'.

---

[111] Burdick, *Germany's Military Strategy*, 27–8.

[112] Ibid. 24–7; from the British point of view—at least after 12 June 1940, when Franco modified Spanish neutrality to non-belligerence—the possibility of Madrid actively intervening in events could no longer be ruled out. The British government, understandably, was not anxious to provoke that step by preventive measures with regard to the Spanish islands in the Atlantic. However, appropriate operations in case the generalissimo should enter the war had been prepared since 22 July 1940; see Butler, *Strategy*, ii. 238–9.

[113] Naval attaché in Rome, B.Nr. g.Kdos. 2250/40 (19 July 1940), to OKM *et al.*, BA-MA RM 7/233. On Italy's conduct of the war see I.III.3 below.

[114] 'Führer Conferences', 120 (25 July 1940); by then the issue was no longer the request for German bases to be established in French North Africa, as that request had already been refused by Vichy on 19 July 1940: Geschke, *Frankreichpolitik*, 42–6.

[115] Halder, *Diaries*, i. 522 (27 July 1940).

Nor did the officers expect any decisive results from an offensive by the Italians alone.[116] They justified this very pessimistic assessment by, among other things, Italy's economic weakness and the difficulties encountered by her military command in translating theoretical ideas into practical operational principles.[117]

As for the German strategic plans, both Halder and Brauchitsch observed at about the same time that the navy 'in all probability will not provide us this autumn with the means for a successful invasion of Britain'. They both agreed on the dangers of such a development: Germany could lose the military and political initiative, while Britain would gain a breathing-space which she would utilize for rearming. Altogether it was not to be expected that by the spring of 1941, the alternative date for the invasion of the British Isles, Germany's military or political position in relation to Britain would have improved. If the idea of an invasion in 1940 had to be abandoned, the following lines of action were open to Germany for maintaining pressure on Britain by means of a peripheral conduct of the war:

(1) Attack Gibraltar (from the landward side, through Spain).
(2) Support Italians with armour in North Africa (Egypt).
(3) Attack British in Haifa.
(4) Attack Suez Canal.
(5) Encourage Russians to drive towards Persian Gulf.[118]

Such reflections necessarily raised the question of what might happen if London not only could not be defeated but actually allied itself with Moscow. In that case Berlin would inescapably be faced with a war on two fronts. But the commander-in-chief of the army and his chief of staff that evening dispensed with an in-depth examination of this problem. Either they were not yet convinced of Hitler's determination to attack or else they were hoping that Germany's political leaders would preserve the friendship of the Soviet Union, if necessary at the price of some concessions in the Balkans and Middle East. In that case they believed they 'could deliver the British a decisive blow in the Mediterranean, shoulder them away from Asia, help the Italians to build their Mediterranean empire, and, with the aid of Russia, consolidate the Reich . . . created in western and northern Europe'. All that, admittedly, would merely ensure the economic prerequisites of 'war with Britain for years', but not victory as such.

These reflections on the part of the generals, who by then were directly concerned with military plans against the USSR, permit of one conclusion only—that they had no intention of encouraging the political leadership to undertake a campaign in the east. This was shown even by the considerably

---

[116] Ibid. 529 (30 July 1940).
[117] Schreiber, 'Les structures', 22–32.
[118] Halder, *Diaries*, i. 529–30 (30 July 1940); this is also the source of the quotations in the following paragraph.

more aggressive 'Thoughts on Russia' formulated by Rear-Admiral Kurt Fricke, chief of the operations department of the naval war staff. The 'chronic danger' of Bolshevism, he argued, had to be 'eliminated soon, one way or another'; the admiral regarded an extension of Germany to a 'line from Lake Ladoga to Smolensk and the Crimea', possibly even the 'capture of Moscow', as feasible, though he did not rule out the possibility that a weak Soviet government might be prevailed upon to concede German wishes by way of negotiation.[119] All this proves that the officers here quoted were familiar—as indeed was everyone who had read *Mein Kampf*—with Hitler's objective of an 'Alexander campaign' in the east, that they adjusted themselves to it, but were in no hurry to put forward any new political objectives of their own.

On 31 July Hitler in a conference with Brauchitsch, Halder, Jodl, Keitel, and Raeder discussed the chances of carrying out Operation Sea Lion after all.[120] It emerged fairly clearly that a postponement of the invasion seemed more probable than its execution. Hitler certainly did not disguise his 'scepticism regarding the technical feasibility'. It was also clear that he regarded the operations envisaged in the Mediterranean area—the capture of Gibraltar and support for the Italian forces in Libya by two German armoured divisions—as diversionary manœuvres and stopgaps.

These remarks by Hitler might, at first glance, be understood in connection with the postponement of Operation Sea Lion. His observation that only the 'attack on England' would produce decisive results also seems to suggest that he was determined to carry out the landing operation. In fact, however, Hitler by then was far more intensively involved in the campaign against the Soviet Union that in the invasion of Britain. This is proved also by his remarks after the departure of the commander-in-chief of the navy. The only 'resolution' he adopted on 31 July concerned his programmatic aggression against the USSR: the 'destruction of Russia's vital strength' in the spring of 1941'. After that, Germany would be 'master of Europe and the Balkans', while Britain would have lost her last potential ally on the Continent.[121]

Evidently as a result of that decision, on 2 August Keitel informed General

---

[119] Salewski, *Seekriegsleitung*, iii. 137–44, No. 6 (28 July 1940); directly on this: ibid., i. 274–5.

[120] Quoted according to Halder, *Diaries*, i. 530–4 (31 July 1940): Maj.-Gen. Jodl was made general of artillery on 19 July 1940; 'Führer Conferences', 122 ff.; *KTB OKW* i. 3 ff. Grand Adm. Raeder left the conference before the subject of the USSR was broached. Whether he was aware of that item on the agenda is uncertain. It is, however, certain that from 21 July 1940 he was informed as to the topicality of the so-called Russian problem (see nn. 110, 119 above). Directly on this: Salewski, *Seekriegsleitung*, i. 275–6; Hillgruber, *Strategie*, 220 ff., 223–6 generally as regards 31 July 1940.

[121] On the binding nature of the decision of 31 July 1940 see Schreiber, 'Mittelmeerraum', 75 ff.; also, on the basis of new sources, Ueberschär, 'Hitlers Entschluß'. Jacobsen, *Deutsche Kriegführung*, 25 ff., believes that the 'really activating element' was not so much 'living-space in the east' as the 'Napoleonic idea of defeating Britain in Russia'. This interpretation seems to lose sight of the basic objective of Hitler's war and policies: the attack on the USSR, ideally with British approval.

of Infantry Georg Thomas, chief of the war-economy and armaments office in the armed forces high command, that the current armament programme would be changed; the relevant directive was issued on 17 August.[122] Henceforth the army was to comprise no longer 120 but 180 divisions. Experts, even if they were not privy to the outcome of the conference on 31 July, concluded from this reorientation that Hitler no longer believed in Britain's collapse in 1940, that he expected the United States to intervene actively in 1941, and that, moreover, his plans implied a change in German–Soviet relations. Accordingly, 120 of the 180 German divisions were earmarked for engagement in the east.[123] By smashing the USSR Hitler intended to deprive Britain of her 'sword on the Continent'. At the same time he hoped to deter the United States from entering the war, because, if his calculations worked out, the Soviet defeat would lead to an 'upward revaluation of Japan in East Asia'.[124]

In Hitler's mind the war was acquiring a global dimension. Everything was subordinated to preparations for an offensive in the east. As the relevant measures had of course to be camouflaged, it was necessary to give the impression that these were activities serving a German–Spanish attack against Gibraltar, a German–Italian action in North Africa, or a landing in England. In parallel with the preparations for aggression against the Soviet Union the generals were in fact discussing the 'setting aside of armoured units' for Mussolini's thrust towards Egypt, Luftwaffe support for the battle for Alexandria, and the Italo-Spanish capture of Gibraltar.[125] Even Operation Sea Lion had not been finally laid to rest. Seen in this light, the meeting of 31 July therefore occasioned no absolute suspension of planning for peripheral warfare. But it resulted in modifications which reflected the qualitative changes the intended operations were then undergoing from Hitler's point of view. Operations along the periphery were no longer related almost exclusively to the conflict with Britain—more particularly to a direct attack on the British Isles—but were increasingly governed by the demands of an attack on the USSR in the spring of 1941. After the failure of the idea of a continental bloc as an interim solution, this was increasingly reflected, roughly from November 1940 onward, in a reduction of the originally intended Wehrmacht engagement in the Mediterranean area, confining it to south-east Europe and the Balkans. Officially, however, the Mediterranean area remained a potential theatre of war for the Wehrmacht in the summer and autumn of 1940, so that relevant planning was allowed to continue.

Following a proposal by the commander-in-chief of the army for an 'expedi-

---

[122] For the tendencies which, soon after the French campaign, were aiming in this direction, albeit semi-officially, see *Das Deutsche Reich und der Zweite Weltkrieg*, iv. 168–89 (Müller).

[123] *KTB OKW* i. 968–9, 'Note on the Development of the Armament Situation in the Summer of 1940'. Chef Wi.Rü.Amt (Gen. of Infantry Georg Thomas) of 20 Aug. 1940. On Operation 'Barbarossa' see *Das Deutsche Reich und der Zweite Weltkrieg*, iv.

[124] Schreiber, 'Mittelmeerraum', 76–7.

[125] *KTB OKW* i. 3 ff. (1 Aug. 1940).

tionary corps' to be transferred to North Africa, and in connection with an estimate of the situation submitted on 30 July by the home-defence department in the Wehrmacht operations staff (Department L), which recommended the dispatch of an armoured corps, since 7 August the Working Party (Army) had been examining the material prerequisites of such an employment in the event of 'Sea Lion' being dropped. On the basis of the findings of Admiral Canaris's reconnaissance trip the Working Parties (Army) and (Navy) simultaneously prepared a study concerned in detail with operational possibilities, questions of chain of command, military strength required, 'reconnaissance tasks to be assigned immediately, establishment of a working-and-command staff, and its tasks'.[126] In addition, the Wehrmacht operations staff directed that the 'whole British Empire' be examined for 'points of attack', other than Gibraltar and Egypt, which would permit a continuation of the war.[127]

In the context of these preliminary studies Major-General Warlimont, head of Department L, in a briefing note to Keitel and Jodl as early as 8 August again recommended the use of German armoured units in North Africa. With the abandonment of 'Sea Lion' these troops had become 'dispensable... until the spring of 1941'. If operations were directed not only against Egypt but also towards a seizure of Gibraltar, the 'British position in the Mediterranean could be destroyed during the winter months'.[128] Shortly afterwards, on 13 August, an estimate was produced by Jodl, based on the views held in the army and navy high commands, on 'the feasibility of a landing in England'.[129] Keitel reported to Hitler the same day on Jodl's conclusions 'in rough outline'.[130] Jodl postulated from the outset that the 'landing operation... must not on any

[126] Ibid. 11 (7 Aug. 1940); according to Halder, *Diaries*, i. 53 (31 July 1940), this expeditionary corps was initially to consist of two armoured divisions.

[127] *KTB OKW*, i. 14–15 (8 Aug. 1940); the explanation given by Halder, *Hitler als Feldherr*, 34, that Hitler was not prepared to commit himself in North Africa until Italy faced defeat there, is objectively incorrect, even though this interpretation is maintained in a recent study: see Gundelach, *Luftwaffe im Mittelmeer*, 35, also 24–41 generally.

[128] *KTB OKW* i. 17 (9 Aug. 1940). Warlimont—like the section heads Army, Air Force, and Navy in Department L—was aware from 29 July 1940 onward of Hitler's intention to attack the USSR. In this connection, as Jodl reported on 29 July, it was by no means a *sine qua non* for Hitler that the fight against England must... first be concluded', though Warlimont and his section heads seemed to have regarded this as necessary, since otherwise there was the risk of war on two fronts. Hence the pressure for Britain to be brought to her knees during the winter of 1940–1: Warlimont, *Inside Hitler's Headquarters*, 110. Warlimont's data also suggest that the 'deliberations on Russia' by the naval war staff on 28 July 1940 (see n. 119 above) can scarcely have been the result of a talk between the LIK, Lt.-Cdr. Junge, and Rear-Adm. Fricke, as assumed by Salewski (*Seekriegsleitung*, i. 275, esp. n. 20, and iii. 137), but that they were prompted by Raeder after his situation report on 21 July, as proved earlier by Hillgruber (*Strategie*, 221). This is confirmed also by the ambivalence in Fricke's minute (see n. 119 above), which was in line with Hitler's exposé ('Führer Conferences', 119–20).

[129] *KTB OKW* i. 30 (14 Aug. 1940) and 31–2, with excerpts from the memorandum which is published in *Dokumente zum Unternehmen 'Seelöwe'*, 353 ff.: Chef WFSt, 13 Aug. 1940, 'Beurteilung der Lage, die sich nach Auffassungen von Heer und Kriegsmarine für eine Landung in England ergibt'. Directly on these 'views': Halder, *Diaries*, i. 547 (12 Aug. 1940). Operation Sea Lion is discussed more fully in vol. ii of the present work; an informative survey in Cigliana, 'La strategia'.

[130] *Dokumente zum Unternehmen 'Seelöwe'*, 355.

2. Ideas on the Continuation of the War

account fail', if only because 'failure... could have political consequences far exceeding the military ones'. This statement was followed by a catalogue of requirements, non-fulfilment of which was bound to turn the landing into a totally unnecessary 'act of desperation'. Seen objectively, the stipulated prerequisites, as Jodl agreed, could not be met by the navy. Moreover—but this the general could not know, as the test still lay ahead—the Luftwaffe was far from being in a position to eliminate the Royal Air Force. However, this argument was not even needed, as the deficiencies of the navy were most probably sufficient to rule out an invasion in the foreseeable future. Proceeding from this argument, the chief of the Wehrmacht operations staff pointed out that Britain could 'be brought to her knees also in another way', given 'closer military co-operation between the Axis powers'. The detailed measures proposed by him closely followed the ideas in his memorandum of 30 June:

Continuation of the air war to the point of the destruction of southern England in terms of her war industry. All Italian air force units not at present employed must be enlisted to this end. . . . Intensification of U-boat warfare from French bases by drawing upon half of all Italian submarines. . . . Seizure of Egypt, if necessary with German assistance, and . . . seizure of Gibraltar in agreement with the Spaniards and Italians. . . . Avoidance of operations which are not necessary for victory over Britain but merely represent desirable objectives, as these can be attained effortlessly after victory over Britain (e.g. Yugoslavia).

Jodl insistently urged that the Axis powers should 'not operate for war objectives but for victory'. According to remarks made by Hitler in the closest circle of his military staff in July 1940 there can be no doubt that Jodl did not expect the war to end with victory over Britain, but that he merely wished to gain freedom in the west for aggression in the east. That was why Britain's 'will to resist' must be broken by the spring of 1941. If this could not be achieved by means of an invasion, then it would have to be done 'by other means'. If the general had been concerned only with the German–British war, then he need not have so persistently emphasized the time factor, any more than Warlimont:[131] for there was nothing except the timing of the attack on the Soviet Union, already fixed by Hitler, that would mark out the spring of 1941 as a final date for peripheral warfare against Britain.[132] Assuming that

---

[131] On Warlimont see n. 128 above. Evidently he seriously thought it possible for Britain to be disposed of by the spring of 1941. At all events, Canaris was instructed not to compromise, by any further reconnaissance trips, Germany's 'own preparations for attack', which Hitler viewed within the framework of his planned aggression against the USSR: *KTB OKW* i. 22 (12 Aug. 1940).

[132] Quoted according to *Dokumente zum Unternehmen 'Seelöwe'*, 353 ff. On the genesis of the memorandum and its place in history see Warlimont, *Inside Hitler's Headquarters*, 108. Gruchmann, 'Die verpaßten strategischen Chancen', 461, points out that Jodl was in favour not of a concentration of Axis operations in the Mediterranean area but of intensified 'air and naval warfare'. Mussolini, who likewise hoped to see the war decided by a direct strike at the British Isles, offered 10 divisions for the invasion, transferred an air corps to Belgium, and stationed 27 submarines at Bordeaux.

Jodl's plan came off, and that the United States did not intervene in the war, the turning against the USSR, following an imposed settlement with London, would then have taken place under the conditions envisaged by Hitler prior to 19 July 1940.

As for the plans, to be examined here, for an employment of the Wehrmacht in the Mediterranean area, on 13 August Hitler, with regard to 'Possible Operations against Gibraltar', favoured a 'major solution', since only that would be acceptable to Franco.[133] The operation was to run in 'four time-phases' as follows:

(1) Binding agreements with General Franco to the effect that Spain, with total camouflage of German participation, ensures the defence against a British thrust or a British landing in the Gibraltar zone.[134]

(2) Surprise attack on the British fleet in the harbour of Gibraltar by strong German air-force formations from Bordeaux, simultaneous transfer of dive-bombers and coastal batteries to Spain.

(3) Destruction of the harbour and expulsion of the British fleet by dive-bombers and coastal artillery.

(4) Seizure of the Rock by an attack from the land and, if possible, also from the sea; for this operation Spanish supreme command would have to be unreservedly acknowledged, though the personality of the German commander must be such as to ensure that practical control of the operations is in German hands.[135]

On this basis the 'Operational Plan for the Attack against Gibraltar' was drawn up.[136]

Despite the imponderables in Hitler's strategic planning, the armed forces high command was vigorously pushing ahead with plans for a peripheral warfare which, at that time, could best be described as an interim strategy. But this did not mean that all the generals unquestioningly accepted the multifarious plans produced by the German staffs. Halder, for instance, who was still earnestly supporting Operation Sea Lion, although the army high command was also working on the campaign against the Soviet Union, noted after a conversation with Brauchitsch about Hitler's instructions:

Pipe-dreams: Spain is to be brought into the war (but the economic consequences for that country are ignored). North Africa is viewed as a theatre of operations against Britain (Egypt, Asia Minor; pushing Britain away from Cyprus and Haifa?!), Romania is to be drawn into our orbit, but in a way that would not rouse Russia too much at this early date (!). We are going to be ready in the north (Petsamo) when Russia attacks

---

[133] *KTB OKW* i. 32 (14 Aug. 1940).
[134] On OKW fears that the British might preventively advance the defence of Gibraltar towards 'the north and west' in order to forestall an attack see *KTB OKW* i. 22 (12 Aug. 1940).
[135] Ibjd. 18 (9 Aug. 1940); Greiner, 'Felix', 2–3, MGFA C-065 h.
[136] Ibid. 40–1 (20 Aug. 1940); Hitler approved the operation plan on 24 Aug. 1940 (Greiner, 'Felix', 3, MGFA C-065 h) because Franco had shown interest. Franco, however, made the condition that his extensive demands for material were met: see Detwiler, *Hitler*, 32–6.

2. Ideas on the Continuation of the War

Finland.[137] And the army is supposed to have everything nice and ready without ever getting any straightforward instructions.[138]

This criticism on Halder's part may reflect a departmental angle, but it also shows that his long-term thinking continued to be orientated towards the conflict with the USSR. Although he rightly expressed a certain hesitation as regards timing, this very reservation clearly shows determination to go ahead with the aggression.

As for Halder's criticism of Hitler's conduct of the war—which after the catastrophe of 1945 he articulated with great vigour, though not always with a sufficiently precise recall as regards his own share of responsibility[139]—the question arises, justified though the criticism was, as to how, during those weeks of strategic dilemma, a set of clear directives could have been produced. The general also evidently failed to understand that Hitler's strategy vis-à-vis Britain was by design bipolar. The road to the east, as Hitler's own relevant measures testify, would clearly be embarked upon sooner or later—probably, after 31 July, sooner. For purely strategic and political considerations it was therefore reasonable somehow to eliminate the enemy in the west beforehand. Yet Germany was unable either to determine the means or to dictate the method of avoiding a war on two fronts. The problems of strategic planning, i.e. Germany's political and economic dependence on other powers, are revealed especially with regard to the Mediterranean area. Hitler was unable, without running incalculable risks, to override Franco's or Mussolini's consent. Particularly with regard to his Axis partner, who was already worried about Pan-Germanism and who also feared that in their western campaign the Germans might, as at the time of the Anschluss, have found documents compromising the Italian government,[140] any independent move by Hitler was liable to strain the German–Italian alliance. Mussolini's indecision in the second half of 1940 counselled prudence. The ambiguity of the Duce's position was reflected, for instance, in the fact that he was over-anxious verbally to affirm his Axis solidarity, while simultaneously, on the basis of his parallel war, practising a policy of refusal vis-à-vis Hitler. From a long-term point of view this policy contained anti-German elements, and Mussolini's occasional hints that he might use Ciano's diary, of whose existence he was aware, though he had no precise knowledge of its contents, against Germany are likewise indications of his unpredictability.[141] From this perspective, Hitler found himself in a situation which virtually ruled out the clear directives his chief of staff would have liked to see. These, it seemed, would only become possible once political relations between Berlin, Madrid, Rome, and Vichy—with special allowance for Franco and Mussolini—were finally clarified and har-

---

[137] Ueberschär, Finnland, 210–13.
[138] Halder, Diaries, i. 564–5 (27 Aug. 1940).
[139] On this see Halder, Hitler als Feldherr.
[140] Palla, 'La fortuna', 40–1.
[141] Ibid. 43.

monized. From a contemporary military point of view this meant that the Reich had to allow time to pass unused—time that would have been valuable, and perhaps even decisive, for the purpose of eliminating Britain before the attack on the Soviet Union.

This was not what Hitler wanted. Indeed he was very ready to support Mussolini's offensive against Egypt by a mixed armoured brigade with the latest equipment.[142] Everything therefore depended on Mussolini's agreement. As early as 21 August the organization department in the OKH had calculated that it would be possible to equip a mobile corps for operation in North Africa within six weeks, both in terms of personnel and equipment, though this did not mean that these troops would therefore be combat-ready.[143]

Immediately afterwards Hitler called for the dispatch of stronger German forces to Libya. He now believed that two armoured divisions were necessary. He thought that the thrust into Egypt[144]—even though it was realized that the Italian command would not launch it until the first German soldiers had landed in Britain[145]—was likely, in conjunction with the seizure of Gibraltar, to 'rob the British of their powerful position in the Mediterranean' and 'moreover create very favourable preconditions' for the naval warfare of the Axis powers. This latter aspect had been brought to Hitler's notice shortly before in a memorandum by Lieutenant-Commander Junge, head of the Working Party (Navy) in the home defence department of the OKW/Wehrmacht operations staff. In it Junge dealt with the 'ratio of strength between the German–Italian and the British fleets', essentially voicing the 'Thoughts on Naval Warfare Options' from the Axis powers' point of view. He also emphasized that only the 'seizure of the Suez Canal and of the bases in Egypt *and* Gibraltar' would enable Italian surface units to operate in Atlantic waters. The lieutenant-commander also left no doubt that the 'economic demands which Spain has made as a condition of her entering the war' should not prevent the attack on the Rock, because these would 'most readily be met by the victory of arms'. To Hitler, who generally agreed with these reflections, the naval officer's uncomplicated solution seemed to be not without its logic.[146] However, it was less convincing to the Spaniards—and they alone mattered here.

At this point the third component in the operational and strategic plans of

---

[142] Halder, *Diaries*, i. 560 (23 Aug. 1940); *KTB OKW* i. 41 (21 Aug. 1940); according to Halder, *Diaries*, i. 564 (26 Aug. 1940), a division was to be dispatched.
[143] Halder, *Diaries*, i. 557 (21 Aug. 1940).
[144] *KTB OKW* i. 54 (30 Aug. 1940).
[145] This had been known since 28 Aug. 1940: *KTB OKW* i. 54, 59 (2 Sept. 1940); 1. Skl., KTB, Teil A, 328 (28 Aug. 1940), BA-MA RM 7/15; see also Hillgruber, *Strategie*, 180 n. 179. According to this Hitler had been in possession of information since 17 July that Mussolini was planning his offensive against Egypt in relation to Operation See Lion.
[146] Schreiber, *Revisionismus*, 285; *KTB OKW* i. 56 (2 Sept. 1940); Halder, *Diaries*, i. 585 (14 Sept. 1940): in full agreement with Junge's suggestions Hitler gave orders to 'promise the Spaniards everything they want, regardless of whether the promises can be kept'.

2. Ideas on the Continuation of the War

the summer of 1940 has to be examined in some detail: the seizure of the Atlantic islands.

The 'question of an occupation of the Azores and/or further Atlantic islands by Germany' was first raised between Raeder and Hitler on 20 June 1940[147] in an exchange of views on the acquisition of bases after the end of the war.[148] On 11 July Hitler returned to the subject. Now he wished to 'acquire' one of the Canary Islands from Spain for the price of French Morocco. The navy was instructed to examine which of the islands, excepting Gran Canaria and Tenerife, would be suitable.[149] In this context Hitler probably thought primarily of the postwar period, which is suggested by the idea of an exchange, even though from 6 July onward Berlin no longer ruled out a British occupation of the islands.[150] This brought to the fore the defensive aspect which subsequently largely dominated discussion of a German landing in the Atlantic islands.[151]

The same line of reasoning was also followed by the naval war staff, who—with knowledge of Hitler's observations on 31 July[152] and the specific ideas of the home-defence department for supporting the Italian offensive against Egypt and the seizure of Gibraltar[153]—stated:

---

[147] Salewski, *Seekriegsleitung*, i. 273, 288.
[148] See I.IV below.
[149] 'Führer Conferences', 115 (11 July 1940); Hillgruber, *Strategie*, 246 n. 22; Salewski, *Seekriegsleitung*, i. 258, 288.
[150] Salewski, *Seekriegsleitung*, i. 289 n. 6.
[151] The following pages examine the role of the Atlantic islands solely in the framework of military planning in 1940–1. It should, however, be remembered that these islands were of interest also with regard to future bases after the war. Both aspects frequently emerge simultaneously in the documents, e.g. in the Spanish foreign minister's talks with Hitler and Ribbentrop in Sept. 1940. The exchange of information between OKW and OKM shows more clearly than do the minutes of the conversations that negotiations were proceeding on 'whether one of the Canary Islands should be made available for German war operations or indeed later as a firm possession'; though the naval war staff wished to acquire 'only one of the two main islands', according to 'Ausarbeitung Vizeadmiral Kurt Assmann, "Die Seekriegsleitung und die Mittelmeerkriegführung"', BA-MA RM 8/1257. See *KTB OKW* i. 80 (17 Sept. 1940): demand for Las Palmas. This is also the meaning of Halder's note that Hitler 'might accept one of the Canary Islands instead of Agadir, or some other base' on the north-west coast of Africa—not, however, by way of leasing but 'to have outright possession of one port' outside any Spanish influence: Halder, *Diaries*, i. 623 (15 Oct. 1940). No doubt Hitler was already envisaging a conflict with the US, to which, in November, he faced up directly. This will be dealt with later. Generally on this complex see *Staatsmänner*, 214–15: conference with Serrano Suñer on 17 Sept.; ibid. 216–20: conversation on 25 Sept. 1940, when Hitler emphasized his idea of a 'European Monroe doctrine'. On the role of the US in Hitler's plans in Aug.–Sept. 1940 and his talks with Serrano Suñer see Burdick, *Germany's Military Strategy*, 44; Detwiler, *Hitler*, 38 ff.; Hildebrand, *Vom Reich*, 679–80; Hillgruber, 'Faktor Amerika', 513; id., *Strategie*, 248 n. 31; Jäckel, *Frankreich*, 110.
[152] 'Führer Conferences', 125 (31 July 1940).
[153] *KTB OKW* i. 17 (9 Aug. 1940), 40–1 (20 Aug. 1940), 48 (24 Aug. 1940). Italy shared the view that Gibraltar must be captured, but the chances of success were regarded sceptically, even though the Italian navy did not rule out a capture of the Rock and the opening of the Suez Canal: 'Memorandum des italienischen Admiralstabes (Übersetzung) über die "Zusammenarbeit der deutschen und der italienischen Marine", Geheim und persönlich! Anlage zu Verbindungsstab beim Admiralstab der königlich Italienischen Marine', B.Nr. g.Kdos. 107/40, (24 July 1940),

In the view of the naval war staff it must be expected that British preparations are being made for an occupation of the islands. However, Britain presumably envisages a capture only in the event of a forced surrender of Gibraltar and of Spain's and/or Portugal's entry into the war. If Gibraltar is lost, an immediate occupation of the islands must be seen as a strategic necessity for Britain. It is therefore necessary, when planning the seizure of Gibraltar by Spain and/or Germany, to consider a sufficient defensive preparedness of the Canary Islands before the event, and/or a pre-emptive or at least simultaneous landing of German forces.[154]

Subsequently, as the danger of a British–American coalition took on clearer outline in connection with the destroyers agreement of 2 September 1940,[155] the naval war staff again stressed the need for occupying the Azores and the Canary Islands, a need that would be even more pressing if Spain or Portugal entered the war. Raeder, in addition, was concerned about Dakar and North-West Africa.[156]

In line with this estimate of the situation the commander-in-chief of the navy reported to Hitler on 6 September.[157] Although Operation Sea Lion had not by then been officially adjourned, Raeder already presented the views of the navy high command on 'operations against Britain in the absence' of an invasion.[158] He was anxious to present Britain's exclusion from the Mediterranean as a measure of 'vital importance', apt to strengthen the position of the Axis powers in south-east Europe, Asia Minor, Arabia, Egypt, and the African area. The navy was looking ahead to guaranteed 'unlimited raw-material sources' and to a new, strategically favourable base for further actions against the British Empire. Sudan, Egypt, and the Arab territories were to be included in the German–Italian economic area. The naval officers' ideas even included the Indian Ocean, where they believed that London's position might be shaken by an attack on the British colonial empire in East Africa and by a threat to India. Moreover, the conquest of Gibraltar would render more difficult British supplies from the South Atlantic, deprive Britain of an

---

BA-MA RM 7/233; but cf. also 1. Skl., KTB, Teil A, 290 (24 Aug. 1940), BA-MA RM 7/15, where it is stated that 'leading Italian circles' regard the capture of Gibraltar as impossible because of the 'free access from the Atlantic'. This was entirely in line with the studies which the Italian navy had undertaken regarding the capture of Gibraltar as early as 1936: see Schreiber, *Revisionismus*, 86–7.

[154] Quoted according to 1. Skl., KTB, Teil A, 329 (28 Aug. 1940), BA-MA RM 7/15; on information about Anglo-American operations against the Azores see also Halder, *Diaries*, i. 560 (23 Aug. 1940); Salewski, *Seekriegsleitung*, i. 278, 290; on British deliberations: Butler, *Strategy*, ii. 239.

[155] The issue of leasing British possessions to the US and the handing over of 50 American destroyers to Britain—dealt with in I.II.3 above—is discussed extensively in Butler, *Strategy*, ii. 243–6. It appears that by the end of 1940 only 9 destroyers had reached the British navy, which was suffering from a shortage of escort vessels.

[156] 1. Skl., KTB, Teil A, 25 (3 Sept. 1940), BA-MA RM 7/16.

[157] 'Führer Conferences', 132 ff., esp. 135; *KTB OKW* i. 63–4 (5 Sept. 1940); see also Ansel, *Hitler Confronts England*, 21; Burdick, *Germany's Military Strategy*, 42; Hillgruber, *Strategie*, 188 ff.

[158] 'Führer Conferences', 132 ff., esp. 134; for a critical assessment of the sources of the memorandum see Schreiber, *Revisionismus*, 272 n. 74.

2. Ideas on the Continuation of the War 213

exceedingly valuable base for her naval warfare, and open up the Atlantic to German shipping even more than the capture of the west coast of France had done. For all these reasons Raeder urged that the realization of these plans be regarded not—as indicated by Hitler at the end of July—as an operation 'of secondary importance' but as 'one of the main blows against England'. It was important to execute it before a possible United States intervention, as America's entry into the war would threaten the Portuguese and Spanish islands in the Atlantic just as much as it would the French colonies in West Africa.[159] Raeder's emphasis on this point differed somewhat from that of the operations department, where the value of the Atlantic islands to the enemy was assessed less highly.[160]

After this report Hitler for the first time expressed the view that 'the Azores, the Canaries, and the Cape Verde Islands must also be taken in hand in good time, in order to forestall the British, and later the Americans, from establishing themselves in these islands'. Department L was to compile the necessary data.[161]

During the ensuing period the army high command therefore studied the 'possibility of a landing of American troops in West African ports and of an American seizure of Atlantic islands'. Halder asked the naval war staff for comment on the questions raised. In reply the navy—predictably after Raeder's report—described both a 'landing' and a 'seizure' as 'no problem' for the United States. Even in the event of a British defeat the United States would still be in a position to preserve the African west coast as a 'strategically important position for the Anglo-Saxon world'.[162] However, there was not always unanimity within the naval war staff on the issue of the Atlantic islands.[163] This had already emerged from the discussions at the end of August and the beginning of September.[164]

---

[159] Raeder emphasized the destroyer agreement which, in the light of long-term British plans (see Butler, *Strategy*, ii. 245), he correctly saw as a milestone in British–American co-operation: 'Führer Conferences', 134.

[160] 'Führer Conferences', 134, 135–6.

[161] Quoted according to *KTB OKW* i. 63–4 (5 Sept. 1940); directly on this ibid. 69 (7 Sept. 1940). A first study was available on 22 Sept. (supplemented by 2 Oct.); on 29. Oct. it served as the basis for detailed examinations of the occupation of the 'Canary Islands, the Azores, Madeira, and the Cape Verde Islands'. See n. 165 below.

[162] Study by Vice-Adm. Kurt Assmann: 'Die Bemühungen der Seekriegsleitung um einen Ausgleich mit Frankreich und um die Sicherstellung des französischen Kolonialreiches in Afrika', 8–9 (10 Sept. 1940), BA-MA RM 8/1209. On the suspense with which developments in the US were followed in Germany see Rosenberg, *Tagebuch*, 143 (12 Sept. 1940). Rosenberg, then head of the foreign-policy department of the NSDAP and Hitler's plenipotentiary for the supervision of ideological training in the NSDAP, noted that an 'invasion of Portugal' and an occupation of the Azores were being considered, with a view to forestalling possible 'American–British foolishness'. On Portugal see also Raeder's situation reports (in 'Führer Conferences') in Nov. 1940.

[163] This emerges clearly from a comparison of the sources quoted so far. A summary of deliberations valid for 1940 is contained in the memorandum of 31 Oct. 1940. See n. 165 below; also the relevant passages from Raeder's reports in Nov. 1940.

[164] See n. 160 above; Raeder's notes on the conference of 6 Sept. diverge considerably from the accounts in *KTB OKW* (see n. 161). According to Raeder, Hitler regarded only the

The authoritative summary of all these reflections within the navy high command is no doubt the memorandum 'Reflections on the Question of the Occupation of Atlantic Islands by Forces of the Wehrmacht',[165] prepared by Admiral Fricke and endorsed by Raeder on 31 October. This will be dealt with in detail as it reflects not only the fundamental problems such an enterprise presented from the viewpoint of the most important service in this operation, the navy, but also because the issue, which has been discussed in the literature from a great many angles, is examined in Fricke's study with close reference to the existing situation and through contemporary eyes.

In line with this memorandum, the naval war staff believed that an occupation of Atlantic islands would be of but slight use to the German war effort, as none of them possessed the qualities of a genuine base; besides, it would scarcely be possible to increase substantially their inadequate defence capabilities by supplies of material. Above all, it seemed out of the question that supplies to the islands could be maintained for any length of time. The Royal Navy, superior in every respect, would prevent any such attempts, as it would also the use of the ports by German naval units. The air war, likewise, would not profit decisively from the possession of the islands, since reconnaissance missions over the Atlantic presupposed supplies of fuel, which were exceedingly difficult. The army, finally, would find any such operation an additional burden, as, once it was concluded, particularly valuable forces would remain tied down at a distant outpost.

The naval staff also examined the advantage which the British might derive from an occupation of the islands, and arrived at the conclusion that possession of the islands would not be 'decisive for the war' either for Germany or for Britain. Another aspect to be taken into consideration was that the countries of North and South America might feel threatened by a German seizure of the islands. The action could therefore provoke anti-German

---

'occupation of the Canary Islands by the Luftwaffe as necessary or possible'. He was also aware of supply problems, especially as submarines could not transport aviation fuel. The C.-in-C. navy suggested as a way out the 'transfer of tankers from Spain to the Canary Islands': 'Führer Conferences', 135 (6 Sept. 1940).

[165] On the study mentioned above (n. 161) see 'LIK, Vortragsnotiz betr. Stützpunkte im östlichen Nord-Atlantik' of 22 Sept. 1940, BA-MA RM 6/73, here 58–67. Among the appendices to these notes there is also 'Beurteilung der atlantischen Inseln vom Standpunkt der Luftkriegführung aus (mit Karte nur an WFSt)', a position paper concerning air-bases in the Atlantic islands, dated 2 Oct. 1940, 70–9. The version of the study of 2 Oct. 1940—'LIK, betr. Kriegführung in Westafrika, Mittelmeer und Atlantik', 75–82 (likewise notes for a report)—was eventually developed into the major study 'Betrachtungen zur Frage der Besetzung atlantischer Inseln durch deutsche Wehrmachtteile' of 31 Oct. 1940 (121–52). This study is misplaced by Salewski, *Seekriegsleitung*, i. 288 ff., who mistakenly dates it to July 1940. Hence his explanation of its genesis is based on false premisses. On the origin of the memorandum see generally *KTB OKW* i. 90 (25 Sept. 1940), 95 (28 Sept. 1940), 102 (1 Oct. 1940), 124 (23 Oct. 1940), 132 (28 Oct. 1940), 135 ff. (29 Oct. 1940). It should be noted that on 22 Oct. 1940 Dönitz emphasized to Hitler the need to gain bases on the islands: see Hillgruber, *Strategie*, 322, *KTB OKW* i. 132; cf. also Besymenski, *Sonderakte Barbarossa*, 286–7: excerpt from the OKW memorandum of 29 Oct. 1940, 'Besetzung der atlantischen Inseln im Rahmen einer späteren Kriegführung gegen die USA'.

political measures both in the United States and in Latin America at a time when these would be undesirable. As for the kind of reaction to be expected from Madrid and Lisbon, the naval staff was in the dark; it lacked detailed information on the nature of political relations between the Reich and the countries of the Iberian peninsula.

From the military point of view, the naval war staff considered it possible to provide support for the transportation of the troops to their landing-points, but it ruled out any possibility of protecting a completed invasion against attacks from the sea. Any such attempt would only result in the loss of German naval units. And as the islands were not 'war-deciding objectives' such a high price was not justifiable. As the navy saw it, the ships employed would have to leave the area of operations immediately after the landing. Altogether, as experience in Norway had shown, it was to be expected that probably twelve, at most twenty-four, hours would be available for disembarkation. After that time British counter-actions must be expected. The Royal Navy was in unchallenged command in the eastern Atlantic, which meant that it would scarcely be possible to ship supplies to the islands on any appreciable scale. This in turn meant that the invasion troops would have to be equipped from the outset in such a way that they could 'hold out in open terrain without supplies for the presumed duration of the war'.

In view of these assumptions the naval war staff rejected the enterprise, as the capture of the islands would saddle the Wehrmacht with a kind of 'permanent Narvik'. If the navy were ordered to provide continuing support for the landed forces, a substantial impairment of the entire naval war against Britain would have to be expected. It was not that the importance of the islands, either to Britain or to Germany, was being underrated—but in the event of an occupation of the Canary Islands, the Azores, the Cape Verde Islands, or Madeira the navy was very clearly aware of the limits of what was feasible.

If, after this digression on the problem of the Atlantic islands, we return to the strategic issues of the summer of 1940, we find that the advocates of a peripheral war waged in and from the Mediterranean area, a view emphatically argued by Raeder on 6 September,[166] recommended that, without detriment to the air and sea war against the British Isles in the form it took at the time,[167] German operations should essentially focus on three major spheres of action: the Near and Middle East as the goal of a German–Italian offensive, with effects deep into the Indian and African areas; the Iberian peninsula, where the seizure of Gibraltar would, or could, directly affect Spain as well as

---

[166] Gruchmann, 'Die verpaßten strategischen Chancen', 462–3.
[167] 'Führer Conferences', 136 (6 Sept. 1940): 'The Allies keep pointing out that the greatest danger to Britain arises from the ruthless conduct of U-boat warfare ... in close conjunction with aerial warfare. The C.-in-C. of the navy therefore believes that this kind of warfare must be pursued with tenacity and energy, without remission, regardless of what other operations are mounted. Führer agrees.'

Portugal; and the Atlantic approaches of Europe and North-West Africa. This meant that, along with the Iberian countries, France too was reassessed in the German debate on the continuation of the war.

The ideas developed in this context seem, as pointed out above, to have become attractive to Hitler from approximately the middle of September 1940, when he was considering the postponement once again of his attack on the Soviet Union in favour of a great continental bloc, though only as an interim solution to German–Soviet relations. In parallel to this political shift the naval war staff now championed a peripheral and Atlantic strategy, which, in line with Jodl's ideas, it proposed with increasing clarity as an alternative to the eastern campaign, or 'Problem S' as it was then called.[168] As recently as 6 September, however, Raeder had raised no objections to the intended aggression; he merely observed that, from the navy's point of view, the 'time after the melting of the snows' seemed appropriate.[169] Hitler was convinced by this point, as he was by the reminder that 'Sea Lion' and 'S' could not be carried out simultaneously. It should be remembered that by then the navy had long regarded an invasion of England, at least in 1940, as unlikely.[170] As for Hitler's reactions to Raeder's reports between the end of September and the middle of November, these have to be viewed against the background of his continental-bloc project. Hitler at that time showed less of a fixation with the east, at least with regard to his timetable. Basically, therefore, he seemed to be more receptive to Raeder's suggestions than might have been expected. This, of course, was due solely to tactical considerations. It would be a mistake to suppose that Raeder's strategic estimate of the situation convinced Hitler that he could dispense with aggression in the east.

In this context it should be noted that theoretical preparatory work for the deployment of army and air-force units in North Africa and Spain received a fresh impetus from the Working Party (Navy)'s memorandum of 26 August. Junge's arguments, especially his idea of employing German and Italian battleships against the British fleet, struck home not only in the Reich chancellery generally but 'evidently also with the Führer'.[171] Hitler at any rate shortly afterwards declared himself in favour, in the event of 'Sea Lion' having to be abandoned, of clearing up the Mediterranean situation before the six winter

---

[168] The designation 'Barbarossa' only came into use with Hitler's Directive No. 21 of 18 Dec. 1940: see *Hitler's War Directives*, 93. Until 16 Dec. 'Problem S' had the code-name 'Fritz': see *KTB OKW* i. 1265.

[169] 'Führer Conferences', 132 ff. (6 Sept. 1940).

[170] The conference at Hitler's HQ on 14 Sept. 1940 was devoted to Operation Sea Lion: see 'Führer Conferences', 137; Halder, *Diaries*, i. 583 ff. (14 Sept. 1940). On 17 Sept. the enterprise was postponed, first 'indefinitely', and on 12 Dec. 1940 until the spring of 1941: see 'Führer Conferences', 142 (26 Sept. 1940). The commitment to 'Sea Lion' was finally dropped in the spring of 1942. At the same time the run-up period for the operation, 'which cannot possibly be carried out in 1942', was fixed at 8 to 12 months: see 'Führer Conferences', 264 (13 Feb. 1942).

[171] *KTB OKW* i. 58 (2 Sept. 1940); quotations ibid. 59 (3 Sept. 1940); directly on this also n. 144 above. For other operational ideas cf. Halder, *Diaries*, i. 569 (31 Aug. 1940); ibid. 572–5 (4–5 Sept. 1940).

months of 1940–1 were out.[172] General Jodl thereupon acquainted the Italian military attaché with these intentions 'in rough outline'. The Germans, of course, realized that the dispatch of troops could not take place at a day's notice, and therefore advised the Italians to launch their Suez offensive even before the arrival of the German units.[173] So as to lose no time, the army high command called for an immediate decision on the start of preliminary work and for the institution of German–Italian consultations in the armed forces.[174] In the mean time the assignment of an armoured corps with two divisions was being considered,[175] but without Franco's and Mussolini's approval it was still impossible to stage anything in the Mediterranean area. For this reason Warlimont wanted Hitler to address himself to Mussolini in 'a more official form' in order to renew Jodl's offer.[176] The OKW preferred first to await the reaction of the general staff in Rome. The Italians, however, were evidently in no hurry. To Badoglio, who appeared to regard the employment of German dive-bombers in Africa as acceptable, the thought of German tanks in Libya held little attraction.[177] At any rate, a full fourteen days after Jodl's initiative —the offensive launched by Mussolini's generals with the greatest reluctance[178] had meanwhile ground to a halt—Berlin was still waiting for a decision.[179]

The scope for political and military action, as seen by the German government, had considerably narrowed down when, with the British–Free French strike against Dakar from 23 to 25 September, German–French relations, until then somewhat static, suddenly came to life. The German war-planners discovered a new perspective, France.[180] Even before this, after the events at

---

[172] *KTB OKW* i. 63 (5 Sept. 1940); Raeder's situation report on 6 Sept. contained no relevant reference, but on 26 Sept. he demanded that the 'Mediterranean problem' be resolved before the end of the winter of 1940–1: 'Führer Conferences', 141.

[173] *KTB OKW* i. 64 (5 Sept. 1940); see also Gruchmann, 'Die verpaßten strategischen Chancen', 461–2; Hillgruber, *Strategie*, 180.

[174] On 5 Sept. OKH (Ops. Dept.) adopted the following position on the dispatch of armoured forces (a mixed brigade): (1) supplies must be a German responsibility and stocking up must be completed prior to the start of operations; (2) readying of the earmarked 3rd Armoured Division (re-equipment, transport, adaptation period) would permit employment at the beginning of December at the earliest. See *KTB OKW* i. 64 (5 Sept. 1940).

[175] Ibid. 68–9 (7 Sept.); cf. ibid. 77 (14 Sept. 1940); the decision on whether an armoured corps or an armoured brigade should be dispatched was thus made dependent on the Italian reply. Halder, *Diaries*, i. 585 (14 Sept. 1940), reports that Hitler had favoured the employment of an armoured corps and had given orders for appropriate preparatory steps. *KTB OKW* i. 78 (14 Sept. 1940) records the same with regard to the dispatch of an armoured brigade.

[176] For further military preparations see *KTB OKW* i. 72 (10 Sept. 1940), 73 (11 Sept. 1940), with detailed data on army and Luftwaffe formations earmarked for Libya. Directly on this Halder, *Diaries*, i. 587 (16 Sept. 1940). On Warlimont's suggestion that Hitler should approach Mussolini directly (*KTB OKW* i. 73) cf. *KTB OKW* i. 77–8 (14 Sept. 1940), to the effect that this was to be done only if the Italian reply was in the negative.

[177] *KTB OKW* i. 81 (20 Sept. 1940); ibid. 83 (21 Sept. 1940).

[178] Ciano, *Diary 1939–1943*, 289–90 (7–14 Sept. 1940); see I.III.3 (*c*). below.

[179] *KTB OKW* i. 83 (20 Sept. 1940); ibid. 84 (21 Sept. 1940).

[180] Studies by Vice-Adm. Kurt Assmann: 'Die Bemühungen der Seekriegsleitung um Ausgleich mit Frankreich und um die Sicherheit des französischen Kolonialreichs in Afrika', 12–19, BA-MA RM 8/1209, and 'Die Seekriegsleitung und die Mittelmeerkriegführung', 20–1, BA-MA RM

Oran in July, various German leaders, even within the navy high command, had called for the safeguarding of France's defence capability. They were concerned primarily about 'those colonies (Dakar, Casablanca)... which belong to the German sphere of interest'. Special attention was focused on tendencies towards a *détente* in British–French relations.[181] Any such indication was taken note of with suspicion. Thus, certain alleviations granted to France after Oran were rescinded again in August. So far neither the political nor the military leadership had any interest in seeing the 'French acknowledged as allies in any form whatever'. In consequence it was urged, among other things, that the French navy should at last be disarmed, as envisaged in Article 8 of the armistice agreement.[182] By the end of the month, however, when virtually the whole of French Equatorial Africa had aligned itself with General De Gaulle's movement, the Germans acted in a more conciliatory manner. They now authorized further cruisers for the sea areas off the African colonies. The navy high command hoped there might be a 'clash between British and French units', which would ultimately be to the advantage of 'German interests in the African area'. About the same time, impelled by the mounting threat to French Morocco, Algeria, and Tunisia from General De Gaulle's activities, the naval war staff urged the OKW to do everything in its power to strengthen Vichy's influence in the overseas territories.[183]

There was a feeling in the navy at the time that the Wehrmacht high command was looking at the problems of North and West Africa from a purely continental angle. Raeder suspected that, both on this issue and on that of German–French co-operation, the OKW was exerting a harmful influence on Hitler. In his opinion it was reluctant to concede 'the predominant importance of sea power in this war—the Mediterranean problem, French collaboration in controlling the North-West African coast including Dakar'. Besides, hints had repeatedly been dropped to the commander-in-chief of the navy that on the Dakar issue, which was of particular importance to his service, Field Marshal Keitel was acting 'obstructively'.[184] In Raeder's view, Hitler had 'not always been correctly advised'. A typical example of this, he believed, was the willingness of the Wehrmacht command to surrender to the Italians the management of the German–Italian Control Commission for Africa. The navy command was unimpressed by the argument that the Mediterranean area was 'the sphere of interest solely' of Italy. The 'Mediterranean and African problem' was of such vital importance to the war that 'Germany must on no

---

8/1257; *KTB OKW* i. 89–90 (25 Sept. 1940); Geschke, *Frankreichpolitik*, 72–7; Jäckel, *Frankreich*, 108.

[181] BA-MA RM 8/1209 (see preceding n.), here 6–7.
[182] Ibid. 2–7, quotation 2.
[183] Ibid. 9; Adès, *L'Aventure*, 19–91, on relations between Vichy and Algiers.
[184] BA-MA RM 8/1209 (see n. 180 above), here annex 3: 'Fragebogen an Großadmiral Dr.h.c. Raeder und dessen Beantwortung' (6 pages).

account allow herself to be pushed into the background in the solution of these problems'.[185]

In putting forward these arguments, the officers of the navy high command had in view the intended campaign against Egypt, the Free French activities in Morocco, the move towards defection in France's Central African possessions, and American interest in West Africa. In their opinion these developments might well require a considerable extension of military operations in the African area, involving potentially vital questions for the Third Reich. The assumption of such a political and military scenario gave rise to problems which, in the opinion of the naval staff, transcended the European dimension of warfare and could 'in no way' be judged 'any longer by the yardstick of continental land war'. Accordingly the demand was raised, as a vital aspect of peripheral warfare, that 'the navy should decisively participate in the supreme command of the Wehrmacht'.[186]

With this request, which was not granted, the navy command once more highlighted fundamental differences in German strategic thinking during the Second World War, which at that time—seen in purely military and operational terms—was still only a conflict between Britain and De Gaulle's Free French on the one side, and Germany and Italy on the other. Whatever one may think of the division of responsibilities within the German war command, the summer of 1940 was certainly not the right moment for a fundamental debate. In another respect, however, a concession was made to the navy in that the Wehrmacht high command, for its part, re-examined the German–French relationship.[187] And its reactions to the French measures at the time of the British–Free French attack against Dakar were certainly within the perspective of the naval war staff's estimate of the situation.

The navy, for its part, was by then even calling for measures[188] which it had rejected prior to Dakar.[189] The reason was obvious. The navy high command was anxious lest the British and Americans should penetrate into the West African and North African area, which would conjure up imponderable

---

[185] Ibid. 10–11.
[186] Quotations ibid., cf. Geschke, *Frankreichpolitik*, 76–7; Jäckel, *Frankreich*, 106 ff., esp. on the control commissions. See also Salewski, *Seekriegsleitung*, i. 281–2; Schreiber, *Revisionismus*, 278–86.
[187] As late as July and August Halder and Brauchitsch, for example, were rather reserved vis-à-vis French overtures: see Jäckel, *Frankreich*, 101–2; Warlimont, *Inside Hitler's Headquarters*, 136–7. On the (pragmatically motivated) change in the attitude of the two generals towards France cf. *KTB OKW* i. 50–1 (29–30 Aug. 1940), 57 (2 Sept. 1940), 61 (4 Sept. 1940), 88 (24 Sept. 1940).
[188] 1. Skl., KTB, Teil A, 317 (24 Sept. 1940), BA-MA RM 7/16. Hitler refused to dismiss the forces in Toulon. Only army, air force, and naval units stationed in Africa were to be made available. This solution did not satisfy the naval war staff—cf. BA-MA RM 8/1209 (see n. 180 above), 13–14—and Raeder reopened the issue in his naval situation report on 26 Sept.: 'Führer Conferences', 141–2.
[189] On Dakar see the detailed study by Marder, *Operation 'Menace'*, 3–192.

dangers for Italy. German air-landing troops and aerial fighting forces were therefore to be dispatched to Casablanca to assist the French. Beyond this, the naval war staff proposed a veritable revolution in relations between Berlin and Vichy, summing up their views as follows:

In the prosecution of the primary war aim of crushing Britain's determination to fight and eliminating Britain from the European area, the naval war staff believes that the time has come to collaborate with the French for the safeguarding of the African colonial empire and its food resources, which are vital to Europe. In the event of a joint conduct of the war with France against Britain—which, after the settling of the final conditions of peace with France (difficulties arising from Italian territorial demands must be liquidated) is definitely considered to be in the realm of the possible—the naval war staff believes that there is a good prospect of forcing Britain out of the Central African area (by the occupation of Freetown) and hence of dealing a decisive blow to her supply organization (convoy traffic from the South Atlantic—South America, South Africa). Attainment of the great operational objective in the Mediterranean—Britain's exclusion from the Mediterranean—will thus be greatly facilitated.[190]

Nothing needs to be added to these suggestions, which were prompted by the attack on Dakar. The naval war staff was convinced that the war against Britain was, by its nature, a war at sea. What distressed them was that the Wehrmacht high command failed to realize this. And the knowledge that, even if Hitler and the Wehrmacht high command had abandoned their continental approach, they would still have been unable to conduct a decisive war at sea must have been frustrating. Germany lacked the military tools, which was why she was looking for 'proxies', or at least powerful partners, for the war at sea. France appeared to have the ideal prerequisites. At any rate the navy—as indeed the armistice commission—recommended a revision of Germany's negative attitude to the Toulon issue, i.e. the release of the French warships lying there. The naval war staff declared itself 'convinced that the future development of Greater Europe' would 'inevitably lead to a kind of collaboration between Germany and France, and moreover, in the event of the United States entering the war, to an alliance of all European countries in a struggle against the Anglo-Saxon world empires'. In September 1940 the moment seemed to have come for 'harnessing France's fighting potential to the German war effort against Britain'.[191]

Raeder's renewed attempt, in his next report to Hitler, took place in a politically favourable situation, in so far as it was correct that questions of German warfare in the Mediterranean were being 'considered following the recent developments closely connected with events in West Africa (Dakar)'. Jodl believed that there had been a 'change of view lately' even on Hitler's

---

[190] See BA-MA RM 8/1209 (n. 180 above), 16–17; directly on this 1. Skl., KTB, Teil A, 331 ff. (25 Sept. 1940), BA-MA RM 7/16.
[191] 1 Skl., KTB, Teil A, 349–50 (26 Sept. 1940), BA-MA RM 7/16.

part, although, in line with Ribbentrop's stance, he had, in conformity with his fundamentally mistrustful attitude towards France, quite recently opposed the release of the French naval forces at Toulon. Jodl realized that the harnessing of France to Germany's war policy meant a rethinking of 'war aims'. And he did not overlook the great difficulties which would result from German–French collaboration, since finding a balance between French interests and those of Italy and Spain would be akin to squaring the circle. Jodl nevertheless intended to induce Hitler to move in that direction. Warlimont fully approved of this intention, which was entirely in line with his own ideas.[192] The same was true of Raeder, who, looking back in January 1944 to his attempt of 26 September 1940, declared that he had been haunted by the anxiety that the war might get shunted on to a 'wrong track, away from the main danger—Britain'.[193]

On 26 September the grand admiral presented his ideas on the future conduct of the war, 'including also matters outside his province'.[194] He immediately placed the Mediterranean area at the focus of his observations, because it was there that Britain was preparing to 'throttle' Italy, although the Italians were unaware of the danger. There was no time to be lost, and Raeder now urged, like Hitler, that the Mediterranean question be cleared up that very winter. He pointed to the threat of American intervention. From that point of view also, Gibraltar, once the Canary Islands had been secured, and the Suez Canal had to be captured. One might even subsequently advance from Egypt via Palestine and Syria as far as Turkey, should this become necessary. Ankara in German hands would lend the 'Russian problem' an entirely 'different aspect'. But the grand admiral believed anyway that the Soviet Union was 'basically afraid of Germany'. The risks of his concept seemed to him slight, and its advantages the greater: there would then possibly be no need to 'move against Russia from the north', Italy's and Spain's supplies would be greatly improved, East Africa would be securely safe-guarded, and the Italians could wage a naval war in the Indian Ocean. However, the situation in North Africa should not be lost sight of. There the British, supported by De Gaulle and possibly also by Roosevelt, were endeavouring to set up 'bases for attack against Italy'. At the same time they were trying to prevent Germany 'from gaining a foothold in the African colonies'. It was all the more important 'to co-operate with France in order to protect North-West Africa after certain concessions have been made to Germany and Italy'. This concept, of course, especially from the aspect of an

---

[192] *KTM OKW* i. 88 ff. (25 Sept. 1940); ibid. 93 (26 Sept. 1940); for a detailed account of the fighting for Dakar from 23 to 25 Sept. 1940 see ibid. 91 ff. On the German–French *rapprochement* see also Hillgruber, *Strategie*, 187–8.

[193] See BA-MA RM 8/1209 (n. 180 above), 20.

[194] 'Führer Conferences', 141 ff. (26 Sept. 1940); also Ansel, *Middle Sea*, 22–5; Burdick, *Germany's Military Strategy*, 46–7; Geschke, *Frankreichpolitik*, 76–7; Gruchmann, 'Die verpaßten strategischen Chancen', 463; Hillgruber, *Strategie*, 188 ff., 241; Salewski, *Seekriegsleitung*, i. 284–5, 291.

American entry into the war, presupposed a different fleet from that of the German navy. Raeder, arguing that after the conquests in the Mediterranean area there would at most be an interim peace, therefore demanded that Germany 'build up her fleet now to the highest possible degree in order to be prepared for the future'. However, this demand could not be met, if only because available shipbuilding capacities were totally taken up by U-boat construction and the building of surface vessels, as well as by repairs. For the moment he therefore had to state that 'lack of an adequate fleet will constitute a continual drawback in the case of further extension of warfare, e.g. with regard to the Canary Islands, the Cape Verde Islands, the Azores, Dakar, Iceland, etc.'.[195] Hitler agreed with this—without, however, crossing the occupation of the Atlantic islands off his list of desiderata[196]—as he did generally with Raeder's exposé. After his impending exchange of ideas with Mussolini he would decide whether 'co-operation with France or with Spain is more profitable'. Judging by his remarks to Raeder, he apparently inclined towards France, 'since Spain demands a great deal but offers little' in exchange. As for an operation across Syria towards Turkey, in order to seize that country and, as Raeder suggested, feign 'an operation against India', Hitler did not rule this out but made it dependent on Vichy's attitude. He also fully shared Raeder's belief that the Soviet Union feared Germany's military strength. Mention has already been made of the fact that Hitler was then toying with the idea of postponing his attack on the USSR, which was why he remarked to Raeder that he intended to induce Moscow to take energetic action against 'the south—Persia, India'.[197]

The advantages of such an interim solution were indisputable: for one thing, Moscow would be so strongly tied down elsewhere that Germany would have no need to hurry with her military preparations for the war with the Soviet Union; and for another, Britain's position in the event of a Soviet thrust towards the Persian–Indian area would be so precarious that she might, after

---

[195] Quoted according to 'Führer Conferences', 141 ff.; on the difficult German–French relationship cf. Halder, *Diaries*, i. 602 (28 Sept. 1940), 605 (1 Oct. 1940).

[196] After his unsuccessful talks with Serrano Suñer, the latest on 25 Sept. 1940, Hitler had ordered the 'plan for a joint German–Spanish attack on Gibraltar not to be further pursued for the time being [sic] in the form hitherto intended', although the 'expulsion of British naval forces from Gibraltar' by the German and French air forces remained under discussion: *KTB OKW* i. 104 (1 Oct. 1940); see also Halder, *Diaries*, i. 604 (30 Sept. 1940), according to which all existing plans were to be kept alive, though 'not yet to be officially discussed'.

[197] 'Führer Conferences', 141–2; see BA-MA RM 8/1209 (n. 180 above), 201; 1. Skl., KTB, Teil A, 352 (26 Sept. 1940), BA-MA RM 7/16; BA-MA RM 8/1257 (n. 180 above), 21–2. Speaking to his naval aide, Capt. von Puttkammer, Hitler remarked that the report of the C.-in-C. navy had 'been particularly valuable to him, by enabling him to check his own view and establish whether he "was on course"' (quoted according to BA-MA RM 8/1209, 20). This did not mean, however, that he actually shared Raeder's opinions. On the interpretation of this remark see Hillgruber, *Strategie*, 190, who reads the passage as referring strictly to the continental-bloc concept and who notes a revaluation of Raeder's exposé. This 'arrangement' of Raeder's ideas by Hitler is opposed by Salewski, *Seekriegsleitung*, i. 285 n. 57, though his organizationally and administratively orientated arguments carry little conviction.

2. Ideas on the Continuation of the War

all, be ready for a compromise with the Reich. In consequence, Hitler would be at an ideal starting-point for, as he was wont to put it, 'settling accounts... with Russia'.[198] Looking back a few weeks before his death, Hitler lamented that he had not had enough time adequately to prepare his 'task', which he thought too great to be accomplished by a single man or in a single generation, viz. 'to form a youth imbued deeply with National Socialist doctrine' or to build up a 'general staff of men moulded from infancy in the principles of National Socialism'.[199] But this was part of Hitler's legend-building: after all, no one had forced him to go to war, nothing put him under pressure of time except his own belief that he had to accomplish his 'programme' in his own lifetime.

The day after Raeder's report, on 27 September, Berlin, Rome, and Tokyo signed the Tripartite Pact.[200] The treaty, like Hitler's comment on Raeder's report, belongs in terms of political history to the concept of a continental bloc.[201] However, as it failed to produce the expected effects on Vichy or Madrid, military planning came no nearer to a realization of the concept.[202] This was virtually self-evident with regard to joint warfare with the French,[203] but it is true also with regard to the German efforts to get Spain to enter the war.[204]

The generals who favoured a German engagement in the Mediterranean area—but not they alone—therefore pinned their hopes on Hitler's meeting with Mussolini at the Brenner on 4 October.[205] Beyond the diplomatic and political results of the meeting it should be pointed out, with regard to military co-operation between the Axis powers, that Mussolini, though not especially enthusiastic, declared himself in basic agreement with the assignment of German forces to the offensive against Egypt.[206] The German side at first envisaged a major, but subsequently only a small, armoured division, to be

---

[198] *Hitler's Testament*, 66 (15 Feb. 1945).
[199] Ibid. 93–5.
[200] See I.III.1 (*b*) above.
[201] *Staatsmänner*, 229. Of a slightly later data is 'Betrachtungen zur Frage: Japan im Dreimächtepakt', Kriegswirtschaftliche Abteilung, BA-MA MBox 1691, PG 33967g (7 pages). This study was mainly concerned with preliminary considerations for the 'orientation of Japan towards the common war aim of overthrowing the Anglo-Saxon coalition'. In this context it was stated (p. 6) that 'In the event of some... Japanese initiative [in the Far East] bringing America into the war on the side of Britain, this would have to be accepted, since, as far as naval operations are concerned, the sum total of advantages outweighs that of disadvantages.'
[202] The entry in Halder, *Diaries*, i. 595 (23 Sept. 1940), is typical: At present [concerning North Africa] 'it is not quite clear what [Hitler] really wants there'.
[203] *KTB OKW* i. 96 (30 Sept. 1940); 102 ff. (1 Oct. 1940).
[204] Ibid. 104 (1 Oct. 1940).
[205] Ibid. 108–9 (2–3 Oct. 1940).
[206] *Staatsmänner*, 230–47 (4 Oct. 1940). Entirely along Raeder's line of argument (26 Sept.), Hitler and Ribbentrop—by then working towards a continental bloc—emphasized that 'the Russians were afraid of Germany' (234). For the third phase of his offensive, 'the fight against Alexandria', Mussolini accepted German help in the form of 'motor-vehicles', 'armoured vehicles', and 'Stukas' (243). See also Halder, *Diaries*, i. 611 (4 Oct. 1940); 622–6 (15 Oct. 1940); *KTB OKW* i. 111 (5 Oct. 1940).

ready for action about the beginning of 1941.[207] But this was too much for Badoglio, who as early as September had objected to the employment of German army formations in North Africa. The marshal tried again on 9 October to limit German involvement to the Luftwaffe.[208] Comparison with his directives on military co-operation with Germany between April and June 1940 shows that nothing had changed as regards Badoglio's mistrust of his Axis partner.

The road to the Mediterranean remained a stony one for the Wehrmacht; under the conditions existing at the beginning of October 1940 it may have been impassable. The more surprising is the confidence with which Hitler seemed to cling to his project. When on 14 October the top commanders of the Wehrmacht again met with him in conference, he held forth about the possible occupation of the 'Canary Islands, Azores, possibly the Cape Verde Islands' and asked if the navy could co-operate by transporting troops and material—which Raeder affirmed, provided that transportation took place before the airborne landing. Hitler thereupon directed that the matter, like so much else during those weeks, be further examined.[209] In fact, scarcely anything was moving forward. Both with regard to employment in Libya[210] and to the capture of Gibraltar, as well as to plans for the control of the Atlantic approaches,[211] the Germans were marking time.

---

[207] A detailed examination of the problems raised by the transport of an armoured division from Italy to Libya in A VI, B.Nr. 2292/40 g.Kdos., an Skl. (I. Skl.), of 7 Oct. 1940, BA-MA CASE GE 1076, PG 33087. Directly on this *KTB OKW* i. 111 (5 Oct. 1940), 115 (8 Oct. 1940); Halder, *Diaries*, i. 611 (4 Oct. 1940), 619 (11 Oct. 1940), 619 (12 Oct. 1940), 633 (23 Oct. 1940).

[208] *KTB OKW* i. 118–19 (10 Oct. 1940); directly on this see BA-MA RM 8/1257 (n. 180 above), 24; Halder, *Diaries*, i. 636–7 (24 Oct. 1940); On Badoglio's tactical moves see Creveld, *Balkan*, 53 ff.

[209] 'Führer Conferences', 143 ff. (14 Oct. 1940), here 145. Directly on this Halder, *Diaries*, i. 634 (24 Oct. 1940): possible air landing on the Canary Islands prior to capture of Gibraltar, but not before the beginning of 1941. Critically on these plans: Ansel, *Middle Sea*, 37.

[210] On preliminary studies up to the beginning of November, when planning was done from new points of view: Halder, *Diaries*, i. 630–1 (21 Oct. 1940), report of Thoma reconnaissance staff, Libya; 632 (23 Oct. 1940), organizational data and timetable in Libya; 636–7 (24 Oct. 1940), Maj.-Gen. Ritter von Thoma on the situation in Libya: Halder considered it unavoidable for Hitler to be informed of the disastrous picture; 637 (25 Oct. 1940), report by Meyer-Ricks (major in the general staff, department 'Foreign Armies West') on the situation in Libya: numerous operational details; 638 (26 Oct. 1940): one armoured division for Libya does not appear to be sufficient, besides Crete has to be captured along with Egypt, and a thrust into Syria, via Bulgaria and Turkey—if need be, by force—has to be allowed for in the plans; 639 (27 Oct. 1940), renewed deliberations concerning plans for Egypt, Crete, and Anatolia/Syria, observation that the attack on the USSR would be impaired by operations in Libya; 640 (28 Oct. 1940), requirements in connection with Libya and a pincer operation from Bulgaria and Libya with a view to closing the eastern Mediterranean; *KTB OKW* i. 124–5 (23 Oct. 1940), readying of 3rd Armoured Division; 126 (24 Oct. 1940), formations envisaged for action in Libya not ready before 28 Oct. 1940, except for Luftwaffe; 126 ff. (25 Oct. 1940), chain-of-command issues in Libya, report by Maj.-Gen. Ritter von Thoma; 129 (28 Oct. 1940), organization of the operation in Libya; 140 (30 Oct. 1940).

[211] The subject of Gibraltar is extensively treated in the sources listed in the preceding n. In very great detail in *KTB OKW* i. 130 ff. (28 Oct. 1940); Halder, *Diaries*, i. 626–7 (16 Oct. 1940); 634–5 (24 Oct. 1940); 638 (26 Oct. 1940). An early detailed account of German political efforts

2. Ideas on the Continuation of the War

The British for their part seemed eager to utilize the inactivity of the Axis powers to consolidate their own position in the Mediterranean area.[212] The German navy feared a British offensive from Egypt and called for the elimination of Malta as well as the occupation of Crete.[213] New plans were made, but in the end everything remained undecided as before. Gradually the impression was gaining ground that the interval since the Hitler–Mussolini meeting was passing unused. By the end of October, for instance, despite agreement on the dispatch of German troops to North Africa, there had still been no discussions between the armed forces high commands.[214] Yet such talks were an indispensable prerequisite of any joint German–Italian operation in Libya. The German high command was aware of this, but, despite the Brenner meeting, could see no 'sufficient basis' for starting them. The only way out were unofficial preparations and contacts. These included a visit to Italy, devoted to technical matters, by Captain von Montigny, the chief of the shipping department in the naval war staff. From his talks it emerged that there would not even be an Italian disembarkation port available for possible German troop transports to Libya. True, on 30 October agreement was reached on Tunis; this, however, did not solve the problem but merely shifted it to the sphere of German–French negotiations.[215] Existing difficulties over obtaining France's consent were not diminished when, shortly after the Italian attack against Greece, vital weaknesses in Axis warfare became obvious.[216]

Added to this was the fact that the mood of the French population by then reflected considerable irritation with the German and Italian commissions working in the country. German officers in the armistice commission never-

---

and military preparations concerning the capture of Gibraltar, for the period from Aug. 1940 to Feb. 1941, in Greiner, 'Felix', MGFA C-065 h.

[212] 1. Skl., KTB, Teil A, 184–5 (16 Oct. 1940), BA-MA RM 7/17.

[213] Ibid. 58–9 (5 Oct. 1940). On Britain see III.iv below (Vogel).

[214] 1. Skl., KTB, Teil A, 267–8 (23 Oct. 1940), BA-MA RM 7/17; see 'Verbindungsstab zur italienischen Luftwaffe', B.Nr. 181/40 g.Kdos., an Luftwaffenführungstab Ic, betr. Unterredung mit Marschall Badoglio am 9. 10. 1940', BA-MA MBox 646, PG 45098; according to this report Badoglio was anxious to have an immediate conference with Keitel, as well as a meeting of the commanders-in-chief of the services, in order to 'determine operation plans for the winter'. See also *KTB OKW* i. 118–19 (10 Oct. 1940), where the letter of the head of the Luftwaffe liaison staff, Lt.-Gen. Ritter von Pohl, is reported in abridged form. On 24 Oct. 1940 Badoglio, through the German military attaché, suggested to OKW the date of 10–11 Nov. for talks with Keitel, to be held at Innsbruck: *KTB OKW* i. 126 (25 Oct. 1940).

[215] BA-MA RM 8/1257 (see n. 180 above), 29–30 (23–30 Oct. 1940). The outcome of the talks is reported in detail in 1. Skl., KTB, Teil A, 371–2 (30 Oct. 1940), BA-MA RM 7/17, report from Montigny and comment by Weichold, who favoured the transfer of German troops to Tunis. The naval war staff concurred and passed on the proposal to OKW for a decision. There it was supported by Warlimont: *KTB OKW* i. 147 (1 Nov. 1940). On 5 Nov., in the course of his talks with Laval, Ribbentrop was to put forward the demand for 'the use of Tunis for the disembarkation of German troops', but these talks did not materialize because of Laval's dismissal in December: L, Vermerk, an I m Asto I (copy Skl., 5 Nov. 1940), BA-MA CASE GE 1076, PG 33087.

[216] 1. Skl., KTB, Teil A, 331–4 (28 Oct. 1940), BA-MA RM 7/17; directly on this *KTB OKW* i. 125–6 (24 Oct. 1940); 129 (26 Oct. 1940); 130–1 (28 Oct. 1940); 138–9 (30 Oct. 1940); see I.III.3 below.

theless believed that officially France desired an 'early peace with alignment towards Germany'. Admittedly, a number of questions would have to be answered first, including the future development of France and the fate of her colonial empire.[217] On these issues all efforts towards German–French collaboration turned into a Gordian knot. What was the use of emphasizing German interest in keeping North and West Africa loyal to the Vichy government when, in the same breath, only Dakar but not French Morocco was recognized as a French possession, to remain as such even after the conclusion of peace? General Noguès, the resident-general of Morocco, was regarded as 'fundamentally anti-German' and would quite certainly have opposed a surrender of territory, just as, out of loyalty to Pétain, he seemed determined to repulse any British or Free French intervention.[218] Military circles in Germany had, from this viewpoint, anxiously followed diplomatic activities in October—Hitler's meetings with Mussolini on 4 and 28 October, with the French deputy premier Laval on 22 October, with Franco on 23 October, and with Pétain on 24 October[219]—only to find to their disappointment that Hitler was 'in principle pursuing the definite policy of keeping France weak in order to eliminate any threat to the Axis powers'.[220]

The Italian campaign against Greece caused a break in German plans for the employment of the Wehrmacht in the Mediterranean area. There had, in fact, been indications even before 28 October that the offensive in Egypt—its resumption had been envisaged for mid-October, but by the end of the month was expected in December at the earliest—was taking second place behind preparations for the attack on Greece. Besides, on the Italian side there clearly existed, quite apart from Mussolini's adventure in the Balkans, some fundamental reservations about advancing beyond the second tactical objective, Marsa Matruh. The scarcely concealed delaying tactics with regard to the participation of a German armoured division in the third phase, the march on Alexandria, confirmed this surmise. Although Italy argued for a pincer movement—the shattering of the British position in the Middle East by means of a synchronized operation from the Balkans and the North African area—a glance at the map showed this excuse for Italian inaction to be untenable. Similar ideas in Germany, also involving the Libya–Egypt and Balkans–Turkey–Syria–Egypt routes, were based on different assumptions.[221] The Italians, moreover, were trying to push the Germans into the western Mediterranean, ostensibly so that they could forestall a threat to the French colonies. All this, of course, suggests that Badoglio assumed that, by the time

---

[217] See BA-MA RM 8/1209 (n. 180 above), 21.
[218] Ibid. 22; *KTB OKW* i. 130–1 (28 Oct. 1940).
[219] See BA-MA RM 8/1209 (n. 180 above), 23–6; *KTB OKW* i. 111 (5 Oct. 1940); 112–13 (7 Oct. 1940); 129 (27 Oct. 1940); 130–1 (28 Oct. 1940); 135 ff. (29 Oct. 1940); 142 (1 Nov. 1940); see also Hillgruber, *Strategie*, 322–3.
[220] 'Führer Conferences', 149 (4 Nov. 1940): conference between Rear-Adm. Fricke, chief I. Skl., and Gen. Jodl, chief WFSt.
[221] Halder, *KTB* ii. 161 (2 Nov. 1940)—not in the English edition—and n. 210 above.

2. Ideas on the Continuation of the War

of his meeting with Keitel in mid-November, he would have established a *fait accompli* in Greece. Such a development, entailing undeniable advantages to Rome, would have transformed the entire situation in the eastern Mediterranean.[222] For the time being, however, the Germans believed, in view of the rather confused situation, that it would be better for the 'question of sending an armoured division to Libya' to be deferred until after the meeting at Innsbruck.[223] They nevertheless informed their Axis partner at the same time that the advance parties for the troop transports would be ready to move from 5 November.[224]

The generals had been aware since 31 October that Hitler, as a result of Mussolini's adventure in Greece, had 'lost any inclination for close military collaboration with Italy'. The employment of German troops in Libya was thus becoming increasingly doubtful. In this situation the greatest importance attaches to the report of General of Mobile Troops Ritter von Thoma, who was entrusted by the army high command with a fact-finding mission. It has to be remembered that, even at that time, an alternative to engagement in Libya was being discussed, viz. a thrust from Bulgaria to the Aegean Sea. In addition, Hitler once more thought about solving the Gibraltar problem: along with Spain but, if possible, without Italy. He even considered the occupation of the Atlantic islands, and possibly also of Portugal.

But this did not seem to satisfy Warlimont. Like Raeder he wanted to see the situation in the entire Mediterranean cleaned up. This, he argued, could be achieved only through the participation of German units in the offensive against Egypt. Skilfully linking his plea with earlier arguments by Jodl and Hitler, he emphasized that only then would the Italian 'battle fleet' be free to operate in the Atlantic. And intensification of the war at sea was doubly important now that the air war against Britain would be affected by weather conditions throughout the winter. Jodl, on the other hand, fully supporting Hitler's ideas, believed that the fall of Gibraltar would have a sufficiently stabilizing effect in the eastern Mediterranean. The Luftwaffe, moreover, with dive-bombers from Syria and by aerial mining of the Suez Canal, would be employed in the Egyptian area anyway. The army high command therefore developed its planning further, while the Luftwaffe refused even to take part in reconnaissance over Gibraltar.[225] Confusion was complete, and Halder now

---

[222] Ausl. Nr. 1024/40 g.Kdos. Ausl. III Org, report memorandum, 1 Nov. 1940 (copy), received by Skl. 2 Nov.; military attaché in Rome, reports in writing (25 Oct.) (received by Abt. Ausl. 1 Nov.), BA-MA RM 7/233. On Innsbruck see also *KTB OKW* i. 126 (25 Oct. 1940).

[223] Halder, *Diaries*, i. 669 (31 Oct. 1940). Detailed account of the meeting in Ceva, 'L'incontro Keitel-Badoglio'.

[224] *KTB OKW* i. 143 (1 Nov. 1940). Badoglio on 30 Oct. stated that at the 28 Oct. meeting Hitler and Mussolini had deferred the question of dispatching German troops till after Innsbruck. There is no mention of this in the German records. According to them, Mussolini kept silent on Hitler's more or less explicit offers: see *Staatsmänner*, 281–94.

[225] *KTB OKW* i. 144 ff. (1 Nov. 1940); see also Halder, *Diaries*, 670 (1 Nov. 1940), 671 (2 Nov. 1940), on the preparations for reconnaissance by Adm. Canaris: discouraging account of the Spanish situation.

called for a 'decision [by Hitler] . . . on the grand objectives to be served by the preparatory work of the army'.[226] After Thoma's report it appeared to be clear, at least, that Hitler had 'written off the Libyan affair'.[227]

Hitler's conference with the principal representatives of the high commands of the army, the navy, and the air force on 4 November disclosed his views on warfare in the Mediterranean and on German-French relations.[228] He would not now send an armoured unit to Libya, as the Italian army—at least for the moment—was incapable of continuing the offensive. This seemed also to be the reason why Italy was not at all keen on the 'employment of a German dive-bomber unit in Egypt'. A weighty argument was the absolutely negative impression conveyed by Ritter von Thoma as to the quality of the Italian officers and men. Nevertheless, Hitler gave orders for 'general preparations for the employment of German forces in Libya to be continued'. Practical measures, however, would become topical only if the Italians took Marsa Matruh.[229] To the Wehrmacht this meant that army units were to be transferred to Libya in the summer of 1941 at the earliest. As for the Luftwaffe units, Hitler intended to make them available after the capture of Marsa Matruh, which was not expected before the end of December.[230] On the other hand, he was now considering generous support for Italy in Greece.[231] The reason was that developments there held considerable dangers following the British occupation of Crete and Lemnos. Hitler was worried about the Romanian oilfields and about Turkey's neutrality. However, he again positively ruled out any 'action against Turkey for the purpose of breaking through to the Suez Canal from the east via Syria'.[232]

---

[226] Halder, *KTB* ii. 159 ff. (2 Nov. 1940)—not in the English edition.

[227] Halder, *Diaries*, i. 672 (3 Nov. 1940).

[228] On the talks on 4 Nov. 1940 see *KTB OKW* i. 148–52; Halder, *Diaries*, i. 672–4 (4 Nov. 1940). The navy, which was blamed a good deal during the conference in connection with the failure of Operation Sea Lion, was not represented; see Engel, *Heeresadjutant bei Hitler*, 90 (4 Nov. 1940). The chief of 1. Skl. was notified the same day of Hitler's 'overall decision on the measures arising from the Italian action against Greece': on this see 'Führer Conferences', 146 ff. (4 Nov. 1940). Extensively on the conference: Ansel, *Middle Sea*, 50–4; Burdock, *Germany's Military Strategy*, 64–5; Detwiler, *Hitler*, 71; Hillgruber, *Strategie*, 323 ff., 335–6, 352–5, where the conference of 4 Nov. is analysed primarily from the point of view of the interrelation of continental bloc and attack against the USSR; Salewski, *Seekriegsleitung*, i. 291, 315.

[229] According to *KTB OKW* i. 149–52 (4 Nov. 1940); Halder, *KTB* ii. 162—not in the English edition.

[230] 'Führer Conferences', 146 (4 Nov. 1940); Halder, *Diaries*, i. 672–3 (4 Nov. 1940), according to which Hitler did not expect the employment of German army formations in Libya until the autumn of 1941.

[231] For details of the Greek campaign see II.III.4 below.

[232] Quoted according to 'Führer Conferences', 146 (4 Nov. 1940); on this point the view of the naval war staff differed radically from Jodl's exposé: see the situation report of 8 Nov. 1940 on the Mediterranean area, 1. Skl., KTB, Teil A, 102–6, here 106, point iv. BA-MA RM 7/18; Halder, *Diaries*, i. 673 (4 Nov. 1940)—although it is stated there that the army 'must make preparations to support a swift march into Turkish Thrace', this operation appears to have been limited, from the outset, to Turkey, in the event of a Bulgarian–Turkish conflict. Directly on this *KTB OKW* i. 150 (4 Nov. 1940).

2. Ideas on the Continuation of the War

Simultaneously with these views on the eastern Mediterranean, possibilities were discussed of improving the position of the Axis in the western Mediterranean and in the Atlantic. Here a lot depended on Spain. Although Hitler, not too amicably, referred to Franco as that 'Jesuit swine',[233] he still considered it possible that the generalissimo might 'within a short time' be prepared to enter the war on the German side.[234] After that the operation against Gibraltar could be launched. At the same time the Canary and Cape Verde Islands were to be occupied by German troops.[235] *Vis-à-vis* Portugal the action would be described as a preventive measure, i.e. it would be claimed that the British were intending to occupy the islands. Moreover, the Portuguese government was to be threatened with invasion by German troops if it supported Britain in any way whatever.[236] Once the operation was completed the Straits of Gibraltar would be closed. This presupposed that German troops and artillery would have crossed over to North Africa (Ceuta). The overall control of defence would have to be in German hands even after the completion of the operation.[237]

General Jodl on the same day informed the head of the operations department of the naval war staff of Hitler's intention. Rear-Admiral Fricke, however, brusquely refused to occupy the Cape Verde Islands, as the naval war staff had, at the end of October, just rejected any such operation in its extensive study 'Reflections on the Question of the Occupation of Atlantic Islands by German Wehrmacht Formations'. However, as Jodl countered by emphasizing Hitler's strong interest, the problem was to be settled by Raeder when he next reported to Hitler. Fricke also warned against an invasion of Portugal, as this would provide Britain with a pretext for occupying the Portuguese islands in the Atlantic.[238]

---

[233] Thus Hitler, after his conversation with Franco in Hendaye on 23 Oct. 1940: Halder, *Diaries*, i. 670 (1 Nov. 1940).

[234] 'Führer Conferences', 146 (4 Nov. 1940).

[235] According to *KTB OKW* i. 151 (4 Nov. 1940); 'Führer Conferences', 147, on the other hand, states:

It must be assumed that our plans will be revealed by the time German troops reach the Spanish border. The following measures are therefore scheduled to begin when army troops are ready to cross the the Franco-Spanish border:

(*a*) Commencement of attacks by the German air force against the British fleet in Gibraltar;

(*b*) Occupation of the Canary Islands . . . ;

(*c*) Occupation of the Cape Verde Islands.

[236] *KTB OKW* i. 151 (4 Nov. 1940); earmarked for the occupation were the 4th Armoured Division and one 'SS Death's Head Division', the so-called Schmidt corps: on this see Halder, *Diaries*, i. 674 (4 Nov. 1940).

[237] 'Führer Conferences', 147 (4 Nov. 1940); Halder, *Diaries*, 673 (4 Nov. 1940).

[238] 'Führer Conferences', 147 ff., esp. 149 (4 Nov. 1940); Jodl instructed OKM to examine the following questions: 'facilities for defence of the Straits of Gibraltar; occupation of the Canary Islands and reinforcement of the defences there; protection of the coastal road along the southern coast of France for transfer of German troops to Spain; occupation of the Cape Verde Islands; the importance of Portugal from the point of view of naval strategy; and release of the French fleet to take over its tasks in the colonies.'

The period of indecision—a symptom of crisis—continued even after 4 November. Directive No. 18, signed by Hitler on 12 November,[239] the day when he had his first conversation with Molotov,[240] still did not provide for any concentration of effort for the German conduct of the war, but was essentially dominated by ideas of employing the Wehrmacht on Spanish and Portuguese territory. Purely formally the problem of France held pride of place.[241] The intention was to use French help against the British, but to recognize them 'for the time being' only 'as a non-belligerent power'. France would have 'to tolerate German war measures and, if necessary, support them by the use of her own means of defence'. Primarily, however, Vichy would have to defend its colonies against the British and the De Gaulle movement. Hitler did not, on principle, seem to rule out that this might 'develop into full-scale participation by France in the war against Britain'. In this connection he entrusted the further development of German–French relations exclusively to the foreign ministry and the armed forces high command, regardless of the duties of the armistice commission.[242]

Wehrmacht intervention in Spain and Portugal—now assigned the cover-name 'Felix'—was to serve the capture of Gibraltar on the one hand, and on the other to prevent the British 'from gaining a foothold at any other point in the Iberian peninsula or in the Atlantic islands'.[243] To that end it was necessary not only to support 'the defence of the Canaries by the Spaniards' but also to achieve possession of the Cape Verde Islands. The armed forces high command, moreover, ordered an examination of the problem of occupying the Azores and Madeira.[244]

---

[239] *Der Zweite Weltkrieg in Bildern und Dokumenten*, i. 280–1; *Hitler's War Directives*, 80–7; additionally *Hitlers Weisungen*, Directive No. 18a—not in the English edition—of 27 Nov. 1940. On the interpretation of Directive No. 18 see also Ansel, *Middle Sea*, 15; Burdick, *Germany's Military Strategy*, 68 ff.; Hillgruber, *Strategie*, 324–5; Rich, *War Aims*, i. 171–2.

[240] *Staatsmänner*, 295–304; on Hitler's scepticism about integrating the USSR in the continental bloc, ibid. 294.

[241] *Hitler's War Directives*, 81–2.

[242] On the deliberations in OKW see *KTB OKW* i. 154 (6 Nov. 1940); on reaction to the French memorandum ibid. 142 (1 Nov. 1940). Warlimont nevertheless refused to make concessions dependent on German counter-claims being met: directly on this BA-MA RM 8/1209 (see n. 180 above), 28–9. Although the naval staff addressed to the French a number of demands of its own—e.g. Tunis as a disembarkation port—it nevertheless supported a generous approval of French requests for rearmament etc.: 1. Skl, KTB, Teil A, 134 ff. (11 Nov. 1940), BA-MA RM 7/18; according to this, Capt. Wever, chief of the navy subgroup in the armistice commission, also favoured a generous treatment of French requests, on practical grounds.

[243] *Hitler's War Directives*, 82; details of the tasks assigned to the three services ibid. 83 ff. On preparations for the capture of Gibraltar during the first half of Nov. 1940 see Halder, *Diaries*, i. 676–7 (6 Nov. 1940); 678 (7 Nov. 1940); 681 (8 Nov. 1940); 683–4 (11 Nov. 1940); 693 (16 Nov. 1940), with examination of the idea of reaching across to North Africa; see also *KTB OKW* i. 166 (10 Nov. 1940).

[244] *Hitler's War Directives*, 84; on the question of occupying the Canary Islands up to 14 Nov. see Halder, *Diaries*, i. 673 (4 Nov. 1940); 681 (8 Nov. 1940); 686 (13 Nov. 1940); and 688 (14 Nov. 1940), according to which the Luftwaffe refused to be used for the occupation of Atlantic islands; see also *KTB OKW* i. 151 (4 Nov. 1940); 169 (11 Nov. 1940); 170 (12 Nov. 1940); 177 (15 Nov. 1940).

2. Ideas on the Continuation of the War

Nothing had changed as regards conditions for German involvement in Libya. German troops were to join the Italian offensive only when it reached Marsa Matruh. But even then Hitler seemed increasingly inclined to confine himself to the employment of the Luftwaffe. This should not be overlooked despite his instructions for a possible intervention in Libya or 'any other North African theatre of war'.

In detail the three services received the following directives: 'Army: One armoured division (composition as already laid down) will stand by for service in Africa. Navy: German ships [in Italian ports][245] will be converted to carry the largest possible forces either to Libya or to North-West Africa.[246] Air force: Plans will be made for attacks on Alexandria and on the Suez Canal to close it to English warships.'[247] The directive further made allowance for military action in the Balkans, to serve as flank cover for 'Barbarossa'; it referred to 'preparations for the east', and mentioned the possibility or necessity of Operation Sea Lion being, after all, executed in the spring of 1941.[248] None of this can be gone into further at this point.

Jodl's conversation with Fricke on 4 November, the unfavourable repercussions of Italian aggression against Greece on the Italian offensive in North Africa (in any case sceptically viewed), and the strengthening of British forces in the Nile delta had induced the naval war staff, even before Directive No. 18 was issued by the armed forces high command, to prepare a comprehensive estimate of the situation in the Mediterranean area.[249] This formed the basis of Raeder's situation report to Hitler on 14 November, which represented a direct reply to Hitler's observations of 4 November.[250] Once more the commander-in-chief of the navy reiterated the arguments put forward in Junge's August memorandum and in the conferences of 6 and 26 September 1940: concentration of the German war effort in the Atlantic and Mediterranean areas.

---

[245] See n. 207, with the navy's study of Oct. 1940, BA-MA CASE GE 1076; also Halder *Diaries*, i. 668 (31 Oct. 1940); *KTB OKW* i. 181 (19 Nov. 1940).

[246] On the problem of shipping German troops to North Africa see Halder, *Diaries*, i. 672, 674 (4 Nov. 1940); 676 (5 Nov. 1940); 676–7 (6 Nov. 1940); 679 (7 Nov. 1940); 681 (8 Nov. 1940); 688 (14 Nov. 1940); *KTB OKW* i. 164–5 (9 Nov. 1940); 171 (13 Nov. 1940); 175–6 (14 Nov. 1940).

[247] *Hitler's War Directives*, 85; on operational details *Hitlers Weisungen*, Directive No. 18a of 27 Nov. 1940 (not in the English edition).

[248] *Hitler's War Directives*, 81–7; on the connections between the plan for the occupation of northern Greece and the pressure on Turkey within the framework of preparations for 'Barbarossa' see Gruchmann, 'Die verpaßten strategischen Chancen', 466.

[249] 1. Skl., KTB, Teil A, 102–6 (8 Nov. 1940), BA-MA RM 7/18; the entries in KTB diverge from annex 3 of the situation report of 14 Nov. (160–3) on only one point. In KTB it is stated, under IV (p. 106): 'Examination of the question of whether an advance by us through Turkey–Syria is possible, or to what extent pressure might be exerted on Palestine–Egypt by an active advance of the French Syrian army.' This item is lacking in the situation report, which instead states under III: 'We shall hardly be spared an advance through Turkey, in spite of all difficulties.'

[250] According to 'Führer Conferences', 149 ff. (14 Nov. 1940); *KTB OKW* i. 174–5 (14 Nov. 1940); 177 (15 Nov. 1940).

The record, in consequence, opens with Raeder's credo about the 'decisive importance for the outcome of the war'[251] of developments in the Mediterranean area—from the British point of view also.[252] The grand admiral observed a stiffening of British determination, which he attributed largely to the invasion that never was, to Italian military failures, and to the scale of American assistance. However, British concern over West Africa and over the position in the Mediterranean played a part.[253] Nevertheless, he believed there was no need for an 'alarming assessment of the situation'. The reason was that the British were not yet capable of an offensive. For Hitler, Raeder's arguments presumably lost some force when he emphasized that Britain was in no position to bring about a 'turn in the military situation' by herself.

What the navy was aiming at, therefore, was not the elimination of an actually precarious situation, but the prevention of 'sources of danger' arising in the Mediterranean and African areas, by means of timely 'political and military precautions and countermeasures'.[254] Such sources of danger seemed to be in the making, which was why the navy wished to deprive the British not only—in line with Hitler's intentions at the time—of their control of the western, but also of the eastern Mediterranean. Such actions would have repercussions of 'war-deciding importance' on the entire African and Middle Eastern region. The Axis should respond to the ever closer *rapprochement* between London and Washington by the creation of a 'European community of states' and the 'conquest of the African area'. The officers of the naval war staff were thinking of cotton, copper, petroleum, and foodstuffs: all these, they believed, a large-scale European–African economic area under German leadership would be able to supply.[255] They of course realized the need to safeguard Germany's position in the Balkans, Asia Minor, Arabia, Egypt, and the Sudan. But there was also talk once more of a 'jumping-off position' for further expansion, for seizing the British colonial empire in East Africa, and for 'threatening India'. In the west the naval staff considered it necessary to control North Africa, thereby winning the much-discussed supply-base both for Spain and for France.

The navy high command aimed at the whole of the Mediterranean area, the possession of which was regarded as 'definitively war-deciding'. Evidently it was seriously expected that this would lead to the collapse of Britain—especially if it proved possible, in parallel with the establishment of German hegemony in the Mediterranean, drastically to impair American support for

---

[251] On the progressive devaluation of 'decisive importance for the war' in the usage of the naval war staff see Salewski, *Seekriegsleitung*, i. 283–4 n. 53. Salewski takes the view that the navy used this term merely in the sense of 'attainment of a better initial situation'.

[252] *Lagevorträge*, 155 (14 Nov. 1940), appendix 1, assessment of the position of Britain, 21 Oct. 1940 (appendix not in the English edition).

[253] Ibid. 156.

[254] Ibid. 157–8.

[255] On the genesis of the German claim to leadership in the Mediterranean area see Schreiber, *Revisionismus*, 277–391; id., 'Italien', 254–67.

2. Ideas on the Continuation of the War

the British. Here the navy pointed to the 'other half' of its military concept: the war against supplies.

With regard to the Mediterranean area the navy assumed that Italy was incapable of fulfilling the necessary conditions. The Wehrmacht would have to do this by itself. That was why all 'operational plans for German warfare' should aim at clearing 'the entire Greek peninsula, including the Peloponnese', of the enemy and occupying all bases.

On these points Hitler largely agreed with Raeder. He was by then considering safeguarding Greece for Germany by independent military action in about three months' time.[256] But unlike the grand admiral, who again advised a thrust against the Suez Canal and believed that 'an offensive through Turkey' could 'scarcely be avoided', Hitler still wished to support the Italian offensive only by his air force. On the issue of Turkey he seems to have remained silent.[257]

No agreement was reached between Raeder and Hitler on the occupation of any Atlantic islands. The navy continued to believe that the Canary Islands would be useful bases for Germany as well as for Britain. That was why their defensive capacity should be increased even before Spain entered the war. Whatever happened, the Wehrmacht must forestall a British occupation. With regard to Portugal and her possessions in the Atlantic, the navy high command again counselled caution. Any violation of Portuguese neutrality would unquestionably provoke a British or American invasion of the Azores, the Cape Verde Islands, and Angola.[258]

Hitler, on the other hand, believed the British would occupy the Azores as soon as the Germans moved into Spain, in order subsequently to hand them over to the United States. He also disclosed the principal reason for his great interest in that island group: the inclusion of the United States in his strategic planning. Hitler was fascinated by the idea that the Azores would provide him with the only facility 'for attacking America, if she should enter the war, with a modern aeroplane of the Messerschmitt type, which has a range of 12,600 km. Thereby America would be forced to build up her own anti-aircraft defence, which is still completely lacking, instead of assisting Britain.'[259]

---

[256] 'Führer Conferences', 156.
[257] Ibid. 156; on such reflections see IV.II.3 below.
[258] 'Führer Conferences', 152; *Lagevorträge*, appendix 4, 'Brief Evaluation of the Cape Verde and Canary Islands', 163–4; and appendix 5, 'Evaluation of the Strategic Importance of Portugal', 164–5 (appendices not in the English edition).
[259] Quoted according to 'Führer Conferences', 152; on this central point in Hitler's strategic plans see also Halder, *Diaries*, i. 694 (18 Nov. 1940); following the Luftwaffe's refusal, capture by the navy was considered; 688 (14 Nov. 1940); also *KTB OKW* i. 177 (15 Nov. 1940), where mention is made of bombers with a 6,000-km. range; see Schreiber, 'Mittelmeerraum', 87 n. 150. Cf. also, Ansel, *Middle Sea*, 59; Burdick, *Germany's Military Strategy*, 75; Compton, *Swastika and Eagle*, 219–20, also on 1941; Hillgruber, 'Faktor Amerika', 512–15, extending to 1941; id., *Strategie*, 326–7, 379–80, esp. nn. 17–18a, showing that between May and July Hitler repeatedly talked about an attack on the US; Thies, *Architekt*, 142–3, 136–47, especially on the long-range bomber project.

Raeder, however, remained sceptical. Although, in line with the above-mentioned results of the study concerning an occupation of the islands, he considered a landing of German troops feasible in extreme circumstances, he stressed the well-nigh insuperable difficulties with regard to their protection and supplies. It was, moreover, most improbable that the islands could be held in the face of massive British attacks. However, in order to gain a realistic picture of the material prerequisites of a German landing, 'an immediate investigation must be made by both a naval and an air officer'. Hitler gave orders for this to be done.[260]

The last, though not the least important, item on the agenda of 14 November concerned the Soviet Union. Raeder was forced to realize that absolutely nothing had changed in Hitler's attitude to the solution of 'Problem S'. A day after Hitler's second conversation with Molotov,[261] Raeder noted that the Führer was 'still inclined to pursue the conflict with Russia'. For departmental reasons the admiral now recommended only a postponement of Operation Barbarossa until after victory over Britain. His reason was that during a German–Soviet conflict 'the area so urgently needed for submarine training in the eastern Baltic would be lost, and submarine warfare thereby adversely affected'.[262] There was no longer any talk of a possible abandonment of the campaign against the USSR, as he had suggested on 26 September.[263]

In point of fact Hitler, in complete conformity with his resolution of 31 July 1940, was now unceasingly pursuing an early military solution in the east. German thoughts on the Mediterranean area played a part in this development, in which the intention to resolve the strategic dilemma in which German warfare had been involved since the summer of 1940 coincided with Hitler's determination to implement his 'programme' for the conquest of living-space in the east.[264] What mattered as regards the Mediterranean was the (repeatedly mentioned) cover of Germany's strategic flank, represented by this area. Germany's insistent efforts, resumed towards the end of 1940, to induce Spain to enter the war were part of an endeavour to stabilize the situation in the Mediterranean and North-West Africa with an eye to the planned war in the east; they also served the purpose—with a westward glance, as it were—of making that area secure against the United States. There is no doubt, however, that the German measures were simultaneously designed to relieve Italy, because the precarious situation in which Mussolini found himself at the end

---

[260] Quoted according to 'Führer Conferences', 153, directly on this *KTB OKW* i. 184 (20 Nov. 1940); 186 (25 Nov. 1940); 193 (30 Nov. 1940); Burdick, *Germany's Military Strategy*, 98 n. 4, with details of the reconnaissance trip to the Canary Islands.

[261] *Staatsmänner*, 304–20.

[262] 'Führer Conferences', 153; *Weizsäcker-Papiere*, 228 (8 Dec. 1940).

[263] Cf. Salewski, *Seekriegsleitung*, i. 316–17, who interprets Raeder's remark as though he had 'emphatically pointed out' that 'Barbarossa' should not take place; in actual fact the text merely says: 'C.-in-C. navy recommends postponement.'

[264] *Das Deutsche Reich und der Zweite Weltkrieg*, iv.

2. Ideas on the Continuation of the War

of 1940 was beginning to act as a brake on Hitler's political and military plans.[265]

The situation in mid-November can therefore be summed up as follows. There was no question of 'fundamental and extensive agreement'[266] between Raeder and Hitler; and although valuable time and effort had been invested in preparatory work on peripheral warfare, Germany was still marking time. As for collaboration with France, no progress was achieved in the military sphere either, because it proved impossible to achieve political agreement between Berlin and Vichy.[267] Seen from within the Axis: although Keitel and Badoglio after their meeting on 14 and 15 November issued an optimistic statement of intent about the intensification of military co-operation, the results of German urgings that Italy be more obliging vis-à-vis French proposals within the armistice commissions remained unsatisfactory. Equally vague was the outcome of talks between the Axis partners on Wehrmacht participation in the offensive against Egypt. Everything depended on a successful Italian advance to Marsa Matruh—which was nothing new. The only clear point to emerge from such verbiage was Mussolini's definite renunciation of participation in Operation Felix.[268]

Military planning for 'Felix' was running at top speed,[269] and preparations for using German divisions to secure the portion of the North African coast facing Europe[270] were also going ahead. Only in the political field was progress slight. The talks with Serrano Suñer on 18 and 19 November yielded no binding promise of Madrid's entry into the war, although the Spanish foreign minister did not positively rule it out either.[271] Hitler even displayed optimism,

---

[265] Hillgruber, *Strategie*, 326–7; Salewski, *Seekriegsleitung*, i. 317.
[266] 1. Skl., KTB, Teil A, 179 (14 Nov. 1940), BA-MA RM 7/18.
[267] See BA-MA RM 8/1209 (n. 180 above), 31 ff.
[268] On the meeting between Keitel and Badoglio on 14–15 Nov. 1940 see n. 223 above; also *KTB OKW* i. 171–2 (13 Nov. 1940); the points for discussion; 173–4 (14 Nov. 1940); 178 (19 Nov. 1940); Halder, *Diaries*, i. 694 ff. (18 Nov. 1940); OKW/WFSt Nr. 9/40 g.Kdos. Chefs. 'betr. Besprechungen Gen. Feldm. Keitel/Marschall Badoglio' (20 Nov. 1940), BA-MA RM 7/233; 1. Skl., KTB, Teil A, 224 (18 Nov. 1940); 270 (21 Nov. 1940); BA-MA RM 7/18; see BA-MA RM 8/1209 (n. 180 above), 30 ff.
[269] On the details see Halder, *Diaries*, i. 694–5 (18 Nov. 1940); Portugal is affected by 'Felix' only in case of emergency; 699 (19 Nov. 1940), data on material; 703–4 (25 Nov. 1940), equipment and transport questions; 707 (26 Nov. 1940), political and military problems; *KTB OKW* i. 177–8, 179–80 (19 Nov. 1940), topical issues 'Marita' and 'Felix', detailed military data; 182 (19 Nov. 1940), political and military implications; 186–7 (25 Nov. 1940), operational matters, results of Adm. Canaris's trip.
[270] Halder, *Diaries*, i. 694–5 (18 Nov. 1940), extension of operations to the North African region; 694 (18 Nov. 1940), batteries for African coastal defence; 700 (20 Nov. 1940), shipping for transports to Tangiers; 703 (25 Nov. 1940), shipping for North African transports; *KTB OKW* i. 187 (25 Nov. 1940), Hitler's intention, following execution of 'Felix', to station one or two divisions in North Africa for insurance; 191 (27 Nov. 1940), transfer of troops to North Africa even before 'Felix' and 'Marita'—on the latter operation see III.III below (Vogel); on military details of 'Felix' cf. Burdick, *Germany's Military Strategy*, 71–2.
[271] On the talks between Hitler and Serrano Suñer on 18 Nov. see *Staatsmänner*, 320–30; on Ribbentrop's talks with Serrano Suñer on 19 Nov. see *DGFP* D xi, No. 357, pp. 619–23

though time—and that was what the Spanish were playing for—was gradually running out.

Meanwhile plans for action in the Balkans for the purpose of securing bases and covering the German flank were competing with those for 'Felix'. Calculations showed that the capture of Gibraltar must be completed before Operation Marita[272] was started, because it would be too difficult for the Luftwaffe to carry out both operations simultaneously.[273] Preparatory studies for 'Felix'[274] moreover revealed that 'the need for rigorous camouflage' did not permit of a lightning war, as thirty-eight days would have to elapse from the crossing of the French–Spanish frontier to the attack on the Rock.[275] Abandonment of camouflage eventually reduced this time-span to twenty-five days.[276] The operation, it was now decided, would start in the spring of 1941. Reconnaissance parties were to travel to Spain on about 6 December.[277]

When the commander-in-chief of the navy reported to Hitler on 3 December[278] it had already been decided that Canaris would go to see Franco to obtain his consent to the entry of German troops into Spain not later than 10 January 1941.[279] Hitler wanted a decision. He must therefore have found it easy to agree with the burden of Raeder's report—clearing up of the situation in the Mediterranean area by the capture of Gibraltar and, if it were still necessary after assumption of 'control of the western Mediterranean', action in its eastern part. The grand admiral also stressed the unique importance of the disruption of British supply-lines in the Atlantic and warned against 'operations entailing too great a risk, since this would tend to prolong the war'. This remark did not indeed refer to 'Barbarossa', but to the occupation of Ireland, an idea which was, at the time, credited by Hitler[280] with 'war-deciding' consequences—though only with regard to the conflict with Britain and not to the intended war against the Soviet Union. According to Raeder

---

(undated); cf. also Burdick, *Germany's Military Strategy*, 65–6; Dankelmann, *Franco*, 149; Detwiler, *Hitler*, 73–9.

[272] This was the code-name for the operations for the capture of the northern Aegean coast and, if necessary, the entire Greek mainland: *Hitler's War Directives*, No. 20, pp. 90–2 (13 Dec. 1940).

[273] *KTB OKW* i. 181 (19 Nov. 1940); at this conference LIL pointed out that 'the 8 Stuka wings envisaged for Operation "Felix" . . . would be needed also for "Marita", which might lead to difficulties in deployment'. Cf. generally also Detwiler, *Hitler*, 80; and Hillgruber, *Strategie*, 328.

[274] Halder, *Diaries*, i. 715 (2 Dec. 1940).

[275] Ibid. 717 (3 Dec. 1940).

[276] *KTB OKW* i. 205–6 (5 Dec. 1940).

[277] Halder, *Diaries*, i. 717, 719 (3 Dec. 1940); *KTB OKW* i. 196 (1–4 Dec. 1940).

[278] 'Führer Conferences', 156 ff. (3 Dec. 1940); *KTB OKW*, i. 197–8 (3 Dec. 1940).

[279] On Adm. Canaris's trip see *KTB OKW* i. 197 (4 Dec. 1940); 219 (8 Dec. 1940): Canaris talked to Franco on 7 Dec. On the fixing of the date, ibid. 206 (5 Dec. 1940), 211 (6 Dec. 1940); cf. also Halder, *Diaries*, i. 721–2 (5 Dec. 1940); Höhne, *Canaris* (trans.), 438 ff.; n. 293 below on Canaris's visit to Spain.

[280] 'Führer Conferences', 156 ff. (3 Dec. 1940), according to which support for Ireland was only to be considered if Dublin asked for it.

2. Ideas on the Continuation of the War

the navy was prepared for the seizure of Gibraltar;[281] and the navy's representatives were meanwhile negotiating with the Spaniards about 'fortification' of the Canary Islands.[282]

On 15 December Hitler discussed the situation with Brauchitsch, Halder, Jodl, and Keitel.[283] He seemed to be confident that Franco was determined to enter the war.[284] He also wished to confine himself entirely to the operations which had been discussed for the western Mediterranean. Participation in the Italian offensive in North Africa was 'out of the question for the time being'.[285]

The high command of the army, its planning long concerned with Operation Barbarossa, envisaged for 'Marita' a date immediately after the spring thaw, i.e. March 1941. It was assumed that by that time any restraints due to Operation Felix would have disappeared, since the capture of Gibraltar, provided it was started as planned, was bound to be completed by the end of February. Hitler did not object, as the seizure of Gibraltar and the employment of the Luftwaffe—from southern Italy—against the Royal Navy would also stabilize the position of Mussolini, whose military failures were having an unfavourable effect on the attitude of the French. Thus Pétain, in order to block Italian demands, was increasingly using the threat that his North African possessions would defect. Largely in order to eliminate that danger, Hitler intended, directly 'Felix' was completed, to transfer German troops to North Africa.[286]

---

[281] Ibid. 157 (3 Dec. 1940); Skl., B.Nr. I. Skl. I op 2465/40 g.Kdos. Chefs., concerning 'Felix' (12 Nov. 1940), BA-MA MBox 57, PG 32087 b.

[282] On the question of an occupation of the Canary Islands, prior to the temporary halt of all fortification and defence plans on 10 Dec. 1940: *KTB OKW* i. 222; *Hitlers Weisungen*, Directive No. 19a (11 Dec. 1940; not in the English edition); see also Halder, *Diaries*, i. 713 (30 Nov. 1940), renunciation of 'Spanish and Portuguese islands' under consideration; 715 (2 Dec. 1940), four batteries earmarked for defence of the Canary Islands; 726 (6 Dec. 1940), the four batteries envisaged for Gran Canaria and Tenerife; *KTB OKW* i. 211 (6 Dec. 1940), batteries for the Canary Islands; 213 (6 Dec. 1940), Canary Islands capable of defence, occupation of Madeira and the Cape Verde islands ruled out, that of the Azores presumably no longer possible—directly on this ibid. 219 (8 Dec. 1940). See also Skl., B.Nr. Skl. I. op 2510/40 g.Kdos. Chefs., on 'Felix' (22 Nov. 1940): enhancement of defensive capacity of the Canary Islands, BA-MA CASE GE 440, PG 32488; ibid. OKW/WFSt/Abt. L Nr. 33395/40 g.Kdos. Chefs. (11 Dec. 1940) to ObdH (Op. Abt.), ObdM. (Skl.), ObdL (Lw.Führ.St.), OKW: WFSt, Abt. L, WNV, Ausl/Abw, Chef Wehrm.Transp.Wesen. On preparatory studies and reconnaissance see B.Nr. AI. I op 2552/40, report to naval staff on the trip of Chef AI (Marinekommandoamt/Kommandoabteilung, later Quartiermeisteramt, Skl/Qu AI) between 15 and 26 Nov. 1940, dated 2 Dec. 1940; BA-MA CASE GE 529, PG 32604.

[283] On this see Halder, *KTB* ii. 211–14 (5 Dec. 1940; not in the English edition); *KTB OKW* i. 203–9 (5 Dec. 1940); Burdick *Germany's Military Strategy*, 98–101; Detwiler, *Hitler*, 80–3; Hillgruber, *Strategie*, 329–30.

[284] It should be noted that, at the same time, Hitler on a different occasion expressed strong doubts about this; his confidence on 5 Dec. was probably deliberately optimistic: cf. Burdick, *Germany's Military Strategy*, 98 n. 5.

[285] *KTB OKW* i. 204 (5 Dec. 1940).

[286] Ibid. 204; on the formations earmarked for Morocco see Halder, *Diaries*, i. 722 ff. (5 Dec. 1940), 727–8 (8 Dec. 1940).

The German generals at the time regarded North-West Africa and West Africa as the 'strategic flank of the entire front' which protected an economic area beyond the reach of the British blockade.[287] They were in agreement with Hitler as to its outstanding importance. But unlike certain officers who advocated concessions to France in order to tie that country closer to Germany,[288] Hitler wanted to eliminate the uncertainties in Africa by the use of bayonets. Thus, the idea of a great continental bloc having been dropped, even the plan for a small bloc confined to western Europe, which in any case was not in line with Hitler's long-term political intentions, seemed doomed to failure.[289] Referring to the entire Mediterranean area, and against the background of his preparations for aggression in the east, Hitler outlined his timetable as follows: '(1) Air war against the British fleet in the eastern Mediterranean from 15 December; (2) attack on Gibraltar, start at beginning of February,[290] end four weeks later; (3) operation against Greece, start at beginning of March, conclusion under favourable conditions end of March, but perhaps not until end of April.'[291]

Under considerable pressure of time the Iberian peninsula was thus to be included 'in the great operational sphere of the Axis powers', and the British fleet was to be driven out of the western Mediterranean.[292]

The labours of German strategists in the summer and autumn of 1940 finally seemed to be approaching their objective when Franco's 'no' dashed all hopes. Hitler and his generals learnt the disappointing truth on 8 December. The Spanish head of state had not allowed himself to be persuaded. He justified his refusal by numerous reasons, but principally by Spain's economic weakness. His suggestion that Germany should carry on with her preparations for the capture of Gibraltar with the 'necessary camouflage' was no more than a diplomatic embellishment of his rejection of the plan. This is confirmed by Franco's reaction to an immediate enquiry by the Wehrmacht high command concerning the 'earliest possible date' he could propose for the execution of 'Felix': the generalissimo declined to commit himself.[293] Madrid did not wish

---

[287] *KTB OKW* i. 196, 200 (4 Dec. 1940), on Warlimont's report to Hitler on 3 Dec.

[288] Halder, *KTB* ii. 212 (5 Dec. 1940; not in the English edition); see BA-MA RM 8/1209 (n. 180 above), 31–4; Warlimont was ultimately unable to get his ideas accepted in the OKW; see also n. 287 above.

[289] See Hillgruber, *Strategie*, 329, and I.III.1(*b*) above.

[290] Agreement was finally reached on 5 Feb. 1940 as the day of the attack: see *KTB OKW* i. 206 (5 Dec. 1940). Detailed information on the intended military operations ibid. 206–7 (5 Dec. 1940), 216 (7 Dec. 1940). Warlimont was to acquaint Franco with the German operations plan in mid-December: ibid. 211 ff. (6 Dec. 1940); directly on this the draft 'Directive No. 19: Operation Felix', *Hitlers Weisungen*, 86–90 (undated, but completed in the afternoon of 7 Dec. 1940; not in the English edition); see *KTB OKW* i. 211 (6 Dec. 1940), 218 (7 Dec. 1940).

[291] *KTB OKW* i. 204–5 (5 Dec. 1940).

[292] *Hitlers Weisungen*, 86 (not in the English edition).

[293] *KTB OKW* i. 219 (8 Dec. 1940), 222 (10 Dec. 1940); Halder, *Diaries*, i. 727–8 (8 Dec. 1940). On Adm. Canaris's mission see Brissaud, *Canaris*, 363–7, stating that Canaris encouraged the Spaniards in their negative attitude; cf. also Burdick *Germany's Military Strategy*, 102 ff.;

2. Ideas on the Continuation of the War

to make the same mistake as Rome. The Caudillo, Canaris reported, 'let it be clearly understood that he could enter the war only when Britain was facing immediate collapse'.[294]

This turn of events deprived German strategic calculations for the Mediterranean area of their basis: without Spain they were unfeasible. As if this were not enough, Berlin feared during those weeks that the separatist movement among the French colonies in Africa—an increasing number of which were switching to De Gaulle's colours—could spread to those French possessions in North Africa which so far had been loyal to Vichy. It could certainly not be ruled out that General Weygand, the delegate-general of the Pétain government for those territories, would proclaim a 'counter-government'. The Germans prepared for that eventuality, and Hitler examined 'extreme consequences'. These were laid down on 10 December in the directive for Operation Attila, whereby, at Halder's suggestion, a defection of the French territories 'controlled' by Weygand was to be countered by the rapid 'occupation of the still unoccupied territory of continental France'. Simultaneously with that invasion the French home fleet and the units of the French air force at home bases were to be brought under German control. The Germans did not expect any concerted opposition from the French forces. Local resistance, which was expected, would be 'ruthlessly' suppressed. Significant and typical of the persistently troubled state of German–Italian co-operation was the explicit order that the Italians were not to be given any information on such preparations or intentions.[295]

But Hitler was already thinking beyond these military measures—initiated in the first ten days of December 1940—as a counter to the defection of French North Africa from Vichy. Franco's intransigence and Italy's military defeats had, in a way, left Germany with greater 'freedom of action *vis-à-vis* the French', which Hitler proposed to 'use for binding them to his policy by the promise to let them keep their African possessions'. Operation Felix therefore seemed to be no longer topical, since, as the directive of 11 December put it, the 'political prerequisites no longer existed'.[296] According to the official formulation, however, the operations were only 'postponed', which meant that 'preparations' were to be maintained.[297]

But in fact German–French *rapprochement* never got beyond the first overtures. The cabinet reshuffle on 13–14 December, which resulted in Laval's

Detwiler, *Hitler*, 123 ff., 'notes on the Franco–Canaris talks on 7 December 1940'; see also n. 279 above.
[294] *KTB OKW* i. 222 (10 Dec. 1940).
[295] Halder, *Diaries*, i. 728 (8 Dec. 1940); *Hitler's War Directives*, No. 19, Operation Attila, 88–90 (10 Dec. 1940). On the hopes of putting the French navy into German service, as well as on the difficulties of getting the units at Toulon into German hands, see Skl. B.Nr. 1, Skl. I op 2603/40 g.Kdos. Chefs. betr. Weisung Nr. 19, Vorg.: OKW/WFst(L) Nr. 33400/40 Chefs. (10 Dec. 1940) to OKW (WFSt) (16 Dec. 1940), BA-MA CASE GE 439, PG 32485.
[296] *Hitlers Weisungen*, No. 19a, p. 901 (11 Dec. 1940; not in the English edition).
[297] Halder, *Diaries*, i. 734 (12 Dec. 1940); id., *KTB* ii. 226 (13 Dec. 1940; not in the English edition); id., *Diaries*, i. 740 (17 Dec. 1940).

dismissal, substantially contributed to this failure.[298] A few days later Hitler once more toyed with the idea of 'making peace with England at the expense of France'.[299]

From the notes made by Weizsäcker on the international situation in December 1940 and January 1941 it emerges that Hitler's tactical manœuvring between Madrid, Rome, and Vichy has to be interpreted against the background of his planned 'spring campaign against Russia', the 'sense' of which the state secretary could not quite see.[300] Remarks about a German–British 'negotiated peace' are probably to be viewed in the same context,[301] i.e. as indications that Hitler was, now and again, still hoping to bring about the ideal jumping-off situation for his attack on the Soviet Union, as originally intended in July. The only important aspect of this is the fact that a political alternative continued to exist for Hitler, thus disproving his official justification for aggression against the USSR. The primary objective, quite simply, was not London but Moscow: it was living-space in the east, it was the realization of his 'programme'.

As for German–Spanish relations, which, at least unofficially, reached a low around the middle of December 1940, it appeared that in view of the 'disorganization' of the Spanish state and Franco's obvious 'incapability' of governing his state even in peacetime, it was 'lucky' that Germany did not have to 'drag this cripple along with her as well'.[302] Soon, however, it became clear how gladly Germany would have taken Gibraltar with the generalissimo's help even in 1941. It was Hitler's grand admiral who once more spotlighted this idea.

The navy high command had for some time been watching with concern the disastrous course of Italy's military operations. A German rescue action seemed to be virtually unavoidable.[303] Both in its estimate of the situation in the Mediterranean of 12 December[304] and in an analysis of 'The Main Problems of the Present Situation' of 20 December[305] the naval war staff reduced its unfavourable impressions to the following formulation. It was 'no longer possible to drive the British fleet from the Mediterranean', although this was 'considered vital for the outcome of the war'; there was doubt about the Italian people's ability to hold out; there was an 'increased danger to German and thus European [sic] interests in general in the African area'; and it had to be admitted that 'the decisive action in the Mediterranean for which we had hoped is therefore no longer possible'.[306] This and other passages of the

---

[298] Geschke, *Frankreichpolitik*, 131–6; Jäckel, *Frankreich*, 140–55; Krautkrämer, 'Entmachtung Lavals'.
[299] Halder, *Diaries*, i. 742 (18 Dec. 1940).
[300] *Weizsäcker-Papiere*, 229 (22 Dec. 1940); 231–2 (16 Jan. 1941).
[301] Ibid. 230 (3 Jan. 1941).
[302] Ibid. 229 (18 Dec. 1940).
[303] Ibid. 229 (22 Dec. 1940).
[304] 1. Skl., KTB, Teil A, 154 ff. (12 Dec. 1940), BA-MA RM 7/19.
[305] Ibid. 234–40 (20 Dec. 1940).   [306] Ibid. 235.

2. Ideas on the Continuation of the War 241

estimate of the situation of 20 December are found verbatim in Raeder's report to Hitler on 27 December.[307]

Hitler seemed to share Raeder's doubts about the Axis partner, but not his pessimism with regard to the overall situation, especially as it was becoming increasingly clear that the Wehrmacht would after all intervene in developments in the Mediterranean area. On 19 November Italy had requested German transport aircraft to relieve the supply situation of the Italian forces in the Balkans. Accordingly, from 9 December onward III Gruppe of 1 Bomber Geschwader (special employment) was flying supply missions from Italy to Albania.[308] On 6 December representatives of the German and Italian air forces negotiated in Rome concerning the employment of X Air Corps in the Mediterranean area. The initiative came from Germany: its goal was in line with the wish expressed by Hitler as early as 28 October. Mussolini approved of the German proposals, and on 10 January X Air Corps flew its first missions from Italy.[309] Militarily those days 'had yielded a net loss' to the Duce.[310] Even before the start of Operation Mediterranean,[311] that is, before the transfer of X Air Corps began, Mussolini felt obliged to enquire in Berlin through the Italian ambassador about indirect flanking measures. Alfieri formulated this very cautiously:[312]

Perhaps it was possible for the Führer, so the Duce had thought, to hit upon a diversionary manœuvre, possibly by bringing Bulgaria to a partial mobilization merely for the sake of effect. In this way also the pressure on the front would be reduced. Another possibility of lessening the pressure he (the ambassador) had already suggested to the Reich foreign minister the day before. It might be possible, by means of a 'journalistic indiscretion', to start a rumour abroad that Germany was concentrating large forces in Romania. All this would, in the opinion of the Duce, contribute to relieving the pressure and splitting the enemy forces. These were, however, only hypotheses that had come up during the conversation, which he (the ambassador) wished to communicate for information; his real specific mission was to request the Führer to bring about a speedy accession of Yugoslavia to the Tripartite Pact.[313]

Soon afterwards Mussolini had to turn to Hitler with extensive and urgent requests for material.[314] On 20 December he not only requested that pressure

---

[307] 'Führer Conferences', 160 ff. (27 Dec. 1940); see on this n. 317 below.
[308] Gundelach, *Luftwaffe im Mittelmeer*, 88–92.
[309] DGFP D xi, No. 452, pp. 789–91 (5 Dec. 1940), letter from Hitler to Mussolini; ibid., No. 460, pp. 798–9 (6 Dec. 1940), report by von Mackensen, German ambassador in Rome, on the results of talks between Field Marshal Milch and Mussolini; directly on this ibid., No. 494, pp. 844–5 (11 Dec. 1940), also the Ambassador's report to the foreign ministry on Milch's visits; in detail on the employment of X Air Corps: Gundelach, *Luftwaffe im Mittelmeer*, 92–9.
[310] *Weizsäcker-Papiere*, 229 (22 Dec. 1940); cf. also Alfieri, *Dictators*, 82–3.
[311] Hillgruber, *Strategie*, 340.
[312] DGFP D xi, No. 477, pp. 817–24 (8 Dec. 1940), talks between Hitler and Alfieri. The suggestion that German help should be asked for came from Ciano: on this Alfieri, *Dictators*, 83. Alfieri had already spoken to Ribbentrop on 7 Dec. (*Dictators*, 85), when the meeting with Hitler was agreed. On its course and on the results reported by Alfieri to Rome see *Dictators*, 85–6.
[313] See III.1.2 below.
[314] DGFP D xi, No. 538, pp. 911–14 (20 Dec. 1940), Hitler–Alfieri conversation on 19 Dec.

be brought upon Greece by stepping up German military and political activity in the Balkans,[315] but also requested through General Cavallero[316] that a German armoured division be made available for operations in Libya. The Italians at that time still intended an active defence of Tripolitania. Moreover, the Germans were to send war material sufficient to equip ten divisions. In addition, Cavallero again pointed out that Italian industry was in need of assistance with raw materials.

Such was the position Italy was in when on 27 December Raeder reported to Hitler on the strategic situation.[317] Hitler observed that there was a 'total lack of leadership' in Italy. With regard to German supporting measures in North Africa, he envisaged action in Tripoli or else from Spanish Morocco, whence the North African area could best be controlled. That was why, in Hitler's opinion, the seizure of Gibraltar was necessary. Raeder welcomed this view. He was 'entirely in agreement' with the Führer, as the navy had always urged that Operation Felix be executed as soon as possible. The navy, quite apart from securing the western Mediterranean and the French colonial empire, was interested also in El Ferrol and Cadiz as bases for battleships and U-boats. But so long as Franco hesitated nothing could be done. However, Hitler agreed to try again to get Spain to enter the war, since a resolution of the precarious situation in North Africa did not seem possible without the conquest of Gibraltar.

On 27 December Raeder justified his 'serious doubts as to the advisability of Operation Barbarossa before the overthrow of Britain' by the indispensable concentration of the war effort upon Britain. Solution of its supply problems was of crucial importance to London, which was why the air and sea war against British imports was the most promising road to victory over Britain. The grand admiral concluded his exposé by demanding priority for aerial and naval armaments. Although Hitler had no fundamental objections to the 'greatest possible progress in submarine construction', in his view, professedly because of military and political realities, the only road to London led via Moscow: first of all it was 'necessary to eliminate at all costs the last enemy remaining on the Continent'. This meant that armaments for the army had priority.[318]

There is no need at this stage to go into the details of military planning and preparations for the engagement of the Wehrmacht in North Africa. Suffice it to point out that with the Italian call for help on 19–20 December—followed on 28 December by the admission that Cyrenaica could not be held, and that without German assistance probably 'the whole of Italian North Africa [would]

---

[315] Ibid., No. 541, pp. 916–17 (20 Dec. 1940), Rome embassy to foreign ministry.
[316] *KTB OKW* i. 241 (20 Dec. 1940); cf. also Gruchmann, 'Die verpaßten strategischen Chancen', 471.
[317] 'Führer Conferences', 160 ff. (27 Dec. 1940).
[318] Ibid., esp. 162.

2. Ideas on the Continuation of the War

be lost'[319]—and with German willingness to employ army formations there,[320] the 'parallel war' concept had become an absurdity. The Mediterranean, for many months sealed off against any German penetration—by Franco in the west and by Mussolini in the east—was now open to Hitler's armies. The generals and the Führer had eventually attained one of their objectives, albeit in totally changed circumstances.

As foreshadowed in conversation with Raeder, Hitler in fact brought Operation Felix once more into German war policy at the end of December. In his letter to Mussolini of 31 December he dwelt at length on Franco's mistaken decision and on the guarantee of success which had existed for the attack on Gibraltar. He was still nourishing a 'faint hope that possibly at the last minute [the generalissimo] will become aware of the catastrophic nature of his own policy' and enter the war.[321]

The following day Hitler conferred with his top commanders. The discussion was essentially about support for Italy, but also touched on French–German relations, on preparations for aggression against the Soviet Union, and on the world-power dimension of National Socialist war policy. From Hitler's viewpoint Germany, after victory in the east, would be in a position 'in future to wage war against continents; she could then no longer be defeated by anyone. When this operation was executed, Europe would hold its breath.'[322]

Hitler and his generals were certainly entitled to expect that effect. Meanwhile, however, allowance had to be made for existing political and military conditions, and these were by no means uncomplicated. The army high command, alarmed by the universally reported shortage of means, believed that the preparatory measures for Operations Felix and Sea Lion would 'have to be held up for a time'.[323] Although Hitler instantly agreed that this was unavoidable, deciding even to cancel Gibraltar altogether,[324] he corrected himself only a few hours later. Berlin would make one last attempt to motivate Madrid to enter the war.[325] In this context the issue of Gibraltar was again brought up. Despite all frustration with the Spaniards, Operation Felix remained at least in the discussion stage, i.e. on the list of desiderata of the German strategists.[326]

---

[319] *KTB OKW* i. 243–4 (28 Dec. 1940), remark by Gen. Marras, the Italian military attaché in Berlin, to chief of OKW.

[320] For a detailed account see V.II below (Stegemann).

[321] *DGFP* D xi, No. 586, pp. 990–4 (31 Dec. 1940); directly on this Burdick, *Germany's Military Strategy*, 114; Detwiler, *Hitler*, 89, 171–2 n. 37.

[322] *KTB OKW* i. 258 (9 Jan. 1941).

[323] 'Führer Conferences', 169 ff. (8–9 Jan. 1941), here 171.

[324] *KTB OKW* i. 225 (9 Jan. 1941).

[325] Ibid. 256 (9 Jan. 1941).

[326] The treatment and assessment of Operation Felix in fact underwent considerable fluctuation during the time that followed. Thus *KTB OKW* i. 260–1 (10 Jan. 1941) records a new impulse for the planning of 'Felix', probably resulting from Raeder's situation report on 27 Dec., which Warlimont tried to support; however, the decision to abandon the operation was announced on 11

When Hitler and Mussolini met in Germany on 19–20 January 1941 for the exchange of ideas repeatedly postponed (by the Italian side) since the beginning of December,[327] Hitler talked at length about the unique importance which Spain's entry into the war would have for the stabilization of the political and military situation in the Mediterranean area.[328] He therefore considered it necessary for Mussolini to appeal once more to Franco's political ambition and to his obligations vis-à-vis the Axis powers. Like Raeder he was not concerned 'only with the occupation of Gibraltar and the strategic advantages of the African territory facing it', but just as much with U-boat bases on the Atlantic coast of Spain. These would be less exposed to British air raids than the bases on the French Atlantic coast. Although time was running short in view of the timetable for Operation Barbarossa, Hitler believed that the units needed for the capture of Gibraltar could be ready for action within twenty days.[329]

The Wehrmacht high command reacted promptly to the talks between Hitler and Mussolini. On 21 January 1941 a directive stated: 'Possible impending changes in political prerequisites render it necessary to amend earlier instructions and to maintain readiness for "Felix" in so far as still possible.'[330] Hope once more sprang up, at least among the champions of an alternative strategy and those who regarded the south-west European area as part of the strategic flank of the eastern campaign.[331] However, on 25 January the army high command felt bound to point out to the chief of OKW that, 'in the event of preparations being resumed on 1 February, the attack on Gibraltar was not possible before the middle of April and that therefore the forces envisaged for this operation would not be available in time for "Barbarossa" '.[332]

At the time the army general staff made this comment, intensive political efforts were still continuing to put Spain under moral pressure. The German ambassador in Madrid went into action on 21 January, and on 24 January Ribbentrop took a hand himself.[333] Both sides were full of accusations, acted disappointedly, and also aggressively. State Secretary von Weizsäcker summed matters up at the end of January: 'The tug-of-war with the Spaniards goes on. Their entry into the war still depends on prior German concessions. But they

---

Jan.: ibid. 262. The Directive No. 22 of 11 Jan. 1941 on 'Assistance of German Forces in Operations in the Mediterranean Area' no longer contains any reference to Gibraltar: *Hitler's War Directives*, 98–100. The abandonment of the idea of capturing Gibraltar against Franco's will dates from 18 Jan. (*KTB OKW* ii. 269), though Halder on that very day noted that Gibraltar could still become a live issue: Halder, *Diaries*, i. 755 (18 Jan. 1941).

[327] *Staatsmänner*, 435–43, conference on 19 Jan.; 443–52, conference on 10 Jan. 1941, attended also by army officers.

[328] Ibid. 438–9 (19 Jan. 1941).

[329] Ibid. 446 (20 Jan. 1941); see also, *Weizsäcker-Papiere*, 234 (24 Jan. 1941).

[330] *Hitlers Weisungen*, Directive No. 22c (21 Jan. 1941; not in the English edition); on Directive No. 22 see n. 326 above.

[331] *KTB OKW* i. 270 (20 Jan. 1941); 271 (21 Jan. 1941); 275 (22 Jan. 1941).

[332] Ibid. 284 (28 Jan. 1941).

[333] Detwiler, *Hitler*, 90 ff.

2. Ideas on the Continuation of the War 245

objected to the suggestion that all they wanted was to be carrion vultures and join in against Britain at the last moment. Not a thing anyone likes to be told.'[334]

Whatever views may be held on German–Spanish relations during those weeks, Hitler certainly believed, even before Mussolini's initiative, that he had to accept that his intended war against Stalin did not allow him time to wait for Franco's decision indefinitely. On 28 January, therefore, when Keitel submitted to him the above-mentioned comment of the army general staff, he gave instructions that 'Operation Felix will have to be dropped because it was impossible to create the political prerequisites.'[335] The conquest of Gibraltar, it was subsequently stated in mid-February, was only to be prepared theoretically, since the forces earmarked for it would be otherwise employed.[336]

When, against this background, Hitler wrote to Franco on 6 February he again listed all the arguments brought out since Hendaye which spoke in favour of Spain's entry into the war. These, admittedly, applied only from the German point of view. He also made it clear to the Caudillo that by his delaying tactics he was backing the wrong horse. In no case must he later assert 'that Spain was unable to enter the war because she received no advance concessions'. This was simply 'untrue'. Hitler basically no longer believed that Franco was willing to fight against 'Jewish-international democracy' at any time. He was by then writing off the Spanish government, which he rather bluntly accused of having played a double game with Germany. He described Madrid's motives as excuses full of contradictions.[337] In addition, however, Hitler's letter was intended as a pre-emptive accusation and self-justification.

The following day Eberhard von Stohrer, the German ambassador in Madrid, received a voluminous memorandum from the Spanish general staff, once more setting out the country's import needs, its shortages with regard to war preparations, and Spain's minimum demands for entering the war.[338] A comment on this document from a competent German source stated: 'The memorandum contains in its main sections such obviously unfulfillable demands that it can only be seen as an attempt at an excuse to avoid entry into the war.'[339]

No one, therefore, could be surprised that Mussolini, when he met Franco at Bordighera on 12 February 1941, was equally unsuccessful in persuading him to enter the war.[340] The Caudillo, according to the Duce, continued to

---

[334] *Weizsäcker-Papiere*, 235 (26 Jan. 1941).
[335] *KTB OKW* i. 284 (28 Jan. 1941); confirmed ibid. 289 (30 Jan. 1941).
[336] Directive OKW, here naval war staff, B.Nr. 1. Skl. I op 140/41 g.Kdos. Chefs. (14 Feb. 1941), 'betr. Unternehmen "Felix". Vorgang: 1. Skl. I op 73/41 g.Kdos. Chefs. vom 23. 1. 1941)', BA-MA CASE GE 529, PG 32604.
[337] *DGFP* D xii, No. 22, pp. 37–42, letter from Hitler to Franco of 6 Feb. 1941; cf. Dankelmann, *Franco*, 160; Detwiler, *Hitler*, 92–3.
[338] *DGFP* D xii, No. 28, pp. 51–3 (7 Feb. 1941).
[339] Ibid., No. 46, pp. 78–9 (12 Feb. 1941), minute by head of the trade-policy department.
[340] Detwiler, *Hitler*, 92.

insist that his country was 'simply not in a position to enter the war on the side of the Axis'.[341] The subject of Spain's belligerence was thereby closed.[342]

3. ITALY'S CONDUCT OF THE WAR BETWEEN THE ARMISTICE WITH FRANCE AND THE ATTACK ON GREECE

(a) Initial Situation, Intentions, and First Results of Naval and Air Warfare

When the Italo-French armistice was signed on 24 June Mussolini had not attained any of his high-pitched war aims. The treaty, signed by Marshal Badoglio and Army General Huntziger, envisaged the following regulation of territorial issues.[343] On French national territory a demilitarized zone was created between the front line resulting from hostilities—in all areas of operation—and a line 50 km. distant from this. In Tunisia the contracting parties agreed analogous arrangements for the territory from the Libyan–Tunisian frontier westward to a depth of roughly 150 to 200 km., thus including in this zone the well-consolidated French defences south of Gabes—the Mareth Line. Along the borders of Algeria and French West and Equatorial Africa, territories likewise bordering on Libya, the French withdrew their troops from a 200-km. wide strip running parallel with the common frontier. In addition, the whole of French Somalia was to be demilitarized for the period of British–Italian hostilities. Italy, moreover, was granted, for the duration of the armistice, the unrestricted right to use the harbour and the port installations of Jibuti. The same applied to the Jibuti–Addis Abeba railway line, which could be used continuously for Italian transports of all kinds.

The military operations which preceded the armistice treaty had taken a most disappointing turn for the Italians. On the Alpine front, perhaps the most unsuitable of all conceivable theatres of operation, the employment of Italian forces convincingly confirmed the inefficiency of the Fascist military machine, an inefficiency which had been feared both in Germany and in Italy. Indeed there were observers who believed that the armistice had come in the nick of time to save Italy from a French invasion.[344] Matters probably were not quite as bad. But the failings in the leadership, training, and equipment of the Italian forces—whose combative efficiency was often overrated, especially

---

[341] *KTB OKW* i. 328 (17 Feb. 1941).
[342] *Weizsäcker-Papiere*, 237 (16 Feb. 1941).
[343] Böhme, *Der deutsch-französische Waffenstillstand*, 368–72, Art. 3; cf. also 82–3; see also vol. ii of the present work, VI.v.4 (Umbreit); Greiselis, *Das Ringen*, 8 ff.
[344] See Smith, *Roman Empire*, 223–4; also the very clear notes in Bottai, *Vent'anni*, 177–8 (17 June 1940), 178–9 (25 June 1940); with considerable divergence Bottai, *Diario*, 194–7 (17 June 1940), 205 (25 June 1940), there also (197–204) daily entries on developments between 18 and 24 June, which *Vent'anni* lacks; Ciano, *Diary 1939–1943*, 270–1 (25 June 1940). On the interpretation of the Italian step with regard to its dependence on the German operations cf. vol. ii of the present work, VI.v.4 (Umbreit); in detail and critically Bocca, *Storia*, 183, 188.

by Germany,³⁴⁵ even after the débâcle on the Alpine front—certainly came as a shock. Casualty figures are eloquent testimony. With 631 servicemen killed, 2,631 wounded, 616 missing, and 2,151 suffering from frostbite on the Italian side, against 37 killed in action, 42 wounded, and 150 missing on the French side, no further comment is needed. Italy's military leaders, however, committed the same frivolous mistakes in the armistice negotiations as they had on the battlefield. Thus they omitted to demand the use of the ports of Tunis and Bizerta. One might explain this restraint by their hope that, after the defeat of France, the war would soon be over anyway—but this omission nevertheless seems ill considered.³⁴⁶ The fact that overland transportation from Tunisia to Libya, because of the great distance and the limited capacity of road and rail links, would also have resulted in risks and bottlenecks is irrelevant in this connection.³⁴⁷ In any event, Tunisian ports would have provided, if not an alternative, then certainly a supplement to Libyan ports.

This brings us to North Africa. Military developments there suffered as unfavourable a start as in the European theatre of war. Air Marshal Balbo, the local commander-in-chief, originally intended to take at least Sollum, to deprive the British of their most advanced post; but Badoglio held him back. Considering the condition of the Italian formations this was possibly a correct decision. After 17 June, when it became clear that there would soon be only one front in North Africa, Balbo displayed optimism. He spoke of an offensive, and Mussolini indicated that, no matter whether or not Egypt was neutral, the marshal always had the green light for an invasion. Balbo, however, demanded that, before any such operation, the equipment of his forces must be completed, especially with anti-tank weapons. Not all the material need come from Italy: pillaging-raids into Tunisia seemed equally suitable for replenishing certain shortfalls. As for a timetable, the air marshal proposed to march on Egypt simultaneously with a German landing in England. Before that, however, he would like to receive some German weapons, especially tanks. Precisely that, however, Mussolini refused. At that time he was still trying to prevent any interference by Hitler in his 'Italian theatre of war'.³⁴⁸ Until the end of 1940 Mussolini clung to his concept of a 'parallel war'—a politico-military construct which reflected mutual mistrust within the Axis partnership, a lack of willingness to co-operate, inadequate information on each other's intentions, and political rivalry. Matters looked much the same on the German side. The 'Thoughts on Wehrmacht Consultations with Italy', formulated in November 1938, for instance, primarily emphasized the diversionary aspect of any co-operation, while ruling out a unified supreme command or a joint German–Italian theatre of war.³⁴⁹ Subsequently, as we

---

³⁴⁵ Cf. Jodl's data in 'Strategy prior to 1944', 3, MGFA, A-914.
³⁴⁶ See Canzio, *La dittatura*, 589–97, esp. 597.
³⁴⁷ Cf. Greiselis, *Das Ringen*, 28.
³⁴⁸ See Knox, *Mussolini*, 130; *Africa settentrionale, La preparazione*, 113–22.
³⁴⁹ *DGFP* D iv, No. 411, 529–32 (26 Nov. 1938), appendix.

have seen, there were certain indications that military realities were ignored. But Hitler himself initially inclined to the concept which Mussolini called a parallel war. When Italy eventually entered the war she did so in line with Mussolini's doctrine and with his generals' understanding of their role: 'not with Germany, not for Germany, but for Italy on the side of Germany'.[350]

There is no doubt that with this formula the Fascist regime was allowing for the easily injured pride of the Italian military leaders. Indisputably it also made allowance for the undeniable anti-German mood of the public. Paradoxically, however, Mussolini, as a result of that attitude—which led to his rejection of the German offer for Italian troops to be employed on the Rhine front—deprived himself of his only realistic chance of achieving (albeit shared) military success.

In the war at sea, likewise, no spectacular actions took place, contrary to the plans[351] proclaimed by Mussolini and the Italian admiralty staff prior to Italy's entry into the war. It may be the case that, in view of developments in France, the Italian admirals saw no reason to embark on any major, let alone risky, enterprises.[352] Their cautious attitude was indeed sensible, as losses would have been difficult to replace.[353] It should also be remembered that—especially as in June 1940 a prolonged war, though no longer expected, could still not be ruled out—the principal task of the Italian navy was the protection of shipping to and from Libya. The fact that between 10 June 1940 and 12 May 1943, the date of the surrender of the Tunisian bridgehead, 1,274 convoys sailed between Italy and North Africa testifies to the priority of that task.[354] Allowing for these conditions and realizing the extent to which Italy was dependent on imports, especially of fuel, the Italian admiralty staff developed the following basic operational concept, which remained essentially valid throughout the war:[355]

- defensive function both in the eastern and in the western Mediterranean, offensive and counter-offensive function in the central Mediterranean;
- prevention of the amalgamation of two large enemy fleets; for this purpose the Italian fleet could utilize its controlling position in the Strait of Sicily;
- attacks on enemy bases with submarines, midget craft, and aircraft;
- operations against the enemy's supply-lines;
- utilization of all combat opportunities when own forces are superior or equal, with co-ordinated employment of submarines and surface units;
- avoidance of conflict with clearly superior enemy forces;

---

[350] Bocca, *Storia*, 156.
[351] Schreiber, *Revisionismus*, 275-6.
[352] Bernotti, *Guerra nel Mediterraneo*, 47-55, here esp. 47-8.
[353] On the concept of the 'fleet in being' cf. Fioravanzo, 'Kriegführung', 19-20.
[354] Cf. Fioravanzo, 'Italian Strategy', 66.
[355] *La marina italiana*, iv. 10-11; ibid. xxi. 353 ff., with reproduction of 'Direttive Navali, o Concetti generali di azione nel Mediterraneo' (29 May 1940).

3. Italy's Conduct of the War

- employment of the bulk of the Italian fleet before enemy forces in the Mediterranean are substantially reinforced; engagements to be accepted as near as possible to Italian bases;
- protection of sea routes to the Italian islands, Libya, and Albania;
- defence of the coasts by minefields, coast artillery, and small units.

Although after Italy's entry into the war the British sought the offensive from the outset, they were beating the air as, for a great variety of reasons, the Italians could not be found. Genoa and Bardia were shelled by Allied units, but, as with the French air raids on Venice, the psychological effects were more important than the physical damage. This was largely also because the Italian navy was seen to be unable to intervene. It is surprising that the numerous Italian submarines, at sea after 10 June, failed to score any major successes against the French or the British. The Italians in fact sank a British light cruiser, three British submarines, and a French submarine. They themselves lost three submarines in the Red Sea and two in the Mediterranean, as well as a small gunboat.[356] The greatest success of the British was probably the capture of the Italian submarine *Galileo Galilei*, because the documents seized in that operation enabled them to operate effectively against Italian units.[357] It should finally be noted that during the first few days of the war Italy lost valuable shipping space through scuttling and enemy action.[358]

Although Mussolini's air force was extremely active—it flew approximately thirty-eight missions against Malta between 11 and 27 June[359]—it failed to score any striking successes. It is significant, on the other hand, that the Italian mainland was subjected to numerous air raids from the very beginning of the war, and that these had their effect on the population. The fact that there was no effective anti-aircraft defence considerably facilitated British— and initially also French—air attacks.[360] During the first weeks of the war the British in North Africa not only operated more aggressively than the Italians,

---

[356] Figures according to *La marina italiana*, iv. 97–8; Playfair, *Mediterranean*, i. 109–12; detailed account of Italian submarine operations in 'Militärischer Bericht Nr. 1. Italienische U-Bootskriegführung' (copy), Chef des Verbindungsstabes beim Admiralstab der Kgl. ital. Marine B.Nr. g.Kdos. 14/40 (5 July 1940), BA-MA RM 7/233. Submarine warfare was particularly difficult in the Red Sea, where average water temperatures of 32 °C resulted in temperatures of 48 °C inside the submarines after six hours of submerged navigation.

[357] Bragadin, *Che ha fatto la marina?*, 32; Playfair, *Mediterranean*, i. 111–12; with its ciphers compromised, the Italian navy was temporarily impeded in its operations: cf. KTB des Chefs des Verbindungsstabes beim Admiralstab der Kgl. ital. Marine, p. 5 (30 June 1940), BA-MA RM 36/1.

[358] According to *La marina italiana*, i. 230, in June 1940 a total of 16 units with 32,835 GRT; in July 10 ships with 31,854 GRT; in August 5 ships with 10,107 GRT; in September 8 ships with 21,705 GRT; in October 8 ships with 20,168 GRT; in November 6 ships with 17,088 GRT; and in December 21 ships with 57,200 GRT.

[359] Attard, *The Battle*, 13–46, lists altogether 80 attacks; Playfair, *Mediterranean*, i. 119 ff., speaks of 38 attacks; for the Italian view up to the end of June see Santoro, *L'aeronautica italiana*, i. 231–46.

[360] Kramer, 'Die italienische Luftwaffe', 268–9.

but also more successfully. The same was finally true in East Africa, despite initial Italian successes.[361]

Before an account is given here of Italian operations from July to October 1940, a few words need to be said about the establishment, at the time of Italy's entry into the war, of German liaison staffs in Italy, each of which had its counterpart institution in Germany.

Before 10 June Marshal Badoglio informed the German military attaché in Rome that, once Italy was in the war, he would regard him as the liaison officer with the Wehrmacht high command. In return he expected Major-General von Rintelen to pass on to him all Wehrmacht information. OKW agreed with this arrangement, and thus at least official contact was established with the Comando Supremo.[362] By contrast, communication with the Italian army command continued to be only at attaché level. A mere two days before Italy's entry into the war Rintelen had to confess that he had no knowledge whatever of the operational intentions of the Italians, and after 10 June the Italian general staff did not inform him until it was clear that the offensive on the Alpine front was making no real headway. Otherwise Rintelen received his information through Major Heggenreiner, one of his assistant attachés, who since 11 June had been serving as the military attaché's liaison officer at army group headquarters in Bra near Turin. From 4 August onward Heggenreiner held the post of liaison officer with the Italian forces in Libya.[363]

Not until 20 September was Rintelen officially designated the 'German General at the Headquarters of the Italian Armed Forces'. Simultaneously he performed the duties of liaison officer between the Italian and German armies. At least he no longer had to communicate with his military superiors through the Rome embassy and the foreign ministry in Berlin, but, having been detached from the embassy structure, as Wehrmacht liaison officer, he could turn direct to the Wehrmacht high command, simultaneously notifying the attaché department of the German army high command.[364]

As a result of this double function, Rintelen was concerned also with the negotiations between Germans, Italians, and French, and progress in the German armistice commission in Wiesbaden and the Italian commission in Turin. Any information he needed in connection with queries from the Comando Supremo or Mussolini he would receive from Colonel von Senger und Etterlin, the German liaison officer with the Italian armistice commission.[365]

The German air force reacted promptly to the changed situation after 10 June. The very next day the establishment of a 'Luftwaffe liaison staff with the

---

[361] Playfair, *Mediterranean*, i. 112 ff.
[362] Rintelen, *Mussolini als Bundesgenosse*, 87; on the problem of military co-operation generally cf. Doerr, 'Verbindungsoffiziere'.
[363] Heggenreiner, 'Operations', 1–2, MGFA, D-216; Rintelen, 'Zusammenarbeit', 18, 22, MGFA, B-495.
[364] Rintelen, *Mussolini als Bundesgenosse*, 96; id., 'Zusammenarbeit', 24–5, MGFA, B-495.
[365] Rintelen, *Mussolini als Bundesgenosse*, 97.

3. Italy's Conduct of the War

Italian air force in Rome' was announced. The new staff, known for short as 'Italuft', came directly under the Luftwaffe commander-in-chief. Its chief, Major-General Ritter von Pohl, presented himself to General Pricolo, chief of staff of the Italian air force, on 15 June. Unlike the arrangement for the army, there continued to be an air attaché alongside Italuft, a fact which—just as in the navy, which chose an analogous solution—soon led to disagreeable relations as a result of ill-defined responsibilities.[366] In retrospect, Rintelen[367] believed 'that the procedure, chosen by the armed forces high command and the army high command, of appointing only one liaison body—moreover the military attaché, who had been in Italy for many years—proved very successful, whereas in the navy and air force a continuous battle was waged between the attachés and the liaison officers. Each of these services had one structure too many.'

Rear-Admiral Weichold, the chief of the 'liaison staff with the admiralty staff of the Royal Italian Navy', arrived in Rome on 28 June.[368] By 2 July his small staff had fully taken over its duties.[369]

The deceptive hope that, after victory in the west, an arrangement would be reached with the British, had not yet evaporated. This was true also on the Italian side, even though, after the armistice with France, the Comando Supremo proclaimed its readiness for battle. Thus its bulletin of 25 June contained the martial pronouncement: 'The war against Britain continues, and it will go on until victory.'[370]

Possibilities for such a continuation of the war were provided by Malta and Gibraltar. As to the Rock, the Italians had agreed with Spain that they would carry out air raids against it. As to Malta, the Italian armed forces command intended to paralyse the island with its air force.[371] But there was no longer any talk at this stage of an invasion of the island, possession of which was not regarded as of decisive importance and would have entailed exceptional risks.[372] It should be noted, however, that at least since 1938 an occupation of Malta had been regarded as a vital prerequisite of any promising military operations in North Africa.[373] There is no point in discussing 'what would

---

[366] Gundelach, *Luftwaffe im Mittelmeer*, 28 ff.

[367] Rintelen, 'Zusammenarbeit', 25, MGFA, B-495.

[368] KTB des Chefs des Verbindungsstabes beim Admiralstab der Kgl. ital. Marine, 2 (28 June 1940), BA-MA RM 36/1.

[369] 1. SKl., KTB, Teil A, 30 (3 July 1940), BA-MA RM 7/14.

[370] *Bollettini di guerra*, 10–11 (25 June 1940).

[371] Knox, *Mussolini*, 134.

[372] *La marina italiana*, xxi. 356–60, study of the conquest of Malta (18 June 1940); the most competent study of the Malta problem from the viewpoint of the Italian armed forces, and richly furnished with documents, is Gabriele, *Operazione C 3*; on 1940 ibid. 47–80. Gabriele (64) concludes that an attack on Malta between 11 and 24 June would have failed. On the Malta–Gibraltar problem cf. records of conferences of the Italian armed forces command on 25 June and 2 July in *Verbali*, i. 62–71.

[373] On this and on the further discussion of a Malta landing cf. Schreiber, *Revisionismus*, 269–70, 351–7.

have happened if'. The decision of the Italian command was in favour of offensive action in North Africa. If the British were defeated there, Malta—that was the assumption—would drop like a ripe plum into Italy's lap.[374]

On 25 June, in connection with preparations for operations in North Africa, Badoglio declared that everything would be done to let Balbo have the equipment he had requested for Libya, and also to reinforce his troops in the future. The seventy medium tanks which the air marshal would receive from the Po army should in particular enable him to control the situation in the field. Badoglio, however, at that time still supported a predominantly defensive strategy. Although he (Badoglio) did not believe that the British were exactly over-brimming with offensive spirit, Balbo's principal task must still be to consolidate his position in such a way that any enemy surprise thrust could be successfully repulsed. Once that had been achieved, he was free to think about offensive action.[375] This was not exactly an invitation for Balbo to march on Egypt. But that arrived the following day. Suddenly time seemed to be pressing, because the Germans, so the Italians believed, would shortly land in England. And Mussolini feared, as Badoglio put it, to stand 'empty-handed' at the conclusion of peace. Balbo was therefore to move eastward as soon as possible.[376] On 28 June, however, when it was obvious that the French North African possessions would not defect from Vichy—which eliminated the danger of a second front in North Africa—Badoglio wrote[377] that Balbo need do nothing other than face east. The Fifth Army, until then stationed on the Libyan–Tunisian frontier, would be able to spare officers, other ranks, and material for the Tenth Army, which was earmarked for the offensive. In any event, the marshal should try to be ready to move off in fourteen days. Balbo's answer never arrived in Rome, for on 28 June he was accidentally shot down by Italian anti-aircraft gunners over Tobruk.[378]

Badoglio states in his memoirs that the Duce received the news of the air marshal's death without showing the slightest emotion. He adds that to Mussolini 'the disappearance of the only one of the Fascist hierarchy who had dared to challenge his supremacy was not altogether unwelcome'. Be that as it may, Marshal Graziani, on Badoglio's recommendation, took over command in Libya. In view of his experience of the Abyssinian campaign and his detailed knowledge of the terrain on the Cyrenaica–Egypt sector—he had been deputy governor and officer commanding the forces in Cyrenaica—Graziani seemed the ideal choice. In retrospect, however, Badoglio observed that in that assumption he had been 'completely mistaken'.[379] The chief of the Comando Supremo may well have been convinced that among the Italian generals

---

[374] See also Bocca, *Storia*, 237 ff., here 239.
[375] *Africa settentrionale, La preparazione*, 94–5.
[376] Ibid. 95–6; cf. also Faldella, *L'Italia*, 206.
[377] *Africa settentrionale, La preparazione*, 96.
[378] Ciano, *Diary 1939–1943*, 272 (29 June 1940); cf. also Knox, *Mussolini*, 135.
[379] Badoglio, *Italy*, 24.

Graziani was the most suitable, even though, from the very outset, Graziani made it clear that he was not enthusiastic about his new appointment. He emphasized, for example, that he was merely obeying orders, but that he was relatively unfamiliar with the situation in North Africa; right up to the armistice with France he had had to concentrate on developments on the Alpine front. Badoglio merely took note of these arguments, while calling for speedy action. Graziani would find all the directives he needed when he got to Libya.[380]

The marshal went to North Africa on 30 June. When on 2 July he read the instructions originally intended for Balbo he was taken aback by the offensive intentions laid down in them. He had left Rome with the conviction that such intentions were not practicable. But the very next day he received orders for his advance on Egypt to start on 15 July.[381]

Badoglio in his memoirs scarcely deals with the actual conditions in Libya, confining himself to exceedingly harsh criticism of Graziani, whom he largely blames for the failure of Italy's high-pitched hopes.[382] Regardless of the question of the usefulness of such personalizations of failure—after all, campaigns and battles in modern wars are rarely decided by the commanders in the field—at the end of June it is a fact that, apart from Badoglio or Mussolini, other senior military figures, as well as the army general staff, were convinced of the excellent prospect of success the Italian forces would have in an attack on Egypt.[383] In view of the conditions existing in the North African theatre as a result of the armistice with France, and bearing in mind Libya's envisaged reinforcement by further army units, the Italian formations were regarded as 'sufficiently strong to mount an offensive against the Anglo-Egyptian forces in Egypt'. It is interesting that this assessment came from the very staff whose chief Graziani remained even after assuming command in Libya. During his absence the business of the army chief of staff was conducted by General Roatta.[384]

Meanwhile Mussolini, back from an inspection tour of the former French–Italian frontier at the beginning of July, rather surprisingly—having before the armistice noted with dejection the failure of his offensive on the Alpine front—now declared his conviction that the Italian troops could have effortlessly broken through the Alpine Maginot Line. As to the 'march on Alexandria', it seemed to him 'a foregone conclusion'. It was probably mainly Badoglio who persuaded Mussolini that, all in all, this undertaking was 'easy and safe'.[385] There was in fact a lot to support that view. The Italians knew

[380] Graziani, *Ho difeso*, 225.
[381] Ibid. 227–8; cf. also Faldella, *L'Italia*, 208.
[382] Badoglio, *Italy*, 24–5.
[383] Knox, *Mussolini*, 136–7.
[384] Rintelen, 'Zusammenarbeit', 31, MGFA, B-495.
[385] Ciano, *Diary 1939–1943*, 273 (2 July 1940); a concise survey of developments from the attack on the Alpine front to the assumption of command in North Africa in Pieri, 'La stratégie', 71–4.

that the British forces consisted essentially of only the 7th armoured division, plus one Indian and one New Zealand division. What the Italians did not suspect was the shortage of equipment these units were suffering from. That was why the Italian generals, while (rightly) not being greatly worried about the combative efficiency of the Egyptian troops, in spite of their own numerical superiority quite unreasonably overrated the British forces.[386]

The Germans learnt details of their Axis partner's intended operation in the course of a conversation between Hitler and Ciano on 7 July 1940.[387] According to the latter, Rome just then regarded the prospects of the 'final blow against Great Britain', which Mussolini wished to see delivered, as extremely favourable. Mussolini, Ciano explained, 'was planning certain military operations in the Mediterranean and in Africa and also desired to participate with Italian land and air forces in the direct blow that Germany would strike against England. For that purpose Italy had already prepared 10 divisions and up to 30 major air-force formations.'[388] In North Africa it was planned to advance on Cairo in order to conquer Egypt, and above all to gain control of the Suez Canal. Preparations for this were in hand. A special problem was the water supply for about 100,000 men on their march through 600 km. of desert. Nevertheless it was intended to mount the offensive against Egypt between 20 and 30 July. According to Ciano, Rome realized the risks involved in this enterprise. However, in view of the urgent need to establish a land link with Abyssinia, Italy believed she must go ahead with it.

In this conversation Ciano also indicated to Hitler that a naval battle between the British and Italian fleets was imminent: the British would no doubt try to intercept a particular convoy destined for North Africa, and the 'entire Italian fleet' had put to sea to protect it.

This reference was to an operation which in fact resulted in an encounter between British and Italian naval forces, the 'battle of Punta Stilo'. Basically, however, there were only four combat contacts between heavy units, as well as operations by the Italian air force and missions by British carrier-borne aircraft. The clash occurred in connection with two convoy operations. For the purpose of supplying Graziani's forces five extensively protected Italian transport vessels had been en route from Naples and Catania to Libya since

---

[386] Playfair, *Mediterranean*, i. 205 ff.
[387] *DGFP* D x, No. 129, pp. 147–55 (8 July 1940).
[388] Ibid., p. 151 (translation adapted); directly on this No. 166, pp. 209 ff. (13 July 1940), letter from Hitler to Mussolini, in which he considers co-operation of the two air forces and navies to be possible, while ruling out any direct participation of the Italian army in operations against the British Isles. On the origin of the Italian offer see Hillgruber, *Strategie*, 131; on operations of Italian submarines in the Atlantic and the resulting co-operation of German and Italian military authorities cf. *La marina italiana*, xii. 25–48; based on German sources: Schreiber, *Revisionismus*, 278–84; between 4 Sept. and 26 Dec. 1940 all 27 submarines originally earmarked for the war in the Atlantic arrived at their base in Bordeaux. The Italian evacuation of Massawa in 1941 meant the addition of another four submarines (figures according to *La marina italiana*, xii. 350–3). On Italian air force operations against Britain see Santoro, *L'aeronautica italiana*, i. 115–24. The 178 aircraft of the 'Corpo Aereo Italiano' flew missions against the British Isles between 24 Oct. 1940 and 3 Jan. 1941. Cf. also Licheri, *L'arma aerea*, 37–40.

3. Italy's Conduct of the War

6–7 July. They had reached their port of destination, Benghazi, when the battle of Punta Stilo began on 9 July.[389]

Britain's Mediterranean fleet was at sea in order to protect two convoys en route from Malta to Alexandria. To that end A Force, B Force, and C Force were operating east of Malta, while H Force had left Gibraltar for a diversionary manœuvre in the western Mediterranean. When on 8 July British aerial reconnaissance established that strong Italian naval formations were protecting a convoy sailing for North Africa, Admiral Cunningham stopped his convoys and tried to force the Italian fleet into an encounter[390] by making for a position between Taranto and the reported Italian units.

Cunningham had three battleships, an aircraft-carrier, five light cruisers, and sixteen destroyers. Admiral Campioni, the Italian commander, had two battleships, eighteen heavy and light cruisers, thirty-three destroyers, and four torpedo-boats. In addition—though only in theory—he could count on the support of the bulk of the Italian air force. Both sides employed submarines, principally for reconnaissance.[391] Both British and Italians sought the engagement as soon as they learnt of each other's presence. The outcome of the so-called battle, which was not fought to the end, satisfied neither Cunningham nor Campioni. The British had not succeeded in destroying the Italian fleet, or even in inflicting serious damage on it,[392] while the Italians had not only not scored any successes but had, moreover, been endangered rather than supported by their own air force, which dropped its bombs more or less indiscriminately on friend and foe.[393]

In the German view Punta Stilo provided all the conditions for an Italian success. The Italians knew their opponent's position, just as they knew his intentions. The Italians operated in the immediate proximity of their bases, weather conditions were perfect, and the Italian units were superior to the British in speed. A weighty disadvantage on their side, admittedly, was that there was no clear delineation between the responsibilities of the naval commander on the one hand and the admiralty staff in Rome on the other. This resulted in delays, misunderstandings, and complications in decision-making. A different question is whether at Punta Stilo the Italian navy really 'missed its decisive moment'.[394] This was suggested by Admiral Weichold,

---

[389] Operations in great detail in *La marina italiana*, iv. 99–159, here mainly 101, 121.
[390] Playfair, *Mediterranean*, i. 150–1, with figures on the British fleet.
[391] *La marina italiana*, iv. 102–3.
[392] Cunningham, *Odyssey*, 263.
[393] Iachino, *Tramonto*, 204–5; Maugeri, *Ricordi*, 34; *La marina italiana*, iv. 140–1; Playfair, *Mediterranean*, i. 154; for an anecdotal but good account by a war reporter who was present at Punta Stilo on board the battleship *Cesare* cf. Cappellini, *Sfida*, 66–73.
[394] Verbindungsstab beim Admiralstab der Kgl. ital. Marine, B.Nr. g.Kdos. 55/40, 'Militärischer Bericht Nr. 2. Operation der italienischen Kriegsmarine zur Überführung eines wichtigen Transports nach Libyen (Bengasi)' (10 July 1940), BA-MA RM 7/233; ibid., Verbindungsstab beim Admiralstab der Kgl. ital. Marine, B.Nr. g.Kdos. 70/40, an OKM/1. Skl., betr. 'Mitteilungen des italienischen Admiralstabes über die Kampfhandlungen am 10. Juli 1940' (12 July 1940).

and naval historians have accepted his hypothesis as though it were an established fact. But what are 'decisive moments'? The British lost far more ships in the war than Cunningham had at his disposal on 9 July, and yet this was not 'decisive'.

What made the engagement off the Calabrian coast remarkable was not the immediate result—damage to a few warships is only of passing significance—but the indirect consequences. During the ensuing period the Italian naval command employed its heavy units even more cautiously,[395] a fact which was not lost on the British. Punta Stilo confirmed them in their offensive tactics.[396]

Italy's admirals, however, were in no way demoralized by the unsatisfactory course of this first major encounter between the British and the Italian fleets.[397] It was only the developments during the next few months that gradually undermined their assurance. One factor in this, no doubt, was an engagement of two light cruisers of the Italian navy, which had sailed into the Aegean for operations against merchantmen. On 19 July they encountered five British destroyers as well as an Australian light cruiser off Capo Spada.[398] The Italians, though superior in heavy guns, did not exactly operate in a brilliant manner: they tried to evade confrontation, and lost one cruiser through action from the pursuing British, while the other, damaged, made for Tobruk.[399] Even Mussolini, who, dazzled after Punta Stilo by totally groundless reports of success by the Italian air force, had boasted of having destroyed some 50 per cent of the British Mediterranean fleet within three days,[400] reacted to Capo Spada in a markedly dejected way.[401]

Generally speaking, it was becoming obvious at that early stage that the war at sea would not yield the hoped-for overwhelming successes either. The Italian submarines, for instance, of which Mussolini was so proud, recorded a very lively activity but achieved only meagre results (Table I.III.1).[402]

When, at the end of July, the Italian navy informed the German navy of its remarkable—though inaccurate—numbers of losses, it explained these by the unexpectedly effective anti-submarine defences of the British, by their efficient aerial surveillance, and by the clarity of the water, which enabled aircraft to detect submerged submarines down to a depth of 40 metres. The Germans

---

[395] Iachino, *Tramonto*, 204–5; Knox, *Mussolini*, 147–8.
[396] Cunningham, *Odyssey*, 265–6.
[397] Bernotti, *Guerra nel Mediterraneo*, 73; Maugeri, *Ricordi*, 34.
[398] *La marina italiana*, iv. 160–80; Bragadin, *Che ha fatto la marina?*, 41–2; Playfair, *Mediterranean*, i. 156–9.
[399] Cunningham, *Odyssey*, 266–7; Potter and Nimitz, *Sea Power*, 620 (the numerical data are incorrect); Maugeri, *Ricordi*, 35–8.
[400] Ciano, *Diary 1939–1943*, 276 (13 July 1940).
[401] Ibid. 278 (22 July 1940).
[402] Unlike the German navy, Italian submarines operated under very strict instructions from the admiralty staff, which governed their tactical movement in the areas of operation. Numerous missions were focused on a specific target, without the best use being made of the cruising endurance of the vessels.

3. Italy's Conduct of the War

TABLE I.III.I. *Italian Submarine Activity, June–October 1940*

Month	Submarines employed	No. of actions	Naval tonnage sunk (t.)	Merchant tonnage sunk (GRT)	Submarines lost	Submarines damaged
June	97	105	4,180	9,920	6	12
July	59	65	1,350	5,141	none	4
Aug.	36	42	uncertain	uncertain	1	none
Sept.	27	32	none	none	1	1
Oct.	27	37	1,475	none	5	none

Source: La marina italiana, xiii. 60, 73, 82, 92–3, 102.

were astonished by the Italian surprise at the efficiency of British submarine-chasing units, considering that the Italians had been kept currently informed of the high standard of the enemy's anti-submarine measures.[403] Broadly speaking, the poor success of the Italian submarines, whose operations of course were not solely concerned with action against British shipping but also included transportation of material to North Africa, reconnaissance missions, and mining operations, may be seen as an indication of the Royal Navy's swift achievement of control over the Mediterranean. It should be noted in this context that, during that initial phase of the naval war in the Mediterranean, the British cryptographers' breaking of the Italian code as yet played no part. The achievements of Bletchley Park did not bear fruit until the end of October 1940.[404]

Two attempted attacks by midget craft[405] against British warships at anchor at Alexandria in August and September 1940 proved unsuccessful. The Italians suffered painful losses.[406] Another failure was a similar operation against Gibraltar at the end of October.[407] The Italians were not very lucky during those months. At the end of August the British were operating both in the eastern and in the western Mediterranean, in order to deliver an aircraft-carrier and an additional battleship to Cunningham, and to get a convoy through to Malta; on 31 August the Italian fleet, which by then possessed four battleships and enjoyed a crushing superiority, set out to find the enemy, but

---

[403] 1. Skl., KTB, Teil A, 347 (29 July 1940), BA-MA RM 7/14.

[404] On this Santoni, 'Einfluß von "Ultra"', 504–5; on the organization of British intelligence in the Mediterranean at the outbreak of the Second World War id., 'Servizio'.

[405] Italian midget combat craft included two-man midget submarines of about 30 t., armed with two torpedoes; super-long-range torpedoes on which two men were seated, who steered the torpedo and attached the explosive charge to the target; explosive boats steered by one man who jumped off about 100 m. before the target; and frogmen as well as motor torpedo-boats from 20 to 28 t.; cf. Iachino, *Tramonto*, 64 ff.

[406] *La marina italiana*, xiv. 33–71.

[407] Ibid. 75–87; Borghese, *Decima Flottiglia*, 67–89.

in the late afternoon, in response to an order from Admiral Cavagnari (never satisfactorily explained), they returned to Taranto.[408]

What remained, and what, in view of Italian intentions in North Africa, was bound to be of major importance, was the securing of supply-routes across the sea. Between Italy's entry into the war and November 1940, 174 transports by merchant ships and 11 by warships were in fact executed. In these operations only one destroyer and four merchantmen were lost.[409]

The war in the air likewise failed to produce any convincing successes between the end of June and the end of October 1940. The Italian air force was good only in parts; generally it was inferior to the Royal Air Force in the Mediterranean in both technology and training. Moreover, operational leadership, especially over the sea, was poor. In view of the fact that on land there were no air-raid shelters and no efficient anti-aircraft defences,[410] it was obvious that no major success could be achieved by the Italian air force either in defensive warfare, i.e. in protecting the population and ground targets against enemy air raids, or in offensive actions.[411] Courage and fighting spirit—and the Italian pilots possessed both—are no adequate substitute for shortfalls in technical quality. This is especially true when the opponent has well-nigh perfect material and outstanding skill.[412] Nevertheless, the hits scored by Italian bombing raids on Malta led Cunningham to abandon the island as a submarine base.[413]

As the use of the air force will be discussed later in conjunction with Italian ground operations in North Africa, this aspect will remain outside our consideration for the moment.

The air war over the sea—even disregarding air-force participation at Punta

---

[408] Thus according to Knox, *Mussolini*, 148–9, where the relevant literature is incorporated. If an encounter had taken place the following units would have faced one another on 31 Aug.: 4 Italian against 2 British battleships, which included an aircraft-carrier; 7 Italian heavy and 6 light cruisers against one British heavy and 4 light cruisers; 39 Italian destroyers against 13 British.

[409] *La marina italiana*, vi. 15; on the total losses of the Italian navy and merchant marine during the period from 10 June to 31 Dec. 1940 see *La marina italiana*, ii and iii. According to this source 71 merchantmen were lost through scuttling or enemy action, 22 were captured or sequestrated. Warships lost irretrievably by Italy were 1 cruiser, 9 destroyers, 6 torpedo-boats, and 19 submarines. An excellent survey of Italian convoy operations 1940–3 and a profound analysis of the conditions under which they were conducted in Gabriele, 'La guerre'.

[410] Delivery of anti-aircraft guns, which Italy had been demanding since 1939, played a major part in German–Italian relations after the outbreak of the Second World War. On developments up to Mussolini's entry into the war and on the volume of German deliveries cf. Schreiber, *Revisionismus*, 244 n. 451.

[411] Characterization according to Kramer, 'Die italienische Luftwaffe', 267–73; on operations see also Belot, *La Guerre*, 63–6.

[412] On the state of training of the Italian air force and air defences from the German viewpoint: Der RdL u. ObdL/GenSt./5. Abt. Nr. 293/39 g.Kdos. (II B), betr. Werturteil über die italienische Fliegertruppe und Flakartillerie (7 Mar. 1939), BA-MA CASE GE 941, PG 32937. Immediately before the outbreak of war the Italian equipment was thought to be 'relatively modern' and the state of training of the fighter pilots was regarded as high, while that of the bomber crews and anti-aircraft artillery revealed marked weaknesses. The tactics of the Italian air force seemed to be generally backward.

[413] Licheri, *L'arma aerea*, 40–1; Playfair, *Mediterranean*, i. 119.

3. *Italy's Conduct of the War*   259

Stilo and Capo Spada—was conducted very actively. Between 17 June and 2 November Italian airmen attacked British naval targets on thirty-three days. In these operations they sank a merchant ship and scored hits on eleven warships and three merchantmen.[414] In addition, in 1940 there were four carefully planned bombing raids on Gibraltar, which, however, caused no damage to the Royal Navy's large units in port. The attacks claimed more casualties among the civilian population on land than they did among servicemen. Apart from Gibraltar the Italian air force also, after the end of June, bombed the port of Alexandria, the oil transshipment centre of Haifa, and the Suez Canal. These actions were fairly sporadic. The Suez Canal, for instance, prior to the arrival of the German X Air Corps in the Mediterranean area, was only once, on 28 August, the target of Italian bombers.[415]

Italian warfare at that time was fragmented predominantly into operations of individual response, characterized by tactical intentions whose realization was only hesitatingly attempted. It suffered conspicuously from a lack of preparation for a major conflict, and showed not even the beginnings of any decision-seeking operations. Where a measure of dynamism seemed to exist, as with Balbo in North Africa, friction at the top command level prevented it from developing. Whenever the Comando Supremo called for speed, the local commander in the field would put on the brakes, as in the case of Graziani; or else the most unfavourable of all conceivable theatres of operations was chosen, as in the case of the attack on the Alpine front.

(*b*) *The War in Italian East Africa*

For a general view of operations see Map I.III.1.

In Italian East Africa, where Prince Amedeo of Savoy, Duke of Aosta and viceroy of Ethiopia, had been primarily concerned over the past few years with controlling the rebels who continued to resist after Italy's victory in the Abyssinian war (in the spring of 1940 he achieved a measure of success), exactly the same conflicting elements of Italian warfare came into play when the duke pressed for an offensive.[416]

The Italians had at least tried not to let the time since the beginning of the war elapse unused. In June 1940 the colonial territory had stocks of foodstuffs and war material sufficient for six or seven months.[417] But what use was that when Ethiopia, Eritrea, and Italian Somaliland all lacked an overland link with Libya? Besides, after 10 June seaborne supplies came to an end because the exits from the Mediterranean were controlled by Britain. Only by long-range

---

[414] Santoro, *L'aeronautica italiana*, i. 545–51, 572–3.
[415] Ibid. 378–91.
[416] A good general view of the situation in Italian East Africa in Knox, *Mussolini*, 150–5; basically on military conditions and developments; *La guerra in Africa orientale*, 15–84 (period up to Dec. 1940).
[417] *La guerra in Africa orientale*, 32–5.

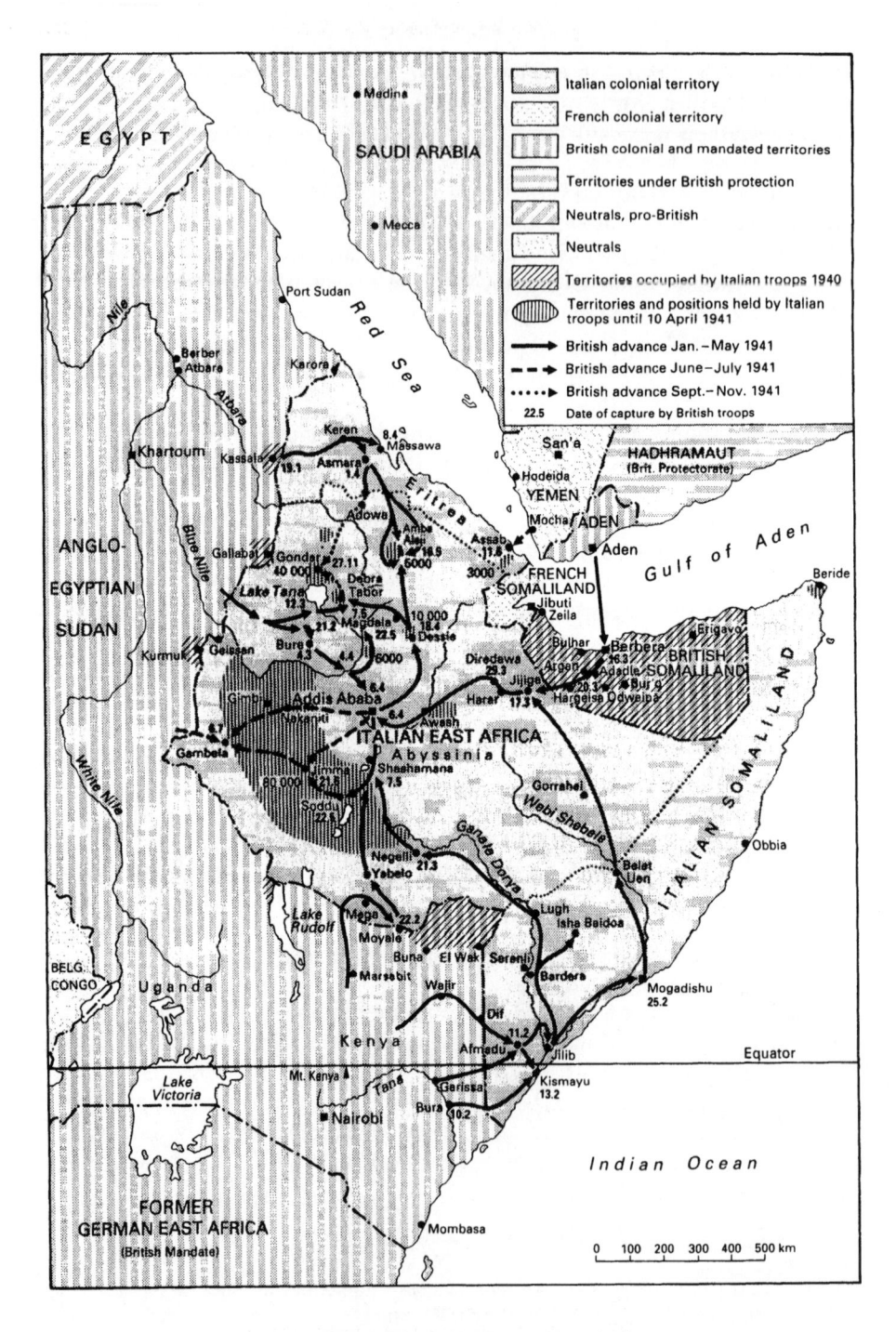

MAP I.III.1. The British–Italian War in East Africa, 1940–1941

3. Italy's Conduct of the War

aircraft, which had to overfly the Anglo-Egyptian Sudan, did supplies now and again reach Addis Abeba; but these were very scant.

For this reason alone it would have made sense to co-ordinate the offensive against Egypt with an Italian advance from Abyssinia towards the Sudan, in order to establish a land bridge. Such a plan had been under consideration since September 1939, but was time and again blocked by different authorities on a variety of grounds.[418] One reason was that the situation in Italian East Africa was regarded as exceedingly unstable. Among leading politicians and military figures in Rome there were some who believed that in the event of war there would be open rebellion there. For this reason also developments between April and July 1940 added to the nervousness of Graziani, Badoglio, and the Duke of Aosta.[419]

As late as the summer of 1939 the British, in view of the shortage of their military forces, were examining the feasibility of provoking a revolt in Ethiopia. In this context it was natural to stress the idea of national liberation. No doubt the measures which soon followed, as well as the intensification of British propaganda after September, initially stemmed from momentary, relatively narrow, opportunistic considerations. However, they marked the beginning, or rather the continuation, of a trend which helped after 1945 to provoke the massive demand of what is now known as the Third World for an end to political tutelage. Thus the end of the colonial empires, one of the beneficial results of the Second World War (which, however, only accelerated rather than caused the process), was thereby brought nearer. Specifically, as early as 11 June the British assured the principal Ethiopian leaders that they would support them with money and weapons; on 3 July the Emperor Haile Selassie was in Khartoum, and from 12 August onward British missions infiltrated into Ethiopia to organize subversive warfare.[420]

At the same time there are good grounds for thinking that, as the situation then was, some resolutely conducted military operations against the British and French possessions in East Africa could have weakened, if not arrested, any potential rebellion. Whatever view one may take of this, it is a fact that a paralysing pessimism kept the Italians from even consistently examining all those openings which their colonial empire offered to the war effort with regard to overall strategic planning by the Axis powers.[421] Although studies were being worked on for an offensive towards the Sudan or Jibuti, the belief that the realization of the plan depended primarily on the domestic situation within the Italian colonial empire made these theoretical operations, at least in the eyes of their planners, almost illusory. Against this background Badoglio's instruction to the chief of the viceroy's general staff, General Claudio Trezzani, to preserve a strictly defensive attitude was scarcely

[418] Knox, *Mussolini*, 150–1.
[419] Playfair, *Mediterranean*, i. 167.
[420] See Merglen, 'Subversiver Kampf', 133–4.
[421] Faldella, *L'Italia*, 355.

surprising. If the marshal did not positively rule out an offensive, this hint of a mere possibility was probably due more to his endeavour to save the face of the high command in Rome than to any genuine intentions on the latter's part.[422]

The Italo-French armistice seemed to put an end to the threat to Ethiopia which had always been apprehended from French Somaliland. However, the situation was not entirely settled until, with effect from 25 July, the pro-British General Paul Legentilhomme was replaced by General Maxime Germain, loyal to Vichy. There was therefore, from a purely formal point of view, no reason for action against Jibuti. Even in the past the Italians had never been anxious for such a move. A penetration into French Somaliland had always been regarded as problematical, both because of the military difficulties and because of possible political consequences. Legentilhomme might have asked the British for help, and Italian intervention, for instance with a view to enforcing the armistice terms, was bound to have an undesirable effect on relations between the Pétain government and the administration of the colony. And that would have run counter to German interests. The French–Italian frontier in Somaliland therefore continued to remain quiet. Nevertheless, the Duke of Aosta suspected, even after July 1940, that French Somaliland might become the bridgehead for a British invasion.[423]

Partly because of these uncertainties, which at first characterized the situation in French Somaliland even after the armistice, at the end of June and the beginning of July Mussolini was disinclined to permit more than limited thrusts along the frontier with the Sudan and with Kenya. Although preparations were started for an offensive against British Somaliland, with Berbera and Seylac as the objectives, the enterprise, originally envisaged for 21 July, was postponed in view of the political situation.

In these circumstances the Duke of Aosta decided to move against Kassala, the communications centre on the frontier between Eritrea and the Sudan, whose capture would provide a base for further-reaching operations. These might be aimed at Khartoum, the political and military centre of the Sudan, or Port Sudan, a valuable port and industrial centre. Useful forays might also be made against Atbarah, an important rail junction.

The operation against Kassala began on 4 July (see Map I.III.I). The following day the town was in Italian hands. The defenders lost 10 men killed, the attackers 117. Parallel to the capture of Kassala the Italians took the town of Qallabat on the Ethiopian–Sudanese border. By 14 July Kurmuk and Qaysan were added. By the successful conclusion of this operation the Italians had quite appreciably improved their jumping-off base for a possible offensive against the Sudan. The successes of the viceroy's troops also had a favourable effect on the native population by enhancing Italian prestige. However—and

---

[422] Ibid. 357; *La guerra in Africa orientale*, 41.
[423] Playfair, *Mediterranean*, i. 167–8; Knox, *Mussolini*, 151–2.

this applies especially to Kassala—there was no apparent anti-British sentiment. On the contrary, throughout the Italian occupation the British were currently supplied with information by sources within the town.

On the Kenya frontier Italian forces occupied a small area along the north-western side of Lake Rudolf; they also captured the British part of Moyale and altogether advanced the front to a line Moyale–Buna–El Wak, the equivalent of a shortening of the front by some 150 to 200 km. No attempt was made to pursue the British troops, who had no intention of holding such an exposed position but, on the other hand, did not abandon it without a fight. This meant, however, that Mombasa, the starting-point of the railway to Nairobi and Uganda as well as being the country's principal port, remained totally unthreatened. Both the railway and the town were too far in the hinterland to be within the attacking range of Italian land operations.

As there were no important military objectives to be defended in northern Kenya, the British had rightly decided not to waste their weak forces, strung out on a long frontier, in pointless engagements with a greatly superior opponent. Kenya, as appeared shortly, provided an ideal area for the careful preparation of a British counter-offensive. Added to this was the fact that the viceroy's forces, cut off from effective supplies, were at no time in a position to continue their expansion. This was one of the reasons why, in February 1941, the British reconquest of all lost territories was successfully mounted from Kenya.[424] All in all, however, their operations against the Sudan and Kenya initially gave the Italians improved positions. That it did not prove possible in the long run to utilize them is another matter. At the time the operations began this could not necessarily have been foreseen. The actions certainly seemed justified and reasonably purposeful.

By contrast, there was scarcely a single convincing reason for attacking British Somaliland, a territory poor in raw materials and communications. This sun-scorched patch of earth was crossed only by a few pitiful tracks; there were no roads worthy of the name. Armoured and motor-vehicles were scarcely able to move in the terrain: they were confined to the tracks.[425] Above all, British Somaliland was surrounded by Italian colonies and by pro-Vichy French Somaliland. As the country's only worthwhile port, Berbera, was not a deep-water harbour, ocean-going vessels had to be unloaded by lighters, a process which could take ten days for a 3,000-ton freighter. Not an ideal spot, therefore, for landing a British expeditionary force so long as Kenya was available. The Duke of Aosta nevertheless assumed that this might happen.[426]

---

[424] *La guerra in Africa orientale*, 41–6; it should be noted that, following Italy's entry into the war, a German company, about 100 strong, was fighting on the Italian side. It was composed of German sailors, whose ships were trapped in Italian ports in East Africa, and of Germans resident in East Africa. See Burdick, *Sonnenblume*, 60. On military events on the frontiers of the Sudan and of Kenya see also Playfair, *Mediterranean*, i. 168–71, 179–82. On the British counter-offensive in 1941 cf. V.I and V.III below (Stegemann).

[425] *La guerra in Africa orientale*, 48–9.

[426] Playfair, *Mediterranean*, i. 173.

His operation, as he saw it, would therefore facilitate the defence of Italian East Africa. His decision, ultimately, was more a question of fancy, based on the obduracy with which he credited the British, than a military necessity. Admittedly a 1,150-km. land front was exchanged for 720 km. of coastline,[427] but in view of British invasion facilities from the Sudan and Kenya this was no reason for sacrificing men and material. One suspects that the wish to hold a colonial pledge in readiness for the apparently imminent peace negotiations may have played some part in the decision. At any rate, Badoglio is said to have informed the viceroy to this effect.[428]

On the British side it was rightly assumed that the Italians, if they attacked, would try to reach Berbera. Operational calculations suggested that approximately five battalions would be sufficient to defend the colony. But when the Italian attack began, the hastily dispatched troop reinforcements had not yet arrived in Somaliland. General Wavell had reacted too late. The units arriving from North Africa and India were, after the loss of British Somaliland, switched to the Sudan.[429] But we are anticipating events.

Since 27 July the Italians, under the command of General Guglielmo Nasi, had been concentrating in their deployment areas. Nasi's forces had an approximately fivefold superiority over the British and also enjoyed control of the air. On 2 August the attackers crossed the frontier. There were three groups, aiming at the following objectives: Seylac (Northern Group under General Bertoldi), Berbera (Central Group under General De Simone), and Ood Weyne (Southern Group under General Bertello)[430]—see Map I.III.2. The fiercest fighting occurred between 11 and 15 August along the Tug Argan line, which followed a dry river bed, between General Godwin-Austen's forces and the Italians. The latter had already taken Seylac on 5 August, so that General Bertoldi was able to push ahead along the coast. On 6 August Ood Weyne was in Italian hands. General Bertello wheeled some of his troops northwards towards Cadaadle, i.e. in the direction of General de Simone, who was advancing in the centre. In view of General Nasi's superiority in artillery and air power the British soon began to wonder whether they should hold Argan at all costs or whether it would not be more sensible, after delaying resistance, to evacuate their troops through Berbera. On 15 August General Wilson, deputizing for Wavell as commander-in-chief, ordered the evacuation, which was successfully completed on 18 August. Including civilians, 7,000 people were rescued by the Royal Navy. The Italians may have won a victory, but they paid for it with 2,052 men killed and with material losses which could not be replaced. The British lost 260 killed.

To the British public the evacuation of Somaliland came as a further shock, which may have been regarded as dangerous by the government. The British

---

[427] *La guerra in Africa orientale*, 47.
[428] Ibid. 47–8 n. 1; Faldella, *L'Italia*, 360–1; Knox, *Mussolini*, 152.
[429] Playfair, *Mediterranean*, i. 175.
[430] *La guerra in Africa orientale*, 52.

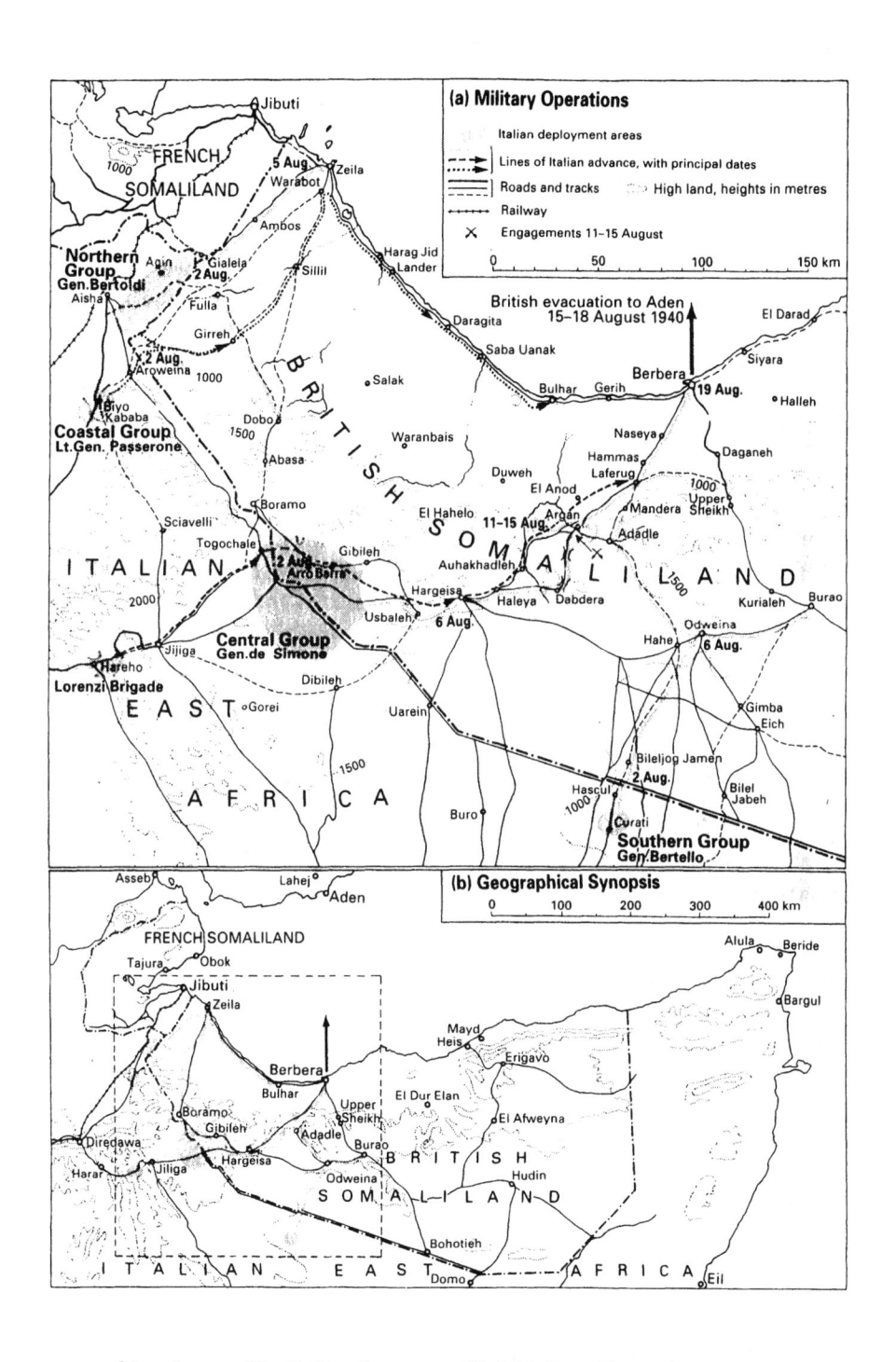

MAP I.III.2. The Italian Conquest of British Somaliland, August 1940

public showed some dismay, but, as was soon to be seen, the country possessed the capability of hitting back.[431]

To the Italians the situation looked different. At the beginning of August their viceroy in East Africa, encouraged by Badoglio, who expected a rapid and decisive Axis victory over Great Britain, still dreamt of the legendary offensive against the Sudan. This would have lent purpose to the war in East Africa, but, especially after the conquest of British Somaliland, was out of the question. Isolated as they were, the Duke of Aosta's forces, in the midst of victory, could expect nothing but defeat: especially if, as became clear in September, if not before, the European war was to continue. At the beginning of that month the Duke of Aosta recognized that unless he received 100 aircraft, 10,000 tyres, and 10,000 t. of fuel—and where were these to come from?—he could only operate defensively. But even defence would be problematical and was becoming more uncertain every day, especially as the Royal Air Force and the guerrilla war were making life difficult for him. Italian East Africa, from whence operations in North Africa were to have been supported, was increasingly dependent, for better or worse, on the course of the offensive against Egypt. Graziani at the Suez Canal might have meant hope, and perhaps salvation, having regard to British troop concentrations along the East African borders.[432]

(c) *The Offensive against Sidi Barrani*

North Africa was without question not only the most important but also the most popular theatre of war for Italy between June 1940 and May 1943, which is not to say that the public was truthfully informed during the war about developments in the Libyan desert. Approximately twenty-six Italian divisions were wiped out in North Africa. The war there consumed nearly the whole of Italy's modest tank production. One half of the Italian air force was, on average, employed in the North African skies. The bulk of the merchant fleet and the navy was engaged in supplying the forces in that theatre.

By now there exists an extensive literature on the course of events. The generals' memoirs, with their transparent intention of assigning to Mussolini the sole blame for the defeat, have gradually been succeeded by more objective critical studies.[433] The turning-point in military historiography on North Africa and on the prehistory of the war in that area came with the still important study of the Ufficio Storico, *In Africa settentrionale: La preparazione al conflitto. L'avanzata su Sidi el Barrani*, which makes available a multitude of sources, either complete or in excerpt.[434] It has to be borne in mind, however,

---

[431] Ibid. 54–66; Playfair, *Mediterranean*, i. 174–9; Maravigna, *Come abbiamo perduto*, 128–32.
[432] Knox, *Mussolini*, 153 ff.
[433] Ceva, 'La guerra italiana', listing some 230 titles without, of course, making any claim to completeness.
[434] *Africa settentrionale, La preparazione*, and now chiefly Montanari, *Le operazioni in Africa*. Also *Diario storico*, i, which could not be considered here in detail.

that the data on the strength of British forces are incorrect, being those issued by the Servizio Informazioni Militari (SIM: military information service). As a corrective, especially for the initial phase of the war, there is the official British work on the war in the Mediterranean.[435] Among comprehensive historical studies mention should be made, above all, of an American study[436] based on research into new sources.

The prospects of an offensive against the Suez Canal were, as observed earlier, viewed with considerable confidence by the Italian generals at the beginning of July. But immediately after Marshal Graziani's assumption of command there began a process of procrastination which was reflected in contradictory instructions and declarations of intent, and in conflicting views between the commander in North Africa and the supreme command in Rome. Mussolini, encouraged by Badoglio and the general staff to mount his attack against Egypt, used political arguments. He was primarily concerned with destroying the British position in the Middle East in order to establish a Fascist empire from Tunisia to the Persian Gulf. Graziani used military arguments, based on strategic and tactical reasoning.[437] That, of course, was his duty, and there are no grounds for criticizing him on that score. He ruled out large-scale actions, but Sollum seemed to him just acceptable as the objective of a military operation in July. Yet even on this point he was contradicted by the commanding officer of the front in question.[438]

Criticism of Graziani is justified mainly on the grounds that he allowed valuable time to be wasted. Instead of concentrating his best forces into the most manœuvrable formation possible, viz. a motorized formation equipped with artillery against British armour and with sufficient stocks of fuel and water, and moving it against the British forces (then by no means strong) in order to reach the Nile, he remained totally wedded to traditional operational doctrine—just as if, since the First World War, there had been no worldwide rethinking about mobile warfare. But basically the marshal probably did not wish to advance; or, if he had to do so, only with his entire army. In this way Graziani condemned himself to immobility. While still in Rome he had sent very different advice to Balbo; but he now refused the mobility he had recommended to his predecessor. Before anything else roads and water pipelines had to be constructed, and his extensive requests for equipment met.[439] The Comando Supremo largely complied with Graziani's demands for equipment, and by the end of July felt entitled to assume that he would launch his offensive in the second half of August. But on 29 July he announced that a 'prolonged and thorough examination of the difficult problem' regrettably

---

[435] Playfair, *Mediterranean*, i. 205–18.
[436] Knox, *Mussolini*, 155–65.
[437] Faldella, *L'Italia*, 208–14; Knox, *Mussolini*, 155–6.
[438] Knox, *Mussolini*, 156–7.
[439] Bocca, *Storia*, 215; Canzio, *La dittatura*, 600, also (599) on Badoglio's and Mussolini's misjudgement of Graziani as a general.

forced him to state unambiguously that both climate and terrain made such an operation impossible. Not till the end of October, when the heat had abated, could the offensive be mounted, and even then it would be very difficult.[440]

Graziani received no answer to this proposal; instead he was instructed to come to Rome. On 5 August a conference was held at the Palazzo Venezia between him, Mussolini, Badoglio, and Soddu.[441] Its outcome was an agreement on a thrust from Giarabub towards the north, in order to harass the British forces on the Egyptian frontier, while simultaneously permission was to be given for an offensive south of Sollum with the 'possible' objective of Sidi Barrani. What Mussolini evidently overlooked was that he had forgotten to commit his commander-in-chief to a definite date.[442] This, of course, was not lost on Graziani, who used his stay in Rome, on the one hand, to undermine Badoglio's position and, on the other, greatly to dramatize the planned offensive in Egypt in discussion with Ciano. In doing so the marshal correctly assumed that Ciano would pass this conversation on to Mussolini. The Duce thereupon personalized the problem: a man like Graziani, who had already achieved everything, should not be made commander-in-chief, because he had no ambition left. The Duce's reaction was in fact visibly one of disappointment. After his conversation with the generals he had supposed that the offensive, which Graziani did not wish to begin sooner than in two or three months' time, if indeed at all, might in fact be launched in a few days.[443]

The fact that Mussolini did not immediately react to Ciano's report was probably due to his hope that Graziani would after all, with a certain delay but within the foreseeable future, move towards Suez, as well as to the circumstance that during those first few days of August the Duce was more concerned with the Greek and Yugoslav questions. Added to this was the fact that certain information from Berlin pointed to a postponement of Operation Sea Lion, which from the Italian point of view made the offensive in North Africa less pressing.[444]

On 18 August, however, it was once more seen how inconsistent Mussolini's actions were, and the extent to which he felt dependent on German policy, to the details of which he was not privy. On the strength of new indications he now believed that the decisive German attack against Britain was imminent. He told Ciano that he expected peace and victory for the Axis powers towards the end of August. The solution of the Egyptian issue must therefore be speeded up.[445] Accordingly a telegram was sent to Graziani explaining to him the advantages of his position, reminding him that time was working against

---

[440] *Africa settentrionale, La preparazione*, 102–3; on Badoglio's and Mussolini's expectations mainly Faldella, *L'Italia*, 215.
[441] *Africa settentrionale, La preparazione*, 103–4.
[442] Knox, *Mussolini*, 160.
[443] Ciano, *Diary 1939–1943*, 281–2 (8 Aug. 1940).
[444] Knox, *Mussolini*, 160–1.
[445] Ciano, *Diary 1939–1943*, 284 (18 Aug. 1940).

Italy, and expressing the view that the conquest of Egypt, which would finally provide Italy with an overland link with Abyssinia, would be the *coup de grâce* for Britain. That was the real dreamt-of objective, even though Mussolini stressed that, for the time being, Graziani should attack the British only when the first German troops landed in England. In order to nip the obviously expected opposition in the bud, Mussolini declared that he would assume personal responsibility for this decision.[446]

It so happened that Graziani had summoned his unit commanders for a conference on the situation on 18 August. Its conclusions were not exactly surprising, considering developments since June 1940. The generals unanimously held the view that an offensive worthy of the name could not, and should not on any account, be opened under the prevailing conditions.[447] Graziani reported this without qualification to Rome, at the same time offering his resignation if this were thought useful to the cause.[448]

Mussolini's telegram, however, pulled the rug from underneath the generals' decision. As the choice of the objective was left to Graziani, and as there was no insistence on Sollum being reached—let alone on an advance to Alexandria—however much this was hoped for in Rome, the marshal was able to override his generals' resolution without losing face. Graziani displayed both spontaneity and a short-lived eagerness to attack. Initially the Italian offensive was to aim at Sollum, and next at Sidi Barrani. In Rome, where there had been some nervousness at the outcome of the conference of 18 August reported by the commander-in-chief, confidence spread after his second telegram, dated 20 August. The marshal had performed an about-turn: he would attack, and this knowledge sufficed for the moment. Graziani now had problems with his subordinates, especially General Mario Berti, commanding the Tenth Army. But after something of a tug of war it seemed, towards the end of August, that all the generals concerned had accepted the decision.[449]

After Italy's entry into the war Mussolini at times found dealings with his generals difficult, just as dealings with his German ally proved far from straightforward. Hitler not only restrained Mussolini in his activities aiming at the Balkans, but also caused him anxiety by the fact that the invasion of Britain was making no progress. Berlin, it was said, preferred a political arrangement with London.[450] If Keitel, as was understood in Rome at that time, had really propagated the view that the capture of Cairo was more important than the fall of London, this could only, from the Italian point of view, mean that 'Sea Lion' had been postponed. In point of fact it is unim-

---

[446] Ibid. 284–5 (19 Aug. 1940); text in *Africa settentrionale, La preparazione*, 105–6.

[447] *Africa settentrionale, La preparazione*, 104–5, 216–21, minute of conference between Graziani and his commanding officers on 18 Aug. 1940.

[448] Ibid. 221–2, Graziani to Badoglio (18 Aug. 1940); cf. Ciano, *Diary 1939–1943*, 285 (20 Aug. 1940), who states clearly that there was only one objective in all such deliberations: Egypt.

[449] Knox, *Mussolini*, 160 ff.

[450] Ciano, *Diary 1939–1943*, 285 (22 Aug. 1940); *DDI*, 9th ser., v, No. 475, pp. 459–60 (23 Aug. 1940), Alfieri to Ciano.

portant whether or not Keitel ever made that remark: Ciano, for instance, did not think so. What is historically relevant is that Mussolini accepted the information at face value. He probably did so because it fitted into his plans. This may be seen as a clear indication of the intensity with which Mussolini was clinging to his expansionist aims (down-played only verbally) in North Africa. Regardless of all tactical and political finessing, such as is frequently reflected in the sources, what he was aiming at was no less than Egypt itself.[451]

This was impressively confirmed by further developments. In a letter which Ciano handed to Hitler in Vienna on 28 August 1940, Mussolini wrote that his troops would attack in North Africa on the same day as the first Wehrmacht soldiers landed in Britain.[452] However, when Ciano, reporting on his talks with the Germans, stated that the invasion was being delayed, Mussolini abandoned the condition he had put forward:[453] Graziani was ordered to move against the British in any case, regardless of whether the Wehrmacht intended a landing in Britain. In this context Mussolini formulated his political calculation with regard to a (possibly limited) offensive: in view of her military action, Italy could not now be disregarded in the event of a German–British arrangement, which could no longer be ruled out. Graziani's forces should be ready for orders to move off between 8 and 10 September.[454]

Mussolini, who was already talking mysteriously to his intimates about his 'premonition' of a new war which would follow the present one,[455] wished to acquire at least such instruments of moral pressure as would later help him assert his material demands. A prolongation of military operations could only serve this intention. The more casualties, he argued, the more justified his extensive claims. Especially if one remembers that Mussolini, like certain groups in Germany in the summer of 1940,[456] was thinking of a kind of interim peace, it will be readily understood what he was really after: an improvement of Italy's geo-strategic starting-position with regard to the next military conflict. The reflection which worried certain German and Italian doubters, that the war might be protracted and would in that case almost inevitably develop to the disadvantage of the Axis powers, does not appear to have been shared by him. It should, however, be noted that Mussolini expected a conclusion of the conflict in the winter. And as he regarded the military and economic development on the British side as unimportant, that time-span did not seem to him to hold any dangers for Italy.[457]

Just then, when everything seemed to have been decided, Graziani suddenly once more urged a postponement of the attack. It was again the vexatious

---

[451] Ciano, *Diary 1939–1943*, 286–7 (28 Aug. 1940).
[452] *DGFP* D x, No. 388, pp. 538–9 (24 Aug. 1940).
[453] *DDI*, 9th ser., v, No. 516, pp. 505–6 (29 Aug. 1940).
[454] *Africa settentrionale, La preparazione*, 107, 230: Badoglio to Graziani (29 Aug. 1940).
[455] Bottai, *Vent'anni*, 191 (29 Aug. 1940), amplified note in id., *Diario*, 224.
[456] Schreiber, 'Kontinuität', 127.
[457] Ciano, *Diary 1939–1943*, 288 (1 Sept. 1940).

problem of equipment, especially of army trucks.[458] But this time Mussolini lost patience. On 7 September he ordered Graziani to start the offensive on the 9th.[459] As for its objective, the marshal himself had defined it a few days earlier: Sidi Barrani.[460] In view of this decision, doubtless no longer expected, the command in North Africa was forced to change its operational plans from top to bottom.

The original plan of 22 August had envisaged only the capture of the area east of Sollum, to a point north of Shawni el Aujerin (see Map I.III.3). Not until 3 September did Graziani emphatically argue for the occupation of Sidi Barrani, originally considered only in the event of favourable progress. The town was to be taken by an outflanking movement. To that end the homeland divisions, i.e. purely Italian units, were to advance along the coast road. On the right, the Libyan divisions and the motorized Maletti detachment were to advance on the Dayr al-Hamra–Bir ar Rabiyah–Bir Enba track. But when Mussolini ordered the beginning of the operation for 9 September, Graziani believed that the material prerequisites underlying his operational plan were still lacking: sufficient motor-vehicles and transport aircraft, as well as command of the air-space.

The marshal thereupon decided to have the bulk of his forces advance along the coast road via Buqbuq to Sidi Barrani. This facilitated the task of the Italian air force. Moreover, Graziani was hoping to surprise the British, who had deployed the bulk of their armoured forces in the direction of Bir Enba–Dayr al-Hamra, because it was there they expected an attack. Most importantly, his decision rendered easier the supply of the Italian formations, especially with water, from the Bardiyah–Capuzzo area.[461]

In view of his shortage of motor-vehicles, Graziani was able to employ only five divisions and the motorized Maletti detachment, which, however, was also slimmed down. These forces formed the XXIII Army Corps under General Annibale Bergonzoli, which comprised the homeland divisions Cirene, Marmarica, and 23 Marzo.

The corps had about 1,000 motor-vehicles at its disposal, which would be used, initially, for moving the two divisions of the first line—non-motorized infantry—and next the reserve division (23 Marzo) by trucks. Added to this were the 1st and 2nd Libyan divisions under General Gallina. They had 650 motor-vehicles. This was sufficient for transporting equipment, guns, and supplies, but the infantry had to march. The Maletti detachment, consisting of three Libyan battalions reinforced by artillery, had 450 motor-vehicles, which was sufficient for transporting the personnel. The XXI Army Corps with the

---

[458] *Africa settentrionale, La preparazione*, 107–8; a very instructive account of the difficult relationship between Badoglio and Graziani in Knox, *Mussolini*, 160–1.
[459] *Africa settentrionale, La preparazione*, 236, Badoglio to Graziani (7 Sept. 1940); cf. also ibid. 108.
[460] Ibid. 231 ff.: Graziani to Badoglio (2 Sept. 1940).
[461] Ibid. 126–30.

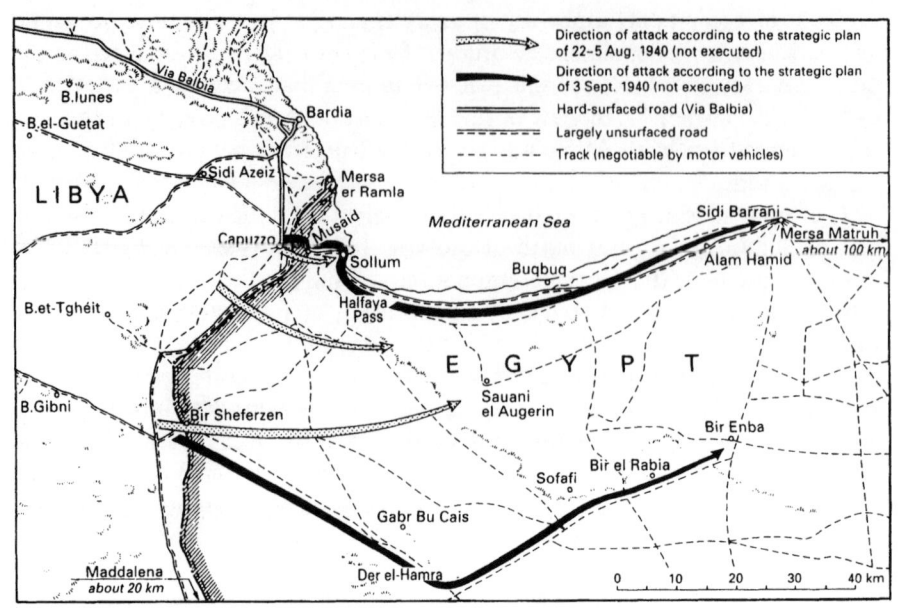

MAP I.III.3. Italian Plans of Attack, August–September 1940

Sirte and 28 Ottobre divisions was held in reserve. The Catanzaro and 3 Gennaio divisions were, because of the necessary reduction in the strength of the attacking units, once more placed under XXII Army Corps in Tobruk.

As for armour, the Italian command decided to concentrate all combat-ready forces under General Valentino Babini. Two armoured detachments were formed, each of one battalion of Model M tanks and three battalions of Model L tanks. In addition there was a mixed battalion and one battalion of light armour. Bergonzoli and Gallina were each assigned one armoured detachment. The mixed battalion joined the Maletti detachment. The light armour battalion was assigned to XXI Army Corps.

These army formations were supported by the 336 aircraft of the Fifth Air Fleet, which comprised 110 bombers, 50 ground-attack aircraft, 170 fighters, and 6 long-range reconnaissance aircraft. At the start of the hostilities another 64 bombers, 75 ground-attack aircraft, and 15 reconnaissance planes were brought in from Italy on 9 September.[462] Apart from attacks against British airfields, supply-centres, and other military targets, the air force was, above all, to provide cover for the Italian troops and attack the British army formations.

On the British side, the forces facing the Italian attackers were relatively

---

[462] Ibid. 122 ff.; different numerical data on the air force in Santoro, *L'aeronautica italiana*, i. 278, who lists the following strength for the start of the offensive: 110 bombers, 135 fighters, 45 ground-attack fighters, 6 long-range reconnaissance planes, and 4 torpedo-carrying aircraft.

weak. Their main task was to intercept and ward off Graziani's expected thrust against Marsa Matruh. All that Wavell had to employ for that purpose was his armoured division, the 4th Indian division, and a few Australian and New Zealand units, all of which suffered from very limited, or even inadequate, equipment. Thus the 7th division at the time had only about a third of its earmarked 200 tanks, and by no means all of them had all the regulation armament. The 4th Indian division was a whole brigade short, and its artillery was also somewhat incomplete. Matters were even worse with the Australians and New Zealanders.[463] The Royal Air Force too was numerically inferior to the Italians. The ratio of fighter aircraft in North Africa, for instance, was 1 to 4.[464]

Under these circumstances the British concentrated the bulk of their armour in the Marsa Matruh area. Advanced cover with occasional nuisance raids was provided by the Seventh Army's support group, which had been stationed since mid-August between Sollum and Rid Maddalena (Quasr ash Shaqqah). The formation had a motorized battalion, artillery, especially anti-tank guns, and an armoured battalion. In addition there were the 11th Hussars, who reconnoitred even further forward and on Italian territory.[465]

It is intriguing, in this situation, to reflect on the German offer, made in the summer of 1940, to transfer armoured units to North Africa.[466] It seems highly probable that in that case the British would have found themselves in serious difficulties, to put it mildly, at a time when all they had in the desert was 85 tanks of 12.5 and 14 t., of which 15 were out of action undergoing repair at the beginning of September.

Before the main features of the Italian advance on Sidi Barrani are set out here, mention should be made of the climatic and geographical characteristics of the theatre of operations.[467] This was a desert, where air temperatures in September reached 50 °C and where no water supplies existed within the area of operations. Movement of vehicles off the tracks was limited. In the event of air attack the troops had no cover; on the other hand, the long valleys of the sand-dunes made it difficult for small units to be spotted in a hurry, so that, provided they were fast and mobile, they stood a good chance during surprise raids. Orientation was difficult in this terrain, at times made even more so by sand-storms. There is a touch of irony in the fact that General Maletti's detachment lost its way hopelessly while still on Italian territory. The general had dispensed with native desert guides. Almost out of water, he was spotted by the Italian air force and set on the right road.

As for the terrain, the Sollum escarpment, roughly 200 metres high, stretches from the Libyan border to Sollum, and thence for approximately 60 km. towards the south-west. The territory between it and the coast could basically be negotiated only by tracked vehicles; even by troops on foot it

---

[463] Knox, *Mussolini*, 155.
[464] Overy, *Air War*, 41.
[465] Playfair, *Mediterranean*, i. 205.
[466] Cf. I.III.2 (*b*) above.
[467] *Africa settentrionale, La preparazione*, 125–6; on Maletti see Knox, *Mussolini*, 164.

could only be traversed with great difficulty. By contrast, the terrain west and south of this natural barrier was easily negotiable by all kinds of motor-vehicles. For anyone coming from the west and wishing to advance in the direction of Sidi Barrani the escarpment could be crossed at three points only: at Sollum, at Halfaya, and near Bir Shaffafah. The easily motorable pass-roads of Sollum and Halfaya ran directly into the coast road; the Bir Shaffafah pass was crossed by a primitive track to Buqbuq. Because of these conditions an advance towards Sidi Barrani from the Marsa ar Ramiya–Rid Capuzzo–Bir Sheferzen area could be effected only via Sollum or Halfaya and along the coast road, or by the track via Jabr Bu Qais, Dayr al-Hamra, Bir ar Rabiyah, Bir Enba. From the frontier this was a distance of 100 or 160 km. respectively. Tactical co-operation between formations moving separately was possible only, at the earliest, in the area of Buqbuq, after the crossing of the escarpment. In the event of the offensive being continued from Sidi Barrani in the direction of Marsa Matruh, about 150 km. distant, there was a good coast road. Marsa Matruh, moreover, was the starting-point of the railway to Alexandria (see Map I.III.4).

From 9 September onwards the Italian forces assembled in their respective deployment areas, at times under harassment from the British air force.[468] On the morning of 13 September the attack, preceded by heavy artillery fire, began at Musaid.[469] At Sollum the British offered virtually no resistance. They had partly destroyed and evacuated the place. At the Halfaya pass the Italians at first encountered stubborn opposition, but by early afternoon the defenders were forced to withdraw towards the east in view of the Italians' crushing superiority in numbers and material. It is interesting that Graziani's formations did not immediately follow up with a pursuit. Not until 14 September was the advance continued, the Italians, according to British accounts, moving at times as if on the parade ground, which of course resulted in unnecessary losses. Generally speaking, the operations resembled a game of chess which avoided the exchange of pieces, while each side's pawns occupied the squares vacated by the opponent. Britain's advanced units, while offering continuous resistance, withdrew by 15 September to Alam Hamid. The following day they stood at Alam el Dab, a few kilometres in front of Sidi Barrani. When the British were outflanked in this position on their left by an Italian combat group consisting of about fifty tanks and motorized infantry, they fell back to positions east of Sidi Barrani. By the same evening the town was in Italian hands. It was therefore clear to the Italian staffs that the British intended to make their decisive stand only in the Marsa Matruh area.

Their operations between 9 and 16 September cost the Italians more than 120 killed and 410 wounded; the British lost fewer than 50 men. There were

---

[468] *Africa settentrionale, La preparazione*, 130 ff.; Playfair, *Mediterranean*, i. 209.

[469] On the development of the operation cf. *Africa settentrionale, La preparazione*, 132–43; Playfair, *Mediterranean*, i. 209 ff.; Heggenreiner, 'Operations', 18–21, MGFA, D-216.

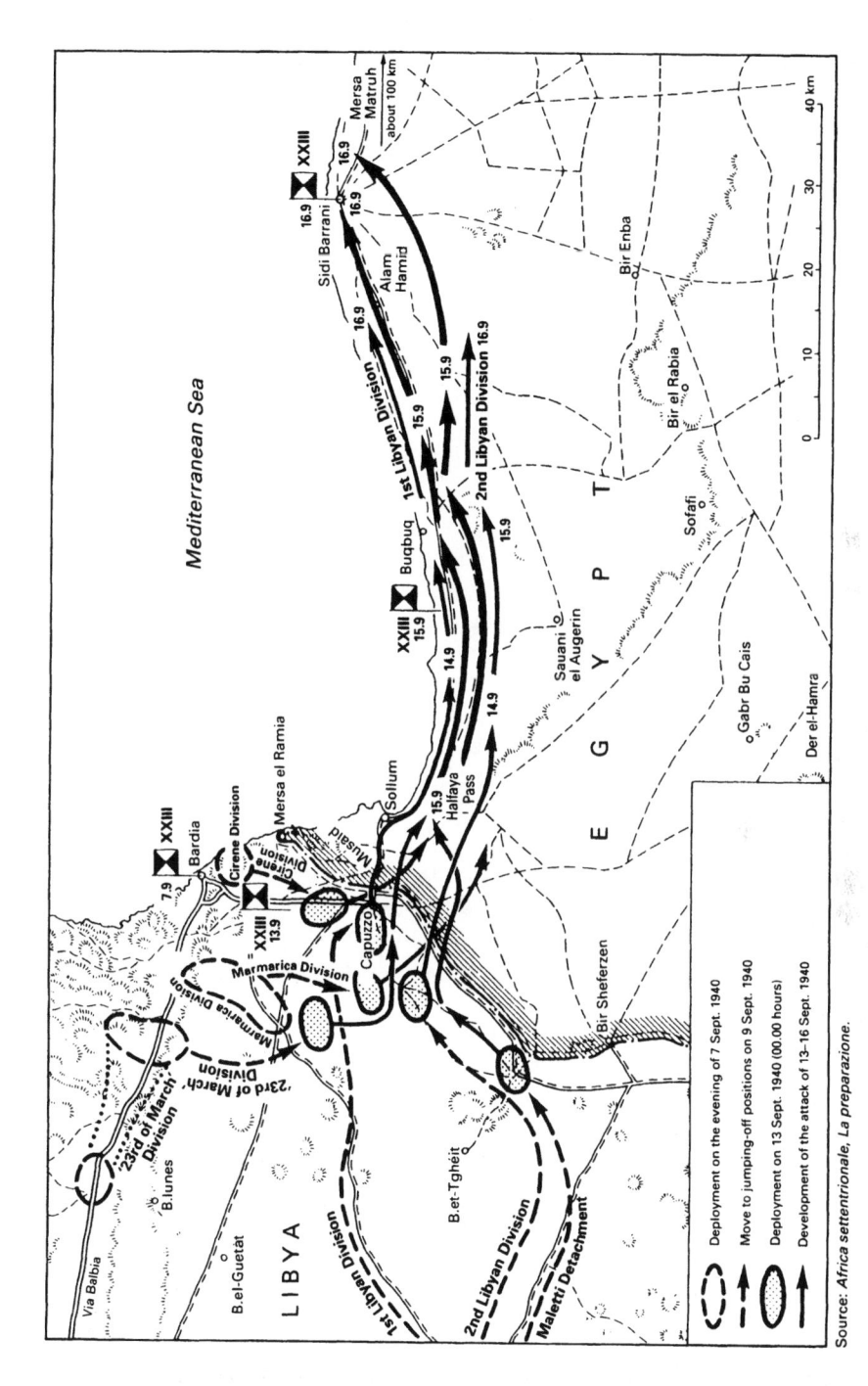

MAP I.III.4. The Italian Offensive against Sidi Barrani, 13–16 September 1940

losses of material on both sides, but their precise extent still does not seem to have been established.[470]

What in fact did the conquest of Sidi Barrani mean? Basically not much for either side, but, from very different viewpoints, certainly more than nothing.

From the British point of view, the loss of an airfield near the Italian border was painful. Bombers could not be escorted by fighters as far as before. The penetration range of reconnaissance planes was also reduced by approximately 150 km. After the loss of this refuelling-base, air attacks on Benghazi became decidedly risky. Fighters, even if equipped with additional fuel-tanks, could no longer reach Malta from land-bases. Henceforward they had to be brought closer by sea transport or by aircraft-carriers. In an emergency this was too time-consuming. Ships shelling the Libyan coast had no land-based air support once off Sidi Barrani. Previously, air cover had extended as far as Bardiyah. Conversely, attacking Italian bombers were now escorted by fighters all the way to Marsa Matruh.[471]

The major threat, however, did not materialize. Very soon it became obvious that, regardless of the urgings and hopes of Mussolini,[472] who felt his judgement had been vindicated by his marshal's successful operation[473]—performed against the generals' estimate of the situation—Graziani had no intention whatever of continuing the offensive at once. Such a follow-up had been expected by the British.[474] On 16 September Graziani reported to Rome that delays would have to be expected because the retreating enemy had filled in the wells in Sidi Barrani, destroyed the barracks, and set fire to the fuel stores.[475] This was true. The British had in fact not only filled in the wells but permanently polluted the water with salt. In addition, the road between Sidi Barrani and the frontier had been destroyed by military action and as a result of the heavy load of traffic during the operations.[476] In these circumstances, on 17 September Graziani declined to follow up the advance. The troops would first have to recover, units would have to be reorganized, the road had to be repaired, and water supplies had to be ensured. Badoglio seems to have agreed with these objections.[477]

Mussolini, on the other hand, had made up his mind, certainly by 14 September, that the advance should proceed to Marsa Matruh. The rapid British retreat encouraged this view; besides, from Marsa Matruh the Italian air force would be able to bomb Alexandria with fighter escort, i.e. also by day.[478] In addition, some generals believed that Wavell in any case would

---

[470] *Africa settentrionale, La preparazione*, 142–3.
[471] Playfair, *Mediterranean*, i. 212.
[472] Rintelen, *Mussolini als Bundesgenosse*, 100.
[473] Ciano, *Diary 1939–1943*, 290–1 (17 Sept. 1940).
[474] Playfair, *Mediterranean*, i. 211.
[475] *Africa settentrionale, La preparazione*, 247, Graziani to the Stato Maggiore Generale (16 Sept. 1940).
[476] Playfair, *Mediterranean*, i. 211.
[477] *Africa settentrionale, La preparazione*, 143–4.
[478] Ciano, *Diary 1939–1943*, 290 (14 Sept. 1940).

3. Italy's Conduct of the War

not stand and fight before Alexandria.[479] This assumption, however, proved incorrect.[480]

From the Italian point of view, the capture of Sidi Barrani, while not immediately decisive, would have made an exploitation of the success possible. In this context it should be noted that, from mid-September to the end of the month, Mussolini did not rule out a thrust into Egypt. As for the delays which were emerging, he blamed these on Badoglio rather than on Graziani,[481] even though the latter, in his telegram of 17 September 1940, had shown little inclination for an advance to Marsa Matruh.[482] Basically, in September 1940 the military and political leadership originally tended to concentrate all available resources in North Africa.[483] Seen thus, the decision to attack Greece,[484] to be discussed later,[485] came as a surprise. It also finally turned the Sidi Barrani offensive into what it threatened to become from the outset: a strategic torso. It could be said that all it did was shift the jumping-off position for the attack against Egypt further east.[486] As Graziani was unable to continue the operation immediately but had to interpose a pause, this was, at best, an ambivalent outcome. The British remained unweakened, while Italian supply-lines were increasingly stretched and supplying the troops had become more problematical. In retrospect it has even been said,[487] in connection with the British counter-offensive in December,[488] that the offensive against Sidi Barrani was one of Italy's most grievous errors in the Second World War. This assessment need not be accepted: a lot of things look clearer in retrospect than they did for the agents at the time. The operations, moreover, confirmed what had been discovered earlier: the Italian army's inability to practise modern armoured warfare, and the difficulties of army–air force co-operation on the battlefield.[489]

German expectations in connection with the Italian advance against Egypt were touched on earlier.[490] What has to be stressed again at this point is that Berlin was aiming at far more than the capture of Sidi Barrani. When it was taken, attentive observers immediately expected that 'a pause of probably several weeks has begun on the Egyptian front',[491] but even that proved over-optimistic. The truth is that, especially after her decision to attack Greece, Italy no longer had the strength, on her own, to launch a second offensive in North Africa.

---

[479] Ibid. 290–1 (17 Sept. 1940).
[480] Playfair, *Mediterranean*, i. 211.
[481] Ciano, *Diary 1939–1943*, 294 (30 Sept. 1940).
[482] Cf. Graziani, *Ito difeso*, 260 ff., with grave accusations against Badoglio; also Salvatorelli and Mira, *Storia d'Italia*, 1047.
[483] Pieri and Rochat, *Badoglio*, 758.
[484] Ciano, *Diary 1939–1943*, 297 (12 Oct. 1940).
[485] See II.III.1 below.
[486] Baum and Weichold, *Krieg der 'Achsenmächte'*, 64; similarly Kesselring, 'Krieg', 69–70.
[487] Faldella, *L'Italia*, 221.
[488] See V.1 below (Stegemann).
[489] Bocca, *Storia*, 217.
[490] See I.III.2(b) above.
[491] KTB des Chefs des Verbindungsstabes beim Admiralstab der Kgl. ital. Marine, 6 (18 Sept. 1940), BA-MA RM 36/8.

IV. Ideas of German Ruling Circles Concerning a Colonial Empire

IN the autumn of 1940 developments in south-east Europe brought about a major change in the role played by the Mediterranean theatre within the strategy of the Axis powers. Before examining this in detail, at least a general look should be taken at the central war aims—which naturally included the Mediterranean area—of the German overseas-minded imperialists: the colonial empire of the European hegemonic power Greater Germany. Victory in the west seemed to have brought these aims within reach. (See Map I.IV.1.)

It is not intended to examine once more the much-researched and convincingly answered question as to whether a Central African colonial empire could, from Hitler's point of view, have offered an alternative to the conquest of living-space in the east.[1] This it certainly could not do, although the problem should not be totally dismissed. In any case, our present intention is to highlight some of the colonial aspirations for which the war provided a vehicle. As stated in the Introduction to Volume I of this work,[2] 'The European war that broke out on 1 September 1939 would not have done so but for Hitler. Very probably, sooner or later, a different war would have broken out with the lines differently drawn.' This thesis is supported by the plans which were updated, though by no means newly conceived, in the summer of 1940. Moreover, the aspirations of German ruling circles at the time are an important guide to the understanding of particular aspects of the war as parts of its overall pattern.[3]

We may begin with a summary of colonial thinking in Germany between the wars, during the era which Wolfgang J. Mommsen, proceeding from global points of view and including the period up to 1945, has defined as the 'era of veiled imperialism'.[4] The term 'veiled' can surely apply only to the imperialism of the European democracies between the wars. Even with regard to them, a better term might be 'moderate' or 'restrained' imperialism, in comparison with its classical phase up to 1918. By contrast, the political have-nots—National Socialist Germany and Fascist Italy—produced 'new outbreaks of overt imperialism of an exceedingly brutal character',[5] such as Mussolini's attack on Abyssinia.[6] This applies especially to Hitler's program-

---

[1] Hillgruber, *Strategie*, 242–55.
[2] p. 8.
[3] Discussed in the context of German imperialist interests in the Mediterranean since the First World War by Schreiber, 'Italien'.
[4] *Der moderne Imperialismus*, 14.
[5] Ibid. 24.
[6] See I.II.2 above.

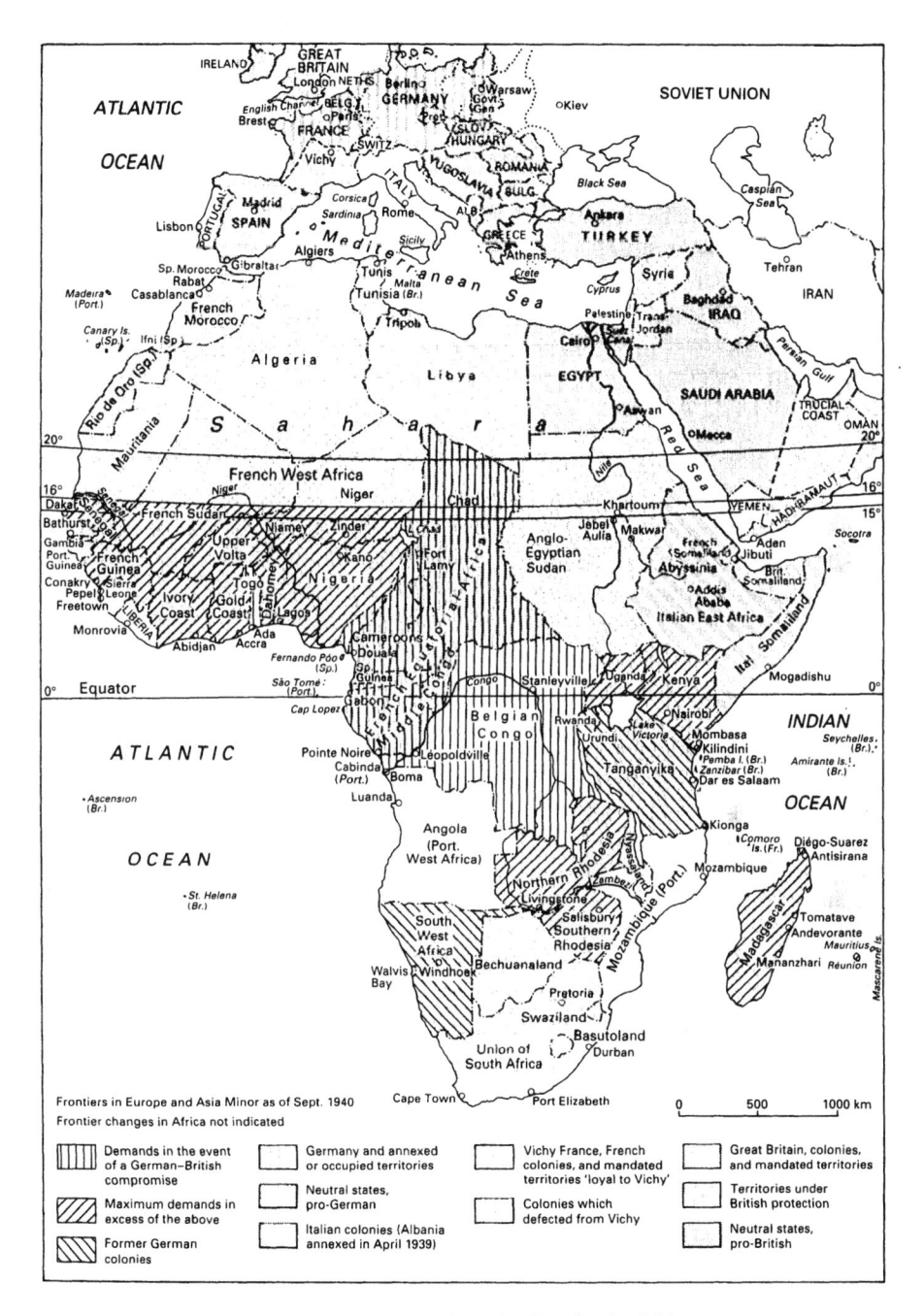

MAP I.IV.1. German Ideas of a Colonial Empire in Africa, 1940–1941

matic expansion towards the east, implemented by the Second World War, and to the annihilation policy of the National Socialist regime which then reached its height. From this point of view the conquest of living-space in the east is certainly unique. Nevertheless, and particularly in view of the changes after the First World War in relations between colonial powers and their colonies, Mommsen's formula is relevant with regard to the overseas aspirations of German imperialists as formulated at that time. But this is to anticipate events.

To begin with, it should be noted that whereas in the public mind of the Western democracies during the 1920s the conviction was gradually gaining ground that 'colonial rule can no longer be justified except when it serves the aim of gradually preparing the natives for emancipation',[7] in Germany there was no such sensitization of public opinion regarding imperialist political ideas.

Certain circles in the Reich cultivated the idea of recovering the colonial possessions lost in the First World War. This went on with varying intensity, but continually. And although the colonial revisionists did not represent a mass movement, they could not be written off as a negligible factor.

Since 1922 there had been the Koloniale Reichsarbeitsgemeinschaft (Colonial Reich Working Community), an umbrella organization for the various colonial organizations. On 20 May 1925 something like a first debate on colonial matters took place in the Reichstag;[8] and a year later a Paris economic journal warned against a 'résurrection du pangermanisme colonial'.[9] This kind of activity is part of the basis and background of the plans of 1940–1.[10]

Hitler, it should be noted, did not steer a steady course in colonial matters. He vacillated, and not only in June 1941, when he declared that 'future German imperialism' would be 'continental-European'—which did not mean, in any case, that he wished to renounce colonies in Africa.[11] Three months later he declared that colonies were 'a questionable possession', whereas 'this soil', the eastern space, was a certainty for Germany.[12] Another six months later he said: 'The day we have firmly organized Europe we shall be able to look out towards Africa. And who knows, perhaps we shall one day be in a

---

[7] *Der moderne Imperialismus*, 23–4.

[8] Hildebrand, *Vom Reich*, 40–247. The study focuses on the interpretation of the attitude of Hitler and the NSDAP towards the colonial question between 1919 and 1945. On the attitude of the public, the political parties, and the Reichstag cf. 56–70. See also Schmokel, *Der Traum vom Reich*, 15–139.

[9] *L'Information*, quoted according to Hildebrand, *Vom Reich*, 70.

[10] On the continuity of the colonial claim see also, along with the studies listed in n. 8, Weinberg, 'German Colonial Plans', 462–8, and especially for the navy Schreiber, 'Reichsmarine'. The navy's views were closely linked with colonial revisionism, even though this aim was not clearly formulated until later. For the viewpoint of Marxist-Leninist historiography cf. Kühne, *Kolonialideologie*, 13–20.

[11] Halder, *Diaries*, ii. 991 (30 June 1940).

[12] Picker, *Hitlers Tischgespräche*, 69 (8–10 Sept. 1941).

position to consider other objectives too.'[13] Five months after that, having in the meantime realized the failure of his plans,[14] he dismissed the whole thing as a project never seriously contemplated: 'He had sought an arrangement with Britain on the basis that colonies were not necessary at all [for Germany]. Even the problem of maintaining communications between Greater Germany and any such colonies, situated for instance in Africa, would cause difficulties.'[15] Hitler by then was already 'building up his legend'.[16]

In contrast to this playing-down of his world-power aspirations, examination of Hitler's strategic plans in the autumn of 1940[17] reveals that he was definitely considering the acquisition of Atlantic bases. These were not only to serve the war against Britain, but, chiefly from a defensive point of view, would prove useful in an extension of the conflict. These ideas, moreover, have to be seen in the context of the long-term objectives which Hitler hoped to achieve by the realization of the second major stage of his programme, viz. overseas expansion. An examination of his foreign policy with regard to the place that colonial plans occupied in it reveals, despite all fluctuations, three major lines of development up to the outbreak of the war.[18]

Between 1925 and 1935 Hitler was emphatically working for a German–British alliance including a worldwide demarcation of interests between Berlin and London. In order to win over the British to this idea he seemed prepared for a long-term, though not a permanent, renunciation of colonies.

In the period from 1935 to 1937 the ambivalent phase of his policy began. This was characterized both by a renunciation of colonial possessions and by the demand for them, used by way of pressure. But regardless of the fact that in March 1935 Britain rejected his idea of an alliance, while the naval agreement of June 1935, to which certain hopes had been attached, was not followed by any substantive political agreement, Hitler continued to pursue his original plans for an Anglo-German alliance.

Not until 1937–9 did Britain become for him the 'hated adversary'. He now intended to implement his programme—which aimed at hegemony in Europe in the short term and overseas world-power status in the long run—no longer only if he came to an arrangement with Britain, but, if necessary, against her. Even the successful realization of the first step would have automatically provided Germany with colonies and brought about a Greater German empire whose 'power [would extend] from the Urals to the Atlantic, from the British Isles to the heart of Africa'.

It can therefore be said (with some over-simplification) that Hitler seems to

---

[13] Quoted according to Hillgruber, *Strategie*, 251–2, remark by Hitler on 22 Feb. 1942.
[14] Ibid. 552–3.
[15] Picker, *Hitlers Tischgespräche*, 465 (26 July 1942).
[16] Hillgruber, *Strategie*, 252; Hildebrand, *Vom Reich*, 713–30, for 1941–3.
[17] See I.III.1(b). I.III.2(b) above.
[18] Quoted according to Hildebrand, *Vom Reich*, 622 ff.; id., 'Deutschland', esp. 412–13; Schmokel, *Traum vom Reich*, 129 ff., especially on the summer of 1939; Weinberg, 'German Colonial Plans', 462–8.

have treated the colonial issue mainly as a tactical one up to the outbreak of the Second World War, with a view to obtaining Britain's agreement to the realization of his continental-European aims. Subsequently—no later than 1938—when it became clear that agreement with Britain on his terms was an unrealistic hope, Hitler gradually determined to solve the British problem after he had established dominion over the Continent, some time in the mid-1940s.[19] Whether such expectations were realistic is of no concern at this point. What interests us here is the nature of Hitler's intentions, because these determined the political line of National Socialism. It is likewise of no concern whether he communicated his intentions at the time to other persons in so many words. It is known, for instance, that between 1935 and 1937 he did not say much about his long-term objectives. And why should be? That those familiar with his ideas believed in their attainability is proved by the preparations put in hand for the seizure of colonial territories, even though this was not envisaged on a major scale until the second phase of his world-power aspirations. These preparations continued even after the outbreak of the war.[20]

The Second World War has rightly been described as the result of Hitler's living-space policy.[21] To many members of German leadership élites, however, it also offered an unexpected opportunity to realize traditional world-power aspirations. This is true especially of colonial demands which had in the past been voiced with relative restraint in diplomatic, economic, and military circles, but which then escalated in the summer of 1940.[22]

At that time Hitler had already decided that 'questions of the recovery of German colonies [should be] examined by the foreign ministry, and the colonial-policy department of the NSDAP [should] make preparations for the administration of the colonies in consultation with the party and state authorities concerned'.[23] On 29 May Ribbentrop thereupon charged Ministerialdirigent Dr Karl Clodius and Dr Karl Ritter, ambassador for special duties, to produce study papers on the future German colonial empire.[24]

Clodius's and Ritter's ideas amounted to a colonial empire which would include all former German colonies, the Belgian Congo, French Equatorial Africa, and possibly also British Nigeria.[25]

---

[19] Hauner, 'World Dominion', 25–8.
[20] On the activities initiated up to May 1940, chiefly though not only by the colonial-policy department of the NSDAP and various colonial movements, see Böhme, *Der deutsch-französische Waffenstillstand*, 280; Hildebrand, *Vom Reich*, 629–41; Schmokel, *Traum vom Reich*, 131 ff.; Schreiber, *Revisionismus*, 286–7; Thies, *Architekt*, 131–2; Weinberg, 'German Colonial Plans', 469.
[21] Schmokel, *Traum vom Reich*, 127; cf. also *Konzept für die 'Neuordnung' der Welt*, 82–5, 92–3.
[22] *Drang nach Afrika*, 327–36; the contribution by Richard Lakowski critically examines the role of scholarship; for the navy, whose leaders were one of the most radical imperialist groups, see esp. Schreiber, *Revisionismus*, 286–300; cf. also *Deutschland im zweiten Weltkrieg*, i. 411–12.
[23] Directive of the Führer's deputy of 23 Jan. 1940: Doc. 59 in Hildebrand, *Vom Reich*, 905.
[24] *DGFP* D ix, No. 367, pp. 496–501 (1 June 1940).
[25] Cf. ibid., No. 354, pp. 476–82 (30 May 1940).

Besides the foreign ministry it was chiefly industrial circles which were interested in the colonial issue. Although the extent of co-operation between German industry and the Reich bureaucracy cannot be traced in all its details, research has firmly established that 'especially during the months of the victorious campaign against France [the two] were co-operating closely'.[26]

The biggest appetite, however, was shown by the navy, whose ideas closely followed the demands of 1916.[27] Since the navy, in a manner of speaking, constituted the lobby of the overseas imperialists, its colonial aspirations will be examined here first. As early as May 1940 Grand Admiral Raeder gave instructions for studies[28] to be put in hand, and on 3 July the first of them was available—a paper by Rear-Admiral Kurt Fricke, chief of the operations department in the naval war staff, on 'Questions of Space Enlargement and Bases'.[29]

The admiral deliberately excluded the numerous political questions which his paper was bound to raise. The navy was primarily interested in the 'strategic possibilities' which might arise from different solutions to the German problem of space. Basically, the 'narrow confines of the German Bight' represented an 'impossible state of affairs' for the navy. Thus the perennial theme of naval planning was addressed: the transformation of narrow confines into an adequate expanse. This was not a new idea, but a traditional demand of the naval command since Tirpitz; it had been kept quiet at times but never abandoned. In the long term it implied conflict with Britain, as was realized by at least some of the planning officers in Imperial Germany, in the Weimar Republic, and in Hitler's Reich. Although material and political conditions in Germany—especially just after the First World War—ruled out public discussion of these matters, this does not mean that the goal as such had altered.[30] The Second World War then brought the expected confrontation with Britain. But since, after the late summer of 1940, total victory by the Wehrmacht could no longer be expected, this meant that the 'final solution of the British problem', as Raeder understood it, had once more to be postponed. The assumption that it would therefore be necessary, within the framework of an interim peace, to negotiate with an as yet undefeated Britain naturally coloured Fricke's reflections.[31]

---

[26] Hildebrand, *Vom Reich*, 646 n. 717; directly on this also Groehler, 'Kolonialforderungen', 554–8, underlining the function of the economy; on details of the plans see *Deutschland im zweiten Weltkrieg*, i. 413–17.

[27] Schreiber, 'Italien', 226; *Weltherrschaft im Visier*, No. 46, pp. 135 ff., letter of 24 Dec. 1916 from Adm. Henning von Holtzendorff, chief of the admiralty staff, to Reich Chancellor Theobald von Bethmann Hollweg on 'war aims of the navy'.

[28] 1. Skl., KTB, Teil A, 260 (26 May 1940), BA-MA RM 7/12.

[29] 1. Skl., KTB, Teil Cb, gKdos. (3 June 1940) (copy, BA-MA RM 7/262; published in Salewski, *Seekriegsleitung*, iii. 106 ff., and *IMT* xxxiv, No. 041-C.

[30] On the problem of world-power tendencies within the navy cf. Schreiber, 'Kontinuität'; on the controversial views on this issue see also the sections by Rahn, Salewski, and Schreiber in *Militär und Militarismus*, 149–92.

[31] The quotations which follow are according to BA-MA RM 7/262 (see n. 29 above).

Specifically the naval staff considered the following ways of changing the intolerable 'position of Germany within the narrow confines of the German Bight and the Baltic, bordered and influenced as it is by a number of states', and of ruling out any 'blockade of Germany from overseas due to natural geographical circumstances'. Denmark, Norway, and northern France were to be kept under occupation, and would be so organized that they would 'count as German possessions in the future'. The extent to which such intentions could be realized was defined by Fricke, quite pragmatically, in terms of the practical enforceability of Germany's demands. As a matter of principle, however, he advised against the establishment of any exclaves, i.e. bases in Europe without direct links with Reich territory. The dimension of his recommendations emerges from the demand that the countries occupied by Germany should be deprived of their independence to a degree which would rule out any military uprising within the 'near or more remote future'. To ensure this, the defeated nations must become, and remain, completely dependent on Germany, politically, economically, and militarily. This intention, to Fricke's mind, would best be implemented by 'smashing France's military strength (population, mineral deposits, industry, armed forces)... so that any future resurgence [might be] regarded as out of the question'. As for Norway, Denmark, and The Netherlands, he advised that, in the event of such a development—'smashing of France, occupation of Belgium and a part of northern and eastern France'—these countries should be left as they were. However, this could be considered only if 'easy reoccupation' were guaranteed through their extreme dependence. Fricke further regarded the possession of Iceland as desirable.

Such alterations of Europe's political geography were directly linked to colonial claims, inasmuch as such a changed situation on the Continent was a prerequisite of safeguarding the colonial empire. In this respect the navy had learnt its lesson from the First World War. As for details of the colonial demands, the naval staff, whose spokesman Fricke was, advised against bases in North or South America, Asia, or Australasia. Like Clodius and Ritter, it called for a continuous zone of Central African possessions. These were to consist of the French colonies south of the parallel running through the estuary of the Senegal river, as well as the former German colonies and the Belgian Congo. In the east the colonial empire would extend as far as (former) German East Africa. German South-West Africa might be bartered against British and Portuguese territories in order to round off the German possessions.[32] Finally the admiral recommended the 'acquisition of one or more bases in the island groups off Africa'. The navy would also have liked to possess Madagascar and the French island groups in the Indian Ocean. But all this was still not a maximum programme, since the 'outcome of the war with Britain might provide the opportunity for extending these demands'.

---

[32] On the question of the renunciation of German South-West Africa cf. Hillgruber, *Strategie*, 145 n. 19 (the subject is not treated exhaustively).

Shortly after Fricke's study Admiral Rolf Carls, then commanding the naval station on the Baltic and simultaneously commander-in-chief of naval group command East, gave answers to a number of questions put by the naval staff, especially on the issue of demands for naval bases.[33] In Carls's view the Second World War was a struggle for 'Germany's rise to world-power status'. Like Fricke he called for final liberation from 'Anglo-French naval encirclement', the 'weakening of France', and—going beyond the chief of the operations department—the 'weakening of the British Empire to the point of an approximate equalization of possessions with Germany'.

For the realization of these ideas the admiral proposed, along with the restoration of former Reich territory and the 'lost colonies', a thorough transformation of the system of European states. Like Fricke, Carls viewed colonial and Reich territory as a single entity. This view was directly expressed in his demands for European and overseas bases. Along her western frontier Germany was to claim a security zone, to run along the Meuse between Liège and Toul, and along the Moselle between Toul and Montbéliard. But that was not all. France would be liquidated as a great power once and for all, and Belgium was to be partitioned. The Walloon parts of the country, together with Picardy, Normandy, Brittany, and Artois, were to become 'demilitarized protectorates' of the Reich. Carls further recommended that Denmark, Norway, Holland, and Flanders be so incorporated into Germany that they would represent only a 'north European union of states or a federal state under German leadership'. Such a dissolution of the old political system would naturally give rise to global colonial demands on Germany's part. The unscrupulousness and brutality with which the groups concerned were planning the destruction of the old Europe is the more remarkable if one remembers the boundless outrage shown by them at the so-called diktat of Versailles.

After the war the French possessions in Africa, among others, were to be shared out between Germany and Italy—and, if necessary, Spain. Provided Germany had sufficient superiority over Britain, the British would have to hand over South Africa and Southern Rhodesia. Only Northern Rhodesia, however, would become a German colony; South Africa and Southern Rhodesia were to become states in their own right. In the event of an unambiguous German victory, Britain would have to cede the Sudan to Italy and, moreover, give up her Egyptian protectorate. The same applied to Malta, Gibraltar, and the Suez Canal; the latter was to be placed under international control, though London and Paris would not, of course, be permitted to retain their right of consultation. In addition to driving Britain out of Africa, the admiral considered it of particular importance for 'all rights in the Persian Gulf and the Anglo-Persian oil installations [to be] ceded to Germany'. Such were the zones

---

[33] 1. Skl., KTB, Teil Cb, Anlage zu OKM I op 941/40 g.Kdos. Chefs., BA-MA RM 7/262. The paper was completed before 13 June 1940, at which date it was on Fricke's desk. The document is published in Salewski, *Seekriegsleitung*, iii. 108–14; quotations according to RM 7/262.

of influence and the territorial expansion aspired to. Another question was the optimal protection of the future colonial empire and its lines of communication with the Reich. As, in the summer of 1940, Carls still assumed that the American and Japanese zones of influence were to be respected, the acquisition of bases had to be primarily at the expense of British and French possessions in Europe and overseas. He was interested in both the European and the overseas sphere.

The commander-in-chief of naval group command East—assuming Germany's position of strength as outlined above—regarded the whole of northern Europe, including Norway, Spitsbergen, Iceland, Greenland, the Faeroe Isles, and possibly also the Shetland Islands, as well as France's Channel coast as far as Brest and Ushant, and the British Channel Islands, as belonging to the German area of dominion. This would certainly have been sufficient to guarantee access to the mid-Atlantic. As Gibraltar would go to Spain after the war, Germany, to protect her sea routes to Africa, would need Casablanca, with the western Moroccan hinterland, as a base of her own. If these demands clashed with Spanish or Italian interests, a naval base in the Canary Islands would be a possible substitute.[34] Further south, Dakar, as suggested by Grand Admiral Raeder after the German–French armistice, might be considered, with Senegal as its hinterland, and possibly also Bathurst. In addition, Carls included German South-West Africa and Walvis Bay with its offshore islands.

For the protection of German maritime transport to the East African coast the admiral suggested the acquisition of Madagascar, the Comoro Islands, the Mascarene Islands (with Mauritius), and the Seychelles. He also proposed Socotra and Aden as suitable bases for the German navy, but noted that the Italians also laid claims to these two bases. This matter, therefore, should be decided at top political level.

Communications with East Asia, where the Reich would gain colonies (the Dutch East Indies) as a result of the 'incorporation of Holland', were to be protected by bases in the Cocos Islands. In addition, to round off German colonial possessions the admiral proposed, if possible, to demand North Borneo from the British. He advised that 'German–Australian and Dutch–Australian possessions east of the Moluccas' should be forgone, to avoid friction with the Japanese. He was concerned principally with Britain, France, and Italy. Once the above-listed German demands were satisfied, these countries would be of about the right strength for their 'existence and measure of power' to be kept within the 'scope desired' by Germany.

These details provide a direct and vivid picture of the power-political claims underlying the German navy's ideas about the establishment of Germany as a great power. As is proved by the comment made on Carls's ideas by representatives of the naval war staff and by Raeder himself, they can in no

[34] Cf. I.III.2 (b) above.

way be dismissed as the untypical ideological or political ramblings of an individual, even though the naval high command made a few amendments to some points in the memorandum.[35]

However, such claims were viewed within the naval command as no more than minimum demands. Without total victory over Britain—which at that stage was not included in the calculations—it was not thought that any more could be expected. Readiness for an interim peace with Britain, however, was by no means an uncontroversial issue within the naval staff. A typical example of the belief that the 'final solution' of the British problem should be brought about once and for all is a memorandum by the officer responsible for operational questions of naval warfare in the Mediterranean, dated 11 July 1940.[36] This stated:

It seems nonsensical to conclude a peace with Britain which means that we must expect to have to face that country again as an enemy in the future, when her chances may be considerably improved by her choice of appropriate allies. Why should Britain be enabled to repeat her war of annihilation against Germany, when we are now in a position—since she is isolated from allies who might help her (Russia and Japan), feebly supported by America, which at this moment is unable, on military and domestic grounds, actively to intervene in the struggle, and abandoned by her former allies whom the German sword has already conquered—so to strike her to the ground that she can never again be a credible opponent?

Within the navy, as in the foreign ministry and in the business world, there were thus convinced champions of those groups of interests which, largely on economic grounds,[37] called for a German colonial empire. These ideas enjoyed a boost in the summer of 1940. Hitler himself, in his efforts to achieve a German–British arrangement, once again concerned himself with this issue. Within the framework of the questions here examined there is no need to go into these details. Suffice it to point out that in Hitler's view, as shown in the detailed studies by Andreas Hillgruber[38] and Klaus Hildebrand,[39] colonies were certainly no alternative to the conquest of living-space in the east.

That said, it can be observed that Hitler gave orders as early as March 1940 'to push ahead vigorously with preparatory studies for a future colonial administration', and that on 15 June he gave urgent instructions 'that preparations for the take-over of the administration' in the colonies be 'completed within the shortest time possible'.[40] At the same time he demanded in his 'guidelines' of 17 June that, with regard to the impending armistice, 'no demands of any kind' must be raised 'at this time, either for the return of

---

[35] Schreiber, *Revisionismus*, 295–6.
[36] Published in Schreiber, 'Kontinuität', 142–7.
[37] On the economic interests cf. mainly Kum'a N'dumbe III, *Hitler voulait l'Afrique*, 123–49.
[38] Hillgruber, *Strategie*, 242–3.
[39] Hildebrand, *Vom Reich*, 648 ff.
[40] Letter from Dr Lammers, Reich minister and head of the Reich chancellery, to the supreme Reich authorities of 15 June 1940, published in Hildebrand, *Vom Reich*, 911.

the former German colonies, or for German occupation of them, or for the establishment of German bases'. Simultaneously he explained the reason for his restraint: such claims at present would 'merely lead to unrest and to the defection of the colonies to the British side'—which was not what Hitler wanted; while, in the event of a French refusal, the German demands could not 'at this time'[41] be enforced.[42]

Viewing Hitler's instruction on the take-over of the colonies and his directives with regard to the armistice, one again realizes how confidently in the summer of 1940 he expected an arrangement between Germany and Britain. Once that was achieved, any consideration *vis-à-vis* France could be dropped. From this point of view the speeding up of colonial preparations made sense. Meanwhile on 20 June Raeder stressed the importance of, for instance, Dakar as a German base. He moreover proposed 'to exchange Madagascar for the northern part of Portuguese Angola'—a suggestion which Hitler, who intended to use the island for the 'settlement of Jews under French responsibility', promised to consider.[43]

We are obliged here to deal, by way of digression, with a macabre aspect of colonial-empire planning against the background of the most shameful chapter of German history: the so-called solution of the Jewish question.[44] On 3 July Legation Secretary Franz Rademacher had drawn up a memorandum, the introduction to which read: 'The imminent victory gives Germany the possibility, and in my opinion also the duty, of solving the Jewish question in Europe. The desirable solution is: All Jews out of Europe.' Ribbentrop approved the proposals worked out on this subject by the German department of the foreign ministry, and they were endorsed as a project by the SS, the ministry of the interior, and various Party authorities.

Under the so-called Madagascar Plan[45] France was to make the island 'available for the solution of the Jewish question'. The matter was to be clarified during the peace negotiations. The approximately 25,000 French nationals who lived on the island, and who would have to leave if it were turned into a Jewish reservation, would naturally have to be compensated. There were also clear ideas on the issue of citizenship. Jews deported from European countries would lose their former nationality and would only be citizens of the German mandated territory of Madagascar, without title to German nationality. In this way the Jews would remain as 'a pledge in German

---

[41] On this set of problems see I.III.1 (*b*) above.
[42] Quoted according to Böhme, *Der deutsch-französische Waffenstillstand*, 22; on Hitler's directives ibid. 20 ff.
[43] 'Führer Conferences', 111 (20 June 1940).
[44] The following data according to *DGFP* D x, No. 101, pp. 111 ff. (3 July 1940); cf. Reitlinger, *Final Solution*, 84 ff.; generally on the anti-Semitic extermination policy in the Third Reich: Dawidowicz, *The War*.
[45] On the Madagascar Plan cf. esp. Browning, *Final Solution*, 35–43, also on the origin of the idea to settle the European Jews in a colony, and on Rademacher's plan, which he had brought up for discussion since the beginning of June; Dawidowicz, *The War*, 118–19.

hands, to guarantee future good behaviour by their co-racialists in America'. In short, it was a plan for the taking of millions of hostages.

Simultaneously there were reflections in Germany on how the island could be put to military use and administered as a mandated territory. The Bay of Diego Suarez and the port of Antsirane would have been at the navy's disposal as bases. If the navy high command wished, it could also use the ports of Tamatave, Andevoranto, and Mananjary. At the same time the carving out of 'suitable parts of the Jewish territory for the purpose of establishing air-bases' was envisaged.

The administration of the Jewish-inhabited part of Madagascar was to be headed by a German police governor, responsible to Himmler's SS. Under this authority the Jews were to be granted a kind of self-administration. As the Jews, moreover, would be responsible for Madagascar as joint debtors, it was envisaged to transfer 'their former European assets, for utilization, to a European bank to be founded'. Compared with the fate which the European Jews were to endure as a result of National Socialist racist mania, even such an arrogant and brutal project as the deportation of several millions of people, on the alleged grounds of their racial inferiority, must still seem humane. One is reminded here of Terezín (Theresienstadt) and the perfidious National Socialist propaganda slogan according to which Hitler 'made a present' of that town to the Jews. The authors of the Madagascar project in 1940 actually included in their calculations a favourable effect on world public opinion. The whole boundless hubris of the Third Reich's leadership, which was by no means confined to the key figures of the National Socialist regime, emerges from the impertinent assertion that Germany's 'sense of responsibility towards the rest of the world ruled out the immediate conferring of an independent state upon a race which for thousands of years' had not possessed 'political independence; for that purpose it still had to prove itself before history'.

However, in the euphoria created by the impending victory in the west reflections of this kind carried little weight among the National Socialist leaders—if indeed they gave them any thought at all. It is therefore largely irrelevant that Britain's determination to continue the war rendered the Madagascar Plan unrealizable in practice.[46] With the attack on the Soviet Union the outlines began to emerge of the kind of 'final solution' which represented Hitler's real attitude to the problem.

When the Madagascar Plan was finally dropped in February 1942,[47] the infamous Wannsee conference, which is indissolubly linked to genocide,[48] had already been held. On 20 January 1942 fifteen senior Nazi officials met at a

---

[46] Browning, *Final Solution*, 42; id., 'Nazi Resettlement Policy', 511–12.
[47] Ibid. 82.
[48] The minutes of the Wannsee conference are published in *Ursachen und Folgen*, xix. 422–30. There is an English trans. in *Document of Distinction: Germany and Jewry 1933–1945*, ed. Raul Hilberg (London, 1972), 89 ff.

villa on the Wannsee in Berlin.⁴⁹ SS-Obergruppenführer Reinhard Heydrich, chief of the Sicherheitspolizei (security police) and of the Sicherheitsdienst (security service), presented an 'overall plan for the physical liquidation of the Jews by means of "natural reduction" through forced labour and any other procedure designed to prevent the resurgence of a Jewish community in Europe'.⁵⁰ Before this, on 1 December 1941, Hitler had already reduced the 'final solution' to a formula in line with his objectives, to the effect that whoever 'destroys life'—as did the Jews in his view—makes himself liable 'to death, and that is precisely what is going to happen [to the Jews]'.⁵¹

The attitude of the German leadership élites towards colonial problems thus encompassed ideas for a Greater German sphere in Europe as well as territorial demands overseas; strategic considerations, such as the acquisition of bases with a view to a future conflict with the Anglo-Saxon powers; and finally racial-ideological components, such as ideas, not confined to Party officials, on the 'Jewish question'.⁵²

Besides the main outlines for Germany's great-power position there were detailed plans. These were primarily concerned with administrative questions concerning the future colonies. Now and again, in this field also, the kind of departmental rivalries appear to have arisen which were typical of the National Socialist system at certain levels. The different departments dealing with this issue were certainly competing with one another to a degree which seemed to fulfil Hitler's principle of divide and rule.⁵³ Military preparations were also making progress. In June 1940, for instance, preparatory work was begun on the raising of colonial troops.⁵⁴ Soon after, on 4 July, Hitler issued a new directive calling for the speedy development of measures for the 'take-over of German overseas territories'.⁵⁵ The following day Halder learnt that von Brauchitsch, the commander-in-chief of the army, had ordered the raising of two battalions of four companies each. The men were to be trained at the army training-ground of Bergen (Hohne) in Lower Saxony. The personnel would be taken from the divisions which would be demobilized in consequence of the expected course of the war until the end of July, as well as from the replacement army. A department for colonial affairs was to be set up at the general army office, and discussions were even taking place about the right kind of motor-car for the colonies.⁵⁶ On the day that Hitler addressed his 'peace offer' to London some 10,000 colonial troops, grouped in ten battalions, half of them motorized, were already envisaged for possible action in the army's plans.⁵⁷

---

⁴⁹ Browning, *Final Solution*, 76–81, on genesis and consequences of the programme.
⁵⁰ Thalmann, 'Das Protokoll', 148.
⁵¹ Quoted according to Picker, *Hitlers Tischgespräche*, 78 (1 Dec. 1941).
⁵² *DGFP* D x, No. 345, p. 484 (15 Aug. 1940); 'Führer Conferences', 111 (20 June 1940).
⁵³ Cf. Hildebrand, *Vom Reich*, 655–9.
⁵⁴ Halder, *Diaries*, i. 474 (19 June 1940); Thies, *Architekt*, 124.
⁵⁵ Hildebrand, *Vom Reich*, 661.
⁵⁶ Halder, *Diaries*, i. 496 (5 July 1940).
⁵⁷ Ibid. 511 (19 July 1940).

All these studies were based on the above-quoted directive of 15 June—that is, they went back to Hitler himself. Nevertheless they did not represent any turning away from his intention of attacking the Soviet Union,[58] as has already been shown.[59] One point, however, deserves renewed emphasis: in the event of a diplomatic settlement of German–British relations, as hoped for by Hitler, the peaceful occupation of colonies would no more have affected his decision in July than did the much-discussed demobilization of parts of the army.[60] Given quiescence in the west, one division of colonial troops would have been neither here nor there in the planning of the attack in the east. And those divisions which were 'being transported home and demobilized' could, in Hitler's opinion, 'be recalled within forty-eight hours and be ready to march' at any time.[61]

As to preliminary work on the subject of colonies, there was produced within the navy, in parallel to the preparations of the army, a paper entitled 'Thoughts of the Naval Staff on the Building up of the Fleet after the War'. The study was submitted in draft to Vice-Admiral Otto Schniewind, the chief of staff of the naval war staff, and to Raeder for examination.[62] On reading it one gains the impression of remarkable political agreement between Hitler— with regard to the second major section of his programme—and the navy command. For the time being the problem of the Soviet Union remained outside consideration; not until the end of the month did the naval staff examine it.

Although in July 1940 the naval staff realized that the situation after the conclusion of the war could not as yet be definitively predicted, it nevertheless proceeded confidently from the following premisses:

(*a*) Germany is the dominant power on the European continent. The economic resources of the north, the west, and the south-east are all equally available to her. A political constellation of the Nordic or the western states (Holland, Belgium, France) against Germany is impossible.

(*b*) Germany dominates a great Central African colonial empire from the Atlantic to the Indian Ocean.

The fate of the British Empire was considered uncertain; it could, however, be assumed—and this agreed very closely with Hitler's thinking at the time— that the British would have to 'waive any interference in Europe and acknowledge German hegemony in Europe'. Admittedly, London in its 'weakness' would 'seek to lean on the United States'. As America would

---

[58] For an overall view of this problem cf. Schreiber, 'Mittelmeerraum'.
[59] See I.III.2 (*b*) above. The present author cannot agree with the interpretation in vol. ii of the present work, end of Part I (Stegemann). Cf. Stegemann, 'Entschluß', and the reply in Hillgruber, 'Hitlers Wendung'. Among the vast literature on this subject see also *Das Deutsche Reich und der Zweite Weltkrieg*, iv. 3 ff., 15 ff. (Förster).
[60] *DGFP* D X, No. 166, pp. 209 ff., Hitler's letter to Mussolini of 13 July 1940.
[61] Ibid. 209.
[62] The memorandum is published in e.g. Salewski, *Seekriegsleitung*, iii. 122–30.

naturally be interested in having a strong Britain in Europe, Germany would 'inevitably have an adversary in the USA'. With an eye, already, to the next conflict, it was stated: 'The two Anglo-Saxon powers will maintain, or else rebuild, their great sea power for the protection of their empire, and will thereby become the prime natural enemies for Germany to consider.' Such arguments—leaving aside the German–Soviet war, which was an axiom to Hitler—were in agreement with his programmatic observations from the 1920s, when he reflected on the struggle between the 'world power USA' and the 'world power Germany'.[63] Günter Moltmann was one of the first historians not only carefully to examine and verify Hitler's idea of world dominion, as manifested in these programmes, but also to place it within the overall pattern of his policies. Moltmann concluded[64] that all three phases of Hitler's policy—the 'seizure of power in Germany, the revision of Versailles, and, thereafter, his imperialist eastern policy as a completion' of continental expansion—'were preparatory steps for a fourth phase in the future, and were from the outset, though not obviously, related to it'.

In the summer of 1941 (to anticipate for a moment), after the attack had been launched against the Soviet Union, the navy command allowed for the new situation by clearly regarding the United States as an adversary.[65] Raeder, for that matter, had included the United States as an enemy power in his strategic situation assessment even before the outbreak of the war in 1939.

Meanwhile, however, on 11 July 1940 the commander-in-chief of the navy, in line with the above-mentioned memorandum, submitted 'Thoughts of the Naval War Staff on the Building up of the Fleet after the War'. Following this exposé Hitler approved the naval construction programme relating to the period after peace with Britain, which was 'largely based on the Z plan of 1938–9'.[66] During that period Raeder and Hitler believed that they would have to face up to 'an ever existing potential hostility on Britain's part'. This fact, together with 'Germany's colonial activity and the resultant vigorous growth of trade, the protection of the colonies and sea routes, and the accession of colonial and overseas bases', would eventually lead the 'Greater German Reich, inescapably and by destiny, on to the road towards becoming a first-

---

[63] Hildebrand, *Vom Reich*, 662–3.
[64] 'Weltherrschaftsideen', 234. A very informative survey of the literature published up to 1970 on Hitler's world-power goals is presented in M. Michaelis, 'World Power Status'. This comes to the conclusion that politically Hitler aimed at world-power status and ideologically at world dominion. This confirms Moltmann's theses just as it does the exhaustive researches of Hillgruber and Hildebrand on this subject. Since the mid-1960s, if not before, it has no longer been possible in the light of current research simply to put forward the minimalization or ignorance theory with regard to the relationship of 'bourgeois historiography' to the 'aggressive colonial policy' of the Third Reich; cf. e.g. Kühne, 'Kolonialpolitik', 515. For argument with 'bourgeois historiography' see also Hass, 'Kriegsziele', 89–102, esp. 92 on plans for world domination.
[65] 'Betrachtungen über die Grundlagen des Flottenaufbaues' (31 July 1941), published in Salewski, *Seekriegsleitung*, iii. 130–5, esp. 131 n. 39.
[66] *Lagevorträge*, 119 (see note 'for report' by G. Wagner, dated 11 July 1940, not in the English edition).

class oceanic naval power'. Although the general situation seemed positively to provoke such ideas, they did not in fact represent any new component in the thinking or the aspirations of the navy command, who merely believed that the moment had come to 'put a final consummation to a development of German sea power which had spanned centuries [sic] and had been subject to numerous mistakes and errors'. However, it was not destiny that led Germany on to the road to dominant sea power, but an aggressive imperialism—long outdated by 1940—which was characterized by the fact that trade was to follow the flag, and not the other way round: first aggression, i.e. the destruction of Europe, and then colonization, i.e. global exploitation.

To sum up, in the summer of 1940 Hitler was faced with three sets of problems which, in the framework of the overall strategy and war aims of the National Socialist regime, have to be seen as interlinked: first the arrangement with Britain, next the conquest of living-space in the east in order to ensure for the Reich a political, economic, and military position of hegemony on the Continent which was scarcely assailable, and—directly linked with this—an overseas expansion to be launched from that favourable position.[67] In the context of these reflections and plans the colonial acquisitions under discussion in the summer of 1940 were aimed, from Hitler's point of view, at the second stage of his programme, i.e. they anticipated partial aspects of German expansion overseas or were directed at the realization of partial projects. At no time, however—and this cannot be emphasized too much—did this project represent an alternative to Hitler's living-space programme.[68] From mid-July, and definitely after the rejection of the so-called peace offer, there could no longer be any question of acquiring colonial possessions by peaceful means. With Hitler's decision of 31 July 1940—the decision to attack the Soviet Union—these plans were finally shelved until such time as the realization of the second phase of the programme was being undertaken.

However, regardless of the dominance of the eastern objective[69] and of the concept of the new order in Europe,[70] which was also at that time being discussed as a long-term policy, organizational and planning preparations for a German colonial empire continued at various political levels and within the departments concerned.

---

[67] The basic lines of Hitler's strategy, which, despite all fluctuations and alternative projects, are to be seen throughout as programme-orientated with regard to politics and warfare, are shown clearly in Hildebrand, 'Deutsch-Mittelafrika'. This is a revised excerpt from Hildebrand, *Vom Reich*.

[68] Hildebrand, *Vom Reich*, 667–8; Schmokel, *Traum vom Reich*, 180.

[69] This is rightly emphasized in the accounts—which pay inadequate attention to the global aspect, though not altogether disregarding it—by Barthel, 'Kriegsziele', 934–52, and Hass, 'Kriegsziele', who deals critically with research in the Federal Republic of Germany and, in so doing, undoubtedly fails to do justice to certain authors. Hass, admittedly, is concerned mainly with the exponents of the war aims, and less with the aims themselves. Specifically on overseas expansion plans see *Deutschland im zweiten Weltkrieg*, i. 411–18.

[70] Cf. Drechsler *et al.*, 'Politik und Strategie', 10; *Deutschland im zweiten Weltkrieg*, i. 385–411; Gruchmann, *Großraumordnung*; Jacobsen, *Teilung der Welt*, 79 ff.

On 8 July the high command of the armed forces issued a Colonial Information Notice,[71] announcing the enactment of a 'Law on the Establishment of a Reich Ministry for the Colonies', to be headed by Infantry General Franz Ritter von Epp. There was also detailed discussion of the 'first occupation of German colonial territory', with Grand Admiral Raeder insisting that the navy should be the first service to set foot on land (the worries of a commander-in-chief in the middle of a war!). There also existed a draft of 'Colonial Regulations for the Wehrmacht'.[72] Like the armed forces high command, interested business circles[73] and the navy were also planning ahead. Very shortly after Admiral Carls's memorandum two further studies appeared on future colonial possessions;[74] these were later incorporated in a study signed by Fricke on 'Bases for the Defence of the Colonial Empire'.[75] Although the paper was passed on to the foreign ministry, there was no direct procedure attached to it. It was simply prepared to show the navy command that 'plans for a future German colonial empire [were] being prepared by various departments'.

In this study the navy had in mind colonial possessions embracing Togo, the Cameroons, and German East Africa, as well as French and Belgian colonies. British territories, on the other hand, were largely left untouched. For the protection of the German colonial empire the following bases were required from France: Dakar, Conakry, Douala, Pointe Noire, Diego Suarez, and the Comoro Islands. Britain was to surrender only those bases which seemed especially suitable for German purposes;[76] in the view of the naval war staff these were Freetown, Zanzibar, Dar es Salaam, Mombasa-Kilindini, St Helena, Ascension Island, Pemba, the Seychelles, and Mauritius. These were not exactly modest demands, and the navy high command was well aware that their fulfilment presupposed a clear British defeat. The system of bases was to be supplemented by Belgian colonial possessions, such as Boma in the Congo, Spanish Fernando Poo, and the Portuguese island of São Tomé, as well as numerous lesser islands 'of great value'.

The German claims during those weeks were for a 'compact East–West African empire',[77] but there were also, simultaneously, further-reaching ideas.

---

[71] Published in Hildebrand, *Vom Reich*, 915–16.

[72] Published ibid. 916–17; see also the article of 15 Sept. 1940 by Rudolf Asmis, head of the Berlin office of the colonial-policy department of the NSDAP Reich directorate, on 'Foundations and Goals of German Colonial Administration', in the periodical *Deutscher Kolonial-Dienst*, published in excerpts in *Weltherrschaft im Visier*, 275 ff.

[73] Groehler, 'Kolonialforderungen', 560; *Deutschland im zweiten Weltkrieg*, i. 417–18.

[74] 'Stützpunkte und Kolonialreich' and 'Gedanken der Seekriegsleitung zur Frage der Stützpunktpolitik', both dating from July 1940; published in Salewski, *Seekriegsleitung*, iii. 114 ff.

[75] The document, dating from 27 July 1940, is published in Salewski, *Seekriegsleitung*, iii. 116 ff.; cf. Hildebrand, *Vom Reich*, 669–70; Hillgruber, *Strategie*, 245; Schreiber, *Revisionismus*, 297.

[76] On Hitler's persistent consideration for the British Empire cf. Hildebrand, *Vom Reich*, 671 ff.

[77] Halder, *Diaries*, i. 560 (23 Aug. 1940), information from Legationsrat Hasso von Etzdorf, the representative of the foreign ministry with OKH.

These examined both the new colonial world order in the event of a peaceful 'partition with England' and also a 'simultaneous partition of the British possessions'.[78] If an arrangement was reached with Britain, Germany would in any case have to acquire the French and the Belgian Congo, the Lake Chad territory, French Equatorial Africa, and the former German colonies. If, however, no arrangement was reached but total victory won, then the following would be added to the above-listed territories: Uganda, Zanzibar, southern Kenya with the capital Nairobi, Nigeria, the Gold Coast, and Dahomey, as well as the bases of Dakar and Bathurst. The navy in addition demanded Ascension Island, Tristan da Cunha, St Helena, the Comoro Islands, the Mascarene Islands, the Seychelles, the Amirantes, and, 'for the Jews', Madagascar. Italy, after the decisive victory over Britain, would take over the latter's protectorate treaties with Arab states and receive the following colonial territories: Tunis, a link to Lake Chad, and one from Libya to East Africa, also British and French Somaliland, the remainder of Kenya, Malta, Aden, and Cyprus. It was also envisaged that the Italians would assume Britain's role in Egypt and the Sudan. Spain could expect to take Morocco, Algeria (as far as Oran and south of the 20th parallel), Gibraltar, and an extension of Spanish Guinea as far as Cape Lopez. Mention was even made of a Thai claim to Laos and Cambodia.

It cannot, of course, be assumed that such maximum demands were in line with Hitler's plans in the summer of 1940, let alone that they had been agreed with him. Hitler at that time, despite his increasing doubts, was basically still hoping for a compromise peace with Britain. In that event the Central African project might have been realized, possibly in modified form, but no more. In his 'peace speech' of 19 July—a misnomer because Hitler regarded any peace solely with a view to a new war, not least as regards relations between Berlin and London—he had displayed remarkable restraint. But the plans drawn up in September were no longer topical for another reason. They would have made sense only with regard to a remote future, whereas the various champions of swift victory over the Soviet Union believed that future to be already within reach in 1941. By the end of October, however, Hitler's concept of an alliance through deception had to be regarded as failed in view of Franco's and Pétain's intransigence, and there could no longer be any question of penetrating into the African sphere by force. The French colonies in Central Africa were defecting, or had already defected, from Vichy. In that situation any serious upheaval would certainly have called into question Pétain's control over France's North African possessions. There it was impossible to establish colonial springboards under the pretext of acquiring military bases. From a historian's point of view the interesting aspect of all these plans is not so much the question of whether they were realistic or unrealistic, but the insight they

---

[78] *DGFP* D xi, No. 16, pp. 20–1 (4 Sept. 1940) (handwritten), notes of the foreign ministry's representative with OKH concerning colonial plans.

provide into the political demands and the minds of German leadership élites. They thus reveal a by no means unimportant aspect of German aggression in Europe, which clearly was not merely Hitler's war.

It should be remembered that the concept of a colonial empire, as it emerged after October 1940, was basically one of those drawing-board designs and sand-table games which no longer bore any relation to Hitler's political and military intentions at the time. This is certain, even though immediately before Molotov's visit to Berlin there was once more a kind of revival of colonial ideas, probably stemming from the consideration at that time of southward expansion in which German, Italian, Japanese, and Soviet interests were expected to harmonize.[79]

A paper of 6 November by Legation Counsellor Ernst Bielfeld examining 'Territorial Demands on France regarding Colonies, within the Framework of Total Demands' summed up the discussion on the hoped-for Central African colonial empire.[80] In it the economic motives once more emerged clearly.

According to this paper, France, Belgium, and Britain, as well as Australia, New Zealand, and the Union of South Africa, would be made to return all former German colonial possessions. With Japan and Portugal there would be an arrangement with regard to the former German Pacific islands north of the Equator and the Kionga (Quionga) triangle in East Africa. The foreign ministry did not wish to take over any French colonies outside Africa. As the ultimate objective Bielfeld spoke of 'providing for 150 million people' and a 'compact colonial empire in Central Africa'. Following the 'establishment of the new order in Europe', the new empire was to supply 'a territory comprising, besides the Greater German Reich, also Scandinavia, Denmark, Belgium, Luxemburg, Holland, Hungary, Slovakia, and other parts of Europe', all of which would 'be incorporated in or affiliated with the Greater European economic sphere', and whose economies would be orientated 'in accordance with the German economy'.

A 'key position' in this project was held by the Belgian Congo. Regardless of Belgium's future form of government, the colony was to come 'under German control in its entirety', as it not only formed the 'natural link between the Cameroons and East Africa', but was so rich in mineral deposits that it could 'satisfy an essential portion of German requirements'. This applied to copper, tin, and cobalt, while German supplies of diamonds, manganese, iron ore, radium, gold, timber, and vegetable fats would also be greatly relieved by the exploitation of that colony. French Equatorial Africa, important both for its geographical position—a hinterland for the Cameroons—and for its agricultural potential, was to be owned by Germany in its entirety. Its frontier with the Italian colonies was to run no further south than the 15th parallel. French Equatorial Africa, however, was still a developing area, for which

---

[79] Hillgruber, *Strategie*, 248–9.
[80] *DGFP* D xi, No. 298, pp. 483–91 (6 Nov. 1940).

reason 'at least part of the economically well developed and therefore especially valuable' British colony of Nigeria should be demanded. Germany must secure, primarily, its palm-oil and tin production. The foreign ministry had already worked out appropriate frontier delineations, and thought had been given to tightening up the somewhat loose British colonial administration. France would further have to give up Dahomey, which formed an economic unit with Togo. She might be compensated for this by west Nigerian territory and the British Gold Coast (Ghana)—though without the port of Ada, which would be attached to German western Togoland. In East Africa the German colonial possessions would be rounded off with Uganda and Kenya. These two colonies, Bielfeld argued, already formed a cultural and economic entity with German East Africa. For strategic reasons the offshore islands of Zanzibar and Pemba 'must not remain in foreign possession'. In line with these ideas, the hinterland of German East Africa would consist of Northern Rhodesia and the northern part of Nyasaland. In East Africa too Germany was interested above all in the gold, tin, copper, lead, zinc, and vanadium deposits, as well as in agricultural produce. From the standpoint of production for military purposes Southern Rhodesia, in Bielfeld's opinion, was 'the most important area of the African continent'—but as it formed part not of Central but of Southern Africa he merely pointed to its importance without claiming it directly for the German-dominated European–African economic sphere.

The foreign ministry also examined the naval staff's demands for bases. The port of Boma in the Belgian Congo was recommended as a base, as were the islands of Zanzibar and Pemba. Instead of Dakar, however, the acquisition of Bathurst with the British colony of Gambia was preferred. Possession of French Guinea, with Conakry as its capital, was regarded as highly desirable. If this demand was not realizable in full, then 'at least the western half as far as the border of the Dabola district' should be insisted on. The French in that case were to be ceded Togo, Dahomey, and western Nigeria. The claim to French Guinea almost inevitably led to that to Freetown. Sierra Leone would have a common frontier with the new German possessions; moreover, the port was just as important as a naval base as neighbouring Pepel was as an ore transshipment point. If, however, the Reich government should not wish to acquire any major part of Guinea, 'the following could be considered: from France, Conakry, with a hinterland to a radius of 50 km.; from England, Freetown, with the peninsula of Sierra Leone'. Nothing had changed by then as regards the intention of making Madagascar a German mandate 'for the purpose of settling the Jews'. The navy, moreover, continued to insist that France cede the island of Réunion and the Comoro Islands.

After the end of July 1940 these ideas for a colonial empire were overshadowed, as mentioned earlier, by preparations for aggression against the Soviet Union. Nevertheless, as the employment of German troops in North Africa was yielding its first successes, the boldest hopes once again flared up in the minds of those who were not primarily looking towards the east. Typical in this respect was a memorandum by the Hamburg professor Franz Heske, dated 22 April 1941, on 'the decisive importance of colonial preparations for the outcome of the war'.[81] The professor justified his assessment by pointing out that 'even after a defeat of Britain in Europe' the United States would 'unquestionably continue all-out, life-and-death economic warfare'. Germany was to be brought to her knees in a prolonged war of attrition by 'shortages of foodstuffs and raw-material supplies'. Heske assumed an 'indirect war, i.e. the war of the time factor': America would try slowly to exhaust the Europeans, instead of fighting them directly. In order to come out victorious in this 'indirect world war' the 'creation of an autarkic Greater European–African sphere' was not only a goal but a positive prerequisite. Referring to the latest developments, the memorandum continued:

The successes of German arms on African soil and the war which has arisen for the Mediterranean have supplied the first preconditions, and will, it is hoped, forcibly open access to the East African area, the most rapid penetration and exploitation of which is of major importance for future supplies for Europe. Conversion of the British-developed 'cotton empire' to foodstuff production is possible provided the elaborate irrigation facilities, especially the dams at Aswan and Makwar, as well as Jabal Awliya, are protected from destruction.

In the present situation the speedy utilization of West African areas depends on the mastery of the Sahara by means of transport technology and the safeguarding of these transport routes. From what has been said it follows that preparations for instant colonial exploitation . . . are of vital and instant importance to the existence of Germany and the Europe controlled by her. That importance will rapidly increase the longer the war continues—even if only as an economic war.

The naval war staff, however, having been questioned in May 1941 by the colonial-policy department of the NSDAP about the navy's wishes with regard to the future colonial empire, declared in August of that year that the 'solution of any kind of colonial policy questions has, for the time being, totally receded into the background'.[82] Developments in the east were engaging its full attention, and by the end of the year there was still little reason to reactivate colonial planning. This was not changed by the circumstance that in October 1941 the 'Reich Group for Industry' believed that the moment had come to 'carry out studies in the field of colonial economy' and actually sent out circulars to various industrial associations.[83] By then these letters were little more than waste paper. The same is true of a study by Under-Secretary of State Ernst Woermann, prepared as a position paper for Ribbentrop at the beginning of 1942, on the 'Question of a Colonial Settlement between Germany, France, and Spain in Africa'.[84] Woermann's ideas should be seen

---

[81] Quoted according to *Weltherrschaft im Visier*, 296 ff.; cf. also *Drang nach Afrika*, 334; directly on 'colonial studies' in Germany, which have to be seen in this context, cf. Kühne, *Kolonialideologie*, 109–13.

[82] Published in Salewski, *Seekriegsleitung*, iii. 118 ff.

[83] *Anatomie des Krieges*, 358–9 (1 Oct. 1941).

[84] *Weltherrschaft im Visier*, 317 ff. (21 Jan. 1942).

against the background of the extension of the war in Europe into a world war. Their historical purport cannot be viewed in isolation from the ideas of the National Socialist regime for a European new order; measured against them, the writer's attitude with regard to France, for instance, was rather pointless, since it did not allow for the view held at the top political level.[85] Altogether the speculations of that time on how, by means of promises of a fair share-out and a colonial transformation of Africa, one might induce France and Spain in particular to give Germany military aid—and this, at least for certain political and military circles, was the essential factor—were rather irrelevant. One statement by Woermann is of interest, because it reflected the fundamentally changed quality of the war compared with its first year: 'The assumption is that Britain loses her African colonial possessions.' In the eyes of the foreign ministry this radical phraseology appears to show that the idea of an interim peace with London had been definitely dropped by the beginning of 1942: there was to be only total victory over the anti-Hitler coalition or total defeat, even though Woermann did not spell this out. Certainly, this cannot be described as the uniform view of the leading echelons of National Socialist Germany. But the under-secretary's interpretation probably agreed fairly closely with Hitler's own estimate of the situation at the time.

In attempting to sum up the findings of the chapters on the strategic dilemma in the second half of 1940 and on the concept of colonial empire among the leading élites, we must first recall the starting-point of Chapter I.III, the chapter on the strategic dilemma. We mentioned there the consequences of the political, military, and economic developments in the second half of 1940, and indicated the relative importance of the different elements in the balance sheet of those months, with regard to the search for a decisive continuation of the war.

The real—strategic—outcome of the historical process between June and December 1940 was that Hitler, in accordance with his programme, at that time took, and kept to, the decision to launch his campaign in the east. Interim solutions, supposed alternatives, and vacillations in Hitler's policies have tempted many a student of those weeks, and no doubt will tempt others, to interpret Hitler's switch from preparatory campaigns to his war proper— i.e. the conquest of living-space in the east and the annihilation of European Jewry—in terms of primarily military or deterrent aspects; but this cannot alter the fact that his decision was ideologically grounded. At the time when military and political activity was stagnating because Britain had resisted both Hitler's violence and his diplomatic overtures—but in a situation, too, when Hitler believed he could count on an overwhelming enthusiasm for the war and a readiness to fight among the German people—he proceeded to implement his programmatic objectives in the face of this paradoxical dichotomy

[85] Gruchmann, *Großraumordnung*, 76–80; on this see *Das Deutsche Reich und der Zweite Weltkrieg* (Umbreit).

between dynamism at home and stagnation abroad. Hitler's decision was in striking conflict with the strategic postulates which had long been a maxim of German warfare: without his rear being covered and without any necessity he turned towards the east in order (if one were to accept his initial, but in fact neither original nor plausible, argument) to 'find the way to London via Moscow'.

It has to be said, however, that the Wehrmacht's military thinking, which after the campaign in France often seemed rather confused, became more systematic after 31 July 1940. In spite of references to 'pipe-dreams', those generals who were privy to Hitler's intentions were undoubtedly, as early as August, basing their operational plans on the date set for 'Barbarossa'. In so doing they seemed to regard the prior elimination of Britain as indispensable if they were to avoid the much-feared war on two fronts. While everything the generals were planning after July 1940 in the way of peripheral warfare was, on the surface, directed against the British, seen strategically these operations were dictated by preparations for the eastern campaign. It is against this background that Jodl's remark that Germany was fighting 'not for war aims but for victory' should be interpreted.[86] 'Britain's will to resist must be broken by next spring', no matter how, because after that—so one might complete the statement—it was the turn of the Soviet Union. The entire spectrum of the debate during these vital months, the arguments advanced, as well as the objections raised against them, all lead to the conclusion that the operations envisaged for the Mediterranean area were to serve only as an interim strategy and not as an alternative one. The timetables laid down in November 1940 definitively confirm this view.[87]

This is not to say that the top leaders of the Wehrmacht unanimously or unreservedly favoured the campaign in the east. But even if its 'purpose [was] not clear' to them[88] they did not oppose it, because ultimately they shared Hitler's underestimation of the Soviet armed forces. Even the navy, the most reluctant of the services as regards the eastern campaign, really only objected to the time-sequence. After a decisive defeat of Britain, Raeder, who had reckoned with the USSR as an adversary in June 1939, would certainly have had no scruples about a blitzkrieg in the east.[89]

Brief reference should be made here to Raeder's much-discussed 'strategic alternative', which, it is argued, would have rendered the attack on the USSR superfluous. Quite apart from the fact that any such interpretation mistakes the essence of Hitler's war plans, the action proposed by Raeder represented, given the existence of the British Empire, merely a single-objective enterprise, which, moreover, was to be carried out in isolation. Even if the operation had

---

[86] *KTB OKW* i. 31 (14 Aug. 1940).
[87] On the dates and interconnections of Operations Barbarossa, Marita, and Felix cf. *KTB OKW* i. 176 (14 Nov. 1940); 180 (19 Nov. 1940); 187 (25 Nov. 1940); 203–6 (5 Dec. 1940); 211 (6 Dec. 1940); see also Halder, *Diaries*, i. 719 (3 Dec. 1940).
[88] Halder, *Diaries*, i. 765 (28 Jan. 1941).
[89] *KTB OKW* i. 228 (12 Dec. 1940).

been concluded successfully—and there were some indications that it would have been, though no certainty—the British would have been struck a painful but not a mortal blow. Germany and Italy would undoubtedly have possessed an expanded war-economic base, especially if the Mediterranean area was, more or less, kept pacified. But victory on Europe's Mediterranean flank did not offer new opportunities for decision-seeking operations. For that the Axis powers lacked the geo-strategic position, adequate weapons, and an appropriate infrastructure. The war against an ocean-spanning empire could not be successfully fought to the end with the means at the disposal of the Axis. Seen in this light, the simple but convincing truth remains that the beginning of the Second World War harboured within itself the German defeat. Many in Germany realized this even before 1939, and officers like Beck, after a misleading period of unexpected victories, soon found their views vindicated. In this context Italian warfare after 10 June 1940 represented a clear piece of writing on the wall. It was, moreover, typical of the total misjudgement of their own position that the maximum demands of the top German leaders were put forward at moments of stagnation: in the summer of 1940 and in the winter of 1941–2.

In reviewing the political and military developments in the Mediterranean area, discussed in the whole of this part of the present volume, the question finally arises as to the turning-point of the war. This is usually given as the campaign against the Soviet Union, the United States' entry into the war, or the battle of Stalingrad. But none of these events is, in its familiar framework, conceivable without the developments during the second half of 1940. It therefore seems justified, for this reason alone, to regard July 1940 as the 'real turning-point in the Second World War'.[90] Another thought that needs recalling in conclusion is the thesis that history is not confined to the dimension of the factual. This belief has quite substantially determined the presentation here, and it is for that reason that ideas and theoretical plans have been given so much space. For 'ideas', Bracher writes in his study of 'problems and perspectives of the interpretation of Hitler', have to be taken seriously, no matter 'how abstruse and remote from all possible realization' they may be.[91] This applies not only to Hitler, and it means not only a rejection of the kind of down-playing of Hitler's programme which has often been, and still is, attempted on the grounds of its remoteness from reality. Instead, Bracher's statement has fundamental validity, and hence applies also to the political and military levels below those of Hitler or Mussolini. As for historical relevance, this stems from the fact that even the most unrealistic planning is, in itself, also real, and that ideas, if given half a chance of realization, seldom remain mere ideas. In other words, they reveal the dimension of volition, i.e. what moves history forward, and usually influence it more powerfully than that which has manifestly taken place.

[90] Hillgruber, 'England', 78.   [91] See Bracher, *Kontroversen*, 99.

PART II

Germany, Italy, and South-east Europe: From Political and Economic Hegemony to Military Aggression

Gerhard Schreiber

PRELIMINARY NOTE

THE following account of relations between Germany, Italy, and the states of south-east Europe is confined almost exclusively to the relationship of the Axis powers with Albania, Bulgaria, Greece, and Yugoslavia. On economic issues, the observations refer back to the account given in Volume I of the present work;[1] where German policy towards Romania, Hungary, and Slovakia is concerned, they are expanded in Volume IV.[2]

To begin with, the legacy of these countries from the war of 1914–18 will be described in terms of the structural problems they faced in social, economic, and political issues. Subsequently, the main features of political development in south-east Europe from the First until the Second World War will be outlined. The rival German and Italian attempts to achieve hegemony in the region will, it is hoped, thereby become clear; similarly, the historical significance of the aggressions of autumn 1940 and spring 1941[3] will be more easily demonstrated.

Such a task can be undertaken only in general terms here. Nevertheless, an excursion into the history of the interwar years remains indispensable, since the events of 1939–40 cannot be adequately understood without it. Despite a large number of studies devoted to individual aspects,[4] the foreign policy of Fascist Italy and National Socialist Germany towards Albania, Bulgaria, Greece, and Yugoslavia remains something of a neglected area in research. This is particularly evident in overall surveys of the period. Over many years, a perspective focusing on Hitler has relegated the countries of south-east Europe to the periphery of historical interest. Firstly, there were no spectacular events to mark German relations with these states; and secondly, they stood in no direct relationship to Hitler's basic programme, which has rightly been at the centre of investigations into the history of the Third Reich. Though it has been observed that 'Berlin's policy towards the south-east European states has

---

[1] See vol. i of the present work, II.VI.6 (Volkmann).
[2] See *Das Deutsche Reich und der Zweite Weltkrieg*, iv.I.v (Förster).
[3] See below, III.II.2–3 and III.III (Vogel).
[4] On Albania see in particular Skendi, *Albania*, 10–17; Rhode, 'Die südosteuropäischen Staaten', 1269–84; Zamboni, *Mussolinis Expansionspolitik*. On Bulgaria see Hoppe, *Bulgarien*, 26–90; id., 'Deutschland', 604–8; Petzold, 'Imperialismus'. On Greece see Richter, *Griechenland*, 31–81; Hering, 'Griechenland', 1314–25. On Yugoslavia see *Osteuropa-Handbuch, Jugoslawien*, 67–98; *Third Reich and Yugoslavia*, 7–422; Rhode, 'Die südosteuropäischen Staaten', 1183–211; Wuescht, *Jugoslawien*, 15–158 (open to criticism as offering something of an apologia for German measures); H.-J. Schröder, 'Hegemonialstellung'. On Italian policy in general see Rusinow, *Austrian Heritage*, 185–280, esp. 226–38. On German–Italian relations with reference to south-east Europe see Petersen, *Hitler—Mussolini*, 74–99, 207–31, 267–327; Stadtmüller, *Geschichte Südosteuropas*, unfortunately ends with the assassination at Sarajevo.

not yet been adequately investigated for the period before 1938–9',[5] the situation has yet to be rectified.[6]

Such neglect is nevertheless surprising in some ways, since the political and economic interest of both Italy and Germany in south-east Europe is apparent on any close examination.[7] The concept of an 'informal empire' has come into use to describe the influence of Hitler's Germany in the region.[8] In the present volume the observations on the policy of Berlin and Rome after the outbreak of war, particularly the sections on the 'Balkan Bloc' and 'Quiet in the Balkans',[9] are linked directly with the German striving for hegemony; the aim, above all, is to make clear the nature of the alliance between Mussolini's Italy and the Third Reich.

In practical terms, Part II of this volume traces the development of the German–Italian relationship during the war and its immediate prelude in a different weather zone of European politics. However, in terms of composition and interpretation it is directly linked with Part I. It concludes with a description of the Italian invasion of Greece, which, though not inevitable, was at least in part a logical consequence of events. Here, the circle is closed: the developments described in the chapter on the 'Strategic Dilemma of the Summer and Autumn of 1940'[10] terminated in a manner which marked the beginning of the end of Italian great-power status. With the entry of the Wehrmacht into the Italian 'sphere of influence'—made possible as a consequence of the abortive military adventure in the Balkans—the complex ties between Mussolini and Hitler turned into a relationship of total dependence. This change is of crucial significance for any understanding of overall developments in the Mediterranean area during 1940–1. Italy was now on the way to becoming a 'confederate province' of the German Reich. Seven months after the intervention of the Wehrmacht, Mussolini himself had recognized the fact. Though not constantly affected by this knowledge during the following period, he nevertheless seems to have understood that the invasion of Greece was his

---

[5] H.-J. Schröder, 'Hegemonialstellung', 757; see also Pacor, 'Italienische Geschichtsschreibung'; Ránki, 'Geschichtsliterarische Fragen'.

[6] The following accounts—and many others which could be cited—begin their description of events in 1939 or 1940: Schramm-von Thadden, *Griechenland*, published in 1955, though this includes a short introductory survey of past developments; Olshausen, *Zwischenspiel auf dem Balkan*, which appeared in 1973; and Breccia's admirable *Jugoslavia* (1978). However, some other studies, concentrating on the interdependence of Germany, Italy, and south-east and eastern Europe from the point of view of ideological affinity, include the interwar years. These are a significant addition to the body of literature on foreign-political and economic issues. See esp. Borejsza, *Il fascismo*; *Native Fascism*; Thamer and Wippermann, *Faschistische Bewegungen*, 84–119. Orlow's *Nazis in the Balkans* provides little information despite its promising title.

[7] See the introduction to H.-J. Schröder, 'Hegemonialstellung', 757–8, esp. n. 1, pp. 757 ff.; Hoppe, 'Balkanstaaten'.

[8] H.-J. Schröder, 'Südosteuropa'; Grenzebach chose an apt title for his comprehensive investigation of relations between Germany, Yugoslavia, and Romania: 'Germany's Informal Empire'.

[9] Below, II.II.2–3.

[10] Above, I.III.

II. Preliminary Note

last genuinely sovereign decision. German 'friends of the Axis' were heard to say that the Duce was to function in future as Hitler's 'Gauleiter for Italy'.[11]

Before 1980 there were already many investigations of the military events to be examined here.[12] All of them suffered, to a greater or lesser extent, from the relatively narrow basis of source materials available. This is now far from being the case.[13] It is particularly fortunate that in 1982 a major study of Italian policy and strategy from 1939 to 1941 was published.[14] Based on a wide range of sources and with a clear judgement of the questions that require answering, it is unlikely to be surpassed in the foreseeable future.

---

[11] Ciano, *Diary 1939–1943*, 383 (13 Oct. 1941).

[12] These include Baudino, *Guerra assurda*; Cervi, *Hollow Legions*; De Loverdo, *Grèce*; Grazzi, *Principio*; Papagos, *Battle*; Prasca, *Grecia*; see also Kehrig, 'Balkan', though only older works are there cited.

[13] Montanari, *Grecia*, i, ii.

[14] Knox, *Mussolini*, 189–285.

I. Unequal Heirs of the First World War

ANY attempt to discuss the legacy of the First World War requires examination of the consequences of the reorganization of Europe which was discussed and decided upon at the peace conference in Paris.[1] A detailed investigation would, however, be outside the terms of this study. Consequently, only some fundamental and general aspects will be outlined.

Even in works of historical scholarship, the peace conference tends to be surrounded by an aura of unease. The reason for this lies mainly in the dismayed reaction of contemporaries and the subsequent development of national resentments. True, the settlement was a rather one-sided arrangement on the part of the victorious states; but there was no conspiracy against the defeated nations. Instead, the peace agreed at Paris should be regarded as a compromise, particularly between American, British, and French objectives, which were often mutually exclusive. London and Washington had already begun to pursue a policy tending towards the construction of a global bloc; in it, west and central Europe, as well as the successor states of the Austro-Hungarian empire, were to form an anti-Communist region with democratic political systems. Such a concept did not permit peace conditions to be too harsh, in order to avoid provoking Germany into making common cause with the Soviet Union. In contrast, Paris was pursuing its own security interests, in which the outlines of an attempt to achieve hegemony could be perceived. This tendency was bound to meet with opposition, not least from the British. In these circumstances, the peace system worked out in Paris inevitably displayed inconsistencies: 'massive efforts to safeguard the victory by military and power-political methods; attempts to prevent the balance of power being disturbed under the new, completely changed conditions; finally the rudiments of a realization of Wilson's ideals,[2] in the first instance the right of self-determination and the organization of collective security in the League of Nations.'[3]

The defeated states regarded the peace terms as a diktat, a denial of the principles of a negotiated peace. Against a background of national outrage fuelled by propaganda, their representatives declared themselves ready to sign the treaties only under intense pressure.[4] Yet there were other points of view:

---

[1] On the peace conference as a whole (18 Jan. 1919–21 Jan. 1920) and its consequences see Schieder, 'Neuordnung Europas' and its many references; also the still very helpful survey of literature in Gunzenhäuser, *Pariser Friedenskonferenz*; specifically on territorial issues, see Schot, 'Selbstbestimmungsrecht'.
[2] See the very thorough account by Schwabe, *Wilson-Frieden*, esp. 298–637.
[3] Schieder, 'Neuordnung Europas', 120.
[4] The treaty of Versailles (Germany) was concluded on 28 June 1919, that of St Germain

terms which the losers regarded as 'too much' actually appeared to most of the victors as distinctly 'too little'. Apart from Britain, none of the victorious powers achieved its war aims in their entirety.

Thus the settlement of 1919–20, which is often judged as one-sided, left as its legacy a number of dissatisfied powers which had not been reconciled to the peace. *De facto*, the new order contained a number of destabilizing factors. In south-east Europe the most significant of these was the problem of national minorities in 'majority national states'. Yugoslavia (10 September 1919) and Greece (10 August 1920) were among the states which were required to conclude treaties on the protection of minorities within their 1919 borders in order to gain recognition under international law. These treaties, endorsed by the League of Nations, theoretically guaranteed the affected groups at least a minimum of equal civil rights and cultural autonomy. However, such rights were difficult to assert in practice in disputed cases.[5]

Momentous consequences for south-east Europe resulted from the disintegration of the Dual Monarchy (Austria-Hungary) and the Ottoman empire. The three primary problems have been summarized as follows:

> the numerous virtually insoluble minority questions arising from the highly controversial drawing of borders; the search for new political and economic relationships in the vacuum left by the old powers, the Habsburg empire and Turkey; and the internal political crises of the new states with their more or less democratically constituted systems, which proved to be scarcely viable, caught between Communist-revolutionary threat and authoritarian-military tendencies towards dictatorship.[6]

The 'cordon sanitaire', the band of national states reaching from the Baltic to the Mediterranean, which had been created by the war as well as by the peace settlement, could not cope with the tasks imposed on it after 1919–20; it could not successfully act as a buffer zone to prevent co-operation between Germany and the Soviet Union, as well as a barrier against Communist expansion into central Europe. Particularly in the south-east, these national states had not achieved stability in either domestic or foreign affairs. Some of the 'unequal heirs' of the war pursued policies aimed at revision of the treaty, while others were anxious to maintain the status quo. Not least because of minority problems which were never brought under control, internal conditions were highly volatile. The new territorial arrangements had actually intensified rather than diminished the economic and social difficulties of these states after the end of the war. There was thus no real balance of power in the region, but only a new political order which was under constant threat. It was already shaken by the war between Greece and Turkey from 1921 onwards,

---

(Austria) on 20 Sept., and that of Neuilly (Bulgaria) on 27 Nov. These treaties came into force respectively on 20 Jan., 16 July, and 9 Aug. 1920.

[5] Schieder, 'Neuordnung Europas', 129–30; Schulz, *Revolutionen*, 239–40; Viefhaus, *Minderheitenfrage*, on the protection agreements in general and on Bulgaria, Greece, and Yugoslavia in particular, 212–23.

[6] Bracher, *Europa in der Krise*, 43.

and a precarious balance of tension was restored only by the treaty of Lausanne (24 July 1923).[7] These developments were accompanied by the Turkish national revolution, which subjected the country to a massive programme of Europeanization. The new Turkish national state of 1923, primarily the work of Mustafa Kemal Pasha (later Kemal Atatürk), now continued the 'cordon sanitaire' as far as Asia Minor.[8] Together with the states of Greece, Bulgaria, Yugoslavia, and Albania, Turkey also constituted a kind of land-bridge between the Black Sea and the Mediterranean. Even though Turkey is not considered separately here, it still played a significant role in the background of developments affecting, in particular, the influence of non-Balkan powers in the region.

1. Albania

Italian claims to hegemony were initially concentrated on Albania, the smallest and least populous of all the Balkan states. The country had freed itself from Turkish rule in the course of the first Balkan war of 1912.[9] As a result of the London conference which settled the conflict, the sovereignty of Albania was recognized with the common consent of Germany, Austria, France, Britain, Italy, and Russia (23 July 1913). However, it was stipulated that Albania, freed from any Turkish influence, should become a neutral power under the protection of those states. As to the form of its neutrality, the definitive borders of the country, and the associated ethnic problems, there was wide disagreement between Vienna, Rome, and Athens. The treaty of Florence (17 December 1913) fixed the borders, but failed to answer the question of how Albania could be helped to achieve internal stability. Events moved quickly. Prince William of Wied, who had been chosen as the ruler of Albania at the London conference, was forced out of his capital, Durrës, after barely seven months. On 3 September 1914 he left for Venice because of internal unrest.[10] But the great European war was then one month old, and conditions in Albania were of interest only to those directly involved. Albania suffered the First World War as a battlefield and under foreign occupation, as a plaything of the various powers and at the mercy of the interests of Serbs, Montenegrins, Greeks, Italians, Frenchmen, and Austrians. At the end of the war the land was occupied by the victorious Allies, with the largest part under Italian control.[11]

The future of Albania appeared most uncertain. Under the provisions of the

---

[7] See e.g. ibid. 46–7; Schieder, 'Neuordnung Europas', 126–34; also the overall description in Parker, *Europe 1919–1945*, 39–40; Schulz, *Revolutionen*, 236–42.

[8] On Kemal's state and its economic and foreign-policy foundations see Onder, *Die türkische Außenpolitik*, 9 ff.

[9] Montanari, *Albania*, 7–21, in detail on the Albania question.

[10] Ibid. 21–9.

[11] Skendi, *Albania*, 10 ff.

1915 treaty of London,[12] which brought Italy into the war, Albania was to be reduced to a rump state after extensive territorial concessions to Italy, Greece, Serbia, and Montenegro. In 1918 Greece and the new 'Kingdom of the Serbs, Croats, and Slovenes' (SHS: Srba, Hrvata i Slovenaca, later Yugoslavia) demanded the territories assigned to them. However, the Italians were content to leave Albania intact provided that the country—within the borders of 1913—became an Italian protectorate.

To complicate matters further, the elements of a national administration were present in both the north and south of the country as a consequence of the rivalry between the Austrians on one hand and the French and Italians on the other. As an occupying power before 1918, each had hoped to draw the country to its own side by means of promises of autonomy. In addition, an Albanian government-in-exile continued to be recognized by Paris.

This is not the place to describe the fluctuating fortunes of the various groups and the many political attempts to find a solution. Ultimately, the future of Albania was decided by the peace conference, to which it sent a representative although he did not receive official recognition. In September 1920, after an arduous and confusing bargaining process, a united state with an autonomous government was created within the borders of 1913. Albania was admitted into the League of Nations as a sovereign state in December of the same year.[13]

Internally the new state was far from secure. Above all, it lacked a working administration, an effective education system, and a regular army. Yet Albania also possessed a number of advantages, notably oil deposits, for which it could grant concessions in return for foreign currency. In domestic politics, men over the age of twenty possessed the vote, though the franchise was indirect. From 1921 Albania had a parliament containing the elected representatives of two parties; one of these represented the conservative owners of large estates, while the other regarded itself as liberal-democratic (although the application of such terms to conditions in Albania remains questionable). The country also had a new capital, Tirana, and a government with Elin Bey Vrioni as prime minister. However, the Vrioni government was overthrown in October 1921 during armed uprisings connected with the Albanian demand that Greece and the Serb-Croat-Slovene kingdom should evacuate those parts of the country which they still occupied.[14]

Bajram Curri, who became prime minister on 16 October 1921, managed

---

[12] On the significance of the treaty of London for Italy and for Italo-Russian and later Italo-Yugoslav antagonism in the Balkans see Muhr, *Deutsch-italienische Beziehungen*, 29–33; on the Albanian question see Montanari, *Albania*, 32–5.

[13] On the above see in detail Zamboni, *Mussolinis Expansionspolitik*, pp. xxv–xxxviii; also Rhode, 'Die südosteuropäischen Staaten', 1273–4; Montanari, *Albania*, 175–230, especially on the military situation in the country after the end of the war, and 231–6 on the political solution from the Italian point of view. On the Albanian question at the peace conference as a whole see Woodall, 'Albanian Problem'.

[14] Rhode, 'Die südosteuropäischen Staaten', 1275–6.

to end the uprising in November. During this process Ahmed Zogu, who was both minister of the interior and minister of war, proved particularly energetic.[15] At the same time, the government in Tirana scored a diplomatic success. The ambassadors' conference in Paris, at which Italy, France, Great Britain, and Japan were represented, confirmed the borders of 1913 with only four minor exceptions. As a result, the troops of Greece and the Serb–Croat–Slovene kingdom were forced to withdraw. However, the end of the occupation did not mean the elimination of border disputes. At least as significant for future developments was the recognition given to the claim that Italy had 'interests in Albania requiring special protection'. Albania, which was after all a member of the League of Nations, naturally rejected this claim. But though there was no recognition of an Italian right of intervention, there can be no doubt that the League helped to bring Albania into the Italian sphere of influence. *De facto*, this decision prejudiced the development of Albanian–Italian relations. For example, the government in Tirana immediately attempted to improve its position by means of a *rapprochement* with London, which was of benefit to the British especially in the economic penetration of the country.[16] By the mid-1920s, however, Albania under Zogu was already drawing perceptibly closer to Italy again.

Zogu was the man with whom the fate of Albania was to be inextricably linked for some fifteen years. During a series of confusing developments in economic, domestic, and foreign affairs, with alternate spells of chaos and relative stability, he served as prime minister from December 1922 to February 1924 before resigning after an apparent assassination attempt which he may actually have staged. Accused of the murder of at least one member of parliament, the former prime minister was forced to flee the country. However, on 24 December 1924 he returned to Tirana with the support of the Serb–Croat–Slovene kingdom and at the head of an army of Albanian, Serbian, and Russian volunteers.[17]

The legal government thereupon fled to Italy, where Mussolini, who had his own plans for Albania, had watched events with relative indifference.[18] With the return of Zogu, the democratic experiment in Albania (1921–4) had failed.[19] From 31 January 1925 he ruled as president, equipped with a vast range of powers. In view of his own career and the turbulent history of Albania, Zogu's decision to have himself proclaimed 'king of the Albanians' (under the name of Zog I) on 1 September 1928 was scarcely surprising. Once the new king was established as sole ruler, the opposition was suppressed and

---

[15] Skendi, *Albania*, 13; Montanari, *Albania*, 237.
[16] Zamboni, *Mussolinis Expansionspolitik*, pp. xl ff.
[17] Montanari, *Albania*, 241; Zamboni, *Mussolinis Expansionspolitik*, pp. xlvii–lix; on Italian policy towards Albania between 1924 and 1927 see also Pastorelli, *Italia e Albania*, interpreting Italian policy as an attempt to reach a stable agreement with Albania.
[18] Zamboni, *Mussolinis Expansionspolitik*, pp. lviii–lxiv.
[19] Skendi, *Albania*, 14.

some of its members murdered. Though elections continued to be held, they were meaningless. Zogu chose the government, he could veto laws passed by the sole remaining chamber, and parliamentary ratification of treaties was no longer necessary.[20]

Despite the undoubtedly repressive nature of Zogu's rule, it cannot simply be described as reactionary. Nor does his regime deserve the label 'fascist'. The government conducted itself in an authoritarian and extremely nationalist way and, especially in the agricultural sector, proved to be dependent on the landowning upper classes. An agricultural reform was introduced in 1930, but the manner of its implementation ensured that there was no threat to the big estates.

In the sphere of justice and public education, however, the Zogu regime introduced genuine changes rather than cosmetic operations. Albania was granted a code of civil law, based on the principles of the French *code civil*; divorce was made legal; the new criminal law was largely based on the Italian model. The modern elements of the system included compulsory schooling, though attempts to enforce it were frequently defeated by the practical problems of daily life in Albania. There was also an extensive administrative reform modelled on the example of Napoleonic France, which Zogu greatly admired.[21] Albania, which had emerged *de jure* from the disorder of the war in 1920, seemed to be evolving into a genuinely sovereign state. Yet the key question was whether it could pursue an independent foreign policy. Here, it quickly became clear that the government's freedom of action at home had to be purchased at the price of concessions in external relations.[22]

Zogu's political calculations were based on comparatively uncomplicated convictions. The strong man in Tirana was faced by the alternative Albanian government under Fan Noli, which had taken refuge on the Italian coast after being driven from office. Zogu could not ignore the fact that Mussolini was at least tolerating its existence. To avoid any dangers and threats, including an Italian intervention in Albania, it therefore seemed necessary to improve relations with the Italians. The first phase of Albanian foreign policy under Zogu, lasting until the beginning of the 1930s, was accordingly marked by a *rapprochement* with Mussolini.[23] This does not, of course, mean that there was no friction between them. Nevertheless, the fundamental direction of Albanian foreign policy was switched from Belgrade to Rome, a process in which pragmatic considerations were decisive. An important role appears to have been played by Zogu's belief that Albanian interests would be served if the hostility between Yugoslavia and Italy was intensified to some extent.[24] However, the *tertius gaudens* policy did not succeed.

[20] Rhode, 'Die südosteuropäischen Staaten', 1278 ff.
[21] Ibid. 1280–1; Skendi, *Albania*, 16–17; on the political system in particular see Borejsza, *Il fascismo*, 59–60; on fascism in Albania see Nolte, *Faschistische Bewegungen*, 196–7.
[22] Skendi, *Albania*, 16.
[23] Rhode, 'Die südosteuropäischen Staaten', 1278; Jacomoni, *Politica dell'Italia*; 18–19.
[24] Zamboni, *Mussolinis Expansionspolitik*, p. lx.

The first steps of Albania towards dependence on Italy cannot be described in detail here.[25] Instead, a number of important points in this process will be noted, with the aim of clarifying the situation as it developed in 1939-40.

Some of the reasons for the turn towards Italy were economic. When Zogu came to power, the Italian market absorbed four-fifths of Albanian exports. There were ties of long standing between businessmen in the two countries.[26] Directly after the establishment of the Zogu regime, Tirana offered Rome a leading position in the economic life of Albania. Without any great activity on his own part, Mussolini's hegemonic ambitions, which included the political and economic penetration of the Balkans, found in Zogu their first, and even willing, victim. At this stage, that was important to the Fascist rulers. They were looking for an easy prey, since they did not yet have the strength for serious conflict.

Specifically, Rome was interested in concessions for the extraction of oil, a trade treaty between the two countries, and the establishment of an Albanian state bank. The oil issue was particularly vital, since Italian intentions here were in conflict with British interests[27] involving the Anglo-Persian Oil Company. However, in March 1925 the desired trade treaty was ratified; at the same time, Italy was granted permission to prospect for oil. A few days later, on 15 March, the Albanians and Italians signed a bank and loan agreement. In the struggle for influence in Albania, Rome had stolen a march on London. After these successes of Italian diplomacy, the conditions had been established which would allow Albania—albeit unofficially—to be treated as an Italian protectorate. By means of financial measures made possible by its banking monopoly, Rome could force any unwanted rival to withdraw; the loans granted to Tirana, which the Albanians were unable to repay, exposed the regime to Italian pressure. The financial policy of the Fascist regime served first and foremost 'to place the Albanian economy and finance under [Italian] control and, through a systematic policy of pauperization', to maintain and increase Zogu's dependence on Italy.[28] Such developments were bound to have a detrimental effect on his internal political aims.

Towards the end of August 1925 Rome and Tirana concluded a secret military agreement. When Albania initially resisted, Mussolini used both economic and military pressure—the latter through a naval show of strength off the Albanian coast—to make his junior partner comply. His conduct revealed that tensions had set in in relations between the two powers at a very early stage. Zogu's policy of *rapprochement* did not come from the heart.

In the August agreements Mussolini committed himself to stand by Zogu if Albania's territorial integrity and sovereignty were threatened. For its part, Tirana undertook to declare war on any Balkan state which attacked Italy, if

---

[25] Ibid. for the following in general.
[26] Jacomoni, *Politica dell'Italia*, 19-24.
[27] For details of the various concessions see Skendi, *Albania*, 174.
[28] Zamboni, *Mussolinis Expansionspolitik*, pp. lxiii ff., quotation p. lxx.

the Italians requested assistance. Zogu also promised not to enter into alliances or military agreements with third parties without the simultaneous participation of Mussolini. On the other hand, the Italian leader was not to negotiate concerning Albanian interests without informing Zogu.[29] In summer 1926 Mussolini made the first attempt to consolidate and extend his economic and financial protectorate by political means. A series of diplomatic interchanges, involving Belgrade and London as well as Rome and Tirana, ended in failure, but not before Zogu had engaged in a number of dangerous manœuvres against Mussolini. However, the Albanians eventually had to agree to the conclusion of the five-year friendship and security pact of 26 November 1926, which became known as the 'first Tirana pact'. Potentially directed against the Serb–Croat–Slovene kingdom, this confirmed the status quo for Albania, including its links with Italy.

The 'second Tirana pact' of 22 November 1927 signified an even clearer move towards dependence on Italy. This twenty-year defensive alliance was primarily Mussolini's response to the *rapprochement* between Paris and Belgrade. Rome and Tirana committed themselves to unconditional mutual assistance in the event of a conflict. Italy subsequently despatched a military mission to Albania; its militia became virtually a suborganization of the Italian army. The Italians had thereby taken over the protection of the country against external threat. Durrës and Vlorë became harbours for Italian warships. However one chooses to explain these developments, by 1927 at the latest Albania had submitted to Italian claims to hegemony. There is thus little point in providing detailed descriptions of the development of political relations thereafter. In the mid-1930s Zogu showed signs of trying to release his country from Mussolini's clutches, but he was not successful. In fact the attempt was largely counter-productive, since it encouraged Mussolini to order the military occupation of Albania. On 7 April 1939, Good Friday, that step was finally taken.[30]

In the interpretation of Fascist foreign policy, the Italo-Albanian relationship is one more proof that Mussolini was by no means an opportunist without a programme. Moreover, the aggression of April 1939 marks a significant stage in the history of south-east Europe, since it completed the transition from penetration by economic and financial means to a policy of military conquest. Italian conduct was a logical consequence of the demand for expansion propagated by the regime, but it also reflected the change in the character of Italian policy in the region as between 1926 and 1939. Of course, such observations must always take account of the international background, and particularly the German aggression against Czechoslovakia in March 1939. Yet it must also be said that at root both methods of Italian foreign policy—however different they appeared to the victims—served the same goal: the

---

[29] Ibid., pp. lxxvii–lxxx.
[30] Rhode, 'Die südosteuropäischen Staaten', 1279.

establishment of hegemony over the Balkans, whether through spheres of influence or through annexations.[31] This will be confirmed in our analysis of Mussolini's relations with the other states in question.[32]

2. YUGOSLAVIA

The expansionist theory of Italian conduct holds that Rome was dedicated to the establishment of an 'Italian system', the creation of a Balkan 'hunting-ground' for the Fascists.[33] Even though Mussolini encouraged the view that he was anxious for settlement or agreement with countries in the area until at least 1924–5, it has thus been argued that his underlying motives were consistently aggressive. In fact, there was at this time no open course of confrontation. Even relations with the Kingdom of the Serbs, Croats, and Slovenes, which had risen from the ashes of the Austro-Hungarian empire to challenge Italian supremacy in the Adriatic, initially revealed a defensive quality in Italian foreign policy.[34] Yet there were other signs which contradicted this impression, one of which was the conflict between Italy and Greece in 1923. Though the immediate issue was Corfu, the unresolved matter of the Albanian border also played a part.[35] For our purposes, the important point is that the Italian government demonstrated aggressive elements in its Balkan policy immediately before the treaty of friendship with Belgrade (1924) and the economic agreements (the Nettuno conventions) which followed in 1924–5.[36]

Within the political triangle formed by Rome, Tirana, and Belgrade, the 'acid test for a friendly relationship between [Italy] and Yugoslavia [was] a reciprocal settlement over Albania'.[37] By 1927 at the latest, the signs were unfavourable. The SHS kingdom now felt threatened at the rear, since Rome and Budapest had concluded a treaty of friendship in April of that year. Moreover, Albania was drawn into extreme dependence on Italy by the second treaty of Tirana (November 1927). Mussolini was clearly attempting to destroy the unity of the South Slav state by exploiting its minority problems.

Since these developments were accompanied by a *rapprochement* between Belgrade and Paris, the conflict of interest in the region acquired a new dimension: increasingly, it was turning into a confrontation between France and Italy. Though the First World War and its aftermath had removed the

---

[31] See also Petersen, 'Gesellschaftssystem', 441, for the 'subversive' Fascist foreign policy in this context. One starting-point was the minority groups. These were 'in Mussolini's view, potential material with which to disrupt the status quo in south-east Europe, and were worth supporting as long as Rome could fully control their freedom of action'; also ibid. 444.
[32] See in particular Carocci, *La politica*, esp. 240.
[33] Zamboni, *Mussolinis Expansionspolitik*, pp. lxxxvii–lxxxviii; also Petersen, 'Außenpolitik', 447; D. M. Smith, *Mussolini*, 154.
[34] Salvatorelli and Mira, *Storia d'Italia*, 296 ff.
[35] Ibid. 293 ff.
[36] Rusinow, *Austrian Heritage*, 185–91.
[37] Petersen, *Hitler—Mussolini*, 4–5.

2. Yugoslavia

powers which had traditionally dominated the region, the fundamental situation remained unchanged. The Balkans remained an object of the ambitions and rivalries of the great powers, for reasons that will be explained.

As reference to the minority issue has already indicated, one of the central problems of the new states was their ethnic heterogeneity. In these circumstances, the history of the South Slav Kingdom (renamed the Kingdom of Yugoslavia in October 1929) was dominated by two opposing tendencies. The first of these was the desire to combine the various elements of the population into the most integrated and unified state possible, while the second was the drive for extensive autonomy for the various groups.[38] These internal political problems were significant in foreign affairs because of their tendency to encourage secession.

Like Albania, though with many differences of detail, the Yugoslav state was a product of the First World War and the events directly preceding it. Between 1900 and 1918 Serbia had developed into the core of a potential South Slav state, a process which contained the seeds of many subsequent developments.[39] These cannot be described in detail here,[40] but a number of structural factors which affected the creation of the South Slav state in 1918 will be summarized.[41]

On 20 July 1917 the 'Corfu Declaration' was issued.[42] Its authors were South Slav emigrants from the (Austro-Hungarian) Dual Monarchy who had formed a 'Yugoslav Committee' in London in 1915, together with the Serbian government, which had been in exile on the island of Corfu since the occupation of Serbia by the Central powers. Among their demands was the establishment of a kingdom of the Serbs, Croats, and Slovenes with the Karadjordjević dynasty at its head. Its borders were to be drawn on the basis of self-contained areas of population and in agreement with the principle of self-determination. A national legislative assembly would work out the details of the future constitution.

From the outset there was disagreement about the nature of the future state. While military developments in the autumn of 1918 made a consensus more urgent, no decision had been taken on whether to have a federation or—as the Serbian government advocated—a centralized unitary state. Another obstacle was the fact that, in foreign affairs, the representatives of the new state had not reached agreement with Italy on territorial questions. The treaty of London (1915) entitled Rome to lay claim to Istria and the Adriatic coast with Fiume

---

[38] Rhode, 'Die südosteuropäischen Staaten', 1184.
[39] Reiswitz, 'Entwicklung Jugoslawiens', 67–70; also relevant passages in *Creation of Yugoslavia*.
[40] See Wuescht, *Jugoslawien*, 20–8; also Kosier, *Großdeutschland*, 232–41, which shows appreciation of Yugoslav nationalism; and, concentrating on the Croats, Kiszling, *Kroaten*, 97–127; also Tomasevich, *War and Revolution*, 3–6.
[41] On the following see esp. Reiswitz, 'Entwicklung Jugoslawiens', 69–72; Rhode, 'Die südosteuropäischen Staaten', 1186 ff.; Schulz, *Revolutionen*, 273–4.
[42] This declaration is also known as the 'Corfu pact'.

(Rijeka), Spalato (Split), and Ragusa (Dubrovnik). If these demands had been fulfilled, the local Slovenes and Croats would have become Italian citizens. Though relations improved somewhat after March 1918, the problem was not resolved. On 6 October 1918 a national council of the Serbs, Croats, and Slovenes was constituted at Zagreb. This set up a government and demanded a 'united independent South Slav national state in all territories inhabited by Slovenes, Croats, and Serbs, without regard for national and provincial borders'.[43] When the designated regent, Prince Alexander of Serbia, arrived in Belgrade on 6 November, his future kingdom consisted, paradoxically, of two separate states. However, representatives of all the groups concerned agreed in Geneva to recognize each other until the creation of a constituent assembly. Existing institutions were thus retained for the time being.

Pressure in foreign affairs—the Italians occupied Rijeka and were marching on Ljubljana—finally brought about unification. On 1 December 1918 Prince Alexander proclaimed the amalgamation of 'Serbia with the lands of the independent state of the Slovenes, Croats, and Serbs' into a united 'Kingdom of the Serbs, Croats, and Slovenes'.[44] A government of national concentration came into being on 29 December. However, Croat protests against the new state had already begun, aroused by fears of Serb domination.[45]

In many respects the SHS kingdom resembled a miniature edition of the old multi-racial Dual Monarchy. It had three religions: Orthodoxy, Roman Catholicism, and Islam. Though the majority of citizens were Serb, Croat, or Slovene, there were numerous minorities: Germans,[46] Hungarians, Romanians, Bulgarians, Greeks, Albanians, and Turks. Nor was the country united culturally. Its diversity reflected the way in which the kingdom had been carved out of many different territories, a fact which also ensured that Belgrade had border disputes with a number of its neighbours. These included the victorious powers of Italy and Romania as well as the defeated states of Austria, Hungary, and Bulgaria (see Map II.1.1). While all the wiles of diplomacy were employed at the peace conference and elsewhere, a number of armed clashes took place, for instance during an unsuccessful attempt by the Yugoslavs to establish the border with Austria north of the Karawanken Mountains. Nevertheless, by the end of 1920 border issues had been resolved, at least to the extent that they were no longer the chief stumbling-block in attempts to consolidate the kingdom.

The country now comprised the following territories: the two former kingdoms of Montenegro and Serbia (the latter comprising Old Serbia and

---

[43] Quoted in Rhode, 'Die südosteuropäischen Staaten', 1187.

[44] Ibid. 1188. Alexander was prince regent from June 1914, and after the death of King Peter I on 16 Aug. 1921 he became official head of state as King Alexander I.

[45] Amoretti, *La vicenda*, p. xiv.

[46] For further details see Wehler, *Nationalitätenpolitik*, 9–39, for the period until Apr. 1941; also Harriman, 'German Minority', for the period after 1941; Paikert, *Danube Swabians*, for the German minorities in Yugoslavia, and also Romania and Hungary. For National Socialist influence on ethnic Germans in Yugoslavia between 1933 and 1941 see Bagnell, 'Influence'.

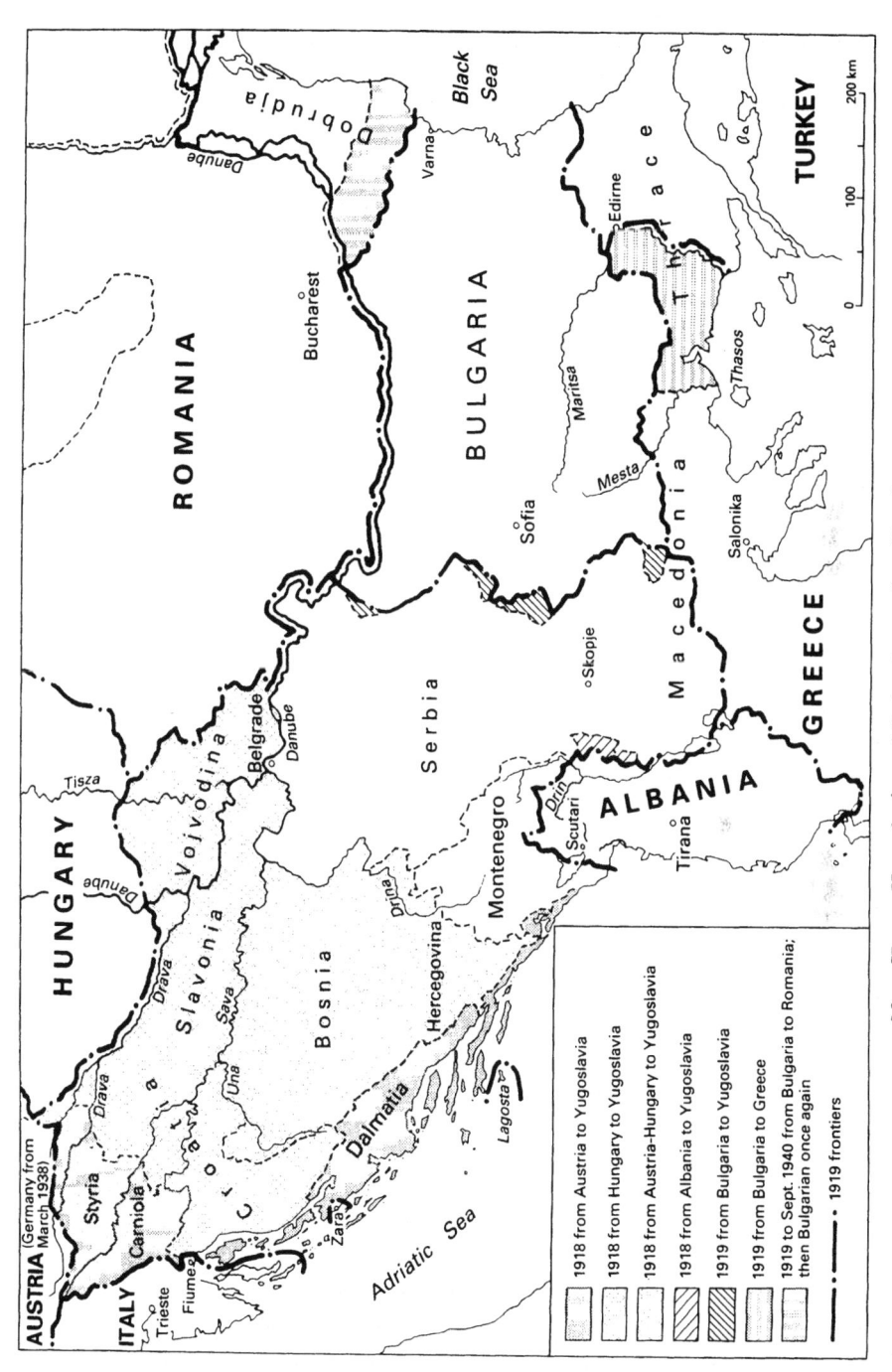

MAP II.1.1. Yugoslavia and Bulgaria, 1918 to March 1941

South Serbia–Macedonia), which were virtually the heartlands of the new state; the newly acquired Vojvodina (with a small section of the Baranja, the western half of the Banat and the Bačka); Croatia-Slavonia; parts of Carinthia, Lower Styria, and almost the whole of the former crown lands of Carniola and Dalmatia; and the province of Bosnia-Hercegovina. All these territories had previously been part of the Austro-Hungarian empire. From Bulgaria, Yugoslavia acquired Caribrod, Bosilegrad, and Strumica. A border strip along the coast south of Prizren was ceded by Albania. Extensive demands for Albanian territory as far as the River Drin, including Scutari (Shkodër), were abandoned after Italy recognized Albanian sovereignty in August 1920.[47]

Next, the urgent domestic political problems of the SHS kingdom came to the fore. Chief of these was the constitutional issue, which involved the need to satisfy Croat interests and thereby safeguard the existence of the state. The necessary majority for a constitution was obtained on 28 June 1921. However, the constitution remained controversial. Though it recognized three Yugoslav ethnic groups, this was little more than lip-service. The country was divided into artificial units of roughly equal size, similar to the French *départements*, which provided a model here as in Albania. These thirty-three units (*oblasti*) were legally constituted in April 1922, and were directly subordinate to the central government in Belgrade.[48]

Unquestionably, the constitutional monarchy of Yugoslavia under the constitution of June 1921 represented a victory of Serbian centralism over a federalism which was historically more appropriate because of the multi-racial nature of the state. The result created deep disillusionment among Croats and Macedonians and encouraged the emergence of separatist movements. Together with irredentist tendencies among the national minorities, separatism was a dangerously explosive element in the domestic affairs of the SHS kingdom.[49]

The tensions produced by unsolved national and religious problems were the root cause of the dissolution of parliament and the establishment of a royal dictatorship in January 1929 in order to maintain both the state itself and its hierarchical structure.[50] At the time, the resulting system was referred to as 'military-fascist' or 'monarcho-fascist'; but even Yugoslav Communists revised this opinion of the governmental system after the war. Despite a certain tendency towards fascism,[51] the royal dictatorship can be more accurately described as a markedly authoritarian regime.[52]

Nevertheless, in general discussions Yugoslavia is frequently bracketed with

---

[47] On territorial questions in particular see Reiswitz, 'Entwicklung Jugoslawiens', 81; Rhode, 'Die südosteuropäischen Staaten', 1189 ff.
[48] Reiswitz, 'Entwicklung Jugoslawiens', 87.
[49] Thamer and Wippermann, *Faschistische Bewegungen*, 91–2.
[50] Hory and Broszat, *Ustascha-Staat*, 16–19; Hnilicka, *Ende auf dem Balkan*, 31; Schulz, *Revolutionen*, 238; for further details see Stoyadinovitch, *Yougoslavie*, 33–7.
[51] Thamer and Wippermann, *Faschistische Bewegungen*, 94–5.
[52] Avakumović, 'Fascist Movements', 136.

2. Yugoslavia

Hungary and Romania[53] as a typical example of fascism in its south-east European manifestation. Admittedly, the term is used more to describe the Ustaša (='Insurgent') regime of Ante Pavelić during the Second World War,[54] after the German invasion and dismemberment of Yugoslavia.[55] The 'Ustaša state' (see below) can justifiably be classified as fascist, but it is debatable whether the term can fairly be applied to Yugoslavia before 1941. Neither Alexander's dictatorship between 1929 and 1934[56] nor the 'royal dictatorship without the king' under the regency of Prince Paul, which followed the assassination of Alexander in Marseilles on 9 October 1934,[57] amounted to a fascist regime. Between 1929 and 1941 there was extensive 'suppression of parties and freedom of the press', but there was no 'popular movement and potential single party, a much more distinctive characteristic' of fascist governments.[58] In these circumstances, the discussion of fascism in Yugoslavia before 1941 must concentrate mainly on so-called fascist organizations or parties; the phenomenological approach[59] seems to provide an appropriate method in this context.

In the case of Yugoslavia, fascism can be described first and foremost as a reaction to certain developments, for instance as an answer to a perceived Communist challenge;[60] as the consequence of the failure of liberal democracy; or as a counter-movement by Croatian circles against the political, economic, and cultural threat they saw in the unitary, Serbian-dominated state of Yugoslavia.[61] This last phenomenon shows that fascism was at least partly associated with the major unresolved problem of Yugoslavia: the conflict between centralism and federalism.[62] It was this conflict which produced the fascist movements we are concerned with here.[63]

These movements are to be sharply distinguished from the numerous nationalist organizations, though some of the latter undoubtedly displayed proto-fascist characteristics, for example an exaggerated nationalism, a belligerent anti-Communism, and a tendency to resort to violence.[64] The Organizacija Jugoslovenskih Nacionalista (ORJUNA), which held the field in the 1920s, refused to accept the label 'fascist'. So did 'Yugoslav Action',

---

[53] On Hungary and Romania see *Das Deutsche Reich und der Zweite Weltkrieg*, iv.I.v (Förster).
[54] Hory and Broszat, *Ustascha-Staat*, 39–174; Thamer and Wippermann, *Faschistische Bewegungen*, 97 ff.
[55] See III.III below (Vogel).
[56] See Kiszling, *Kroaten*, 138; Alexander decided on this after Stjepan Radić, the leader of the Croatian Peasants' Party, was fired at by a Serbian deputy in parliament on 20 June 1928. He died of his wounds in August.
[57] Rhode, 'Die südosteuropäischen Staaten', 1204–11.
[58] Nolte, *Three Faces of Fascism*, 14.
[59] Ibid. 20–30; Wippermann, *Faschismustheorien*, 77–88.
[60] Tomasevitch, *War and Revolution*, 11–12, on the Yugoslav Communist Party.
[61] Avakumović, 'Fascist Movements', 136.
[62] Nolte, *Faschistische Bewegungen*, 200.
[63] Djordjević, 'Fascism', 130.
[64] Avakumović, 'Fascist Movements', 136–7.

founded in 1930 and initially dedicated to the service of the royal dictatorship. This movement was banned in 1934 after its leaders quarrelled with the regime. Its programme contained corporatist, anti-parliamentary, and anti-Communist elements as well as ideas of a planned economy.[65]

Only in the 1930s did two organizations come into being in Yugoslavia which deserved the label 'fascist'. These were the Zbor party (Yugoslav patriotic unity movement), founded in 1935 by the Serb Dimitrije Ljotić, and the Ustaša movement of Ante Pavelić. Zbor was organized on strictly hierarchical lines, cultivated the leadership principle, and promoted corporatist views. The core of the party was recruited from the extreme right wing of 'Yugoslav Action' and, not surprisingly, it supported the centralist unitary state at all costs.[66] Zbor played no significant role in Yugoslavia before the German invasion; after it, however, party adherents were among the most reliable supporters of the National Socialist conquerors.[67]

Considerably more important from a historical point of view was the second fascist movement, the Ustaša. Its ideological roots lay in the 'greater Croatian' nationalism of the pre-1914 era. Ustaša was persistently anti-Yugoslav and was founded as a direct reaction to the royal dictatorship. In ideology and intent, the Ustaša—an insurgent movement, as its name denotes—reached back beyond the fascist era. Since the nineteenth century the original version of both movements had been dedicated to the 'establishment of an independent Croat state'.[68] In the 1930s the Ustaša was profoundly affected by 'the fascist climate of the age'. For Pavelić, the Freemasons, liberals, Jews, and Bolshevists were the deadly enemies of his idea, which found an appropriate counterpart in the 'blood and soil' ideology of the National Socialists.[69] Nevertheless, his ideology differed from Hitler's National Socialism as well as from Mussolini's Fascism in respect of its commitment to the Catholic faith. Pavelić's ideas can best be compared with those of the Spanish Carlists, to whom he was originally closer than to Hitler and Mussolini.[70] But his movement was unquestionably fascist. It became significant, however, only when Pavelić was handed governmental power by the Germans and Italians after the destruction of the Yugoslav state.[71]

Even sympathetic interpretations of Croatian nationalism[72] are forced to allow that the Ustaša, which was founded in 1929, had the declared aim of fighting against the Yugoslav state with illegal methods. Pavelić's struggle was

---

[65] Djordjević, 'Fascism', 130–1.
[66] Ibid. 131; Avakumović, 'Fascist Movements', 137–8; Borejsza, *Il fascismo*, 57–8.
[67] Thamer and Wippermann, *Faschistische Bewegungen*, 93–4; Matl, 'Jugoslawien im Zweiten Weltkrieg', 108–12; Wuescht, *Jugoslawien*, 58, which interprets Ljotić more as a Serb nationalist than as a convinced collaborator with the Fascists.
[68] Thamer and Wippermann, *Faschistische Bewegungen*, 95–6.
[69] Nolte, *Faschistische Bewegungen*, 201.
[70] Thamer and Wippermann, *Faschistische Bewegungen*, 97–8.
[71] Hory and Broszat, *Ustascha-Staat*, 13.
[72] Fricke, *Kroatien*, 10–14; Omrčanin, *Geschichte Kroatiens*, 189.

2. Yugoslavia

not only against the internal stabilization sought by Alexander.[73] The destructive activity of the Ustaša reached a peak with the assassination of the king in October 1934, but this was only the most spectacular of a series of murders in which the movement was involved. In the rigidly hierarchical Ustaša, the struggle against the Serbs was seen as a kind of continuation of the wars against the Turks. Such views could be shared only by Croat nationalists, whereas international public opinion condemned the murder of the king as terrorism. Even Mussolini, previously Pavelić's chief supporter, kept his distance. After the Italo-Yugoslav friendship treaty of 25 March 1937 had settled outstanding disputes, the Fascists actually interned on the Lipari Islands those Ustaša members who were living in Italy. Pavelić suddenly found himself isolated. For the Ustaša, the period later called 'the era of great silence' had begun.[74]

All this gives the impression that fascism had few adherents in Yugoslavia during the interwar years. This can partly be explained by the authoritarian political structure of the country, which allowed only those parties that supported the existing constitution to take root.[75] Until political relations between Belgrade and Rome were normalized, which occurred only in 1937–9, political parties dependent on the support of Mussolini were not popular with the Yugoslavs. Furthermore, irredentist groups in Hungary, Bulgaria, and Albania, as well as Austria—which were more or less hostile to the Yugoslav state—sympathized with the revisionist tendencies of Italian policy; Mussolini's great-power ambitions might therefore encourage movements in the region which were distinctly undesirable from a Yugoslav point of view. It is also to be noted that the Yugoslav fascists offered hardly any themes which had not been taken up by other parties long before—except for anti-Semitism, which had few supporters. In this sense there was no need for fascist politics.[76] Nevertheless, the growing strength of National Socialism in Germany clearly stimulated fascism in Yugoslavia. Zbor in particular modelled its party organization and much of its foreign policy on the example of Germany.[77] In the 1930s, and before the coup of March 1941, Yugoslavia's official foreign policy likewise drew closer to the Third Reich, and there were many indications that the country would follow increasingly in the German wake.[78]

In internal affairs, the proclamation of the royal dictatorship on 6 January 1929 was the great turning-point in the political development of Yugoslavia after the First World War. There were no more genuinely free or secret elections thereafter. Democracy had been defeated; the South Slav kingdom, however, was not the first to turn its back on the parliamentary system.

[73] Borejsza, *Il fascismo*, 57.
[74] Hory and Broszat, *Ustascha-Staat*, 19–26; on the murder of King Alexander see also Stoyadinovitch, *Yougoslavie*, 38 ff.
[75] Nolte, *Faschistische Bewegungen*, 199–200.
[76] Avakumović, 'Fascist Movements', 141–2.
[77] Nolte, *Faschistische Bewegungen*, 200.
[78] See also III.1.2 below (Vogel).

Neither at home nor abroad was there any great protest at the turn of events. The population came to terms with the regime. Executive power was controlled by the king; the government was responsible to him alone.[79] At least until a new constitution came into force, the legislature was also completely under his control. No freedom of the press existed, and unwanted opposition of all kinds was forcibly repressed. Alexander intended to compel his subjects into unity. The change of name on 30 October 1929, from the 'Kingdom of the Serbs, Croats, and Slovenes' to the 'Kingdom of Yugoslavia', was a reflection of this goal. Numerous measures were introduced internally in the hope of achieving it. Yet the internal balance of forces did not initially alter; for example, the first cabinet in April 1929 consisted of ten Serbian ministers, four Croats, and one Slovene.[80]

Also at the heart of the royal reforms was a territorial reorganization of Yugoslavia. Instead of the previous thirty-three departments, nine regions or banats were created on a geographical basis: Drava, Sava, Vrbas, Primorje (the coastal region), Drina, Zeta, Danube, Morava, and Vardar. Here too historical links were deliberately ignored. But the real, structural significance of the reorganization lay in the fact that the Serbs, though only 45 per cent of the total population, were in a majority in six of the nine banats.[81]

From 3 September 1931 the country had a new constitution, which guaranteed civil rights but continued the prohibition against the formation of political parties. When a new Skupština (assembly) was elected on 8 November, the vote was not secret. Though such measures ensured that the royal power was not threatened, the state continued to be shaken by internal unrest. At the beginning of the 1930s there was not the slightest prospect that conflicting group interests could be satisfied. Somewhat surprisingly in these circumstances, the murder of Alexander at Marseilles in 1934 initially had a unifying effect. However, prospects in foreign affairs were grave, since the regime lacked a competent successor; eventually the uncertainty was likely to have unfavourable consequences at home also. Alexander's son, King Peter II, was only eleven years old when his father was killed. Prince Paul, a cousin of the dead ruler, was therefore appointed head of a regency council. He proved unable to cope with a constitutional position which had been designed for a head of state ruling as a dictator. Paul, apparently much influenced by liberal ideas, was quickly pushed into the background by Milan Stojadinović, who became prime minister in the summer of 1935.[82]

---

[79] Until 4 Apr. 1932 General Živković was prime minister, then—until 2 July 1932—Vojislav Marinković. He was followed until 26 Jan. 1934 by Dr Milan Srškić, until 19 Dec. 1934 by Nikola Uzunović, and then until 20 June 1935 by Boguljub Jevtić, who was succeeded by Stojadinović. For details of these governments see Reiswitz, 'Entwicklung Jugoslawiens', 84–93.

[80] Rhode, 'Die südosteuropäischen Staaten', 1201–2.

[81] Reiswitz, 'Entwicklung Jugoslawiens', 84.

[82] Rhode, 'Die südosteuropäischen Staaten', 1202–5; also (writing with knowledge as Prince Paul's confidant) Stoyadinovitch, *Yougoslavie*, 41–6.

2. Yugoslavia

Stojadinović, the champion of a *rapprochement* with Rome, was, however, removed from office without much ado on 4 February 1939, when he was in difficulties over the Croat question.[83] This fact indicates how little tendency there was to follow German or Italian models in domestic policy,[84] despite the country's *rapprochement* with Germany and Italy in respect of foreign affairs: we shall return to the latter point.

Dragiša Cvetković, successor to Stojadinović as prime minister, remained in office until anti-Axis coup led by General Dušan Simović on 27 March 1941.[85] It was Cvetković who finally managed to reconcile the Croats to the Yugoslav state in an agreement of 26 August 1939, the Sporazum.[86] The interests of the Croats were represented by the leader of the Croatian Peasant Party, Vladimir Maček.[87] In April 1939 the Italians had occupied Albania. Under the impact of this development, and after Maček had played the Italian card with great skill and taken the risk of making close contact with Rome, the government in Belgrade was prepared to make substantial concessions to the Croats.[88]

Under the Sporazum, the central government in Belgrade retained responsibility for foreign policy, defence, the postal service, and transport policy. The Croats, whose banat was to consist of the regions of Sava (Croatia) and Primorje (coastland), plus the districts of Dubrovnik, Travnik, Fojnica, Derventa, Gradačac, Brčko, Ilok, and Šid, were to have their own government in Zagreb and extensive autonomy. However, only days after the conclusion of this far-reaching agreement the Second World War broke out. The measures which would have transformed Yugoslavia into a federal state remained in abeyance. The implications and consequences of the conflict between Germany and Poland—Belgrade mobilized its army and faced a grave situation in foreign affairs—ultimately prevented the Sporazum from being implemented. This was welcome to the Serbs, but there was bitter disappointment and distrust among the Croat population. Domestic stability was further undermined by the propaganda influence of the war parties.[89] Tensions became intolerable with Mussolini's unsuccessful invasion of Greece in October 1940. Almost all the Balkan states now faced the crucial problem of deciding which side to take.[90] Should the Yugoslavs follow the example of the Greeks or, leaving aside the Romanians and Hungarians, follow the example of Bulgaria, which is of particular interest to us here?

---

[83] On this remarkable event see Breccia, *Jugoslavia*, 1–5, and 6–13 on the foreign-policy implications; also Tasso, *Italia e Croazia*, i. 130–9.
[84] Rhode, 'Die südosteuropäischen Staaten', 1205.
[85] For details see III.II.1 below (Vogel).
[86] On the Sporazum see Kiszling, *Kroaten*, 159–60; Tomasevitch, *War and Revolution*, 22–5.
[87] Reiswitz, 'Entwicklung Jugoslawiens', 96 ff.
[88] Hory and Broszat, *Ustascha-Staat*, 33–4.
[89] Details in Reiswitz, 'Entwicklung Jugoslawiens', 96; also Rhode, 'Die südosteuropäischen Staaten', 1206–7.
[90] See Rich, *War Aims*, ii. 240–1.

3. BULGARIA

During the interwar years the interests of Bulgaria, unlike those of Albania and Yugoslavia, were restricted exclusively to the Balkans.[91] However, this did not mean that the country remained unaffected by the designs of the European great powers.

The Bulgarian 'bridge to the east' played a constant role in the expansionist ambitions of the German ruling élite. This was true of the Kaiser's Germany, and equally of Hitler's. Bulgaria was a country which it was desirable to win over in order to establish a dominant position in the Near East with a secure hinterland. In so far as the Germans adhered to such ideas,[92] they were concerned partly with military-strategic objectives and partly with economic goals.[93]

Within this complex situation it is difficult to recognize absolute priorities. For example, the genesis of the German–Bulgarian alliance of 6 September 1915 demonstrates how economic relations paved the way for political and military penetration, or were mainly used to facilitate it. In 1915-16 the Bulgarians fought against Serbs and Romanians alike under German supreme command. Their national war aim was the revision of the treaty of Bucharest (1913), which had confirmed the defeat of Bulgaria in the second Balkan war. Victory for the Bulgarians enabled them to achieve this goal, but the triumph was short-lived. To achieve it, they had linked themselves for better or worse with the military fortunes of Germany and Austria. When the weakness of the Central powers was unmistakable and there was no longer any hope of victory, the objective became merely to achieve the best possible peace settlement. In these circumstances, Bulgaria's fate was sealed even before the German defeat. Sofia was forced to sign an armistice on 29 September 1918. A few days later King Ferdinand abdicated and was succeeded by his son Boris.[94]

Accordingly, the second major difference between Bulgaria on the one hand, and Albania and Yugoslavia on the other, was that Sofia was among the losers of the First World War. When the last German forces left the Bulgarian capital on 10 October, their place was taken by French troops, who occupied the city in accordance with the armistice agreement.[95]

The peace treaty was signed by the Bulgarian prime minister Alexandur Stamboliiski at Neuilly on 27 November 1919. Stamboliiski, leader of the Peasants' League, had been a strong opponent of Bulgarian war policy before 1918. Though the treaty can fairly be described as 'less drastic than the other

---

[91] See Rhode, 'Die südosteuropäischen Staaten', 1241-2.
[92] Among those most interested were the representatives of the German naval command, whose generally anti-British thinking almost inevitably led them to aim at the establishment of German hegemony in the eastern Mediterranean; see Schreiber, 'Italien', *passim*.
[93] Petzold, 'Imperialismus', 65 ff.
[94] Hoppe, 'Deutschland', 605.
[95] Id., *Bulgarien*, 26.

3. Bulgaria

European treaties',[96] that was not how it appeared to the Bulgarians.[97] The country lost approximately 8 per cent of the territory it had held in 1913; after 1919 it comprised only 103,146 km.² Its territorial losses included part of Macedonia, the Dobrudja, and western Thrace. Strumica and Caribrod were handed over to Yugoslavia, and in 1920 western Thrace was finally ceded to Greece, depriving Bulgaria of its access to the Aegean. But it was not only the loss of territory which damaged the country: Sofia was also burdened with reparations to the tune of 2,250 million francs, to be paid within thirty-eight years. In addition, universal military service was to be abolished, the Bulgarian army was limited to 20,000 men, and the possession of tanks and aircraft was forbidden.[98]

According to the calculations of the victorious powers, Bulgaria was to have a significant role in plans to contain the Communist threat to Europe. However, the terms of the peace treaty initially aroused revisionist sentiments in wide circles of the population. Such a reaction might well have an effect on the Western policy of 'containing' Bolshevism by means of a *cordon sanitaire* in eastern Europe. It was even more likely to make the Bulgarians susceptible to the revisionist propaganda which was intensified after 1922 in Fascist Italy, and after 1933 in National Socialist Germany.[99]

Other consequences of the treaty of Neuilly contributed to Bulgarian discontent. The economy was not damaged by reparations alone; the flood of unemployed also had an exceptionally disruptive effect. In part, increased unemployment was a consequence of the rapid and complete demobilization of the armed forces, but it was also the result of the wave of refugees caused by the loss of territory.[100] The associated problem of the protection of minorities and the exchange of population, which played an important role at the peace conference, further damaged Bulgaria's relations with Greece and Yugoslavia.[101] This was of major significance in the creation of political groupings in the Balkans. When Mussolini's troops launched their attack on Greece in autumn 1940, the dictator had good reason to hope for Bulgarian support.

Political and economic conditions in Bulgaria during the immediate postwar period thus led to a process of radicalization in domestic affairs. A situation was created which in many respects was comparable with that in the Weimar Republic at the time of the world depression. After the end of the war,

---

[96] Parker, *Europe 1919–1945*, 30.

[97] Miller, *Bulgaria*, 2–3; Rhode, 'Die südosteuropäischen Staaten', 1244, points out that it was the 'harshness' of the peace terms which caused the Bulgarian prime minister Todor Teodorov to refuse to sign them.

[98] More details in Drake, 'Bulgaria', *passim*; Hoppe, *Bulgarien*, 26–7.

[99] See Rhode, 'Die südosteuropäischen Staaten', 1242; the revisionist aims of Bulgaria extended to parts of Yugoslavia, Romania (the southern Dobrudja), and Greece. See also Hoppe, 'Balkanstaaten', 169; and Collotti, 'Il ruolo', 53.

[100] Hoppe, *Bulgarien*, 27.

[101] Viefhaus, *Minderheitenfrage*, 212–23; on the numbers and the actual exchange quotas see Rhode, 'Die südosteuropäischen Staaten', 1246.

Bulgarian political life was turbulent. It was marked by revenge on those who had led the country into war, the domination of class interests, and terror on the political scene as a whole. A first climax came at the end of 1919 with the transport workers' strike, which lasted for two months. It led to arrests, not least of functionaries of the Communist Party of Bulgaria, which had won a clear victory at the local elections shortly before. Parliament was dissolved on 20 February 1920. However, the new elections resulted in significant gains for the Communists and the Peasants' League at the expense of the Socialists. Over the following years the Peasants' Party—Zemledeltsi—was to become the decisive political force.[102]

Alexandăr Stamboliiski thereupon formed his second cabinet, a purely 'agrarian government' which he led from May 1920 until June 1923. It followed an extreme anti-bourgeois, anti-urban, and anti-capitalist policy.[103] Stamboliiski's agrarian reform was intended to make social conditions in Bulgaria reflect the real structure of society, which was 80 per cent peasant. The big landowners, unlike their counterparts in Albania, had to pay the price. Alongside these measures, Stamboliiski introduced universal labour service for both men and women, though not for the same length of time.

Although the Peasants' League represented rather more than half of all Bulgarians, the government's actions did not make it universally popular. A number of factors combined to produce an explosive situation: the economic and internal policy of the government, rigorously directed towards farming interests; its terroristic methods of rule, based on the strong-arm 'Orange Guard' from the Peasants' Party; and Stamboliiski's flirtation with the Soviet Union in foreign affairs despite his harsh treatment of the Communists at home. Moreover, Stamboliiski had his own dreams of a Greater Slav state, rooted in the conviction that he could unite all the southern Slavs into one state. The idea was not exactly timely; the Yugoslav government in particular had little sympathy for the proposed confederation of Balkan peasant states. Internally, moreover, Stamboliiski's notions eventually provoked the hostility of the Internal Macedonian Revolutionary Organization (IMRO).

In Bulgaria after 1919 IMRO, originally a terrorist anti-Turkish organization, constituted 'a regular state with . . . a legislature and an executive, differing from other states only in that it possessed no fixed location'. It was headed by a three-man central committee, responsible to the congress of the organization. Within it there were sanctions and punishments, dues were paid, and there was a form of finance and economic policy. There was even a 'school authority for secret education in the oppressed territories'. Altogether, IMRO became the most powerful terrorist movement in the Balkans and an important political factor. In Bulgaria, with a population of approximately 250,000 Macedonians, it had a large base from which to foment constant unrest.[104]

---

[102] Rhode, 'Die südosteuropäischen Staaten', 1244–5; Nolte, *Faschistische Bewegungen*, 194–5.
[103] Hoppe, *Bulgarien*, 27.
[104] Id., 'Deutschland', 605; quotation from Nolte, *Faschistische Bewegungen*, 308 n. 6.

3. Bulgaria

Against this background and with the sanction of the king, various opposition groups staged an uprising against the government at the beginning of June 1923. Participants included the conservative officer corps (especially reserve officers), bourgeois intellectuals, and IMRO. Some were motivated by Stamboliiski's talk of a republic and the elimination of the monarchy, while others rebelled against his fantasy of a Greater Southern Slav empire. All the groups had reason for satisfaction with the outcome: the prime minister was overthrown, and murdered.[105]

An attempted counter-revolt by the Communists ended in failure and the brutal persecution of the party. Georgi Dimitrov, its leader, went into exile along with various members of the Peasants' League. However, calm was not restored over the next two years. In April 1925 an attack on the king in Sofia's Sveta Nedelja cathedral claimed 125 lives. Boris III survived, but there followed what the Communists called a 'fascist bloodbath'.[106] The regime took harsh measures: a state of emergency until October 1925, a temporary increase in the size of the army to 30,000 men, and death sentences for anybody held guilty of participation in the coup. Furthermore, the Communist Party, officially banned from 1924 onwards, lost much support in the population. Even the Peasants' League, actually its companion in misfortune, was careful to distance itself from the Communists.[107]

If one attempts to characterize Bulgarian governments in the period between the coup of 1923 and the next internal turning-point of 1934, it may first be said that up to 1925 they were comparatively stable, despite their heterogeneous composition and the chaotic state of domestic affairs. But this stability, like the parliamentary majority of the rulers, rested on repressive measures. This fact did not escape public notice at home and abroad; as a result of its domestic policies, the government in Sofia failed to gain any significant support. In fact, its isolation had at least one positive effect in helping to prevent the establishment of a full-blown dictatorship, since the regime felt compelled to observe at least a modicum of restraint.[108]

The political leadership of Bulgaria cannot be designated simply as fascist either before or after 1925, as contemporary Communist propaganda alleged. For example, there was still a form of parliamentary opposition. After 1927 it again included Communists, though under the name 'Independent Workers' Party'. There were even elections, which though not genuinely free were also not completely manipulated.[109] The population thus had some prospect of exerting influence on politics. The government was not truly fascist, although the Democratic Alliance which stood behind the regime included the National Association, which had been founded in 1922 and was ideologically close to the

---

[105] Borejsza, *Il fascismo*, 43–4.
[106] Nolte, *Faschistische Bewegungen*, 195.
[107] Rhode, 'Die südosteuropäischen Staaten', 1245–6.
[108] Borejsza, *Il fascismo*, 44.
[109] Nolte, *Faschistische Bewegungen*, 195.

Italian Fascist party.[110] There were also a number of fascist movements surrounding the Democratic Alliance itself. These, though not controlling the political life of Bulgaria, were not without influence.[111]

Among the fascist groups (as opposed to those which were simply right wing or extreme nationalist) was the Rodna Zashtita (Defence of the Fatherland), which had been created as an illegal organization even before the coup of 1923. The objectives of Rodna Zashtita were anti-agrarian in the party-political sense, anti-Communist, and anti-Semitic. Its members made no distinction between Bolsheviks, Freemasons, and Jews. They held that the political parties should be disbanded and replaced by a parliament organized on a corporative basis. Supporters of Rodna Zashtita adopted the fascist salute, wore black shirts, and relied on highly emotional and hackneyed propaganda themes, revolving around love for Bulgaria, willingness to make sacrifices for it, and the desire for its aggrandizement. Yet these themes cannot be described as specifically fascist, since they were shared, with only slight variations, by what the press and political jargon had come to label brown (fascist), black (clerical), and red propagandists.

Apart from the Rodna Zashtita, particular attention must be paid to the Natsionalna zadruga fashisti (National Community of Fascists), which unreservedly took Italian Fascism as its model, and the Natsionalnosotsialisticheska bulgarska rabotnicheska partiya (NSBRP), the counterpart to Hitler's NSDAP. Yet neither the Bulgarian Fascists nor the Bulgarian National Socialists achieved genuine significance. In contrast, the Social National Movement, founded in 1931 and also modelled on the NSDAP, managed to obtain between 10 and 20 per cent of the vote at elections and was a more serious force in Bulgarian political life.[112] It may have been concern about a possible fascist uprising which persuaded King Boris to transform the constitutional monarchy into an authoritarian monarchy in 1934. In any case, the move spelt the end for the fascist movements, which were disbanded.

The world economic crisis can be regarded as the trigger for the developments which began in early summer 1934. Bulgaria, a predominantly agricultural country, had suffered greatly from the collapse in farm prices. Tobacco, the main export product, had been especially hard hit. As in other countries, the value of money had declined, real wages had fallen in value, and unemployment had increased. Strikes had broken out and public discontent had steadily mounted. In this situation, the elections of 1931 had brought the opposition National Bloc to power.

This victory can be taken as evidence that the elections were free (although

---

[110] Borejsza, *Il fascismo*, 43–4; instead of 'Democratic Alliance', the terms 'Democratic Unity' (Hoppe) and 'Democratic Union' (Nolte) are also used.

[111] On the following descriptions of fascist groups in Bulgaria see Borejsza, *Il fascismo*, 44–5; Miller, *Bulgaria*, 4–5; and esp. Nolte, *Faschistische Bewegungen*, 195–6.

[112] Both Nolte and Borejsza (see n. 111 above) interpret the role of the Social National Movement in this sense, while Hoppe, *Bulgarien*, 45, plays down its significance.

it is arguable that the electoral manipulation by the Democratic Alliance had simply been too inefficient). At any rate, Sofia was now ruled by a highly disparate coalition of democrats, radicals, left liberals, and moderate agrarians. In Bulgaria, in contrast to elsewhere, the economic depression actually brought victory to democracy and the parliamentary system. However, the triumph was short-lived. The new regime failed to deal with outstanding political and economic problems, and opinions on the left and right of the political spectrum became increasingly radicalized. The situation was made more difficult because successes in foreign policy, which might have diverted attention from domestic hardship, eluded the regime. In particular, the Balkan pact of February 1934, involving Ankara, Athens, Belgrade, and Bucharest, made it clear that Sofia had been unable to escape its isolation; the pact was manifestly intended to thwart Bulgarian revisionist claims.[113]

By May 1934 the National Bloc was in disarray. Conflicts over cabinet posts resulted in a governmental crisis and an upsurge of popular discontent. A relatively small clique of officers exploited the general confusion to organize a *putsch* on 19 May, supported mainly by the reserve officers' league and the eighty-strong political group known as Zveno—'the Link'. In truth, the putschists were an individualistic group which was held together chiefly by its rejection of existing political conditions. Beyond that, the rebels were animated by nationalist and authoritarian tendencies. Zveno's proximity to fascism was expressed in anti-liberal ideas, the cult of the élite, and support for a corporate state. Yet it differed from fascism in its rejection of a mass movement, its lack of a racial ideology, and the repudiation of extreme nationalist and revisionist objectives.[114]

The leader of Zveno, General Kimon Georgiev, took over as head of a cabinet which was right-wing in domestic politics but largely drawn towards Moscow (Bulgaria's traditional protector) in foreign affairs. Though he was anxious to end the isolation of Bulgaria, Georgiev's first move was to change the domestic situation. Sections of the 1879 constitution were rescinded, the bloated administrative apparatus was reduced, press censorship was imposed, and IMRO was destroyed by the army in what was virtually a war. Political parties were banned. From 31 August 1934 a decree for the protection of the state permitted the regime to take arbitrary action against anything that appeared in any way to threaten it.[115] But this political experiment also failed, despite some initial encouraging signs of stability or improvement in economic and political conditions at home and in foreign relations.

Tensions within the government, with royalists and republicans intriguing against each other, persuaded Boris III to dislodge the prime minister on 22 January 1935. He thus engineered a coup from above against a regime which lacked mass support. The Bulgarian royal dictatorship had begun. Yet though

---

[113] Hoppe, *Bulgarien*, 29 ff.   [114] Ibid. 31–2.
[115] Rhode, 'Die südosteuropäischen Staaten', 1250.

political parties were still forbidden, in March 1938 the Bulgarians elected individual candidates to a parliament of 160 seats. The royalists managed to obtain a majority in parliament only after the outbreak of the Second World War, when new elections were held. Though the powers and function of the parliament are still a matter of controversy, there is no doubt that deputies were able to express strong criticism of the government.[116] In Bulgaria under the royal dictatorship people were certainly not free, and opponents could be sent to concentration camps. But at least its citizens were not subjected to constant ideological indoctrination. Within limits—and if the term is ever valid—this was a liberal dictatorship. In the years preceding the outbreak of war, the political strategy of Boris III involved an attempt to provide stabilization at home, national independence in foreign affairs, and close economic cooperation with Germany without dependence on Hitler.[117] Sofia was forced to change course only in 1940, after the Italian invasion of Greece. Here Bulgarian revisionist demands against Athens, which had never been abandoned, played a significant role.

4. GREECE

For Greece, unlike Albania, Bulgaria, and Yugoslavia, the historical and political turning-point of the interwar years came in 1923 rather than 1918. It then became apparent that many of the objectives for which the Greeks had striven at the peace negotiations in 1919–20, and which had been expressed in the treaties of Sèvres and Neuilly, could not be achieved. The effects on both the internal and foreign politics of Greece were considerable.

In particular, the provisions of the treaty of Sèvres, which was signed on 10 August 1920 but not ratified by the Turkish parliament, were overturned.[118] The treaty had stipulated that eastern Thrace as far as the Chatalja line, as well as the islands of Imbros and Tenedos, should be ceded to Greece. Turkish territory in Europe was thus reduced to a relatively narrow strip of land west of the Straits. Italy, which along with Greece, Britain, and France hoped to profit from the break-up of the Ottoman empire, was awarded the Dodecanese. Greek administrative authority was recognized in the zone of İzmir (Smyrna); after five years the inhabitants were to be given the chance to unite with Greece on the basis of a plebiscite.[119]

At the peace negotioations Greece also secured parts of southern Albania and what was formerly Bulgarian southern Thrace. The Greek decision to enter the war on the side of the Allies, taken on 2 July 1917, thus seemed to have been fully vindicated. Only at that stage had the struggle between King Constantine I, who wanted to follow a pro-German course of neutrality, and

---

[116] Ibid. 1251.
[117] Ibid. 1252; Hoppe, *Bulgarien*, 34.
[118] Keskin, *Türkei*, 51–2.
[119] Schulz, *Revolutionen*, 249–64; also for the treaty of Sèvres and its consequences.

the pro-British prime minister Eleftherios Venizelos,[120] been resolved in favour of intervention.

By mid-1917 the dispute had resulted in unrest akin to civil war, with two Greek governments in being and with a call by Venizelos, encouraged by the British, for revolution. The issue was finally resolved by the Allies with an ultimatum to the king, to abdicate or risk the bombardment of Athens. Constantine I went into exile in June 1917, though he did not formally abdicate. His place on the throne was taken by his second son Alexander instead of the crown prince, who was regarded as pro-German.[121]

By 1920 the fact that Constantine had not officially stepped down became significant. When Alexander died in October and his younger brother Paul refused to accept the crown, the November elections turned into a vote on the return of Constantine. The population was deeply divided between royalists and supporters of Venizelos. However, a majority supported the relatively unambitious arguments of the royalists, with their support for demobilization, a period of peace, and moderation in territorial matters.[122] In December a plebiscite smoothed the way for Constantine's return to Athens.[123]

This event had serious consequences, mainly in foreign affairs. Efforts to implement the Allied war aims had led to a partial occupation of Turkey, which was shaken by internal unrest stoked up from abroad. Greek soldiers invaded Anatolia in June 1920, ostensibly to restore order.[124] Bursa and Edirne (Adrianople) were occupied without significant resistance. However, subsequent military developments were to damage Greek finances as well as the national morale. The position quickly deteriorated to a dramatic degree.

Developments were triggered, if not actually caused, by the return of Constantine. London and Paris, long weary of the conflict, distanced themselves from Greek affairs. War loans were cut off. The French supported Turkey directly by sending military equipment and staff officers. Though British conduct was more restrained, the lifting of the naval blockade against Turkey and the halting of weapons deliveries to Greece made the British attitude clear.[125]

The royalists then chose to adopt the Greater Greek slogans of Venizelos, though their election victory and the popular approval for the return of the king had been based on the belief that peace would at last be secured. They were thus steering a war course which had lost all prospects of success now that Britain and France had changed their approach towards the Turkish question. None the less, in March 1921 the Greeks launched an attack on Kemal Atatürk's troops.[126] After an initial retreat, the Turks launched a

[120] Richter, *Griechenland*, 29 ff.
[121] *Südosteuropa-Handbuch, Griechenland*, 16.
[122] Richter, *Griechenland*, 31.
[123] Manousakis, *Hellas*, 122.
[124] Jäschke, 'Osmanisches Reich', 544–5.
[125] Manousakis, *Hellas*, 122–3.
[126] On Atatürk's policy and strategy see also Keskin, *Türkei*, 55–8.

devastating counter-offensive in 1922 which virtually threw the Greek forces into the sea.[127]

It has been rightly observed that the 'collapse of the Greek army in Asia Minor [was . . .] the greatest turning-point in modern Greek history' after the war of independence (1821–30).[128] The Greek presence in Asia Minor, a tradition dating from antiquity, was ended. King Constantine was forced to abdicate for good, to be followed, for a short period, by George II. The treaty of Lausanne, though failing to fulfil all the Turkish demands, made the provisions of Sèvres a dead letter. Turkey held on to the Straits as well as its former possessions in Europe and Asia Minor; this was the chief result of the terms of 24 July 1923.[129] Furthermore, the Turkish victory led to massive shifts in population, reflecting the efforts of Kemal Atatürk to establish the new Turkey as a national state, limit its territory to Anatolia and Thrace, and abandon all claims to Arabia. In the resulting 'Turkization' many crimes were committed against Greeks, Armenians, and Kurds.[130] For Greece itself, Lausanne meant the loss of eastern Thrace, Smyrna, and certain islands. Apart from the Dodecanese—ceded to Greece by Italy only in 1947—the boundaries of the modern Greek state were thereby established.[131] Immediately after the Graeco-Turkish war Athens was confronted with a wave of ethnic Greek refugees from Asia Minor. This was mainly the result of an agreement of January 1923 between Greece and Turkey, providing for an exchange of Muslim citizens of Greece for Greek Orthodox citizens of Turkey.[132] Taking 1919 as the benchmark, the influx of refugees and immigrants from Turkey, Bulgaria, and the Soviet Union led to a population increase of 28 per cent.[133] In an agricultural country such circumstances inevitably raised the issue of land reform. The peasants, working on farms which were too small and were handicapped by the prevailing monoculture, remained a factor of unrest.[134]

For our purposes, the political consequences of the débâcle in Asia Minor are especially significant. At first there were brutal acts of revenge against the opponents of Venizelos, who were held responsible for the disaster. After bitter political conflict a republic was proclaimed on 25 March 1924. The army, which had a great deal of influence, had forced King George II into exile beforehand. A plebiscite in April brought an overwhelming majority for the republic. Yet its foundations remained insecure, since the regime was stubbornly rejected by the conservatives.[135]

The instability of the political system can be demonstrated by a few facts: between 1924 and 1928 Greece experienced eleven governments, eleven military coups, three elections, and two military dictatorships.[136] Hostility between

---

[127] Richter, *Griechenland*, 31–2.   [128] Hering, 'Griechenland', 1314–15.
[129] Schieder, 'Neuordnung Europas', 129.
[130] Schulz, *Revolutionen*, 261.   [131] Richter, *Griechenland*, 32.
[132] Jäschke, 'Türkei', 1340–1.   [133] Hering, 'Griechenland', 1315.
[134] Further details on economic issues in Richter, *Griechenland*, 32–41.
[135] Manousakis, *Hellas*, 123–37.   [136] Richter, *Griechenland*, 42.

republicans and conservatives (or, more accurately, royalists) was not about democracy as a political system in itself, which had been emerging gradually since the last quarter of the nineteenth century. Instead, it revolved around the issue of the head of state. The supporters of the republic wanted a president elected for a limited period, to prevent abuses of power such as had been practised by Constantine I during the First World War.[137] In contrast, the royalists valued the monarchy as a stabilizing factor.

Greek domestic politics in these years thus contained a number of dangerously unstable factors.[138] Nor was calm restored in foreign affairs after the defeat in Asia Minor. In the late summer of 1923 tensions were provoked by the Italian invasion of Corfu, an act represented by the Fascists as retaliation for the murder in obscure circumstances of the Italian member of the commission set up to regulate frontier issues between Athens and Tirana.[139] The occupation came to an end after a few weeks, since Mussolini was as yet unable to defy international opinion.[140] However, other dangers remained. In October 1925 war with Bulgaria seemed likely when the military dictatorship under General Theodoros Pangalos ordered Greek troops into Bulgarian territory on account of a frontier incident. Since Bulgaria was demilitarized, the argument of the Pangalos regime—that Bulgaria had been about to attack—appeared ludicrous. Athens was rightly ordered by the League of Nations to withdraw its troops and pay compensation.[141]

Foreign relations became more stable only after the treaties of friendship with Italy in September 1928, with Yugoslavia in March 1929, and with Turkey in October 1930. The success of this diplomatic offensive, particularly the almost revolutionary improvement in Graeco-Turkish relations, was due to Venizelos, who, amid chaotic internal conditions, had again become prime minister in July 1928.[142]

Venizelos was less fortunate in domestic politics. When Greece began to suffer severely from the world depression at the beginning of the 1930s, the head of government fell. He was paying the price for the decline in agricultural exports, the collapse of the main earner of foreign exchange, viz. revenue from merchant shipping, the rapid fall in the value of the currency, and all those shortcomings in the wake of the depression which led to deteriorating living conditions, discontent, and protest strikes. It mattered little that the economic crisis had an international dimension and that not all these problems were home-grown. From late summer 1932 until March 1933 the republicans fought to retain their hold on power. Though their conduct was sometimes unscrupulous, it was ultimately futile; the March election was won by the royalists. Even then domestic tranquillity was not restored. The notorious cycle of Greek politics in the postwar years began afresh: attempted coups and

---

[137] Hering, 'Griechenland', 1316–17.
[138] Manousakis, *Hellas*, 138.
[139] Hering, 'Griechenland', 1317.
[140] Salvatorelli and Mira, *Storia d'Italia*, 293–6.
[141] Hering, 'Griechenland', 1320.
[142] Richter, *Griechenland*, 42.

assassinations, and repressive measures by the party in power. By June 1935 the royalists had prevailed. However, conflict now broke out between the moderate and extreme factions among them, culminating in the triumph of the extremists in November. King George II was able to return from exile on the basis of a plebiscite which was manifestly and unashamedly rigged.[143] The new monarchy was based on fraud.

Irrespective of this fact, George II and the royalists soon faced other problems, which were ultimately suppressed, though not eliminated, by the dictatorship. One difficulty was that the king, who was initially anxious for a reconciliation between the opposing parties, remained a foreigner in his own country. Moreover, the Greek army, purged of liberal and republican elements, was rightly regarded as thoroughly royalist, which removed some of the credibility from the king's efforts to reach a settlement. In January 1936 elections were held; the royalists, confident of the king's authority over the population, did not manipulate the results. However, the election revealed that the republicans were as strong as the monarchists. With the aid of deputies from the people's front, which was regarded as Communist, the liberal forces appeared on the verge of forming a government. The army turned to the king, who in turn put pressure on the liberals; the result was the creation of a 'non-political' government under Konstantinos Demertzis. But the new premier died suddenly at the beginning of April 1936, and George II took the fateful step of appointing the former army minister, General Ioannis Metaxas, as prime minister. At the outset Metaxas used emergency decrees to allow him to rule until the end of November. Members of parliament went on forced leave, not, as originally planned, until November 1936, but until the end of the Second World War.[144]

The route to dictatorship was far from original: suppression of strikes which had their roots in social problems; police terror; arrest and deportation of union leaders; purging the army of remaining liberal elements; preparation of the armed forces for a coup; and—always a major argument of authoritarian 'saviours of the fatherland'—invocation of the Communist peril. Too many people allowed themselves to be duped, although a Communist danger to the state existed only in the fantasies of the royalists. Ultimately, democracy was sacrificed to liberate Greece from a fictitious threat. The general moved to incapacitate parliament when workers organized strikes to protest against developments. In May 1936 a general strike broke out in Salonika; Metaxas deliberately exaggerated its significance and provoked a climate akin to that in Germany after the Reichstag fire. The king was persuaded to agree to a dictatorship.[145]

George II appeared to hesitate at first. But although liberal politicians and

---

[143] Hering, 'Griechenland', 1322 ff.; Manousakis, *Hellas*, 143–4; Richter, *Griechenland*, 42–6; in contrast Nolte, *Faschistische Bewegungen*, 193, seems to regard the results of the plebiscite as genuine.

[144] Hering, 'Griechenland', 1324.

[145] Richter, *Griechenland*, 46–53.

other groups offered him a democratic alternative on 3 August, he proclaimed the dictatorship on the following day.[146] This was

> exclusively an anti-constitutional action on the part of the king and Metaxas. Neither the parties nor the military... had played an active role. The domestic political instability of the republic (between 1924 and 1936 there were 21 changes of government) had contributed to a situation in which nobody offered resistance [*the present author would say* 'resolute resistance'] to Metaxas on 4 August. The presence of his friends in leading military positions tipped the balance towards unresisting acceptance of the dictatorship by the people and the parties, whose leaders were arrested and banished.[147]

There has been some dabate about whether George II 'opened the door to fascism' with his decree of 4 August 1936. Can the period between 1936 and 1941 accurately be described as 'monarcho-fascist'?[148] Some historians have argued that the Metaxas regime was initially influenced by 'the German model', but thereafter emerged as a typical 'royal and military dictatorship'. Subscribers to this view concede that there were fascist movements, such as the Ethnikē Enosis Ellados, the Greek National Socialist Party, the Sidera Irini, and the Pan-Student Association. However, these are regarded merely as 'semi-fascist' organizations. If they had been genuinely fascist they would have been unsuited to the national character of the Greeks, a people 'quick to rouse and also quick to tire'. These historians also claim that 'tensions with Italy and the traditional Western orientation of the country' made it difficult for fascism to gain ground in Greece.[149] Though such arguments cannot be dismissed entirely, they are less than convincing in view of the experience of Italy. And as far as relations between Greece and Italy are concerned, there was also the friendship treaty of 1928. Another theory sees Metaxas as the 'pupil of Mussolini', at least in his basic political principles. His regime, based on the army and police, had modelled itself in its 'outward forms' on the Fascist example.[150]

It seems beyond doubt that Metaxas at least tried to apply fascist forms of government in Greece. But this does not in itself prove that his regime was actually fascist. Though there were fascist and National Socialist influences on the dictator, he and his followers did not possess any specific 'totalitarian ideology'. Moreover, there was no fascist mass movement; the 'Organization of Youth' (EON) cannot be regarded as an adequate counterpart. Furthermore, while Metaxas used repressive measures at home to guarantee a superficial calm and order, brutalities of this kind are not the sole prerogative of fascism.[151]

A more sophisticated view seems appropriate to Greek conditions in those years. In foreign policy, it has been demonstrated[152] that although Athens never co-operated closely with Rome, at the official level it did everything

---

[146] Hering, 'Griechenland', 1324.   [147] Manousakis, *Hellas*, 144–5.
[148] Richter, *Griechenland*, 55; Cliadakis, 'Metaxás', 21–35.
[149] Nolte, *Faschistische Bewegungen*, 193–4.
[150] Schramm-von Thadden, *Griechenland*, 8–9.
[151] Manousakis, *Hellas*, 146–7.   [152] Borejsza, *Il fascismo*, 61–4.

possible to avoid unnecessary friction. However, the Greek population flatly rejected fascism. Fear of the expansionist ambitions of an apparently powerful Italy played a part here, alongside the individualism of the Greeks themselves. The totalitarian state was alien and unattractive to them, or at least to the majority; the fascist or semi-fascist movements—chauvinist, anti-Communist, and anti-Semitic—were virtually associations of outsiders. But the attitude of the population was not identical with that of the Metaxas regime. Its record was unenviable: murders and deportations in large numbers; censorship and the prohibition of opposition parties; the establishment and operation of a secret police modelled on that of totalitarian states; the ruthless involvement of the heads of local administration in the service of the regime; and the organization of young people on the model of the Hitler Youth. Attempts were also made to adopt the leadership cult of Italy and Germany. These facts argue strongly against a sympathetic view of the Greek dictator,[153] portraying him as a devoted father of his nation. Such arguments are reminiscent of descriptions of Hitler by his inner circle, where the mass murderer appears in a petty bourgeois milieu. During the rule of Metaxas, Greeks were subjected to arbitrary deportation, imprisonment, and murder—approximately 50,000 of them, according to some estimates. Books were also burnt, a process which brings discredit on any regime which orders it. Authors treated in this way included not only Marx and Engels but Sophocles and Thucydides, Goethe, Heine, Shaw, Freud, and Fichte. The youth organization encouraged its members to adopt the mindless and totalitarian slogans of 'one people, one king, one leader, one youth'. Here the models were the Germans and Italians—not surprisingly, since Metaxas showed himself eager to ape the conduct of Hitler and Mussolini.

Admittedly, Metaxas also introduced a number of progressive social measures: the eight-hour day, a minimum wage, and state job-creation schemes. But at the same time he forged increasingly close links with Nazi Germany from 1937 onwards. After the outbreak of the Second World War he made vain attempts to avoid a conflict with the Axis by pursuing an opportunistic policy of accommodation. But by 1940 at the latest, as we shall see, Mussolini actually wanted war.

In summary, it seems clear that Metaxas had strongly fascist inclinations. If he did not succeed in turning Greece into a genuinely fascist state, this was owing to the recalcitrance of the Greeks themselves and not to any reluctance on the dictator's part.[154] Metaxas failed to make headway on many issues. Yet what distinguished his dictatorship from its predecessors was the fact that it was 'not intended as an emergency solution for a transition period, nor did it seek opportunities for pseudo-democratic legitimation like the Pangalos government. [Instead it desired] to establish a fascist state on a permanent

---

[153] See Schramm-von Thadden, *Griechenland*, 9.
[154] Borejsza, *Il fascismo*, 64.

4. Greece

basis and a "third Greek civilization", a successor to classical antiquity and Byzantium.'[155]

Recent historians have refused to accept palliative descriptions of the Metaxas regime. Sympathetic interpretations were based either on the myth that Metaxas had saved Greece from the Communist threat, or on the fact that the dictator, whose foreign policy had previously oscillated between Berlin and London, memorably defied his former mentor Mussolini on 28 October 1940. Yet this conduct does not affect the assessment of his regime. It is not tenable to weigh his domestic policies against his subsequent opposition to Fascist Italy and even National Socialist Germany in foreign affairs; the existence of the latter does not diminish the significance of the former.

Metaxas can fairly be regarded as a favourite of Constantine I, and a man driven by egotism and plagued by complexes. During the interwar years he was 'involved in every conspiracy and attempted coup by the extreme right'. Twice sentenced to death and pardoned, at the beginning of the 1920s Metaxas was in exile in Italy. From this period dates his sympathy for fascism as a political system.[156] By now there is broad agreement about the character of his rule in Greece.[157] Particularly significant is the determination of historians to refute any notion that it was simply a military or royal dictatorship; instead, there is an insistence on the fascist nature of the regime. The evidence used to support the argument is convincing, provided it is recognized that, on account of the unique features of the Greek party system, a mass party was not a *sine qua non* of fascist rule or a fascist seizure of power. Many other characteristics of fascism were apparent: glorification of the nation; emphasis on the external enemy; propaganda for the strong state; a moral code based on military thinking; the leadership principle; the ideology of the 'national community'; job creation by means of labour service in paramilitary organizations; a large degree of immunity for the economic oligarchy; pseudo-socialist tactics in dealing with the workers; anti-Communism and terrorist methods in internal affairs.[158]

The question of whether the dictatorship of General Metaxas was fascist, semi-fascist, or less than that cannot be answered definitively here. It must suffice to bear in mind the wide variety of opinions on the subject, ranging from absolute assertion to an equally clear denial of its fascist character.

Any attempt to summarize developments in south-east Europe during the interwar years must take into account a number of factors.

The aim of the peace settlement after the First World War—involving, among other things, the inclusion of the countries of south-east Europe in a zone of democratic and anti-Communist states—could not be realized.

To explain this failure, account must be taken of the historically rooted

---

[155] Hering, 'Griechenland', 1325.
[156] Richter, *Griechenland*, 55.
[157] Ibid. 56–61.
[158] Ibid. 61–4.

ethnographic, territorial, religious, and economic structures of these countries, on which internal political conditions were directly dependent.

Tensions which had emerged before the First World War, or broke out at its end, continued to affect multilateral relations in the interwar years. There was one perspective of the victors and another of the vanquished; but hardly anywhere was there a genuine commitment to peace. Both revisionist ambitions and attitudes in support of the status quo had a more or less direct influence on internal politics. Factors such as the world economic crisis or the war between Greece and Turkey served to intensify or accelerate the process of destabilization.

One consequence was that the democratic and parliamentary states of south-east Europe were transformed fairly rapidly into authoritarian systems of government after 1919. Though these systems cannot be described as wholly fascist, they revealed a more or less marked affinity with fascism in their forms of rule.

Finally—and most significantly, as will be seen in the next chapter—all these states lacked genuine independence in terms of power politics. This factor contributed greatly to their internal instability. In fact, structural conditions in Albania, Bulgaria, Greece, and Yugoslavia after the First World War made such independence impossible to achieve; dependence on one or other of the European great powers was the result. In the political interplay between Athens, Belgrade, Sofia, and Tirana on the one hand, and Berlin, Rome, London, and Paris on the other—to name only the most important political centres—economic conditions, which we have so far touched on only lightly, further restricted the political freedom of manœuvre of the states of south-east Europe.

II. German and Italian Policy towards the States of South-east Europe

BOTH before and after 1933 economic needs determined the relations between Germany and south-east Europe. In market terms, the countries of the region satisfied German requirements to a great degree; they were equally suitable as an outlet for German products and as an area from which Germany could import materials it lacked. According to a brief study of 1941 by Ulrich von Hassell, the special position of south-east Europe for the foreign economic needs of Germany rested on three circumstances:

1. a broad, multi-faceted, and expandable agricultural foundation;
2. a considerable wealth of the most varied mineral resources, not yet fully ascertained;
3. a general agricultural and social primitiveness, somewhat varying in degree but common to the whole region, due to shortage of capital.[1]

It should be remembered that, geographically, the region was adjacent to Germany in the latter's borders of 1938. It was also an advantage that from a certain stage it became possible to use German export goods as direct payment for imports from south-east Europe.

Von Hassell, who renewed his interest in the south-east in January 1941, had acquired an intimate knowledge of conditions there as minister in Belgrade (1930–2), as ambassador to Italy (1932–7), and finally as a member of the executive board of the Central European Economic Forum.[2] Particularly during his years in Italy, he became the advocate of a special concept of south-east Europe within German foreign policy;[3] this, as will be seen, had its effect on German–Italian relations.

If the aims of Italian policy in the region are examined against the background of German interests, it is clear that south-east Europe provided another field of conflict for German–Italian relations. For Italy, the states in question formed an important market, by no means fully developed. Partly to ensure their dominance, the Fascists intended to pursue a rigorous policy of penetration vis-à-vis these countries. Such a policy was intended to block British, and especially French, influence on the Balkan peninsula, and also to put a stop to German penetration of the region.[4]

---

[1] Hassell, 'Deutschland', quotation p. 322; slightly abridged text in *Zeitschrift für Politik* under the title 'Wirtschaftliche Interessen'.
[2] *Hassell Diaries*, 5–6, 37.
[3] Petersen, *Hitler—Mussolini*, 77–80.
[4] Collotti, 'La politica dell'Italia', 5–6; also D. M. Smith, *Mussolini*, 154; and especially Rusinow, *Austrian Heritage*, 226–32, for an excellent survey of the economic aspects.

1. POLITICAL AND ECONOMIC DEVELOPMENT IN THE INTERWAR PERIOD

At the beginning of the 1920s Germany set about intensifying its trade relations with the states of south-east Europe. As a parallel development, there was an escalation of German–Italian rivalry in the region. German export policy had previously been concentrated mainly on overseas lands; the reason for the new direction was that from the middle of 1929 overseas exports were declining rapidly. To counteract the resulting trade deficit and the growing crisis in foreign trade, Germany sought to develop new outlets in continental Europe.[5]

However, the problem was still unsolved when the National Socialists came to power in Germany. Hjalmar Schacht, president of the Reichsbank, became *de facto* minister of economics on 30 July 1934 and was officially appointed minister on 31 January 1935. He had become convinced that, compared with German import requirements, the volume of exports was completely inadequate. His deliberations culminated in the 'new plan'. Schacht's solution to the chronic shortage of foreign exchange was more complex than can be described here, but at its centre was the following basic idea:

If a country has insufficient foreign exchange to permit it to buy what it needs anywhere and everywhere, then the question of cheapness ceases to be of interest, and the main question becomes whether it is possible to obtain the desired goods anywhere at all, even at high prices. Might it not therefore be possible to find countries which would be willing to sell their goods not against payments in their own currency, but against some other consideration? This other consideration... could only be German goods. Thus I had to look around for agricultural and raw material producing countries which would be willing to take German goods in exchange for the foodstuffs and raw materials they produced. Bilateral commercial agreements with such countries were the solution.[6]

Particularly in south-east Europe and South America, there were enough states prepared to accept an opening of the German market for their goods on the terms established by Schacht. The 'new plan' was astonishingly successful. The German trade balance went into the black, the import of foodstuffs and raw materials increased, that of finished products declined by two-thirds.[7] Over these years, the economic relations of Bulgaria, Greece, and Yugoslavia with Germany underwent a considerable change; the German share of their trade rose appreciably.[8]

German–Albanian trade relations were much less significant. Germany

---

[5] Petersen, *Hitler—Mussolini*, 50–1.
[6] Schacht, *Account Settled*, 80–1.
[7] Ibid. 12–13; on economic questions in general see vol. i of the present work, II.IV–VI (Volkmann).
[8] See e.g. the report by the president of the German–Bulgarian chamber of commerce and the Bulgarian consul-general von Brandenstein, PA, HaPol. IVa, Bulgarien, Akten betr. Handelsbeziehungen zu Deutschland; also *Griff nach Südosteuropa*, 25. As the calculations produce very different results, no details will be given here.

was not even mentioned in surveys of Albanian exports. In 1937–8 Albania obtained most of its imports from Italy, and sent an even greater proportion of its exports to that country.[9] The figures serve to confirm that, economically and politically, Albania was virtually an Italian protectorate from the end of the 1920s. However, as regards the development of trade with Bulgaria, Greece, and Yugoslavia between 1929 and 1937, it is clear that Italy was outstripped by Germany.[10]

Even in comparison with Britain, France, and the United States, Germany established a clear lead in trade with south-east Europe.[11] From 1934 onwards the states of south-east Europe were increasingly drawn into the German economic orbit. Almost inevitably, such great reliance on one trading partner impaired the activity of Bulgaria, Greece, and Yugoslavia on the world market and thus produced dependence on Germany. Only the Greeks proved able to withstand the economic pull of the Third Reich. As was recognized, for example, in London by the mid-1930s, Berlin exploited the economic terrain in order to establish a hegemonic political position in the south-east. A number of factors assisted the Germans in accomplishing these changes in their foreign-trade policy and thus initiating political penetration: the economic structures of the states involved; international market conditions; and the inability of the democracies to offer an alternative.[12]

Now that the basic outline of relations between Germany, Italy, and southeast Europe has been delineated—anticipating the historical course of events—we shall describe the German–Italian relationship regarding policy towards south-east Europe as a background against which to interpret relations with the individual states of the region.

Within the framework of German–Italian relations as a whole, the particular problems of the south-east had caused concern in Rome even before the Nazi seizure of power. At the end of 1932 Mussolini proposed an economic and political co-operation in which Germany and Italy would share the south-east European market. Though the German foreign ministry regarded the suggested agreement on detailed trade questions as of little use since it could scarcely be realized, it favoured the creation of a relationship of trust in trade policy, based on reciprocal information. However, Baron Constantin von Neurath, the Reich foreign minister, knew that every attempt to reach agreement in the past had failed owing to genuine differences as well as mistrust and technical difficulties. In February 1933 he assured the Italians that Germany did not desire a special political relationship with the states in ques-

---

[9] Skendi, *Albania*, 226.
[10] See n. 1 above.
[11] Ibid.; also Günzel, 'Wirtschaftliche Entwicklung', 225; Wuescht, *Jugoslawien*, 92; Hoppe, *Bulgarien*, 50–1; *Griff nach Südosteuropa*, 25; Wendt, 'England', 499; Milward, 'Reichsmark Bloc', 404.
[12] Still highly informative in this context is an investigation based on detailed evaluation of contemporary literature by Treue, 'Das Dritte Reich', 47–64; see also Avramovski, 'Isolation', 261.

tion. There could therefore be 'no idea of any political "expansion towards the south-east"'. Berlin was simply concerned 'to work for a gradual loosening-up and, if possible, the eventual breakup of the Little Entente'. The plan was primarily anti-French; Paris had been the dominant force in the alliance system of 1920–1, which was directed against revisionist objectives and in which Czechoslovakia, Yugoslavia, and Romania had united fairly clearly against Hungary, Bulgaria, and Austria. However, Neurath also thought that his plan would serve Italian interests. Germany, he declared, was in agreement with Italy's plans to achieve 'predominance in the Danubian basin'. The only differences between them concerned Austria.[13]

Shortly afterwards, Under-secretary Gerhard Köpke, head of department II (western, southern, and south-eastern Europe) in the foreign ministry, described the situation bluntly to the ambassador in Rome, Ulrich von Hassell.[14] He argued that German and Italian interests in the Danube region did not run parallel. 'Unreserved collaboration', he believed, was only conceivable in certain specific circumstances, though he was basically in favour of co-operation with Italy. Köpke seems to have had a precise knowledge of the economic and political value of south-east Europe to Germany.

In contrast, von Hassell believed that a settlement with Italy was essential to the success of German policy in the south-east. He did not think it sensible to try and convince Mussolini that Germany had no thought of an 'expansion towards the south-east'. The Italians knew as well as the Germans that the region was of interest to both states and could thus 'some day' lead to conflicts.[15] Hassell had a number of objectives in view: if not political hegemony in the south-east, then at least a dominant position for Germany; a weakening of France, which would be achieved by German–Italian agreement on outstanding questions; and steps towards a new development of German power, in which south-east Europe had its own assured position.[16] Such concepts underpinned his continued insistence on closer German–Italian co-operation in the region.[17]

By the end of October 1933 German–Italian relations had deteriorated considerably, mainly as a consequence of German withdrawal from the League of Nations.[18] Hassell, however, again proposed to Neurath that Berlin should adopt an accommodating approach to Mussolini's policy in the Danube area.[19]

---

[13] *DGFP* c i, No. 14, pp. 29–34 (7 Feb. 1933).
[14] Ibid., No. 27, pp. 57–60 (20 Feb. 1933).
[15] Ibid., No. 35, pp. 74–8 (23 Feb. 1933).
[16] On this subject see Petersen, *Hitler—Mussolini*, 77–80.
[17] *DGFP* c i, No. 51, pp. 106–11 (6 Mar. 1933); No. 64, pp. 128–9 (8 Mar. 1933); No. 388, pp. 715–16 (3 Aug. 1933); No. 397, p. 731 (8 Aug. 1933); No. 448, pp. 838–40 (24 Sept. 1933); No. 485, pp. 893–7 (6 Oct. 1933). In these documents Hassell's ideas, already mentioned, were repeated, amended, and given more precise form, particularly in a 'five-point programme' for German–Italian co-operation in the Danube region.
[18] See vol. i of the present work, IV.II.3 (Messerschmidt).
[19] *DGFP* c ii, No. 28, pp. 43–6 (25 Oct. 1933); on the Italian government's memorandum of 29 Sept. 1933, with concrete proposals for an improvement of the economic situation of the Danube states, see *DGFP* c i, No. 485, pp. 893–7, here 896–7 n. 5, of 6 Oct. 1933.

The foreign ministry now appeared sympathetic, if not to this recommendation itself, then at least to the ambassador's plea that German–Italian policy should at last be put on a mutually agreed basis.[20]

At the beginning of December Hassell and Mussolini exchanged views about international developments. Their conversation included the complex 'general problem' of the Danube, which was of crucial importance for the German–Italian relationship in the early years of Hitler's dictatorship.[21] The ambassador submitted a five-point programme he had drafted, which Berlin had been aware of for some time; in Hassell's view this offered a suitable basis for the co-ordination of German–Italian policy in the south-east, at least in the early stages.[22] Hassell argued that German–Italian support for the Balkan states should at first be concentrated on Bulgaria and Hungary. He regarded bilateral negotiations with the various governments as essential, partly to prevent the creation of blocs and circumvent existing ones. Trade policy towards the countries of the Little Entente should be agreed in order to bring them to 'the same common denominator'. On the basis of these general guidelines, he hoped to bring about a comprehensive agreement on the economic activity of Germany and Italy in the south-east.

In theory the proposal seemed likely to have a positive effect on the German–Italian relationship. But at a second glance it was obvious that their relations in the south-east could not be interpreted as purely economic or seen in isolation. Without going into too much detail, it must be remembered that all these issues depended on two major factors: first, on the role of the south-east in international politics;[23] and second, on the conflict of interest between Rome and Berlin over relations with Austria.[24] In the early 1930s, therefore, the relationship between Germany and Italy was less harmonious than might have been expected, given the ideological affinity between Fascism and Nazism.

In mid-February 1934, Hassell submitted a political report which drew attention to Italian plans for a customs union between Rome, Vienna, and Budapest. His comments gave some indication of the difficulty in obtaining genuine German–Italian co-operation in the south-east;[25] equally, it was clear to initiates that Rome was playing the Hungarian–Austrian card against Berlin. Although the Italians denied any anti-German intentions, the ambassador emphasized that the Fascists were gradually developing their economic relations with the Hungarians and Austrians in the direction of a firm economic

---

[20] *DGFP* c ii, No. 67, p. 123–5 (13 Nov. 1933).
[21] Ibid., No. 104, pp. 181–3 (17 Dec. 1933).
[22] Ibid. i, No. 485, pp. 893–7 (6 Oct. 1933), here 896.
[23] Still important here are Hillgruber, *Südost-Europa*, 11–35; Wendt, 'England', 483–512; Schröder, *Deutschland und die Vereinigten Staaten*, 265–83; Teichova, 'Wirtschaftsinteressen'; and in particular Wendt, 'Strukturbedingungen'.
[24] Still unsurpassed for an overall view is Petersen, *Hitler—Mussolini*, passim.
[25] *DGFP* c ii, No. 257, pp. 487–91 (15 Feb. 1934).

community of interests. 'In the final analysis', this would come close to the 'idea of the customs union'.²⁶

It must be borne in mind that such plans were developing in Italy alongside the intensifying German–Italian antagonism over the Austrian question. Even in 1933 Hassell had repeatedly warned of the 'increasing' danger of an 'Italian economic policy in the Danube region which would block off' Germany. The Italians remained fearful of 'the victory of National Socialism in Austria in the foreseeable future'; in February 1934 this anxiety seemed to arouse their desire for specific economic agreements to strengthen Vienna's will to resist any Anschluss attempt, whether begun internally or from outside. Once again the ambassador described his concern lest Italian fears of an overwhelming German drive to the south-east—after union with Austria—might lead to political hostility between Berlin and Rome. To avoid such an outcome, Hassell recommended a concerted German–Italian economic policy towards the states of south-east Europe.

However, any political design was complicated by the Balkan pact of 9 February 1934 between Greece, Yugoslavia, Romania, and Turkey, which faced Italy with a completely new situation. In the pact the signatories gave reciprocal guarantees of their common borders and—in the German interpretation—*all* one another's frontiers. They also agreed to co-ordinate their policy towards those Balkan states which did not belong to the pact, by means of an early and reciprocal exchange of information on intended measures. It was clear enough that the agreement was directed against Bulgarian revisionism, and was therefore likely to increase tensions in the south-east.²⁷

As regards the issue of a customs union, the Germans assumed that neither Austrian nor Hungarian economic circles were in favour of the project, since the farmers' interests would be damaged by the creation of an economic bloc of this kind. That was certainly the case, and even in Italy the project had few supporters in economic circles. The union would undoubtedly have brought political advantages by turning Austria and Hungary into clients of Italy, but it offered no prescription for remedying the serious Italian trade deficit with these two countries. Hassell remained convinced that Mussolini had no desire for an open and serious breach in German–Italian relations; he therefore assumed that, despite all friction, the goal of Italian policy in the south-east was restricted 'to maintaining Austria and Hungary economically and politically independent, while protecting Italian influence and preventing too great a slide into the German sphere of influence'.²⁸

German discussions concerning Mussolini's current and future intentions were unexpectedly interrupted by the Rome protocols of 17 March 1934. In these treaties Italy, Austria, and Hungary agreed on measures of political and

---

²⁶ On the tradition of such ideas see Petersen, *Hitler—Mussolini*, 80–3.
²⁷ *DGFP* c ii, No. 246, pp. 463–4 (10 Feb. 1934).
²⁸ See n. 25 above; also *DGFP* c ii, No. 292, pp. 549–50 (10 Feb. 1934).

economic co-operation. Rome thereby secured political dominance within the triangle, but had been forced to make major economic concessions to achieve it. Mussolini was probably prepared to do so because of his direct, long-term political objective of tying Vienna into close association with Rome. This policy, clearly aimed against Berlin, had serious implications for the development of German–Italian relations. In the course of the negotiations over the three protocols he therefore gave a guarantee to Austria which was itself a slap in the face for Hitler. Though policy towards Austria cannot be described in detail here, for both Italy and Germany it was a central element in relations with the states of south-east Europe. Vienna was at the hub of Italian calculations, since Austria's independence of Nazi Germany was an essential precondition for the success of Italian plans to prevent German penetration of the south-east.

The Germans were well aware of the situation in general. Yet there had been no overt change in German–Italian relations, so that the signing of the Rome protocols came as a shock to the foreign ministry. The diplomats in the Wilhelmstrasse regarded the agreement, in the words of State Secretary Bernhard von Bülow, as directed against Germany 'in the whole way it came about and in its political motives'. Hitler's foreign policy had suffered an obvious setback. Nevertheless, Berlin continued to adopt a restrained and considerate policy towards Rome. Such conduct was required by the real objectives of the Nazi regime,[29] which prohibited a confrontation with the power which, apart from Germany itself, was most committed to revisionist goals.

For the Germans 1934 had begun badly. Subsequently, in the summer of the same year, the murder of the Austrian chancellor, Dollfuss, led to a crisis in German–Italian relations. The Stresa front of 1935 revealed that these tensions had not eased.[30] It took the Abyssinian conflict to normalize German–Italian relations and point the way to closer co-operation. Ultimately, as a consequence of this development, the political balance in the south-east likewise altered.[31]

In his political report on Germany and the Abyssinian conflict[32] Hassell argued that one favourable effect of the changed international situation was that the African conflict was shifting 'the main thrust of Italian policy away from Austria to the Red Sea'. Moreover, Mussolini's adventure had also diverted attention from Germany at a time which was particularly useful for the latter's purposes. As regards the outcome of the diplomatic struggle and the military hostilities, the ambassador saw various possibilities with different consequences for Germany. There seemed little danger of an outright triumph for Italy, which would 'increase her great-power megalomania in Europe'.

---

[29] Petersen, *Hitler—Mussolini*, 319–27, quotation p. 326.
[30] See vol. i of the present work, IV.IV (Messerschmidt).
[31] Funke, *Sanktionen*, 45 ff.
[32] *DGFP* C iv, No. 360, pp. 744–7 (17 Oct. 1935).

Italian defeat appeared more likely. Yet Germany could not desire this, since the resulting tremors and internal changes within Italy might ultimately rob Germany of its chief revisionist partner in Europe. A compromise which did not genuinely satisfy Mussolini would also cause problems. 'Particularly if Italy, with the help of France, were to some extent to succeed in saving face, a very possible result would be increased dependence on Paris, and at the same time a resumption of the thrust towards the Brenner on the basis of a Franco-Italian agreement over the Danubian region.' Fear of possible co-operation between France and Italy against Germany persuaded Hassell to warn against forcing the pace in the Austrian question. This was far from a matter of course, since in the existing situation he was basically in favour of obtaining an assurance of Italian 'non-interference in the internal affairs of Austria'.

At the same time Franz von Papen, the German minister in Vienna, recommended a patient wait for further developments on the Austrian scene. The 'shift of forces on the European chessboard' would soon enable Germany 'actively to tackle the question of our obtaining influence in the south-east'.[33] There were both positive and negative signs to justify these views; and Hitler's uncommonly cautious conduct towards Italy reveals that they were shared at the highest levels.[34] Though the dictator's main desire was to solve the Austrian problem, he also wanted a more general change in the south-east.

In July 1936 a German–Austrian agreement provided a *modus vivendi* for the difficult political relationship between Berlin, Vienna, and Rome.[35] Henceforth, Germany and Italy moved towards an alliance, which took the form of the Axis[36]—not inevitably, but to some extent as a logical development.[37] Hassell once more took up the theme of south-east Europe in a political report of mid-July 1936, for the 'first time since his reports during 1933 and 1934 on the necessity of a German–Italian agreement of a political and, above all, of an economic kind in the Danubian basin'.[38] The ambassador claimed that Germany's present political and economic situation had much improved her negotiating position. While Italy's situation in the markets of the south-east had suffered as a consequence of League of Nations sanctions owing to the war in Abyssinia, the position of Germany had been strengthened in Italy and the south-east alike.

Neurath was even more specific at the end of August,[39] when he referred directly to Hassell's report. At the outset, the foreign minister outlined the success of the policy Berlin had pursued over the past few years. It had strengthened Germany's position in the Danube region by integrating the

---

[33] Ibid., No. 363, pp. 751–3 (18 Oct. 1935).
[34] Petersen, *Hitler—Mussolini*, 444–50.
[35] See vol. i of the present work, IV.v.1 (Messerschmidt).
[36] Schreiber, *Revisionismus*, 85.
[37] See vol. i of the present work, I.v.4 (Messerschmidt).
[38] *DGFP* c v, No. 457, pp. 774–9 (17 July 1936); for a survey of the period 1933–6 see Ádám, 'Pays danubiens'.
[39] *DGFP* c v, No. 523, pp. 936–42 (31 Aug. 1936).

1. Interwar Politics and Economics

economies of the south-eastern states with that of the Reich. Apart from direct benefits, the policy of economic penetration had also done much to promote political *rapprochement*. According to Neurath, important milestones on the route had been the trade treaty with Bulgaria,[40] concluded as early as 24 June 1932, and its counterpart with Yugoslavia on 1 May 1934.[41]

Thanks to the improved negotiating position, Berlin expected to reap advantage from German–Italian agreements over future economic and political conduct in the south-east. Now that the acute problems in German–Italian relations had been eliminated by the settlement of the Austrian question, a favourable moment for such agreements seemed to have arisen. Nevertheless, there were conditions to be met on the German side. For example, the Italians must accept that Berlin would continue to oppose and combat collective agreements, which included the Rome protocols as well as the treaty network of the Little Entente. The latter, indeed, was a primary target of German political and economic strategy. Germany was not even prepared to enter into trade discussions with such groups of states. Of course, aggressive intentions lay behind these fears of contact. German policy was framed in the hope that an attitude of extreme intransigence would prevent the emergence of similar groups and potential 'bridges to the creation of political blocs' with anti-German tendencies. Such aims were also behind the general demand that economic treaties by other states concerning south-east Europe should 'not be directed politically against third countries'. Beyond that, Berlin was willing to sanction such treaties only if it was 'asked for its agreement before their conclusion'. The German government justified its demands by reference to the conclusions of the Stresa conference of September 1932 (not to be confused with the 'Stresa front' of 1935). There the representatives of fifteen European states had concluded a treaty aimed at providing economic support for the countries of south-east Europe through a system of preferential tariffs based on bilateral treaties.[42] But in 1936 the Germans used the economic agreement of 1932 simply as a lever with which to realize objectives that were rooted in power politics.

Mussolini was attracted by the German ideas when Hassell presented them to him in autumn 1936. Admittedly, there were some differences on issues of detail. For example, Berlin advocated the establishment of good relations with Yugoslavia because Belgrade was not yet dependent on the Soviet Union;[43] Rome, on the other hand, had adopted a hostile approach to the Yugoslavs as a result of its involvement in Albania and its strong support for Hungary's

---

[40] Hoppe, *Bulgarien*, 37–8.
[41] *DGFP* c ii, No. 318, pp. 592–6 (12 Mar. 1934), for the preparations for the trade treaty; and ibid. iii, No. 23, pp. 54–6 (21 June 1934), on the assessment of the treaty and the official guidance. Details are discussed below.
[42] See in particular *DGFP* c v, No. 129, p. 169 n. 6, on the Stresa conference (5–20 Sept. 1932).
[43] Ibid., No. 534, pp. 962–3 (12 Sept. 1936).

revisionist claims. However, these tensions had eased somewhat in comparison with previous years.⁴⁴ When Ciano spoke to Neurath in October he mentioned that he had an 'improvement in relations between Italy and Yugoslavia so much at heart because Yugoslavia was at the moment one of the strongest bulwarks against Bolshevism in south-eastern Europe'. (Ciano was nothing if not an expert in the echo effect.) Moreover, Italy was determined to oppose the British 'encirclement policy in the Mediterranean'. Rome would therefore attempt to resolve its differences with Belgrade and even try to make relations with Yugoslavia as good as possible.⁴⁵ At the same time, despite his threatening gestures, Mussolini was striving for good relations with Britain; his tactical manœuvring in that direction must always be taken into account in interpreting the Italian *rapprochement* with Germany.⁴⁶

The aftermath of the Abyssinian conflict, the events of the Spanish civil war, and a diplomatic offensive in the south-east—all these factors provided the background for the convergence of German and Italian policy. In October 1936 Ciano finally visited Berlin,⁴⁷ where a protocol, the details of which had been worked out beforehand, was signed on the 23rd.⁴⁸ The event gave rise to Mussolini's famous statement in Milan on 1 November 1936:⁴⁹ 'this agreement, which has been fixed in special procès-verbaux, duly signed, this vertical line between Rome and Berlin, is not a dividing-line but rather an axis around which all European states animated by the will to collaboration and peace can collaborate.' As regards the south-east, however, the October agreements merely contained a few general phrases. At most, they can be regarded as non-binding declarations of intent:⁵⁰

The German and Italian governments will keep each other currently informed of the basic principles governing their commercial policies in the Danubian region.

While the two governments recognize the value of such co-operation, they reserve the right to have its nature and extent studied and fixed by their respective technical bodies.

The two governments confirm their opposition, both now and in the future, towards all endeavours to set up in the Danubian region, without the simultaneous participation of Germany and Italy, new economic organizations—such as, for example, economic integration of the Little Entente, or an economic integration in the sense of the Tardieu plan.⁵¹

---

⁴⁴ Ibid., No. 572, pp. 1041–5 (5 Oct. 1936).
⁴⁵ Ibid., No. 618, pp. 1125–30 (21 Oct. 1936).
⁴⁶ De Felice, *Mussolini il duce*, ii, esp. pp. 344–58.
⁴⁷ See *DGFP* c v, No. 583, pp. 1061–2 (12 Oct. 1936); No. 588, p. 1065 (12 Oct. 1936); No. 593, pp. 1072–3 (13 Oct. 1936); No. 597, p. 1075 (14 Oct. 1936); No. 603, pp. 1090–1 (15 Oct. 1936).
⁴⁸ Ibid., No. 624, pp. 1136–40 (23 Oct. 1936).
⁴⁹ Ibid. vi, editors' note, 1; see De Felice, *Mussolini il duce*, ii. 353–4; Petersen, *Hitler—Mussolini*, 490 ff.; Wiskeman, *Rome–Berlin Axis*, 68.
⁵⁰ *DGFP* c v, No. 624, pp. 1136–40 (23 Oct. 1936), here 1137.
⁵¹ The plan by André Tardieu, the former French prime minister and foreign minister, which was discussed at the beginning of the 1930s, was designed to alleviate the economic crisis in south-east Europe, but also possessed clear foreign-policy implications directed not least against Hungary.

Historians have criticized the protocol as representing no real progress.[52] It is rightly judged to 'give a clear insight into the real aversion of Rome and Berlin to codified treaties at this stage'.[53] On the other hand, the protocol must be seen against the background of the conversation between Ciano and Hitler on 24 October.[54] During Ciano's visit to Berlin, Germany and Italy had given 'a first institutional guarantee' of their co-operation and articulated their desire to regard the 'Axis'—though the term was not yet used—as a 'loose alliance formed for [a] war of expansion'.[55]

In the October talks Hitler described the Mediterranean as 'an Italian sea' in which the interests of Italy must be given precedence, while Germany reserved the right to 'freedom of action in the east'.[56] But this did not mean—any more than the constant emphasis of both parties on anti-Communism meant—that Germany and Italy were abandoning their 'mutually competing' interests in the Danube region.[57] These played an important political role for the Italians, who had both expected and feared the 'return of Germany to the south-east European region'[58] even before 30 January 1933. Hitler's somewhat patronizing advice to Ciano on Italian conduct in the south-east is significant in this context.[59] Furthermore, before the German–Italian negotiations, Göring, who was appointed plenipotentiary for the Four-year Plan in October, warned that the agreements would oblige the German government to inform the Italians in detail of their economic and trade policy. The foreign ministry reassured him, however, that the wording offered the desired security.[60]

The main outline of German policy towards Italy down to autumn 1936, as far as south-east Europe was concerned, can be summarized as follows: without prejudice to their own economic policy, the Germans aimed at preventing other states from playing off Italy against Germany within the framework of attempts at a new economic settlement. The achievement of this goal was to lead to the increasing integration of Rome in German calculations and thus to a weakening of Mussolini's position *vis-à-vis* Hitler. Berlin was successful in this, thanks in part to the international situation. The Italians were forced to accept obvious breaches in their policy of preventing German penetration of the south-east, particularly in Austria. After 1935 neither Berlin nor Rome adopted political tactics which would exclude the possibility of joint actions; nevertheless, in the south-east each country was determined to get the better of its ostensible partner and thereby achieve its own goals without conflict. It is therefore no surprise that the south-east remained a problem area in

---

[52] Borejsza, 'Rivalität', 600; De Felice, *Mussolini il duce*, ii. 353.
[53] Funke, 'Deutsch-italienische Beziehungen', 833–4.
[54] Published in *Ciano's Diplomatic Papers*, 56–60.
[55] Thus Petersen, *Hitler—Mussolini*, 502; see also ibid. 490 ff.
[56] *Ciano's Diplomatic Papers*, 57.
[57] Funke, 'Deutsch-italienische Beziehungen', 835.
[58] Petersen, *Hitler—Mussolini*, 80.
[59] *Ciano's Diplomatic Papers*, 58–9.
[60] *DGFP* c v, No. 618, p. 1129 n. 9 (21 Oct. 1936).

German–Italian relations even after October 1936. Significantly, after his return to Rome Ciano seems to have made optimistic remarks about almost every issue he had discussed with Hitler; on the subject of relations with the states of south-east Europe, however, he kept silent.[61]

In December 1936 Germany and Italy finally signed a protocol on co-operation in the Danube region, which referred specifically to point 8 of the agreement of 23 October. The two countries agreed to keep each other informed about their economic policy towards 'a Danubian state' and to assist each other in implementing it. However, this decision related only to Yugoslavia.[62]

Italy abided by the agreement.[63] Yet it was apparent that, in contrast to the development of German–Yugoslav relations, the search for an Italo-Yugoslav *rapprochement* was seriously hindered by the Albanian question. The Yugoslavs wanted Albania to be completely independent of Italy.[64] However, despite Ciano's announcement of a readiness to negotiate, the Italians were never genuinely willing to contemplate this prospect. It should be pointed out here that in 1939 the Italians reacted extremely negatively to the slightest suggestion of a German involvement in Albania. Politely, but with absolute determination, Ciano stressed that all matters concerning Albania were regarded as 'a purely Italian family affair'. Though not yet in a legal sense, the country was *de facto* an Italian 'province'. The enormous sums which Rome had invested there prevented Mussolini from allowing any other power, even Germany, from entering into competition with Italy.[65]

With his policy towards Yugoslavia, Mussolini intended to integrate the country into the German–Italian sphere of influence, to destroy the alliance system created by France in south-east Europe, and to frustrate the objectives of Franco-Soviet policy in the region. Certain sacrifices were justified to achieve these goals. Yet the project appeared so ambitious that German scepticism about prospects for its success were understandable.[66] However, in March 1937 Yugoslavia and Italy signed a political and an economic agreement, both of which were made public, and in addition a secret exchange of letters in which Rome recognized Albanian independence. In fact this was doubtless mere lip-service. More significant, however, was the secret understanding over the treatment of terrorists and Croat *émigrés*.[67] In the German

---

[61] Ibid. vi, No. 14, pp. 31–3 (6 Nov. 1936): report from an informant of the German ambassador.
[62] Ibid., No. 86, pp. 162–3 (10 Dec. 1936).
[63] Ibid., No. 138, p. 282 (12 Jan. 1937).
[64] Ibid., No. 143, pp. 294–5 (14 Jan. 1937).
[65] Ibid. D iv, No. 449, pp. 578–9 (10 Feb. 1936); and No. 450, pp. 704–5 (11 Feb. 1939), in which the Germans profess both their surprise at Italian sensitivity and their own innocence.
[66] See n. 64.
[67] *DGFP* C vi, No. 291, pp. 593–4 (23 Mar. 1937); directly on this subject see Bauer, 'Italien', here pp. 112–13; Meneghello-Dinčić, 'Politique étrangère', 58; Tasso, *Italia e Croazia*, i. 98–104; *Ciano's Diplomatic Papers*, 98–105, conversation with Stojadinović on 26 Mar. 1937.

foreign ministry the Italo-Yugoslav treaties were viewed with favour. It was thought that they would bring peace and a reduction of tension in Europe, as well as strengthening the principle of bilateral treaties as against the collective system. Moreover, they also meant that 'two anti-Bolshevik states have linked themselves more closely together'.[68]

Hitler's policy towards Austria was naturally a constant factor in all these changes. In view of the intended Anschluss, Berlin was bound to welcome signs of strain within the Little Entente (the alliance between Czechoslovakia, Romania, and Yugoslavia). The dictator's long-term policy towards Czechoslovakia was also in line with this.[69]

During the pact negotiations, the Italian government had put fresh life into its policy of *rapprochement* with Yugoslavia, which had tended to stagnate since 1928.[70] Rome had good reason to be content with the general outcome. Ciano believed that the French alliance system and the Little Entente had been 'seriously shaken'. As regards the difficult political relationship between Hungary and Yugoslavia on one hand, and Italy and Romania on the other, Rome now hoped to see some improvement without damage to Italian relations with Hungary.[71]

An impression of Italo-German agreement, willingness to co-operate, and community of interest had been created. But this was an illusion. Italian policy under Ciano pointed the way to a double game motivated by continuing fear of the German drive to the south-east. Hassell was aware that German–Italian relations were excellent for the present but could not be described as permanently stabilized. In a report of February 1937 he pointed out several potential dangers to the relationship. Among them was the problem of the Italians' reaction if the Abyssinian conflict should be settled by the League of Nations. It was also unclear how Mussolini would respond in the event of a seizure of power by the French right or the termination of the Spanish civil war. Equally, the current friendship might be destroyed by a political 'row' over Austria or 'a clash between German and Italian activity in the Danube region'.[72]

Shortly afterwards, the German minister in Belgrade, Viktor von Heeren, informed the foreign ministry of Ciano's remarks to Jovan Dučić, the Yugoslav minister in Rome, during the prelude to the pact negotiations with Yugoslavia. According to Heeren, Ciano had recognized the Anschluss as an inevitable development which the Italians could at most delay. Consequently, the German 'drive to the south' would have to be dealt with before long. This process, Ciano had said, 'would affect Yugoslavia as much as Italy. Germany was dangerous as an enemy, difficult as a friend.' Neither Rome nor Belgrade

---

[68] *DGFP* C vi, No. 297, p. 607 (28 Mar. 1937).
[69] See Blasius, *Großdeutschland*, 33.
[70] On the Yugoslav perspective see Hoptner, *Yugoslavia 1934–1941*, 61–85; for the Italian view Tasso, *Italia e Croazia*, i. 29–104.
[71] *DGFP* C vi, No. 298, pp. 608–9 (29 Mar. 1937).
[72] Ibid., No. 216, pp. 457–61 (18 Feb. 1937).

could abandon the desire for co-operation with Germany, but if this became impossible then the creation of a bloc by Italy, Yugoslavia, Bulgaria, and Romania was desirable. When Ciano added that this grouping should not be directed a priori against Germany,[73] this was only half the truth. Indirectly, through the establishment of a barrier somewhat further off than Austria—which would soon lose its blocking function—a proposal of this kind inevitably contained anti-German features.

When asked by the foreign ministry to ascertain whether Ciano had actually spoken along these lines, the German ambassador in Rome was unable to do so; but he believed that Heeren's report accurately reflected Ciano's views. Hassell had in the past frequently stressed that, for Italy, fear of the German 'drive to the south' was 'the very crux of the Austrian problem'. It could be no surprise if Ciano hoped to take precautionary measures in case co-operation with Germany ended in failure; in such a situation Rome was anxious 'not to be outdone' by Germany in relations with the south-east, Hassell regarded some of Ciano's reported comments to Dučić as highly significant, particularly his hints at a definite Italo-German understanding over spheres of influence. The suggestion was that Bulgaria and Yugoslavia, like Hungary and Romania, had been awarded to Italy. Since this was not the case, the ambassador regarded it as an attempt (clearly unsuccessful) to sow mistrust between Berlin and Belgrade.[74]

After the conclusion of the Italo-Yugoslav treaties in March 1937, in view of the 'vigorous Italian activity' in the Danube basin Hassell believed that the danger of a German–Italian conflict of interest in the region was increasing.[75] Italian activity was being stepped up perceptibly. Against British resistance, the Italians were attempting to reach an understanding with Turkey modelled on their treaties with Yugoslavia; furthermore, they hoped to include Greece in a 'Mediterranean agreement'. However, London managed to thwart all these efforts.[76] Barely a year later—on 20 April 1938, after the Anschluss—the new German ambassador in Rome, Hans Georg von Mackensen, reported to Weizsäcker, secretary of state in the foreign ministry, that discussions in the Palazzo Chigi (the Italian foreign ministry) were revolving around the question of how Hitler would solve the 'German question'. This was regarded not merely as a problem of space, but primarily as the need to secure resources which would guarantee Germany's economic, and therefore also political, independence'. Italian politicians saw two possible solutions for Germany: 'either by way of Russia, or else by way of the old *Drang nach Südosten* in the direction of Constantinople, Baghdad, and the Persian Gulf.' If Berlin chose the second route, it would inevitably lead to confrontation with Italy's many

---

[73] Ibid., No. 254, pp. 515–16 (8 Mar. 1937); on the Anschluss issue in the context of the south-east see *Anschluß 1938, passim*.
[74] *DGFP* c vi, No. 274, pp. 559–61 (15 Mar. 1937).
[75] Ibid., No. 312, pp. 641–3 (12 Apr. 1937).
[76] Ibid., No. 354, pp. 726–7 (4 May 1937).

1. Interwar Politics and Economics

interests 'in the Balkans, in the Mediterranean, and in the Near East'. Conflict would then become a possibility. Some circles in the Palazzo Chigi evidently feared that 'from Constantinople Germany will, so to speak, press on Italy's flank in the Mediterranean'.[77] Once again, Italian diplomats were facing the problem that was to exert a decisive influence on the Italo-German alliance during the Second World War.[78] But in 1938, despite all premonitions, future developments could not be predicted accurately. Here as elsewhere, events were not predetermined; there was only a certain probability that relations would develop in the manner suggested.

In this complex situation the Anglo-Italian agreements of 16 April 1938 were signed shortly after the Anschluss. To attentive observers it must have seemed that Italy had re-established 'greater freedom of movement in questions of central and south-eastern Europe' by means of her *détente* with London. Furthermore, there was anxiety in Berlin that relations between Germany and Italy might deteriorate. Since the disagreement between Britain and Italy over Italian aggression in Abyssinia had been ended by diplomatic means, Mussolini felt less exclusively dependent on Hitler's support.[79] At least in theory, he now had the chance to concentrate on regaining the influence in the south-east which Italy had lost during the Abyssinian conflict.

Developments in the south-east continued to indicate fierce German–Italian competition and the danger of a deterioration in relations. In the first half of 1939, when Hitler disposed of rump Czechoslovakia, Mussolini sought to emulate German success by occupying Albania; the areas of friction within the Axis, long perceptible in outline, were once more manifest. For the time being, however, the two partners remained dependent on each other. For that reason Mussolini was unable to play the British card. On 6–7 May 1939, virtually on the eve of the Pact of Steel,[80] there was a further exchange of views between Ciano and Ribbentrop. At this meeting in Milan south-east European issues were discussed for the last time before the outbreak of war.[81]

Italy now declared itself prepared to respect the status quo in Yugoslavia, but reserved the right to alter its position in the event of a major crisis in that country. The minority question thus had not been eliminated as the vehicle of Italian policy towards the Balkans. Berlin was chiefly interested in ensuring Yugoslav neutrality in wartime, and Belgrade had already announced that it would provide economic support to the Axis powers in the event of conflict.

---

[77] Ibid. D i, No. 745, pp. 1082–3 (20 Apr. 1938).
[78] Schreiber, 'Italien', 255–67.
[79] Memorandum of 27 Apr. 1938, *DGFP* D i, No. 755, pp. 1097–11.
[80] See vol. i of the present work, IV.VI.2 (Messerschmidt); still unsurpassed is the investigation by Toscano, *Origins*; comprehensive treatment in De Felice, *Mussolini il duce*, ii. 613–25, paying particular attention to the role of the 'disposal' of rump Czechoslovakia and the conquest of Albania; also D. M. Smith, *Mussolini*, 231–7.
[81] *DGFP* D vi, No. 341, pp. 450–2 (18 May 1939); *Ciano's Diplomatic Papers*, 283–6, discussion of 6–7 May 1939; Ciano's position according to *DGFP*, Ribbentrop's according to *Ciano's Diplomatic Papers*, quotations from *DGFP*.

Otherwise, the Germans made no objection to Italian ambitions. Ribbentrop accepted as a matter of course that Italy's dominant influence in the region must be secured in the event of the internal disintegration of Yugoslavia. Since the occupation of Albania, Ciano had regarded Greece as fully integrated into the Italian sphere of influence. Ribbentrop was in full agreement; indeed, he was eager to exploit the chaotic internal situation in Greece to depose the Greek king, who was hostile to the Axis. As regards Bulgaria, both sides agreed to do all they could to prevent the country from responding to constant promptings from the Western powers and Turkey and joining the Balkan pact. In other words, the Germans and Italians intended to provide unconditional support for the regime in Sofia. Though all Ciano's remarks on such occasions need not be taken at face value, he revealed a tendency of Italian foreign policy by observing that 'for an armed conflict, we must have our way clear over the Balkan states. These states must either agree to a disarmed neutrality or be occupied.' Before 28 October 1940 (the Italian attack on Greece) the issue really appeared as simple as that. And the Italian foreign minister also let slip Mussolini's version of the future policy of the Axis: 'Toujours parler de la paix et préparer la guerre.'

In this outline of developments in German–Italian relations concerning south-east Europe it is clear that in 1937–8 there was, if not an outright diplomatic offensive, at least a renewal of Italian efforts to achieve predominance in the region. We shall now attempt to describe the relationship of the Axis powers with the individual states of south-east Europe. German–Italian interests in the area will act as a criterion for organizing the material, always with the aggressions of autumn 1940 and spring 1941 in mind. However, the account must also be extended back to cover the 1930s. Within this analysis, Albania is a special case. It will therefore be described at the end of the section; this will allow the Albanian experience to provide a transition to the phase of German–Italian policy in south-east Europe after the outbreak of war, and gives the opportunity for an assessment of British and French reaction to the events of March and April 1939.

(a) Bulgaria

At the beginning of 1934 Bulgaria found itself more obviously isolated than before. Its government had clung, not always intelligently, to its revisionist demands at the four Balkan conferences between 1930 and 1933. As we have seen, on 9 February 1934 Greece, Yugoslavia, Romania, and Turkey finally concluded the Balkan pact in Athens. The treaty was directed unequivocally against Bulgarian revisionism,[82] stating that the 'maintenance of the present

---

[82] Rhode, 'Die südosteuropäischen Staaten', 1248; *DGFP* c ii, No. 246, pp. 463–4 (10 Feb. 1934), for the official German verdict on the Balkan pact, which on the whole was sceptical or even hostile.

territorial order in the Balkans is irrevocable for the treaty partners'. The meaning was unmistakable.

Almost inevitably, Bulgaria's isolation led it to move towards even closer cooperation with Germany and Italy. Rome had already paid much attention to Bulgaria in the 1920s, since the country appeared as a potential ally within the framework of Mussolini's revisionist policy. Besides the existing common ground in foreign affairs and ideology, the Fascist regime also took advantage of economic factors to establish the best possible relationship with Bulgaria. One starting-point in attempts to extend Italo-Bulgarian economic cooperation was the fact that Bulgaria's ties to the Central powers had been greatly damaged by the conclusion of the First World War. Nevertheless, the Bulgarian market remained what it had traditionally been—linked with, and dependent on, Germany. The country was only fourth among Italy's trade partners in the Balkans, after Yugoslavia, Romania, and Greece. Of course, trade balances do not in themselves say anything definitive about capital investment and its associated economic and political influence. As Italian capital was more comprehensively committed than German, Rome certainly played a greater role than Berlin in Bulgarian economic life.[83] If the enterprises concerned were unable to bring about a reorientation of Bulgarian trade policy, this was probably due to the structure of the market.

Germany, to which Bulgaria had first drawn close in the 'wake of Austria-Hungary',[84] remained an extremely important partner for the country after 1918. Though the Bulgarians were aware that they remained partly dependent on the Germans, they did not abandon the pursuit of an autonomous policy. It was entirely possible that some cracks would appear in the German–Bulgarian community of interest. France and Britain attempted to drive a wedge between the two states, but made their efforts too late.[85] In any case, they faced serious difficulties. The ties between Germans and Bulgarians, who liked to refer to themselves as the 'Prussians of the Balkans', were many, and were not based on calculation alone.[86] Such factors must be taken into account in any consideration of developments. Moreover, the country remained fragmented internally; only Boris III, who appeared to emerge strengthened from every crisis, represented at least an element of calculability in its affairs.[87]

However, the king did not enter blindly into a German–Bulgarian alliance. Instead he was anxious to move cautiously and steer a neutral course, a task which proved difficult both for complex domestic reasons and because of the external situation. Boris himself described his political tightrope act very vividly: 'My army is pro-German, my wife is Italian, my people pro-Russian, and I am the only one in this country who is pro-Bulgarian.'[88] Bulgarian foreign policy after the National Socialist seizure of power in

[83] See in particular Collotti, 'Il ruolo', 54–9; also the survey in Cohen, 'Pillage', 43.
[84] Hoppe, *Bulgarien*, 24.   [85] Stefanov, 'Politique', 1–4.   [86] Miller, *Bulgaria*, 7.
[87] Gorneski and Kamenov, 'Politique', 23–4.
[88] Quoted in Hoppe, *Bulgarien*, 44.

Germany has been described as the attempt to obtain 'the greatest possible gain for the country with the least possible commitment, by means of a cautious *rapprochement* with the Third Reich'.[89]

In this process, a development occurred which was of great significance for German policy in the south-east, as the king emerged as the mediator between Germany and Yugoslavia. Boris himself was especially anxious for an understanding with Yugoslavia, which he regarded as essential if his country was to be stabilized economically. To achieve it he was even ready to make painful concessions on the Macedonian issue, a course which involved great personal risks at home. During talks on this question, held in the first instance with King Alexander of Yugoslavia, the Yugoslavs aked Boris to inform the Germans of their desire for a German–Yugoslav *rapprochement*.

Subsequently, there emerged a degree of economic and political co-operation between Berlin, Belgrade, and Sofia which seemed likely to change the balance of power in the region.[90] Boris III left no doubt about the anti-French, and also anti-Italian, objective of this policy. Alexander for his part hoped to draw closer to Hitler in order to shake off, or at least reduce, the burdensome patronage of France; while Boris wanted to establish a pro-Bulgarian German–Yugoslav spearhead to provide effective resistance to the Italians, who were attempting to make use of his country to achieve their anti-Yugoslav objectives.

Largely as a consequence of the murder of Alexander in Marseilles in October 1934, agreement between the two states became more difficult to reach. However, on 24 January 1937 a Yugoslav–Bulgarian friendship and non-aggression treaty was finally signed in Belgrade.[91] This agreement, avowing 'inviolable peace and heartfelt, eternal friendship',[92] was to acquire particular significance for Bulgaria with regard to the German aggression against Yugoslavia in the spring of 1941.[93]

In 1937 German politicians welcomed the *rapprochement* between Bulgaria and Yugoslavia, since it appeared to undermine the collective alliance system in general and the Balkan pact, which the Germans opposed, in particular.[94] Such trends appeared to be confirmed by the conclusion of the Italo-Yugoslav agreements of March 1937. Of course, it could also be argued that the Bulgarian–Yugoslav pact actually strengthened the Balkan pact by achieving a *rapprochement* between Bulgaria and one of its members.[95] But after weighing both sides of the question, one must conclude that the treaties of January and March 1937 weakened rather than strengthened the collective alliance system; they demonstrated a trend towards disintegration rather than stability.

---

[89] Rhode, 'Die südosteuropäischen Staaten', 1251.
[90] *DGFP* c ii, No. 291, pp. 547–8 (1 Mar. 1934).
[91] Ibid. c vi, No. 132, pp. 264–5 (8 Jan. 1937).
[92] Rhode, 'Die südosteuropäischen Staaten', 1251.
[93] See III.II.2 below (Vogel).
[94] Hoppe, 'Balkanstaaten', 170.
[95] Hoppe, *Bulgarien*, 47, claims also to recognize an element in the Bulgarian–Yugoslav *rapprochement* which was directed against the predominance of the Axis.

1. Interwar Politics and Economics

Parallel to these movements in foreign policy, the Germans after 1933–4 achieved a steady improvement in their economic position in Bulgaria. Some fluctuations in the trade balance occurred, but these did not signify any break in the process, or affect the central issue of the economic integration of Bulgaria with Germany. Consequently, Germany accounted for a much larger proportion of Bulgarian imports and exports than was the case inversely.[96] The situation was thus one of Bulgarian dependence, highly advantageous to Berlin.

On 12 March 1938, as Hitler ordered the Wehrmacht into Austria,[97] Germany and Bulgaria signed a 'secret protocol' on the delivery of German war materials (except aircraft) to Bulgaria. Arms purchases worth approximately RM30m. were agreed, to be delivered 'as soon as practicable, but at the latest within two years'. Sofia was given five years to repay the 6 per cent loan, beginning in 1942, with an option for extension of the repayment period.[98] At first glance the two sides had finally concluded a matter which had been the subject of inconclusive negotiations in 1935, 1936, and 1937. But the Bulgarians were not fully satisfied, since they had expected to get much more.[99]

Nevertheless, the affair had made it clear that Boris III did not intend to become a satellite of Hitler. The Bulgarians remained eager to maintain their freedom of decision in foreign affairs and occasionally warned the Germans to respect this position.[100] Yet they were still conciliatory, offering recognition and sympathy for the German cause. This attitude was displayed after the Anschluss and during the crisis between Germany and Czechoslovakia in May 1938.[101] But Boris made it clear that he objected to foreign duress. When the Italians made a clumsy attempt to apply such pressure, he declared to the Axis representatives in Sofia that 'Bulgaria wished to conduct her foreign policy without any fixed commitments, and that such an independent policy was precisely in the interests of the "Axis", rightly understood.'[102]

In August 1938 the Bulgarians concluded a credit agreement with a French banking group for the delivery of goods such as 'railway equipment and armaments', which were traditionally German exports. As far as the Germans were concerned, this was taking Bulgarian independence a little too far. When the subject was broached, the Bulgarians innocently maintained that 'the agreement with France was modelled on the agreement of 12 March 1938 with Germany'.[103] To avoid other 'surprises', they informed the Germans that the

---

[96] Ibid. 38, 48–9; very informative on German–Bulgarian trade relations between 1931 and 1941 is Habedank, 'Eingliederung'.
[97] See vol. i of the present work, IV.v.7(a) (Messerschmidt).
[98] *DGFP* D v, No. 181, pp. 254–5 (12 Mar. 1938).
[99] Ibid. c iv, No. 14, pp. 17–18 (5 Apr. 1935); No. 48, pp. 83–4 (25 Apr. 1935); No. 481, pp. 961–3 (2 Jan. 1936); No. 557, pp. 1128–30 (12 Feb. 1936); vi, No. 559, p. 1075 (22 Sept. 1937).
[100] Ibid. D v, No. 202, pp. 278–9 (13 May 1938).
[101] Ibid., No. 206, pp. 283–4 (31 May 1938).
[102] Ibid., No. 210, pp. 286–8 (22 June 1938).
[103] Ibid., No. 217, pp. 296–7 (10 Aug. 1938).

British were also eager to provide them with a loan. Boris was much in demand; he was well aware that London and Paris were offering attractive bait in an attempt to weaken Bulgaria's links with Germany. Following strong German hints, the Bulgarian minister in Berlin attempted to calm the situation. His country, he assured the Germans, had 'made no commitments of any kind and would not sell her friendship with Germany for the mess of pottage represented by this loan'.[104]

Comments of this kind were welcome to the Germans, and were probably truthful. However, the Bulgarians were applying some pressure of their own; the Germans had been told more or less directly that it was up to them to provide more loans and to deliver more goods more quickly. They could then make the orders in France a triviality. Eugen Rümelin, the German minister in Sofia, therefore recommended an additional loan of up to RM45m.[105] The sum was discussed and accepted by the economic-policy department of the foreign ministry on the grounds that it offered a 'further improvement of Germany's economic position in the Balkans' as desired by Berlin. Besides, it would presumably prevent the Bulgarians from trying to obtain further loans from the Western powers in future. The Third Reich also had a clear interest in 'completing Bulgaria's rearmament with German arms and excluding other countries from participating in it'.[106]

The arguments of Emil K. J. Wiehl, head of the trade and economic-policy department, were not without force. His recommended solution was such as to encourage a relationship of political dependence. Of course, there were some unknown quantities, due to the absolute priority attached to Germany's own war preparations. Accordingly Wiehl added various reservations to his remarks. However, at the beginning of 1939 the Germans were inclined to make concessions to the Bulgarians, while telling Sofia in no uncertain terms that Bulgaria would be expected to toe the line politically in return for an 'increase in the armaments credit to Bulgaria'.[107] Shortly afterwards the foreign ministry informed the finance ministry that it was considered 'absolutely essential, for political considerations' to comply with the urgent Bulgarian request for more war materials. Wiehl then recommended a loan of RM20–2m. on the same terms as on 12 March 1938. Göring's consent was dependent on 'an appropriate share in the exports of desired raw materials from Bulgaria',[108] while the Reich minister of economics supported the loan without objections.[109]

However, the Bulgarian response was one of disappointment that the

---

[104] Ibid., No. 222, pp. 301–2 (31 Aug. 1938).
[105] Ibid., No. 226, pp. 306–7 (26 Sept. 1938).
[106] Ibid., No. 250, pp. 333–4 (15 Nov. 1938).
[107] Ibid., No. 301, p. 401 (23 Feb. 1939); No. 302, p. 402 (24 Feb. 1939); No. 303, pp. 402–3 (24 Feb. 1939).
[108] Ibid., No. 315, pp. 416–17 (15 Mar. 1939).
[109] Ibid., No. 314, pp. 415–16 (15 Mar. 1939).

loan was so small.[110] The government in Sofia pressed for more; ideally it would have liked equipment for two divisions from the material seized in Czechoslovakia. Pointing to the 'threatening situation' in which Germany found itself in international affairs,[111] the Bulgarians argued that it was in the German interest to comply with their requests. Ribbentrop now endorsed a loan of RM45m.[112] On 21 April 1939 Germany and Bulgaria signed a second 'secret protocol' embodying the same financial conditions as in March 1938. As a side-effect, these conditions enabled the Germans to intervene even more decisively in the Bulgarian economy. To ensure that sufficient mineral resources would be extracted to cover the required part of the loan, German specialists were to be brought into the country, German industry was to be enlisted 'first of all', and the raw materials themselves were to be delivered to Germany on a preferential basis.[113]

The Bulgarians, currently worried by the Anglo-Turkish *rapprochement* and made insecure by border incidents in the Dobrudja and by problems on the Greek–Bulgarian frontier, continued to press for the delivery of seized Czech weapons.[114] Boris III asserted that the country had enough weapons and materials to wage a war lasting exactly two weeks. In May 1939 he even asked for the accelerated delivery of small submarines (of 250 t.) from Germany for the defence of his Black Sea coast.[115] Over the following months the Bulgarians pressed repeatedly for concessions.[116] The Germans were generally prepared to satisfy Bulgarian wishes,[117] though not for submarines, since Hitler had specifically forbidden it.[118] Bulgaria was already in a difficult position in foreign affairs: there were tensions with Romania over the Dobrudja; Bulgarian demands for treaty revision in eastern Thrace had created ill feeling with Turkey; the same was true of relations with Greece over western Thrace; finally, Yugoslavia would be an uncertain neighbour in time of crisis, now that conditions in Macedonia appeared more unstable following the resignation of the Stojadinović government on 4 February 1939.[119] This was the political background against which Berlin decided to deliver small arms, machine-guns,

---

[110] Ibid. vi, No. 17, pp. 17–18 (17 Mar. 1939); No. 63, pp. 73–4 (21 Mar. 1939).
[111] Ibid., No. 218, p. 268 (17 Apr. 1939).
[112] Ibid., p. 268 n. 3.
[113] Ibid., No. 243, p. 303 (21 Apr. 1939); also directly relevant is No. 566, pp. 785–6 (24 June 1939).
[114] Ibid., No. 392, p. 514 (16 May 1939).
[115] Ibid., No. 415, pp. 547–8 (21 May 1939); this was a question of two submarines which were to be delivered to Bulgaria before the completion of the submarines ordered in Germany: see No. 728, p. 1005 (27 July 1939) and vii, No. 12, p. 11 (10 Aug. 1939).
[116] Ibid. vi, No. 480, pp. 645–6 (6 June 1939); No. 500, p. 687 (9 June 1939); No. 656, pp. 904–5 (12 July 1939).
[117] Ibid., No. 508, pp. 698–700 (12 June 1939); No. 659, pp. 908–9 (12 July 1939); vii, No. 11, p. 10 (10 Aug. 1939), on the delivery of machine-guns; also No. 12, p. 11 (10 Aug. 1939).
[118] Ibid. vii, No. 33, pp. 31–2 (11 Aug. 1939); No. 34, p. 33 (11 Aug. 1939).
[119] Ibid. vi, No. 673, pp. 923–6 (14 July 1939); on the aims of Bulgarian revisionism and their adaptation to political developments in the first half of 1939 see also No. 67, pp. 75–6 (22 Mar. 1939); No. 320, pp. 415–16 (3 May 1939).

and armoured cars from Czech stocks to Sofia. For the time being, because of Germany's own needs, U-boats were not supplied.[120]

It is not the case that in the last months before the war Germany seriously intended to demand that Bulgaria join the anti-Comintern pact in return for the military assistance she had received. The idea was considered, but not adopted.[121] However, Rome and Berlin agreed that Bulgaria must draw even closer to the Axis and abandon its tactical manœuvres. The chances of achieving such a situation were quite good, but the issue did not seem urgent, either in Rome or in Berlin. The time for definite moves to fulfil Bulgarian territorial demands did not appear to have arrived. For one thing, Bulgaria was not yet adequately armed; and secondly, the relationship of the Axis powers with Bulgaria's neighbours compelled restraint.[122]

The Bulgarians probably took a similar view. However, they desired to counter the attempts of other powers to drive a wedge between Germany and the Balkan countries after the outbreak of war; in other words, Bulgaria would pursue a pro-German policy.[123] After the conclusion of the non-aggression treaty between Germany and the USSR,[124] the Bulgarian foreign minister, Georgi Kioseivanov, claimed that it 'had convinced even those who had so far opposed co-operation between Bulgaria and Germany of the rightness of the Bulgarian government's policy'.[125] The Bulgarian government was able to consolidate its domestic political position as a result of the Germany–Soviet pact. The pro-Western liberals were weakened and the pro-Soviet groups gradually came over to the side of the government. After the pact was signed (on 23 August 1939), the danger of a Balkan enterprise by the Allies—together with Turkey—seemed to have receded. For the time being, Bulgaria's situation seemed easier than before.[126]

(b) *Yugoslavia*

The Yugoslavs had no real interest in a revision of the Versailles peace settlement, certainly not one achieved outside the League of Nations. In this context, their main concern was with the attitude of Italy.[127] After the National Socialists came to power, the Yugoslavs grew increasingly anxious that a German–Italian *rapprochement* might encourage Mussolini to embark on an

---

[120] Ibid. vii, No. 78, pp. 86–7 (16 Aug. 1939); also No. 1, p. 1 (9 Aug. 1939); No. 60, p. 66 (14 Aug. 1939); No. 101, pp. 109–10 (17 Aug. 1939); vi, No. 508, pp. 698–700 (12 June 1939); No. 617, pp. 847–52 (5 July 1939); No. 618, pp. 852–8 (6 July 1939); No. 656, pp. 904–5 (12 July 1939).
[121] Ibid. vi, No. 479, pp. 644–5 (5 June 1939).
[122] Ibid., No. 476, pp. 640–1 (5 June 1939).
[123] Ibid. vii, No. 168, pp. 177–8 (21 Aug. 1939).
[124] See vol. i of the present work, IV.VI.4 (Messerschmidt).
[125] *DGFP* D vii, No. 314, pp. 320–1 (26 Aug. 1939).
[126] Hoppe, *Bulgarien*, 67 ff.
[127] *DGFP* C i, No. 99, pp. 182–3 (16 Mar. 1933).

aggressive policy.¹²⁸ The Yugoslavs deliberately took an intransigent approach to the issue of treaty revision whenever the Germans and Italians raised it. For example, in May 1933 Berlin sought to discover how Yugoslavia would react to the question of a return of the territories it had been awarded in the peace treaty.¹²⁹ Not surprisingly, the German minister reported that Yugoslavia would reject any such request out of hand.¹³⁰

Unlike the relationship between Bulgaria and the Third Reich, German–Yugoslav relations were complicated by a divergence of interest over a central foreign-policy objective of Berlin, the revision of the Paris peace treaties. The problem inevitably affected German policy towards the other states of south-east Europe. In the words of Franz von Papen, German minister in Vienna from the end of 1934, south-east Europe was 'the natural hinterland of Germany as far as the Turkish border'.¹³¹ But in order to achieve its political aims in that area, Berlin had to proceed with the utmost care.

What were these aims? They involved the achievement of control and hegemony, not necessarily by means of aggression, though this was discussed even before the outbreak of the war. Initially, as the example of Bulgaria also demonstrates, the Germans attempted to destabilize international relations. The aim was to play off the individual states against each other;¹³² to undermine the collective-pact system by means of bilateral treaties; to isolate the states of the region, partly by means of economic penetration; and then to exploit the situation to establish the supremacy of Germany.¹³³ In German–Italian relations it became apparent that although the Nazis and Fascists both advocated treaty revision, their interests concerning individual questions were often opposed. The policy of the two states towards Yugoslavia reveals this fact clearly.¹³⁴

Economic agreements, while naturally of intrinsic value in ensuring the supply of raw materials and foodstuffs to Germany,¹³⁵ also served as a vehicle for political penetration.¹³⁶ Such penetration is the ruling theme of German diplomacy towards Yugoslavia. It has been argued that the objective underlying the south-east policy of the Third Reich was 'to amalgamate the national economies in this area under German leadership into a greater economic area, on the basis of equal partnership and recognition of the political sovereignty of

---

¹²⁸ Ibid., No. 279, pp. 508–12 (1 June 1933). Italo-Yugoslav relations are considered in detail in the collected volume *L'imperialismo italiano*: for the interwar years and World War II, pp. 179–602.
¹²⁹ *DGFP* c i, No. 266, p. 495 (27 May 1933).
¹³⁰ Ibid., No. 345, pp. 617–19 (30 June 1933).
¹³¹ *IMT* xxviii, doc. 1760-PS, p. 272: affidavit of 28 Aug. 1945 by the former US consul-general in Vienna, here relating to a statement by Papen in 1934; on sources of similar tenor see Schröder, 'Südosteuropa', 243–4.
¹³² Cf. Zografski, 'Macedonia', 383 ff.
¹³³ Collotti, 'Penetrazione', 284; Schröder, 'Südosteuropa', 243.
¹³⁴ Schumann, 'Aspekte', 222.
¹³⁵ Schönfeld, 'Rohstoffsicherungspolitik', 215–29.
¹³⁶ Cvijetić, 'Yugoslavia', 185.

these states'.[137] Such views are entirely unrealistic, and have rightly been rejected.[138] The prevailing view of foreign trade was that it was essential to create organized economies which covered large areas and gave priority to autarky over global trade with all its incalculable elements; but the idea was accompanied by a conviction that great powers such as Germany must dominate the small and medium-sized states which were more or less dependent on them. In such a view of policy, as Wilhelm Treue pointed out in 1953, 'freedom' boiled down to the privilege of the great powers. For these privileged states, economic independence was a vital component of sovereignty. But at the same time the number of truly sovereign states was inevitably reduced to a quite small group.[139] The south-east European countries were certainly not among them.

Yugoslavia was a classic example of the translation of these economic ideas into practical politics, and one in which the striving for autarky betrayed the predominance of military motives. In a ministerial conference on 7 April 1933 the German foreign minister, Neurath, had emphasized that the aim was to provide economic support for Yugoslavia for two reasons:[140] first, 'in order to gain political influence'; and secondly, to preserve this 'important market' for German exports. German policy towards Yugoslavia then developed with great consistency along these lines, with all their economic and political implications.[141]

In the prelude to negotiations for the trade treaty of 1934 it was indicated, for example, that Berlin was ready to make concessions to Yugoslavia in the field of financial policy. The German approach was based partly on the purely economic desire to increase German exports. More important, however, was the declared aim 'to establish a strong trading-base within the economic sphere of the Little Entente'. In the long term German policy was directed against two centres of international trade, represented by Rome on the one hand and Paris and Prague on the other. Berlin had already succeeded in finalizing economic agreements with Hungary to frustrate the Italian attempt to secure an 'exclusive economic position' within the group formed by Italy, Austria, and Hungary. Now Yugoslavia would serve to drive a wedge into the economic circle of the Little Entente. The actual occasion for efforts in this direction was provided by discussions between the Italian and French governments. In German eyes the latter's objective was 'to reconcile the conflicts and tensions in the Danube basin with respect to commercial policy under the leadership of these two governments, with Germany being excluded from these talks, and German economic interests in the Danube basin being ignored'. Neurath therefore described it as one of 'the most important tasks of German foreign

---

[137] Wuescht, *Jugoslawien*, 251.
[138] Collotti, 'Penetrazione', 279.
[139] Treue, 'Das Dritte Reich', 61.
[140] *DGFP* c i, No. 142, pp. 256–62, here 259 (7 Apr. 1934); see Mitrović, 'Ergänzungswirtschaft', 20 ff.
[141] Schröder, 'Hegemonialstellung', 759 ff.; Mitrović, 'Ergänzungswirtschaft', 20 ff.

trade policy' to construct 'firm commercial footholds in the Danube basin in the face of these Franco-Italian attempts'.[142]

German–Yugoslav economic relations were also under discussion at that time because the trade treaty of October 1927 had expired in March 1933. It was followed in July of that year only by a temporary agreement.[143] When this arrangement expired in May 1934, the lack of a treaty threatened to accelerate the decline in mutual trade which was a consequence of the world depression.[144] Such a situation was to be avoided if possible.

This was the background against which Germany and Yugoslavia concluded a new commercial treaty on 1 May 1934.[145] Understandably, the German foreign ministry regarded it as highly significant both politically and economically. The basis for trade between the two countries was considerably extended, and Germany kept open a number of promising possibilities for development in the Yugoslav market. Most important of all, Germany obtained the desired commercial foothold within the economic circle of the Little Entente. Berlin now had an instrument it could use to prevent Yugoslavia from becoming economically bound up with other countries. By means of camouflaged trade preferences, the Germans made their market virtually indispensable for Yugoslav exports. The price Belgrade paid for German concessions was indirect political dependence on the Third Reich.

It must be remembered that the treaty also brought Germany solid economic privileges and advantages, though the hoped-for trade surplus in Germany's favour failed to materialize. In fact the opposite was the case. In both 1934 and 1935 Germany's trade balance with Yugoslavia showed a considerable deficit. However, the Germans did not intend to eliminate this by reducing their imports from Yugoslavia. Since they could not afford to dispense with Yugoslav goods, the problem was to be solved by an increase in exports. On the other hand, Belgrade's hands were tied, since Yugoslavia was unable to reduce its exports to Germany to any great extent. The principle underlying the 'new plan' worked perfectly: Yugoslav freedom of action was clearly narrowed by its political and economic agreements with Germany, as that of the other Balkan states had been. Using the instrument of bilateral treaties, German trade policy created an interrelation of imports and exports which made it almost impossible for its partners to trade wherever they wished. In the period before 1936, in order to reduce the imbalance in German–Yugoslav trade, Yugoslavia was forced to bring its foreign-trade policy closer to the German system of import controls with a clear preference for German firms. The consequence was exactly what the Germans had wanted—the consolidation of their economic position in Yugoslavia.[146]

---

[142] *DGFP* C ii, No. 318, pp. 592–6 (12 Mar. 1933), quotation pp. 577–8.
[143] Schröder, 'Hegemonialstellung', 759.
[144] Šimončić, 'Influence', 363 ff.; but especially Schröder, 'Südosteuropa', 244–5.
[145] *DGFP* C iii, No. 23, pp. 54–6 (21 June 1934).
[146] Schröder, 'Hegemonialstellung', 762 ff.

Between 1933 and 1936 Yugoslav imports from Germany increased significantly.[147] The rise in the country's exports to the Reich was equally impressive. This development concluded the 'first stage in the intensification of German–Yugoslav economic relations begun in May 1934, and the associated extension of the German hegemonic position'.[148] This impression was confirmed by the conduct of the Yugoslav government, which refused to extend the treaties with France into a 'general treaty of alliance' towards the end of 1936. Belgrade had already rejected an attempt by the Czechs to extend the Little Entente in this way. Informing the German envoy of this, Stojadinović, the prime minister, pointed out that 'both these plans he regarded as being aimed against Germany'.[149] The Germans had every reason to be satisfied, since that was exactly the conduct they required. Having taken the place of Italy—until 1935 the main recipient of Yugoslav goods[150]—the Germans now actually felt confident enough to encourage a *rapprochement* between Belgrade and Rome.[151]

In November 1936 the Yugoslavs were convinced that Mussolini remained a serious danger, despite some signs of a reduction in tension between the two countries. They regarded themselves as adequately protected against Hungarian and Bulgarian revisionism by the defensive alliances of the Little Entente and the Balkan pact. However, these offered no reliable defence against Italy. Alliances with the British or French would undoubtedly have provided the required security; but even if the Western powers could have been persuaded, the Yugoslavs preferred treaties which allowed them to maintain their policy of neutrality. This concern led the Yugoslavs to be sceptical about the value of closer ties to the democracies. Such alliances might embroil the country in conflicts in which it had no interest. The antagonism between Paris on one side, and Berlin and Rome on the other, may have played a part in these deliberations. Besides, according to the impression of the German envoy, Heeren, Yugoslavia wanted to ensure good relations with Germany 'not only for economic but also for political reasons'.[152] A *rapprochement* with London, let alone Paris, would not have helped to achieve this.

A combination of factors thus persuaded the Yugoslavs to accept a *rapprochement* with Italy. Its agreements with the other Balkan states offered no security against Italian aggression. Neither Germany nor Britain nor France was a potential protector against Mussolini; this was ruled out by complex political entanglements reflecting the national objectives of Belgrade, Berlin, London, Paris, and Rome. Furthermore, both the Italian aggression in Abyssinia and Hitler's reoccupation of the Rhineland in March 1936 demon-

---

[147] See above, II.II.1, first two pages, and literature cited in n. 11 above.
[148] Schröder, 'Südosteuropa', 251.
[149] *DGFP* c vi, No. 19, pp. 43–4 (9 Nov. 1936); No. 309, pp. 633–5 (9 Apr. 1937).
[150] Hoptner, *Yugoslavia*, 98.
[151] *DGFP* c vi, No. 20, p. 44 (9 Nov. 1936).
[152] Ibid., No. 27, pp. 53–4 (12 Nov. 1936).

1. Interwar Politics and Economics

strated that the League of Nations was powerless against the aggressors. Belgrade became convinced that a settlement between Yugoslavia and Italy was essential to safeguard its own international position.[153] The Italo-Yugoslav treaties were finally signed in March 1937. These agreements did not add up to an alliance. Asked for their advice, the Germans had warned emphatically against it,[154] particularly as similar offers from Rome and Paris had indicated some form of competition for the favour of the Yugoslavs. At the same time, the incident revealed the extent of influence Berlin already possessed.

It was in Germany's interest that the Yugoslav government had extended its freedom of manœuvre *vis-à-vis* its Little Entente partners by the treaties with Italy and also the agreements with Bulgaria at the beginning of the year. At the Little Entente conference of April 1937 the Yugoslavs demonstrated their ability to use this new freedom in the manner intended by Berlin by stubbornly resisting all the plans of the French and Czechs for an alliance. Yet this foreign-policy aspect was only one side of the coin. Internally, the move away from its former partners was not popular in Yugoslavia and was likely to cause problems for Stojadinović. Heeren therefore urged his government to emphasize that the development of Yugoslav foreign policy was 'in no way an option for the Rome–Berlin Axis with a renunciation of the Paris–London axis'. Instead, it should be regarded as a demonstration of the national independence and autonomy of the country.[155]

It is important to emphasize that the Stojadinović government also concluded the agreement with Italy chiefly in order to obtain freedom of manœuvre in its relationship with France. The Yugoslavs had no illusions about the real attitude of Italy. It was indicated that, on the Serbian side, the 'guns on the coast of the Adriatic' would not be removed.[156] This hardly suggested a love-match. Ciano, who thought that Italy would soon take the place of France in Yugoslav foreign policy, was no doubt over-optimistic.[157] Such an assessment is supported by the economic facts. In the two periods 1931–5 and 1936–9 France roughly maintained its share of total Yugoslav exports, at 2.4 per cent and 2.8 per cent respectively. In contrast, Italian imports from Yugoslavia fell from 21.4 per cent to 7.4 per cent. The export figures were only slightly less unfavourable for Italy. In the same two periods France supplied 4.5 per cent and 2.3 per cent of Yugoslav imports compared with 12.9 per cent and 7.8 per cent from Italy.[158] In other words, Italian exports to Yugoslavia declined by 39.5 per cent and French by about 49 per cent. As usual, the only winner in this development was Germany.

---

[153] Hoptner, *Yugoslavia*, 59–86, for extensive coverage of developments leading to the pact; and Wheeler, *Britain*, 9.
[154] *DGFP* C vi, No. 295, p. 601 (25 Mar. 1937).
[155] Ibid., No. 309, pp. 633–5 (9 Apr. 1937).
[156] Ibid., No. 410, pp. 832–5 (7 June 1937).
[157] *Ciano's Diplomatic Papers*, 105.
[158] Hoptner, *Yugoslavia*, 95–6.

After the conclusion of the first phase of German penetration in the south-east, lasting until 1936, a second stage began, consisting largely of an attempt to consolidate and extend the position which had been achieved. Following the Anschluss in 1938, the German 'drive to the south-east' then entered its third phase; this was 'profoundly influenced by the German armaments economy, and in its course Yugoslavia was drawn increasingly into the direct political wake of Hitler's Germany'. However, some qualification of this assessment is necessary. Developments were not predestined and did not occur without friction. For example, there were financial problems which caused protracted disputes between German and Yugoslav negotiators. Furthermore, after 1936–7 the states of the south-east made numerous attempts to escape from the German wake and prevent the economic link from turning into political dependence. Moreover, among the leaders of economic policy, and in private business circles in Germany itself, there were clear conflicts of interest and differences of opinion about the best course. In policy towards south-east Europe as elsewhere, there were confusing and inhibiting conflicts of authority at the various levels of decision-making.[159] There was thus some justification for the British misjudgement of German involvement in Yugoslavia, which was assessed from a purely economic perspective and underestimated the political dimension.

For the Germans the issue was further complicated by the fact that London and Paris exercised the decisive influence in the south-east as regards the supply of capital. The intention was to prevent German expansion, which might very well take military form, or at least assist in barring it if necessary. The British and French assumed that they would be able to use interlocking capital arrangements to paralyse the German war-machine, for example by blocking German supplies from the south-east. Only after the Anschluss and the occupation of Prague in March 1939 did Berlin achieve a significant increase in its 'influence on investment capital in the economy of the south-east', by exploiting the existing links of Austria and Czechoslovakia with the states of south-east Europe. A leading expert on economic relations in this area has trenchantly observed that 'between 1918 and 1938 the British, French, and American governments and capitalists [unintentionally] helped to develop and finance the potential (e.g. oil) which allowed the Reich to overcome the weakness of its war economy and hold out until 1945'.[160]

The Germans used selective economic operations to eliminate the barriers to attainment of a dominating position in the south-east. Their great opportunity came during the world economic depression. The south-east European nations lacked export markets, while France and Britain could not import the necessary volume of products from south-east Europe because of their internal economic

---

[159] Schröder, 'Hegemonialstellung', pp. 769–70, quotation p. 769; Treue, 'Das Dritte Reich', 51–7.
[160] Wendt, 'England', 494–5, quotation p. 495.

1. Interwar Politics and Economics 369

situation and basic foreign-trade requirements. The Germans, by contrast, opened their market to countries such as Bulgaria and Yugoslavia on the conditions mentioned above. Then and later, London and Paris did not fully understand that the issue involved 'not merely economic but high policy'.[161]

As early as the beginning of 1938 the German view was that the Yugoslavs had little interest in maintaining the Little Entente, and that the country's membership of the Balkan pact was of a purely formal nature. Stojadinović, it was thought, would continue as far as possible to manœuvre between London, Rome, and Paris without commitment and to avoid tying himself to Berlin; but he was anxious to maintain 'extremely friendly relations with Germany, which not only are based on the highly developed exchange of goods but also have an ideological foundation'.[162] Intensive German efforts to expand 'economic and thereby also political relations' with the states of south-east Europe after 1933 had in the case of Yugoslavia been successful. Italy had been replaced by Germany as Belgrade's most important trading partner. The Reich obtained cereals, livestock, animal products, hides, skins, bauxite, copper, and timber, in return for machines, products of the iron industry, coal, coke and chemical and pharmaceutical produce.[163] Though the Yugoslav *rapprochement* with Germany was always pursued with caution, it reached a superficial climax with the long-expected visit[164] of Stojadinović to Berlin, 15–22 January 1938.[165] The Germans were satisfied with the outcome. Stojadinović assured his gratified hosts that his country would 'never under any circumstances' join a pact or alliance against Germany. For their part, the Germans showed restraint and did not embarrass the prime minister by making awkward offers of alliance.[166] At that stage the Yugoslav role appeared to be accepted in Berlin. The relationship was made easier by a declaration from Stojadinović that the Yugoslavs regarded the impending solution of the Austrian question as an 'internal German affair'.[167] Indeed, the Anschluss liberated the Yugoslav government from the lingering fear of a restoration of the Habsburg monarchy,[168] and Hitler's entry into Vienna was generally welcomed by the Yugoslav government. However, there was unrest in Slovenia, where the population was increasingly fearful of the 'German drive towards the Adriatic'.[169] For this reason, after the liquidation of Austria the

---

[161] Treue, 'Das Dritte Reich', 47–52, quotation p. 51.
[162] *DGFP* D v, No. 158, pp. 215–17 (3 Jan. 1938).
[163] Ibid., No. 159, pp. 217–19 (7 Jan. 1938).
[164] Survey in Reiswitz, 'Entwicklung Jugoslawiens', 95.
[165] *DGFP* D v, No. 163, pp. 222–9 (17 Jan. 1938): record of talks between Stojadinović and Hitler.
[166] Ibid., No. 165, pp. 230–1 (22 Jan. 1938).
[167] Ibid., No. 174, p. 242 (4 Mar. 1938).
[168] Ibid., No. 163 (see n. 165), pp. 222–9; see also Reiswitz, 'Entwicklung Jugoslawiens', 95; and Avramovski, 'Isolation', 274.
[169] *DGFP* D v, No. 185, pp. 259–60 (17 Mar. 1933).

government in Belgrade wanted assurances from Hitler about the inviolability of the German–Yugoslav border.[170] And in Berlin words were cheap.

Yugoslavia's skilful foreign policy in the years between 1935 and 1939 was largely the work of Stojadinović, its prime minister and foreign minister. When he resigned in February 1939, for reasons already described,[171] the Germans were naturally concerned about the immediate future of relations between the two countries. Hitler was already planning the 'disposal' of rump Czechoslovakia; since the Yugoslavs regarded the Czechs as a 'sister nation',[172] it was conceivable that Belgrade would distance itself from Germany.

That did not happen immediately. Yet whatever one thinks about the influence of personalities on history, it is at least arguable that the departure of Stojadinović was fateful for Yugoslavia.[173] Of course, account must also be taken of the interplay of domestic and foreign policy in Yugoslavia, and the actions and reactions in international politics. For example, there was a direct correlation between the separatist movements within Yugoslavia on the one hand and Italian power politics on the other; these could have provoked developments which even a Stojadinović would have found it difficult to master.

For the Germans the change of government in Yugoslavia did not at first have dramatic consequences. The new prime minister (and minister of the interior) was Dragiša Cvetković, who hastened to assure Berlin that the new government wanted to strengthen its relations with Germany. Yugoslav entry into the anti-Comintern pact would also be considered sympathetically.[174] The appointment of the former minister in Berlin, Cincar-Marković, as Yugoslav foreign minister can also be interpreted as an attempt to reassure the Germans.[175] Furthermore, in February 1939 Prince Regent Paul and Dušan Simović, chief of the general staff, requested large-scale arms supplies from Germany.[176] This indicated a desire for a further *rapprochement*, since political involvement went hand in hand with military co-operation. These factors throw further doubt on the unsubstantiated assertion that, after the Anschluss, Germany rather than Italy had become 'enemy number one' in the eyes of the Yugoslav general staff.[177]

After the resignation of Stojadinović, Yugoslav policies towards Germany developed even more clearly in the direction of *rapprochement*. Yet in Germany

---

[170] Ibid., No. 184, pp. 257–9 (17 Mar. 1933); Hitler also gave this explanation: Hoptner, *Yugoslavia*, 113.
[171] See II.1.2 above.
[172] *DGFP* D v, No. 232, p. 315 (7 Oct. 1938).
[173] Reiswitz, 'Entwicklung Jugoslawiens', 96.
[174] *DGFP* D v, No. 285, pp. 385–6 (7 Feb. 1939).
[175] Ibid., No. 291, pp. 390–1 (11 Feb. 1939); and No. 300, pp. 400–1 (22 Feb. 1939); No. 307, pp. 408–9 (27 Feb. 1939); No. 308, pp. 409–10 (27 Feb. 1939); and vi, No. 620, pp. 860–2 (5 July 1939): secret protocol on terms of a loan to Yugoslavia for armament purchases in Germany.
[176] Ibid. v, No. 296, pp. 396–7 (17 Feb. 1939).
[177] Wuescht, *Jugoslawien*, 41.

itself the response was less marked. Against the background of internal Yugoslav disputes between centralists, federalists, and separatists,[178] the Germans began to abandon their restraint on the Croat question.[179] Berlin was inclined to support the Croat demand for self-determination, which was highly destabilizing to the Yugoslav state.[180] The German decision was apparently linked with reflections on the future of Yugoslavia which went beyond the constitutional decisions reached in the Sporazum of August 1939. But these remained within the realms of theory, as the extremely sensitive reaction of the Italians, especially after Hitler's occupation of Prague, quickly led Berlin to declare its lack of interest in the Croat issue.[181]

In the last six months before the outbreak of war German–Yugoslav relations involved a number of open questions. These concerned the loan for war material; the unresolved issue of aircraft supplies; Germany's anxiety that Yugoslavia might drift into the Western camp; the German–Italian attitude towards the internal stabilization of Yugoslavia; the implications of the minorities issue; and Yugoslavia's possible withdrawal from the League of Nations and its accession to the anti-Comintern pact. In retrospect, the general impression is of insecurity and occasionally even a distinct coolness between the two countries.[182]

A new phase of Yugoslav foreign policy began, at the latest, after the Italian invasion of Albania. This enterprise gave Victor Emmanuel III the title of 'King of Italy and Albania, Emperor of Ethiopia', but brought only problems for Italy. Faced with this demonstration of the Fascist lust for expansion, the Yugoslavs attempted from then on to play the Axis powers off against one another. From Hitler they hoped for support against Mussolini's revived plans for the division of their country; this inevitably meant closer ties with the Reich. Unforeseen developments then made the Yugoslav position much more difficult: Britain and France gave guarantees to Greece and Romania on 13 April; Turkey was drawn more closely into the plans of the Western powers by the British and French declarations of assistance on 12 May and 23 June; and on 22 May Germany and Italy concluded the 'Pact of Steel'. Belgrade, anxious to protect its neutrality, was thereafter forced to manœuvre between increasingly hostile power-blocs, both in overall policy and in regional affairs.[183]

Within this framework the government pursued a policy of limited *rapprochement* with Germany, which was extremely risky both domestically and in foreign affairs. On one hand, the Yugoslavs hoped to avoid too close a link with the Third Reich; on the other hand, the policy enabled the country to distance itself from the Western powers without provoking an outright break.

---

[178] See II.1.2 above.
[179] See Hory and Broszat, *Ustascha-Staat*, 29 ff.
[180] *DGFP* D v, No. 310, pp. 411–12 (7 Mar. 1939); No. 311, pp. 412–13 (7 Mar. 1939).
[181] Hory and Broszat, *Ustascha-Staat*, 31–4; Kljaković, 'German–Italian Agreement', 137 ff.
[182] See *DGFP* D vi and vii under 'Yugoslavia'.
[183] See here especially Breccia, 'Le potenze', 107–29.

Characteristically, the government did not desire, and even prevented, a guarantee from Britain and France. After 1 September 1939 German military successes quickly restricted Yugoslavia's remaining freedom of action to a drastic degree.[184] All that was left was the unpopular policy of manœuvring and waiting, unless the government was ready to risk the existence of the state itself.[185] As a consequence of its political and socio-economic structure, Yugoslavia was simply too weak and dependent. When the government showed signs of wanting to maintain a 'strictly neutral attitude' at the start of the war, the Germans immediately made it clear that they expected a policy of 'benevolent neutrality' instead.[186]

(c) *Greece*

Greek foreign policy in the 1930s was clearly affected by political and economic trends in south-east Europe as a whole, particularly by the growing involvement of Bulgaria and Yugoslavia with the Rome–Berlin Axis. However, certain constants must be taken into account in any assessment of Greek policy during these years. Among them was the traditional convergence of interests between Greece and Britain. In part this was the result of British naval strategy, in which a stable and pro-British Greek state was regarded as a vital support of the British maritime position in the Mediterranean. Consequently, the British did not see relations with Greece as an ideological issue first and foremost, but as a matter to be approached in a 'businesslike' fashion.[187] As long as the Greek government was not anti-British, London was largely indifferent to the country's political system. The common interests of Greece and Britain were reflected in the Greeks' desire for British assistance in safeguarding the northern border against threats from Yugoslavia or Bulgaria, since both these countries were pursuing ambitions which directly affected Greek territory. A further constant element in Greek foreign policy was fear of Italian expansionism in the Balkans. The government's preventive measures inevitably influenced Greek relations with the Axis powers.[188]

The attitude of the Greek government to the various treaty systems must be assessed against this background. The Balkan pact of February 1934, in which Turkey, Greece, Yugoslavia, and Romania united to oppose alterations to Balkan borders in general and Bulgarian revisionism in particular, was conceived as a defensive alliance which guaranteed protection only against attack by a Balkan state: it did not oblige the signatories to intervene if one of them was attacked by another power, such as Italy.[189] Moreover, collective security in the Balkans was largely undermined by a series of events in the 1930s. In the first place, Turkey decided to base its policy more on Britain than on its

---

[184] Reiswitz, 'Entwicklung Jugoslawiens', 97; Rhode, 'Die südosteuropäischen Staaten', 1207.
[185] Hoptner, *Yugoslavia*, 134–5.
[186] *DGFP* D vii, No. 532, p. 508 (1 Sept. 1939).
[187] Koliopoulos, *Greece 1935–1941*, 1.
[188] Richter, *Griechenland*, 68–9.   [189] Papagos, *Battle*, 34 ff.

Balkan partners: a shift signalled by the Montreux convention of July 1936, which permitted Ankara to fortify the Black Sea straits and even close them under certain circumstances. Secondly, Yugoslavia's treaties of 1937 with Bulgaria and Italy seemed to ensure that Belgrade was no longer a target for Italian ambitions, a development far from welcome to the Greeks. Finally, Romanian foreign policy temporarily switched towards a pro-Axis course. Hopes of extending the collective-security system to non-Balkan powers appeared more unrealistic than ever. For Greece, one reason for entry into the Balkan pact had been the desire to prevent the threat to its northern border; now, the *rapprochement* of Bulgaria and Yugoslavia with Italy appeared to make the danger more acute. Though Greece remained within the Balkan *entente*, after the summer of 1936, and especially in 1937, the government moved closer to Britain.[190] A complicated period in Greek foreign policy began, since there were also increasing economic links between Athens and Berlin. The British recognized the danger of a Greek slide into dependence on Germany and made efforts to ward it off, not least by economic means. But in May 1938 London rejected an offer of alliance from the Metaxas regime involving a British guarantee of the Greek frontiers. The British government was still afraid of the incalculable implications of such obligations. Consequently, 1938 came to an end without the British guarantee for which the Greeks had been working.[191]

The unsettled quality of Anglo-Greek relations ensured that Metaxas, who had no ideological qualms about close contacts with National Socialism,[192] attempted to pursue a balanced foreign policy until well into the war. He hoped to keep his country out of the conflict of interest between Britain and Germany, and at the same time to counterbalance the threat from Italy by means of a calculated *rapprochement* with the Third Reich.[193] This will be seen as our account proceeds.

After the Nazis came to power, Graeco-German relations were generally good. Arms deals were discussed at an early stage at both official and unofficial level, although by the outbreak of war the Greeks still had not acquired all the weapons they would have liked.[194] At the time of international concern over the German entry into the demilitarized Rhineland, the Greek government adopted a neutral attitude which was actually of benefit to Hitler.[195] Then, when Hjalmar Schacht, the minister of economics, paid a visit to Athens in June 1936, he was able to adopt a confident tone during his talks with the

---

[190] Koliopolous, *Greece 1935–1941*, 34 ff., 59–63; Richter, *Griechenland*, 69–70; especially on the effect and assessment of the agreement over the Dardanelles see *DGFP* c v, No. 482, pp. 832–4 (27 June 1936).

[191] Comprehensive treatment in Koliopoulos, *Greece 1935–1941*, 84–96.

[192] Cliadakis, 'Metaxás', 21–35. [193] Richter, *Griechenland*, 71.

[194] See *DGFP* c ii, No. 289, pp. 542–4 (28 Feb. 1934); iv, No. 312, p. 669 (30 Sept. 1935); No. 369, p. 762 (21 Oct. 1935); No. 459, pp. 908–12 (12 Dec. 1935); No. 539, pp. 1089–93 (4 Feb. 1936); v, No. 383, pp. 624–6 (18 June 1936); D vi, p. 418 (4 Apr. 1939).

[195] Ibid. c v, No. 110, pp. 149–50 (14 Mar. 1936).

king. Germany was Greece's most important export market, with a trade surplus of RM30m. in Greece's favour. However, as Germany was not prepared to pay foreign currency for the produce it obtained, Greece would have to import more German goods to reduce the surplus. Here, as elsewhere, the system of the 'new plan' functioned like clockwork: Germany's trade partner became a virtual dependant. Schacht also made it clear to the king that Germany wanted to import raw materials as well as currants and tobacco. The Greeks should therefore adapt 'more than hitherto' to the German market, which was the only one of genuine significance for all the countries of south-east Europe.[196] If necessary, German firms could become more directly involved in the Greek economy. Subsequently Schacht described his role during his trip to the south-east, which also took him to Sofia, Belgrade, Vienna, and Budapest, as that of a 'hawker';[197] but this is not an accurate description of his conduct, towards the Greeks at least. In May 1937 the German minister in Athens, Prince Viktor zu Erbach-Schönberg, observed that the German position in Greece had been consolidated with unexpected rapidity over the last two years. Germany was not only the most important provider and recipient of merchandise, but had also caught up with Britain and France in the cultural sphere. All in all, the prince thought that the 'similarity in our ideologies and our joint interest in combating Communism' had greatly improved the German political position in Greece. Metaxas appeared confident that Hitler had no power-political ambitions of his own in the eastern Mediterranean. Thus, at any rate, the German minister explained the conspicuous Greek preference for German rather than British, French, or Italian assistance, as shown for example in the fact that German officers were constructing Greek naval fortifications and German coastal artillerymen were equipping them with guns. German companies were also heavily involved in the extension of the Greek railway network. Yet despite obvious signs of *rapprochement* with Germany, the prince warned against too optimistic a view. Athens continued to regard Britain as a 'kind of protecting power'. If the Greeks had to choose in the event of conflict, Berlin must assume that the Greek government would comply with London's wishes. As regards overall Greek relations with the Axis powers, the minister thought that the relaxation of tension between Italy and Greece would bring economic disadvantages and no political benefits for Germany. To promote further improvement in Graeco-German relations, he considered that an understanding between Berlin and London would offer much better prospects.[198]

Following the Metaxas government's conduct during the Sudetenland crisis, the Germans came to believe that in a European war Greece would quickly abandon its neutral stance and would—in fact must—take the side of the

---

[196] Ibid., No. 383, pp. 624–6 (18 June 1936).
[197] See Treue, 'Das Dritte Reich', 50.
[198] *DGFP* c vi, No. 396, pp. 810–12 (29 May 1937).

Western powers. Metaxas was thus a prisoner of public opinion, in that 'the pro-German attitude displayed by many during good times' had not 'stood the test' during the Sudeten crisis.[199] The Greeks had good reason for their attitude towards Germany, since Hitler's annexationist policies had put him firmly at the head of all the revisionist powers. Every success he gained was thus bound to damage Graeco-Bulgarian relations, at least indirectly, and certainly made the situation in the Balkans more difficult.[200]

This point remains valid despite the fact that on 31 July 1938 Bulgaria concluded the Salonika agreement with Greece and her partners in the Balkan pact. In the negotiations the Bulgarians secured the lifting of the arms restrictions of the treaty of Neuilly, as well as permission to occupy the demilitarized zone on the Graeco-Bulgarian border.[201] But the Greeks had not forgotten the further Bulgarian demand for access to the Aegean. The nationalist wave which swept Bulgaria after the fulfilment of German and Hungarian revisionist claims against Czechoslovakia at the end of 1938 was thus observed with concern in Athens.[202] At this time, on 15 November, the Greek government signed a temporary commercial agreement with the United States. Though it was not the result of the developments outlined above, the agreement would certainly help to free the Greeks from the German economic embrace.[203]

All these events demonstrated the fundamental problem faced by Metaxas in the Balkans. His balancing-act was in danger of collapse as soon as the European great powers became involved in a conflict. After Hitler's troops marched into Czechoslovakia in March 1939, and Mussolini sent his armies into Albania in April, Britain and France finally gave the guarantees which offered the Greeks—fearing Hitler's economic pressure as well as Mussolini's army in Albania—some breathing-space.[204] Metaxas took pains to reassure the Germans,[205] presenting the guarantees as a Franco-British offer which had not been expected but could not be refused. However, there are many indications that, from the middle of May 1939, he expected a European war in the long term.[206] Metaxas had no doubt that if Greece was drawn into the conflict, its enemies would be Germany, Italy, and Bulgaria, despite their ideological affinities with his regime.[207]

This conviction determined the political course adopted by Metaxas in the last weeks before the war. He avoided giving unnecessary provocation to Hitler or Mussolini.[208] At the end of June the Greek government was still trying to persuade the Germans that Athens would maintain strict neutrality in

---

[199] Ibid. D v, No. 233, pp. 316–18 (8 Oct. 1939).
[200] Ibid., No. 262, pp. 349–51 (6 Dec. 1938).
[201] Hoppe, *Bulgarien*, 53; on developments after 31 July see also the reports of the American ambassador in Athens: MacVeagh, 135–8 (22 Aug. 1938).
[202] *DGFP* D v, No. 262, pp. 349–51 (6 Dec. 1938).
[203] MacVeagh, 138–42 (22 Nov. 1938).
[204] Ibid. 158 (17 Apr. 1939).
[205] *DGFP* D vi, No. 231, pp. 287–8 (19 Apr. 1939).
[206] MacVeagh, 159–60 (15 May 1939).   [207] Hering, 'Griechenland', 1325–6.

the event of a conflict, and that no attention should be paid to any sign that the Balkan countries were being drawn into the group of so-called encirclement powers (which included Turkey).[209] But two months later, as the political crisis of summer 1939 mounted to a climax, Metaxas replied frankly to an enquiry from the American ambassador concerning the position of Greece: 'We are with the western powers, because it is to our own interest, and because of our allies [the Turks].'[210]

Metaxas did not necessarily believe that war was imminent, but he no longer excluded the possibility that it would break out soon. In response to the concentration of Italian troops in Albania, he ordered Greek troops to the northern border as a precautionary measure. After the conclusion of the Nazi-Soviet non-aggression pact in August 1939 there was also a general fear that the Balkans might be handed over to the Red Army.[211]

In August 1939, therefore, Metaxas deliberately played the American card.[212] Understandably in view of the prevailing international climate, the Americans were prepared to ignore the fact that Greece was ruled by a dictatorship; what counted was her intention to support the British.[213] Despite increases in the number of troops on the Albanian border, there was a superficial relaxation of tension between Greece and Italy.[214] However, it should not be supposed that Mussolini's restraint, forced on him by Italian military weakness, meant that he had abandoned his aggressive designs.[215]

Since the Italian invasion of Albania, most contemporaries had understood that Greece would stand with the Western camp if it was forced to take sides in a European war. As far as Axis policy was concerned, therefore, the sensible course was to avoid any step which would push the Greek government further in that direction.

(d) Albania

This is not the place for another summary of the events leading to the Italian aggression against Albania in April 1939, which has already been dealt with elsewhere.[216] Nor should too much attention be devoted to a military operation which took place before the Second World War, and which one expert described as so simple that it could not possibly fail.[217] In fact the invasion did reveal deficiencies in organization, logistics, and, above all, communications,

---

[208] Schramm-von Thadden, *Griechenland*, 21.
[209] *DGFP* D vi, No. 550, pp. 752–3 (20 June 1939).
[210] MacVeagh, 161–2 (21 Aug. 1939).
[211] Schramm-von Thadden, *Griechenland*, 22–3.
[212] MacVeagh, 165 (31 Aug. 1939).
[213] Ibid. 162–5 (31 Aug. 1939).
[214] Koliopoulos, *Greece 1935–1941*, 114–15.
[215] Very good on this subject are Knox, *Mussolini*, 52, and D. M. Smith, *Mussolini*, 234–5.
[216] For details see Jacomoni, *Politica dell'Italia*, 78–138, though with all the reservations that normally apply to memoirs.
[217] Montanari, *Albania*, 278; also pp. 250–78 for the planning and execution of the military operation as a whole.

which in the opinion of some military and political witnesses might well have endangered General Guzzoni's advance on Tirana. But in the kingdom of the blind the one-eyed man is king, and the Albanian troops were unable to offer resolute resistance.[218] Italian losses—twelve dead and eighty-one wounded— were caused more by equipment failures than by enemy action. As we have seen, there was no genuine reason for an attack on Albania, since the country had long been virtually an Italian protectorate. But it was soon clear that to Mussolini protectorates were not enough.

The whole affair provided further military confirmation of a fact which had first been revealed in Ethiopia and Spain: the utter failure of political and military leadership in Italy. Politically, the model for the Italian attack was provided by the German invasion of rump Czechoslovakia. Ciano himself observed that, by invading Albania, the Fascists were seeking compensation for the humiliation they had suffered over Hitler's move.[219] It should also be noted that Mussolini, who thought the time for action not yet ripe, was hesitant at first. It was Ciano who forced the pace.[220]

The invasion of Czechoslovakia by the Wehrmacht thus provided the occasion, but not the actual cause, for Mussolini's decision. As we have seen, Italian conduct was the result of the aggressive expansionist ideology of the Fascist regime; the general plan dated back to the 1920s, while discussions on the best way to implement it had been held at least as early as 1938. Ciano suggested to Mussolini that the annexation of Albania would bring the Straits of Otranto under Italian control, thereby turning the Adriatic into an Italian sea;[221] it would also constitute an Italian counter-move to the Anschluss. Ciano planned to launch the invasion, on the pretext of an uprising to be staged by paid henchmen, in or about May 1939. Mussolini fully concurred with his son-in-law's suggestions. He even seems to have believed Ciano's assertion that Albania, previously an area requiring economic subsidy, would suddenly be transformed into an ideal supplementary territory after the occupation.[222]

After the conquest of Albania the Italians did not remain in the country long enough to verify this belief. Only Italian exporters did good business there. Moreover, any profit they made was at the expense of the Italian state, which was forced to subsidize the Albanian economy. Ciano, the figurehead of an interest-group, had once again been indulging in fantasy. So also did Mussolini when—after the event—he maintained that Albania was the 'Bohemia' of the Balkans and the key to mastery of south-east Europe. 'Whoever holds Albania holds the Balkans.' This assertion, made to the Fascist Grand Council on 13 April 1939,[223] was graphic and assured of approval, but it was no more than empty rhetoric.

---

[218] Bottai, *Vent'anni*, 126 (13 Apr. 1939); Ciano, *Diary 1939–1943*, 66–7 (8 Apr. 1939); see also D. M. Smith, *Roman Empire*, 152–3.
[219] Ciano, *Diary 1939–1943*, 44–6 (15 Mar. 1939).
[220] Ibid. 46 (16 Mar. 1939).   [221] Skendi, *Albania*, 18.
[222] Collotti, 'La politica dell'Italia', 7–8; D. M. Smith, *Roman Empire*, 149 ff.
[223] Bottai, *Vent'anni*, 126–7 (13 Apr. 1939); see D. M. Smith, *Roman Empire*, 156 ff.

One of the reasons for Mussolini's hesitation in March 1939 was his fear that the Germans might attempt to interfere in Croatia.[224] Less convincingly, Rome later justified its aggression to the British and French by arguing that the invasion had forestalled a German advance on the Balkans in the aftermath of the destruction of Czechoslovakia.[225] The Germans promptly denied the charge: they had no ambitions of any kind regarding Croatia; talk of Croat autonomy as a Nazi protectorate was a fiction; Germany would not intervene in Yugoslavia.[226]

Mussolini was naturally delighted by this professed lack of interest.[227] In any case, he always tended to pay attention to things he wanted to hear. A new war now seemed possible, promising easy victory, military fame, and personal prestige. Apart from Mussolini's craving for glory, Albania could also serve as the base for a subsequent attack on Yugoslavia and Greece.[228] These were the underlying motives for the invasion of a small country which, in truth, served only to extend southern Italy—and all the problems that region caused for the Italian state—to the other side of the Adriatic.

At the beginning of April 1939 *agents provocateurs* were dispatched to Albania to provoke the disturbances which would be used to justify the Italian occupation.[229] King Zog was handed an ultimatum at the end of March, virtually demanding that he surrender the independence and sovereignty of his country voluntarily. No answer had reached Rome when the ultimatum expired at midday on 6 April 1939.[230] The die was cast. After the farce was concluded on 9 April, General Guzzoni used the customary glowing phrases to announce the Italian victory, while Mussolini subsequently spoke of the 'Fascist strength of purpose' behind the action. He even boasted of the 'striking-power of the Italian fighting forces',[231] as if this could have been genuinely put to the test in Albania.

Berlin found out about the Italian plans only at the beginning of April, from informants.[232] But it was enough. The German ambassador was instructed, even before he received official information,[233] to indicate to the Italians that they would receive full German support.[234] After the invasion, the task of conveying Germany's gratification was entrusted by Hitler to Field Marshal Göring, a man thoroughly at home with every manifestation of Roman baroque, verbal and otherwise. He spoke of German pleasure and satisfaction,

---

[224] Knox, *Mussolini*, 40–1.
[225] For a refutation of this claim see Catalano, *Trionfo dei fascismi*, 261–2.
[226] *DGFP* D vi, No. 15, pp. 15–16 (17 Mar. 1939); No. 45, pp. 45–6 (20 Mar. 1939).
[227] Bottai, *Vent'anni*, 124 ff. (21 Mar. 1939).
[228] D. M. Smith, *Mussolini*, 230–1.
[229] Ciano, *Diary 1939–1943*, 61 (2 Apr. 1939).
[230] Canzio, *La dittatura*, 494; De Felice, *Mussolini il duce*, ii. 607–8.
[231] Catalano, *Trionfo dei fascismi*, 261.
[232] *DGFP* D vi, No. 150, pp. 752–3 (20 June 1939).
[233] Ibid., No. 170, p. 207 (6 Apr. 1939).
[234] Ibid., No. 158, p. 194 (5 Apr. 1939); No. 171, pp. 207–9 (7 Apr. 1939).

and of the growth of Axis power and strategic gain, and offered the congratulations of the Reich.[235] Mussolini too was gratified. He enjoyed the role of *condottiere*, especially when successful. Difficult tasks or easy ones—profit was what counted, however small.

But this, as we have seen, was not the German view. Within his inner circle Hitler was contemptuous; but he was also concerned about the possible repercussions of the affair. Germany's opponents could no longer be expected to tolerate every coup by the Axis. The 'taking possession of rump Czechoslovakia' —to use the euphemism of State Secretary Weizsäcker—had finally mobilized the 'counter-forces' to German aggression which could be dangerous to Hitler. According to Weizsäcker, the 'acquisition of Albania by Italy' had done the rest: matters were now 'half-way towards war'.[236] Certainly the rape of Czechoslovakia and the attack on Albania, taken together, formed an important milestone in the development of the anti-Hitler coalition.

On 15 April President Roosevelt demanded a promise from Hitler and Mussolini that they would not attack any of twenty-nine states enumerated by him, at least for the next ten years. With some skill, Berlin and Rome used the opportunity to win a cheap propaganda victory. But in the long term the more significant fact was that the American president had intervened decisively in European politics. Furthermore, after their guarantee to Poland, Britain and France also issued guarantees to Greece and Romania. The British introduced conscription,[237] and continued their treaty negotiations with Turkey in a stronger position after Mussolini's Balkan adventure.[238] On 12 May it was announced that Turkey and Britain were ready to work together and provide each other with all possible assistance in the event of a war in the Mediterranean involving acts of aggression.[239]

In Anglo-Italian relations the conquest of Albania produced effects in stark contrast to the moderate tone which had dominated the discussions of British and Italian diplomats in April. Chamberlain and the Foreign Office now recognized that Mussolini could not be trusted; like Hitler, the Italian head of government was to be regarded as a potential enemy. Yet London was not certain what decision Mussolini would reach in the event of conflict, because too many tactical factors were involved. This uncertainty led the British government to maintain its policy of restraint towards Mussolini; it was, after all, in the British interest not to drive the Italians further into the German embrace.[240] On 1 September 1939 it became apparent that, at least for the time being, the British had not miscalculated. As we have seen, Mussolini initially kept out of the war.

---

[235] Ibid., No. 205, pp. 248–53 (15 Apr. 1939).
[236] *Weizsäcker-Papiere*, 154 (18 June 1939).
[237] D. M. Smith, *Roman Empire*, 156; Salvatorelli and Mira, *Storia dell'Italia*, 1007.
[238] *DGFP* D vi, No. 259, p. 323 (25 Apr. 1939).
[239] Ibid., No. 259, editors' note.
[240] De Felice, *Mussolini il duce*, ii. 609–10, and 606–12 on Albania in general.

2. Moves Towards a New Policy after the Outbreak of War The 'Balkan Bloc' Project

After the outbreak of war all the Balkan states made efforts to stay out of a conflict involving the great powers on which they had traditionally been dependent. This applied to Germany, Britain, France, and Italy, as well as the Soviet Union. The Balkan countries' hopes were not entirely unrealistic, since Italy did not enter the war immediately, and the Mediterranean thus did not become a theatre of operations. Mussolini's decision had a direct influence on the interests of the belligerents in south-east Europe. Neither the Germans nor the Western Allies were averse to the idea of keeping south-east Europe out of the conflict, despite the differences in their motives and underlying ideas: Berlin, for instance, supported the concept of individual neutrality on the part of each state, while London and Paris hoped for a bloc neutrality of the Balkan countries.[241] Though the issue is exceptionally complex and much was uncertain at the time, this at least seems clear.

The idea of creating a bloc of neutral Balkan states opened up new political perspectives for Italy. Some of those concerned, particularly in circles close to Ciano, were tempted to exploit German commitments in the north of Europe in order to regain the influence in the Balkans which Italy had lost during the war in Abyssinia. But it must be remembered that Italian foreign policy did not always speak with one voice. In principle Mussolini was still determined to enter the conflict as soon as the strategic situation seemed favourable.[242]

Plans for a Balkan bloc of neutral states took shape in the second half of 1939 in three proposals or suggestions, all of which were based on the neutrality of Italy.[243] The Allies, and some British representatives in particular, were sympathetic to proposals of this kind; they had not yet abandoned the idea that Italy might function as a bulwark against both German and Soviet expansion in the Balkans.[244] Definite suggestions on the subject were first made by Ciano in September and October 1939.[245] At virtually the same time the Romanian foreign minister Grigore Gafencu[246] discussed the issue with his Yugoslav counterpart, Aleksandr Cincar-Marković, at Jebel on 19 September.[247] Finally, Gafencu took the initiative once again in November of the same year,[248] thus launching the most ambitious approach of all. However, to all intents and purposes the plan had to be written off after December

---

[241] Woodward, *British Foreign Policy*, i. 22–3.
[242] Onder, *Die türkische Außenpolitik*, 52, makes accurate reference to this matter.
[243] Marzari, 'Projects', 771.
[244] Onder, *Die türkische Außenpolitik*, 52–3.
[245] Siebert, *Italiens Weg*, 376–80.
[246] In his memoirs of this period (Gafencu, *Prelude*) such activities are not mentioned, save for a fleeting reference on p. 260.
[247] Breccia, *Jugoslavia*, 208–28; Hoptner, *Yugoslavia*, 164–5.
[248] Krecker, *Deutschland*, 68–71, in this connection draws attention to the justified suspicion that the links between Turkey and the Western powers were damaging the prospects of the plans for a Balkan bloc, and at least making Ankara lose credibility as an 'advocate of a Balkan union'.

2. The 'Balkan Bloc' Project

1939–January 1940, when Mussolini finally rejected it.[249] Subsequent discussions[250] were on a very different basis, since they assumed that Italy would not be involved. The British, whose first plans were based largely on the pre-war structure of the Balkan Entente, did not abandon their ideas concerning a bloc until April 1941, but by the end these had been reduced to a project involving only two states.[251] In practice all hope was destroyed by the defeat of France. This was indirectly confirmed by the 'Vienna award' of August 1940,[252] which consolidated Axis dominance in south-east Europe.

What political factors led to the plan for a Balkan bloc? Firstly, it reflected the fear of some Balkan states, and also of Italy, that the military conflict might be extended to south-east Europe. The Germans quickly offered reassurance with the declaration that Berlin wanted nothing more than quiet in the region.[253] Ciano used this opportunity to stress yet again that such calm could be ensured only by Italian non-belligerence.[254] However, when war broke out there were still a number of open questions in the region: the attitude of the revisionist states of south-east Europe; the Soviet claim to Bessarabia; and the Polish–Romanian mutual-assistance pact. The last of these was quickly settled. As it rapidly became clear that the Polish situation was hopeless, Bucharest and Warsaw renounced their treaty obligations to each other when the Red Army marched into Poland on 17 September and occupied, with some extensions, the territories which Moscow had lost to the new Polish state by the treaty of Riga in 1921. These developments had some favourable repercussions for Italian foreign policy; Rome could now offer itself as a protecting power to the Balkan states, and particularly Romania. It is reasonable to assume that Ciano in particular thought along these lines. During the early months of the war he pursued a distinctly anti-German course and attempted to establish Italian neutrality on a permanent basis.[255]

At least on the surface, Mussolini seemed sympathetic to these ideas. Thus, as early as 9 September he emphasized to Rintelen, the German military attaché in Rome, that the Italian attitude would enable Turkey, Greece, Romania, Yugoslavia, and Egypt to refrain from providing direct assistance to Britain.[256] On the morning of 11 September he even appeared anxious to further the plan to gather the states of south-east Europe into a neutral bloc. However, the initiative was postponed on the evening of the same day; Mussolini wanted to wait until German–Polish hostilities were at an end. He still hoped that a system of collective security and a relatively durable *Pax*

---

[249] Schreiber, *Revisionismus*, 196–7.
[250] Campus, 'Balkanblock', 20 ff., interprets the whole project as anti-Soviet; evidence to support the idea of lasting Italian interest is lacking.
[251] Barker, *British Policy*, 11 ff.
[252] See *Das Deutsche Reich und der Zweite Weltkrieg*, iv. 333 ff. (Förster).
[253] DDI, 9th ser., i, No. 58, p. 34 (6 Sept. 1939).
[254] Ibid., No. 89, p. 61 (8 Sept. 1939).
[255] Schreiber, *Revisionismus*, 192; Siebert, *Italiens Weg*, 376–7.
[256] DGFP D viii, No. 38, pp. 35–6 (9 Sept. 1939).

Mussoliniana could be established in Europe within the framework of an international conference. Ciano's telegram to Attolico, the ambassador in Berlin, written after Mussolini's comments that morning, was therefore not sent.[257]

Three days earlier the embassy in Berlin had reported that Göring thoroughly approved of the Italian attitude. He too believed that Italy's non-belligerence would help Germany to exploit the Balkan countries for its war effort, and also restrict British and French freedom of action in the Mediterranean.[258] After a conversation with Weizsäcker, Attolico judged Göring's remarks to be 'important'; this is debatable, but in any case they were what he wanted to hear. Attolico therefore advised Ciano to encourage the creation of a third force, consisting chiefly of the smaller neutral states and Italy. Particularly if the United States stayed out of the war, Attolico believed that an association of this kind might even succeed in compelling the belligerents to make peace at some future date.[259] Attolico's plans thus had implications reaching far beyond the Mediterranean; indeed, they were apparently based on a wildly optimistic assessment of Italian freedom of action and influence. Yet even these ideas involved the notion of a limited bloc, and served to keep the project for a Balkan bloc alive as an object of discussion in terms of Italian political objectives. In the middle of September, however, Mussolini's hesitation apparently cast doubt over such plans for the time being.

It was the entry of Soviet troops into eastern Poland which gave the matter fresh impetus. Bulgaria, Greece, Romania, and Turkey then signalled more or less directly that they wanted an association of the Balkan states under Italian leadership.[260] Ciano's interest in the bloc project was probably revived by these developments. At any rate, on 23 September he gave Attolico permission to sound out the German government on the issue. He did not mention the possible Soviet threat to south-east Europe, however; given the close cooperation between Berlin and Moscow, this would not have been regarded as a convincing argument. Instead Ciano drew attention to the threat to Germany posed by a reportedly imminent Anglo-French move to undermine the neutrality of the states of south-east Europe and the Balkans. Italy therefore thought it advisable to unite these states into a neutral bloc under its own leadership. Such a move would allow greater resistance to Allied pressure, and could also serve major economic objectives and (undefined) political goals. Naturally, the project would take account of the needs of the German war effort. If the Germans agreed, Rome would take the initiative. In this way

---

[257] Ciano, *Diary 1939–1943*, 152 (15 Sept. 1939).
[258] *DDI*, 9th ser., i, No. 170, pp. 104–9, here 108 (12 Sept. 1939): conversation between Göring and the Italian minister, Count Massimo Magistrati.
[259] Ibid., No. 258, pp. 158–61 (16 Sept. 1939); Ciano also regarded the conversation between Göring and Magistrati as highly significant: see Ciano, *Diary 1939–1943*, 152 (14 Sept. 1939).
[260] Marzari, 'Projects', 771–2; on Soviet interests see also H. Weber, *Bukowina*, 11–12.

2. The 'Balkan Bloc' Project

Italy could offer decisive opposition to the British plan to induce the Balkan countries to take an anti-German line.[261]

Attolico thought the time was ripe to approach the German foreign ministry. He was careful to use the economic arguments to which Berlin was bound to be sympathetic: Weizsäcker on a previous occasion had urged the Italians to lead the neutral states in their resistance to British economic pressure. In the Mediterranean Attolico was now proposing to do just that. Weizsäcker also stated that the Germans did not object to the formation of such an economic group by the neutrals, but he wished to consult with the foreign minister to make sure.[262] Four days later he informed Attolico that Berlin had 'nothing against Italy's assuming leadership of the resistance against Anglo-French economic pressure in the countries of south-east Europe'. But Weizsäcker made an important condition, which limited Italian freedom of action: Germany would take a direct interest in the matter as soon as it 'touched upon the political'.

The Germans were aware of the political opportunities offered by the proposal. Besides, they knew as well as the Italians that Turkey was attempting—in parallel, so to speak, with the Italian plan—to create a neutral bloc containing Romania, Yugoslavia, and perhaps also, at a political price, Bulgaria. A bloc of this kind, on lines foreshadowed in the Jebel discussion between Romania and Yugoslavia, would have committed the Balkan states 'to joint defence of neutrality towards the north'. The Germans were naturally opposed to the plan and its political implications. If Italy could use economic means to counteract it, this could only be welcome to Berlin. Since Attolico took pains to emphasize that Italy was concerned only with 'defence against economic blockade measures', the Germans had good reason to be satisfied.[263] After 27 September Attolico—like Ciano, anxious to keep Italy out of the war—felt that his sanguine first impressions had been confirmed.[264]

It is likely that the meeting between Hitler and Ciano on 1 October had a decisive influence on the fate of the Italian project for a Balkan bloc. During these talks Hitler raised the issue of his own accord. He was by no means unsympathetic towards the plan, but Ciano must have realized that Hitler's ideas were very different from his own. Hitler expected that Mussolini's involvement with a bloc of neutral states would lead him into difficulties with the Allies and even closer ties with Germany. In any case, he made no bones about his belief that the destiny of Italy was inseparable from that of Germany. Hitler saw Italian entry into the war as virtually unavoidable. Even more important from Ciano's point of view, Hitler was willing to grant Italy a preferential position only in those Balkan states which bordered directly on the Adriatic or the Mediterranean.

---

[261] *DDI*, 9th ser., i, No. 394, pp. 239–40 (23 Sept. 1939).
[262] *DGFP* D viii, No. 128, p. 126 (23 Sept. 1939).
[263] Ibid., No. 145, pp. 150–1 (27 Sept. 1939).
[264] *DDI*, 9th ser., i, No. 407, p. 245 (23 Sept. 1939).

For a number of reasons, Ciano could scarcely be happy with the course of the discussion: first, he was anxious to keep Italy out of the war; second, he was pursuing a policy of *rapprochement* with Britain; and third, the political ambitions of the Fascist regime were not limited to the states adjoining the Mediterranean, as indicated by Hitler.[265] We have no concrete evidence concerning the effect of Hitler's statements of 1 October on Mussolini. But in October all the plans hatched by Ciano and Attolico were dropped, evidently on the basis of a decision by the dictator. This also meant the failure of British and French calculations that Italy could be drawn gradually to their side through the Balkan project; that a bulwark could thereby be created in the south-east against German and/or Soviet expansionism; and that undefined concessions in the region could divert Mussolini from his ambitions in Corsica and Tunis.

With hindsight, it may appear that 'in the Balkans Mussolini was at the crossroads of his entire policy'.[266] But Mussolini does not seem to have taken this view. In his opinion there was never any real alternative to entry into the war on the German side.[267] We have already seen that this did not mean an unconditional commitment to Hitler, but was a consequence of Mussolini's own political objectives. The Duce would not allow lesser aims to divert him from his ambition to establish an *imperium*. He took steps, promptly and emphatically, to repudiate the rumour that Italy would assume the leadership of a neutral bloc and detach itself from Germany. In October Ciano emphasized to the German ambassador that such claims 'were false'. 'The idea of a bloc of Balkan states under Italian leadership had been aired already in conversations in Berlin, and the Duce had pondered it long and in detail but had definitely decided against it, although the Balkan capitals had clearly shown sympathy for such a project.' The foreign minister thought that Mussolini now 'detested' the word 'neutral', since he was doing all he could to he ready to enter the war 'at the proper moment'. 'Leadership of a bloc of neutral Balkan states would mean a tie for him that might prove embarrassing some day.'[268] Whatever the fluctuations in Mussolini's attitude—and they continued after October 1939—the idea of a Balkan bloc had been resolved. In truth, Mussolini had probably never considered it as a genuine option because of the incalculable political factors involved. His approach was therefore always hesitant, and German military successes were not calculated to increase his sympathy for such plans. However, his decision of 17 October was not relayed to the capitals of the interested Balkan states, where hopes of a bloc under Italian leadership continued. Dominated as they were by often con-

---

[265] *DGFP* D viii, No. 176, pp. 184–94 (2 Oct. 1939); for interpretation and further sources see Marzari, 'Projects', 773; and Schreiber, *Revisionismus*, 194 ff.
[266] Siebert, *Italiens Weg*, 379.
[267] This theory is expressed with emphasis by e.g. Knox, *Mussolini*; D. M. Smith, *Mussolini*; and Schreiber, *Revisionismus*.
[268] *DGFP* D viii, No. 266, p. 305 (17 Oct. 1939).

flicting national objectives, manifested in minority issues and territorial demands, these states needed a great power around which they could rally and which would protect their neutrality. Only Italy was neutral; only Italy could function as a focus for the Balkan states, bridge inner Balkan rivalries, and offer protection against external pressures. This latter goal in particular would have required close association of the Balkan states on the principle that 'unity is strength'.

Romania was the moving spirit in further attempts to create a bloc of neutral Balkan states. The country's primary concern was to safeguard Bessarabia against an attack from the Soviet Union, which appeared possible after the outbreak of the Russo-Finnish war. The Allies, who continued to encourage plans of this kind, were also interested in the possibility of opening a second front against Germany. Gafencu thought that Italy's first function would be to hold the USSR in check. If this did not succeed, Bucharest hoped that the Western powers would be able, after a settlement between Bulgaria and Romania, to establish a defensive position stretching from Syria to the Carpathians. This scenario implied a *rapprochement* between Italy and the Allies which would inevitably bring Rome into conflict with Berlin. Such a bloc would also, in the event of a Romanian–Soviet conflict, have given Paris and London the opportunity to open a front against Germany. The plan was therefore unacceptable to Mussolini, and in his speech of 16 December, already mentioned, Ciano indicated that Italy did not regard the formation of a neutral Balkan bloc as helpful. Mussolini's basic political objectives strengthened his resolve to adhere to the decision of October 1939. This is shown, for example, by the fact that the Fascist regime considered intervening in Croatia at the end of December.[269]

In military and political terms Mussolini's rejection of the Balkan project was in harmony with German plans for the south-east. Any kind of action over Croatia, however, was wholly undesirable to the Germans. At the suggestion of Ribbentrop, the Wehrmacht high command therefore drew up a preventive study at the beginning of 1940, written entirely on the basis that there must be no instability in the Balkans.[270] The German military leadership had no desire to allow unrest to develop there, since this might have affected the circumstances, which were then favourable, for the coming campaign in the west: Germany would very possibly have to transfer military forces to the south-east and even be obliged to fight on two fronts, contrary to existing plans. The Wehrmacht leaders argued, ambiguously, that the region must stay neutral at least as long as it provided what the Germans required as an economic supply-base. Above all, it was vital 'not to draw Italy into the war through military action in the south-east', no matter who provoked it. Furthermore, the 'over-

---

[269] Marzari, 'Projects', 775–87; Schreiber, *Revisionismus*, 196–7; Siebert, *Italiens Weg*, 380 ff.; Campus, 'Balkanblock', 16–20.
[270] *DGFP* D viii, No. 514, pp. 631–3 (8 Jan. 1940); in this context see also the Wehrmacht high command study referred to in I.II above, n. 326.

lapping of interest' between Rome and Moscow, which could not then be ruled out, would endanger the relationship between Germany and Italy. The Third Reich, and here is the main line of German policy in the south-east from January until October 1940, wanted to maintain the status quo, which guaranteed Germany both political influence and economic advantage.

Developments of this kind clearly demonstrate the insincerity of statements in the secret supplementary protocol to the German–Soviet non-aggression pact, according to which Germany had 'no political interest' in south-east Europe. Ribbentrop was well aware that his country was pursuing important economic interests there, and these were *ipso facto* political; if he had stated that Germany had no 'territorial' interest, that would have been more credible. Moreover, after August 1939 the Germans interfered regularly in the affairs of the south-east European states. As Hitler's conversation with Ciano on 1 October reveals, it even allocated spheres of influence in the Balkans, while the study produced by the Wehrmacht high command considered ways of diverting the Soviet Union from the Balkans to the Middle East. Like the Nazi–Soviet pact as a whole, the section relating to the Balkans was no more than a tactical manœuvre.

3. 'QUIET IN THE BALKANS'?

In August 1939 Hitler prepared to attack Poland, thus launching himself on the 'old Germanic trail to the east' which he regarded as essential for 'economic reasons'.[271] At this stage he had two conversations with the Italian foreign minister, in which it became apparent that the Balkans had a military as well as an economic role in German strategic thinking. Furthermore, it was clear that the region would, or at least could, be treated as a variable quantity in German political calculations. Should there be an attempt to realize the regime's overriding plans for *Lebensraum*, 'quiet in the Balkans' would not be a *sine qua non* of the German war effort. Only this fact can explain Hitler's conduct in mid-August when, though still anxious not to allow the conflict with Poland to escalate into a major European war, he bluntly urged his Axis partner to 'give Yugoslavia the *coup de grâce* as soon as possible'.[272]

At first sight this advice to Mussolini directly contradicts every principle of German policy towards south-east Europe in the 1930s. It is true that, as soon as it became clear that Mussolini did not intend to enter the war immediately, the Germans adopted policies which would have been equally appropriate for the so-called status quo powers in south-east Europe. In August 1939, though, Hitler's calculation was apparently a different one. As we have seen, the Yugoslavs had rejected the British and French offer of a guarantee. An attack on Yugoslavia would therefore not put

---

[271] *DGFP* D vii, No. 47, pp. 53–6, conversation between Hitler and Ciano at Obersalzberg on 13 Aug., quotation p. 55.

[272] Ciano, *Diary 1939–1943*, 124 (12 Aug. 1939); see the record—in this context corroborative—of the talks in *DGFP* D vii, No. 43, pp. 39–49 (12 Aug. 1939), here 40–1, and

3. 'Quiet in the Balkans'?

the Allies under overwhelming psychological pressure to intervene, but would nevertheless force them to keep strong forces in the Mediterranean, since it would not be possible to predict the extent of hostilities. In this situation the British and French would have been unable to concentrate all their military strength on Germany's western frontier. Hitler may have hoped that this would cause the Allies to stay out of the German–Polish conflict altogether, or at least wait until it had been resolved. Much of this remains speculative, although it is theoretically compatible with the strategic concept Hitler had espoused since 5 November 1937, to which many references have been made. In any case, Hitler seems to have regarded Yugoslavia as no more than a pawn: he was little interested in its continued existence. This view is supported by his willingness to sacrifice the country in August 1939, and again during his discussions with Ciano in October, when he seemed ready to hand it over to Italy. A comment by the chief of the army general staff in December 1938 also points strongly in this direction. Halder then reportedly described Yugoslavia as a country which would be among the victims of German expansion.[273]

On the other hand, there is no evidence in either the German or the Italian record of the August discussions[274] that Hitler then advised Mussolini in favour of aggression against Greece.[275] In view of the guarantees Athens had received, such a move would have tended to escalate rather than limit the European conflict. After Ciano's visit to Berlin, however, Mussolini assumed that Italy would probably be drawn into the war; and in the middle of August he ordered Marshal Badoglio to draw up a plan of attack against both Greece and Yugoslavia. However, he intended to take action against Greece only if the Western powers forced him to enter the war. A move against Yugoslavia would also depend on an increase in internal unrest there (Croatia). The Italian generals did not have to start from scratch in their plans, since they had begun to prepare operational studies for an invasion of Greece directly after the attack on Albania.[276] Irrespective of the fluctuations in relations between the

---

No. 47 (see n. 271 above), pp. 53–6 (13 Aug. 1939); *Ciano's Diplomatic Papers*, 297–304, including the notes of his talk with Ribbentrop on 11 Aug. at Salzburg (297 ff.) as well as the conversation with Hitler; also directly relevant is *IMT* iii. 126–7, 309, proceedings of 4 and 7 Dec. 1945.

[273] *IMT* xxviii, doc. 1759-Ps, pp. 238–9; affidavit by the former US consul in Berlin, Raymond H. Geist, of 28 Aug. 1945. According to this, Halder showed a remarkable knowledge of Hitler's programme, to which he referred directly. Hence it is basically unnecessary to speculate on why the chief of the army general staff ordered preparations for war against the Soviet Union in summer 1940, even before Hitler ordered it. For Halder, working from Hitler's programme, the attack in the east was the obvious next step after victory in the west. Nor was the extent of Halder's knowledge surprising. Hitler made no secret of his intention 'to destroy the Communists by conquering Russia', and Maj.-Gen. Walter von Reichenau gave F. W. Winterbotham, later head of 'Ultra', 'details of the German plans against Russia' as early as 1934; see Winterbotham, *The Ultra Secret*, 5.

[274] See n. 272 above.

[275] *Hellēnikos stratos*, i. 79–83.

[276] Montanari, *Grecia*, i. 30–1: Badoglio's information communicated to the commanders of the Wehrmacht services dates from 17 Aug. 1939. On the Greek side also the Italian conquest of

two countries,[277] an Italian attack on Yugoslavia had also been a constant possibility.[278]

The first results of these deliberations were submitted on 31 August. They indicated that an offensive against Greece could not be considered until Italy had repelled the expected dual onslaught from France, in Europe and in North Africa. Only on that basis could realistic plans be made. On the other hand, an attack on Yugoslavia could be contemplated, providing that the country was disintegrating from within. Such scepticism appears to have convinced even Mussolini, who by 17 September was no longer calling for an attack on Greece. Graeco-Italian relations had improved, at least superficially,[279] and in any case Greece was such a wretched prey that its acquisition was not worth the bones of a single Sardinian grenadier.[280]

On 19 September Ciano told the German ambassador in Rome that relations with Greece were decidedly improving. The country was not 'set across Italy's course', which as far as the Balkans were concerned was to be found 'more in the direction of Yugoslavia'. If Greece were less poor, the situation would be different. As things stood, Rome would aim to conclude a 'pact of neutrality, non-aggression, and consultation' with Athens in the near future.[281] However, no genuine settlement was achieved in the following months. Moreover, Mussolini never gave up the idea of launching an invasion of Greece, despite the passing notion that the country could be turned into an Italian satellite by political means. This idea did much to explain the temporary restraint shown towards Athens after the outbreak of the German–Polish war, which tied in with efforts to loosen Greek ties with Britain and France. Nevertheless, the existence of an Albanian irredentist movement enabled Rome to keep all its options open. The minority problem was a card Mussolini could play if his political efforts to subject Greece to Italian hegemony ended in failure.

In the foreground, however, was Yugoslavia. At the end of September military preparations began afresh. Italy provided financial support to the Croat separatists, while unrest provoked by the Communists might also serve as an excuse for intervention.[282] The Italians were prepared to exploit any opportunity that presented itself. Their interest in the Yugoslav question

---

Albania set off a process of military planning which—taking account of the Allied promise of assistance, but not dependent on it—envisaged the resolute defence of the country against Italy initially, and then, after the outbreak of a general war, against Germany also.

[277] See here Tasso, *Italia e Croazia*, i, with a useful division of Italian–Yugoslav relations into phases on pp. iii–vi.

[278] D. M. Smith, *Roman Empire*, 22.

[279] Knox, *Mussolini*, 52; thorough coverage for the entire period 1939–40 in Grazzi, *Principio*, 45–105.

[280] Montanari, *Grecia*, i. 32.

[281] *DGFP* D viii, No. 96, pp. 98–9 (19 Sept. 1939): Ciano here closely follows the argument used by Mussolini to his inner circle in Sept. 1939; see Grazzi, *Principio*, 80; Montanari, *Grecia*, i. 19.

[282] Knox, *Mussolini*, 52 ff.; also Baudino, *Guerra assurda*, 92.

increased after the start of 1940, along with Mussolini's own desire to enter the war. Nevertheless, the plans continued to be pursued in a highly casual manner.[283]

The Germans had been satisfied by the failure of the projected Balkan bloc, partly because its realization might have brought developments unfavourable to German interests in the south-east. Basically, after 1 September 1939 Berlin wanted to keep the region quiet.[284] The status quo was the most reliable guarantee of Germany's hegemonic position in south-east Europe, based on bilateral economic and political agreements. The existing network of relations enabled the Germans to use economic pressure to prevent penetration by third parties. Uncontrolled involvement by another power in the region, even if the power was Italy, would bring undesirable risks. All these assessments led the Germans to place great emphasis, vis-à-vis the Italians, on preserving the status quo in the south-east. Hitler's letter to Mussolini at the beginning of March 1940 stressed that it was in the interest of both countries not to 'set a fire' there.[285] There were good reasons for this fear. On the German side the memory of the Salonika front in the First World War lived on. Moreover, it was an open secret that between September 1939 and June 1940 the Allies, particularly the French, often discussed the possibility of opening a Balkan front.[286] Consequently, the army high command submitted various plans for the defence of Germany's southern borders in such an eventuality.[287]

By the end of May 1940, however, the campaign in the west had destroyed any prospect of a British and French intervention in south-east Europe. The German foreign ministry and the army high command then became concerned that 'Italy's attitude' might cause 'chaos in the Balkans'. Furthermore, they assumed that Italian action against Yugoslavia would provoke Russian intervention in Bessarabia.[288] (In fact the Soviet Union incorporated Bessarabia and the northern Bukovina into its territory at the end of June 1940.) Prior to that, Hitler apparently wanted 'to limit Russian ambitions in the direction of Bessarabia'.[289] However, the commander-in-chief of the army was sceptical about the prospects for doing so; as General Brauchitsch rightly suspected, the territory had already been allocated to the Soviet Union during the German–Soviet discussions in August 1939. Inevitably, this fact limited German efforts

---

[283] Warner, 'Politique', 514–17.
[284] See the excellent description in Collotti, 'La politica dell'Italia', 11–15, esp. p. 15.
[285] *DGFP* D viii, No. 663, pp. 871–80 (8 Mar. 1940), quotation p. 879.
[286] Highly informative is the overview in Barker, *British Policy*, 13–19; see also *Weizsäcker-Papiere*, 178 (14 Oct. 1939): 'For a while we had to consider that our enemies would establish a southern front—a new Salonica. Attempts of this kind are still under way today.'
[287] GenStdH No. 100/39 g. Kdos. of 21 Dec. 1939, BA-MA RH2/v. 390.
[288] *DGFP* D ix, No. 328, p. 446 (27 May 1940); for a chronological assembly of all the information received by German authorities concerning Italian intentions in the Balkans from the beginning of April 1940 see Schramm-von Thadden, *Griechenland*, 42–5.
[289] Presseisen, 'Prelude', 359; see also *Das Deutsche Reich und der Zweite Weltkrieg*, iv. 332–3 (Förster).

in that direction.²⁹⁰ Whether desirable or not, there was no chance of preventing the Soviet absorption of Bessarabia.

German anxieties were eased by Mussolini's letter of 30 May, claiming that he fully shared Hitler's desire to prevent the extension of the war to the southeast. Italy, he observed, was dependent, like Germany, on the Balkans for supplies which could no longer be brought in through the Strait of Gibraltar once Italy entered the war.²⁹¹ In his letter Mussolini suggested a declaration which would calm the fears of Greece and Yugoslavia. On 10 June, when he took Italy into the war, such a declaration was made.²⁹² Consequently, Mussolini's threats against Yugoslavia in May²⁹³—admittedly made only within his inner circle—appeared irrelevant. The Duce seemed to be inspired by German triumphs in the west as though they were his own; in the middle of May he told Ciano that he would not wage war on Yugoslavia, as this would be a 'humiliating expedient', but on Britain and France. There was no time to lose. Ciano, recognizing that his father-in-law had made up his mind, stopped arguing; Mussolini, he wrote, 'has decided to act, and act he will'.²⁹⁴

Mussolini was as capable of grandiose statements as Hitler, but he generally lacked the means to put them into effect. There is an Italian proverb that saying and doing are oceans apart, which sums up the Italian attack on the Allies. At any rate, Greece, the 'wretched prey', gained sudden powers of attraction for Mussolini; he also cast his eyes on Switzerland and, of course, Yugoslavia.²⁹⁵ At this juncture discussions concerning the Balkans were somewhat awkwardly linked with the war effort against Britain.

There is no point in detailing all the 'incidents' which soon caused relations between Athens and Rome to deteriorate. At root these were no more than excuses which allowed Mussolini to push on with a process he had begun with the occupation of Albania, and which now became the object of military planning once again: the establishment of Italian hegemony in south-east Europe.²⁹⁶

When Ciano visited Albania at the end of May, cheering crowds were mobilized on the streets of Tirana to demand the acquisition of Kosovo from Yugoslavia and the Çamüria region from Greece. But Ciano told his inner

---

²⁹⁰ *DGFP* D ix, No. 328, p. 446 (27 May 1940).
²⁹¹ *DDI*, 9th ser., iv. No. 646, p. 500 (30 May 1940); directly relevant is *DGFP* D ix, No. 360, pp. 489-90 (1 June 1940). In conversation with Ambassador von Mackensen Mussolini stressed that he was 'not contemplating any action against Yugoslavia and Greece' (p. 489); also No. 373, p. 505 (2 June 1940), an incomplete translation of the letter of 30 May 1940 (see *DDI* reference above).
²⁹² On the guarantee for Greece and Yugoslavia see Collotti, 'La politica dell'Italia', 21.
²⁹³ See Knox, *Mussolini*, 100.
²⁹⁴ Ciano, *Diary 1939-1943*, 249 (13 May 1940).
²⁹⁵ Tasso, *Italia e Croazia*, ii. 3-4. On this subject and the further development of Italo-Yugoslav relations see Breccia, *Jugoslavia*, 278-312, for the period from Italian entry into the war until the beginning of May 1940; also the different view of Sala, 'Jugoslavia', 85-105.
²⁹⁶ Collotti, 'La politica dell'Italia', 22-3; Knox, *Mussolini*, 139-40; Schramm-von Thadden, *Griechenland*, 46-59.

3. 'Quiet in the Balkans'?

circle that the Albanians would have to limit their revisionism to Çamüria 'for the moment'.[297] Greece, not Yugoslavia, was next in the Italian programme of expansion. On the evening of 23 May he instructed General Carlo Geloso to modify the military plans, which had been directed primarily against Yugoslavia; as a consequence of Italian entry into the war, the conquest of Greece was more urgent. When Geloso predicted problems, mentioned obstacles, and created the impression that he was not ready to proceed, he was replaced on 5 June as commander-in-chief of Italian troops in Albania by General Sebastiano Visconti Prasca.[298]

The rapid German victory in the west, the subsequent armistice with France, and the expectation of an imminent peace caused Mussolini to hesitate over any military adventure for the moment. When the Soviet ambassador asked Ciano about the Italian attitude to the Balkans, the latter assured him that the Fascist regime wanted only to maintain the status quo.[299]

It is noteworthy that it was Hitler who gave fresh impetus to Italian ambitions in the region, ambitions which had stagnated although they had never been abandoned. In a discussion with the Italian ambassador, Dino Alfieri, on 1 July[300] Hitler mentioned the secret documents of the French general staff which had been found at La Charité-sur-Saône,[301] and which provided the Axis with interesting information about the attitude of the Balkan states in the current conflict. Hitler now advised the greatest caution towards Yugoslavia, and pointed out that the Greek prime minister had even declared himself 'in agreement with a landing by the Allies at Salonika'.[302]

Alfieri, whose report to Ciano was similar in tone to the German memorandum, firmly endorsed Hitler's opinion of Yugoslavia. The French documents, he declared, had revealed the 'ambiguous and hostile' attitude of that country towards the Axis. Rome would therefore have to 'settle and clarify many matters' with Belgrade 'at the right moment'.[303] Alfieri's report can scarcely be regarded as a direct call for an active policy, since it spoke of action at a suitable time. But who was to decide when such a time had arrived? Nevertheless, Mussolini seems to have gained the impression that Hitler had given him a free hand against Belgrade. On the eve of Ciano's trip to Berlin, which was designed mainly to co-ordinate Italian and German policy towards France, he gave his foreign minister precise instructions.[304]

---

[297] Jacomoni, *Politica dell'Italia*, 225–6.
[298] Montanari, *Grecia*, i. 34–5; Prasca, *Grecia*, 1 ff.
[299] Ciano, *Diary 1939–1943*, 269 (22 June 1940).
[300] *DGFP* D x, No. 73, pp. 79–83 (1 July 1940); on Mussolini's reaction see Armellini, *Diario*, 49 (3 July 1940).
[301] On this and on the German 'White Books' on the subject see *DGFP* D x, No. 111, pp. 124–5 (4 July 1940) and editors' note.
[302] See n. 300 above, here p. 81; also directly relevant is the Wehrmacht high command study cited at I.II n. 326 above. For international policy towards Yugoslavia after Italy's entry into the war cf. Knoll, *Jugoslawien*, 35–138.
[303] *DDI*, 9th ser., v, No. 161, pp. 147–50 (1 July 1940), here 148–9.
[304] Ciano, *Diary 1939–1943*, 275 (5 July 1940).

Ciano fulfilled these to the letter.[305] During his conversation with Hitler on 7 July he accused Greece of supporting Britain and declared that Italy would occupy the Ionian Islands, Corfu, and the adjacent islands, because Athens was only 'waiting impatiently for the moment when she would be violated by England'. He then came to the subject of Yugoslavia. Italy now had proof that Belgrade's policy was insincere; Prince Paul was behaving like a slave of the British; whatever else the Yugoslavs might be, they were certainly not pro-German or pro-Italian. The Duce therefore no longer shared the view that 'the Balkans should be left in peace as much as possible'. Instead, he believed that he would be forced to settle the Yugoslav question in approximately one month. Rome's intention was clearly to truncate and redistribute Yugoslav territory. The moment seemed favourable, because since the armistice with France Italy had had 'only one land frontier to defend'. Ciano also described his plan for allocating German and Italian spheres of interest in the Balkans: the Adriatic to Rome, Romania and the Black Sea area to Berlin.

According to the German record, Hitler did not reply directly to Ciano's remarks on the subject of Greece. Nevertheless, he made no objection to them, and his reference to the documents discovered at La Charité could even be taken to signify agreement. Ciano's report to Mussolini is rather more detailed.[306] According to this, Hitler fully concurred with Ciano's assessment, i.e. he appreciated the danger that the British might eventually occupy the Ionian Islands and 'transform them into anti-Italian bases'. He was even openly in favour of an Italian preventive action. Furthermore, according to Ciano, Hitler emphasized that everything which affected the Mediterranean and the Adriatic was a purely Italian affair in which he did not intend to intervene. In this way, or so the Italian foreign minister interpreted it, 'he sanctioned a priori any decision and any action ordered by the Duce'. However, Ciano then contradicted his own remarks: though Hitler had declared himself in agreement with a solution to the Yugoslav question in the manner required by Italy, he insisted that it should not take place until the time was ripe. Hitler remained anxious about the possibility of 'setting a fire in the Balkans'. A move against Yugoslavia might lead to intervention from the Soviet Union and perhaps bring about an Anglo-Soviet solidarity of interests. However, these objections would disappear if ever a Balkan war broke out for other reasons; then, of course, Italy must move against Yugoslavia.

Taking the two positions into account, and subject to the approval of Mussolini, the following points were established:

(1) agreement that Yugoslavia could have no place in a new Europe created by the Axis and that the Yugoslav question must be solved in the interests of Italy;

(2) understanding that Italy would not take any initiative for the moment,

---

[305] *DGFP* D x, No. 129, pp. 147–55 (8 July 1940), esp. pp. 152–3.
[306] *DDI*, 9th ser., v, No. 200, pp. 186–90 (7 July 1940), here 188.

3. 'Quiet in the Balkans'?

but would make strategic preparations, assembling the means and military forces to enable rapid action to be taken as soon as an appropriate opportunity occurred;

(3) awareness that this 'appropriate opportunity' could be created by disturbances in the Balkans, or by the imminent collapse of Britain.

Hitler agreed, claiming that this was exactly the policy he recommended to Mussolini. He emphasized again that he had no doubt that the time chosen by the Duce for Italy's intervention would be the correct one. If he really spoke in such terms, they were somewhat optimistic.

However, the German record[307] indicates that Hitler's objections to the extension of war to the Balkans were much more emphatic. It also reports the Italian foreign minister as declaring that he 'fully and completely shared the Führer's reasoning and he was certain that the Duce would also take this attitude'. The Yugoslav matter could be postponed until the 'war with England was settled'. According to this version, Ciano accepted Hitler's views entirely, while the latter gave the following assurance as regards future developments: 'The questions raised by Count Ciano were no problem at all once England was broken or if there was peace with England.'

Nevertheless, it is important to bear in mind that Hitler raised direct objections only to Italian action against Yugoslavia. It was on this question alone that Ciano agreed that Rome would take action when Berlin thought the 'moment had come'. Of course, it could be argued that Greece was part of the Balkans and that, even if he did not refer to it directly, Hitler's interest in keeping the region free from conflict applied to Greece as well as Yugoslavia. But he did not expressly forbid Italian action against Greek territory.[308] Greece and the Balkans were perhaps not regarded, in the last analysis, as forming an indissoluble unit.[309] For example, towards the end of May 1940 some German circles believed that Greece would not enter the war over Italian military measures in the region, 'even if the Gulf of Patras and Crete should be affected'.[310]

Following these discussions, which took place early in July 1940, German ideas for Axis policy in the south-east within the foreseeable future became clear. The Italians were able to perceive their main lines after Hitler's letter to

---

[307] See n. 305, here p. 153.

[308] There is no evidence in the minutes of the talks to support Hitler's statement, cited in Halder, *Diaries*, i. 506 (13 July 1940), that he had attempted to 'interest the Italians in Crete and Cyprus', but that the Italians had rejected the idea. In so far as it is a reliable record the passage confirms Hitler's very open attitude to the Greek question. That apart, Crete in particular had a certain traditional role in German thinking on Italian entry into the war. See ibid. 331 (24 Apr. 1940), not only mentioning the prospect of a Balkan war and Hitler's recommendation of theoretical preparation for it, but also mooting the idea of an attack on Crete; also ibid. 340 (4 May 1940); ibid. 409 (19 May 1940), apparently expecting German occupation of 'Greek islands including Crete'; and ibid. 413 (21 May 1940).

[309] See Schramm-von Thadden, *Griechenland*, 57.

[310] Halder, *Diaries*, i. 413 (21 May 1940).

Mussolini on 13 July.[311] In it, Hitler rejected the Italian offer of extensive support with land forces for the attack on Britain (though air-force assistance was eventually accepted).[312] He also reminded the Italians of their proper military objectives, namely Egypt and the Suez Canal! The refusal undoubtedly vexed Mussolini,[313] although outwardly he professed understanding for a decision taken on account of technical and organizational problems.[314]

Hitler's call for an active Italian policy in North Africa was not basically new, but was meant as an additional hint. A few days later, however, he put the matter more clearly. On 19 July Ciano was in Berlin to hear Hitler's Reichstag speech, calling on Britain to come to terms on the basis of the conditions created by the Wehrmacht in Europe.[315] Ciano then discussed the issue with Ribbentrop, who made it clear that the Germans had no expectation whatever that the British would respond to this 'final appeal'.[316]

In a conversation on 20 July Hitler left Ciano in no doubt that he regarded quiet in the Balkans as essential.[317] The direct cause of his remarks was the problem of Hungarian and Bulgarian revisionist claims against Romania, but Italy was also affected, since Mussolini now wanted war 'more than ever'. Mussolini feared that Hitler's speech, which he considered much too conciliatory, might actually ruin his plans. Contrary to German expectations, the British might seize upon it as an excuse to enter into negotiations.[318] Considering Italy's military situation at the time, this anxiety appears fantastic. According to Ciano, the Italian air force had lost 250 aircraft in the first month of war, as many as the national aircraft industry was able to produce per month;[319] moreover, the inner circles of the Fascist leadership were aware that the Italian position would become untenable if the war lasted more than a year. Italian tank production was in equally dire straits. Even assuming that the necessary raw materials were available, ony thirty armoured vehicles, at most, could be produced by Italian industry each month. That was fewer than 400 tanks per year: an absurdly small total, and certainly not enough.[320]

Yet this was a period when Mussolini had begun to talk of another conflict to follow the one now under way. In four or five years' time there would be a

---

[311] *DGFP* D x, No. 166, pp. 209–11 (13 July 1940).
[312] Ibid., No. 26, p. 27 (26 June 1940); No. 73, pp. 79–83 (1 July 1940); No. 129, pp. 147–55 (8 July 1940).
[313] Ciano, *Diary 1939–1943*, 277 (16 July 1940).
[314] *DGFP* D x, No. 185, pp. 242–3 (17 July 1940).
[315] Ciano, *Diary 1939–1943*, 276–7 (15, 18, 19 July 1940).
[316] *DDI*, 9th ser., v, No. 272, p. 254 (20 July 1940); the view that Hitler's speech was not understood by either side as a serious offer seems to have been quickly accepted by the Italian leaders: see Armellini, *Diario*, 52 (21 July 1940).
[317] *DDI*, 9th ser., v, No. 272, p. 254 (20 July 1940); also Ciano, *Diary 1939–1943*, 277 (20 July 1940); the Italian record of the conversation has been published in English translation in *Ciano's Diplomatic Papers*, 381–2.
[318] Ciano, *Diary 1939–1943*, 278 (22 July 1940); see also Bottai, *Vent'anni*, 188 (24 July 1940).
[319] Ciano, *Diary 1939–1943*, 278 (26 July 1940).
[320] Bottai, *Vent'anni*, 189–90 (10 Aug. 1940).

new struggle, the 'war of the continents', and even this would not be the last. Mussolini thought that, in future, military conflicts would be an increasingly frequent element in international politics. It was therefore necessary to devote more attention to organizing for war than to preparing for peace.[321] Italy had the right soldiers, he believed, but not yet the right generals. Here he may have been thinking enviously of Hitler, since Italian war reporters were quick to claim that the German army and its leaders were eager for battle,[322] while the Italian generals stared at the enemy like rabbits at a snake. Mussolini demonstrated his indignation at the generals' persistent hope that everything could be settled 'at the political level'.[323]

In July 1940, then, the Italians must have been aware that the Germans did not desire any unrest in the Balkans. In particular, they were completely opposed to an attack on Yugoslavia. Despite this, and to some extent contravening Ciano's instructions to the Italian commander in Albania, preparations for war between Italy and Yugoslavia continued. At the beginning of July a study by General Mario Roatta, deputy chief of the army general staff, argued that operations against Yugoslavia could succeed, especially if the Yugoslav defensive positions could be circumvented by means of an attack from Austria and if, at the same time, the Italians advanced over the Julian Alps. To that end thirty-nine divisions were to be concentrated in the eastern part of the Po valley by 27 August. It was estimated that it would take them between two and four weeks to move into attacking positions in Austria and on the Italian–Yugoslav border.[324]

The Comando Supremo accepted the plan on 20 July. It proposed a frontal attack by two armies over the Julian Alps, and an assault by another army from southern Austria. Only two days later Roatta asked the German military attaché to request information from the German general staff about Yugoslav fortifications on the German–Yugoslav border.[325] Initially the high command appears to have made no objection to handing over the information.[326] But on 9 August Rintelen had another conversation with Roatta,[327] which provoked this angry comment from Halder: 'Italians propose to invade Yugoslavia, and want German help: German transport for the build-up, German supply organization, 5,000 trucks, etc. What incredible nerve!'[328] Rintelen had immediately informed Roatta that such an action was not in the German interest, to which the soothing reply was that the matter involved no more than 'preparations by the general staff for an operation that might become

---

[321] Ibid. 191 (7 Sept. 1940).
[322] Ibid. 186–7 (14 July 1940).
[323] Ibid. 192 (19 Oct. 1940).
[324] Knox, *Mussolini*, 165; Roatta, *Otto milioni*, 117 ff.
[325] Rintelen, *Mussolini als Bundesgenosse*, 105.
[326] *KTB OKW* i. 33 (14 Aug. 1940); Halder, *Diaries*, i. 540 (5 Aug. 1940), 544 (9 Aug. 1940); apparently the use which was to be made of the information was not initially understood.
[327] Rintelen's report is published in *DGFP* D x, No. 343, pp. 481–3 (14 Aug. 1940); the report itself is dated 9 Aug. 1940.
[328] Halder, *Diaries*, i. 549 (14 Aug. 1940).

necessary'.[329] But as Roatta well knew, since Mussolini's decision of 8 August this was no longer the case. The operation was intended to be feasible at any time after the end of August, with a preparation time of fifteen days.[330]

Hitler demonstrated a total lack of interest in the Italian proposal. He wanted quiet on Germany's southern border, warned against giving the British an opportunity to gain a foothold in Yugoslavia, and rejected both Rome's request for German–Italian staff discussions and the delivery of information on Yugoslav border fortifications by the army high command.[331] Rintelen then informed Roatta of this decision;[332] the German military could only concern themselves with the matter once the 'political side' was clarified.[333] By now Italian plans for operations in the Balkans were in a state of some confusion. On 8 August Mussolini even ordered preparations for a solution of the Greek question, as the Germans were aware by the middle of the same month at the latest.[334]

It should be noted that since 16 July the Italian general staff had also been discussing an offensive against both Yugoslavia and Greece, launched from Albanian territory. Independently of these deliberations, the navy was planning the seizure of the Ionian Islands. From early August 1940 the Italians were obviously attempting to intimidate the Greeks with a series of provocative acts, including some of a military nature. On 10 August Mussolini spoke of a surprise attack on Greece at the end of September, while Ciano envisaged it taking place even sooner. The press duly reflected the tougher line of Italian foreign policy. On 11 August Visconti Prasca and Francesco Jacomoni di San Savino, the Italian governor of Albania, were informed officially that Mussolini had decided to occupy the Çamüria for political reasons.

The participants in all these discussions seem to have been making very different assumptions, and to have had varying amounts of information concerning the intentions of the political leadership. This was true of Badoglio, Roatta, Soddu, and Visconti Prasca. No one really knew the true state of affairs. Nevertheless, three basic designs can be recognized: Ciano and Visconti Prasca inclined towards a surprise attack on Epirus and Corfu before Greece had a chance to mobilize; at the same time both Ciano and Mussolini seem to have believed that Greece could be intimidated into making concessions; finally, there was also Mussolini's personal opinion. He tended to favour a surprise attack, but also wanted to make use of intimidatory tactics even though these were bound to reduce the element of surprise. Mussolini calculated that the time to attack would come at the end of September, particularly if Britain had collapsed by then. During this period, therefore, it seems that Mussolini wanted to move against Greece and Yugoslavia at the same time.[335]

---

[329] *DGFP* D x, No. 343 (see n. 327).
[330] Knox, *Mussolini*, 166–7.
[331] *KTB OKW* i. 36 (15 Aug. 1940).
[332] Rintelen, *Mussolini als Bundesgenosse*, 105–6.
[333] *DGFP* D x, No. 343 (see n. 327).
[334] Halder, *Diaries*, i. 550 (15 May 1940).
[335] Knox, *Mussolini*, 167–72.

3. 'Quiet in the Balkans'?

In the middle of August, in parallel, so to speak, with their refusal to agree to an Italian attack on Yugoslavia, the Germans began to clarify the 'political side' of the affair.

Italian–Soviet relations played a role in this process which can only be described briefly here. In June the Italian ambassador had returned to Moscow and the Soviet ambassador to Rome. Thereafter, both sides demonstrated a desire to improve the political climate, which had deteriorated since the outbreak of the Russo-Finnish war.[336] Stalin's chief concern was to consolidate Soviet influence around the Black Sea, while Mussolini was eager for a *rapprochement* which would prevent strong links between Yugoslavia and the Soviet Union. He hoped that a spectacular agreement with the Soviets, modelled on the Nazi–Soviet non-aggression pact of August 1939, would persuade Stalin to abandon Yugoslavia to Italian ambitions, and would also strengthen his position *vis-à-vis* Berlin.[337]

Mussolini had become suspicious that Italy would come off second best in the formation of the 'new order' in Europe.[338] Ciano, apparently informed of Mussolini's intentions on 4 August,[339] wrote on that day a summary of the most important events in Italian–Soviet relations during June and July 1940. He urged Mussolini to tell the Germans about Italian intentions towards the USSR.[340] Ciano assumed that, as Hitler did not want unrest in the Balkans, he would veto Italy's plan to attack Yugoslavia. Partly for that reason, he regarded Mussolini's proposal for a far-reaching *rapprochement* with the Soviet Union as premature.[341] In any case, he contacted the German ambassador in order to sound out the German attitude.[342]

The German government was not opposed to a general improvement in Italo-Soviet relations, but advised the Italians not to discuss the Balkans or the Straits with Moscow.[343] For Ciano this was welcome news.[344] The Italians continued to handle the whole affair in a desultory fashion, despite evidence in September of Soviet irritation at the lack of response.[345] Subsequently, when the Italians tried to organize fresh talks with the Soviet Union at the end of 1940 and the beginning of 1941, in the hope of obtaining supplies, the Germans strictly forbade it. Moscow, Ribbentrop warned on 19 January 1941, was not 'trustworthy'—and Ciano did not protest any longer.[346] In view of Hitler's decision to attack the Soviet Union, taken at the end of July 1940, the

---

[336] Schmitt, 'Italian Diplomacy', 167–8.
[337] Breccia, *Jugoslavia*, 321–2; Knox, *Mussolini*, 166.
[338] *DGFP* D x, No. 243, pp. 331–2 (27 July 1940); *DDI*, 9th ser., v, No. 341, pp. 312–16 (1 Aug. 1940).
[339] Ciano, *Diary 1939–1943*, 280 (4 Aug. 1940).
[340] *DDI*, 9th ser., v, No. 356, pp. 345 ff. (4 Aug. 1940).
[341] Ciano, *Diary 1939–1943*, 281 (6 Aug. 1940).
[342] *DGFP* D x, No. 290, pp. 416–19 (6 Aug. 1940).
[343] Ibid., No. 348, pp. 486–7 (16 Aug. 1940).
[344] Ibid., No. 357, pp. 501–2 (17 Aug. 1940).
[345] Ibid. xi, No. 42, pp. 54–6 (10 Sept. 1940).
[346] Toscano, *Mancata intesa*, 85–132, quotation p. 108.

German attitude was not surprising. At this stage the Italians had not yet been informed of the decision officially, though they had begun to feel its effects.

As regards Italian relations with Greece and Yugoslavia, on 14 August 1940 Ribbentrop pressed for clear information on the extreme tension between Athens and Rome.[347] The Italians claimed that they were interested only in precautionary measures in case the British gained a foothold in Greece.[348] When Ambassador Alfieri held further discussions with Ribbentrop on 16 August, the latter again gave detailed reasons for the German decision on the Yugoslav question. It was clear that Berlin did not want conflict with either Belgrade or Athens. Quiet in the Balkans should be maintained. Alfieri thereupon handed over a document which was subsequently seen by Hitler, in which the Italians explained that they did not intend to start 'action of any sort' against Yugoslavia; moreover, they were striving to 'transfer the dispute with Greece to the diplomatic plane'. Their only military action would be to send another three divisions to reinforce the six already in Albania.[349]

Alfieri told Ciano that the German attitude towards both Greece and Yugoslavia was dominated by their preoccupation with the decisive struggle against Britain; they had therefore emphasized yet again that this required an Italian victory in North Africa.[350] Directly afterwards, the Italians reaffirmed their intention to behave with restraint towards Greece and Yugoslavia, and to concentrate military resources on the defeat of Britain. There were also renewed assurances that military discussions and decisions involved preventive or contingency measures rather than preparations for an attack.[351] But when Alfieri presented the Italian position officially on 20 August, Ribbentrop stressed that war should not be started in the Balkans under any circumstances. Berlin evidently still did not trust the Italian attitude towards Greece.[352]

At this time Mussolini in fact ordered his military commanders to complete the movement of forces to the Yugoslav border by 20 October (previously 20 September), and to the Albanian–Greek border by the end of September (previously the end of August). An attack was only to be considered if the other side became aggressive. North Africa was to have priority.[353] But this did not reassure the Greeks, who turned to the Germans for more information.[354] German mistrust had not disappeared[355] when Mussolini finally wrote to Hitler on the subject.

---

[347] *DDI*, 9th ser., v, No. 413, p. 396 (14 Aug. 1940).
[348] Ibid., No. 420, p. 402 (15 Aug. 1940).
[349] *DGFP* D x, No. 353, pp. 495–6 (17 Aug. 1940); see on this subject No. 383, p. 534 (23 Aug. 1940).
[350] *DDI*, 9th ser., v, No. 431, pp. 414–15 (17 Aug. 1940).
[351] Ibid., No. 435, pp. 418–19 (17 Aug. 1940); *DGFP* D x, No. 357, pp. 501–2 (17 Aug. 1940); also No. 367, pp. 512–13 (19 Aug. 1940).
[352] *DDI*, 9th ser., v, No. 451, pp. 435–6 (10 Aug. 1940).
[353] Ibid., No. 467, pp. 452–3 (22 Aug. 1940); No. 469, p. 454 (22 Aug. 1940).
[354] Ibid., No. 467, pp. 452–3 (24 Aug. 1940); *DGFP* D x, No. 338, pp. 538–9 (13 Aug. 1940).
[355] *DDI*, 9th ser., v, No. 490, p. 475 (25 Aug. 1940).

3. 'Quiet in the Balkans'? 399

In his letter Mussolini briefly summarized his view of the international situation. As regards south-east Europe, he still maintained the position which had been agreed in Berlin and Rome, according to which Italy remained determined to keep the region out of the conflict. Once again, he claimed that Italian measures on the borders with Greece and Yugoslavia were purely precautionary and were justified by the fact that both countries were deeply hostile to the Axis and were only waiting for a favourable opportunity to fall on Germany and Italy from the rear. There was evidence that Greece was still an accomplice of the British, since Greek ports were being used as British bases. Nevertheless, Italy would advance against Egypt unless unforeseeable circumstances intervened; Marshal Graziani had already received the order to go into battle on the same day that the German army invaded the British Isles. Mussolini was not to know that this signified the Greek calends.[356]

However, Mussolini's explanation still failed to reassure the Germans. On 27 August Alfieri reported that senior German military figures and politicians, including Ribbentrop, were still warning Italy more or less directly not to unleash war in the Balkans. The ambassador regarded this fear as genuine, and based on the fact that the Germans did not yet have their hands free; as soon as they did, the situation would change. Germany, he thought, had nothing against a settlement of Balkan affairs as such and would then co-operate with Italy, but would also take care to safeguard its own, extensive interests in the region.[357]

In Alfieri's view there was logic in German pressure for restraint. For the moment the Germans wanted to prevent the extension of the war, and in the long term they wished to prevent the Italians gaining an advantage over them in the south-east. Significantly, Berlin did not offer Athens any opportunity to play the Axis powers off against each other. The Greeks were consistently informed that Germany did not approve of their links with the British; they were warned not to use the Italian measures as an excuse for mobilization;[358] and they were bluntly told that the Germans believed the word of the Italians rather than that of the Greek government.[359] The German attempt to maintain quiet in the Balkans had nothing to do with sympathy for the Greeks.

As part of the negotiations which led to the second Vienna arbitration on 30 August 1940 and ended the danger of hostilities between Hungary and

---

[356] *DGFP* D x, No. 388, pp. 475–6 (24 Aug. 1940); identical to *DDI*, 9th ser., v, No. 484, pp. 469–70. In his reply of 17 Sept. Hitler stated that the attack on Britain would begin as soon as the weather allowed: *DGFP* D xi, No. 68, pp. 102–5.
[357] *DDI*, 9th ser., v, No. 506, pp. 490–1 (27 Aug. 1940); see also No. 508, pp. 491–2 (27 Aug. 1940): report from Alfieri to Ciano on a conversation with Field Marshal von Brauchitsch. For similar reports indicating that Germany wanted Greece for itself, see Cliadakis, 'Neutrality and War', 186.
[358] *DGFP* D x, No. 363, p. 509 (18 Aug. 1940); No. 372, p. 520 (21 Aug. 1940); No. 377, p. 525 (22 Aug. 1940); No. 386, p. 536 (24 Aug. 1940); No. 387, pp. 537–8 (24 Aug. 1940); No. 391, p. 541 (25 Aug. 1940); No. 394, pp. 544–5 (27 Aug. 1940).
[359] Ibid., No. 334, pp. 472–3 (13 Aug. 1940).

Romania,³⁶⁰ Hitler and Ciano again exchanged views on the situation in south-east Europe and the Balkans.³⁶¹ Basically they thought alike. Hitler accepted Mussolini's view that Greece and Yugoslavia, and even Romania, were 'fundamentally foes of Italy and Germany'. Greek and Yugoslav conduct was dictated purely by expediency.³⁶² On the other hand, German and Italian interests required that war should not break out in the region at present, since it was needed as a source of supplies. Ciano agreed without reservation: 'The outbreak of a conflict had to be avoided at all costs, since its effects on Italian supplies, especially of petroleum, would be extremely serious.'

In the three weeks following this exchange of views, concrete Italian plans to invade Yugoslavia were virtually abandoned. Moreover, military plans for a campaign in the Balkans remained largely theoretical or preparatory. However, these facts do not support the conclusion that Mussolini's restraint towards Greece was anything other than temporary.³⁶³ The Germans had certainly won a temporary success. No one appeared more relieved by this than Badoglio, who considered that Italian plans to attack Yugoslavia and Greece had been 'quashed' by the German prohibition.³⁶⁴ September passed in relative calm. Despite continued harassment of the Greeks, there were no grave provocations as there had been in the past.³⁶⁵ Significantly, Hitler's letter of mid-September referred to the German 'potato, turnip, and cabbage crop', but not to the Balkans.³⁶⁶ Yet the sense of relaxation was not complete, at least not everywhere. To return to the theme of this section, there was no genuine 'quiet in the Balkans' in September 1940.

---

[360] Ibid., No. 407, pp. 566–70 (28 Aug. 1940).
[361] Ibid., No. 413, pp. 581–7 (30 Aug. 1940).
[362] This claim was not new; see ibid., No. 121, pp. 133–6 (5 July 1940); No. 215, pp. 282–3 (23 July 1940).
[363] Knox, *Mussolini*, 175–9.
[364] *KTB OKW* i. 175–9.
[365] Schramm-von Thadden, *Griechenland*, 87–8; G. Vogel, 'Überfall', 3393–4.
[366] *DGFP* D xi, No. 68, pp. 102–5 (17 Sept. 1940).

III. Mussolini's Invasion of Greece The Beginning of the End of Italy's Great-power Status

IT is sometimes difficult to distinguish between fact and appearance in history. In the case of the Balkans, this is particularly true of Ribbentrop's discussions with Mussolini and Ciano in Rome between 19 and 22 September 1940. One of the most controversial questions of Italo-German relations in the last four weeks before the Italian invasion of Greece concerns the German attitude at this meeting. Did the Germans on this occasion give the Italians a free hand in the Balkans, notwithstanding their sustained efforts to keep control over developments there during the previous weeks? These meetings certainly have a very important place in any assessment of the attack on Greece; in historiographical terms, they reflect the gradual Italian shift from obedience to the German veto on disturbance in the south-east to independent action.

1. THE POLITICAL DECISION

The main purpose of Ribbentrop's visit to Rome on 19 September was not to discuss the Balkans. Instead, the talks must be seen in the context of plans for the Tripartite Pact,[1] in connection with which Ribbentrop gave the Italians another detailed account of the German view of the state of the war and the general situation.

First, the German foreign minister discussed 'the struggle against Britain' with Mussolini. The Germans maintained that the only factor which had so far prevented final victory was the weather. Ribbentrop spoke of reducing London to ruins, of damaging attacks on British armament factories, of crippled ports, of German air superiority—though not supremacy—and of the fact that there were no usable airfields left between the capital and the south coast. If Ribbentrop was to be believed, the Luftwaffe had carried all before it.[2] Only the weather was outside German control, and it had saved Britain for the time being. The war—and Ribbentrop was not the only one to proclaim this—was virtually over; only its formal conclusion remained.

Such optimism was agreeable, but it was vexing that the British appeared equally confident of victory. The Germans thought they knew why Britain was

---

[1] See I.III.1 (b) above. The Italians were again surprised at the state of affairs: see Ciano, *Diary 1939–1943*, 291 (19 Sept. 1940).
[2] See vol. ii of the present work, IX.II–IV (Maier), esp. III.3 at nn. 88–9.

fighting on; the British were hoping 'to be rescued by America and Russia'. Ribbentrop therefore had some good news: if Mussolini agreed, within a few days the Axis powers could conclude a military alliance with Japan, which should keep the United States out of the war. The Germans were aware of the danger that Stalin might react by coming to an understanding with Churchill and Roosevelt, but believed that, all things considered, the Soviet Union would not alter its course.

After some remarks on Anglo-Bulgarian relations, the conversation turned to Yugoslavia and Greece. Ribbentrop stated that it was better for 'Italy's plans for the future regarding Yugoslavia' to keep the Soviet Union out of the region. Apart from that, the German record reads as follows: 'Regarding Greece and Yugoslavia, [the foreign minister] emphasized that this concerned Italian interests exclusively, the settlement of which Italy alone should decide, in which it could be sure of sympathetic support from Germany. However, the Germans thought it better not to touch on the problem at this time, but to concentrate all forces on the destruction of England.'[3]

As to this point,[4] Mussolini declared that he would 'make no military move against either [Greece or Yugoslavia] for the present'. Italian troop concentrations on the borders with these countries were purely precautionary. The record continues: 'The internal situation of Yugoslavia was bad, while the Greeks were playing the same role in the Mediterranean that the Norwegians had played months ago as accomplices of England. If Italy conquered Egypt, the British navy could not remain in Alexandria and would possibly seek refuge in Greek ports.' To minimize the danger Mussolini was describing, Ribbentrop noted that British ships would then be easier to attack. His comment can be regarded as evidence that he would have been opposed to any military over-reaction in such circumstances. Finally, Mussolini agreed that 'at the moment the main thing was the war against England, that he would therefore conduct himself calmly towards Yugoslavia and Greece, and intended first to carry out the conquest of Egypt'.

According to the Italian record,[5] Ribbentrop stated that his government's only interest in Yugoslavia was in the district of Maribor. Otherwise Germany regarded Greece and Yugoslavia as a purely Italian sphere of influence, and it was for Mussolini alone to find suitable solutions to unresolved questions. However, Ribbentrop stressed yet again that the military efforts of the Axis must now be directed against Britain. The indication is clearly that, though Germany was promising support for any policy that Italy thought it necessary to pursue against Greece and Yugoslavia, this was not a blank cheque which could be cashed at any time. Nevertheless, the Italian record does not give the war against Britain the same unequivocal priority as does the German. The

---

[3] *DGFP* D vi, No. 73, pp. 85–7, quotation p. 87 (20 Sept. 1940).
[4] Ibid. 87.
[5] *DDI*, 9th ser., v, No. 617, pp. 598–601 (19 Sept. 1940), here 599.

significance of such differences should not, of course, be exaggerated, since the texts are not verbatim transcripts; they record only the points which the respective minute-takers regarded as significant. However, such an explanation does not suffice in this instance, since the Italian version of Mussolini's remarks on the Greek–Yugoslav problem differs so clearly from a number of points in the German text.[6] The Italian record states that Italy must 'proceed ... to liquidate Greece'. This decision is represented as the consequence of the statement, which also appears in the German version, that 'Greece represents for Italy what the Norwegians meant for Germany before the action in April'. Mussolini's supposition that the British fleet might take refuge from Alexandria in Greek ports was only an additional reason for Italy to move against Greece, and not a requisite condition for the launching of an Italian attack. Nevertheless, it is not certain that Mussolini was using these speculative remarks to prepare the way for a specific course of action. Whatever the truth of the matter, in the context of the record as a whole one thing is evident: Mussolini's agreement that the 'major concern' of the Axis war effort was 'to defeat England' did not necessarily mean that he was abandoning his ambitions in the Balkans.

Comparison of the German and Italian records raises further problems. The German minute shows Ribbentrop, following the discussion with Mussolini, informing the Italians about the dispatch of a German military mission to Romania at the latter's request. German troops were to provide the Romanians with 'certain military backing ... because of the Russians', and to protect the oilfields.[7] Neither the Italian record nor Ciano's diary (which, it must be emphasized again, is not entirely reliable as a source) contains any such reference.

A comparison of the two records, therefore, reveals that only the Italian version contains any mention of the 'liquidation of Greece'; only here does Ribbentrop describe the Greek–Yugoslav region as an exclusively Italian sphere of influence in which Mussolini could do as he pleased. On the other hand, the Italian text contains no reference to the need for success in North Africa before an operation in the Balkans. There is also no clear promise from Mussolini that he would act against Greece and Yugoslavia only when Egypt was conquered or Britain defeated. Finally, the Italian record makes no mention of the sending of a German military mission to Romania.

However incredible it may be, it seems that Mussolini was not told about Ribbentrop's news concerning the military mission.[8] Ciano, none the less, received this information officially and at an early stage. We cannot know why Ribbentrop did not give Mussolini the information direct, but he was under no obligation to do so. Problems of internal communication in Italy apparently

---

[6] Ibid. 600.
[7] See n. 3, here p. 87; on the military mission see *Das Deutsche Reich und der Zweite Weltkrieg*, iv. 335 ff. (Förster).
[8] Schramm-von Thadden, *Griechenland*, 89.

prevented the German move from being accurately assessed, but the Germans can scarcely be blamed for that. It is clear that, as regards the Balkans, Ribbentrop was talking only about political measures. Perhaps that was not how he was understood by the Italians. However, when Mussolini claimed that Italy might be provoked into action if the British fleet sought refuge in Greek ports, Ribbentrop's response indicates, at least, that he considered major land operations to be neither appropriate nor necessary. He thought the Italian response should be limited to air raids. This, at least, is the objective analysis of what took place. Subjectively, despite his leisurely handling of Balkan issues over the following days, Mussolini seems to have thought that Hitler had given him a free hand in both Greece and Yugoslavia.[9]

At the end of Ribbentrop's visit there was thus confusion on both sides about the extent and binding nature of guidelines for Axis policy towards the Balkans. This was not immediately apparent. But when the differences emerged, both the Germans and the Italians (as is usual in such cases) could produce good reasons to support their own interpretation of the discussions.

On 22 September, the day of Ribbentrop's departure, Mussolini told Badoglio of his satisfaction that the war would continue for some time, since a rapid end to hostilities would harm Italy's prospects of achieving its war aims.[10] The Duce was playing for time. The knowledge that the Wehrmacht was not on the point of invading Britain gave Rome some breathing-space. There no longer seemed to be a direct pressure for immediate success. Mussolini could proceed to capture pawns in his own time. There were many indications that this new sense of timing played an important role in the days after his talks with Ribbentrop.

Three days after the conversation with Badoglio, the latter ordered a meeting of Italian military leaders in the Comando Supremo and gave them details of the latest developments.[11] On the basis of this discussion, the generals could assume that Italian troops were unlikely to intervene in Yugoslavia. Invasion would be most likely after an internal uprising, and there seemed no prospect of this in the foreseeable future. Furthermore, Badoglio stressed that it was in the interests of both Italy and Germany that the situation in Yugoslavia should not change, because the country was supplying the Axis with many raw materials. On the Greek–Albanian border the Italian government intended to deploy nine divisions by the end of the month. According to the marshal, that would be sufficient to hold the Greeks in check. Most remarkable, perhaps, was his assertion that the fate of Greece and Yugoslavia would be settled at the peace conference, making resort to war unnecessary.[12]

In view of this discussion by the commanders in chief, it has rightly been

---

[9] Knox, *Mussolini*, 190.
[10] Armellini, *Diario*, 91 (23 Sept. 1940).
[11] Montanari, *Grecia*, ii, doc. 29, pp. 96–7 (25 Sept. 1940).
[12] According to Armellini, *Diario*, 94–5 (25 Sept. 1940), Badoglio quoted Mussolini in his reference to the peace negotiations.

1. The Political Decision

stated that 25 September 1940 'marked the end of the first phase of Mussolini's war against Great Britain'.[13] In fact, where the Balkans were concerned there were clear signs of a relaxation of tension in Rome. On the other hand, the impression in Albania itself was that the action against Greece might begin at any moment. It appears that, perhaps again as a result of inadequate communication, General Visconti Prasca had not understood the implications of recent developments.[14]

One further measure was taken which was later to hinder the Italian campaign against Greece. In autumn 1940 large parts of the Italian army were demobilized. The order for demobilization appears at first sight to be evidence that in late September and early October Mussolini did not intend to launch an attack. In this context it must be remembered that the Italian army had been partly mobilized in September 1939, demobilized again in October and November of that year, and then, in February 1940, had been almost fully mobilized. Subsequently, in July, economic conditions had necessitated another partial demobilization which left utter confusion in its wake. No army in the world could have emerged unscathed from this merry-go-round of mobilization and demobilization. In October a combination of economic facts and psychological calculations—the Italian population had to be persuaded that the situation was normal—led to further changes. Mussolini ordered that 600,000 out of 1,100,000 soldiers were to be sent home with effect from 10 October. The effect was all the more serious because the demobilization was organized by age-group, which meant that almost every unit lost men. A limited demobilization, restricted to specific units, would have been less damaging.[15] In addition, the measures meant that large-scale troop transfers had to be undertaken in the various units, because the release of reservists required a redistribution of personnel and material. This made such demands on the military machine that an *ad hoc* mobilization was impossible for the time being. In his protest against demobilization, which was originally due to be completed by 15 November, General Roatta declared that it would take months to restore the army to combat-readiness. Mussolini's decision meant that any major offensive operation was out of the question for the foreseeable future.[16]

The Italian war effort and military planning at the beginning of October 1940 can be summarized as follows. Priority was given to the offensive in North Africa. Rome hoped to solve the Greek–Yugoslav problem within the framework of general peace negotiations, though these were not regarded as imminent. However, this did not mean a definite abandonment of military action. Mussolini's statements must be interpreted mainly as implying a temporary postponement of long-term plans to attack Greece or Yugoslavia. He had no qualms about raising hopes when the moment seemed opportune,

---

[13] Knox, *Mussolini*, 192.
[14] Montanari, *Grecia*, i. 60 ff.
[15] Ibid. 63–70; Knox, *Mussolini*, 193 ff.
[16] Faldella, *L'Italia*, 246.

and in these weeks it was expedient to play down the danger of a Balkan war. At the same time he was no doubt influenced by the conviction that Italy would gain military success in North Africa, by the unpopularity of a Balkan adventure among many of his military leaders, and by the objections of the Germans. Yet what did Mussolini's 'decision' actually entail? Remarkably, the preparations for 'Case G' continued,[17] though with the proviso that its execution was 'postponed for the moment'.[18] Phrases of this kind will bear almost any interpretation.

With hindsight, it is possible to say that ambiguity was a major characteristic of developments during this period. Optimistic military assessments held that 'Case G'—the conquest of Epirus, and the occupation of Corfu (Kerkira) and some of the Ionian Islands—could be carried out with the forces which had been transferred to Albania since the beginning of October, plus the Bari Division, which would be ordered to capture Corfu from southern Italy. Italian planning thus assumed that, under favourable conditions, the big demobilization need not prevent an attack on Greece. In other words, Mussolini had not really committed himself. The most that can be said is that in late September and early October he did not intend to move against Greece or Yugoslavia immediately. Badoglio, who was not exactly a fire-eater, may have recognized this fact and tried to exploit the hour of indecision. Though Roatta and other generals protested against demobilization, the old marshal did not do so, apparently because, given his pessimistic assessment, it would prevent an extension of the war.[19]

Did all this mean that Mussolini intended to maintain 'quiet in the Balkans'? If this were the case, it might explain why the region is not mentioned in the records of his conversation with Hitler at the Brenner on 4 October 1940.[20] Unlike Hitler, the Duce had travelled without his military commanders; he was anxious to play his favourite role of great military strategist—in North Africa—and to gratify an almost pathological desire to be regarded as an 'all-round genius'.[21] However, the record of the meeting is misleading as far as the Balkans are concerned. Recent research has shown that Greece, Yugoslavia, and Romania were all discussed at the Brenner, and Mussolini certainly thought he had been given a free hand in Greece. Doubtless Hitler did not urge him to take action, since this continued to be contrary to German interests. Instead, the talk seems to have been of operations without a definite

---

[17] Numerous documents relating to 'Emergenza G' (Case G) are published in Montanari, *Grecia*, ii, docs. 17, 18, 25–8, 31–2, 34–5, dealing with the period from the end of August to the beginning of October.
[18] Ibid., doc. 35, p. 112 (3 Oct. 1940).
[19] Knox, *Mussolini*, 194–5; Faldella, *L'Italia*, 246.
[20] *DGFP* D xi, No. 149, pp. 245–59 (4 Oct. 1940); *DDI*, 9th ser, v, No. 677, pp. 655–8 (4 Oct. 1940).
[21] Armellini's comments on this were published in 1946: Armellini, *Diario*, 102–3 (4 Oct. 1940). Yet the legend persists that Mussolini 'did not imagine himself to be a military leader': see Kuby, *Verrat*, 138.

time-scale; the capture of Marsa Matruh appears to have been used as a form of marker for the Italian action.[22]

Since the defeat of Britain in the Mediterranean played an important part in plans to secure Germany's strategic flank for the Russian campaign, Hitler could have little objection to the elimination of Greece, whose attitude he mistrusted. However, it was essential that such a project should offer good prospects of success, which the Germans thought would be the case after an advance to Marsa Matruh and beyond. The British would then continue to be tied down in North Africa.

A suggestion of this kind was actually due to be made to the Italians on 28 October, when Hitler and Mussolini met in Florence. As we know, by that time it was already too late.[23] The same idea, however, was contained in a letter which Mussolini sent to Badoglio the day after his return from the Brenner. 'When we get to Marsa Matruh we shall see which of the two pillars of the Mediterranean will be the first to fall: the Egyptian or the Greek.'[24] Coincidence? Hardly. General Armellini described Mussolini's change of opinion after his conversation with Hitler, noting that 'the reappearance of the action against Greece seems to be designed not to achieve Albanian irredentist goals, but to eliminate a support of England. It is no longer about Çamüria, but directly about Salonika and the Greek naval bases, i.e. the whole of Greece.'

We must therefore investigate the reasons which subsequently persuaded Mussolini not to follow this proposed sequence of events, but to attack Greece while Marsa Matruh was still in British hands. The Romanian affair seems to have played a key role in this development. After Ribbentrop's earlier remarks about the establishment of a German military mission in Romania, Italy had received no further official information on the subject. However, on 8 October a report arrived in Rome from Pellegrino Ghigi, the Italian minister in Bucharest, stressing that the arrival of German troops was imminent and would complete German hegemony over Romania. The government in Bucharest, he added, was well aware of this, and hoped for greater Italian activity in Romania to create a barrier against German influence.[25] Meanwhile, the United Press agency—wrongly, as it turned out—had reported the actual arrival of German troops in Romania.[26] Mussolini was apparently indignant that German soldiers alone were to be stationed at the centre of the German–Italian oil-supply network.[27] Ghigi was immediately instructed to persuade the

---

[22] Creveld, *Balkan*, 33–9; Knox, *Mussolini*, 200–3; on 29 Sept. 1940 State Secretary von Weizsäcker noted Ciano's warning as to the need not only to think of Egypt, but also 'to obtain guarantees in Greece soon as well', which seems to imply that the issue had been mentioned at the Brenner: *Weizsäcker-Papiere*, 220.

[23] *KTB OKW* i. 131–2 (28 Oct. 1940).

[24] Armellini, *Diario*, 105–6 (5 Oct. 1940).

[25] *DDI*, 9th ser., v, No. 676, p. 654 (4 Oct.1940).

[26] Knox, *Mussolini*, 206.

[27] Ciano, *Diary 1939–1943*, 469 (8 Oct. 1940).

Romanians to ask for a contingent of troops, albeit a smaller one, from Italy,[28] but the Romanians regarded the demand as too risky.[29] Rome and Berlin, they argued, must first agree between themselves. These discussions were then overtaken by events when the Germans felt obliged to inform the Italians of what was happening.[30]

Berlin instructed its embassy to remind Ciano on 10 October that, during Ribbentrop's visit to Rome, he had been told of the request made by General Ion Antonescu, head of the Romanian government, for the 'dispatch of German military units to Romania'. The German government had acceded to this request. After a second request from the Romanians, these troops would now be accompanied by a contingent of the Luftwaffe. The whole arrangement would be in the Italian interest no less than the German. Ciano was asked to give Mussolini this information, as he no doubt had the first. The Italian foreign minister listened to Ribbentrop's message 'without comment'. Some days later Mackensen told Weizsäcker that the Italians were still greatly put out; it would be desirable for a smaller Italian force to be sent along with the German troops, since that was what the Italians wanted.[31] On the same day the ambassador told his foreign minister that 'the question of a showdown with Greece, which was put aside for the time being last August, still engrosses minds here, and powerful forces, including Count Ciano, are working to reach a solution of the Italian–Greek problem'. Mackensen had learnt that military action at the end of October or in the first half of November could not be ruled out. However, unless any new factors had emerged at the Brenner meeting, it could be assumed that Mussolini would not march against Greece until after a British surrender.[32] What had actually happened?

It must be remembered that on 5 October Mussolini had ordered Marshal Graziani to attack in North Africa between 10 and 15 October.[33] He was unimpressed by the objections of his military leaders, who regarded the time-scale as impossible. Clearly, the Duce was willing to pay almost any price for a success which could be exploited for the purposes of domestic propaganda, and would also show that Hitler's insistent offer to send German troops to North Africa was unnecessary.[34] However, Marshal Graziani made a strong case[35] for delaying the offensive. In his view the proposed date was completely unrealistic. This was already known to Mussolini on 12 October,[36] when

---

[28] *DDI*, 9th ser., v, No. 694, pp. 669–70 (8 Oct. 1940).
[29] Ibid., No. 714, pp. 686–7 (12 Oct. 1940); No. 720, pp. 692–3 (13 Oct. 1940).
[30] *DGFP* D xi, No. 167, p. 277 (9 Oct. 1940).
[31] Ibid., No. 192, pp. 324–5 (18 Oct. 1940).
[32] Ibid., No. 191, pp. 322–3 (18 Oct. 1940).
[33] Armellini, *Diario*, 105 (5 Oct. 1940).
[34] Faldella, *L'Italia*, 248; on the Germans' desire to take part in the war effort in North Africa in the second half of 1940, see I.III.2 above.
[35] On the subject as a whole—communication between Mussolini, Badoglio, and Graziani in connection with the offensive of October 1940—see *Prima offensiva*, i. 29–35.
[36] Ciano, *Diary 1939–1943*, 297 (12 Oct. 1940).

German troops entered Bucharest, reportedly to shouts of 'Heil!' from the population.[37]

In view of Mussolini's reaction, it is largely academic to enquire how much knowledge the Italians had, or could have had, of German activity in Romania before 12 October, and what effect this had as regards the Italian attack on Greece. Ciano gives a very precise account of Mussolini's indignation at the 'German occupation of Romania'. The event had a deeply damaging effect on public opinion in Italy, and Mussolini feared that it might even demolish his image as a great military leader and politician. After the Vienna arbitration, he had not expected Hitler to act alone in such a matter. As it was, this latest affront was the last straw. The stationing of German troops in Romania was not the actual cause of the Italian invasion of Greece; but it provided the background against which a project long desired for its own sake, but temporarily postponed, was set in motion. While Graziani was unable to advance on Marsa Matruh, Mussolini was no longer prepared to respect Hitler's wishes concerning the sequence of Italian operations. Mussolini himself summarized the practical consequences of developments in Romania in a famous outburst: 'Hitler keeps confronting me with a *fait accompli*. This time I shall pay him back in his own coin; he shall learn from the newspapers that I have occupied Greece. Thus equilibrium will be restored.'[38] The decision was undoubtedly taken on the spur of the moment, as the military leadership only found out about it later. This fact is yet more evidence that Mussolini, who like Ciano thought the operation would be easy, regarded himself as a gifted strategist.

At least some Italian leaders knew from 13 October that the invasion of Greece was now due to begin on the 26th. But the objective was no longer the one prepared for in 'Case G', the conquest of Epirus as far as the River Arakhthos. Instead—though Badoglio, Roatta, and Soddu did not discover this until 14 October at the earliest—the plan was to conquer the whole of

---

[37] Knox, *Mussolini*, 208.
[38] Ciano, *Diary 1939–1943*, 297 (12 Oct. 1940); the above interpretation of Mussolini's decision to attack Greece draws on various studies. It is largely in agreement with Knox, *Mussolini*, 208–9. However, the idea of a dual offensive against the British position in the eastern Mediterranean, which was entertained on the Italian side, is not given the same significance here as by Knox. Ultimately it was Mussolini who had talked of Egypt or Greece. Graziani's decision not to attack did not arrive in Rome in its definitive form until after 15 Oct., but the trend was known. In the interpretation given here, it is expressly accepted that the project was not improvised but reflected long-term Italian aims, and that it should also be seen in the context of Italo-German rivalry in south-east Europe; cf. Cervi, *Hollow Legions*, 60, and Collotti, 'La politica dell'Italia', 24–5. On the place of the aggression in Fascist imperialism see Bocca, *Storia*, 247; Catalano, *Trionfo dei fascismi*, 291 ff.; Canzio, *La dittatura*, 601–2. The setting-up of the German military mission is also interpreted as a tactical move by Mussolini in Hillgruber, *Strategie*, 282, and Tasso, *Italia e Croazia*, ii. 154–7; it is given greater importance by Jacomoni, *Politica dell'Italia*, 247, and by Salvatorelli and Mira, *Storia d'Italia*, 1052. The effect of the military mission seems to be overemphasized in Cruickshank, *Greece*, 34; Presseisen, 'Prelude', 361; Wiskemann, *Rome–Berlin Axis*, 230. It is also given too much stress as a decisive factor in Schramm-von Thadden, *Griechenland*, 96–7, despite a detailed description of the origin of the decision, in which the Brenner meeting is still interpreted as though the Balkans were not mentioned there.

Greece. Of course there were protests and references to the changed conditions created by this new objective. In their attempt to respond, the generals turned to the 1939 Guzzoni–Pariani plan for the conquest of Greece. This plan called for the assembly of twenty divisions, on the assumption that the Bulgarians would, as Mussolini believed, tie down between six and eight Greek divisions. Three months would be needed to ship the necessary twelve divisions from Italy to Albania, along with strict restrictions on civil transport. It thus emerged that the Italian troops would be in position and ready to attack at a time when conditions in Albania were suitable perhaps for skiing, but certainly not for major military operations.[39]

On 15 October the decisive discussion concerning the invasion took place.[40] Apart from Mussolini, it was attended by Ciano (foreign minister), Badoglio and Soddu (commander and deputy commander of the Italian armed forces), Jacomoni (Italian governor in Albania), Roatta (deputy army chief of staff), and Visconti Prasca (commander-in-chief in Albania). Surprisingly, there were no representatives of the air force or the navy. Roatta arrived very late because he had not been informed in time. Moreover, he was still under the impression that the issue would boil down once again to 'Case G'. However, on 15 October he wrote to Graziani that the situation had changed since the previous day, and that the aim now was to launch an operation on 26 October 'with the objective of occupying the whole of Greece'.[41] This was indeed the case. Mussolini proposed a two-phase plan, whose first stage would consist of 'Case G', the second being the Guzzoni–Pariani plan of 1939.[42]

Mussolini opened the meeting by providing general directions for the attack on Greece. He indicated that in its first phase the action would pursue both naval and territorial goals. The achievement of its objectives on land would guarantee Italian control of the southern Albanian coast. Furthermore, the Ionian Islands of Zakinthos, Kefallinia, and Corfu must be occupied and Salonika captured, thus considerably improving Italy's position *vis-à-vis* Britain. As a second step, or possibly at the same time as the operations of the first phase, the whole of Greece was to be occupied and the country taken out of the war permanently. Moreover, Greece must then be kept in the Italian 'political-economic sphere of influence' at any cost.

Mussolini emphasized that he had planned the project even before the

---

[39] Schramm-von Thadden, *Griechenland*, 101–2.
[40] The record of this meeting has been published on a number of occasions: *DDI*, 9th ser., v, No. 728, pp. 699–705; Faldella, *L'Italia*, 753–9; Grazzi, *Principio*, 206–15; Montanari, *Grecia*, ii, doc. 52, pp. 159–67; Schramm-von Thadden, *Griechenland*, 209–17; Cervi, *Hollow Legions*, doc. 41, pp. 311–20.
[41] Quoted in Knox, *Mussolini*, 211.
[42] The following is based on *DDI*, 9th ser. (see n. 40); detailed comments on the discussion in Cervi, *Hollow Legions*, 67–71; Knox, *Mussolini*, 211–14; Montanari, *Grecia*, i. 77–84; Schramm-von Thadden, *Griechenland*, 103–6. Note also the observations of a contemporary: Jacomoni, *Politica dell'Italia*, 254–8, who also refers to the overall character of the discussions and to the imprecise arguments of the participants.

1. The Political Decision

outbreak of the European war, and was thus realizing a long-term goal. He then sketched in the political background. He saw no problem in the north, since Yugoslavia would keep quiet as long as it was not attacked. Nor were the Turks a danger, because the Germans now had troops in Romania, and Bulgaria was thus strengthened. Sofia could now be used as Mussolini had hoped, as a pawn in the Italian game. Finally, Bulgaria had no doubt made its own definite claims on Greek Macedonia and for access to the sea.

Jacomoni then presented his own analysis, which Mussolini undoubtedly found agreeable. The governor stressed that the Albanians were positively eager for war and full of enthusiasm for military action. Consequently, less significance was attached to his other comments: the road network was insufficient to ensure supplies, and the port of Durrës was a problem because the supply-chain running through it was vulnerable to attack from the air.

The discussion then turned to the Greeks themselves. Mussolini dismissed the idea that the British would be able to help them. Jacomoni believed that the Greeks would resist, particularly if Italian troops failed to advance rapidly and on a broad front. He also thought that a partial occupation of the country might allow the British to gain a foothold. As Jacomoni saw, this argument did not please Mussolini. When the governor was asked once again about Greek morale, he was quick to say what Mussolini wanted to hear: the population appeared 'deeply depressed'. Ciano argued that only a very small and wealthy upper class would be ready to defend itself, while the mass of Greeks were completely indifferent. This would be the case, he thought, even in the event of an Italian invasion. Events were soon to prove him wrong.

Visconti Prasca's assessment of the situation was recklessly optimistic. The general thought the Greeks had no stomach for a fight; on the other hand, his own troops, allegedly well prepared in every respect, were thirsting for battle. Given the superiority in numbers—as 70,000 Italians against 30,000 Greeks—he could win the battle in ten to fifteen days. The date of 26 October would be a good choice for launching the attack, because it left enough time to prepare. Visconti Prasca was confident that he could bring off a major encirclement operation, and his chief concern was with the enemy air force. The remaining Greek troops would be forced to fight mainly in isolation, since geographical factors made it extremely difficult to move reinforcements to the Epirus region. Only with regard to the march on Salonika did the Italian commander in Albania show a degree of caution, and even then because of the weather rather than the Greeks: he was concerned about the imminent rainy season. Nevertheless, Mussolini insisted on this objective because of his desire to prevent British forces from gaining a foothold in Salonika. It was roughly 300 km. from Durrës to Salonika and, according to Visconti Prasca, the operation would require approximately two months. His argument did not win agreement, because Salonika was important to Mussolini. Finally, the participants agreed on the 'incidents' which were to act as an excuse for the Italian invasion. The provocation was scheduled for 24 October.

Badoglio wanted the operation in Greece to be launched at the same time as Graziani's advance to Marsa Matruh. This would certainly have suited Mussolini, but who could seriously believe it to be a practical proposition given the suggested starting date of 26 October? Perhaps Badoglio did; he even demanded that the campaign should go on until Crete and the Peloponnese were in Italian hands, since only that would signify that the occupation was complete. If the marshal meant what he said, then the idea was reasonable from the ideal military viewpoint. But objectively—that is, in the light of Italy's military weakness and the state of preparation of the project—Badoglio's proposal was completely unrealistic. Like the entire discussion of 15 October, it merely serves to illustrate the military incompetence of the participants. The plan for a dual offensive against the British positions in the eastern Mediterranean was wholly impracticable, given Graziani's obvious endeavours to gain time and delay the attack in North Africa. Mussolini had apparently recognized this before 18 October, when he told Graziani that he should take whatever time he considered necessary. In reality, this meant that, if things went according to plan, the Greek campaign would be over by the time Graziani arrived in North Africa.[43]

The need now, Badoglio reminded Mussolini, was for concrete preparations, including the twenty divisions necessary to enable the operation to be carried out within three months. However, the Guzzoni–Pariani plan assumed three months for the transportation of these troops. During the discussion of this problem, Roatta produced the inspired suggestion that the troops which had not yet reached Albania by the start of the first phase should be transported there as the struggle for Epirus got under way. These troops would then be available when required for the assault on the Greek heartland. Assuming that the operations in Epirus could be concluded by 15 November, this left one month in which to land the extra divisions in Albania. This was truly unadulterated 'ideology of the will', or what Mussolini called 'Fascist resolution'.

Throughout the meeting, difficulties were light-heartedly brushed aside. Major geographical problems were ignored, almost as though Italian troops could fly. Roatta considered that two divisions would be sufficient to threaten Salonika; Badoglio saw no danger of a landing there by the British. For his part, Visconti Prasca reckoned that five or six divisions would have no difficulty in marching to Athens as soon as his troops had won the battle for Epirus. When Roatta reminded Visconti Prasca that the Pindus mountains were a formidable barrier to an advance on Athens, the discussions showed signs of degenerating into farce. The commander in Albania actually purported to solve the problem by claiming that the Pindus was full of mule-tracks which he knew very well; he foresaw no difficulty in getting his divisions to Attica, like a modern Hannibal. Yet only a few minutes before the

[43] *Prima offensiva*, i. 32–5.

same chain of mountains had been used as evidence that the Greek troops in Epirus would be virtually cut off from their supplies. Visconti Prasca, Mussolini's specialist on Albania, swept aside further problems in an equally bewildering fashion. Asked about the mountain divisions which would be needed as reinforcements for the second phase, he argued that these could be disembarked at Preveza, the harbour for Arta, in a single night.

For the general, the conquest of Epirus seemed to be the solution to every problem. Nobody argued. Even Badoglio was silent when, after about ninety minutes, Mussolini declared that every aspect of the campaign had been adequately discussed. The marshal promised to finalize the military details. Mussolini's summary was short and concise: 'offensive in Epirus, observation and pressure on Salonika, and, as a second step, march on Athens.' Such was the planning of an entire military campaign.

What did the Germans know of these goings-on? Almost everything, but nothing decisive. Between 16 and 24 October Berlin obtained abundant information about the imminent aggression from its various military and civilian offices in Italy, Albania, and Greece. By 18 October the Germans knew the original date set for the attack, which was later put back from 26 to 28 October. However, the Italians in conversation issued various denials, describing the reports as empty scaremongering. The Germans eventually accepted these, and made no serious attempt to investigate more thoroughly. Many regarded the rumours as altogether implausible; after all, it was these same Italians who had signally failed to demonstrate any military prowess against France or in North Africa. The foreign ministry, the Wehrmacht high command, the army high command, and the navy all discussed the danger of a Graeco-Italian war. Yet when they received news of Mussolini's letter to Hitler—some on 24 October, the others a day later—and were thus supplied with concrete evidence, the Germans were taken by surprise that their allies really seemed determined to attack.[44]

Hitler received Mussolini's letter on the way back from his meetings with Franco, Laval, and Pétain. He must have learnt of its contents some time between midnight and midday on 25 October. He did not react at once: he was in any case preparing for a new exchange of views with Mussolini to settle certain differences of opinion on Axis policy in Europe, and particularly on the role of France. This, however, was not too urgent. Not until supplementary information was received from the foreign ministry, reporting that the date of the attack on Greece had been quite definitely fixed for 26 or 27 October, did Hitler decide to travel to Florence rather than Berlin.[45]

It is certain that differences of opinion on policy towards France were not the main reason why Hitler ordered his train to change course. The balance

---

[44] First full account in Schramm-von Thadden, *Griechenland*, 110ff.; discussed, with an assessment of all relevant sources and literature, in Knox, *Mussolini*, 223–6.

[45] Knox, *Mussolini*, 227–8.

was tipped by the increasing threat of a premature Italian invasion of Greece. Ribbentrop now telephoned Ciano to request a meeting, which the Italians, without enthusiasm, agreed to hold on 28 October. As Ciano's reaction suggests, the Italians probably had no fear that Hitler would thwart Mussolini's plans for Greece, because it would already be too late by the time the meeting took place in Florence. They were more anxious lest the Germans should present them with a 'cup of hemlock' as regards the Italian demands on France. Ciano felt that this would be a more bitter disappointment for the Italian people than even the treaty of Versailles had been.[46]

In fact Hitler had no intention of treating Mussolini in this way. Towards the end of October State Secretary Weizsäcker actually believed that Germany did not intend to prevent the Italian attack on Greece at any price.[47] However, this opinion probably reveals the confusion surrounding political assessments in the Reich leadership rather than reflecting Hitler's real intentions. In truth, he would no doubt have been only too eager to dissuade Mussolini from launching his attack; but Hitler could scarcely believe that the dates given by the foreign ministry, 26 or 27 October, were definite. Only this can explain his vehement reaction to the Italian invasion when he received news of it in Tuscany in the early hours of 28 October. According to Army Adjutant Engel, Hitler was beside himself with fury:

F[ührer] raging when he hears of the Italian attack on Greece. Complains about Gmn. liaison staff and attachés, who only 'went to lunch-parties' and were not proper spies... Judges that the Duce is afraid of our economic influence in the Balkans, and doubts whether Italians can defeat Greece as the Greeks are not bad soldiers in themselves. The F. says verbatim: 'This is their revenge for Norway and France.' But he, F., had been forced to act secretly, since every second Italian was a traitor or a spy. Angry words about Rintelen, who let himself be conned. Only advantage is that now the British will be forced to stand their ground there too.... Greatly alarmed that Italy's action may involve the entire Balkans and give the British a welcome excuse to set up an air-base there.[48]

The Germans arrived in Italy too late to prevent the Greek campaign. But this did not mean that the meeting, originally planned to discuss Hitler's ideas for an anti-British continental bloc, had 'lost its point'.[49] Here we must bear in mind the 'latent opposition' between the Axis powers which was always revived by the issue of France,[50] and which dated from before the war. As Italo-German relations developed after the armistice with France, Mussolini could not be persuaded that Hitler's dealings with the Vichy government were dictated primarily by tactical considerations.

Furthermore, the Italians attached great weight to the fact that Pétain was

---

[46] Ciano, *Diary 1939–1943*, 300–1 (25 Oct. 1940).
[47] *Weizsäcker-Papiere*, 221 (21 Oct. 1940).
[48] Engel, *Heeresadjutant*, 88 (28 Oct. 1940).
[49] Kuby, *Verrat*, 141.
[50] *Weizsäcker-Papiere*, 221 (25 Oct. 1940).

1. The Political Decision

strongly influenced by Germany in his ideas on the future of France. In his eyes, Berlin rather than Rome was the really important power with which to maintain relations. As Pétain's convictions became increasingly apparent, these cast great doubt on Mussolini's hope, entertained when Italy entered the war, that France could be persuaded to support the Italians against German interests.[51] Mussolini's letter to Hitler[52] certainly reflected this change in the situation as seen from Rome, although its first objective was to provide information about the imminent invasion of Greece. The letter called in question the entire German strategy in the Mediterranean and North Africa, as this had been conceived and discussed in the context of the 'strategic dilemma' in the second half of 1940. Mussolini sought to frustrate Hitler's plans by means of a political manœuvre, the main aim of which was to impair relations between Germany and France. For this purpose it was necessary to confront the Vichy government with the final demands of the Axis powers at a peace settlement. The underlying idea accurately reflected Mussolini's calculations in June 1940; he hoped to convince the French that only Germany posed a threat to the existence of France, while Italy would be satisfied with superficial adjustments.

In his letter Mussolini referred adroitly to the meeting at the Brenner: he had, he said, reflected deeply on this, and had formed conclusions that he must not withhold from Hitler. He first examined the relationship between the Axis powers and France, where, according to his information, Germany and Italy were intensely hated. Opinion in that country was so pro-British as to make French collaboration in the war against Britain inconceivable. But, unlike the German diplomats, Mussolini did not even want such collaboration to occur. He frankly advised Hitler not to make further attempts to establish co-operation of this kind. The French, 'after having denied [the reality of] their defeat, would believe and cause others to believe that the victory over Great Britain was due to them, and to them only, and they would be capable of presenting us [the Axis] with the bill'.

In this way Mussolini sought to prevent a Franco-German *rapprochement* which would further damage the political and military influence of Italy. With his unequivocal demand for the abandonment of any idea that France would join the continental bloc, Mussolini was using the general situation in France to disguise his own objectives. As camouflage the argument was not unskilful, and the next step had a certain logical consistency. If things were really as

---

[51] See I.II.2 above.

[52] *DGFP* D xi, No. 246, pp. 411–22 (19 Oct. 1940); *DDI*, 9th ser., No. 753, pp. 720 ff. On the interpretation of and background to the letter see also Creveld, *Balkan*, 39–48, who thinks that the passages concerning France caused Hitler's sudden decision to travel to Florence. The importance of these passages is beyond doubt, but they could also have been discussed later, so that this interpretation must give way to the belief that Hitler's decision was based on Weizsäcker's telegram. However, this is only true of the timing of the meeting, and not the need for it against the background of the developments outlined above. Hitler's fit of rage when he discovered he was too late is also evidence that Greece, at that moment, was being given priority.

Mussolini said, it was not necessary to waste time in 'defining the shape of the metropolitan and colonial France of tomorrow'. In that case the task was what Hitler 'justly wished', i.e. to reduce French territory in such a way that the French would never again dare 'to dream of expansion and hegemony'. Here Mussolini was deliberately reminding Hitler of his declarations of intent at the Brenner. However, he also made it clear what the Italians wanted: German demands should destroy any French illusions and make them realize that they had no chance of reaching an agreement with the Germans which would allow France to retain its status as a great power. By contrast, Mussolini himself would make only modest demands on France. Besides some reparations, he would be content with the acquisition of Nice, Corsica, and Tunis. He would also keep hold of Somaliland, of course, but that was only a desert and of little value.

Thus, in the middle of October, Mussolini was apparently again determined to keep further developments in the Mediterranean in his own hands. Naturally he invited Hitler's comments, but the letter had increased the obstacles confronting German attempts to create an anti-British European bloc. Rome was not only opposing the entry of Vichy France into the continental bloc, but was proposing that the Pétain government should be informed of the final peace terms. That was just what the French were expecting, and Hitler had no intention of doing.

This was not all: Mussolini was even working to create further difficulties. He maintained categorically that Spanish non-belligerence was considerably to the advantage of the Axis. It might well be that 'tendencies hostile to the Axis' had weakened in Spain, but the economic weakness of the country remained. In other words, the Italian government was not impressed by German plans for the conquest of Gibraltar. Regarding France, the continental bloc, Spain, and Gibraltar, Mussolini's letter amounted to a catalogue of rejection.

Even at the heart of the letter, this independence of view was maintained. Here Mussolini mentioned the need, in the longer term, to destroy 'the remaining English positions on the European continent'. He regarded this as essential if victory was to be achieved. Portugal, Yugoslavia, Greece, Turkey, Egypt, and Switzerland were touched on here. Of these states, Portugal was neutralized by Spain, and the Turks would not dare to intervene because of the German 'occupation forces' in Romania. Switzerland was a somewhat different matter, since neither the British nor the Germans regarded Switzerland as an 'English position', given its geographical situation and the power-political state of Europe after the fall of France. Nevertheless, Mussolini declared in Sibylline fashion that Switzerland's 'incomprehensibly hostile attitude' towards the Axis had brought the country's existence into question. Yugoslavia, as he knew Hitler agreed, was described as hostile to the Axis and as a 'bad neighbour' to Italy; in the long term, burdened by the antagonism between Serbs and Croats, 'she cannot exist as she is'. Nevertheless, Rome did not intend for the time being to alter its attitude towards

1. The Political Decision

Belgrade, marked by 'watchful vigilance'. These last remarks were sincere, because Mussolini was now turning his attention towards Greece, that puny adversary which had once not been worth the sacrifice of a single Sardinian grenadier, but was now to claim the lives of thousands of Italian soldiers. In this context Mussolini emphasized his determination to act 'very quickly'.[53] Greece remained a cornerstone of British naval strategy in the Mediterranean, its people as a whole were profoundly anti-Italian, and the government in Athens was allowing the British to use Greek air-force and naval bases. In short—and this was not new—Greece was the Norway of the Mediterranean and would therefore share its fate.

Mussolini then turned to the offensive against Egypt which the Germans were so eager to see. In reality, the date for the attack on Greece was now fixed, and it was equally certain that Graziani would not make an appearance in North Africa for some considerable time, if at all. Hence Mussolini's comment that he still hoped to move against Greece and Egypt simultaneously may be dismissed as pure camouflage to disguise the timing of the Balkan campaign. More significant was the clear statement that the 'co-operation' of German armoured forces in the struggle for Egypt would only be 'considered' after the capture of Marsa Matruh. To say the least, this was not in harmony with the German desire to deploy the Wehrmacht in Egypt.

Many issues had been raised to justify a meeting between the two leaders, which finally took place on 28 October. By the time Hitler's special train arrived in Florence at 11 a.m., the dictator had regained his self-control. Had Mussolini, who was waiting to greet him on the platform, been afraid of this meeting?[54] Previously he had shown considerable self-assurance, and had even enjoyed preparing to provoke his ally. Whatever the atmosphere, attacks were launched in Albania while the two men spoke in the historic Palazzo Vecchio. In the first instance they discussed the results of Hitler's talks with Pétain, Laval, and Franco.[55] Regarding the Balkan war, Hitler merely indicated that 'Germany could make available for the military operations against Greece, especially for the protection of Crete against occupation by the English, a division of airborne troops and a division of parachute troops, for which North Africa would be the proper starting-base.'[56] This did not eventuate. In the course of the conference, which was really another of Hitler's monologues, the subject appears not to have been dealt with in more detail.

The Italian record concludes with the comment that the two sides reached agreement 'on all points'.[57] Ciano at least thought so, noting with great

---

[53] The following is cited from *DDI* (see n. 52), as the translation in *ADAP* contains some significant inaccuracies.
[54] Kuby, *Verrat*, 141–2, on the atmosphere in which the meeting took place.
[55] See I.III.1 (*b*) above.
[56] *DGFP* D xi, No. 246, pp. 411–22 (28 Oct. 1940), quotation p. 411; *DDI*, 9th ser., v, No. 807, pp. 771–5 (28 Oct. 1940).
[57] *DDI*, 9th ser. (see n. 56), 775.

satisfaction that Florence had demonstrated the unimpaired solidarity between the German and the Italian leadership.[58] The fact that Germany did not break off diplomatic relations with Greece (she only did so in 1941) evidently did not affect Ciano's assessment. For their part the Germans thought that everything 'went off smoothly', and that Mussolini now fully accepted the Franco-German relationship.[59] According to Weizsäcker, Hitler had pulled off his usual trick of beguiling Mussolini, whose 'forceful letter' had left no trace behind it.[60]

On the surface this was true, but it soon became clear that the demonstration of Italian weakness in the Balkans was to some extent dimming the radiance of German military victories. The two were allies, and Italian defeats inevitably cast a shadow on the German position.[61] For some time Hitler remained personally vexed by Mussolini's display of independence. He had no desire to send German troops to Libya or to Albania[62] (and indeed, at that stage they were not asked for). However, the German attitude changed very quickly. From 4 November onwards preparations were made 'in case of need, together with the Bulgarians and in co-ordination with the Italian operations in Greece, to take possession of Greek Macedonia and Thrace' in order to protect the Romanian oil-producing areas.[63]

By that time the Italian troops in Albania had begun their attempt to scale the Balkan heights. Initially they made rapid advances, but their progress soon slowed down and finally stopped altogether. Early in November the extent of this setback was clear:[64] one step forward was to be followed by two steps back. Gradually the Italians were forced back down the mountains, and by the middle of February 1941 they had lost one-third of Albania to the Greeks. But this is to anticipate developments. Why and how did this disaster occur?

2. Italy's Plan of Operations

It has rightly been observed that after the discussions in the Palazzo Venezia on 15 October Badoglio first approved of the entire enterprise, then opposed its implementation, and finally, after an unsuccessful attempt to stop it, consented once again.[65] There is no doubt that he had agreed to the Greek operation on 15 October. Next day, however, Admiral Cavagnari presented

---

[58] Ciano, *Diary 1939–1943*, 301 (28 Oct. 1940).
[59] Halder, *Diaries*, i. 669 (31 Oct. 1940); Halder, however was inaccurately informed when he believed that the Greek affair had 'not even been touched on'. In any case this shows that the chief of the army general staff had not been informed about Hitler's offer of military intervention.
[60] *Weizsäcker-Papiere*, 223 (6 Nov. 1940).
[61] Thackrah, 'Italian Invasion', 340–3, 347–8.
[62] Halder, *Diaries*, i. 671 (1 Nov. 1940); see also *KTB OKW* i. 144 (1 Nov. 1940).
[63] *KTB OKW* i. 150 (4 Nov. 1940); details in III.1.2 below (Vogel); Fabry, *Balkan-Wirren*, 34–5.
[64] Ciano, *Diary 1939–1943*, 301–4 (28 Oct.–8 Nov. 1940).
[65] Cervi, *Hollow Legions*, 77.

2. Italy's Plan of Operations

him with the navy's verdict on the discussions, stating that it would be impossible to land the troops at Preveza, a base which would be acquired with the conquest of Epirus. The admiral also feared that the British would establish air and naval bases on Greek territory as a consquence of the Italian attack. This could threaten Taranto and force the withdrawal of the fleet stationed there.

At a meeting with Marshal Badoglio, General Roatta, and General Pricolo on 17 October, Cavagnari stressed that the plan to land three divisions at Preveza in a single night was unrealistic. His view was that it would take three months to get them to Arta. Furthermore, he referred again to the threat to Taranto and the possible damage to Italian naval strategy. General Roatta declared himself astonished that the operation was to be carried out under current conditions, while General Pricolo demanded at least a week's delay to give time for the air-force units to be made at least partly ready.[66]

Badoglio was very receptive to these arguments. He and General Soddu went to report to Ciano, as Mussolini was away from Rome. There is evidence that the marshal expected Ciano to be a useful ally; obviously he did not know his foreign minister, or he would not have been so trusting. However, Badoglio was extremely adaptable, as he proved yet again when the matter was put before Mussolini on 18 October. It was fairly clear to the marshal that Mussolini was already in an exceptionally bad mood because of Graziani's delaying tactics over North Africa. He even appeared ready to put an end to any confrontation by dismissing Badoglio if necessary. The latter therefore made a complete about-turn, presenting himself to Mussolini as a compliant strategist. All that was achieved was a postponement of the date of the attack from 26 to 28 October. Cavagnari's protest had been futile. After 18 October the orders for the war against Greece were issued without further counter-proposals.[67]

The plans and preparations developed 'rapidly' and 'chaotically',[68] and need not be described in every detail. Nevertheless, it would be going too far to claim that enthusiasm for the war led Mussolini to 'forget' that demobilization had been ordered.[69] The army general staff appealed to the minister of war for the order to be rescinded, without notable success. In fact, the remobilization of the army was not ordered until 26 November, when the Greek campaign had already turned into a disaster.[70]

On 20 October, nevertheless, the operational plans for the campaign against Greece were ready.[71] In line with the discussions of 15 October, these pro-

---

[66] Montanari, *Grecia*, i. 85–6; ii, doc. 53, p. 168.
[67] Ibid. i. 86 ff.
[68] Ibid. 88–96, very thorough on the preparations for the attack, and 109–24, on the preliminary operational studies. Also Knox, *Mussolini*, 217–21, quotation p. 217.
[69] D. M. Smith, *Mussolini*, 257.
[70] Schramm-von Thadden, *Griechenland*, 108.
[71] For further details see esp. the documents in Montanari, *Grecia*, ii (cited in the following notes as *M.G.Doc.*).

posed an army offensive in Epirus; this part of the plan, based largely on 'Case G', appeared to have some prospect of success. However, the plan to threaten Salonika, and particularly with an attack by only two divisions, was wildly unrealistic. The Greek troops in that region—five combat-ready divisions and three reserve divisions—would have had little difficulty in dealing with the Italians. The Italian plans were probably intended to indicate that the Macedonian flank must be covered. The only completely new part of the project was the advance on Athens, to be carried out in a second stage.[72]

However, in these plans of 20 October[73] (see Map II.III.1) the conquest of Epirus was itself extended. Previously 'Case G' had provided for an advance to a line roughly corresponding to the course of the Arakhthos river. Now the plan was to capture certain positions south and east of the Gulf of Arta (Amvrakia), enabling the Italians to control the gulf itself and land the required reinforcements. Parallel to the offensive in Epirus, the Bari Division was to land on Corfu. As soon as this objective was achieved, Visconti Prasca would be given control of this unit also.

While these operations were being carried out, the Italian troops in the Korçë (Koritsa) region on the Graeco-Albanian border were to adopt a position of active defence in order to tie down the enemy. All incidents on the border with Yugoslavia were to be avoided.

As soon as the planned reinforcements arrived, the march from Epirus to Athens was to begin. The invasion of the Greek heartland was to be carried out in two great movements: one involved fanning out in the north through Arta–Lamia–Tanagra, with a vital role for flank cover in the direction of Thessaly; the other would come through Arta–Agrinion–Mesolongion in the south. A strip of territory south of the Corinthian Canal was also to be seized.

At the same time as the above operation, the units transferred to Korçë were also to launch an offensive in the general direction of Florina and Kastoria. The objective was to tie down the Greek forces in the area, to force the Greek high command to withdraw more units from Thessaly and eastern Greece, and to achieve favourable starting-positions for an eventual attack on Salonika.

The entire plan could be changed suddenly if the situation developed exceptionally favourably as a result of the internal collapse of Greece and the cessation of significant resistance. In that case the advance on Athens and the strategic movements round Korçë would begin even if the expected reinforcements had not yet arrived.

Furthermore, on 20 October the army general staff named the large units which, though still stationed in Italy, were to be deployed against the Greeks. These were:

- the motorized Trieste Division, which, it was hoped, would be transported to Albania by 15 November (in fact only the divisional command

[72] Montanari, *Grecia*, I, 124–5.
[73] *M.G.Doc.* 70, pp. 219–22 (20 Oct. 1940): army general staff to C.-in-C. in Albania.

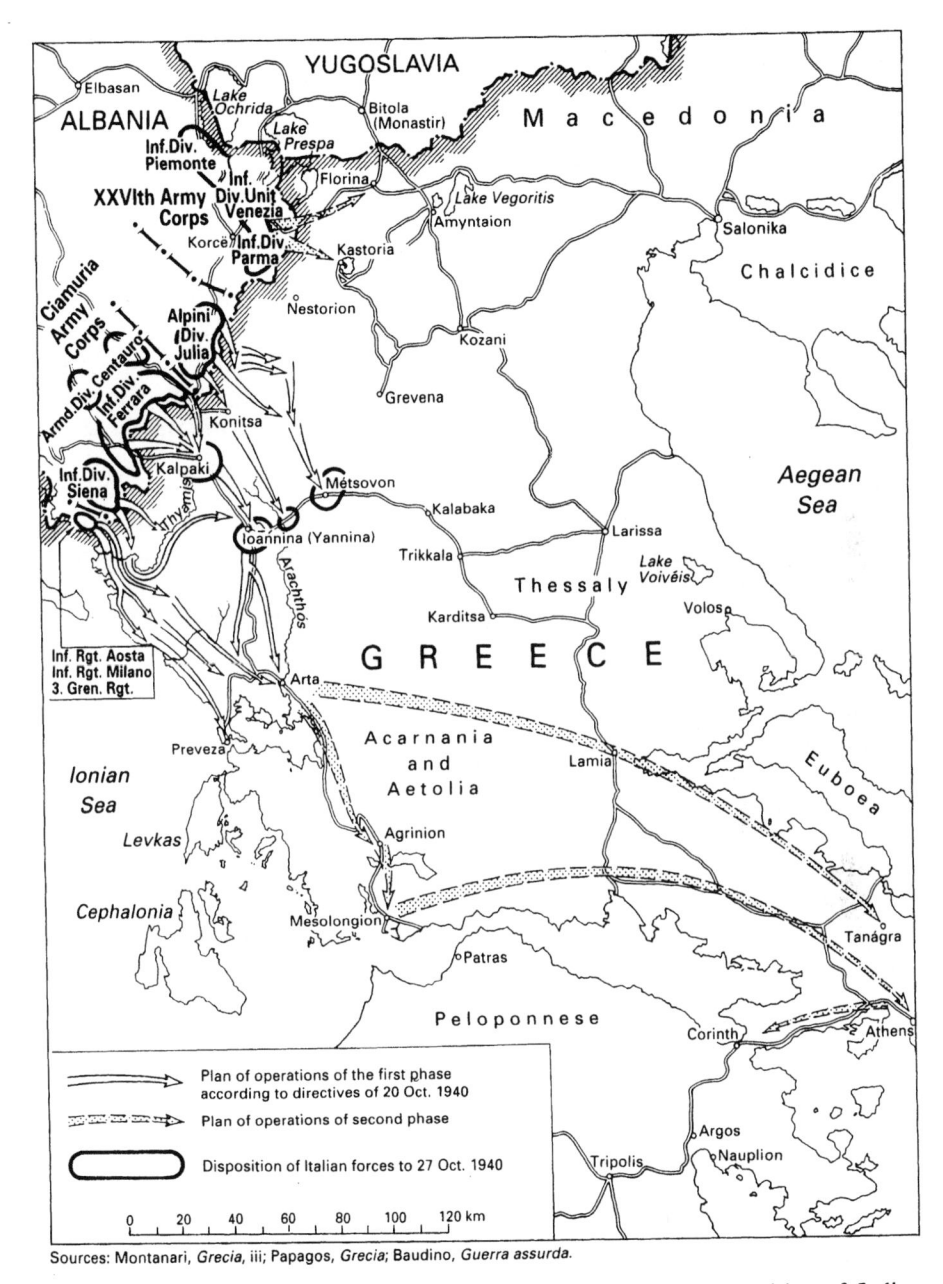

MAP II.III.1. The Italo-Greek War: Plan of Operations and Disposition of Italian Forces at End of October 1940

and a few artillery units reached Albania on schedule because of a lack of transport capacity);
- an infantry division to be deployed in the hills or a pure mountain division, though the means of transporting it to Albania were not specified;
- three divisions suitable for mountain duty, but which were still in the process of formation;
- a mobile division, which likewise had yet to be formed.

On 23 October the Comando Supremo summarized its plans under 'Case G'. These also involved the landing on Corfu, and an order to Marshal Graziani and the commander in the Dodecanese, General De Vecchi, to engage the British on land and sea on the day of the attack.[74] Graziani was to make particular use of his tanks; De Vecchi was to attack British warships and merchant ships with surface vessels and submarines.

Next day the chiefs of the Italian armed forces held a meeting with Badoglio to discuss the plan for the last time.[75] By now the marshal knew that King Boris of Bulgaria had no intention of playing the part the Italians had wanted; Sofia would not intervene.[76] However, Badoglio does not seem to have been unduly worried by the elimination of a significant element in the Italian battle plan.[77] The important thing was that the Greeks believed in the Bulgarian threat, as the deployment of their troops on the Bulgarian border revealed.

That apart, Badoglio concentrated on the discussion of three strategic questions. First, it was agreed that the invasion of Corfu should take place if possible at three locations, and at least at two. The project depended mainly on the weather. Badoglio, Cavagnari, and Roatta decided that the landing would have to be called off if conditions at sea meant that troops could be landed at only one place.[78] The participants also quickly agreed their approach to the Kefallinia landing: because of serious problems in ensuring supplies for the 2,400 men who would be involved in the operation, it was postponed until further notice. Exactly when it would be implemented was not specified. The chief of the Comando Supremo then turned his attention to the plan of operations itself.

---

[74] *M.G.Doc.* 74, pp. 227 ff. (23 Oct. 1940): Comando Supremo.

[75] Ibid. 75, pp. 230–3 (24 Oct. 1940). Participants: Gen. Ubaldo Soddu (ministry of war), Adm. Domenico Cavagnari (C.-in-C. of the navy); Gen. Francisco Pricolo (C.-in-C. of the air force), Gen. Mario Roatta (deputy chief of army general staff), Adm. Edoardo Somigli (deputy chief of naval staff), Gen. Giuseppe Santoro (deputy chief of air force general staff), Gen. Quirino Armellini (Comando Supremo).

[76] Montanari, *Grecia*, i. 130; on this development see *DDI*, 9th ser., v, No. 757, pp. 727–30 (20 Oct. 1940); *Ciano's Diary 1939–1943*, 298–9 (19 Oct. 1940); Armellini, *Diario*, 122 (25 Oct. 1940).

[77] Statements according to the minutes of the meeting (n. 75 above); see also commentary in Faldella, *L'Italia*, 289 ff., who writes that Badoglio miscounted the troops in the sector of operations, since there were only five divisions available in Epirus.

[78] Details of operational planning for the landing on Crete in *M.G.Doc.* 74, pp. 227–8 (23 Oct. 1940).

2. Italy's Plan of Operations

Badoglio did not believe that the Greeks would be able to revise their troop deployments at short notice. The difficult countryside, inadequate communications, and transport shortages all militated against this. It could therefore be assumed that six Greek divisions would remain tied down in Thrace, and that another six would engage the Italian invaders. Visconti Prasca would have at his disposal six divisions which would arrive by 28 October; another two were in position along the Albanian–Yugoslav border; and a further division would concentrate on Salonika. After the first days of the war it would be clear that neither the Yugoslavs nor the Turks wanted to take sides; two of these divisions could then be deployed to secure the left flank of the Epirus offensive. In other words, the marshal did not exclude the possibility of a Greek counter-offensive in that area. Nevertheless, he was already thinking of the second stage of the conquest of Greece.

That was the last discussion in the Comando Supremo before the invasion. After the meeting, Badoglio claimed, 'the facts will speak for themselves'. Astonishingly, there had been no realistic and detailed comparison of the relative strength of the opposing forces. Yet the Italian minister in Athens, Emanuele Grazzi, had reported both the steady call-up of Greek reservists and the transfer of troops from the Peloponnese to northern Greece; he calculated that the Greek government had some 300,000 men under arms on 21 October. Three days later, the war diary of the Comando Supremo estimated the number of Greek soldiers at between 320,000 and 350,000 men. The divisions based in Patras and Navplion (northern and eastern Peloponnese) were concentrated almost exclusively on the Graeco-Albanian border in Epirus.[79]

Visconti Prasca began to prepare for the attack according to his instructions of 20 October.[80] For the coastal sector (where the Italian attack had some initial success after 28 October) a special tactical command was established.[81] On 22 October its commander, along with the commanders of the Çamüria Army Corps, the XXVIth Army Corps, and the individual divisions, as well as the various support units subordinate to Visconti Prasca, received detailed orders for the offensive in Epirus and the defensive operations on the Macedonian border.[82] Preparations were also made to regroup the units which were to be used to strengthen the left flank.[83] Furthermore, the commander in Albania issued guidelines for the strategic support which would be required of the air force during the battle for Epirus.[84]

On 27 October Visconti Prasca reported that preparations to implement the orders or proposals from Rome were complete.[85] He had already received a

---

[79] Montanari, *Grecia*, i. 131–2; Cervi, *Grecia*, 131–2.
[80] *M.G.Doc.* 70, pp. 219–22.
[81] Ibid. 77, p. 235 (22 Oct. 1940).
[82] Ibid. 78, pp. 236–45 (22 Oct. 1940).
[83] Ibid. 79, pp. 246–7 (26 Oct. 1940).
[84] Ibid. 80, pp. 248–9 (26 Oct. 1940).
[85] Ibid. 81, pp. 250–1 (27 Oct. 1940).

letter from Mussolini,[86] informing him that he was being retained as supreme commander in Albania despite attempts to remove him. Success against Greece, he was told, would undoubtedly justify this decision. Mussolini advised Visconti Prasca to proceed as rapidly as possible, since victory depended largely on the speed of the Italian advance. Mussolini, as he had often emphasized, wanted to wage a lightning war. But his comments were also designed to stiffen the commander's resolve. A certain psychological pressure, in the form of personal obligation, therefore seemed appropriate. After all, the Duce already had experience of the enthusiasm for battle, or lack of it, of his generals.

In fact Visconti Prasca was scarcely in need of additional motivation. An ambitious officer who had not yet reached the peak of his military career, he responded exactly as Mussolini wanted. His conduct, as we shall see, was very different from that of Graziani, the 'Cunctator' in North Africa. Visconti Prasca's memoirs reveal that since 26 October the weather in Albania had been unusually bad, with continuous rain. Because of the almost total absence of paved roads, the roads to the front and connections with the rear were virtually impassable. Small river-courses, easy to ford under normal conditions, were being transformed into raging torrents which posed a considerable danger to troops attempting to cross them. As the waters had also destroyed many bridges, the movement of troops had become even more difficult. Yet the offensive could not be called off on the eve of the attack. Orders to that effect would have had to be dispatched by runners, who could not have reached the advanced lines in time. Furthermore, Visconti Prasca knew that an ultimatum was to be delivered to the Greek government, as a matter of form, immediately before the outbreak of hostilities. What would happen if the ultimatum was sent but the Italian troops then proved incapable of launching their attack? In these circumstances General Francesco Rossi's proposal for a postponement of the attack had no chance of being accepted. Visconti Prasca consoled himself with the belief that the weather conditions would make life equally difficult for the enemy.[87] The commander radiated confidence. His telegram to Mussolini in Rome stated that the morale of the Italian troops was 'extraordinarily high' despite the rain, storms, and floods.[88] Mussolini's own mood, which Ciano described as excellent on 28 October, may have been improved still further by such optimism.[89]

3. Greek Countermeasures

The Italian attack did not take the Greeks by surprise. For some time there had been numerous indications of Italian intentions, in addition to the re-

---

[86] Published in Montanari, *Grecia*, i. 132.
[87] Prasca, *Grecia*, 89–90.
[88] Montanari, *Grecia*, i. 133, for Visconti Prasca's telegram.
[89] Ciano, *Diary 1939–1943*, 301 (28 Oct. 1940).

3. Greek Countermeasures

peated provoking of incidents. Events during the year had led the Greek government to conclude that Rome was only seeking an excuse to declare war. Despite the constant calls for secrecy, much information reached Greece directly from the Italian capital. For example, on 23 October, only eight days after the crucial meeting in the Palazzo Venezia, the Greek ambassador in Rome reported that all the signs pointed to an attack some time between 25 and 28 October.[90] The impending campaign against Greece was an open secret on the banks of the Tiber.

Before giving details of Greek strategic planning, we must first briefly examine that country's military potential in October 1940. After a period of lethargy following the catastrophic defeat of 1921–2 in Asia Minor, a programme to modernize and rearm the forces had been introduced in the mid-1930s and was due to be completed by 1944. In 1936 Metaxas altered the original concept, dispensing with some of the plans and concentrating all resources on the achievement of the remainder. In 1937 he made the proud and entirely inaccurate boast that the original version of the plan (dating from 1935) had been implemented. Only dictators can utter such falsehoods without fear of contradiction. It remains true, however, that within a short period of time the Greek armed forces had greatly improved in terms of combative readiness and effectiveness.[91]

In 1939 the Greek army consisted of fourteen infantry divisions and one cavalry division, distributed between five army corps with headquarters in Athens (I), Larisa (II), Salonika (III), Kovalla (IV), and Alexandroupolis (V). Within the framework of Greek defensive strategy, the task of defending the Graeco-Albanian border fell to II Corps in Larisa and to 8 Infantry Division, which had its own command in Yannina (Ioannina). In the event of mobilization, a high command, two army commands, and a 'divisional group command' would be established. Furthermore, the remaining military command authorities and the divisional personnel were to be brought up to war strength, and four brigades and three regiments created to defend the coast. In the second phase, four new infantry divisions were to be mobilized.

Each Greek division consisted of approximately 18,500 men. Unlike the two-part Italian divisions (12,000–14,000 men), it had a three-part structure, although the third infantry regiment was not always available. Some of the artillery and infantry weaponry was obsolescent, but this was a handicap shared with the Italians. The Greek army had no tanks at all, and very few anti-tank weapons. The Greeks were inferior to the Italians in terms of heavy guns (a disadvantage partly offset by the fact that they were on the defensive). On the other hand, they had a clear superiority in machine-guns. Further-

---

[90] The various reports which arrived in Athens concerning Italy's preparations for the aggression are summarized in *Hellēnikos stratos*, i. 98–120, here esp. 118–20; see also Papagos, *Battle*, 17–33.

[91] Montanari, *Grecia*, i. 145–50, on the following as a whole. See *Hellēnikos stratos*, ii. 22, on Greek technical terms.

more, after 28 October a number of important Italian misjudgements became apparent: they had seriously underestimated the morale of the Greek soldiers, and overestimated the venality of the Greek politicians and generals.[92]

By comparison with the Italian navy, Greek naval forces were extremely modest.[93] After the Italian submarine *Delfino* had sunk the light cruiser *Helli* (a veteran of the First World War which had been turned into a mine cruiser) on 15 August, the following vessels were available to the Greeks on 28 October:

- 1 armoured cruiser, completely obsolete;
- 10 destroyers, 4 of which dated from the First World War;
- 13 torpedo-boats, all built between 1905 and 1915;
- 6 submarines, all of which entered service in the second half of the 1920s;
- 4 motor torpedo-boats;
- 4 small minesweepers and 4 small minelayers.

One vital potential task for this small and ageing fleet would be to guard troop transports to north-west Greece. In such circumstances the warships could also be used to transport material at the same time. In addition, the naval leadership would hope to attack Italian convoys to Durrës and Vlorë (as did indeed occur), using the five submarines which were fit for service. To anticipate events, before April 1941 the Greeks were to sink four Italian transport ships amounting to 21,386 GRT.

The Greek air force[94] possessed some 300 aircraft, of which 180 were obsolete. In terms of modern machines there were:

- 44 fighter aircraft;
- 16 reconnaissance planes;
- 46 bombers;
- 21 aircraft for naval reconnaissance.

As regards strategic planning,[95] in May 1939 the military commanders in Athens developed Operations Plan IB as a direct consequence of the Italian occupation of Albania (see Map II.III.2). This was based on the assumption that Greece would have to fight against Italy or Bulgaria or both. In such a situation Greece could reckon on support from both Britain and France under

---

[92] D. M. Smith, *Mussolini*, 258; also André, 'La politica estera', 64.

[93] Simpsas, 'Griechische Marine', 627–31. The defeat of Greece having become inevitable after the intervention of the Wehrmacht, up to the end of Apr. 1941 the armoured cruiser *Averoff*, 6 destroyers, 3 torpedo-boats, 5 submarines, and a number of auxiliary vessels sailed to Alexandria in order to continue the war on the British side: ibid. 632.

[94] Montanari, *Grecia*, i. 150; in contrast, the official Greek work on the Graeco-Italian war gives the following figures: 38 fighters, 9 light bombers and reconnaissance aircraft, 18 bombers, and 50 reconnaissance aircraft; under repair, 15 reconnaissance aircraft, 6 bombers, and 7 fighters (from *Hellēnikos stratos*, ii. 16). The Greeks were supported by the RAF from November onwards, though its operations did not meet with conspicuous success. On the British effort as a whole see Higham, 'Generals and Guarantees', 5–8, 10–11.

[95] Montanari, *Grecia*, i. 150–69; *Hellēnikos stratos*, ii. 20–3.

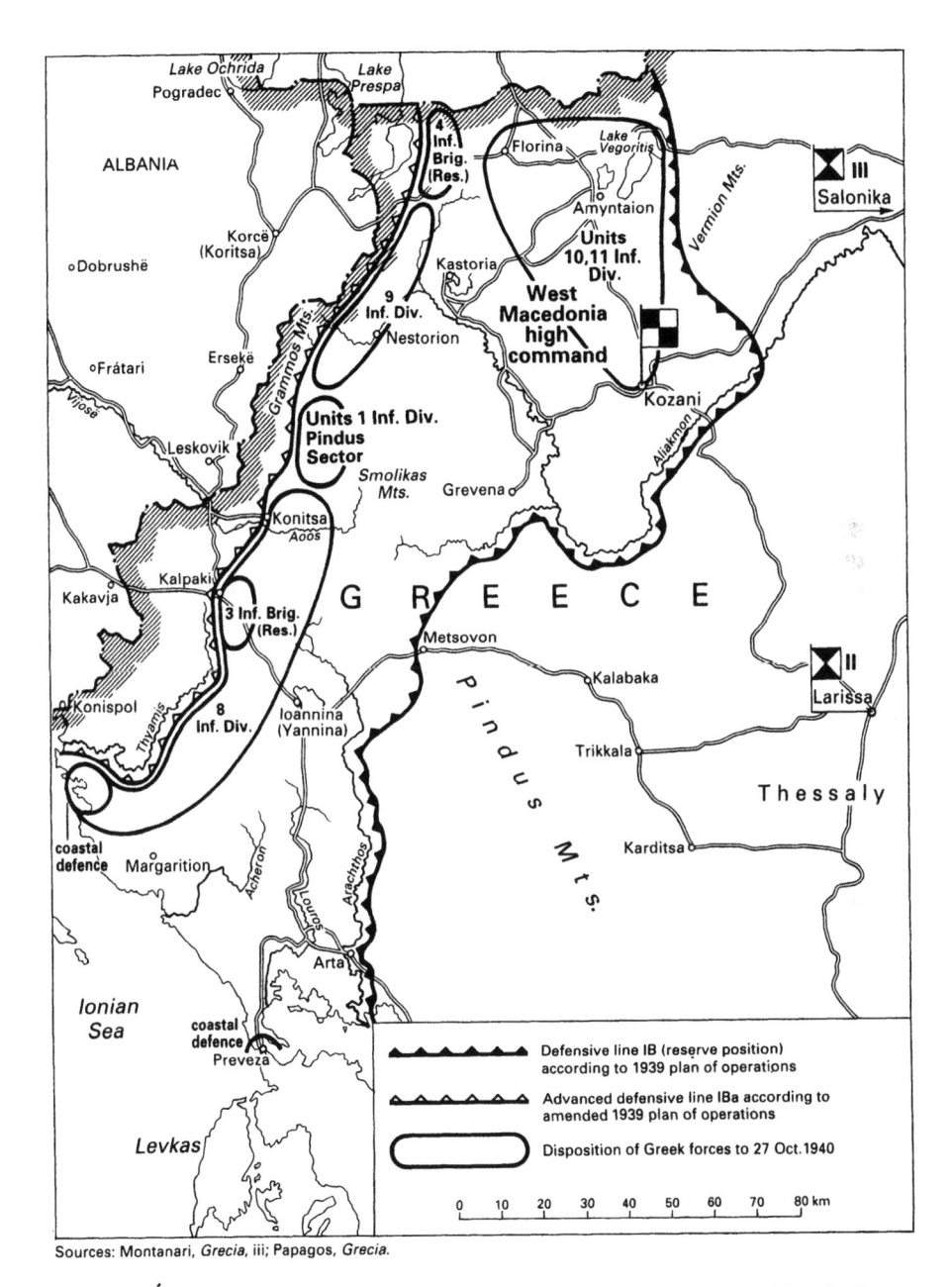

MAP II.III.2. The Italo-Greek War: Defensive Lines and Disposition of Greek Forces on 27 October 1940

the guarantees of April 1939. However, the actual extent of British and French assistance remained an unknown quantity and would largely depend on the international political situation. The Greek government assumed that, of the neighbouring states, Greece could rely on the sympathetic attitude of Turkey. The Yugoslav attitude was uncertain, since the country was geographically so exposed between Albania and Bulgaria that it would scarcely be able to resist Italian or Bulgarian demands for free passage for their troops. Athens also had to consider that the members of the Balkan pact were not obliged to intervene in the event of conflict between Italy and Greece, or between Greece and an Italo-Bulgarian alliance.

The Greeks were fully aware of Bulgarian revisionist demands. Consequently, in May 1939 they assumed that war would be on two fronts, and developed their strategic planning on that basis. The fundamental design was for a defensive operation against a Bulgarian attack in Macedonia, plus a waiting defensive on the Graeco-Italian front in northern Greece. It was accepted that the main Italian attack would come in the area round Korçë. In Epirus the unfavourable terrain led the Greek military to consider a major Italian offensive unlikely. Nevertheless, they intended to evacuate the area as far as a defensive line running along the Arakhthos river. This rear position, laid down in Plan IB, stretched to the north through Metsovon, diagonally across the Pindus and along the Vermion Mountains, and past Lake Vegorritis as far as the Yugoslav border. The Greeks divided the Albanian theatre of operations into the sectors of west Macedonia and Epirus, linked by the Pindus front.

Similarly, the Bulgarian theatre of operations was divided into the operational sectors of west Thrace and east Macedonia. The generals in Athens knew that the Bulgarians held the initiative. It was likely that Bulgarian military leaders would be able to choose their moment and gain the advantage of surprise, and their situation was also superior in terms of mobilization, which took longer in Greece than in Bulgaria. Resolute action would enable the Bulgarians to reach the Aegean without undue difficulty, thus cutting off west Thrace from Macedonia.

In such a situation the Greek army was forced to restrict itself to preparations for a decisive battle on the River Nestos, which had fortifications on its west bank. Nevertheless, the Greeks in west Thrace would also attempt to hold bridgeheads at Alexandroupolis and Pithion. The Greek position would be considerably improved if Bulgaria did not enter the war, since extra units could then be transferred to the Albanian theatre. Depending on political developments, the Greek high command would then gain a certain freedom of action.

Plan IB was thus framed with the primary objective of enabling the available forces to hold up an Italian offensive in front of the Greeks' defensive positions until general mobilization was completed. The Greek general staff had assumed that there would be no possibility of halting the advancing Italians before line IB without sustaining unacceptable losses. However, the mobilization in August 1939, staged specifically for the Albanian border region, led to some shift in opinion. Some of the earlier calculations were no longer valid; it seemed that previous estimates of the situation had been too pessimistic.

Though there were no major geographical barriers between Albania and northern Epirus, in the south-west the River Thiamis lay near the Albanian border. In autumn and winter in particular, this was a barrier which could be crossed only at a few points and with great difficulty. Especially on its steep left bank, it was easy to defend. At the same time, the position of the Thiamis enabled more troops to be concentrated in the north, in the region round Korçë where the main Italian thrust was expected.

Consequently, the new strategic thinking led to the creation of Plan IBa in September 1939, and to the establishment of a new zone of defence in front of line IB. Its most advanced line, IBa, ran from the Thiamis through Kalivakia to the north as far as Lake Prespa. The line thus lay between the Graeco-Albanian border and the towns of Yannina, Nestorion, and Kastoria. In this area, between lines IB and IBa, the majority of combat-ready Greek troops were to be deployed. Units mobilized at a later date would then take up position behind line IB. The Greeks also intended to retain control of the island of Corfu, parallel with line IBa, for as long as possible.

There were two particularly significant elements in Plan IBa. The first was a refusal to accept the loss of national territory, which required a major defensive effort on the Greek border. Secondly, the plan left the Greek high command the whole of I Corps, consisting of three infantry divisions, the 5th Infantry Division, the cavalry division, and the 3rd Brigade, as an operational reserve. These troops might prove extremely important in the event of a counter-attack, should that prove possible, since it would mean that relatively fresh troops could then be brought to the front. Initially, however, the prospects for the Graeco-Italian war were clear: an Italian offensive in Epirus, and a Greek defensive action along the entire front. In October 1940 the Greeks could also rely on the strict neutrality of Yugoslavia, thus relieving the right flank of the Greek defensive position in the Albanian theatre, and removing the threat to the rear of the units in east Macedonia.

4. MILITARY DEVELOPMENTS BETWEEN OCTOBER 1940 AND MARCH 1941

On 27 October both sides were in position. Greece had mobilized some weeks before, although the government did not order general mobilization until the day of the attack.[96] The Italians were more or less prepared to launch their attack with the troops which had been stationed in Albania for some time.

[96] *M.G.Doc.* 90, pp. 278–84 (undated).

What were the forces on both sides? (See Maps II.III.1 and II.III.2; also Map II.III.3 for communications in the area.)

In Epirus the Italian commanders intended to advance on Yannina with the mass of their troops, and then to move on to Arta. For that purpose Visconti Prasca had the following big units at his disposal:

Ciamuria Army Corps, consisting of the infantry divisions Siena and Ferrara and Centauro Armoured Division. Centauro and Ferrara Divisions were given the objective of capturing the transport junction of Kalivakia, while Siena Division was to cross the Thiamis in the south and subsequently march to Yannina along the road on the left bank of the river. There the army corps would regroup for the attack on Arta.[97]

The *Alpini Division Julia*, to the north of Ciamuria Army Corps, was to march on Metsovon and capture it. The objective was to prevent the Greek forces slipping away to the east, and to block off the influx of reinforcements from Thessaly. Furthermore, the passes in the Pindus Mountains were to be occupied as swiftly as possible.[98]

The *coastal detachment*, consisting of three infantry regiments which, like the other Italian units, had been strengthened, was to attack between Konispol and the sea, to cross the Thiamis, and to advance by the direct route on Preveza, Louros, and Arta.[99]

At first glance the plan was not obviously flawed. However, the Italian forces would be widely dispersed, creating problems of control for the high command. Inadequate communications between the units exacerbated this difficulty. Problems might also develop as soon as reinforcements were required, since these could only be obtained by moving troops from other sectors of the front.

In Macedonia there was XXVI Army Corps, but this was still in the process of being assembled. It consisted mainly of Parma Infantry Division, strengthened by units of Venezia Infantry Division. Piemonte Infantry Division was also deployed in the area round Korçë, but was, at least in theory, regarded as a high-command reserve division. Visconti Prasca made some concessions to the precarious position of XXVI Army Corps by placing the Piemonte and the Venezia wholly under its command.[100] Immediately beforehand, the commanding general of the corps, General Gabriele Nasci, had given him a graphic description of the problems of defence in the sector. In truth, the weakness of the corps virtually invited a counter-offensive. The situation was unchanged when war broke out, since on 28 October units of the Venezia and the entire Arezzo Division were still at the Yugoslav border.

---

[97] Ibid. 83, pp. 257–61 (25 Oct. 1940).
[98] Ibid. 84, pp. 262–6 (25. Oct. 1940).
[99] Ibid. 85, pp. 267 ff. (27 Oct. 1940).
[100] Ibid. 86, pp. 270–3 (25 Oct. 1940); 87, pp. 274–5 (27 Oct. 1940); 88, p. 276 (28 Oct. 1940).

MAP II.III.3. The Italo-Greek War: Lines of Communication Albania–Northern Greece, October 1940

Sources: Montanari, *Grecia*, iii; Papagos, *Battle*.

In total, including Venezia and Arezzo, the Italian commander had at his disposal eight divisions and one combat group, i.e. approximately 140,000 men. The combat units were at 100 per cent of their wartime effective strength, but had only 75 per cent of the vehicles or animals necessary to transport men and equipment. Also damaging, it later proved, was the fact that the Italians had insufficient guns in relation to the area to be conquered. Moreover, it rapidly became clear that the Italian guns were inferior to the French 10.5-cm. guns used by the Greeks. The Greek troops under General Alexandros Papagos were also able to make use of fortifications to assist their defensive operations. Statistically, the Italians had superiority in tanks and aircraft. Analysts of the Italian defeat therefore tend to emphasize the fact that the Greeks had not a single tank compared to an Italian total of 160. However, it must be remembered that the Italian vehicles were not genuine battle tanks and the Greeks did not require a Maginot Line to stop them. As regards the air force, on the other hand, Italian failures cannot be explained by reference to technical inadequacies.[101]

On 28 October the Italian units attacking Epirus were initially confronted solely by Greek covering forces deployed between defensive lines IBa and IB. Their objective was to hold the region until general mobilization was completed in approximately three weeks' time. The military leadership in Athens regarded the plan as realistic, and events after the launch of the Italian offensive were to prove them correct.[102]

As a preparatory measure, from August 1940 onwards the Greek high command had sent reinforcements to the Epirus area of operations. Some of the units along the Bulgarian border were also to be transferred to that area as soon as the neutrality of Sofia was assured. But once hostilities had begun that would not be easy. In particular, any attempt to move troops to Epirus could encounter great difficulties if the Italians, as seemed likely, had complete mastery of the skies, because every single transport route was vulnerable to attack from the air. From the outset the Greeks had to calculate that their troops in Epirus might be cut off. For that reason the reinforcements sent to the west Macedonian front had a dual function: they increased the defensive capability in that sector and also created the conditions for a relief or counter-attack.[103]

The front in west Macedonia stretched, along the Greek defensive positions, from Lake Prespa to the Smolikas Mountains, a chain of hills belonging to the

---

[101] See Montanari, *Grecia*, i. 139 ff.; Bocca, *Storia d'Italia*, 251 ff., is very critical, and takes issue with certain theories in the Italian literature. As almost always occurs when numbers are involved, the figures vary considerably. Thus Cervi, *Grecia*, 133–6, gives figures very different from those of Montanari. Centauro Division had only ten- or even twenty-year-old model 21 and CV 35 tanks before Dec. 1940, and only the latter saw service in Greece. Once the M 13 medium tank was ready for front-line service, the Centauro received it on 1 Dec. 1940. However, when this tank was deployed in January in a frontal attack on the Greek artillery at Klisoura, Greek fire decimated the Italian armoured vehicles: see Sweet, *Iron Arm*, 179.

[102] Montanari, *Grecia*, i. 169–70.   [103] *Hellēnikos stratos*, ii. 9.

4. Military Developments

Pindus massif and lying north of the River Aoos. To secure the territory between Lake Prespa and the Grammos Mountains along the Graeco-Albanian border, the Greeks had the 9th Infantry Division and 4th Infantry Brigade, which had been reinforced with several infantry battalions and some light and heavy artillery. The 'Pindus detachment', composed of three infantry battalions and a mountain artillery battery, was to defend the sector between the Grammos and Smolikas hills, i.e. the border strip west of Konitsa and Nestorion. For operational purposes these troops were placed under the west Macedonian high command (army high command), which took control over all units of II and III Army Corps after the general mobilization.[104]

The Epirus front was defended by the 8th Infantry Division, reinforced by 3rd Infantry Brigade and a number of small units including heavy mountain artillery, which took up position between Kalivakia and the Thiamis river. In total these forces were protecting a front line stretching from the Ionian Sea to the Smolikas Mountains, 100 km. as the crow flies. To that end the troops were drawn up in two echelons. Their objective was to delay the Italian advance in the border region and bring it to a halt as quickly as possible in order to protect Thessaly, Aetolia, and Akarnania.[105]

According to the figures of the Greek general staff, on 28 October there were approximately 35,000 men in Epirus, ranged in 39 infantry battalions and 40.5 batteries.[106] For their attack in Epirus the Italians brought 55,000 men to the front, with 268 guns, 16 anti-tank guns, 32 anti-aircraft guns, and 163 tanks. In the first line on the Greek side there were 15 infantry battalions, a reconnaissance group, and 16.5 batteries, of which 2 were heavy batteries. The Italian side threw 22 infantry battalions, 3 cavalry regiments, 61 batteries, including 18 heavy batteries, and 90 tanks into the fighting.[107]

When these units met in battle, the Greeks were able to fight with the protection of fortifications. These were not always complete, but—as in the area round Kalivakia (also called Elea), where the roads from Perat and Kakavi met en route to Yannina—they were highly effective. To capture Yannina the Italians would have to take Kalivakia, a crucial outpost. Among the defences facing them was a trench system 66 km. in length, 31 artillery positions which could withstand 10.5-cm. shells, and approximately 290 machine-gun nests trained on the infantrymen of Siena and Piemonte Divisions and the tanks of Centauro Division.[108]

The area of operations (see Maps II.III.1 and 2) was bounded in the north by the line Durrës–Tirana–Dibrës–Prilep, in the east by the line Prilep–Bitola–Florina–Kozani–Volos, in the south by the connection between Volos and Arta, and in the west by the coast of the Adriatic and the Ionian Seas. In general it was not especially suited to military operations (see also Map

---

[104] Papagos, *Battle*, 239; also *Hellēnikos stratos*, ii. 204–7; Montanari, *Grecia*, i. 172–3.
[105] *Hellēnikos stratos*, ii. 10; Papagos, *Battle*, 239; Montanari, *Grecia*, i. 171–2.
[106] *Hellēnikos stratos*, ii. 12.   [107] Ibid. 13; Cervi, *Hollow Legions*, 103–4.
[108] Montanari, *Grecia*, i. 171–2.

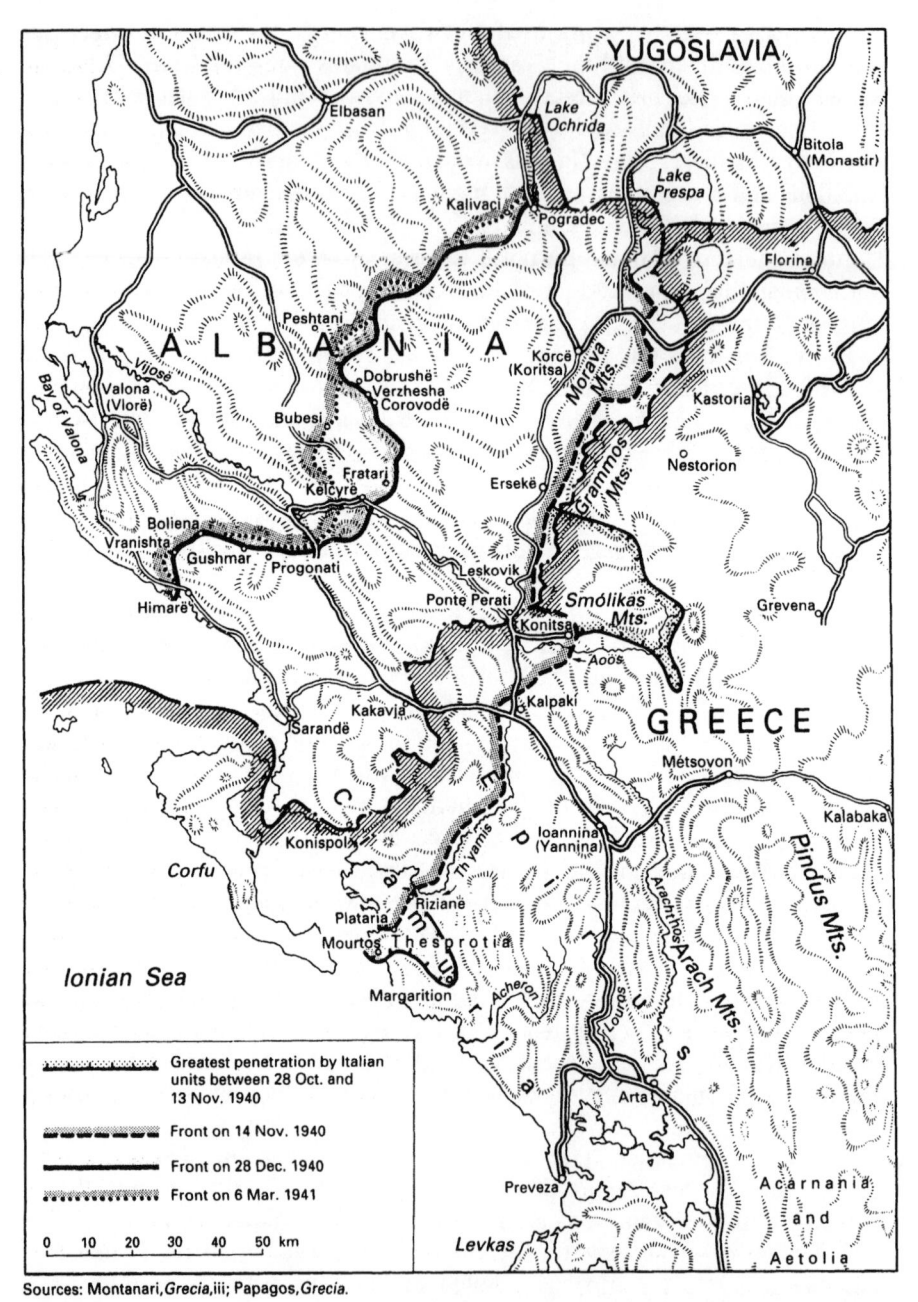

MAP II.III.4. The Italo-Greek War: Changes in the Front, October 1940 to March 1941

4. Military Developments

II.III.4). An area some 250 km. long and 180 km. wide, it was divided into numerous mountain chains, running mainly north-west and south-east. To name only two obstacles, the Italians were confronted by the Grammos Mountains in the north-west of the Pindus massif, and by the River Thiamis. Furthermore, the autumn brought heavy rain and winter was extremely cold; consequently, the Italians would face enormous problems both in moving their troops and in living off the land.

In Albania and Greece alike, there were simply not enough serviceable roads: it was thus clear from the outset that the movement of units would be extremely difficult. From Durrës to the Greek frontier, under normal conditions, it took lorries three days to cover 300 km. The harbours of Vlorë and Sarandë (Santi Quaranta) were closer to the front, but had a smaller unloading capacity and worse road connections with Greece. In autumn 1940 the Italians managed to unload 50 lorries and 1,000 t. of material a day in Durrës, the only harbour with wharfs; in Vlorë the figure was approximately 250 t., and in Sarandë 150 t. In this situation, the fact that there were no effective or even continuous railway links in the area of operations became even more significant.[109]

This was the region in which hostilities began on 28 October. At 3 a.m. the Italian minister in Athens had delivered an ultimatum, due to expire three hours later, to the Greek prime minister.[110] Metaxas recognized the ultimatum for what it was, a virtual declaration of war which left the Greeks no choice.[111] The perfidy of the Italian action needs no emphasis. The Fascists in Rome wanted war, which they imagined would bring them easy victory; an uncontested entry into Greece, had it been conceivable, would not have suited them at that time.[112] Nevertheless, the feeling that the war was unnecessary, senseless, and even dangerous was widespread, not least among Italian military leaders. In retrospect it appears that many generals and admirals completed their preparations for the conflict, the seriousness of which was still open to doubt after 15 October, in an atmosphere of unreality. How else can we explain the fact that both Pricolo, chief of the general staff of the air force, and Somigli, deputy chief of the naval staff, asked in the Comando Supremo on the eve of the attack whether the war against Greece was actually to begin next day, and whether it would be extended to the whole country?[113] In fact the

---

[109] Ibid. 97–108; Scala, *Storia delle fanterie*, 433 ff.; in this context see also *M.G.Doc.* 66, pp. 189–95 (2 Dec. 1940), a letter from Benini, the under-secretary for Albania, to Gen. Soddu, describing the state of the road network in Albania, after much complaint by Soddu.

[110] *DDI*, 9th ser., v, No. 789, pp. 753 ff. (26 Oct. 1940); published according to the press release in English in *Mediterranean Fascism*, 217 ff.

[111] *DDI*, 9th ser., v, doc. 803, p. 768 (28 Oct. 1940).

[112] Schramm-von Thadden, *Griechenland*, 114–17.

[113] Armellini, *Diario*, 124–8 (26 Oct. 1940), esp. p. 127; it emerges from the content that the entries relate to 27 Oct. 1940. On the attitude of the Italian military, whose 'lack of courage to contradict' is explained by the disintegration of rationally based moral courage under conditions of dictatorship, see André, 'La politica estera', 63–4.

war began at 5.30 a.m. on 28 October, when the Italians crossed the Graeco-Albanian border half an hour before the ultimatum was due to expire.[114]

The Italian campaign against Greece before the intervention of the Wehrmacht can be divided into three main phases. The first of these lasted from 28 October until 13 November and, in operational terms, was marked by the Italian offensive. The second phase, between 14 November and 28 December, was dominated by the Greek counter-attack. In the third phase, lasting from 29 December 1940 until 26 March 1941, events were dominated by the local efforts of both sides to launch an attack and by the Italian offensive (ultimately unsuccessful) in March.[115] (See Map II.III.4.)

Italy's attack in Epirus began to falter on the second day. Italian units became stranded in the area in front of Kalivakia and on the bank of the Thiamis, where the Greeks had succeeded in dynamiting all but two of the remaining bridges (others had already been swept away by the floods) before the Italians could reach them. As their commander was aware beforehand, the Italian offensive lacked the essential element of surprise.

Between 31 October and 8 November the tanks of Centauro Division and the infantry of Ferrara Division made a great effort to capture Kalivakia. However, the attempt was in vain, because the superior Greek artillery gave them no real chance. In the south, Siena Division was equally unsuccessful at first, although its advance failed as a result of technical deficiencies rather than the Greek defence. The division was simply not properly equipped for operations in mountainous terrain.

The front line now measured about 140 km. On 5 November the Italians renewed their attack. No progress was made in the region round Kalivakia, but in the south Siena Division established a bridgehead on the left bank of the Thiamis. This was immediately extended, and on the evening of 6 November the division occupied Riziani. At this stage the army corps gave the order, comprehensible only in view of the crisis in the northern sector, to halt the advance. Until that stage the operations of the troops advancing in the

---

[114] The description of the course of operations during the campaign is based—apart from other occasional sources—primarily on the following works: Bocca, *Storia*, 257–302; Cervi, *Grecia*, 159–323; Faldella, *L'Italia*, 288–314, 335–40; Canzio, *La dittatura*, 606–13; Cruickshank, *Greece*, 40–51; Prasca, *Grecia*, 97–168; Knox, *Mussolini*, 232–60; Montanari, *Grecia*, i. 177–627; D. M. Smith, *Mussolini*, 256–66; Vernier, 'La guerre italo-grecque', 15–36; also a highly informative and, as regards details, generally accurate description by the German military attaché in Athens: 'Der Krieg Griechenlands 1940–1941', a study by von Hohenberg, c.1942, BA-MA N 449/7; a shorter version, 'Kurzer Überblick über den italienisch-griechischen Krieg 1940/41 und seine Vorgeschichte', written by von Hohenberg c.1941, BA-MA N 449/4. On military developments from 28 Oct. 1940 to 25 Mar. 1941 see also Destopoulos, 'La guerre gréco-italienne', 5–21.

[115] This division follows the official work by the Greek general staff, which was also used by the German military attaché in his account (n. 114 above). Montanari, *Grecia*, divides the phases of the war somewhat differently: (1) Italian offensive from 28 Oct. to 9 Nov. 1940; (2) Greek counter-offensive from 10 Nov. to 3 Dec. 1940; (3) trench warfare from 4 Dec. to 31 Dec. 1940; (4) battle of Berat in Jan. 1941; (5) battle of Tepelenë, Feb.–Mar. 1941; (6) Italian offensive in Mar. 1941.

4. Military Developments

coastal sector had been successful; here too the Thiamis had been crossed. Thereafter the attacks of the three advancing regiments had proceeded more or less according to plan. Mourtos (Sivota) (Aosta Regiment), Plataria (3rd Grenadier Regiment), and Margarition (Milano Regiment) were taken. However, the offensive strength of these units was apparently exhausted. Visconti Prasca even ordered that the Milano and Aosta Regiments should be withdrawn to a line level with Plataria.[116]

Meanwhile the Julia Division of Alpini had advanced on the left flank towards the Pindus Mountains in an attempt to capture the pass at Metsovon, and thereby to break the connection from the Greek hinterland to Yannina and Kalivakia. At first the Greeks withdrew, allowing the Alpini—among the best of the Italian troops—to climb towards disaster. On 3 November the Italian spearhead was surrounded by the Greeks, who attacked from all sides. The commander of Julia Division requested relief attacks, and General Nasci threw his reserves into the battle. They were unable to break through; the Alpini were isolated. They attempted to break out and away from the enemy, but sustained such heavy losses that the division was virtually wiped out. The trap at Metsovon snapped shut. Less than two weeks later the surviving troops—they could hardly be called a division—were in roughly the position they had occupied on 28 October. The infantrymen of Bari Division, originally intended to land on Corfu, filled the gaps in this sector of the front, where their commander took overall command.[117]

The Greek forces had thus successfully beaten back the Italian offensive. Any danger that the units in Epirus would be stranded by the operations in the Pindus was over; Visconti Prasca was forced to go on the defensive in every sector. As before, the front in the central sector ran in front of Kalivakia and along the Thiamis. Only in southern Thesprotia were the Greeks forced to withdraw their troops to the line of the River Akheron. Furthermore, the Greeks had finally decided to launch an offensive which had been announced in the first days of the campaign, viz. to attack in north-west Macedonia in order to capture the transport junction at Korçë.[118] On the Albanian front as a whole, Papagos, the chief of the Greek general staff, commanded eleven infantry divisions, one cavalry division, and two infantry brigades with 232,000 men, 556 guns, and 100,000 animals. On the border with Bulgaria there were four more divisions, with about 57,000 men and 20,000 animals.[119]

In this situation the Greek high command decided to begin major offensive operations in north-west Macedonia on 14 December. The counter-offensive was to be continued in the Pindus, and in Epirus the intention was to throw the Italians back over the border.[120] Highly significant for the success of Greek countermeasures was the Italian air force's failure to disrupt the mobilization

---

[116] Montanari, *Grecia*, i. 177–92.
[117] Bocca, *Storia*, 261–2, 264–5.
[118] *Hellēnikos stratos*, ii. 244.
[119] Ibid. 246–7.
[120] Ibid. 245–6.

and deployment of the Greek troops. For this reason alone, the geographical and technical difficulties faced by the Greeks in transporting men and materials did not have catastrophic consequences. The railway network was inadequate, and the lines terminated a long way from the front; in Epirus too the assembly-point had to be moved considerably to the west, involving various units in foot-marches of between 250 and 400 km. through countryside vulnerable to air attack.[121]

This was the situation at the end of the Italian offensive. But what was the reaction in Rome as events unfolded and the scale of the disaster began to emerge? On 29 October General Armellini had already felt a sense of unease, when he prayed that Mussolini's serene confidence would not prove unfounded.[122] That same day an optimistic Ciano travelled to Albania,[123] apparently intending to take personal charge of a campaign of which he, more than anyone else, had been the advocate.[124] Only two days later he wrote his father-in-law a long letter, accusing the Stato Maggiore Generale of responsibility for all the difficulties encountered by Italian troops. Badoglio emerged as the chief whipping-boy in these complaints; the charge was that the marshal, convinced that the Greek affair would eventually be settled at the peace negotiations, had failed to make adequate preparations for the military campaign. For example, three extra divisions had been promised, but had yet to arrive.[125]

To those marching in the Albanian mud, many things no longer appeared as they had done during the light-hearted discussions in palaces before 28 October. The assessments in the Comando Supremo and the top Italian leadership had been confused, to say the least, and one inside observer claimed that nobody would believe the true version of events if it were ever told.[126] At the end of October there were already signs of crisis, which although no one was yet prepared to admit the position openly, was first manifested in attempts to shift the blame. However, there were also concrete indications of the real situation. On 31 October, for example, the decision was taken to postpone the landing on Crete.[127] The precarious position in Albania was also revealed by the results of a discussion of the situation in the Italian high command on 1 November.[128] Here the chiefs of the armed forces confirmed that the Bari Division was to be sent to Albania instead of making a landing on Corfu. Above all, it was essential to step up reinforcements to Visconti Prasca. As a result of developments so far, the Albanian theatre of operations now received

---

[121] BA-MA N 449/7 (see n. 114 above). The work is obviously based on captured Greek material.
[122] Armellini, *Diario*, 130 (29 Oct. 1940).
[123] Ciano, *Diary 1939–1943*, 301 (29 Oct. 1940).
[124] Armellini, *Diario*, 130 (30 Oct. 1940).
[125] Ciano, *Diary 1939–1943*, 302 (31 Oct. 1940).
[126] Armellini, *Diario*, 130 (30 Oct. 1940).
[127] Ibid. 131–2 (31 Oct. 1940).
[128] *M.G.Doc.* 93, pp. 292–6 (1 Nov. 1940); 94, p. 297 (1 Nov. 1940).

unconditional priority, even over North Africa. In the succinct words of General Armellini: 'Everything for Albania, nothing more for Cyrenaica.'[129]

Yet on 1 November Roatta felt able to describe the position of the Italian troops in Albania as generally good, and Visconti Prasca behaved as though he had no need for reinforcements. The decisions of the Comando Supremo, however, were more realistic. Bari Division would only be the beginning; further transports of men and materials must follow. To accelerate the process, the Germans should be asked to place their merchant ships in Italian ports at the disposal of the Italians.[130] Such a move also seemed appropriate because the Italians no longer wished to discuss an existing plan to transport a motorized German division in these ships.[131] By the beginning of November North Africa played only a peripheral role in the plans of the Comando Supremo. According to Badoglio, it was of little consequence whether Italy attacked Marsa Matruh in December or in January. A much more urgent and important problem was Greece.[132]

Mussolini endorsed all these recommendations and ideas,[133] since it was obvious that the campaign in Greece was proving more difficult than expected. In order to 'set in motion the divisions that were marking time' before the Greek defensive line, Mussolini proposed in a memorandum to Badoglio on 3 November that the enemy should be attacked from the rear. Exploiting Italian naval and air superiority as well as a spell of relatively good weather, a Bersaglieri regiment should make a surprise landing at Preveza for this purpose.[134]

That same day, representatives of the armed services met Badoglio to examine these suggestions.[135] Badoglio referred openly to the threat in the Korçë region, where strong Greek pressure was to be countered by the concentration of the Parma, Piemonte, Venezia, Arezzo, and Bari Divisions. From 4 November Taro Division would also be ready for transportation to Albania. That apart, the discussions dealt exclusively with Mussolini's idea. The proposal as it stood was rejected, because more troops—at least three regiments—would be required. But Roatta also made it clear that the general staff had fundamental objections to a landing at Preveza: it was not enough merely to establish a new front; it would also have to be supported. And the Italians were already fully stretched in their efforts to hold the existing sectors.[136]

Reference was made to the problems created by the geographical conditions

[129] Armellini, *Diario*, 133 (1 Nov. 1940).
[130] See Schreiber, *Revisionismus*, 210–11, 231, 235–9.
[131] *M.G.Doc.* 93, p. 293 (1 Nov. 1940); however, the Wehrmacht high command and the naval war staff continued to discuss this plan: see *KTB OKW* i. 143 ff. (1 Nov. 1940).
[132] On the above text see *M.G.Doc.* 93, pp. 292–6.
[133] Armellini, *Diario*, 133 (1 Nov. 1940).
[134] Montanari, *Grecia*, i. 217–18.
[135] *M.G.Doc.* 95, pp. 298–302 (3 Nov. 1940).
[136] Ibid. 302.

of the area of operations. The railway lines stopped some hundreds of miles away from the Albanian ports, and there were insufficient lorries and mules (for transport in impassable mountainous regions of the front)—the latter providing practically the only means of transport for weapons, munitions, provisions, and the wounded.

Next day, after the staffs of the armed forces had examined the proposal once again, Badoglio explained their objections to Mussolini, who agreed to abandon the operation. His thinking had been based on premises which were insufficient to ensure success, and other demands by the military could not be met quickly enough. Mussolini therefore proposed that every effort should now be devoted to reinforcing the troops on the existing fronts.[137]

Alongside this development there were personnel changes, caused more by the failure of the offensive than by the proposed re-forming of the Italian troops in Albania. The most important of these was in the high command. General Soddu, who had used the turn of events for his own advantage with much skill,[138] took command of the Italian troops in Albania on 9 November.[139] The Albanian theatre of operations was thereby perceptibly upgraded. Soddu was commander of an army group comprising 9th and 11th Army. Until the middle of March, Visconti Prasca continued to command the field army in Epirus, but he was then replaced and pensioned off. At the outset, 9th Army contained the Piemonte, Arezzo, Parma, and Venezia Divisions, and, as a reserve in the Korçë region, an Alpini division. In the Pindus sector were the remainder of the Julia Division and Bari Division. In total, seven divisions or sixty-three battalions were under the command of General Mario Vercellino from mid-November onwards. For the entire winter, 9th Army was to maintain its defensive position in the Korçë area and in the Pindus. However, there might be changes if the Bulgarians decided to intervene in the conflict. The 11th Army, under Visconti Prasca's successor General Carlo Gelaso, consisted of the Ferrara, Siena, and Centauro Divisions and the 'Littorale' coastal detachment, now also classified as a big unit akin to a division. Six new divisions were also to be added to this army. A total of seventeen divisions would then be in position on the Greek front in Albania, while a further three would be held in Italy as operational reserve.[140] It should also be noted that General Soddu was to make some further changes to the two armies in mid-November.

Against this background, on 10 November Mussolini held discussions with

[137] Montanari, *Grecia*, i. 218–19; Armellini, *Diario*, 136 (4 Nov. 1940).
[138] Knox, *Mussolini*, 234–5.
[139] *M.G.Doc.* 97, p. 307 (9 Nov. 1940); 98, pp. 308–9 (9 Nov. 1940); see also Prasca, *Grecia*, 163. On 16 Nov. Visconti Prasca was also relieved as commander of the Epirus army, and replaced by Gen. Geloso: see Montanari, *Grecia*, i. 246.
[140] *M.G.Doc.* 100, pp. 319–20 (9 Nov. 1940); the figures cited there were amended in the course of detailed examination; see Montanari, *Grecia*, i. 228. In this altered form they are used in the above text.

4. Military Developments

Badoglio, Cavagnari, Pricolo, and Roatta.[141] The scapegoats for the disaster on the Greek front were identified: Visconti Prasca and Jacomoni. It was agreed that they had made inaccurate predictions and that the estimated requirement of forces had been much too low. Yet anyone acquainted with the proceedings of the grotesque council of war on 15 October must have known that this was a one-sided verdict. The truth—and Badoglio and Roatta at least must have been aware of it—was rather different. But Badoglio's own comments reveal that he too was unwilling or unable to face the facts. Now that the Italian war effort in Albania was grinding to a halt, Badoglio summoned the courage to engage in open opposition before the assembled military leaders. His main aim was to exonerate himself and Roatta. Perhaps he even intended, as Armellini thought possible,[142] to provoke his own dismissal. However, Mussolini did not do him this favour, at least not yet.[143]

Mussolini appeared full of optimism that day.[144] He hoped to have six new divisions transported to Albania within twenty-five days. The new commander, General Soddu, would be the right man to eliminate the chaos in the command structure of the Italian forces and get a grip on the situation. Nor should the army be too downhearted by its failure to break through the Greek defences. From 5 December onwards the army must and would be ready to launch further attacks in the southern sector of the front. Mussolini also threatened to resort to area bombing in Greece: every town with more than 10,000 inhabitants would be razed to the ground. To ensure that the threat was taken seriously—which, given the previous performance of the air force, was doubtful—Mussolini stressed that he had just given a 'direct order' to that effect.[145]

The longer the Duce spoke, the more he lost touch with reality. Finally he referred to the general strategic position as reflected in the political situation, and used the opportunity to claim that this 'could not be more advantageous' for Italy. The claim was ludicrous, and demonstrated that things Mussolini did not like were treated as if they did not exist. In particular, this applied to the

---

[141] The record of the talks has been published, e.g. as *M.G.Doc.* 99, pp. 310–18 (10 Nov. 1940). In the course of the meeting Mussolini also read out the 'Nota per lo Stato Maggiore Generale' (see n. 140 above). Faldella, *L'Italia*, 296, points out that Badoglio said considerably more than would appear from Mussolini's amended version of the record. Interestingly, Knox, *Mussolini*, 236, quotes from the original the remark about the destruction of Greek towns, which does not appear either in Faldella, *L'Italia*, 760–7 (here 764), or in *M.G.Doc.* 99 or 100, from which Mussolini read on that occasion. Reference is made to area bombing and terror attacks on the population, but not to the addition (Knox, p. 236): 'All urban centres of over 10,000 population must be destroyed and razed to the ground. This is a direct order.'

[142] Armellini, *Diario*, 147 (11 Nov. 1940).

[143] Ciano, *Diary 1939–1943*, 305–6 (13 Nov. 1940), reports that Mussolini was just beginning seriously to mistrust Badoglio.

[144] On the following see *M.G.Doc.* 99, pp. 310–18 (10 Nov. 1940); and additional information in Knox, *Mussolini*, 235 ff.

[145] See n. 141. Quotation in Knox, *Mussolini*, 236.

nightmare prospect that the world might come to believe that the Italians were incapable of defeating the Greeks. It was entirely typical that, at the very moment when the attacking-strength of the Italian forces was spent,[146] and they were already awaiting the Greek counter-attack in an exhausted and demoralized state, Mussolini was hoping that it was Metaxas's soldiers who were in that condition.[147]

On 10 November the military leaders insisted that, before any date was fixed for a renewed offensive, it must be calculated how much time was required for the preparations, troop transports, etc. After that, Mussolini could set a date for the attack. But from the middle of November the initiative had already been forfeited to the Greeks. Furthermore, investigations by the army and navy revealed that it would take between two and three months to transport the big units required.[148]

The relative strength of the two sides was to become obvious at the start of the second phase of the war. Directly beforehand, however, the British Mediterranean fleet dealt another painful blow to Italy's damaged prestige. In the night of 11–12 November twenty aircraft from a British combat group, consisting of the aircraft-carrier *Illustrious*, the heavy cruisers *Berwick* and *York*, the light cruisers *Glasgow* and *Gloucester*, and four destroyers, attacked the Italian fleet at Taranto.[149] There have been many detailed descriptions of this operation.[150] Contemporaries on the British side portrayed the attack with understandable pride,[151] the Italians with bitterness or resignation,[152] and the Germans with a touch of malice.[153]

On 12 November, which Ciano described as a 'black day', although Mussolini

---

[146] Armellini, *Diario*, 138 (7 Nov. 1940).

[147] *M.G.Doc.* 99, p. 315; also Ciano, *Diary 1939–1943*, 304–5, expressing the opinion that both sides lacked the strength for an offensive.

[148] Armellini, *Diario*, 147 (11 Nov. 1940). Statistical information of this kind always involves an element of uncertainty. However, the statistics of the official Italian study of the naval war (*La marina italiana*, i. 160–1) give some idea of naval transports to Albania and the Dodecanese for the Italian army between Nov. 1940 and Mar. 1941. They reveal that the majority of Italian transports were destined for Albanian ports. In November warships and merchant ships took 59,604 men to the region, in December 80,282, in January 94,397, in February 79,283, and in March 107,464. At the end of November, under the impact of developments in Greece, Mussolini ordered general mobilization.

[149] On the place of the attack in history and on the most important sources see Knox, *Mussolini*, 238–9; Schreiber, *Revisionismus*, 300–1. The event is dealt with in every work on the war in the Mediterranean in 1940.

[150] Operation Judgement is given the most thorough coverage in *La marina italiana*, iv. 213–57, which also assesses the consequences for Italian naval operations.

[151] Cunningham, *A Sailor's Odyssey*, 273, 283–90; *Keyes Papers*, 118 (3 Dec. 1940).

[152] Bernotti, *Guerra nel Mediterraneo*, 103–9, a mainly factual description but one which also evaluates the possibilities of the Italian fleet before Taranto; Bragadin, *Che ha fatto la marina?*, 58–67, with a strong element of apologia; most critical of the Italian naval leadership is Iachino, *Tramonto*, 233–43.

[153] War diary of the head of the liaison staff attached to the naval staff of the royal Italian navy, 35–42: 'Kurze, zusammenfassende Abschlußbetrachtung der engl. Mittelmeer-Operationen vom 7.–13.11.40', BA-MA RM 36/11; the tone is even more pronounced in 1. Skl., KTB, Teil A, 159 ff. (12 Nov. 1940), BA-MA RM 7/18.

did not appear excessively disturbed by the events of the night,[154] the battleships *Littorio*, *Duilio*, and *Cavour* were hit by torpedoes. Only the last of these, which was sunk, was damaged beyond repair. The heavy cruiser *Trento* and a destroyer also suffered slight damage from unexploded bombs. The British lost two aircraft. They could not have escaped so lightly if the Italians had had enough anti-aircraft guns and more practice in co-ordinating their spotlights and flak. The battleships were not adequately protected by torpedo-nets, because even here there were bottlenecks in production in Italy as well as doubts about their usefulness. Yet the most astonishing thing was that the British had been able to attack the Italian fleet in Taranto harbour at all. During discussions before the invasion of Greece, Admiral Cavagnari had argued that the fleet would have to be withdrawn from Taranto, since the ships would be extremely vulnerable to RAF operations from Greek bases. An agitated Badoglio reminded Ciano of this on 12 November. But the Palazzo Chigi was hardly the right target for his reproaches, quite apart from the fact that the British had not needed to use Greek bases for their attack. Ciano was justified in asking why, if the military considered the transfer so necessary, it had not taken place in the fifteen days since the opening of hostilities, and especially in view of the full moon.[155]

In the long term, this spectacular British success did not have major strategic repercussions on the war in the Mediterranean. True, the Italian navy was even more cautious after Taranto than it had been before. Its significance as a 'fleet in being', i.e. more important because of its sheer existence than because of its actual operations, had been diminished. On the other hand, engagements between the two navies since June 1940 had already shown the British the real worth of the Italian fleet, its lustre dimmed by its poor performance. However, the damage inflicted on the Italian warships reassured the British that their support for Greece on the ocean was less seriously threatened than ever. This was a fortuitous result of the manœuvre; Operation Judgement was not part of a co-ordinated action within the context of developments in the Balkans. Admiral Cunningham had originally intended to carry out the attack on Trafalgar Day, 21 October, when war had not yet broken out between Italy and Greece, but had been forced to abandon the idea because of technical difficulties. The genesis of the plan in fact went back to 1938.[156] It was one of a series of measures which figured in basic plans for any military conflict between Britain and Italy, rather than relating to any specific situation.

Following the first phase of hostilities and operational plans, the further course of the Graeco-Italian war can be described in general terms. Military developments were greatly influenced by the terrain, the weather conditions, the infrastructure of the region, the strategic military leadership and its

---

[154] Ciano, *Diary 1939–1943*, 305 (12 Nov. 1940).
[155] Ibid. 306.   [156] Knox, *Mussolini*, 238.

organization, the pyschological condition and military training of the soldiers, and of course their equipment. It cannot be said that either side was superior in every respect. Nevertheless, in general the Greeks dealt with the problems with more skill. Their leaders proved more effective, their soldiers coped with the terrain better, appeared better trained, and fought with greater resolution. Otherwise it would be difficult to explain why the Greeks demonstrated much greater attacking-power and considerably superior stamina under similar conditions.

The situation in the other two sectors of the Graeco-Italian war contained no new elements. It must be emphasized that the Italians did not enter the field with an attacking force of sufficient quality on 28 October. Yet even in numerical terms conditions changed in favour of the Greeks after the failure of the Italian offensive in early November, at least temporarily. The threat to the flank disappeared; the Greeks were quickly able to reinforce the front and bring up fresh troops; and they even created a clear superiority in strategic forces for the prospective main points of attack in their counter-offensive.

Once forced on to the defensive, the Italian troops defended themselves courageously. They did not make things easy for the Greeks. But in the end they were forced inexorably backwards, hoping only that a slow retreat would allow most of the heavy equipment and guns to be taken with them. It now became vital to establish strong defensive positions in Albania. The Italians could only hope that the attacking-strength of the Greeks would at some stage reach its limits. This was in fact what happened; when, some time later, the Germans finally attacked, the Italians remained in a precarious position, but they had not been thrown into the sea. By that time the two sides in Albania were exhausted. But this is to anticipate developments, which unfolded broadly as follows.

The second phase of the Graeco-Italian war opened with a major Greek offensive on 14 November. At this stage the Greeks had clear numerical superiority (see Table II.III.1). As time passed, both sides received significant reinforcements. Eventually eleven infantry divisions, two infantry brigades, and one cavalry division on the Greek side were confronted by fifteen infantry divisions and one tank division on the Italian side.[157] Although comparisons of this kind are of limited value in assessing actual relative strengths, it should be remembered that Italian divisions comprised two infantry regiments and Greek divisions three. In Albania the Italians were unable to exploit to the full the greater mobility of their smaller divisions. The reasons were obvious: difficult terrain, lack of proper roads, inadequate means of transport. On the other hand, it was clear that the process of thinning out had greatly diminished the divisions' powers of resistance. This must always be taken into account in any assessment of the conduct of Italian units in battle.[158]

In the second phase of the war the Italians lived from hand to mouth. Their

---

[157] Papagos, Battle, 273–4.   [158] See I.1.4(a) above.

4. Military Developments

TABLE II.III.1. *Strengths of Greek and Italian Forces, mid-November 1940*

Front sector	No. of soldiers		No. of guns	
	Italy	Greece	Italy	Greece
Korçë	45,000	80,000	208	198
Ersekë–Leskovik	23,000	32,000	112	114
Epirus	47,000	80,000	248	184

Source: Montanari, *Grecia*, i. 261–2.

air-lift to Tirana, which moreover virtually put an end to the already sporadic supply of East Africa, was suitable only for the transport of men.[159] But these men, whether they arrived in Tirana or in one of the ports, were then dispatched to the front in an unsystematic and disorganized fashion.[160] In consequence, they were of little help to the war effort. Under normal conditions military units are experienced bodies of troops, which cannot be separated or too often enlarged with impunity. When their command structures are removed they lose their powers of resistance, which is the result of a solidarity based on common training and experience. That was what happened with the Italian divisions in Albania. Nor was it sensible to dispatch big units to the front bit by bit. As the soldiers assembled over an extended period, they ceased to be an integrated division. Furthermore, the units which had freshly arrived in Albania rarely came to the front with full equipment.

One significant operational factor was the relative ease with which the Greeks were able to infiltrate between the Italian troops, who were spread out too thinly along the front, and then to attack them from the rear or on the flanks. Among milestones in the Greek counter-attack the following may be mentioned: the breaching of the line at Ersekë, which separated the Italian 9th and 11th Armies from each other; the eight-day battle for the Mali i Moravës massif, followed by the capture of the important transport junction at Korçë; and the pushing-back of the Italians over the Thiamis, followed by the capture of Sarandë.

During the first phase of their counter-attack the Greeks concentrated on the northern sector. When Greek troops made more rapid progress than expected, the high command was faced with a choice at the end of November: to advance through Korçë to Elbasan, or southwards towards Vlorë. Papagos decided on the south, where there were more roads and the climate was milder than in the north, particularly in winter, and where the capture of Sarandë would provide a port nearer to the front. The fact that the north was easier to defend was, of course, also taken into account.[161]

[159] Knox, *Mussolini*, 237–8.
[160] Montanari, *Grecia*, i. 249–50.
[161] 'Der Krieg Griechenlands 1940–1941', 21 ff., BA-MA N 449/7.

On 9 December the Greeks were firmly in control of the plateau of Korçë. Pogradec had fallen to them on 4 December following bitter fighting. The Greeks secured the strategic link between this port and Kalivakia by means of strategic thrusts which enabled them to occupy a line north of the Sarandë–Kakavi route.[162] On 28 December (significant changes to the front had occurred only in the southern and central sectors) Metaxas's troops held the following line:[163] north-west of Himarë–Vranisht–Bolenë–Gusmar–north of Progonat–Mt. Bus Devrit–south-east of Këlcyrë–east of Frátar–Çorovodë–Verzhezhë–Dobrushë–Peshtan–south-east of Kalivac–north-west of Pogradec. The Greeks were first forced to halt their advance by the unfavourable weather conditions and the difficulties caused by their constantly lengthening lines of supply.

Since we have described the conditions in which Italian troops were supplied, a glance should also be directed at the situation faced by the Greeks. The solution of the supply question was one key problem, if not the principal one, of waging war in Albania and Greece. Success or failure depended largely on the ability to provide a reliable and adequate supply of men, weapons, munitions, means of transport, and food to the front lines. For the Greek fighting forces, there were the following possibilities.[164]

In Epirus the troops were supplied by lorries from the port of Preveza, where goods arrived by ship. Land connections as far as Mesolongion were used almost exclusively to transport the wounded, since the sea route was more vulnerable. Lorry capacity was not sufficient to transport equipment by this route as well. The units in the northern Pindus could utilize the railway for the route to Amindaion and Florina. Then the material was loaded on to lorries, and subsequently on to pack animals. In the southern Pindus the supply-lines ran from the railway station at Kalabaka by lorry to Metsovon and Grevena. From here supplies had to be carried on pack animals. When the Italians were forced to retreat, supplies for these Greek units could be taken from Yannina to Konitsa by lorry.

Despite large-scale requisitions, the Greeks, like the Italians, suffered from a serious shortage of lorries. Trucks manufactured abroad began to arrive in Greece in January 1941, but by the end of March there were only three hundred. In these circumstances it is easy to understand why the port of Sarandë became so vital for the Greek high command. For the Greek offensive to be continued, lorries would have to be brought closer to the front, and land connections to the rear would have to be shortened to supply it. If the lorries continued to be forced to travel to Preveza, there would be insufficient capacity to supply the front line, which was now beyond the Graeco-Albanian border. Control of Sarandë meant a considerable reduction of the distance between

---

[162] Ibid. 25–30.
[163] Papagos, *Battle*, 290; Montanari, *Grecia*, iii, map 92.
[164] 'Der Krieg Griechenlands 1940–1941', 23, BA-MA N 449/7.

4. Military Developments

the disembarkation-point and the fighting forces intended for Vlorë. In consequence, land transport between the landing-point and the destination-point could, without additional need for lorry capacity, attain the frequency essential to meet requirements.

Thus, though Greek troops had penetrated deep into Albania by the end of December 1940, the military leadership was unable to exploit this success fully. The Greek army was not sufficiently mobile to allow it to go in hot pursuit or outflank the enemy. The Greeks had no tanks with which to attack the retreating Italians in the plains, and they lacked enough anti-tank guns to ward off Italian tanks advancing in the flat countryside. These factors delayed the advance, as the Greek troops were often forced to take evasive action on relatively protected side-roads.

The leaders in Rome were astounded by developments in Greece after 14 November. General Roatta pressed for general mobilization, to which Mussolini agreed on 22 November. Fifty divisions were now to be created. According to the Duce, the thirty divisions intended for Albania were to be given absolute priority.[165] At the end of November Mussolini and Badoglio parted company. Under the impact of military defeats and various intrigues, their relationship had been less and less tolerable since the middle of the month.[166] General Ugo Cavallero was appointed supreme commander of the Italian armed forces in Badoglio's stead.[167] From 28 December onwards he also led the Italian troops in Albania.[168]

By this time the situation, which had caused both Mussolini and Soddu to lose their heads on 4 December, had calmed down. Previously the Greeks had broken through at Pogradec, and Mussolini, misunderstanding Soddu's appeal for a political solution, had for a short time contemplated asking Hitler to mediate an armistice with Metaxas. Ciano resolutely opposed this idea.[169] By next evening such a drastic solution no longer appeared necessary. Italy seemed capable of holding Albania, at any rate for the time being.[170] That did not mean, however, that the Italian army's position had been stabilized.

In the third phase of the conflict the Greeks continued their attack, with the sector Këlcyrë–Bubq becoming the main centre of events. Greek troops finally captured the important transport junction of Këlcyrë. Consequently the front there was pushed considerably, and in other places less dramatically, to the north-west or west. Thereafter the Italians attempted a counter-attack in the region; this ended in failure, as did another counter-offensive ordered insistently by Mussolini in March 1941.[171] He had hoped to achieve at least a

---

[165] Montanari, *Grecia*, i. 333.
[166] Thorough coverage of the affair in Knox, *Mussolini*, 243–9; Montanari, *Grecia*, i. 324–45.
[167] From 4 Dec. 1940 Cavallero was to all intents and purposes in charge in Albania together (and in competition) with Soddu; cf. Cavallero, *Comando Supremo*, 8–44 (4–31 Dec. 1940).
[168] Cavallero, *Comando Supremo*, 40–1 (29 Dec. 1940); Montanari, *Grecia*, i. 456 n. 176.
[169] Ciano, *Diary 1939–1943*, 313 (4 Dec. 1940).
[170] See the thorough description in Montanari, *Grecia*, i. 346–58.
[171] 'Der Krieg Griechenlands 1940–1941', 34–44, BA-MA N 449/7.

local success before the intervention of the Wehrmacht.[172] In fact, the changes to the front were minimal.

This failure confirmed what had long been obvious: the Italians were unable to change the aspect of the Balkans on their own. It must have been profoundly humiliating for Mussolini to find himself so publicly dependent on Hitler's help. More generals and admirals were dismissed at roughly the same time as Badoglio,[173] but the appointment of new men to senior ranks in the hierarchy was not enough to guarantee success when the other causes of failure remained. By the end of 1940 it was too late.

Finally we must examine the price paid by the Italian people for the campaign in Greece, before and after the German intervention. This price, first and foremost, involved the men who were killed, missing in action, or wounded. By 23 April 1941 Italy had deployed 29 divisions in this theatre. At the middle of the month there were 20,813 Italian officers and 470,918 NCOs and men there, plus 487 officers and 11,231 NCOs and men of Albanian origin. During the Greek campaign 50,874 of all these were wounded, 52,108 were put out of action at least temporarily through illness, 12,368 suffered from frostbite, and 38,832, most of whom fell in battle, did not return. Some divisions, such as Julia with 3,754 dead and Ferrara with 3,331, lost almost one man in three.[174] All these losses were incurred in a war against a country which, in Mussolini's contemptuous words, was not worth the life of a single Sardinian grenadier.

Italy also paid a political price, which is touched on in the title of this chapter. The conflict with Greece—and, of course, the failures in North Africa—demonstrated Italy's bankruptcy as a great power. The country became totally dependent on National Socialist Germany. Though the façade of equal partnership was maintained, from 1941 onwards the war in the Mediterranean developed into an Anglo-German conflict in which Mussolini was involved only as Hitler's vassal.[175] These developments evolved with a certain iron logic after Italy's entry into the war, when her claim to greatpower status, which had been conceded up until June 1940, was put to the test. From the point of view of armaments, military capability, and industrial capacity, the country was unable to satisfy the requirements of such status. This fact, no more and no less, was made manifest in the course of Mussolini's 'parallel war'.

[172] Knox, *Mussolini*, 260.
[173] *DGFP* D xi, No. 519, pp. 876–8 (14 Dec. 1940), foreign ministry information on 'changes in the high command of the Italian army and navy'.
[174] Figures from Montanari, *Grecia*, i. 938–43.
[175] See V.1 below (Stegemann).

PART III

German Intervention in the Balkans

Detlef Vogel

I. Germany's Balkan Policy in the Autumn of 1940 and the Spring of 1941

1. THE GENERAL AIMS OF GERMAN POLICY IN SOUTH-EAST EUROPE

As has been seen in the preceding chapters,[1] Hitler's expectation that he would be able to force Britain to accept an armistice or even peace with Germany after the defeat of France had not been fulfilled. On the contrary, the British government left no doubt that now more than ever they intended to keep on fighting until the final defeat of Germany.[2] Although this situation was incompatible with the conditions Hitler had originally considered essential in his calculations for a war with the Soviet Union, namely a secure front in the west in order to concentrate his forces in the east, he nevertheless decided to begin the war with that country, which he had already planned for ideological reasons.[3] To the German leaders a victory over the Soviet Union seemed to be the only way to resolve the strategic dilemma of the summer of 1940, after the alternatives of defeating Britain or at least forcing her out of the war had proved to be unfeasible.[4]

Lacking a complete rear cover in the west for the imminent war in the east, the German leaders were determined not to leave their flanks in northern and southern Europe unsecured. In the autumn of 1940 Hitler therefore included Finland and the eastern part of Norway as well as Romania in his preparations for the war against the Soviet Union.[5] In south-east Europe as a whole, the German government sought to increase the already considerable German influence in order to be able to use the Balkans in its plans.[6]

As in northern Europe, the main aim of German policy in the countries of south-east Europe was to secure their economic resources for Germany's future plans.[7] Even before the outbreak of the war, Germany had succeeded in

---

[1] Cf. I.III.1 (*b*) and I.III.2 (*b*) above (Schreiber); also *Das Deutsche Reich und der Zweite Weltkrieg*, iv. 3 ff. (Förster).
[2] Churchill, *Second World War*, ii. 191; OKW/A Ausl/Abw/Abw I No. 0982/40 geh., Außen- und militärpolitische Nachrichten (31 Aug. 1940), BA-MA RW 5/v. 354; Hillgruber, *Strategie*, 274.
[3] Halder, *Diaries*, i. 517 (22 July 1940); i. 533–4 (31 July 1940); Hillgruber, *Strategie*, 353–4.
[4] Cf. I.III.2 above (Schreiber); Schreiber, 'Mittelmeerraum', 76–7; *Das Deutsche Reich und der Zweite Weltkrieg*, iv. 13 ff. (Förster).
[5] On northern Europe cf. *Das Deutsche Reich und der Zweite Weltkrieg*, iv. 365 (Ueberschär); on Romania ibid. 338–9 (Förster); on the danger to the northern and southern flanks in general cf. Simović, 'Memoari', *Politika* (8 Sept. 1970).
[6] Cf. II.II.1 above (Schreiber); Hillgruber, *Strategie*, 460–1.
[7] On northern Europe cf. *Das Deutsche Reich und der Zweite Weltkrieg*, iv. 371–2 (Ueberschär); on the Balkans cf. *Griff nach Südosteuropa*, 29–31, 118 ff.

binding the Balkan countries to herself as important producers of food and raw materials.⁸ The economic ties between Germany and south-east Europe continued during the first year of the war, e.g. in the conclusion of an 'oil-for-arms' pact between Germany and Romania. Even countries such as Yugoslavia and Greece, which had previously pursued policies favourable to Britain and France, were no longer able, especially after the defeat of France, to avoid becoming politically and economically dependent on Germany.⁹

Using these economic ties, Hitler also sought to bind south-east Europe to Germany politically. In the autumn of 1940 Germany and Italy strove to draw the Balkan countries into the Tripartite Pact, directed initially against Britain and, when Molotov's visit to Berlin in mid-November produced no results, against the Soviet Union.¹⁰ Wherever these aims could not be realized, e.g. in the case of Greece because of the constant tension between Athens and Rome, German diplomacy attempted at least to weaken existing ties with Britain and induce the country concerned to pursue a policy of friendly neutrality towards Germany.¹¹

Although Mussolini and Hitler were both interested in expanding the Tripartite Pact (to include Hungary, Romania, Slovakia, and Bulgaria), it was clear that the two dictators were pursuing different objectives with regard to Yugoslavia and Greece. Because of this rivalry, Hitler was quite prepared to present his Italian ally with *faits accomplis* whenever an opportunity or need presented itself to strengthen Germany's influence in south-east Europe. When he decided to grant Romania's request for the sending of a German military mission to that country in September 1940, he took this decision without sufficiently consulting Italy, which caused Mussolini to feel that he had been deceived.¹²

The official reason for sending German soldiers to Romania in October 1940 was to train the Romanian armed forces. But this action also served to protect the important oilfields around Ploeşti from destruction or capture. As indicated above, Hitler also wanted the military mission to prepare the participation of the Romanian armed forces with Germany in the attack on the Soviet

---

⁸ Vol. i of the present work, II.vi.6 (Volkmann); II.ii.1 (*a*)–(*c*) above (Schreiber); *Innen- und Außenpolitik*, 161; Schönfeld, 'Rohstoffsicherungspolitik', 215–31.

⁹ *DGFP* D ix, No. 338, pp. 459–60 (28 May 1940); Förster, 'Rumäniens Weg', 47–8. In accordance with the 'oil-for-arms pact' Germany delivered military equipment in exchange for oil, which Romania was obliged to sell at low prices.

¹⁰ Hillgruber, *Strategie*, 337. The Tripartite Pact was concluded between Germany, Italy, and Japan on 27 Sept. 1940: *DGFP* D xi, No. 118. Hungary joined on 20 Nov. 1940 and Romania on 23 Nov: Olshausen, 'Die deutsche Balkanpolitik', 713. On the Italian side cf. *DDI*, 9th ser., v, No. 745, p. 716 (18 Oct. 1940), and No. 760, p. 731 (21 Oct. 1940).

¹¹ OKW/A Ausl/Abw/Abw I, No. 01200/40 geh., 'Außenpolitische Übersicht', 7 Oct. 1940, pp. 6–7, BA-MA RW 5/v. 350; on Greek policy after 1939 cf. Koliopoulos, *Greece 1935–1941*, 109–10.

¹² *DGFP* D xi, No. 192, pp. 324–5 (18 Oct. 1940); details in II.iii.1 above (Schreiber); on German–Italian relations in general cf. Hillgruber, *Strategie*, 282–3.

1. General Aims in South-east Europe

Union.[13] The military mission to Romania, which marked, for the time being, the high point of Germany's efforts to increase her influence in the Balkans, was incompatible with the non-aggression pact of 23 August 1939 between Germany and the Soviet Union, in which Ribbentrop had declared Germany's complete lack of political interest in these areas.[14] As the Soviet Union had also long considered south-east Europe to be in its sphere of influence, Hitler feared that his actions might cause the Soviet government to intervene in the Balkans at the first opportunity. To avoid giving Stalin such an opportunity, he employed diplomacy to settle peacefully military and political conflicts among the Balkan states. Although in the late summer and autumn of 1940 the German policy of balancing the diverging interests of the countries of south-east Europe was successful in several cases, fear of Soviet involvement remained, as will be shown, an element in German planning.[15]

On the whole, Hitler's main aim in the autumn of 1940, until the Italian attack on Greece, was to prevent the Balkans from becoming involved in political and military conflicts. Only in this way was Germany able to derive the greatest possible benefits from her economic ties with south-east Europe.[16] For the time being the use of military force to achieve German aims there did not seem necessary, as Germany's dominant position was sufficient to safeguard her interests through political, economic, and, if necessary, military pressure. Nevertheless, the use of force definitely remained a possibility, as Germany was dependent on Romanian oil and would become even more so if Soviet deliveries were to stop. For this reason Hitler closely followed all Soviet and British activities in the Balkans which might endanger the position Germany had achieved there.

Italy's military weakness in the Mediterranean presented an additional problem in the defence of German interests in south-east Europe. It was to be feared that, in the further course of the war, Britain would definitely be in a position to intervene militarily in the Balkans.[17] However, Hitler did not consider it possible at that time to achieve a rapid change in the situation in the Mediterranean, which he regarded as dangerously unstable, as Mussolini was able to prevent any German involvement there.[18]

---

[13] On the sending of the military mission: *KTB OKW* i. 56 (2 Sept. 1940) and 81 (18 Sept. 1940); teletype message OKH/Att. Abt. No. 3290/40 geh. (8 Sept. 1940) to OQu IV, Frd H Ost, BA-MA RH2/v. 2954; Förster, 'Rumäniens Weg'; on Hitler's plans to occupy Romania for fear of a Soviet invasion cf. *Das Deutsche Reich und der Zweite Weltkrieg*, iv. 17 (Förster).

[14] *DGFP* D vii, No. 229, pp. 246–7; the Axis powers had also issued a guarantee declaration for Romania on the conclusion of the Vienna Award, 30 Aug. 1940. Cf. ibid. x, No. 413, pp. 581–7.

[15] Ibid.

[16] Hillgruber, *Strategie*, 335; Papagos, *Griechenland*, 171–2.

[17] Cf. III.1.2 below.

[18] Creveld, *Balkan*, 53–5; Halder, *Diaries*, i. 668–9 (30 Oct. 1940).

2. GERMAN POLITICAL AND MILITARY PREPARATIONS FOR THE INVASION OF GREECE

Mussolini's attack on Greece from Albania on 28 October 1940 seriously disrupted the peace and stability Germany had sought to maintain in the Balkans. An Italian victory would certainly have been in Germany's interest, but within a few days after the start of the attack the Wehrmacht high command no longer expected a decisive Italian success.[19] Britain reacted to Mussolini's attack with military measures, and this fact itself posed a danger for Hitler's further aggressive plans. Prime Minister Metaxas of Greece immediately asked the British government to support his country with air and naval forces.[20] As Britain had guaranteed the independence of Greece on 13 April 1939, the British government immediately promised help, although it was able to provide little real assistance. The British commanders-in-chief in the Middle East were also of the opinion that significant help for Greece should be provided only when the Italian offensive against Egypt, which had already been halted, had collapsed completely.[21] Nevertheless British troops occupied parts of Crete as early as the beginning of November. Britain sent a naval mission to Athens on 2 November and transferred the first Royal Air Force squadrons to the Greek mainland a little later.[22] Admiral Chatfield, who considered Italy to be the Achilles' heel of the Third Reich, believed that Britain now had the opportunity to defeat Hitler in the Mediterranean if she could force the Duce to his knees.[23] In any case, after British aircraft attacked units of Mussolini's fleet in Taranto on 11 and 12 November 1940, it hardly seemed possible that Italy would be able to interfere seriously with British actions in the eastern Mediterranean.[24] Because of the weak Italian position in the Mediterranean, German military leaders believed that the British were capable of sending at least three divisions to the Aegean within a very short time.[25]

---

[19] *KTB OKW* i. 162 (9 Nov. 1940); the Germans were informed of Mussolini's planned attack at the end of October. Cf. Greiner's notes of 24 and 26 Oct. 1940, pp. 92 ff., BA-MA RW 4/v. 42; Hillgruber, *Strategie*, 285.

[20] Butler, *Strategy*, ii. 365; Greiner, 'Balkan', 1, MGFA C-065 g.

[21] *PWT*, Middle East I, Hist (B) 1, No. 7, pp. 6–7 (30 Nov. 1940); Churchill's promise in his speech of 5 Nov. 1940. Cf. 1. Skl., KTB, Teil A, 63 (6 Nov. 1940), BA-MA RM 7/18. For more details of British policy in south-east Europe cf. Knoll, *Jugoslawien*, 35 ff., and Richter, *Griechenland*, 91.

[22] On the occupation of Crete: *PWT*, Middle East I, Hist (B) 1, No. 6, p. 5 (1 Nov. 1940), and Schramm-von Thadden, *Griechenland*, 121; on the naval mission in Athens cf. 1. Skl., KTB, Teil A, 34 (3 Nov. 1940), BA-MA RM 7/18; on the RAF build-up in Greece: Higham, 'Generals and Guarantees'.

[23] Cf. the reference in 1. Skl., KTB, Teil A, 3 (1 Nov. 1940), BA-MA RM 7/18. Chatfield was Admiral of the Fleet and Minister for the Co-ordination of Defence; the war diary of the Skl. refers here to information provided by the Marinenachrichtendienst (naval intelligence department).

[24] Ibid. 159 (12 Nov. 1940), BA-MA RM 7/18. On the Italian losses cf. Hillgruber and Hümmelchen, *Chronik*, 50.

[25] 1. Skl., KTB, Teil A, 37 (4 Nov. 1940), BA-MA RM 7/18.

2. Preparations for Invasion of Greece

In their planning, however, the British at first attached greater importance to air support for Greece. Air Marshal Longmore, the commander-in-chief of the Royal Air Force in the Middle East, was in complete agreement with Churchill in his intention to strengthen air units in Greece as soon as possible.[26] In addition to making it easier to reach the eastern coast of Italy and to intervene in the fighting on the Albanian front, bases in Greece would also enable the British to bomb the Romanian oilfields.[27] To support these military plans, British diplomats continued their policy of trying to find more allies against the Axis powers among the Balkan states. According to the German ambassador in Ankara, the British hoped to win Yugoslavia and Turkey for this purpose and also to obtain Soviet approval for their plans.[28] Hitler feared that these British efforts could jeopardize his further war plans by creating a new front, in south-east Europe, before or during his war in the east.[29] Equally dangerous from the German point of view were British plans to bomb the Romanian oilfields. In November 1940 reports of constant reinforcement of British air power on the Greek mainland as well as Crete and Lemnos made this danger seem more threatening. Fearing German retaliation, however, Metaxas forbade the establishment of Royal Air Force bases in Macedonia or the Thracian plain.[30] How seriously Hitler took the threat represented by British air units can be seen in the German request to the Bulgarian government of 6 November 1940 to set up an air-raid warning service along the frontier between Bulgaria and Greece in order to detect British air attacks as early as possible. The Bulgarian government agreed to this request and the warning service began operations at the end of the month.[31]

Seen from Berlin, the Italian attack on Greece seemed, already after the failure of the first offensive, to endanger the dominant position of the Axis in south-east Europe and to further weaken Italy's military position in the Mediterranean. For this reason and with his future war plans in mind, Hitler began very early to consider using military force to resolve the Greek situation in favour of the Axis. The intention of the German leadership to reach the Aegean Sea through Bulgaria was discernible as early as 1 November 1940.

---

[26] *PWT*, Middle East I, Hist (B) 1, No. 4, p. 4 (31 Oct. 1940), and No. 5, p. 4 (1 Nov. 1940).

[27] Woodward, *British Foreign Policy*, i. 518; Col.-Gen. Fromm, BdE, 'Bericht zur allgemeinen Lage' (no date), 2, BA-MA RW 5/v. 7.

[28] OKW/A Ausl/Abw/Abw I No. 01442/40 geh., 'Außenpolitische Übersicht' (4 Nov. 1940), 7, BA-MA RW 5/v. 350; OKW/A Ausl/Abw/Abw I No. 0129/40 geh., Außen- und militärpolitische Nachrichten (17 Oct. 1940), BA-MA RW 5/v. 354. As early as Jan. 1940 the German legation in Athens had informed Papagos of the fears of the German government: Papagos, *Battle*, 149–50. *Griechenland, 1940–1941*.

[29] Förster, 'Rumäniens Weg', 54; Olshausen, 'Die deutsche Balkanpolitik', 712. On 19 Nov. 1940 Hitler planned to attack the Soviet Union on 1 May 1941 (*KTB OKW* i. 176); on 6 Dec. 1940 the earliest date was the middle of May 1941 (ibid. 211).

[30] Higham, 'Generals and Guarantees'. On British plans to bomb the oilfields cf. COS (40) 13 (0), Foreign Office proposal, PRO, CAB 80/56 (16 Oct. 1940), and ibid., Prem. 3,374/13a (28 Nov. 1940). There were no RAF aircraft on Lemnos.

[31] *DGFP* D xi, No. 345, pp. 591–2 (16 Nov. 1940); *KTB OKW* i. 187 (25 Nov. 1940).

Three days later the army high command was instructed by the head of the Wehrmacht operations staff to make preparations to occupy Greek Macedonia and Thrace.[32] With this action Hitler wanted to create the basis for the use of German fighter units against British air attacks on the Romanian oilfields. At the same time force requirements and operations necessary for such a campaign were considered.[33] In Directive No. 18 of 12 November 1940 it was assumed that a German military intervention in the Balkans should be limited and only resorted to 'if necessary',[34] in order to keep the forces used as small as possible and avoid time-consuming operations. But neither the Luftwaffe nor the navy leaders agreed to these objectives. In their view the military objective should include the occupation of the Greek mainland and the Peloponnese.[35] At the end of November the Wehrmacht operations staff were also inclined to accept this view, after Hitler had observed that any British attempt to gain a foothold in Greece would be 'intolerable for Germany'.[36] Although it became clear at the same time that Greece only intended to permit British operations against Italy, Hitler's attitude did not change. For him the mere possibility that the British might be able to deliver painful blows to the 'soft under-side'[37] of the area under German–Italian domination was decisive. When Italy suffered defeats in Greece and, in December, in North Africa,[38] the German leadership concluded that Germany would have to support Italy. While assistance for Italy in North Africa included early military help, Hitler told Ciano on 18 November 1940 that Germany would be able to intervene in the Balkans only in the spring.[39] In answer to Italian requests in December, however, he stated that he was prepared to help Italy with diplomatic moves and weapons deliveries.[40]

Although Hitler had basically decided, for the reasons mentioned, to intervene in the Balkans, he expressed the hope at the beginning of December 1940

---

[32] *KTB OKW* i. 144 (1 Nov. 1940) and 150 (4 Nov. 1940). Cf. also Donlagić *et al.*, *Jugoslawien im Zweiten Weltkrieg*, 28.

[33] Halder, *Diaries*, i. 673 (4 Nov. 1940), 678–9 (7 Nov. 1940).

[34] *Hitler's War Directives*, No. 18, p. 42, and Jodl's assessment of the situation in *KTB OKW* i. 171 (13 Nov. 1940).

[35] On the Luftwaffe: *KTB OKW* i. 179–80 (19 Nov. 1940) and Greiner, 'Balkan', 1, MGFA C-065 g. On the navy: 1. Skl., KTB, Teil A, 102 (8 Nov. 1940), BA-MA RM 7/18.

[36] *DGFP* D xi, No. 326, pp. 541 ff. (16 Nov. 1940), here 545; *KTB OKW* i. 188 (25 Nov. 1940).

[37] Barker, *British Policy*, 101. The quote is from Leo Amery (secretary of state for India) on 1 Dec. 1940. Cf. also Knoll, *Jugoslawien*, 65–6. On the reservations of the Greek government regarding the use of the RAF cf. OKW/A Ausl/Abw/Abw I No. 01585/40 geh., Außen- und militärpolitische Nachrichten (26 Nov. 1940), BA-MA RW 5/v. 354.

[38] Butler, *Strategy*, ii. 375. On the Italian defeat in December cf. V.1 below (Stegemann).

[39] *DGFP* D xi, No. 353, pp. 606 ff. (19 Nov. 1940), here 607; on assistance in North Africa ibid., No. 452, pp. 789–91 (5 Dec. 1940).

[40] Ibid., No. 538 (20 Dec. 1940). Among other things Mussolini had asked that, to put pressure on Greece, Germany should openly announce that German troops were in Romania: ibid., No. 477, p. 820 (8 Dec. 1940); II.III.4 above (Schreiber). On the plans to support Italy in Albania: Burdick, 'Operation Cyclamen', 24 ff.; Ciano, *Diary 1939–1943*, 312 (1 Dec. 1940).

2. Preparations for Invasion of Greece

that the Greek government might decide to ask the British to leave Greece.[41] In that case, he observed, there would be no reason for Germany to attack Greece.[42] Nevertheless, preparations for the operation with the cover-name 'Marita' were to continue; the units deployed against Greece could just as easily be used in the war in the east.[43]

As a first measure against the British gaining a foothold in Greece, the German military leaders had ordered a strengthening of the military mission to Romania on 4 November.[44] As early as the middle of October contingents of the German army had been in Bucharest, and even before the start of the Italian attack on Greece, Luftwaffe units arrived in Romania.[45] In his Directive No. 18 of 12 November Hitler considered a strengthening of the military mission necessary to guarantee that the ten German divisions envisaged for the campaign in Greece would be able to move from Hungary through Romania to the Danube without difficulty.[46]

With the permission of the Bulgarian government, a German advance group under the command of Colonel Kurt Zeitzler was sent to Bulgaria. Its task was to ensure the further movement of the German units to the Greek frontier by carrying out appropriate infrastructure measures.[47] The Wehrmacht high command planned the start of the attack for the beginning of March.[48] Because of the poor roads in Bulgaria it did not seem advisable to begin the attack before then; this view was supported by Zeitzler's reports. The command of the units planned for the attack was entrusted to the headquarters staff of the Twelfth Army under Field Marshal Wilhelm List. The German troops were to reach the Greek frontier from Germany in three echelons with a total of five army corps (XI, XIV, XVII, XXX, and XXXX).[49] For air support VIII

---

[41] Halder, *KTB* ii. 212 (5 Dec. 1940; not in trans.). Hitler expressed this hope because he believed that the German threat would have the desired effect in Athens.

[42] Halder, *KTB* ii. 212 (5 Dec. 1940; not in trans.).

[43] *KTB OKW* i. 204 (5 Dec. 1940). On the deployment directive for 'Marita' cf. Halder, *Diaries*, i. 727–8 (8 Dec. 1940).

[44] *KTB OKW* i. 150 (4 Nov. 1940). Cf. also Creveld, *Balkan*, 96; one mountain battery and one mountain battalion were envisaged.

[45] Lfl.Kdo. 4, KTB, Fü.Abt. Ia op 2, p. 24 (19–21 Nov. 1940), BA-MA RL 7/668. In the middle of November four fighter and two reconnaissance Staffeln were in Romania: *KTB OKW* i. 168 (11 Nov. 1940).

[46] *Hitler's War Directives*, No. 18, p. 43 (12 Nov. 1940). On 19 Nov. 1940 Hitler ordered two additional divisions to be included in the attack on Greece: *KTB OKW* i. 179 (19 Nov. 1940); in the middle of December 16th Armoured Division was already being transported to Romania: ibid. 235 (18 Dec. 1940).

[47] Halder, *Diaries*, i. 734 (12 Dec. 1940), and Hoppe, *Bulgarien*, 108.

[48] *KTB OKW* i. 204 (5 Dec. 1940).

[49] Ibid. 224 (11 Dec. 1940) and 240 (20 Dec. 1940). In the end it was planned to use 2 armoured and 2 motorized infantry, 3 mountain and $4\frac{1}{2}$ infantry divisions: supplementary directive of the OKH for 12th Army of 22 Mar. 1941, Annex 2, BA-MA RH 6/v. 3; originally 4th Army headquarters (under FM Günther von Kluge) was intended to direct the operations: *KTB OKW* i. 208 (5 Dec. 1940).

Flying Corps was assigned to Twelfth Army and placed under the command of Air Fleet Four in Vienna.[50]

In Hitler's Directive No. 20 (Operation Marita) of 13 December 1940, which described the tasks of the army and Luftwaffe units, operations in northern Greece were mentioned, as they had been in the first planning in November. Additional actions to occupy the mainland of Greece as far as Corinth were, however, also indicated as a possibility. Evidently Hitler and his generals still wanted to avoid becoming too deeply involved in Greece in order to be able to withdraw the assigned units quickly 'for new tasks'.[51] But at the same time they made the necessary organizational preparations for an advance further south.

The German government attempted to prevent possible Soviet intervention against the deployment of German troops in the Balkans by carefully directed information. The foreign ministry was instructed to inform Romania's northern neighbour about German intentions before the sending of a military mission to Bucharest. Nevertheless, State Secretary von Weizsäcker considered the measures taken by Hitler, above all the sending of German troops to Romania and the German guarantee for that country, to be extremely dangerous. In his opinion it was important to 'spread the necessary autumn fog for the Russians'[52] in order to be able to conceal Germany's further intentions. With the same aim Hitler informed General Erik Hansen, head of the German military mission to Romania, that he should avoid anything that might awaken Moscow's distrust. Ribbentrop also instructed German diplomatic missions to refrain from any remarks that might be interpreted as anti-Soviet in connection with the presence of German troops in Romania.[53]

Such diplomatic moves could not, however, completely overcome Stalin's distrust. Fourteen days after the arrival of the first German contingents in Romania the Soviet government sent several officers to Bucharest to observe the activity of the German military mission.[54] And, as expected, during his visit to Berlin Molotov objected to the German moves in Romania. When the Soviet foreign minister sought to ascertain further German intentions by enquiring how Germany would react in the case of a Soviet guarantee for Bulgaria, Hitler avoided giving a clear answer, with good reason. He feared that Soviet diplomatic involvement in Bulgaria would endanger his plans to send troops through that country. He attempted instead to calm Molotov with

---

[50] Gen.Kdo. VIII. Fl.Korps, Ic No. 1990/41 geh. (30 Apr. 1941), 1, BA-MA RL 8/245. Cf. Deichman, 'Balkanfeldzug des VIII. Fliegerkorps', 1, BA-MA RL 8/238.

[51] This meant, of course, against the Soviet Union. Cf. *Hitler's War Directives*, No. 20; also deployment order for 12th Army, 9 Dec. 1940, pp. 5–8, BA-MA RH 6/v. 3.

[52] *Weizsäcker-Papiere*, 219 (27 Sept. 1940). On the instructions to the foreign ministry cf. *KTB OKW* i. 99 (20 Sept. 1940).

[53] On the conversation between Hitler and Hansen cf. *KTB OKW* i. 105 (1 Oct. 1940); Ribbentrop's order in *DGFP* D xi, No. 169, p. 279 (10 Oct. 1940).

[54] *KTB OKW* i. 130 (28 Oct. 1940).

2. Preparations for Invasion of Greece

the assurance that possible German actions would be directed solely against the British presence in Greece, which had to be eliminated by whatever means were necessary.[55] Even if Molotov accepted Hitler's arguments, he must also have realized that the German measures in the Balkans represented a considerable danger for the Soviet Union. If Hitler could drive the British out of Greece, he would be in a position not only to plan further military operations in the Mediterranean, but also to use south-east Europe as a power-base against the Soviet Union. And the German measures represented an insurmountable obstacle to the realization of Stalin's plans to draw the Balkan states into his sphere of influence.

At the beginning of December Hitler did not expect the Soviet Union to intervene if Germany attacked Greece,[56] but he nevertheless continued his information policy and let the Soviet government know at that time of the envisaged transports of Twelfth Army. At the same time Berlin assured the Soviet government that the concentration of German military units in southern Romania did not represent a danger for the Soviet Union and that neither Turkey nor Yugoslavia would be involved in the imminent operations.[57] To be prepared for all eventualities, however, the German military mission in Romania was instructed to plan defensive measures against a Soviet intervention.[58]

In the following months the German government was mainly concerned with bringing the policies of friendly countries in south-east Europe more closely into line with German intentions. The success of German plans against Greece depended on the political good will and the functioning infrastructure of the Balkan states as a transit and deployment area. Moreover, long-term German plans still envisaged maintaining political stability in those states in order to bind the Balkans more closely to Germany economically.

Hungary soon acquired a special significance in German military preparations for the war against Greece, as it began to be evident as early as the end of 1940 that Yugoslavia would not permit German troops to pass through her territory to attack Greece.[59] The Hungarian decision to join the Tripartite Pact on 20 November 1940 provided favourable conditions for the realization of German intentions. The Hungarian government had already permitted the passage of transports of the German military mission in Romania a month earlier, and, in mid-January 1941, agreed to the passage of troops for Operation Marita through Hungary.[60] The Wehrmacht high command was also able to start drawing up a timetable to give priority to carrying out the large

---

[55] *DGFP* D xi, No. 326, pp. 541 ff. (16 Nov. 1940), here 545.
[56] Halder, *KTB* ii. 213 (5 Dec. 1940; not in trans.).
[57] *KTB OKW* i. 237 (18 Dec. 1940) and 995.
[58] DHM Rumänien, Abt. Ia, No. 75/40 g.Kdos., 23 Oct. 1940, BA-MA RH 27-13/2.
[59] Halder, *Diaries*, i. 676 (5 Nov. 1940).
[60] OKW/A Ausl/Abw/Abw I No. 01264/40 geh., Außen- und militärpolitische Nachrichten (12 Oct. 1940), BA-MA RW 5/354.

troop movements in January 1941.[61] In addition to the arrangement between Hungary and Romania achieved in the Vienna Award, the German government attempted to protect Germany's plans politically by improving relations between Hungary and Yugoslavia. Hitler obviously wanted to eliminate the danger that Yugoslavia might create difficulties for the German deployment against Greece. With German encouragement, a treaty of friendship was concluded between Hungary and Yugoslavia in December 1940, although it did not contain a Hungarian renunciation of claims to certain areas of Yugoslavia (the Mur area, the Baranya triangle, the Bačka, and the eastern Banat).[62] In March 1941, however, Hitler clearly indicated to the Hungarian foreign minister Bardossy that, for the time being, he considered Hungary's territorial claims to be satisfied, although Germany did not intend expressly to guarantee Yugoslavia's frontiers.[63] At this meeting Hitler also spoke of the economic importance of Hungary for Germany and underlined the need for Hungary to meet her delivery commitments of important raw materials and foodstuffs. Admiral Horthy, the Hungarian regent, agreed to the economic and military wishes of his German ally because he hoped to play a leading role in south-east Europe after the war and expected further territorial gains.[64] The German interest in maintaining stability in Hungary was due to the fact that Hungary was an indispensable link between Germany and the Balkan states for military movements and shipments of important goods such as Romanian oil. It was also intended to use Hungary as a deployment area for the attack on the Soviet Union.[65]

Military and economic interests also determined German policy towards Romania at the end of 1940 and the beginning of 1941. The main economic aim was to increase the production of the Romanian oilfields and to protect the storage areas against foreign attacks. It was certainly to the advantage of Germany that all high-ranking British employees of the oil companies who were suspected of sabotage had been arrested by Romanian officials and put on trial at the end of September 1940.[66] The German government sought to increase its influence on Romanian oil production with the help of mixed companies and the participation of German capital.[67] In March 1941 Göring, in his capacity as plenipotentiary for the Four-year Plan, suggested to the

---

[61] Halder, *Diaries*, i. 742 (18 Dec. 1940).

[62] *DGFP* D xi, No. 431, p. 758 (30 Nov. 1940), and No. 478, p. 824 (9 Dec. 1940); Olshausen, *Zwischenspiel auf dem Balkan*, 32.

[63] *DGFP* D xii, No. 191, pp. 331 ff. (23 Mar. 1941).

[64] OKW/A Ausl/Abw/Abw I No. 01516/40 geh. and No. 0480/41 geh., Außen- und militärpolitische Nachrichten (17 Nov. 1940 and 2 Mar. 1941), BA-MA RW 5/v. 354.

[65] On political and economic relations between Hungary and Germany cf. *Das Deutsche Reich und der Zweite Weltkrieg*, iv. 347 ff. (Förster); Borus, 'Ungarn', 46 ff.; Schumann and Wappler, 'Südosteuropa', 112–13.

[66] OKW/A Ausl/Abw/Abw I No. 01442/40 geh., 'Außenpolitische Übersicht' (4 Nov. 1940), 5, BA-MA RW 5/v. 350.

[67] *DGFP* D xi, No. 663, pp. 1113–14 (16 Jan. 1941); *Griff nach Südosteuropa*, 70 ff.

2. Preparations for Invasion of Greece

Romanian leader Antonescu that he should use German capital and technical know-how to increase production and to drill new wells. The German government also wanted to keep a check on Romanian oil exports to third countries. Romania reacted positively to the German demands and promised to give the German government the greatest possible say in matters concerning oil production.[68] Antonescu also complied with Hitler's wishes concerning the military protection of the oilfields, pipelines, and storage areas. German projects for the construction of underground oil-storage facilities and an extensive anti-aircraft and coastal defence system could accordingly be carried out.[69]

Romanian economic co-operation with Germany was based on the integration of Romanian policy and German interests mentioned above. Romanian compliance with Hitler's wishes did not date from the arrival of the German military mission. As early as 7 September 1940, only one day after the abdication of King Carol, Marshal Antonescu let Hitler know that he wanted to 'co-operate one hundred per cent with Germany'.[70] And in January he stated that his country had completely abandoned neutrality.[71] The extent to which the German government sought to determine Romanian foreign policy was evident in the reaction of the Romanian government to the request of the American special representative William Donovan to visit the country at the end of that month on a fact-finding trip. After the German government had indicated its disapproval of the proposed visit, Romania refused to grant Donovan a visa.[72] With his policy of close co-operation with Germany, Antonescu clearly wanted to secure the independence of his country and obtain the greatest possible protection with regard to the Soviet Union. Moreover, as was the case with Admiral Horthy, a basic ideological affinity made it easy for him to co-operate with Hitler.

Thus the situation in Romania was ideal for the realization of German military plans against Greece; at the end of 1940 and the beginning of 1941 the responsible German officers were able to devote their complete attention to the planning and execution of the deployment north of the Danube. With Antonescu's express approval two armoured divisions (5th and 11th) and two infantry divisions (72nd and 164th), in addition to the headquarters staff of Twelfth Army, the command of Armoured Group 1, and the corps commands

---

[68] *DGFP* D xii, No. 126, pp. 221 ff. (8 Mar. 1941). Antonescu was only concerned that the low 'special price' that Germany paid for the oil should not be passed on to third countries.

[69] Cf. 1. Skl., KTB, Teil A, 325–6 (24 Jan. 1941), BA-MA RM 7/20, and Skl. B.Nr. 1, SKL I, op. 218/41 g.Kdos., Chefs. (26 Feb. 1941), 4 ff., BA-MA MBox 57, P632087c.

[70] OKH/army general staff/Att.Abt. No. 3290/40 geh. (8 Sept. 1940), BA-MA RH 2/v. 2954. On Romanian policy in general cf. *Das Deutsche Reich und der Zweite Weltkrieg*, iv. 327 ff. (Förster).

[71] *DGFP* D xi, No. 661, pp. 1109 ff. (15 Jan. 1941).

[72] OKW/A Ausl/Abw/Abw I No. 0208/41 geh. (27 Jan. 1941) (reports from the German minister in Bucharest of 25 and 26 Jan. 1941), BA-MA RW 5/v. 354; 1. Skl., KTB, Teil A, 386 (29 Jan. 1941), BA-MA RM 7/20.

XIV and XXX with all corps and army troops, reached the Romanian Dobrudja by the end of January.[73]

Although the German government informed Romania of the individual military movements, Antonescu was kept ignorant of the total strength of the German units. When he asked how many German soldiers were actually in his country at the end of the month, he was given the exaggerated figure of 500,000. This more or less agreed with the figure of 680,000 men the German ambassador in Moscow gave the Soviet government at the end of February. The purpose of such exaggerations was no doubt to make resistance in Greece seem senseless and to deter the Soviet Union from intervening in Romania. The Greek military attaché in Bucharest, however, accurately estimated the total strength of German forces in Romania on 18 January 1941 at about 180,000 men.[74] It can therefore be assumed that Soviet military officers in Bucharest were also not deceived by the German figures.

Like the Wehrmacht operations staff, in December 1940 the Romanian government considered a Soviet intervention quite possible as a consequence of the German deployment in southern Romania.[75] A month later Hitler seemed to share this concern and wanted at least to delay the whole operation.[76] At the end of January 1941, however, Halder was informed by the Wehrmacht high command that the risk of a Soviet attack had to be accepted.[77] As it had done at the end of 1940, the German government still tried to present its military aims as directed exclusively against Britain.

While the Romanian government especially feared a Soviet intervention, the Germans considered the danger of a British operation during their deployment on the Danube to be very great. The head of the Luftwaffe mission to Romania believed that the most probable time for a British operation would be the expected severing of diplomatic relations between Britain and Romania in mid-February.[78] But these concerns did not disrupt German military prepara-

---

[73] On the organization of the army units in Romania cf. AOK 12, Ia, No. 9M/41–11M/41 (2 Jan. 1941), 20–2, BA-MA RH 31-I/v. 23; *KTB OKW* i. 279 (25 Jan. 1941), 292 (31 Jan. 1941).

[74] *PWT*, Middle East I, Hist (B) 1, No. 58, p. 33 (18 Jan. 1941). On the exaggerated figures cf. OKH/Att.Abt. (Grote), Funkspruch an DHM, No. 248 (29 Jan. 1941), 46, BA-MA RH 31-I/v. 23; *DGFP* D xii, No. 70, pp. 126–7 (22 Feb. 1941).

[75] *KTB OKW* i. 995 (21 Dec. 1941); 1. Skl., KTB, Teil A, 327–8 (24 Jan. 1941), BA-MA RM 7/20; Churchill, *Second World War*, iii. 29.

[76] Halder, *Diaries*, i. 759 (23 Jan. 1941). Here Halder speaks of an order from the OKW to halt all visible preparations on the Danube; on 20 Jan. 1941 Hitler called Mussolini's attention to the danger posed by the 34 Soviet divisions along the Romanian border: *DGFP* D xi, No. 679, pp. 1145–51 (21 Jan. 1941), here 1146.

[77] Halder, *Diaries*, i. 765 (28 Jan. 1941).

[78] DLM, Niederschrift 2. Kdr.-Besprechung Bucharest (10 Feb. 1941), 11–12, BA-MA RL 9/85. On the British plans cf. COS to Churchill, end of Feb. 1941, PRO, Prem, 3,374/13a. Because of bad weather and the lack of heavy bombers, operations against Romania were repeatedly postponed: *PWT*, Middle East I, Hist (B) 2, No. 57, p. 33 (28 Feb. 1941). On the refusal of the Greek government to permit British air attacks cf. ibid., No. 88, p. 47 (6 Mar. 1941).

2. Preparations for Invasion of Greece

tions in Romania. Although poor roads and bad weather slowed the deployment in the following weeks and required constant revision of the schedules for military movements, by the end of February the German military had been able to mass undisturbed the following forces north of the Danube for a crossing: two mountain, three armoured, one motorized, and four infantry divisions; one corps command, the command of Armoured Group 1, and corps and army troops.[79]

After the order had been given with Directive No. 18 of 12 November 1940 to prepare Operation Marita, in the following weeks and months the German government strove to remove all diplomatic obstacles to the passage of German troops through Bulgaria. Hitler would have preferred to see Bulgaria join the Tripartite Pact in November 1940, as Hungary, Romania, and Slovakia had done, in order to create the political conditions for carrying out his plans. In several conversations the German government sought to persuade Bulgaria that joining that pact early would protect Bulgaria from pressure from other states.[80] On 23 November 1940, however, Parvan Draganov, the Bulgarian minister in Berlin, explained to Hitler why his government still hesitated to join the pact. But he did not permit any doubt to arise that, in principle, Bulgaria was prepared to take that step.[81] According to Draganov, the Bulgarian government feared that not only the Soviet Union but also Turkey would object to such an action. On the basis of the Balkan pact of 9 February 1934, Turkey had the possibility of intervening together with Greece and Yugoslavia. Draganov also pointed out that sympathy for Russia was traditionally strong in Bulgaria, which made joining the Tripartite Pact unwise at the present time.[82] And, after the Italian attack on Greece, the presence of British military forces in the Aegean had to be considered.[83] The situation was dangerous for Bulgaria because the country was poorly armed and had received little support from Germany. Although Hitler promised quick deliveries of vital military equipment for Bulgaria, he could not convince Draganov of the need for Bulgaria to join the Tripartite Pact as soon as possible.

The position of the Bulgarian government did not change until the end of January 1941, although Hitler held out the prospect of a land link to the Aegean in the near future.[84] On the other hand, Bulgaria was prepared to fulfil

---

[79] Wisshaupt, 'Balkanfeldzug', 7, BA-MA RH 20-12/129. Cf. also 'Balkanfeldzug der 12. Armee', map of 1 Mar. 1941, BA-MA 75090/1.

[80] *DGFP* D xi, No. 378, pp. 651–3 (22 Nov. 1940), and No. 384, pp. 672–8 (23 Nov. 1940). On German–Bulgarian relations cf. Gornenski, *Hitleristkata politika*, 117 ff.

[81] *DGFP* D xi, No. 384, pp. 672–8 (23 Nov. 1940). Cf. also Hoppe, *Bulgarien*, 101.

[82] OKW/A Ausl/Abw/Abw I No. 01767/40 geh., Außen- und militärpolitische Nachrichten (20 Dec. 1940), BA-MA RW 5/v. 354. Cf. also Hoppe, *Bulgarien*, 112.

[83] On 13 Jan. 1941 the Bulgarian government again informed Germany that it feared British moves in the Aegean: *DGFP* D xi, No. 648, pp. 1080–1.

[84] *Weizsäcker-Papiere*, 233 (19 Jan. 1941). On Bulgaria's refusal cf. also Hoppe, *Bulgarien*, 109–10.

German wishes as far as possible; because of the military situation in Europe a policy of neutrality no longer seemed to be a real option.[85] Good relations with Germany offered not only the prospect of territorial acquisitions but would also preserve limited sovereignty for Bulgaria.[86] For this reason King Boris supported the reconnaissance operations by German soldiers in Bulgaria in November and granted German troops the right to pass through the country to Greece.[87] The Bulgarian government was also prepared to co-ordinate to a considerable degree its foreign policy with that of Germany. The main aim in these efforts was to develop a policy based on the interests of both countries towards the Soviet Union, which had undertaken numerous initiatives at the end of 1940 and the beginning of 1941 to keep Bulgaria from moving closer to Germany.

In his conversation with Hitler on 12 and 13 November 1940, Molotov had pointed out that the German military presence in Bulgaria represented a difficult problem for the Soviet Union.[88] Several days later he expressed his reservations about Bulgaria joining the Tripartite Pact to the Bulgarian minister in Moscow. He promised to take Bulgaria's territorial and economic wishes into consideration and offered the Bulgarian government a guarantee.[89] On 25 November 1940 the Soviet Union again made clear to the German government that Bulgaria was in the Soviet security zone and that it wanted to ratify a mutual-assistance pact with that country.[90] In agreement with Germany, however, the Bulgarian government rejected closer ties with the Soviet Union, but assured the Soviet government nevertheless that Bulgaria placed great value on friendly relations with that country.[91]

Like the Soviet initiatives, efforts by the British and American governments in January 1941 were also aimed at drawing Bulgaria away from Germany. The Bulgarian government, however, rejected the wish of Roosevelt's special representative, Colonel Donovan, that it should actively oppose Hitler's policies. It also resisted the urging of the British government to issue a statement that Bulgaria was not planning any action against Greece.[92]

Although these efforts of other countries in Sofia did not achieve their aim, they did cause the Bulgarian government repeatedly to put off joining the Tripartite Pact. On 13 January 1941 the prime minister of Bulgaria, Bogdan Filov, observed that this step could only be taken after Germany had provided

---

[85] Miller, *Bulgaria*, 38.
[86] OKW/A Ausl/Abw/Abw I No. 01804/40 geh., Außen- und militärpolitische Nachrichten (29 Dec. 1940), BA-MA RW 5/v. 354.
[87] Miller, *Bulgaria*, 36; Hoppe, *Bulgarien*, 108.
[88] *KTB OKW* i. 174 (14 Nov. 1940).
[89] *DGFP* D xi, No. 379, pp. 653–4 (22 Nov. 1940); the talk took place on 18 Nov. 1941.
[90] Ibid., No. 404, pp. 714–15 (26 Nov. 1940). The Soviet government thus expressed its particular interest in participating in the solution of the Dardanelles question.
[91] Ibid., No. 430, pp. 756–7 (30 Nov. 1940), and No. 433, pp. 759–60 (1 Dec. 1940). On the relations Bulgaria desired in future cf. ibid., No. 536, p. 908 (19 Dec. 1940).
[92] On Donovan's trip cf. 1. Skl., KTB, Teil A, 271 (21 Jan. 1941), BA-MA RM 7/20; on the British demands cf. ibid. 188 (15 Jan. 1941), and Miller, *Bulgaria*, 41–2.

2. Preparations for Invasion of Greece

sufficient military protection.[93] In the opinion of the German government, however, the German troop concentrations north of the Danube in January should have eliminated any ground for concern on the part of Bulgaria. In view of the growing German strength in southern Romania, the German leadership began to increase pressure on the Bulgarian government. On 15 January 1941 the foreign ministry informed the German legation in Sofia in a telegram that it would point out to Bulgaria the 'serious consequences' if that country refused to comply with German wishes. On the other hand, the German government suggested starting conversations at general-staff level with Bulgaria to find solutions for all problems arising from German troop movements through that country.[94] The Bulgarian government thereupon made the successful conclusion of the military consultations a condition for joining the Tripartite Pact. Until this point Bulgaria sought to realize as many of its wishes as possible in agreement with Germany. In addition to a written confirmation of the promise (previously only oral) of territorial gains in Greece, Bulgaria also wanted financial and economic aid. Moreover, the Soviet Union should be informed of all further German steps in Bulgaria.[95] In fact, Ribbentrop informed the Soviet foreign minister of German plans to begin constructing bridges over the Danube on 28 February 1941, and also announced Bulgaria's decision to join the Tripartite Pact.[96]

To prevent any danger to troop movements in Bulgaria from Turkey, the German government attempted as early as November 1940 to induce the two countries to conclude a non-aggression pact. However, as Bulgaria had recently rejected a Soviet offer of assistance, the Bulgarian foreign minister felt that his country could only agree to a declaration with Turkey that the two countries would refrain from aggression against each other.[97] After the exchange of friendship and non-aggression declarations between Bulgaria and Turkey on 17 February 1941, the German foreign ministry believed that all speculation about a Turkish intervention in the event of a German attack on Greece could be dismissed as unfounded.[98] The German government also countered the danger of Turkish intervention with assurances that the German troop deployment in Romania would not lead to any action against Turkey. Hitler underlined his desire to avoid alienating Turkey by ordering the German units in the eastern Dobrudja to avoid the area of the frontier with Turkey when entering Bulgaria.[99]

---

[93] *DGFP* D xi, No. 648, pp. 1080–1.
[94] Ibid., No. 660, pp. 1106–9 (15 Jan. 1941); *Griff nach Südosteuropa*, 112–13.
[95] *DGFP* D xi, No. 693, pp. 1171–2 (23 Jan. 1941); xii, No. 30, pp. 54–6 (8 Feb. 1941), No. 41, pp. 73–5 (10 Feb. 1941).
[96] Ibid. xii, No. 99, pp. 182–3 (27 Feb. 1941).
[97] Ibid. xi, No. 413, p. 725 (28 Nov. 1940), No. 433, pp. 759–60 (1 Dec. 1940).
[98] 1. Skl., KTB, Teil A, 225 (18 Feb. 1941), BA-MA RM 7/21; *DGFP* D xi, No. 714, pp. 1203–4 (27 Jan. 1941). Cf. also Hillgruber, *Strategie*, 427.
[99] On the German statement to Turkey cf. 1. Skl., KTB Teil A, 91 (8 Jan. 1941), BA-MA RM 7/20. The order to German troops is in *DGFP* D xii, No. 51, pp. 99–100 (14 Feb. 1941), and Greiner, 'Balkan', 31–2, MGFA C-065g.

Efforts of British military representatives and diplomats in Ankara to induce the Turkish government to take measures against the German actions were unsuccessful. Turkey was prepared to act only if events in Bulgaria endangered its own territory.[100]

With the exchange of friendship and non-aggression declarations between Sofia and Ankara in February, the ability of the Soviet Union to influence developments in Bulgaria in its own favour declined rapidly. Conferences between German and Bulgarian military representatives, such as took place at the end of January and the beginning of February in Predeal (Romania), made such steps impossible.[101] At these conferences, representatives of the Bulgarian general staff and the German Twelfth Army reached agreement not only on the details of German troop movements in Bulgaria but also on the tasks of Bulgarian forces during the German invasion of Greece. Bulgaria was to provide only covering forces against Yugoslavia and Greece but would deploy six divisions as a defence on the Turkish frontier. Germany promised to provide the necessary supplies for the Bulgarian troops and to transfer strong Luftwaffe and air-defence units to Bulgaria at the latest when German troop movements through that country began.[102] In the following days the date for bridging the Danube was postponed from 15 to 21 February and then set for 28 February. Organizational and weather problems, as well as the Bulgarian wish not to begin the invasion before that date because of the Soviet expressions of concern, were probably responsible for the delays.[103]

After the bridging of the Danube at three separate points on 28 February, the German troop movements through Bulgaria began on 2 March 1941, at first primarily with fast units (three armoured and one motorized division) and parts of a mountain division. VIII Air Corps under Luftwaffe General Wolfram Freiherr von Richthofen moved most of its fighters to Bulgarian airbases by 2 March. Because of bad weather and roads, the accompanying ground personnel reached their operational areas several days later.[104] While the armoured divisions quickly reached the Varna–Burgas–Yambol–Stara Zagora line, in order if necessary to provide support for Bulgarian troops there, the infantry and mountain divisions crossed the river. In spite of the months of preparations by German soldiers in Bulgaria, the march to the quartering areas on the frontiers with Greece and Yugoslavia was not without difficulties. The weather and the low capacity of the rail lines in those areas

---

[100] OKW/A Ausl/Abw/Abw I No. 0519/41 geh., Außen- und militärpolitische Nachrichten (8 Mar. 1941), BA-MA RW 5/v. 354.
[101] *KTB OKW* i. 1001–4 (2 Feb. 1941), 283 (28 Jan. 1941); Fabry, *Balkan-Wirren*, 139–43.
[102] *KTB OKW* i. 311 (8 Feb. 1941).
[103] AOK 12, Ia, Organisation Balkan, No. 0112/41 (22 Feb. 1941), BA-MA RH 20-12/60; 1. Skl., KTB, Teil A, 149 (12 Feb. 1941), BA-MA RM 7/21; Halder, *Diaries*, i. 782 (14 Feb. 1941).
[104] AOK 12, Ia, Organisation Balkan, 17 Mar. 1941, BA-MA RH 20-12/60. VIII Air Corps had to transport a total of 2,700 vehicles over the Danube to Bulgaria. Cf. also VIII. Fl.Korps/Ia, draft of an operation experience report (no date), 5, BA-MA RL 8/241.

2. Preparations for Invasion of Greece

also slowed the advance of the German troops.[105] Nevertheless, the deployment of most of Twelfth Army could be considered ended by 25 March; the date of the attack on Greece was set for the first days of April.[106] By 28 March a total of fourteen German divisions and an infantry regiment had been drawn together in Bulgaria; their main forces were on the frontier with Greece. In addition, armoured units secured the frontiers with Turkey, and two fast divisions of Armoured Group 1 protected the front in the west against Yugoslavia. Three additional divisions (a mountain division and two infantry divisions) were still north of the Danube.[107]

These units, together with the two fast divisions of the German military mission in Romania, seemed adequate protection against a possible military intervention by the Soviet Union. The Soviet reaction to the announcement of the German troop movements into Bulgaria showed that the hostility of the Soviet government towards the German plans had not changed, but in the Soviet statements there was no threat to use military force. And on 1 March 1941, when the German ambassador in Moscow, Friedrich Werner Graf von der Schulenburg, informed Soviet Foreign Minister Molotov officially of the movement of German troops into Bulgaria, Molotov did not indicate that this action would have any lasting effect on German–Soviet relations. He merely stated that the Soviet Union regretted the German action and could not support it in any way. Schulenburg did not have the impression after this conversation that the Soviet Union would undertake concrete steps against Germany in the foreseeable future.[108]

In contrast, Britain reacted to the movement of German troops into Bulgaria by recalling her minister from Sofia on 5 March 1941 and, at the same time, broke off economic relations with Bulgaria.[109]

Although the military and diplomatic preparations for the planned operation against Greece dominated German–Bulgarian relations at the beginning of 1941, the long-term economic interests Germany pursued in Bulgaria should not be overlooked. On 31 January an agreement was concluded which not only regulated supplies for German troops in Bulgaria but also promised measures

---

[105] On the activity of German soldiers in Bulgaria before the larger German units entered the country cf. Spaeter, *Brandenburger*, 125; on the German advance cf. Donlagić et al., *Jugoslawien im Zweiten Weltkrieg*, 28.

[106] Wisshaupt, 'Balkanfeldzug', 13–14, BA-MA RH 20-12/129.

[107] AOK 12, Ia, KTB, evening report (28 Mar. 1941), BA-MA RH 20-12/62; Balkanfeldzug der 12. Armee, maps of 25 and 28 Mar. 1941, BA-MA 75090, 1.

[108] In this regard the somewhat sharp words of the Soviet Union towards Bulgaria did not change anything. Cf. OKW/A Ausl/Abw/Abw I No. 0489/41 geh., Außen- und militärpolitische Nachrichten (4 Mar. 1941), BA-MA RW 5/v. 354; and Miller, *Bulgaria*, 46. On Schulenburg's conversation with Molotov cf. *DGFP* D xii, No. 108, p. 195 (1 Mar. 1941); No. 121, pp. 213–16 (3 Mar. 1941).

[109] Huene, German minister in Lisbon, to Amt Ausl/Abw, telegram No. 467 (8 Mar. 1941), BA-MA Wi/IC 5/36. Cf. also Woodward, *British Foreign Policy*, i. 531.

to support the Bulgarian economy.[110] The purpose of this policy was to make Bulgaria, like the other states of south-east Europe, a supplier of raw materials at low prices for Germany. In order to increase the production of precious metals, representatives of the Mitteleuropäischer Wirtschaftstag (Economic Committee for Central Europe) sought to expand the involvement of German firms in Bulgaria in February 1941;[111] as a result, Germany's share of Bulgarian exports increased considerably from 1940 to 1941.[112]

The German military and political steps in Romania and Bulgaria had not escaped the attention of the Greek government, which, however, still attempted to avoid a military conflict with Italy's Axis ally. Especially when it became clear in the first days of November that Mussolini would suffer a defeat on the Albanian front, Greece tried to maintain contact with Germany. The Greek government repeatedly assured Germany that British help did not include any British troops on the Greek mainland and that British air support was directed against Italy.[113] In January 1941 Greece informed Germany that, as soon as the military situation permitted, it would renounce British assistance and request German arbitration in the conflict with Italy.[114] Greece would even be prepared to accept an armistice with Italy on the basis of the original frontier.[115] But Hitler did not want to accept this offer, as he feared that it would mean a diplomatic defeat for his Axis partner. The suggestions of the German negotiators in Athens were aimed therefore at a 'peaceful capitulation', in which important areas of Greece would be occupied by German forces. On 19 February, however, the Greek government rejected these demands.[116] German diplomatic representatives abroad were instructed in a circular from State Secretary von Weizsäcker to contradict denials by Greek diplomats of the frequent rumours about British troop movements to the Aegean. German military attachés and diplomats were to refer to supposedly more accurate German sources of information when talking with Greek representatives. In his circular Weizsäcker was able, however, to cite

---

[110] Hoppe, *Bulgarien*, 113.

[111] *Griff nach Südosteuropa*, 119–20; Fabry, *Balkan-Wirren*, 149–50. The Mitteleuropäischer Wirtschaftstag co-ordinated German government economic interests in south-east Europe with the aims of German investors. For the negotiations on exchange-rate regulations cf. the report of Oberstlt. (Lt.-Col.) Drews (liaison officer of the Wehrmacht high command at the Reichsbank), Berlin, of 18 Oct. 1940, BA-MA Wi/IC, 5/36.

[112] Hoppe, *Bulgarien*, 202; Miller, *Bulgaria*, 7.

[113] *DGFP* D xi, No. 106, pp. 185–6 (25 Sept. 1940), No. 248, pp. 423–4 (29 Oct. 1940), No. 395, pp. 701–2 (25 Nov. 1940).

[114] OKW/A Ausl/Abw/Abw I No. 081/41 geh., Außen- und militärpolitische Nachrichten, 11 Jan. 1941 (report of 4 Jan. 1941), BA-MA RW 5/v. 354. According to *Hellēnikos stratos*, iv. 30, senior Greek officers even discussed stationing German troops between Italians and Greeks on the Albanian front, but in the end this idea was rejected by the government in Athens.

[115] OKW/A Ausl/Abw/Abw I No. 081/41 geh., Außen- und militärpolitische Nachrichten, 11 Jan. 1941 (report of 4 Jan. 1941), BA-MA RW 5/v. 354; *Weizsäcker-Papiere*, 555 n. 28.

[116] *Hellēnikos stratos*, iv. 30–1, and *Weizsäcker-Papiere*, 236 (7 Feb. 1941), 239 (23 Feb. 1941). Unofficial talks between Greece and Germany also failed to produce any positive results: cf. *DGFP* D xi. 929–30.

2. Preparations for Invasion of Greece

only Churchill's speech of 19 December 1940 as proof of the presence of British troops on the Greek mainland. Churchill had mentioned the transfer of British units from North Africa to the Aegean.[117] The Greek government then offered to permit the German military attaché to travel freely within the country, so that he could convince himself that the rumours were without foundation. At the end of February, however, Jodl rejected this offer without giving a reason.[118]

An agreement between Greece and Germany was prevented not only by Hitler's desire to eliminate the danger to the Romanian oilfields, but also by the German promise of access to the Aegean for Bulgaria. At the beginning of March 1941 Weizsäcker was of the opinion that putting this promise in writing had excluded any possibility of reaching a peaceful arrangement with Greece.[119]

In view of the efforts of the Greek government to keep its country out of the war, it is understandable why Greece at first accepted only British air support in the conflict with Italy. Greece was prepared to agree to the sending of British troops to the Greek mainland only if German troops first crossed the Danube and thus made Germany's aggressive intentions clear.[120] For the British, however, such support created considerable problems, as it coincided with the main British military effort in North Africa. In a telegram of 21 January 1941 the British commander-in-chief in the Middle East, General Wavell, informed the government in London that he wanted to capture Benghazi first and not divide his forces between Europe and Africa.[121] Wavell's reservations were strengthened by the Greek military plans: Prime Minister Metaxas requested at least nine divisions from Britain to support Greece. He viewed Wavell's offer of two to three divisions with mistrust, because these forces would merely give Germany a pretext to invade Greece but would not secure the defence of the country.[122] At the beginning of February, after the capture of Benghazi, the British government decided, however, to support Greece.[123] Churchill abandoned his original plan to push on to Tripoli in North Africa and decided to send the troops thus made

---

[117] *DGFP* D xii, No. 77, pp. 138–9 (23 Feb. 1941).

[118] Cf. *KTB OKW* i. 334 (24 Feb. 1941) and OKW/A Ausl/Abw/Abw I No. 0454/41 geh., Außen- und militärpolitische Nachrichten (24 Feb. 1941), BA-MA RW 5/v. 354.

[119] *Weizsäcker-Papiere*, 239 (5 Mar. 1941).

[120] Papagos, *Griechenland*, 83, 161; Woodward, *British Foreign Policy*, i. 520. According to Halder's information of 15 Feb. 1941, the strength of the RAF in Greece was 120 bombers and transport aircraft and 60 fighters: Halder, *Diaries*, ii. 806 (21 Feb. 1941). According to Higham ('Generals and Guarantees'), in February 7 RAF squadrons were in Greece and it was planned to have up to 16 there in March: 130–220 aircraft.

[121] *PWT*, Middle East I, Hist (B) 1, No. 68, p. 38 (21 Jan. 1941); Playfair, *Mediterranean*, i. 343.

[122] Barclay, *Their Finest Hour*, 61–2. Metaxas died on 29 Jan. 1941; his successor was Alexandros Koryzis.

[123] Churchill, *Second World War*, iii. 9, 13–14; Jukić, *Yugoslavia*, 39; Ovelmen, 'British Decision', 15, 22–3, 44–5.

available to the Aegean.[124] In this decision the British pursued the aim of keeping Greece's neighbours from co-operating with Germany and of winning them as allies for Britain. Moreover, Churchill expected that a refusal to abandon Greece without a fight would strengthen Britain's prestige with the Dominions. He also hoped that British help for Greece would have a positive influence on America's attitude towards Britain.[125]

The British government believed that the prospects for successful resistance against a German invasion of Greece would be especially good if Yugoslavia and Turkey supported the British plans. In February 1941 the British were still trying to create an alliance between those two countries and Greece.[126] While Yugoslavia's attitude remained uncertain, Turkey indicated at the beginning of March that it did not want to participate in any operation against Germany.[127] At a conference with Eden and the chief of the British general staff, Sir John Dill, at the end of February in Cairo, the commanders-in-chief of the British forces in the Middle East also intimated that they had doubts about the success of the operation. But in the end they believed that they could accept the risk involved in transferring troops to the Aegean.[128] At the beginning of March even Churchill observed that the loss of Greece and the Balkans as a whole would be very unpleasant, but not a catastrophe, if only Turkey remained genuinely neutral.[129]

After the Greek government had declared its readiness to accept British aid, in spite of the promise to send little more than three divisions to Greece, negotiations began on the basic features of a defence of the country on 22 February 1941.[130] The British military leaders preferred the 'Aliakmon line', extending from Kaïmakchalan over the Vermion Mountains to the Aegean, to avoid the danger of being encircled in a defensive position close to the frontier.[131] General Papagos, chief of the Greek general staff, however, wanted to withdraw troops from the frontier with Bulgaria only when Yugoslavia's position had become clear. Because of the exhaustion of the Greek divisions on the Albanian front (the Epirus and West Macedonian Armies), Papagos viewed with scepticism the suggestion of strengthening the Aliakmon line with units

---

[124] Richter, *Griechenland*, 95.
[125] On 20 Feb. 1941 Col. Donovan, Roosevelt's representative, had talks on these aspects of the war with Eden, Dill, and Wavell in Cairo. Cf. Richter, *Griechenland*, 96–7; *PWT*, Middle East I, Hist (B) 1, No. 39, p. 21 (9 Jan. 1941).
[126] Donlagić et al., *Jugoslawien im Zweiten Weltkrieg*, 29; Churchill, *Second World War*, iii. 16–19.
[127] *Weizsäcker-Papiere*, 239 (23 Feb. 1941); cf. also I.II.4 (*d*) above and IV.II.2 below (Schreiber).
[128] Lewin, *The Chief*, 97, and Ovelmen, 'British Decision', 219 ff. At the conference of 20 Feb. 1941 all commanders-in-chief in the Middle East (Wavell, Longmore, and Cunningham) as well as Dill (chief of the Imperial General Staff) were present.
[129] *PWT*, Middle East I, Hist (B) 2, No. 78, p. 43 (6 Mar. 1941). Cf. also Lawlor, 'Greece, March 1941', 940.
[130] *Hellēnikos stratos*, iv. 245–6. The talks took place near Athens.
[131] Cruickshank, *Greece 1940–1941*, 140; *Hellēnikos stratos*, iv. 62. Cf. also Map III.III.1.

2. Preparations for Invasion of Greece

from that area. And he wanted to avoid giving Italy an unexpected advantage by withdrawing from that front.[132] On 5 March 1941, however, Sir Michael Palairet, the British minister in Athens, was able to report to his government that a compromise had been reached.[133] The Aliakmon line was to be occupied by British and Dominion troops and the newly formed Central Macedonian Army (three weak divisions with reduced fighting power). While defence units were envisaged for western Thrace east of the Nestos, most of the East Macedonian Army remained in positions on the Bulgarian frontier (the Metaxas line). Papagos planned to withdraw these units to the Aliakmon line if Yugoslavia remained neutral and the Germans attacked from Bulgaria.[134] The British accepted his plans with serious doubts, as they left the Aliakmon line inadequately defended. Because of this development, on 5 March Churchill still had not decided definitely to transfer British troops to the mainland.[135] His scepticism was certainly strengthened by statements of Greek generals of the Epirus and West Macedonian Armies on the Albanian front, opposing the decision by Athens to resist Germany. The next day, however, Churchill came to the conclusion that the bilateral military agreements and the readiness of the Greek government to resist a German invasion left the British no choice but to come to their aid.[136]

In spite of all disagreements in the Allied camp, the British began the transfer of Empire units (Operation Lustre) to the Greek mainland as soon as German troops had crossed the Danube. The first contingents arrived in Piraeus on 7 March; by 25 March the German military attaché in Athens estimated that between 30,000 and 35,000 men had arrived in Greece and were moving north.[137]

Although the Greek government had decided no longer to do without British divisions on the mainland after German troops entered Bulgaria, it continued its efforts to reach an agreement with Germany. Around the middle of March influential Greek officers attempted to obtain German mediation in the conflict with Italy. One of the Greek commanders in the north even wanted to stop fighting if the Italians were replaced by German troops.

---

[132] *PWT*, Middle East I, Hist (B) 2, No. 73, pp. 39–40 (5 Mar. 1941). Cf. Papagos, *Griechenland*, 89 [88].

[133] *PWT*, Middle East I, Hist (B) 2, No. 77, p. 42 (5 Mar. 1941). On the differences of opinion between Athens and London cf. Kitsikis, 'La Grèce 1940/41', 203.

[134] Papagos was of the opinion that, if Yugoslavia joined the Allies, the units along the Aliakmon line should be transferred to the East Macedonian Army: Papagos, *Griechenland*, 92.

[135] On the military agreement with Greece: *PWT*, Middle East I, Hist (B) 2, No. 73, pp. 39–40 (5 Mar. 1941); on Churchill's reservations: ibid., No. 78, p. 43 (6 Mar. 1941). Cf. also Lawlor, 'Greece, March 1941', 940.

[136] *PWT*, Middle East I, Hist (B) 2, No. 79, p. 44 (6 Mar. 1941). Cf. also Lawlor, 'Greece, March 1941', 941. On the ideas of the Greek generals cf. Richter, *Griechenland*, 105. Although several of these officers were replaced, the opposition to the continuation of the war, now against Germany, could not be eliminated.

[137] A total of 24,200 British, 17,100 Australian, and 16,700 New Zealand troops landed in Greece: *Hellēnikos stratos*, iv. 62.

German diplomats in Salonika were assured that Greek army leaders would then demand that the British forces leave the country.[138] Although the German government rejected these suggestions, Greek representatives continued their attempts, through various diplomatic channels, to persuade Germany that Greece was merely reacting to Italian and German military moves.[139] The German response to these efforts remained, however, extremely reserved, and in the end Germany rejected all Greek requests to establish contacts. Ribbentrop did not want to make it possible for anyone to assert later that Greece had officially approached the German government in an effort to end the conflict peacefully.[140] Hitler's decision, reaffirmed on 17 March, was final: all of Greece was to be conquered in order to force the British out of the Aegean area.[141]

Since Hitler had considered the possibility at the beginning of November 1940, because of the Italian defeats in Albania, of helping Mussolini if necessary by invading Greece, Germany's relations with Yugoslavia also acquired a special significance. Quite apart from the strategic and economic role of Yugoslavia with regard to preparations for the war against the Soviet Union, because of her geographical position her attitude was of decisive importance for the planning of the attack on Greece. The government of Yugoslavia was able to influence both the conflict in Albania and the planned deployment of German troops in Bulgaria. Immediately after the beginning of hostilities between Italy and Greece, however, the German minister in Belgrade reported to his government that Yugoslavia wanted to stay out of that conflict. The Yugoslav government therefore refused to permit Italian troop transports through its territory.[142] In November Yugoslavia indicated to Germany that she would also refuse passage for German troops.[143]

Reports of a mobilization of Yugoslav units in Macedonia, provided by the German air attaché in Belgrade in the middle of March, made the German government aware of the urgency of an arrangement with Yugoslavia.[144] Unlike Mussolini, who wanted to put pressure on the Yugoslav government if it did not immediately comply with the wishes of the Axis powers, Hitler at first considered it more important to win Yugoslav support for his aims through negotiations.[145] He was obviously interested in continuing good

---

[138] *DGFP* D xii, No. 155, pp. 279–80 (12 Mar. 1941), and n. 114 above.
[139] Ibid., No. 180, pp. 316–17 (18 Mar. 1941).
[140] Ambassador Ritter's note: ibid., No. 189, p. 325 (21 Mar. 1941).
[141] Halder, *KTB* ii. 322 (18 Mar. 1941) n. 7 (not in trans.).
[142] OKW/A Ausl/Abw/Abw I No. 01379/40 geh., Außen- und militärpolitische Nachrichten (29 Oct. 1940), BA-MA RW 5/v. 354. Cf. also Olshausen, *Zwischenspiel auf dem Balkan*, 30–1.
[143] Memorandum by Kramarz, 26 Nov. 1940, PA, Büro St.S., Jugoslawien, i.
[144] German air attaché in Belgrade to Reich Ministry of Aviation, telegram No. 828 (12 Nov. 1940), PA, Büro St.S., Jugoslawien, i. In the air attaché's opinion, Yugoslavia had mobilized these troops because of the Italian attack on Greece. On Italian intentions cf. Armellini, *Diario*, 139 (7 Nov. 1940).
[145] *KTB OKW* i. 185 (22 Nov. 1940); Baar, *Jugoslawienpolitik 1935–1941*, 182. At the same

2. Preparations for Invasion of Greece

economic relations with Yugoslavia and therefore wanted to avoid anything that might lead to instability in that country or in her foreign policy. At the beginning of November 1940 the Yugoslav military attaché in Berlin, Vauhnik, had indicated a possible starting-point for bilateral talks when he enquired what quid pro quo Germany would demand for supporting Yugoslavia's claim to the port of Salonika.[146] On 28 November Hitler assured the Yugoslav foreign minister, Cincar-Marković, that Germany would support Yugoslavia in this question and demanded in return the conclusion of a non-aggression pact between Italy, Germany, and Yugoslavia. In addition, Yugoslavia should demilitarize the Dalmatian coast as a gesture towards Italy and later make Salonika her main naval base.[147] Hitler added that Germany was not interested in territorial gains in the Balkans and wanted to maintain stability in south-east Europe. Germany's efforts to improve her good economic relations with Yugoslavia were closely related to these aims. In Hitler's view Yugoslavia should continue to provide raw materials, while Germany would deliver industrial goods.

However, many observers in Belgrade considered the one-sided orientation of Yugoslav economic policy towards Germany to be the main cause of many of their country's economic problems, as trade between the two countries was determined not by Yugoslavia's own needs, but by conditions dictated by Germany. But an alternative trade policy was not possible; the war in the Mediterranean increasingly isolated Yugoslavia from the world market. Germany was prepared to contribute to the economic development of the country with greater investment, but that would make Yugoslavia's monetary and trade policy even more one-sided.[148]

At the beginning of December 1940 Yugoslavia agreed to Hitler's suggestion that she should conclude a non-aggression pact with the Axis powers, although some differences had developed in relations between the three potential treaty partners. Yugoslavia rejected Italy's demand that she should transport Italian lorries through her territory to Albania. As a counter-move, Germany then

---

time, however, Italy was conducting secret negotiations with Yugoslavia on a practical arrangement. Ciano, *Diary 1939–1943*, 304–5 (11 Nov. 1940).

[146] Draft of a telegram from Ritter to Heeren of Nov. 1940, PA, Büro St.S., Jugoslawien, i; *DGFP* D xi, No. 320, p. 525 (11 Nov. 1940). The friendship treaty between Yugoslavia and Hungary offered a further possibility for the Axis powers to improve relations with Yugoslavia. Cf. n. 62 above.

[147] *DGFP* D xi, No. 417, pp. 728–35 (29 Nov. 1940). Ciano had discussed Italy's demands with Hitler on 18 Nov. 1940: ibid., No. 353, pp. 606–10 (19 Nov. 1940). On 22 Nov. the Duce even demanded that the Adriatic be demilitarized and that Yugoslavia join the Tripartite Pact: cf. ibid., No. 383, pp. 671–2. Cf. also Knoll, *Jugoslawien*, 59–60, and Olshausen, *Zwischenspiel auf dem Balkan*, 31.

[148] Hassell's report (as representative of the Mitteleuropäischer Wirtschaftstag) of 25 Nov. 1940, PA, Büro St.S., Jugoslawien, i. On the conclusion of the economic negotiations cf. Weizsäcker's teletype message to the foreign minister of 10 Jan. 1941: ibid. ii. On German economic policy in south-east Europe in general cf. Treue, 'Das Dritte Reich', 54–5, 60 ff.; Förster *et al.*, 'Jugoslawien und Griechenland', 358–9.

refused to export to Yugoslavia material for the construction of aircraft.[149] At about the same time the German government began to consider rejecting the idea of a simple non-aggression pact and demanding that Yugoslavia join the Tripartite Pact. Yugoslavia reacted to this change with surprise, as the demand to conclude a non-aggression pact had come from Hitler himself and further-reaching commitments had not been discussed on 28 November 1940.[150] The German minister in Belgrade, von Heeren, also had the impression in January 1941 that the Yugoslav government was trying to avoid becoming involved in the imminent conflict. Cincar-Marković informed Heeren on 5 January that he welcomed the increase in the number of Wehrmacht troops in southern Romania, but Heeren received reports at the end of the month that Yugoslavia would resist with military force any attempt by German troops to pass through her territory.[151] The German government was therefore able to conclude that Yugoslavia approved of the German actions in other countries of south-east Europe but was not prepared to support them herself, which would have been a precondition for joining the Tripartite Pact.[152]

Nevertheless, in January and February 1941 Yugoslavia rejected all American and British demands to oppose Hitler's aggressive plans.[153] At the end of January the Yugoslav government indicated to the American representative Colonel Donovan that Yugoslavia would not intervene if German troops entered Bulgaria. The Yugoslav regent, Prince Paul, also rejected a suggestion that he should agree to a Balkan front against Germany. In his opinion the German military threat was too close to be eliminated by vague American promises of help. The Yugoslav government also attempted to play down the importance of the talks with Donovan and for that reason restricted public reports of his visit.[154] The efforts of Anthony Eden and the American minister in Belgrade, Arthur Lane, in February 1941 to encourage the prince regent and members of the Yugoslav government to resist Germany were equally unsuccessful.[155]

Because of the antidemocratic and anti-Communist direction of its policies at home as well as the increasingly close economic ties with Germany, the Yugoslav government tended instead to pursue a policy of cautiously im-

---

[149] *DGFP* D xi, No. 465, pp. 803–4; No. 467, pp. 805–6; No. 471, pp. 810–11 (7 Dec. 1940).
[150] *DGFP* D xi, No. 549, pp. 927–8 (21 Dec. 1940), No. 551, p. 930 (23 Dec. 1940). Cf. also *Weizsäcker-Papiere*, 227 (3 Dec. 1940); Krizman, 'Tripartite Pact', 401, and Knoll, *Jugoslawien*, 95.
[151] Heeren to foreign ministry, 5 Jan. 1941, and telegram No. 42 (30 Jan. 1941), PA, Büro St.S., Jugoslawien, ii.
[152] Bulgaria's hesitation about joining the Tripartite Pact probably encouraged the Yugoslav government to resist German pressure. Cf. Hillgruber, *Strategie*, 338.
[153] Maček, *Struggle for Freedom*, 207, and Wheeler, *Britain*, 42–3.
[154] Heeren to foreign ministry, telegram No. 22 (25 Jan. 1941), PA, Büro St.S., Jugoslawien, ii.
[155] *FRUS* (1941), ii. 943, 945–6 (11 and 18 Feb. 1941); Papen to foreign ministry, telegram No. 190 (28 Feb. 1941), PA, Büro St.S., Jugoslawien, ii.

2. Preparations for Invasion of Greece

proving relations with that country. At his own request the Yugoslav prime minister met Hitler on 14 February 1941 at the Berghof. Cvetković stressed the good relations between their two countries and pointed to their many common characteristics and mutual interests in domestic and foreign policy. After condemning Britain's intention to gain a foothold on the Continent, he suggested to Hitler a pact between Yugoslavia, Turkey, and Bulgaria. The purpose of this alliance would be to defeat any British attempt to land in south-east Europe. Hitler, however, indicated that he was pessimistic about the prospects of success for such an undertaking. Above all, he did not believe that Turkey could be separated from Britain. For his part he demanded that Yugoslavia, 'in her own interest', should immediately join the Tripartite Pact. Cvetković and his foreign minister then promised to arrange a meeting between Prince Paul and Hitler.[156]

This meeting took place on 4 March 1941 at the Berghof, at a time when the first German units had already entered Bulgaria and in south-east Yugoslavia three divisions had been mobilized to protect the country against Bulgaria.[157] In his talk with Hitler, Prince Paul made no secret of his personal sympathy for Greece and Great Britain on the one hand and his loathing for Italy on the other. He feared domestic difficulties if Yugoslavia immediately joined the Tripartite Pact and did not exclude the possibility of a *coup d'état*. Hitler, however, was not persuaded by such fears and pointed to the serious consequences if Yugoslavia did not take advantage of the first opportunity to come to an agreement and sign a treaty with Germany and Italy.

The massive pressure to which Hitler and Ribbentrop subjected Prince Paul at this meeting probably caused the Yugoslav government, in spite of serious reservations, to declare its readiness to join Germany and Italy several days later.[158] In deference to public opinion, however, the government raised demands for joining the Tripartite Pact which were intended to affect the independence of the country as little as possible. With an eye to his future military plans, Hitler declared his readiness to fulfil most of Yugoslavia's conditions.[159] The territorial integrity of the country was to be guaranteed and demands for a passage of German troops through Yugoslavia were dropped. The Axis powers also did not demand any support from Yugoslavia in their conflict with Greece. Moreover, Ribbentrop declared his readiness to permit

---

[156] Telegram No. 56, Hitler to German ambassador in Rome (14 Feb. 1941), PA, Büro St.S., Jugoslawien, ii. Cf. also Maček, *Struggle for Freedom*, 207, and Matl, 'Jugoslawien im Zweiten Weltkrieg', 99. Hitler also tried to interest Italy in a new pact with Yugoslavia, but this was turned down by Ciano, who pointed to Italy's treaty with Belgrade of 1937: *DGFP* D xii, No. 117, pp. 206–10 (2 Mar. 1941).

[157] Feine, Belgrade, to foreign ministry, telegram No. 185 (4 Mar. 1941), PA, Büro St.S., Jugoslawien, ii. On Hitler's meeting with Prince Paul cf. *DGFP* D xii, No. 130, pp. 230–2 (7 Mar. 1941), and Knéjévitsch, 'Prince Paul', 43.

[158] *DGFP* D xii, No. 131, pp. 232–3 and n. 5 (7 Mar. 1941); No. 138, p. 247 (8 Mar. 1941). Cf. also Simović, 'Memoari', *Politika* (8 Sept. 1970).

[159] *DGFP* D xii, No. 138, p. 247 (8 Mar. 1941).

the Yugoslav government to publish these parts of the treaty. A further undisputed provision of the treaty was Germany's promise, of course still secret, to support Yugoslavia's claim to Salonika. On the other hand the German government refused to state publicly that it would not request military assistance from Yugoslavia in future. However, on 9 March Ribbentrop instructed the German minister in Belgrade to inform the Yugoslav government confidentially that Germany would very probably renounce the right to make such a request.[160] In spite of new reservations, which Foreign Minister Cincar-Marković explained to the German minister in Belgrade on 10 March, it was finally agreed that, in a secret note to the Yugoslav government, Germany would promise not to demand military support. In this way Germany countered fears that Yugoslavia could become involved in a war with the United States or the Soviet Union.[161]

In Yugoslavia the compromise, in so far as it became known, did not enjoy general support. As early as 1 March a rumour that Germany had demanded in the form of an ultimatum that Yugoslavia join the Tripartite Pact created considerable agitation in Belgrade. It was supported by British and American press reports calling for resistance to Germany's plans. The German minister in Belgrade had the impression that opposition to the government's policy was growing and that for that reason the government wanted to delay joining the Tripartite Pact.[162]

Undoubtedly Prince Paul and his government decided to comply with Germany's wishes because of the hopeless military situation, which the minister of war, Petar Pešić, described to the cabinet in a very realistic fashion. In his judgement, the Yugoslav army would be able to resist a German attack for more than four weeks only in the inaccessible regions of Bosnia and Hercegovina. All other parts of the country would be occupied by the Germans within a few days.[163] The mission of Lieutenant-Colonel Miloslav Peresić to Athens at the beginning of March 1941 to explore the possibilities of a common Greek–Yugoslav–British front produced a similar assessment of the military situation.[164] The resources of the Greek army were already under such a strain that, with the few British units available, it would probably be able to do little more than carry out defensive operations.

The decision of the Yugoslav government to join the Tripartite Pact was finally approved by the ministers by a vote of sixteen to three on 21 March. The three cabinet members opposed to joining the pact then announced their

---

[160] Ibid., No. 144, pp. 255–6 (9 Mar. 1941). Cf. also Krizman, 'Tripartite Pact', 407.
[161] *DGFP* D xii, No. 145, pp. 257–8 (10 Mar. 1941), No. 149, pp. 269–70 (11 Mar. 1941), and No. 173, pp. 303–4 (17 Mar. 1941). The Italian government was informed about the negotiations between Germany and Yugoslavia on 18 Mar. 1941: *DGFP* D xii, No. 178, pp. 312–15.
[162] Ibid., No. 151, pp. 271–2 (11 Mar. 1941); Krizman, 'Tripartite Pact', 420.
[163] Maček, *Struggle for Freedom*, 211.
[164] Papagos, *Griechenland*, 92; Baum and Weichold, *Krieg der 'Achsenmächte'*, 145. Peresić's mission seems quite inconsistent with other aspects of Yugoslav policy, e.g. the efforts to acquire Salonika.

resignations. This act seemed to endanger again the conclusion of the treaty with Germany, because Prime Minister Cvetković wanted to postpone the signing until new ministers could be appointed.[165] Ribbentrop, however, reacted to the domestic political difficulties in Yugoslavia with annoyance and instructed the German minister in Belgrade to inform the Yugoslav government that Germany would be prepared to sign the treaty only until 25 March.[166] The Yugoslav prime minister was able to complete his cabinet and to initial the treaty in Vienna on 25 March 1941, but the signs of strong opposition in the country could not be ignored. The opposition was strengthened by the fact that the government generally neglected to inform the public about its intentions.[167] Nevertheless, the German minister in Belgrade believed that Prince Paul and Prime Minister Cvetković had the situation under control and that significant opposition to the treaty, carried on by small groups, would not last long.[168] At the end of March 1941 the German government seemed on the whole not only to have succeeded in removing the last uncertainty with regard to the imminent invasion of Greece, but also to have harnessed Yugoslavia more than ever before to the aims of National Socialist foreign policy.

The above account shows that German policy in south-east Europe from October 1940 until the end of March 1941 pursued the aim of binding the countries of that region politically and economically to Germany. After Mussolini's attack on Greece and the appearance of British soldiers in the Aegean area, German moves in the Balkans were intended to drive the British from the mainland in order to secure the southern flank of Europe for the imminent attack on the Soviet Union.[169] After it became clear that Mussolini would suffer a defeat in Greece, Hitler was determined to support the Italian dictator, if necessary with military measures. The planned German intervention in the Balkans would also make it possible to exploit south-east Europe economically for future German war plans. The erratic German decision-making process in the case of the attack on Greece can be explained by the belief of the German leaders that the use of force in the Balkans could endanger the economic and political stability of the region and lead to an overextension of German military forces. At first Hitler wanted to achieve his aims in south-east Europe by diplomatic means or, if political pressure did not suffice, to occupy only certain parts of Greece. But as the date for the attack on the Soviet Union drew nearer, Hitler inclined more to destroy completely

---

[165] Heeren to foreign ministry, telegram No. 254 (21 Mar. 1941), PA, Büro St.S., Jugoslawien, ii.

[166] *DGFP* D xii, No. 192, pp. 335–6 (22 Mar. 1941).

[167] Feine to foreign ministry, *DGFP* D xii, No. 211, p. 364 (26 Mar. 1941). A short time before, Cvetković's government had stated its intention to continue the policy of neutrality: ibid.

[168] Ibid. and Heeren's telegram to foreign ministry, No. 268 (26 Mar. 1941), PA, Büro St.S., Jugoslawien, ii.

[169] Hillgruber, *Strategie*, 460–1.

the foothold the British had now established in Greece.[170] During the period considered here, German policy towards south-east Europe changed only in so far as its emphasis shifted from political, economic, and military intimidation to the open use of force.

[170] On the importance of the Balkans for the planned war in the east cf. Creveld, *Balkan*, 93.

II. From the Coup in Yugoslavia to the Outbreak of War on 6 April 1941

1. THE COUP IN YUGOSLAVIA

THE signing of the Tripartite Pact by the Yugoslav government on 25 March 1941, which took place under considerable political pressure from Germany, was greeted with scepticism in many parts of the country. The growing distrust in Serbian circles of the policies of the Cvetković government, which was considered to be dominated by Croats, was expressed in demonstrations against the treaty. As early as October 1940 the German legation in Belgrade had reported to Berlin rumours that Serbian generals were preparing a coup.[1] The opposition was directed against the attempt to bind Yugoslavia more closely to the Axis powers, but the leaders of the revolt also wanted to increase the influence of the Serbians in the multinational state.[2] The initialling of the Tripartite Pact with Germany and Italy in Vienna[3] helped the groups supporting a coup to gain the upper hand. Only two days after the signing of the treaty pro-Western officers, mostly in the air force, forced the Cvetković government to resign in a bloodless coup. Air Force General Simović became head of the government, and King Peter II, who was still in his minority, ascended the throne. The new rulers placed Prime Minister Cvetković and Foreign Minister Cincar-Marković in temporary custody and called upon Prince Paul to leave the country.[4] After initial difficulties, Simović succeeded in forming a cabinet consisting of representatives of the various ethnic groups in the country. The German foreign ministry regarded Simović as an enlightened personality who would support a Serbo-Croatian understanding.[5]

---

[1] OKW/A Ausl/Abw/Abw I No. 01366/40 geh., Außen- und militärpolitische Nachrichten (26 Oct. 1940), BA-MA RW 5/v. 354. On the situation in Belgrade before the coup cf. also Heeren to foreign ministry, telegram No. 268 (26 Mar. 1941), PA, Büro St.S., Jugoslawien, ii. For a more detailed analysis of the coup cf. Knoll, *Jugoslawien*, 139 ff.

[2] It was a significant indication of the changed political situation that the pro-German former prime minister Stojadinović was forced to leave the country in the middle of March. Cf. *DGFP* D xii, No. 226, pp. 399–400 (28 Mar. 1941).

[3] Ratification by the Yugoslav parliament and the consent of Prince Paul were still necessary to complete Belgrade's accession to the Tripartite Pact.

[4] On the course of the coup cf. especially Heeren's reports to the foreign ministry of 27 Mar. 1941, *DGFP* D xii, No. 221, p. 385; telegram No. 276, PA, Büro St.S., Jugoslawien, ii. Cf. also Dongalić et al., *Jugoslawien im Zweiten Weltkrieg*, 30; Hoptner, *Yugoslavia 1934–1941*, 247 ff.; Vauhnik, *Memoiren*, 172 ff.; Cvetković, 'Prince Paul', 466–8; Sundhaussen, *Geschichte Jugoslawiens*, 106–7.

[5] Memorandum by Kramarz of the foreign ministry (27 Mar. 1941), PA, Büro St.S., Jugoslawien, ii. On the formation of the government cf. Simović, 'Memoari', *Politika* (21 Sept. 1970).

Especially in Belgrade, the revolt was accompanied by demonstrations against the signing of the Tripartite Pact. Isolated excesses against German institutions and individuals, as well as the temporary arrest of pro-German journalists in the capital, caused the German legation to protest to the new government. In reply Simović assured the German minister that he would use all means at his disposal to prevent a repetition of such incidents.[6]

The anti-German tendency of the coup caused the German government to suspect that it had been directed from London. Britain had indeed condemned the expected Yugoslav signing of the Tripartite Pact and had warned the Yugoslav government that such a step would have serious consequences after the war.[7] On 26 March Churchill ordered the British minister in Belgrade to do everything possible to prevent Yugoslavia joining the pact. Two days before the signing, Eden even authorized British diplomats in Yugoslavia to support all efforts to organize a *coup d'état*. But what help was Britain able to offer Yugoslavia to resist intimidation and perhaps attack by the Axis powers? Apart from the prospect of very limited material support, Britain only promised vaguely to change the frontier with Italy in Istria in favour of Yugoslavia after the war.[8] And the actions of the new government in Belgrade for several days after the coup do not indicate that Britain had any significant influence on the course of events. Simović refused to take concrete steps in the direction of closer co-operation between his country and Britain.[9]

In London the British government nevertheless welcomed the coup in Belgrade because they hoped it would enable Britain, together with Yugoslavia, to fight Germany in south-east Europe with good prospects of success. Churchill's statement that 'the Yugoslav nation found its soul' was accompanied by the expectation that the new rulers in Belgrade would turn away from Germany. More cautious observers interpreted the revolt there as a return to strict neutrality, as the new government hesitated to take the final steps in joining the Tripartite Pact. Generally the belief was widespread in the West that the coup in Belgrade represented a serious setback for Hitler's aggressive plans in south-east Europe.[10]

---

[6] Heeren to foreign ministry, *DGFP* D xii, No. 214, p. 368 (27 Mar. 1941), and telegram No. 303 (29 Mar. 1941), PA, Büro St.S., Jugoslawien, ii. The German consulate at Ljubljana reported smaller demonstrations in Maribor: telegram No. 7 (28 Mar. 1941) to foreign ministry, ibid.

[7] Heeren to foreign ministry, telegram No. 288 (28 Mar. 1941), PA, Büro St.S., Jugoslawien, ii. In this telegram Heeren refers to a British protest note that had come to his knowledge. Cf. also Wheeler, *Britain*, 45.

[8] Woodward, *British Foreign Policy*, i. 541–2; Churchill's general promise of help in his speech of 27 Mar. 1941 in Churchill, *The Unrelenting Struggle*, 88. On British influence on the events of 27 Mar. 1941 cf. Hinsley, *British Intelligence*, i. 369–70.

[9] Cf. below at nn. 26, 27. Speculation (e.g. in Wuescht, *Jugoslawien*, 172–3) that the Soviet Union was involved in the preparations for the coup has not been confirmed.

[10] Churchill, *The Unrelenting Struggle*, 87–8, and *PWT*, Middle East I, Hist (B) 3, No. 3, p. 2 (28 Mar. 1941). According to Reuter the First Lord of the Admiralty remarked that the coup was an extremely serious political defeat for Hitler: OKW/A Ausl/Abw/Abw I No. 0671/41 geh., Außen- und militärpolitische Nachrichten (30 Mar. 1941), BA-MA RW 5/v. 354.

1. The Coup in Yugoslavia

Not least because of the reaction in the West, the German government interpreted the events of 27 March in Belgrade as an affront. The arrest of Cvetković and Cincar-Marković, who had just signed the Tripartite Pact in Vienna, was viewed in Berlin as an action directed against the Axis by anti-German, mainly Serbian, groups. Simović's order of 28 March for all persons liable to military service to report to the registration offices made Hitler even more distrustful.[11] The conjecture of the German minister in Belgrade that the first stage of the ordered mobilization was possibly due to domestic political reasons went unnoticed in Berlin.[12]

Shortly before noon on 27 March, only a few hours after the coup in Belgrade, Hitler summoned his military leaders and informed them that he was determined to crush Yugoslavia and eliminate her as a state as soon as possible. Even if the Yugoslav government should issue a 'declaration of loyalty', the country was to be attacked without an ultimatum or a declaration of war. As a direct retaliation, the Luftwaffe was to destroy Belgrade as soon as the weather permitted.[13] The reason for Hitler's uncompromising and swift reaction was very probably that he feared lest the events in Belgrade would lead to a considerable loss of prestige for his policies in the eyes of the entire world.[14] Moreover, a rapid German advance into Yugoslavia would prevent possible alliances directed against Germany in the Balkans and thus also the loss of secure sources of raw materials. An invasion of Yugoslavia would also facilitate the campaign against Greece. Hitler's decision required the Twelfth Army to regroup part of its forces and deploy them for an attack in the west; at the same time, however, an attack on the southern part of Yugoslavia would make it possible to circumvent the impassable mountain-chain along the frontier between Greece and Bulgaria.[15]

The time was also favourable for an attack on Yugoslavia. The deployment for the campaign against the Soviet Union had only begun and units were thus available to invade Yugoslavia from the north. On the other hand, Hitler's plan to conclude the preparations for the war in the east by the middle of

---

[11] *KTB OKW* i. 369 (28 Mar. 1941); Jodl's testimony: *IMT* xv. 386–7; Ribbentrop's testimony: ibid. x. 374–5; Weizsäcker's telegram of 28 Mar. 1941 to all German diplomatic missions, PA, Büro St.S., Jugoslawien, ii; Under-Secretary of State Woermann's memorandum of conversation with foreign diplomatic representatives, ibid., Pol. No. 245 (29 Mar. 1941).

[12] Heeren to foreign ministry, telegram No. 279 (27 Mar. 1941), PA, Büro St.S., Jugoslawien, ii.

[13] *Hitler's War Directives*, No. 25, p. 61; *KTB OKW* i. 368 (27 Mar. 1941). According to Jodl's testimony to the International Military Tribunal, he tried in vain to persuade Hitler to send an ultimatum to Yugoslavia: *IMT* xv. 387.

[14] Hassell, *Diaries*, 170 (7 Apr. 1941).

[15] Hitler also wanted to forestall the Yugoslav mobilization and relieve the pressure on the Italians in Albania: Weichs papers, 'Erinnerungen', iv. 41, BA-MA N19/8; Müller-Hillebrand, 'Improvisierung', 24, MGFA, P-030. On the possibilities of a bloc being formed against Germany cf. the report of the Wehrmacht high command, report of Legation Secretary von Grote of 3 Apr. 1941, PA, Büro St.S., England, iv. On the effects on the attack on Greece cf. Jodl's testimony: *IMT* xv. 386–7.

May did not permit possibly time-consuming diplomatic negotiations with Belgrade.[16]

In addition to pragmatic reasons, Hitler's decision of 27 March 1941 to smash Yugoslavia was influenced by ideological factors, which showed his long-held antipathy towards that country. His aim was to completely reverse the results of the First World War and above all to eliminate Serbian influence in Yugoslavia. He and his followers obviously believed that there was a connection between Serbian policies and anti-German conspirators. To reinforce this claim, National Socialist propaganda even asserted that the assassination of Archduke Franz Ferdinand at Sarajevo in 1914 was proof of a Serbian tradition of terror directed against Germany.[17] On the other hand, the German minister in Belgrade, von Heeren, observed that the coup had been carried out by a few individuals and that the majority of Serbs were by no means hostile to Germany. It would, he argued, be a serious mistake to subject Yugoslavia to a punitive action. State Secretary von Weizsäcker agreed with this assessment, but he considered it futile to attempt to dissuade Hitler and Ribbentrop from attacking Yugoslavia.[18]

Having decided to wage a war against Yugoslavia, the German leaders sought to weaken the country from within in order to achieve an early victory. For this purpose they attempted to exploit the conflict between the Serbian and Croatian ethnic groups, as Italy had also done in her policies against Yugoslavia.[19] The foreign ministry had been informed that the coup in Belgrade did not enjoy the undivided support of the Croats, who were prepared to co-operate with the new government under General Simović only if certain conditions were fulfilled.[20] This seemed to present a favourable opportunity for Germany to promote the separation of Croatia from the rest of Yugoslavia. On 31 March Ribbentrop informed the Croatian leaders confidentially that Germany intended to create an independent Croatian state after smashing Yugoslavia. Maček, the influential leader of the Croatian peasant party, was in particular urged to avoid any ties with the government in Belgrade and to co-operate with the Germans. As a reward the German government promised to make him the leader of an independent Croatia.[21] After some hesitation, however, Maček emphatically rejected the German plans for a Greater Croatia

---

[16] Müller-Hillebrand, 'Improvisierung', 24, MGFA, P-030. On the timetable for Barbarossa cf. *Das Deutsche Reich und der Zweite Weltkrieg*, iv. 31 ff. (Förster).

[17] *Ursachen und Folgen*, xvi. 472, 476; *Weizsäcker-Papiere*, 566 n. 132; Olshausen, 'Die deutsche Balkanpolitik', 720.

[18] Heeren's memorandum: *DGFP* D xii, No. 259, pp. 444–6 (3 Apr. 1941); *Weizsäcker-Papiere*, 564 n. 114.

[19] *Weizsäcker-Papiere*, 564 n. 113. Cf. II.I.2 and II.II.1 (*b*) above (Schreiber).

[20] 'Meldungen über Jugoslawien', Berlin (30 Mar. 1941), PA, Büro St.S., Jugoslawien, ii. According to these reports the Croats demanded that Yugoslavia should join the Tripartite Pact and that a general settlement be reached between Croatia and Serbia.

[21] *DGFP* D xii, No. 238, p. 424, and No. 239, p. 425 (31 Mar. 1941). Cf. also Olshausen, *Zwischenspiel auf dem Balkan*, 93.

independent of Belgrade and for the cession of Slovenia to Germany. Instead he attempted to influence Yugoslav foreign policy in such a way that a peaceful solution of the conflict with Germany would be possible.[22] For this reason and after coming to an agreement with the new rulers in Belgrade, he joined Simović's government as vice-premier. After the attempt to separate Croatia from Serbia with Maček's help had failed, German representatives in Zagreb began to support groups opposed to both Maček and Simović.[23] With their help it was possible in the end to encourage many Croatians in their rejection of Belgrade's authority to such an extent that they refused to obey Simović's call-up order.

Like Maček, the Simović government was aware from the very beginning of the great importance of the coup of 27 March. On the same day the new Yugoslav foreign minister, Momčilo Ninčić, explained that the overthrow of the Cvetković government was essentially due to domestic political factors. The new government hoped to continue close co-operation with Germany and would be prepared to fulfil all obligations assumed under the Tripartite Pact. In a conversation with Heeren on the evening of 27 March Simović repeated the words of his foreign minister and promised that there would be no repetition of the anti-German incidents. Heeren believed that the new government enjoyed a much broader base of popular support than had its predecessor. Of course a return to a policy of strict neutrality was possible, but Simović would nevertheless strive to establish good relations with Germany.[24] In contrast, the German military attaché in Belgrade, Colonel Rudolf Toussaint, reported two days later that the mood in the Yugoslav capital was still anti-German. Although he considered it possible that the coup was due primarily to domestic political factors, he doubted whether its political aims could ever be determined, given the 'stubbornness and stupidity of Serbian officers'. And he pointed out that the new government had not succeeded in putting an end to British propaganda in Yugoslavia.[25] In fact, however, on the day of the coup Simović attempted to persuade the British to refrain from tendentious radio broadcasts. On 27 March he also informed the American and the British minister in Belgrade that there would be no change in Yugoslavia's foreign policy.[26] In the following days, in order to counter rumours that the coup in

---

[22] *DGFP* D xii, No. 241, pp. 425–6 (1 Apr. 1941); ibid., No. 262, C.-G. Freundt, Zagreb, to foreign ministry (3–4 Apr. 1941). Maček had suggested offering Germany satisfaction for all anti-German incidents.

[23] Ibid., No. 243, pp. 427–8 (1 Apr. 1941).

[24] Heeren to foreign ministry, telegram No. 282 (27 Mar. 1941), PA, Büro St.S., Jugoslawien, ii; *DGFP* D xii, No. 225, pp. 398–9 (28 Mar. 1941). Cf. also Cruickshank, *Greece 1940–1941*, 125.

[25] OKW/A Ausl/Abw/Abw I No. 0675/41 geh., Außen- und militärpolitische Nachrichten (31 Mar. 1941), BA-MA RW 5/v. 354; Memorandum by Legation Secretary von Grote (29 Mar. 1941), PA, Büro St.S., Jugoslawien, ii.

[26] Heeren to foreign ministry, telegram No. 286 (28 Mar. 1941), PA, Büro St.S., Jugoslawien, ii.

Belgrade would lead to a new Balkan alliance, he also refused to confer with the British foreign secretary Eden.[27] However, this attitude of the Yugoslav government could not change Hitler's decision to attack Yugoslavia, but only reduced the ability of the countries threatened by Germany to defend themselves.

The German government considered Simović's efforts to steer a neutral course friendly towards Germany as an attempt to win time to mobilize and to form alliances.[28] As the decision had already been taken to refrain from any diplomatic efforts to settle the conflict, the foreign ministry announced the recall of almost all German government employees from Yugoslavia. Heeren's place would be occupied by legation officials merely authorized to receive communications. On 2 April the legation was ordered to prepare to destroy its files and leave the country. The German government called upon Germany's allies to follow her example.[29] On 29 March the German foreign ministry ordered all its departments and agencies to react to any Yugoslav feelers with the utmost reserve in order to stop all diplomatic contact. German diplomats and other officials of the foreign ministry would have to claim to be busy or otherwise unavailable if Yugoslav representatives should try to approach them.[30] Ribbentrop ordered the German diplomatic personnel still in Belgrade to inform the foreign ministry immediately of all acts against German nationals and institutions. The information was to be used to prepare the German public for the attack on Yugoslavia.[31]

The Yugoslav government considered the steady reduction of the German diplomatic presence in Belgrade to be a serious danger. For this reason it clearly stated again on 30 March its intention to fulfil all its obligations as a member of the Tripartite Pact and its desire to maintain friendly relations with Germany as well as Italy. Ribbentrop, however, informed Ciano the same day that Germany had no intention of answering this statement or even publishing it. He referred instead to Hitler's letter of 27 March to Mussolini, in which the former had demanded the use of military force against Yugoslavia.[32]

---

[27] The Yugoslav government did agree to a visit by the chief of the British general staff, Dill, which, however, did not produce any significant results. Cf. Cruickshank, *Greece 1940–1941*, 136. On the possibility of a new Balkan alliance cf. Halder, *Diaries*, ii. 848 (1 Apr. 1941).

[28] *KTB OKW* i. 371 (31 Mar. 1941).

[29] Foreign ministry to legation at Belgrade, telegram No. 379 (29 Mar. 1941), PA, Büro St.S., Jugoslawien, ii; foreign minister to chargé d'affaires in Belgrade, *DGFP* D xii, No. 248, pp. 431–2 (2 Apr. 1941).

[30] Foreign ministry to legation at Belgrade, *DGFP* D xii, No. 232, p. 412 (29 Mar. 1941); *Weizsäcker-Papiere*, 244 (6 Apr. 1941) and 564 n. 116.

[31] The regional leader of the NSDAP in Styria especially distinguished himself with such reports, which he received primarily from the German consulate in Zagreb. Cf. *Dokumente zum Konflikt mit Jugoslawien und Griechenland*, 129–30, 132–3. On the propaganda in Germany cf. Vauhnik, *Memoiren*, 153.

[32] Cf. Yugoslav statement of 30 Mar. 1941 to the Italian minister in Belgrade, PA, Büro St.S., Jugoslawien, ii; Ribbentrop's telephone conversation with Ciano, *DGFP* D xii, No. 237, p. 423 (30 Mar. 1941); Hitler to Mussolini, ibid., No. 224, p. 397 (27 Mar. 1941).

Nevertheless, in his efforts to obtain a hearing in Berlin, Simović attempted to persuade Italy to act as an intermediary. Italy was, however, quite unsuited for such a role, as the prospect of subjugating Yugoslavia seemed to offer Mussolini a chance to realize long-held imperial ambitions. After the coup in Belgrade relations between the two countries remained tense, especially when, according to the Italian minister in the Yugoslav capital, Simović threatened on 29 March to take military action in Albania if Germany occupied Salonika.[33] As was to be expected, the Italian government turned down the Yugoslav request for mediation on 3 April.[34] Even after this new failure of its efforts to achieve an understanding, the Yugoslav government tried to negotiate with Germany at the highest level on the day before the start of hostilities. Foreign Minister Ninčić let the German government know that he was prepared to come to Berlin immediately to achieve an improvement in relations between the two countries.[35] The German government, however, did not answer Ninčić's offer. After Hitler's decision of 27 March, Berlin gave no serious consideration to avoiding a war with Yugoslavia.

2. The German Deployment against Greece and Yugoslavia

Although as early as February 1941 the army high command had concluded that a war with Yugoslavia was possible, Hitler's decision of 27 March nevertheless required considerable changes in German military planning.[36] Twelfth Army was now to be used not only against Greece, but also against southern Yugoslavia. Moreover, according to Directive No. 25, a unit of shock troops was to be formed in Styria and Hungary to attack Yugoslavia from the north. These troops would consist of forces from the army and the Luftwaffe which were either still fighting against Britain (the Luftwaffe), preparing to take part in Barbarossa, or serving as occupation forces in western Europe.

On 27 March Hitler had informed his allies of his plan to invade Yugoslavia and had given each of them very specific tasks. Together with units of the German military mission, Romania was to provide protection against the Soviet Union. Bulgaria continued to refuse to participate in the imminent hostilities, although Hitler offered it Yugoslav parts of Macedonia in a talk with the Bulgarian minister in Berlin, Draganov, on 27 March. The German government was only able to persuade Bulgaria to leave defensive forces on the

---

[33] Heeren to foreign minister, telegram No. 311 (29 Mar. 1941), PA, Büro St.S., Jugoslawien, ii. However, Heeren did express considerable doubt as to whether Simović's threats were supported by the whole cabinet. Cf. Heeren to foreign minister, telegram No. 315 (30 Mar. 1941), *DGFP* D xii, No. 235, pp. 421–2 n. 3. Cf. also Breccia, *Jugoslavia*, 613–14.

[34] Feine to foreign ministry, *DGFP* D xii, No. 253, p. 437 (3 Apr. 1941); Hillgruber, *Strategie*, 464. On the first Italian military plans cf. Cavallero, *Comando Supremo*, 76–7 (27–30 Mar. 1941).

[35] Feine to foreign ministry (5 Apr. 1941), *DGFP* D xii, No. 271, pp. 462–3 (5 Apr. 1941).

[36] Cf. *KTB OKW* i. 1002 (8 Feb. 1941); Creveld, *Balkan*, 145.

Turkish frontier.³⁷ In contrast, the Hungarian leader Horthy promised at first to support Germany militarily and to move against Yugoslavia in the area of the Yugoslav Banat which was claimed by Hungary. After the suicide of the Hungarian prime minister Teleki—itself a reaction to Horthy's intention to wage war against a neighbouring state with which Hungary had a treaty of friendship—the general mobilization in Hungary was rescinded. The Hungarian government informed Germany that it would be able to intervene militarily only when Yugoslavia had officially ceased to exist as a state. Nevertheless, Horthy permitted the deployment of German troops in his country.³⁸ In contrast, Mussolini was prepared to make all necessary preparations and invade Yugoslavia immediately when Hitler informed him of his intentions. A conference between Italian and German representatives on the details of the attack took place two days after the coup in Belgrade.³⁹ However, as Halder did not expect Germany's Axis partner to be ready to intervene in good time, Italy was given the tasks of first merely providing increased security in northern Albania and of invading Slovene territory only if German troops advanced without difficulty in northern Yugoslavia.⁴⁰

After Germany's allies had been drawn into the invasion plans, the German military leaders concentrated on the supplying and redeployment of their own forces against Greece and Yugoslavia. Twelfth Army had been redeploying its units since 28 March, when it received new orders from Berlin. According to an order of the army high command of 22 March, the command staff of Armoured Group 1 was to be withdrawn and transferred via Vienna to Breslau. The army high command also announced that Twelfth Army would now receive only three divisions from the third deployment echelon. In addition, the armoured divisions near the frontier between Bulgaria and Turkey were to prepare to return to Romania and wait there with the remainder of the last deployment echelon.⁴¹ The planned reduction of the units originally envisaged for the invasion of Greece indicates that the German government now considered Turkish military intervention to be highly improbable. Moreover, it

---

³⁷ Hitler's War Directives, No. 26, p. 63 (3 Apr. 1941). On the informing of the Romanian government cf. *DGFP* D xii, No. 249, p. 433 (Apr. 1941); conversation between Hitler and Draganov, ibid., No. 216, pp. 371–2 (28 Mar. 1941). Bulgaria refused to take military action against its neighbours because of the Balkan pact of 1934.
³⁸ Halder, *Diaries*, ii. 843 (28 Mar. 1941). Cf. also *Das Deutsche Reich und der Zweite Weltkrieg*, iv. 353 (Förster). On Teleki's suicide (3 Apr. 1941) cf. Halder, *Diaries*, ii. 851–2, 856 (3 and 5 Apr. 1941); Hillgruber, 'Deutschland und Ungarn', 661–2.
³⁹ On Mussolini's assent cf. *DGFP* D xii, No. 226, pp. 399–400 (28 Mar. 1941). On the agreements between Germany and Italy cf. Jukić, *Yugoslavia*, 67.
⁴⁰ Weichs papers, 'Erinnerungen', iv. 43–4, BA-MA N 19/8; Halder, *Diaries*, ii. 847 (30 Mar. 1941).
⁴¹ AOK 12, Ia, No. 0184/41 g.Kdos. Chefs., Befehlsregelung (22 Mar. 1941), BA-MA RH 20-12/60; Pz.Gr. 1, KTB 115–23 (21–8 Mar. 1941), BA-MA RH 21-1/40D. According to Hinsley (*British Intelligence*, 371), the British government learnt of the planned withdrawal on 26 Mar. 1941.

2. Germany against Greece and Yugoslavia

was assumed that a smaller German invasion force would be sufficient to deal with the technically inferior Greek army and the small British expeditionary corps. Considerations of time and space thus caused the German leaders to remove all divisions they considered superfluous from the Balkans and deploy them for the attack on the Soviet Union. Three army corps were left for the invasion of Greece: XVIII Mountain Corps (two mountain divisions, one infantry division, and one infantry regiment) in the extreme south-western part of Bulgaria and XXX Corps (two infantry divisions) north of Xanthi; the divisions of XXXX (motorized) Army Corps were held in reserve near Plovdiv.[42]

But before these planned measures could be put into effect, events in Belgrade forced a new transfer of units and commands; for the attack on southern Yugoslavia parts of Twelfth Army had to be redeployed. Directive No. 25 set the priorities for this action as well as the general distribution of forces under the command of Field Marshal List.[43] The deployment of XVIII Mountain Corps and XXX Army Corps was not changed significantly; the divisions of XXX Corps were still to advance to Xanthi and Komotini on the Aegean. The task of XVIII Mountain Corps remained to capture the Rupel Pass in a direct attack. Moreover, an armoured division was added to the large unit to advance through Yugoslav territory (Strumica) in the direction of Salonika and Edessa. With this manœuvre the German military leaders intended to attack the strongly fortified Metaxas line from the flanks and the rear.[44] While the planning of the operations of these two corps did not create any problems, List and the chief of the army general staff had different ideas about the main objectives on the frontier between Yugoslavia and Bulgaria. List wanted to continue to give priority to the attack on Greece and for this reason attempted to keep Armoured Group 1, which had been ordered back to the Balkans, as small as possible in order to strengthen the forces attacking Greece.

On the other hand Halder, the chief of the army general staff, intended to assign many divisions to the command staff of Armoured Group 1. He believed that this would make possible a strong thrust in the direction of Niš and could lead to the collapse of the south-east Yugoslav front. XXXX Army Corps (motorized), advancing from the area south-west of Sofia, was to help secure this success. With its help, the German military leaders intended to push on to the Albanian frontier via Skopje in order to prevent a possible link-up between Greek and Yugoslav forces and to relieve the pressure on the Italian units in Albania.

---

[42] Balkanfeldzug der 12. Armee, map of 25 Mar. 1941, BA-MA 75090/1.
[43] *Hitler's War Directives*, No. 25, pp. 61–2 (27 Mar. 1941); Halder *Diaries*, ii. 841 (27 Mar. 1941).
[44] Cf. Wisshaupt, 'Balkanfeldzug', 17, BA-MA RH 20-12/129, 'Metaxas-Linie'; cf. Map III.III.1.

After some discussion, Hitler agreed with Halder.[45] Kleist's Armoured Group 1 was ordered to deploy a total of four divisions (two armoured, one mountain, and one infantry division) north-west of Sofia. For the drive via Niš to Belgrade, Armoured Group 1 could count on the support of XXXXI (motorized) Army Corps, which was to attack towards Belgrade from Timişoara.[46]

Both armoured divisions of Kleist's group (5th and 11th) had to be withdrawn from the areas where they had originally been stationed to provide protection against a possible Turkish intervention. Their tasks were taken over by an armoured division of the German military mission in Romania, which was assigned to List for this purpose. The army high command transferred XI Corps with two infantry divisions, which had also been in Romania, across the Danube to Twelfth Army command in the area east of Armoured Group 1.[47] The bulk of XXXX Army Corps mentioned above moved in stages, an armoured and an infantry division at a time, from Plovdiv and Stara Zagora to its operations area south of Kyustendil.[48] As a reserve, List still had L Army Corps with one infantry division. On 5 April these forces were half-way between Plovdiv and Pazardzhik (west of Plovdiv) and were to follow the divisions of XXXX (motorized) Army Corps into Yugoslavia.[49]

Thus, after the coup in Belgrade German troop movements were in two main directions: from east to west, from the area of the Turco-Bulgarian frontier to west of Sofia; and from north to south, from Romania across the Danube. The German military leaders attempted to correct the partial exposure of Romania by the transfer of individual units. The 'General Göring' regiment, originally assigned to XXXXI (motorized) Army Corps, was reassigned by the army high command to the Luftwaffe mission in Bucharest. Hitler decided that at least one armoured division should remain in Romania.[50]

The date of attack for most of Twelfth Army (XVIII Mountain Corps, XXX Corps, and XXXX (motorized) Army Corps) was set for 6 April. Armoured Group 1 was to begin operations two days later, and XXXXI (motorized) Army Corps only on 12 April, because German troops in Hungary, Styria,

---

[45] Halder, *Diaries*, ii. 844 ff., 854–5 (29–30 Mar. and 4 Apr. 1941); Pz.Gr. 1, KTB 125 ff. (29 Mar.–4 Apr. 1941), BA-MA RH 21-1/40 D.

[46] Teletype message AOK 12, Ia, No. 0217/41 (31 Mar. 1941), to Pz.Gr. 1, BA-MA RH 20-12/60. XXXXI (mot.) Corps, assigned to Armoured Group 1, was to be completely assembled near Timişoara on 11 Apr. 1941. Cf. also Röhricht, 'Balkanfeldzug', 218–20. Moreover, 60th Inf. Div. (mot.), which was south of Sofia on 8 Apr. 1941 (the day of attack for Armoured Group 1), was assigned to 12th Army.

[47] Balkanfeldzug der 12. Armee, map No. 9, BA-MA 75090/1.

[48] There was also SS Leibstandarte Adolf Hitler, which originally was supposed to be sent to Romania: teletype message AOK 12, Ia, No. 0217/41 (31 Mar. 1941), to Pz.Gr. 1, BA-MA RH 20-12/60.

[49] Teletype message AOK 12, Ia, No. 715/41 (6 Apr. 1941), to Gen.Kdo. L. AK, BA-MA RH 20-12/60. On the organization of 12th Army cf. Table III.II.1 and Map III.III.1.

[50] On the assignment of the 'General Göring' Regiment cf. teletype message AOK 12, Ia, No. 0233/41 (4 Apr. 1941), to Pz.Gr.1, BA-MA RH 20-12/60; for Hitler's demands cf. *Hitler's War Directives*, No. 25, pp. 61–2 (27 Mar. 1941).

TABLE III.II.1. *Organization of the Twelfth Army on 6 April 1941*

Corps cmds.	Divisions	Area	Remarks
XXX	164th and 50th Inf. Divs.[a]	North of Xanthi	
XVIII Mtn.	2nd Armd. Div.,[b] 5th and 6th Mtn. Divs., 72nd Inf. Div., 125th Inf. Regt.	Between the Mesta (Nestos) and the Struma (Strimon)	
XXXX (mot.)	9th Armd. Div., 73rd Inf. Div., SS Leibstandarte Adolf Hitler	Kyustendil	
Armd. Gp. 1	XIV (mot.) Army Corps with 5th and 11th Armd. Divs., 4th Mtn. Div., 294th Inf. Div., 60th Inf. Div. (mot.)[c]	North-west of Sofia	As of 12 Apr. (minus 5th Armd. Div.) assgnd. to Second Army HQ
XXXXI (mot.)	SS-Div. Das Reich, Inf. Regt. Großdeutschland	Near Timişoara	As of 12 Apr. assgnd. to Second Army HQ
XI	198th and 76th Inf. Divs.	Between Botevgrad and Pleven	
L	46th Inf. Div., 16th Armd. Div.	West of Plovdiv. Around Yambol	16th Armd. Div. from Ger. military mission in Romania

[a] An infantry division had between 15,000 and 18,000 men (3 infantry regiments and 1 artillery regiment).
[b] An armoured division had about 15,000 men (between 150 and 300 armoured vehicles).
[c] An infantry division (motorized) had about 14,000 men (2 infantry regiments and 1 artillery regiment).

and Carinthia had not all reached their deployment areas.[51] The army high command intended that as far as possible all units directed against Belgrade should advance at the same time.

The formation of a group of sufficiently strong forces north of the Yugoslav frontier proved to be much more difficult than the redeployment of Twelfth Army. As no units able to conduct operations over large areas were available in the German frontier area or western Hungary, a completely new attack

[51] AOK 12, Ia, KTB, evening report (5 Apr. 1941), BA-MA RH 20-12/62; Halder, *Diaries*, ii. 847 (30 Mar. 1941). Cf. also Maps III.III.1, 2.

group had to be created. Serious delays seemed inevitable because numerous motorized formations were being redeployed and all divisions ready for combat were far from the northern Yugoslav frontier. Moreover, the planned operation against Yugoslavia disrupted the movement, which had just begun, of German forces from west to east for the attack on the Soviet Union.[52] An advantage in the creation of an attack group on the Yugoslav frontier was, however, that Second Army headquarters was located in Munich and was responsible only for training programmes. The command staff under Colonel-General Maximilian Freiherr von Weichs was therefore placed in charge of the newly created Second Army.[53] The army high command decided to draw the units to be placed under Second Army headquarters primarily from southern Germany and German forces stationed in France. The movements of those units to their operations areas on the Yugoslav frontier were to be carried out mainly by rail but in particular cases by lorry. However, the limited capacity of the railway lines south of Vienna in the direction of Graz and Hungary forced most of the units to cover that part of their journey using other forms of transportation (see Table III.II.2).[54]

For the coming battles in northern Yugoslavia, the army high command intended to use a total of four corps commands with eleven divisions.[55] Second Army headquarters deployed three fast divisions in south-west Hungary (near Nagykanizsa) under the command of XXXXI (motorized) Army Corps (two armoured and one motorized infantry division). The main forces were to capture Drava crossings and attack between the Sava and the Drava towards Belgrade. There they would link up with Kleist's troops.[56]

An armoured division of the corps was to advance rapidly to Zagreb. It was intended to meet Hungary's condition for participating in military events, by capturing Zagreb and proclaiming the establishment of a separate Croat state. The army high command was therefore determined to have strong units of XXXXVI (motorized) Army Corps attack before the date at first set for 12 April.[57] As an immediate advance by Hungarian units was not expected, the German military leaders planned to use XXXXI (motorized) Army Corps mentioned above. Its units, grouped around Timişoara, received the order to attack east of the Tisza in the direction of Belgrade.[58] South of Graz, LI Army

[52] However, only one division, which fought with 2nd Army, had to be redirected south after the start of its movement to the eastern frontier. Cf. Creveld, *Balkan*, 153.
[53] Müller-Hillebrand, 'Improvisierung', 46, MGFA, P-030.
[54] Annex 4 to AOK 2, Ia, No. 35/41g.Kdos. (4 Apr. 1941), BA-MA RH 20-2/140; AOK 2, KTB 23 (1 Apr. 1941), BA-MA RH 20-2/130. Cf. also Greiffenberg, 'Die Invasion in Jugoslawien', 9, MGFA B-525.
[55] AOK 2, KTB 20 (31 Apr. 1941), BA-MA RH 20-2/130; Halder, *Diaries*, ii. 843 (28 Mar. 1941). Cf. also Map III.III.2. On the deployment of 2nd Army cf. Maydell, 'Balkanfeldzug', 32 ff.
[56] Cf. AOK 2, KTB 17–18 (30 Mar. 1941), BA-MA RH 20-2/130.
[57] Deployment order for Operation 25, AOK 2, Ia, No. 35/41 (4 Apr. 1941), 1, BA-MA RH 20-2/140; Halder, *Diaries*, ii. 857 (5 Apr. 1941), 859 (6 Apr. 1941). Halder finally set 10 Apr. 1941 as the date of the attack.
[58] Greiffenberg, 'Die Invasion in Jugoslawien', 9, MGFA, B-525. For this purpose XXXXI (mot.) Army Corps was assigned to 2nd Army (Armd. Grp. 1) on 12 Apr. 1941.

2. Germany against Greece and Yugoslavia

TABLE III.II.2. *Organization of the Second Army on 6 April 1941*[a]

Corps cmds.	Divisions	Area	Remarks
XXXXVI (mot.)	8th and 14th Armd. Divs.,[b] 16th Inf. Div. (mot.)	South-west Hungary	On 10 Apr. most units in operat. area; on 13 Apr. to Second Army (Armd. Gp. 1)
LI	132nd and 183rd Inf. Divs., 101st Lgt. Div.[c]	South of Graz	Two-thirds unloaded on 6 Apr.; to Second Army on and after 11 Apr.
XXXXIX Mtn.	1st Mtn. Div., 79th Inf. Div.[d]	South-east of Klagenfurt	On and after 12 Apr. to Second Army
LII[e]	125th Inf. Div.[d]	Orig. planned east of LI A.Co.	Assgnmt. to Second Army planned as of 13 Apr.
Armd. Gp. 1	XIV Army Corps (mot.) with 11th Armd. Div., 4th Mtn. Div.; 294th Inf. Div., 60th Inf. Div.	North-west of Sofia	On 12 Apr. assgnd. to Second Army HQ
XXXXI (mot.)	SS-Div. Das Reich, Inf. Regt. Großdeutschland	Near Timişoara	Until 12 Apr. assgnd. to Twelfth Army

[a] The 197th, 179th, 20th (mot.), 169th, and 100th Inf. Divs. and the 4th, 12th, and 19th Armd. Divs. were planned as reserves, but the army high command stopped their transport to the Balkans on 12 Apr.

[b] 14th Armd. Div. was placed directly under Second Army HQ on 10 Apr.

[c] Advanced to the Sava by 14 Apr.; on 18 Apr. north of Maribor; light division: in equipment and weapons between an infantry division and a mountain division, later renamed *Jäger-Division*.

[d] Did not reach Yugoslavia during the fighting.

[e] On 15 Apr. the Corps Cmd. LII A.Co. took over command of the 125th Inf. Div. and parts of the 101st Lgt. Div.

Corps assembled three infantry divisions to advance to the south-east via Maribor.[59] Finally, on the right flank of Second Army, east of Klagenfurt, XXXXIX Mountain Corps was deployed with one mountain division, later followed by an additional infantry division. The planned attack was to take the corps via Celje to the heights around the Croatian capital.[60] The north-west part of Slovenia was to be taken by the Italian Second Army. The army high command itself assumed the direction of the two armies to be used in south-

[59] Deployment order for Operation 25 (cf. n. 57 above).
[60] AOK 2, KTB 50–1 (8 Apr. 1941), BA-MA RH 20-2/130.

east Europe. For this purpose a forward headquarters was established in Wiener Neustadt, which was ready for operation on 9 April 1941.⁶¹

Hitler's decision to conquer Yugoslavia resulted in a considerable expansion of Luftwaffe support for the army units involved in the campaign. The previous mission of the units of VIII Flying Corps, to support mainly XVIII Mountain Corps in its attack on the Metaxas line, was not changed after 27 March. But the Luftwaffe was now also to support the attack of XXXX (motorized) Army Corps near Kyustendil. The commanding general of VIII Air Corps, Richthofen, decided to integrate half his ground units into the marching units of the divisions of the corps in order to facilitate co-operation between the army and Luftwaffe units. The expanded mission of the Luftwaffe did not require the construction of new airfields.⁶² On 2 April Richthofen received reinforcements for his air corps in the form of three additional Gruppen of dive-bombers, which, however, were transferred without ground units to Bulgarian airfields.⁶³ The withdrawal of supply and maintenance units to XXXX (motorized) Army Corps, as well as the arrival of new air formations without ground units in Bulgaria, placed a considerable strain on the logistical system of VIII Air Corps for the coming operations.

The Wehrmacht high command envisaged the formation of a second Luftwaffe attack group in the area south of Vienna. For this purpose, on 27 and 28 March Göring ordered the transfer of numerous bomber and fighter units (about 500 aircraft) from France and northern Germany and the reinforcement of Air Fleet Four under Luftwaffe General Alexander Löhr.⁶⁴ These units were first to destroy Belgrade and the ground organization of the Yugoslav air force and later to support the attack of Second Army. In Croatia the Luftwaffe was forbidden to carry out any bombing on its own and was restricted to intervening in the ground fighting.⁶⁵ In this way losses among the civilian population were to be avoided as far as possible. To achieve the greatest possible effect in the imminent battles, Löhr transferred all Luftwaffe formations that were to participate in the ground fighting to the Yugoslav frontier. On the other hand the operational bomber formations were stationed in rear areas and, in the area of Air Fleet Four, had to take off for their attacks from airfields south of Vienna. For this purpose VIII Flying Corps concentrated its bombers near Plovdiv. Air Fleet Four received additional

---

⁶¹ Ibid. 24 (2 Apr. 1941), BA-MA RH 20-2/130. Cf. also Müller-Hillebrand, 'Improvisierung', 30, MGFA P-030.

⁶² It was, however, necessary to establish communication links with XXXX (mot.) Army Corps. Cf. Meister, 'Der Einsatz des VIII. Fliegerkorps', Teil I, 25, BA-MA RL 8/237. Richthofen had transferred the close-support units to airfields on the frontier between Bulgaria and Yugoslavia.

⁶³ Deichmann, 'Balkanfeldzug des VIII. Fliegerkorps', 16–17, BA-MA RL 8/46. For 'Gruppen' and related terms see the Glossary. Richthofen had a total of 400–500 aircraft in this area.

⁶⁴ *KTB OKW* i. 369 (27 Mar. 1941). Cf. also Gundelach, *Luftwaffe im Mittelmeer*, 162.

⁶⁵ Deployment order for Operation 25 (see n. 57 above), 5.

2. Germany against Greece and Yugoslavia

support, especially for the fighting in Greece and southern Yugoslavia, from X Air Corps, which was to fly missions from Sicily. For airborne operations XI Flying Corps was available near Bucharest.[66] Altogether the German military planned to use a quarter of its Luftwaffe units, a total of about 900 aircraft, in the attack on Greece and Yugoslavia.[67]

3. THE MILITARY REACTIONS OF YUGOSLAVIA, GREECE, AND BRITAIN TO THE EVENTS OF 27 MARCH 1941

The Yugoslav rejection of the Greek and British plans for a political alliance was not without effect on the military co-operation between the three countries. During his visit to Belgrade on 31 March, the chief of the Imperial General Staff, General Dill, found Simović reluctant to commit himself: he promised Yugoslav military support only in the event of an Axis attack on Salonika. The Yugoslav government was not even prepared to establish a liaison staff with Greece and Britain until the fighting started.[68] A meeting of Generals Wilson, Papagos, and Janković at Kenali on the frontier between Greece and Yugoslavia on 3 and 4 April 1941 was equally unproductive.[69] Janković wanted to negotiate primarily about measures to be taken in the event of a German attack on Salonika. Otherwise the three generals merely discussed the possibility of joint advances by Greek and Yugoslav forces into Albanian territory. Janković considered unacceptable Papagos's suggestion of concentrating Yugoslav forces in the south-east of the country, thus leaving the north exposed to attack.

In contrast to Churchill, who wanted to encourage the Yugoslav government to undertake rapid operations against the Italians in Albania, Simović tried to avoid taking a decision. The hope that the Axis powers would respect Yugoslavia's efforts to remain neutral was probably his main reason for not agreeing to the British and Greek demands.[70] This general uncertainty in assessing Yugoslavia's political possibilities also influenced the mobilization of its armed forces. Simović's government did not decide to call up reservists until three days after the coup, with the result that only parts of most units had reached their wartime strength at the outbreak of hostilities.[71] It was planned to use them in all frontier areas. Each of the seven Yugoslav armies

---

[66] Gundelach, *Luftwaffe im Mittelmeer*, 163. A part of this corps was transferred to Plovdiv.

[67] Lecture on the combat-readiness of the air units (8 Apr. 1941), Gen.Qu., 6. Abt. (I), Stand 5 Apr. 1941, BA-MA RL 2 III/712. In addition there were 140 reconnaissance aircraft. On the strength and organization of the Luftwaffe cf. Maydell, 'Balkanfeldzug', appendix A4.

[68] *PWT*, Middle East I, Hist (B) 3, No. 39, pp. 16–17 (4 Apr. 1941).

[69] Ibid., No. 46, p. 19 (4 Apr. 1941). Cf. Long, *Greece, Crete and Syria*, 26–7. Papagos was chief of the general staff and C.-in-C. of the Greek army; Wilson was commander of the imperial forces in Greece; and Janković was deputy chief of the Yugoslav general staff.

[70] Churchill, *Second World War*, iii. 153–4. Cf. also Woodward, *British Foreign Policy*, i. 546.

[71] The deployment was to be concluded on 12 Apr. 1941. Cf. Papagos, *Griechenland*, 104; Donlagić *et al.*, *Jugoslawien im Zweiten Weltkrieg*, 33. The final mobilization of the Yugoslav armed forces was ordered only after the German attack began. Cf. 'Überblick über die Operationen des jugoslawischen Heeres', Teil I, 276–7.

(comparable to German army corps), a total of thirty-six divisions, had its own reserves, but a sufficiently large strategic reserve in the interior of the country was lacking.

The deployment of the Yugoslav forces was concentrated mainly around Belgrade and in the south-eastern part of the country. Only the divisions confronting the Italians on the Albanian frontier were ordered to attack; all other divisions were to go on the defensive in the event of an advance by the Axis forces.[72] The unfavourable initial position of the Yugoslav armed forces, e.g. with regard to mobilization and deployment, was made even worse by the lack of anti-tank and anti-aircraft units.[73] As will be seen, the conflict between Croats and Serbs also had a negative effect on the fighting value of the Yugoslav army. Moreover, many officers in the general staff, above all those of Serbian origin, did not accept the measures of the new government. Instead, they supported a common front with the Greeks and the British, which Simović had rejected for political reasons.[74] An additional disadvantage was that, through agents, deserters, and diplomatic personnel, the Germans were informed about the attack plans, areas of concentration, and deployment of the Yugoslav armed forces.[75]

As in Germany, the events in Belgrade also caused the Greek government and the British to change their joint defence strategy. Immediately after learning of the successful coup, Foreign Secretary Eden and General Dill flew to Athens. There Papagos explained to them his new plan for the defence of Greece. It called for the Greeks and the British to establish a continuous front from the Adriatic to the Turkish frontier. Papagos planned to assign to the Yugoslav forces the task of carrying out an offensive against Albania and Bulgaria.[76] The British leaders, however, expressed serious reservations about the Greek plans, as they were not certain how energetically the Yugoslav forces would oppose a German attack.[77] They therefore refused to plan new defensive

---

[72] On 6 Apr. 1941 only the 3rd and 5th Yugoslav armies in the south-eastern part of the country had completed their deployment. Cf. Matl, 'Jugoslawien im Zweiten Weltkrieg', 101; Report from Toussaint and Feine, Belgrade, to the army high command, Att.Abt. (4 Apr. 1941), PA, Büro St.S., Jugoslawien, ii.

[73] According to *Deutschland im zweiten Weltkrieg*, i. 542, the Yugoslav army had approximately 200 tanks, assigned to cavalry units; the Yugoslav air force had about 300 combat-ready aircraft of German and Soviet production.

[74] Telephone call from military attaché in Bucharest to foreign ministry, 30 Mar. 1941, PA, Büro St.S., Jugoslawien, ii.

[75] Teletype message Lw.Fü. St./Ic No. 316/41 g.Kdos. (4 Apr. 1941), PA, Büro St.S., Jugoslawien, iii. The British secret service also knew about German preparations for attack; cf. n. 86 below.

[76] Papagos, *Griechenland*, 103 ff.; Woodward, *British Foreign Policy*, i. 542–3. Cf. also III.1.2 above. The units of the 'W Force' (the Central Macedonian Army and the expeditionary corps) on the eve of the German attack were: 1st British Armoured Brigade, 2nd New Zealand Division (4th, 5th, and 6th brigades), 6th Australian Division (16th brigade; parts of 19th and 17th brigades were still in Alexandria); 1st Australian Corps Cmd.; 20th and 12th Greek Divisions; in the area of the East Macedonian Army: 18th, 14th, and 7th Divisions and the 'Nestos Brigade'; in addition, 19th (mot.) Division (of the Central Macedonian Army).

[77] *PWT*, Middle East I, Hist (B) 3, No. 3, p. 2 (28 Mar. 1941).

positions on the northern frontier of Greece beyond the recently established Aliakmon line. General Wilson considered the danger of a German encirclement too great. He did, however, approve the reinforcement of the East Macedonian Army with a Greek division to prevent the expected German attempt to break through and advance past Lake Doiran to Salonika.[78]

A closer analysis of the situation showed, however, that the difficulty of drawing Yugoslavia into the Allied camp represented a serious military problem for the defence of Greece. Instead of having to attack the heavily fortified Metaxas line on the frontier between Bulgaria and Greece from the front, the German forces could now use two open gates to the south, the Vardar (Axios) valley and Florina, if they could overcome Yugoslav resistance. An attack near Florina would in particular constitute a serious danger for the British expeditionary corps and the Central Macedonian Army (both combined as the W Force), because their defensive positions would then be threatened on the flank and in the rear. At the same time, a German attack at this point would be able to cut off the greater part of the Greek army (fourteen divisions), which was to attack the two Italian armies in Albania, from their rear communications. Papagos, however, and probably also the British, hoped for a determined Yugoslav offensive against the Italians and, for that reason, assigned relatively weak forces to the area around Florina.[79] The British and Greek military leaders even thought that Yugoslav successes would make it possible to withdraw troops of the West Macedonian Army from Albania and transfer them to the central Macedonian front.

The Greek army consisted largely of infantry units, of which only a small part were motorized. Because of its lack of anti-aircraft and anti-tank guns and other kinds of artillery, German military leaders considered the Greek army to be quite backward, although they acknowledged the great stamina and courage of the individual Greek soldier.[80] The units fighting against Italy in Albania had several months of combat experience; however, the resulting personnel and material losses had also reduced their effectiveness. The barely three divisions of the British expeditionary corps were, on the other hand, equal to the German forces in their equipment and fire-power. The addition of an armoured brigade and numerous anti-tank weapons in particular made it possible to use them against the fast German formations.[81] Originally it was

---

[78] 'Überblick über die Operationen des griechischen Heeres', Teil I, 79; Woodward, *British Foreign Policy*, i. 542–3.

[79] *Hellēnikos stratos*, iv. 2, 100; Playfair, *Mediterranean*, ii. 80; Papagos, *Griechenland*, 104. Before 6 Apr. 1941 a total of 4–5 battalions were sent into action around Florina.

[80] OKH/army general staff/Op.Abt. (I) No. 704, Annex 1, 3 (9 Dec. 1940), BA-MA RH 6/v. 3. According to this report the Greek forces had about 60 tanks. Cf. also *Hellēnikos stratos*, iv. 124, and II.III.3 above (Schreiber).

[81] *Hellēnikos stratos*, iv. 123. Wilson had more than 100 tanks at his disposal. Cf. Barclay, *Their Finest Hour*, 109. *Hellēnikos stratos* (iv. 62) gives the total of imperial troops in Greece as 58,000 men, as does Playfair (*Mediterranean*, ii. 105). Woodward (*British Foreign Policy*, i. 551) gives 62,000 and Churchill (*Second World War*, iii. 205) 53,000.

intended to strengthen the expeditionary corps even more with Polish and additional Australian brigades from Egypt, but Rommel's offensive in Cyrenaica thwarted these plans.[82] As of 5 April 1941, also because of the German attack in North Africa, Britain had transferred only about eighty usable combat aircraft to Greece.[83] The task of the Royal Air Force was made substantially easier by the Greek government's removal of almost all previous restrictions. After the coup in Belgrade, the Royal Air Force could also use bases in central Greece. This would make it possible to attack the rear communications of the advancing German forces during the expected attack. Moreover, the Greek government agreed to the use of bases in Greece by the Royal Air Force even if Germany should at first attack only Yugoslavia.[84]

A comparison of the opposing armies shows that the Germans disposed of a considerably larger number of armoured vehicles and aircraft.[85] Moreover, German technical equipment and weapons were more modern than those of most of the Greek and British units. This enabled the German forces to fight with greater speed and mobility. In addition to the deficiencies and problems already mentioned, which reduced the fighting value of the Greek and Yugoslav armies, the British, Greek, and Yugoslav forces suffered from the disadvantage of having to wait for the Axis attack. The time and place for the start of the attack would be determined by the German military leaders. However, knowledge obtained by the British secret service about German military preparations provided some indications of when the German forces in the Balkans would be able to start their offensive.[86]

---

[82] Playfair, *Mediterranean*, ii. 82; Woodward, *British Foreign Policy*, i. 550; V.II and III below (Stegemann).

[83] *Hellēnikos stratos*, iv. 123, *PWT*, Middle East I, Hist (B) 3, No. 8, p. 4 (29 Mar. 1941). Cf. also Macmillan, *Royal Air Force*, iii. 85. For individual missions several bomber formations from Egypt were available to the British troops in Greece; the Greek army had 44 fighters and 46 bombers and reconnaissance aircraft; the Italians had 160 combat aircraft stationed in Albania. Cf. Playfair, *Mediterranean*, ii. 81, and 'Überblick über die Operationen des griechischen Heeres', Teil I, 73.

[84] *PWT*, Middle East I, Hist (B) 3, No. 30, p. 13 (2 Apr. 1941).

[85] On the number of tanks used by the German forces cf. Hillgruber and Hümmelchen, *Chronik*, 66, who give a total of 1,200. Calculations based on the known figures for an armoured division in 1941 also produce a total of about 1,200 for the 2nd and 12th Armies. Cf. Müller-Hillebrand, *Heer*, ii. 107. Barclay (*Their Finest Hour*, 109) gives a figure of 800 tanks in Greece alone. According to AOK 12, Ia, Kriegsgliederung 12. Armee (31 Mar. 1941), BA-MA RH 20-12/397, 2nd, 9th, 11th, and 5th Armoured Divisions had a total of 501 tanks ready for action.

[86] Santoni, 'British Knowledge', 3 ff. According to Simović ('Memoari', *Politika* (3 Oct. 1970), 11), Vauhnik, the Yugoslav military attaché in Berlin, received very precise information about the time of the German attack from an anonymous source on 28 Mar. 1941.

III. The German Attack on Yugoslavia and Greece

ON the morning of Palm Sunday, 6 April 1941, the German minister in Athens presented a note to Alexandros Koryzis, the Greek prime minister, in which his government purported to justify the attack on Greece that was to begin a few hours later. The note consisted largely of accusations against the Greek government because of its co-operation with Britain. Not being able to tolerate the creation of a second front in south-east Europe, Hitler had decided to invade Greece. Nevertheless, the minister untruthfully emphasized, the German attack was directed against Britain and not against Greece. Koryzis replied that he refused to accept an occupation of his country without fighting and that Greece would resist the German attack.[1]

In contrast, the attack on Yugoslavia was launched without any previous announcement. As retaliation for the coup of 27 March 1941, Hitler ordered operations to be started with the bombing of Belgrade under the name 'Strafgericht' (Retribution). For this purpose Air Fleet Command Four provided about 500 aircraft, which were to attack the Yugoslav capital in waves day and night.[2] Although Colonel-General Löhr, the chief of Air Fleet Four, issued the order to attack for the Geschwader under his command on 31 March 1941, as late as 5 April the final decision to bomb Belgrade had not been taken in Berlin.[3] The reason for this indecision was perhaps that, two days before the start of hostilities, the Yugoslav government had declared Belgrade to be an open city. The German legation also reported that the city had no anti-aircraft defences and that possible movements of Yugoslav troops would not come near it.[4] But on 5 April Hitler's hatred of Yugoslavia overcame any reservations he may have had; the order to bomb Belgrade was not rescinded.[5] Publicly the German government attempted to justify the attack on an almost defenceless city by speaking of operations against 'Fortress Belgrade' after the first bombs had been dropped.[6] The air attacks, which were

---

[1] Hillgruber, *Strategie*, 466 n. 42, and De Loverdo, *Grèce*, 219–23. Text of German note in *Ursachen und Folgen*, xvi. 467–70.
[2] Lfl.Kdo. 4, Ia Op No. 1000/41 (31 Mar. 1941), 2–12, BA-MA RL 7/657.
[3] *KTB OKW* i. 375 (5 Apr. 1941).
[4] Toussaint and Feine, telegram No. 368 (4 Apr. 1941), to foreign ministry, PA, Büro St.S., Jugoslawien, ii. On 4 Apr. 1941 a state of war with Germany did not yet exist; as a precaution the Yugoslav government declared that Belgrade would be an open city in the event that hostilities should actually begin. It was also intended to declare Ljubljana and Zagreb open cities.
[5] *KTB OKW* i. 375 (5 Apr. 1941).
[6] OKW report, Balkanfeldzug der 12. Armee, Deutsche Wehrmachtberichte und englische Rundfunkpropaganda, 1 (6 Apr. 1941), MGFA.

continued on 7 April, not only claimed many victims among the civilian population,[7] but also paralysed the command and operations centres of the state and the armed forces. The Yugoslav air force fought as best it could against the superior Luftwaffe, but within a few days it had been eliminated, either at its bases or in the air. After the first attack by the Luftwaffe, Simović was forced to leave Belgrade and was not able to establish continuous contact with his military staffs and other institutions. In order to prevent a collapse of resistance to the invader, he issued an order 'to all units' to act according to their own judgement, even without direct instructions.[8]

In his desperate situation Simović could have expected help only from the Soviet Union or Turkey, both of which were bound by treaties to help Yugoslavia. Turkey was a party to the Balkan pact of 1934, and a Yugoslav–Soviet non-aggression pact was signed at the eleventh hour before the German attack.[9] Immediately before the start of hostilities, therefore, German diplomatic activity was directed against possible Soviet efforts to help Yugoslavia. Several hours before the attack on Belgrade, Ribbentrop instructed Schulenburg, the ambassador in Moscow, to inform Molotov of German intentions, giving the British presence in south-east Europe as the main reason for the attack. After the end of operations the German troops would be withdrawn, as Germany was not pursuing any territorial interests in the Balkans.[10] In reply Molotov did not mention the pact just concluded between his country and Yugoslavia, but merely remarked that he considered the spread of the war 'extremely regrettable'.[11] Two days later, when State Secretary von Weizsäcker met the Soviet ambassador in Berlin, Soviet treaty obligations towards Yugoslavia were not mentioned either, and the ambassador refrained from any criticism of the German action.[12] Clearly the Soviet government was mainly concerned with avoiding anything that might worsen its relations with Germany or even lead to a war. In its desire to maintain good

---

[7] The figures for the number of persons killed vary between 1,500 and 30,000. Cf. Donlagić et al., *Jugoslawien im Zweiten Weltkrieg*, 33; Hillgruber, *Strategie*, 466 n. 42; Diakow, 'Der Luftkrieg im jugoslawisch-griechischen Feldzug 1941', 7, Löhr papers, KA, Vienna, B 521, No. 29. On the other hand, in his biography of Löhr (*Generaloberst Alexander Löhr*, 38 ff.) Diakow writes that on Löhr's orders only military targets were attacked. Nevertheless, the report of one Geschwader stated: 'Judging by aerial photographs and ground observation, the effect was excellent. The 50-kilo demolition bomb, used with the incendiary bomb, really proved its worth as a weapon for destroying large parts of cities.' See. KA, Vienna, B 521, No. 20, operation experience report, KG 2, Ia No. 1206/41 (9 May 1941).

[8] Cf. AOK 2, KTB 68 (10 Apr. 1941), BA-MA RH 20-2/130. On the transfer of the government from Belgrade cf. Dedijer, 'Sur l'armistice germano-yougoslave', 1.

[9] On the Yugoslav–Soviet non-aggression pact: *DGFP* D xii, No. 265, pp. 451–2 (4 Apr. 1941). After the German attack Yugoslavia had requested help from Turkey as well as from the Soviet Union. Cf. 'Überblick über die Operationen des jugoslawischen Heeres', Teil I, 288.

[10] *DGFP* D xii, No. 284, pp. 479–80 (6 Apr. 1941, 4.30 a.m.).

[11] Ibid., No. 288, p. 484 (6 Apr. 1941).

[12] Ibid., No. 294, pp. 490–1 (8 Apr. 1941). Halder did not consider the Soviet troop concentrations observed in the Ukraine as evidence of an imminent Soviet intervention: Halder, *Diaries*, ii. 859 (6 Apr. 1941).

relations with Germany, the Soviet government also insisted on antedating the non-aggression treaty with Yugoslavia of 6 April 1941 to 5 April, so that it would not be seen as a reaction to German aggression.[13]

On 6 April, in order to forestall a possible Turkish intervention against the German attacks on Greece and Yugoslavia, Germany addressed to the Turkish government a note almost identical with the one handed to the Soviet government in Moscow. Moreover, two days later Ribbentrop assured Gerede, the Turkish ambassador in Berlin, that Germany recognized Turkey's sovereignty over the Dardanelles and that Hitler was even prepared to guarantee it in writing. Thereupon Gerede promised to do everything to promote political cooperation between the two countries.[14]

While these efforts seemed to secure the German attack on its left flank, Hungary, as an ally of Germany, was subjected to considerable pressure from Britain as well as the United States. Both countries warned Hungary not to attack Yugoslavia. Britain even threatened to react to such an attack by declaring war and bombing Hungary.[15] Although Britain broke off diplomatic relations on 7 April because the Hungarian government permitted its territory to be used as a base for the German attack on Yugoslavia, the British threats had no significant effect. The German government had undoubtedly informed Hungary of the weakness of the British forces in Greece; Hungary was therefore prepared to invade Yugoslavia after the proclamation of a separate Croatian state, whenever Germany asked it to do so. At first, however, no significant military action took place along the frontier between Hungary and Yugoslavia, as the German leadership had decided to assign the main role in the attack to Twelfth Army in Bulgaria.[16]

1. The Attack of Twelfth Army on Greece and Southern Yugoslavia

(See Map III.III.1)

For their operations in northern Greece and southern Yugoslavia, the units under List's command had to pass through terrain poorly suited to a rapid advance of fast troops. A mountain-chain along the frontier between Bulgaria and Greece practically excluded the use of motorized formations; in Yugoslav Macedonia the mountains greatly restricted their movements. A rapid advance was possible only in the larger valleys in the frontier area between Greece and

---

[13] Cf. n. 9 above and Erickson, *Soviet High Command*, 574.

[14] *DGFP* D xii, No. 303, pp. 504–5 (10 Apr. 1941); *Weizsäcker-Papiere*, 247 (14 Apr. 1941) and 567 n. 138; text of German note to the Turkish government: *DGFP* D xii, No. 285, p. 481 (6 Apr. 1941).

[15] *DGFP* D xii, No. 287, pp. 483–4 (6 Apr. 1941), and No. 296, pp. 493–5 (9 Apr. 1941). On 8 Apr. 1941 Roosevelt described the German attack as a 'criminal assault'. Cf. telegram No. 955 (8 Apr. 1941), PA, Büro St.S., Jugoslawien, iii.

[16] On the timing of the stages of the attack cf. III.II.2 above at n. 51; on the deployment of the German forces cf. ibid. at n. 56.

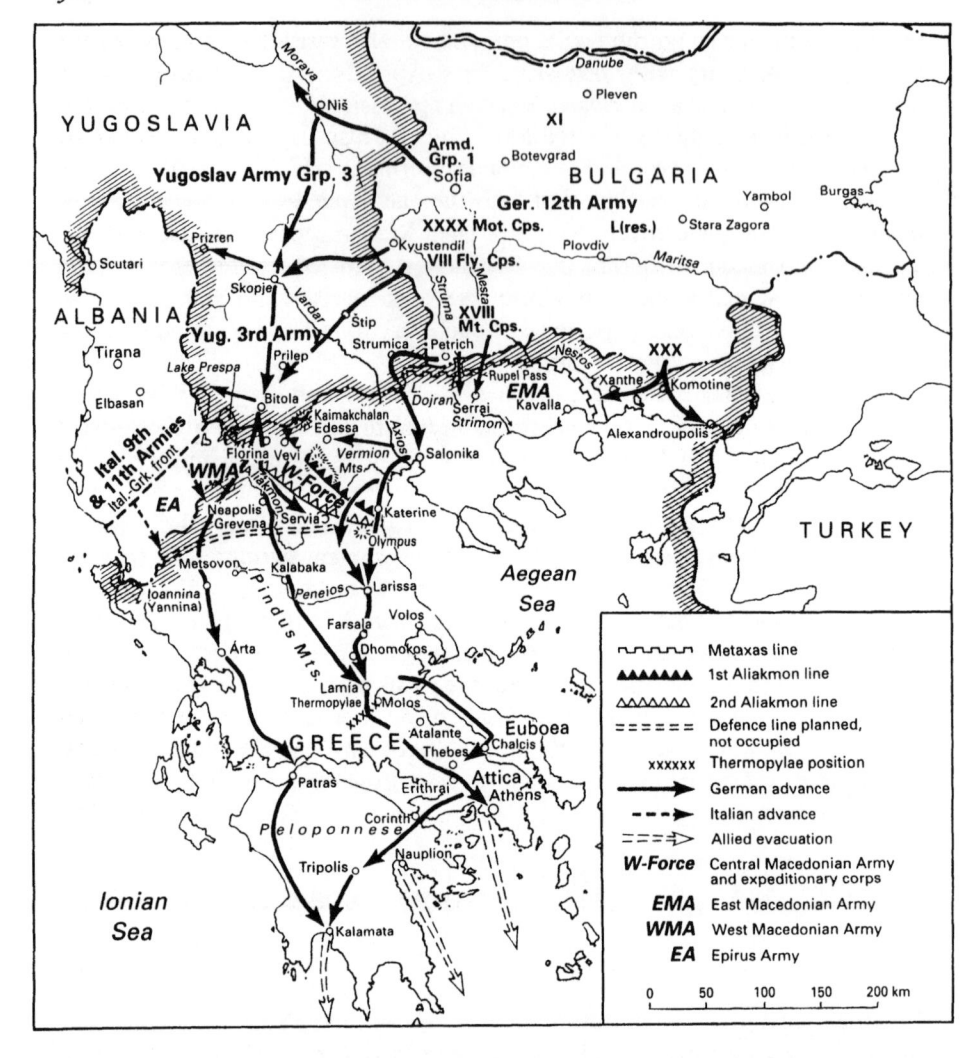

MAP III.III.1. Operations in Southern Yugoslavia and Greece, 6–30 April 1941

Yugoslavia. And during its further drive into Greek and Yugoslav territory, Twelfth Army had to overcome rugged terrain with few roads, which offered the defenders numerous opportunities to oppose the German advance from favourable positions.

The German invasion of Greece began on the morning of 6 April with fierce bombing attacks on the strongly fortified Metaxas line along the northern Greek frontier. Aircraft of VIII Air Corps and army artillery concentrated on destroying fortifications on both sides of the Rupel Pass in order to achieve a breakthrough to the Strimon valley and open the way to the Aegean. At the same time units of the Luftwaffe attacked traffic junctions and military installations in rear areas of the East Macedonian Army.[17] In spite of this intensive preparation, the formations of XVIII Mountain Corps achieved only modest success, although the Greek forces were hardly able to defend themselves against German air attacks.[18] The Royal Air Force repeatedly attacked cities and military installations in the German deployment area in Bulgaria but, because of its numerical inferiority, was not able to interfere seriously with the German advance.[19] Because of the strength of the Greek fortifications, the attacks of VIII Air Corps proved relatively ineffective. Only with the help of artillery and anti-aircraft guns were the Germans able to penetrate the Greek defence system at a few points. This enabled 5th Mountain Division, though with heavy casualties, to circumvent the Rupel Pass near Petrich and attempt to open it from the south. The hard fighting caused the commander of the division to remark sarcastically: 'It seems the Greeks are prepared to fight to the last man for England's sake.'[20]

The commander of XVIII Mountain Corps undoubtedly found the progress achieved by 72nd Division, which was attempting to break through to the Strimon valley via Serrai, equally unsatisfactory. After two days of fighting, the spearheads of the division were still twenty kilometres north-east of the town. XXX Army Corps with two infantry divisions, on the other hand, was at first more successful east of the Nestos. On 6 April units of the corps were able to cut the rail line between Komotini and Xanthi. After the fall of both towns on 7 and 8 April, the defenders withdrew across the Nestos, which at that point formed the eastern end of the Metaxas line.[21] Greek resistance along this natural obstacle was, however, so strong that the Germans were not able to advance further west until 9 April.[22]

While the German advance on the left flank, along the frontier between Greece and Bulgaria, was slow and difficult, units of XVIII Mountain Corps on the right wing of the attack were more successful. As early as 6 April 2nd

---

[17] Deichmann, 'Balkanfeldzug des VIII. Fliegerkorps', 18 ff., BA-MA RL 8/46; *PWT*, Middle East I, Hist (B) 3, No. 61 (6 Apr. 1941), 25; Papagos, *Griechenland*, 110. VIII Air Corps had more than 400 aircraft at its disposal in Bulgaria to support the attack of 12th Army. Cf. Gundelach, *Luftwaffe im Mittelmeer*, 172.

[18] AOK 12, Ia, KTB, evening reports (6, 7, 8 Apr. 1941), BA-MA RH 20-12/62; AOK 12, Ic, Verhör von Kriegsgefangenen [interrogation of prisoners of war] (8 Apr. 1941), BA-MA RH 20-12/397.

[19] Meister, 'Der Einsatz des VIII. Fliegerkorps', Teil I, 30, BA-MA RL 8/237.

[20] 5. Geb.Div., Fü.Abt., KTB, 7 Apr. 1941, p. 39, BA-MA RH 28-5/1. On the fighting cf. Buchner, 'Metaxas-Linie', 727–8. Between 6 and 10 Apr. 1941 XVIII Mountain Corps lost 480 men dead, 1,750 wounded, and 70 missing. Cf. AOK 12, Abt. IVb, progress report on the campaign in the south-east (16 June 1941), BA-MA RH 20-12/356.

[21] Cf. OKH/army general staff/Op.Abt., situation report (6 Apr. 1941), 2, BA-MA M VII e 17; Papagos, *Griechenland*, 111. Some of the 'Nestos' Brigade located there retreated to Alexandroupolis: *PWT*, Middle East I, Hist (B) 3, No. 73 (8 Apr. 1941), 30.

[22] AOK 12, Ia, KTB, evening report (9 Apr. 1941), BA-MA RH 20-12/62. According to this report only the advance units of XXX Army Corps reached the west bank.

Armoured Division, with Luftwaffe support, captured Strumitsa in Yugoslavia and was able to repel attacks by units of the Yugoslav Third Army Group, which had been brought up from Shtip.[23] Those who had not been taken prisoner attempted in the following days to cross the Vardar (Axios) to the west and establish a new line of defence there.[24] The armoured units of XVIII Mountain Corps then turned south and reached the frontier between Greece and Yugoslavia near Lake Doiran on the second day of the attack.[25] This surprising development seriously endangered the East Macedonian front, as no natural obstacles now separated the attackers from Salonika. Lieutenant-General Nikos Bakopoulos, the commander-in-chief of the East Macedonian Army, decided to place motorized forces (the Greek 19th Division) between Lake Doiran and the Axios to prevent the threatening encirclement of his army. However, the Germans had already shifted the main weight of their air support to the right wing of XVIII Mountain Corps and, by means of constant air attacks, were able to prevent the Greek troops south-west of Lake Doiran from establishing defensive positions in time.[26] For this reason the Greek 19th Division, which was still not completely assembled, came under heavy attack by 2nd Armoured Division and had to withdraw with heavy losses in the direction of the Strimon valley.[27] The demolition of the bridges over the Axios by units of the British armoured brigade prevented a German drive against the Aliakmon line, but the way to Salonika was now open. By the evening of 8 April advance units of 2nd Armoured Division were only a few kilometres from the city.[28]

As no Greek units were available around Salonika to stop the German advance, Bakopoulos considered withdrawing his army to the south and subsequently evacuating it by sea. But, in agreement with the Greek commander-in-chief, this plan was abandoned as neither sufficient ships nor adequate air cover was available. It was also argued that the operation would have no chance of success because there was no preventing 2nd Armoured Division from pushing further east.[29] Moreover, the Greek generals were aware that the Yugoslav troops east and west of the Vardar were no longer able to attack the division on the flanks or in the rear.[30] On 8 April the Greek army command in

---

[23] Halder, *Diaries*, ii. 860 (6 Apr. 1941); AOK 12, Ia, KTB, evening report (6 Apr. 1941), BA-MA RH 20-12/62.

[24] They were supposed to stop the advance of XXXX Motorized Army Corps: Operationstagebuch des jugoslawischen Heeres, 10 (7 Apr. 1941), BA-MA RH 20-2/1085.

[25] AOK 12, Ia, KTB, evening report (7 Apr. 1941), BA-MA RH 20-12/62; OKH/army general staff/Op.Abt., situation report (7 Apr. 1941), 2, BA-MA M VII e 17.

[26] On the shift of the main effort: Deichman, 'Balkanfeldzug des VIII. Fliegerkorps', 24, BA-MA RL 8/46; on the transfer of the Greek 19th Motorized Division cf. Papagos, *Griechenland*, 115, and *PWT*, Middle East I, Hist (B) 3, No. 64 (7 Apr. 1941), p. 27.

[27] Papagos, *Griechenland*, 118–19.

[28] Long, *Greece, Crete and Syria*, 42; *Hellēnikos stratos*, iv. 203–4. The British armoured units retreated west to Edessa.

[29] *Hellēnikos stratos*, iv. 82, 201–2.

[30] Operationstagebuch des jugosl. Heeres, 20 (8 Apr. 1941), BA-MA RH 20-2/1085, and 'Überblick über die Operationen des jugoslawischen Heeres', Teil I, 286.

Athens and Bakopoulos therefore decided that their troops east of the Axios should remain in their positions and offer to surrender. After German troops entered Salonika, the surrender took place the following day.[31] All Greek forces east of the Axios, about 60,000 men, laid down their weapons.

The Wehrmacht high command ordered that the captured Greek soldiers should be treated well. The Greek police were even permitted to bear arms while on duty, as the Germans did not want to leave large forces of their own in the conquered areas.[32] Out of consideration for Turkish reactions, Hitler ordered that Bulgarian units, which could have been used as occupation forces, should not enter north-east Greece for the time being.[33]

In retrospect, it may be asked why Twelfth Army command was prepared to pay such a high price for victory over the Greek forces in eastern Macedonia while it was possible to reach positions behind and on the flanks of the Metaxas line quickly and with relatively small losses.[34] Certainly the attackers did not expect that the Greeks, who had been fighting the Italians in Albania for months, would offer such fierce resistance in that area. And the relative ineffectiveness of the air attacks on the Greek fortifications could not be foreseen.[35] German ability to outflank the Metaxas line depended largely on the strength of Yugoslav resistance in the south-eastern part of their country. Twelfth Army command could not assume from the very beginning that the Yugoslav forces there could be decisively defeated and that it would then be possible to turn south. The lack of agreement among the Greek, Yugoslav, and British military leaders was an additional factor hastening the collapse of the Yugoslav defence.[36]

While the operations of XVIII and XXX corps were aimed at reaching the Aegean quickly and establishing a good position for an attack on the British and Greek forces along the Aliakmon river, the task of XXXX (mot.) Army Corps was to smash all resistance in the south-eastern part of Yugoslavia and thus take pressure off the Italians in Albania. At first the commander of the corps, which began its advance on the morning of 6 April, intended to reach the main road from Skopje to Bitola in order to prevent an organized defence by Yugoslav units in the Third Army Group. For that purpose the corps concentrated its attack in the areas assigned to 9th Armoured Division and SS Leibstandarte Adolf Hitler, which were to cross the frontier near Kyustendil and capture Skopje. Other divisions of XXXX Corps were to advance via Shtip and capture the town of Prilep.

---

[31] Memorandum by Kramarz (11 Apr. 1941), 22, PA, Büro St.S., Griechenland, ii. Cf. also Koliopoulos, *Greece 1935–1941*, 264.

[32] Memorandum by Kramarz (11 Apr. 1941), 23, PA, Büro St.S., Griechenland, ii. On the surrender cf. Creveld, *Balkan*, 159; on the treatment of the Greeks cf. Halder, *Diaries*, ii. 865 (9 Apr. 1941).

[33] Ibid. 867 (10 Apr. 1941).

[34] Hepp, 'Die 12. Armee', 207.

[35] Operation experience report, VIII. Fl.K., Südosten (10 May 1941), 14, BA-MA RL 8/242.

[36] Churchill, *Second World War*, iii. 195–6; 1. Skl., KTB, Teil A, 99 (8 Apr. 1941), BA-MA RM 7/23.

In spite of energetic resistance, the German armoured units succeeded in penetrating deep into Yugoslav territory on the first day of the attack.[37] The arrival of a Yugoslav reserve division in the area north-east of Skopje with orders to close the resulting breach could not prevent the Germans from capturing the city the next day.[38] With similar swiftness units of 73rd Infantry Division reached Shtip, and on 8 April advance units threatened Prilep, only fifty kilometres from the frontier between Yugoslavia and Greece.[39] With this rapid advance XXXX (mot.) Army Corps was able to eliminate most of the units forming the east front of the Yugoslav Third Army Group or force them back across the Vardar to the west. German observers believed that signs of disintegration were already becoming evident in parts of the Yugoslav army: while Serbian units continued to fight, Macedonian and Croatian soldiers surrendered in increasing numbers.[40]

The quick successes of the army units in southern Yugoslavia were also due to the constant support of VIII Air Corps, which was able to achieve air supremacy on the first day of the campaign by uninterrupted attacks on Yugoslav airfields. Richthofen's Geschwader then concentrated on demoralizing Yugoslav troops by strafing columns, supply installations, and staff headquarters.[41] Through the Greek high command, the Yugoslav government requested British air support at least for the area around Skopje. But, as had already been the case in the area of the East Macedonian Army, the Royal Air Force was able to provide little help because of the limited number of aircraft at its disposal.[42] The units of 9th Armoured Division were thus able to exploit their success around Skopje and secure their breakthrough with drives on a broad front to the north and west. The remainder of the forces from the Yugoslav Third Army Group then withdrew in the direction of Montenegro and Serbia.[43]

South of Skopje, motorized units of XXXX Army Corps pushed on to Bitola on 10 April, captured Florina in Greece, and threatened Vevi the next day. There, however, they encountered determined resistance from Greek and British forces, which prevented their further advance to the south.[44] This halt

---

[37] On 6 Apr. 1941 9th Armoured Division reached Stracin, east of Skopje: AOK 12, Ia, KTB, evening report (6 Apr. 1941), BA-MA RH 20-12/62.
[38] OKH/army general staff/Op.Abt., situation report (8 Apr. 1941), 3, BA-MA M VII e 17. On the advance of XXXX Motorized Army Corps cf. Operationstagebuch des jugoslawischen Heeres, 4 (6 Apr. 1941), BA-MA RH 20-2/1085.
[39] AOK 12, Ia, KTB, evening report (8 Apr. 1941), BA-MA RH 20-12/62; Halder, *Diaries*, ii. 860 (6 Apr. 1941). Most of 73rd Inf. Div. and the Leibstandarte were located south-west of Shtip.
[40] On the fighting: 'Überblick über die Operationen des jugoslawischen Heeres', Part I, 282.
[41] Report Gen.Kdo. VIII. Fl.K., Ic, 1 (30 Apr. 1941), BA-MA RL 8/245; Deichmann, 'Balkanfeldzug des VIII. Fliegerkorps', 22 ff., BA-MA RL 8/46.
[42] Operationstagebuch des jugoslawischen Heeres, 8, 10 (7 Apr. 1941), BA-MA RH 20-2/1085.
[43] Ibid. 38–9 (11 Apr. 1941). Cf. also Matl, 'Jugoslawien im Zweiten Weltkrieg', 101.
[44] AOK 12, Ia, KTB, evening report (10 Apr. 1941), BA-MA RH 20-12/62; Halder, *Diaries*, ii. 866 (10 Apr. 1941).

was also due to Hitler's order to divert strong units from 9th Armoured Division and the Leibstandarte to the west towards Albania in order to establish contact with the Italian forces there as soon as possible.[45] Against the wishes of Halder, who would have preferred to concentrate all available troops to continue the advance to the south, parts of XXXX Army Corps fought their way to the Albanian frontier on 10 and 11 April.[46] The manœuvre enabled them to attack from the rear and partially eliminate Yugoslav forces of the Third Army Group which had been engaging the Italian forces in eastern Albania near the frontier since 7 April. Only in the area of Prizren could the German push westward be stopped temporarily. But this required the withdrawal of Yugoslav forces of the Third Army Group, which had penetrated Albania from the north. Nevertheless, the Yugoslavs continued their attacks with their remaining forces north of Scutari, without, however, being able seriously to threaten the city. Because of the German successes in southern Yugoslavia on 8 April, Halder no longer expected the Italians in Albania actually to be endangered.[47] Such a development was all the more improbable as the German advances prevented any co-operation between the Yugoslav troops and the Greek and British forces.[48]

After the East Macedonian Army had been eliminated and serious resistance was no longer expected in southern Yugoslavia, the German attack concentrated on the Greek and British forces in central Macedonia. XVIII Mountain Corps was to cross the Axios, push the W Force back over the Vermion Mountains, and then proceed along the coast to Larisa in the Thessalian plain. By 12 April motorized units of the corps were near Edessa. As the British covering forces had already withdrawn to the west, they did not encounter significant resistance. In the following days the Germans turned south with the aim of circumventing Mount Olympus in the east. Difficulties in maintaining supplies of fuel, however, prevented a rapid attack, especially in the armoured units of XVIII Corps.[49]

XXXX Motorized Corps, on the other hand, was to attack the Aliakmon line from the north and also drive past Mount Olympus into the Thessalian plain. The attacks by these large units had two decisive aims: to cut off the Greek forces in Albania from their rear communications and thus make possible an Italian attack against Greece from the north-west, and to encircle

---

[45] Halder, *Diaries*, ii. 865 (9 Apr. 1941). On the advance across the frontier between Greece and Yugoslavia cf. also Richter, *Griechenland*, 108.

[46] Halder, *Diaries*, ii. 865 (9 Apr. 1941).

[47] Ibid. 863–4 (8 Apr. 1941). On the fighting between the Yugoslavs and Italians cf. Operationstagebuch des jugoslawischen Heeres, 19 (8 Apr. 1941), BA-MA RH 20-2/1085, and Loi, *Jugoslavia*, 74–98. Originally the Italians had considered withdrawing their troops and abandoning Scutari. Cf. Cervi, *Hollow Legions*, 268.

[48] Churchill, *Second World War*, iii. 197.

[49] AOK 12, Ia, KTB, evening report (10 Apr. 1941); morning report (11 Apr. 1941), BA-MA RH 20-12/62. On the advance of XVIII Mountain Corps cf. 'Balkanfeldzug der 12. Armee', map of 11 Apr. 1941, BA-MA 75090/1.

the W Force.⁵⁰ Hitler attached the greatest importance to preventing the British from withdrawing from Greece by annihilating all their forces in the north.⁵¹

The troops of the Leibstandarte Adolf Hitler were, however, evidently too weak to break through the Greek and British defensive positions south of Florina. The attempt to push on in the west in the direction of the frontier between Greece and Albania on 11 April was also unsuccessful.⁵² For this reason the command of XXXX (mot.) Army Corps was forced to bring up 9th Armoured Division, whose advance units arrived in Bitola on 12 April. Field Marshal List also ordered elements of an additional division (Kleist's 5th Armoured Division) to be brought up via Niš. Halder estimated that it would take several days for these units to join XXXX Corps.⁵³ Because of the poor roads near the frontier between Greece and Yugoslavia, the organization of an efficient supply-system and the construction of suitable airfields proved to be difficult.⁵⁴ But List insisted that effective air support was indispensable for a successful attack.

Until the arrival of the German forces in Florina, the Greek and British units in central Macedonia and Albania had only been involved in small engagements. Papagos, the Greek commander-in-chief, had launched an attack against the Italians on the west Macedonian front on 7 April, but his troops made very little progress, although Yugoslav units attacked at the same time towards Elbasan. But they too were unable to achieve a decisive breakthrough. Because of the unfavourable developments in southern Yugoslavia, Papagos broke off the attack of the Greek divisions the next day.⁵⁵

The German advance towards Florina and the appearance of units of XVIII Corps east of the Axios constituted a serious threat to the Allied forces in central Macedonia. As the German intention to encircle the W Force was clear, Wilson and Papagos, the British and Greek military leaders, decided to partially regroup their forces, the larger part of which were still in Albania (the West Macedonian and Epirus Armies with approximately fourteen divisions) and between Mount Olympus and Vevi (the W Force with four and a half divisions). Around the lakes in northern Greece there was thus a gap between

---

⁵⁰ *KTB OKW* i. 379 (13 Apr. 1941) and AOK 12, Ia, KTB, evening report (10 Apr. 1941), BA-MA RH 20-12/62.

⁵¹ *Hitler's War Directives*, No. 27, pp. 65 ff. (13 Apr. 1941); report Gen.Kdo. VIII. Fl.k., Ic, 2 (30 Apr. 1941), BA-MA RL 8/245. A corresponding order was given to 12th Army headquarters on 12 Apr. 1941: OKH/army general staff/Op.Abt. (I) No. 1018/41 g.Kdos. (12 Apr. 1941), to AOK 2 and AOK 12 (p. 156), BA-MA RH 6/v.3.

⁵² OKH/army general staff/Op.Abt., situation report (12 Apr. 1941), 11, BA-MA M VII e 17. Cf. also Long, *Greece, Crete and Syria*, 58.

⁵³ 5th Armoured Division (minus one regiment) was withdrawn from Armoured Group 1 and reached the area around Bitola only on 15 Apr. 1941: Pz.Gr. 1, KTB (11 Apr. 1941), BA-MA RH 21-1/40 D.

⁵⁴ Wisshaupt, 'Balkanfeldzug', 32, BA-MA RH 20-12/129.

⁵⁵ Long, *Greece, Crete and Syria*, 40; Cervi, *Hollow Legions*, 269, 277; Montanari, *Grecia*, i. 777–8. Italian attacks on the Greek positions had been repelled. Cf. *Deutschland im zweiten Weltkrieg*, i. 546.

the main Allied forces that was inadequately secured, primarily occupied by troops of the West Macedonian Army. In their intention to reinforce these units significantly, the British and Greeks were seriously hampered by the poor roads, the lack of transport on the Greek side, and the expected attacks by VIII Air Corps. As early as 6 April the Luftwaffe had demonstrated by a heavy attack on Piraeus, the most important Greek port, that the Royal Air Force in Greece hardly represented a serious danger.[56] But in the following days unfavourable weather prevented German aircraft from disrupting the movements of Allied troops. Moreover, Richthofen's Geschwader were not able to mount night attacks.[57] For this reason the British and Greeks succeeded in massing troops south of Florina and were thus able to stop the German thrust southward until 12 April.[58]

Wilson and Papagos, however, realized that the forces at their disposal could not guarantee a lasting success, especially if the Germans were able to bring up additional armoured units and construct more bases near Bitola for the close-support aircraft of VIII Air Corps. Moreover, the concentration of British and Greek forces south of Florina had seriously weakened the central Macedonian sector of the front. For parts of the Australian divisions envisaged for the W Force had not reached the Aliakmon sector and were still moving from Athens to northern Greece. The Greek high command therefore decided, in agreement with Wilson, to withdraw all troops to the line Mount Olympus–Servia–Lake Prespa. This move was intended to enable the West Macedonian Army to withdraw in an orderly fashion from Albania to the upper Aliakmon valley. The Allied leaders intended to establish a new, shorter defensive line there from Mount Olympus around the bend in the Aliakmon river to Albania. The Epirus Army was ordered to occupy the left flank of this shorter, east–west front.[59]

The necessity of a withdrawal from Albania, however, not only confronted the Greek military leaders with logistical and organizational difficulties, but also seriously affected the morale of the troops on the Albanian front and their officers. For months they had resisted the Italian invaders and even pushed them far back into Albania. Now they were most unwilling to leave the field to the enemy without a fight. They therefore attempted to hold the Albanian front until German units threatened them from the rear, in order to demonstrate that only the German advance had forced them to evacuate the conquered areas.[60] Several Greek commanders on the Albanian front actually

---

[56] The port was largely destroyed: *PWT*, Middle East I, Hist (B) 3, No. 74, p. 31 (8 Apr. 1941).
[57] Operation experience reports, VIII. Fl.K., Südosten, 66, BA-MA RL 8/242. There was no equipment for night flights at the forward airfields.
[58] *PWT*, Middle East I, Hist (B) 3, No. 206, p. 89 (26 Apr. 1941). Cf. also Cruickshank, *Greece 1940–1941*, 144–5.
[59] Long, *Greece, Crete and Syria*, 46. On 12 Apr. 1941 a division of the Epirus Army was already marching towards the Metsovon pass. On the planned retreat cf. Butler, *Strategy*, ii. 456.
[60] Koliopoulos, *Greece 1935–1941*, 265; Cervi, *Hollow Legions*, 279.

argued that a withdrawal was no longer possible.[61] For this reason Papagos ordered the West Macedonian and Epirus Armies to retreat from Albania only on 12 April, when the German forces had already penetrated northern Greece.[62]

In the meantime the units of the W Force had already begun to occupy their new positions to protect this retreat. While the Empire units reached their assigned areas in the southern foothills of Mount Olympus and near Servia relatively quickly, the movement of Greek units to the area east of the upper Aliakmon valley was delayed significantly because of bad weather. When Wilson gave the order to withdraw the covering forces south of Vevi and transfer them to Grevena on the evening of 12 April, large parts of the Greek divisions (12th and 20th) could not reach their new positions on the Aliakmon in time.[63] They broke up during the march or were taken prisoner in the following days by units of 9th Armoured Division, which was able to break through the defile south of Florina and push on in the direction of Servia on the evening of 12 April. It was prevented from starting another drive to the south only by a lack of fuel and ammunition.[64]

Wilson's decision to carry out such a rapid withdrawal from the area around Florina was probably due to his fear that List's armoured formations might be able to encircle the entire W Force or at least the British parts of it in the west and thus prevent any withdrawal to the south. However, this step taken by the British commander-in-chief endangered the withdrawal of the West Macedonian divisions from the Albanian front. The passes on the upper Aliakmon, the only possibility of avoiding an encirclement, were secured only by weak Greek units of the W Force.

At first, however, the German armoured formations advanced along the road to Servia, took Ptolemais against considerable resistance by the British 1st Armoured Brigade, and reached the north bank of the Aliakmon near Servia on 14 April. There they found the well-prepared positions of the Australians, which they were not able to take in the following days in spite of intensive close support by the Luftwaffe. In the meantime the British 1st Armoured Brigade, facing the units of XXXX Motorized Army Corps, had withdrawn to Kalabaka.[65]

---

[61] Koliopoulos, *Greece 1935–1941*, 267. One such officer was Gen. Tsolakoglou, C.-in-C. of the West Macedonian Army.

[62] Papagos, *Griechenland*, 131; Playfair, *Mediterranean*, ii. 87. On the Italian planning for the advance cf. Montanari, *Grecia*, i. 780–8 (9th Army), 788–800 (11th Army).

[63] Tippelskirch, 'Balkanfeldzug', 63. According to Papagos (*Griechenland*, 133), the Greeks were informed of the British plans either too late (12th and 20th Divs.) or not at all (the cavalry div. south of Florina).

[64] Creveld, *Balkan*, 162. On the retreat of the Greek sections of W Force cf. *Hellēnikos stratos*, v. 76.

[65] AOK 12, Ia, KTB, evening reports (13 and 14 Apr. 1941), BA-MA RH 20-12/62. According to Long (*Greece, Crete and Syria*, 90), the British 3rd Armoured Regiment still had 6 out of 52 tanks.

At the same time another group of attackers, composed of soldiers from the Leibstandarte Adolf Hitler, forced their way into the upper Aliakmon valley after hard fighting with Greek units. With strong support from the Luftwaffe, German units also captured the passes east of the river and the towns of Neapolis and Grevena by 17 April. As mentioned above, troops of the Central and West Macedonian armies had not been able to defend these passes adequately and now attempted to escape through the foothills of Mount Olympus to the south-west.[66] Their aim was to establish contact with the divisions of the Epirus Army. Lack of supplies and unhindered attacks by the Luftwaffe, however, caused many of the retreating units to break up.[67]

With the capture of the upper Aliakmon valley, List was able to cut the line of retreat of the units of the West Macedonian Army still in the north and push them into the impassable Pindus Mountains. The German advance also frustrated the intention to establish a common Allied front at the Aliakmon bend, as troops could not be moved to the left flank fast enough. This development represented a serious danger for the Epirus Army, which began its retreat on 14 April, because German units were rapidly approaching the roads it would have to use to reach central Greece.[68]

Using armoured and mountain infantry units, XVIII Mountain Corps had been able to push New Zealand rearguard units at the eastern end of the Aliakmon front rapidly back to Katerini. And the first positions of the Australian–New Zealand divisions, now renamed the Anzac Corps, did not long withstand the German attacks east of Mount Olympus. On 17 April the German units reached the Tempe gorge on the lower Pinios.[69] At the same time a battle group of armoured and infantry units from the same corps was able to skirt Mount Olympus in the north-west from Katerini and advance to within twenty kilometres of the road from Servia to Larisa.[70]

This situation seemed to offer Twelfth Army the opportunity to encircle the Aliakmon front and the British expeditionary corps there as planned. The continued stubborn resistance of the British and Australians near Servia now had no purpose, as the Germans were threatening their positions from the

---

[66] *Hellēnikos stratos*, v. 76. Units of the German 9th Armoured Division had pushed on to Grevena on 16 Apr. 1941: AOK 12, Ia, KTB, evening report (16 Apr. 1941), BA-MA RH 20-12/62. On the use of the Luftwaffe cf. Bericht Gen.Kdo. VIII. Fl.K., Ic (30 Apr. 1941), 2, BA-MA RL 8/245.

[67] Koliopoulos, *Greece 1935–1941*, 269–70. Isolated groups reached the British positions or withdrew to Kalabaka. Cf. *Hellēnikos stratos*, v. 76.

[68] *PWT*, Middle East I, Hist (B) 3, No. 105, P. 45 (14 Apr. 1941); 'Überblick über die Operationen des griechischen Heeres', Teil II, 173. On 20 Apr. 1941 SS Leibstandarte Adolf Hitler reached the Metsovon pass. On the Greek retreat cf. also 'Der Krieg in Griechenland 1940–1941', 63 ff., Papers of Clemm von Hohenberg, BA-MA N 449/7.

[69] OKH/army general staff/Op.Abt., situation report (15 Apr. 1941), 20, BA-MA M VII e 17. The renaming of the Australian–New Zealand divisions as the Anzac Corps recalled the joint operations of 1915 on the Gallipoli peninsula in Turkey. Cf. Barclay, *Their Finest Hour*, 113.

[70] OKH/army general staff/Op.Abt., situation report (17 Apr. 1941), 25, BA-MA M VII e 17; 'Balkanfeldzug der 12. Armee', maps 14–18 Apr. 1941, BA-MA 75090/1.

rear. Wilson, the British commander-in-chief, had, however, recognized the German objectives in time and taken precautionary measures for a further withdrawal. He considered this all the more inevitable as no support could now be expected from the Greek divisions in the north-west. As early as 14 April, before the last British units had reached the south-western sector on the Aliakmon, he decided to order a retreat to positions at Thermopylae. On 16 April Papagos agreed to the British plans.[71]

Although most of the expeditionary corps was supposed to retreat at night (between 17 and 19 April) because of the danger of air attacks, many movements of covering and rearguard troops had to be carried out during the day to ensure the security of the retreating units. And because of the considerable distance (100 to 150 kilometres) not all transfers could take place at night. For this reason Wilson's troops were in danger of being annihilated by the Luftwaffe during their withdrawal to the south, especially as weather conditions no longer restricted the use of aircraft and only a few roads were available for the withdrawal.[72] The Royal Air Force was able to provide only limited protection: after a German attack on the airfield at Larisa, the British air command in Greece had decided to move its aircraft to Crete.[73] Under these very unfavourable conditions the British abandoned their positions and, moving in three groups, reached the new defence line at Thermopylae on 20 April.[74]

Armoured and mountain infantry units of XVIII Corps were then able to advance rapidly, taking Larisa on 19 April and eliminating New Zealand covering forces on the way south before moving on towards Farsala and Dhomokos in the following days.[75] While the German units around Servia were able to advance against the British rearguard only slowly because of the demolition of numerous bridges, units of 5th Armoured Division, which had now arrived, took Kalabaka on 19 April and approached Lamia one day later.[76] When advance detachments of this division started an attack towards Thermopylae from Lamia on 21 April, they were repulsed.[77]

Richthofen's Geschwader supported the German advance with numerous air attacks, but they were not able to disrupt the movements of the Anzac

[71] Butler, *Strategy*, ii. 456; Churchill, *Second World War*, iii. 199. According to Hinsley (*British Intelligence*, i. 409), Wilson received timely information from the British secret service regarding German plans to turn the flank of his troops in the east.

[72] Deichmann, 'Balkanfeldzug des VIII. Fliegerkorps', 35, BA-MA RL 8/46. On the retreat of the expeditionary corps cf. Long, *Greece, Crete and Syria*, 98 ff.

[73] Ibid. 83. On 16 Apr. 1941 the British still had 46 combat-ready aircraft in Greece. Cf. Gundelach, *Luftwaffe im Mittelmeer*, 182.

[74] Papagos, *Griechenland*, 140; Playfair, *Mediterranean*, ii. 91. A small part of the Empire troops withdrew to Volos.

[75] 'Balkanfeldzug der 12. Armee', maps 14–18 Apr. 1941, BA-MA 75090/1; OKH/army general staff/Op.Abt., situation report (22 Apr. 1941), 34, BA-MA M VII e 17.

[76] AOK 12, Ia, KTB, evening reports (19, 20 Apr. 1941), BA-MA RH 20-12/62. The demolitions carried out by the British led to considerable traffic congestion and long queues of German vehicles. Cf. Cruickshank, *Greece 1940–1941*, 148.

[77] Buchner, *Griechenland-Feldzug*, 184.

units, let alone annihilate the entire expeditionary corps. One reason for the Luftwaffe's lack of success was the shortage of fuel;[78] another was the skilful British use of camouflage and dispersed marching order to keep losses low. Moreover, Richthofen had shifted the focus of his attacks.[79] The frustration of British plans to evacuate troops from Greece, and not support for the army units, was now the main objective. The Empire troops had been able to avoid being encircled on the Aliakmon front, but Richthofen was determined to give them no opportunity to escape by sea.

On 14 April the British government had ordered the high command in Cairo to make preparations for a possible evacuation of the expeditionary corps.[80] Two days later, on his own initiative, General Papagos suggested that Wilson consider evacuating his troops in order to spare Greece further destruction. Churchill and Wavell thereupon stated that they did not wish to leave their forces in Greece against the will of the Greek government. In his capacity as commander-in-chief for the Middle East, Wavell then decided not to send any more supply-ships to the Aegean.[81]

Papagos's suggestion of a withdrawal of the British forces was certainly also due to the situation of the Greek armies in the north-west of the country. One day after the start of the retreat from Albania, the commander of the Epirus Army, General Pitsikas, urged his commander-in-chief to begin armistice negotiations with the Germans as soon as possible. Otherwise, he feared, the unity of the armed forces would be endangered. Papagos, however, refused to surrender as long as the expeditionary corps was still in Greece. The king and the government supported him.[82] The Greek commanders repeatedly appealed in vain to Papagos to prevent the disintegration of their units and their possible capture by the Italians. Finally, without waiting for the approval of the Greek government, General Tsolakoglou, who had declared himself spokesman for the commanders on the Albanian front, sent a request for an armistice to the Germans on 20 April. The next day sixteen Greek divisions which had reached the area around Yannina surrendered to the German Twelfth Army. The Italian forces in Albania were now also able to reach the Greek frontier.[83]

---

[78] According to Deichmann ('Balkanfeldzug des VIII. Fliegerkorps', 34, BA-MA RL 8/46), the allocation of tanker vehicles even led to arguments between the chief of staff of 12th Army and Richthofen.

[79] Long, *Greece, Crete and Syria*, 130.

[80] *PWT*, Middle East I, Hist (B) 3, No. 116, pp. 50–1 (16 Apr. 1941). The expected surrender of Yugoslavia also played a role in this decision.

[81] Ibid., No. 118, pp. 51–2 (16, 17 Apr. 1941). Cf. also Woodward, *British Foreign Policy*, i. 551. Gen. Blamey, commander of the Anzac Corps, also agreed to the evacuation. Cf. Butler, *Strategy*, ii. 456.

[82] Koliopoulos, *Greece 1935–1941*, 271 ff.; Papagos, *Griechenland*, 141, 180.

[83] OKH/army general staff/OQu IV-Abt Fr.H.Ost (I) No. 1558/41 geh., situation report east, No. 23/41 (23 Apr. 1941), BA-MA RH 20-2/137; AOK 12, Ia, KTB, evening report (21 Apr. 1941), BA-MA RH 20-12/62. As had been done with the East Macedonian Army, the Greek soldiers were disarmed and released. On the Italian advance cf. Cervi, *Hollow Legions*, 287.

During the surrender negotiations considerable differences emerged between the Italian and the German negotiators and between Field Marshal List and the Wehrmacht high command. Tsolakoglou had demonstratively directed his request for an armistice to the German side and had made no mention of Italy. The commander-in-chief of Twelfth Army and Hitler at first accepted this procedure. List even called upon General Cavallero, the Italian commander-in-chief in Albania, to halt his advance in order not to endanger the armistice negotiations with the Greeks.[84] Cavallero reported this unpardonable insult to Italian honour, as he saw it, to the Duce in Rome. After Mussolini had complained to Hitler, the latter sent General Jodl to Greece to ensure Italian participation in the armistice.[85] List protested against this action, as it represented a humiliation for him as well as for the Greeks. His protests were, however, unavailing. On 23 April, without List but in the presence of Italian military representatives, Jodl accepted the final Greek capitulation in Salonika. To avoid any further offence to Italian arms, the Wehrmacht high command issued guidelines for press and military attachés forbidding any mention of these events.[86]

The end of Greek resistance had serious consequences on the Greek and British side. The hopeless situation of his country had caused Prime Minister Koryzis to commit suicide on 18 April. Only after repeated attempts was the king able to form a new government under Emanuel Tsouderos, with the aim of continuing Greek resistance from Crete.[87]

The political and military developments on the Greek side naturally led to a process of rethinking among the British. Shortly before Tsolakoglou's capitulation became known, Wavell and Wilson were still planning to hold Thermopylae as long as possible. They assigned to the Greek forces the task of securing the south-western sector of the defence line; the Anzac troops would occupy the eastern part on both sides of Molos as far as the sea. The British 1st Armoured Brigade, weakened by considerable losses, set up its defensive positions on the coast near Atalandi.[88] The British plan to resist energetically a further German advance at Thermopylae had two objectives: to secure the evacuation (Operation Demon) and to halt for as long as possible the German drive to the south. The British military leaders considered the continuation of resistance in Greece to be important in order to keep the Luftwaffe away from the North African theatre.[89]

---

[84] Rintelen's report to foreign minister, 23 Apr. 1941, PA, Büro St.S., Griechenland, ii. 57; KTB OKW i. 383 (21 Apr. 1941). On the Italian advance cf. OKH/army general staff/Abt. Fr. Heere West (IV), situation report west, No. 471 (25 Apr. 1941), BA-MA RH 2/v. 1497.

[85] Warlimont, *Headquarters*, 130–1; *DGFP* D xii, No. 379, p. 601 (22 Apr. 1941).

[86] Memorandum by Kramarz (28 Apr. 1941), 77, PA, Büro St.S., Griechenland, ii. On the surrender cf. Hillgruber, *Strategie*, 466–7; for the Italian viewpoint cf. Montanari, *Grecia*, i. 809–22.

[87] *Hellēnikos stratos*, v. 238–9.

[88] *PWT*, Middle East I, Hist (B) 3, No. 149, pp. 64–5 (19 Apr. 1941). Cf. also Long, *Greece, Crete and Syria*, 141.

[89] *PWT*, Middle East I, Hist (B) 3, No. 130, p. 56 (18 Apr. 1941).

After the Greek leaders had indicated that they would no longer be able to support the expeditionary corps and would only help with the evacuation, Wavell and Wilson decided to defend Thermopylae only as long as might be necessary to carry out Operation Demon.[90] It was important to start evacuation measures early, as the Luftwaffe had established airfields near Larisa and was able not only to mount heavy attacks from there against the Empire troops at Thermopylae, but also to attack British ships with dive-bombers.[91] The RAF inflicted heavy losses on the Luftwaffe during various German attacks on airfields in Athens on 19 and 20 April, but its own losses were so high that Longmore withdrew all remaining British aircraft from Greece. The RAF was instructed to cover Operation Demon only from Crete and Egypt.[92] Under these conditions it was certainly no understatement when the British calculated that they would be able to evacuate only 30 per cent of their troops and no equipment from Greece.[93]

The Luftwaffe attacks on concentrations of Allied ships even before the start of the evacuation seemed to confirm this pessimistic prediction. On 21 and 22 April alone, Richthofen's aircraft sank twenty-three British and Greek ships in the Aegean.[94] In agreement with the commander of the evacuation, Vice-Admiral Pridham-Wippell, Wilson then planned to load the ships only at night. After the battles of the past fourteen days, the British were aware that the Luftwaffe was not able to mount night attacks. The ships of the Royal Navy therefore had to arrive in Greek ports around eleven o'clock at night and leave by three the next morning in order to cross the thirty-seventh parallel in darkness. South of that point the Royal Air Force, operating from bases in Egypt and Crete, was able to protect them.[95] At first Wilson and Pridham-Wippell planned to start the evacuation from ports on the coast of Attica on 28 April. But the incessant Luftwaffe attacks and the Greek capitulation forced them to bring the date forward to 24 April. Moreover, more areas along the eastern and southern coasts of the Peloponnese were to be used in order to decentralize Operation Demon and shorten the distance for the ships.[96]

The ability of the British expeditionary corps to keep enemy units away from the loading-areas as long as possible and to disengage unnoticed was of decisive importance for the success of the evacuation. The New Zealanders

---

[90] Ibid., No. 157, p. 68 (20 Apr. 1941); Cervi, *Hollow Legions*, 286. The final Greek and British decision to evacuate was taken on 21 Apr. 1941. Cf. Butler, *Strategy*, ii. 456.

[91] Report Gen.Kdo. VIII. Fl.K., Ic (30 Apr. 1941), 3, BA-MA RL 8/245; *PWT*, Middle East I, Hist (B) 3, No. 157, p. 68 (20 Apr. 1941).

[92] The last British aircraft left Greece on 24 Apr. 1941: *PWT*, Middle East I, Hist (B) 3, No. 162, pp. 69–70 (21 Apr.), and No. 195, p. 84 (24 Apr. 1941). Cf. also Gundelach, *Luftwaffe im Mittelmeer*, 187.

[93] Cruickshank, *Greece 1940–1941*, 149.

[94] Macintyre, *Battle*, 61; Cunningham, *A Sailor's Odyssey*, 352.

[95] *PWT*, Middle East I, Hist (B) 3, No. 193, p. 83 (24 Apr. 1941); Cunningham, *A Sailor's Odyssey*, 353.

[96] Wilson's order to evacuate, 23 Apr. 1941: Long, *Greece, Crete and Syria*, 143, 151; *PWT*, Middle East I, Hist (B) 3, No. 190, p. 81 (24 Apr. 1941).

and Australians were in fact able to hold the Germans at Thermopylae until their planned withdrawal date of 24 April. The 5th Armoured Division in particular had attempted to force a breakthrough near Molos. Only by using mixed formations of armour, infantry, and mountain infantry were the Germans able to push the Anzac troops back to the south end of the Thermopylae pass on 24 April. In the meantime Wilson had been able to withdraw most of his units towards Thebes or to collection-areas on the coast. The Germans fought only the rearguard.[97] The sending of fast German groups via Euboea in a thrust from Khalkis to cut the retreat route of the Anzac units therefore failed to achieve any operationally significant results.[98]

The British covering forces around Khalkis were able to stop the Germans until most of the Empire troops and passed through the city and moved on to the south-east. Because of the numerous demolitions along the road from Molos to Athens, units of 5th Armoured Division reached Thebes only on the evening of 25 April and encountered the last rearguard of the expeditionary corps near Erithrai not far from the capital the next day.[99]

To defeat the British troops, who had been able to escape all previous attempts to encircle them, the German military leaders planned to occupy the isthmus of Corinth with airborne units. This operation was intended to prevent a further withdrawal of the expeditionary corps to the Peloponnese. The Germans also hoped to capture the Corinthian Canal undamaged and thus keep the oil-supply route from Romania to Italy open.[100] The order from the Wehrmacht high command of 23 April to capture the isthmus with airborne forces did not, however, meet with the approval of all German commanders in Greece. While List believed that the operation would have a positive influence on the future course of the fighting, Richthofen thought that it would impair his ability to attack concentrations of British ships, as the necessary additional supply-flights would reduce the already limited logistical capacity of his air corps.[101] Göring, however, supported List, and in agreement with Twelfth Army command the operation was set for the morning of 26 April.[102]

Air Fleet Four transferred the necessary paratroop units from Plovdiv in Bulgaria to Larisa in order to have them as close to the objective as possible on the day of the attack.[103] On 25 April several attacks by German dive-bombers

---

[97] On the fighting at Thermopylae cf. AOK 12, Ia, KTB, evening report (24 Apr. 1941), BA-MA RH 20-12/62. On the British retreat cf. OKH/army general staff/OQu IV-Abt. Fr. Heere Ost (I) No. 1558/41 geh., situation report east, No. 23/41 (23 Apr. 1941), BA-MA RH 20-2/137.

[98] Spaeter, *Brandenburger*, 133. The group consisted largely of motor-cycle riflemen.

[99] *Hellēnikos stratos*, v. 262.

[100] AOK 12/Ia (23 Apr. 1941), BA-MA RH 20-12/105. Cf. Also Götzel, 'Korinth', 202.

[101] AOK 12/Ia (23, 24 Apr. 1941) (see previous n.). Cf. also Gundelach, *Luftwaffe im Mittelmeer*, 191.

[102] Deichmann, 'Balkanfeldzug des VIII. Fliegerkorps', 47, BA-MA RL 8/46. According to Deichmann, Göring's support was decisive for the carrying out of the operation.

[103] In Plovdiv parts of 7th Air Division were standing by. In addition to these units, one reinforced paratroop regiment, which was to carry out the operation, was transferred. Cf. Gundelach, *Luftwaffe im Mittelmeer*, 191.

of VIII Air Corps almost completely destroyed British anti-aircraft defences near Corinth. Wilson was left with only two weak battalions to defend the isthmus.[104] Nevertheless, the German paratroops suffered considerable losses when they captured the positions of the British Empire troops the next day. The attempt to take the only bridge over the canal intact failed: it was demolished at the last minute.[105] After the conclusion of the operation around Corinth on 26 April, only remnants of the expeditionary corps were still north of the canal. Most of its units had already reached the Peloponnese or had been evacuated from various ports during the previous two nights.[106] Even the units still north of Corinth were able to reach the loading-areas in southern Attica without difficulty and were then evacuated.[107]

Although Richthofen had known since 25 April that the British were waiting to be evacuated in collection-areas near the coast, in the following days his aircraft were not able to disrupt Operation Demon. The loading-places were too widely scattered, and the soldiers of the expeditionary corps camouflaged themselves too well during the day. By 1 May more than 50,000 of the approximately 62,000 men of the expeditionary corps had been picked up by ships of the Royal Navy.[108] Compared with the original pessimistic predictions, this was a highly satisfactory result, even considering the loss of all equipment and heavy weapons.

During the operation the Germans were only twice able to interfere seriously with the evacuation. On 27 April Richthofen's aircraft sighted and sank at the thirty-seventh parallel three ships that had left Navplion too late.[109] And on 28 April German advance units reached the evacuation port of Kalamata and, although unable to capture the town at first, prevented the embarkation of several thousand soldiers.[110]

On the previous day German armoured units had taken Athens and crossed the isthmus of Corinth, using an improvised bridge. At the same time, the Leibstandarte Adolf Hitler, coming from Arta, reached the Gulf of Patras,

---

[104] *Hellēnikos stratos*, v. 261; Long, *Greece, Crete and Syria*, 153, 166.

[105] The canal remained impassable until the middle of May: Götzel, 'Korinth', 203. German losses were 63 dead, 158 wounded, and 16 missing: battle report, XI. Fl.K., Einsatz Kreta (11 June 1941), BA-MA RL 33/98.

[106] Pridham-Wippell's ships evacuated over 16,000 men in the first two days of the evacuation. Cf. *Hellēnikos stratos*, v. 261 ff.; Cunningham, *A Sailor's Odyssey*, 353.

[107] Long, *Greece, Crete and Syria*, 165. 6 British light cruisers, 20 destroyers, 7 other warships, 19 transport ships, and numerous smaller ships participated in Operation Demon. Cf. Hümmelchen and Rohwer, 'Vor zwanzig Jahren', 122.

[108] Playfair, *Mediterranean*, ii. 105; Long, *Greece, Crete and Syria*, 182–3. Some of the troops were evacuated to Egypt; most of them, however, were first evacuated to Crete. German bombers from Plovdiv could not effectively attack the landing-places in Soudha Bay in Crete. Cf. report Gen.Kdo. VIII. Fl.K., Ic (30 Apr. 1941), 4, BA-MA RL 8/245.

[109] Macintyre, *Battle*, 63; Cunningham, *A Sailor's Odyssey*, 354. 500 Allied soldiers died; 2 destroyers and 1 transport ship were sunk during the evacuation: ibid.

[110] Although the Germans were thrown back, the evacuation ships left the port empty, as the British believed that the Germans had already occupied Kalamata. Cf. Cruickshank, *Greece 1940–1941*, 105–6.

crossed the strait there, and advanced along the west coast to the south without encountering much resistance. On the other hand, 5th Armoured Division had to fight remnants of the Anzac troops near Navplion and Tripolis before it could continue the drive towards Kalamai on 29 April.[111] When German troops reached the southern tip of the Peloponnese on 30 April and occupied all important islands except Crete by 3 May, the campaign in Greece was over.[112]

At this time the divisions of XXX Army Corps were still in eastern Macedonia and western Thrace, reinforced by numerous units of the Bulgarian Second Army, which occupied the coastal area between the Strimon and Alexandroupolis. Bulgarian divisions had also marched into Yugoslavia to take possession of the frontier area between the upper Morava and Vardar. Two German infantry divisions were in northern Greece near Neapolis and Katerini; after the fighting around Servia, 9th Armoured Division assembled near Larisa. XXXX Motorized Corps and XVIII Mountain Corps concentrated their units along the Attic peninsula and near Corinth and Patras. Italian forces advanced to a point north of the Metsovon pass and Yannina.[113]

In accordance with Hitler's orders, only two or three German divisions were to remain in Greece, around Athens and Salonika. Parts of Twelfth Army were withdrawn as early as the end of April and the beginning of May and replaced by Italian troops. The obvious aim of these measures was to strengthen Mussolini's position in south-east Europe and at the same time withdraw as many German units as possible for Hitler's war plans elsewhere.[114]

The king of Greece, George II, and the government of Prime Minister Tsouderos had already left the mainland for Crete on 23 April.

2. THE CONQUEST OF THE REST OF YUGOSLAVIA

(*See Map* III.III.2)

The rapid advance of the German XXXX Motorized Army Corps in the first two days of the campaign not only took pressure off the Italians and prevented any military co-operation among the Allies, but also made the imminent attack by Armoured Group 1 considerably easier. When Kleist's units crossed the

---

[111] AOK 12, Ia, KTB, evening report (28 Apr. 1941), BA-MA RH 20-12/62; OKH/army general staff/Op.Abt., situation report (30 Apr. 1941), 48, BA-MA M VII e 17. Cf. also last n.

[112] Reports OKW (30 Apr. 1941), 125. The losses of the expeditionary corps were: 11,800 men, including 3,480 dead or wounded, 200 aircraft, and 100 tanks; 3 cruisers and 6 destroyers were sunk; numerous other ships were damaged. Cf. Barclay, *Their Finest Hour*, 141.

[113] 'Balkanfeldzug der 12. Armee', maps 21, 25, 30 Apr. 1941, BA-MA 75090/1.

[114] *Hitler's War Directives*, No. 27, pp. 65 ff. (13 Apr. 1941); No. 29, pp. 69 ff. (17 May 1941); No. 31, pp. 74 ff. (9 June 1941). In accordance with Directive No. 27, it was intended to withdraw the air-defence and air units earlier; parts of the army troops were transferred only at the end of May and the beginning of June: OKH/army general staff/Op.Abt. (I S) No. 42090/41 g.Kdos. to AOK 12 (2 May 1941), BA-MA RH 20-12/60.

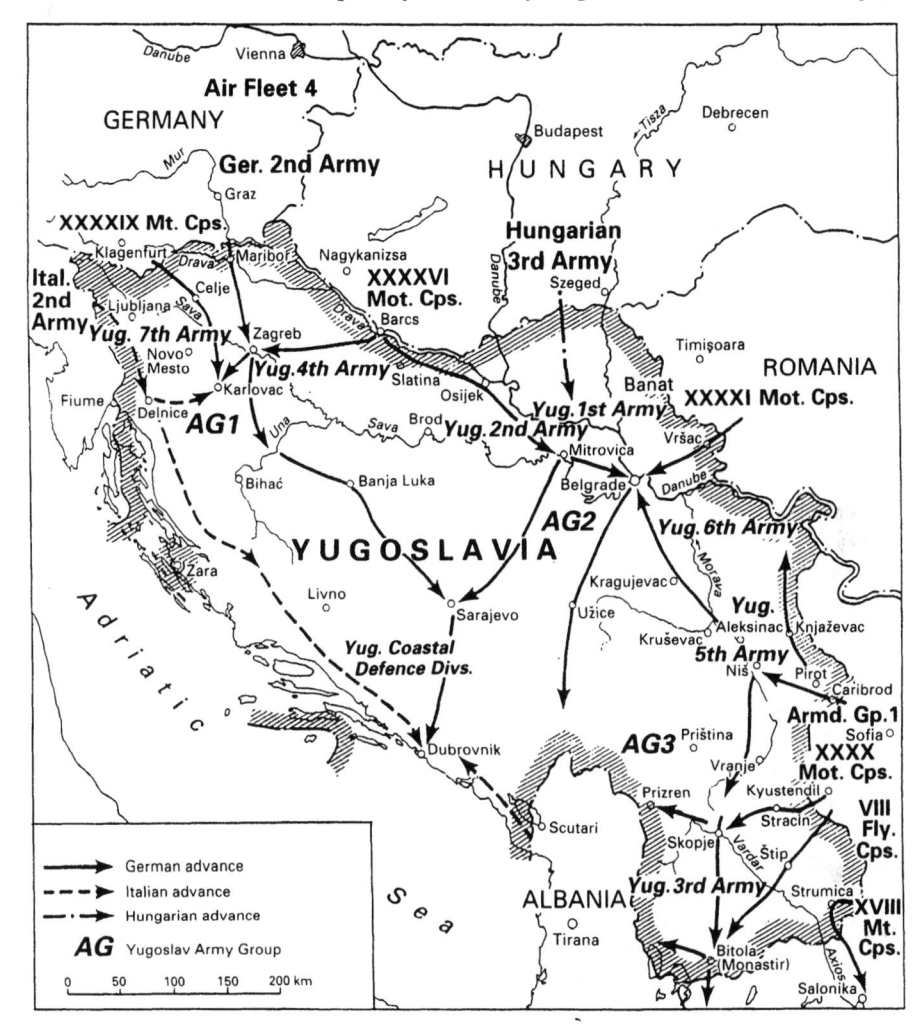

MAP III.III.2. Operations in Yugoslavia, 6–17 April 1941

frontier between Bulgaria and Yugoslavia near Caribrod on 8 April, the successes of XXXX Corps had already secured the far left flank of the attack. Together with Second Army and XXXXI Motorized Army Corps in Romania, Armoured Group I was to take Niš and advance towards Belgrade.[115] However, large parts of the Yugoslav Third and Fifth armies north of Priština delayed this plan.

At first Kleist's 2nd Armoured Division encountered stubborn resistance from parts of the Fifth Army along the road to Niš. But the Yugoslav units

---

[115] The attack by 2nd Army and XXXXI Motorized Army Corps was originally planned for 12 Apr. 1941: cf. n. 125 below. On the deployment of the units cf. Table III.II.2.

were not able to withstand the massed use of armour and aircraft. They had to withdraw to the left bank of the Morava, which left the way to Niš open on 9 April.[116] The next day 2nd Armoured Division maintained the momentum of its attack; its advance units reached the half-way point between the frontier and Belgrade by evening.[117]

But the much slower supply-units and the mountain and infantry forces, which were supposed to secure the flanks of the armoured troops, were not able to keep up with the rapid advance. Units of 6th Mountain Division were able to go little further than Pirot on 10 April and reached Knjaževac only on the next day.[118] Bad weather made almost all secondary roads useless, which forced the Germans to move along the main routes. This led to the formation of long columns of mixed units between the Bulgarian frontier and the spearheads of Armoured Group 1, which still had to deal with determined Yugoslav resistance.[119]

In this situation Kleist requested that the order of the army high command to transfer 5th Armoured Division to the south be rescinded. He intended to use it to secure the flanks of the attack of 2nd Armoured Division far to the north-west. Against List's wishes, who, as described above, wanted to use 5th Armoured Division in northern Greece, the army high command permitted Kleist to keep one armoured regiment of the division, which he then used to push back units of the Yugoslav Fifth Army threatening his rear communications from the north near Aleksinac.[120] Moreover, the advance of the two other regiments of 5th Armoured Division, which attacked from Niš in the direction of Priština, secured part of Kleist's open left flank. This movement also prevented parts of the Fifth Army from establishing positions on the west bank of the Morava between Vranje and Kragujevac.

In this situation the Yugoslav army command was forced to withdraw the units of the First and Sixth Armies around Belgrade back across the Danube to the south on 12 April. There it was intended to have them take up defensive positions together with remnants of the Fifth Army in the triangle Lake Shkodër–Kruševac–Belgrade. The bad weather and poor roads, however, made rapid movements impossible.[121]

The withdrawal of Yugoslav forces across the Danube to the south and Kleist's rapid advance caused the army high command to change its previous

---

[116] Pz.Gr. 1, KTB 142, 144 (8, 9 Apr. 1941), BA-MA RH 21-1/40 D. Cf. also Deichmann, 'Balkanfeldzug des VIII. Fliegerkorps', 25, BA-MA RL 8/46.

[117] Near Kragujevac. Cf. OKH/army general staff/Op.Abt., situation report (10 Apr. 1941), 7, BA-MA M VII e 17.

[118] Pz.Gr. 1, KTB 146 (10 Apr. 1941), BA-MA RH 21-1/40 D.

[119] On 11 Apr. 1941 a line of vehicles extended from the Bulgarian frontier to Niš; the average speed was only 2.5 km./h. Cf. Bericht über die Erfahrungen im Feldzug gegen Jugoslawien, 60. Inf.Div. (mot.), Abt. Ia No 125/41 geh. (11 May 1941), 2, BA-MA RH 20-2/149.

[120] Pz.Gr. 1, KTB 148, 150–1 (10, 11 Apr. 1941), BA-MA RH 20-1/40 D; AOK 12, Ia, KTB, evening report (11 Apr. 1941), BA-MA RH 20-12/62.

[121] 'Überblick über die Operationen des jugoslawischen Heeres', Teil II, 390 ff.; Hnilicka, *Ende auf dem Balkan*, 36.

2. Conquest of the Rest of Yugoslavia

schedule. XXXXI Motorized Army Corps, grouped around Timişoara, was ordered not to wait until 12 April to begin its attack towards Belgrade, but to start as soon as possible.[122] Thereupon units of the corps crossed the frontier between Yugoslavia and Romania on 11 April and, without encountering significant resistance, took Vršac on the same day. On 12 April they were already approaching the Yugoslav capital.[123] In the meantime, after hard fighting around Kragujevac, Kleist's forces succeeded in taking the heights south-east of Belgrade.[124]

The successes in south-eastern Yugoslavia also affected the schedule of the corps of Second Army in Carinthia and southern Hungary, not yet completely assembled. On 9 April the army high command ordered the attack date for Weichs's units to be moved up to 10 and 11 April respectively, although their deployment had not been completed and the flow of supplies could not yet be guaranteed.[125] Second Army had already been able to improve decisively its starting-position for the imminent attack by carrying out isolated thrusts into Yugoslav territory. The passes in the Karawanken, as well as all important crossings on the Mur and the Drava, fell into German hands with little resistance from Yugoslav defence forces by 9 April. The Germans were also able, before the outbreak of hostilities, to secure the transport of raw materials on the Danube by carrying out a special operation, involving SS men wearing Hungarian uniforms, to prevent the demolition of a bridge at the Iron Gate, which would have blocked the river.[126]

In these operations the Germans realized that they would encounter far less resistance in the north-western parts of Yugoslavia than in the south-east. This assumption proved to be correct. Because of the belated Yugoslav mobilization, Second Army faced few enemy units in the northern part of the country at the start of its attack. Yugoslav staffs also reported to the army command cases of insubordination and even fighting between Croatian troops and those of other ethnic groups. The attacks of Air Fleet Four on military installations and troop concentrations contributed to the disintegration of Yugoslav morale.[127] For these reasons, on 8 April the army command was forced to

---

[122] There were already indications of this on 9 Apr. 1941. Cf. Pz.Gr. 1, KTB 145, BA-MA RH 21-1/40 D.

[123] Here too the bad roads caused delays: AOK 12, Ia, KTB, evening report (12 Apr. 1941), BA-MA RH 20-12/62.

[124] OKH/army general staff/Op.Abt., situation report (11 Apr. 1941), 9, BA-MA M VII e 17; Pz.Gr. 1, KTB 152 (12 Apr. 1941), BA-MA RH 21-1/40 D.

[125] AOK 2, KTB 57–8 (9 Apr. 1941), BA-MA RH 20-2/130. XXXXVI Motorized Army Corps was to attack on 10 Apr., the LI on 11 Apr., and XXXXIX Mountain Corps as soon as all mobile parts were available. The original attack date for Weichs was 12 Apr. 1941. Cf. also Krumpelt, *Material*, 158.

[126] Loßberg's lecture, 5 May 1941, 22, BA-MA RW 4/v. 662. On the fighting before 10 Apr. 1941 cf. AOK 2, KTB 36 ff. (6 Apr. 1941), BA-MA RH 20-2/130.

[127] On the effectiveness of the Luftwaffe cf. Tagebuch der jugoslawischen Obersten Heeresleitung, 8 (7 Apr. 1941), BA-MA RL 7/656; Operationstagebuch des jugoslawischen Heeres, 16, 24, 30 (7, 8, 9 Apr. 1941), BA-MA RH 20-2/1085.

order the retreat of the troops of the First Army Group around Ljubljana to the south-east.[128]

When Second Army began its attack on 10 April, it was therefore able to achieve decisive gains within a few days. XXXXVI Motorized Army Corps passed the already occupied Drava crossings on the frontier between Hungary and Yugoslavia and, together with 14th Armoured Division, captured the Croatian capital of Zagreb against weak resistance from the Yugoslav Fourth Army. In the next two days the division reached Karlovac, south-west of Zagreb, and established contact with the Italian Second Army. At the request of the Germans, the Italians had also moved up the date of their attack and had advanced from Friuli and western Slovenia via Ljubljana to Delnice (east of Fiume/Rijeka) on 11 and 12 April.[129] For future fighting the Germans agreed to leave the Italians a strip of the Dalmatian coast between fifty and eighty kilometres wide.[130]

In the meantime 8th Armoured Division of XXXXVI Motorized Army Corps had used the Drava crossing at Barcs to advance along that river to the south-east. On the third day of the attack, against the resistance of the Yugoslav Second Army, the first units of the armoured formations reached the Sava near Mitrovica via Slatina and Osijek.[131]

The attack of XXXXIX Mountain Corps and XXXXI Army Corps against the retreating units of the Yugoslav First Army Group in the north was equally successful. By 12 April two infantry divisions and one mountain division had crossed the Sava and were pushing on towards Karlovac and Zagreb. There they relieved 14th Armoured Division, which had been ordered to advance to the Una in Bosnia.[132] The occupation of Zagreb on 10 April had been followed on the same day by the proclamation of a separate Croatian state under the fascist leaders Pavelić and Kvaternik.[133] The collapse of the Yugoslav state made it possible for the Hungarian government to abandon moral reservations about military intervention in a neighbouring country: on 11 April Hungarian military units began to occupy the area between the Tisza and the Drava, without being significantly hindered by Yugoslav forces. The Germans were, however, very careful to prevent their ally from advancing towards the Sava in

---

[128] This affected the Yugoslav 7th Army: 'Überblick über die Operationen des jugoslawischen Heeres', Teil I, 288.

[129] On the advance of XXXXVI Motorized Army Corps (14th Armd. Div.) cf. AOK 2, KTB 65-6, 74 (10, 11 Apr. 1941), BA-MA RH 20-2/130. On the Italian advance cf. Doerr, 'Verbindungsoffiziere', 275; Loi, *Jugoslavia*, 58-66; and the Weichs papers, 'Erinnerungen', iv. 43, BA-MA N 19/8. According to Weichs, the C.-in-C. of the Italian troops, Gen. Ambrosio, had ten divisions at his disposal.

[130] AOK 2, KTB 76 (11 Apr. 1941), BA-MA RH 20-2/130. Novo Mesto, Bihać, and Livno were to be at the frontier.

[131] AOK 2, KTB 65-6, 79 (10, 12 Apr. 1941), BA-MA RH 20-2/130. Cf. also Henrici, 'Sarajewo 1941', 198.

[132] AOK 2, KTB 64, 74 (10, 11 Apr. 1941), BA-MA RH 20-2/130.

[133] *Ursachen und Folgen*, xvi. 481. Cf. also Hillgruber, 'Deutschland und Ungarn', 662.

2. Conquest of the Rest of Yugoslavia

the south or over the Tisza to the east. Antonescu had threatened in that event to attack Hungary, as he claimed the Banat for Romania.[134]

In the meantime the disintegration of the Yugoslav units had reached threatening proportions. While the Fourth Army around Zagreb stopped fighting on the day the Croatian separatist movement declared the independence of Croatia, there were mutinies in the First and Seventh armies and the divisions on the coast. The Second Army, in the area of Slatina-Brod, was able to carry out the withdrawal ordered to the south across the Sava only with the strength of a weakened division. All other units had already disintegrated or had fallen victim to the German attacks.[135]

Strong resistance was only to be expected from the Yugoslav units around Belgrade, which had withdrawn into the Serbian and Bosnian mountains in the south-west when confronted by Armoured Group 1. Their retreat made it possible, however, for Kleist to occupy the capital without fighting on 13 April.[136]

After the fall of Belgrade, the Germans concentrated on defeating the remnants of the Yugoslav army with as few forces as possible and on quickly occupying centres important to the supply of raw materials.[137] The drive against Sarajevo was to be carried out from two directions. While 16th Motorized Infantry Division was to attack in a southerly direction from the lower Sava, 14th Armoured Division, its flanks protected by the infantry units of Second Army, would advance via Banja Luka from the west. At the same time it was planned to use 8th Armoured Division to pursue the Yugoslav Sixth and First Armies, which were retreating south of Belgrade, in order to secure the attack on Sarajevo in the east. In spite of the occasionally strong resistance, the attackers were able to occupy Sarajevo on 15 April and reach the Adriatic two days later. There they established contact with the Italians, who had in the meantime advanced along the coast to Dubrovnik.[138]

Faced with an increasingly hopeless situation, the Yugoslav high command ordered all army and army group commands to establish contact with the Germans in order to agree on an armistice.[139] At first, however, the Germans

---

[134] On the Hungarian attack: OKH/army general staff/Op.Abt., situation report (11 Apr. 1941), 8; (13 Apr. 1941), 14, BA-MA M VII e 17. On Romanian and Hungarian differences cf. *DGFP* D xii, No. 321, pp. 525–6 (12 Apr. 1941). On the Hungarian army, cf. *Das Deutsche Reich und der Zweite Weltkrieg*, iv. 354–5 (Förster).

[135] 'Überblick über die Operationen des jugoslawischen Heeres', Teil II, 392, 394; Operationstagebuch des jugoslawischen Heeres, 31, 45 (10, 12 Apr. 1941), BA-MA RH 20-2/1085.

[136] Pz.Gr. 1, KTB 154 (13 Apr. 1941), BA-MA RH 21-1/40 D. The Yugoslav army command had not envisaged a defence of Belgrade.

[137] Hitler attached great importance to occupying the copper-mining area between the Morava and the Danube. Cf. *Hitler's War Directives*, No. 27, pp. 65 ff. (13 Apr. 1941). The Yugoslavs were, however, able to blow up the mines: OKH/army general staff/Op.Abt., situation report (15 Apr. 1941), 19, BA-MA M VII e 17.

[138] On the fighting in Serbia cf. AOK 2, KTB 88 ff. (13–17 Apr. 1941), BA-MA RH 20-2/130. On the Italian advance cf. Loi, *Jugoslavia*, 63–4.

[139] Cf. Operationstagebuch des jugoslawischen Heeres, 53, 55 (14 Apr. 1941), BA-MA RH 20-2/1085; Dedijer, 'Sur l'armistice germano-yougoslave', 5–6.

rejected such requests.[140] The fighting continued. Only after several Yugoslav divisions had capitulated and German troops had taken the Yugoslav high command prisoner near Sarajevo on 15 April was Second Army command prepared to accept the request for an armistice. The surrender was signed in Belgrade on 17 April by the former foreign minister Cincar-Marković and Lieutenant-General Janković in the presence of Colonel-General Freiherr von Weichs.[141] With British assistance, King Peter and Prime Minister Simović had already left the country.

In the last days before the capitulation only a few German units were still fighting against Yugoslav troops. When the army high command was informed that little resistance was now to be expected, it stopped the planned transfer of reserves to Yugoslavia on 12 April. At the same time the commands of Second Army and Armoured Group 1 were ordered to concentrate all units no longer needed in rest areas.[142] In this way the army leaders wanted to be able to transfer fast units, army troops, and command staffs quickly to the east in the coming days.[143]

According to Hitler's decision of 16 April, only two divisions were to remain in the future occupied territory of Old Serbia, and only one division in the copper-mining area between the Morava and the Danube. Hitler also decided that it was important to leave Luftwaffe forces in the Balkans in order to be able to continue the war against British installations in the eastern Mediterranean.[144] The planned withdrawal of the mobile units from Yugoslavia was largely carried out between the end of April and the middle of May 1941. In May the army high command also withdrew the infantry and mountain infantry divisions remaining in Yugoslavia.[145]

After the Yugoslav capitulation, the aggressor states agreed on the following partition of the conquered country (see Map III.III.3): Germany received northern Slovenia and occupied Old Serbia and the Banat. Hungary was given

---

[140] The reasons for this refusal are not quite clear. While Halder noted on 15 Apr. 1941 (*Diaries*, ii. 876) that several generals of the Yugoslav 2nd and 5th armies had been rejected because they had no authority to negotiate, the German chargé d'affaires in Belgrade reported on the same day that Weichs had stated that he would not negotiate with Yugoslav politicians, who were evidently also trying to start armistice negotiations, but would only accept representatives of the Yugoslav army: Feine, telegram No. 6, PA, Büro St.S., Jugoslawien, iii. Cf. also Olshausen, *Zwischenspiel auf dem Balkan*, 115–16.

[141] The Italian military attaché signed for Italy. Cf. Weichs papers, 'Erinnerungen', v. 4, BA-MA N 19/9. On the surrender cf. also the Böhme papers, Aufzeichnungen, 21 (beginning of May 1941), KA, Vienna, B/556, No. 47. According to this source, casualties were: 1,100 dead, 3,750 wounded, and 390 missing; XVIII Mountain Army Corps alone suffered 2,854 dead, wounded, and missing: ibid. 111.

[142] OKH, army general staff/Op.Abt. (I) No. 1018/41 g.Kdos. (12 Apr. 1941) to AOK 2 and AOK 12, BA-MA RH 6/v. 3.

[143] Among the army troops the army high command attached special importance to an early transfer of the bridging columns: AOK 2, KTB 107 ff. (16 Apr. 1941), BA-MA RH 20-2/130, and Pz.Gr. 1, KTB 171 (22 Apr. 1941), BA-MA RH 21-1/40 D.

[144] OKW/WFst/Abt. L No. 44545/41 g.Kdos. Chefs. (18 Apr. 1941), BA-MA RW 4/v. 588.

[145] AOK 2, Ia, No. 350/41 g.Kdos. (7 May 1941), BA-MA RH 20-2/140.

MAP III.III.3. The Partition of Yugoslavia and Greece after the Balkan Campaign, 1941

the area west of the Tisza as far as the Danube and the Mur area east of Maribor. Italy took southern Slovenia and Montenegro as well as western Macedonia, and Bulgarian units moved into the eastern areas of Macedonia. The new state of 'Greater Croatia' became an area of Italian influence.[146] Hitler had realized in full his intention to smash Yugoslavia as a state. Even the Fascist-ruled state of Croatia, which comprised former Croatian and Bosnian areas,[147] was under the control of Italian or German occupation troops. In Athens, on the other hand, Hitler permitted the formation of a Greek government under the pro-German General Tsolakoglou. The final decision on the fate of the country was to be taken after the end of the war.

In the Balkan campaign the Axis powers had achieved their objectives with remarkable swiftness. Neither the army nor the Luftwaffe had been able to eliminate the British expeditionary corps, but they had been able to force Britain out of the Balkans and the Aegean. The successful campaign also strengthened the position of Italy in south-east Europe and bound her more closely to Germany.

For the war against the Soviet Union the southern flank now seemed to be militarily, politically, and economically secure. Hitler, however, believed that the Royal Air Force could still launch attacks against the Romanian oilfields from bases in Crete. Although the idea of conquering Crete assumed a more concrete form in German military thinking in the final phase of the Balkan campaign, at first no further operations in the eastern Mediterranean were planned. It was intended to use the conquered territory in south-east Europe as a springboard to the Middle East only after the conclusion of the campaign against the Soviet Union.[148]

In Britain the unsuccessful operation in the Balkans was followed by a post-mortem. In the secret session of the House of Commons on 5 and 6 May the political decision to help Greece was in itself hardly criticized. Most members took the view that Britain had had a moral obligation to assist the Greeks. Moreover, it was hard to gainsay Churchill's claim that the American president would be more prepared to support Britain if she did not retreat without a fight.[149] The prime minister did, however, have to answer embarrassing questions about the preparations for Operation Lustre. It became clear that British diplomats and the intelligence services had performed poorly in south-east Europe. Reports on conditions in the Balkan countries before the start of the

---

[146] AOK 2, Ia, KTB, Annex 1, undated map, BA-MA RH 20-2/149. Cf. also Hillgruber, *Strategie*, 469.

[147] The coastal region of Dalmatia, which Italy claimed, was not assigned to the new state of Croatia. Cf. *Das Deutsche Reich und der Zweite Weltkrieg*, v/1.I.II (Umbreit); Sundhaussen, *Geschichte Jugoslawiens*, 116–17; Loi, *Jugoslavia*, 107–16.

[148] Warlimont, *Headquarters*, 130. On German thinking about conquering Crete cf. III.IV below.

[149] Bryant, *Turn of the Tide*, 248 ff.; Churchill, *Second World War*, iii. 207. On the debate on 5 and 6 May 1941 cf. Butler, *Strategy*, ii. 459–60. On the attitude of the United States cf. I.II.3 above (Schreiber).

2. Conquest of the Rest of Yugoslavia

campaign had not always been realistic.[150] The resulting mistakes were all the more serious in that exactly one year earlier Britain had experienced a similar fiasco with the evacuation of troops from Norway. British plans had probably depended too much on support by the Royal Air Force, which, in spite of its superb performance in defending the homeland, had not been able to cope with the overwhelming numerical superiority of the Luftwaffe in south-east Europe. Generally, however, the view prevailed that the defeat suffered in Greece was only an episode and that the defence of Egypt and the Suez Canal still had priority.[151]

Hitler and his generals, however, turned their attention to the east. On 28 March 1941 Halder had assumed that the Balkan campaign would delay the start of the war against the Soviet Union by about four weeks.[152] But the rapid success of the operation permitted an early withdrawal of the divisions used in Yugoslavia and Greece and made unnecessary the planned transfer of reserves to south-east Europe. It is therefore probable that the final decision to set the attack on the Soviet Union for 22 June was due primarily to the fact that severe flooding in eastern Europe prevented wide-ranging military movements there before the middle of June.[153]

More serious were the long-term consequences of the German attack on Yugoslavia and Greece. The harsh German treatment, of the Serbian population in particular led immediately to a bitter guerrilla war which made considerably more difficult the economic exploitation of Yugoslavia, so important for the future conduct of the war in general. The partisan movement in Yugoslavia also tied down increasingly large German forces.[154]

The war in south-east Europe was reminiscent of the Polish campaign as regards Berlin's hatred of the Serbs and Hitler's decision to destroy Yugoslavia as a state. In this respect it differed from German conduct in western and northern Europe. After the coup in Belgrade, the long-smouldering German hostility towards Serbia came to the surface in the behaviour of the leadership. Hitler (the Austrian) was convinced that Serbia was guilty of having started the First World War, was a centre of terrorist movements in Europe, and was prone to co-operate with Britain to harm Germany.[155] In addition to this hostility, the attitude of many German diplomats and officers towards

---

[150] Butler, *Strategy*, ii. 459; Cruickshank, *Greece 1940–1941*, 153–4.

[151] Butler, *Strategy*, ii. 460; Overy, *Air War*, 41.

[152] From the end of May (planned in Dec. 1940) until the end of June. Cf. Halder, *Diaries*, ii. 843 (28 Mar. 1941).

[153] Müller-Hillebrand ('Improvisierung', 78, MGFA P-030) estimates the time lost at not more than one or two weeks. Cf. id., 'Zusammenhang zwischen Balkanfeldzug und Invasion in Rußland', MGFA C-101; Hillgruber, *Strategie*, 504 ff.; comprehensive discussion in Zapantis, *Greek–Soviet Relations*, 498 ff. On 17 Feb. 1945 Hitler stated that the delay caused by the war in the Balkans was the reason for the failure of the attack on the Soviet Union: *Hitler's Testament*, 72–3.

[154] Cf. *Das Deutsche Reich und der Zweite Weltkrieg*, v/1.I.II (Umbreit), and vii; Donaglić et al., *Jugoslawien im Zweiten Weltkrieg*, 35; Fleischer, *Griechenland 1941–1944*.

[155] *Ursachen und Folgen*, xvi. 470 ff.

Yugoslavs was marked by a pronounced feeling of superiority which occasionally extended to outright disdain.[156] This helps to explain the bombing of Belgrade as well as the later treatment of the Serbs. Even before the start of hostilities German soldiers were given a leaflet in which Serbian soldiers in battle were described as 'tough, brutish, and callous' and, for that reason, 'any leniency—even with prisoners' was to be avoided.[157] Moreover, the army high command planned to apprehend all 'especially important individuals' after the start of the fighting. Included in this group were *émigrés* and Jews as well as Communists, saboteurs, and terrorists. The capture of such individuals was to be carried out by the police and the security service in co-operation with the intelligence and counter-intelligence departments of the German army commands.[158] Like German behaviour in Poland, these plans provided a preview of the atrocities which were to be inflicted on Yugoslavia and the Soviet Union.[159]

---

[156] For example, Bernhard von Loßberg, Lt.-Col. of the general staff in the Wehrmacht operations staff, described the Yugoslav generals as 'clowns' (*Weihnachtsmänner*): lecture, 5 May 1941, p. 23, BA-MA RW 4/v. 662. On the other hand, the attitude of Heeren, the German minister in Belgrade, was quite different.

[157] Richtlinien für das Verhalten der Truppe in Jugoslawien (no date), BA-MA RH 20-12/397. According to an order from the Wehrmacht high command, Serbian officers were to be 'treated in the worst possible manner': Halder, *Diaries*, ii. 865 (9 Apr. 1941).

[158] OKH/army general staff/GenQu/Abt. Kriegsverwaltung No. II/0308/41 (2 Apr. 1941) to AOK 2 and AOK 12, regarding the use of the security police and the security service in Operation Marita and Operation 25, BA-MA RH 31-I/v. 23.

[159] Cf. *Das Deutsche Reich und der Zweite Weltkrieg*, iv. 413–47, 1030–78 (Förster).

IV. The Capture of Crete

1. THE PLACE OF CRETE IN GERMAN AND BRITISH MILITARY PLANNING, 1940–1941

DURING the Balkan campaign, especially as it became increasingly clear that the Allies would be defeated in Greece, German military leaders began to consider the possibility of using the Luftwaffe to destroy British military bases on Crete and Malta or even to occupy those islands. The bases on Crete and Malta enabled the British, in spite of the German victories in the Balkans, to continue attacks on Axis shipping to North Africa and, especially from Crete, to carry out naval thrusts into the Aegean. Moreover, Hitler feared that during the war against the Soviet Union air attacks on the Romanian oilfields could be mounted from bases on Crete.[1]

The German leaders began to consider the possibility of occupying Crete for the first time when Hitler learnt of Italian plans to invade Greece at the end of October 1940. The German government believed that the British could use the Italian attack on Greece to justify taking the island in a surprise attack. On 10 September 1940 the head of the German naval liaison staff in Rome had already expressed the view that Mussolini should forestall such a British move by landing Italian troops on Crete.[2] In addition to the importance of Crete during the war in the east, mentioned above, the island was also interesting for the war the Axis powers were fighting in the Mediterranean. The occupation of Crete would be an important additional conquest after a possible drive by the Italians towards Marsa Matruh in North Africa. The Wehrmacht operations staff therefore ordered a more detailed study of the strategic importance of the island.[3] Within the framework of their plan for a strategy along the periphery of the main theatres of operations, the naval war staff in particular welcomed all ideas for military measures against British positions. In their view it was essential for the further conduct of the war against Britain to drive the British out of the Mediterranean.[4]

After the Italian attack on Greece on 28 October 1940, the German government expected that the British would immediately take measures to occupy Crete. Because of this, the Wehrmacht operations staff assumed that Italy's

---

[1] Hillgruber, *Strategie*, 467, and Mühleisen, *Kreta 1941*, 15.
[2] 1. Skl., KTB, Teil A, 58–9 (5 Oct. 1940), BA-MA RM 7/17. Cf. also Baum and Weichold, *Krieg der 'Achsenmächte'*, 61; Ansel, *Middle Sea*, 191; Weichold, 'Seestrategie', 165.
[3] *KTB OKW* i. 129 (26 Oct. 1940), 131–2 (28 Oct. 1940). In Halder's view a German thrust through Turkey and Syria to the Suez Canal would require the conquest of Crete at the same time. Cf. Hillgruber, *Strategie*, 342.
[4] Salewski, *Seekriegsleitung*, i. 315; 'Führer Conferences', 141–3 (26 Sept. 1940). On the 'peripheral' conduct of the war cf. Hildebrand, *Foreign Policy*, 116, and I.III.2 above (Schreiber).

lines of communication with Libya were now exposed to an additional threat. On the same day, at his meeting with Mussolini in Florence, Hitler offered to send two German paratroop or two airborne divisions to take Crete for the Axis. Mussolini, however, declined Hitler's offer, obviously wishing to keep Germany from gaining any influence on the conduct of the war in the Mediterranean. But Italy did not try to occupy Crete on her own. General Roatta, the deputy chief of general staff of the Italian army, rejected German suggestions to this effect, as Italy did not have the military means to carry out such an operation.[5] German fears were confirmed only a few days later: Royal Air Force and British army units began to land in Crete on 1 November.[6]

The establishment of air-bases not only in Crete but also in Greece itself substantially improved Britain's military position in the Aegean. More important, however, was the fact that the failure of the Italian offensive against Greece from Albania seemed seriously to weaken Italy's position in south-east Europe and the eastern Mediterranean. On 19 November Hitler bluntly told Ciano at a meeting on the Obersalzberg that the changed situation was also beginning to affect Germany's interests. He pointed out that bombing attacks on the vital Romanian oilfields were now to be expected from the British air-bases on the Greek mainland and in the Aegean.[7] After the start of Wavell's offensive in North Africa in December 1940, Hitler believed that the British could now attempt to inflict painful blows on the weaker Axis partner.[8]

Although Hitler planned to help Italy in the Balkans only in the spring of 1941, he decided around the turn of the year to help Mussolini, who was hard pressed on all sides, in Libya as soon as possible.[9] He feared, however, that the British bases on Malta would continue to disrupt shipping to North Africa necessary for carrying out such an operation.[10] In mid-February the Wehrmacht high command was of the opinion that Malta would remain a significant factor in the conduct of the war by the Axis in the Mediterranean, even if North Africa should be completely lost. According to Warlimont's memoirs, the Wehrmacht operations staff also produced a study arguing that the conquest of Malta would most probably make it possible to disrupt British shipping to the Middle East and at the same time block British operations against Axis positions in southern Europe. For the first time the Wehrmacht high command considered a landing operation in Malta.[11] The realization of

---

[5] *KTB OKW* i. 131 (28 Oct. 1940); Halder, *Diaries*, i. 640 (28 Oct. 1940). Hitler's offer to Mussolini: *DGFP* D xi, No. 246, pp. 411–22 (28 Oct. 1940), here 411. Cf. also Gundelach, *Luftwaffe im Mittelmeer*, 200.

[6] Cf. I.2 above and Cruickshank, *Greece 1940–1941*, 162.

[7] *DGFP* D xi, No. 353, pp. 606 ff. (19 Nov. 1940). Cf. also Salewski, *Seekriegsleitung*, i. 317; Ciano, *Diary 1939–1943*, 307 ff.

[8] Halder, *KTB* ii. 226 (13 Dec. 1940; not in trans.). The British offensive began on 9 Dec. Cf. Hillgruber, *Strategie*, 290.

[9] Hillgruber, *Strategie*, 340, 346–7; V.II below (Stegemann).

[10] Cf. Stegemann, loc. cit.

[11] Cf. Warlimont, 'Kriegführung', 323–4, MGFA P-216/I-III; *KTB OKW* i. 309 (6 Feb. 1941).

1. Crete in German and British Planning

this plan would certainly have excluded any operation to conquer Crete in the following months. Germany did not have the means to carry out both operations at the same time, and the campaign in the Soviet Union was imminent.

On 22 February 1941, however, the Wehrmacht high command informed the naval war staff that Hitler had now planned the conquest of Malta for the autumn of 1941, after the conclusion of the war in the east.[12] Although Raeder advocated conquering the island in a discussion of the situation on 18 March 1941, Hitler did not abandon his reservations. Moreover, he informed Raeder that the Luftwaffe had expressed doubts about the technical feasibility of an operation against Malta.[13]

There were also several indications that the situation in the eastern Mediterranean and especially the British presence in the Aegean required Hitler's attention: he repeatedly urged Mussolini and Ciano not to abandon the Dodecanese.[14] And Raeder even encouraged the Italians to attack British naval forces in the eastern Mediterranean.[15] At the same time the German military leaders decided to assemble paratroop units in Bulgaria in order, if necessary, to occupy important islands in the Aegean.[16] As had been the case six months earlier, Hitler's efforts were now obviously aimed at excluding any threat from the British air force. After the capture of suitable airfields on the Greek mainland, and possibly Crete, the Luftwaffe would also be able to paralyse British shipping through the Suez Canal.[17] The plans of the naval war staff went beyond this objective: as in November 1940, they indicated that such a development would create the conditions for further operations against Britain in the eastern Mediterranean.[18]

The German victories in Greece represented, among other things, an important step towards being able to carry out these plans. As mentioned above, concrete planning was now begun for an operation to capture Crete. In mid-April 1941 senior Luftwaffe officers were especially concerned with working out plans to occupy the island. In several discussions, in which Göring occasionally participated, they envisaged the possibility of using airborne and paratroop units to conquer the island.[19] The naval war staff agreed to these

---

[12] 1. Skl., KTB, Teil A, 295 (22 Feb. 1941), BA-MA RM 7/21. Cf. also Salewski, *Seekriegsleitung*, i. 330.

[13] 'Führer Conferences', 185.

[14] *DGFP* D xii, No. 110, pp. 197–9, Hitler's letter to Mussolini (28 Feb. 1941), and No. 117, pp. 206–10, Hitler's talk with Ciano (2 Mar. 1941).

[15] Cf. Salewski, *Seekriegsleitung*, i. 327.

[16] *KTB OKW* i. 366 (22 Mar. 1941) and 369 (28 Mar. 1941); *Hitler's War Directives*, No. 25 (27 Mar. 1941).

[17] Warlimont, 'Mittelmeer', 368, MGFA P-216/I-III.

[18] 1. Skl., KTB, Teil A, 354 (26 Feb. 1941), BA-MA RM 7/21; 'Führer Conferences', 154–6 (14 Nov. 1940), annex 3.

[19] Lfl. 4, No. 6340/41 g.Kdos., Bericht Kreta (28 Nov. 1941), here p. 1, BA-MA RL 7/463; Löhr's letter of 8 Dec. 1942, p. 1, in Diakow, 'Unternehmen Kreta im Mai 1941', Löhr papers, KA, Vienna, B 521; Gen.Kdo. XI. Fl.K, No. 2980/41 g.Kdos. (11 June 1941), Einsatz Kreta, 2, BA-MA RL 33/98. Cf. also Götzel, *Student*, 198. Jeschonnek (chief of the Luftwaffe general staff), Löhr, Student (commanding general of XI Air Corps), Süßmann (commander of 7th Air

plans, but pointed out that it was necessary to see Crete as a link in the chain of British bases extending all the way from Gibraltar to Alexandria. For this reason the capture of Malta remained an essential prerequisite for a successful war against Britain in the Mediterranean.[20] In view of the sinking by the British, near the Kerkenna (Qirqinah) Islands, of ships carrying supplies for Rommel's troops in North Africa on 15 and 16 April, the Wehrmacht operations staff also argued, as in February 1941, in favour of capturing Malta.[21]

When Hitler decided on 21 April 1941 at a conference with representatives of the Luftwaffe to conquer Crete nevertheless, this was probably due primarily to his desire to eliminate any possible threat to south-east Europe by British air or naval forces. He made it clear that he would consider the capture of Crete to be a good conclusion of the Balkan campaign. On the other hand, he explained, the Luftwaffe should continue to attack British forces on Malta.[22] The next day the naval war staff also concluded that the conquest of Malta should be postponed until Crete had been taken and, if necessary, until the Axis threat to Egypt had begun to have an effect on strategy.[23] Halder was of the opinion that the conquest of Crete would be the best way to support Rommel and the Italians in North Africa. The Superaereo (Italian air force command) agreed with him, as it believed that the fall of Crete to the Axis would make it much easier to master the pressing supply problems in the Mediterranean theatre.[24]

The need of senior Luftwaffe officers to re-establish prestige may also have played a marginal role in the decision to conquer Crete with airborne and paratroop forces. After their failure to defeat the Royal Air Force over Britain, they were eager to win laurels in other theatres of the war.[25]

During the conference of 21 April Hitler gave his permission to prepare the operation against Crete, which was to be planned for the middle of May because of the approaching attack on the Soviet Union. In Directive No. 28 (Merkur), issued only four days later, the priority of the war to be fought in the east was again clearly underlined: Merkur must not delay the start of the war against the Soviet Union.[26] Clearly the capture of Crete was to be the last German military operation in the eastern Mediterranean for the time being.

Division), Korten (chief of staff of Air Fleet 4), and Schlemm (chief of staff of XI Air Corps) participated in the discussions.

[20] 1. Skl., KTB, Teil A, 264-5 (18 Apr. 1941), BA-MA RM 7/23.
[21] On the Kerkenna Islands sinkings cf. 1. Skl., KTB, Teil A, 230 (16 Apr. 1941), BA-MA RM 7/23. On the problem presented by Malta cf. Warlimont, *Headquarters*, 131; Weichold, 'Seestrategie', 167-8.
[22] Lfl. 4, Bericht Kreta, 1, BA-MA RL 7/463. Cf. also Müller-Hillebrand, 'Merkur', 41, MGFA C-100. It can be assumed that even before this conference Göring had spoken with Hitler about the decision to conquer Crete.
[23] 1. Skl., KTB, Teil A, 317 (22 Apr. 1941), BA-MA RM 7/23.
[24] Verbindungsstab Italuft No. 1529/41 g.Kdos. (16 May 1941), 5, BA-MA RL 2/II/38. On the importance of Crete for Rommel cf. also Halder, *Diaries*, ii. 887 (24 Apr. 1941).
[25] Götzel, *Student*, 199.
[26] *Hitler's War Directives*, No. 28 (25 Apr. 1941).

1. Crete in German and British Planning

For the coming months more extensive actions, such as those desired by the navy leaders, were not planned. At most it was in the German interest to secure what had already been won and, if possible, to weaken Britain's naval position in that area. The decision to conquer Crete and pin down the British forces on Malta with air attacks again made it clear that the Mediterranean theatre was of secondary importance compared with Hitler's dominant aim to attack and crush the Soviet Union.

As early as the beginning of 1940 the British had devoted considerable attention to the geographic situation of Crete in a future war in the Mediterranean. Crete could provide a base for thrusts into the Aegean and, in the view of the British leaders, forces there would also be better able to protect Egypt and Malta. At the same time the British government believed that occupying the island would make it possible effectively to counter operations by Italian air and naval forces from nearby Rhodes.[27] At the end of April 1940 the chiefs of staff therefore decided to occupy Crete if Mussolini entered the war on the side of Germany. The British intended to carry out this operation jointly with French troops.[28] The fall of France caused the British government temporarily to abandon the plans to occupy Crete, but they were taken up again after the Italian entry into the war at the end of June 1940. However, Britain still hesitated to violate Greek neutrality by landing military forces in Crete, and for the time being restricted herself to logistic preparations for the operation.[29] This self-restraint ceased, however, on 28 October 1940, when Italy attacked Greece and the Greek government requested British military assistance. As early as 1 November British advance parties arrived in Crete from Alexandria. In the following months they were joined by a weak infantry brigade and air-defence units. Moreover, Air Marshal Longmore, the Royal Air Force commander, intended to use Soudha Bay as a stopover point for convoys from Egypt to Malta. British naval aircraft at nearby Maleme were to provide air protection for the naval base.[30]

At the beginning of November, when the Greek government transferred its military units stationed on the island to the Epirus front, Churchill suggested sending significant reinforcements to Crete. Wavell was, however, extremely sceptical about the wisdom of such an action. He did not want unnecessarily to split up his few divisions in Egypt, which were still fighting the Italians.[31] In addition, because of the great distance from Egypt, a defence of the island with air and naval forces would be difficult. The War Office feared that, in the event of fighting, the Royal Air Force units envisaged for Crete would suffer

---

[27] Churchill, *Second World War*, iii. 238–9; Baldwin, *Battles*, 63–4.
[28] Davin, *Crete*, iii. 3. The consent of the Greek government to the occupation of Crete by British and French forces was received on 21 May 1940: Ansel, *Middle Sea*, 80.
[29] Ibid. 80–1.
[30] Thomas, *Crete 1941*, 114. On the occupation of the island cf. *PWT*, Middle East I, Hist (B) 1, No. 3, p. 4 (28 Oct. 1940), and No. 6, p. 5 (1 Nov. 1940); Playfair, *Mediterranean*, ii. 121.
[31] Cruickshank, *Greece 1940–1941*, 158–9; Gundelach, *Luftwaffe im Mittelmeer*, 208.

heavy losses, as the Italian bases on Rhodes were much nearer than the British airfields in North Africa. It was also a disadvantage that landing possibilities were available for the Royal Navy only on the northern coast of Crete, and it would be difficult to provide sufficient protection with submarines and fighters. In any case, the British leaders in Cairo and London wanted to avoid any further reduction of their already weak air units in Egypt.[32]

After the Italian setback in Greece had become evident at the beginning of November, Wavell came to the conclusion that the troops already envisaged were, at the moment, sufficient to defend Crete.[33] In the following months this judgement changed very little in principle, even though at Churchill's urging army reinforcements arrived in Crete and three landing-strips had been built for Royal Air Force units by February 1941.[34] The attack of the German and Italian units in North Africa in March 1941, the British military engagement in Greece, and the limited military forces at Britain's disposal in the Middle East made it quite impossible to reinforce the defences of Crete to any significant extent.[35] Moreover, the events in Iraq, Ethiopia, and Syria also required Wavell's attention and placed a great strain on his military resources in April and May 1941.[36]

However, when it became clear in mid-April that the Greeks and the British would suffer a defeat in the Balkan campaign, the British government was forced to consider new possibilities for defending Crete. There was no doubt that the troops already on Crete would not be able to repel an invasion. As early as the end of March 1941, after the transfer of parts of XI Air Corps to Bulgaria had become known, the War Office in London surmised that Hitler intended an airborne operation in south-east Europe. The British government did not yet consider this action to be preparation for an attack on Crete, but the sending of about 250 transport aircraft to Plovdiv in mid-April gave reason to expect a large-scale airborne attack. This assumption was strengthened a few days later when British intelligence learnt that after the operations by German paratroops near Corinth, on 26 April, the units involved had not left Greece.[37] But, in spite of these intelligence successes, the British remained for some time uncertain about the actual German objectives. The military staffs in Cairo and London believed that the Germans would most probably attack Crete, as all preparations that had become known seemed to indicate, but

---

[32] *PWT*, Middle East I, Hist (B) 1, No. 6, p. 5 (1 Nov. 1940), and No. 7, p. 6 (3 Nov. 1940).

[33] Ibid.; also Davin, *Crete*, iii. 12.

[34] At Maleme, Rethimnon (not usable for combat aircraft), and Heraklion. Cf. Macmillan, *Royal Air Force*, iii. 93. The reinforcements were air-defence units in Dec. 1940 and an infantry battalion in Mar. 1941. At the beginning of 1941 there were 1,000 Greek soldiers in Crete: Long, *Greece, Crete and Syria*, 203.

[35] Playfair, *Mediterranean*, ii. 125; Stewart, *Struggle for Crete*, 29.

[36] Cf. IV.II.2 below (Schreiber); *PWT*, Middle East I, Hist (B) 3, No. 136, p. 58 (18 Apr. 1941); Churchill, *The Unrelenting Struggle*, 164–5, 168. In view of the numerous other difficulties the British were facing in the Middle East it is not surprising that between Nov. 1940 and Apr. 1941 the British forces on Crete had five different commanders. Cf. Butler, *Strategy*, ii. 510.

[37] Cf. Hinsley, *British Intelligence*, i. 415–16.

I. Crete in German and British Planning

landings in Cyprus and Syria could not be completely excluded. The British military leaders also considered it possible that the planned conquest of Crete was only the start of a greater offensive, whose interim objective was to threaten Egypt.[38]

Because of the assumed German intentions, the British military staffs developed plans, even before the Balkan campaign, to secure Crete not only against Italian, but also against German attacks. These plans began to assume concrete form, however, only when Britain decided to withdraw her troops from Greece. On 17 April Churchill ordered Wavell to send part of the expeditionary corps to Crete to guarantee at least a sufficient number of soldiers for an effective defence of the island.[39] Churchill also believed that strong Greek forces on the island, with the moral support of the king, had to be in a position to assist the Empire troops. Only one day later, however, Churchill indicated in a telegram to the British high command in Cairo that in his view, because of Britain's limited resources, Crete was of only secondary importance in the war in the Middle East as a whole. His main priority, even before the withdrawal of British troops from Greece, was to achieve victory in Libya. Crete, he informed the commanders in Cairo, was to serve for the time being only as a catch-basin for units evacuated from Greece. Only later would Britain concentrate on preparing Crete for defence.[40]

As at the end of 1940, the commanders-in-chief in the Middle East again pointed to inadequate British military resources and expressed fundamental reservations about trying to defend Crete. At the end of April the Admiralty in London expressed the view that it might be more advantageous to concentrate all available Royal Air Force and air-defence units in North Africa in order to recapture Benghazi. From this point of view it was unimportant whether Crete was occupied by the Germans or by the British.[41]

Churchill, however, decided to defend Crete at the end of April, in spite of all reservations. As he informed Wavell, he believed that such a defence would give Britain the opportunity to inflict heavy losses on the German paratroops and would have a favourable effect on Turkey and the Middle East as a whole.[42]

---

[38] *PWT*, Middle East I, Hist (B) 3, No. 191, p. 82 (23 Apr. 1941), and Hist (B) 4, No. 106, p. 45 (15 May 1941); Lewin, *The Chief*, 128. The British government knew the details of the German measures early, as British intelligence had already broken the German radio codes: Hinsley, *British Intelligence*, i. 415 ff.

[39] *PWT*, Middle East I, Hist (B) 3, No. 119, p. 52 (17 Apr. 1941); Cruickshank, *Greece 1940–1941*, 166. On British defence plans in Mar. 1941 cf. Long, *Greece, Crete and Syria*, 197.

[40] *PWT*, Middle East I, Hist (B) 3, No. 136, p. 58 (18 Apr. 1941); Playfair, *Mediterranean*, ii. 124.

[41] *PWT*, Middle East I, Hist (B) 3, No. 231, p. 99 (29 Apr. 1941). On the reservations of Wavell and the RAF and Royal Navy commanders, Longmore and Cunningham, cf. ibid., No. 162, p. 70 (21 Apr. 1941), and No. 191, p. 82 (23 Apr. 1941). In Apr. 1941 Longmore had only 90 bombers and 43 fighters in Egypt. Cf. Thomas, *Crete 1941*, 115.

[42] *PWT*, Middle East, Hist (B) 3, No. 222, p. 96 (28 Apr. 1941). Cf. also Churchill, *Second World War*, iii. 250–1.

2. Preparations for Operation Merkur and British Defence Measures

The planning for the conquest of Crete was based on Directive No. 28 and subsequent individual orders. Hitler entrusted to Göring the general direction of the operation. Göring then gave the task of preparing and carrying out Merkur to Air Fleet Four in Vienna. For this purpose XI Air Corps (commanded by General Student) with its airborne and paratroop units was placed under Luftwaffe General Löhr. The fighter and bomber units of VIII Air Corps under General von Richthofen assumed the task of providing escorts. Parts of 5th Mountain Division of Twelfth Army in Greece in particular were to be used to reinforce XI Air Corps. To secure lines of communication between the Greek mainland and Crete and supply the units of the army and the Luftwaffe on the island, the Wehrmacht operations staff planned to use the navy. However, as no significant German naval units were present in the Mediterranean, Italy was asked to help.[43]

The operation, therefore, was to involve participation of all the Wehrmacht services under the general authority of the Luftwaffe command. Halder had reservations about this solution because it envisaged the use of ground troops without the participation of the army high command. In the end, however, he could not change the decision already taken.[44]

As a result, only Luftwaffe officers were involved in the discussion about how Crete could be conquered most quickly. The geographical position of Crete, which forms a bar 260 kilometres long and 15 to 60 kilometres wide south of the other Greek islands, played an important role in their planning. Because of the very steep mountains along the south coast, the main towns of the island as well as the east–west roads and all important landing-places for ships were located on the north coast. Only a few primitive roads in poor condition connected the south coast with the rest of the island on the other side of the mountains.

Because of these geographical conditions, Löhr intended first to conquer Khania, the capital of Crete, and the largest airfield on the island at Maleme, and subsequently to attack along the main road to the east. XI Air Corps, on the other hand, suggested capturing all important points on the island from the air at the same time. After this surprise attack, army units would land

---

[43] *Hitler's War Directives*, No. 28 (25 Apr. 1941), pp. 68–9; Lfl. 4, Bericht Kreta, pp. 1 ff., BA-MA RL 7/463. At first it was planned to use 5th Mountain Division as a replacement for the envisaged 22nd Infantry Division, which had been trained for airborne operations and was stationed in Romania. But because of the lack of adequate transportation the army high command rejected this plan. Cf. OKW/WFSt/Abt. L (I op) No. 00785/41 g.Kdos. to ObdL and others (30 Apr. 1941), BA-MA RM 7/940. A total of 23,000–25,000 paratroopers and mountain infantry were assembled. Cf. 5th Geb.Div., annex 481 to KTB (16 May 1941), BA-MA RH 28-5/3b; Müller-Hillebrand, 'Merkur', 48, MGFA C-100, pp. 264–5.

[44] Halder, *Diaries*, ii. 909 (8 May 1941).

2. Preparations for Operation Merkur

at the two occupied airfields and conquer the rest of the island.[45] Richthofen, however, was strongly opposed to this plan proposed by Student and his staff, as he did not believe that the fighter units of VIII Air Corps would be able to protect a large number of landing-places simultaneously. Presumably as a result of mediation by the Luftwaffe operations staff and Göring, it was finally agreed to attack only four points, one after the other, from the air in order to have the full support of VIII Air Corps for each attack.[46] As in Löhr's original plans, it was intended to occupy the area around Maleme and Khania with a first wave of paratroopers and airborne troops in the early morning on the day of attack. A second wave would occupy Rethimnon and Heraklion on the afternoon of the same day.[47]

As mentioned above, on 21 April Hitler had chosen 15 May as the date of the attack. But Halder as well as Löhr assumed in the first days of May 1941 that they would be able to start the attack as early as 10 May. This assumption was based on reports of an imminent withdrawal of British troops from Crete for service in Iraq. The German military leaders believed that if these reports were true, the defenders of Crete would not be able to offer protracted resistance.[48]

The start of the attack, however, depended to a considerable degree on how much time the German troops needed to prepare themselves in Greece for the battle of Crete. Two main problems emerged: transporting personnel and equipment of XI Air Corps to the assembly areas and supplying the troops. While parts of XI Air Corps (the Süßman detachment, which belonged to 7th Air Division) had been in Bulgaria and Greece since the end of March,[49] other units of the corps had to be transferred to Romania by rail. From there they reached the envisaged operational bases in Attica and Boeotia by lorry only on 14 May. By that date the transport aircraft of XI Air Corps to be used for the flight to Crete (about 500 Ju 52s) had reached their bases in this area.[50] The Staffeln of VIII Air Corps had to share their airfields in Attica with the units of XI Air Corps. However, depending on their range, the fighters and bombers also had bases in Bulgaria and the Peloponnese. Moreover, the Italians had

---

[45] Lfl. 4, Bericht Kreta, 7–8, BA-MA RL 7/463. Cf. also Ansel, *Middle Sea*, 211, 218. Student's suggestion was probably based on the belief that his paratroops were good jumpers, but less good as infantry soldiers.

[46] Gen.Kdo. XI. Fl.K., Einsatz Kreta, 12, BA-MA RL 33/98. On Richthofen's doubts and the compromise cf. Lfl. 4, Bericht Kreta, 7, BA-MA RL 7/463; Götzel, *Student*, 227.

[47] Gen.Kdo. XI. Fl.K. No. 40/41 g.Kdos. Chefs. (4 May 1941), Absichten für die Besetzung der Insel Kreta, 1–3, BA-MA RL 33/34.

[48] KTB Adm. Südost, 15 (4 May 1941), BA-MA RM 35 III/3; Halder, *Diaries*, ii. 912–13 (9 May 1941). On the fighting in Iraq cf. IV.II.2 below (Schreiber).

[49] For the planned airborne landing on Lemnos and the operation to capture Corinth the Süßmann Detachment was stationed near the city in the first days of May: Gen.Kdo. XI. Fl.K., Einsatz Kreta, 4, BA-MA RL 33/98.

[50] Tagebuch Sturmregiment, 12 ff. (7–15 May 1941), BA-MA RL 33/31; Gen.Kdo. XI. Fl.K., Einsatz Kreta, 5–6, BA-MA RL 33/98.

TABLE III.IV.1. *Forces of XI and VIII Flying Corps Planned for Operation Merkur*

XI Air Corps (Student)[a]
  1 reconnaissance Staffel
  10 'special duty combat Gruppen', Ju 52s (in total about 500 aircraft)[b]
  7th Air Div. with 3 paratroop regiments
  Corps troops: 1 shock regiment (equipped and trained as paratroops), various support troops
  Reinforced 5th Mountain Div. with 3 regiments
  Motor-cycle riflemen, armoured and anti-aircraft units
  Parts of 6th Mountain Div. as reserve

VIII Air Corps (Richthofen)[c]
  280 bombers
  150 dive bombers
  180 fighters
  40 reconnaissance aircraft

In addition, 62 Italian combat aircraft in the Dodecanese[d]

[a] Figures from Gen.Kdo. XI. Fl.K., Einsatz Kreta, 5 ff., BA-MA RL 33/98, and Lfl. 4, Bericht Kreta, 11–12, BA-MA RL 7/463.
[b] Plus about 80 gliders.
[c] Figures according to Deichmann, 'Balkanfeldzug des VIII. Fliegerkorps', 26, BA-MA RL 8/238.
[d] According to Greiner's memorandum, p. 107, BA-MA RW 4/v. 42. Domeniko ('Die Eroberung Kretas aus der Luft', 3, BA-MA ZA 3/21) mentions 21 bombers and reconnaissance aircraft and 24 fighters and torpedo-bombers.

planned landing facilities for German formations on the island of Karpathos and stationed some of their own aircraft on Rhodes.[51] The troops of 5th Mountain Division and support units of Twelfth Army occupied their assigned areas around Athens without serious difficulties.[52]

Upon their arrival at the designated airfields the responsible officers of the air units learnt that existing installations in Greece were completely inadequate for the kind of attack planned against Crete. A total of 1,280 aircraft were to take part (see Table III.IV.1). Significant improvement could not be achieved to make up for the lack of sufficient ground-support units, communications links, and means of transport because the necessary units and equipment had

[51] Cf. Müller-Hillebrand, 'Merkur', 49, MGFA C-100; Lfl. 4, Bericht Kreta, annex 4, BA-MA RL 7/463. On the stationing of the Italian aircraft cf. also Santoni and Mattesini, *La partecipazione tedesca*, 82.
[52] 5. Geb.Div., Div.-Befehl No. 15 (5 May 1941), BA-MA RH 28-5/3a. In case of need, parts of 6th Mountain Division were to be used. Cf. Gen.Kdo. XI. Fl.K., Einsatz Kreta, 5, BA-MA RL 33/98. The headquarters of all units was in Athens.

2. Preparations for Operation Merkur

already been designated for the attack on the Soviet Union. Moreover, the poor taxi-strips and the large numbers of aircraft using the few airfields gave the operation against Crete the appearance of improvisation from the very beginning.[53]

This impression was strengthened by the fact that supplies for the units involved in the attack on Crete had to be delivered under considerable pressure of time. It was almost impossible to move adequate quantities of supplies through a country whose road system was still destroyed in many places after the recent fighting. As alternatives, two main supply-lines were established: one through Romania to the Black Sea and then by ship to Piraeus; the other through Italy and from there by sea to Patras, Corinth, and Piraeus by sea.[54] 'Admiral South-east' (Admiral Karlgeorg Schuster) used, in addition to Bulgarian, Romanian, and Italian ships, twelve steamers of a contingent intended for Rommel.[55] Italy assumed the duty of protecting the transports at sea and placed several warships under the command of 'Admiral South-east'. When he heard of the planned operation against Crete at the end of April or the beginning of May, Mussolini even offered to provide troops; however, Göring rejected this suggestion.[56] The Duce was interested in the smooth functioning of the supply-lines through Greece because Italy received the oil important for her war effort from Romania. While the eastern supply-line was soon functioning relatively efficiently, the section of the western line from Italy to Greece presented considerable difficulties, as the Corinthian Canal could not be reopened before 16 May, and then only for small ships. Minefields and British submarines also occasionally prevented regular shipping traffic.[57]

The difficulties in the supply-system repeatedly forced the staffs of the units involved in preparing the operation against Crete to revise their schedule. While according to the planning of 5 May the attack was to begin between the 16th and 18th of the month, Admiral Schuster and Major-General Korten, chief of staff of Air Fleet Four, feared five days later that they would have to postpone the attack until the 19th. Because of the considerable delays with

---

[53] The individual Gruppen were stationed up to 150 km. apart. Cf. Ansel, *Middle Sea*, 219. On the organizational problems cf. XI. Fl.K., preliminary operation experience report, 3–4 (11 June 1941), BA-MA RL 33/116. On the use of the aircraft cf. Deichmann, 'Balkanfeldzug des VIII. Fliegerkorps', 26, BA-MA RL 8/238.

[54] 1. Skl., KTB, Teil A, 436 (30 Apr. 1941), BA-MA RM 7/23 and operation experience report Merkur (Adm. Schuster), 1, Löhr papers, KA, Vienna, B 521, No. 25.

[55] These losses were, however, offset by the use of Italian ships. Cf. Skl., A VI, 2261/41 g.Kdos. (2 May 1941), to OKW/WFSt and others, BA-MA RM 7/940.

[56] Cf. Rintelen, *Mussolini als Bundesgenosse*, 141; Bernotti, *Guerra nel Mediterraneo*, 170–1. On Italian support with warships cf. OKW/WFSt/Abt. L (I Op) No. 44708/41 g.Kdos. Chefs., annex (12 May 1941), BA-MA RW 4/v. 588.

[57] Gen.Kdo. XI. Fl.K., Einsatz Kreta, 7, BA-MA RL 33/98; KTB Adm. Südost, 8 (18 May 1941), BA-MA RM 35 III/4. According to this source the first ships arrived in Piraeus on 18 May 1941.

shipments of fuel, the start of the attack was finally postponed until 20 May 1941.[58]

In addition to the supply problems, Admiral Schuster also had to provide shipping space for the transport of personnel and materials to Crete. This was necessary because, in the opinion of the Luftwaffe officers involved, the aircraft of XI Air Corps alone would not be able to bring sufficient reinforcements for the airborne and paratroop units to Crete. At the end of April, however, the naval war staff pointed out that, because of the British naval supremacy, it was absolutely essential to supply the German units in Crete by air after the initial attack. In mid-May the chief of staff of the naval command in Greece again pointed out the high risk involved in transporting personnel and supplies to Crete by ship. Thereupon XI Air Corps decided to bring most personnel to Crete by air.[59] Nevertheless, 'Admiral South-east' made every effort to assemble an adequate number of ships, which were to sail from Greek ports if the situation developed favourably. Providing sufficient transport capacity and ship's personnel, however, turned out to be an extremely difficult task. The German military authorities were forced to resort to a large number of small, powered sailing-ships and to fly some of the necessary personnel to Greece from Germany.[60] 'Admiral South-east' finally succeeded in assembling two groups of about sixty powered sailing-ships, which were loaded with soldiers and various kinds of material.[61] The Italians declared their readiness to escort this improvised fleet from Greece via the island of Melos to Crete.[62]

At first the departure of the two groups of ships was planned in such a way that the first would reach Crete on the evening of the first day of the attack; the second group was to arrive near Heraklion the following day. The ships with heavy equipment were to leave on 22 May at the earliest.[63] At the urging

---

[58] KTB Adm. Südost, 15 (5 May 1941), 26 (10 May 1941), BA-MA RM 35 III/3; Gen.Kdo. XI. Fl.K., Einsatz Kreta, 8, BA-MA RL 33/98. Cf. also Forbes, 'Crete', 22. On the evening of 19 May some of the aircraft had still not been fuelled, partly because no fuel was available for the second attack: notes of the commander of 7th Flying Division in W. Hornung, 'Kreta', 10–11, BA-MA ZA 3/19.

[59] KTB Adm. Südost, 39 (15 May 1941), BA-MA RM 35 III/3; 1. Skl., I Op 547/41 g.Kdos. Chefs., Stellungnahme zum Plan der Luftwaffe, Besetzung Kretas (24 or 25 Apr. 1941), 11, BA-MA RM 7/940. Cf. Baum and Weichold, *Krieg der 'Achsenmächte'*, 155.

[60] KTB Adm. Südost, 43–4 (29 Apr. 1941), BA-MA RM 35 III/2. On the withdrawal of the Greek fleet to Alexandria cf. II.III.3 n. 93 above (Schreiber).

[61] In addition there were 7 freighters. Cf. Lfl. 4, Bericht Kreta, 5–6, BA-MA RL 7/463. On the loading of the ships cf. 5. Geb.Div., annex 488 to KTB, 36–7 (17 May 1941), BA-MA RH 28-5/3b; KTB Marinebefehlshaber A, 29 (9 May 1941), BA-MA M 721. Khalkis and Megara were ports of embarkation.

[62] Mar.Verb.Stab Rom, No. 2444/41 g.Kdos., to OKM/Skl. (15 May 1941), BA-MA CASE GE 1084, PG 33101. According to this source the Italians provided 2 destroyers, 3 or 4 torpedo-boats, and several patrol-boats. It was planned to assign one torpedo-boat to protect each group of ships. Anti-aircraft units being transported by the sailing vessels were also to be used against enemy aircraft and ships.

[63] Operation experience report Merkur (Adm. Schuster), 4, Löhr papers, KA, Vienna, B 521, No. 25; operational order No. 1 for Operation Merkur (17 Apr. 1941) from Adm. Südost, BA-MA CASE GE 1084, PG 33101.

2. Preparations for Operation Merkur

of XI Air Corps, however, all these operations were postponed by one day shortly before the start of the attack, as it was not certain that the paratroop and airborne units would be able to capture the landing-places in Crete on 20 May. And because of the Italian refusal to send ships to engage the British fleet west of Crete, it seemed advisable to await developments in the area north of the island before sending transport ships across the sea to Crete.[64]

This decision, however, did not change the plan of Air Fleet Four to shift the main area of attack to the area between Soudha Bay, Khania, and Maleme. The staffs of the participating units assumed that the British had assembled their main forces in this area. But neither agents in Crete nor air reconnaissance were able to provide a clear picture of British defence preparations. More or less exact information was available only as regards the strength of the Royal Air Force units at the three airfields on Crete. In the first half of May Richthofen's formations mounted such strong strikes against the approximately forty aircraft stationed there—of which at times only about twenty were ready for action—that because of heavy losses the British decided to withdraw all remaining aircraft to Egypt shortly before the start of the German attack.[65] XI Air Corps had thus achieved absolute air supremacy over Crete. German reconnaissance and combat aircraft were also able to recognize several anti-aircraft and defence installations near Khania, Heraklion, and the Royal Air Force bases, but the Germans were still unable to obtain exact knowledge of the actual disposition and strength of the British troops. Attempts to improve this situation by continued air attacks on located and assumed enemy positions produced only meagre results.[66] As late as 19 May, therefore, one day before the start of the attack, Air Fleet Four assumed that the German forces would encounter only an infantry division reinforced by remnants of the expeditionary force and some Greek units in Crete. It was also believed that the British expected the main attack by sea.[67]

A central task of VIII Air Corps was the locating and sinking of enemy supply- and warships near Crete. As early as the first days of May German aircraft intensified attacks on enemy ships and convoys, which forced the British to carry out supply operations for Crete primarily at night.[68] When, in

---

[64] Operation experience report Merkur (Adm. Schuster), 4, Löhr papers, KA, Vienna, B 521, No. 25. On the timing and the Italian refusal cf. 1. Skl. to Adm. Südost, No. 676/41 g.Kdos. (20 May 1941), BA-MA CASE GE 1084, PG 33101. The refusal of the Italian government was due to the need to use warships to escort convoys to North Africa. It was planned to bring a total of 6,000 men, many of them soldiers of 5th Mountain Division, to Crete by ship. Cf. Forbes, 'Crete', 56.

[65] *PWT*, Middle East I, Hist (B) 4, No. 77, p. 34 (11 May 1941). Cf. also Butler, *Strategy*, ii. 512. On the results of German reconnaissance cf. Halder, *Diaries*, ii. 908 (7 May 1941).

[66] Lfl. 4, Bericht Kreta, 8–9, BA-MA RL 7/463. Cf. also Forbes, 'Crete', 58, 62.

[67] KTB Adm. Südost, 10 (19 May 1941), BA-MA RM 35 III/4. On German estimates of the strength of British troops on Crete cf. 5th Geb.Div., annex 1 to KTB, 54 (18 May 1941), BA-MA RH 28-5/3b.

[68] Lfl. 4, Bericht Kreta, 4, BA-MA RL 7/463. According to this source, 27 ships were sunk or damaged by 20 May 1941. On the other hand, Cunningham ('The Battle', 3105) mentions 8 ships sunk, and Long (*Greece, Crete and Syria*, 217) 19 damaged or destroyed in Soudha Bay.

the following days, German reconnaissance aircraft sighted almost no British ships, Air Fleet Four concluded for a time that the British would evacuate Crete in stages.[69] But at the latest when Richthofen's and Student's aircraft discovered strong formations of the Royal Navy south and west of Crete a few days before the start of the German attack, the German military leaders realized that the British had understood their intentions and would do everything to defend the island.[70]

The British had already taken concrete measures to defend Crete at the end of April, when the government in London decided, in spite of the requirements of other theatres, not to abandon Crete without a fight.[71] Significant progress was made in defence preparations, under the code-name 'Scorcher', only after General Freyberg, who had commanded the New Zealand troops in Greece, took command of British forces in Crete on 30 April. There was no lack of soldiers: by the end of April 30,000 men of the expeditionary corps had reached Crete. There were also 5,000 men from the original contingent on the island and 7,000 Greek soldiers.[72] The condition of these troops was not, however, satisfactory. Having left much of their equipment in Greece, they had only light weapons. Some of the troops of the expeditionary corps were only auxiliary personnel and would be more of a hindrance than a help in the defence of the island.[73] Freyberg, who at first considered the situation rather depressing, nevertheless did everything to provide his forces with weapons and other essential material, to evacuate unnecessary personnel to Egypt, and to organize the remaining troops for battle. The original intention, to send all units of the expeditionary corps to Egypt and replace them with completely equipped units, was abandoned because of the lack of time and shipping space.[74]

In his efforts Freyberg could now count on the complete support of the commander-in-chief in the Middle East, General Wavell, who during the following weeks, in co-operation with the Royal Navy, supplied Crete with anti-aircraft weapons and artillery in the first place, as well as tanks. Freyberg had also persuaded the New Zealand prime minister to apply diplomatic pressure in London in order to obtain even more help from Churchill. Churchill

---

[69] KTB, Adm. Südost, 23 (8 May 1941), BA-MA RM 35 III/3.

[70] South of Crete, German reconnaissance found 1 aircraft-carrier, 2 battleships, 3 cruisers, and 12 destroyers; and west of Crete 2 battleships, 1 cruiser, and 2 destroyers: 1. Skl., KTB, Teil A, 276–7 (19 May 1941), BA-MA RM 7/24. On the number of British ships cf. n. 82 below.

[71] Cf. end of IV.1 above. The British code-name for Crete was 'Colorado'; the designation for the British Empire troops in Crete was 'Creforce'.

[72] PWT, Middle East I, Hist (B) 3, No. 233, p. 99 (29 Apr. 1941). Cf. also Forbes, 'Crete', 38; Long, *Greece, Crete and Syria*, 207; there were also 2,500 Cretan gendarmes.

[73] Forbes, 'Crete', 38. The Greek troops were poorly equipped and most of them were recruits. Cf. ibid. 182 and PWT, Middle East I, Hist (B), 3, No. 238, p. 101 (29 Apr. 1941).

[74] Until 5 May 1941 the British secret service assumed that the German attack was imminent. On 6 May the British learnt that the provisional date for the attack was 17 May 1941: Hinsley, *British Intelligence*, i. 418. On the decision to send no further troops to Crete cf. PWT, Middle East I, Hist (B) 4, No. 68, p. 28 (10 May 1941).

2. Preparations for Operation Merkur

then promised to order the urgently needed Royal Air Force units to Crete, but only by 25 May.[75] Wavell and the commander-in-chief of the Royal Navy in the Mediterranean, Admiral Cunningham, also promised all possible support from the British fleet, which had already assumed the duty of protecting supply shipments from Egypt to Crete. In spite of the attacks of the Luftwaffe on British ships, Cunningham was able to overcome the most serious shortages of weapons and equipment of Creforce, as it was called, to transport approximately 2,000 men as reinforcements to Crete, and to evacuate about 7,000 men who were not needed on the island.[76]

Freyberg's deployment of his remaining troops was determined by the geography of Crete and by the assumed plans of attack of the Germans. As a result of information provided by the British secret service, he was aware of German military preparations in Greece and the probable organization and main objectives of the coming attack. He could thus assume that a combined air and sea attack was imminent which would be aimed primarily at the western part of Crete.[77] He therefore placed most of his troops in the area around Maleme, Khania, and Soudha Bay, with orders to hold the capital, the airfield, and the most important port against sea and air landings. It was mainly New Zealanders and British soldiers who took up positions in this area, while Australians defended the area east of Rethimnon and the neighbouring airfield. British units were stationed around Heraklion and its airfield. Greek units reinforced the imperial troops in all sectors.

In the four main defence zones on Crete there were:

Maleme: 11,500 men (2nd New Zealand Division with 4th, 5th, and 10th brigades, and 3,500 Greeks);

Khania and Soudha: 17,400 men (various British and Australian units, and 930 Greeks);

Rethimnon: 4,800 men (19th Australian Brigade, and 3,200 Greeks);

Heraklion: 8,100 men (14th British Brigade, and 3,200 Greeks).

The British, New Zealand, and Australian units included 6,000 'service hands'.[78]

The original pessimism with which Freyberg viewed the coming battle was replaced in the first half of May by a cautious optimism. This change was mainly due to the progress that he had made in arming, supplying, and equipping his troops, as well as to the superiority of the naval forces under Cunningham's command. On the other hand the weakness of the Royal Air Force units in Crete and Egypt was a cause for concern. During the day the

---

[75] PWT, Middle East I, Hist (B) 4, No. 8, p. 4 (1 May 1941). On Freyberg's efforts cf. Ansel, *Middle Sea*, 232.

[76] PWT, Middle East I, Hist (B) 5, No. 73, p. 29 (4 June 1941); Davin, *Crete*, iii. 47. However, over 5,000 auxiliaries remained in Crete. Cf. Stewart, *Struggle for Crete*, 92–3. There were also 16,000 Italian prisoners of war on the island. Cf. Macmillan, *Royal Air Force*, iii. 94.

[77] Cf. Hinsley, *British Intelligence*, i. 417–18; Long, *Greece, Crete and Syria*, 210.

[78] According to Ansel, *Middle Sea*, 235–6. Cf. also n. 76 above.

Luftwaffe was able to attack Freyberg's positions almost unhindered and keep the ships of the Royal Navy away from the island. Only excellent camouflage enabled Creforce to avoid significant losses before the start of the main German attack.[79] Knowledge of the German guidelines for airborne operations and the schedule of Air Fleet Four also played a useful role in the defence of Crete. After 6 May the British military leaders not only knew that Löhr at first wanted to start the attack on 17 May; they were also informed of every postponement. Freyberg was therefore able to base his defence preparations on a knowledge of the exact date of the attack and avoid having to keep his soldiers in a constant state of alert.[80]

The British also used their knowledge of the stationing of units of XI Air Corps at Greek airfields to carry out several night attacks from Egypt against the German jump-off bases. Because of the weakness of the Royal Air Force units in the Middle East, however, these raids did not have any decisive effect.[81]

The lack of suitable Royal Air Force units also forced Cunningham to restrict the operations of his naval forces in order to avoid heavy losses through German air attacks. Nevertheless, to be ready to intervene quickly in the sea around Crete and prevent a German landing on the island, British naval forces took up positions south and west of Crete on 15 May. Rapid thrusts to the north were possible from there, and British aircraft from bases in Egypt were able to provide protection for the ships at least part of the time. Cunningham had also chosen his position west of Crete in order to intercept possible Italian attacks. Although most of his ships had to return to Egypt because of a lack of fuel immediately before the German attack, almost all were able to return to their positions by the evening of 19 May.[82]

On the eve of the battle of Crete the German side possessed overwhelming air supremacy, but the British dominated the sea. However, the British navy was able to operate only at high risk during the day because of its lack of air cover. While Freyberg and the British military leaders in Cairo knew the details of German planning and the exact attack date, Löhr and his staff possessed only fragmentary information about the measures the British had taken to defend Crete. Moreover, the improvised nature of the German preparations in a country without an adequate infrastructure inevitably had an adverse effect on an operation so heavily dependent on modern transportation and technology.

---

[79] K.G. 2, Ia, No. 1439/41 geh., annex 1 (1 Jan. 1941), 19, BA-MA RL 8/243. On the problem of stationing RAF units on Crete cf. *PWT*, Middle East I, Hist (B) 4, No. 30, pp. 13–14 (5 May 1941). On Freyberg's optimism cf. Ansel, *Middle Sea*, 233.

[80] Hinsley, *British Intelligence*, i. 418 ff.

[81] Only one RAF attack on the Athens airfield succeeded (during the night of 16–17 May 1941). Six German aircraft were destroyed and several others damaged: AOK 12, Ia, KTB, evening report (17 May 1941), BA-MA RH 20-12/62.

[82] Thomas, *Crete 1941*, 126; Cunningham, *A Sailor's Odyssey*, 366–7. On the disposition of the British fleet cf. Roskill, *War at Sea*, i. 440–1. According to Forbes ('Crete', 63), Cunningham had 1 aircraft-carrier, 4 battleships, 11 cruisers, 30 destroyers, and auxiliary ships.

3. THE BATTLE FOR CRETE

(See Maps III.iv.1 and 2)

To prepare the way for the landing of paratroops and airborne units, formations of VIII Air Corps concentrated their attacks in the early morning of 20 May 1941 on the Creforce units around Khania. The heavy bombing caused considerable casualties among the British anti-aircraft units and destroyed a large part of their communications links, but it did not effectively paralyse the fighting power of the British forces in this area.[83]

To effect a rapid defeat of the enemy units on the ground, XI Air Corps used transport gliders (mostly carrying soldiers of the shock regiment), some of which landed in enemy positions south of Maleme. Only thereafter did the paratroopers arrive to capture, together with the units of the shock regiment, the town of Khania and the landing-places for ships in Soudha Bay (the first wave numbered between 5,000 and 6,000 men).[84] However, technical problems and the readiness of the New Zealand, British, and Greek defenders in this sector resulted in heavy losses in the first landing operation of XI Air Corps. Several of the gliders crashed on the way to Crete, and others did not reach the designated landing-area or were shot down by the Creforce defenders. The paratroopers following also suffered heavy casualties because they landed in defensive positions, as they carried only light weapons and could not quickly reach the containers of heavier weapons which were dropped at the same time. For this reason the paratroopers of Group Centre, who had been dropped south of Khania, could not occupy Khania and Soudha Bay, their objectives, and had to go on the defensive towards evening. Only in the Tavronitis valley were units of Group West able to reassemble after being dropped and attempt an attack on the commanding heights south of the airfield of Maleme, although their commander was seriously wounded and many other officers had been killed.[85] But the New Zealanders on the heights defended their positions successfully during the day and also prevented the German troops from using the airfield at Maleme. During the evening and the night, however, the local New Zealand commander, owing to inadequate communications, formed the mistaken belief that his units had been so weakened that they would not be able to hold their positions against German air attacks the following day. In agreement with his brigade commander he therefore decided to withdraw to a line three to four kilometres further east.

---

[83] The positions near Heraklion and Rethimnon were also attacked: Lfl. 4, Bericht Kreta, 13 ff., BA-MA RL 7/463; *PWT*, Middle East I, Hist (B) 4, No. 153, p. 63 (20 May 1941).

[84] Gen.Kdo. XI. Fl.K., Einsatz Kreta, 15 ff., BA-MA RL 33/98. Cf. also Ansel, *Middle Sea*, 283. The first landings began around 7 a.m. German time. Figures according to H. Neumann, 'Ärtzliche Versorgung', 9, BA-MA ZA 3/19.

[85] The glider with the commander of 7th Air Division (who was also the commander of Group Centre) and almost his whole staff had crashed while approaching the landing-area: AOK 12, Ia, KTB, evening report (20 May 1941), BA-MA RH 20-12/62. On the losses and their causes cf. operation experience report, XI. Fl.K., 7–8 (11 June 1941), BA-MA RL 33/116.

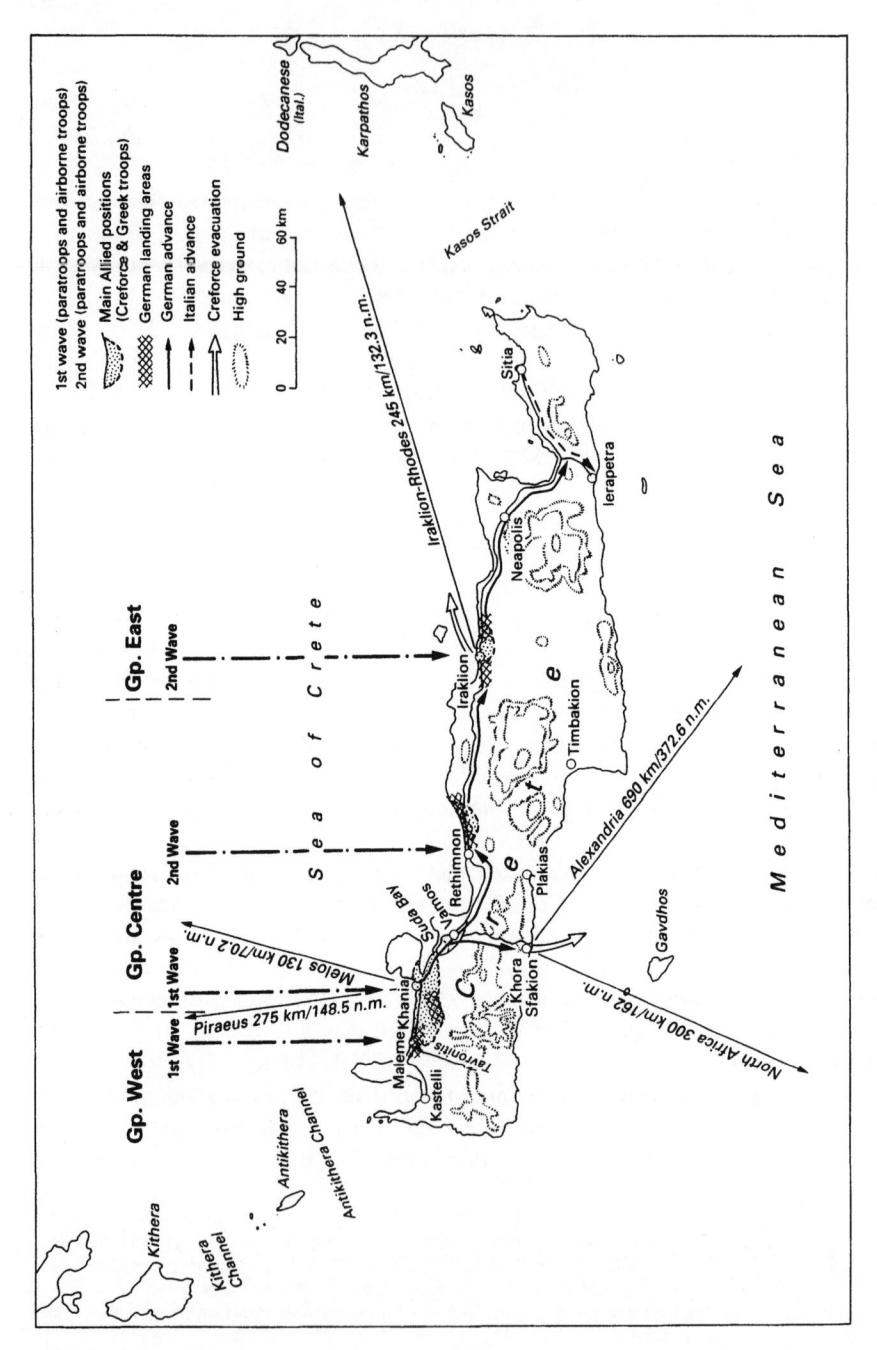

MAP III.IV.1. The Battle of Crete, 20 May–1 June 1941

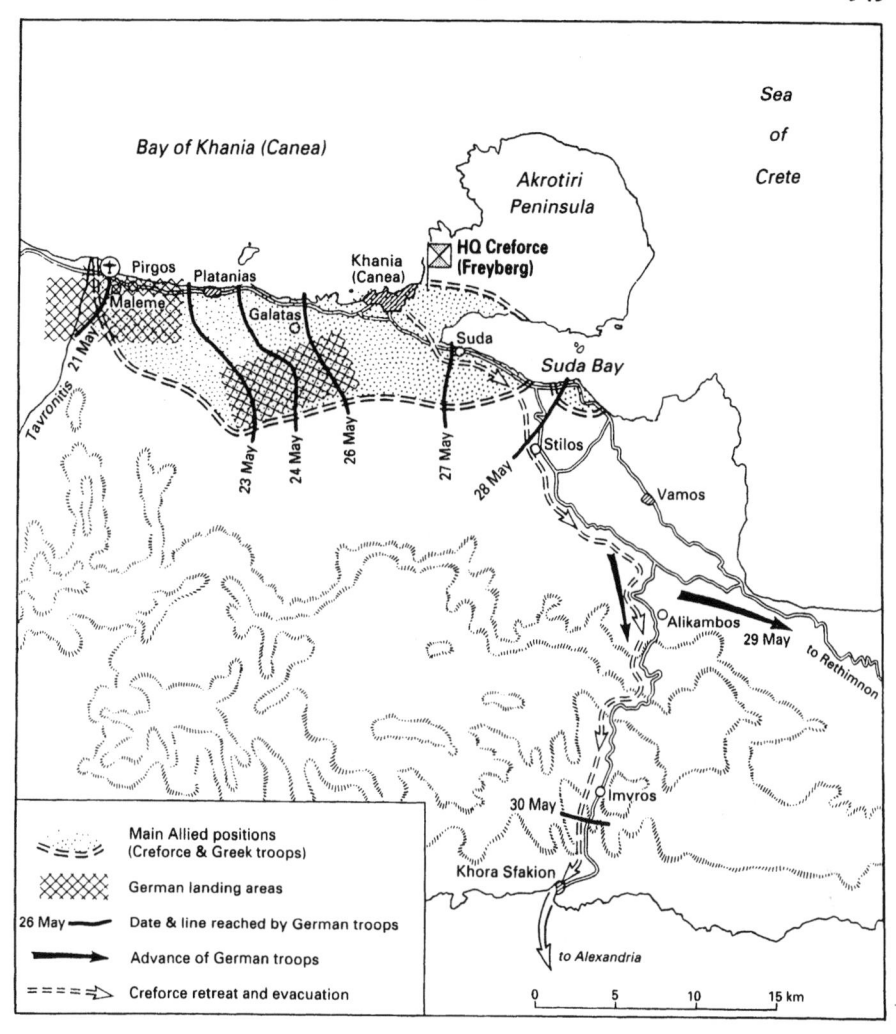

MAP III.IV.2. The Fighting in the West of Crete

The German units were thus able to pursue him closely and capture parts of the airfield and the heights to the south during the night. On the morning of 21 May, however, the landing-place was still within range of British artillery and infantry weapons.[86]

The German troops who had landed had not been able to establish radio

---
[86] On the fighting around Maleme cf. Gen.Kdo. XI. Fl.K., Einsatz Kreta, 20, 38 (11 July 1941), BA-MA RL 33/98; combat report, Sturmregiment (7 June 1941), 24, BA-MA RL 33/31; *The Second World War*, i. 184.

contact with the staffs in Athens and report on the situation. As a result, German military leaders there assumed at first that the operation was proceeding satisfactorily. Only during the afternoon, when contact had been established, did the command in Athens learn the approximate extent of the reverses and losses. It was, however, too late to adapt the orders of the second wave of attack to the new conditions. There was not sufficient contact with the Geschwader of VIII Air Corps, because several communications links with the airfields had been interrupted. Moreover, the transport units could not start at the time envisaged because of various problems such as the poor condition of the taxi-ways and the slow fuelling of the aircraft. Together with Italian aircraft, Richthofen's formations thus attacked targets in the middle and eastern sectors (primarily near Rethimnon and Heraklion), but, contrary to plan, the transport aircraft did not follow them immediately. As a result, the paratroops of the second wave were often dropped unprotected and, because of the large dust-clouds at the Greek airfields, with considerable delays. For these reasons the units of the second wave suffered even higher losses than those of the first on 20 May. Almost half of the paratroops were killed when they jumped or on the ground shortly thereafter. Neither in Rethimnon nor in Heraklion was it possible to make significant progress. Everywhere the German units still able to fight were forced to go on the defensive.[87]

In the evening of the first day of the attack Löhr, Student, and Richthofen had to admit that they had failed to reach any of their objectives because of the unexpectedly determined resistance of Creforce. Most seriously, none of the airfields on Crete had been captured; it was impossible to fly in reinforcements for the weakened paratroop and shock units, which were still separated from one another and could therefore provide no mutual support. The situation at Maleme was the most favourable. There the German units had at least succeeded in reaching the airfield. This was no longer possible in Rethimnon and Heraklion. The commanders of the corps involved and Löhr agreed to drop more paratroops to reinforce Group West the following day in order to capture the airfield at Maleme for the landing of troops of 5th Mountain Division. At the same time an attempt was to be made to land mountain infantry in the west of the island with 1st Glider Staffel by evening.[88]

On the morning of 21 May several transport aircraft were able to land between Maleme and the coast with urgently needed weapons and ammunition

---

[87] On the action of the second wave: Lfl. 4, Bericht Kreta, 17 ff., BA-MA RL 7/463; operation experience report, XI. Fl.K., 3, BA-MA RL 33/116; Mühleisen, *Kreta 1941*, 50. Near Rethimnon the commander of the German paratroop regiment fighting there was taken prisoner. Cf. Götzel, *Student*, 257.

[88] Löhr, Richthofen, and Student all claimed to have been responsible for the decision to leave Groups Centre and East to their fate for the time being and stake everything on consolidating the position of the German forces around Maleme. Cf. Löhr's letter of 8 Dec. 1942, p. 2 in Diakow, 'Unternehmen Kreta im Mai 1941', Löhr papers, KA, Vienna, B 521; Gen.Kdo. XI. Fl.K., Einsatz Kreta, 22–3, BA-MA RL 33/98. Cf. also Lewin, *The Chief*, 132–3; Gundelach, *Luftwaffe im Mittelmeer*, 213.

for Group West, and in the afternoon several companies of paratroops were dropped in this area. While some of them landed near Pirgos in the defenders' positions and only a few were able to escape, those dropped west of Maleme suffered only light losses. With the help of these units Group West was able to capture the airfield; the first transport aircraft with mountain infantrymen landed a few hours later. Aircraft losses were, however, heavy, as the airfield was still under British fire. By the evening of 21 May more than eighty destroyed or damaged German aircraft littered the airfield.[89] Personnel losses were, on the other hand, light. Group West was therefore able to begin pushing east. By the evening of 21 May, however, the attack had been stopped near Pirgos by the stubborn resistance of 5th New Zealand Brigade.[90]

Like the commanders of the New Zealand brigades, Freyberg had at first underestimated the importance of the battles in the western part of the island, as he had expected the main German attack to be by sea. For this reason he did not at first withdraw troops from positions near the coast to attack the Germans near Maleme. Instead he did everything to isolate the groups of paratroops. In this effort he was successful near Khania, Rethimnon, and Heraklion. After fighting which in some cases took a heavy toll, the paratroops in these areas were still unable to make any significant progress on 21 May.[91] Freyberg's expectations of an attack by sea were also confirmed: on the same day Admiral Schuster began to transport soldiers, weapons, and equipment to Crete by ship. But the first group of twenty-five motorized sailing-ships, accompanied by an Italian destroyer, failed to reach Crete before nightfall and was intercepted north of the island by British warships, which had patrolled the area the previous night. In spite of a fierce defence by the destroyer, the Royal Navy sank some of the sailing-ships and forced the survivors to head for Melos. The failed operation cost the lives of approximately 300 mountain infantrymen; almost all of the weapons and equipment on the ships were lost.[92] An attempt to reach Crete the following day with an even greater number of ships failed twenty nautical miles south of Melos. There the second group of transport ships encountered British cruisers and destroyers which had come from the direction of Heraklion during the morning. The transport group escaped the fate of the first group only because it was bravely covered by an Italian warship and the Luftwaffe finally forced the British ships to turn

---

[89] Figures according to Fl.Fü. 7. Fl.Div., W. Hornung, 'Kreta', 17, BA-MA ZA 3/19. On the landings cf. Gen.Kdo. XI. Fl.K., Einsatz Kreta, 40, BA-MA RL 33/98; Merglen, *Luftlandetruppen*, 45.

[90] Baldwin, *Battles*, 83–4.

[91] Gen.Kdo. XI. Fl.K., Einsatz Kreta, 42 ff., BA-MA RL 33/98. The supplying of the paratroops in this area was difficult because some of the ground panels they laid out fell into British hands: AOK 12, Ia, KTB, morning report (25 May 1941), BA-MA RH 20-12/62. On Freyberg's assumptions about the point of main effort of the German attack cf. *PWT*, Middle East I, Hist (B) 4, No. 160, p. 65 (21 May 1941); Davin, *Crete*, iii. 215.

[92] 1. Skl., KTB, Teil A, 313–14 (21 May 1941), BA-MA RM 7/24. Cf. also Roskill, *War at Sea*, i. 441.

away. The motorized sailing-ships were then able to return to the Greek mainland. Under constant attack by the Luftwaffe, the British ships turned towards the Kithira Channel, where another group of Royal Navy ships came to their aid. Nevertheless, the British fleet suffered considerable losses in this first great sea–air battle of the Second World War. On 23 May alone Richthofen's aircraft sank 3 warships (2 cruisers and 1 destroyer) and heavily damaged several others.[93]

The forays of Cunningham's ships north of Crete, which were also carried out during the day on 22 May, caused the German military staffs to assume that the British would accept any risk to prevent a landing on Crete from the sea. Löhr therefore decided to entrust the transport of soldiers and equipment to Crete to XI Air Corps until further notice.[94]

On the British side, however, the heavy losses of the Royal Navy—in the first three days of the battle of Crete alone 6 British warships were sunk and 7 others heavily damaged—caused Cunningham to ask the Admiralty to desist in future from any attempt to operate during the day in areas within the range of the Luftwaffe. At first the British government did not wish to grant this request, but they could not refute Cunningham's and Wavell's argument that further naval losses would endanger Britain's predominant position in the eastern Mediterranean. Without waiting for the decision of his government, Cunningham recalled almost all British ships to Alexandria on 23 May and, in agreement with Wavell, ordered that, to avoid German air attacks, Freyberg's troops were to be supplied only at night, using the fastest ships available.[95]

In Freyberg's headquarters the danger presented by the loss of the airfield at Maleme had now been recognized. On 21 May, therefore, 5th New Zealand Brigade was ordered to retake the lost positions around Maleme at nightfall. Although the attack began only after a considerable delay in the early hours of 22 May, the New Zealanders were able to advance rapidly at first. In the south they almost reached the Tavronitis river, and in the coastal sector one group even succeeded in pushing forward to the edge of the airfield. When, however, German resistance stiffened at sunrise and the Luftwaffe intervened, the attackers were unable to advance further. German counter-attacks forced them to withdraw to their old positions east of Pirgos, then to Platanias, and finally to Galatas the next day to escape German attempts at encirclement. This

---

[93] On the fighting at sea on 22 May cf. operation experience report Merkur (Adm. Schuster), 7–8, Löhr papers, KA, Vienna, B 521, No. 25; Unternehmen Merkur, 8–9, BA-MA RM 35 III/120; Playfair, *Mediterranean*, ii. 137. Richthofen's aircraft also attacked Italian warships several times by mistake. Cf. KTB Adm. Südost, 18, 30 (22, 24 May 1941), BA-MA RM 35 III/4.

[94] The Italian government did not comply with Göring's request the same day to send fast transport aircraft to Greece: Adm. Südost, Op 415 g.Kdos. to OKM/Skl., 22 May 1941, BA-MA CASE GE 1084, PG 33101. On Löhr's decision cf. operation experience report Merkur (Adm. Schuster), 8–9, Löhr papers, KA, Vienna, B 521, No. 25.

[95] *PWT*, Middle East I, Hist (B) 4, No. 186, p. 73 (23 May 1941), No. 190, p. 75 (23 May), and No. 204, p. 80 (24 May). Cf. also Butler, *Strategy*, ii. 512. On 23 May 1941 two more destroyers in a group of ships coming from Malta were sunk south of Crete. Cf. Roskill, *War at Sea*, i. 443.

3. The Battle for Crete

success also enabled Major-General Ringel, who had assumed command of the German forces in the western part of Crete on 22 May, to link up with the paratroops south-west of Khania, who had been isolated.[96] Moreover, the airfield at Maleme was now beyond the range of British artillery.

Löhr was mainly concerned about reaching Soudha Bay in order to cut the British supply-line and then relieve the paratroops in Rethimnon and Heraklion. Ringel therefore ordered mountain infantry to bypass the enemy troops in the south and at the same time attacked along the coast with all other available forces.[97] While the south wing of the German attack made only very slow progress in the impassable terrain, the attack on the carefully constructed positions of the New Zealanders around Galatas at first came to a stop. Only on 26 May, after incessant attacks by the Luftwaffe, were Ringel's forces able to break through Freyberg's defensive positions and reach Khania the next day.[98]

When the German attack around Galatas stalled and the attackers suffered high losses, on 26 May the Wehrmacht operations staff requested Mussolini to send army units to Crete and thus take some of the pressure off the German forces there. Mussolini immediately agreed, and two days later an Italian regiment, reinforced with armour and artillery, landed near Sitia in the eastern part of the island. By the end of the month these formations reached Ierapetra on the south coast without encountering significant resistance.[99]

The German request for Italian assistance was also due to the fact that attacks by the Royal Air Force for a time seemed to threaten the ability of XI Air Corps to deliver supplies to the airfield at Maleme. On 23 May British fighters and bombers appeared over Heraklion and carried out several successful attacks on German aircraft at Maleme in the following days.[100] In this situation Löhr decided to drop paratroops near Heraklion in order to capture the airfield there at last. Although the reinforced German troops were still not able to occupy the airfield, for a time the operation brought the taxi-ways within range of German guns. Finally, further British successes at Maleme

---

[96] Gen.Kdo. XI. Fl.K., Einsatz Kreta, 46 ff., BA-MA RL 33/98; *PWT*, Middle East I, Hist (B) 4, No. 180, p. 71 (22 May 1941). Cf. also Davin, *Crete*, iii. 196–7, 222. By 27 May all combat troops of 5th Mountain Division and parts of 6th Mountain Division had landed in Maleme: Gen.Kdo. XI. Fl.K., Einsatz Kreta, 47, BA-MA RL 33/98.

[97] 5. Geb.Div., Fü.Abt., KTB (22 May 1941), BA-MA RH 28-5/1. Cf. also Ansel, *Middle Sea*, 366–7.

[98] On the fighting around Galatas cf. 5. Geb.Div., KTB, annex 783 (map of 26 May 1941), BA-MA RH 28-5/3b; Stewart, *Struggle for Crete*, 403.

[99] There they were supposed to disrupt possible British evacuation measures: KTB, Adm. Südost, 38 (28 May 1941), BA-MA RM 35 III/4. On the German requests for help and the Italian reaction cf. Abt. Ausland No. 178/41 g.Kdos. Chefs. Ausl. III Org (27 May 1941), BA-MA RL 2 II/38; Bernotti, *Guerra nel Mediterraneo*, 174–5. After the conquest of Crete the eastern part of the island was occupied by Italian troops: 5. Geb.Div., Fü.Abt., KTB (28 May 1941), BA-MA RH 28-5/1.

[100] Operation experience report, J.G. 77, 41 (1 June 1941), BA-MA RL 8/243; AOK 12, Ia, KTB, morning report (23 May 1941) and evening report (25 May 1941), BA-MA RH 20-12/62.

were prevented by the dispatch of larger numbers of fighters from VIII Air Corps to protect the airfield there.[101]

After the fall of Khania, Freyberg, with the help of fresh troops from Egypt, was able to establish a new front along the road to Soudha and inflict heavy losses on the German attackers, but he realized that he would be able to hold this new defensive position for only a limited time. On 26 May he therefore informed his commander-in-chief in Cairo that, primarily because of the German air attacks and the dwindling quantities of supplies he was receiving, his troops had now reached the limit of their endurance. With the consent of Wavell and Churchill, he decided the next day to withdraw to Khora Sfakion on the south coast and attempt an evacuation by sea.[102] The British units in central and eastern Crete were to be picked up by ships of the Royal Navy from Heraklion and Plakias (on the south coast). Although on 25 May Cunningham had claimed that the crews of his ships had also reached the limits of their endurance, he was prepared to make every effort to save as many soldiers of Creforce as possible from being taken prisoner.[103]

Two days after Freyberg decided to evacuate his forces, Ringel's units broke through the stubbornly defended positions south-east of Khania and occupied Soudha Bay. The next day (29 May) they linked up with the decimated paratroop units near Rethimnon and at the same time pushed Creforce back to the east and south. However, the German commanders failed to notice that most of Creforce were withdrawing towards Khora Sfakion and not, as it had appeared, along the coastal road. For this reason Ringel sent only weak forces towards Khora Sfakion and ordered his main units to continue their advance eastward.[104] This mistake enabled Freyberg's rearguard to give the retreating troops of Creforce enough time to carry out their evacuation. Ringel's mistake is all the more surprising as, thanks to their total air supremacy, the Germans seemed to be aware of almost all important moves by the defenders of Crete. The explanation for Ringel's seeming misjudgement of the situation is probably that he and Löhr gave top priority to relieving the hard-pressed paratroops near Rethimnon, whose fate was still unknown.[105]

---

[101] Operation experience report, J.G. 77, 41 (1 June 1941), BA-MA RL 8/243. Cf. also Baldwin, *Battles*, 90 ff.

[102] On the new front between Khania and Soudha cf. Gen.Kdo. XI. Fl.K., Einsatz Kreta, 52, BA-MA RL 33/98; Stewart, *Struggle for Crete*, 419. On the plans to withdraw to Khora Sfakion for evacuation cf. *PWT*, Middle East I, Hist (B) 4, No. 229, p. 90, No. 232, p. 91, and No. 235, p. 92 (27 May 1941); Playfair, *Mediterranean*, ii. 141.

[103] *PWT*, Middle East I, Hist (B) 4, No. 221, p. 87 (26 May 1941). Cf. also Butler, *Strategy*, ii. 513–14.

[104] On Ringel's advance cf. AOK 12, Ia, KTB, evening report (28 May 1941), BA-MA RH 20-12/62, and ibid., morning report (30 May 1941).

[105] The high losses of the Luftwaffe as a result of crashes, enemy fire, and insufficient maintenance may also have been a reason why the British withdrawal to the south coast was not discovered in time. In many combat units of the Luftwaffe the number of aircraft ready for action sank to less than half the full numerical strength: K.G. 2, Ia, operation experience report Merkur (1 June 1941), 26, BA-MA RL 8/243.

3. The Battle for Crete

When Ringel's forces had linked up with these troops, they pushed on towards Heraklion and forced the units of the Creforce east of Rethimnon to surrender on 30 May. The Australian battalions there had been supposed to withdraw to the south coast of Crete, but Freyberg's order to retreat did not reach them in time.[106] Quite unnoticed by the Germans, on the other hand, the Creforce units in Heraklion (about 4,000 men) were picked up by British warships on the night of 28–9 May. Thereupon the paratroops of Group East occupied the area around Heraklion without a struggle and linked up with Ringel's troops approaching from the west on 29 May.[107]

The evacuation of the British troops, which began during the night of 28–9 May to avoid German air attacks, at first encountered serious difficulties. When the force coming from Heraklion was held up by the inability of a ship to manœuvre and could not pass the Strait of Kasos east of Crete under cover of darkness, German aircraft appeared and inflicted serious losses on the evacuation ships. Royal Air Force aircraft supposed to protect the group were unable to find them because of the resulting delay.[108] The evacuation on the south coast of Crete proceeded more smoothly. In four nights, up until 1 June, the Royal Navy was able to evacuate a total of 13,000 soldiers from Khora Sfakion to Egypt. The success of this operation was primarily due to the fact that the few long-range squadrons available to the Royal Air Force were able to prevent German aircraft from attacking the ships still within their range after sunrise.[109] They would have had serious difficulties fulfilling this task if heavy wear and technical problems had not begun to impair the fighting ability of the Luftwaffe units operating in Crete. The constant sorties and the lack of maintenance caused many breakdowns.[110] Nevertheless, when Wavell and Cunningham ended the evacuation on 1 June, the German mountain troops around Khora Sfakion were still able to take 9,000 Creforce soldiers and 1,000 Greeks prisoner. In spite of objections from London, the commanders-in-chief in Cairo refused to continue the evacuation after 1 June, as the remaining troops on Crete were no longer able to defend themselves against the approaching German mountain infantry.[111]

---

[106] AOK 12, Ia, KTB, evening report (29 May 1941), BA-MA RH 20-12/62. Cf. also Davin, *Crete*, iii. 390.

[107] XI. Fl.K., Einsatz Kreta, annexes, 44, BA-MA RL 33/99. Cf. also Davin, *Crete*, iii. 387–8.

[108] Cunningham, 'The Battle', 3114, 3116. The Luftwaffe sank 1 cruiser and 1 destroyer. Of the 4,000 evacuated men aboard, 800 were killed, wounded, or taken prisoner. Cf. Baldwin, *Battles*, 99.

[109] *PWT*, Middle East I, Hist (B) 5, No. 43, p. 17 (31 May 1941). Cf. also Cunningham, *A Sailor's Odyssey*, 388. On the evacuation figures cf. *PWT*, Middle East I, Hist (B) 5, No. 76, p. 30 (4 June 1941).

[110] Cf. n. 105 above. There were no reports of attacks by Italian submarines, which were supposed to disrupt the British evacuation attempts. On the sending of Italian submarines to the south coast of Crete cf. Verbindungsstab (liaison staff) Rom to Adm. Südost, No. 2648/41 g.Kdos, 27 May 1941, BA-MA CASE GE 1084, PG 33101.

[111] Gen.Kdo. XI. Fl.K., Einsatz Kreta, 54, BA-MA RL 33/98. On the advance towards Khora Sfakion cf. *PWT*, Middle East I, Hist (B) 5, No. 44, p. 17 (31 May 1941), decision to end the evacuation; Eden, *The Reckoning*, 283, for the British government's objections.

The fighting with Creforce on the island ended with the capture of Khora Sfakion, but not the operations of the German units against the Cretans themselves, who, unlike the Greeks on the mainland, had at times actively supported the Allies as partisans. As the Germans had received information that Greek officers had helped to arm the Cretans, all Greek soldiers on the island were taken prisoner and not, as had been done on the mainland, released after being disarmed.[112] Student also ordered harsh retaliatory measures against Greek civilians who had participated in the fighting and 'committed atrocities'. The German units concerned were to return to the respective villages, exterminate the male population, and demolish or burn down all the houses. Student expressly ordered the officers concerned not to wait for a special military court, but to set a warning example.[113] He believed that in this way he could create the best conditions for his work as future Wehrmacht commander on the island.

The German units involved did not report how many Greek civilians fell victim to these massacres. In contrast personnel and material losses in the battle of Crete were recorded in detail. Considering the short duration of the operation (twelve days), they were extremely high, especially among the paratroops and the airborne units. In many units more than half of the soldiers were dead, missing, or wounded.[114] Total casualties of XI Air Corps were approximately 6,000; moreover, a considerable number of aircraft had been destroyed. When the fighting on Crete ended, Student had only 185 aircraft at his disposal; 150 had been completely destroyed and 165 heavily damaged.[115] In view of these high losses it is astonishing that, in his order of the day on 12 June 1941, Löhr promised: 'True to our oath to the Führer and supreme commander of the Wehrmacht, we stand ready for new tasks.'[116] This was clearly impossible in the near future, as the best fighting units, and in particular their officers, had suffered the most serious losses.

Allied losses were also considerable.[117] However, the British succeeded, as

[112] 5. Geb.Div., KTB, annex 1199 (3 June 1941), BA-MA RH 28-5/4.

[113] 5. Geb.Div., Fü.Abt., KTB (2 June 1941), BA-MA RH 28-5/1, and KTB, annex 1192, Befehl XI. Fl.K. (31 May 1941), BA-MA RH 28-5/4; mission completion reports, ibid., annex 1211 (5 June 1941). Cf. also Austermann, *Eben Emael*, 62. On violations of international law by the Cretans cf. OKW, Wehrmachtuntersuchungsstelle für Verletzungen des Völkerrechts, BA-MA RW 2/v. 138; Zayas, *Die Wehrmacht-Untersuchungsstelle*, 262 ff.

[114] Combat report, 2./Sturm-Rgt. (8 Aug. 1941), 28, BA-MA RL 33/36. According to this report, the company of 150 men had suffered 85 casualties.

[115] Breakdown according to Notizen Fl.Fü. 7. Fl.Div., in W. Hornung, 'Kreta', 38, BA-MA ZA 3/19: 143 complete losses, 8 missing, 120 with considerable and 85 with medium and light damage. Richthofen's losses were 200–300 men and 50–70 aircraft. Luftwaffe general staff/ Gen.Qu. 6. Abt. (Ic) No. 2836/41, g.Kdos., report (1 June 1941), BA-MA RL 2 III/957. Cf. also Forbes, 'Crete', 157.

[116] AOK 12, Abt. IIa (5 June 1941), BA-MA RH 20-12/93 D.

[117] The figures vary between 10,000 men (*PWT*, Middle East I, Hist (B) 5, No. 73, P. 29 (4 June 1941)) and 14,000; 11,000–12,000 of these were prisoners (mostly non-combatants), 1,740 dead, and 2,200 wounded. In addition, the losses of the Royal Navy were 1,800 dead and 200 wounded. Cf. Cruickshank, *Greece 1940–1941*, 173; Playfair, *Mediterranean*, ii. 147; Long, *Greece, Crete and Syria*, 316. Greek losses were 1,500 dead and 5,000 taken prisoner. Cf. Ansel, *Middle Sea*, 419.

3. The Battle for Crete

they had on the Greek mainland, in evacuating large parts of their best fighting units to Egypt, where in the following months they were sent into action against the Axis in North Africa.[118] For the British government and the military commanders in Cairo, the losses of ships were the most painful aspect of the battle of Crete. German aircraft had sunk six warships and heavily damaged seven others. However, as Halder himself admitted, the remaining ships of the Royal Navy in the eastern Mediterranean were sufficient to maintain Britain's dominant position there.[119]

Nevertheless, Hitler had succeeded with a triphibious operation (mainly carried out, however, by the Luftwaffe and the army) in conquering a large island from the air for the first time. The capture of Crete secured the supply-lines from the Black Sea to Italy and took the military pressure off Germany's Axis partner. Moreover, the German government could now assume that Turkey would be less inclined than ever to enter into an alliance with Britain. In retrospect, however, it seems doubtful that the conquest of Crete was necessary to secure south-east Europe completely against British attacks. From the Dodecanese, in Italian possession, it would have been possible to maintain constant surveillance of the airfields on the island.[120] The original Axis expectation that the conquest of Crete would make it possible to relieve supply problems in North Africa proved to be unfounded. The transportation network in Greece and the shipping space available to Germany and Italy were barely adequate to supply the troops remaining on the island. As a result, the main supply-line for North Africa continued to pass close to Malta, held by the British.[121] Mussolini's prediction to Hitler that the conquest of Crete would cause Britain to abandon Alexandria, leaving Gibraltar as the only refuge for the British fleet in the future, proved to be completely groundless.[122]

Although Hitler did not contradict his Italian ally, more realistic considerations determined further German aims in the Mediterranean. Two factors were especially important in this regard: the high losses of the airborne units could not be simply ignored, and, on the other hand, a clear decision had to be made about the future geographical area of main effort in the war. Hitler was of the opinion that the high material and personnel losses on Crete prohibited further use of large airborne units. He therefore rejected Mussolini's idea of conquering Cyprus as the next British bastion and thus seizing the key to

---

[118] There was one exception: the infantry units of the Australian contingent near Rethimnon were all taken prisoner. Cf. Long, *Greece, Crete and Syria*, 316.

[119] Halder, *KTB* ii. 442 (4 June 1941). According to Baldwin (*Battles*, 102–3), the following ships were still available in Alexandria (some of them, however, required extensive repairs): 1 aircraft-carrier, 2 battleships, 2 cruisers, and 13 destroyers. According to Long (*Greece, Crete and Syria*, 320), the figures were: 1 aircraft-carrier, 2 battleships, 3 cruisers, and 17 destroyers.

[120] Cf. Baldwin, *Battles*, 109–10. On the conclusions based on the conquest of Crete cf. *Lagevorträge*, 258 ff. (6 June 1941).

[121] Cf. Warlimont, 'Kriegführung', 369, 371, MGFA P-216/I-III.

[122] *DGFP* D xii, No. 584, pp. 940 ff. (3 June 1941), here 945, conference with Hitler on 2 June 1941.

further operations in the Middle East. Hitler argued that such an operation was not feasible at that time because of the short range of German fighters, which would not be able to use Turkish bases. Nevertheless, Keitel suggested at a conference with leading representatives of the Italian armed forces general staff that, using the Dodecanese, Italy herself should conquer Cyprus with the support of the Luftwaffe.[123]

Like Mussolini, the naval war staff and representatives of the department of home defence in the Wehrmacht operations staff argued for a continuation of the offensive in the Mediterranean. Raeder in particular considered the prestige of the British Empire to be inseparably linked with Britain's influence in the Middle East. He concluded that a continuation of the German–Italian offensive in that area and the Mediterranean was of decisive importance for the war. On no account, he argued, must the war against the Soviet Union delay this development.[124]

Hitler, however, was still convinced that the war against the Soviet Union would be decisive and that Germany clearly did not have sufficient resources to conduct it and the war in the Mediterranean at the same time with equal intensity. In Directive No. 31 of 9 June 1941 Hitler's intention to begin an offensive air war against the British in the eastern Mediterranean with X Air Corps, transferred to Greece at the beginning of the month, was clear. But at the same time he explained that 'at the present time' he only wanted to organize the future 'Fortress Crete' for this task. After several operations by X Air Corps shortly after its arrival, German air units on Crete confined their activities to securing the conquered territory.[125]

After the fall of Crete, the British at first expected Hitler to exploit his success and set his sights on other objectives in the Mediterranean and the Middle East. The War Office therefore established a list of priorities, the war in North Africa being considered the most important theatre. While the British government considered reinforcing the Allied position in Syria, the weak garrison in Cyprus was to be given no additional support for the time being.[126] Realistically assessing German possibilities, the British had considered how to improve security at airfields in the area under their control, and how to provide better protection for surface ships, but they did not believe that Hitler, as was sometimes suggested, would try to carry out airborne

---

[123] Niederschrift WFSt, No. 44872/41 g.Kdos., 3 June 1941 (conference, 2 June 1941), BA-MA RL 2 II/38. On Mussolini's intention cf. Dt.Gen. beim H.Q. d. ital. Wehrmacht to Chef Amt. Ausl. Abw. No. 178/41 g.Kdos. (27 May 1941), ibid. On Hitler's opinion cf. *DGFP* D xii, No. 584, pp. 940 ff. (3 June 1941); Hillgruber, *Strategie*, 468; Merglen, *Luftlandetruppen*, 46.

[124] 1. Skl., KTB, Teil A, 454–5 (30 May 1941), BA-MA RM 7/24; 1. Skl., KTB, Teil C, XIV, Deutsche Kriegführung im Mittelmeer, 18 ff. (1 June 1941), BA-MA RM 7/234. Cf. also Creveld, *Balkan*, 170.

[125] Cf. Ansel, *Middle Sea*, 432; *Hitler's War Directives*, No. 31, pp. 74–7 (9 June 1941). In addition to the units of X Flying Corps and the Italian troops, parts of 5th Mountain Division also remained on Crete. Cf. Baum and Weichold, *Krieg der 'Achsenmächte'*, 167.

[126] *PWT*, Middle East I, Hist (B) 5, No. 7, p. 4 (28 May 1941); Außen- und militärpolitischer Kurzbericht No. 154 (3 June 1941) (BBC broadcast), BA-MA RW 5/v. 354.

3. The Battle for Crete

operations against Britain herself. The superiority of the Royal Air Force in the skies over Britain and the heavy losses suffered by German airborne units in Crete were sufficient reasons to consider such operations highly improbable.[127] After the initial shock of the new defeat, the British realized that German possession of Crete would not have a decisive effect on the war in the Mediterranean and the Middle East. In retrospect it was even suggested that the German decision to conquer Crete and not Malta had perhaps had a favourable effect on the course of the war in North Africa from the British point of view.[128] The first indications of this could be seen in the following months, when the transfer of X Air Corps from Italy to Greece significantly improved the British position around Malta and the Axis supply-lines to North Africa became increasingly vulnerable.

The spectacular conquest of Crete, the capture of a large island without using significant naval forces, did not change the fact that this operation did not involve a decisive battle.[129] The really important events took place elsewhere. By mid-1941 Britain was able to regain the upper hand in East Africa (Ethiopia) and the Middle East (Iraq and the Levant). These successes enabled the British to concentrate their resources on the war in North Africa. Although Churchill's assessment of the situation in his speech to the House of Commons on 10 June 1941 contained elements intended to restore Britain's shaken self-confidence, he was right when he asserted that, on the whole, the situation in the Mediterranean and the Middle East was far more favourable for Britain than it had been a year earlier.[130]

[127] Churchill, *The Unrelenting Struggle*, 163. Cf. also Stewart, *Crete*, 477.
[128] Cf. Roskill, *War at Sea*, i. 449; Playfair, *Mediterranean*, ii. 148 ff.; Stewart, *Crete*, 477 ff.
[129] e.g. Gundelach, 'Kreta'.
[130] Churchill, *The Unrelenting Struggle*, 167–8. On the situation in the Middle East and East Africa cf. IV.II.2 below (Schreiber).

PART IV

Politics and Warfare in 1941

GERHARD SCHREIBER

I. The Anglo-American Association and its Consequences for British Strategy

THE United States presidential election took place on 5 November 1940. Although it was known in Britain that, over and above party conflicts, both the president in office and his opponent, Wendell Willkie, were alike resolved that America should furnish material and political support to the British, Churchill nevertheless received the report of Roosevelt's re-election with 'indescribable relief'.[1] Indeed, no other president would have secured to the same extent the stability of the American–British relationship, based essentially on the personal links between the two statesmen,[2] and no politician fresh at the helm could have guaranteed, as did the experienced Roosevelt, the continuity of an active foreign policy embracing equally the European–Atlantic and the Pacific–East Asian areas. This was decisive, for, irrespective of agreement about material aid,[3] readiness to accept involvement in both hemispheres was then by no means unquestioned among American politicians.[4]

Doubts about such a double burden, which, if it came to the test, seemed likely to exceed America's military potential, were also reflected in a memorandum, known under the code-name 'Plan Dog', which was submitted on 4 November by Admiral Harold R. Stark, Chief of Naval Operations of the US Navy.[5] This represented the first attempt, after the change of situation due to the conclusion of the Tripartite Pact,[6] to analyse every aspect of American military strategy in order to achieve a realistic concept for military planning. Stark's investigation assumed the imminent entry of the United States into the war and presupposed unlimited co-operation between British and American forces. In addition, the admiral established a direct dependence between

---

[1] Churchill, *Second World War*, ii. 489. The congratulations (6 Nov. 1940) are printed in *Churchill and Roosevelt*, C-37x, p. 81.
[2] On the relationship between Churchill and Roosevelt cf. e.g. Lash, *Roosevelt and Churchill*; also the introduction to F. D. Roosevelt, *Roosevelt and Churchill*, 3–88.
[3] Churchill, *Second World War*, ii. 490.
[4] Hillgruber, *Strategie*, 310; cf. also Divine, *Reluctant Belligerent*; Doenecke, 'Non-interventionism'. On Roosevelt's policy, particularly in relation to Germany, see e.g. Bailey and Ryan, *Hitler vs. Roosevelt*, 31–47 and 99–116 on lend-lease; Dahms, *Roosevelt*; Divine, *Roosevelt*; Fehrenbach, *Undeclared War*; Greenfield, 'Hauptentscheidungen'; Gruchmann, 'Völkerrecht'; Junker, *Roosevelt*; also Link's bibliographic survey, 'Das nationalsozialistische Deutschland'; Moltmann, *Amerikas Deutschlandpolitik*; Sniegoski, 'Die amerikanische Reaktion'.
[5] On Plan Dog cf. e.g. Hillgruber, *Strategie*, 310–11; Matloff and Snell, 'Strategische Planungen', 66–9; eid., *Strategic Planning*, 25–8; Morison, *The Battle*, 42 ff.; Sherwood, *Roosevelt and Hopkins*, 271–2; Watson, *War Department*, 118 ff.; Stoler, *Second Front*, 7, 10–11.
[6] Cf. I.III.1 (*b*) above.

PRELIMINARY NOTE

THE dominant themes of 1941 were Operation Barbarossa, the war of destruction, inspired by racialist ideology, against the Soviet Union;[1] the United States as the arsenal of British resistance, which after the armistice between France and the Axis powers was of vital significance in defeating Hitler's strategic calculations; and the extension to the military sphere of the US–Japanese dispute.[2] This completed the broadening of the European conflict into a world war, in which such contrasting social systems as the Western democracies and the Stalinist dictatorship were linked in defence against the global aggression of Germany, Italy, and Japan.[3] All these developments were more or less to be expected as Hitler's programme took effective shape. Admittedly this is a highly simplified view of the historical process, for Japan had, since the 1930s, conducted a completely autonomous policy[4] aimed at the 'greater East Asian co-prosperity sphere'. But from the point of view of German aspirations and their fulfilment this view is indeed correct. In this context it should be recalled that in mid-July 1941 Hitler tried to form an alliance with Japan, the aim of which, after the achievement of the German continental empire, was to be the destruction of their main enemy, the United States.[5] And it was the latter's increasing readiness in 1941 to play a military role in events which supplied the counterpoint to Hitler's hegemonic design.

[1] On this whole theme see *Das Deutsche Reich und der Zweite Weltkrieg*, iv.
[2] Ibid., vol. vi; cf. also Herde, *Pearl Harbor*; Libal, *Japans Weg in den Krieg*; Lehmann, 'Leitmotive'.
[3] See esp. Harris, *Shifting Winds*; Knipping, *Amerikanische Rußland-Politik*, esp. 117–99; Langer, 'Formulation'; among the older Literature McNeill, *America, Britain, and Russia*; Weinberg, *World*, 27–52.
[4] See e.g. Herde, *Pearl Harbor*; Libal, *Japans Weg in den Krieg*; Martin, 'Deutsch-japanische Beziehungen', 454–70; id., *Deutschland und Japan*; id., 'Japans Weltmachtstreben'; Meskill, *Hilter and Japan*; Presseisen, *Germany and Japan*; Schroeder, *Axis*; Sommer, *Deutschland und Japan*; also Krebs, 'Japans Deutschlandpolitik', probably the best investigation of this theme so far. The author was able to make full use of Japanese literature and sources in the original.
[5] Cf. the excellent summary of the programmatic and situational factors in Hitler's calculations in the summer of 1941 in Hillgruber, *Zenit*, here esp. pp. 16 ff.

American military capabilities and the possible defeat of Great Britain and the destruction of the Empire. For, should the British Empire no longer exist, not only would the western hemisphere be open to direct attack, but the consequent loss of exports could lead indirectly to the weakening of American armament. Stark was therefore of the opinion that the United States, 'in the event of Great Britain achieving a decisive victory over Germany, could be victorious everywhere, but that should Great Britain lose, [the Americans] would face a very severe problem. [They] could then indeed not lose everywhere but might nowhere win.'

For the operational planning of the American conduct of war in the Atlantic and Pacific areas, Plan Dog recommended a 'strictly defensive' attitude in the Pacific. For a limited offensive there—at immeasurably high cost—would not lead to the defeat of Japan, but would remove the United States' freedom to transfer their fleet at need from the Pacific to the Atlantic Ocean; it could also escalate at any time to an unlimited engagement of the United States. It was this in particular that Admiral Stark wished to avoid. For, basically, Stark did not believe that the British were capable of maintaining their empire. It could perhaps not be taken for granted that they could defend their islands. Above all, Stark regarded Britain as unable to carry out the land offensive which, in his view, was alone capable of deciding the war. The United States must therefore be prepared for large-scale landing operations in the Atlantic area. For, after American entry into the war, they would not only have to employ their navy in support of Britain but would also have 'to send strong land and air forces to Europe or Africa, perhaps to both continents'.[7] In essence Stark's arguments amounted to the following demands: the reorientation of American foreign policy in the Far East, in order to lessen the Japanese threat,[8] and the building up of strategic concentrations of forces in the Atlantic area with the aim of overcoming the Axis powers ('Germany first') on land. In order to make this possible, not only the island realm but also the British positions in Egypt, Gibraltar, and West and North-West Africa would have to be maintained.

The American general staff agreed wholeheartedly with the Admiral's plan. Roosevelt's detailed comments, when the memorandum was made known to him in mid-November, are not on file, but he tacitly allowed Stark's project to be pursued.[9] It seems clear, however, that the president, at least until March 1941, did not feel committed to such a strategy. This showed, for instance, in his unchanged policy in East Asia.[10] As to the key question of whether the fleet should have its main operational area in the Atlantic or the Pacific, the president decided on 16 January 1941 that, in a basically defensive stance, it should remain stationed in Hawaii. At the same time Roosevelt committed

---

[7] Matloff and Snell, 'Strategische Planungen', 68.
[8] On the Japanese viewpoint cf. Libal, *Japans Weg in den Krieg*, 88–97, for the period autumn 1940 and winter 1940–1.
[9] Matloff and Snell, 'Strategische Planungen', 74 n. 16.
[10] Hillgruber, *Strategie*, 312–13.

himself to according Great Britain every possible material assistance.[11] He had previously agreed to Stark's proposals for secret but official American–British staff talks. This intention was known in London on 30 November 1940. The subject of the negotiations was to be full military co-operation, in the event of American entry into the war, on the basis of Plan Dog, i.e. war against Germany and Italy, while everything was to be done to keep Japan out of the conflict.[12] The delegations met on 29 January 1941, and the result of their consultations formed the central provisions of the subsequent joint strategy.

Before these military agreements are treated in greater detail, however, consideration must be given to the origins of the Lend-Lease Act and the German reaction to it. This law placed America's material aid to Britain on a completely new basis.[13] It accorded, on the one hand, with the main precondition of any continuation of the war against the aggressors, namely the speedy and comprehensive supplying of Britain with war material,[14] and, on the other, with the desperate financial situation of the British.[15] Churchill expressed his views on this in a very frank and comprehensive letter to Roosevelt dated 8 December 1940.[16] The importance of this letter is undisputed.[17] The prime minister described the difficult situation in which Great Britain would find herself in 1941, with the question of the dollar at the root of all problems. Until November 1940 the British had paid cash for everything the Americans delivered. This amounted to $4,500m.; the British still had a reserve of something over $2,000m., chiefly in investments which were not readily saleable. London's financial capacity was gradually being exhausted. Even if all investments abroad and cash reserves had been realized, they would not have sufficed to pay for even half of the material already ordered, not to mention that the extension of the war made it necessary to raise orders tenfold.[18] Thus for London the previous practice of 'cash and carry' had become an impossibility.[19]

Roosevelt received Churchill's letter on board the heavy cruiser *Tuscaloosa* during a cruise in the Caribbean in the course of which he visited the new

---

[11] Butler, *Strategy*, ii. 424.
[12] Ibid. 423; Watson, *War Department*, 120.
[13] On the lend-lease law, mentioned in all the relevant studies, cf. e.g. Butler, *Strategy*, ii. 418–23; Carl, *Leih- und Pacht-Gesetz*; Churchill; *Second World War*, ii. 488–508; Hillgruber, *Strategie*, 313 ff.; Kimbal, *The Most Unsordid Act*; Krüger, 'Das Jahr 1941'; Marshall *et al.*, *War Report*, 481 ff., 115–16, 311; Playfair, *Mediterranean*, ii. 231 ff.; Schlauch, *Rüstungshilfe* (covering the whole period of the war); Snell, *Illusion*, 73; Stettinius, *Lend-Lease*, 71–108; Woodward, *British Foreign Policy*, i. 388–97.
[14] Butler, *Strategy*, ii. 418.
[15] Stettinius, *Lend-Lease*, 69–74.
[16] Churchill, *Second World War*, ii. 494–501.
[17] Ibid. 493; repr. in Woodward, *British Foreign Policy*, i. 388–95. There is a detailed commentary on the genesis of this letter in *Churchill and Roosevelt*, C-43x, pp. 87–111, with copies of all its drafts from 12 Nov. to 7 Dec. (later dated 8 Dec.) 1940; correction of 20 Dec. 1940, p. 111.
[18] Churchill, *Second World War*, ii. 493–4, 501–2.
[19] On the 'cash and carry' system cf. Stettinius, *Lend-Lease*, 11–23.

naval bases leased from the British.[20] At a press conference on 17 December, the day after his return, he referred for the first time to his plan 'to eliminate the dollar sign' from American support for Great Britain, setting out the principles of his new idea with the now famous illustration of the garden hose. The president said:

> Suppose my neighbour's house catches fire and I have a length of garden hose four or five hundred feet away. If he can take my hose and connect it up with his hydrant, I may help him to put out the fire. Now what do I do? I don't say to him before that operation 'Neighbour, my garden hose cost me fifteen dollars; you have to pay me fifteen dollars for it!' No. What is the transaction that goes on? I don't want fifteen dollars—I want my garden hose back after the fire is over![21]

That was the principle of 'lend-lease'.

Roosevelt, as Churchill records,[22] had pondered for longer over the effective public presentation of his idea than over its basic principle. The latter was by no means a novelty, and the president had for some time been considering a solution of this sort for the British payments problem. It was suggested to him by the fact that since 1892 there had been a law in the United States whereby army property 'not required for state purposes' could be leased for a prescribed period 'for the benefit of the community'. Doubtless one of the impulses for lend-lease derived from this. Moreover, in the National Defence Council in the late summer of 1940, when the British shortage of shipping space and the resulting supply difficulties were discussed (it was known that the British lacked the money to order sufficient new shipping), Roosevelt had expressed the view that it was not absolutely necessary to sell ships to Great Britain: there was no obstacle to leasing tonnage simply 'for the duration of the emergency'.[23] On 17 December, too, the president had in mind basic aspects of American defence strategy. As long as she was able to defend herself, Britain was the most direct and effective protection for the United States. It was therefore in the American interest for quite pragmatic, indeed self-centred, motives to help the British in every way. In addition there was of course the traditional bond with Britain in the struggle for the 'survival of democracy throughout the world'. All in all the satisfaction of British needs represented a vital concern of the American people. The material produced should, however, only be leased, not sold.[24]

Roosevelt had already given signs of adopting such a course immediately after his re-election. On 8 November he had ordered that war material produced, particularly aircraft, should in future be divided approximately equally between American and British forces. At the same time American industry

[20] Ibid. 78; Sherwood, *White House Papers*, i. 221–2.
[21] Cited from Churchill, *Second World War*, ii. 502; cf. Butler, *Strategy*, ii. 420–1; Sherwood, *White House Papers*, i. 223–4; Stettinius, *Lend-Lease*, 62 ff.
[22] Churchill, *Second World War*, ii. 502.
[23] Stettinius, *Lend-Lease*, 75.
[24] Ibid. 75; Woodward, *British Foreign Policy*, i. 395.

accepted orders for a further 12,000 aircraft in addition to the 11,000 already ordered.[25] However, the still limited capacity of the aircraft industry placed relatively tight restraints on the completion of these orders; of the 23,000 machines, the British had received only 2,100 by 1 December 1940.[26]

A few days after Roosevelt's press conference, the White House gave notice of a 'fireside chat' on matters of national defence.[27] Now that the election campaign was over, the president was free to reject unambiguously any thought of appeasement. Roosevelt left no doubt that in his opinion there must be no negotiated peace with Hitler.

A nation can have peace with the Nazis only at the price of total surrender. . . . Such a dictated peace would be no peace at all. It would be only another armistice, leading to the most gigantic armament race and the most devastating trade wars in history. . . . All of us, in all the Americas, would be living at the point of a Nazi gun loaded with explosive bullets, economic as well as military.[28]

At the end of his talk Roosevelt summed up his views on the future policy of the United States in the striking demand: 'We must be the great arsenal of democracy.'[29] That was much more than the simple transition from 'cash and carry' to 'lend-lease'. The president in fact showed himself determined to place America with all her economic resources in support of the battle against the aggressors.[30]

The first draft of the lend-lease bill was ready on 2 January 1941. After various consultations and amendments it was presented to the Senate and House of Representatives on 10 January.[31] The debate on the bill, which received the 'historic' number 'H.R. 1776', lasted over two months.[32] Finally, on 11 March, the law 'to promote the defence of the United States' was passed by 317 votes to 71.[33] It entitled the president to use all the resources of the

---

[25] Butler, *Strategy*, ii. 422; Hillgruber, *Strategie*, 314.

[26] Stettinius, *Lend-Lease*, 62.

[27] On the 'fireside chat' of 29 Dec. 1940 cf. esp. Sherwood, *White House Papers*, i. 224 ff.; Stettinius, *Lend-Lease*, 67, 73.

[28] Cited from Sherwood, *White House Papers*, i. 225; cf. also Butler, *Strategy*, ii. 421.

[29] This was not an original formulation by Roosevelt, as it appeared in various newspapers before his speech. It probably originated with William S. Knudsen or Jean Monnet. There was for some time discussion in the White House as to whether such a satement was opportune, as it might block or at least call in question American aid to non-democratic states. However, the president succumbed to the attraction of the phrase—'it was too good': Stettinius, *Lend-Lease*, 67.

[30] Hillgruber, *Strategie*, 313.

[31] Stettinius, *Lend-Lease*, 73-7.

[32] Ibid. 77-85; 4 July 1776 is the date of the Declaration of Independence of the then thirteen United States and the first formulation of human rights and the right of resistance which was derived therefrom. Cf. also Sherwood, *White House Papers*, i. 227-8.

[33] Printed in full in Stettinius, *Lend-Lease*, 335-9 (app. 1). Extracts in Jacobsen, *Der Zweite Weltkrieg*, 129-30. Cf. also Gilbert, *Finest Hour*, 1031 ff. The Senate passed the law on 8 Mar. 1941 by 60 votes to 31. On 11 Mar. 1941 it was once again presented to the House of Representatives for agreement to certain amendments. The House had already approved the law in principle by 260 votes to 165 on 8 Feb. 1941. See also *DGFP* D xii, No. 34, pp. 60-2 (7 Feb. 1941); No. 88, pp. 161-4 (25 Feb. 1941); and No. 141, pp. 251-2 (9 Mar. 1941).

state within the framework of lend-lease measures to support the government of any country in so far as he regarded the protection of that country as 'vital to the defence of the United States'.[34] On the following day Roosevelt asked Congress to grant $7,000m. for the manufacture of aircraft, armoured vehicles, guns, industrial plant, and food production, as well as the procurement of raw materials, in order to aid nations whose defence was thought necessary: in the first instance, Greece and Britain.[35] For Yugoslavia an emergency programme of material aid was drawn up after 6 April, but it came too late, as did the consignments for Greece. The first lend-lease programme therefore did not affect operations in the Balkans.[36]

How did the German leadership react to these developments across the Atlantic? Hans Thomsen, the chargé d'affaires in Washington, interpreted Roosevelt's re-election as an expression of the will of the American nation to aid Britain by every means, but did not expect the United States to enter the war soon. It had to be assumed that under Roosevelt the American government would be much more ready than under Willkie to support Britain even at the expense of the national armament effort, and perhaps even by direct military action.[37] However, Roosevelt's 'garden hose' speech of 17 December was interpreted by the embassy as intended basically to ensure that he retained freedom of decision. For this reason the president had also proposed that the United States government should in future treat all British orders as their own. This meant in practice that—unlike the position under an aid agreement of the traditional type, which would have provided American credits to remedy Britain's inability to pay—as things were London could neither determine the extent of deliveries of raw materials nor use American dollars, which it could probably never repay, to build aircraft works, munitions factories, and shipyards. In the present case the American government was investing in its own country, and the newly created armaments industry remained under national control. Thomsen quite rightly supposed that Roosevelt's plan was also based on the belief that whether the British could really hold out would not be apparent for some weeks. If they did, a long war was to be expected, and Britain would become steadily stronger thanks to increasing American help. The American arms industry would then have time to achieve a volume of production that would make a British victory possible. It was thus a question of a relatively slow-working, long-term calculation, with the advantage that if Britain were defeated the whole of America's productive capacity could be applied without difficulty to her own needs.[38]

---

[34] Stettinius, *Welt in Abwehr*, 417, § 3 (a) (i) (not found in *Lend-Lease*).
[35] Stettinius, *Lend-Lease*, 85–6; Butler, *Strategy*, ii. 422.
[36] Stettinius, *Lend-Lease*, 90–2; Playfair, *Mediterranean*, ii. 231.
[37] Chargé d'affaires in Washington to foreign ministry, 6 Nov. 1940, *DGFP* D xi, No. 292, pp. 476–7. Cf. the state secretary's circular of 8 Nov. 1940 concerning the language to be employed in the context of Roosevelt's re-election, ibid. No. 305, p. 499.
[38] Chargé d'affaires in Washington to foreign ministry, 19 Dec. 1940, ibid., No. 534, pp. 905–6.

The German embassy regarded the 'fireside chat' of 29 December as a further step towards intensive aid to Britain. The president evidently wished to mobilize all the nation's resources so as to overcome the backwardness of American armaments as quickly as possible. The response to his words had shown that American public opinion sympathized with his intention, as people believed firmly in what he had called 'Hitler's plans for world conquest and the threat to America'. Altogether Roosevelt's words were 'an open challenge to the totalitarian states' and a 'proclamation of the greatest historical importance'.[39] In any case it was less feasible than ever to rule out the official entry of the United States into the war. The German ambassador (who was at that time in Berlin) warned against the view occasionally put forward in Germany that it was rather a matter of indifference whether the United States entered the war against Germany or not, as they were already giving the British all the help they could, and their entry into the war 'would not represent any essential change'.[40] The foreign ministry for its part feared that American intervention would put an end to any hope that, after the collapse of Britain, an arrangement might be arrived at with the American isolationists, who would then presumably be stronger, whereby 'America would sacrifice England and withdraw from the affair with her own gains'.[41]

Thus when the lend-lease law was passed by the Senate on the night of 8–9 March 1941 (the vote in the House of Representatives on 11 March was purely a formality),[42] the German ambassador hoped that the Wehrmacht would soon inflict a decisive defeat on Britain, as in that case Roosevelt would hardly dare to intervene militarily against the will of 70 or 80 per cent of the American electorate. If, on the other hand, the German–British contest dragged on indecisively for a long time, there was 'a considerable danger that public opinion will develop in the direction of a growing willingness to enter the war'. At present, however, 85–90 per cent of Americans approved only of a policy 'short of war'.[43]

On the other hand, on the very day when the president's 'enabling law' entered into force, General Boetticher, the German military attaché, reported that the war preparations of the American armed forces were fully under way and that from the summer of 1941 arms-production capacity must be expected to increase rapidly. Nevertheless, the competition inherent in the lend-lease law between the needs of national rearmament and aid to Britain could probably only be harmonized 'to some degree' by 1942, so that in this sense Germany had time to spare. But even this confident officer, who in general

---

[39] Chargé d'affaires in Washington to foreign ministry, 31 Dec. 1940, ibid., No. 583, pp. 989–90.
[40] Memorandum by ambassador to the US (Dr Hans Heinrich Dieckhoff), 9 Jan. 1941. ibid., No. 633, pp. 1061–3.
[41] Memorandum by state secretary, 16 Jan. 1941, ibid., No. 666, p. 1117.
[42] See n. 33 above.
[43] Memorandum by Ambassador Dieckhoff, 10 Mar. 1941, *DGFP* D xii, No. 146, pp. 258–9.

argued as a good Nazi and anti-Semite, could not help hinting that in the final analysis time was working against the Third Reich. Every day brought an increase in American land-armaments and war-industry capacity and success in the creation of a 'really modern air force'. In any case the United States would be fully ready for war in 1942.[44] Shortly afterwards, however, as he had done previously,[45] the general characterized Roosevelt's actions as a bluff. The president's moves, he said, were merely designed to hide the fact that 'the United States today is not yet capable of giving help that could decisively influence the course of the war', for the huge $7,000m. programme could, given the conditions of production, certainly not be achieved before 1942.[46]

Basically this prediction was not far wrong; nevertheless, after March 1941 American deliveries of material to Britain increased enormously. In each month from March to June shipments were two and a half times greater than for the whole period from September to December 1940. Certainly these were still mainly purchased under 'cash and carry' agreements.[47] The difficulties of lend-lease transactions, which could not be overlooked, were partly due to poor organization,[48] but in part simply to the fact that the arms industry was not producing enough. Thus, for example, in March 1941 America supplied only 16 tanks, 283 bombers, 223 fighters, and 630 training or civil aircraft. Only part of these deliveries went to Britain, where it was expected that lend-lease would only begin to ease the situation from October onwards. Of 2,400 aircraft supplied between 11 March and 31 December 1941, fewer than 100 were lend-lease machines. The situation was better as regards tanks: 951 were delivered, including 786 under lend-lease. This was far from meeting British needs, but American tank production got under way rather slowly. The British, however, received 13,000 trucks, including 4,000 under lend-lease. These deliveries made a substantial contribution to halting Rommel's advance in the summer of 1941 and thus making possible the Operation Crusader counter-offensive in the late autumn of that year.[49]

In June nine American supply-ships entered Middle East ports of importance to the war in North Africa; in July thirty-two ships carrying armaments, and in the following months until the end of 1941 an average of sixteen cargo vessels with war supplies, arrived in the Middle East. These deliveries represented infringements of the 'cash' as well as the 'carry' principle. At the end

---

[44] Artillery Gen. Friedrich v. Boetticher, German military and air attaché, to foreign ministry, 11 Mar. 1941, ibid., No. 148, pp. 266–9; on Boetticher's reporting cf. Compton, *Hitler und die USA*, 103 ff.; Hillgruber, *Strategie*, 399–400.

[45] Compton, *Swastika and Eagle*, 112 ff.

[46] Washington embassy to foreign ministry, 26 Mar. 1941, *DGFP* D xii, No. 212, pp. 364–6; on further reports by Boetticher cf. Friedländer, *Prelude to Downfall*, 172 ff.

[47] Butler, *Strategy*, ii. 422; Playfair, *Mediterranean*, ii. 231–2; Stettinius, *Lend-Lease*, 93.

[48] Butler, *Strategy*, ii. 422–3; Stettinius, *Lend-Lease*, 95 ff.; and, on the organization of the American arms economy, Junker, 'Struktur', covering 1939–45.

[49] Stettinius, *Lend-Lease*, 93–6; for the operation cf. V.vi below (Stegemann); cf. also Roosevelt's pledges about war material intended for delivery to Great Britain, including 4,500 aircraft, in *Churchill and Roosevelt*, R-30x, p. 154 (29 Mar. 1941).

of July, when the military decision in North Africa was in the balance, the British forces received 10,000 trucks, 84 light tanks, 164 fighter aircraft, 10 bombers, and 23 anti-aircraft guns, as well as much other equipment and spare parts.[50] In this case it was of no importance whether the material was supplied under 'cash and carry' or lend-lease.

Altogether, in 1941 it was American aid as such rather than lend-lease that affected the course of the war. The full effect of the latter did not come into play until 1942.[51] It must not be overlooked, however, that the material aid furnished in 1941 already enabled Britain's war industry to concentrate on certain areas of production, such as the manufacture of aircraft. Even in 1941, Britain produced 20,100 aeroplanes, far exceeding the German output of 11,030. In that year Germany did produce 5,000 tanks as against Britain's 4,855; but the 951 tanks supplied by the United States gave Britain a slight superiority in this respect also, at least in terms of simple figures.[52]

Not all the German military underrated the change in American foreign policy. The Wehrmacht high command described Roosevelt's address on the entry into force of the new law as a 'war speech'.[53] Hitler, who had emphasized to Jodl on 17 December 1940 that Germany must 'solve all her problems on the continent of Europe in 1941, because the Americans could interfere from 1942 onwards',[54] wanted for good reason to avoid anything that might provoke the United States into entering the war before he had been able to defeat the Soviet Union.[55]

On 14 March 1941, after the German ambassador reported that Roosevelt was planning to send a convoy of approximately 120 ships under American protection to a point near Iceland, where the Royal Navy would then assume the task of escorting it to British ports, Hitler indicated that the German operational area around Britain should be extended to include Iceland.[56] However, he did not accept Raeder's proposal that Germany should cease to recognize the Pan-American neutrality zone (see front endpaper map) or should do so only up to a distance of 300 nautical miles from the American coast.[57] This is clear from the directive of the Wehrmacht high command of 25 March, whereby 'as a countermeasure against the expected effects of the aid-to-England law . . . as well as to keep pace with the northward shift of

---

[50] Playfair, *Mediterranean*, ii. 232–3.
[51] Butler, *Strategy*, ii. 422; Stettinius, *Lend-Lease*, 99–108.
[52] Hillgruber, *Strategie*, 400; for the whole picture also Overy, 'Mobilisierung'; Leighton, 'Les armes'; Smith, 'La mobilisation'.
[53] *KTB OKW* i. 360 (17 Mar. 1941); cf. Sherwood, *White House Papers*, i. 265 ff. Cf. also Churchill's enthusiastic comments on Roosevelt's speech of 14 Mar. 1941 in *Churchill and Roosevelt*, C-68x, p. 148 (17 Mar. 1941).
[54] *KTB OKW* i. 996 (21 Dec. 1940): on German–American relations in general also Frye, *Nazi Germany*; H.-J. Schröder, 'Das Dritte Reich'; Hass, *München*.
[55] Hillgruber, *Strategie*, 401 ff.
[56] *DGFP* D xii, No. 167. pp. 295–6 (14 Mar. 1941).
[57] 'Führer Conferences', 184 (18 Mar. 1941); Hitler himself had initially considered that only the three-mile limit should be respected (ibid.).

British import traffic, the hitherto existing area of operations in the Atlantic and the North Sea is extended'.[58] One of the most important effects of the lend-lease act, the unrestricted use of American dockyards for the repair of British warships, could not be prevented by the German measures, nor could many other consequences.[59] As a counter to the extension of the German operational area Roosevelt sequestrated German, Italian, and Danish merchant vessels in American ports: these ships finally became American property in June 1941.[60] In April the United States established bases in Greenland to strengthen their position in the Atlantic. The naval war staff saw it as only a matter of time before American units relieved the British troops who had occupied Iceland on 10 May 1940; this duly happened on 7 July 1941.[61]

Raeder now urged more strongly that, over and above the unrestricted use of weapons of war in the operational area round Britain and Iceland,[62] German naval forces should be permitted to 'operate freely in the western part of the Atlantic Ocean up to the customary international three-mile zone': this of course would have meant disregarding the Pan-American security zone. At first he demanded the 'cancellation of the preferred position which American merchant ships have enjoyed so far in the conduct of our naval warfare', having regard only to the sparing of American lives.[63] Ribbentrop was not averse to this, but Hitler thought the proposal disadvantageous on balance.[64] He even made no objection when, on 18 April, the Americans extended to 30° W. the 'western hemisphere' security zone within which no warlike operations were to take place, according to the Panama conference of 3 October 1939.[65] This was at the time when German successes in south-east Europe seemed to have caused an 'undecided attitude' in the United States, and the last thing Hitler wanted to do was to provoke Washington.[66]

Here we must revert to the other central event for British strategy at the turn of 1940-1, the secret British-American staff talks. They were especially

---

[58] OKW directive of 25 Mar. 1941, *DGFP* D xii, No. 210, p. 363; *KTB OKW* i. 1006-7 (25 Mar. 1941). On the new operational area cf. the front endpaper map 'Europe and the Atlantic and Mediterranean Areas (1 September 1939-25 March 1941)'.

[59] Sherwood, *White House Papers*, i. 271; Hillgruber, *Strategie*, 399.

[60] Hillgruber, *Strategie*, 401-2.

[61] Ibid. 403; Salewski, *Seekriegsleitung*, i. 492. On the various agreements relating to the takeover by the US of the defence of Iceland cf. *Churchill and Roosevelt*, C-93x, pp. 201-2 (29 May 1941); C-100x, pp. 208-9 (14 June 1941); and R-51x, p. 222 (19 July 1941) (consequences for naval warfare).

[62] Memorandum by Karl Ritter, ambassador on special assignment, 1 Apr. 1941; in particular *DGFP* D xii, No. 244, p. 428 n. 2.

[63] State secretary to foreign minister, 12 Apr. 1941, ibid., No. 316, p. 519.

[64] Minister Emil v. Rintelen (political department) to the foreign ministry, 12 Apr. 1942, ibid., No. 325, pp. 529-30.

[65] Hillgruber, *Strategie*, 402.

[66] 'Führer Conferences', 192-3 (20 Apr. 1941); on the continuing but unsuccessful efforts to persuade Hitler to change his mind cf. Salewski, *Seekriegsleitung*, i. 492-5; memorandum by Ambassador Ritter of 9 June 1941, *DGFP* D xii, No. 608, pp. 987-8. Hitler forbade naval actions which might provoke the Americans, as he wished at all costs to avoid 'incidents with the United States'.

significant for the transition to a war alliance, although the latter did not exist *de facto* until December 1941.[67] Conversations between the two delegations began in London on 28 January 1941 and ended on 27 March.[68] They resulted in what was called the ABC-1 report, which, long before Washington entered the war, formed the basis of a joint Anglo-American strategic conception. The Americans had no intention of committing themselves irrevocably—and they made this clear to the British at the outset—but they indicated that they would not, without agreement, undertake any future 'adaptation of American military planning to the strategic requirements of the Second World War'.[69] As a result of the talks, the Americans achieved a 'strategic preparedness' for their possible involvement in a conflict, on a scale probably never before attained by a non-belligerent power.[70]

On the assumption that America would enter the war, agreement was reached on the scope of future coalition warfare in the European–Atlantic and the East Asian–Pacific areas. It was accepted without question that in case of a war against Germany and Japan the maxim of 'Germany first' should prevail. A delaying war of attrition was to be waged in the Far East until Germany was defeated. These intentions were in accord with domestic American considerations and with the guidelines of British policy hitherto, in which safeguarding the Atlantic supply-routes had always played a dominant role. Accordingly, it was planned to use the American navy as early as possible in the Atlantic theatre of war, while the Royal Navy would concentrate on the Mediterranean. The United States army was to occupy the Atlantic islands—primarily the Azores, Cape Verde, and Iceland—and would send some units to Britain. The British Isles were to form the base for a land offensive, which was regarded as decisive. The extension and consolidation of Allied deployment areas in the Mediterranean were related to plans for invading south-east Europe. Plans provided for a supreme war council, to be advised by the chiefs of staff of the two countries; a tightening of the blockade; and intensification of bombing, subversive activities, and propaganda, so as to exert stronger military, economic, diplomatic, and financial pressure on Germany. Among measures to be taken immediately was the establishment of military missions in London and Washington (these eventually developed into the Combined Chiefs of Staff, known before American entry into the war as the Joint Staff Mission; the calling of a conference of commanders-in-chief in the Far East, including the Dutch; the preparation of operational plans; and an agreed pro-

---

[67] On the background cf. Butler, *Strategy*, ii. 423 ff.; Sherwood, *White House Papers*, i. 271–2; Matloff and Snell, *Strategische Planungen*, 70 ff.

[68] Butler, *Strategy*, ii. 425 ff.; Hillgruber, *Strategie*, 405 ff.; Matloff and Snell, *Strategic Planning*, 32–48.

[69] Matloff and Snell, 'Strategische Planungen', 72.

[70] Sherwood, *White House Papers*, i. 273.

cedure for the allocation of American war material before and after American intervention in the conflict.[71]

The British government at once endorsed the proposed guidelines and measures. Roosevelt made no official comment on the recommendations—from the purely formal point of view, the agreements were non-political—but assumed that they would be followed in the event of war.[72] Indeed Case Rainbow 5, which came very close to the ABC-1 report—it assumed a war on two fronts, and also advocated a decision in Europe first and a defensive stance to begin with in the Far East—was treated after 27 March 1941 as the war plan of the American armed forces, and continued essentially to be such throughout the war.[73]

The ABC-1 agreement did not confirm Hitler's view that the Soviet Union was the Allies' 'sword on the continent' of Europe. The Americans and British had worked out their strategy for fighting the aggressors before 22 June 1941.[74] This of course said nothing as to the date on which America would enter the war, which Roosevelt could not decide without taking account of public opinion. Until about November 1941 the statement made by the American delegation on 29 January seemed valid: 'The American people as a whole wish to keep out of the war and supply Britain only with economic and material help. As long as that remains their attitude, it must be supported by the responsible army and navy authorities.'[75] In his speech of 27 May 1941 Roosevelt spoke of an 'extreme national emergency',[76] but the only concrete effect was the tightening of the American organization for war production.[77] Thus, for example, the prerequisites were created for the building of 'liberty ships', which subsequently did much to relieve the Allies' shortage of tonnage.[78] The Germans attributed Roosevelt's reserved attitude towards military intervention partly to the influence of the general staff (they were probably wrong in this) and partly to the country's external and internal difficulties,

---

[71] Butler, *Strategy*, ii. 424 ff.
[72] Ibid. 426.
[73] Hillgruber, *Strategie*, 92, 407.
[74] Ibid. 408. German–American relations beyond May 1941 are not dealt with here, as developments in the second half of 1941 were dominated by the German attack on the USSR and the extension of the European conflict into a world war: cf. *Das Deutsch Reich*, iv and vi respectively.
[75] Cited from Matloff and Snell, 'Strategische Planungen', 72. The political and diplomatic developments in the last weeks before America's entry into the war are, like the entry itself, still among the debated themes of the Second World War. Cf. e.g. (in addition to titles previously mentioned) Hillgruber, *Kriegsziele und Strategie*, 82–7; Martin, 'Amerikas Durchbruch'; Murdock, 'Eintritt'; and Small, *Was War Necessary?*, 226–65.
[76] Chargé d'affaires in Washington to foreign ministry, 28 May 1941, *DGFP* D xii, No. 560, pp. 901–2.
[77] Medlicott, 'Economic Warfare', here 23 ff., for the first half of 1941.
[78] Hillgruber, *Strategie*, 399.

viz. the uncertain situation in the Far East and the American people's lack of enthusiasm for the war.[79] These were indeed the central problems in Roosevelt's strategic calculation; they were solved in an unexpected manner by the Japanese attack on Pearl Harbor on 7 December 1941.[80]

[79] Notes of 6 June 1941 by Ambassador Dieckhoff on a report by the military attaché, *DGFP*, D xii, No. 600, pp. 973–4.
[80] Prange, *At Dawn*.

II. Hitler's Strategic Deliberations in Connection with the Attack on the Soviet Union

At his conference with the top-ranking officers of the Wehrmacht and army high commands on 9 January 1941 Hitler presented a picture of the general situation in which he once again justified the attack on the Soviet Union on the ground that the British, who had put their trust in the United States and the Soviet Union, would give in after Germany's victory in the east. That victory would also enable Japan to concentrate all her forces against the United States and thus prevent the latter from entering the war. As often, Hitler was arguing from hypotheses which he does not seem to have fully believed himself. His doubts were shown in the remark that 'either the British would then give in, or Germany could continue the fight against Britain under more favourable circumstances'. We may probably interpret in a similar way his idea that after a victory in the east Germany would be in a much better position from the point of view of its war economy and 'in future would be able to fight against whole continents'. As Germany would supposedly then be in control of all Europe, the remark can only be taken as referring to the United States. Here again there seems to be some uncertainty on Hitler's part as to his prophecy that the Japanese threat would keep America out of the war. In fact he by no means excluded the idea of a showdown with the United States, at a later date but definitely during the present war.[1]

Such was the context of the military planning directly dependent on Operation Barbarossa and connected with the continuation of the war and a possible front against the United States. The capture of Gibraltar, envisaged for the autumn of 1941, to be followed by the creation of a North-West African

---

[1] *KTB OKW* i 257-8 (9 Jan. 1941); on the spelling-out of these ideas in July 1941 cf. Hillgruber, *Zenit*, 16-19. On 23 Feb. 1941 Ribbentrop tried to persuade Ambassador Oshima that Japan should attack Singapore but not the Philippines. The seizure of the British base would not bring the US into the war—on the contrary. Cf. *DGFP* D xii, No. 78, pp. 139-151 (conversation Ribbentrop-Oshima, 23 Feb.). It should be noted that Hitler and Mussolini in their conversations with Oshima and Matsuoka, the Japanese foreign minister, held respectively in Feb. and Mar.-Apr. 1941, were concerned as far as possible to keep the US from entering the war. However, the German leaders were prepared, if it came to the worst, to accept the risk: *DGFP* D xii, No. 218, pp. 376-83 (conversation Ribbentrop-Matsuoka, 27 Mar.); No. 230, pp. 405-9 (conversation Ribbentrop-Matsuoka, 28 Mar.); No. 233, pp. 413-20 (conversation Ribbentrop-Matsuoka, 29 Mar.); No. 266, pp. 453-8 (conversation Hitler-Matsuoka, 4 Apr.); No. 278, pp. 469-74 (conversation Ribbentrop-Matsuoka, 5 Apr.). The progress of these conversations and of the plan for a Japanese attack on Singapore—from German and Japanese viewpoints—is examined expertly and in detail by Krebs, *Japans Deutschlandpolitik*, i. 511-24.

barrier against the American–Atlantic area, presupposed the success of the campaign against the Soviet Union, as did the operations developing from the Caucasus, south-east Europe, and North Africa and designed to threaten India and British possessions in the Middle East.

On the other hand, the efforts which began before June 1941 to secure a forefield in the west, as well as the operations in the Middle East and the endeavour in May 1941 to push the Japanese in the direction of Singapore (while avoiding any provocation to the Americans), were all designed, in the broadest sense, to safeguard the operation against the Soviet Union. They were preventive measures which were sometimes handled in a dilatory fashion, because Germany did not expect Washington to intervene before 1942 at the earliest; by then the eastern campaign must be concluded. This was not achieved, as the Russians withstood the German onslaught; and when the United States entered the war in December 1941, Hitler's hopes of a good starting-position for a war between the continents were definitely thwarted.[2]

1. Attempts to Create a Forefield in the West

After the Montoire meeting between Hitler and Pétain,[3] efforts to achieve German–French co-operation also led to closer contacts at the military level. The focus of common interest was the securing of those colonies that had not yet broken away from Vichy and the reconquest of those that had joined de Gaulle. The Vichy government worked out a general plan for military operations, which it wished to discuss at the end of November 1940 with Wehrmacht representatives.[4] Shortly after the French approach Hitler sent General Warlimont to Paris to conduct the talks under the embassy's aegis.[5]

On 29 November Warlimont met the war minister, General Charles Huntziger, and the minister of the navy, Admiral Jean-François Darlan. The French produced a plan aimed primarily at 'strengthening means of defence to preserve the integrity of French North Africa, French West Africa, and Syria', and in addition they discussed offensive action against the colonies that had defected to de Gaulle: this might take place in the autumn of 1941. In this connection Pierre Laval, the vice-premier and foreign minister, who seemed disappointed by the caution of the French military, stated that Britain would probably oppose by force any attempt by the French fleet to leave its present

---

[2] Cf. Hildebrand, *Vom Reich*, 700 ff.; id., *Foreign Policy*, 113 ff.; Hillgruber, 'Faktor Amerika', 513 ff.; id., *Strategie*, 364–5.

[3] Cf. I.III.1 (*b*) above. On German–French military contacts in the period between Montoire and 23 Nov. 1940 see Jäckel, *Frankreich*, 126–7, 129 n. 68.

[4] Embassy in Paris to foreign ministry, *DGFP* D xi, No. 385, pp. 678–9 (23 Nov. 1940); also memorandum of 26 Nov. 1940 by Ambassador Ritter on a message from Jodl that the French wanted to speak to German military officials about the situation in Africa. This was, however, impossible because of Hitler's directive that only the foreign ministry was competent for such negotiations: ibid., No. 408, p. 720.

[5] Foreign minister's office to embassy in Paris, *DGFP* D xi, No. 410, p. 722 (27 Nov. 1940).

1. Attempts at a Western Forefield

bases. Action by Vichy against the defecting colonies would probably also lead to a conflict with Britain.[6] Such a development would have been fully in accord with the ideas of the German naval war staff, who were keenly interested in a clash between the British and French and who had recommended both actions to the foreign ministry as 'necessary'.[7] The Germans, however, were mainly disappointed by the timing suggested by the French. Ambassador Otto Abetz frankly pointed out to General Huntziger the disadvantages that delay might mean for Vichy: the war would probably be decided by autumn, and then Germany would only have to make terms with the British as regards territorial questions in Africa. But this threat was of no avail; Huntziger remained obdurate, invoking his 'military conscience' as an argument against the premature execution of any of the plans under discussion.[8]

On 2–3 December Warlimont reported the results of the Paris meeting to Hitler, the foreign ministry, and the Wehrmacht high command, emphasizing that despite the unsatisfactory outcome it was in Germany's interest to continue the discussions, as nothing less than the safeguarding of the 'strategic flank of the whole front' was involved, a function which essentially could be performed only by the French themselves.[9] With this in mind he had accepted Huntziger's proposed timetable. He thought it more important to check the trend towards defection and to secure the areas that were still loyal than to recover immediately the territories that had gone over to de Gaulle.[10] On 5 December a report arrived from Abetz proposing that the talks with Laval and Huntziger should continue on 10 December. Hitler agreed that Warlimont should return to Paris to get a direct impression of the conclusions arrived at by the French cabinet within the context of internal discussions regarding extended plans in Africa.[11]

Five French and nine German experts accordingly met on 10 December,[12] when the French submitted an elaborate plan to strengthen the French

---

[6] Ambassador Abetz to foreign ministry, ibid., No. 428, pp. 752–3 (27 Nov. 1940); directly relevant is KTB OKW i. 195 (2 Dec. 1940). For interpretation see also Geschke, Frankreichpolitik, 130; Jäckel, Frankreich, 137–8; Hillgruber, Strategie, 332; Warlimont, Headquarters, 122.

[7] Memorandum by Ambassador Ritter of 30 Nov. 1940 on the proposal by Admirals Fricke and Schniewind that 'if the occasion arises, the entire French naval forces should be deployed against de Gaulle and England': DGFP D xi, No. 432, p. 759.

[8] Ambassador Abetz to foreign ministry, ibid., No. 434, pp. 760–2 (1 Dec. 1940).

[9] KTB OKW i. 195–6 (1–4 Dec. 1940); Warlimont, Headquarters, 124.

[10] KTB OKW i. 200 (4 Dec. 1940).

[11] Ibid. 210 (6 Dec. 1940), 216 (7 Dec. 1940): Lt.-Col. Hans Speidel, chief of general staff of the military commander in France, mentioned that in a conversation on 4 Dec. Laval had expressed Pétain's dissatisfaction with Huntziger's conduct of the negotiations on 29 Nov. The marshal did not agree with the proposed operational plan. For his own part, Laval wished 'to attack de Gaulle and consequently England in order to reconquer the lost territories'. This should certainly not be delayed for 6–12 months.

[12] KTB OKW i. 984–94 (13 Dec. 1940): record of discussions on 10 Dec. 1940. On the significance of the meeting cf. Böhme, 'Deutschland und Frankreich' (B 31), 19; Geschke, Frankreichpolitik, 131; Hillgruber, Strategie, 332–3; Jäckel, Frankreich, 138; Warlimont, Headquarters, 124.

defences in West Africa, especially near Dakar, although that port now seemed capable of resisting stronger attacks than the raid it had beaten off in September. Offensive operations in the area by de Gaulle's forces were already thought to be impossible. The Vichy troops were being regrouped to secure the line Niger–Zinder–Lake Chad, and preparations had been made for an offensive against the area held by de Gaulle around Lake Chad. The operation was to be started as early as March 1941 from Niamey against Fort Lamy and other bases, skirting British Nigeria to the north.[13] The deployment for this would probably be completed by mid-February. Vichy would then issue an ultimatum, and if it were rejected the bombardment of Fort Lamy would begin on 1 March.[14]

Of course Vichy expected this to provoke reactions from the British, who had threatened them often enough. If it came to a clash, the following countermeasures would be taken: an air attack on Kano in northern Nigeria, the capture of Bathurst in British Gambia, an offensive by all three service branches against Freetown, and further 'operations outside the West African area, depending on capabilities and opportunities', e.g. air raids on Gibraltar. The French regarded it as an essential condition for carrying out their plans that the Germans should release from captivity a sufficient number of colonial soldiers of all ranks to bring the African troops completely up to strength. Berlin must also provide Vichy with the necessary quantities of fuel and permit it to manufacture aircraft, bombs, and munitions and to train pilots. Italian opposition was to be taken care of by the Germans.[15]

The French now played the British card. Laval emphasized that 'France wanted to reconquer her colonies and would accept a war with Britain in Africa to achieve that aim',[16] but he suggested that the German government for its part should issue a declaration that it had 'no intention of annexing any territory in Black Africa'.[17] This was the guarantee of France's colonial empire which Hitler had always refused to give. If the French insisted on having it, the inevitable result would be a deadlock in the negotiations.

None the less, Abetz and Warlimont were at first highly pleased with the meeting. In the first place, French readiness for action had 'received a decisive impetus'; and secondly there was no doubt of the sincerity of Pétain's professions of his military intentions.[18] The French plans, moreover, 'were entirely in accord with German wishes as far as space and time were concerned'.[19] Jodl urged that the German side should 'strike while the iron was

---

[13] Minute by the chief of the *OKW* home defence department on the second Paris conference of 10 Dec. 1940, *DGFP* D xi, No. 506, pp. 860–3 (12 Dec. 1940); also in *KTB OKW* i. 982 ff.

[14] Ambassador Abetz to foreign ministry, on the conference of 10 Dec., *DGFP* D xi, No. 490, pp. 839–41 (11 Dec. 1940).

[15] Ibid., No. 506, pp. 860–3.

[16] Record of the second Paris conference, *KTB OKW* i. 984–94 (13 Dec. 1940), here 989.

[17] Ibid. 990.

[18] *DGFP* D xi, No. 506, pp. 860–3 (see n. 13).

[19] *KTB OKW* i. 225 (11 Dec. 1940).

1. Attempts at a Western Forefield

hot'.[20] All this sounded very promising, but Hitler was still deeply mistrustful of France,[21] and when Laval was unexpectedly dismissed on 13 December there ensued a pause in the attempts at German–French *rapprochement*, which in any case were not especially lively.[22]

In December 1940, when German thinking was dominated by Operations Barbarossa (the Soviet Union) and Marita (Greece), Hitler was certainly no longer occupied with first seeking a decision in the western Mediterranean and Africa; he continued to think of that area as a defensive glacis.[23] But even within that modest framework the problems of the west and south—the German rear area and flank respectively—could not be solved by the date set for the attack on the Soviet Union. As France and Spain, despite diplomatic niceties, finally refused to fulfil German wishes, no progress could be made. Accordingly Operation Marita and the plans in Hitler's directive No. 22 concerning 'German support for [Italian] battles in the Mediterranean area',[24] involving Tripoli ('Sunflower') and Albania ('Alpine Violet'),[25] were concerned for the most part with protecting the Romanian oilfields, stabilizing the position in the south-east, and thus generally safeguarding the German flank in the eastern Mediterranean. Political, military, and psychological motives played a role difficult to evaluate in detail in the related decisions. Apart from Operation Attila (occupation of unoccupied France), envisaged as a reaction to a breakaway by the colonies under General Weygand, and which soon came to be considered as a single entity with Operation Camellia (the plan to occupy Corsica),[26] France received little attention between 13 December 1940 and April–May 1941 and was not even considered in Hitler's comprehensive assessment of the situation of 5 February 1941.[27] Evidently Berlin was keeping Vichy at arm's length: until 'clarification of the effects of Laval's forced resignation', the armistice agreement was to form the sole basis of mutual relations. Its execution by France was again to be closely supervised, and all French requests for a 'strengthening of the military potential of the troops stationed in metropolitan France or the African colonies' were to be refused.[28]

---

[20] Ibid. 229 (13 Dec. 1940); cf. Warlimont, *Headquarters*, 124.
[21] See I.III.1 (*b*) above.
[22] In detail: Geschke, *Frankreichpolitik*, 131–6; Jäckel, *Frankreich*, 140–56.
[23] On this whole question see I.III.2 above.
[24] *Hitler's War Directives*, No. 22, pp. 53–4.
[25] See *Hitlers Weisungen*, No. 22a, p. 110 (14 Jan. 1941); No. 22b, p. 111 (28 Jan. 1941); No. 22c, pp. 112–13 (21 Jan. 1941); No. 22d, pp. 114ff. (Feb. 1941) (not in trans.). On Operation Marita cf. III.II.2, 3 and III.III above (Vogel).
[26] *KTB OKW* i. 303 (4 Feb. 1941); 326 (15 Feb. 1941); 350 (8 Mar. 1941). The preparation of Operation Attila was ordered in Dec. 1940: see *Hitlers Weisungen*, No. 19b, pp. 91ff. (10 Dec. 1940; not in trans.).
[27] *KTB OKW* i. 297–302 (3 Feb. 1941). On the German–French relationship between Dec. 1940 and May 1941, described below, cf. Melka, 'Darlan', 66–9.
[28] *KTB OKW* i. 310 (8 Feb. 1941). Cf. memorandum by Ambassador Ritter, *DGFP* D xi, No. 690, p. 1169, according to which Hitler had forbidden official discussions with prominent Frenchmen; also foreign ministry memorandum about the OKW order of 8 Feb. containing

If, nevertheless, German–French collaboration reached a far higher level than ever before in the course of 1941, this was primarily due to Admiral Darlan. As Laval's successor he was in charge of the ministries of home and foreign affairs and of information, while remaining commander-in-chief of the navy.[29] He soon endeavoured to bring about a thaw in relations between Berlin and Vichy, at first without success.[30] A change came as a result of several concurrent circumstances. There was good co-operation with Ambassador Abetz in Paris, and the German military were anxious for their unsecured southern flank. The developments in the Middle East, which we shall describe, may have made Hitler and his advisers more sympathetic. No doubt also the material requirements of the German Africa Corps played a decisive part.

Rommel's offensive strength was impaired not least by insufficient transport capacity. The French had large stocks of lorries in North Africa: why not buy these up, relieving German production and avoiding the risky sea crossing? Vichy, not wishing to endanger the prospects of improvement in its relations with Germany, showed itself compliant. The relevant agreement was not signed until June 1941, but the Germans relaxed their attitude of reserve towards the French at an earlier date.[31] On 26 April Abetz, from the Reich foreign minister's special train, informed his embassy in Paris that Hitler had decided to receive Darlan, the 'French deputy head of state', at Munich in the first or second week of May.[32]

The German government had good reason for hastening to show itself accommodating towards Darlan. On 28 April Ribbentrop had informed Keitel that Germany was interested both in supply-bases for U-boats and merchant vessels on the west coast of Africa and in the delivery to Iraq of French arms stored in Syria, as well as in any other help to the anti-British regime in Iraq. Berlin therefore wished the French to allow the delivery of war material via Syria. In addition the Luftwaffe required permission for German aircraft intended for Iraq to make intermediate landings on Syrian territory. Ribbentrop also spoke of possible concessions in return. To keep the whole matter strictly secret, however, it should not be dealt with by the armistice commission but

---

'Directives for the Negotiations of the Armistice Commission', ibid. xii, No. 50, pp. 98–9 (14 Feb. 1941).

[29] Jäckel, *Frankreich*, 158–9.

[30] Ambassador Abetz to foreign ministry, *DGFP* D xi, No. 736, p. 1234 (31 Jan. 1941). On Darlan's role in regard to Vichy's relations with Berlin as well as with Washington and London cf. Melka, 'Darlan', 57–80, esp. 64–78; and Funk, 'Negotiating', esp. 83–8.

[31] Jäckel, *Frankreich*, 159–63. On the *détente vis-à-vis* Germany which resulted from the development of the truck question see the telegram from the office of the foreign ministry representative with the German armistice commission in Wiesbaden to the foreign ministry, *DGFP* D xii, No. 417, pp. 659–61 (28 Apr. 1941). On the delivery of the trucks cf. Halder, *Diaries*, ii. 1188–90 (19 Aug. 1941). According to this, only 28% of the trucks from Tunis were usable for the establishment of the planned motorized battalions. On this matter in general see also Greiselis, *Das Ringen*, 29 ff., 42; V.iv below (Stegemann).

[32] *DGFP* D xii, No. 462, p. 721 n. 2.

first of all in talks between Darlan and Abetz.³³ On 3 May Abetz was again instructed to 'give foremost attention to the question of arms shipments from Syria to Iraq'; he spoke to Darlan accordingly on the same day. Artillery General Oskar Vogel, then chairman of the armistice commission, held himself in readiness to reach agreement on the military details.³⁴ Although Darlan allegedly had his difficulties at Vichy, he was finally able to inform Abetz of the 'virtual agreement' of Pétain and the other cabinet members involved.³⁵

Thereupon negotiations took place in Paris on 6–7 May between Darlan, the finance minister Yves Bouthillier, Abetz, General Vogel, and the German diplomatic minister Johannes Hemmen. The French offered the following military and political concessions:

(1) release of French weapons stocks under Italian control in Syria for transport to Iraq;
(2) support in further transport by land or sea of arms deliveries of other origin arriving in Syria for Iraq;
(3) permission for intermediate landings and refuelling in Syria of German aircraft destined for Iraq;
(4) turning over to Iraq of reconnaissance, fighter, and bomber aircraft and bombs of the air force permitted in Syria by the armistice agreement;
(5) making available in Syria an airfield reserved especially for intermediate landings by German aircraft;
(6) until the airfield was available, ordering all airfields in Syria to provide support for intermediate landings by German aircraft.

As a quid pro quo the German government permitted the rearming of seven French torpedo-boats and made several concessions as regards the demarcation-line, in particular its general opening for goods traffic and currency transfers. Moreover, it was planned to begin immediately negotiations on reduced payments for the occupation costs. But the Germans demanded additional French co-operation, especially before they were prepared to make concessions on this last point, e.g. the creation of additional German and Italian control organs at the frontiers of Vichy France with third countries; the assigning of commissars to supervise the Bank of France and the currency transactions of the finance ministry and the ministry of trade; the delivery of large quantities of alumina and aluminium; and the immediate payment of part of the reduced occupation costs in gold or foreign currency and securities.³⁶ On 9 May Senior Legation Counsellor Rudolf Rahn arrived in Syria to carry

---

[33] Ibid., No. 421, pp. 663–4 (28 Apr. 1941).
[34] Memorandum by the director of the political department, ibid., No. 442, p. 695 (3 May 1941).
[35] Ambassador Abetz to foreign ministry, ibid., No. 459, pp. 718–20 (5 May 1941).
[36] Memorandum by the director of the economic policy department, ibid., No. 475, pp. 740–2 (8 May 1941). Cf. also Halder, *Diaries*, ii. 909–12 (8 May 1941), the details in which do not tally with the actual outcome of the discussion.

out the agreements reached with regard to Iraq in co-operation with the French high commissioner there, General Henri Dentz.[37]

Darlan was now finally permitted to undertake his long-planned trip to Germany. On 11 May he first saw Ribbentrop,[38] and conferred with Hitler in the afternoon.[39] The atmosphere of the talks may have suffered from the fact that Rudolf Hess, Hitler's deputy, had undertaken his bizarre flight to Britain the day before in a personal attempt to achieve peace, which, however, was quite in accord with Hitler's original programmatic aims.[40] The results of the negotiations of 11 May can be described as a declaration of intent to achieve co-operation on a 'give and take' basis; in future relations would be based exclusively on mutual concessions.[41] For the time being, however, Darlan seemed to be satisfied that the talks with the Germans had not been broken off. In any case, he indicated his readiness in principle to pursue a policy directed against Britain if Germany agreed to appropriate concessions. However, details were not clarified during his visit; that was to be done in conversations with Ambassador Abetz.[42]

In accordance with the principle agreed upon on 11 May, to make concessions to the French only if they were prepared to provide quid pro quos useful in Germany's war against Britain, Abetz worked out a very detailed programme for the forthcoming French–German negotiations.[43] He wanted to advance the *rapprochement* in four steps. In particular Abetz was first concerned with French lorries loaded with supplies for the Africa Corps. Vichy's readiness to ship the supplies to North Africa from ports in unoccupied France and turn over the vehicles to the Germans should be rewarded with the release of 1,000 French prisoners of war; Darlan could provide a list of names. As for the rest, the French had already been granted concessions at the demarcation-line and permitted to rearm the seven torpedo-boats. Moreover, as regards French readiness in principle to resupply German U-boats and merchant ships in French Morocco and French West Africa, the possibility was being considered of permitting the French to place six destroyers back in service. In

---

[37] Memorandum by director of political department, *DGFP* D xii, No. 476, pp. 742–3 (8 May 1941). For Iraq see further IV.II.1, 2 below.
[38] Ribbentrop–Darlan conversation at Fuschl, ibid., No. 490, pp. 755–63 (11 May 1941).
[39] Hitler–Darlan conversation at the Berghof, ibid., No. 491, pp. 763–74 (11 May 1941).
[40] Cf. *Weizsäcker-Papiere*, 225–6 (19 May 1941); Ciano, *Diary 1939–1943*, 352 (2 June 1941); Jäckel, *Frankreich*, 165; Martin, 'Das "Dritte Reich"', 538–9. On the interrogation of Hess in England cf. *Churchill and Roosevelt*, R-40x, p. 187 (14 May 1941); C-87x, pp. 187ff. (17 May 1941).
[41] For details of the discussions, including the second conversation with Ribbentrop on the following day, see Jäckel, *Frankreich*, 166–7.
[42] Tête-à-tête conversation Darlan–Ribbentrop at Fuschl, *DGFP* D xii, No. 499, pp. 781–2 (12 May 1941). The record states: 'The conversation ended with the position on both sides having been made completely clear, i.e. that Darlan was resolved to take the clear course of entering the war against England in the near future.' Of that, however, there could be no question, since, on his return to Vichy, Darlan in cabinet frankly excluded the possibility of Anglo-French hostilities: cf. Melka, 'Darlan', 70.
[43] Abetz to foreign ministry, *DGFP* D xii, No. 520, pp. 823–5 (15 May 1941).

I. Attempts at a Western Forefield

addition, Abetz suggested, as a visible sign of willingness to accommodate Darlan and as a reaction to his clear readiness to co-operate with Germany, considering the granting of leave to 80,000 French prisoners of war, the relaxation of controls at the demarcation-line, and the facilitation of travel to the northern departments and the restricted area. It might be possible to achieve comprehensive German participation in 'agricultural and raw-material production in North Africa', which could be repaid with reduced occupation costs. Abetz's most radical suggestion was that the German government should call upon Vichy openly to support German conduct of the war against Britain. In his view it was realistic to demand the use of the two French divisions in Syria to aid the rebels in Iraq and to expect that France should 'provide North African troop units and weapons for the operations of the Africa Corps against the Suez Canal'. French naval units could support German operations against the Canary Islands and Gibraltar. After all, Abetz argued, one had only to think of the already prepared French offensive against Bathurst and Freetown. As the realization of such plans would obviously lead to open war between Britain and Vichy, Germany must be ready to make important concessions. Abetz therefore recommended the incorporation of the northern departments into the military administration in France,[44] a realistic determination of occupation costs based on the actual burden, a liberal opening of the demarcation-line for civilian passenger traffic, and a release of all prisoners of war over forty years of age. Remaining prisoners should be freed in so far as the German economy could do without their labour.

Such a far-reaching inclusion of France in German strategy did not, however, reflect the views of the German government; the question of open 'support of German war measures against England' was put aside.[45] The guidelines for the German–French negotiations, which Hitler and the Wehrmacht high command issued on 19 May, took many of Abetz's suggestions into consideration but contained only cautious references to direct military co-operation. In the talks to be conducted by General Warlimont the main aim was to achieve a use of French installations and bases for the German conduct of the war and, in connection with this, to re-establish French sovereignty in the French colonies under de Gaulle's control.[46] This was an expression of the changed, purely defensive role now assigned to North-West Africa. The Germans wanted to be certain that the French would protect that area during Operation Barbarossa.[47] They were therefore most ready to make concessions which would strengthen French defences. Direct French military action

---

[44] For details cf. Umbreit, *Militärbefehlshaber*, 79 ff.; a reincorporation of this area, which was subordinate to the military commander in Brussels, did not take place.

[45] *DGFP* D xii, No. 520, p. 825 n. 9, on Ribbentrop's decision of 17 May 1941. In the negotiations of 20–8 May Abetz touched on this theme only to the extent of telling the French that they should not instigate any warlike actions against Great Britain: see ibid., No. 546, pp. 867 ff., (24 May 1941), here 870.

[46] Jäckel, *Frankreich*, 168–9.

[47] Warlimont, *Headquarters*, 125–6.

against the British was not envisaged; the possibility of a confrontation with them was therefore left to chance. Nor did the Wehrmacht high command mention direct French military assistance in Iraq, North Africa, or in the Atlantic approaches. It did, on the other hand, demand indirect support for Iraq through the use of Syria, West African bases for Germany, the availability of North African ports for German supply transports, and the turning over to Germany of French merchant ships.[48]

The negotiations in Paris from 20 to 28 May 1941 immediately followed those begun on 6 May.[49] Agreement on Syria, Iraq, and North Africa was achieved on 23 May.[50] But the difficult questions concerning French West and Equatorial Africa were still open. The French government signed an agreement that, among others, had the following practical effects: up to 75 per cent of the war material stored in Syria could be sold to Iraq; German and Italian aircraft were to be permitted to make intermediate landings in Syria; the Vichy government placed an airfield north of Aleppo at the disposal of the Luftwaffe. The Axis powers were to be able to use transport routes and facilities for supplies destined for Iraq. Moreover, French ships would assume the task of protecting German supply transports east of Cyprus. The French wanted to train Iraqis to use the weapons to be turned over to them in Syria. The Germans intended to provide the French high command with intelligence on British forces and 'war measures' in the Middle East.

The negotiations within the framework of the discussion about French West and Equatorial Africa were extremely difficult, as the French demanded political concessions in view of the planned strengthening of ties with Germany. Vichy was not prepared at that point to risk its entire colonial empire simply because the German government promised to assume a benevolent attitude in talks about a peace treaty. Against this background Darlan desired not only the military measures already mentioned to strengthen the protection of French colonies; he also pressed for a concrete agreement as regards further talks on unsettled political and economic questions. For this reason he signed a military protocol with Warlimont on the night of 27–8 May, while he signed an additional, political agreement, called the Paris Protocols, with Abetz.[51] In assessing the significance of these arrangements, however, it should be remembered that these protocols were not in fact signed but only initialled and still required the approval of the German and French governments.

As regards Syria, Iraq, and North Africa, the agreements were confirmed in the preliminary negotiations, in which mainly technical details were given

---

[48] Jäckel, *Frankreich*, 168–9.
[49] Ibid. 169 ff., presenting the negotiations on the basis of French documents.
[50] Abetz to foreign ministry, *DGFP* D xii, No. 546, pp. 857–70 (24 May 1941); for details of the agreements on North Africa cf. V.IV below (Stegemann).
[51] The negotiations are described in detail in Jäckel, *Frankreich*, 169 ff.; cf. also Böhme, 'Deutschland und Frankreich' (B 31), 23 ff.

concrete form.[52] In the draft for an agreement[53] on West and Equatorial Africa[54] the French government stated its readiness to make Dakar available as a base for German war and merchant ships. The Luftwaffe would also be given a base in this area. During a first period, beginning on 15 July 1941, the agreement would have permitted German U-boats to be replenished by a German supply-ship in the harbour of Dakar. It was also planned to permit German merchant ships to stay there temporarily. Additional possibilities for Germany, such as the use of the base at Dakar by surface ships of the German navy and the general use of the port facilities and the airfield, were to be regulated by agreements set down in the additional protocol. As France was to assume the defence of all installations that Vichy wanted to make available to the Wehrmacht, the French understandably presented extensive military demands. The Germans took note of them without making any promises and stated only that they were prepared to let the armistice commission deal with the details of the measures already laid down or under consideration.

In the additional protocol signed by Darlan and Abetz, the French assumed that the support they were expected to give Germany in West and Equatorial Africa could lead to an armed conflict with Britain or the United States, and they based their demands on that assumption: it was therefore important to prepare adequately for such eventualities. In so far as the German government actually wanted the French to provide the agreed support, it must not only approve in advance the military assistance necessary for a 'state of increased defence in West and Equatorial Africa'; it must also make political and economic concessions to enable the French government convincingly to justify to the French public such a conflict with the British or the Americans.

When Warlimont reported the results of the negotiations in Berlin, neither the Wehrmacht high command nor Hitler nor Ribbentrop showed any interest in them. As time had already grown short, the German leaders had definitely postponed further consideration of the French problem until after Barbarossa.[55] Shortly thereafter developments in Iraq and then in Syria made the concrete agreements irrelevant.[56] By 1 June Abetz already knew that Ribbentrop no longer placed any value on the close collaboration with the French which he, Abetz, had been trying to achieve.[57] The price seemed too high. Moreover, the Germans assumed that smaller sources of friction and conflict between Vichy and Britain would be sufficient to cause the French to defend the southern

---

[52] *DGFP* D xii, No. 559, pp. 892–900. The protocols are arranged in four groups: (1) Agreements on Syria and Iraq; (2) Agreements on North Africa (both documents initialled on 27 May); (3) Draft of an agreement on West and Equatorial Africa; (4) supplementary protocol (the last two signed on 28 May).
[53] Jäckel, *Frankreich*, 171.
[54] Cited from *DGFP*, No. 559 (see n. 52).
[55] Warlimont, *Headquarters*, 125–6.
[56] Cf. IV.II.2 below.
[57] Abetz, *Das offene Problem*, 190–1.

flank adequately. After the war against the Soviet Union it would be possible to clarify the situation without difficulty.

However, it would not have been possible to find a broad base of support in France for the kind of collaboration Darlan seemed to want to achieve. On 7 June Vichy presented additional, revealing demands. Pétain wanted nothing less than the complete restoration of French sovereignty, with the exception of a separate arrangement for Alsace-Lorraine. The exchange of views continued in the following weeks, but under such conditions merely assumed the appearance of negotiations. In this respect the now awakened interest of the Wehrmacht high command in reaching an agreement with Vichy, caused by developments in North Africa, did not change anything.[58]

Against the background of the changed military situation in the Mediterranean, and tired of the endless haggling, the French finally presented a *note verbale* in which they summarized developments in German–French relations since 11 May. In this note Darlan observed soberly that the armistice was not a suitable platform for Franco-German relations, as the possibilities of cooperation so far discussed could not be realized on that basis. He therefore urged that the German–French as well as the French–Italian negotiations must aim at 'an immediate and definitive settlement of certain vital questions, and at replacing the armistice regime by one founded on the sovereignty of the French state and a sincere collaboration by France with Germany and Italy'.[59] But, in view of previous experience in this regard, the Vichy government can hardly have entertained any illusions that these proposals would be accepted. In fact the German foreign ministry refused to take official note of them.[60]

The resulting deadlock in German–French relations was overcome around the middle of August 1941 at the urging of the Wehrmacht high command. The military leaders wanted to achieve advantages and ease the pressure on the Axis in North Africa through direct or indirect French support. However, as Hitler's attitude towards France had not changed, all attempts to reach a breakthrough were doomed to failure. The collapse of the German offensive against Moscow and the entry of the United States into the war meant that the developments of May 1941 would remain only a brief episode.[61] At the end of 1941 the naval war staff noted: 'It can be assumed from discussions with French cabinet members that, after the entry of the United States into the war and our reverses in Russia, Vichy is no longer as convinced of the final victory of the Axis powers as it was.' This was evident in, among other areas, the behaviour of the French delegation towards the armistice commission, whose members insisted 'with increasing stubbornness on the acceptance of their

---

[58] Jäckel, *Frankreich*, 172–8.
[59] Memorandum by Ribbentrop for Hitler, *DGFP* D xiii, No.113, pp. 142–9 (16 July 1941), enclosing the French *note verbale*. Cf. Hillgruber, *Strategie*, 452–3; Jäckel, *Frankreich*, 178.
[60] Embassy in Paris to foreign ministry, *DGFP* D xiii, No. 162, pp. 231–3 (30 July 1941).
[61] Böhme, 'Deutschland und Frankreich' (B 31), 25–9; Jäckel, *Frankreich*, 199–217; Warlimont, *Headquarters*, 126.

1. Attempts at a Western Forefield

political and economic counter-demands'.[62] Now that the myth of German invincibility had begun to fade, however, the foreign ministry was forced to admit that a French–German *rapprochement* was becoming increasingly urgent, as the world was dividing into two camps. If, in this situation, Germany continued to wait, it would 'perhaps have to be more forthcoming with the French'.[63]

In addition to such political efforts to construct a defensive position in the west and south-west for the duration of the war against the Soviet Union, various military plans were developed which were conceived primarily as reactions to measures the enemy might take. Altogether they were intended to secure completely the south coast of Europe, including offshore islands, and the Portuguese and Spanish Atlantic coast. Operation Attila has already been mentioned in this connection. If the French possessions in North Africa from Morocco to Tunis went over to de Gaulle, the immediate occupation of Vichy France would ensure that the French coast facing that area was firmly in German hands.[64] When the dismissal of Laval in December 1940 led to increased tension between France and Germany, the possibilities of carrying out such an operation were examined very closely.[65] Since March 1941, as the deployment in the east assumed an increasingly dominant role, the German military had come to consider Attila difficult to carry out.[66] Nevertheless Hitler, whom Raeder had informed on 8–9 January that France would have to be 'crushed completely' if the French became troublesome and that the French fleet must not be allowed to escape,[67] insisted that it must be possible to carry out Operation Attila at any time, even if this could be done only on a limited scale.[68] This was quite in agreement with earlier guidelines of the Wehrmacht high command.[69] When German–French relations seemed temporarily to improve in April and May 1941, Hitler's readiness to occupy the part of France under Vichy control did not change.[70]

---

[62] Assmann, 'Bemühungen der Seekriegsleitung', BA-MA RM 8/1209, here i. 109–10. The themes of Assmann's study (both vols.) are noted, without any real interpretative comment, by Meyer-Sach, 'Bemühungen'.

[63] *Weizsäcker-Papiere*, 282 (26 Dec. 1941).

[64] Cf. IV.II.1 below; directly relevant is: German armistice commission, Chefgr., Ia No. 12, 40 g.Kdos., IV. Ang. Chefs. (21 Dec. 1940), to naval operations staff, on operation Attila, BA-MA CASE GE 439, PG, 32485.

[65] *KTB OKW* i. 253 (8 Jan. 1941); 254–5 (9 Jan. 1941); 269 (18 Jan. 1941); 270 (20 Jan. 1941), where it is stated that Italy, after the Hitler–Mussolini conversation, wanted in the right circumstances to take part in Attila.

[66] Ibid. 299 (3 Feb. 1941).

[67] 'Führer Conferences', 169–72 (8–9 Jan. 1941). For the further deliberations within the navy as regards the seizure of the French fleet cf. Skl., I op 85/41 g.Kdos. Chefs. (27 Jan. 1941), to OKW/WFSt on Attila, BA-MA CASE GE 439, PG 32485.

[68] *KTB OKW* i. 303 (4 Feb. 1941).

[69] OKW/WFSt 140/41 g.Kdos. (13 Feb. 1941), to the naval war staff, referring to Skl. 85/41 g.Kdos. (see n. 67); and OKH/GenStdH/OP.Abt. (IIa) No. 420008/42 g.Kdos. (8 Mar. 1942), to OKM/Skl. This letter cancelled the state of readiness as from Mar. 1942: BA-MA CASE GE 439, PG, 32485.

[70] 'Führer Conferences', 193 (20 Apr. 1941).

Afraid that the unfavourable development of the military situation in North Africa could lead to a direct threat to Italy, the Wehrmacht high command discussed possible countermeasures at the beginning of 1941. These were intended not only to protect Italy, but also to tie down strong enemy forces in the Mediterranean. Among the moves considered were the establishment of bases on the French Mediterranean coast, the occupation of Corsica, and the conquest of Malta.[71] The operation against Malta soon came to be regarded as no longer necessary,[72] an indication of the underestimation of the island's importance on the part of the German military; but planning for an operation to occupy Corsica continued.[73] Preparations, under the code-name 'Camellia', had been in progress since 8 March.[74] The Wehrmacht high command assumed that the occupation of the island should take place at the same time as Attila or as a measure to forestall British landing operations. Of course the Italians would have to carry out these measures, as most German forces would probably be tied down in the east until the autumn of 1941. This meant that only X Air Corps was available in the Mediterranean. In any case, the study of Camellia should be communicated to the Italians to influence their preparations in the desired direction.[75]

Such deliberations show the concern of the Wehrmacht leaders lest the British should launch an offensive in the south and south-west when most German forces were tied down in the east. Surprisingly, such fears received new support at the moment of German successes in south-east Europe. At that time the British government in fact considered, in addition to diplomatic actions and economic sanctions, offensive military measures against Spain. The British believed it possible that Franco would definitely side with the Axis in the near future, and they had good reasons for this assumption: they had received their information from usually reliable sources close to the Spanish foreign minister. According to these sources, Franco only wanted to wait until Suez had fallen before entering the war. Nevertheless, British policy towards Spain was still basically defensive. As far as possible, Britain wanted to keep Franco out of the war by peaceful means.[76] As, on the other hand, the British press publicly discussed preventive measures Britain might take if

---

[71] *KTB OKW* i. 312 (8 Jan. 1941).

[72] Ibid. 335 (26 Feb. 1941).

[73] Ibid. 344 (4 Mar. 1941); 346 (6 Mar. 1941); 347 (7 Mar. 1941); according to these, the home defence department of the OKW/WFSt was also concerned in the operation.

[74] Ibid. 350 (8 Mar. 1941).

[75] OKW WFSt/Abt. L (I Op.) No. 44283/41 g.Kdos. Chefs. (23 Mar. 1941), to ObdM, ObdL, ObdH on Corsica; and 1/Skl. I op 376/41 g.Kdos. Chefs. (31 Mar. 1941), to OKW on the study 'Camellia' (the navy's comment on the WFSt/Abt. L paper signed by Jodl was exclusively concerned with German–Italian chances of preventing the French fleet from putting to sea by blockading Toulon): BA-MA CASE GE 439, PG 32485. On Italian plans relating to Corsica cf. memorandum by Ambassador Ritter (undated), *DGFP* D xii, No. 82, pp. 155–6 (24 Feb. 1941). Cruccu, 'L'Italia e la Corsica', 16, mentions that the Italian views were not conveyed until June 1941; cf. also Schreiber, *Revisionismus*, 305 n. 281.

[76] Woodward, *British Foreign Policy*, i. 499–500.

1. Attempts at a Western Forefield

the Wehrmacht moved against Gibraltar and Spanish Morocco via Spain, the Germans for their part thought in terms of a British threat to Spain.

Because of the very reserved attitude of the Spanish government since December 1940, in February 1941 Operation Felix (the attack on Gibraltar) had definitely been postponed until after the conclusion of Barbarossa. Germany was unable to act; exploratory talks with a view to an operation in the autumn were to be continued,[77] but because of the disappointing results in recent months[78] Ambassador Stohrer was forbidden to take the initiative on the question of Spain entering the war.[79] For the time being the Germans could only wait and maintain a sceptical vigilance. This also determined the course of a conversation between Hitler and the Spanish ambassador in Berlin, General Eugenio Espinosa de los Monteros, which the former had scheduled because of his concern about possible British operations during the war against the Soviet Union.[80] He openly expressed his suspicion that the inaccurate British propaganda reports about German military activities in Spain were in reality only intended to provide a pretext for British operations against Spain or Spanish Morocco.[81]

Espinosa asserted that Britain would not dare to carry out such operations, but Hitler was not reassured. Of course he used the opportunity to point out again how unwise it had been of Spain to frustrate the realization of Operation Felix. If Franco had been prepared to enter the war, Spain would now possess Gibraltar and German troops would be in Morocco. That would have made the position of the British in the Mediterranean untenable. Now it had to be expected that the enemy would attempt to 'establish himself in North Africa, occupy the Portuguese islands, and overthrow Franco'.[82] In Spain such suppositions raised the disturbing possibility that the Germans themselves

---

[77] *KTB OKW* i. 331 (18 Feb. 1941); Chef OKW 44197/41 g.Kdos. (20 Feb. 1941) (p.p. Warlimont), BA-MA CASE GE 440, PG 32488: 'The seizure of Malta [*but cf.* n. 72 above] is planned to take place after the completion of Operation Barbarossa... The execution of Operation Felix may become necessary about the same time—New orders to issue in good time.' Cf. also I.III.2 (*b*) above.

[78] Cf. also Hitler's letter to Franco of 6 Feb. 1941, *DGFP* D xii, No. 22, pp. 37–42; ambassador in Madrid to foreign ministry on the Spanish general staff memorandum justifying the country's non-participation in the war, ibid., No. 28, pp. 51–3 (7 Feb. 1941); and Wiehl's comments, ibid., No. 46, pp. 78–9 (12 Feb. 1941). Also ambassador in Madrid to foreign ministry, reporting Franco's views on Hitler's letter, ibid., No. 32, p. 58 (8 Feb. 1941); and Franco's official reply, ibid., No. 95, pp. 176–8 (26 Feb. 1941).

[79] Ribbentrop to Stohrer, ibid., No. 73, pp. 131–2 (21 Feb. 1941).

[80] *DGFP* D xii, No. 422, pp. 664–6 (28 Feb. 1941); *KTB OKW* i. 389 (30 Apr. 1941); Halder, *Diaries*, ii. 894–6 (30 Apr. 1941): the sensitive points in relation to the feared British invasion were Gibraltar and the north coast of Spain. A landing in Spanish Morocco was likewise not to be excluded. On the press campaign in Britain and the United States cf. Burdick, *Germany's Military Strategy*, 132.

[81] See *DGFP* D xii, No. 422, pp. 664–6 (28 Feb. 1941).

[82] *KTB OKW* i. 389 (30 Apr. 1941) records as Hitler's reaction to such fears: 'The Army must make preparations to release 8–10 divisions to support Portugal and Spain in throwing out troops landed.'

would resort to military action to forestall British operations.[83] Because of Barbarossa, however, at the end of April Germany was no longer in a position to take such steps. But even earlier they would hardly have accorded with Hitler's intentions. German troops were to march into Spain against Franco's will only if such action were absolutely necessary, e.g. to repel a possible enemy landing on the Iberian peninsula.

Hitler's speculation at the discussion on 30 April about measures the enemy might take on the Iberian peninsula or in Africa[84] caused Keitel to issue a directive on 1 May instructing the army and the Luftwaffe to prepare operations with the aim of driving enemy troops into the sea after a landing and of occupying strategic points on the Spanish and Portuguese coasts.[85] By 4 May discussions about such an operation were far advanced,[86] and three days later the army high command issued the directive for Operation Isabella, i.e. German intervention in the Iberian peninsula.[87]

The army high command continued to assume that in the summer of 1941, when most of the German army was tied down in the east, Britain would attempt to carry out a landing on the peninsula to prevent Franco from joining the Axis, recover lost prestige, make it easier for Roosevelt to enter the war, seize important locations along the coast for the Royal Navy, establish more bases for the use of the Royal Air Force, and extend British control of the land approaches to Gibraltar. The army high command expected the landing itself to be carried out in Portuguese ports. It considered an invasion of France at the same time improbable. Much would depend directly or indirectly on the behaviour of the states involved. The Germans expected France to adopt a wait-and-see attitude, while Portugal would make a more or less serious protest and then resist Wehrmacht units crossing its frontiers if the British invasion force were strong enough to have a good chance of success. Spain would probably want to resist a British invasion, but Franco's forces were hardly strong enough to withstand attack. If Germany should be forced to carry out Operation Isabella under such conditions, it would also have to prepare the way for Operation Felix, which was planned for the autumn. Operation Isabella would be carried out via unoccupied southern France. The necessary six to eight divisions were to be provided by the Commander-in-Chief West, who would also be in charge of preparations and execution of the operation. Moreover, planning should be done in such a way that Operation

---

[83] Stohrer's telegram of 1 May 1941, *DGFP* D xii, No. 422, pp. 664–6 n. 3; also Stohrer to foreign ministry on the Spanish foreign minister's expectation that the Wehrmacht would not march in without Franco's consent, ibid., No. 453, p. 711 (4 May 1941).

[84] Halder, *Diaries*, ii. 894–6 (30 Apr. 1941); *KTB OKW* i. 389–90 (30 Apr. 1941).

[85] Jacobsen, *1939–1945*, 213–14; cf. Halder, *Diaries*, ii. 896–7 (1 May 1941); Jäckel, *Frankreich*, 157.

[86] Halder, *Diaries*, ii. 901 (4 May 1941).

[87] *DGFP* D xii, No. 469, pp. 731–3 (7 May 1941). On 'Isabella' see Burdick, *Germany's Military Strategy*, 133–54; Seraphim, '"Felix" und "Isabella"', 73–82.

Isabella or Attila could be carried out as circumstances might require.[88] On 9 May 1941 the army high command issued a supplementary order.[89] After July the possibility of combining Operations Felix and Isabella was considered; all these deliberations took place within the framework of planning for the time after Barbarossa.[90]

2. CHANCES AND DANGERS FOR GERMAN STRATEGY IN THE MIDDLE EAST

Germany's relations with the countries of the Middle East were dominated by uncertainty at the end of 1940.[91] In Tehran irritation towards Germany prevailed when, after Molotov's visit in Berlin, British propaganda claimed that Germany wanted to sell Iran to the Soviet Union. Clearly Britain wanted to create tension in German–Iranian relations, which had until then been generally free of friction, although geographical factors, if not others, made it impossible to develop their relationship as they might have preferred. At the same time the British sowed mistrust between Tehran and Moscow.[92] The German government attempted to exercise a calming influence on Iran. It did not want to and could not cast doubt on its own superficially harmonious relations with the Soviet Union, but it assured the Iranian government that Iran had not been mentioned in Berlin.[93]

At approximately the same time the government of Iraq under Rashid Ali al-Gailani pressed the Axis powers to provide propaganda, economic, and military support to enable it to offer better resistance to British pressure. The Italian government had serious doubts in this regard, as the difficulties of providing any practical assistance were obvious.[94] The German government, on the other hand, promised at least to undertake diplomatic and propaganda actions friendly to Iraq, as previous public statements of sympathy for Arab liberation movements had evidently made a very good impression in Arab countries. Moreover, Berlin wanted to take pressure off the Gailani government,[95] which had received clear warnings from the British and the Americans not to endanger its neutrality by resuming diplomatic relations with the Third Reich. In this regard Iraq was even worried about the possibility of hostile

---

[88] *DGFP* (as n. 87).
[89] Jacobsen, *1939–1945*, 214–15; cf. *Hitler's War Directives*, No. 42, pp. 121–3 and n.
[90] See IV.II.3 below.
[91] On the background see I.II.4(*d*) above.
[92] Erwin Ettel, minister in Tehran, to foreign ministry, *DGFP* D xi, No. 350, p. 597 (18 Nov. 1940). On German–Iranian relations cf. esp. Hirschfeld, *Deutschland und Iran*, 211–51; B. P. Schröder, *Deutschland und der Mittlere Osten*, 37–8, also 232–40.
[93] *DGFP* D xi, No. 364, p. 632 (20 Nov. 1940); on the Persian reaction Hirschfeld, *Deutschland und Iran*, 251–2.
[94] Memorandum by director of political department, *DGFP* D xi, No. 482, pp. 829–31 (9 Dec. 1940).
[95] Memorandum by Legation Counsellor Melchers (pol. dept.), ibid., No. 496, pp. 846–7 (11 Dec. 1940).

action by Turkey.⁹⁶ In the not very confident hope that no obstacles remained to a resumption of normal diplomatic relations,⁹⁷ Berlin sent Baghdad a statement, already broadcast on German radio, about the Arab independence movement.⁹⁸

A little later the Iraqi government did seem prepared to enter into close co-operation with the Axis powers, but by then Gailani's position and that of his party were endangered by, among other things, the British successes in North Africa.⁹⁹ Around the end of January 1941 developments in Iraq were marked by a rapid succession of events. On 21 January the Anglophile foreign minister Nuri as-Said had to resign, which led the German ambassador in Ankara to hope for great things in German–Iraqi relations,¹⁰⁰ but on 31 January the pro-British party was able to bring about Gailani's fall.¹⁰¹ This development was quite the opposite of what had been expected, and it is therefore not surprising that Hitler decided not to answer for the time being a letter of 20 January from Haj Amin al Husseini, the Grand Mufti of Jerusalem, in which the latter attempted to give fresh impetus to German–Arab relations.¹⁰²

Ribbentrop—who, unlike other voices in the foreign ministry,¹⁰³ as late as the beginning of February still wanted to develop German policy towards Arab countries only with special consideration of Italian interests—remained very reserved. Germany should take the initiative only in 'suitable cases' and even then only after consultation with the Italians. Ribbentrop's attitude towards arms deliveries to Iraq, which were still being discussed in spite of Gailani's resignation, was equally cautious. Transports via the Soviet Union were now out of the question. Ribbentrop approved the examination of other possibilities, but he rejected a proposal by Admiral Canaris to deliver the weapons camouflaged in shipments of other goods. Although Ribbentrop's position in fact excluded large-scale actions to help Arab independence movements, discussions of the Arab question continued between the foreign ministry and the Wehrmacht high command.¹⁰⁴

---

⁹⁶ Memorandum by director of political department, ibid., No. 578, pp. 976–7 (29 Dec. 1940).
⁹⁷ Ibid. 977: Woermann's view was that Gailani, as a result of American–British pressure, was no longer particularly interested in a resumption of relations between Baghdad and Berlin.
⁹⁸ Ambassador in Ankara to foreign ministry, ibid., No. 596, pp. 1004–5 (2 Jan. 1941).
⁹⁹ Memorandum by director of political department, ibid., No. 601, pp. 1012–13 (3 Jan. 1941); ambassador in Ankara to foreign ministry, ibid., No. 722, p. 1215 (28 Jan. 1941).
¹⁰⁰ Ibid., No. 722.
¹⁰¹ On the fall of Gailani, for the British view cf. Woodward, *British Foreign Policy*, i. 571 ff. The new premier was Gen. Taha al-Hashimi, who had been war minister in Gailani's cabinet. See also B. P. Schröder, *Irak*, 30 ff., on the political background: he is very critical of the British. Tillmann, *Deutschlands Araberpolitik*, 211, emphasizes on the other hand that 'since the autumn of 1940 and particularly in the early months of 1941 there had been increasingly intensive efforts by German imperialists to bring about an armed conflict between Iraq and Great Britain'.
¹⁰² *DGFP* D xi, No. 680, pp. 1151–5; cf. Hillgruber, *Strategie*, 474.
¹⁰³ Tillmann, *Deutschlands Araberpolitik*, 188–9.
¹⁰⁴ *DGFP* D xii, No. 12, pp. 18–19 (4 Feb. 1941); on the planning of the intelligence department in the OKW cf. Hillgruber, *Strategie*, 474.

2. German Strategy in the Middle East

The views of the Wehrmacht high command as regards the German role in the Middle East differed considerably from those of the foreign minister. The military leaders were convinced that the German decision to 'give the Italians a free hand as regards their policies in the Mediterranean' should, with reference to the Arab countries, be re-examined. It was obvious, they argued, that Italy's lack of interest in independent Arab states—a result of Mussolini's imperialistic aims—had not only created difficulties but had led to a breaking off of valuable ties with Arab countries. The enemy had skilfully exploited this situation. To counteract it, the Wehrmacht high command proposed that in future political activity in the Middle East should be controlled from Germany. Quick and energetic action was required. The independence of the Arab countries must be recognized as an Axis war aim. Apart from that, experts should examine the question of whether Germany should publicize specific ideas about the future states in the Middle East. Germany was already in an advantageous situation because it could make any concession to the Arabs as regards the 'Jewish question in Palestine'.

Saudi Arabia was considered especially important. Unlike the Italians, who were hardly interested in having a powerful state under Ibn Saud opposite their possessions in East Africa, the Wehrmacht high command believed that the king, whom German officers wanted to make a central factor in efforts to increase German influence in the Middle East, must at least be offered the prospect of a free hand in south-west Arabia and corrections of his frontier with Transjordan. If the German government seriously intended to play an active role in that area, it was most important to develop contacts with Ibn Saud. In addition to territorial promises, it was therefore necessary to plan weapons deliveries to him at a later date.

Of course all these plans were evolved within the framework of the continuing conduct of the war against Great Britain. At the beginning of 1941 the Wehrmacht high command recommended that Germany should play the Saudi Arabian card,[105] to which the foreign ministry had attributed little significance since diplomatic relations had been broken off in September 1939.[106] And indeed, a certain change did take place in this regard: although at the official level negotiations were conducted with Iraqi contacts,[107] Ribbentrop was also

---

[105] Memorandum by Legation Counsellor Kramarz (pol. dept.) enclosing an OKW memorandum, *DGFP* D xii, No. 18, pp. 30–2 (5 Feb. 1941).

[106] Cf. I.II.4(*d*) above (text to nn. 396–9).

[107] Memorandum by director of political department of a conversation between the Grand Mufti's private secretary and Italian government representatives, *DGFP* D xii, No. 68, p. 121 (21 Feb. 1941); memorandum by Woermann on his conversation with the private secretary in Berlin, ibid., No. 92, pp. 168–9 (26 Feb. 1941). The armistice between Germany and France naturally featured in these conversations. Possible German support for a Greater Arab realm, which was also mentioned, affected the French position in Syria and could provoke, at least among the French, anxiety which must have its effect on the Vichy government. See also Woermann to Ambassador Abetz, ibid., No. 83, pp. 156–7 (25 Feb. 1941); Abetz to foreign ministry, ibid., No. 103, pp. 188–9 (28 Feb. 1941). It was feared that Syria would fall to the de Gaulle movement; but de

interested in a general activation of German policy in the Middle East with the aim of re-establishing ties with Iraq and Saudi Arabia and creating difficulties for the British in that area.[108]

This tendency in German policy was strongly reflected in a study by the foreign ministry on the possibility of drawing the Arab countries into the conflict with Britain. The importance of those countries resulted from their geographical situation: the Suez Canal; the land-bridge between Africa and India; the land supply-routes for British troops in Egypt through Iraq, Transjordan, and Palestine; the possible land connection between Britain and the Soviet Union; and the oil pipelines from Mosul to the Mediterranean coast. However, Ernst Woermann, the director of the political department in the foreign ministry, who was in charge of the study, assumed that as long as Turkey remained neutral direct military intervention in that area would not be possible for the Axis powers. This meant that in the final analysis German chances of overcoming British influence in the Arab countries were extremely small. But Woermann was of the opinion that even such small chances should be used. In this regard Egypt offered no possibilities, but, in addition to Iraq, Saudi Arabia might become a partner for Germany, as could the Grand Mufti, whose authority was, however, disputed among the Arabs.

Woermann considered the following possible instruments for German policy in the Middle East: propaganda, sabotage, and revolts; the proclamation of a great Arab confederation with unrestricted sovereignty as an Axis war aim; support with weapons and munition; financial aid; an attempt to induce Iraq to enter the war; the establishment of a mission in Syria, and the 'removal of de Gaulle's followers in key positions' in that country. The German government could try to make use of all these possibilities, but in fact only financial aid, the removal of de Gaulle's supporters, and the establishment of a German mission at the Italian control delegation in Syria could be realized.[109]

State Secretary von Weizsäcker was in agreement with Woermann's views; but he thought that nothing short of drawing the Soviet Union into the Middle East would seriously endanger Britain's position there. As, however, 'military decisions of a different kind' had already been taken with regard to the Soviet Union, there remained only 'the supplying of some arms, some money, and good words, the effect of which on the Arab movement should not be over-

---

Gaulle himself was being urged by the British to promise Syria and the Lebanon independence. This was in fact proclaimed by the high commissioner, Gen. Georges Catroux, for Syria (see IV.II.2 below) on 27 Sept. and for the Lebanon on 26 Nov. 1941; cf. Woodward, *British Foreign Policy*, i. 569-70.

[108] *KTB OKW* i. 327 (15 Feb. 1941). As regards the directly linked arms deliveries in Iraq, cf. esp. Tillmann, *Deutschlands Araberpolitik*, 187-8, on a corresponding trend of thought dating from Dec. 1940; and, for 1941, Hillgruber, *Strategie*, 474 ff.

[109] Memorandum by Woermann on the 'Arab question', *DGFP* D xii, No. 133, pp. 234-43 (7 Mar. 1941); on the political background and possible proposals cf. B. P. Schröder, *Deutschland und der Mittlere Osten*, 64-5.

2. German Strategy in the Middle East

estimated'.[110] Ribbentrop also agreed in principle with Woermann's views and added only a few remarks about details.[111]

A few days after these discussions, a completely new situation arose in Iraq, as Rashid Ali regained power in a bloodless coup on the night of 1–2 April 1941. This development was at least indirectly affected by the situation in North Africa. However, the British setbacks there were not the cause but at most an important contributing factor in the revolt. Rommel had begun his offensive in North Africa on 30 March, the Wehrmacht was deployed in southeast Europe, and the Italians had not lost the Dodecanese. The German actions seemed to indicate a shift of the main Axis war effort to the Mediterranean.[112] Moreover, at the beginning of April Hitler finally ordered the Grand Mufti's letter of 20 January to be answered.[113]

In spite of the above-mentioned German actions, it can be assumed that the changes in Iraq came too early for the Axis, for German deliberations about the Middle East all centred on the time after Barbarossa. But German diplomats sought to adapt their diplomacy to the new situation. In addition to many polite expressions of support, Weizsäcker wrote that Germans and Arabs had common enemies in the 'British and the Jews'. Berlin was ready 'to enter into friendly co-operation with the Arabs and, as far as possible, to give them military and financial support when they are forced to fight Britain to achieve their national aims'. The Germans wanted to deliver war material immediately if a way could be found to transport it. This letter has with good reason been termed a 'blank cheque for starting a revolt'; at least in the eyes of the Arab nationalists it was such.[114]

Nevertheless, this does not mean that Hitler expected Gailani to start a revolt soon, let alone that he desired such an action at that time. He considered developments from the perspective of their long-term significance for the German conduct of the war and therefore only wanted, for the time being, to prepare the ground for the period after Barbarossa. This was also evident in an oral report by Woermann to Ribbentrop on 9 April.[115] Woermann's remarks indicate that the German government assumed that the new Iraqi cabinet would resist British demands to be permitted to station troops in Iraq or for British units to be given permission, without any restrictions, to march through Iraqi territory. This was very important for the conflict in North

---

[110] *DGFP* D xii, No. 159, pp. 284–5 (12 Mar. 1941); also *Weizsäcker-Papiere*, 239 ff. (6 Mar. 1941).
[111] *DGFP* D xii, No. 188, pp. 323–5 (21 Mar. 1941).
[112] Hillgruber, *Strategie*, 475; Playfair, *Mediterranean*, ii. 177 ff.; also Al-Qazzaz, 'Iraqi–British war'; numerous details in B. P. Schröder, *Deutschland und der Mittlere Osten*, 74–8; id., *Irak*, 32–7, where developments seem to be interpreted according to the view that Britain and the US deliberately brought about the conflict with Iraq.
[113] *DGFP* D xii, No. 293, pp. 488–9 (8 Apr. 1941).
[114] Hillgruber, *Strategie*, 475.
[115] *DGFP* D xii, No. 299, pp. 497–9 (9 Apr. 1941); cf. also Tillmann, *Deutschlands Araberpolitik*, 215–16.

Africa. If the Iraqis acted as Berlin assumed and hoped, the British reaction could easily be predicted.

Immediate support for Gailani would have been the logical reaction for the German government, but apparently Berlin overestimated the ability of the Iraqi army to withstand a British attack. In any case the measures the Germans took do not indicate that they felt themselves to be under pressure of time. Weapon deliveries were envisaged and even discussed with the Japanese. Afghanistan also indicated a readiness to help. When Hitler stated on 10 April that 'weapons of all kinds can be provided',[116] German help for Iraq seemed indeed to be only a question of transport possibilities and routes. It was, however, indicative of the time-frame of German planning when Ribbentrop stated that, should Britain not be defeated in 1941—and most informed persons did not expect her to be—questions of the Near East' could 'assume a decisive importance from about autumn onwards'.

Woermann was instructed to take a special interest in the 'Near East, extending all the way to Afghanistan and India on the one hand and to North Africa on the other'. This agreed completely with the strategic objectives of Hitler's instructions of 17 February 1941,[117] which received final form in Directive No. 32,[118] to be examined in detail below. At that time the German government intended to confine itself to the establishment of a military intelligence service and acts of sabotage in Palestine, Transjordan, and Iraq. Moreover, Germany would intensify its activities in the Arab countries and in Africa in general, especially in French Morocco, Algeria, and Tunisia. These plans were also an indirect indication of intentions to be realized after the war with the Soviet Union.

That same day the Italians, who still maintained a legation in Baghdad, informed the German government that developments in Iraq were moving towards a military conflict.[119] Thereupon Italy and Germany agreed on a joint statement concerning the events in Iraq. The Axis powers affirmed that they were following Gailani's activities with the 'greatest sympathy'; they also advised him, rather cautiously, to take up armed resistance against Britain as soon as the relative strength of the forces involved offered a promise of success.[120] Under such conditions it would have been best for Gailani not to count on significant help from Germany and Italy.

---

[116] *DGFP* D xii, No. 299 (see previous n.) n. 4, p. 497. The quotation refers to information from Ribbentrop and to his conversation with Hitler.
[117] *KTB OKW* i. 328 (17 Feb. 1941); also IV.II.3 below.
[118] *Hitler's War Directives*, No. 32, pp. 78–82; 'Preparations for the period after Barbarossa'.
[119] B. P. Schröder, *Deutschland und der Mittlere Osten*, 77. On British measures cf. Rondot, 'Les mouvements', 657 ff.; Woodward, *British Foreign Policy*, i. 574–81 (these two titles also cover the suppression of the revolt).
[120] Memorandum by director of political department, *DGFP* D xii, No. 322, pp. 526–7 (12 Apr. 1941). B. P. Schröder's interpretation in *Irak*, 63, is incorrect where (probably by a printer's error) *solange* ('so long as') appears instead of *sobald* ('as soon as'), thus reversing the meaning. Cf. also Tillmann, *Deutschlands Araberpolitik*, 205, 218 ff., on the events leading up to the German–Italian offer, the content of which, however, is not very clearly dealt with.

2. German Strategy in the Middle East

For the moment the British neither recognized nor refused to recognize Gailani's new government, an attitude which inevitably had a direct effect on British–Iraqi relations. After the First World War Iraq had been the first former Turkish province to be given independence. Since 30 June 1930 it had been allied with Britain through a mutual-assistance pact. The pact defined the relationship between the *de jure* sovereign state, which had been admitted to the League of Nations in 1932, and the former British mandatory power; it was certainly not the result of negotiations between equal partners, but it obligated Iraq to help Britain in the event of war, by providing all possible support and making available to the British all transport routes, ports, and airfields within its frontiers. Even in peacetime British troops were to be permitted to pass through Iraqi territory; but since 1937, with the exception of the British forces at the air-bases of Shaybah near Basra and Habbaniyah on the Euphrates, which secured the line of communication with India, no British soldiers had been stationed in Iraq. In analysing the attitude of the British government in 1941, however, it must be remembered that, although Britain had made concessions to the Iraqi government in day-to-day relations over the years by not exploiting all possibilities under the treaty, she had never renounced her full rights guaranteed by it.[121]

At the start of the war in 1939 and again after Italy's entry into the conflict it became evident that Iraq had no intention of fulfilling all of its obligations under the treaty. Diplomatic relations with Italy were not broken off; and the rapid succession of German victories in Europe gave fresh impetus to anti-British tendencies in the country. Britain thus had good reason to view domestic developments in Iraq with concern. As early as July 1940 London intended to transfer troops guarding the Anglo-Iranian oilfields to Basra. But, to avoid creating additional tension, the units were sent to the Sudan and Egypt, where they were also needed.[122] However, this did not lead to a relaxation of the tense situation in Iraq. In January 1941 the change of government threatened to bring on a civil war, and the revolt in March seriously endangered British interests in the country. For Britain, Iraq possessed a key strategic position, not only because of the communication links and pipelines to Haifa in Palestine and Tripoli in northern Lebanon, but also because of the growing importance of Basra since the end of March as a possible discharging port for deliveries of American war material, especially aircraft.[123]

Because of these factors, the chiefs of staff and the joint planning staff (but not the commanders-in-chief, who were already fighting on two fronts against the German invasion of Greece and Rommel's offensive in North Africa, and wished to avoid a third) recommended on 8 April that Britain should intervene

---

[121] B. P. Schröder, *Irak*, 36, sees non-recognition as a deliberate measure to complicate the situation further; cf., on the other hand, Woodward, *British Foreign Policy*, i. 573–4. On the treaty see Schröder, 20–1.
[122] Playfair, *Mediterranean*, ii. 177–8.
[123] Butler, *Strategy*, ii. 460; on the delivery of US aircraft cf. Ray, 'Takoradi Route'.

militarily in Iraq. This plan quickly received Churchill's approval. Indian troop contingents intended for Malaysia were redirected to Basra on 10 April after talks with the viceroy of India, the Marquess of Linlithgow. On 12 April a transport with 3rd Field Regiment and 20th Indian Infantry Brigade put to sea and arrived at Basra on 18 April. The 1st King's Own Royal Regiment had been flown from Karachi to Shaybah a day earlier.[124]

On the evening of 16 April the British ambassador in Baghdad, Sir Kinahan Cornwallis, informed Gailani of the imminent arrival of the Indian units;[125] but rumours about the transports had leaked out earlier. The Iraqi government raised no objections to the landing of the troops in itself, but it demanded that they immediately move on to their destination in Egypt. Additional units were to be permitted to leave their ships in Basra only when the troops which had embarked on 18 April had already left Iraq. The British, of course, had no intention of meeting this wish and, after their request had been refused, they declared that Gailani was a usurper, with whom they would not negotiate. At the same time the British government accelerated the transfer of additional troops from India to Iraq. The British intended to establish a strong base in Basra; if necessary they were prepared to use force to stabilize the situation within the country and keep the Axis out. By 19 April at the latest Gailani's government knew of the British plans to convert Basra into a strong base. The British also offered to recognize the new government, as Gailani had demanded at the beginning of April; but he insisted on an early withdrawal of British troops. When, on 28 April, he was informed that an additional 2,000 soldiers would arrive in Iraq, he refused to permit them to land. Cornwallis then warned him not to oppose the landing, as the British government was determined to carry it out, although this was contrary to the treaty of 1930—which, however, Iraq itself had broken long before. But Gailani's attitude remained so hostile that the British evacuated women and children from Baghdad to Habbaniyah.[126]

In judging Gailani's aims, it is important to note that, immediately after being informed of the British troop movements, and using Italy as an intermediary, he sent a message to the German government asking for air support, weapons, and munitions deliveries from the Axis powers. He stressed that his government was determined to defend the country and requested financial help and numerous other forms of assistance for which Iraq had previously asked.[127]

---

[124] Churchill, *Second World War*, iii. 225–6; Butler, *Strategy*, ii. 460–1; Playfair, *Mediterranean*, ii. 178–9.

[125] Chargé d'affaires in Rome to foreign ministry, *DGFP* D xii, No. 372, pp. 857–8 (19 Apr. 1941); also Playfair, *Mediterranean*, ii. 179; Woodward, *British Foreign Policy*, i. 576.

[126] In detail in Woodward, *British Foreign Policy*, i. 576 ff.; Churchill, *Second World War*, iii. 226; an earlier detailed account of these events in Buckley, *Five Ventures*, 8–12; a partly divergent view in B. P. Schröder, *Deutschland und der Mittlere Osten*, 79–83; id., *Irak* 37 ff., with a summary of developments from 7 to 30 Apr.

[127] *DGFP* D xii, No. 372, pp. 587–8 (19 Apr. 1941); B. P. Schröder's interpretation (*Irak*, 38) is markedly pro-Iraq. Cf., however, also Tillmann, *Deutschlands Araberpolitik*, 218, and the analysis of the whole Iraqi episode in Hirszowicz, *The Third Reich*, 134–7.

2. German Strategy in the Middle East

It was typical of the difficult communications between the German foreign ministry and the different departments of the Wehrmacht that Woermann noted: 'The German military authorities have not yet been informed about Iraq's request. Please send instructions as soon as possible indicating whether this is to be done here or at your end [the office of the foreign minister].'[128] More important than the delays that may have resulted from this poor communication[129] was the fact that the British intercepted and easily deciphered Gailani's message transmitted by the Italian legation in Baghdad, and thus knew of his request for assistance soon after it was sent.[130] The Germans knew that Italian communications between the legation in Baghdad and Rome were not secure. When Ribbentrop submitted a memorandum to Hitler on 21 April concerning Germany's capacity to help Iraq, he emphasized that because of this fact the element of surprise had been lost. It seemed possible to deliver weapons by air via Syria, but few aircraft were available for such an operation. The land route was blocked by Turkey, but the Turkish government would permit transit shipments if the declared destination of the material were Afghanistan. The foreign ministry was now trying to obtain Kabul's consent. But no fast aid could be sent to Iraq this way, as the procedure would require weeks. And weapons shipments via Japan, which had been discussed at the beginning of April but which the Japanese government continued to reject, would require too much time. In the discussion of various ways to help Iraq, it became evident that the German government was sceptical about the will of the Iraqis to fight the British. Berlin wanted first to be sure that any assistance would not be wasted, which of course required even more time.[131]

Meanwhile, the Iraqi government seemed irritated that its request for support by the air forces of the Axis powers had still not been answered. In view of the strong British forces in Iraq, Baghdad soon found itself in a very uncomfortable position. This situation would become critical when additional British units, reported to be already on the way, arrived in the coming days. It quickly became clear that Gailani had overestimated Hitler's and Mussolini's power to help Iraq. Even the Axis propaganda support did not meet Iraqi expectations.[132]

Hitler still hesitated as the foreign ministry was discussing military assistance for Iraq with the Wehrmacht high command on 26 April. As the British had already landed troops in Iraq, he believed that the moment for support

---

[128] *DGFP* D xii, No. 372, p. 587 n. 4.
[129] On 21 Apr. the Luftwaffe had turned down an operation in Iraq as the aircraft range was inadequate. There was moreover a shortage of transport aircraft; cf. B. P. Schröder, *Deutschland und der Mittlere Osten*, 84.
[130] *DGFP* D xii, No. 377, pp. 592–4 nn. 4, 8 (21 Apr. 1941).
[131] Ibid., No. 377; on planned deliveries of weapons and ammunition see Tillmann, *Deutschlands Araberpolitik*, 217–22.
[132] Ambassador in Rome to foreign ministry on a conversation of the Italian minister in Baghdad with Gailani and the Grand Mufti, *DGFP* D xii, No. 401, pp. 634–5 (25 Apr. 1941); on German considerations concerning material support cf. B. P. Schröder, *Irak*, 64–5.

actions was already past. The fact that the figures reported by the Wehrmacht department dealing with foreign armies were too high, as the foreign ministry suspected, was not important in this regard; the Wehrmacht high command showed little inclination to become involved. Only on 28 April was Keitel prepared, in response to a request from Ribbentrop, to explain a possible action by the Luftwaffe to Hitler.[133] The army high command was now concentrating its attention on the most important objective of the German war effort, Barbarossa.[134]

When the calls for help from Baghdad became more urgent, the foreign ministry proposed to send Fritz Grobba, a Middle East expert who had been German minister in Iraq until 6 September 1939, to Ankara as a special representative to begin direct negotiations with the Iraqi military.[135] The Iraqis were again assured of German sympathy for their cause; more important, the German government promised them financial assistance. Deliveries of weapons and munitions were, however, still being considered. The transport routes were a considerable problem in this regard.[136]

The Germans considered providing the following forms of support for Iraq.[137] Arms deliveries for Iran were to be held back in Iraq; 500–600 tonnes of *matériel* were available. However, such an action would have required several weeks. Arms shipments with Afghanistan as their declared destination offered similar possibilities; but here too the action would require two or three months. As had already been mentioned in the Franco-German negotiations in May, it was also possible to provide weapons from stocks, now under Italian control, taken from the French army formerly under General Weygand in Syria. Since the beginning of April the Italians had been making preparations for an action to bring the arms to Iraq via Syria in the course of a 'corsair operation' at sea. Weapons could also be transported to Iraq by the Luftwaffe. If Hitler gave his consent, such an operation could be prepared to the point that it would require only an order at the proper moment.

Ribbentrop emphasized the great importance of Iraq's fate for the situation of the Axis in North Africa. A use of German forces other than the Luftwaffe, e.g. via Syria, depended primarily on the development of German–French relations. But Ribbentrop was not thinking of operations to be realized in the short term; first it had to be ensured that Gailani would attack the British only when Iraq was able to stand its ground because of support provided by the Axis powers.

---

[133] Memorandum by director of the political department to the foreign minister's office recording conversation with Col. Fritz Brinckmann of the OKW foreign department, *DGFP* D xii, No. 407, pp. 641–2 (26 Apr. 1941).
[134] Halder *Diaries*, ii. 889–91 (26 Apr. 1941).
[135] *DGFP* D xii, No. 412, p. 652 (27 Apr. 1941); cf. Grobba, *Männer und Mächte*, 224–5.
[136] Foreign minister to Rome embassy, *DGFP* D xii, No. 413. p. 653 (27 Apr. 1941).
[137] Memorandum by Ribbentrop for Hitler dated 27 Apr. 1941, submitted 28 Apr.: ibid., No. 415, pp. 655–6; cf. B. P. Schröder, *Deutschland und der Mittlere Osten*, 86. A detailed account of these problems in Hirszowicz, *The Third Reich*, 147–50.

2. German Strategy in the Middle East

The following day Ribbentrop informed the head of the Wehrmacht high command about the agreement planned with the French. Vichy was prepared, within the framework of the German–French agreements, to supply arms for Iraq from its own stocks in Syria. It would also allow German aircraft flying to Iraq to make intermediate landings in Syria.[138]

The fighting between Iraqi and British forces began on 2 May, before German preparations had been concluded. The events cannot be described in detail here, but it should be mentioned that the Iraqi government ordered the British air-base at Habbaniyah to be surrounded on 29–30 April. After negotiations failed to produce any improvement of the situation, the British attacked the besiegers on 2 May. Gailani immediately broke off diplomatic relations with Britain and asked Germany to send Grobba to Baghdad and provide fast military assistance, especially in the form of Luftwaffe operations and arms deliveries for the Iraqi army.[139]

In Iraq itself the imminent struggle was clearly one-sided.[140] Gailani's 'Iraqi National Army', based on universal conscription, consisted of five divisions with about 50,000 men. The Iraqi air force possessed fifty-six aircraft, all of which, with the exception of several acquired in Italy, were obsolete. Most of the aircraft were fighters; personnel totalled 1,000 men. Anti-aircraft defences were lacking. The Iraqi navy was able to send four river gunboats against the British. In the course of the fighting British strength in Iraq reached 23,450 men. About 3,500 were already in the country before the crisis became acute at the beginning of April. Between 18 and 29 April 14,000 men of 10th Indian Division (motorized infantry) arrived in southern Iraq from Karachi. The rest followed by 13 May from India and Transjordan. Each side had sixteen tanks. The British troops were generally better motorized; this was especially true of the intervention force assembled in Transjordan for the relief of Habbaniyah, known as Habforce, which consisted of 1,500 men of the Arab Legion, 400 men and 8 tanks of an air force armoured battalion, 2,700 men of 4th Cavalry Brigade (motorized), 800 men of Essex Regiment (two infantry battalions), a battery (200 men) of 60th Field Artillery Regiment, and an anti-tank and a sapper group of 100 men each, making a total of 5,800 men. The Royal Air Force in Iraq, reinforced with units from India and Egypt, including those of the carrier *Hermes* in the Persian Gulf, enjoyed absolute air supremacy with a total of 252 fighter and bomber aircraft. Although the British air units in Iraq suffered considerable losses at the beginning of the conflict, the number of their aircraft remained above 200 during the entire month of May.

---

[138] Cf. IV.II.1 above, esp. *DGFP* D xii, No. 442, p. 695 (3 May 1941), and No. 459, pp. 718–20 (5 May 1941). On the German decision to deliver weapons cf. also Hirszowicz, *The Third Reich*, 150–3; Hitler had consented on 3 May.

[139] Chargé d'affaires in Ankara to foreign ministry, *DGFP* D xii, No. 432, p. 686 (2 May 1941). On the military events cf. Buckley, *Five Ventures*, 11–38; Playfair, *Mediterranean*, ii. 182–97; B. P. Schröder, *Deutschland und der Mittlere Osten*, 87–141; id., *Irak*, 46–58.

[140] B. P. Schröder, *Irak*, 41–6.

To return to the decision-making process in Germany, at the beginning of May Ribbentrop recommended that Grobba should be sent to Baghdad, accompanied by a Luftwaffe officer and an army officer. Ribbentrop was determined to find out whether the Luftwaffe should prepare to transport war material to Iraq and whether Hitler intended to send a bomber Geschwader and a fighter Geschwader there. He believed it to be quite possible to establish a base in Iraq for the war against Britain. Moreover, he was thinking of a decisive German thrust against Egypt in the course of a great Arab revolt.[141] Hitler basically agreed to such plans, but as regards the transfer of Luftwaffe units, i.e. concrete action, he was extremely sceptical, especially because of the uncertain fuel situation in Iraq.[142]

The Iraqi government again pointed out that German assistance was urgently needed, as time would play an important role in further developments.[143] The already mentioned French readiness to co-operate seemed to offer Hitler a solution in this situation. Perhaps it would be possible in this way, with little direct German involvement, to enable Iraq to offer armed resistance against the British on a long-term basis.[144] After the agreement between Darlan and Abetz, Legation Counsellor Rahn was sent as German representative to the Italian control delegation in Syria[145] to ensure that the agreements would be carried out quickly. In spite of the German–French agreements, the French continued to be rather reserved towards the Italians. This again became obvious when the Italian government requested permission to use Syrian airfields for Italian aircraft which were to fly to Iraq.[146]

Grobba arrived in Iraq on 10 May and had his first talks with Gailani and the Iraqi foreign minister. He then advised the foreign ministry in Berlin that it was necessary to send German aircraft to Iraq for military and political reasons, although such a gesture would mainly have propaganda value.[147]

---

[141] Memorandum by Ribbentrop for Hitler, *DGFP* D xii, No. 435, pp. 688–9 (3 May 1941).

[142] Record of Hitler's comments by Minister Hewel, ibid., No. 436, p. 690 (3 May 1941); cf. also director of political department to Ankara embassy, ibid., No. 441, pp. 694–5 (3 May 1941); B. P. Schröder, *Deutschland und der Mittlere Osten*, 91–5.

[143] Minister in Tehran to foreign ministry, *DGFP* D xii, No. 457, pp. 716–17 (5 May 1941).

[144] See n. 138, and cf. *KTB OKW* i. 392 (7 May 1941): 'According to Ambassador Ritter and Abetz the French have made air landing-places available. Ibn Saud's attitude is not yet clear. An officer in disguise to be sent as arms dealer to Syria to purchase French arms for Iraq.' Cf. also Warlimont, *Headquarters*, 131–2; according to B. P. Schröder, *Irak*, 66, Hitler required a 'heroic gesture' in Iraq.

[145] *DGFP* D xii, No. 476, pp. 742–3 (8 May 1941). On German involvement and the military events cf. also the account based on personal experience in Moellhausen, *Giuoco*, 90–117, who was Rahn's colleague in the Near East.

[146] Memorandum by Woermann, *DGFP* D xii, No. 479, pp. 744–5 (9 May 1941), who believed that the Italian action could endanger the German one. After 11 May the foreign ministry had Darlan informed that Italian aircraft were 'to be treated in the same way' as the German. On the employment of the Italian air force cf. Ciano, *Diary 1939–1943*, 350 (30 May 1941). A month after the beginning of the conflict the Italian aircraft had still not taken part—further evidence of inadequate preparation for war.

[147] Grobba to foreign ministry, *DGFP* D xii, No. 493, p. 775 (11 May 1941); cf. Grobba, *Männer und Mächte*, 234–7, and *KTB OKW* i. 393 (8 May 1941).

2. German Strategy in the Middle East

Indeed, on 6 May the Luftwaffe operations staff and the Wehrmacht high command had already decided to send a group of Me 110s and a group of He 111s—twin-engine fighters and medium bombers—to Iraq.[148] The Wehrmacht high command also formulated instructions for operations in the Middle East.[149] These were followed on 23 May by Hitler's directive No. 30,[150] which, however, came much too late to initiate any action that might have helped the Iraqis. It must be pointed out again that Hitler was still interested only in temporary measures. In his directive he clearly stated: 'I have decided to accelerate the progress of developments in the Middle East by supporting Iraq. Whether and how the British position between the Mediterranean and the Persian Gulf—in connection with an offensive against the Suez Canal—is to be finally destroyed will be decided only after Barbarossa.' Operation Barbarossa was the centre of German strategy. This was true in two respects, for on the one hand it was intended to create the preconditions for future operations, and on the other hand it limited for the time being the strategic possibilities open to the Axis powers.

German military aid was sent to Iraq in the middle of May, but it retained its stopgap character. The German military accepted this situation, as they believed that the operation in Iraq was important even if 'in the long term it should not be completely successful'. The activities of the Luftwaffe formed the largest single part of the German engagement. On 16 May the 'Air Leader Iraq', Colonel Werner Junck, had twelve Me 110s and five He 111s under his command. A transport Staffel consisting of Ju 52s and Ju 90s was to shuttle between Athens, Rhodes, Syria, and Baghdad to bring supplies. Sea routes were also to be used. The army wanted to send only a military mission consisting of weapon specialists and general staff officers to Iraq. The navy was given the task of blocking the Shatt al Arab with German merchant ships lying in Bandare Shahpur to slow the flow of British supplies to Basra.[151]

On 15–16 May the German aircraft intervened in the fighting,[152] but after two days they were no longer serviceable. On 28 May only one He 111 was able to take off in Mosul.[153] The inadequately prepared operation had to be considered a failure. That events would take this course had become evident

---

[148] Gundelach, *Luftwaffe im Mittelmeer*, 238; *KTB OKW* (as n. 147).

[149] Warlimont, *Headquarters*, 132.

[150] *Hitler's War Directives*, No. 30, pp. 72–4, 'Middle East'; Jacobsen, *1939–1945*, 217–18; Hillgruber, *Strategie*, 478; B. P. Schröder, *Deutschland und der Mittlere Osten*, 127 ff.

[151] Memorandum by Legation Counsellor Kramarz on the state of military aid for Iraq, *DGFP* D xii, No. 528, pp. 833–5 (16 May 1941). On support by the Luftwaffe cf. esp. Gundelach, *Luftwaffe im Mittelmeer*, 238 ff., from which the above figures derive; see also *KTB OKW* i. 395 (13 May 1941). For details concerning the decision on 21 May to establish a military mission under Air General Hellmuth Felmy in Iraq see B. P. Schröder, *Deutschland und der Mittlere Osten*, 127 ff. The tasks of 'Special Staff F' (which was never of practical importance) were laid down in Directive No. 30; on military aid see Schröder, ibid., 107–11.

[152] Gundelach, *Luftwaffe im Mittelmeer*, 241–50.

[153] On German casualties see *KTB OKW* i. 396–7 (19, 20, 21, 28 May 1941); Hillgruber, *Strategie*, 479; B. P. Schröder, *Deutschland und der Mittlere Osten*, 126.

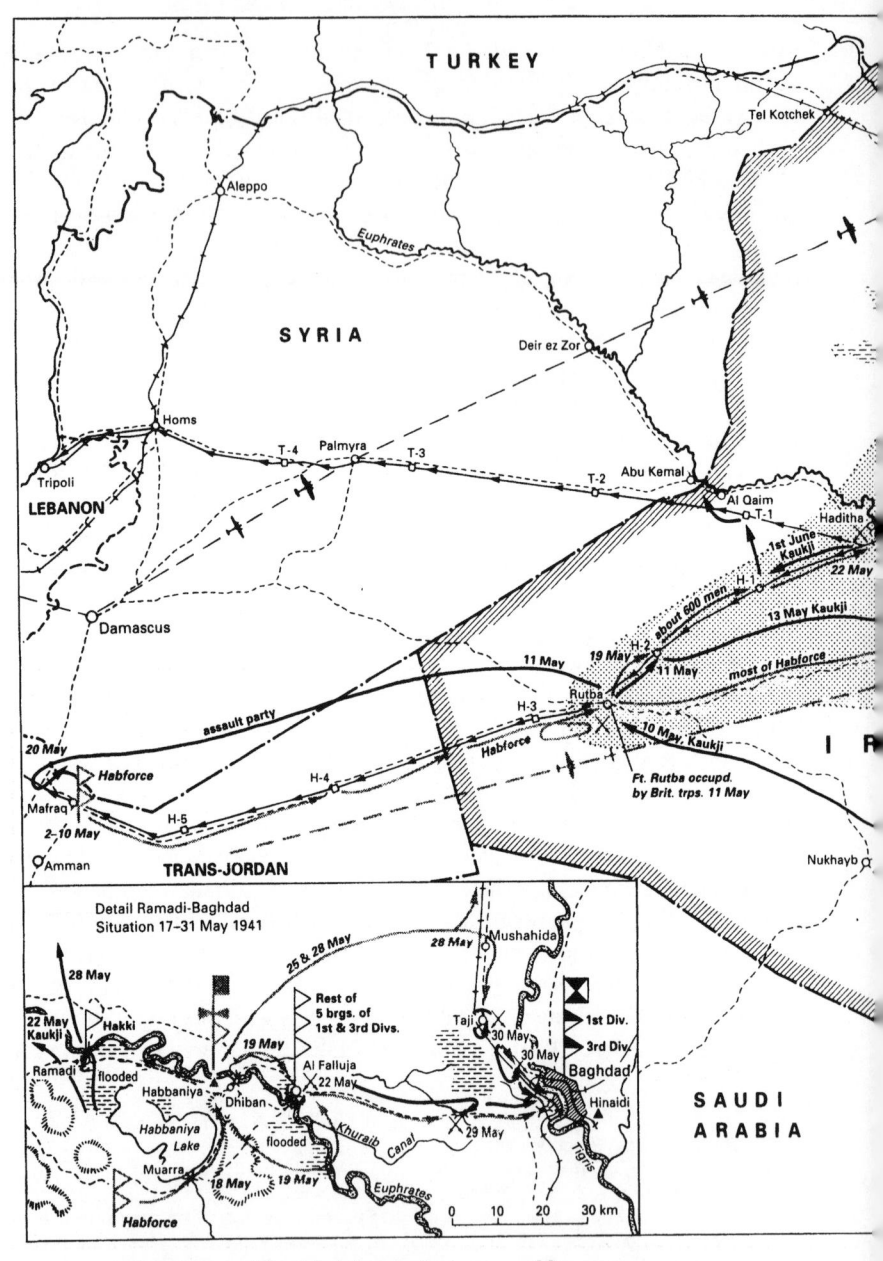

MAP IV.II.1. The Fighting in Iraq, 2–31 May 1941
Detail Ramadi–Baghdad: Situation 17–31 May 1941

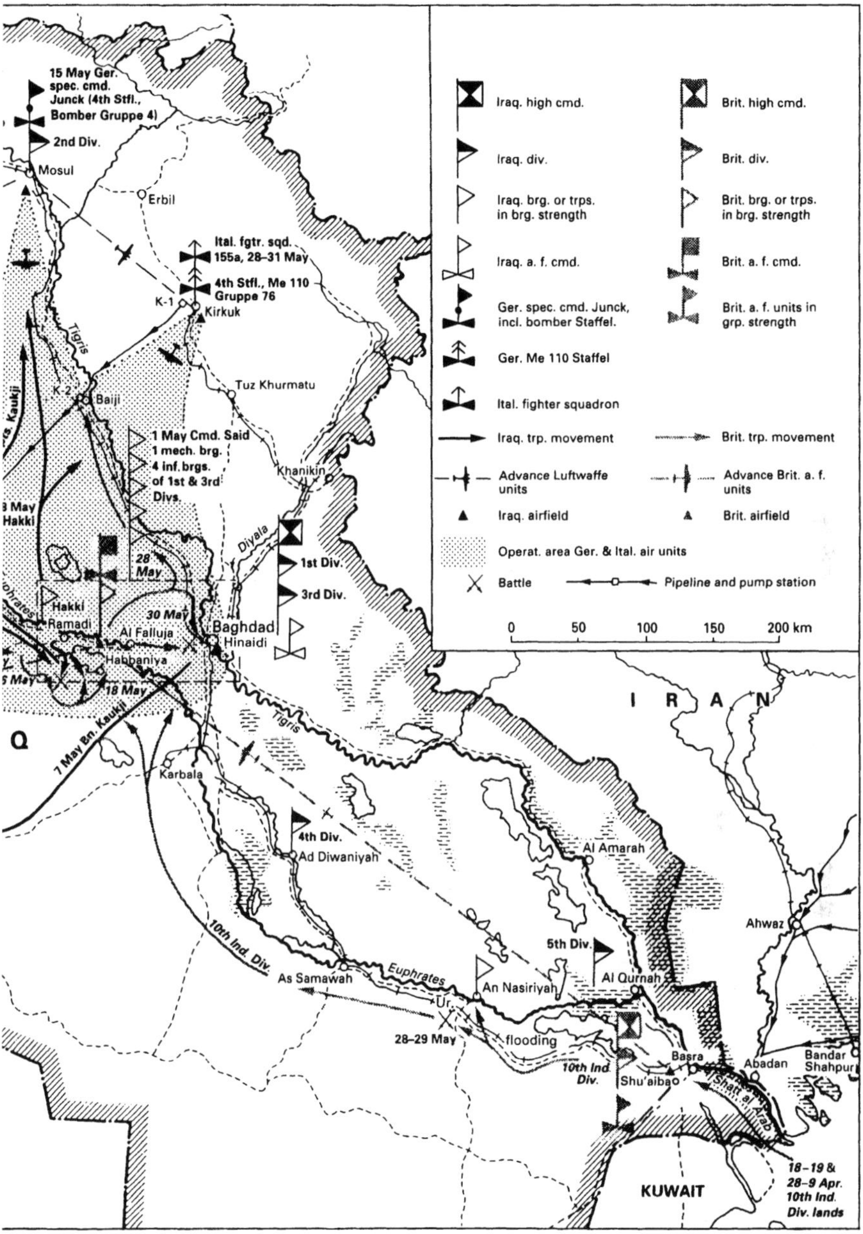

15 May Ger. spec. cmd. Junck (4th Stfl., Bomber Gruppe 4)
2nd Div.
Mosul
Erbil
Ital. fgtr. sqd. 155a, 28–31 May
4th Stfl., Me 110 Gruppe 76
K-1
Kirkuk
Tigris
K-2
Baiji
Tuz Khurmatu
1 May Cmd. Said 1 mech. brg. 4 inf. brgs. of 1st & 3rd Divs.
Khanikin
Hakki
28 May
Diyala
1st Div.
3rd Div.
Hakki
Ramadi
30 May
Baghdad
Al Falluja
Hinaidi
Habbaniya
18 May
7 May Bn. Kaukji
Q
Tigris
Karbala
4th Div.
Ad Diwaniyah
Al Amarah
I R A N
Ahwaz
10th Ind. Div.
5th Div.
As Samawah
Euphrates
An Nasiriyah
Al Qurnah
Ur
28–29 May
flooding
10th Ind Div.
Basra
Shu'aiba
Abadan
Bandar Shahpur
Shatt al Arab
KUWAIT
18–19 & 28–9 Apr. 10th Ind. Div. lands
Iraq. high cmd.
Brit. high cmd.
Iraq. div.
Brit. div.
Iraq. brg. or trps. in brg. strength
Brit. brg. or trps. in brg. strength
Iraq. a. f. cmd.
Brit. a. f. cmd.
Ger. spec. cmd. Junck, incl. bomber Staffel.
Brit. a. f. units in grp. strength
Ger. Me 110 Staffel
Ital. fighter squadron
Iraq. trp. movement
Brit. trp. movement
Advance Luftwaffe units
Advance Brit. a. f. units
Iraq. airfield
Brit. airfield
Operat. area Ger. & Ital. air units
Battle
Pipeline and pump station
0 50 100 150 200 km

early, as it had not been possible to disrupt the flow of British reinforcements. On 6 May the Iraqis had to abandon the plateau of Habbaniyah. For the British it was extremely advantageous that they were able to eliminate the Iraqi air force early. By 3 May the Iraqis had lost half their aircraft, and twelve days later the Iraqi air force had ceased to exist (see Map IV.II.1).

In the course of the fighting, as a result of an attack by shock troops, Fort Ar Rutbah fell to the British on 11 May. Two days later Habforce was at the frontier of Iraq. On 15 May most of its units reached the area of Ramadi, where Iraqi forces had been drawn together for defence. The British advance slowed, as the Iraqis had opened the sluice-gates of the dams on the Euphrates and flooded the approaches to Habbaniyah between the lake of the same name and the river at Ramadi, making them impassable for Habforce. The British had to turn south and captured the Mujarra bridge on 18 May, thus opening the way to Habbaniyah.

At the same time other parts of Habforce advanced from Ar Rutbah to the pipeline centre Al Hadithah. Although they were occasionally slowed by Iraqi resistance, the operation was concluded by 22 May.

Between 19 and 22 May, after they had circumvented the flooded area west of Al Fallujah in the west and south, the British conquered the approaches to the Iraqi capital between Habbaniyah and that city, where fighting had been going on since 6 May. The capture of the bridge over the Euphrates at Al Fallujah intact greatly facilitated the deployment for the attack on Baghdad. By 28 May the British had concentrated 3,500 men for the attack, which was carried out from two directions. The city was defended by more than twice as many Iraqis, who, however, had no effective weapons against British air power. This fact contributed decisively to the favourable development of the situation for the attackers.

The 10th Indian Division made no significant contribution to the British victories. It had been tied down by unrest among the population of Basra, where Iraqi troops also blocked its advance by opening the sluice-gates of the dams on the Euphrates. After the division had left Shaybah on 27 May, it was involved in fighting with the Iraqi 5th Division near Ur on 28–9 May. Thereafter the advance went according to plan, but units of 10th Division arrived near Baghdad only after the battle for the city had already been decided.[154] In view of the military situation, it is not surprising that the Grand Mufti expressed his concern about Gailani's position on 27 May and urged the Axis powers to send more assistance.[155] On 29 May Grobba even advocated more missions by the Luftwaffe to relieve Baghdad, but, as mentioned above, the German air units in Iraq now had only one aircraft fit for action.[156] The

---

[154] B. P. Schröder, *Irak*, 46–57; Buckley, *Five Ventures*, 13–34.
[155] *DGFP* D xii, No. 557, pp. 890–1 (27 May 1941).
[156] Ibid., No. 568, p. 917 (29 May 1941). Grobba stayed a little longer in Iraq, where it appeared at first as if resistance could be mobilized in the north of the country. On 2 June he arrived in Aleppo, returning to Berlin on the 4th: Grobba, *Männer und Mächte*, 245–8.

next day Grobba moved to Mosul, as the situation of Baghdad was hopeless. Gailani, the Grand Mufti, various ministers, and high-ranking officers went into exile in Iran. After 2 June Jamil al-Midfai was the new leader of Iraq.[157] On 31 May the British had signed an armistice with the Iraqi armed forces. The Iraqi army was permitted to keep its weapons, while British forces were granted unrestricted freedom of movement within the country.[158] The British victory meant the end of German hopes of achieving a diversionary effect by supporting Iraqi resistance to British domination, and it also had far-reaching effects in the Arab world at the moment of the Axis conquest of Crete.

As the revolt in Iraq reached its climax, the Afghan economics minister, Abdul Majid Khan, who was spending several weeks at a German health resort at the time, advocated, though without authorization, comprehensive co-operation between his country and the Third Reich.[159] Clearly he saw a chance to achieve extensive changes of Afghanistan's frontiers under Germany's aegis, especially with regard to India.[160] After the collapse of resistance in Iraq, however, he persistently avoided giving a clear answer to German requests for Afghan support for anti-British propaganda to be directed at India. As Weizsäcker observed, the latest developments in Iraq had clearly had their effect. Abdul Majid Khan, who as recently as 20 May had promised to support a guerrilla war to be instigated by Germany along the Afghan–Indian frontier,[161] now refused to have anything to do with such plans. He mentioned instead that the British for their part were mobilizing the mountain tribes against Kabul; he advised caution, and even described the defeat in Iraq as an advantage, for sufficient time would now be available to create the indispensable firm foundation for German–Afghan co-operation.[162]

Shortly after the start of the war against the Soviet Union, Berlin knew definitely that Kabul intended to observe strict neutrality. The exposed position of Afghanistan between the Soviet and British spheres of influence clearly made such a policy advisable. This attitude showed that neutral powers had obviously recognized the extent to which Hitler, by starting Operation Barbarossa, had made the realization of his strategy against Britain dependent on victory over the Soviet Union. But no later than the spring of 1941 the decision to attack the Soviet Union had limited Germany's capacity to wage war in other areas. In the months before June 1941 German policy and military actions were completely determined by the *sine qua non* for all future

---

[157] B. P. Schröder, *Irak*, 58; only in October was he replaced by Nuri as-Said.
[158] Buckley, *Five Ventures*, 34 ff.; Woodward, *British Foreign Policy*, i. 580–1.
[159] See Glasneck and Kircheisen, *Türkei und Afghanistan*, 224–5; Hillgruber, *Strategie*, 386–7.
[160] Memorandum by Weizsäcker recording conversation with Abdul Majid, who was mainly concerned about territorial claims west of the Indus, *DGFP* D xii, No. 467, pp. 728–9 (6 May 1941).
[161] Hillgruber, *Strategie*, 386–7.
[162] *DGFP* D xii, No. 598, pp. 971–2 (6 June 1941): memorandum by state secretary of conversation with Abdul Majid.

operations, the successful conclusion of the war against the Soviet Union.[163]

This was clear not least from Hitler's reaction to developments in the Middle East. On 24 April he again reproached the diplomats of the foreign ministry for, as he claimed, not having informed him accurately or in time about the situation there; but he did this in order to shift the blame for the fiasco. He himself identified the real reason for the half-hearted German engagement: 'In itself the Middle East would present no difficulty if other plans [Barbarossa] were not irrevocable.'[164] Moreover, and this perspective dominated Hitler's long-term strategic deliberations: 'Success [in the Soviet Union] will open the gate to the Orient.'

What was true of Afghanistan and the Arab countries was also true of India. Even before 1941 any planning of Hitler in this regard was directly affected by the development of German–Afghan relations. German policy towards India was marked by an absence of clear, consistent aims,[165] although the leader of the Indian nationalists, Subhas Chandra Bose, had tried to develop contacts and ties with the National Socialists, as well as the Italian Fascists, while living in European exile in the early 1930s. The Third Reich was at that time interested in India primarily for reasons of economic and cultural policy. Support for anti-British or other anti-colonial national movements was, on the other hand, incompatible with Hitler's intentions and preferred policy towards Britain.[166]

Bose's experience with the National Socialist regime was generally negative. Nevertheless, although he detested the racist arrogance which prevailed in the new Germany, and which Indians living there experienced personally, he never condemned unequivocally the aggression of the Third Reich in Europe.[167] His nationalist aims doubtless forced him to judge the situation pragmatically. Because of the difficulty in judging German policy towards Britain, in 1938 Bose, who was president of the Congress Party at the time, enquired at a secret meeting with representatives of the British-India and Ceylon chapter of the organization for NSDAP members abroad whether Germany, should the occasion arise, would actually want to prop up the British Empire, which was moving towards collapse; he also complained about anti-Indian excesses in Germany. But he did not receive any official answer

---

[163] For details see *Das Deutsche Reich und der Zweite Weltkrieg*, iv. 3–37 (Förster).

[164] Engel, *Heeresadjutant bei Hitler*, 101–2 (24 Apr. 1941).

[165] Voigt, in 'Hitler und Indien', tries very convincingly to define the historic significance of India in Hitler's strategic calculations. The view that India, before the outbreak of war in 1939, was of minor importance in the strategic calculations of the National Socialist regime is also supported by Hauner, 'Deutschland und Indien', 430; this includes arguments from the same author's comprehensive study, *India*.

[166] Hauner, 'Deutschland und Indien', 433–8, makes it clear that the attitudes of the National Socialist leadership were not uniform. Hitler saw India as a component of his policy towards England; his attitude to Indians as a race was pejorative. Hitler's attitude to India is well outlined in Voigt, *Indien*, 101.

[167] Thierfelder, 'Begegnungen', 154 ff.: Bose's letter of 25 Mar. 1936.

2. German Strategy in the Middle East

to his question: the foreign ministry was not interested.[168] At the end of April 1939 Bose, whose general ideology was influenced by Communism and Fascism, had to resign as president of the Congress Party. His resignation possibly prevented a nationalist revolution in India at the beginning of the Second World War,[169] which he considered 'a golden opportunity' for his country.[170] In Indian domestic politics, however, Bose's influence declined after he resigned his offices in the Congress Party. His 'Forward Bloc' movement was dissolved and he himself placed under house arrest on 2 July 1939 for continuing to advocate the use of force in the struggle against Britain. This development led for the time being to his complete political isolation.[171]

Bose's escape from India on 17 January 1941[172] marked, in a sense, the birth of German policy towards India in the Second World War. Bose arrived in Afghanistan on 1 February, where, however, he remained only for a short time, as he was in danger of being arrested there. With the help of the German foreign ministry, he finally reached Berlin via Moscow.[173] Arriving on 2 April,[174] he spoke with Woermann in the foreign ministry the next day, with whom he discussed in a noncommittal way a 'programme for the immediate future'. As regards India, the Germans thought mainly in terms of propaganda, but Bose developed concrete political plans. He proposed to organize an Indian government in exile in Germany, if the Axis powers gave their consent. Moreover, he wanted to instigate uprisings in India. He even spoke of German and Italian troops intervening there. Woermann showed a certain sympathy for such ambitious ideas, but recommended a talk between Bose and Ribbentrop.[175]

A few days later Bose submitted a memorandum containing a 'plan for co-operation between the Axis powers and India'.[176] His deliberations centred on the demand for freedom for India. This required that 'Britain should be completely defeated in this war and the British Empire broken up.' To achieve this co-operation it was necessary to concentrate on Europe, Afghanistan, and

---

[168] Hauner, 'Deutschland und Indien', 439–40.

[169] Ansperger, *Auflösung der Kolonialreiche*, 50–1; on the resignation cf. also Werth, *Tiger Indiens*, 95–6.

[170] Bose, *The Indian Struggle*, 339. After Sept. 1939 Bose repeatedly called on his countrymen to rise against Britain in her time of difficulties; cf. Voigt, *Indien*, 100, and Werth, *Tiger Indiens*, 101 ff.

[171] Hauner, 'Deuschland und Indien', 440.

[172] For details see Toye, *The Springing Tiger*, 57–60; Werth, *Tiger Indiens*, 107–13.

[173] Director of political department to Moscow embassy, *DGFP* D xii, No. 36, pp. 63–4 (9 Feb. 1941). According to Glasneck and Kircheisen, *Türkei und Afghanistan*, 236, the Germans already knew by 1 Feb. that Bose wanted to come to Berlin. On the escape from Kabul to Berlin see Werth, *Tiger Indiens*, 113–18.

[174] Memorandum by director of political department recording first conversation with Bose, *DGFP* D xii, No. 257, pp. 442–3 (3 Apr. 1941).

[175] Ibid.; cf. also Hillgruber, *Strategie*, 482.

[176] *DGFP* D xii, No. 300, pp. 499–502 (9 Apr. 1941); Glasneck and Kircheisen, *Türkei und Afghanistan*, 236; Hauner, 'Deutschland und Indien', 443; cf. also Voigt, 'Hitler und Indien', 52–3.

India. Bose envisaged subversive and propaganda measures for India and Afghanistan—from radio broadcasts to attacks on British military installations, from strikes to open revolts. Such actions were to be developed in phases. Activities in Europe could at first be limited to the founding of a 'Free Indian Government', which would sign a treaty with Berlin and Rome. Among other aims, the treaty would proclaim freedom for India in the event of an Axis victory. Bose intended then to establish diplomatic missions with all friendly European governments. With such steps he hoped to convince his countrymen that India's freedom would be guaranteed after the victory of the Axis powers and that the latter had already recognized her independence.

In addition to political matters, Bose also examined financial and military questions. Assuming that the British disposed of, at most, 70,000 loyal troops in India, he believed that 50,000 German and Italian troops could defeat them there, if the Axis forces were equipped with the most modern weapons and the Indian troops were prepared to revolt against Britain, which could hardly be predicted with any degree of certainty; on this point, however, Bose was very optimistic.

The German foreign ministry did not share Bose's optimism and viewed his programme with unconcealed scepticism.[177] Indeed, there was hardly any reason to proclaim immediately the liberation of India from British colonial domination as a German war aim. In addition, Bose's Forward Bloc was a left-wing organization, and the establishment of an Indian government under Bose in Berlin would mean German recognition of the Forward Bloc as the exponent of a future India. This would inevitably lead to difficulties with Mohandas Gandhi and Jawaharlal Nehru, Indian leaders no less prominent than Bose. The foreign ministry saw no reason to take a clear position with regard to Bose, as indicating a preference for him would not only offer no political advantages but would also produce a negative reaction in many circles in India. On the other hand, the ministry had no objection to the intended propaganda and subversive activity. It also advocated generous financial support, but advised against pursuing the question of a 'military expedition to India'.

When Bose met Ribbentrop on 29 April, the two men discussed the situation in India at length.[178] Bose criticized Gandhi's accommodation with the British and informed Ribbentrop about the military situation in India, the Nationalist Party organization, the attitude of the officer corps and the maharajas, and India's relations with Japan, Afghanistan, and the Soviet Union. Because of the anti-imperialistic attitude of the Indians, many of them viewed the last-mentioned country with a certain sympathy. In any case the Soviet Union was more popular than Germany. In India, according to Bose,

---

[177] Memorandum by director of political department for Ribbentrop, *DGFP* D xii, No. 323, pp. 527–8 (12 Apr. 1941).

[178] Ibid., No. 425, pp. 670–8; Bose was able to speak to the foreign minister in Vienna, but his request for an interview with Hitler was not granted: Voigt, 'Hitler und Indien', 53.

2. German Strategy in the Middle East

people had the (quite accurate) impression that the National Socialists and Fascists only wanted to dominate other races.

In reply, Ribbentrop again predicted the end of Britain and explained Hitler's plans 'for a new Europe without Britain', which meant in fact unlimited German hegemony. He considered it 'very probable that India would achieve its independence in the course of the war', and he described at great length the development of German policy towards Britain—of course presenting the situation of the British in very dismal terms in order to make Germany appear all the more impressive and powerful. In short, he offered the standard German picture of the international political and military situation; but his response to Bose's grandiose plans was very reserved, which was hardly surprising in view of Woermann's memorandum of 12 April. In the end Bose received only the promise that Germany would support propaganda and subversive activities in India.

Nevertheless, on 10 May, after consultation with Ribbentrop, Hitler approved in principle the issuing of an official German statement supporting a free India, which was still a matter of dispute in the foreign ministry.[179] An appropriate text was drafted on 19 May, a few days before Hitler's Directive No. 30 was issued and shortly after German aircraft had arrived in Iraq.[180] This decision must be considered one of the erratic acts typical of the reaction of the German leaders to developments in the eastern Mediterranean and the Middle East in May 1941; for on 24 May, when Gailani's defeat in Iraq had become certain, Ribbentrop again wanted to 'postpone somewhat the deadline for releasing the declaration on a free India', as being no longer relevant to the current situation. Only activities connected with the establishment of a central office for Free India were to be continued. Bose, who had just been invited to Rome, raised no objections to this decision.[181]

Bose's talks in the Italian capital were, for him, totally unsatisfactory.[182] When he returned to Germany in July, the war against the Soviet Union had already begun. He seemed profoundly shocked,[183] for he knew that the 'feelings of the Indian people' in that war would be 'definitely on the Russian side', as Germany was obviously the 'aggressor and thus also for India a dangerous imperialistic power'. Even a total German victory over the Soviet

---

[179] Director of political department to foreign minister, *DGFP* D xii, No. 553, pp. 878–9 (25 May 1941), here 878 n. 1.

[180] Hauner, 'Deutschland und Indien', 445 n. 88.

[181] *DGFP* D xii, No. 553, p. 878; on 27 May Ribbentrop did not want Bose to travel to Italy. There was concern lest he might speak with Mussolini, which would have placed Hitler, who had avoided meeting Bose and would probably continue to do so, in something of a dilemma; cf. ibid. 879 n. 2. See also ibid., No. 561, pp. 902–3: telegram of 28 May 1941 from director of political department to Rome embassy on Bose's flight to Rome, where he arrived on 29 May 1941. On his stay cf. Ciano, *Diary 1939–1943*, 354–5 (6 June 1941). The Italian foreign minister regarded with considerable reserve Bose's notions about an uprising in India.

[182] Memorandum by Woermann on his conversation with Bose, *DGFP* D xiii, No. 120, pp. 165–7 (17 July 1941), here 165 n. 1.

[183] Hauner, 'Deutschland und Indien', 446.

Union would hardly change that attitude. Moreover, as Britain was in the process of introducing reforms, it even had to be expected that, contrary to Bose's earlier conviction, a German advance towards India would cause the Indians to support the British. It was therefore all the more urgent to issue the official declaration on a free India as soon as possible. But the German government still did not want to set a definite date.[184] On 18 August, after the situation in India had clearly developed unfavourably for the Axis, Bose insisted again on a declaration.[185] But Hitler decided on 6 September that the time was not propitious to issue such a statement, as this would give the British a pretext to invade Afghanistan.[186] Two days later Ribbentrop added by way of explanation[187] that the German government continued to be interested in Bose's plans, but the situation as a whole required caution until German operations in the east began to 'have a stronger impact on the situation in the Middle East and southern Asia'. In fact this meant that further consideration of the matter would be postponed indefinitely, although most persons on the German side did not take this view at the time.

On 29 November Ribbentrop provided more details regarding the issuing of the declaration Bose desired. In his view, the proper time for it would be when German troops had crossed the Caucasus.[188] Even if the planned Reich Commissariat for the Caucasus, which was to extend to the northern frontiers of Turkey and Iran, had not remained an unfulfilled dream of National Socialist megalomania—in other words, if the Wehrmacht had reached Baku and Tbilisi—Hitler would presumably have considered only threatening India, although in October 1941 he still spoke of a campaign against that country.[189]

In this situation, the importance of Bose and his Free India varied. On 30 September, for example, Weizsäcker thought that, after the collapse of the Soviet Union, which he expected soon, Germany would perhaps form a counter-government for India under Bose. Until that point Berlin had carefully avoided such a move in order not to exclude completely the possibility of eventually coming to terms with Britain.[190] And Weizsäcker's remark did not mean that in such a situation Germany wanted to renounce a settlement with Britain. Berlin would then have been able to negotiate from a different position and would probably have done so; but it was indicative of the German attitude that on 13 November Ribbentrop wrote in a note for Hitler that a declaration on a free India should only be issued 'when it is clearly discernible

---

[184] *DGFP* D xiii, No. 120, pp. 165–7 (17 July 1941).
[185] Ibid., No. 213, pp. 328–31 (18 Aug. 1941): memorandum by Woermann on conversation with Bose, who on this occasion delivered a letter for the foreign minister.
[186] Ibid., No. 286, p. 461 (6 Sept. 1941).
[187] Ibid., No. 296, p. 472 (10 Sept. 1941).
[188] Conversation Bose–Ribbentrop, *DGFP* D xiii, No. 521, pp. 896–900 (29 Nov. 1941).
[189] *Staatsmänner*, i. 636: conversation Hitler–Ciano (25 Nov. 1941), pp. 626–38; cf. Hauner, 'Deutschland und Indien', 447–8: Hillgruber, *Strategie*, 483–4.
[190] *Weizsäcker-Papiere*, 272 (30 Sept. 1941).

that England does not manifest any willingness to make peace even after the final collapse of Russia'.[191]

Hitler shared this view. In his strategic thinking Bose was a completely insignificant, basically superfluous pawn. This was reflected in the fact that in Directive No. 32 of 11 June 1941 on 'preparations for the period after Barbarossa'[192] no mention was made of any desire that Britain should give up India, as Ribbentrop had implied to Bose in April. On the other hand, Hitler never completely abandoned the idea of attacking India militarily.[193] This indicates that such an operation remained a possibility, although in Hitler's policies and conduct of the war as a whole a rather improbable one.

At the end of May and the beginning of June, while the Wehrmacht was preparing intensively for the attack on the Soviet Union, the Middle East again became the centre of political and military events. On 31 May Iraq concluded an armistice with Britain. This placed Syria in a precarious situation, for French co-operation in helping Germany to provide assistance for Gailani now became a dangerous boomerang. Neither French material aid nor the participation of the completely inadequate German forces in the fighting had been able to prevent the collapse of Iraqi resistance. For the British, who had attacked and destroyed German aircraft at the airfield at Palmyra on 14 May,[194] the French action provided a welcome occasion for the conquest of Syria, which had been considered increasingly urgent since March and acquired even greater strategic importance after the fall of Crete. The British government feared that the Germans could establish a bridgehead in Syria for attacks on Cairo and the oil refineries of Abadan as well as the lines of communication in Iraq and Palestine.[195]

After the end of the fighting in Iraq, the Vichy government was justifiably worried about British actions and attempted to save the situation. On 1 June Darlan asked the Germans to remove their military personnel returning from Iraq as soon as possible from Syria in order to deprive the British of any pretext for intervention.[196] On this question there was some discussion

---

[191] *DGFP* D xiii, No. 468, pp. 774–9 (13 Nov. 1941).

[192] Cf. IV.II.3 below.

[193] Glasneck and Kircheisen, *Türkei und Afghanistan*, 237. On Axis policy towards India in 1942 cf. *KTB OKW* ii. 21 ff., intro. by Andreas Hillgruber; also Voigt, *Indien*, 148–55: 'A joint Axis declaration on India failed to come about because of the opposition of Hitler, whose Indian policy was still governed by respect for Britain and by the illusion of a possible British readiness for peace. He gave priority to these considerations and hopes over any support of Japanese policy towards India' (p. 154).

[194] Gundelach, *Luftwaffe im Mittelmeer*, 240–1; Playfair, *Mediterranean*, ii. 201.

[195] Gruchmann provides a very compressed survey in *Der Zweite Weltkrieg*, 166 ff.; on British deliberations before the attack, not covered in detail here, cf. Barclay, *Their Finest Hour*, 130–1, 145 ff.; Churchill, *Second World War*, iii. 287–97; Butler, *Strategy*, ii. 519 ff.; Lewin, *The Chief*, 138–9; Playfair, *Mediterranean*, ii. 199–205; B. P. Schröder, *Deutschland und der Mittlere Osten*, 151–4; Woodward, *British Foreign Policy*, i. 563.

[196] *DGFP* D xii, No. 581, pp. 936–7 (1 June 1941); on views held on the French side—which were neither taken into account by Darlan nor endorsed by Dentz—that Syria could be held by a speedy and massive employment of the Wehrmacht, and that accordingly the German military

between Berlin and the German agencies involved abroad.[197] On 8 June, when the attack by British and Free French forces on Syria had already begun, Hitler decided to withdraw the Germans, as the Vichy French would very probably not be able to repel the attack. Ribbentrop agreed with this assessment of the situation; but Rahn, the German representative, was instructed to remain in Syria for the time being. Jodl, although he considered the situation by no means so urgent, also supported a withdrawal, but on the condition that the French would not ask for help again a week later. The foreign ministry was able to reassure him in this regard, as it had now realized that Germany could not provide significant military assistance in Syria: 'An insufficient or merely symbolic commitment of German forces would encumber the political situation of France more than it would help.'[198] It was assumed that the French shared this view; but the staff under General Felmy in Athens, which concerned itself with 'purely military tasks of the future', and the one under Fritz Grobba, responsible for all foreign-policy questions relating to Iraq, were to be kept together for possible later operations in the Middle East.[199]

General Henri Dentz, the French high commissioner in Syria, requested Luftwaffe support for his troops on 8 June. He also demanded reinforcements from France and French North Africa.[200] But off the coast of Syria the aircraft of X Air Corps, which took off from bases in Greece or the Dodecanese, had to fight at the extreme limit of their combat range, and this meant that their chances of success were minimal from the very beginning.[201] Attacks by German aircraft were limited essentially to Haifa in Palestine, the terminal of the important pipeline from Iraq, and the coast of Syria. Even the naval war staff—which in the first days of the fighting in Syria and in keeping with its tradition had pointed out the 'very special importance' of the eastern Mediterranean and had urged that, in spite of the immediate requirements resulting from preparations for Barbarossa, Germany should try to support the French, who were determined to resist, with all available means—had to admit that the possibilities of providing assistance were limited.[202]

In practice the Germans were able to help the French only by permitting them to transfer reinforcements to Syria. On 12 June French anti-tank and

missions should only be recalled if such an engagement proved impossible, cf. ibid. 937 n. 3; also Assmann, 'Bemühungen der Seekriegsleitung', i. 54, BA-MA RM 8/1209.

[197] *KTB OKW* i. 400 (3 June 1941), 401 (5 June 1941); cf. also B. P. Schröder, *Deutschland und der Mittlere Osten*, 155 ff.

[198] *DGFP* D xii, No. 606, pp. 983–4 (8 June 1941). The instruction that Rahn should remain in Syria was sent on 3 June: cf. ibid., No. 587, p. 953 (foreign minister to Rahn).

[199] Memorandums by ambassador Ritter, ibid., No. 606, p. 984 n. 4 (9 and 19 June 1941).

[200] *KTB OKW* i. 402 (9 June 1941). On 11 June Darlan sought the employment of the Luftwaffe: Gundelach, *Luftwaffe im Mittelmeer*, 253; on the question of German support see also Hirszowicz, *The Third Reich*, 182, whose account differs in part as *KTB OKW* was not available to him.

[201] Warlimont, *Headquarters*, 132. France did not make available the requested 'intermediate landing-grounds' but only 'emergency' ones: *KTB OKW* i. 404 (16 June 1941); for details cf. Gundelach, *Luftwaffe im Mittelmeer*, 252–3.

[202] Assmann, 'Bemühungen der Seekriegsleitung', i. 55–6, BA-MA RM 8/1209.

2. German Strategy in the Middle East

anti-aircraft units were to be sent to Salonika in seven trains and then to Syria by sea.[203] Hitler permitted the use of rail lines through France and southern Germany as well as the transfer of French naval and air units. The latter were able to use the Greek islands as bases for their operations.[204] But in the end neither the Germans nor the French succeeded in breaking the British blockade off the Syrian and Lebanese coast. Thus the only possible supply-line was the land route through Turkey, but the Turkish government obstinately refused to abandon its policy of strict neutrality in the British–French conflict.[205] Under these circumstances the resistance of the French Levant Army, with its inadequate and obsolete equipment,[206] was from the very beginning more a question of prestige than a serious attempt to hold Syria and Lebanon with any chance of success. This is true even if one considers that the British also cited supply and equipment problems to explain difficulties arising in the course of the operations.[207]

The fighting within the framework of Operation Exporter, the code-name for the occupation of the French mandate areas Syria and Lebanon, lasted five weeks (see Map IV.II.2). The British employed 2 brigades of 7th Australian Division; 2 regiments, one motorized, of 1st British Cavalry Division; 5th Indian Infantry Brigade (which came directly from Eritrea after the Duke of Aosta had surrendered there); several special armoured and air units of the British 6th Division; a commando unit especially equipped for seaborne landings (C Battalion of the Special Service Brigade); and 1st Free French Division, which, however, consisted of only 6 battalions, 1 battery, and 20 tanks. Arriving from Egypt on 17 June, 16th Infantry Brigade of the British 6th Division was able to participate in the second phase of the operations, between 14 and 22 June. The failure of Battleaxe, the operation in North Africa in mid-June, permitted a reinforcement of the British ground and air units in Syria. This change made itself clearly felt in the third phase of the fighting. Not only 2nd Brigade of 6th Division, but also Habforce and 10th Indian Division, advancing from Iraq, took part in the fighting.

At the start of Operation Exporter—the code-name for the capture of French-mandated Syria and Lebanon—these units were supported by only fifty or so aircraft of the Royal Air Force, primarily fighters. Twenty additional aircraft in Iraq and Cyprus were instructed to co-operate with the

---

[203] *KTB OKW* i. 403 (10 June 1941); Hirszowicz, *The Third Reich*, 182, states that the trains crossed the demarcation-line on 11 June and arrived in Salonika on 17 June.

[204] Warlimont, *Headquarters*, 132: Playfair, *Mediterranean*, ii. 214: on 27 June one battalion and several train-loads of weapons and material left France, destined for Salonika.

[205] *KTB OKW* i. 409 (22 June 1941), according to which transports through Turkey of arms (but not of fuel) were refused by Ankara: Papen to foreign ministry, *DGFP* D xii, No. 651, p. 1056 (20 June 1941). The ambassador stressed that there would be no point in a *démarche*. On Turkey's attitude to this question cf. Hirszowicz, *The Third Reich*, 181–4, with details of the considerations about a move of Turkish troops into northern Syria. Some at least of the German aircraft fuel which had been stored in Turkey since June did therefore reach Syria (ibid. 182).

[206] Mockler, *Our Enemies*, 74–7; B. P. Schröder, *Deutschland und der Mittlere Osten*, 159.

[207] Playfair, *Mediterranean*, ii. 205 ff.

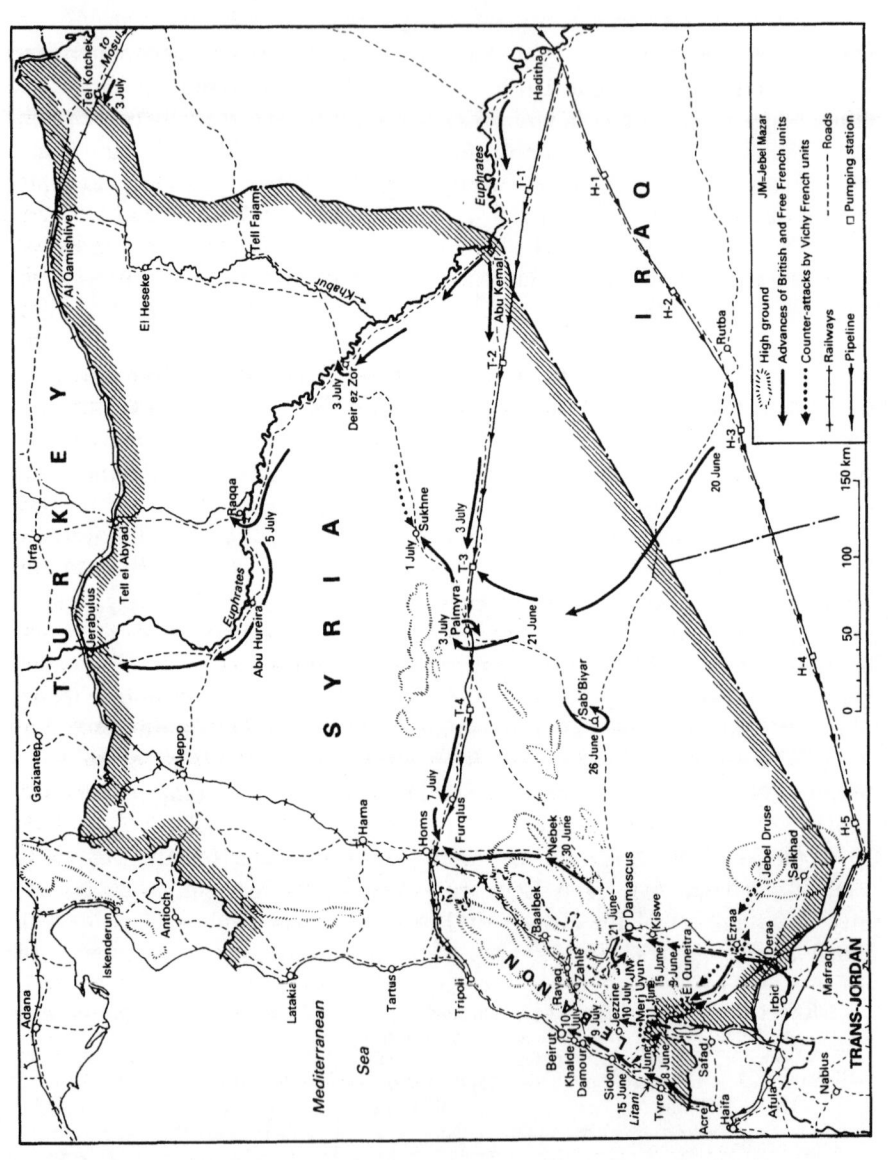

MAP IV.11.2. The War in Syria, 8 June–14 July 1941

units involved in Operation Exporter. But in this area too the situation of the British forces improved during the third phase of the campaign. Two fighter squadrons and one bomber squadron were transferred to the battle area after the failure of Battleaxe.

The Royal Navy was clearly superior to the units of the French navy loyal to the Vichy government. The sea flank of the British advance against Syria was secured by 15th Cruiser Squadron, consisting, apart from supported units, of at first three and later five cruisers, eight destroyers, and a landing-ship for C Battalion.

The Vichy forces under General Dentz (whose death sentence in April 1945 for resistance to the Allies was later reduced to imprisonment) had between 35,000 and 45,000 men organized in 120 battalions. Dentz also had about 90 tanks and 120 artillery pieces at his disposal. At the start of the fighting his air units had 30 bombers and 60 fighters, figures which were later almost doubled by transfers from North Africa. The only important Vichy naval units in the area were two destroyers and three submarines, all in Beirut. Of two additional destroyers sent to Lebanon, one was sunk by British torpedo-bombers and the other reached Beirut heavily damaged. In the following weeks the French navy was unable to transfer army reinforcements that had arrived in Salonika—one battalion, anti-aircraft units, ammunition, and replacement parts—to Tripoli on the Lebanese coast. When the fighting stopped, the submarines went to Bizerta and the three partially damaged destroyers sailed to Toulon; the remaining ships were interned in neutral ports.[208]

The British and Free French troops crossed the frontiers of Lebanon and Syria on 8 and 9 June.[209] Their offensive unfolded in three directions: in the west along the coastal road from Acre via Tyre and Sidon to Beirut, in the middle sector in the Lebanon Mountains towards Marj Uyun and Riyaq, and in the east from Irbid towards Qunaytirah and Damascus. Tyre fell on 8 June; the attackers crossed the Litani river four days later. Then the advance slowed; in the mountains, where the resistance of the Vichy units was especially strong, Marj Uyun fell on 11 June. In the east on 9 June the Allies were already only twenty kilometres from Damascus. Thus, at the conclusion of the first phase of the campaign the position of the British and Free French was satisfactory only in the east.

In the second phase of the conflict Sidon was taken on 15 June. But at the same time the troops under General Dentz undertook a counter-attack against the Allied units that had reached Al Kiswah in their advance towards Damascus. The Vichy forces captured Izra, on the rail line from Amman to

---

[208] For details of strengths cf. Butler, *Strategy*, ii. 219–20; Churchill, *Second World War*, iii. 295–7; Playfair, *Mediterranean*, ii. 200, 204, 207, 211, 215.
[209] On the military operations cf. Buckley, *Five Ventures*, 63–135; Mockler, *Our Enemies*, 73–193; Playfair, *Mediterranean*, ii. 207–21; B. P. Schröder, *Deutschland und der Mittlere Osten*, 162–76; on the employment of the French naval forces cf. Auphan and Mordal, *Marine française*, 312 ff.

Damascus, and Qunaytirah. Marj Uyun was also retaken. The next day Izra and Qunaytirah were again occupied by the British and the Free French, but for the time being the offensive against Damascus came to a halt. After the failure of Operation Battleaxe on 17 June, additional British troops were free to be transferred to Lebanon and Syria. They joined the attack on Damascus, among other actions, and the city fell on 21 June after the Allies had succeeded in cutting its rail and road supply-routes from Beirut.

In Lebanon the Allies were now only twenty kilometres from Beirut. With the push towards Palmyra, Operation Exporter developed a new front. In the course of this thrust Habforce was employed again. Threatening the communication lines with Damascus and Homs, it advanced on Palmyra on 21 June, but the planned surprise attack was not successful. The Vichy French put up a stubborn defence and the British troops lacked air support. At the end of the second phase of the war in Syria and Lebanon, Damascus and Sidon were also captured, and all counter-attacks by General Dentz's troops were repulsed. Qunaytirah and Izra were retaken. But Marj Uyun was still held by Vichy units, and Habforce found itself in a difficult situation. Accepting a certain amount of damage to its ships, the Royal Navy provided considerable support on the sea flank for the land forces. Especially important was the fact that the aircraft supporting the Vichy forces began to show signs of wear.

The final phase of the fighting lasted from 23 June to 12 July. The fact that the reinforcements and supplies that had now arrived in Salonika could not be transported to Lebanon and Syria seriously affected the fighting ability of the forces under General Dentz, as Turkey refused permission for the use of the land route and available Vichy naval forces were too weak to provide adequate protection for sea transports. Moreover, British air attacks on Tripoli and Beirut, as well as on the airfield at Aleppo and maritime traffic in the entire eastern Mediterranean, contributed to the worsening supply situation of the Vichy troops in Syria and Lebanon. As early as 22 June Dentz was forced to describe the situation of his forces as hopeless.[210] This problem became even more serious as the British reinforced their air units in the area.

By 24 June the British had also recaptured Marj Uyun, but they were unable to take Riyaq. They could not exploit the capture of Damascus as they were not able to hold a strategic hill between Riyaq and Damascus that commanded the area around Riyaq. This forced a postponement of the planned attack on Zahla, between Beirut and Riyaq.

On 3 July Palmyra finally surrendered, and at about the same time new British forces arrived in Syria from Iraq, one group of which, coming from Baghdad, had already reached the important transportation centre of Dayr az Zawr on the Euphrates on 1 July, while the other advanced along the rail line Baghdad–Mosul towards Tall Kushik. This frontier town was taken without

---

[210] Assmann, 'Bemühungen der Seekriegsleitung', i. 57, BA-MA RM 8/1209.

difficulty, and on 3 July Dayr az Zawr was also occupied. Two days later parts of these units pushed on towards Raqqah. They and the troops advancing via Tall Kushik now threatened Jarabulus on the Turkish frontier and Aleppo. In the meantime the Vichy French and the Allies were massing their forces for a decisive battle on the Damur river a few kilometres south of Beirut.

Geographical conditions offered the defenders certain advantages when the fighting began in the night of 5–6 July, in which the British fleet also bombarded the defenders' positions. After the town of Damur had been captured on 9 July, the Vichy troops attempted to establish a new defence line at Khaldah, about seven kilometres south of Beirut; but they were able to hold this for only a few hours. General Dentz had lost the battle of Beirut. Further inland his soldiers still fought on near Jazzin and in the Jebal Mazar, but they were now completely exhausted. Their situation was clearly hopeless; and the British were now able to mount incessant air attacks on airfields, ports, and communication lines. They would soon launch an offensive against Homs and Aleppo. Dentz thereupon requested a cease-fire on the evening of 11 July. Three days later the British and Vichy French signed an armistice in Acre. Syria was placed under General de Gaulle's authority; it could no longer be considered a potential base for the Axis in the Middle East.

Outwardly the German government acted as if the loss of Syria were almost an advantage for the Axis; now Germany would not have to consider Vichy interests in its support for the Arab independence movement.[211] In this regard German propaganda—and German support for Arab efforts to achieve independence was for the time being limited to propaganda—had always had to exercise restraint in the past. As recently as 21 June the Vichy government had enquired whether, if it requested help through German military action in Syria, the German reply 'might be combined with a declaration that, in contrast to England, Germany does not call in question French rights in Syria'. Had Germany granted the French request, it would probably have lost the sympathy of the Arabs, who would then have had to assume that Syria would remain under French rule indefinitely. A German refusal of the request, however, would have made the French suspicious of German intentions.[212] Developments in the Middle East saved the German government from having to take a decision, but at a high price.

A report by the German representative at the Italian control delegation, Rahn, on his activities between 9 May and 11 July provided a detailed account of events in Syria. In his opinion fifty transport aircraft would have been sufficient to bring the five French battalions waiting in Salonika to Aleppo. This would have made it possible to hold Beirut and Aleppo for six more weeks and thus provide decisive help for Rommel in Africa. In view of the fact that the British were able to withdraw troops from North Africa after the

[211] Cf. also Hillgruber, *Strategie*, 481.
[212] *DGFP* D xiii, No. 19, pp. 22–3 (25 July 1941).

failure of Battleaxe, this argument is not very convincing. On the other hand, Rahn was quite right in his opinion that Turkey had made an indirect but decisive contribution to the British victory by its intransigent attitude in the transit question.[213]

German efforts to weaken Britain's position in the Middle East of course affected Turkish interests. This had already become clear during the preparations for the attack on Yugoslavia and Greece, when Hitler was forced to calm Turkish fears regarding German military intervention in the Balkans by a letter of 1 March 1941. He informed İsmet İnönü, the president of Turkey, that the German steps were in no way directed against Turkey's territorial or political integrity. He had given orders that German units entering Bulgaria should remain at a sufficient distance from the Turkish frontier so that no mistaken conclusions could be drawn as to the reason for their being there, unless the Turkish government itself saw fit to take measures aimed at forcing Germany to alter this attitude.[214]

It is not in dispute that this letter was suggested by Franz von Papen, the German ambassador in Ankara, in view of Operation Marita. But Hitler's warning and reassurance were also a reaction to Eden's visit to Ankara, which took place at the same time.[215] Together with the chief of the general staff, General Sir John Dill, the foreign secretary had arrived in Ankara on 26 February 1941 to discuss with the Turkish government the possibility of aid for hard-pressed Greece. He had also conducted or intended to conduct talks on the same subject with the governments of Greece, Yugoslavia, and Egypt.[216] Turkey, however, emphatically refused to enter the war, as it was in no way prepared. The British representatives were divided in their opinion of the validity of the Turkish arguments, but Britain had no suitable means of applying pressure to Turkey to force it to change its mind.[217]

The German government also had its doubts about Turkish reliability, but assumed for the time being that Ankara would stay out of the conflict. Hitler, however, remarked in a letter to Mussolini, in which he also informed the latter of his letter to İnönü, that he saw no danger as long as Eden did not succeed in diverting the Turkish statesmen and soldiers from a 'sober evalua-

---

[213] Ibid., No. 165, pp. 236–65 (30 July 1941); cf also Rahn, *Ruheloses Leben*, 152–81, on this whole development. While the top leadership of the Wehrmacht in those days concentrated completely on developments on the eastern front and apparently paid hardly any attention to Syria, the naval war staff 'attached great significance to the collapse of the French position in Syria'. In the OKM 'the British position on the land-bridge to India was regarded as secured against an attack from the east, and it was feared that the forces released there would be used for a decisive thrust against the German–Italian position in North Africa': Assmann, 'Bemühungen der Seekriegsleitung', i. 64, BA-MA RM 8/1209.

[214] *DGFP* D xii, No. 113, pp. 201–3 (1 Mar. 1941); cf. Ackermann, 'Türkei', 501; Glasneck and Kircheisen, *Türkei und Afghanistan*, 67; Krecker, *Deutschland*, 138–9.

[215] Krecker, *Deutschland*, 135–6, 155; Papen, *Memoirs*, 473.

[216] Woodward, *British Foreign Policy*, i. 525–9.

[217] Ibid. 539 ff.

2. German Strategy in the Middle East

tion of their own interests'.[218] He thus added a note of caution to his optimism of January 1941, when, in a talk with Mussolini, he had flatly rejected the idea that Turkey might enter the war.[219] The more cautious view of the situation was also evident in Hitler's efforts of February and March, including the letter to İnönü, to secure German operations in the Balkans through a political arrangement with Ankara.[220]

İnönü received Hitler's letter on 4 March and his reaction was very positive. He did not dwell on the subject of improving German–Turkish relations, raised by the German ambassador, which had not been discussed since the turn of the year 1940–1,[221] but he approved the establishment of contacts for this purpose and also indicated that Turkey, in spite of its obligations under the Anglo-Turkish treaty of 1939, would 'do everything to avoid a conflict with Germany'.[222] However, İnönü did not take kindly to Hitler's intimation that in the event of Turkish countermeasures with regard to the intended operations, German forces would no longer remain at the promised distance from the Turkish frontier. The Turkish government suspected that even their own troop movements might be interpreted as countermeasures directed against the Wehrmacht. Ambassador von Papen thereupon assured İnönü categorically that Hitler's remarks referred only to a Turkish attack or clearly aggressive intention towards Germany—an assurance which the Turks accepted with great satisfaction.[223]

In a letter to Ribbentrop, however, Papen indicated the limits of Turkish reliability. Although Hitler's letter was doubtless a cause of great relief for Turkey, the planned occupation of Greece and the intended closing of the Aegean would, if the operation were to affect the Suez Canal, make further steps necessary and confront Turkey with new and difficult decisions. In this connection Papen quoted the Turkish foreign minister Saracoğlu: 'By June or July it will be evident whether the Axis is capable of delivering a decisive blow against England, a blow which will paralyse American aid and make the victory of the Axis probable. Until that moment it will remain Turkey's most important rule not to commit herself to either side.' Papen also mentioned another possible problem for Germany: an extension of German power to the coast of the Black Sea might cause Turkey and the Soviet Union to move closer together. Moreover, Britain would probably attempt to draw Moscow into the Anglo-Turkish alliance as soon as German–Soviet relations worsened. Papen did not exclude an even closer *rapprochement* between Britain and Turkey if Britain and the Soviet Union were to offer Turkey pledges with

---

[218] *DGFP* D xii, No. 110, pp. 197–9 (28 Feb. 1941).
[219] Ibid., xi, No. 679, pp. 1145–51 (20 Jan. 1941), here 1150.
[220] Krecker, *Deutschland*, 134–41.
[221] Cf. ibid. 144–5.
[222] *DGFP* D xii, No. 122, pp. 216–17 (4 Mar. 1941).
[223] Ibid., No. 137, p. 246 (8 Mar. 1941): conversation between Papen and Turkish foreign minister.

regard to the Dardanelles and the Turkish economy. He therefore urged immediate measures to bind Turkey to the Axis.[224]

On 17 March the Turkish ambassador in Berlin, R. Hüsrev Gerede, brought Hitler İnönü's answer.[225] The Turkish president described as the maxim of his policy the 'protection of Turkish independence in its most absolute sense and peaceful development without interference with the rights of others'. Since September 1939 Turkey had based its policy on these principles. Turkey was also determined in future not 'to consider her territory and her integrity from the standpoint of political and military combinations between one or the other group of powers'. İnönü stressed the defensive character of Turkish policy, but also Turkey's determination resolutely to oppose any aggressor. He countered Hitler's warning with the self-confident remark that Turkey would not undertake any actions against the German troops 'as long as the government of the German Reich does not take measures which could compel the government of the Republic to change this attitude'.[226]

Hitler had already included Turkey in his plans for the time after Barbarossa. As a reward for helping Germany, Turkey was to receive, among other things, territory in the Caucasus, which, however, Germany would exploit.[227] Reports, received before İnönü's letter, about a Turkish–Soviet *rapprochement* must also have disturbed Hitler. The generally cool answer of the Turkish president probably strengthened Hitler's intention to inform the Turks of Soviet ambitions in the Dardanelles, to which Molotov had referred in November 1940. He now told Gerede that the Soviet foreign minister had spoken not only of Red Army garrisons in Bulgaria, but also of establishing bases on the Dardanelles in Turkish territory. Hitler claimed that his refusal had 'prevented the liquidation of the Balkans and Turkey by Russia'.[228]

This information had the desired effect. The fact that Germany had rejected Stalin's terms for a Soviet accession to the Tripartite Pact—viz. Soviet access to the Dardanelles—made a strong impression in Ankara. Papen considered the conversation between Hitler and Gerede a 'historical turning-point' in German–Turkish relations.[229] In Turkish eyes Hitler's calculated indiscretion indicated a German preference for good relations with Turkey, but this did not cause Turkey to change its official policy. For Turkey a compromise peace between the Axis and Britain would have been the best solution. The Turkish government hoped that the war would end without the complete defeat of one

---

[224] Ibid., No. 154, pp. 276–9 (11 Mar. 1941).
[225] Ibid., No. 161, pp. 286–7 (12 Mar. 1941); on Hitler's conversation with Gerede cf. ibid., No. 177, pp. 308–12 (18 Mar. 1941).
[226] Ibid., No. 161.
[227] Halder, *Diaries*, ii. 830–3 (17 Mar. 1941), with Hitler's statement: 'Caucasia will eventually be ceded to Turkey, but must be exploited by us.'
[228] *DGFP* (see n. 225), No. 177.
[229] Ibid., D xii, No. 220, pp. 384–5 (27 Mar. 1941).

side or the complete victory of the other, and was still not prepared to adopt a policy of even benevolent neutrality towards Germany.[230]

In March, however, the British government reacted with concern to the German–Turkish contacts, fearing that Turkey might in the end be drawn into the enemy camp. The British tried to forestall such a development by promoting better relations between Turkey and the Soviet Union. Any reduction of the Soviet danger, in Turkish eyes, would reduce the supposed need to move closer to the Axis, a step which would by no means have been popular with Turkish public opinion.

British diplomatic activity with the object of improving Turkish–Soviet relations began on 9 March. On 25 March a Turkish–Soviet declaration of neutrality was signed; it was directed against Germany, and this was also understood in Berlin.[231] But British attempts—such as Churchill's urgent letter of 27 March, written under the impression of the conclusion of the deployment of Twelfth Army in Bulgaria on 17 March and the coup in Belgrade on the 27th—to persuade the Turkish government to join a common Balkan front[232] were unsuccessful.[233] It was, however, only the British political leaders, especially Churchill, who seemed interested in persuading Turkey to enter the war. They hoped that such a development would deter Germany from attacking Yugoslavia or at least delay such an attack. British military leaders in the Middle East, on the other hand, advised against such a step. They were aware of the inadequacies of the Turkish armed forces and thus also of the problems a Turkish entry into the war would create for Britain. After the German attacks in the Balkans began on 6 April, the British government stopped trying to persuade Turkey to enter the war, but Turkey was still urged to break off diplomatic relations with Germany. However, the Turkish government saw little purpose in such an action, which would have been incompatible with the basically wait-and-see attitude Turkey had assumed. Thereupon the British abandoned their efforts.[234]

The course of events in the Balkans quickly made it clear that a Turkish intervention would have contributed nothing to a stabilization of the situation. But apart from that, the Turkish government saw no reason to intervene. Immediately before the start of operations in the Balkans, the Germans had again assured Ankara that they would undertake no action against Turkey.[235] On 8 April Papen once more took the initiative in the question of a German–Turkish non-aggression pact or 'similar instrument'. Papen's action was

---

[230] Memorandum by Papen of conversation with Numan Menemencioğlu, secretary-general of the Turkish foreign ministry, ibid., No. 231, pp. 409–12 (28 Mar. 1941).
[231] Extensively treated in Krecker, *Deutschland*, 141–6; also Keskin, *Türkei*, 110–11.
[232] Cf. III.II.2 above (Vogel).
[233] Ackermann, 'Türkei', 503–4; Glasneck and Kircheisen, *Türkei und Afghanistan*, 145–6; Woodward, *British Foreign Policy*, i. 546 ff.
[234] Woodward, *British Foreign Policy*, i. 548–9.
[235] *DGFP* D xii, No. 268, pp. 460–1 (5 Apr. 1941); ibid., No. 269, p. 461 (5 Apr. 1941); ibid., No. 285, p. 481 (6 Apr. 1941): exchanges between Ribbentrop or the foreign ministry and Papen.

motivated by the belief that the war had entered a new, decisive phase, at the end of which, as he had implied earlier, the Turks might begin to suspect that Germany intended to bring the Dardanelles and the Bosporus under its control. That could lead to an improvement of relations between Turkey and the Soviet Union, which had hitherto not been marked by mutual trust. And precisely this development had to be prevented.[236]

Papen was called to Berlin on 15 April;[237] he returned to Ankara on 12 May. At this time Iraq was at war with Britain, and Papen's task was not only to prepare the treaty with Ankara mentioned above, but also to arrange for the transport of arms shipments for Gailani through Turkey. His first report on this question was very optimistic, as the Turkish president and the foreign minister seemed receptive.[238] In reality, however, the Turkish government had not changed its reserved attitude.[239] This became clear immediately when Ribbentrop revealed that Germany actually wanted two treaties. At the same time as the official treaty a secret agreement was to be concluded granting Germany the right to 'unlimited transit of arms and war material through Turkey', including troop transports. To persuade Turkey to sign such an agreement the German government intended to offer 'rectification of its frontier near Edirne to an extent yet to be determined and, possibly, an island in the Aegean Sea'.[240]

It has already been pointed out that the Turkish government did not react favourably to the German requests as regards transit. On 27 May, when the end of Iraqi resistance was already in sight, Papen had to admit finally that German efforts to obtain permission for arms transports through Turkey had reached a deadlock.[241] A few days later, after the collapse of the Gailani government, the German foreign ministry concluded that, as 'the question of the transit of war material through Turkey has lost current interest for us', the signing of a political treaty need no longer depend on a transit agreement.[242] Nevertheless, it was not until 18 June that the 'Turkish–German friendship treaty' was signed.[243] It came into effect on the date of signature and was to remain in force for ten years; it expressly took into account the 'present

---

[236] *DGFP* D xii, No. 295, pp. 491–3 (8 Apr. 1941).
[237] Ibid. n. 8.
[238] Ibid., No. 514, pp. 812–17 (13 May 1941); cf. also Krecker, *Deutschland*, 155–8.
[239] Papen to foreign ministry, *DGFP* D xii, No. 523, pp. 282–9 (16 May 1941); on Turkish policy concerning Iraq cf. esp. Onder, *Die türkische Außenpolitik*, 109–14; and, very comprehensively, F. G. Weber, *Evasive Neutral*, 82–106, where the politics of the Arab world are treated as a whole.
[240] *DGFP* D xii, No. 529, pp. 836–7 (17 May 1941).
[241] Ibid., No. 556, pp. 738–41 (27 May 1941); on the transit question cf. Krecker, *Deutschland*, 159 ff. As already mentioned, Ankara allowed German petrol through to Syria. As far as transport of arms and material was concerned, Turkey—still allied with France, although the latter was now opposed to Britain—permitted the passage of three trains from Aleppo to Mosul, which involved the crossing of Turkish territory. Cf. also Onder, *Die türkische Außenpolitik*, 109–11, 117.
[242] *DGFP* D xii, No. 582, pp. 937–8 (1 June 1941); cf. Krecker, *Deutschland*, 161–2.
[243] Ackermann, 'Türkei', 504 ff.

2. German Strategy in the Middle East

obligations' of the two countries. With this proviso, which was important primarily with regard to the agreements between Turkey and Britain,[244] Ankara and Berlin promised 'mutually to respect the integrity and inviolability of their territories and not to take measures of any sort aimed directly or indirectly against the other contracting party'. The two governments also promised friendly consultations on all questions affecting their mutual interests.[245]

What were the motives of Turkey and Germany in concluding such a treaty?[246] In the view of the Turkish government, the treaty was completely consistent with the basic line of its foreign policy since September 1939, whose primary aim was to preserve neutrality as long as it remained unclear how the war would end. Turkey was able to maintain its position in October 1939 and in the treaty of 18 June 1941, while at the same time obtaining valuable reassurances with regard to the Soviet Union. The conclusion of treaties with Germany and Britain was also appropriate from a domestic point of view, as the Turkish population was by no means united in its attitude towards one or the other warring state. An additional motive for Turkey was presumably to block a German–Soviet settlement at Turkey's expense. However, in view of Hitler's obsession with his aims in the east, the Turkish leaders attributed too much importance to the treaty if they considered it a decisive factor in prompting the German attack on the Soviet Union.

Germany for its part also had several reasons for signing the treaty. An immediate motive, soon overtaken by events, was the intention to transport arms and troops through Turkey to Iraq. In addition Germany wanted to obtain advantages in the use of the Straits, and of course hoped eventually to gain Turkey as an ally. When all these aims proved to be illusory, the short-term political and psychological effects of the treaty on the scene in Europe moved into the foreground. The economic agreements connected with the treaty also played a certain role. Not least, the treaty contributed to maintaining the function of Turkey as a barrier preventing direct communication between the British in the Middle East and the Soviet Union. From the point of view of the imminent German attack on the Soviet Union, the treaty doubtless represented an important measure to relieve pressure on Germany's southern flank. But in the operations planned for the period after Barbarossa the German leaders had no intention of continuing to respect Turkish wishes, if they still persisted in the matter of neutrality.

---

[244] Krecker, *Deutschland*, 173 ff., on the British government's measured reaction.

[245] *DGFP* D xii, No. 648, p. 1051 (18 June 1941); the Turkish national assembly ratified the treaty on 25 June and the instruments of ratification were exchanged on 5 July. For the genesis and assessment of the treaty cf. Glasneck and Kircheisen, *Türkei und Afghanistan*, 69–75; Krecker, *Deutschland*, 153–75; Onder, *Die türkische Außenpolitik*, 121–6; Ulman, 'La neutralité', 559–62 (this takes the interests of the US especially into account).

[246] Cf. Ackermann, 'Türkei', 506–7; Glasneck and Kircheisen, *Türkei und Afghanistan*, 74–5; Hillgruber, *Strategie*, 497–8; Keskin, *Türkei*, 111; Krecker, *Deutschland*, 170–5; Onder, *Die türkische Außenpolitik*, 124 ff.

3. Planning for the Period after Barbarossa

The following remarks are limited to the deliberations within the German military leadership regarding operations in the Middle East, the Mediterranean, and Africa after the conclusion of the war against the Soviet Union. Placed in connection with the colonial ideas already described, they provide noteworthy indications of the extent of the territorial designs or spheres of influence of the Axis powers and the consequences of a victory over Britain, which the conduct of the war after Barbarossa was intended to make possible. Organizational and administrative preparations for German rule in the territories yet to be conquered, which, in a relatively modest form, were started at this time, cannot be considered here, nor can the internal discussions about the organization of the planned colonial empire.[247]

Since the late autumn of 1940 departments and sections within the Wehrmacht had concerned themselves with the future conduct of the war after the victory over the Soviet Union. Barbarossa seemed indeed to be the only way to solve the strategic dilemma resulting from the fact that Germany was able to vanquish Britain neither in the air nor at sea.[248] But in fact the decision to launch the campaign in the east, and hence the whole development that began in the summer of 1940, was the result of a number of interrelated ideological, economic, political, and military factors which together formed the basis of Hitler's obsession with the east. In analysing German operational planning, it should be emphasized that the decision to attack the Soviet Union itself disregarded the principle of not starting any new action against a great power 'before getting rid of other enemies'.[249] The deliberations regarding Germany's conduct of the war after the defeat of the Soviet Union assumed a no less dangerous situation: Hitler and his advisers were prepared to risk a global escalation of the war, a confrontation with the United States, even before their conquests in the east could be digested. They did not seek a confrontation in such circumstances, but would accept it if need be.

The calculations of the German leaders contained defensive and offensive elements. The fact that they still had not completely abandoned the hope of reaching some kind of compromise peace with Britain did not constitute a contradiction. Hitler never discarded this basic principle of his policy. But his efforts to achieve a settlement with the 'island cousins' changed as a result of strategic developments: he did not intend to seek an understanding at any price after Barbarossa, even if this meant that the Americans could no longer be kept out of the war.[250]

---

[247] On the colonial aspect of German global aspirations after the attack on the USSR cf. Hildebrand, *Vom Reich*, 711–44; on Hitler's visions of Germany as a world power cf. Thies, *Architekt*, 149–82; Hillgruber, *Faktor Amerika*, 513 ff.

[248] *Weizsäcker-Papiere*, 238 (16 Feb. 1941). Cf. Hillgruber, *Kriegsziele und Strategie*, 48–9.

[249] *Weizsäcker-Papiere*, 232 (16 Jan. 1941); also esp. 239 ff. (6 Mar. 1941), 249–50 (28 Apr. 1941).

[250] Cf. Hildebrand, *Foreign Policy*; 113 ff.; id., *Vom Reich*, 701; Hillgruber, *Strategie*, 364–5.

3. Planning for Post-Barbarossa Period

All these factors show that in German planning it was intended to intensify the war in the Mediterranean only after a victory over the Soviet Union. An early indication of the operations planned for that time[251] was contained in Hitler's order of 17 February 1941 to prepare a study for a deployment in Afghanistan against India following Barbarossa.[252] At the same time operations against Gibraltar were discussed,[253] as were the conquest of Malta and attacks on Egypt from North Africa.[254] Hitler's thinking with regard to India was dominated not so much by the desire to conquer that country as by the intention to threaten it in order to force Britain to come to terms.[255] As he was never in a position to attack India, however, a definite answer to the question of his designs with regard to that country is not possible.

In April 1941 the organization department of the army general staff analysed the demands that were to be made of it after the conquest of all of Europe.[256] The department assumed that no country with which the Third Reich would then have common frontiers would possess numerically equal armed forces. Greater Germany's military sphere of influence would then extend to the frontiers of Europe. German domination would be secured by occupation forces and treaty links or economic dependence. Against this strategic background the further conduct of the war would be marked by a reduction of the strength of the army and a greater concentration on operations by the Luftwaffe and the navy.

After the establishment of German domination over all of Europe it was planned to use the army exclusively in 'theatres outside Europe', which, because of their particular geographical and climatic conditions, would place special demands on the army organization. German conduct of the war would then have to take into consideration the following characteristics of the new operations areas. Firstly, there would be a great expansion of the theatres, which would require the development of operations along transport arteries. This would permit the enemy to withdraw into impassable terrain. It would be possible to achieve the conditions for a 'final victory' only by locating and defeating him there. The shortage and inadequate capacity of road and rail systems would create additional problems. Moreover, the Wehrmacht would

---

[251] The interrelation between Hitler's instruction of 17 Feb. and preparations for the conduct of the war after Barbarossa—subsequently embodied in Directive No. 32—was already pointed out by Warlimont (*Headquarters*, 133). Cf. also Besymenski, *Sonderakte Barbarossa*, 284.

[252] *KTB OKW* i. 238 (17 Feb. 1941); Halder, *Diaries*, ii. 810 (25 Feb. 1941).

[253] OKW WFSt/Abt. L (I Op) No. 44197/41 g.Kdos. Chefs. (20 Feb. 1941) to ObdH (Op.Abt.), ObdL (Fü.Stab Ia), ObdM (1. Skl.), BA-MA CASE GE 440, PG 32488. This stated: 'The seizure of Malta is expected in the autumn of 1941 after the completion of Operation Barbarossa'; and: 'The execution of Operation Felix may become necessary at about the same time.'

[254] Halder, *Diaries*, ii. 810 (25 Feb. 1941); also Glasneck and Kircheisen, *Türkei und Afghanistan*, 234; Hildebrand, *Foreign Policy*, 109; Moritz, 'Planungen', 324.

[255] Hildebrand, *Vom Reich*, 703; Hillgruber, *Strategie*, 383.

[256] Moritz, 'Planungen', 326–9, doc. 1: OKH/GenStdH/Org.Abt. (1), No. 507/41 g.Kdos. Chefs. (7 Apr. 1941), note for oral report.

occasionally have to fight in terrain with all the features of high mountain regions. Climate and weather would have a great effect on operational and tactical conduct of the war. In addition, in future operational areas it would not be possible to supply the army from the regions themselves, as the necessary goods were lacking. This was true of North Africa, where the Wehrmacht now had considerable experience, but it also applied to the southern and eastern parts of the Middle East. Maintaining an adequate water supply for large formations in these areas presented especially difficult problems.

For all these reasons it was most important that the German army should possess a sufficient number of mobile units to fulfil its tasks in the domination of Europe and the conduct of the war in countries outside Europe. These units would have to be able to operate in difficult terrain and co-ordinate their actions with the Luftwaffe over great distances, at least in certain cases. They would also require adequate transport capacity to ensure the rapid establishment of a supply-system and the reliable flow of supplies in operations covering large areas. It was therefore necessary to endow such units with a high degree of motorization and to create special units for operations in mountainous terrain or other impassable areas as well as for airborne operations. Sufficient troops also had to be available for occupation duties.

The size of this army of the future was estimated at thirteen or fourteen motorized corps with at least twenty-six armoured and thirteen motorized divisions, no fewer than ten mountain, and perhaps four airborne divisions. The army general staff estimated requirements for operations areas outside Europe at ten armoured and three infantry divisions. These were counted among the thirty-nine mobile divisions mentioned above, which were to be kept as small as possible to facilitate command and supply. Moreover, they were to be equipped with special all-terrain vehicles suitable for use in the tropics. The soldiers for these divisions were also to be carefully selected.

Colonel-General Halder gave his views on the proposals of the organization department on the same day that they were presented to him.[257] He agreed with the basic idea but made numerous technical suggestions and expressed the view that the mobile formations should consist of twenty-four armoured and twelve motorized divisions. Troops envisaged for service in the tropics should be called 'light armoured divisions' and 'light motorized divisions'. In view of the tasks with which the Wehrmacht would be confronted in North-West Africa, North Africa and Egypt, the Middle East, and Afghanistan—perhaps all at the same time—Halder considered the following organization of the army appropriate: 24 armoured divisions, including 10 light divisions; 12 motorized divisions, including 5 light divisions; 66 normal infantry divisions, including 6 trained and equipped for air transport and 10 suitable for service

---

[257] Cf. Table IV.II.1 and Halder, *Diaries*, ii. 845–7 (30 Mar. 1941), 860–3 (7 Apr. 1941), 946 (4 June 1941); also Besymenski, *Sonderakte Barbarossa*, 284; Glasneck and Kircheisen, *Türkei und Afghanistan*, 234–5.

3. Planning for Post-Barbarossa Period

TABLE IV.II.1. *Structure of the Future German Army Proposed by Colonel-General Halder, April 1941*

Area of use	Mobile units	Mobile infantry divisions	Mountain divisions	Normal infantry divisions	Vehicle transport groups
West		6		24	2
North			2	6	
East	6	6	2	20	2
South-east				6	
Operational groups					
Spain–Morocco	3	2		2	1
North Africa–Egypt	6	2			1
Anatolia	6	4		4	
Afghanistan	3	4	6	4	
TOTAL	24	24	10	66	6

Source: Moritz, 'Planungen', 329–30, doc. 2: Chef GenStdH No. 124/41 g.Kdos. Chefs. (7 Apr. 1941), comment on work referred to in n. 256.

in the tropics; 10 mountain divisions; 24 infantry divisions suitable for motorized transport, including 6 equipped for service in the tropics; 6 motor-vehicle transport regiments for operational purposes; and 2 air-transport Staffeln, each with sufficient capacity to transport an infantry division. Halder's plan to distribute these units, based on a rough calculation of requirements, is presented in Table IV.II.1. The excess divisions would form the army high command reserve in Germany itself.

The army general staff knew, of course, that a large-scale offensive in North Africa,[258] as well as the envisaged conquest of Gibraltar, could only be carried out after Barbarossa,[259] but it already had relatively concrete ideas about the dates for these operations. As early as the end of February 1941 Hitler had ordered a resumption of preparations for the conquest of the Rock. On 10 March he received a final report on the plan, which was temporarily named 'Felix-Heinrich'.[260] The attack was set for 15 October 1941. Halder then became more cautious and made the operation conditional on the course of the war against the Soviet Union. It was now to begin 'three months after the withdrawal of the [necessary] forces from the east'.[261] The draft plan for

---

[258] Halder, *Diaries*, ii. 816–18 (3 Mar. 1941), 918–23 (14–15 May 1941), according to which it was accepted in May that 4 armoured and 3 motorized divisions would be required for the continuation of the offensive against Egypt; cf. *KTB OKW* i. 1010 (3 Apr. 1941).

[259] Halder, *Diaries*, ii. 845–7 (30 Mar. 1941).

[260] Burdick, *Germany's Military Strategy*, 122; subsequently the code-name 'Felix' was again employed.

[261] Halder, *Diaries*, ii. 830 (16 Mar. 1941).

the continuation of the war in the south-west was, however, ready; the fact that it was completed early should not be interpreted as an indication that it merely involved provisional, preliminary deliberations. In March the German military leaders were undoubtedly convinced that they could carry out such plans. However, as they gradually realized, especially after the setbacks in Iraq and Syria, that campaigns outside Europe could not be improvised, they began to adapt their long-term plans to the requirements of such operations.[262]

In the final analysis the Third Reich began to prepare the second phase of the war, to secure the conquest of Europe achieved in the first phase, before the latter had actually been completed. Britain was also to be 'finished off' in 1941, in Hitler's view as noted by Weizsäcker, 'with or without Russia'. The war against the Soviet Union began the 'final round' of the first phase. During this phase of aggression on the European continent Hitler wanted to stop short of a war with the United States.[263]

But already on 22 May, during a situation report by Raeder, Hitler insisted on the occupation of the Azores—which Raeder had rejected—in order to be able to operate long-range bombers from there against the United States. This occasion 'might arise by the autumn'.[264] After several months of silence Hitler thus returned to his ideas of 1940. It is possible that this development was prompted by his talk with Darlan on 11 May,[265] which would permit the conclusion that his calculations were primarily defensive. At that time even the Spanish government feared Allied operations against Spain's islands in the Atlantic. In fact, from May to September 1941 the British kept a force of 10,000–20,000 men ready to occupy the islands, but only as a reaction to the expected German push into south-west Europe.[266]

It is, however, very probable that Hitler's thoughts also implied offensive operations.[267] In this connection it is not important that the Luftwaffe still did not have the aircraft necessary to pose a serious threat to the United States.[268] This fact is relevant only to the feasibility of such operations, and not to the question of what Hitler actually wanted, with which the present analysis is primarily concerned. Hitler was considering contingencies and repeated on 25 July that America's entry into the war had to be prevented if at all possible 'while the eastern campaign is still in progress', but he reserved the right to

---

[262] Warlimont, *Headquarters*, 132.
[263] *Weizsäcker-Papiere*, 325–6 (1 May 1941).
[264] 'Führer Conferences', 199 (22 May 1941).
[265] *DGFP* D xii, No. 491, pp. 763–4 (11 May 1941); pp. 770–1: Darlan's reference to the importance of the islands for British strategy. The navy, with reference to a communication from the foreign ministry, indicated, not quite correctly, that Darlan had recommended the 'occupation of the Canary Islands before military operations against Gibraltar' and had referred to the 'particular importance of the Azores': Assmann, 'Bemühungen der Seekriegsleitung', i. 47, BA-MA RM 8/1209.
[266] Ruhl, *Spanien im Zweiten Weltkrieg*, 33–4.
[267] Hildebrand, *Vom Reich*, 709; Hillgruber, *Strategie*, 380.
[268] Hillgruber, *Strategie*, 380, n. 17.

3. Planning for Post-Barbarossa Period   629

take 'strong action' against that country after Barbarossa.[269] The question of how this was to be done remained open.

All of this confirmed once again that the centre of all German planning was the war against the Soviet Union. This was also true as regards the German assessment of the situation in Spain. Since 22 February 1941 the German government had forbidden any official exchange of ideas about that country entering the war.[270] Eberhard von Stohrer, the German ambassador in Madrid, pointed out as early as April that Berlin should not renounce all attempts to influence Spain politically, or to achieve possible agreements on future co-operation.[271] This had to be avoided if only because it was becoming increasingly evident that Serrano Suñer, the Spanish foreign minister, as well as the Spanish generals, wanted to participate actively in the conflict. But such suggestions made no impression in Berlin. State Secretary von Weizsäcker observed that 'Germany and not Spain should determine the date of Spain's entry into the war', but, like Stohrer, he advised against forcible intervention in Spain.[272] At the end of May, under the impression of the very tense domestic situation in Spain, which seemed to involve the danger of a coup that would strengthen the position of the war party even more, Stohrer considered political precautions indispensable so that Germany would be able to react to a shift in the power situation.[273] But on 7 June Ribbentrop decided that Stohrer should not approach the Spanish government, as the Spanish 'appetite for war' could hardly be taken seriously.[274]

As far as the Iberian peninsula was concerned, German military staffs, as mentioned above, concentrated primarily on Operation Isabella, i.e. measures with which Germany would react to British operations in the area of Spain and Portugal. These preparations were concluded by 15 June.[275] Thus Hitler

---

[269] 'Führer Conferences', 222 (25 July 1941), also 221 (9 July 1941). At the time Hitler was seeking to put off American entry into the war 'by another 1–2 months', because on the one hand Barbarossa would tie down the air force designated for the operation and, on the other, victory in the east would no doubt affect the attitude of the US. Any incident at sea was therefore to be avoided in the meantime.

[270] *DGFP* D xii, No. 73, pp. 131–2 (22 Feb. 1941). On Spain's domestic crisis, which, since the beginning of April 1941, had led to tension between the foreign minister and old Falangists or the military, see ibid., No. 21, pp. 36–7 (6 Feb. 1941); No. 386, pp. 611–15 (22 Apr. 1941): both from Ambassador in Madrid to foreign ministry. On subsequent developments cf. also Ruhl, *Spanien im Zweiten Weltkrieg*, 29–32.

[271] *DGFP* D xii, No. 386, pp. 611–15 (22 Apr. 1941), here 615.

[272] Ibid., No. 492, p. 774 (11 May 1941).

[273] Ibid., No. 574, pp. 928–30 (30 May 1941).

[274] Ibid. 930 n. 15. One day after the completion of Directive No. 32, Ribbentrop had Stohrer informed that Berlin regarded the 'speedy and complete restoration of the railway bridge at Hendaye' as of such importance that he should discuss the matter with the Spanish government. At the time the primary German concern was to be able to use the bridge for possible countermeasures in the event of a British action against Portugal or Spain, but it was also important in view of Operation Felix. The Spaniards promised to repair it as quickly as possible: *DGFP* D xii, No. 619, pp. 1017–18 (12 June 1941); *KTB OKW* i. 405–6 (17–18 June 1941).

[275] Halder, *KTB* ii. 479–80 (undated, beginning of June 1941; not in trans.); cf. *KTB OKW* i. 413 (2 and 6 June 1941); 407 (20 June 1941).

postponed the solution of all major problems still facing Germany in the west, the south, the Mediterranean, and Africa until after victory over the Soviet Union. The preliminary deliberations in this regard[276] were summarized in Directive No. 32 of 11 June 1941 on 'Preparations for the Period after Barbarossa'.[277] This directive, of which a draft has been preserved, was never signed by Hitler, but that is relatively unimportant. For on 19 June it was sent to the high commands of the Wehrmacht services and was used thereafter as a basis for their decisions.[278] This shows that the Wehrmacht services considered Directive No. 32 binding; and the fact that Hitler signed the order of the Wehrmacht high command concerning personnel and material preparations of the Wehrmacht referring to it[279]—together with the corrections of 30 June to Directive No. 32, which were also sent to the Wehrmacht services,[280] and the Service Regulation for Special Staff F (Luftwaffe General Felmy) of 21 June[281]—leaves no doubt that the failure to sign the draft directive was a mere accident.[282]

What in fact were Hitler's plans for the period after Barbarossa?[283] Directive No. 32 assumed that, after the Soviet armed forces had been 'smashed', the Axis powers would completely dominate Europe with the exception of, for the time being, the Iberian peninsula. As their position on the Continent would then be impregnable, it was possible to plan a reduction of the army and a concentration of arms production on the needs of the Luftwaffe and the navy.[284] Closer German–French co-operation was to tie down British forces, eliminate any possible threat in the rear area of the German and Italian troops in North Africa, reduce the freedom of movement of the British fleet in the western Mediterranean, and 'protect the deep south-west flank of the European theatre, including the Atlantic coast of North and West Africa, against Anglo-American intervention'. Then it was intended to put to Spain the crucial question: Franco would have to decide definitely whether to par-

---

[276] Halder, *KTB* ii. 442 ff. (4 June 1941; not in trans.); *KTB OKW* i. 400–1 (4 June 1941); *Lagevorträge*, 258–62 (6 June 1941; not in trans.); Klee, 'Der Entwurf', 138; Hillgruber, *Strategie*, 379, 382; Warlimont, *Headquarters*, 133.

[277] *Hitler's War Directives*, No. 32, pp. 78–82, with relevant supplements (of which only one is in the English edition: for the remainder see *Hitlers Weisungen*, 133–6). Also *DGFP* D xii, No. 617, pp. 1012–16 (11 June 1941); Klee, 'Der Entwurf', 133–7.

[278] Warlimont, *Headquarters*, 132–3; cf. also 1. Skl., KTB, Teil A, 283 ff. (23 June 1941): situation conference with chief of naval war staff, here 'Ia's report on the draft of Führer Directive No. 32 . . .', BA-MA RM 7/25.

[279] *Hitler's War Directives*, No. 32a, pp. 82–5 (14 July 1941).

[280] *Hitler's War Directives*, 81 n.

[281] *Hitlers Weisungen*, 157 ff. (not in trans.).

[282] Klee, 'Der Entwurf', 131–2, 140; Besymenski, *Sonderakte Barbarossa*, 282 ff.

[283] *Hitler's War Directives*, 78–82; for interpretation cf. Burdick, *Germany's Military Strategy*, 124–5; Hildebrand, *Vom Reich*, 710–11; Hillgruber, *Strategie*, 378–82; Hirszowicz, *The Third Reich*, 198–9. For previous considerations on similar lines, though based on quite different premisses, cf. I.II.4 (*d*) and I.III.2 (*b*) above.

[284] However, reservations prevailed in the naval war staff. The tasks foreseen for the army certainly did not justify any assumption that there could be an acceleration in the armament of the navy: 1. Skl., KTB, Teil A, 284 (23 June 1941), BA-MA RM 7/25.

3. Planning for Post-Barbarossa Period

ticipate or not in the 'expulsion of the British from Gibraltar'. Moreover, the German government hoped that, as a result of the opportunities to exert pressure on Turkey and Iran after the conclusion of Barbarossa, it would be able to use these two countries directly or indirectly in the war against Britain. Against this strategic background the Wehrmacht had to assume that it would have two main tasks in the late autumn of 1941 and during the following winter. One of these was the organization, protection, and economic use of the new territories conquered in the east; the other was the 'continuation of the war against Britain in the Mediterranean and the Middle East'. It was planned to carry out 'concentric attacks from Libya through Egypt, from Bulgaria through Turkey, and possibly from Transcaucasia through Iran'.

On 18 June the Wehrmacht high command ordered the establishment under Major-General Hans Rhode, the German military attaché in Ankara, of an agency to gather intelligence on all military, infrastructure, and geographical matters relating to the eastern Mediterranean and the Middle East, so as to provide a realistic foundation for studies to be produced by the general staff. Such studies were concerned with the 'Attack on the Suez Canal from the North (Anatolia), Including the Area of Mosul, Baghdad, and Basra', the 'Attack against Baghdad–Basra from the Caucasus, Using the Route via the Caspian Sea', and 'Operations against the Middle East via Iran and Afghanistan'.[285] Of course preparations for the offensive from Cyrenaica also continued, but at this time the Germans favoured an operation via Anatolia, while North Africa, where the conduct of the war was dependent on transport of supplies by sea and was subject to 'incalculable vicissitudes', was to be left essentially to the Italians.[286] When, in July 1941, Hitler concerned himself with the transfer of an armoured division to the Bulgarian–Turkish frontier, his main aim was to warn the Turks, who were again 'getting above themselves', but he also intended to use the transferred troops in a later attack on the 'British land route in the Middle East'.[287]

---

[285] Moritz, 'Planungen', 330–1, No. 3: Chef GenStdH/OQu IV/Abt. Fremde Heere Ost No. 84/41 g.Kdos. Chefs. (18 June 1941), tasks for military attaché in Ankara; also ibid. 331–2, No. 4: OQu I des GenStdH No. 430/41 g.Kdos. Chefs. (3 July 1941), 'Preparation of operations for the period after Barbarossa'. OQu I at the time was Lt.-Gen. Friedrich Paulus. On 21 June 1941 tasks similar to those of the military attaché in Ankara were taken on by 'Special Staff F', which was to co-operate closely with the military representatives in Ankara and Tehran: *Hitlers Weisungen*, 134–6 (not in trans.). Tehran was dropped after the arrival of British and Soviet troops in Iran on 25 Aug. Three days later the government was reorganized and resistance by Iranian forces ceased: cf. Buckley, *Five Ventures*, 141–61; Hirschfeld, *Deutschland und Iran*, 282–95. Both the German and the Italian legations were closed on 9 Sept. 1941; Hirschfeld, 252–66, on Iran's role in the planning for the period after Barbarossa. Germany's long-term interest was to draw Iran into the Axis camp, possibly by means of an uprising. No action was taken on this because of the earlier lack of success and in order to avoid an untimely crisis: German troops must first reach the Caucasus. Moreover, political relations between Berlin, Tehran, and Rome were very difficult owing to numerous differences of interest.

[286] Halder, *Diaries*, ii. 998–1002 (3 July 1941); *KTB OKW* i. 433 (13 July 1941).

[287] Halder, *Diaries*, ii. 1014–18 (8 July 1941).

The progress of the attack on the Soviet Union in July 1941 produced euphoric expectations of victory in the German military staffs. Under the impression of the initial, brilliant successes of the German army in the east, Halder noted 'It is thus probably no overstatement to say that the Russian campaign has been won in the space of two weeks', although he expected the Soviet army to continue fighting for several weeks longer.[288] July 1941 also marked the high point of Hitler's boldest hopes and plans. On 23 July he assumed that his troops would reach the Volga by the beginning of October and the area of Baku and Batumi by November.[289]

Hitler's guidelines for personnel and material preparations of the Wehrmacht[290] were dated 14 July. The United States were also mentioned in them. The navy, whose armament plans were limited to the current U-boat construction programme, was instructed to take as its point of orientation the conflict with Britain and the United States.[291] This is surprising, but Hitler had drawn very individual conclusions from the course of the war hitherto. The original armament priorities laid down in Directive No. 32 had been overtaken by events. After the victory in the east the army was indeed to be greatly reduced, but the number of armoured units was to be increased. However, the main emphasis of armament programmes was to be shifted to the Luftwaffe, which would be greatly expanded. Hitler now expected the strengthening of the armament of his Wehrmacht as a whole essentially to come about from the realization of the air-armament programme already approved.[292] In this respect German armament plans seemed to become more assimilated to the ideas of General Douhet; and Hitler's discussions of the situation with Raeder,[293] as well as his offer to the Japanese ambassador in Berlin, General Oshima, to wage a joint struggle against the United States for world domination, indicate that in July 1941 the defeat of that country con-

---

[288] Ibid. 998–1002 (3 July 1941). About a month later it was clear to Halder that the economic and organizational as well as the military strength of 'the Russian colossus' had been underestimated: ibid. 1170–1 (11 Aug. 1941).

[289] Ibid. 1070–1 (23 July 1941), esp. n. 12; cf. Hillgruber, *Zenit*, for assessment of the whole month of July.

[290] *Hitler's War Directives*, No. 32a, pp. 82–5; Halder, *Diaries*, ii. 1043–8 (15 July 1941); Moritz, 'Planungen', 332–3, No. 5: Abt. L No. 441187/41 g.Kdos. Chefs. (I. Op) (11 July 1941), 'Distribution of army forces after conclusion of the eastern operations'. Although Transcaucasia was not mentioned in this document, cf. the undated but certainly subsequent plan (see *KTB OKW* i. 433–4, 13–14 July 1941) for the 'Operation proceeding from northern Caucasia via the Caucasus and north-west Iran to seize the passes Rawanduz and Khanaqin on the Iranian–Iraqi border': *KTB OKW* i. 1038 ff. For the operation, which was to be conducted in six stages, 'a probable duration from November 1941 to September 1942' was estimated.

[291] See *KTB OKW* i. 1047–54: discussion between Chief OKW and heads of services about 'The consequences of the Führer's directives of 14 July 1941 and the feasibility of the new programme of priorities arising from them'.

[292] *Hitler's War Directives*, No. 32a, pp. 82–5; on Hitler's change of emphasis cf. Hillgruber, *Strategie*, 381.

[293] 'Führer Conferences', 222–5 (9 July 1941), 271 (25 July 1941).

3. Planning for Post-Barbarossa Period

stituted a concrete war aim in his view, although he did not set an exact date for the start of the conflict.[294]

These ideas had no influence on the preparatory planning of the military staffs. Apart from current operations, the planners concentrated for the time being on the conduct of the war after Barbarossa within the framework of Directive No. 32. By the end of July the army general staff had already drawn up a schedule for the various operations.[295] Continued Luftwaffe attacks on Malta to keep the British from using the island as a base, an attack on Gibraltar, and the capture of Tobruk were planned for the autumn of 1941. In the winter of 1941–2 it was planned to obtain Turkish permission to send forces through the passes in the Taurus mountains in order to attack Syria and Palestine before pushing on towards Egypt. Depending on how this operation developed, an offensive could be started against Egypt from Cyrenaica. The concentric attack towards the Persian Gulf from Transcaucasia and Anatolia would begin in the spring of 1942, if Turkey were prepared to co-operate. If Turkey refused, one part of the attack would be carried out against Thrace and Anatolia and then further in the direction of Egypt, while other forces would advance from Transcaucasia through northern Iran to the Persian Gulf.

But only two days later, on 30 July, Directive No. 34 indicated that the war against the Soviet Union was not developing as the German leaders had expected.[296] This inevitably cast uncertainty upon the ambitious plans of 11 June and subsequent planning,[297] for early success in the east was the essential precondition for their realization. But for the time being the discussion of the general plan continued, although it was clearly increasingly restricted to objectives in the west.

There Directive No. 32 called for the closing of the Mediterranean. It had been planned to start intensive preparations for Operation Felix (the attack on Gibraltar) as soon as the fighting in the east approached an end. The Wehrmacht high command obviously assumed that the French would then be more prepared to collaborate.[298] The German military therefore expected in June that they would be permitted to send supply transports through the unoccupied part of France, if not troops. The idea of participation by the French air force and navy in the war against Britain was also revived. In that event, it would have only been necessary to transfer German army units to

---

[294] For differing views on this question cf. Besymenski, *Sonderakte Barbarossa*, 289–90; Hildebrand, *Foreign Policy*, 112–13; Hillgruber, 'Faktor Amerika', 518–21; Thies, *Architekt*, 161–2.

[295] Cf. ObdM, Skl. Ia op 1335/41 g.Kdos. Chefs. (28 July 1941), memorandum on army operations, BA-MA RM 7/234. The Skl. study referred to two letters from the general staff of the army to the OKW, commenting on 'Army operations after "Barbarossa"'.

[296] *Hitler's War Directives*, No. 34, pp. 91–3.

[297] See n. 295; also *KTB OKW* i. 446 (28 June 1941). At the beginning of September the army general staff assumed that Felix would not be carried out before Dec. 1941 or Jan. 1942: Halder, *Diaries*, ii. 1217–18 (5 Sept. 1941).

[298] On scepticism in the foreign ministry about collaboration with France cf. *Weizsäcker-Papiere*, 261 (24 June 1941); also *Hitler's War Directives*, No. 32, pp. 78–82.

Spanish Morocco to secure the Strait of Gibraltar. On the other hand, the Wehrmacht high command wanted to leave the protection of the African Atlantic coast and the reconquest of the Gaullist French colonies to the French themselves. This did not mean, however, that Germany renounced the use of these areas for the further conduct of the war. The Germans assumed that it would not be difficult to persuade the French to accept the demands of the Luftwaffe and the German navy for bases in West Africa when Wehrmacht units were deployed at the Strait of Gibraltar. Then it would also be possible to reconsider the occupation of the Atlantic islands.[299]

Felix was thus the most important of the measures being considered in the western Mediterranean. Halder wanted to defer preparations until Germany would be able actually to start the attack on Gibraltar,[300] but, because of logistical problems to be expected during the transfer of units from the east front to the French–Spanish frontier, long-term planning was essential.[301] The navy at first refused to support Felix with sea transports from southern France to Spain, as it considered the risk in an area dominated by the British fleet to be too great.[302] But on 22 July, when plans for carrying out the operation in October 1941 began to assume concrete form, Rear-Admiral Fricke produced a detailed analysis of the possibilities for the navy to support the operation and the advantages which the capture of Gibraltar would have for Germany in the war at sea.[303] The army calculated that the return of the troops from the Soviet Union would require about three months. Nevertheless, in any case Felix was to begin in 1941.[304]

The related planning was intensified even more in July and August 1941. But two important factors could not be calculated in advance: Franco's consent to the operation, and developments in the east. The first came to be considered increasingly improbable[305] as the outcome of the Russo-German war became more and more uncertain after August 1941.[306] On 22 August Raeder again vigorously pointed out the importance of capturing Gibraltar and enumerated all the advantages which, in his opinion, military co-operation with Spain would have for Germany: possession of the Strait of Gibraltar, domination of the western Mediterranean, a reduction of the importance of Malta, the use of El Ferrol and Cadiz as bases for the battle of the Atlantic, and the possibility of transferring German war and merchant ships to the Mediterranean, which could ease the situation there for the Axis. But Hitler,

---

[299] Cf. comments on Directive No. 32, n. 283 above.
[300] Halder, *Diaries*, ii. 1018–22 (9 July 1941).
[301] Burdick, *Germany's Military Strategy*, 125–6.
[302] 1. Skl. I op 1267/41, g.Kdos. Chefs. (17 July 1941), commenting on OKH/GenStdH/Op.Abt. IIa No. 1348/41 g.Kdos., BA-MA RM CASE GE 529, PG 32087 d.
[303] Naval war staff, B.Nr. 1. Skl. I Op 1302/41 g.Kdos. Chefs. (22 July 1941), to Skl. Qu.A, on Operation Felix (no file reference), BA-MA CASE GE 529, PG 32604.
[304] Burdick, *Germany's Military Strategy*, 127.
[305] Ruhl, *Spanien im Zweiten Weltkrieg*, 127 ff.
[306] On this interrelationship see Burdick, *Germany's Military Strategy*, 127 ff.

3. Planning for Post-Barbarossa Period

while agreeing completely with Raeder's remarks, was no longer disposed to set an exact date for Felix.[307] Three days later, in a conversation with Mussolini, he showed that he had given up hope of obtaining Spanish co-operation.[308] However, Franco's disinclination to co-operate was not the decisive factor in Hitler's eyes. For the Germans developments in the east now made operations on the Iberian peninsula 'undesirable'.[309]

By the end of September 1941 Operation Felix had receded into the background.[310] At the end of the year no possibility was open even of improving German–Spanish military relations. The head of the Wehrmacht high command now forbade enquiries in Spain by the Wehrmacht services or discussions of military subjects. The same applied to discussions of joint military operations and the question of Spain's entry into the war.[311] When, on 7 December, the Spaniards took the initiative in bringing up the subject of the capture of Gibraltar, Hitler replied that at the moment he could do nothing in that direction, adding with regret that Franco alone was responsible for the failure to take the opportunity to capture Gibraltar in the spring of 1941.[312] It should, however, be remembered that in December 1941 the Spanish government, General Moscardó's remarks notwithstanding, was not seriously interested in closer military co-operation, let alone joint operations.[313]

It was doubtless the naval war staff that most regretted the disappointing development of relations with Spain. In an analysis of 2 December, 'Thoughts on the Importance of Gibraltar', the staff wrote that the operation against Gibraltar was worth the necessary withdrawal of troops and materials from the eastern front: for after a victorious operation in Spain they would be able once again to make 'manifold contributions to the war effort in the east'.[314] In view of this statement in December 1941, it seems justifiable to wonder whether the navy high command really understood the nature of the war in which Germany was involved.

In connection with the planning and deliberations initiated by German military staffs for the continuation of the war, several other studies should be mentioned in which the Wehrmacht and navy high commands raised basic questions of strategy.

Since May 1941 in particular, as a result of various statements by Hitler, the

---

[307] 'Führer Conferences', 225–30 (22 Aug. 1941).
[308] *DGFP* D xiii, No. 242, pp. 383–8 (25 Aug. 1941).
[309] Chief of OKW to foreign ministry, ibid., No. 314, pp. 498–9 (10 Sept. 1941).
[310] Burdick, *Germany's Military Strategy*, 129–30. Similar action was taken in relation to Isabella: the operation was officially kept in being, but from the beginning of 1942 at the latest it was an illusion (ibid. 147–54).
[311] Director of political department to the embassy in Madrid, *DGFP* D xiii, No. 467, p. 774 (13 Nov. 1941).
[312] Ibid., No. 555, pp. 971–2 (9 Dec. 1941): Hitler's conversation on 7 Dec. 1941 with Gen. Ituarte José Moscardó, chief of Falange militia and chief of Franco's military cabinet.
[313] Ruhl, *Spanien im Zweiten Weltkrieg*, 39.
[314] OKM/Skl. B.Nr. 1. Skl. I opa 2120/41 g.Kdos. Chefs. (2 Dec. 1941), observations on the importance of Gibraltar, BA-MA RM7/234.

navy had the impression that after the end of the war, Germany might become involved in a confrontation with the United States, with Britain on the side of America. In these strategic deliberations the naval war staff did not exclude even the possibility of a war between Germany and Japan.[315] With a view to conflicts thus escalating towards a struggle for world domination, appropriate plans for naval construction were made at the end of July.[316] But these represented in the final analysis merely a 'first requirement'. The long-term aim, discussed at the time in the navy high command, envisaged a battle fleet many times the size of the 'first requirement': 28 battleships, 8 aircraft-carriers or cruisers with flight-decks, 50 cruisers, and 400 U-boats. To this was to be added a fleet to protect German trade with a core of 50 cruisers, plus home-fleet forces of 150 destroyers, 50 torpedo-boats, 250 minesweepers, 100 fast patrol-boats, 20 minelayers, 20 flak cruisers, and 100 submarine chasers. This construction programme was to be completed over twelve or, at most, thirteen years. The armament guidelines for the period after Barbarossa originally implied in Directive No. 32 probably encouraged the navy leaders to make even more ambitious plans. But the priority of the air war, mentioned in the guidelines of the Wehrmacht high command for material and personnel preparations, should have been a warning to the navy high command. For in them Hitler, who remained convinced of the possibility of conflict between Germany and America, had assigned the decisive role to the Luftwaffe, with all the resulting consequences for the navy. This set of priorities—and other signs supported this view—could lead to a weakening of the naval components of German armament programmes even in the present, and possibly even to a decision not to wage a naval war against the Anglo-Saxon powers. All these factors, and developments in the battle of the Atlantic, finally caused the naval war staff to present its views in a comprehensive 'Memorandum on the Present State of the Naval War against Britain in July 1941'. In addition to taking stock, the memorandum was also intended to present again the navy's own conception of German strategy.[317]

In the introduction to its memorandum the naval war staff stressed that 'overpowering Britain' must be the main objective for Germany.[318] This would be achieved by 'eliminating Britain as an enemy, or as a deployment base for her ally, the United States'. This objective could be achieved by bombing, resulting in the complete destruction of British supply and armament installations, or by cutting Britain's sea routes. But in recent months experience had

---

[315] 'Observations on the basic principles of the expansion of the fleet', memorandum of July 1941, printed in Salewski, *Seekriegsleitung*, iii. 130–5.

[316] Ibid. 135–6; on supplementary considerations in the naval war staff see Schreiber, 'Thesen', 273–4.

[317] The memorandum is printed in Salewski, *Seekriegsleitung*, iii. 192–210; cf. also 'Führer Conferences', 222 ff. (25 July 1941), and Halder, *Diaries*, ii. 1085–8 (30 July 1941). The latter describes the naval war staff's paper as 'very gratifying, but also sober, in its appraisal of the situation'.

[318] See Salewski, *Seekriegsleitung*, iii. 192–210.

3. Planning for Post-Barbarossa Period

shown that only the battle of the Atlantic offered a real chance to defeat Britain. At the conclusion of a detailed analysis of the situation in the war against the Soviet Union and in the Mediterranean, and of the attitudes of the United States, France, and Japan, as well as the war at sea, the naval war staff observed that in its opinion

> the collapse of the Soviet Union will not change the British will to resist; even a defeat of the British forces in Africa will not force the British to yield, as they are convinced that only through victory can they recover all the positions they have lost. The extraordinary concentration of all British and American forces on the battle of the Atlantic clearly shows the decisive importance of the final phase of the struggle there.

Britain would be prepared to accept a negotiated peace only if she had to admit defeat at sea. Otherwise she would continue to pursue her 'final aim', the 'destruction of Germany's position on the Continent'. The naval war staff could hardly imagine that Britain would be able to achieve this objective after the German victory over the Soviet Union. But it did not exclude the possibility that 'a comprehensive, large-scale offensive operation by the United States, with the occupation of the Atlantic islands as an intermediate base to provide more extended protection in the Atlantic, together with the occupation of the French colonies in Africa as a strategic starting-position', could create a situation which would influence the course of developments and prolong the war.

Under the impression of the recent replacement of British occupation forces in Iceland by Americans, the naval war staff considered it probable that London and Washington would occupy the Azores, the Cape Verde Islands, Dakar, and Casablanca.[319] In connection with these operations, an Anglo-American offensive would presumably be launched against the still relatively weak position of the Axis in North Africa. After that the Allies would try to put things in order in the eastern Mediterranean. It was therefore necessary to meet this threat in time, but this could not be done with purely defensive measures, by which an attack could perhaps be warded off. Rather the effort must also be made to defeat the enemy clearly in the Atlantic in order to create the conditions for subduing Britain. This aim could be achieved through: '(a) the mobilization of all forces and an extraordinary effort in all areas to disrupt supplies for Britain in the battle of the Atlantic, (b) keeping the positions in North and West Africa in the German sphere of influence, and (c) drawing the Iberian peninsula, including Gibraltar, into that sphere.'

This plan would require military co-operation with France, even at the price of making significant political concessions and accepting temporary disadvantages to improve German–French relations. Spain and Portugal had to be induced to resist resolutely any British–American attempt to land on their

---

[319] Regarding Allied planning in the period 1940–3 there were in existence 21 different case-studies for the seizure of the Azores, the Cape Verde Islands, or Madeira: cf. Siedentopf, *Die britischen Pläne*.

coasts or on the Atlantic islands, and to take the necessary military precautions at once.[320] Political means should be used to prompt Italy to wage war more energetically. Moreover, it was important to induce Japan to take political and military action that would relieve the pressure on the German navy in the Atlantic. It was most important, however, that 'permission should be given for a war against US merchant shipping according to prize rules as soon as the conclusion of the campaign in the east [permitted] this political decision'.

From a purely military point of view the naval war staff considered it essential to intensify submarine warfare in the Atlantic as far as personnel and material resources permitted. To support the U-boats, Geschwader of long-range aircraft had to be formed. The air war should concentrate on British supplies in the Atlantic and along the coasts of Britain. For this purpose it was advisable to create special Atlantic Geschwader. It was also proposed to use more air-dropped mines, to carry out systematic attacks on British ports and warships, to integrate France with all its bases and naval forces into the battle of the Atlantic, and to make preparations to defend Casablanca and Dakar with Luftwaffe and army units if necessary.[321]

Copies of the naval war staff's memorandum of 21 July were sent to, among others, the foreign ministry and the Wehrmacht high command,[322] where Major-General Warlimont, the head of Department L (Home Defence), found it 'very good' and suggested making it the basis for a 'brief strategic survey' for Hitler after obtaining the opinions of the army and Luftwaffe high commands. Like the naval war staff, Warlimont wanted to make clear to Hitler the 'key position' which France should have in German strategy.[323] By 6 August he had written a 'Brief Strategic Survey on the Continuation of the War after the Campaign in the East'.[324] This can be considered a preliminary study for

---

[320] On these problems *DGFP* D xiii, No. 157, pp. 222–4 (27 July 1941); 'Führer Conferences' 198 (22 May 1941), 225–30 (22 Aug. 1941), 244–5 (12 Dec. 1941); for relevant items not printed in 'Führer Conferences' see *Lagevorträge*, 303 (27 Oct. 1941) 312 (13 Nov. 1941). After American entry into the war Raeder no longer expected an imminent landing on the islands or an attack on Dakar, as the Americans would in the coming months have to concentrate on the Pacific area. Britain, in Raeder's opinion, could not afford any greater risks. Cf. also Salewski, *Seekriegsleitung*, i. 441. Raeder, however, rejected a German occupation—e.g. of the Azores, as mooted by Dönitz on 11 July 1941—as he was primarily interested in strengthening the defensive readiness of the Atlantic islands.

[321] On the question of Dakar cf. 'Führer Conferences', 244–5 (12 Dec. 1941); *Lagevorträge*, 238–9 (22 May 1941); 265, 268–71 (21 June 1941).

[322] On the distribution see Salewski, *Seekriegsleitung*, iii. 190 n. 5.

[323] Ibid. 190.

[324] Abt. L—Chef—No. 441339/41 g.Kdos. Chefs. (6 Aug. 1941), Skl.'s copy, BA-MA RM7/258. In his introduction Warlimont stipulated that 'the Wehrmacht leadership must accept that in the east the operation goals—viz. the Caucasian oil regions, the Volga, and Archangel—will not be completely reached. A fluid front there would have to be taken into account; apart from the defence and securing of the occupied areas, this would tie up additional forces for the continuation of operations in 1942.' One of the conclusions reached was: 'Operations in the eastern Mediterranean area only after reaching Transcausasia.' The 'Caucasian oil', i.e. control of its disposition, was the precondition for the realization of planning in accordance with Directive No. 32.

3. Planning for Post-Barbarossa Period

the memorandum of 27 August by the Wehrmacht high command on 'The Strategic Situation in Late Summer 1941 as a Basis for Further Political and Military Plans', which Hitler approved.[325]

In contrast to the situation in July 1941, the memorandum by the Wehrmacht high command did not assume that the war against the Soviet Union would develop as originally planned, and this removed one of the main assumptions on which the memorandum of the naval war staff was based.[326] The Wehrmacht high command observed cautiously[327] that it could no longer be predicted 'how many forces can be made free in the east at the onset of winter and how many will still be necessary for the conduct of operations next year'. This admission that it was impossible to break Soviet resistance in the foreseeable future inevitably had far-reaching and manifold effects on the general situation. The German military had to assume now that the hoped-for Japanese intervention would be long in coming. Soviet–British co-operation in Iran had to be expected. In view of the British position in Iraq and Syria as well as the attitude of Turkey, Germany had no effective means to oppose such a development and was not able to put pressure on the Turkish government to change its policy. In August the Wehrmacht high command did not expect the military situation in the Mediterranean to change significantly in Britain's favour, but neither was it expected to change in favour of the Axis. And time was working against the aggressors. It was indicative of the altered military situation that the Axis's potential allies, Spain and Vichy France, were already showing rather openly that they wanted to await further developments in the east before committing themselves. The Wehrmacht memorandum then dealt in detail with the Axis's own possibilities and those of the enemy.[328]

For the German conduct of the war the overriding strategic principle[329] had to continue to be achieving the collapse of the Soviet Union by the 'use of all forces which can be spared from other fronts'. In so far as this aim could not be achieved in 1941, continuation of the war against the Soviet Union would also have top priority in 1942. Conquering more territory on the southern flank would indeed have important political and economic effects, and for this reason Germany should try to bring about a change in Turkey's attitude; but the 'battle of the Atlantic and the Mediterranean' could be waged with full strength only after the 'elimination of Russia as a power factor'. Even if it should still be possible to 'subjugate most of the Soviet Union this year', the army and the Luftwaffe would hardly be available for 'decisive operations in

---

[325] The memorandum is printed e.g. in *DGFP* D xiii, No. 265, pp. 422–35 (27 July 1941); cf. also Halder, *Diaries*, ii. 1228–34 (13 Sept. 1941); for its interpretation see Hillgruber, *Strategie*, 548–9; Warlimont, *Headquarters*, 192–3; on military planning and development in August cf. *Das Deutsche Reich und der Zweite Weltkrieg*, iv. 508–13 (Klink).

[326] Cf. Salewski, *Seekriegsleitung*, iii. 191.

[327] *DGFP* D xiii, No. 265 (n. 325 above).

[328] These were also set out in detail by Warlimont (n. 324 above), who concentrated on France, the western Mediterranean, and a possible landing in England in 1942.

[329] Warlimont, *Headquarters*, 192.

the Mediterranean, the Atlantic, and mainland Spain before the spring of 1942'. Until then the Wehrmacht would at most be able to carry out support operations, such as the transfer of naval forces to the Mediterranean.[330] The high command continued to place its hopes in the French will in North-West Africa. Axis operations in the eastern Mediterranean could only be expected when German forces reached Transcaucasia.

In the memorandum of 27 August 1941 Hitler's 'improvised war plan' dating from late autumn 1940, with its operational sequence Soviet Union–Middle East–North Africa, was formulated for the last time.[331] In a conference in the office of the assistant chief of staff (operations) on 24 October it was noted that: 'Because of the course of the campaign in the east, the development of the supply situation in Africa, and the still unclear attitude of Turkey, of the three possible operational directions for the attack on the Middle East (Egypt, Anatolia, and Caucasus–Iran), at the present time the attack via the Caucasus is the most obvious choice.'[332] The concentration on the west mentioned above was thus only an interlude; of the three great pincer movements originally planned, only one was still discussed. Shortly thereafter the dogma that a decisive success against the Soviet Union would solve all Germany's problems came to dominate the strategic thinking of the German military.[333] To the degree that a victory over the Red Army became improbable, discussion of the conditions for the operations once planned for the period after Barbarossa became irrelevant. After December 1941 they definitely belonged to the past, for, although some observers did not realize it at the time, the German failure in the battle of Moscow also marked the irreversible defeat of Hitler's master strategy of autumn 1940.[334]

---

[330] Schreiber, *Revisionismus*, 315–23, esp. 322.
[331] Hillgruber, *Strategie*, 549 n. 69.
[332] *KTB OKW* i. 1072–3 (24 Oct. 1941); cf. *Weizsäcker-Papiere*, 275 (30 Oct 1941): 'There is no question at present of an offensive against Egypt from Libya. Whether by way of Iran or Turkey will become apparent. The oil in Iraq is also attractive, perhaps India too; Gibraltar has been missed, must be left to its own devices.'
[333] Warlimont, *Headquarters*, 193.
[334] Reinhardt, 'Scheitern', 119.

PART V

The Italo-German Conduct of the War in the Mediterranean and North Africa

BERND STEGEMANN

I. The British Take the Offensive in North and East Africa

WHEN, after the fall of France, it became clear that Britain was determined to continue the war alone if necessary, German leaders developed numerous plans, as alternatives or interim strategies, to shift the main war effort to the Mediterranean and Africa in order to destroy the British position there. In contrast to these ideas for large-scale, sweeping operations, Italian military activity in Africa remained within modest limits until the autumn of 1940. The offensive by Marshal Graziani, begun on 13 September, came to a stop five days later with the conquest of Sidi Barrani.[1] The Italian commander-in-chief in East Africa, the Duke of Aosta, captured only some of the border towns in the Sudan and Kenya, but he was able to drive the British out of their colony of Somaliland and to occupy the port of Berbera on 19 August.[2] Including native troops, the strength of his forces at the start of the campaign, which the British soon estimated correctly, was 255,950 men.[3] Together with the 215,554 Italian soldiers in Libya, these troops represented, in terms of simple numbers, a considerable threat to the British position in Egypt.

The British commander-in-chief in the Middle East, General Sir Archibald Wavell, was, moreover, not only in charge of the defence of Egypt. According to his instructions of 24 July 1939,[4] in peacetime his command authority included the Sudan, Palestine, Transjordan, and Cyprus. In wartime he was also responsible for land operations in British Somaliland, Aden, Iran, and on the coasts of the Persian Gulf. To carry out his duties he was dependent on co-operation with the commander-in-chief of the Royal Navy in the Mediterranean, Admiral Sir Andrew Cunningham, the commander-in-chief of the Royal Air Force in the Middle East, Air Chief Marshal Sir Arthur Longmore, and local British commanders. He also had to bear in mind that, formally, Egypt and Iraq were sovereign states.

Wavell's instructions also required him to co-operate with the French military in North Africa, Syria, and French Somaliland as well as with the Turkish general staff and, possibly, the general staffs of Greece and Romania. As of 25 June 1940, however, France had ceased to be an ally, and the French armed forces in North Africa and Syria remained loyal to the Vichy government. This development removed a threat in the west for the Italians in Libya,

---

[1] Cf. I.III.3(c) above (Schreiber).
[2] Cf. I.III.3(b) above (Schreiber).
[3] Cf. *L'esercito italiano tra la 1ª e la 2ª guerra*, 332; Playfair, *Mediterranean*, i. 93; also Table I.1.1 above.
[4] Printed in Playfair, *Mediterranean*, i. 457-9.

while Syria now represented a potential new danger for Wavell in the east. In the summer of 1940 Romania had requested the sending of a German military mission, and it was to be expected that the Romanian general staff would now work closely with the German armed forces. On the other hand, after the Italian attack on Greece from Albania on 28 October, the Greek general staff was prepared to co-operate with Britain. But this meant at first that Wavell had to send Royal Air Force units to protect Crete,[5] so that his combat units in Egypt had a strength of only 36,000 men, who, moreover, were not completely equipped. In the south, on the southern frontier of the Sudan, Wavell had only 4,500 men until he was able to order the stationing of 5th Indian Division there in August.[6] In Kenya two African divisions were assembled and 1st South African Division brought up.[7] In Palestine Wavell had mixed units with a strength of 27,500 men; most of them, however, including two Australian brigades, were still not operational.[8]

At Churchill's request, Wavell flew to London on 8 August 1940 to discuss Britain's problems in the Middle East. Although the Battle of Britain had just started and the British army, after the material losses in France, was still not properly equipped to repel a German invasion, Churchill decided to send Wavell more reinforcements, as he feared that, after a failed invasion of Britain, or in place of such an attempt, the German leaders would press Italy to attack Britain's position in Egypt and would vigorously support such an effort. In this respect he considered the month of September to be especially dangerous.[9]

Churchill's plan to reinforce the British army in Egypt was, however, difficult to carry out: the sea route through the Mediterranean could only be used in exceptional cases. Convoys from Britain therefore had to take the long route round the Cape of Good Hope, which on average required six weeks. Moreover, many of the troops had to disembark in South Africa, as the fast transport ships were especially needed in the U-boat-infested areas of the North Atlantic. Troops from Australia and New Zealand made an intermediate stop in Bombay, where the reinforcements from India also embarked for Egypt. Aircraft were sent by ship to Takoradi in the Gold Coast (now Ghana) and flown from there almost 6,000 kilometres across Africa to Egypt. By the end of October 1943 the British alone had sent over 5,000 aircraft to Egypt by this route. By the start of the British offensive in December 1940 about 126,000 men had been sent to Egypt by ship, an average of over 1,000 a day.[10]

This steady stream of reinforcements did not, however, necessarily mean

---

[5] Cf. III.1.2 above (Vogel).
[6] Playfair, *Mediterranean*, i. 169, 187.
[7] Ibid. 181.
[8] Ibid. 93.
[9] Churchill, *The Second World War*, ii. 396–7.
[10] Playfair, *Mediterranean*, i. 195 ff., 244–7.

that the strength of the combat troops in Egypt had increased proportionately. As Churchill later observed angrily in a telegram to Wavell on 7 January 1941, the ration strength of his troops had reached 350,000 men,[11] while only two divisions were fighting the Italians in Cyrenaica. Churchill's mistrust of Wavell was not new. He had considered relieving him in August 1940, when the two men met in London, but had not found sufficient reason to do so. Churchill's critics believed that the prime minister had little understanding of the logistical problems of modern armies, which were even more serious if they had to fight in Africa. His ideas of warfare were dominated by memories of the Boer War. Thus in his understandable desire to put the only troops confronting an enemy into battle he did not realize that many of them were not adequately trained and equipped, that transport and repair facilities were lacking, and that men and equipment could not be sent into battle immediately after arrival.[12]

The relations between the commander-in-chief Middle East and the prime minister were further strained by the fact that, for fear that Churchill would intervene, Wavell did not inform him of his plans to attack the Italians in North Africa. On 11 September, even before the Italian invasion of Egypt, he had ordered a study of the problems involved in a British penetration of Cyrenaica. During the Italian offensive he had prepared the Western Desert Force for a possible counter-attack if the Italians advanced to Marsa Matruh. A month later he concluded that he need not wait for the Italian forces to advance further, and ordered the commander of British troops in Egypt, Lieutenant-General H. Maitland Wilson, to prepare suggestions for an attack of four to five days' duration, which was given the name 'Operation Compass'.[13]

Wavell even refrained from informing Anthony Eden, British secretary of state for war and a close friend of Churchill, who had been in the Middle East since 4 October, about his intentions. After the Italian attack on Greece on 28 October 1940, Eden pressed Wavell to send the Greeks weapons and other equipment. Believing that this would endanger the chances of achieving a military success in North Africa, Wavell finally told Eden of his plans.[14]

Churchill was delighted when, after returning to London on 8 November, Eden explained Wavell's strategy, but he soon began to urge Wavell to carry out Operation Compass in the first half of December at the latest. He feared a German intervention in Greece via Bulgaria and hoped in that case to be able to win Turkey and Yugoslavia as new allies. All British forces in the Middle East would then be needed in Europe.[15]

The units actually available to Western Desert Force under Lieutenant-General R. N. O'Connor were 7th Armoured Division, 4th Indian Division,

---

[11] *PWT*, Middle East I, Hist (B), 1, No. 33, p. 18 (7 Jan. 1941).
[12] Cf. Jackson, *Campaign*, 25–5, Pitt, *Crucible*, 61–6.
[13] Playfair, *Mediterranean*, i. 258–9; Pitt, *Crucible*, 81.
[14] Pitt, *Crucible*, 82; Jackson, *Campaign*, 33–4.
[15] *PWT*, Middle East I, Hist (B) 1, No. 24, p. 14 (22 Nov. 1940).

7th Royal Tank Regiment, and the garrison at Marsa Matruh. O'Connor, however, did not know that after the operation, which Wavell estimated would require four or five days, 4th Indian Division would be transferred to the Sudan for the planned campaign in East Africa. In view of the difficult transportation situation, Wavell wanted to take advantage of the opportunity to transfer the division using the ships of a convoy scheduled to return to Britain empty around the Cape of Good Hope. He envisaged 6th Australian Division as a replacement, although it was still not completely trained and equipped.[16]

Facing Western Desert Force was the Italian Tenth Army, since 25 November under General Italo Gariboldi, in several fortified camps south of Sidi Barrani. Subordinate to Tenth Army was Libyan Division Group, which consisted of 1st and 2nd Libyan Divisions and 4th Militia Division '3 Gennaio'. These units held the camps in Sidi Barrani, Maqtalah, Tummayr East and West, and at Point 90. The group also included Twenty-first Army Corps with the Maletti Detachment near Nibeiwa and the partially motorized Cirene Division in the area of Rabiyah and Shaffafah in four camps, as well as the partially motorized Catanzaro Division south-east of Buqbuq.[17]

O'Connor planned to use the 24-kilometre-wide gap in the Italian defences between Nibeiwa and Rabiyah to penetrate the Italian positions and attack the camps at Nibeiwa, Tummar East, and Point 90 from the rear with 4th Indian Division and 7th Royal Tank Regiment, while 7th Armoured Division was to shield the attackers in the direction of Buqbuq and Shaffafah. The Indian division would then advance against Sidi Barrani. The Royal Navy planned to support Operation Compass by bombarding Italian positions near the coast between Sollum and Maqtalah. Against the 327 largely obsolete combat-ready aircraft of the Regia Aeronautica (the Italian air command), the Royal Air Force had only 192 aircraft. Because of Britain's decision to help Greece, Longmore was unable to provide more, although he had largely stripped other areas of his command of air cover. However, among his aircraft were two squadrons of Hurricane fighters, which gave the British air supremacy.[18]

As the railway line from Alexandria ended at Marsa Matruh, and O'Connor did not have sufficient vehicles to transport his troops and their supplies the remaining 160 kilometres to the Italian positions, he ordered two supply-

---

[16] Cf. Playfair, *Mediterranean*, i. 259, 265. On Wavell's decision to start the campaign in East Africa and the influence of the fighting in North Africa cf. Lewin, *The Chief*, 74–6.

[17] Moreover, XXIII Army Corps was subordinate to Tenth Army; it included 1st Militia Division '23 Marzo' in Bardia, 2nd Militia Division '28 Ottobre' in the area of Sollum–Halfaya, and Marmarica Division between Sidi Umar and Jabr Bu Faras, which had pushed advance units to the escarpment south of Halfaya. Cf. Playfair, *Mediterranean*, i. 265; *Prima offensiva*, i. 77–84, 93–8. The new, revised edition by Mantonari, *Le operazioni in Africa settentrionale*, is based largely on *Prima offensiva* but devotes more space to the relevant literature. For the deployment and subsequent movements cf. Map V.I.1.

[18] Playfair, *Mediterranean*, i. 260–4; *Prima offensiva*, i. 84–7. On the Italian air force during the British offensive cf. Santoro, *L'aeronautica italiana*, i. 292–323.

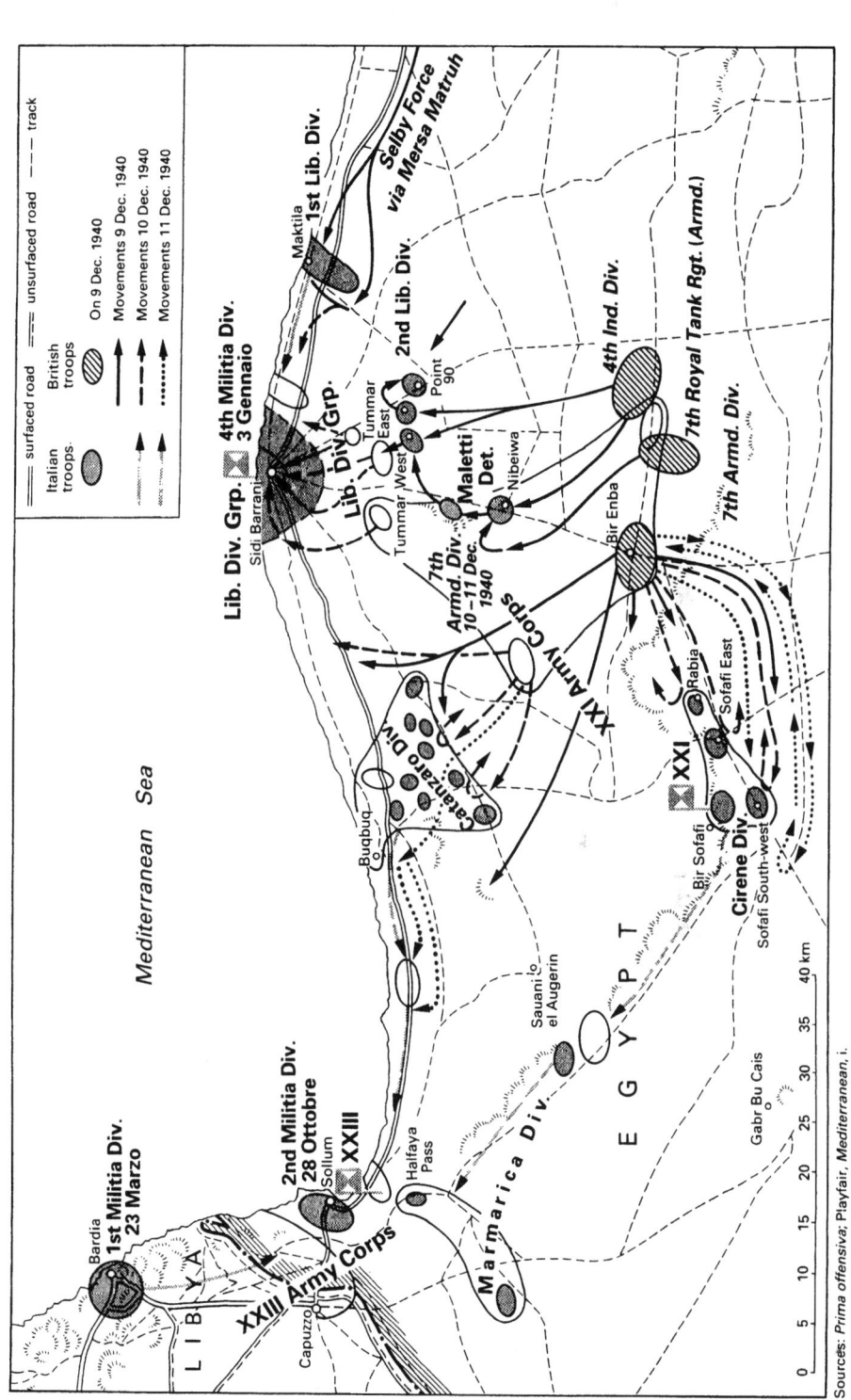

MAP V.I.I. The Battle of Sidi Barrani, 9–11 December 1940

Sources: *Prima offensiva*; Playfair, *Mediterranean*, i.

depots to be constructed approximately eighty kilometres west of Marsa Matruh, although this increased the danger that the Italians might discover his intentions, while the success of Operation Compass was wholly dependent on achieving initial surprise. Nevertheless, by means of considerable activity on the ground and in the air as well as extensive security measures, O'Connor was able to prevent the enemy from gaining any insight into his preparations.

The morale of the British troops was good and they were generally well equipped. Their 25-pounder gun (102 mm.) was clearly superior to the 75-mm. gun of the Italians. The forty-eight Matilda close-support tanks of 7th Royal Tank Regiment gave the British a special advantage, as the Italians had no effective defensive weapons against them. Apart from light armoured reconnaissance vehicles, the British distinguished between two types of tank—the fast but lightly armoured Cruiser[19] and the slower but heavily armoured close-support or infantry tank.[20] O'Connor, Wilson, and Wavell placed their hopes in the Matildas.[21]

The British attackers achieved complete tactical and operational surprise. The Italians had indeed noticed several of the British preparations but had interpreted them wrongly and did not expect an attack at that time.[22] Western Desert Force was able to reach its line of departure without being discovered and to pass through the gap between Nibeiwa and Rabiyah unnoticed in the night of 8–9 December. While Selby Force from Marsa Matruh, supported by the coastal bombardment of the Royal Navy, attacked Maqtalah from the east, the attack of the Matildas from the west, supported by units of the Indian division, began along the unmined access-road to the camp at Nibeiwa at 7.15 a.m. As expected, the Italians were not able to mount an effective defence and had to stop fighting after four hours. Using the same tactic the British captured Tummayr West in the afternoon; Tummayr East fell the next morning.[23]

In the meantime, the armoured division secured the flank of the attack in the direction of Rabiyah and Shaffafah and cut the coastal road west of Sidi Barrani. Together with parts of the Indian division it was able to capture that town on 10 December. The Italian forces further east surrendered the next day. On 11 December the armoured division was able to capture the Italian camps in the area of Buqbuq. While most of Catanzaro Division was taken prisoner, Cirene Division was able to withdraw to the west in time from the area of Rabiyah and Shaffafah. The first phase of Operation Compass was

---

[19] Cruiser tank Mark I (A9): 18.5 t., armour 6–14 mm., 150 hp, 38 km./h. max. speed, 1, 2-pounder anti-tank gun; 3 machine guns, 6-man crew.
[20] Infantry tank Mark II (Matilda II): 26.5 t., armour 20–78 mm., 174 hp, 24 km./h. max. speed, 1, 2-pounder anti-tank gun, 1 machine-gun, 4-man crew.
[21] Cf. Jackson, *Campaign*, 29–30; Pitt, *Crucible*, 86–7.
[22] Cf. Hinsley, *British Intelligence*, i. 375.
[23] For details of the fighting cf. Playfair, *Mediterranean*, i. 266–75; Pitt, *Crucible*, 102–17; *Prima offensiva*, i. 102–6.

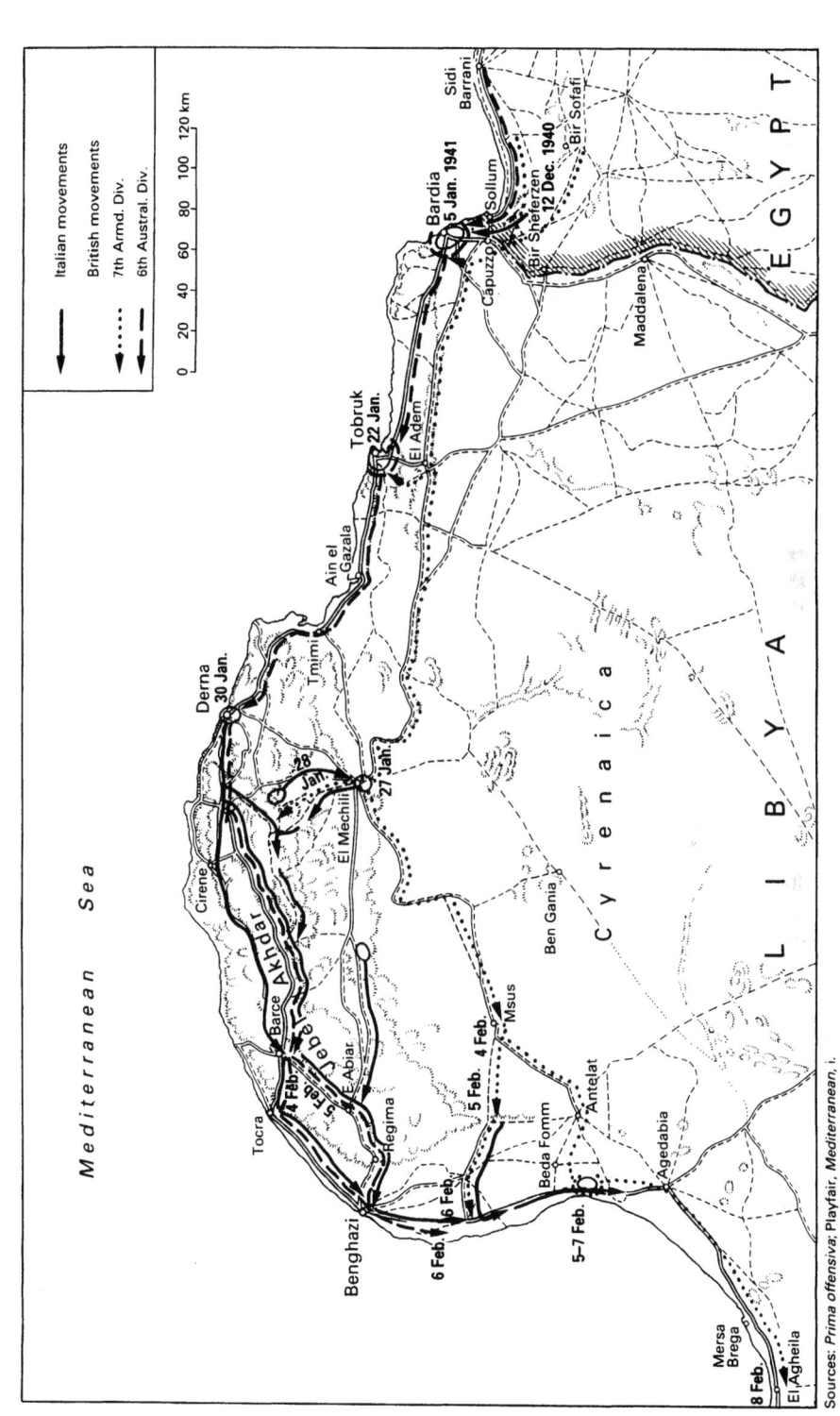

MAP V.I.2. The British Advance to Al Uqaylah, 12 December 1940–8 February 1941

successfully concluded: O'Connor's forces had taken 38,300 Italians prisoner and captured 237 artillery pieces, 73 tanks, and over 1,000 lorries, at a cost of only 624 British casualties. At the same time O'Connor was surprised to learn that 4th Indian Division, except its 16th Infantry Brigade, would be transferred to the Sudan to take part in the campaign in East Africa and that, to make up for this reduction of his forces, he would be given 16th Australian Infantry Brigade as the first part of 6th Australian Division. Nevertheless, he was determined to continue the offensive into Cyrenaica. In this decision he was supported not only by his commander-in-chief in Cairo, but also by Churchill, who expected great things from a continuation of the offensive.[24]

The objective of the subsequent operation was the port of Bardiyah, but first the supply-system had to be organized over the constantly increasing distance from the original line of departure. New supply-depots were established along the escarpment and the coast, and the small port of Sollum, which the Italians had evacuated, was put back into operation. Nevertheless, the supply situation remained strained, especially as regards water.

Marshal Graziani had at first ordered Tenth Army to defend Bardiyah and Tobruk, but then he concluded that it would be better to concentrate his forces in Tobruk, which had been strongly fortified. Mussolini, however, insisted on stopping the British as far to the east as possible in order to be able to send new units to North Africa from Italy.[25] For this reason XXIII Corps under General Annibale Bergonzoli was to defend Bardiyah with four divisions: 1st and 2nd Militia Divisions, '23 Marzo' and '28 Ottobre', and the two partially motorized divisions Marmarica and Cirene, a total of approximately 45,000 men with 430 artillery pieces of various sizes and twelve M 13 medium tanks.[26]

General O'Connor, who estimated Italian strength to be half this level, brought up 16th and 17th Australian Brigades west and south of Bardiyah, while 7th Armoured Division secured the north-west approaches, ready to half the Italians if they tried to break out to the west. The attack began on 3 January, again supported by air attacks and coastal bombardment. Although it was not against field fortifications and the British now had only twenty-three Matilda tanks, the Italians in Bardiyah had to surrender after three days of fighting. XIII Corps, the new designation for Western Desert Force since 1 January, suffered only 130 dead and 326 wounded.[27]

While the fighting in Bardiyah was continuing, 7th Armoured Division pushed on to Al Adam on 5 January in order to cut Tobruk off from the west. The Australians reached the eastern front of Tobruk on the morning of

---

[24] *PWT*, Middle East I, Hist (B), 1, No. 29, p. 16 (17 Dec. 1940). On the development of the fighting cf. *Prima offensiva*, i. 109–15.

[25] *Prima offensiva*, i. 133–4, 315 ff.

[26] Cf. Playfair, *Mediterranean*, i. 281–2; Jackson, *Campaign*, 54; *Prima offensiva*, i. 127 ff., 143 ff.; see also Map V.I.2.

[27] Taysen, *Tobruk*, 39; *Prima offensiva*, i. 145–54.

V.I. The British Take the Offensive in North and East Africa

7 January; the fortress was encircled. O'Connor prepared his attack, but Churchill's intentions in Greece now began to endanger his further plans. If the Greek government accepted the British offer to transfer Royal Air Force and army units, including tanks and artillery, to Greece, that would mean the end of the offensive in Cyrenaica. On 11 January Churchill informed Wavell that Tobruk must be captured, but thereafter help for Greece would be given priority over operations in Libya.[28] At a conference in Athens on 13 January the Greeks fortunately declined such British help; Wavell's suggestion that the British forces in North Africa should push on to Benghazi was therefore accepted.[29]

First, however, the British captured Tobruk and took 25,000 Italians prisoner. They also captured 208 guns and 87 tanks, while suffering just over 400 casualties.[30] The 7th Armoured Division continued its advance westward towards Zawiyat Al Mukhayla. One day earlier Wavell had been informed by the chiefs of staff in London that the capture of Benghazi was of the utmost importance. It was to be turned into a strongly defended naval and air-base. Moreover, Wavell was instructed to prepare the capture of Rhodes in order to deprive the Luftwaffe of the ability to operate in the eastern Mediterranean from the Dodecanese. He was also to form a strategic reserve of four divisions in order, if necessary, to be able to help Greece and Turkey. In addition, the defence of Malta continued to be the primary task of the Royal Air Force.[31] Two days later Wavell was instructed to work out plans and make preparations to occupy Sicily, possibly after the operation against Rhodes.[32]

But Wavell hardly had time to concern himself with such unrealistic instructions, which completely ignored the actual relationship of forces in his theatre. He also had to keep an eye on the campaign against the Italians in East Africa. The liberation of Ethiopia was not merely a desirable objective in itself. The British government also hoped that it would have a deterrent effect on the Japanese and greatly simplify the transport of supplies to Egypt if the Red Sea were no longer a war-zone and was therefore open to American ships. In January the British noticed that the Italians had begun to withdraw from the frontier with the Sudan. In view of the Italian defeats in North Africa, the Duke of Aosta believed that his troops would not be able to hold their forward positions against a British attack. Wavell therefore ordered operations in East Africa to be started early, on 19 January, to block the Italian withdrawal.[33] As he was constantly being given new tasks and changing priorities, it is understandable that Wavell found it difficult to discern a clear direction and objectives in Churchill's policy and thus to allocate his limited forces wisely

---

[28] *PWT*, Middle East I, Hist (B) 1, No. 44, pp. 24–5.
[29] Ibid., No. 59, pp. 33–4. Cf. also Lewin, *The Chief*, 82–5; III.I.2 above (Vogel).
[30] Playfair, *Mediterranean*, i. 293. On the battle of Tobruk cf. *Prima offensiva*, i. 169–94.
[31] *PWT*, Middle East I, Hist (B) 1, No. 62, p. 35 (21 Feb. 1941).
[32] Ibid., No. 65, p. 36 (24 Jan. 1941).
[33] Cf. Playfair, *Mediterranean*, i. 391–6; Jackson, *Campaign*, 62–3.

and conclude his operations successfully. This is especially important in analysing the conquest of Cyrenaica by General O'Connor and the end of the operations there.

After the fall of Tobruk, the Italian Tenth Army still had approximately 5,000 men near Darnah and 14,000 men with 254 guns and 57 medium tanks—most of them in two infantry regiments, a motorized unit, and an armoured brigade—in the Al Qubbah–Al Mukhayla sector.[34] Units of the British 7th Armoured Division encountered this brigade north of Al Mukhayla on 24 January. O'Connor now planned to encircle and annihilate the Italians, but General Babini, the brigade commander, was able to withdraw his forces to the north-west in the night of 26 January. Derna was attacked by the Australians and, after hard fighting, abandoned by the Italians on 29 January.

O'Connor was now approaching the mountainous region of Jabal Akhdar and paused to consider how to continue his operations. He ordered one brigade to be detached from the Australians, who were to continue the direct advance to Benghazi in the coastal region. With the armoured division and the detached Australian infantry brigade, he wanted to push 200 kilometres through the desert to Zawiyat Masus and either attack Benghazi from the south or, if the Italians attempted to evacuate Cyrenaica, to block their retreat along the coastal road. The drive was to begin between 10 and 12 February, but first the supply-system via Tobruk had to be organized and new depots established. Moreover, O'Connor was waiting for two regiments of 2nd Armoured Division; 7th Armoured Division now had only fifty Cruisers, all of which were in need of maintenance.[35]

In the meantime Marshal Graziani had realized how dangerous the situation in Cyrenaica had become for his troops. On 1 February he informed Mussolini of his decision to withdraw to Sirte in Tripolitania. He placed General Tellera, who had been commander-in-chief of Tenth Army since 23 December 1940, in charge of carrying out the retreat and transferred his own headquarters from Benghazi to Tripoli two days later. Additional factors that influenced his decision were the appearance of British and Free French forces in southern Libya, concern over the attitude of the Vichy French in North Africa, and fears that the British might land in the French possessions there.[36]

On 2 February the Royal Air Force reported the Italian withdrawal, which forced O'Connor to take a new decision. He could wait no longer and therefore ordered 7th Armoured Division to advance through the desert on the morning of 4 February. At noon on 5 February the vanguard of the division reached the coastal road south-west of Bayda Fumm, just in time to stop a withdrawing Italian column. In the subsequent fighting, which continued until the morning of 7 February, the Italians, in spite of several attempts, were not able to break

---

[34] *Prima offensiva*, i. 208–10.
[35] Playfair, *Mediterranean*, i. 354–6.
[36] *Prima offensiva*, i. 230–1; Taysen, *Tobruk*, 49–50.

V.I. The British Take the Offensive in North and East Africa 653

through the British position in large numbers, although the British, whose stocks of ammunition and fuel were low, were several times in danger of being overrun by the sheer numbers of the enemy. When the fighting stopped, 7th Armoured Division had only twelve Cruisers fit for action,[37] but the Italian Tenth Army had been destroyed. Only 8,300 Italian soldiers, carrying only light weapons, were able to fight their way through to Tripolitania.

Since the initial attack near Sidi Barrani on 9 December, XIII British Corps with two divisions had defeated ten Italian divisions, taken 130,000 prisoners, and captured 180 medium and more than 200 light tanks as well as 845 medium and heavy artillery pieces. British losses were 500 dead, 1,373 wounded, and 55 missing.[38] Moreover, the British had now reached Tripolitania. The question presented itself whether Wavell and O'Connor would be permitted to continue their offensive and drive the Italians completely out of North Africa. O'Connor in any case wanted to take advantage of the opportunity and extended his reconnaissance to Tripolitania. In the course of this action he captured El Uqaylah on 8 February. But Churchill's decision to halt operations in North Africa temporarily and assemble forces to intervene in Greece had already been taken.[39]

This decision was to have very serious consequences, for the forces sent to Greece were too weak to stop the German invasion of that country, and in trying to do so they lost the greater part of their equipment, as had the British troops in Norway and France. Moreover, Churchill's decision gave the Germans the opportunity to intervene successfully in North Africa, and two years were to pass before the British, together with the Americans, were able to achieve the final victory there which had been so near in February 1941.[40]

The success of Operation Compass and the elimination of the Italian Tenth Army did, however, create the decisive conditions for an offensive against the Italians in East Africa. On 19 January the troops of Major-General W. Platt, including 4th Indian Division, had begun their attack from the Sudan. They were so successful that Wavell ordered them on 3 February to capture the strategic towns of Keren and Asmera. On 21 January Emperor Haile Selassie returned to his country to lead the resistance against the Italians, while Major-General Alan Cunningham began the offensive from Kenya with the capture of Afmadow on 11 February.[41] This event marked the beginning of the end of Italian rule in East Africa. As relief was no longer possible from Libya, to say nothing of co-ordinated operations against Egypt from the south and west, it was only a question of time before the Duke of Aosta's isolated troops would have to lay down their arms.

---

[37] Cf. Taysen, *Tobruk*, 52.

[38] Figures according to Playfair, *Mediterranean*, i. 362. The Italians suspected that the figure of 130,000 prisoners included civilians. Cf. *Prima offensiva*, i. 280.

[39] Cf. III.I.2 above (Vogel); Pitt, *Crucible*, 192–3; Taysen, *Tobruk*, 52–3.

[40] On the criticism of Churchill's decision and Wavell's change of mind cf. Barclay, *Their Finest Hour*, 61–83; Lewin, *Churchill*, 55–7, 65–7; id., *The Chief*, 92–116.

[41] Playfair, *Mediterranean*, i. 400–1, 406, 412. Cf. also Map I.III.2.

II. German Intervention and its Effects on the Naval and Air War in the Mediterranean

THE German decision to intervene in the Mediterranean had a varied history, reaching back to the summer of 1940; it has been presented in detail elsewhere.[1] Plans for the Luftwaffe were developed first, even before the British began their offensive in North Africa. On 5 December 1940, during a discussion of the situation, Hitler informed the commander-in-chief of the army, Field Marshal von Brauchitsch, that he wanted to transfer two Gruppen of Ju 87s and two of Ju 88s to Sicily and southern Italy to attack the British fleet in the eastern Mediterranean, starting on 15 December. On the other hand, at that time he no longer planned to send German army units to North Africa.[2]

But the Italian defeats in North Africa and Mussolini's urgent requests for assistance caused Hitler to revise his judgement of the situation. On 9 January at the Berghof he revealed to the senior officers of the Wehrmacht his intention to help the Italians by sending an armoured blocking force to Libya. The first units of this force were to leave on 22 February.[3] Hitler did not regard the threatened loss of Libya as a serious military setback, but he did fear that its effect on public opinion in Italy could lead to the fall of Mussolini and the end of the Axis.

Hitler believed that the Italian defeats in North Africa were due to the lack of modern armour-piercing weapons; consequently the German force was to consist of anti-tank, armoured, and engineer troops. X Air Corps under Luftwaffe General Hans Geisler, which was transferred to Sicily, was ordered, in addition to attacking British naval forces and east–west sea routes, to provide direct support for the Italians in North Africa by attacking British unloading-ports and supply-bases near the coast in western Egypt and Cyrenaica.[4] But the establishment of the necessary ground-support organization and the transfer of 14,385 men and 307 aircraft required more time than expected: on 9 January, one day before the first attacks were flown, only 156 German aircraft had arrived in Italy.[5]

---

[1] See I.III.2 above (Schreiber).
[2] Cf. *KTB OKW* i. 204; Halder, *KTB* ii. 211 (5 Dec. 1940; not in trans.); Greiner, *Oberste Wehrmachtführung*, 324.
[3] *KTB OKW* i. 253–4; Halder, *Diaries*, i. 752 (16 Jan. 1941). For details of the changing and divergent objectives of the leading German government agencies and the military services with regard to North Africa cf. Reuth, *Entscheidung*.
[4] *Hitler's War Directives*, No. 22, pp. 53–4 (11 Jan. 1941).
[5] Cf. Gundelach, *Luftwaffe im Mittelmeer*, 97–9; Santoni and Mattesini, *La partecipazione tedesca*, 28–33.

The situation in North Africa deteriorated rapidly; British forces were already attacking Darnah and Zawiyat al Mukhayla. Cyrenaica fell to the British much sooner than expected, and it seemed doubtful that German help would arrive in time to defend Tripolitania effectively. On 1 February Major-General Hans von Funck, commander of 5th Light Division, which it was planned to send to Libya as the blocking force, reported to Hitler on his impressions during a visit to his future operational area. In Tripolitania Marshal Graziani now had only four divisions, without artillery, which were occupied with building defensive positions around Tripoli. He considered a defence further east impossible.[6] In view of this situation, Funck did not think his light division would be sufficient to prevent a catastrophe in Libya. He demanded at least one armoured division in order to conduct his defence by attacking the enemy and reconquering Cyrenaica. On the other hand, he believed that the German forces would arrive in North Africa too late.

Hitler also believed that a defence limited to the area around Tripoli would be impossible. Before taking a final decision, he wanted to know what the Luftwaffe would be able to do to slow the British advance in Cyrenaica and how the Italian high command itself judged the situation in North Africa: what forces it wanted to use, what orders Marshal Graziani had received, and how he intended to carry them out. Hitler stopped all transports to Naples and from there to Tripoli until he received answers to his questions.

On 3 February, at a conference with representatives of the Wehrmacht, the army, and the Luftwaffe high commands,[7] Hitler announced his decision. First he explained that the loss of Libya would be militarily bearable, but he feared that Italy might then leave the war, which would free the strong British forces in the Mediterranean for duty in other areas and reduce Germany's position there to the south coast of France. For these reasons it was necessary to help the Italians in North Africa. Success there might even make a campaign in the Balkans unnecessary.

It was envisaged to establish a corps command for Libya, to which the mobile Italian forces would also be subordinate. Nothing was known of Marshal Graziani's orders and intentions, but the Italians had informed Hitler that Tripolitania could be defended with the forces planned. As far as possible the Luftwaffe should intervene immediately in North Africa, protect transports to that theatre, and attempt to put Malta out of action as a British base. The army was ordered to speed up the transport of the blocking force, which was to be strengthened by the addition of an armoured regiment, and to prepare to send an armoured division later. Brauchitsch pointed out that the division would then not be able to take part in the planned campaign against

---

[6] *KTB OKW* i. 292–4; Halder, *Diaries*, i. 769–70 (1 Feb. 1941). Graziani's 5th Army consisted of X Army Corps, with the Bologna and Savona Divisions, and XX Army Corps, with the Brescia and Pavia Divisions. For details cf. *Prima controffensiva*, 7–10.

[7] Cf. *KTB OKW* i. 300–2; Halder, *Diaries*, i. 770–1 (3 Feb. 1941).

the Soviet Union.[8] This remark raised a basic question, as to which, however, Hitler and the army high command were of the same opinion at that time. As long as it was believed that the conquest of the Soviet Union would be a decisive turning-point in the war, it was only natural and logical to concentrate all available forces on achieving that objective and to minimize as far as possible German involvement in secondary theatres.

The same day, 3 February, Lieutenant-General Erwin Rommel was named 'commander of German army troops in Libya'.[9] On 6 February Hitler and Brauchitsch briefed him on his new tasks.[10] He and Major-General von Rintelen were given the same guidelines for their conferences with the Italian high command and Marshal Graziani. The German leaders rejected the defence of a fortified camp near Tripoli as futile and did not want to provide any forces for such an effort. Instead, most of the Italian infantry divisions should be used to establish a defensive front near Buyarat on the Gulf of Sidra (Sirte), behind whose right wing the German and Italian mobile units would be assembled to repel any further British advance with the support of the Luftwaffe and the Italian air force.

These guidelines also formed the basis for the 'Order for the Transfer of Army Troops to Tripolitania', which the army high command issued on 10 February after the Italian government had expressed its agreement with the German plans.[11] Tactically the German troops in Libya would be directly subordinate to the Italian commander-in-chief there; otherwise their subordination to the commander-in-chief of the German army did not change. Their commander was instructed to co-operate with X Air Corps, which itself remained directly subordinate to the commander-in-chief of the Luftwaffe.

On 10 February Rommel arrived in Rome, where the Italians again confirmed Mussolini's acceptance of the German plans. After X Air Corps had agreed to carry out stronger attacks on the British units south of Benghazi, Rommel landed in Tripoli on 12 February, one day after the first German sea-transport group had arrived. General Gariboldi—successor to Marshal Graziani, who had resigned as commander-in-chief in Libya—did not agree at first to the German defence plan and accepted it only when General Roatta brought him a direct order from the Comando Supremo.[12] Finally, it was agreed to expand the defensive position further east near Sirte and to extend reconnaissance to An Nawfaliyah.[13]

---

[8] As early as 27 Jan. Halder expressed the view with regard to Libya that 'we cannot cut any further into resources for Barbarossa': Halder, *Diaries*, i. 762.

[9] Cf. Taysen, *Tobruk*, 47–8.

[10] Ibid. 53–4; *KTB OKW* i. 308; Halder, *Diaries*, i. 772–3 (7 Feb. 1941). According to Halder, the conference with Rommel took place in the office of the C.-in-C. of the army on 7 Feb. 1941.

[11] Cf. *KTB OKW* i. 321; Taysen, *Tobruk*, 54.

[12] Cf. Rommel, *Papers*, 100–1.

[13] Rintelen to army general staff/Att.Abt., 14 Feb. 1941, BA-MA H 27/43. On the change in the Italian high command on 10 Feb. 1941 cf. *Prima controffensiva*, 8.

Major-General Johannes Streich was appointed the new commander of 5th Light Division, and on 19 February the Wehrmacht high command ordered that the armoured corps to be sent to Libya should be given the name 'Deutsches Afrika-Korps' (German Africa Corps). This marked the completion of preparations for German intervention in Africa, which received the name 'Unternehmen Sonnenblume' (Operation Sunflower). A battle with shifting fortunes began for North Africa, in which Rommel and the Africa Corps were to play a dominant role.[14]

The Mediterranean was no longer only an Italian theatre of war, but the joint strategy was limited to defence. The German Balkan campaign and the engagement in North Africa had become necessary because the Italians had completely misjudged the situation in their decisions of summer and autumn 1940, and it was evidently not possible to prevent the loss of these areas to the British in any other way.[15] At the end of 1940 and the beginning of 1941, however, Hitler and the Wehrmacht and army high commands were primarily interested in the campaign against the Soviet Union, which had already been decided upon. Rommel, on the other hand, expressed the view later that the Balkan campaign would have been superfluous if the army and Luftwaffe units committed there had been sent to North Africa. With strong motorized units he wanted to drive the British from the coasts of the Mediterranean and secure the Middle East as a source of oil and a base for the attack on the Soviet Union.[16]

In this regard it should be noted that the German military leaders intended to use the bulk of the army and Luftwaffe units assembled for the Balkan campaign later in the Soviet Union. Had they been tied down in North Africa and the Middle East, it would not have been possible to start Operation Barbarossa. Moreover, in Libya only the port of Tripoli was available at first, and its capacity was limited. For this reason, in January 1941 the army high command calculated the time required to transport 5th Light Division to North Africa at forty-two days.[17]

Benghazi and Tobruk had even less unloading capacity than Tripoli, and at that time they were in British hands. Clearly an enormous transport operation was required, the difficulty of which would increase in proportion to the number of German troops sent to Africa and the distance they advanced eastward. And the British would certainly not have watched such an operation without intervening. Fifty-eight thousand British and Empire troops were transferred from Egypt to Greece in March 1941 only because German armies

---

[14] On Rommel's arrival in North Africa cf. Taysen, *Tobruk*, 55–6; Behrendt, *Afrikafeldzug*, 34–7.
[15] Cf. Rintelen, *Mussolini als Bundesgenosse*, 127.
[16] Cf. Rommel, *Papers*, 119ff., 514–15.
[17] OKM/A VI s 283/41 g.Kdos. (27 Jan. 1941) to Mar.Verb.-Stab, Rom, Seetransportchef Italien, BA-MA CASE GE 1793, PG 33092. On the transport and supply problems in the Africa campaign in 1941 in general cf. Creveld, *Supplying War*, 182–92.

had been deployed along Greece's northern frontier and not, as Rommel desired, sent to the Libyan desert.

But even the transport of an initial single division, as envisaged in the concrete German plans, required extensive preparations. They had been started in the autumn of 1940, when Hitler wanted to support the expected Italian advance to the Nile with an armoured division.[18] The 3rd Armoured Division, which was chosen for this task, calculated its transport requirements at sixty freighter loadings for approximately 18,000 men and 4,087 vehicles.[19] Moreover, the Luftwaffe had its own assumed transport requirements for 10,516 men and 1,672 vehicles with a total weight of about 130,000 GRT.[20] The Italian navy was not able to provide this capacity, as most of its transport ships were being used to carry supplies to Italian troops in Albania and Libya. The German navy therefore wanted to use German freighters in the Mediterranean that had taken refuge in Italian ports at the beginning of the war. In October the navy high command had selected seventeen ships which the Italians were to prepare for the planned operation.[21] To clarify the related problems a naval commission under Captain von Montigny was sent to Rome and negotiated with representatives of the transport office of the Italian navy high command from 28 to 30 October 1940.[22] In the negotiations it became clear that only two German ships could be unloaded at a time in Tripoli, a process which took approximately two days. The Italians suggested that the Germans should request permission from the Vichy government to use the port of Tunis, although that would lengthen the supply-lines in North Africa itself by 600 kilometres. This idea was taken up again later, and German units actually landed in Tunis on 9 November 1942, but under completely changed conditions: by that time the Allies had landed in Morocco and Algeria.

On 9 January 1941, when Hitler decided to send a blocking force to North Africa to defend Tripoli instead of the originally envisaged help for the advance to Egypt, the earlier plans and preparations greatly facilitated the rapid realization of the necessary measures. The navy expanded its organization in the Mediterranean by establishing transport offices in Brindisi, Durrës, Naples, and Tripoli under a 'head of transport offices abroad' and liaison officer with the naval liaison staff in Rome.[23] It was now planned to carry out the transfer of 5th Light Division to North Africa with sixteen ships. A group of four ships would have to leave Naples every three days; then the transfer could be completed within forty-five days from the first loading until the return of the last ship. It was calculated that a crossing would require three

---

[18] Cf. I.III.2 (*b*) above (Schreiber).
[19] 3. Pz.Div., Ia No. 01269/40 g.Kdos. (1 Nov. 1940), to OKM, Abt. A VI, BA-MA CASE GE 1793, PG 33092.
[20] Ibid., ObdL, Gen.Stab, Gen.Qu. 4. Abt. (III) No. 5824/40 g.Kdos. (24 Oct. 1940), to OKW/1. Skl.
[21] Ibid., OKM, A VI s, 2460/40 g.Kdos. (25 Oct. 1940), to Skl.
[22] Ibid., Montigny to Skl. with final protocol (31 Oct. 1940) (15948/40 g.Kdos.).
[23] Ibid., OKM, A II ao 89/41 g.Kdos., express letter (23 Jan. 1941).

days and an unloading in Tripoli three days more, with the simultaneous use of two berths (one and a half days for every two ships).[24] The first group put to sea on 8 February.

At that time, however, it was already known that the transfer would not be completed with the return of the tenth sea-transport group. The transfer of an armoured regiment and the units assigned to it to North Africa, ordered by Hitler on 3 February, required five additional groups of ships.[25] And the sending of an entire armoured division was not even considered in these calculations. Thus the number of transports required continued to rise. On 25 February the first five groups of ships brought 7,232 men, 2,366 vehicles, and approximately 4,000 tonnes of cargo to Tripoli; in the meantime the numbers of men and vehicles scheduled to be sent to North Africa had risen to 22,626 and 5,827 respectively.[26] With the arrival of the ninth group of ships in Tripoli on 10 March, the total transport figures rose to 12,920 men, 4,074 vehicles, and 10,560 tonnes of supplies.[27] The transfer of 5th Light Division was finally concluded at the beginning of April.

The protection provided by the German navy for the ships was limited to equipping each of them with two 20-mm. anti-aircraft guns.[28] Otherwise the Italian navy, supported by the Italian air force and X Air Corps, was generally responsible for protecting the convoys.[29] Rear-Admiral Weichold, head of the naval liaison staff in Rome, soon complained that the necessary close co-operation between the Italian navy and air force and X Air Corps had not been achieved; for this reason aerial reconnaissance for the protection of the German convoys remained completely inadequate. In his view this situation was due to the weakness of the Italian naval air arm, the heavy demands made on X Air Corps by actual combat missions, and the engagement of the Italian air force in Albania and Greece.[30] It proved rather difficult to provide constant cruiser protection against attacks by enemy surface ships, and the Luftwaffe as well as the Italian air force considered it impossible for fighters to defend the convoys against night attacks by torpedo-aircraft.[31] The protection provided for the convoys against enemy submarine attacks, as a rule three torpedo-boats or destroyers, was also quite inadequate.

For these reasons the success of the sea transports to Africa depended to a

---

[24] Ibid., OKM, A VI s 283/41 g.Kdos. (27 Jan. 1941), to Mar.Verb.-Stab Rom, Seetransportchef Italien.
[25] Ibid., OKM/Skl./A VI B. No. 533/41 g.Kdos. (13 Feb. 1941), to OKH/army general staff/Op.Abt. II.
[26] Ibid., Skl./A VI s 767/41 g.Kdos. (25 Feb. 1941), to Skl. (1. Skl. I m).
[27] Ibid., Skl./A VI s 1032/41 g.Kdos. (11 Mar. 1941), to Skl. (1. Skl. I m).
[28] FS Neu Skl./A VI No. 393/41 g.Kdos. (3 Feb. 1941), to Mar.Verb.-Stab Rom, Seetransportchef Rom, ibid.
[29] Ibid., liaison staff with the staff of the Royal Italian Navy to OKM-Skl. (7 Feb. 1941), also 5 Feb. 1941, Weichold papers, BA-MA N 316/v. 36.
[30] KTB Chef des Verb.-Stabes beim Admiralstab der Kgl. ital. Marine (8 Mar. 1941), BA-MA RM 36/16. Cf. Baum and Weichold, *Krieg der 'Achsenmächte'*, 126–8.
[31] Weichold papers (Feb. 1941), BA-MA N 316/v. 36.

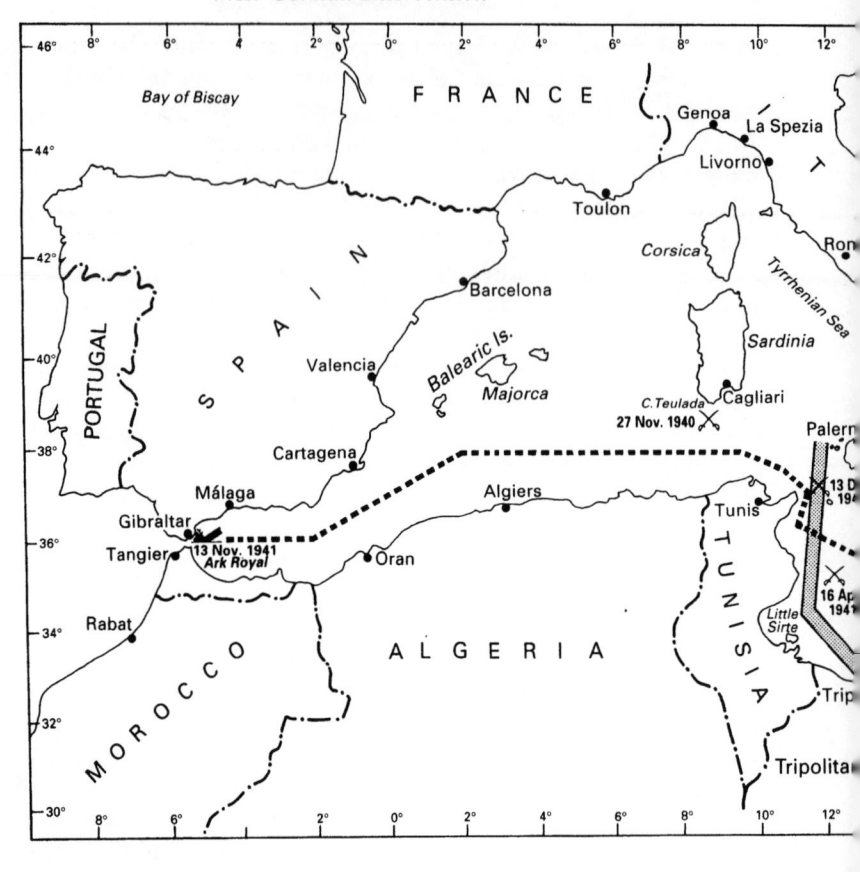

MAP V.II.1. The Mediterranean: General Map Showing Main Events, 1940–1941

considerable degree on the inactivity of the enemy. In practice the transports were stopped when approaching enemy forces were discovered and reported in time, which, however, was often not the case because of inadequate reconnaissance. Whether X Air Corps would be able to eliminate Malta as a base for the Royal Air Force as well as British surface ships and submarines and to deter the British Mediterranean Fleet from operations in the central Mediterranean was another question. The final answer was not so clear as the Axis or the British wished. (For an overview of the problems both sides faced and of events in the Mediterranean in 1940–1 cf. Map V.II.1.)

On 6 January 1941 the British began Operation Excess, in which it was intended to send three ships from Gibraltar to Piraeus and one to Malta. At the same time Admiral Cunningham wanted to send two light cruisers with reinforcements and two freighters with supplies from Alexandria to Malta and bring eight empty freighters back.[32] Protection for the convoys was to be provided by H Force with the battleships *Renown*, *Malaya*, and the aircraft-carrier *Ark Royal*, and the Mediterranean Fleet with the battleships *Warspite* and *Valiant* and the aircraft-carrier *Illustrious*.

In the eastern as well as the western Mediterranean, the British ships were soon discovered by Italian reconnaissance aircraft. Air, torpedo-boat, and U-boat attacks on them on 9 and 10 January, however, resulted only in the loss of an Italian torpedo-boat. In its first appearance in the Mediterranean, X Air Corps was, on the other hand, more successful. Ju 87 dive-bombers achieved six hits on the *Illustrious*, forcing her to seek safety in the harbour at

---

[32] Cf. Roskill, *War at Sea*, i. 421–2; Gundelach, *Luftwaffe im Mittelmeer*, 99–100. On the supplying of Malta and its   for the war against German and Italian supply transports to North Africa cf. Lutton, 'Malta'.

Malta. In the afternoon of 11 January aircraft of X Air Corps damaged the light cruiser *Southampton* so heavily that she had to be abandoned.[33]

In the next two weeks the Luftwaffe attempted to destroy the *Illustrious* in Valletta but was able to achieve only two additional hits. On 23 January the ship, which had been partially repaired, was able to leave Malta and sail via Alexandria to the United States, where she spent the next several months in a shipyard. Although the *Illustrious* had escaped the Stuka dive-bombers and the British had been able to resupply Malta, the Luftwaffe leaders considered the first operations of X Air Corps in the Mediterranean a success. It had indeed been made clear to the British that the air war there had entered a new phase.[34]

That the possibilities of the Luftwaffe in the Mediterranean were not unlimited became clear in the first air attack on the Suez Canal, which was carried out by eight He 111 aircraft from Martubah near Benghazi to relieve pressure on the Italian front. The aircraft did not find the reported convoy, and only one of them returned from the improvised mission without damage.[35] In any case, grand Admiral Raeder's demand that the British fleet had to be 'driven out of the whole Mediterranean, and as far as possible destroyed'[36] could not be fulfilled with the available Axis forces. The Royal Navy soon demonstrated that it was still able to carry out successful and impressive operations in the central Mediterranean.

On 6 February H Force, with the battleship *Malaya*, the battle cruiser *Renown*, the aircraft-carrier *Ark Royal*, the light cruiser *Sheffield*, and ten destroyers, left Gibraltar for the Gulf of Genoa. The departure of the ships was quickly reported, and two days later British carrier-aircraft were sighted 100 kilometres south of Minorca. The Italian naval high command therefore ordered the Italian fleet to put to sea, but air reconnaissance in the central and western Mediterranean provided no new information, as H Force did not steam east, as expected, but took a north-easterly course. The Italian navy least expected an attack on Genoa, and did not even anticipate an operation to resupply Malta. It was assumed that the British would attempt to transport aircraft to the island or repeat the air attack on the dam at Tirso on Sardinia. (The first attack, during the night of 1–2 February, had failed.[37])

Admiral Iachino put to sea from La Spezia with the battleships *Vittorio*

---

[33] For details of the operation see Fechter and Hümmelchen, *Seekriegsatlas*, 30–2; Rohwer and Hümmelchen, *Chronik*, 94–5; Bernotti, *Guerra nel Mediterraneo*, 125 ff.; Santoni and Mattesini, *La partecipazione tedesca*, 33 ff.

[34] Cf. Gundelach, *Luftwaffe im Mittelmeer*, 99–100; Santoni and Mattesini, *La partecipazione tedesca*, 36–7.

[35] Cf. Gundelach, *Luftwaffe im Mittelmeer*, 101; Santoni and Mattesini, *La partecipazione tedesca*, 37–8.

[36] 'Führer Conferences', 155 (14 Nov. 1940) (trans. amended).

[37] For details cf. KTB Chef des Verb.-Stabes Marine, 75–80 (8 and 9 Feb. 1941), BA-MA RM 36/16; 1. Skl., KTB, Teil A, 112–13 (9 Feb. 1941), 125–7 (10 Feb. 1941), BA-MA RM 7/21; Fechter and Hümmelchen, *Seekriegsatlas*, 32; *Marina italiana*, iv. 338–81, esp. 348–9; Bernotti, *Guerra nel Mediterraneo*, 129–36.

Veneto, *Andrea Doria*, and *Giulio Cesare*, escorted by 10th and 13th Destroyer Flotillas. On the morning of 9 February, north-west of Sardinia, he was joined by 3rd Division from Messina, consisting of the heavy cruisers *Bolzano*, *Trento*, and *Trieste* and three destroyers. Earlier, however, H Force had reached its attack position and began to bombard the city and harbour of Genoa. Aircraft from the *Ark Royal* mined the entrance to La Spezia and bombed Livorno. Few military objectives were hit, but Genoa itself suffered considerable damage. More important, because of fog and light haze, Italian aerial reconnaissance was not able to find the British ships when they withdrew towards Gibraltar. Additional confusion was caused by a French convoy headed for Corsica, which at first was assumed to be the British force. And seventy aircraft of X Air Corps, which had set out from Sicily, were also unable to find the enemy before nightfall.

In terms of concrete results, the attack by H Force on Genoa was not a great success for the British; even the dry-docked battleship *Gaio Duilio* remained undamaged. But the psychological effect on the Italians was considerable, as they had just lost Cyrenaica to the British. The German military took advantage of the opportunity to point out to the Italians the chances they had missed; later their failure was even elevated to the level of a supreme mistake.[38]

Rear-Admiral Weichold was not the only German critic. The naval war staff also tried to persuade the Italian naval staff to conduct a more offensive war in the Mediterranean. This was the aim of a meeting with the Italian naval staff scheduled to take place at Merano. As new officers were appointed to the senior positions in the Italian naval staff—Fleet Admiral Riccardi as head of the staff and Admiral Campioni as his deputy—the meeting had to be postponed until 13–14 February.[39] The change in the leadership did not, however, mean a change in the Italian view of the military situation in the Mediterranean. Riccardi was also of the opinion that the Italian navy could not simply adopt without hesitation lessons learnt from Germany's experience in the war. In view of the superior strength of the Royal Navy, Italy had to give priority to defence in order not to endanger the supply-lines of the armies in Greece and North Africa. Riccardi argued that the Italian fleet could only become more active when the Balkan campaign had been concluded and the Italian battleships damaged at Taranto were again ready for action. Moreover, Italian aerial reconnaissance was not sufficient for offensive operations. Riccardo was mainly interested in obtaining material help from the German navy, while Raeder and Fricke, the German naval representatives at the meeting, attempted to persuade the Italians to adopt their idea of offensive operations. And they believed that their efforts had not been completely in

---

[38] Cf. KTB Chef des Verb.-Stabes Marine, 131–2 (21 Feb. 1941), BA-MA RM 36/16; Baum and Weichold, *Krieg der 'Achsenmächte'*, 117–18.

[39] On the talks at Merano cf. Salewski, *Seekriegsleitung*, i. 323–4; Schreiber, *Revisionismus*, 300–92; *Marina italiana*, iv. 382–92; Santoni and Mattesini, *La partecipazione tedesca*, 69 ff.

vain: in their opinion the meeting in Merano gave reason to hope that 'in future Germany will be able to influence naval operations in the Mediterranean more strongly'.[40] German pressure did in fact affect Italian tactics, but the result was exactly the opposite of what the naval war staff wanted to achieve.

Independently of the discussions in Merano, the commander-in-chief of the Italian fleet, Admiral Iachino, had been considering the possibility of attacking British shipping bound for Greece by advancing with a fast naval force to the line between Benghazi and Crete.[41] When the British began to transfer troops from Egypt to Greece on 5 March (Operation Lustre), German pressure on Italy to conduct a more offensive naval war in the Mediterranean increased. Riccardi argued that, at the time, an offensive operation was out of the question, because only one fast battleship was ready for action, Taranto could still not be used as a base, and aerial reconnaissance was still inadequate. Instead, he was considering sending a light cruiser to reinforce the German navy in its cruiser war in the Atlantic.[42] This idea was especially noteworthy, as immediately before the meeting at Merano the German naval war staff had considered sending a heavy cruiser to the Mediterranean; it was hoped that this would motivate the Italians to pursue a 'more active conduct of the war'.[43] Both navies evidently considered it their duty to support each other in their respective theatres.

But after the crews of two He 111s of X Air Corps erroneously reported the torpedoing of two British battleships on 16 March, the naval war staff believed the situation in the Mediterranean to be 'more favourable for the Italian fleet than ever before', and suggested an operation south of Crete 'seriously to disrupt British transport routes and perhaps stop the transports altogether'.[44] The Italians, who actually wanted to undertake an operation, accepted the German assessment of the situation and informed the Germans on 24 March that they had ordered a sweep with one battleship, six heavy and two light cruisers, and three destroyer flotillas in the direction of Crete. X Air Corps was requested to provide support and air cover for the ships on the way to and from the operations area; the Italian air force in the Dodecanese was responsible for air cover in the operations area itself.[45]

The British were not yet able to decipher Italian radio messages at the start of the operation. But from other sources, among them the radio traffic of the

---

[40] 1. Skl., KTB, Teil A, 324 (24 Feb. 1941), BA-MA RM 7/21.
[41] *Marina italiana*, iv. 393.
[42] KTB Chef des Verb.-Stabes Marine, 63–4 (13 Mar. 1941), BA-MA RM 36/16.
[43] 1. Skl., KTB, Teil A, 214 (17 Feb. 1941), BA-MA RM 7/21. On the difficulties of the German and Italian navy leaders in agreeing on an effective conduct of the war at sea cf. Schreiber, *Revisionismus*, 309–29.
[44] KTB Chef des Verb.-Stabes Marine, 31 (19 Mar. 1941), BA-MA RM 36/19. Additional literature and source references in Baum and Weichold, *Krieg der 'Achsenmächte'*, 118–24.
[45] Cf. Salewski, *Seekriegsleitung*, i. 327–9; Gundelach, *Luftwaffe im Mittelmeer*, 114–15. For an italian account cf. *Marina italiana*, iv. 392–512; Santoni and Mattesini, *La partecipazione tedesca*, 71–2.

Luftwaffe, they had learnt that an operation was planned in the eastern Mediterranean for 28 March. They did not, however, know any details. Admiral Cunningham was warned, and he stopped all convoys to Greece, sent a cruiser force to the area south of Crete, and ordered the Mediterranean Fleet to put to sea on the evening of 27 March.[46]

The units of the Italian fleet involved in the operation put to sea on 26 and 27 March and assembled east of Sicily in two groups the next morning. The first group included the battleship *Vittorio Veneto*, the heavy cruisers *Trento*, *Trieste*, and *Bolzano*, and seven destroyers; the second consisted of the three heavy cruisers *Pola*, *Zara*, and *Fiume* with the two light cruisers *Garibaldi* and *Abruzzi* and six destroyers. This cruiser force was sighted and reported by a British Sunderland flying-boat at 12.35 p.m. The message was, however, intercepted by the Italians and passed on to the commander-in-chief of the fleet, Iachino, the same evening. The operation could no longer be successfully carried out, as a surprise attack on the convoys from Egypt to Greece was no longer possible, and countermeasures had to be expected from the British Mediterranean Fleet. Moreover, according to Iachino, before the Italian fleet put to sea on 26 March X Air Corps had informed the Italian naval high command that aerial photographs had shown the Mediterranean Fleet, with three battleships and an aircraft-carrier, to be off the coast of North Africa on 24 March. But the Italian naval high command evidently did not realize the importance of this report; in any case the commander-in-chief of the fleet was not informed. And neither the Italian naval high command, nor the commander-in-chief of the fleet, nor the German naval war staff considered the report on the position of the Italian cruiser force to be a sufficient reason to cancel the operation.[47]

On 28 March at 6.35 a.m. a seaplane from the *Vittorio Veneto* sighted B Force, the British cruiser force under Vice-Admiral Pridham-Wippell with four light cruisers—*Orion*, *Ajax*, *Perth*, and *Gloucester*—and four destroyers. But A Force under Admiral Cunningham, with three battleships—*Warspite*, *Valiant*, and *Barham*—the aircraft-carrier *Formidable*, and nine destroyers, was not discovered. Iachino pursued the British cruisers, which turned eastward. A running battle at long range followed, without, however, producing any results. Finally the Italians turned around at 8.51 a.m., followed by the British ships, which maintained visual contact. At 11.00 a.m. Iachino reversed his course again and attempted to open fire on the British ships from two

---

[46] Cf. Hinsley, *British Intelligence*, i. 404–6.

[47] Cf. Maugeri, *From the Ashes*, 22–3; Baum and Weichold, *Krieg der 'Achsenmächte'*, 121; 1. Skl., KTB, Teil A, 384 (27 Mar. 1941), BA-MA RM 7/22. For the view of the C.-in-C. of the Italian fleet on this question cf. Iachino, *Tramonto*, 137–8, 257–61; id., *Sorpresa*. In fact the British had intercepted two radio messages on 26 Mar., in which 'Rome' informed the Italian fleet that two battleships were at sea near Crete (12.00 a.m.) and then changed the number to two or three near Marsa Matruh (6.00 p.m.). Cf. Santoni, *Ultra*, 98, 316–17. For the subsequent development of the operation see Map V.II.2.

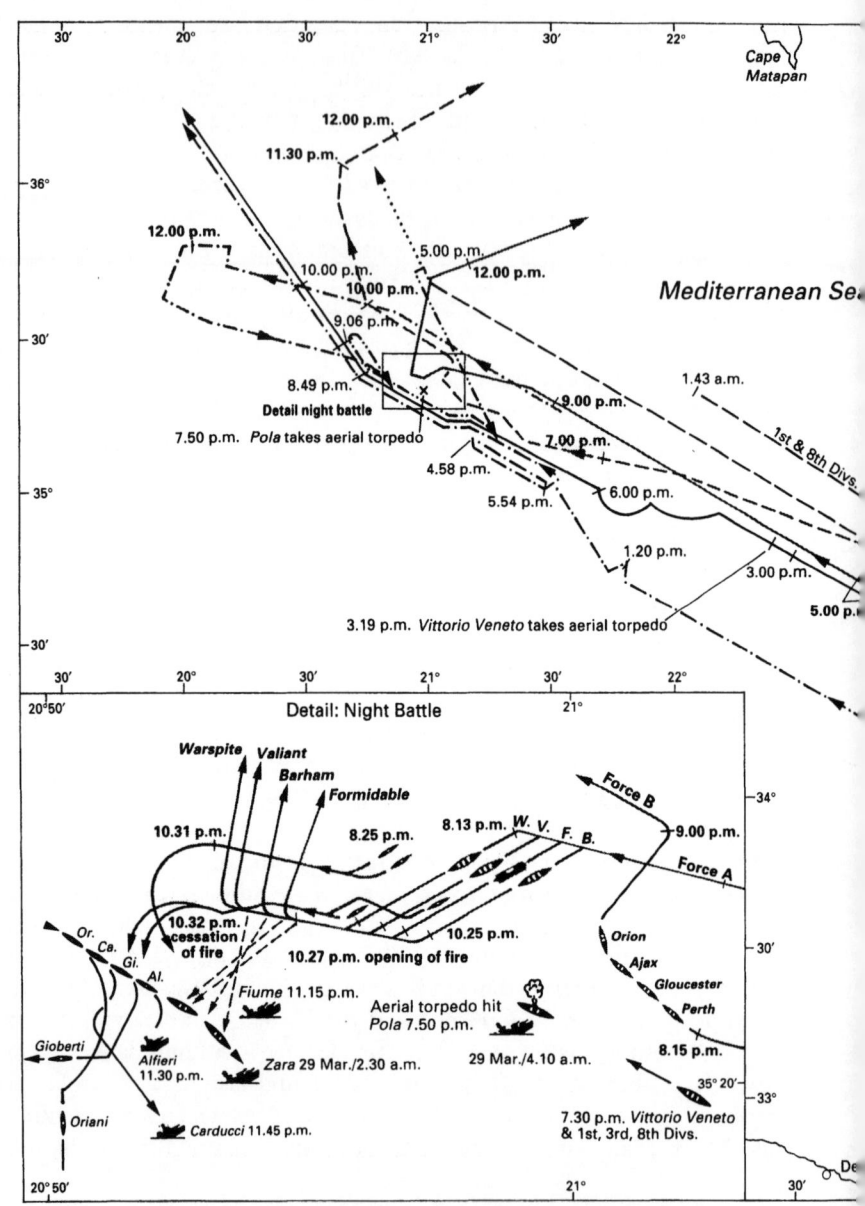

MAP V.II.2. The Battle of Cape Matapan, 28 March 1941

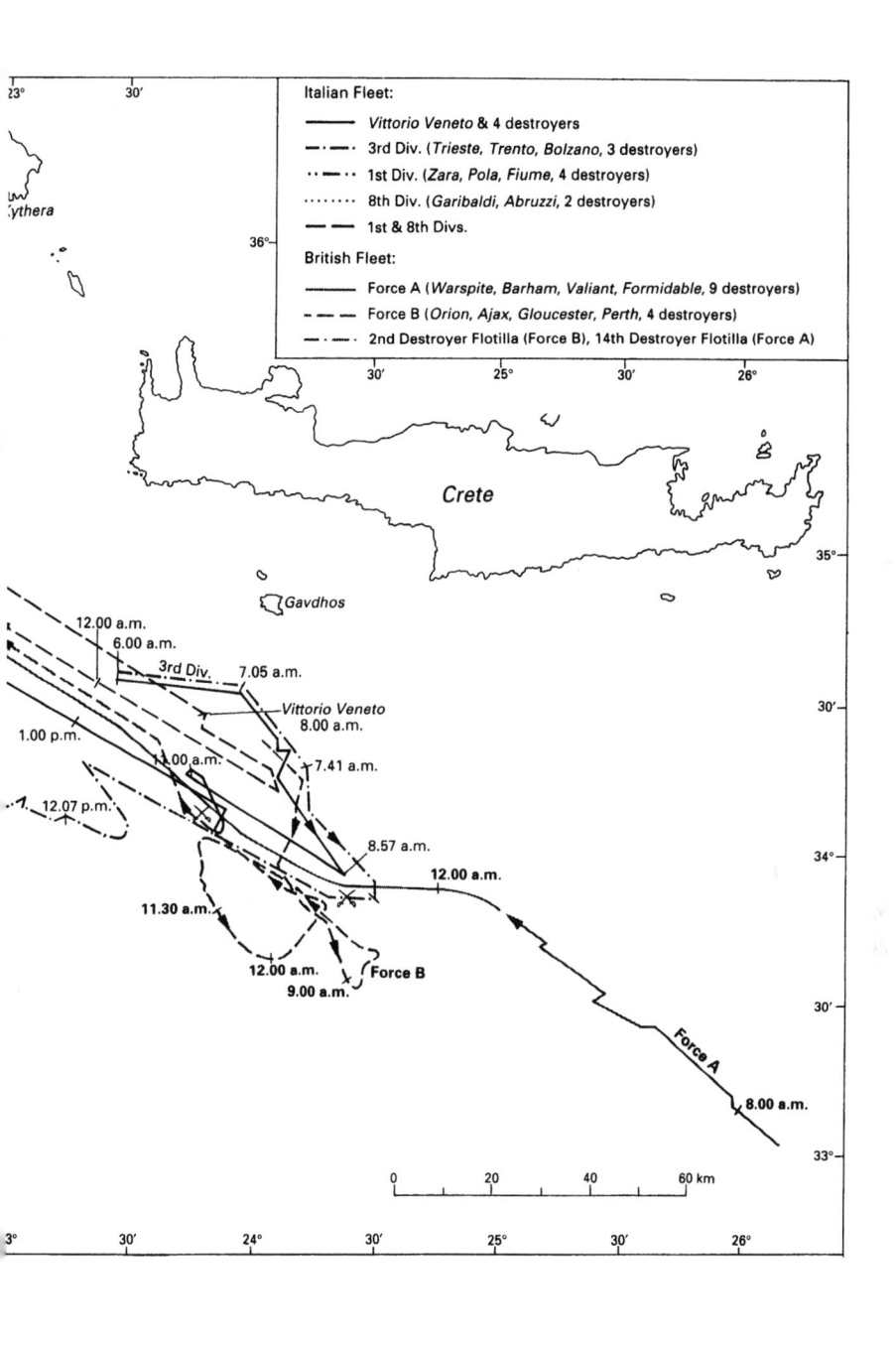

Italian Fleet:

——— *Vittorio Veneto* & 4 destroyers
—·—· 3rd Div. (*Trieste, Trento, Bolzano*, 3 destroyers)
··—·· 1st Div. (*Zara, Pola, Fiume*, 4 destroyers)
········ 8th Div. (*Garibaldi, Abruzzi*, 2 destroyers)
— — 1st & 8th Divs.

British Fleet:

——— Force A (*Warspite, Barham, Valiant, Formidable*, 9 destroyers)
— — — Force B (*Orion, Ajax, Gloucester, Perth*, 4 destroyers)
—·—·— 2nd Destroyer Flotilla (Force B), 14th Destroyer Flotilla (Force A)

sides. But Pridham-Wippell withdrew under cover of fog, and the Italian manœuvre was ended by the first attack of aircraft from the *Formidable* on the *Vittorio Veneto*. Other British aircraft, from Maleme in Crete, continued the attacks, attempting to reduce the speed of the *Vittorio Veneto* so that Cunningham with his three veteran ships of the First World War would be able to catch up with her.

More successful was the second attack by torpedo-aircraft from the *Formidable*, which scored a hit on the Italian battleship at 3.15 p.m. The ship took on about 4,000 tonnes of water and was able to reach a speed of nineteen knots only two hours later. However, this success did not affect the further course of the battle, as British reconnaissance was unable to find the *Vittorio Veneto* during the following night.

The third attack by British torpedo-aircraft had more serious consequences. At 7.50 p.m. the Italian heavy cruiser *Pola* was immobilized by a torpedo hit.[48] Over an hour later, at 9.00 p.m., 1st Division, with the cruisers *Zara* and *Fiume* and four destroyers, received the order to turn back to aid the helpless ship. At about the same time the *Pola* was discovered by Pridham-Wippell's B Force, and Admiral Cunningham was approaching to examine the unknown immobilized ship. He arrived on the scene at the same time as the completely unsuspecting 1st Division approached in line ahead with the destroyers at their rear. Using their radar, the British battleships opened a devastating fire shortly before 10.30 p.m.[49] Only two Italian destroyers, one of them damaged, escaped. The hulks of the cruisers were sunk by British destroyers, as was the *Pola*, after the remaining crew members had been taken off. The operation was a clear victory for the British, who lost only one aircraft, although Cunningham greatly regretted that the *Vittorio Veneto* had escaped.[50]

German criticism began even before the Italian operation had been concluded. On 29 March the head of the navy liaison staff in Rome observed: 'Neither the strategic idea of the offensive nor, as far as is known, the operational plan determined the result, but rather the tactical execution and the difference in the skill with which formations, ships, and weapons were used by either side.'[51] He repeated the suggestion he had made at the beginning of the year and recommended that 'officers of the German navy should take over or participate in some form in the command of the Italian navy, including front staffs'. The naval war staff supported this unqualified criticism: 'That this first offensive operation was such a disaster must be attributed solely to the complete failure of the Italian navy as regards tactical

---

[48] Times according to *Marina italiana*, iv. According to Roskill (*War at Sea*, i. 429), the third attack took place at 7.30 p.m.
[49] Cf. Roskill, *War at Sea*, i. 430.
[50] Ibid. 430–1.
[51] Weichold papers, BA-MA N 316/v. 36.

execution, command of formations and ships, and training in the use of weapons.'[52] The naval staff realized, however, that Weichold's suggestions could not be put into practice, and concluded with resignation: 'After the complete failure of the Italian navy, the naval war staff must refrain from any suggestions for an offensive conduct of the war in future.'

On several points Weichold agreed with Riccardi. Both men were of the opinion that the mistaken report by X Air Corps about the torpedoing of two British battleships had contributed to the decision to undertake the unsuccessful operation, and that the reconnaissance for and protection of the fleet provided by the Italian air force and the Luftwaffe had been inadequate. Because of heavy rain German long-range fighters had not found the Italian ships on 27 March, and on 28 March they were able to protect the fleet only from 6.00 p.m. to 6.30 p.m. The British, on the other hand, had the advantage that their fighters and torpedo-bombers were able to operate from aircraft-carriers and, above all, that their ships were equipped with radar. The Italians had no comparable equipment of their own, such as the German DT (*Dezimetertelegrafie*) devices.[53] Moreover, criticism of the tactical decisions of the Italian commanders, which led to the annihilation of 1st Division, was certainly justified.[54] But in all their criticism, justified or not, the Germans failed to understand that the starting-point of the entire operation, as they themselves had demanded it, had been mistaken. Because of the inadequate intelligence about the British convoys, the success of the operation was heavily dependent on chance from the very beginning. The risk was, however, perhaps acceptable as long as it was possible to surprise the enemy. In the final analysis, the question whether the British Mediterranean Fleet had one battleship ready for action, or three, had no effect on the result of the operation. Under the actual conditions, one battleship would have been sufficient to destroy the two cruisers of 1st Division. The danger from the air, especially from the carrier-based aircraft, was, however, decisive. And even perfect cooperation between the Italian air force, the Luftwaffe, and the fleet, attempted here for the first time, would not have been able to overcome this difficulty, given the relationship of forces and their geographical positions. Iachino did not have to fear the British battleships themselves, for this superior speed enabled him to avoid a battle with them. Thus when it eventually became clear that surprise was no longer possible—and this was known in Rome and Berlin—the only sensible decision would have been to cancel or break off the operation. Because this was not done, the Italian fleet suffered a serious defeat, for which the Germans were blamed. Thereafter the Italian navy refused to bring the fleet into action without cover by Italian fighters, which meant that

---

[52] 1. Skl., KTB, Teil A, 407–8 (29 Mar. 1941), BA-MA RM 7/21.
[53] 'Unterlagen zur Urteilsbildung über die Schlacht bei Matapan' (10 Nov. 1943), Weichold papers, BA-MA N 316/v. 36.
[54] Cf. Schreiber, 'Seeschlacht von Matapan'.

operations by the fleet could be carried out only within 110 kilometres of the coast. The German navy was thenceforth very cautious about making demands or giving advice, not because the Germans accepted responsibility for the Italian defeat, but because they did not want to be held responsible for the Italian failure.[55]

The battle of Cape Matapan, as the encounter between the Italian and British fleets on 28 March was called, clearly showed that the Italian fleet was not able to operate against the Mediterranean Fleet in the eastern Mediterranean; and the transfer of X Air Corps to Sicily had not basically changed this situation. This of course did not mean that the Italians had to remain completely inactive. On 26 March six Italian explosive boats penetrated Soudha Bay in Crete and damaged a British tanker and the heavy cruiser *York*. The *York* had to be grounded and later abandoned; the tanker sank in heavy seas while being towed to Alexandria.[56]

Against Operation Excess in January X Air Corps had been able to demonstrate its abilities, but its successes were not sufficient to make the central Mediterranean impassable for the Royal Navy and establish an effective blockade around Malta. Between 19 and 24 March, immediately before the Italian operation in the waters south of Crete, Admiral Cunningham had even been able to send a convoy to Malta without its being noticed by the Italians or the Germans.[57]

For the third task of the Italian navy and the Luftwaffe in the Mediterranean, the transfer of army troops and securing an uninterrupted flow of supplies to North Africa, the fighting strength of the British forces on Malta represented the most difficult problem. In this respect the strength of H Force in Gibraltar and the Mediterranean Fleet in Alexandria was less important, as, in spite of their superiority at sea, they were unable to operate for long periods of time in the central Mediterranean. As a base of operations for torpedo-bombers and other bomber aircraft, light surface vessels, and submarines, Malta represented a much greater danger for the German and Italian convoys. For this reason, on 3 February 1941 Hitler ordered X Air Corps to protect the transports to North Africa and to destroy British air power on Malta.[58]

At first the idea of conquering Malta in order to secure the sea routes to North Africa did not arise in connection with the German intervention there. Instead, the occupation of the French Mediterranean coast, as well as Corsica and Malta, was considered an alternative if Tripolitania should also be lost to the British. Göring was asked whether it would be possible for the airborne

---

[55] On the consequences of the battle of Cape Matapan cf. Baum and Weichold, *Krieg der 'Achsenmächte'*, 124–5; Salewski, *Seekriegsleitung*, i. 325–7; Schreiber, *Revisionismus*, 308–9.

[56] Cf. Rohwer and Hümmelchen, *Chronik*, 113; Bernotti, *Guerra nel Mediterraneo*, 141–2; *Marina italiana*, xiv. 91–8. This was the first important success of the midget naval units, which acquired considerable significance in the course of the war.

[57] Cf. Rohwer and Hümmelchen, *Chronik*, 111; Roskill, *War at Sea*, i. 423.

[58] *KTB OKW* i. 301. Cf. the beginning of the present chapter.

corps to occupy Malta before the start of Operation Barbarossa.[59] When, in an oral situation report on 18 March, Raeder pointed out the importance of occupying Malta to protect transports to North Africa, Hitler had already lost interest in such a project, as the Luftwaffe had emphasized the great difficulties of carrying out an airborne landing operation against the island because much of it was covered with walls.[60] A month later the naval war staff submitted a pessimistic assessment of the chances of success of a landing operation. In a memorandum on the study 'Malta' by the army general staff of 15 April, the navy advocated waiting to see how the occupation of Greece and Crete and the threat to Egypt[61] would affect the British position in the eastern Mediterranean. The memorandum came to the hardly surprising conclusion that increased activity by the Royal Navy in this area would make the planned operation more difficult, but a withdrawal of the Mediterranean Fleet to the Red Sea would facilitate it.[62]

Thus Malta did not have to fear an invasion for the time being and only had to defend itself against the attacks by X Air Corps, which had begun in January. These attacks, however, reached such intensity that the Royal Air Force transferred its Sunderland flying-boats and Wellington bombers stationed on Malta to Egypt in the first weeks of March. The British fighter defence force on Malta, however, withstood all attacks, as it constantly received new aircraft from carriers in the western Mediterranean.[63] X Air Corps was nevertheless able to counter the threat of air attacks from Malta on the convoys to North Africa. From February until April only one ship was lost to enemy aircraft from the island. British submarines stationed in Malta represented a far more serious danger; in addition to several freighters, they also sank the Italian light cruiser *Armando Diaz* during this period.[64]

Churchill and Wavell were very anxious about the almost uninterrupted flow of reinforcements for Rommel and his Africa Corps, for in April the German and Italian forces began their advance in Cyrenaica, while the British reserves were still tied down in Greece. The British leaders were agreed that attacks on the supply-convoys had to be increased and that the unloading port for the

---

[59] *KTB OKW* i. 326 (15 Feb. 1941). The German and Italian staffs had, of course, concerned themselves with the problem of Malta much earlier. Cf. Warlimont, 'Malta'; Weichold, 'Seestrategie'; Schreiber, *Revisionismus*, 269, 351–7. On the time before the German intervention cf. I.I.3 and I.III.3 (*a*) above (Schreiber).

[60] 'Führer Conferences', 185.

[61] An advance unit of 15th Armoured Division had captured Sollum on the frontier between Libya and Egypt on 13 Apr.

[62] 1. Skl., KTB, Teil A, 318–19 (22 Apr. 1941), BA-MA RM 7/23; 1. Skl. to army general staff/Op.Abt. (22 Apr. 1941), BA-MA RM 7/945, p. 11. Cf. also Salewski, *Seekriegsleitung*, i. 329–31.

[63] When the German attacks started 12 fighters, 5 flying-boats, 4 reconnaissance aircraft, 12 bombers, and 10 torpedo-bombers were stationed on Malta. At the end of April the number of fighters had risen to more than 40. Cf. Playfair, *Mediterranean*, ii. 45, 48; Santoni and Mattesini, *La partecipazione tedesca*, 44–8.

[64] Cf. Playfair, *Mediterranean*, ii. 55, 58; Rohwer, 'Nachschubverkehr'; ch. v below.

convoys, Tripoli, had to be put out of action. But there was disagreement on the question of how these objectives should be achieved. Wellington bombers were again transferred to Malta, and Cunningham sent four destroyers, but for an attack on Tripoli he demanded the stationing of long-range bombers in Egypt.[65] The Admiralty in London, on the other hand, preferred to blockade or bombard Tripoli, using the Mediterranean Fleet. Cunningham rejected this idea for good reason, as the losses to be expected would be out of all proportion to the results of the operation.[66]

At first, however, 14th Destroyer Flotilla, which had been transferred to Malta, achieved a spectacular success. On 16 April, after several fruitless attempts, it surprised the twentieth sea-transport group off the Tunisian coast near the Qirquinah Bank—aerial reconnaissance by X Air Corps had been cancelled the day before—and, in a night battle between 2.20 and 3.20 a.m., sank five freighters and two of the escorting Italian destroyers while losing only one destroyer itself.[67] At the same time, however, the Admiralty continued to urge Cunningham to carry out an operation against Tripoli, and he finally decided to combine a bombardment of the port with a resupplying of Malta.[68] On 18 April he put to sea with the Mediterranean Fleet and reached Tripoli unnoticed on the morning of 21 April. Starting at 5.00 a.m., he bombarded the port for an hour, after it had already been attacked by aircraft stationed on Malta. But the bombardment and the bombing attacks achieved no significant results. The feared losses did not materialize, but Cunningham was nevertheless not prepared to repeat the operation.[69]

The German naval staff again complained about the Italian navy's lack of operational foresight and purposeful action,[70] as it had been pointing out to the Italians the importance of mine-barrages to protect Tripoli since the beginning of February. But the laying of the mines had been repeatedly postponed; it was finally carried out on 1 May. After the success of 14th Destroyer Flotilla, the British attempted to station more destroyers and light cruisers in Malta; but the German air attacks and the evacuation of British troops from Greece, which required all available light surface ships, prevented the realization of these plans.[71] This did not, however, eliminate the threat from Malta to the supply-convoys, and losses in May—eleven ships, 47,507 GRT—reached a new high.[72]

---

[65] *PWT*, Middle East I, Hist (B) 3, No. 87, p. 36 (10 Apr. 1941). Cf. also Roskill, *War at Sea*, i. 431–3.
[66] *PWT*, Middle East I, Hist (B) 3, No. 88, pp. 36–7 (11 Apr. 1941), No. 115, pp. 49–50 (16 Apr. 1941).
[67] Cf. Playfair, *Mediterranean*, ii. 54; 1. Skl. KTB, Teil A, 230–2 (16 Apr. 1941), BA-MA RM 7/23.
[68] The telegrams cited by Roskill (*War at Sea*, i. 431–2) are not printed in *PWT*, Middle East I.
[69] Bernotti, *Guerra nel Mediterraneo*, 164–7; Playfair, *Mediterranean*, ii. 112–13.
[70] 1. Skl., KTB, Teil A, 312 (21 Apr. 1941), BA-MA RM 7/23.
[71] Cf. Playfair, *Mediterranean*, i. 54–5; Roskill, *War at Sea*, i. 433–4.
[72] Cf. Playfair, *Mediterranean*, ii. 58. Cf. also ch. v below.

III. The Reconquest of Cyrenaica and the Failure of the Attacks on Tobruk

THE first German combat troops in North Africa, Reconnaissance Battalion 3 and Tank Destroyer Battalion 39, arrived in Tripoli with the second German sea-transport group on 14 February 1941. Rommel immediately sent them to Sirte, which they reached on 16 February. The same day Generals Gariboldi and Roatta agreed to his suggestion to send a fighting unit to An Nawfaliyah, which had been reported to be free of enemy troops. The newly arrived units of 5th Light Division were brought up, and on 29 February Rommel ordered the occupation of the Mugtaa defile, which was formed by the sea and a saltmarsh. This pushed the front back to 700 kilometres from Tripoli and only twenty-five kilometres west of Al Uqaylah, which was occupied by the British. Rommel was also able to persuade Gariboldi to place Ariete Armoured Division and the partially motorized Brescia Division under his command and to send them to the front.[1] At the same time X Air Corps transferred two Gruppen of dive-bombers and a Staffel of twin-engine fighters to North Africa. Major-General Fröhlich was named Fliegerführer Afrika (Air Leader Africa) and assigned to the air corps. A Staffel of close-reconnaissance aircraft was placed under the direct tactical command of the Africa Corps.[2]

But even at this time Rommel was not satisfied with expanding his defensive position as far as possible. He already planned to begin his attack on Tobruk on 8 May. For this purpose, however, he needed more divisions than merely 5th Light Division and 15th Armoured Division, which he was scheduled to receive at that time; he especially needed more transport capacity. Hitler and the army high command agreed that the defensive front should be pushed forward and that an offensive operation should be prepared to take advantage of the situation in the event that the relative strength of the combatants in North Africa changed in Rommel's favour;[3] but an armoured corps for an attack on Egypt was to be provided only after Operation Barbarossa and after the end of the following winter. For the time being there could be no question of additional reinforcements for the Africa Corps, and Rommel would not be

---

[1] Cf. Taysen, *Tobruk*, 56–61; Kriebel, 'Nordafrika', 30–5, MGFA T3, vol. i.
[2] Gundelach, *Luftwaffe im Mittelmeer*, 109–10. Taysen (*Tobruk*, 56) mentions a Gruppe of Me 110s and a fighter Staffel; Kriebel ('Nordafrika', 36, MGFA T3, vol. i) a Gruppe of Me 110s. The decision to send aircraft to Africa made it necessary to reinforce X Air Corps with aircraft stationed in western Europe to enable it to fulfil its other tasks. As a result its strength rose to approximately 510 aircraft.
[3] The army high command estimated that there were still 15 British divisions in Egypt and Libya.

able to use the port of Tunis for his supplies.[4] He was unable to change these decisions in spite of personal talks with Hitler and the army high command on 20 and 21 March, and was merely given permission to carry out limited offensive operations to capture the approaches to Ajdabiya and prepare an attack in the direction of Tobruk by autumn.[5] These limitations were defined in a directive of the army high command of 21 March, and on 2 April Hitler again clearly stated that a large-scale offensive should not be undertaken even after the arrival of 15th Armoured Division.[6]

A further advance eastward by Rommel's forces was indeed not without difficulties. The army high command had at first assumed that the blocking force near Buyarat would have to be supplied from Tripoli, 380 kilometres to the west, which required two supply-columns with a capacity of 750 tons. Since German troops had reached the Mugtaa defile, however, the distance had almost doubled, and the Italians had to help with additional transport capacity. In addition, a modest coastal shipping system was established from Tripoli to Buyarat and Ras al Ali, but available transport capacity was still not sufficient. On the one hand, the assistant chief of staff of the Africa Corps was concerned with making optimum use of the available berths assigned to him in Tripoli, unloading the supply-ships in the endangered port as rapidly as possible, and distributing the supplies to depots near the city, which required a large part of the transport capacity and the supply companies. On the other hand, the supplies in Tripoli did not help 5th Light Division, which also needed transport capacity to supply its units and build up a base in Al Qaws on the border between Tripolitania and Cyrenaica in order to ensure its mobility in large-scale operations.[7] Soon it became clear that the delivery of foodstuffs, which the Italians had taken over, was inadequate and that the fuel they provided was not suited to the German vehicles, which resulted in new supply problems. The composition of rations was not adapted to the African desert climate, which led to a great increase in the number of personnel reporting sick. As the German units had no previous knowledge of the North African theatre and the information provided by the Italians was quite unsatisfactory, the equipment the Germans had brought with them was often not up to the demands of the new situation. For example, the standard German air filters could not cope with the desert sand, which reduced the average life of a motor by half.[8] Under these conditions a tank required an overhaul after between 1,000 and 1,500 kilometres;[9] thus the German tanks had to use most of their combat range between overhauls to move from Tripoli to Mugtaa.

---

[4] Halder, *Diaries*, ii. 827 (12 Mar. 1941), 829 (14 Mar. 1941); *KTB* ii. 314–15 (16 Mar. 1941, not in trans.), and *Diaries*, ii. 833 (17 Mar. 1941).
[5] Rommel, *Papers*, 105–6; Halder, *Diaries*, ii. 835–6 (20, 21 Mar. 1941). Cf. also Taysen, *Tobruk*, 68–9.
[6] Warlimont, 'Kriegführung', 344–5, MGFA P-216/I-III.
[7] Cf. Kriebel, 'Nordafrika', 46–53, MGFA T3, vol. i; Taysen, *Tobruk*, 61–4 and annex 8, pp. 365–73. On the following account cf. also Valentin, 'Ärzte im Wüstenkrieg'.
[8] Taysen, *Tobruk*, annex 7, pp. 360–4.
[9] Kriebel, 'Nordafrika', 33, MGFA T3, vol. i.

V.III. Reconquest of Cyrenaica and Failure of the Attacks on Tobruk

Operations into Cyrenaica would inevitably aggravate these problems: longer supply-lines would require additional transport capacity and personnel, increase fuel and foodstuff consumption, and result in greater wear and tear on vehicles and motors. The problems Rommel faced were not due only to the fact that the army high command and initially Hitler wanted, for good reasons, to avoid a deeper involvement in North Africa, but also to the need to transport personnel and material for the Africa Corps across the Mediterranean. It had already become evident that this would inevitably lead to losses and delays: supply capacity was limited and the transport route was constantly threatened by the enemy. In his planning, however, Rommel did not consider the strategic situation in the Mediterranean or in North Africa. 'Rommel himself was not at all interested in the supply question. For him the supply-system was simply part of the rear area, and he took its smooth functioning for granted.'[10]

On 24 March Rommel returned to his headquarters from Germany after having stopped in Rome and Tripoli for talks with Mussolini and Gariboldi. He had been informed that Gariboldi was not permitted to advance eastward beyond Al Uqaylah. On the same day 5th Light Division took the town against only weak resistance. This gave Major-General Streich the chance to extend his reconnaissance to the defile at Marsa Burayqah, which did not seem to be occupied by strong enemy forces. Streich also secured an airfield and additional water sources by taking the oasis of Maradah. With this action the Africa Corps had reached the limits of its advance approved by the high commands in Rome and Berlin. It is uncertain whether Rommel intended from the very beginning to ignore these limits. According to his own account, he feared that, if he waited to seize the approaches to Ajdabiya until 15th Armoured Division was completely assembled in May, the British would be able to make their position at Marsa al Burayqah almost impregnable. Marsa al Burayqah also offered 'a suitable assembly and forming-up area for the May attack' and an abundant water supply.[11]

On 31 March 5th Light Division began its attack and was able to take the position near Marsa al Burayqah after heavy fighting. The next day an advance unit was supposed to maintain contact with the retreating enemy and reconnoitre the area in the direction of Ajdabiya; but Major-General Streich ordered the whole division to follow, and in the afternoon of 2 April the advance unit captured the town with Rommel's consent. Rommel wanted to bring up the motorized parts of Brescia Division, but Gariboldi was strongly

---

[10] Ibid. 50. Cf. also Irving, *Rommel*, 67. To Halder's question how Rommel wanted to maintain and supply the two additional armoured corps he demanded, Rommel replied: 'That's quite immaterial to me. That's your pigeon.'

[11] Rommel, *Papers*, 107. Cf. also Kriebel, 'Nordafrika', 57–8, MGFA T3, vol. i; Taysen, *Tobruk*, 70; Pitt, *Crucible*, 253: 'Rommel... proceeded to disobey his orders with a diligence which compels the admiration of all who have ever cocked a snook at Authority.' According to Schmidt (*Afrika*, 14), Rommel had already said in Tripoli that he wanted to advance to the Nile and then reconquer the Italian possessions in East Africa.

opposed to this idea. On the evening of 3 April he came to Rommel and a violent argument ensued between the two men. Gariboldi pointed to the insecure supply situation; he demanded that Rommel break off the operation, which was in defiance of the orders of the Italian high command, and refrain from carrying out any further troop movements without marching orders. Rommel, on the other hand, insisted that he should be free to react as he thought necessary to the changing situation; he considered Gariboldi's misgivings about the supply situation to be unfounded.

At this point a message arrived from the Wehrmacht high command which referred to Hitler's directive of the day before, warned Rommel not to advance further, pointed to other commitments of the Axis, and announced delays in the transport of 15th Armoured Division to North Africa. The message concluded: 'A further advance of the German Africa Corps is therefore only possible if it can be determined beyond any doubt that the enemy is withdrawing most of his mobile units from Cyrenaica. Written order follows.'[12] Thereupon Rommel announced that the Wehrmacht high command had granted him complete freedom of action. Gariboldi abandoned his opposition, although Rommel was formally his subordinate. 'He soon transformed the role which the Italian high command wanted to assign to him—commander of a mobile reserve behind the front—into that of commander of all units on the fighting front.'[13]

In March 1941 the main task of the British commander-in-chief in North Africa was the transfer of the expeditionary corps to Greece. For that purpose units of the army and squadrons of the Royal Air Force had to be withdrawn from Cyrenaica, while the Royal Navy had to cope with the transport tasks involved. The staff of XIII Corps had been disbanded. Lieutenant-General O'Connor had taken over the command of the British troops in Egypt, and Lieutenant-General Neame in Al Marj had become head of the Cyrenaica command as military governor. This command was intended to replace the civilian administration, but did not have a staff suitable for directing mobile units in a war of movement. Naeme's command included 2nd Armoured Division and 9th Australian Division. At the end of March Wavell sent him his only reserve unit, 3rd Indian Motor Brigade. At the beginning of January 2nd Armoured Division had arrived from Britain and disposed of little more than a weak armoured brigade, with tanks whose tracks and motors had reached the end of their service life. And 9th Division had so little transport capacity that it had had to leave a brigade in Tobruk. For this reason the

---

[12] On 3 Apr. and previous developments cf. Irving, *Rommel*, 71; Rommel, *Papers*, 111–12; Taysen, *Tobruk*, 81–3; *Prima controffensiva*, 73–87. Late in the evening Gariboldi received an order from the Italian high command permitting a continuation of operations if the situation were favourable.

[13] Kriebel, 'Nordafrika', 55, MGFA T3, vol. i. On relations between the 'Comandante del Corpo Tedesco in Afrika' (Rommel) and the 'Comandante Superiore italiano A.S.' (Gariboldi), cf. *Prima controffensiva*, 86–7.

Australians had not been able to occupy the favourable defensive position west of Al Uqaylah. General Wavell had accepted this exposure of Cyrenaica for the campaign in Greece because he did not expect any serious threat from the German troops in Africa before May. Both his new divisions were scheduled to complete their training and be fully equipped by then. Wavell also hoped to be able to transfer one or two additional divisions from East Africa after the expected decline in the fighting there.[14]

Wavell underestimated the possibilities open to Rommel, but this was not due to a lack of reliable information about the enemy. At this time the British could not yet decipher the radio traffic of the German army and were therefore dependent on the radio messages of X Air Corps and the Air Leader Africa, which after 28 February they were able to decipher within twenty-four hours, for information about enemy transport movements. But even the situation assessments and orders from Hitler and the Wehrmacht and army high commands, if Wavell had known them at this time, would only have confirmed the views he already held. Wavell's difficulties resulted from the fact that Rommel judged the situation differently and frequently disregarded the orders he received from Berlin.[15]

In the event of a limited German advance, which Wavell expected, he planned to withdraw to Benghazi and, if necessary, to evacuate the city. The first suitable defensive position for the Australian infantry was located further north, at the escarpment between Tocra and Er Regima. The British armoured units were to assemble in the area of Antelat and attack the enemy on the flanks and in the rear, regardless of whether the main direction of his advance was towards Benghazi or Tobruk. In any case, the defence was to be mobile and avoid the danger of a serious defeat.[16] To achieve this, Wavell had to interfere with the tactical dispositions to the Cyrenaica command, which had caused him great concern. He returned from a visit to the front with forebodings and shaken confidence.[17]

Churchill also watched Rommel's advance with growing uneasiness. On 26 March he wrote to Wavell: 'I presume you are only waiting for the tortoise to stick his head out far enough before chopping it off. It seems extremely important to give them an early taste of our quality. What is the state and location of the 7th Armoured Division?'[18] Churchill must have known that the withdrawal of troops for the campaign in Greece had left very little 'quality' in Cyrenaica.[19] Wavell's answer was therefore not surprising:

I have to admit to having taken considerable risk in Cyrenaica after the capture of Benghazi in order to provide maximum support for Greece.... I have one brigade of

---

[14] Playfair, *Mediterranean*, ii. 1–5; Pitt, *Crucible*, 251–2.
[15] Cf. Hinsley, *British Intelligence*, i. 390–2; Lewin, *The Chief*, 122–3.
[16] Playfair, *Mediterranean*, ii. 7.
[17] Pitt, *Crucible*, 249–50.
[18] Churchill, *Second World War*, iii. 178–9; PWT, Middle East I, Hist (B) 2, No. 141, p. 73.
[19] Cf. PWT, Middle East I, Hist (B) 2, No. 35, pp. 19–20 (21 Feb. 1941).

2nd Armoured Division in Cyrenaica, one in Greece. 7th Armoured Division is returning to Cairo and, as no reserve tanks were available, is dependent on repair, which takes time. Next month or two will be anxious, but enemy has extremely difficult problem and am sure his numbers have been greatly exaggerated.[20]

In this last assumption Wavell was certainly right, but his overall estimate of the situation was still not sufficiently realistic. As late as 30 March he believed that Rommel would not be able to start a large operation before the end of April.[21]

But on 2 April, when the German 5th Light Division advanced towards Ajdabiya and the commander of the British 2nd Armoured Division, Major-General Gambier-Parry, ordered a retreat to Antilat, Wavell realized the seriousness of the situation and flew to Lieutenant-General Neame in Al Marj. Gambier-Parry had also withdrawn to Antilat the support group securing the road to Benghazi in order not to divide the forces of his armoured division. Wavell ordered the support group to continue to slow the German advance along the coastal road, at first together with 3rd Armoured Brigade, which then, further east, was to withdraw to the area south of Al Abyar to protect the left flank of 9th Australian Division. He obviously assumed that Rommel's offensive was only a limited advance to capture Benghazi. This analysis of the situation was a mistake; in addition, with his orders and counter-orders, which in some cases reached the troops not at all or only too late, Wavell contributed greatly to the confusion on the British side in the next hours and days. His decision to replace Neame with O'Connor, who then persuaded him to leave Neame in command and himself, O'Connor, as his adviser, was equally unfortunate.[22] Rommel was aware of the crisis in the enemy camp, and on 3 April he therefore decided to attempt to conquer all of Cyrenaica. He first ordered advance detachments to be formed in order to cause the British to continue their withdrawal by applying constant pressure. The same day a detachment composed largely of Italians was sent via Bin Ghaniyah to reconnoitre the way to Zawiyat al Mukhayla, while Reconnaissance Battalion 3 entered Benghazi, which had already been evacuated. The following morning the first detachment received the order to push on to Al Tamimi and conduct reconnaissance in the direction of Tobruk. A group from Ariete Division was sent towards Zawiyat al Mukhayla via Bin Ghaniyah, and a German advance unit along the same road to the coast at Darnah. The motorized parts of Brescia Division advanced to Benghazi to enable Reconnaissance Battalion 3 to push on further to Zawiyat al Mukhayla via El Abiar. A group with 5th Armoured Regiment at its centre was sent towards Zawiyat al Mukhayla via Zawiyat Masus. Finally, Major-General Streich was to break through to the

---

[20] Churchill, *Second World War*, iii. 179; *PWT*, Middle East I, Hist (B) 2, No. 144, pp. 74–5 (27 Mar. 1941).
[21] Lewin, *Rommel*, 46.
[22] Cf. Playfair, *Mediterranean*, ii. 20–1; Jackson, *Campaign*, 100–1; Lewin, *Rommel*, 47–8; Taysen, *Tobruk*, 78. On the geographical situation cf. Maps V.I.1 and 2 and V.VI.6.

V.III. Reconquest of Cyrenaica and Failure of the Attacks on Tobruk

coast between Darnah and Tobruk with the few units still not engaged and cut the retreat route of the enemy.[23] The march through the unknown desert placed extraordinary demands on the units involved. Individual vehicles and entire groups lost their bearings, got stuck, or ran out of fuel. Rommel was constantly on the move to keep his scattered troops moving in the right direction and to urge them on. Supply problems had to be solved in unusual ways by improvisation. For example, 5th Light Division sent all of its wheeled vehicles back to Al Qaws to bring up supplies, although this meant that it would be immobilized for twenty-four hours. To supply the advanced groups, a column of approximately 800 vehicles was formed on 5 April and reached Zawiyat al Mukhayla on 7 April after driving through the desert via Antilat and Zawiyat Masus. But another week passed before the last vehicles lost in the desert could be salvaged.[24]

Lieutenant-General O'Connor had sent 3rd Indian Motor Brigade to Zawiyat al Mukhayla, where a large supply-depot was located. The brigade was able to defend its position against the first German units, which arrived on 6 April. Gambier-Parry was to support the defenders, but he reached Zawiyat al Mukhayla without 2nd Armoured Division: because of counter-orders and a lack of fuel, the support group and 3rd Armoured Brigade had joined the retreat of the Australians from northern Cyrenaica after having destroyed the supply-depot near Zawiyat Masus too early. The division had lost all its tanks, less as a result of enemy action than because of mechanical failures and a lack of fuel. After an unsuccessful attempt to break out on the morning of 8 April, most of the defenders of Zawiyat al Mukhayla were taken prisoner.

The advance unit sent to Darnah was at first too weak to block the Australian retreat, but it was able to take O'Connor and Neame prisoner, as their driver had missed the road to Al Tamimi. On the morning of 8 April the unit occupied the road, the airfield, and the city of Darnah. That evening, when the first elements of Brescia Division arrived, Rommel ordered reconnaissance to be extended in the direction of Al Tamimi and Tobruk and, using the parts of 5th Light Division that had already arrived, formed a new battle group under the commander of 15th Armoured Division, Major-General von Prittwitz und Gaffron, which was also to advance against Tobruk.[25]

The following day Rommel also decided to attack and destroy the enemy at Tobruk. Reconnaissance reports that the British had withdrawn into the heavily fortified port and that a large number of ships were assembled in the harbour evidently caused him to conclude that an evacuation was being prepared, as had already been done several times in 1940.

---

[23] Cf. Playfair, *Mediterranean*, ii. 26–7; Rommel, *Papers*, 109–13; Taysen, *Tobruk*, 78–85; *Prima controffensiva*, 89–92.
[24] Kriebel, 'Nordafrika', 70–75 g, MGFA T3, vol. i.
[25] On the fighting in Cenaica cf. Playfair, *Mediterranean*, ii. 27–33; Jackson, *Campaign*, 103–6; Rommel, *Papers*, 113–18; Taysen, *Tobruk*, 85–94; *Prima controffensiva*, 92–111.

V.III. Reconquest of Cyrenaica and Failure of the Attacks on Tobruk

The reconquest of Cyrenaica in less than a week was undoubtedly a notable achievement, although Rommel had not been able to cut off the enemy's retreat. The main cause of this failure was the continued resistance of the Indian brigade in Zawiyat al Mukhayla. However, it may be asked whether he would have achieved this objective if he had concentrated his forces in an attack on the coastal road further east near Ayn al Ghazalah.[26] While it cannot be said with certainty that the annihilation of 9th Australian Division in Cyrenaica would have made a defence of Tobruk or even Egypt impossible, Rommel was in any case not able to take Tobruk as long as it was defended by the Australians.

Although Rommel's victory was no Cannae, the German advance did place General Wavell in a most unpleasant situation, as it threatened the base of the British expeditionary corps in Greece at the very moment when the German attack in the Balkans began. This was not the result of rational calculation by the Wehrmacht leaders but rather a consequence of Rommel's unauthorized actions—which, however, did not make the threat any less serious for Wavell. He stopped the planned transport of 7th Australian Division to Greece and ordered the transfer of its 18th Infantry Brigade to Tobruk on 5 April. The next day Eden, Dill, Longmore, and Cunningham agreed in Cairo to hold Tobruk if at all possible; Churchill was also of the opinion that Tobruk had to be held. Major-General Morshead, the commander of 9th Australian Division, was appointed commander of Tobruk on 8 April and organized the defence. Three brigades occupied the fortifications of the outer defence belt, while the fourth was held in reserve behind the defences. In the meantime the Royal Navy brought in reinforcements of tanks, artillery, and anti-tank and anti-aircraft guns. South of Tobruk near Al Adam, to protect the desert flank, a Mobile Force was formed around the support group of 2nd Armoured Division. Lieutenant-General Sir Noel Beresford-Peirse was given command of the newly created Western Desert Force, which disposed of two incomplete divisions in Egypt (7th Australian and 6th British Division); 22nd Guards Brigade was sent to defend the western frontier of Egypt.[27] Wavell was not able to do more at the moment, for at the same time the fighting in East Africa reached a climax (though not an end), with the capture of Keren on 27 March and Asmara on 1 April, while in Iraq a new crisis arose with the coming to power of Rashid Ali al-Gailani in Baghdad.[28]

As late as 10 April Rommel had not recognized the measures and intentions of his enemy. He wanted to pursue the retreating British forces and prevent a break-out from Tobruk; his final objective was to capture the Suez Canal. The previous day he had wanted to advance with the Italian units along the coastal road while 5th Light Division circumvented Tobruk to the south. At first,

---

[26] Cf. Kriebel, 'Nordafrika', 76–8, MGFA T3, vol. i; Irving, *Rommel*, 76–8.
[27] Cf. Pitt, *Crucible*, 269–72; Playfair, *Mediterranean*, ii. 35–7; Taysen, *Tobruk*, 96–8.
[28] Cf. IV.II.2 above (Schreiber).

however, only the advance unit under Prittwitz was available, and Prittwitz was killed when he unwittingly drove into the Australians' field of fire. Such incidents were to occur frequently, as the Africa Corps did not know the type and location of the fortifications built earlier by the Italians.[29]

The reinforced Reconnaissance Battalion 3 was ordered to advance on Bardiyah via Akramah and Al Adam and reached Bardiyah on 12 April. The Mobile Force was able to stop the Germans at Al Adam but then withdrew to the Egyptian frontier. Another advance unit had already reached the coastal road east of Tobruk the day before and thus cut the main approach to the town from that direction. Brescia Division took over the western siege front and 5th Light Division assembled its forces between Al Adam and Tobruk for an attack on the fortress. However, these forces consisted only of Machine-gun Battalion 8 supported by twenty-five tanks and ten anti-tank guns on self-propelled mounts. It was typical of Rommel's complete misjudgement of the situation that he ordered such forces to attack a fortress defended by 24,000 combat troops with strong artillery support. The attack, in the afternoon of 11 April, was soon stopped by an anti-tank ditch and the troops had to pull back after taking losses.[30]

The next day Rommel ordered a second attack by 5th Light Division to capture Tobruk; this, however, was slowed by a sandstorm and then stopped by enemy artillery fire. But even this setback did not impress Rommel, who prepared his main attack for 14 April. In his estimate of the situation, the enemy was still too weak to stop a German drive towards Egypt. Until Rommel was able to send forward his main forces, advance units were to defeat one after another the reserve units brought up by the enemy. For this reason Tobruk had to be captured as soon as possible. It not only tied down a substantial part of the fighting power of the Africa Corps, but also blocked the coastal road and thus supplies for the advance units pushing towards the Egyptian frontier. Rommel therefore had good reason to attack the fortress, but he underestimated the defenders and, in blaming supposedly faulty leadership of 5th Light Division for the failure of the attacks, failed to understand the actual situation.[31]

During the night of 13-14 April Machine-gun Battalion 8 succeeded in crossing the anti-tank ditch, in penetrating the outer area of the fortress, and, in heavy fighting, in defending its bridgehead until the following morning. Then 5th Armoured Regiment joined the attack with thirty-eight tanks and attempted to widen the penetration. But the tanks soon came under defensive fire from artillery and anti-tank guns and had to withdraw after suffering a total of seventeen losses. The machine-gun battalion remained alone and had to cease fighting after expending all its ammunition. It had lost 280 men dead or

---

[29] According to Irving (*Rommel*, 77) and Taysen (*Tobruk*, 99–100), Rommel showed no interest in the fortifications.
[30] Cf. Playfair, *Mediterranean*, ii. 37; Taysen, *Tobruk*, 102–3; Map V.III.1.
[31] Rommel, *Papers*, 123–4; Taysen, *Tobruk*, 105.

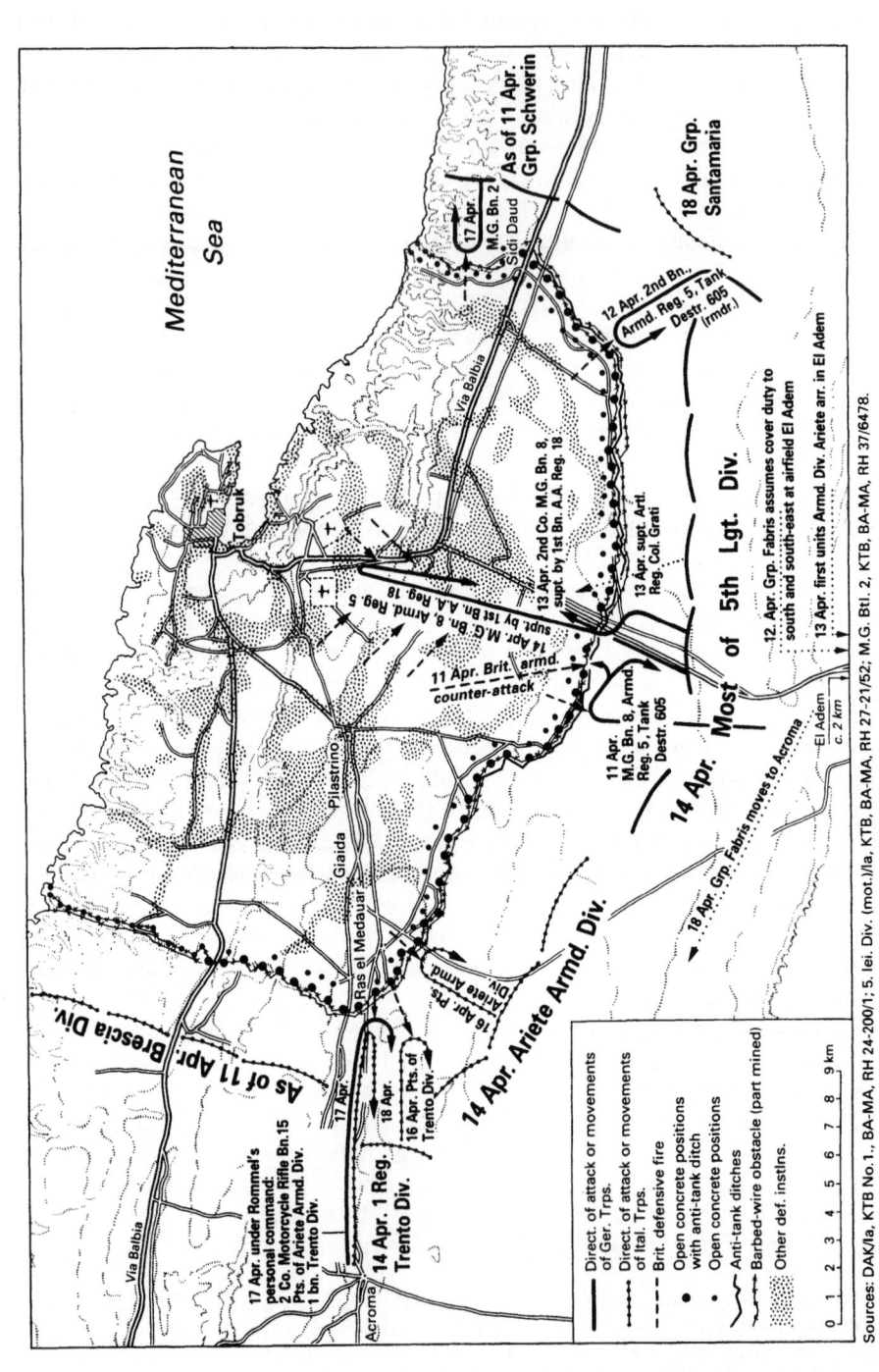

MAP V.III.I. Tobruk: The Attacks of 11–18 April 1941

V.III. Reconquest of Cyrenaica and Failure of the Attacks on Tobruk

taken prisoner. But even after this failure Rommel could not be persuaded that he did not have the necessary forces to renew the attack immediately.[32]

On 16 and 17 April Rommel directed new attacks against the commanding heights of Ras al Mudawwarah in the south-west sector of the belt of fortifications. From this position the British were able to shell the bypass road east of Akramah, the supply lifeline to the Egyptian frontier, as the Via Balbia through Tobruk was still blocked. The attack was to be carried out by Ariete Armoured Division, reinforced by several German and other Italian units. With the exception of two companies of motor-cycle riflemen, no German forces were available for the operation. Rommel had wanted to use Ariete Division on 14 April to deepen and expand the penetration of the fortification belt achieved by 5th Light Division, but it had not reached the battlefield in time. As was to be expected, the British were able to repel the attacks by Ariete, and even to take numerous Italian prisoners in a counter-attack.[33]

Rommel then decided to wait for the arrival of additional troops before launching new attacks. He explained his failure as being primarily due to the poor training and equipment of the Italian units: 'It made one's hair stand on end to see the sort of equipment with which the Duce had sent his troops into battle.'[34] This insight, however, had not prevented Rommel himself from sending the Italians to assault the British defensive ring after his better-equipped and -trained German troops had repeatedly failed to achieve a breakthrough.

With his over-hasty attacks on Tobruk, Rommel had seriously weakened his limited forces and created a situation which fairly invited a British counter-attack. Major-General Morshead understood well the tactical implications of the situation, but he, and Wavell in Cairo, assumed that many more Germans were in North Africa than had actually landed; for this reason he contented himself with limited counter-attacks in order not to weaken the defensive strength of the fortress.[35] This tactic resulted in limited crises for the Germans, which were overcome, but Rommel's tactics came under heavy criticism, not only from Berlin but also from officers of the German units under his command. Colonel von Herff, at that time commander of the troops on the Sollum front, observed:

Nobody here understood these first attacks on Tobruk: although the strength of the garrison and fortress were known, each newly arrived battalion was sent into attack and naturally enough didn't get through. The result is that there isn't a unit at Tobruk that

---

[32] Irving, *Rommel*, 81–4; Playfair, *Mediterranean*, ii. 38; Rommel, *Papers*, 124–8; Taysen, *Tobruk*, 106–11; *Prima controffensiva*, 117–21. On Rommel's behaviour cf. also Schmidt, *Afrika*, 52–3.
[33] *Prima controffensiva*, 122–5. Playfair (*Mediterranean*, ii. 38) gives a figure of 26 officers and 777 men on 16 Apr. Taysen (*Tobruk*, 112) mentions over 1,100 prisoners on the same day.
[34] Rommel, *Papers*, 127.
[35] Cf. Playfair, *Mediterranean*, ii. 38–9; Taysen, *Tobruk*, 113–14.

hasn't taken a mauling. . . . A lot of the more impulsive commands issued by the Africa Corps we junior officers just don't make head or tail of.³⁶

When, because of the situation he himself had created at Tobruk, Rommel absurdly demanded additional forces, the army high command responded with harsh criticism. Although Hitler was evidently inclined to send him an additional motorized regiment, and Göring wanted to support his advance to the Suez Canal with the Luftwaffe, Brauchitsch, referring to the general situation, refused Rommel's request. Because of the approaching campaign against the Soviet Union no more forces could be diverted to other theatres; their transfer to North Africa would in any case only be possible after the arrival of 15th Armoured Division, whose core units were scheduled to reach Tripoli by 5 May. Sufficient transport capacity and fuel were not available for such an operation, and the further the German troops advanced against Egypt, the fiercer British resistance would become. The army high command therefore considered a raid against Egypt to be the most that could be attempted.³⁷ Halder reacted to Rommel's calls for help after the failed attack of 14 April with sarcasm: 'Now at last he is constrained to state that his forces are not sufficiently strong to allow him to take full advantage of the "unique opportunities" afforded by the overall situation. That is the impression we have had for quite some time over here.'³⁸

The Italian high command also rejected Rommel's request for two divisions in line to free Brescia and Ariete Divisions for another attack on Tobruk. He also wanted to occupy the area around Bardiyah and Sollum with Trento Division. The lack of transport capacity made it impossible to bring up the two divisions, and, after the successful British forays, Rommel had to station most of Trento Division on the fortress front. Only a reinforced battalion could be transferred to Bardiyah. For the time being, only the two exhausted advance units of 5th Light and 15th Armoured Divisions were available on the Egyptian frontier to secure the triangle Bardiyah–Sollum–Capuzzo. Facing them, 22nd Guards Brigade secured the coastal plain, while the Mobile Force operated on the desert plateau, which it reached via the Halfaya pass. In addition to the coastal road between Upper and Lower Sollum, where the hostile armies confronted each other, the Halfaya pass was, at this point, the only way of reaching the desert plateau from the coastal plain or, conversely, of reaching the plain from the plateau, which gave it considerable military significance.³⁹

On 23 April a British attack on Fort Capuzzo was repelled, but it nevertheless caused great concern in the German command, for, as a result of a

---

³⁶ Irving, *Rommel*, 90; Kriebel, 'Nordafrika', 92–4, MGFA T3, vol. i. Cf. also Schmidt, *Afrika*, 51.
³⁷ Halder, *Diaries*, ii. 868 (11 Apr. 1941); 872 (13 Apr. 1941); 873 (14 Apr. 1941).
³⁸ Ibid. 875 (15 Apr. 1941).
³⁹ Taysen, *Tobruk*, 124–6.

transmission error in the report to the Africa Corps, the enemy force was described as having sixty tanks, which threatened the rear communications of the German units in the area of Sidi Aziz. Although the enemy had almost completely disappeared by next morning, Rommel ordered reconnaissance to be carried out to the south and south-east and the defence to be conducted in the form of attacks. On 26 April, after an unsuccessful attack, the Germans were able to penetrate the British positions above the Halfaya pass. Because of the unclear situation they withdrew during the night, but the British overestimated the capacity of their enemy and withdrew to Buqbuq, whereupon the Germans occupied the pass the next day and extended their protective forces to the south to Sidi Umar and Sidi Sulayman. The troops who had carried out the attack on the pass were withdrawn to the front around Tobruk during the night.[40]

Although the threat to the German position on the Egyptian frontier had disappeared on the morning of 24 April, Rommel sent alarming reports to the army high command and demanded additional forces, the reinforcement of the Luftwaffe in North Africa, especially with fighter bombers, and the sending of U-boats to the coast of North Africa. The previous day Halder had complained that he was not receiving any clear reports from Rommel, who, he thought, was unequal to the demands of his position as commander of the Africa Corps. From reports from German officers in Africa, Halder had received the impression that no one had an overview of the widely scattered German troops, whose fighting ability had declined considerably as a result of the numerous partial advances. It was decided that the assistant chief of staff for operations in the army general staff, Lieutenant-General Paulus, would attempt to clarify the situation in North Africa, as he was on good terms with Rommel and 'is perhaps the only man with enough personal influence to head off this soldier gone stark mad'.[41]

Basing his judgement on reports from Rommel, Halder believed that a crisis had arisen, not in Tobruk, but near Sollum, because the enemy was reinforcing his troops there. A retreat from the Egyptian frontier and abandoning the siege of Tobruk were quite undesirable, primarily for propaganda reasons. This dangerous situation would not change until 5 May, because only then were most units of 15th Armoured Division scheduled to arrive in Africa. Halder considered airborne troops to be worthless in Africa, as they were immobile and too little fuel was available to reinforce the Luftwaffe there. Paulus's task was to explain to Rommel the very limited help the army high command could offer him and to find out what Rommel's intentions were under the existing circumstances. At the same time, however, five additional battalions, an engineer assault battalion, and two coastal artillery battalions were assembled for use in North Africa, rail transports to

---

[40] Ibid. 127–30.
[41] Halder, *Diaries*, ii. 885 (23 Apr. 1941).

Naples were accelerated; and the use of air-transport groups was requested from the Wehrmacht high command.[42]

On 26 April the Luftwaffe transferred two additional air-transport Gruppen from the Balkans to southern Italy, which flew 800 men to Africa the following day. However, this lightning action led to delays of the sea transports, as the transport aircraft had to be escorted by Me 110s, which were thus not available to protect the convoys. For this reason the Italians refused to let the ships put to sea.[43]

But this was not the only additional burden for the Luftwaffe resulting from Rommel's campaign. In April a Gruppe of Me 109 fighters from the Balkans and an additional Gruppe of dive-bombers from Sicily were transferred to North Africa to compensate for Rommel's lack of artillery. During a visit to the front on 18 April, the head of the Luftwaffe operations staff, Major-General Hoffmann von Waldau, realized that the Air Leader Africa urgently needed reinforcements to fulfil his numerous tasks. While Rommel complained about a lack of support in the fighting around Tobruk and on the Egyptian frontier, the Luftwaffe still had to protect the transports to North Africa, the unloading ports, coastal shipping, and the entire, greatly expanded rear area, and, at the same time, prevent supplies from reaching the defenders of Tobruk. It was unable to prevent the annihilation of the twentieth sea-transport group on 16 April or the bombardment of Tripoli on 21 April, but it did force Royal Air Force fighters to leave Tobruk, achieve air supremacy, and inflict heavy losses on transports to and from Tobruk.[44]

However, the Luftwaffe did not intend to continue fulfilling these varied tasks in the Mediterranean. After the Balkan campaign its first priority was to transfer X Air Corps to Greece to be able to attack British naval forces and supply shipments in the eastern Mediterranean, especially in the Nile delta and the Suez Canal. On 18 April the Wehrmacht high command informed the Italian high command of German plans and wishes, for the Luftwaffe also needed airfields in certain areas of Greece to be occupied by the Italians. Three days later, returning from his visit to Rommel, Hoffmann von Waldau met General Pricolo in Rome and worked out the details with him. While the Air Leader Africa was also to have strong formations in future—a Gruppe of Ju 88s, two or three Gruppen of Ju 87s, a Gruppe of Me 109s, a Gruppe of Me 110s, a long-range reconnaissance Staffel, and a transport Gruppe of Ju 52s—the Luftwaffe wanted to leave only one Gruppe of Ju 87s and one of Me 110s in Sicily, where the Italian air force was to resume its previous tasks. Then, however, the Luftwaffe leadership decided to transfer these two Gruppen to Greece and informed the Italian air force in a detailed letter of 6 May how it could fulfil its tasks in the central and western Mediterranean.[45]

---

[42] Ibid. 885–7 (24 Apr. 1941). Cf. also Taysen, *Tobruk*, 130–3.
[43] Cf. Gundelach, *Luftwaffe im Mittelmeer*, 138; Taysen, *Tobruk*, 132.
[44] Gundelach, *Luftwaffe im Mittelmeer*, 135–8; cf. Santoni and Mattesini, *La partecipazione tedesca*, 55–62.
[45] Gundelach, *Luftwaffe im Mittelmeer*, 224–9.

V.III. Reconquest of Cyrenaica and Failure of the Attacks on Tobruk 687

General Pricolo urgently requested that the German aircraft be left in Sicily, as he did not have any suitable aircraft for attacking ships, for anti-submarine defence, for laying mines near Malta, and for dealing with the Hurricane fighters over the island. He was supported by the German liaison staffs in Rome, who warned that the German plans would have serious consequences for the transport situation in the Mediterranean. They did not limit their criticism to the material shortcomings of the Italian air force, and pointed out that the Italians were not in a position to take over the tasks of protecting the transports to North Africa and containing the British forces on Malta.[46] The 'complete inactivity of the Italian armed forces' gave reason to fear that 'a rejection of the Italian request would not only seriously endanger the convoy movements, but, given the known attitude of the high command of the Italian navy, the possibility exists that the convoy traffic itself would come to a standstill'.[47]

The naval war staff noted that between 8 February and 1 May 1941 33,549 men, 11,330 vehicles, and 36,332 tonnes of equipment and supplies had been transported to Libya; but in the same period, of the twenty-nine ships in service, with a total displacement of 129,837 GRT, twelve, with 47,000 GRT, had been lost and five, with 28,628 GRT, were out of service indefinitely. The total loss thus amounted to 59 per cent. In the view of the naval war staff this situation required the 'aggressive, active use of the Italian navy and air force', the improvement of the anti-aircraft defences and air protection of Tripoli and Benghazi, and the 'elimination of Malta and Crete [as British bases] by occupying them with German troops'.[48] These suggestions were an attempt to place the blame for the situation in the central Mediterranean on the Italians; the demand that Malta and Crete should be occupied was more a form of words, not directed to anyone in particular. Two weeks earlier, the naval war staff itself had expressed doubts about a landing on Malta and had suggested waiting to see what effects the conquest of Crete and the resulting threat to Egypt would have on the situation in the Mediterranean.[49] It emphasized the seriousness of the situation in Africa and took note of Rommel's requests, which fortunately were not directed to the naval war staff but to the Italian navy, the Luftwaffe, and the Italian air force; but it accepted of course the decision of the Wehrmacht high command that 'for the time being preparations for Merkur [the capture of Crete] must be given priority'.[50]

After the transfer of X Air Corps to Greece had been ordered in Hitler's Directive No. 29 of 17 May 1941,[51] Raeder again emphasized to Hitler the importance of bases in Greece as a strategic starting-point for a successful

---

[46] Ibid. 226; Baum and Weichold, *Krieg der 'Achsenmächte'*, 163.
[47] 1. Skl., KTB, Teil A, 78–9 (6 May 1941), BA-MA RM 7/24.
[48] Ibid. 91 (7 May 1941).
[49] Cf. V.II above.
[50] 1. Skl., KTB, Teil A, 138 (10 May 1941), BA-MA RM 7/24.
[51] *Hitler's War Directives*, No. 29, pp. 69–71 (17 May 1941).

tactical use of the X Air Corps, and demanded that the bases in question 'should be firmly held by German forces... until British operations in the eastern Mediterranean, including Alexandria and Suez, have been eliminated'.[52]

Clearly the naval staff saw here an opportunity to conduct a successful naval war from the air and was therefore not prepared to support the warnings against a transfer of X Air Corps. Without an influential ally, the Italians were not able to prevent the withdrawal of the Luftwaffe from the central Mediterranean. Further discussions with the Germans concerned only the delimitation of operational areas and the placing of Italian air-force units in the German operational area under German command, which, however, the Italians were able to avoid. On 26 May Generals Pricolo and Geisler agreed on a dividing-line from Cape Matapan to Darnah, which, however, only applied to reconnaissance activity. The Nile delta—with Alexandria, Cairo, and the Suez Canal—was reserved as an operational area for X Air Corps.[53]

Although the reorientation of the activity of the Luftwaffe gave reason to expect a worsening of the transport situation in the Mediterranean, Rommel continued to prepare a new attack on Tobruk. However, the Germans still encountered difficulties not only with transports across the sea to North Africa, but also on land. Capacity was not sufficient to move normal supplies —as well as large quantities of ammunition for the attack and the newly arrived troops—the 1,500 kilometres from Tripoli to Tobruk. The Air Leader Africa considered the use of airfields near the front to be too dangerous.[54] However, when Lieutenant-General Paulus, in his capacity as representative of the army high command, arrived to visit Rommel on 27 April, his host described the supply situation, especially as far as ammunition was concerned, as quite satisfactory. He also rejected other reasons to postpone the attack, e.g. the suggestion of 15th Armoured Division to attack two days later than planned, when it would actually be possible to make use of the recently arrived reinforcements. Rommel professed to fear that it would then no longer be possible to surprise the enemy, who could bring in reinforcements by sea more quickly than the Germans could bring them up by land. Paulus, however, while pointing out that he had the authority to give orders to the Africa Corps, reserved his judgement of the situation until he had gained an impression on the spot. He raised objections to the withdrawal of German forces from the front near Bardiyah and Sollum, but he approved the planned attack on 29 April, after General Gariboldi had given his approval the previous day.[55]

Rommel intended, after dive-bomber attacks and artillery preparation, to penetrate the fortification belt with shock troops on the evening of 30 April near Ras al Mudawwarah and, from the bridgehead thus established, to

---

[52] 'Führer Conferences', 199 (22 May 1941).
[53] Gundelach, *Luftwaffe im Mittelmeer*, 228–30.
[54] Cf. Taysen, *Tobruk*, 136–40.
[55] Ibid. 141–4.

penetrate the fortress itself with all German and Italian attack forces on the following day. German forces were placed in the centre to capture Ras al Mudawwarah and attack Fort Pilastrino: parts of 5th Light Division under Major-General Kirchheim (Major-General Streich had become *persona non grata* for Rommel) were on the right flank; 15th Armoured Division was on the left. Further to the right Ariete Armoured Division was to attack, further to the left Brescia Infantry Division. The main force in Kirchheim's group was a detachment of seventy-four tanks; in addition the group had a platoon of tank-destroyers as well as a machine-gun battalion, an engineer battalion, and an anti-aircraft battalion. As its tanks had not yet arrived, 15th Armoured Division was able to deploy only a tank-destroyer battalion, two rifle battalions, one motor-cycle-rifle battalion, and an engineer battalion.[56]

The attack began as planned on 30 April at 6.15 p.m. The shock troops were able to penetrate the fortification belt, and during the night the two shock regiments were brought forward. But 15th Armoured Division suffered heavy losses: the units brought to Tobruk by air went into battle without rest or rations and were quite ignorant of the terrain and the plan of the bunkers they were supposed to capture. Rommel had forbidden any reconnaissance, to avoid alerting the enemy, but Kirchheim's group had ignored this prohibition. For this reason it was able to advance most rapidly eastward, until its tanks encountered a minefield shortly after 8.00 a.m. Supported by one of Kirchheim's tank companies, 15th Armoured Division, which had been halted by the fortification belt, was also able to move forward. Rommel, who as usual was near the front, had at first ordered the Kirchheim group to resume its attack eastward when he received the report, in the meantime overtaken by events, that 15th Armoured Division had not succeeded in breaking through the fortification belt. He was concerned about securing the penetration, broke off the attack in the east, and ordered the armoured detachment to attack to the south-west to support Ariete Armoured Division in penetrating the fortification belt from the west. However, this decision actually meant the end of the attempt to break through to the port and capture Tobruk, although the two battalions of the Kirchheim group were left in their forward positions. Apparently Rommel wanted to go over to the defensive only temporarily and resume the attack in a few days, but he had to accept the actual conditions and the orders of Paulus and the army high command.[57]

On the morning of 1 May Paulus had been optimistic about the chances of success of the attack on Tobruk, but during the day, at the point where a

---

[56] Cf. ibid. 142–3; Kirchheim, 'Angriffsgruppe', 6–7, MGFA D-350. Cf. also text to nn. 30–1 above and Map V.III.2.

[57] On the course of the fighting cf. Holtzendorff, 'Angriff', 6–10, MGFA D-087; Kirchheim, 'Angriffsgruppe', 7–13, MGFA D-350; Taysen, *Tobruk*, 145–8; *Prima controffensiva*, 137–45. Rommel (*Papers*, 134) wrote about the situation in the newly captured positions: 'Many men had dysentery and the conditions were frightful.' Nevertheless, he refused to withdraw the two battalions of the Kirchheim group in the fortification belt. Cf. Map V.III.3.

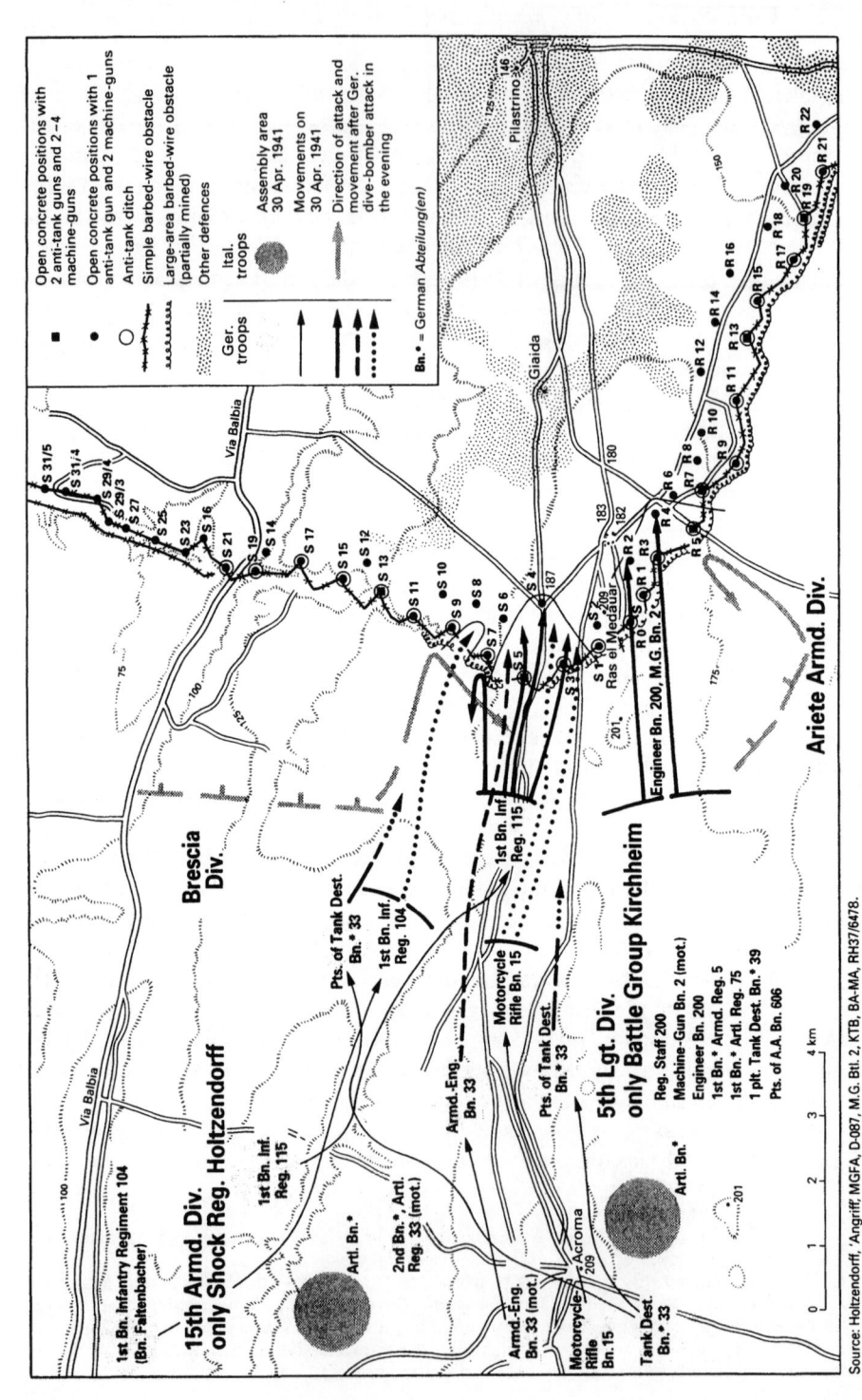

MAP V.III.2. Tobruk: The Night Attack on Ras al Mudauwwarah, 30 April–1 May 1941

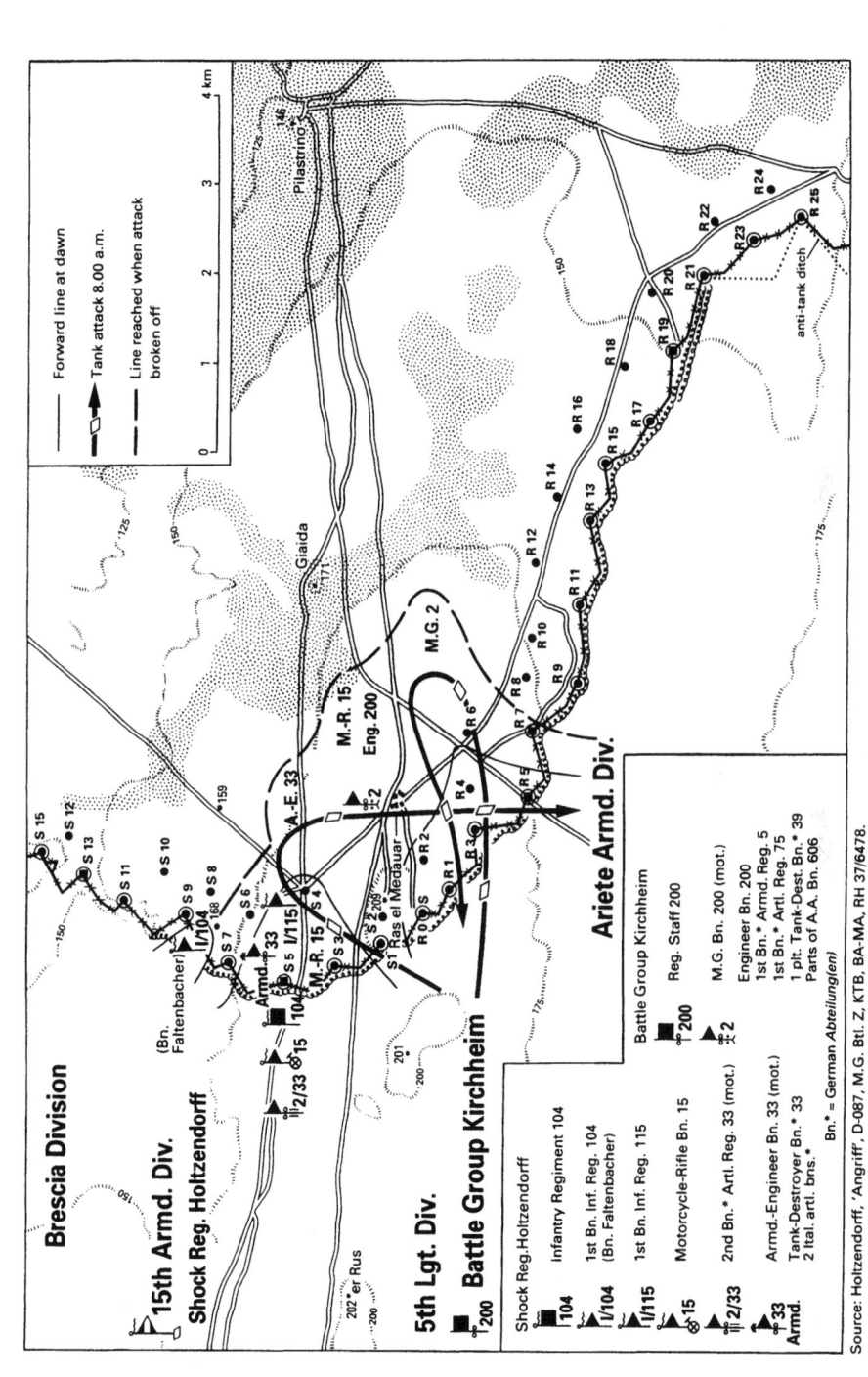

MAP V.III.3. Tobruk: The Course of the Attack on 1 May 1941

penetration of the fortification belt had been achieved, he came to the conclusion that a continuation of the attack before fresh troops and sufficient ammunition had been brought up would not lead to success. Rommel therefore decided not to order a resumption of the attack, even on 2 May. In the afternoon of 2 May Paulus gave Rommel a written order in which he expressed his view that the Africa Corps did not have sufficient forces to break the resistance of the enemy. The attacks were to be resumed only if the enemy withdrew. The main task of the Africa Corps was to hold Cyrenaica, with or without Tobruk, Bardiyah, and Sollum.[58] Rear-area defensive positions were to be prepared along the line Ayn al Ghazalah–Ghwat al Ahmar. Whether the attack on Tobruk could be resumed after the arrival of most of 15th Armoured Division would depend on the development of the situation.

Paulus's order was confirmed by the army high command the next day, with the restriction that 'before any resumption of the attack seeking a decision at Tobruk, even after the arrival of the rest of 15 Armoured Division and additional reinforcements, the approval of the army high command must be obtained'.[59] First, however, the attackers had to repel the counter-attacks of the Australians, who, on the evening of 1 and 3 May, attempted in battalion and brigade strength to recapture Ras al Mudawwarah, but failed to do so.[60] At this point the lack of ammunition on the German side made itself strongly felt. Paulus also noticed that, contrary to Rommel's original description, the ammunition situation had become extremely critical. After he had ended his visit to the Africa Corps on 7 May, Paulus had talks with the commanding general of X Air Corps and the quartermaster of the Africa Corps. He telephoned his impressions to the army high command: 'The crux of the problem in North Africa is not Tobruk or Sollum, but the organization of supplies.'[61]

Paulus also talked with the Italian high command in Rome about the problems in North Africa, but the promises he was given could not, of course, offset the withdrawal of X Air Corps, for which the Italians could not be held responsible. Even Rommel now thought it necessary to call the attention of the army high command to his supply problems: 'Because of concentrated enemy pressure on ships and ports, with present protective measures arrival of supplies by ship cannot be guaranteed.'[62] Halder was certainly right when he wrote on 11 May, after Paulus had returned and reported to him: 'Situation in North Africa unpleasant. By overstepping his orders Rommel has brought about a situation for which our present supply capabilities are insufficient. Rommel cannot cope with the situation.'[63]

---

[58] Halder, *Diaries*, ii. 899 (3 May 1941). Cf. also Taysen, *Tobruk*, 149–50.
[59] Ibid. 150.
[60] Playfair, *Mediterranean*, ii. 156.
[61] Halder, *Diaries*, ii. 912 (8 May 1941) (trans. amended).
[62] 1. Skl., KTB, Teil A, 138 (10 May 1941), BA-MA RM 7/24.
[63] Halder, *Diaries*, ii. 915 (11 May 1941).

V.III. Reconquest of Cyrenaica and Failure of the Attacks on Tobruk

The capture of Tobruk was an essential precondition for an attack on the Suez Canal and the British position in Egypt. But the Wehrmacht and army high commands did not plan to carry out such an operation in 1941, nor were sufficient forces available for it. The defence of Cyrenaica was possible, however, without the occupation of Tobruk. The criticism of his conduct of the campaign was aimed less at Rommel's attack on Tobruk than at its preparation and execution, and at the high losses he accepted.[64] Rommel himself explained the losses as a typical consequence of 'changing from a war of movement to positional warfare'. He did not mention that a large part of the troops had had to attack at night shortly after arriving and without knowledge of the battle area: 'The high casualties suffered by my assault forces were primarily caused by their lack of training.'[65]

When Major-General Streich, whose removal Rommel had requested after the failure of the first attack on Tobruk, reported to him before leaving, an argument developed between the two men. Rommel reproached Streich, who had disobeyed his completely unrealistic attack orders: 'You were far too concerned with the well-being of your troops'; Streich replied: 'I can imagine no greater words of praise for a division commander.'[66] Major-General Kirchheim, who had commanded parts of 5th Light Division in the attacks on Tobruk at the end of April, also expressed criticism after the war: 'I do not like to be reminded of that time, because so much blood was needlessly shed.' But he clearly did not want to criticize Rommel; his reasons and his explanation of Rommel's reputation are instructive:

Regarding Rommel, my view is that thanks to the propaganda, first by Goebbels, then by Montgomery, and finally, after he was poisoned, by all the former enemy powers, he has become a symbol of the best military traditions. His qualities of leadership are glorified, as are those of his character, especially his chivalry, goodness, and modesty.... Any public criticism of this already legendary personality would damage the esteem in which the German soldier is held.[67]

Rommel, however, demanded senseless sacrifices not only in the attacks on Tobruk. After these were stopped, his troops were by no means in a favourable position, while the British position in Tobruk offered considerable advantages. The British were able to make effective use of the extensive system of fortifications and their superiority in infantry and artillery, which was made even greater by the artillery left behind by the Italians. At the same time, the weakness of their armoured forces[68] was not as significant as it would

---

[64] According to Rommel's report to the army high command (9 May 1941), losses were 53 officers and 1,187 men: Halder, *Diaries*, ii. 912–13 (9 May 1941). Cf. also Holtzendorf, 'Angriff', MGFA D-087.

[65] Rommel, *Papers*, 133.

[66] Quoted according to Irving, *Rommel*, 97.

[67] Correspondence between Streich and Kirchheim in 1959, quoted in Heckmann, *Rommels Krieg*, 120–1. On the glorification of Rommel's conduct of the war in North Africa in National Socialist propaganda cf. Reuth, *Erwin Rommel*, 84–6.

[68] Cf. Playfair, *Mediterranean*, ii. 159.

have been in a war of movement in the desert. The question remains whether it would not have been possible and better for the British to establish a similarly favourable defensive position at El Alamein, where they enjoyed the advantage of not having to move supplies by sea, while Rommel lacked the fuel and transport capacity to maintain close contact with the enemy. But Churchill would probably have had as little patience with such a rational strategy as did Hitler with similar German tactics.

IV. The Fighting on the Sollum Front

IN April 1941, because of the strained transport situation in the Mediterranean, which threatened to become worse after the withdrawal of X Air Corps, and the shortage of transport capacity in North Africa, German and Italian military leaders again became interested in Tunisia. To begin with, the Germans negotiated with the French through the armistice commission about the purchase of field kitchens and lorries, which were at the same time to transport foodstuffs from Algeria and Tunisia. At the beginning of May General Guzzoni, the deputy chief of the Italian general staff, stated in a memorandum that, in his opinion, the transport situation was such that it was not possible to hold Libya, much less prepare an offensive. He therefore demanded the use of the port of Tunis.[1] This question was also discussed during the same month in the negotiations in Paris between the Wehrmacht and the French army. Within the framework of the agreements on military co-operation in Syria, West Africa, and Equatorial Africa[2] agreements were also concluded on Tunisia, according to which Bizerta could be used as an unloading port for German supplies and transports; the latter could also be carried out from Toulon to Bizerta using French ships. Moreover, French ships were to be chartered for transports across the Mediterranean and for North African coastal traffic. The Germans wanted to buy heavy artillery and coastal guns and the appropriate ammunition. In addition to the purchase of 1,100 lorries, 300 cars, 300 motor-cycles, 30 buses, and 10 vehicle workshops in North Africa, 400 lorries were to be bought in France itself.[3]

However, the agreements were not carried out, because Hitler was not prepared to pay the political price the French demanded, and because he believed that he would be able to achieve his aims without important concessions after the campaign against the Soviet Union. Under these conditions, Germany purchased only several artillery pieces and took delivery of 1,500 lorries, of which, however, only about 400 could actually be put to limited use. A total of seventeen different makes and fifty-eight models were involved; most of them could be used only in the ports.[4] This result was quite modest, but an improvement of relations between Germany and the Vichy government would not have changed the situation of the Africa Corps significantly.[5] Using

---

[1] Cf. Greiselis, *Das Ringen*, 29–30; Halder, *Diaries*, ii. 905 (6 May 1941). For the Italian view cf. *Prima controffensiva*, 164 ff.; Cavallero, *Comando supremo*, 105 (26 May 1941).
[2] Cf. IV.II.1 above (Schreiber).
[3] Protocols signed in Paris on 27 and 28 May 1941: *DGFP* D xii, No. 559, pp. 892–900.
[4] Cf. Greiselis, *Das Ringen*, 34; Taysen, *Tobruk*, 200.
[5] On the general prospects of a Franco-German co-operation in Africa cf. Warlimont, 'Kriegführung', 390–9, MGFA P-216/I-III.

Bizerta as a supply-port would have considerably lengthened the German supply-routes, and from there supplies could be moved by railway only to Qabis. Available lorry transport capacity was sufficient to move only half of the necessary supplies between Tripoli and Tobruk, the other half being moved by coastal shipping.[6] Moreover, as an air attack on the port of Sfax on 28 May 1941 demonstrated,[7] the British had no intention of tolerating sea transports along the Tunisian coast or to Bizerta if they carried supplies for the Axis troops in North Africa. For this reason, in his answer to the memorandum by General Guzzoni Major-General von Rintelen rejected the idea of opening a supply-route via Tunisia and recommended the conquest of Malta to the Italian high command as the best way to protect transports to North Africa.[8] Nevertheless, the Germans and Italians continued their attempts to make use of the route via Tunisia and to replenish equipment and supplies for their troops through French deliveries from North Africa. While German and Italian leaders had come to consider the supply question as the central problem of the war in North Africa since the end of April, Churchill was determined to use all available means to interrupt the flow of supplies to Axis forces there. General Wavell in Cairo had an additional problem: after sending the British expeditionary corps to Greece and withdrawing from Cyrenaica, he had very few tanks with which to repel a possible German advance into Egypt. He could not count on a return of the tanks sent to Greece, and he would receive only thirty or forty tanks from the repair shops before the end of May. As he reported to the British government on 18 April, the situation seemed all the more threatening when he realized that the second German division to arrive in Libya was not an additional 'colonial division', but 15th Armoured Division, whose strength was (erroneously) assumed to be over 400 tanks.[9] Churchill decided to act immediately and send a convoy with tanks through the Mediterranean to Egypt, in spite of the risk, and not around the Cape of Good Hope. The shorter route would save forty days. He assumed, however, that the British 7th Armoured Division would then resume its victorious advance and drive the Germans from Cyrenaica by the end of June.[10]

The operation, under the code-name 'Tiger', was carried out between 6 and 12 May. Together with the battleship *Queen Elizabeth* and two light cruisers, sent as reinforcements for Admiral Cunningham, five fast transport ships carrying 295 tanks and 53 Hurricane fighters put to sea under the protection of H Force from Gibraltar.[11] The Mediterranean Fleet, which was to take over protection of the convoy south of Malta, used the opportunity to escort two

---

[6] Taysen, *Tobruk*, 156.
[7] Greiselis, *Das Ringen*, 32.
[8] Gundelach, *Luftwaffe im Mittelmeer*, 140.
[9] *PWT*, Middle East I, Hist (B) 3, No. 140, p. 60. Cf. Hinsley, *British Intelligence*, i. 395–6.
[10] Churchill, *Second World War*, iii. 217–20.
[11] Playfair, *Mediterranean*, ii. 114–19. The number of tanks differs in Churchill (n. 10 above) and Taysen (*Tobruk*, 158).

convoys to the island. On the morning of 8 May, on the way to Malta, and on 11 May shortly after midnight, on the way back to Alexandria, light British surface ships bombarded Benghazi. Although they captured two Italian ships after the bombardment on 8 May, they were driven off by a dive-bomber attack on 11 May. A transport ship of the Tiger convoy sank with fifty-seven tanks and ten fighters after hitting two mines; returning to Gibraltar, a destroyer was struck by a bomb. But, favoured by thick weather, the British suffered no other losses. The convoy with H Force was discovered only on the morning of 8 May north of the Algerian coast: 'As a result of the well-known inactivity of the Italian navy, German–Italian countermeasures against the enemy transport operation were limited to the use of air units.'[12] This presumption of the naval war staff was not quite accurate: a force of Italian cruisers and destroyers did leave Palermo, but it remained in the area north of Sicily, where contact with the enemy was hardly to be expected.[13] As no Italian battleships were ready for action, except for the modernized *Cesare* and *Doria*, the Italians rightly considered their forces inferior to those of the Royal Navy in the Mediterranean. And after the engagements off Cape Matapan and near the Qirquinah Bank the Italians had no illusions about successfully attacking the British ships at night with light forces.

In the meantime the British had intercepted and deciphered the report by Lieutenant-General Paulus on the situation in North Africa and his instructions to the Africa Corps, which had been transmitted by the Luftwaffe. Churchill had sent the information gained to Wavell in Cairo, with the demand that he take immediate action. 'Those Hun people are far less dangerous once they lose the initiative.'[14] Wavell then decided to take advantage of the situation before 15th Armoured Division reached the battle area in full strength. He ordered Brigadier W. H. E. Gott to start an offensive in the area of Sollum with all available tanks as soon as Operation Tiger had been successfully concluded, but without waiting until the newly arrived tanks were ready for action. Churchill and the British military leaders completely approved of this 'Operation Brevity' and expected it to have a great effect on the situation in Iraq, where fighting had begun on 2 May, as well as on the situation in Syria and Palestine.[15]

For his operation, which was intended if possible to relieve the garrison of Tobruk and lead to a further, joint operation westward, Brigadier Gott had only weak forces available, which he divided into three groups. On the desert flank in the west 7th Armoured Brigade Group was to advance from Bir al

---

[12] 1. Skl., KTB, Teil A, 106 (8 May 1941), BA-MA RM 7/24.

[13] *Marina italiana*, v. 7–8. According to Iachino (*Tramonto*, 266) and Bragadin (*Che ha fatto la marina?*, 140–1), the Italian fleet did not put to sea.

[14] Churchill, *Second World War*, iii. 299; *PWT*, Middle East I, Hist (B) 4, No. 50, p. 22 (7 May 1941). Cf. also Hinsley, *British Intelligence*, i. 396–7.

[15] Churchill, *Second World War*, iii. 299–300; *PWT*, Middle East I, Hist (B) 4, No. 62, p. 26 (9 May 1941), No. 100, p. 43 (14 May 1941).

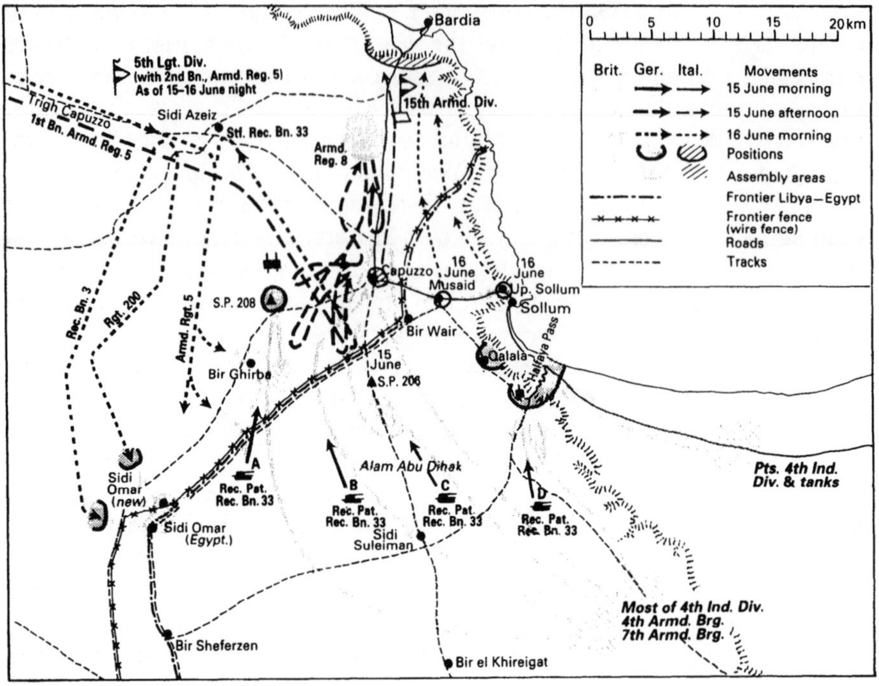

Bardia
0 5 10 15 20 km
Brit. Ger. Ital. Movements
15 June morning
15 June afternoon
16 June morning
Positions
Assembly areas
Frontier Libya—Egypt
Frontier fence (wire fence)
Roads
Tracks
5th Lgt. Div. (with 2nd Bn., Armd. Reg. 5) As of 15–16 June night
Trigh Capuzzo
1st Bn. Armd. Reg. 5
Sidi Azeiz
Stf. Rec. Bn. 33
Armd. Reg. 8
15th Armd. Div.
Capuzzo
16 June Musaid
16 June Up. Sollum
Sollum
S.P. 208
Rec. Bn. 3
Rgt. 200
Armd. Rgt. 5
Bir Wair
Bir Ghirba
15 June
S.P. 206
Qalala
Halfaya Pass
Pts. 4th Ind. Div. & tanks
Alam Abu Dihak
A
Rec. Pat. Rec. Bn. 33
B
Rec. Pat. Rec. Bn. 33
C
Rec. Pat. Rec. Bn. 33
D
Rec. Pat. Rec. Bn. 33
Sidi Omar (new)
Sidi Omar (Egypt.)
Sidi Suleiman
Most of 4th Ind. Div. 4th Armd. Brg. 7th Armd. Brg.
Bir Sheferzen
Bir el Khireigat

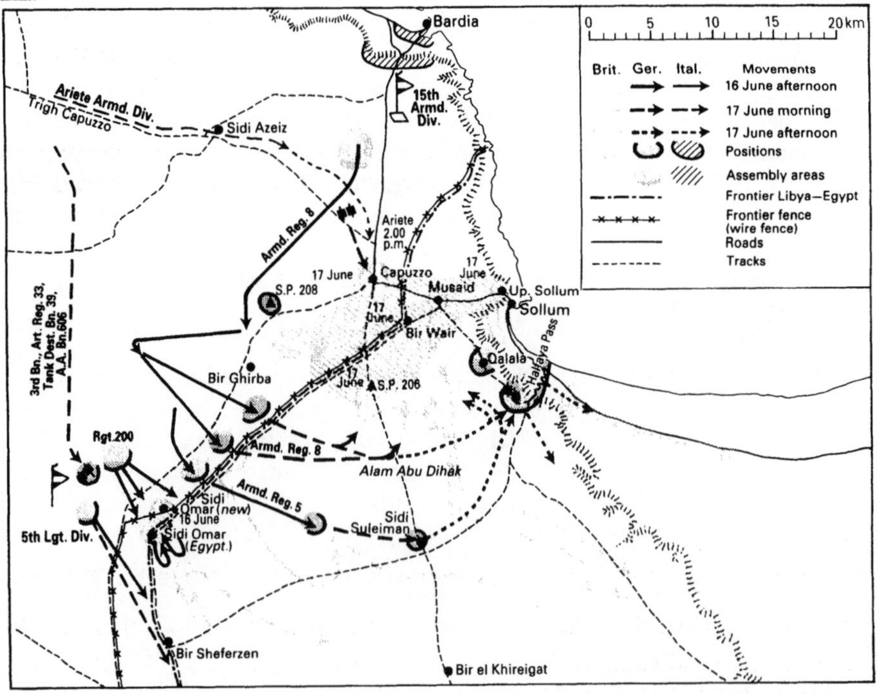

Bardia
0 5 10 15 20 km
Brit. Ger. Ital. Movements
16 June afternoon
17 June morning
17 June afternoon
Positions
Assembly areas
Frontier Libya—Egypt
Frontier fence (wire fence)
Roads
Tracks
15th Armd. Div.
Ariete Armd. Div.
Trigh Capuzzo
Sidi Azeiz
Armd. Reg. 8
Ariete 2.00 p.m.
17 June
Capuzzo
17 June
Musaid
Up. Sollum
Sollum
S.P. 208
17 June
Bir Wair
Qalala
Halfaya Pass
Bir Ghirba
17 June
S.P. 206
3rd Bn., Art. Reg. 33, Tank Dest. Bn. 39, A.A. Bn.606
Rgt.200
Armd. Reg. 8
Alam Abu Dihak
Armd. Reg. 5
Sidi Omar (new)
16 June
Sidi Omar (Egypt.)
Sidi Suleiman
5th Lgt. Div.
Bir Sheferzen
Bir el Khireigat

V.IV. The Fighting on the Sollum Front

Khuyraygat to Sidi Aziz with twenty-nine Cruiser tanks. In the centre above the escarpment 22nd Guards Brigade Group, with the support of twenty-four infantry tanks, was to take the upper end of the Halfaya pass, secure Fort Capuzzo, and advance northward, while Coastal Group had the task of occupying the lower end of the Halfaya pass and Sollum with an infantry brigade and an artillery regiment.[16]

On the German side, Colonel von Herff commanded a company of motor-cycle riflemen and a company of tank destroyers, a motorized reconnaissance battalion, an anti-aircraft battalion, and an Italian battalion. On 8 May he received an armoured battalion from Rommel as a reserve, as various signs indicated that a British attack was imminent. On 11 and 12 May, however, reconnaissance produced little concrete information. As a result, the German commanders on the Sollum front were at first surprised when the British attack began on the morning of 15 May.[17] Initially the attack was successful. The 7th Armoured Brigade Group reached Sidi Aziz, Centre Group captured Fort Capuzzo and the position above the Halfaya pass, and by evening Coastal Group had taken the lower end of the Halfaya pass. But a counter-attack by the German armoured detachment on Capuzzo forced the guards brigade group to withdraw with heavy losses. Brigadier Gott then decided to withdraw to the Halfaya pass, while leaving Western Group to provide cover at Sidi Aziz. Herff considered this force especially dangerous, and he therefore withdrew westward during the night in order, together with an armoured battalion provided by Rommel, to attack from the south on the morning of 16 May. Contact was established with the enemy only near Sidi Sulayman, as Brigadier Gott had withdrawn his forces and still held only the Halfaya pass.[18]

Even Churchill's attempts to put a good face on the results of Operation Brevity could not conceal the fact that it was clearly a failure, although the Halfaya pass remained in British hands for the time being. Wavell quickly recognized the cause: the underestimation of the enemy's strength.[19] At the

---

[16] Playfair, *Mediterranean*, ii. 160. On the fighting cf. Maps V.IV.1 and 2.
[17] Kriebel, 'Nordafrika', 135–7, MGFA T3, vol. i.
[18] Cf. Playfair, *Mediterranean*, ii. 160–2; Taysen, *Tobruk*, 160–3; *Prima controffensiva*, 155–8.
[19] Churchill, *Second World War*, iii. 302–3; *PWT*, Middle East I, Hist (B) 4, No. 126, pp. 53 (17 May 1941), 128 (18 May 1941).

MAP V.IV.1. Operation Battleaxe, 15 June 1941 (Morning)–16 June 1941 (Afternoon)

Sources: 15 P2. Div./Ia, KTB, BA-MA RH 27-15/4; 5 lei. Div. (mot.)/Ia, KTB, BA-MA RH 27-21/52; Kriebel, 'Sollum', MGFA D-121; Playfair, *Mediterranean*, ii.

MAP V.IV.2. Operation Battleaxe, 16 June 1941 (Afternoon)–17 June 1941 (Evening)

Sources: 15 P2 Div./Ia, KTB, BA-MA RH 27-15-4; 5 lei. Div. (mot.)/Ia, KTB, BA-MA RH 27-21/52; Kriebel, 'Sollum', MGFA D-121; Playfair, *Mediterranean*, ii.

same time, however, he made a new mistake when he concluded from the experience of the operation that German tanks were cautious about attacking British armoured units. This conclusion was correct, but it was due only in part to respect for British tanks. The main reason for the German tactic was the doctrine that fighting enemy tanks was the task of anti-tank units. Only much later did the British realize that the main cause of their tank losses was the superiority of German anti-tank defences, especially use of the 88-mm. anti-aircraft gun for ground fighting, and not the superiority of German tanks themselves.[20] But the British attack clearly revealed the weakness of the German position on the Sollum front. Rommel immediately took action to correct this situation and transferred most of his mobile units there on 16 May. This enabled Group Herff to begin the reconquest of the Halfaya pass on 26 May. Three armoured battalions, protected by two reconnaissance battalions on the desert flank, advanced eastward in the afternoon, while a reinforced infantry battalion attacked the defenders of the Halfaya pass above and below the escarpment. On the morning of 27 May a combined infantry and tank attack finally completed the reconquest of the pass.[21]

The Germans immediately began to fortify the Halfaya pass and points 206 and 208 in a circular arc between Halfaya and Sidi Aziz as strong points. They were equipped for a defence in all directions and so designed that the enemy would not be able to recognize them easily. Further west a second line of strong points—Capuzzo, Musaid, and Upper Sollum—were occupied by Italian troops. As a mobile reserve the armoured regiment of 15th Armoured Division was assembled west of the Via Balbia between Bardiyah and Capuzzo. On 14 June its commander, Major-General Neumann-Silkow, had taken over the Sollum front. His intention was to let the enemy exhaust his energy attacking the strong points in the forward line, to inflict heavy losses on the enemy forces with armour-piercing weapons and artillery further to the rear, to force the enemy tanks to divide into several columns, and to attack and destroy those columns one after the other with the mobile reserve.[22] The haste with which 15th Armoured Division made its defensive preparations was necessary. Churchill was already pressing Wavell to send into battle the tanks he had received during Operation Tiger. As a result of the haste with which the operation had been improvised, many of the tanks were not fit for action when they were unloaded in Egypt. Moreover, some of these tanks were a new model, the Crusader, with which the soldiers of the British 7th Armoured Division still had to familiarize themselves, apart from the fact that they had not had any opportunity to train since returning to Egypt without their tanks after their victory over the Italians at Bayda Fumm. And Churchill's demand that British units should start moving into Syria on 8 June made it difficult for

---

[20] Cf. Jackson, *Campaign*, 121–2.
[21] Cf. Playfair, *Mediterranean*, ii. 163; Taysen, *Tobruk*, 164–5.
[22] Cf. Taysen, *Tobruk*, 165–6; Kriebel, 'Sollum', 3–4, MGFA T3, vol. i; *Prima controffensiva*, 172 ff.

V.IV. The Fighting on the Sollum Front

Wavell to assemble sufficient forces for an attack by Western Desert Force. The reservations Wavell therefore expressed about a military intervention in Syria caused Churchill to decide definitively to relieve him of his command at the next opportunity. The forces Wavell was able to assemble were in fact too weak to force the French in Syria to capitulate quickly: although reinforcements were sent to Syria after the end of the fighting on the Sollum front, the campaign there required five weeks.[23]

Under these circumstances, Wavell had only limited forces available for Operation Battleaxe. Two divisions were placed under the command of Western Desert Force under Lieutenant-General Beresford-Peirse: 4th Indian Division with 11th Indian and 22nd Guards Brigades, which were to be supported by 4th Armoured Brigade of the 7th Armoured Division, equipped with close-support tanks. The division was still lacking two of its own brigades; one had been sent to Syria, and the other was in the process of being transferred to Egypt from East Africa. The 7th Armoured Brigade of 7th Armoured Division consisted of only two, instead of three, regiments. One was equipped with overhauled Cruisers, and the other with new Crusaders. Various units of the division's support group were also lacking. But these were not the only reasons Wavell considered it necessary to inform Churchill that

> the measure of success which will attend this operation is in my opinion doubtful. . . . Our infantry tanks are really too slow for a battle in desert, and have been suffering considerable casualties from the fire of the powerful enemy anti-tank guns. Our Cruisers have little advantage in power or speed over German medium tanks. Technical breakdowns are still too numerous. We shall not be able to accept battle with perfect confidence in spite of numerical inferiority, as we could against Italians.[24]

Beresford-Peirse's operational plan for Battleaxe was a new, enlarged version of Brevity, with divisions in place of brigades and brigades in place of battalions.[25] In the first phase of the operation 11th Indian Infantry Brigade was to take the Halfaya pass with the help of several close-support tanks. The 4th Armoured Brigade and 22nd Guards Brigade would attack Point 206 and Capuzzo. To their left, 7th Armoured Brigade would advance north via Strong Point 208, and the support group would cover the flank in the direction of Sidi Umar. If, as Wavell hoped, the German tanks attacked 7th Armoured Brigade and a general tank battle seemed likely, 4th Armoured Brigade would join 7th Armoured Division. The British had a total of 100 close-support and ninety Cruiser tanks, opposed to more than fifty combat-ready medium tanks on the German side of the front and sixty-seven near Tobruk. In the air the 203 aircraft of the Royal Air Force enjoyed a clear supremacy over the forces available to the Air Leader Africa, of whose 156 aircraft only 101 were ready

---

[23] Cf. IV.II.2 above (Schreiber).
[24] Churchill, *Second World War*, iii. 304; *PWT*, Middle East I, Hist (B) 5, No. 11, pp. 5–6 (28 May 1941).
[25] Jackson, *Campaign*, 126.

for action. During the fighting, however, he did receive reinforcements from X Air Corps.[26]

The British attack, which the Germans recognized in time, began on 15 June. The British were not able to reach their objectives on both wings. At the Halfaya pass they lost fifteen of eighteen close-support tanks, and at Point 208 by evening the defenders reduced 7th Armoured Brigade to forty-eight Cruisers still capable of fighting. In the centre, on the other hand, the British attack was more successful and was able to overrun most of the German artillery positions there. The 15th Armoured Division was then forced to send its 8th Armoured Regiment into battle earlier than planned to relieve Strong Point 206 and recapture the lost artillery. Rommel, who had remained at the front around Tobruk to repel an expected foray by the British garrison, sent 5th Light Division via Kambut to Sidi Aziz at noon. The reinforced 1st Battalion of 5th Armoured Regiment was able in the evening to intervene in the fighting around Strong Point 208 and force the British back in the direction of Sidi Umar. In the centre, however, 8th Armoured Regiment was pushed back to the north-east by the British 4th Armoured Brigade and could not prevent the fall of Strong Point 206 and Fort Capuzzo during the afternoon. South of Bardia the Germans were able to establish an improvised defensive front only with difficulty. The 4th Indian Division intended to advance further towards Bardiyah and finally take the Halfaya pass on 16 June. The 4th Armoured Brigade was then to return to the command of 7th Armoured Division in order, together with 7th Armoured Brigade, to defeat the German tank forces near Strong Point 208.[27]

The 15th Armoured Division wanted to continue the attack on Capuzzo with 8th Armoured Regiment and 1st Battalion of 5th Armoured Regiment on 16 June, but the commander of 5th Light Division ordered the armoured battalion to join his division in an attack via Sidi Umar and Sidi Sulayman against the enemy's flank. As a result, 4th Indian Division was able to turn back the attacks of the German 8th Armoured Regiment and also to capture Musaid and Sollum. However, this action prevented the British 4th Armoured Brigade from joining 7th Armoured Brigade at Strong Point 208. At 11.00 a.m., after three futile attacks on Capuzzo, 15th Armoured Division finally decided to withdraw most of its mobile forces and move them south-westward to join the attack of 5th Light Division on the enemy flank. The 5th Light Division was able to overcome the resistance of the British 7th Armoured Brigade, which by evening had only twenty-one tanks still in action, and reach the area west of Sidi Sulayman. On 17 June Rommel ordered it to push on to the Halfaya pass via Sidi Sulayman, while 15th Armoured Division was to

---

[26] Playfair, *Mediterranean*, ii. 165–6; Taysen, *Tobruk*, 167–8; Gundelach, *Luftwaffe im Mittelmeer*, 143–4.

[27] On the course of the fighting cf. Kriebel, 'Nordafrika', 153–91, MGFA T3, vol. i; id., 'Sollum', MGFA D-121; Playfair, *Mediterranean*, ii. 167–74; Taysen, *Tobruk*, 170–82; *Prima controffensiva*, 176–82; Maps V.IV.1 and 2.

reach the same objective via Alam Abu Dihak. When the British commander, General Beresford-Peirse, visited his two division commanders in the afternoon of 16 June, he saw no reason to change his plans for the following day. These called for 4th Armoured Brigade to be added to 7th Armoured Division in order to destroy the German tank forces. On the morning of 17 June, however, the division commanders realized the threat to their flanks, while they still had only twenty-one Cruiser and seventeen close-support tanks. When Wavell reached the command post of 7th Armoured Division with Beresford-Peirse to decide on further tactics, the commander of 4th Indian Division, Major-General Messervy, had already ordered the withdrawal of 22nd Guards Brigade.

This step enabled the British to withdraw their troops to the south in time before the first units of the two German divisions reached the Halfaya pass at 4.00 p.m. Rommel was annoyed because he had not been able to surround the enemy. He blamed tactical mistakes by his commanders for this failure, which was not completely justified.[28] Certainly the German commanders, especially the two new division commanders Major-Generals von Ravenstein and Neumann-Silkow, did not have sufficient experience, but more important was the fact that, in spite of completely inadequate communications, Rommel had tried to direct the two divisions from Tobruk instead of appointing one of their commanders to take charge of all operations on the Sollum front. Moreover, German movements during the entire operation were seriously hampered by the Royal Air Force, which mounted very successful attacks against German rear communications and supply-columns. In contrast, co-operation between German ground forces and the Air Leader Africa was inadequate. As there were no Luftwaffe liaison officers with the Africa Corps or its divisions, operations of the Luftwaffe units could not be co-ordinated sufficiently with those of the German ground forces.[29] However, on balance the result of the fighting was positive for the Germans: while the British lost 33 fighters and 3 bombers, total German losses amounted to only 10 aircraft.[30]

British tank losses were also significantly greater than those of the Germans: 27 Cruiser and 64 close-support tanks compared with German losses of 5 light and 7 medium tanks. Including Italian losses, total Axis casualties were higher than those of the British: 586 dead and missing and 691 wounded, while the British suffered 381 dead and missing and 588 wounded.[31]

A few days after the end of the fighting, on 21 June, the unfortunate Wavell was relieved of his command and appointed commander-in-chief in India, while the previous commander-in-chief in India, General Sir Claude Auchinleck, succeeded him as Commander-in-Chief Middle East. Churchill had been

---

[28] Rommel, *Papers*, 145.
[29] Cf. Gundelach, *Luftwaffe im Mittelmeer*, 146.
[30] Cf. ibid. 145; Taysen, *Tobruk*, 180.
[31] Cf. Playfair, *Mediterranean*, ii. 171; Taysen, *Tobruk*, 181; *Prima controffensiva*, 183.

considering removing Wavell since August 1940. He blamed Wavell for the loss of Cyrenaica, which in his opinion had led to the failure of the British campaign in Greece. The failure of Battleaxe and the accompanying loss of so many tanks sent to Egypt at such high risk and cost were only the final factors in Churchill's decision to remove a man who had not been able to transform his (Churchill's) military wishful thinking into reality. Air Chief Marshal Longmore, who like Wavell had pointed out the gap between the bold plans made in London and the forces available in North Africa, had been unexpectedly removed from his command a month earlier when he was in London for consultation, without having an opportunity to hand over to his successor and previous deputy, Air Marshal Tedder. Nevertheless, it had come to be realized in London that the British military organization in the Middle East was inadequate and that Wavell was simply overworked. On 28 June Oliver Lyttelton, as permanent representative of the War Cabinet, was appointed Minister of State in the Middle East. The newly created Intendant-General of the Army of the Middle East, who was to direct all support agencies, was placed under his authority. However, this office was made superfluous by the creation in October of a 'Principal Administrative Staff Officer to the Commander-in-Chief Middle East'. The support units of the Royal Air Force were also reorganized, which led to a significant increase in the number of combat-ready aircraft in the autumn.[32]

Changes were also made in the organization of the Axis forces in North Africa. Under the impression of Paulus's report on conditions in North Africa, Halder had suggested to the commander-in-chief of the army the creation of an office of commander of German troops in North Africa, to which Rommel was to be subordinate. But Hitler was especially concerned that Rommel should not be restricted by being given a subordinate position; instead he wanted to assign a German chief of staff to the commander-in-chief of Axis forces in North Africa, Army General Gariboldi.[33] The Wehrmacht and army high commands finally agreed to assign a German liaison officer, with a staff of 42 officers and 120 men, to the Italian high command in North Africa, although a lieutenant-colonel from the staff of the German general at the headquarters of the Italian armed forces was already serving as liaison officer there. Mussolini and the Italian high command at first agreed to the new measures, but when Major-General Gause, the new liaison officer, reported to Gariboldi on 10 June, the latter refused to accept the German staff, which neither he nor Rommel had requested. He pointed out to the Italian high command the danger that the new staff could be intended to prepare the way for German supervision of the Italian command in North Africa. This

---

[32] Cf. Churchill, *Second World War*, iii. 308–14; Pitt, *Crucible*, 309–10; Playfair, *Mediterranean*, ii. 235–46.
[33] Halder, *Diaries*, ii. 915–16 (12 May 1941); 920–1 (15 May 1941); 928 (19 May 1941). Cf. also Taysen, *Tobruk*, 183–8; *Prima controffensiva*, 167 ff.

reopened the discussion about the command organization in North Africa and gave Rommel an opportunity to resolve the question in accordance with his own wishes. On 23 June he pointed out to the army high command that the Italians intended to establish corps staffs for their troops around Tobruk and near Sollum, which, with their six divisions together with the two divisions of the Africa Corps, were to be under his command. He then suggested placing the new staff at his disposal to help him cope with his new duties until a commander-in-chief of the now necessary German army headquarters staff could be appointed.

General Gariboldi rejected the very idea of a German army headquarters staff; the head of the Italian high command, General Cavallero, wanted to accept it, but only with Rommel or an Italian as commander-in-chief. Halder and Paulus then considered forming an Armoured Group Rommel under an Italian supreme command.[34] The German liaison officer with the Italian high command in North Africa, Major-General Gause, was ordered to come to Berlin to discuss this solution with the army high command. His report confirmed Halder's negative image of Rommel: 'Rommel's character defects make him extremely hard to get along with, but no one cares to come out in open opposition because of his brutality and the backing he has at top level.... This obviously bungled situation might be rectified by modifying the mission of Gause's staff in the process of changing the command set-up (the formation of an Armoured Group Rommel).'[35] Thus the situation developed in accordance with Rommel's wishes, for originally the army high command had wanted to create an armoured group as an instrument for controlling Rommel. On 1 June he was appointed General der Panzertruppe (general of the armoured troops), and on 31 July the army high command ordered the previous liaison staff to be reorganized as the command of the Armoured Group Africa, whose chief of staff Gause now became. Rommel's successor as commanding general of the Africa Corps was Lieutenant-General Crüwell. Army General Gariboldi, Rommel's adversary, was replaced by Army General Bastico on 18 July.

The result of all these changes was the exact opposite of what Halder had actually intended. Instead of creating an instrument to control Rommel, Halder had unintentionally greatly strengthened Rommel's position. The reason for this development was certainly not only the respect Rommel enjoyed in the Italian high command after the battle at Sollum, but Hitler's favour, to which, by Rommel's own admission, he owed his most recent promotion.[36] Hitler had good reason to treat Rommel well: the victory at Sollum eliminated the British threat to Libya for the foreseeable future and thus ensured that events in North Africa would not disturb the German

[34] Halder, *Diaries*, ii. 984 (28 June 1941).
[35] Ibid. 1010 (6 July 1941). The C.-in-C. of the army then reprimanded Rommel for his treatment of his commanders. Cf. Irving, *Rommel*, 102–3; Heckmann, *Rommels Krieg*, 119. On the reorganization of the command structure cf. *Prima controffensiva*, 229–33.
[36] Cf. Irving, *Rommel*, 101.

campaign against the Soviet Union, which began on 22 June. The fighting in North Africa also helped divert attention from the final German preparations for the war in the east.

On the other hand, Libya was now completely overshadowed by the war against the Soviet Union. On 28 June the army high command asked Rommel to submit an operational draft for an offensive against Egypt; but it was to be launched only in the autumn of 1941, after the fighting in the Soviet Union had been concluded, as a simultaneous German advance was planned against the Suez Canal from the north-east, through Turkey, Syria, and Palestine.[37] When Rommel's then chief of staff, Lieutenant-Colonel Klaus von dem Borne, had presented his views to Hitler and the army high command at the beginning of June, he brought back to Africa a good impression. Rommel therefore now hoped that at least two additional German divisions would be placed at his disposal for the offensive. But on 3 July the army high command informed him that he was mistaken: even for the autumn offensive it was not intended to transfer additional large German formations to North Africa.[38] For an attack on Tobruk alone the Africa Corps needed twenty-six units. The army high command calculated that twelve ships would be required to transfer them to North Africa and that deliveries of supplies would have to be increased by 20,000 tons. To prepare for an offensive against Egypt after the fall of Tobruk, 40,000 tons of supplies and twenty shipments would be necessary for the additional troops. For this reason the army high command expected to be able to start an attack on Tobruk at the beginning or in the middle of September 1941, and an offensive against Egypt at the beginning of 1942. At the same time Halder demanded the use of the new transport routes from Toulon to Bizerta and from Italy and Greece to Benghazi and, 'at the latest after the conclusion of operations in the east', the transfer of Luftwaffe units to Sicily 'to repel British attacks from Malta on the sea route to Tripoli, which are becoming stronger with every passing day'.[39]

At the end of August the quartermaster-general listed a number of conditions for an attack on Egypt on 15 March 1942 which could hardly be fulfilled, and mentioned 15 June 1942 as the more probable date for the operation.[40] However, the most important condition, a simultaneous advance by German forces through Turkey and Syria, became increasingly unlikely. On 1 September, in a memorandum on the strategic situation in the late summer of 1941, the Wehrmacht high command described the effect of a failure to break Soviet resistance that year, which now had to be expected. Turkey would

---

[37] OKH, army general staff, Op.Abt. (IIb), No. 1299/41 g.Kdos. (28 June 1941), to the Africa Corps, BA-MA RH 2/v. 460.
[38] Ibid., army general staff, Op.Abt. (IIb), No. 1292/41 g.Kdos. (3 July 1941), to the Africa Corps.
[39] Ibid., OKH, army general staff, OQu I (Op.Abt. IIb), No. 1380/41 g.Kdos. (21 July 1941), to OKW/WFSt/L.
[40] Ibid., Gen.Qu. Qu 1/I, 22 Aug. 1941, to Op.Abt. (II).

remain neutral, but its voluntary assistance was a prerequisite for the success of German plans for the Middle East; military action against Turkey would only create additional problems. The high command concluded: 'Without a serious German threat from the direction of Syria–Iraq, the English position on the Suez Canal will constantly get firmer.'[41]

Moreover, the Wehrmacht high command demanded the concentration of all available forces on the elimination of the Soviet Union as the next, decisive objective and concluded that, even if this should be largely achieved in 1941, the army and the Luftwaffe would hardly be available for other large-scale operations before the spring of 1942. As the only additional support for Axis forces in the Mediterranean theatre it announced the transfer of minesweepers, motor torpedo-boats, and U-boats there as soon as possible.[42] These priorities meant not only the end for the time being of the dream of an advance to the Nile; they also made it uncertain whether Rommel would at least receive the forces he needed for a new attack on Tobruk and whether he would be able to withstand a second British offensive on the Sollum front.

[41] *DGFP* D xiii. No. 265, pp. 422–33, here 424.
[42] Ibid. 431.

V. The Naval and Air War in the Mediterranean and Supplies for the North African Theatre

THE effects of the transfer of X Air Corps to Greece in May 1941 on the position of the Axis in the central Mediterranean did not make themselves clearly felt at first, as the last ten days of that month were dominated by the battle of Crete, in which the British Mediterranean Fleet suffered serious losses. With its reduced forces it then had to transport supplies to Tobruk and support British army operations in Syria. However, the Mediterranean Fleet was less of a threat to German and Italian supply transports to North Africa than were the British forces on Malta. In May forty-eight Hurricane fighters flew to Malta from H Force operating south of Sardinia. In June four similar operations delivered 142 additional fighters to the island. At the beginning of August, in spite of heavy losses, British air strength on Malta was 75 fighters, 20 torpedo-bombers, 20 other aircraft for attacks on ships, 12 bombers, and 10 reconnaissance aircraft.[1] British surface ships had not returned to Malta, but around the middle of the year ten submarines of 10th Flotilla operated from the island, supported by 8th and 1st Submarine Flotillas in Gibraltar and Alexandria.[2]

The Italians faced these British forces alone; since the end of the fighting around Sollum, X Air Corps had concentrated its attacks on the Nile delta and the Suez Canal. But on average it had only forty aircraft ready for action, too few to achieve any significant effect in such a large target area at ranges of 600–1,000 kilometres. In particular, it did not have enough aircraft to perform adequate reconnaissance between Crete and Africa, the area it had claimed for its operations in the negotiations in the middle of May, and had to ask the Italians to take over this task.[3] But the Italians themselves did not have sufficient forces for the tasks they had had to assume in the central Mediterranean after the transfer of X Air Corps. In Sicily their air force had 65 bombers and 120 fighters, which were hardly able to protect the transports to North Africa, let alone reduce British strength on Malta sufficiently to eliminate any threat from the island. And the Italian air force could not afford to carry out large-scale operations, with the danger of heavy losses, as it received too few replacements from the domestic aircraft industry.[4]

In view of this considerably worsened situation in the central Mediterranean, it is not surprising that the Italians did not succeed in seriously inter-

---

[1] Playfair, *Mediterranean*, ii. 280.   [2] Rohwer and Hümmelchen, *Chronik*, 136.
[3] Gundelach, *Luftwaffe im Mittelmeer*, 273.   [4] Ibid. 284.

fering with additional supply operations for Malta. On 21 July H Force, reinforced by units of the Home Fleet, put to sea from Gibraltar to escort six freighters and a troop transport ship to Malta. The next day it, but not the freighters, was discovered by Italian reconnaissance aircraft south of the Balearic Islands. The Italian navy high command therefore assumed that the British were only taking additional aircraft to Malta, and the Italian fleet was not ordered to put to sea. Italian submarine and air attacks sank one British destroyer and damaged two others and a light cruiser before the actual convoy was discovered on 23 July. Italian motor torpedo-boats were only able to damage one freighter. Of seven empty ships that left Malta at the same time to be escorted back to Gibraltar by H Force, only one was damaged, by an Italian aerial torpedo. On 27 July Operation Substance was successfully concluded, apart from the fact that 1,750 Royal Air Force personnel destined for Malta were still at Gibraltar: the troop transport had run aground putting to sea, and many of them had been transferred to warships which, damaged by Italian air attacks, had had to return early before reaching Malta. Between 31 July and 4 August these men were sent to Malta in an additional operation ('Style') on two light cruisers, a fast minelayer, and two destroyers. During the operation an Italian submarine was also sunk. After these two operations the garrison of Malta had a strength of 22,000 men, with 230 anti-aircraft guns and 103 guns for coastal defence. Supplies were now sufficient for eight to fifteen months.[5] In the night of 25–6 July the Italians attempted to penetrate Valletta harbour with eight explosive boats and two human torpedoes to destroy the transport ships that had reached Malta, but the attempt failed completely and all the attackers were either killed or captured.[6]

The next British operation, 'Mincemeat', produced no results for either side. On 22 August the fast minelayer *Manxman* left Gibraltar to lay mines off Livorno, while Admiral Somerville put to sea with H Force in the western Mediterranean and carrier-aircraft attacked targets in northern Sardinia. Assuming that the British would make another attempt to break through to Malta, the Italian navy put to sea with a large force: the two modern battleships *Littorio* and *Veneto*, four heavy and two light cruisers, twenty-five destroyers, eight submarines, and eight motor torpedo-boats. The Italians wanted to challenge the British covering force south-west of Sardinia. The light cruisers were to intercept the convoy in the strait of Sicily. But Admiral Somerville, with his weaker force, had in any case no intention of seeking a battle with the Italians, who, moreover, remained under the protection of their fighters. He therefore considered an attack by torpedo-bombers from the *Ark Royal* senseless and returned to Gibraltar. The Italians thought that the British had broken off the operation because of the appearance of the Italian fleet. They did not discover the minelayer *Manxman*, but they did find the mines it

---

[5] Cf. Playfair, *Mediterranean*, ii. 266–9; *Marina italiana*, v. 11–14.
[6] Playfair, *Mediterranean*, ii. 270–2; *Marina italiana*, xiv. 113–31.

had laid, which therefore caused no damage. However, they did not even tell their German allies that their fleet had put to sea.[7]

Although Malta had only recently received supplies in Operation Substance, the chiefs of staff decided on 28 August to send an additional supply convoy to the island. They feared that the Luftwaffe might return to the central Mediterranean and wanted to be prepared for such an eventuality. On 24 September nine large transport ships entered the Mediterranean, protected by the strengthened H Force, which consisted of three battleships, the *Ark Royal*, five light cruisers, and eighteen destroyers. Nine submarines took up positions off the Italian coast. Parts of H Force were discovered by Italian reconnaissance aircraft on 26 September; the Italians then stationed eleven submarines off the African coast and motor torpedo-boats near Pantelleria, and the Italian fleet put to sea for the area south of Sardinia with two battleships, three heavy and two light cruisers, and fourteen destroyers on the evening of the same day. A shortage of oil prevented other ships from leaving port. Admiral Iachino was to keep his ships under the protection of fighters stationed on Sardinia and only attack if his own forces were clearly superior to those of the British. But because of British feints the Italians did not know the actual strength of H Force.

On the afternoon of 27 September the British battleship *Nelson* suffered a hit from an Italian torpedo-bomber, which reduced her speed to fifteen knots, but otherwise co-operation between the Italian air force and navy was inadequate. Iachino received too few reconnaissance reports and, as he missed the expected fighter protection for his ships, he broke off his advance shortly before encountering H Force. Admiral Somerville had sent his two undamaged battleships, two cruisers, and two destroyers to meet the Italians, but when he was informed that they had reversed course, he ordered his ships to return to the convoy. For this reason Iachino did not find the enemy when, before sundown, he again turned south after receiving a report that the British force consisted of only one possibly damaged battleship.

Before the convoy and its escort of five cruisers and nine destroyers reached Malta on 28 September, it lost one transport ship in a night attack by Italian torpedo-bombers; a British cruiser bombarded Pantelleria. The Italian motor torpedo-boats and the British submarines had no opportunity to carry out attacks. But on 30 September an Italian submarine was sunk off the African coast in an attempt to attack the British ships on their way back to Gibraltar. Moreover, three empty transports from Malta reached Gibraltar without escort. These were the most important events and results of Operation Halberd, as the British action was named. The Italians had not been able to prevent the resupplying of Malta, and it did not seem as if they would be able to do so in future.[8]

---

[7] Cf. Playfair, *Mediterranean*, ii. 272–3; *Marina italiana*, v. 17–30; 1. Skl., KTB, Teil A, 428 (6 Aug. 1941), BA-MA RM 7/27.

[8] Cf. Bragadin, *Italian Navy*, 120–4; Fechter and Hümmelchen, *Seekriegsatlas*, 53–4; Playfair, *Mediterranean*, ii. 274–6.

German and Italian military leaders were very much aware that the transport situation in the Mediterranean for their forces in North Africa was deteriorating steadily as a result of the constant attacks carried out by British aircraft and submarines from Malta. On 4 July the naval war staff informed the Wehrmacht operations staff that, in its opinion, the planned transfer of Italian air units to the eastern front should be reconsidered. The Italians should use all their forces to master the situation in the central Mediterranean.[9] In a section he contributed to a letter from Hitler to Mussolini, Raeder analysed the situation and summarized his demands for the conduct of the war in the Mediterranean. He then remarked: 'The Italian armed forces, especially the navy and the air force, will have to bear the main burden of the battle for the central Mediterranean and the transports [to North Africa].' But Raeder did not want to leave the Italians completely to their own devices; he generously offered to make German experience in the war available to them: 'It is suggested that the head of the naval liaison staff in Rome should join the working staff of the Italian naval command in order to give him the chance to assume a responsible role in the present joint, if limited, task.'[10] Raeder expressed the same views in a letter to Fleet Admiral Riccardi and expanded his offer of help: it was planned to transfer motor torpedo-boats and R-boats (minesweepers) to the Mediterranean after the conclusion of the fighting in the east; preparations had already started.[11]

The department of home defence in the Wehrmacht operations staff had already pointed out the only possible realistic solution to the supply problems in the Mediterranean in view of the war situation as a whole: 'If, because of other tasks for the Luftwaffe ... it is not possible to begin the conquest of Malta, as a less satisfactory, temporary solution a strong Luftwaffe force must be transferred back to Sicily to put Malta out of action as an air-base more completely than the Italians have been able to do.'[12] Considerable time passed before the naval war staff came to the same conclusion. In the middle of June Raeder still entertained fantastic expectations when he wrote to Riccardi: 'The operations of the naval forces must be supplemented by strong attacks of German and Italian air units, using the heaviest bombs and torpedoes, against the British fleet in the eastern Mediterranean and its bases in order systematically to destroy battleships, aircraft-carriers, and installations.'[13] Of course it was not easy to renounce the prospect of such impressive successes and demand the return of X Air Corps to Sicily only because the Italians were not concentrating their forces on protecting the supply shipments to North Africa. However, as the German liaison staff with the Italian air force reported, the

[9] 1. Skl., KTB, Teil A, 34–5 (4 July 1941), BA-MA RM 7/26. Cf. also *Das Deutsche Reich und der Zweite Weltkrieg*, iv. 898–9 (Förster).
[10] The C.-in-C. of the navy and head of the naval war staff to OKW/WFSt/L: B.Nr. 1. Skl. Im 1248/41 op. Chefs. (5 July 1941), BA-MA RM 7/234.
[11] Ibid., B.Nr. 1. Skl. Im 1260/41 op. Chefs. (12 July 1941). On co-operation between the German and Italian navies until the end of 1941 cf. Schreiber, *Revisionismus*, 309–29.
[12] Note for an oral report (10 July 1941), BA-MA RM 7/234.
[13] Ibid., B.Nr. 1. Skl. Im 986/41 g.Kdos. Chefs. (14 June 1941).

Luftwaffe units in Africa were also suffering from the supply shortage. The staff called for the immediate transfer of Me 110 units to Sicily to protect the convoys, for losses had reached a frightening level: 'From 27 January to 20 August 1941 in the transports between Italy and North Africa a total of 33 ships with 156,819 GRT were sunk; 26 ships with 98,676 GRT were damaged. In coastal shipping between Tripoli and Benghazi 19 ships with 28,064 GRT were sunk, and 12 with 11,372 GRT were damaged.'[14]

Ten days later, on 13 September, the naval war staff came to a realistic assessment of the situation. In reference to a situation report by the German general assigned to the headquarters of the Italian armed forces, it described the transfer of German air units back to Sicily as 'absolutely necessary.... Even the effects of German air attacks on the Suez Canal are far less important than protecting the sea transports, as strengthening our position in North Africa must have top priority.'[15] The same day Hitler decided that the main task of the Luftwaffe in the Mediterranean, X Air Corps, was the protection of the convoys to North Africa. He also pressed for early attacks by the six U-boats assigned to the Mediterranean, which of course did not achieve any immediate improvement of the situation. Moreover, Göring was able to persuade Hitler to change his order in a way that in effect almost completely revoked it: X Air Corps was to assume only the task of guarding the seldom used sea route from Greece to Cyrenaica and had to provide additional protection only for convoys for Tripoli which, in its own judgement, were especially important. Raeder intervened in the Wehrmacht high command and emphasized again the effects of the military setbacks threatening in North Africa unless the operational order for X Air Corps were changed or new forces from the eastern front were transferred to Sicily.[16] Two days later the Wehrmacht high command informed him of the reasons for Hitler's decision. X Air Corps had withdrawn its ground-support units in Sicily, and the airfields were now occupied by Italian units. Large German forces could therefore not operate from them. If strong forces were transferred to Sicily, it would not be possible to defend the Aegean area against enemy sea and air forces or to support the Africa Corps in Cyrenaica. Raeder's suggested alternative was decisively rejected: 'Weakening of east front suggested by naval war staff is contrary to all principles for conducting war. Air units in the east are barely sufficient to support operations there, to reach objectives set for this year. But that is prerequisite for [improvement of] general situation.'[17]

After this clear rejection, Raeder refrained for the time being from further efforts to change Hitler's decision and instructed Hitler's naval adjutant not to

[14] Ibid., liaison staff with the staff of the Royal Italian Navy to OKM-Skl., B.Nr. 1. Abt. Skl. 20517/41 g.Kdos. (3 Sept. 1941).
[15] Ibid., Skl. to OKW/WFSt, B.Nr. 1. Skl. 1515/41 g.Kdos. Chefs. (13 Sept. 1941) (printed in 'Führer Conferences' as annex 2 to oral report of 17 Sept. 1941).
[16] Ibid., Skl. to OKW/WFSt, B.Nr. 1. Skl. Ia 1551/41 g.Kdos. Chefs. (19 Sept. 1941).
[17] Ibid., OKW/Chef WFSt to OKM/Skl.: No. 441573/41 g.Kdos. Chefs. (21 Sept. 1941). On these disagreements cf. also the account by Gundelach, *Luftwaffe im Mittelmeer*, 288–92.

submit an additional letter on the subject which he had written earlier.[18] Finally, Hitler changed his assessment of the situation and his opinion about the necessary measures. In the middle of October he wrote in the draft of a letter to Mussolini: 'The fate of your and my troops fighting in Africa and the continuation of the war against the British in Libya and the eastern Mediterranean depend on the flow of supplies to Africa.' Mussolini was to be offered strong Luftwaffe units for use in the Mediterranean to secure the sea routes to North Africa, eliminate Malta as a British base, stop British transports from west to east, and support the attack on Tobruk.[19] Even the naval war staff were not certain what had caused Hitler to change his mind and had to resort to conjecture: 'It seems quite possible that the Führer himself read the last teletype message from the commander-in-chief of the navy and that it influenced him to write the present letter.'[20] In any case Hitler now considered a shift of the main German war effort to the Mediterranean to be imperative. And, as he informed the chief of staff of the naval war staff on 27 October, the navy itself would have to send more U-boats to the Mediterranean.[21] He gave as his reasons the threat to the supply-routes for the German forces in North Africa and his old worry about the domestic situation in Italy, which could not bear additional strain. A change of government in Italy would mean the end of Fascism there and Italy's going over to the side of Germany's enemies.

In the letter, which Mussolini received on 31 October, Hitler of course did not mention these fears. Instead he wrote of the German success in the campaign against the Soviet Union, which had caused this 'only remaining, last great hope of the British on the Continent' to collapse, and of the futility of possible British offensives to take the pressure off the Soviet Union. Finally, Hitler spoke of the need for Germany to offer better protection of the supply transports to North Africa, to eliminate the threat from Malta, and to drive the British from the central Mediterranean. To achieve these aims he offered the help of the Luftwaffe and U-boats.[22] The subsequent negotiations were concluded a month later, and on 2 December 1941 Hitler issued Directive No. 38, in which he ordered the transfer of an air corps from the eastern front to southern Italy and North Africa and appointed General Field Marshal Kesselring Commander-in-Chief South. But Kesselring was in direct command only of the Luftwaffe forces in the Mediterranean. To use German naval

---

[18] The C.-in-C. of the navy and head of naval war staff, express letter to Hitler's field headquarters: B.Nr. 1. Skl. Ib 1563/41 g.Kdos. Chefs. (23 Sept. 1941): 'For Captain von Puttkamer. To be submitted to the Führer', BA-MA RM 7/234 (printed in *Lagevorträge*, 299–300; not in trans.); handwritten additional note: 'On orders from C.-in-C. of the navy to Captain von Puttkamer, not to be submitted for the time being, as, given views of Führer and Wehrmacht high command, it cannot be expected that this request would be approved at present.'

[19] Ibid., Abt. Landesverteidigung (IL op), 1941 (no day or month), signed on 16 and 17 Oct.

[20] Ibid., p. 3, note Ib.

[21] *Lagevorträge*, 301–4 (not in trans.). On the use of German warships in the Mediterranean cf. Schreiber, *Revisionismus*, 321 n. 376; Santoni and Mattesini, *La partecipazione tedesca*, 115–37.

[22] *DGFP* D xiii, No. 433, pp. 709–16. Cf. also *Das Deutsche Reich und der Zweite Weltkrieg*, iv. 900 (Förster).

forces there he could issue orders to the Navy Group South and to the German admiral assigned to the Italian navy high command. This officer also served as an intermediary to convey Kesselring's requests regarding the operations of the Italian navy.[23]

Thus Kesselring's command authority was rather limited, although Göring had wanted to give the Commander-in-Chief South full responsibility for supply transports to North Africa and command of German and Italian forces assigned to protect them. Göring had even informed Hitler that he considered the extension of operations in the east beyond the Caucasus to secure sufficient oil reserves more important than overcoming the difficulties the Axis powers were experiencing in the Mediterranean.[24]

While Göring could not persuade Hitler and the Wehrmacht high command to accept his views, Raeder did not even try again to defend his own objectives, although he had argued that 'it is not possible to send U-boats into the Mediterranean, as this would handicap operations in the Atlantic. Moreover, British submarines and aircraft are the forces used in the Mediterranean to attack transports, and these cannot be combated with U-boats.'[25] Now twenty-four U-boats were to be stationed permanently in the Mediterranean, and Raeder had to accept this decision, 'against which, because of the Führer's clear decision regarding the general situation, there can be no protest, especially as the Führer is prepared practically to abandon the U-boat war in the Atlantic in order to deal with our problems in the Mediterranean'.[26]

Hitler's decisions also showed the importance he now attributed to the Mediterranean theatre, although the individual steps in this process of strategic reorientation of the main German war effort cannot be reconstructed in detail. Since September 1941 at the latest, the Wehrmacht high command had expected the war against the Soviet Union to continue into 1942 and therefore demanded that all available forces should be concentrated in that theatre.[27] In the middle of October, when Hitler made his offer of assistance to Mussolini, the battle of encirclement near Vyazma and Bryansk had already been decided and the order to continue operations in the direction of Moscow already issued.[28] But Hitler's order of 10 November to transfer Luftwaffe units from the eastern front to Italy[29] did not involve any cessation of army operations in the east. Halder even wanted to push on to Vologda and Stalingrad to secure important positions for the campaign in 1942. Hitler gave his permission for

---

[23] *DGFP* D xiii, No. 535, pp. 938–9.
[24] The Reich Marshal of the Great German Reich (Göring), No. 01559/41 g.Kdos. (Ia), 20 Oct. 1941, to the Führer and supreme cmdr. of the Wehrmacht, BA-MA RM 7/234. Cf. also Gundelach, *Luftwaffe im Mittelmeer*, 329–38.
[25] 'Führer Conferences', 224 (25 July 1941) (trans. amended).
[26] 1. Skl., KTB, Teil A, 498–9 (29 Oct. 1941), BA-MA RM 7/29. On Hitler's decision and Raeder's attitude cf. also Salewski, *Seekriegsleitung*, i. 474–9.
[27] Cf. end of Ch. IV above.
[28] *Das Deutsche Reich und der Zweite Weltkrieg*, iv. 575–8 (Klink).
[29] Gundelach, *Luftwaffe im Mittelmeer*, 339.

this 'supreme effort', but only on condition that 'troops going into battle in subzero temperatures must not lose contact with their supply-base if snowdrifts endanger supply transports again'.[30]

Thus Hitler clearly rejected the demand of the Wehrmacht high command to concentrate all available forces to conclude the campaign against the Soviet Union in 1941 as a precondition for the successful continuation of the war against Britain and, later, also against the United States. He knew that the war against the Soviet Union was not over when he ordered the shift of the main German war effort to the Mediterranean. However, he probably did not foresee the dramatic change which was imminent in the east. According to information from the army high command, more divisions—a total of 109—would be necessary there in 1942 than had been originally planned, but no one doubted that operations could be successfully continued. The transfer of II Air Corps and the creation of a Commander-in-Chief South were therefore not isolated actions to overcome a momentary crisis, but the first step in a new phase of the war 'after Barbarossa'. This thesis is also supported by German planning for the future: 'Operations beyond the Caucasus against Egypt will probably have to be supported by additional forces.'[31]

It is hardly possible to determine the influence on Hitler's decision of the constant warnings, especially those from the naval war staff, about the deterioration of the situation in the Mediterranean and the effects to be feared on the general conduct of the war. Nevertheless the loss figures for the convoys to Africa were helpful, as the dramatic increase in losses obviously gave the naval war staff the most important argument in its attempts to achieve a shift of the main German war effort to the Mediterranean (see Table V.v.1).

Around 8 May 1941 X Air Corps had begun to transfer ground-support units to Greece by sea and on 5 June, after withdrawing its units from Sicily, had officially taken over the 'war against the British in the eastern Mediterranean'.[32] Losses of ships on the transport routes to North Africa did not, however, begin to rise only after X Air Corps had turned over the task of protecting the convoys to the Italians; a clear increase had become evident as early as April, when the Luftwaffe still 'dominated' the central Mediterranean. The further increase in May can be easily explained, for, while the Luftwaffe left Sicily, the Italians were able to occupy the airfields and transfer forces there only gradually to take over the task of protecting the convoys. It is, however, surprising that losses declined sharply in June. The reports of the naval war staff that 'the worsening of the situation coincided with the transfer of X Air Corps to the eastern Mediterranean'[33] were therefore completely baseless.

---

[30] OKW/WFSt/Abt. L (IOp.) 441 888/41 g.Kdos. Chefs. (11 Nov. 1941), to OKH, Op.Abt., BA-MA RM 4/v. 578.
[31] Ibid., p. 3.
[32] Gundelach, *Luftwaffe im Mittelmeer*, 231–2; Santoni and Mattesini, *La partecipazione tedesca*, 109–13.
[33] 1. Skl., Ia 1551/41 g.Kdos. Chefs. (19 Sept. 1941), to OKW/WFSt/L, BA-MA RM 7/234.

TABLE V.v.1. *Losses and Shipments to North Africa in 1941*
[Cf. explanations following table]

Month	Losses (GRT)				Loads (t.)			
					For the Wehrmacht		Total	
	(A)	(B)	(C)	(D)	Shipped	Unloaded (E)	Shipped	Unloaded (F)
January	3,950	7,331	14,537	—	632	0	50,505	49,084
February	2,365	8,452	6,027	—	25,276	24,102	80,352	79,183
March	10,194	13,839	10,194	1,927	43,424	41,149	101,800	92,753
April	20,183	25,611	23,371	32,159	33,808	28,504	88,597	81,472
May	29,172	40,162	47,507	31,308	24,294	24,294	75,367	69,331
June	13,989	15,356	16,956	—	37,848	37,848	133,331	125,076
July	23,222	23,829	28,070	19,776	39,512	32,784	77,012	62,276
August	31,007	31,007	35,126	36,126	34,170	27,372	96,021	83,056
September	62,431	63,624	64,954	49,373	34,552	27,723	94,115	67,513
October	33,471	33,471	33,471	18,818	24,358	15,723	92,449	73,614
November	54,011	54,990	59,052	26,744	13,531	5,138	79,208	29,813
December	37,747	38,757	38,757	13,000	11,793	10,275	47,680	39,092
TOTAL					323,198	274,912	1,016,442	853,193

Sources:

(A) *La marina italiana*, i. 116–17.

(B) *La marina italiana*, vi. 436–50: Aldo Cocchia, 'La difesa del traffico coll'Africa settentrionale'; condensed in Rohwer, 'Nachschubverkehr', 106.

(C) Playfair, *Mediterranean*, ii. 58, 281; iii. 107 (compiled from Italian postwar and German war records).

(D) Oberkommando der Kriegsmarine, Skl.: Qu.A VIsa 4765/43, 26 May 1943, 'Seetransportleistungen der Kriegsmarine 1941 und 1942', BA-MA RM 8/1166.

(E) and (F) *La marina italiana*, i. 132–3.

Explanations of Table V.v.1

The figures under (A) are the most recent, published in 1972 by the Ufficio Storico della Marina Militare, but unfortunately without any reference to the sources on which they were based. The figures under (B), from 1958, are based on a loss-list of ships in the convoys to North Africa—with date, ship type, name, tonnage, nationality, route, position, and cause of loss—which seems to be a very reliable source. At the beginning of the list is a summary (pp. 341–434) of the convoys to North Africa with dates and times of departures and arrivals, names of the transport ships and escort vessels, and finally remarks about enemy attacks and resulting losses. In this summary losses of ships are noted which are not included in the loss-list. For example, in the figures for April three ships are not mentioned which are listed as lost in the summary and in German records.[a] In the summary there are no data about tonnages, whereas in the German records only the tonnages of German ships are given.[b] For this reason it is

[a] 1. Skl. Im, Kriegsakte, xiv, Deutsche Dampfer und Transporte in Italien (Mar.–June 1941), BA-MA PG 33097, Case GE 1794.

[b] Ibid. xxxiii (June 1941–Jan. 1942), BA-MA PG 33122, Case GE 1080.

possible to say with certainty only that the loss of the ship *Samos* (2,575 GRT) should be added to the figures for April in the table under (B).

Differences in the data for other months are much more serious. The loss-list contains nine ships' names for September; in the summary two additional names are mentioned. In the German records,[c] however, a total of sixteen ships are listed as lost, with names and in some cases the exact cause of loss, but without any tonnage data. These vessels were clearly Italian ships. It can therefore be assumed that losses were generally higher than the figures under (B) indicate. For this reason doubts about the most recent figures, under (A), seem to be justified, as, with the exception of those for August and October, they are lower than the figures in the other columns, although the differences for the second half of 1941 are small. The generally higher figures in British accounts, under (C), would seem to be the most reliable, but, in view of what has already been said about losses in April, the surprisingly low losses they indicate for the months February to April can hardly be accurate.

In a second edition, with notes, the British authors explain which 'Italian postwar records' they used to compile their figures: *La marina italiana*, iii. *Navi perdute* (Rome, 1952).[d] Here ship losses are listed chronologically but not by theatre, and without information on mission or destination. For February, however, losses of convoys to North Africa can be determined with considerable accuracy by referring to the positions of the sinkings. This method indicates that fifteen ships with 12,583 GRT were lost in that month. Column (B) (8,452 GRT), in contrast, lists only three ships lost as a result of direct enemy action, without scuttlings and losses due to accidents as well as losses of sailing vessels and powered sailing vessels. How the figure in column (C) was calculated (6,027 GRT) cannot be determined, nor can the figure for February in column (A). This sample, however, confirms the suspicion that losses of the convoys to North Africa were actually greater than indicated in the table.

The figures under (D), compiled by the naval war staff in May 1943, are, on the other hand, completely unreliable. As they do not agree with reports in the files for 1941, they must be rejected. Although (A), (B), and (C) do not provide exact loss figures, the similar development of the loss curve they indicate does permit certain conclusions.

[c] Ibid.   [d] Playfair, *Mediterranean*, ii. 74 n. 78.

Losses continued to rise in the following months, but even in August they did not reach the level of May (except according to source (A), Table V.v.1). In September losses reached a record high, but even these figures must be seen in perspective. In that month three large passenger ships were used to transport troops to North Africa, of which two were torpedoed in the same attack by the submarine *Upholder*. These two ships alone represented a loss of 38,731 GRT. It should also be noted that the quantity of supplies received by German troops in North Africa was not smaller than in the previous month. The increase in losses affected shipments of supplies for Italian troops. This, however, does not mean that complaints about the supply situation were unjustified. At that time the ongoing monthly requirements for the German army troops in Africa alone were calculated at 25,000–30,000 tonnes.[34] Only in October did the quantity of supplies transported for the Africa Corps decline, because the Italians dispatched fewer loads for the Germans and German losses were disproportionately high. On the whole, however, losses declined to the level of August, and the quantity of supplies transported rose again. In November the situation did in fact become extremely serious, for the Royal Navy was again in a position, as it had been in April, to station surface ships in Malta.

Simultaneously with the sending of Swordfish torpedo-bombers to Malta, K Force, which consisted of the light cruisers *Aurora* and *Penelope* and two modern destroyers of the L class, had been transferred there. It was discovered on 21 October by Italian reconnaissance aircraft. Thereupon the Italians discontinued convoy traffic to Tripoli and continued to use only the limited unloading facilities in Benghazi. On 7 November the fifty-first sea-transport group left Naples, after the Italians had provided an escort force of two heavy cruisers and ten destroyers. K Force was ordered to put to sea the next day; since summer the British had been able to decipher Italian radio traffic concerning shipping in the Mediterranean. To avoid arousing suspicion, a reconnaissance aircraft was sent out from Malta to 'discover' the convoy. With the help of radar the British ships were able to approach the convoy unseen at the moment when the escorting cruisers were changing course and were behind the freighters. Shortly before 1.00 a.m. on 9 November the British ships opened fire and in slightly more than half an hour destroyed all seven freighters, with 39,787 GRT, and a destroyer. A second Italian destroyer, occupied with saving survivors, was lost the next day to a submarine attack. The Italians were unable to inflict any losses on the enemy; attacks by torpedo-bombers as the British ships were returning to Malta were also unsuccessful.[35]

The German naval staff was quick to express its indignation: 'Even the reports already received show that the destruction of this convoy, which, after waiting for weeks, dared, under the protection of a superior escort, to run the blockade of traffic to Tripoli by two British light cruisers, can only be explained by the inexcusable blunder of the Italian naval forces. The importance and consequences of this defeat must be considered extremely serious.'[36] Moreover, the staff viewed the destruction of the convoy as a justification of its efforts to strengthen its influence on the command of the Italian navy. In a memorandum the question was again discussed of whether it was possible virtually to take command of the Italian navy by assigning

---

[34] Taysen, *Tobruk*, 366–7.
[35] Hinsley, *British Intelligence*, ii. 22, 319–20; Playfair, *Mediterranean*, iii. 103–5; *Marina italiana*, vii. 43–71. The official Italian designation for the convoy was BETA; in English and German historical literature it is referred to as the *Duisburg* convoy, after one of the German freighters sunk. According to Santoni (*Ultra*, 125–8), the deciphering of Italian radio traffic did not play a role in this operation.
[36] 1. Skl., KTB, Teil A, 175 (9 Nov. 1941), BA-MA RM 7/30.

V.v. Naval and Air War in Mediterranean

German officers to Italian naval-force staffs and even to individual ships. In this regard the naval war staff even considered taking heavy German surface ships out of commission and disbanding fleet and force staffs in order to provide the necessary personnel. The idea of sending German surface ships to the Mediterranean also came up again. The most noteworthy suggestion was probably the proposal, in a marginal note, to purchase Italian warships and man them with German personnel. This would require much time, but the question should be examined 'if an Italian collapse should ever become imminent'.[37] But the memorandum did not suggest any measures which would be immediately effective. If the heavy German surface ships in Brest[38] were to be taken out of service, they would have to be brought back to Germany, and that could not be done before the winter of 1942. A transfer of the group to the Mediterranean would not have been possible before February or March 1942, and even then the ships would only have been a burden, as they would have required their own defence forces, of which the Axis already had too few in the Mediterranean. Destroyers, however, had such a restricted cruising range that they were unable to reach Italian bases in the Mediterranean without being refuelled. In the end the naval war staff could only offer the well-meant suggestion that Germany should comply with Italian wishes regarding the delivery of oil for the Italian navy.

After the destruction of the convoy on 9 November the Italians stopped all traffic to Tripoli and continued to send ships only to Benghazi. Of course this situation could not be permitted to become permanent, especially after the British started their offensive in North Africa, 'Operation Crusader', on 18 November. In a complicated operation between 19 and 22 November the Italians sent a light cruiser, with a load of fuel, and thirteen transport ships to North Africa. The cruiser and six of the transport ships reached their destinations. The other ships had to abandon the breakthrough attempt after the heavy cruiser *Trieste* of the covering force had been torpedoed by the submarine *Utmost* on 21 November and the light cruiser *Duca degli Abruzzi* took an aerial torpedo hit the following day. K Force, which had left Malta, and the Mediterranean Fleet, which had put to sea to provide support, found no targets to attack.[39]

A convoy consisting of two German steamships was less fortunate when K Force again put to sea. The British ships were reported, but the convoy received no order to take refuge in the nearest port and was surprised and sunk on the way to Benghazi on 24 November. But the British losses in this operation were even more serious. As early as 13 November German U-boats

---

[37] 'Entwicklung der Lage im mittleren Mittelmeer', Ia, initialled on 11 Nov., BA-MA RM 7/234. Cf. also the detailed account in Salewski, *Seekriegsleitung*, i. 480–1, and Schreiber, *Revisionismus*, 321–7.
[38] The battleships *Scharnhorst* and *Gneisenau* and the heavy cruiser *Prinz Eugen*.
[39] Cf. Hinsley, *British Intelligence*, ii. 320; *Marina italiana*, vii. 100–1; Rohwer and Hümmelchen, *Chronik*, 189.

had made their presence felt in the Mediterranean, when the *U-81* torpedoed the aircraft-carrier *Ark Royal* returning to Gibraltar with H Force after taking thirty-seven Hurricane fighters to Malta. The ship sank the next day, only twenty-five nautical miles from Gibraltar, while being towed. Two British freighters which were supposed to reach Malta unescorted during this operation were intercepted and sunk by Italian torpedo-bombers off the Tunisian coast. The Mediterranean Fleet was also affected. On 25 November north of Bardiyah the *U-331* torpedoed the battleship *Barham*, which immediately capsized and exploded.

In spite of these losses, Admiral Cunningham sent B Force with the light cruisers *Ajax* and *Neptune* and two K-class destroyers to Malta as reinforcements on 27 November. This forced the Italians to strengthen their covering forces for the convoy operations. When on 28–9 November four freighters put to sea for Benghazi and on 30 November a tanker and a freighter sailed for Tripoli, the covering force consisted of a battleship, four light cruisers, and nine destroyers. While the Italians were delayed by the engine problems of a light cruiser, K Force attacked the convoy with four light cruisers and three destroyers. They sank one freighter and the tanker, which was already sinking after an air attack, together with its escorting destroyer. British aircraft also sank a second freighter and forced a third to turn back. In the end only one freighter reached Tripoli and Benghazi respectively. At the same time, however, four destroyers transported fuel to Benghazi and Darnah, and two freighters took advantage of the opportunity to return from Tripoli to Naples unescorted while the British were concentrating on intercepting ships on the way to North Africa.[40]

The Italian stopgap measure of using warships for transport tasks had until now functioned smoothly. In May and June 1941 submarines were used regularly to bring ammunition to Darnah, and after the beginning of August they transported fuel to Bardiyah. The development of the transport situation in the Mediterranean forced the Italian navy high command to start using three destroyers to bring fuel to North Africa as of 15 October. On 21 November the light cruiser *Cardona* was put into service as a tanker to Benghazi; the transport programme drawn up by the Italian navy high command at the end of November called for two other light cruisers, the *Da Barbiano* and the *Di Giussano*, to take over fuel transports on the Taranto–Tripoli route.[41] On the evening of 12 December, accompanied by a torpedo-boat, both ships put to sea with a cargo of fuel. In the afternoon of the same day Italian aerial reconnaissance had reported three British and one Dutch

---

[40] Cf. Playfair, *Mediterranean*, iii. 105–6; Rohwer and Hümmelchen, *Chronik*, 193–4; *Marina italiana*, vii. 121—38, 158, 379–83; Santoni, *Ultra*, 134–7. Because in the British account a water tanker intended for Crete was reported damaged, while the arrival of one ship at Tripoli and the return of two others from there, as well as the transport operations of the four destroyers, were not noted, the results of the operation seemed much less favourable for the Italians.

[41] *Marina italiana*, vii. 533–4. A first attempt, on 9 Dec., was broken off when the ships were 'discovered' north of Pantelleria by British aerial reconnaissance.

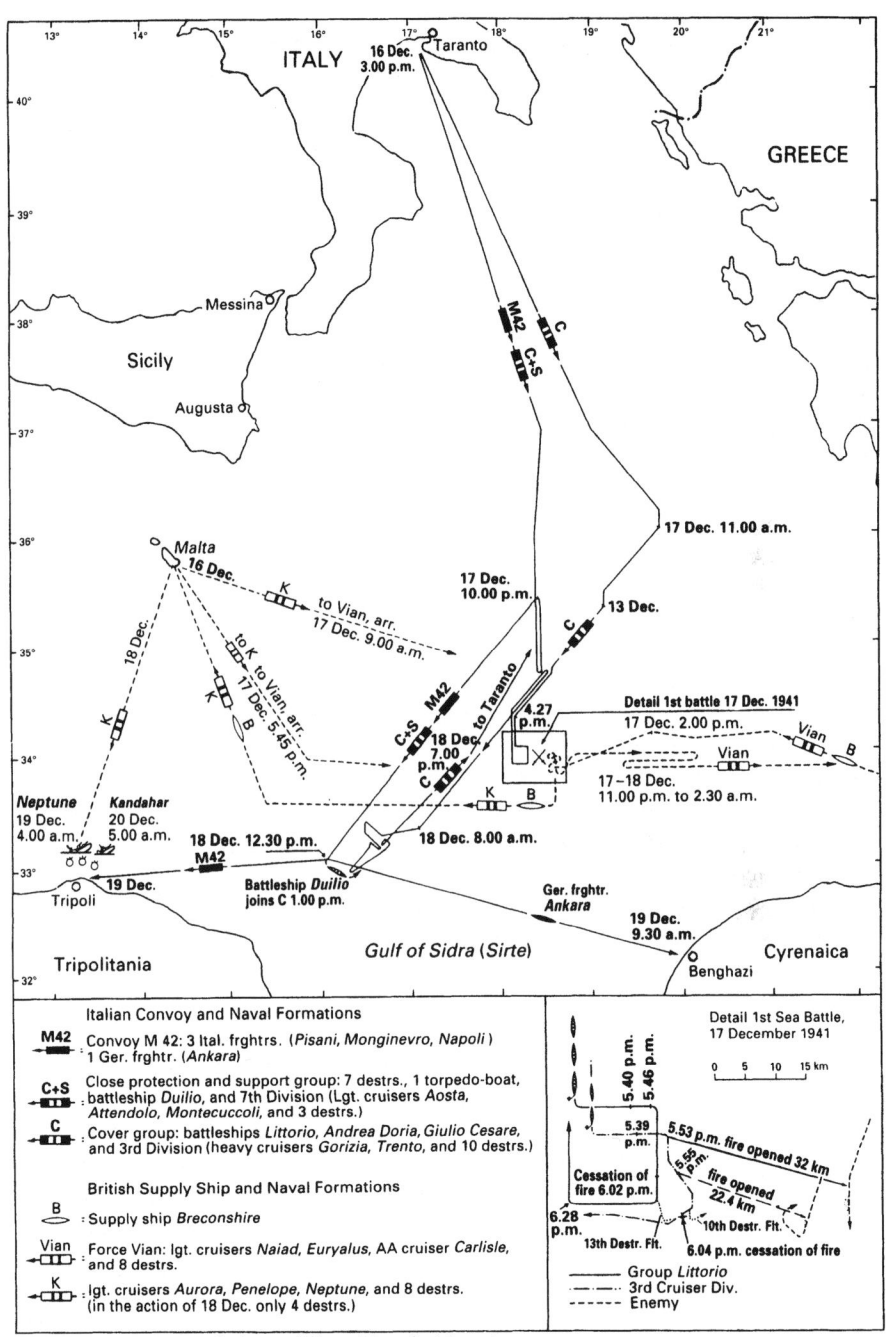

MAP V.V.I. The First Battle of Sirte

destroyer off the Algerian coast steaming eastward at a speed of twenty knots. The Italian navy high command calculated that the cruisers had a sufficient lead to pass Cape Bon even if the destroyers increased their speed to twenty-eight knots. In fact, however, the cruisers were one hour behind schedule and the destroyers had increased their speed to thirty knots when they sighted the Italian ships at 3.00 a.m., shortly before the latter disappeared behind Cape Bon on a south-eastward course. Twenty minutes later, however, the Italian division commander, Admiral Toscano, reversed his course and thus quickly encountered the destroyers, which, using torpedoes, sank his ships with their highly explosive cargo in a short battle. Toscano and his entire staff were killed; only the torpedo-boat escaped, slightly damaged. Historians have usually assumed that Toscano turned back because his ships were sighted by British aerial reconnaissance at 2.45 a.m., but this does not explain why he hesitated so long.[42]

In the evening of the same day on which the two Italian cruisers were sunk off the Tunisian coast, a large-scale operation, 'M 41', was begun to transport supplies to North Africa. Six freighters in three groups put to sea for Benghazi with a total escort of four battleships, one heavy and four light cruisers, twenty-four destroyers, and two torpedo-boats. Admiral Cunningham understood the significance of preparations for this operation and sent only Rear-Admiral P. L. Vian from Alexandria with three light cruisers, which were to join the cruisers and destroyers stationed in Malta. To deceive the Italians, Cunningham then used radio traffic to simulate the sailing of the entire Mediterranean Fleet. The Italians thereupon broke off the operation and Vian returned to Alexandria with his cruisers, where, however, the *Galatea* was sunk by *U-557*. The Italian battleship *Vittorio Veneto* suffered heavy damage in a torpedo attack by the British submarine *Urge*.[43]

The Italians refused to be discouraged and began Operation M 42 on 16 December, in which it was planned to send three freighters to Tripoli and a German steamship to Benghazi. Seven destroyers and a torpedo-boat were to provide close-range protection; a battleship with three light cruisers and three destroyers formed the support group; the more distant cover group consisted of three battleships, two heavy cruisers, and ten destroyers. The previous day Rear-Admiral Vian had also put to sea with his two remaining light cruisers, an anti-aircraft cruiser, eight destroyers, and the supply-ship *Breconshire* with fuel for Malta. When the British realized that the Italians were again attempting to carry out a large-scale operation, Admiral Cunningham decided to continue the operation with the *Breconshire*. All available ships were to sail

---

[42] Hinsley, *British Intelligence*, ii. 322; Playfair, *Mediterranean*, iii. 109–10; *Marina italiana*, vii. 166–89; Santoni, *Ultra*, 137–42. Times are given according to the Italian account.

[43] Hinsley, *British Intelligence*, ii. 322–3; Playfair, *Mediterranean*, iii. 110; *Marina italiana*, vii. 185–90. For the following account cf. Map V.v.1. According to Santoni (*Ultra*, 142), the decision to break off the operation was taken after Italian aircraft reported sighting the Mediterranean Fleet at sea.

from Malta to support Vian in a night attack on the Italian convoy. Only the slow anti-aircraft cruiser was sent back to Alexandria. Cunningham himself was not able to put to sea with his two battleships, because he had no destroyers to provide protection. On the morning of 17 December two light cruisers and six destroyers were thus on their way to join Vian's cruisers. They were followed that evening by another light cruiser and two more destroyers.

German and Italian aerial reconnaissance erroneously reported the *Breconshire* as a battleship. This caused Admiral Iachino, the commander-in-chief of the Italian fleet, to misjudge the actual purpose of the British operation and to assume that its only objective was to attack his convoy. While he tried to make contact with the British ships before sundown, Vian sought to avoid a battle until the *Breconshire* had safely arrived in Malta. Shortly before nightfall anti-aircraft fire enabled Iachino to find the British ships. But the resulting battle, which began at 6.00 p.m., was short and without results. Vian sent the *Breconshire* south and carried out diversionary manœuvres, during which he not only lost contact with the enemy but also for a time with his own ships. On Cunningham's orders he then attempted until 2.30 a.m. to intercept the part of the Italian convoy destined for Benghazi, and finally returned to Alexandria. In the meantime the *Breconshire* continued on to Malta under the protection of K Force with two additional destroyers.

Until this point the Italians had not lost any transport ships, but the British refused to give up. British aircraft attacked Tripoli and mined the entrance to the harbour. This action prevented the Italian ships from entering the harbour. On the evening of 18 December Captain R. C. O'Connor left Malta with the light cruisers *Neptune*, *Aurora*, and *Penelope* and four destroyers to destroy the Italian convoy directly before it reached its destination. Half an hour past midnight, however, O'Connor encountered a previously unknown Italian minefield. His ship the *Neptune* and a destroyer were sunk; the *Aurora* was heavily and the *Penelope* lightly damaged.

The convoys of both parties reached their destinations without losses; but the result of the operation was a clear fiasco for the British, since the threat which the British cruiser force in Malta constituted to supply-convoys to North Africa had been eliminated for the near future.[44] The most important result of the first battle of Sirte, as the encounter was called, was undoubtedly the strengthening of Italian self-confidence, as even the official British account recognized. With considerable effort the Italians had succeeded in completing their operations in spite of the threat from Malta. Even Rear-Admiral Weichold in Rome had words of praise for their achievement: 'The convoy reached its destinations without losses. The task has been completed and the critical supply situation in North Africa has improved considerably, although by no means decisively. . . . It is to be hoped that this success will have an advantageous effect on the greatly weakened self-esteem of the Italian navy and its

---

[44] On the course of the operations as a whole cf. Bragadin, *Italian Navy*, 146–51; Hinsley, *British Intelligence*, ii. 323–4; *Marina italiana*, vii. 193–214; Playfair, *Mediterranean*, iii. 110–14.

commanding officers and will favourably influence future convoy operations to Tripoli.'[45]

Almost at the same time as the losses suffered by K Force, the self-confidence of the Italians was also greatly strengthened by a considerably more serious defeat they were able to inflict on the British. Although the Mediterranean Fleet had been warned by the Admiralty in London, three Italian human-torpedo crews dropped off by the submarine *Scire* were able to penetrate the harbour at Alexandria in the night of 18–19 December and attach explosive charges under the battleships *Queen Elizabeth* and *Valiant* and under a Norwegian tanker. All three ships were so seriously damaged that they settled on to the floor of the harbour. A destroyer alongside the tanker was also heavily damaged.[46]

The ships were out of action for months; the Mediterranean Fleet was without aircraft-carriers, battleships, or heavy cruisers. As the war against Japan in the Far East had just begun and Japanese naval aircraft had sunk the battleship *Prince of Wales* and the battle cruiser *Repulse* on 10 December, no replacements were available for the large ships in the Mediterranean. Other types of ship also had to be sent to the Far East; Admiral Cunningham's forces were temporarily reduced to three light cruisers and ten destroyers ready for action. At this time Admiral Somerville's H Force in Gibraltar consisted of only the battleship *Malaya*, the *Argus* (the oldest and smallest aircraft-carrier of the Royal Navy), a modern light cruiser, and a few destroyers. While Eighth Army was able to relieve Tobruk in Operation Crusader and force Rommel to retreat from Cyrenaica, the strength of the Royal Navy in the Mediterranean fell to the lowest level ever, endangering plans for the conquest of Tripolitania and the invasion of French North Africa. With its few remaining ships the Mediterranean Fleet was unable to support and protect from the sea a further westward advance of Eighth Army, nor could it blockade the Italian ports in North Africa with surface ships. But in the final analysis the subsequently planned operation did not fail because of the temporary weakness of the Royal Navy. The chiefs of staff in London and General Auchinleck and the other two British commanders-in-chief in Cairo were agreed that there could be no question of withdrawing army or Royal Air Force units from North Africa if that would endanger the continuation of the offensive to the Tunisian frontier. But this plan could not be maintained in view of the military disasters the British suffered in the Far East. In fact British forces originally intended for North Africa were diverted to the Far East, and the withdrawal of units already in action in North Africa became inevitable, with the result that the Axis powers were again able to seize the initiative there.[47]

[45] Chief of German naval cmd. in Italy to OKM/Skl.: B.Nr. g.Kdos. 8188/41 (19 Dec. 1941), BA-MA M Box 629, PG 39972 NID. Later Weichold modified his judgement: 'In the convoy operation from Alexandria to Malta it [the British fleet] was lucky, because the Italians, as they have done so often, let a favourable opportunity slip away': Baum and Weichold, *Krieg der 'Achsenmächte'*, 194.   [46] *Marina italiana*, v. 78–118; Playfair, *Mediterranean*, iii. 115.
[47] Cf. Playfair, *Mediterranean*, iii. 117–33.

VI. Operation Crusader

IN July 1941 the German army high command expected to be able to start a new attack on Tobruk at the beginning or in the middle of September. This, however, was based on the assumption that it would be possible to increase the volume of supplies transported to North Africa.[1] In contrast, the Wehrmacht high command was not interested in the North African theatre at this time and considered the protection of transports there to be the task of the Italians.[2] In fact, however, the Italians were not able to increase the quantity of supplies sent to North Africa. It had reached a record level in June, but then sank by November to the lowest figure ever recorded.[3] This forced a postponement of the date of attack, for without reinforcements, adequate preparations, and sufficient supplies, even Rommel did not want to make a new attempt to take Tobruk. He thus found himself in a dilemma: while the flow of supplies and reinforcements slowed and shrank, he could assume that the British were strengthening their forces more or less undisturbed in Egypt.

Rommel of course did not expect that the enemy would remain inactive on the Sollum front when the Germans attacked Tobruk again. He therefore wanted to avoid any battles involving heavy casualties and to achieve a decisive success within two days in order to be able to repel British relief attacks with his still relatively fresh forces. The question was, however, whether the enemy would seize the initiative and launch a new offensive on his own, to relieve Tobruk and destroy German and Italian armoured forces in North Africa before Rommel had concluded his preparations for a new attack. When Rommel set the date of attack for 21 November, he had already lost the race with the enemy. Three days earlier the British Eighth Army had crossed the frontier between Egypt and Libya. The waiting of the past few weeks had not given Rommel any advantages, as the Italians had not sent any transports to Tripoli since 21 October, when K Force began operating from Malta. Armoured Group Africa was forced to consume parts of its reserve supply stocks.[4]

On the eve of the next cycle of battles in North Africa the German and Italian forces possessed impressive strength only on paper. The Italian XXI Army Corps under General Navarini with the three partially motorized divisions Bologna, Pavia, and Brescia, which were stationed on the Tobruk front, was subordinate to the Armoured Group Africa. The latter also included the

---

[1] Cf. end of ch. V.IV above.
[2] Halder. *Diaries*, ii. 1085 (29 July 1941).
[3] Cf. Table V.V.1, p. 716 above.
[4] Taysen, *Tobruk*, 211; Kriebel, 'Nordafrika', MGFA T 3, ii. 50–1.

Africa Corps under Lieutenant-General Crüwell, which had grown to four divisions. Among them were now two armoured divisions; in addition to 15th Armoured Division, 5th Light Division had been reorganized and renamed 21st Armoured Division on 15 August. The Division for Special Tasks Africa—at the end of November renamed 90th Light Division—had been created using various units sent to Africa in the summer and autumn. It consisted primarily of 155th Infantry Regiment; 361st Africa Regiment, made up of former members of the Foreign Legion; a light artillery battalion (*Abteilung*); and five oasis companies of volunteers. These troops were deployed against Tobruk and on the Sollum front. The partially motorized Italian Savona Division was also stationed on the Sollum front and, together with German units, had constructed a line of strong points extending forty-five kilometres from Sollum to Sidi Umar. An additional, motorized corps, the 'corpo d'armata di manovra', was formed with Ariete Armoured Division and Trento and Trieste motorized divisions. It was directly subordinate to the Italian high command in North Africa under Army General Bastico. His chief of staff, General Gambara, was at the same time commanding general of the corps. He was therefore not responsible to the command of Armoured Group Africa, but had agreed with Rommel to advance with his corps to the area of Bir al Ghabi in the event of a British attack.[5]

In October the German army troops in Africa reached a ration strength of 48,500 men, but, owing in part to malnutrition, the number reported sick was 11,066.[6] The division for special tasks lacked all communications equipment and supply facilities; the forces besieging Tobruk and the two armoured divisions were still waiting for the arrival of artillery and other units. Both armoured divisions received a total of only 44 Mark III and sixteen Mark IV tanks as replacements by the end of the year.[7] Before the fighting began they had 249 tanks, of which, however, 70 were Mark IIs. In addition, the Italian Ariete Armoured Division had 137 M 13/40 tanks.[8] The situation of the Luftwaffe was no better. On 15 November the air leader, Major-General Fröhlich, had only 140 aircraft at his disposal, of which only 76 were ready for action. For fighter protection he had only 35 Me 109F4s (27 ready for action) and 12 Me 110s (7 ready for action). However, the Italian Fifth Air Fleet had approximately 290 aircraft in Cyrenaica and Marmarica, of which 154 were fighters. X Air Corps in Greece, with 181 aircraft (104 ready for action), was also able to provide some assistance.[9]

---

[5] *Seconda offensiva*, 21–4; Cmd. of Armoured Group Africa, Abt. Ia No. 31/41 g.Kdos. Chefs. (6 Sept. 1941), to OKH, army general staff/Op.Abt., BA-MA RH 2/v. 460. Cf. the differing accounts by Kriebel, 'Nordafrika', MGFA T 3, ii. 29–30, 32–3, and Taysen, *Tobruk*, 197–8, 201–2.
[6] Cf. Taysen, *Tobruk*, 359.
[7] Ibid. 195–7, 368.
[8] Figures according to *Seconda offensiva*, 29, 33. Cf. also Playfair, *Mediterranean*, iii. 30.
[9] Gundelach, *Luftwaffe im Mittelmeer*, 303–5.

The British were much better equipped for the coming battles. The Commander-in-Chief Middle East, Auchinleck, had created Eighth Army under Lieutenant-General Sir Alan Cunningham, the victor in East Africa. Western Desert Force under Lieutenant-General A. R. Godwin-Austen was placed under Cunningham's command and given its old name, XIII Corps. Most of the armoured forces were combined in the new XXX Corps—which included 7th Armoured Division, 4th Armoured Brigade Group, and, to provide cover in the rear and on the flanks, 1st South African Division and 22nd Guards Brigade—and were finally placed under the command of Major-General C. W. M. Norrie. The New Zealand Division, 4th Indian Division, and 1st Army Armoured Division were placed under XIII Corps.[10]

The garrison of Tobruk under Major-General Scobie consisted of 70th Division, 32nd Army Armoured Brigade, and a Polish infantry brigade group. At the request of the Australian government, the original garrison, 9th Australian Division, had been relieved. Evacuating the Australians was an additional burden for the Mediterranean Fleet, which had transported 34,113 men to Tobruk during the siege (11 April–10 December 1941) and removed 47,280 (including prisoners) from the fortress. A total of thirty-four ships had been lost in these operations, and thirty-three others had been damaged.[11]

The 29th Indian Infantry Brigade Group and 6th South African Armoured Regiment were assembled near the oasis of Al Jaghbub to secure a temporary airfield 160 kilometres further west, from which the Royal Air Force wanted to attack the coastal area south of Benghazi. It was planned to capture Jalu subsequently and disrupt the rear communications of the Axis troops. The main objective was, however, to create the appearance of a strong threat from the south and divert attention from the main actual effort of the British attack.[12] The 2nd South African Division was to be held in reserve.

The main question for the British was how much time would be available to prepare the operation. While Churchill wanted to take advantage of the concentration of the German war effort on the campaign in the Soviet Union and considered it intolerable that the British 'Middle East armies have had to stand for four and a half months without engaging the enemy', Auchinleck, like Wavell before him, did not want to start an offensive before his preparations were completed and his troops had finished their training and received all their equipment.[13] In this respect, in contrast to Rommel's situation, he considered every postponement of the start of the operation to be a gain. By the end of October his troops had received approximately 300 Cruiser tanks,

---

[10] Playfair, *Mediterranean*, iii. 37.
[11] Ibid. 22–6.
[12] Ibid. 8, 38.
[13] Churchill, *Second World War*, iii. 481–2. Moreover, Auchinleck wanted first to strengthen his position in Iraq, Syria, and Cyprus, as he considered a German attack through Anatolia possible after August. As the most important front might develop there, he intended to refrain from attacking in North Africa before the end of 1941. Cf. Hinsley, *British Intelligence*, ii. 278–9.

300 American Stuart light tanks, 170 infantry close-support tanks, 34,000 lorries, 600 field-guns, 80 heavy and 160 light anti-aircraft guns, 200 anti-tank guns, and 900 mortars.[14] At the start of the offensive XXX Corps had a total of 477 tanks, including 94 older Cruisers and 173 Stuarts. XIII Corps had 1st Army Armoured Brigade with 3 Cruisers and 132 infantry close-support tanks, of which approximately half were new model Valentine tanks. In addition, 32nd Army Armoured Brigade in Tobruk had 32 Cruisers, 25 light tanks, and 69 Matilda close-support tanks. Apart from reserves, the British thus had 738 tanks against 386 for the Germans and Italians.[15]

The situation of Western Desert Air Force was equally favourable. It had reached a strength of 650 aircraft (550 ready for action). In addition, 74 aircraft (66 ready) were stationed on Malta.[16] More important than mere numerical superiority was, however, the fact that sufficient fuel, ammunition, and spares were available for these aircraft. In the air offensive preceding the actual ground attack they flew almost three thousand sorties, an average of eighty a day, between 14 October and 17 November, not counting those against German and Italian sea transports, and achieved clear air supremacy.

Supplying their advancing army again presented a great problem for the British, at least in the first days of the offensive. The sea route could not be used as long as Tobruk had not been reached and Sollum and Bardiyah were still in enemy hands. Among the extensive preparations made for this reason were the lengthening of the water-conduit from Alexandria to Marsa Matruh and of the railway to Mishfah. Forward supply-depots were established near Sidi Barrani, Mishfah, and Al Jhagbub and, west of them, six field maintenance centres. The 7th Support Group and 22nd Guards Brigade protected these preparations until units of 4th Indian Division advanced into the frontier area.[17]

The Germans were aware of the constant flow of British forces and supplies to Egypt, but no attack preparations or changes on the Sollum front were detected. At the end of August the Luftwaffe reported four possible forward supply-depots in the area of Bir al Khuraygat, Bir Dignash, and Bir Habatah, but doubts arose as to whether the depots were full. Finally, 21st Armoured Division was ordered to destroy the enemy covering forces on the plateau and attack 7th Armoured Division near Bir Habatah on 14 September. This operation was, however, a complete failure, as the German division remained immobile on the battlefield for several hours because of a lack of fuel and was subjected to fierce attacks by the Royal Air Force. The attack on the enemy near Bir Habatah was delayed so long that it had to be broken off without achieving any results. No enemy supply-depots were found.[18]

---

[14] Playfair, *Mediterranean*, iii. 4.
[15] Ibid. 30.
[16] Ibid. 15. Gundelach (*Luftwaffe im Mittelmeer*, 303) gives a total figure of 750 aircraft.
[17] Playfair, *Mediterranean*, iii. 9–11.
[18] Cf. Kriebel, 'Nordafrika', MGFA T 3, ii. 25–6; Taysen, *Tobruk*, 203–4.

The results of this reconnaissance strengthened the belief of Rommel and the armoured group command that an enemy attack in the immediate future was not to be expected. The movement of enemy reinforcements to the front was even explained as a reaction to the advance by 21st Armoured Division. The British organized and concealed their deployment so well that even the day before the attack the Germans expected at most only efforts to relieve Tobruk and not an attempt to launch a decisive offensive, for they knew that the enemy was aware of their own preparations to attack the fortress.[19] Rommel was, however, somewhat concerned about reports of enemy activity and ordered 21st Armoured Division to assemble south of Kambut.[20]

The basic objective of the British operational plan was to advance with the mass of British tanks in XXX Corps towards the north-west in order to defeat the enemy's tanks and subsequently break through to Tobruk. XIII Corps was to attack and cut off the German units on the Egyptian frontier and then advance westward. In spite of outward appearances, however, XXX Corps was not especially well prepared for its task. The experienced 7th Brigade of 7th Armoured Division was equipped with older-model Cruiser tanks in need of repair, while 22nd Armoured Brigade, just arrived from Britain, had new Crusader tanks but no time to prepare itself for a war in the desert because its tanks first had to be refitted in Alexandria for such combat. The 4th Armoured Brigade Group was the first unit to use the American Stuart, whose qualities were generally praised but which, with a weight of 13.5 tonnes, was only a light tank. Finally, 1st South African Division had proved its worth in the campaign in East Africa, but the losses suffered there had not yet been replaced, with the result that it started the offensive with only two instead of three brigades, which, moreover, had not completed their training for the new theatre.[21] Far more serious than these problems was, however, the fact that the British commanders down to brigade level still had not realized that at this time their most effective weapon against German tanks was not their own armour, but rather their artillery. Even worse, the British operational plan was based on wishful thinking, When XXX Corps reached the area of Qabr Salih, only a point in the desert, on the evening of the first day of the attack, it was assumed that the Africa Corps would move eastward and accept a battle, although there was not the least necessity for it to do so. As Rommel was concentrating all his attention on preparing an attack on Tobruk and expected at most diversionary operations on the Sollum front, the British plan was doomed to failure.

The concealment of the British attack was greatly aided at the last moment by the weather. A sandstorm developed on 16 November, and in the night of 17–18 November a violent thunderstorm swept over Cyrenaica and Marmarica.

---

[19] Cf. Behrendt, *Afrikafeldzug*, 125–7.
[20] Taysen, *Tobruk*, 210.
[21] Cf. here and for the following account Pitt, *Crucible*, 342–6.

Cloudbursts flooded the roads, and many troop units were surprised in the wadis where they had set up their positions. Most important, however, was the fact that for several days the airfields in the area were unusable, while the Royal Air Force was able to continue operating without interruption from Egypt. On 18 November XXX Corps advanced without difficulty ninety kilometres from Maddalena to Qabr Salih, while protective forces reinforced with tanks, artillery, and anti-tank guns pushed the German reconnaissance battalions 3 and 33 back to the north and north-west. General Cunningham accompanied the headquarters of XXX Corps to be able to give quick orders when reports on the movements of the Africa Corps were received. Difficulties arose because the Africa Corps still had not changed its position by evening. Finally, 4th Armoured Brigade was ordered to remain near Qabr Salih, and protect the left flank of XIII Corps and the right flank of 7th Armoured Division. The 22nd Armoured Brigade was to advance on Bir al Ghabi, where Ariete Armoured Division was deployed, and 7th Armoured Brigade was ordered to push on to the escarpment near Sidi Rizq and if possible capture the heights there. Lieutenant-General Norrie had suggested from the beginning ordering the entire corps to advance to Sidi Rizq, because the Tariq Capuzzo and the bypass road around the besieged fortress passed below the heights there, and capturing them would cut off the German and Italian troops between Tobruk and the Sollum front from their supplies and establish a direct link with Tobruk. But his suggestion was accepted and implemented in such a way that it would inevitably lead to a breakup of the concentration of British armoured forces.[22]

The following day, 19 November, 22nd Armoured Brigade attacked the Italian Ariete Armoured Division near Bir al Ghabi but broke the attack off after losing twenty-five of its 136 modern Crusader tanks; the Italians lost thirty-four tanks. The 7th Armoured Brigade was more successful, advancing to Sidi Rizq, occupying the airfield there, and capturing nineteen aircraft on the ground. It was then able to threaten the Division for Special Tasks Africa, which formed part of the siege front around Tobruk, from the rear. The division was forced to establish an improvised defensive front towards the south. The British 4th Armoured Brigade also became involved in combat. Lieutenant-General Crüwell, who unlike Rommel believed that the British had begun a major offensive, was finally able to obtain permission to put 15th Armoured Division on alert and advance with the armoured battle group of 21st Armoured Division to Qabr Salih to restore the situation. This forced 4th Armoured Brigade, which lost twenty-three of its Stuart tanks, to withdraw. The battle was not decided before nightfall, but the Germans, who had lost only three tanks, had achieved a clear success.[23]

The next day began with a German setback. After the armoured group

---

[22] Cf. Playfair, *Mediterranean*, iii. 38–9; Taysen, *Tobruk*, 225–7; Map V.VI.1.
[23] Cf. Jackson, *Campaign*, 157; *Seconda offensiva*, 45–9; Map V.VI.2.

command had realized the extent of the British offensive, the Africa Corps wanted first to destroy the enemy forces which had driven Reconnaissance Battalion 3 back to the north and then attack eastward with both armoured divisions. The 15th Armoured Division was to advance via Sidi Aziz towards Capuzzo; 21st Armoured Division would advance north of the Trigh el Abd towards Sidi Omar. But only enemy reconnaissance units were found, and 21st Armoured Division was immobilized by a lack of ammunition and fuel. During the day Crüwell realized that enemy units were moving west along the Tariq al Abd and for that reason attacked 4th Armoured Brigade again near Qabr Salih. The brigade lost ten more Stuart tanks and withdrew further. The British 22nd Armoured Brigade arrived from Bir al Ghabi too late to intervene.

In the meantime 1st South African Division had advanced towards Bir al Ghabi, and near Sidi Rizq 7th Support Group had reinforced 7th Armoured Brigade. Rommel now realized[24] that this development constituted the main danger for the siege front around Tobruk, and ordered the Africa Corps to disengage itself from the British 4th Armoured Brigade in the night and attack in the direction of Belhamid, a ridge six kilometres north of the airfield at Sidi Rizq, on 21 November. In spite of the adverse outcome of the tank battles, Cunningham considered his situation to be unusually favourable. On the basis of various reports he concluded that the German armoured group had begun to withdraw to the west. Near Sidi Rizq in particular the enemy seemed to be so weak that the break-out from Tobruk was prepared for 21 November, although the destruction of the German and Italian tank forces, according to British plans the prerequisite for such a move, had not yet been achieved. To support the break-out, 7th Armoured Division was ordered to attack near Sidi Rizq and was strengthened by the addition of 5th Brigade and 1st South African Division. The 4th and 22nd Armoured Brigades were ordered to attack and destroy the Africa Corps near Qabr Salih.[25]

The break-out attempt from Tobruk began on the morning of 21 November with heavy losses on both sides. Around noon Major-General Scobie ordered the attacks to be stopped and went on the defensive, as 7th Armoured Division had not succeeded in reaching the heights of Al Dudah north-west of Sidi Rizq. Units of the division were able to dislodge the Germans and Italians from the edge of the heights north of the airfield at Sidi Rizq, but in the following attempt to continue the attack along the Tariq Capuzzo to the north a battalion of 7th Armoured Brigade lost three-quarters of its tanks. This Axis defensive success was shared by the siege artillery originally assembled to support the attack on Tobruk and Reconnaissance Battalion 3, which Rommel

---

[24] In its evening news broadcast BBC Cairo reported that 8th Army had opened a large-scale offensive with the object of destroying the German and Italian forces in Africa. Cf. Irving, *Rommel*, 121–2; Map V.vi.3.

[25] Playfair, *Mediterranean*, iii. 41–4; Taysen, *Tobruk*, 232–6; *Seconda offensiva*, 49 ff.; Map V.vi.4.

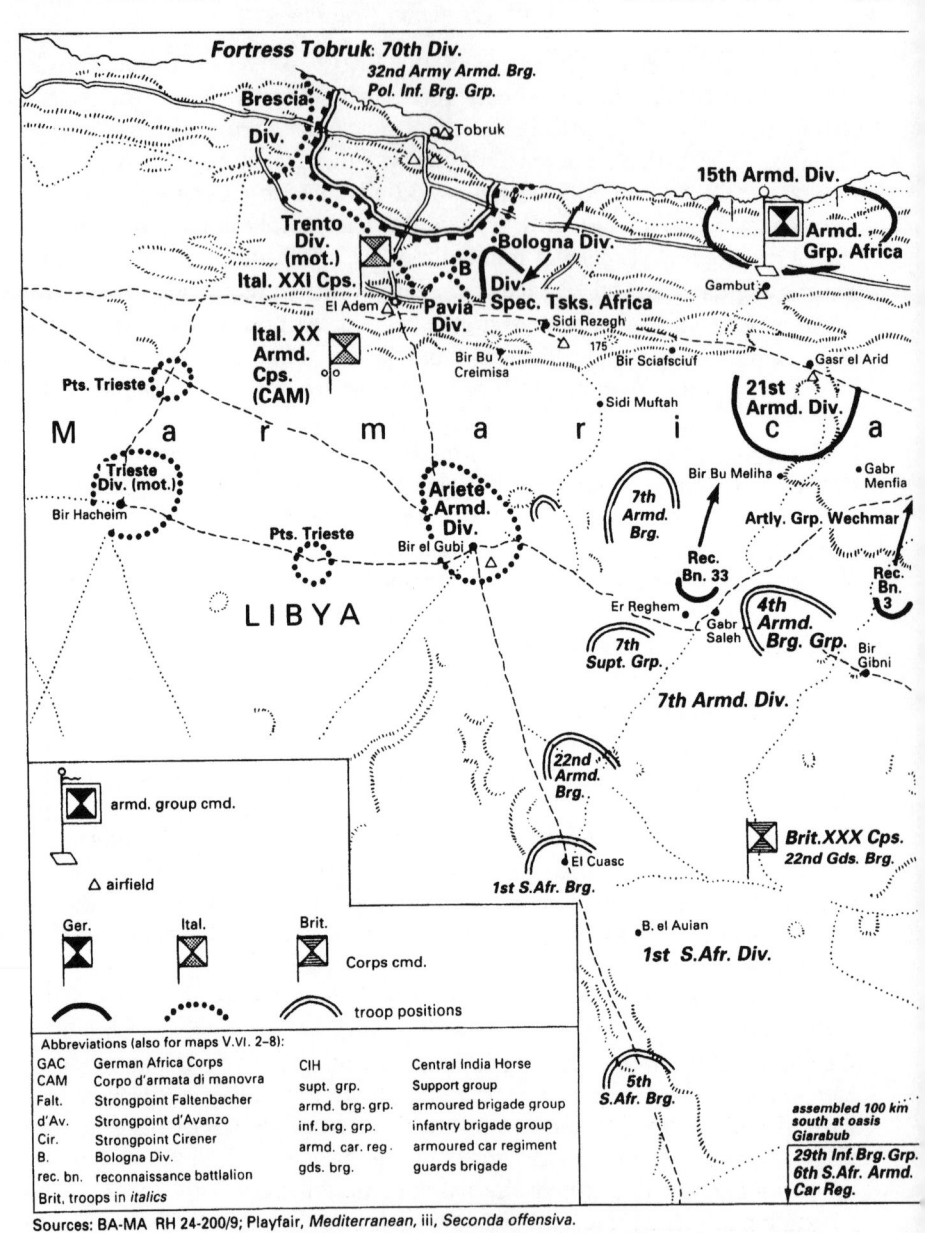

MAP V.VI.1. Operation Crusader: Deployment, 18 November 1941

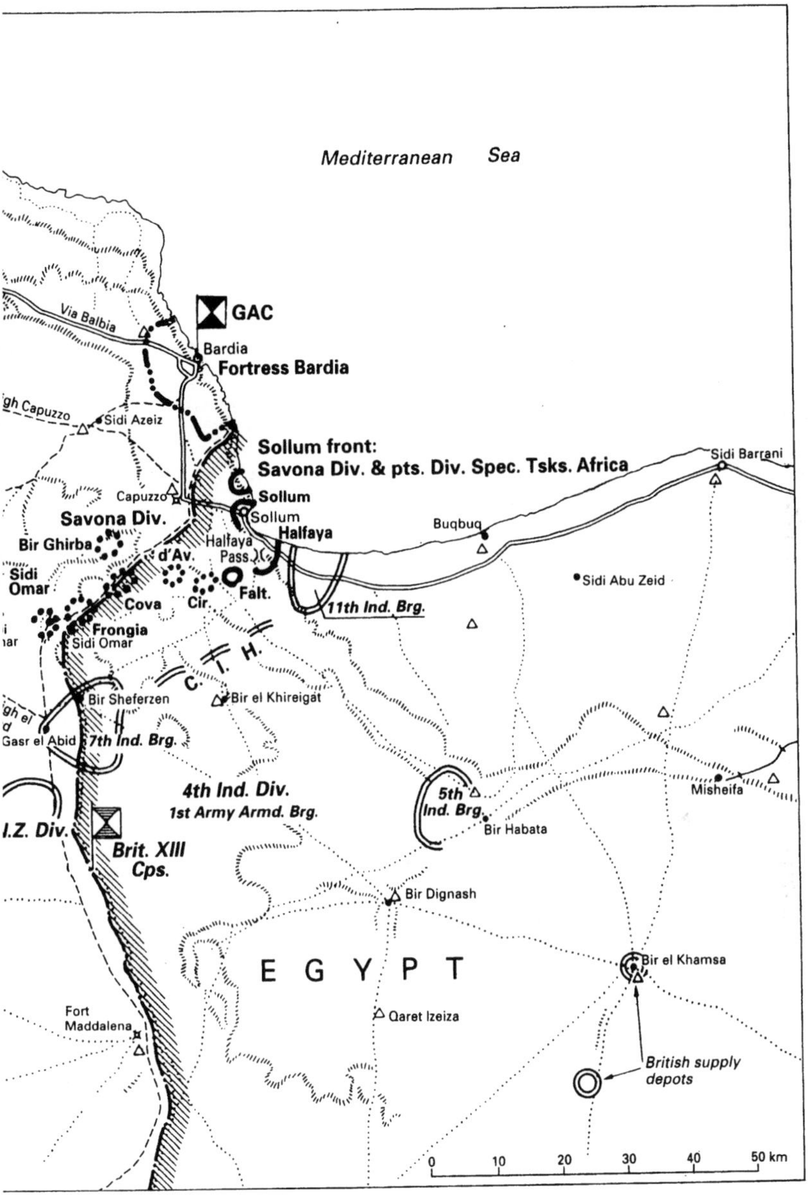

Mediterranean Sea
GAC
Via Balbia
Bardia
Fortress Bardia
gh Capuzzo
Sidi Azeiz
Sollum front:
Savona Div. & pts. Div. Spec. Tsks. Africa
Sidi Barrani
Capuzzo
Sollum
Sollum
Savona Div.
Halfaya
Buqbuq
Halfaya Pass
Bir Ghirba
d'Av.
Sidi Omar
Sidi Abu Zeid
Falt.
Cova
Cir.
11th Ind. Brg.
Frongia
Sidi Omar
C. I. H.
Bir Sheferzen
Bir el Khireigat
Gasr el Abid
7th Ind. Brg.
4th Ind. Div.
1st Army Armd. Brg.
5th Ind. Brg.
Misheifa
Bir Habata
I.Z. Div.
Brit. XIII Cps.
Bir Dignash
E G Y P T
Bir el Khamsa
Fort Maddalena
Qaret Izeiza
British supply depots
0 10 20 30 40 50 km

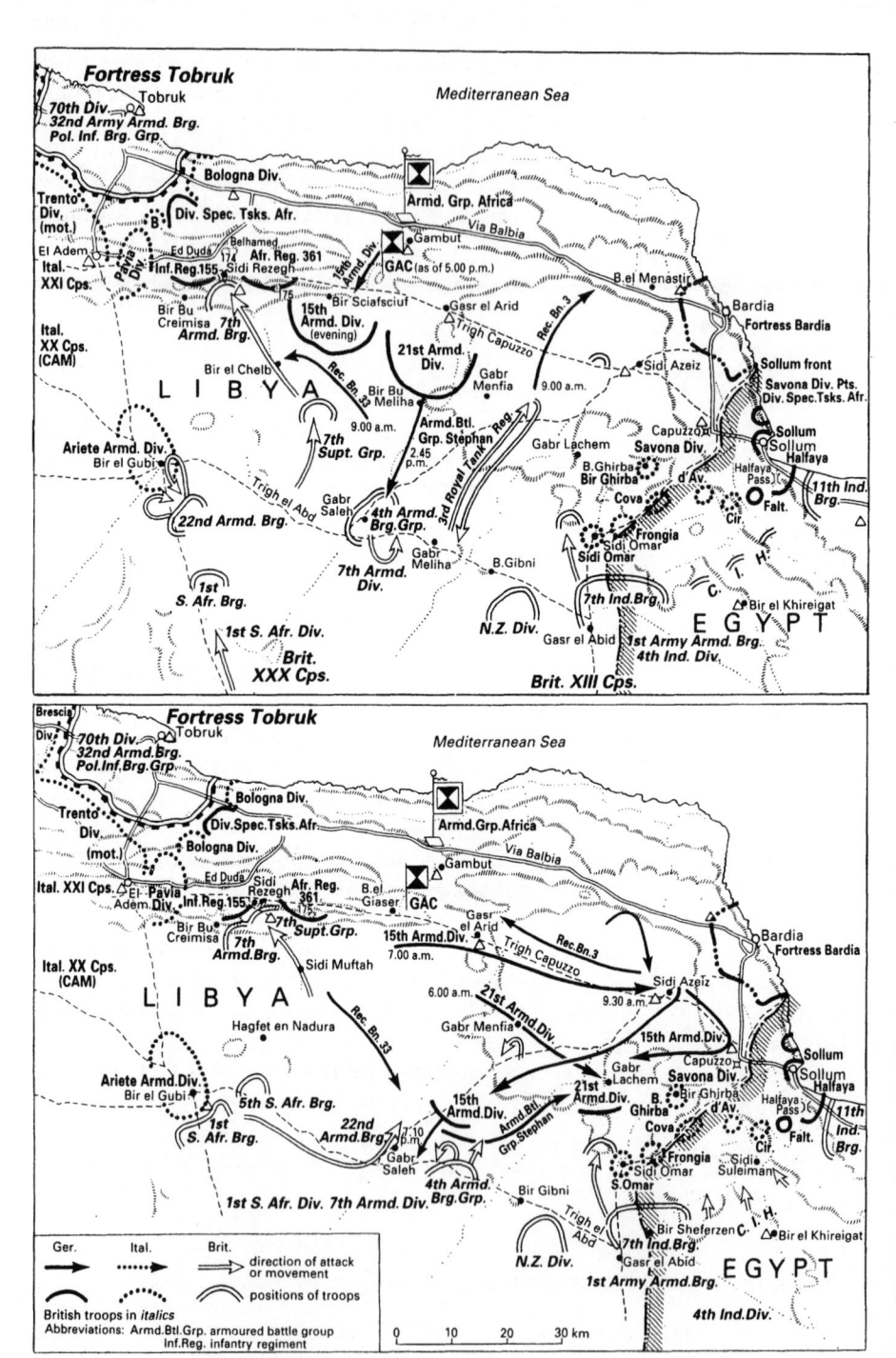

Sources: BA-MA RH 24-200/9; Playfair, *Mediterranean*, iii; *Seconda offensiva*.

had strengthened with 88-mm. anti-aircraft guns. To oppose the two German armoured divisions approaching from the south-east, 7th Armoured Division had only two battalions, which were quickly pushed back to ten kilometres south-east of Sidi Rizq. In the evening 7th Armoured Division had only twenty-eight tanks still ready for action. The 22nd Armoured Brigade, which had attacked the flank of the German 15th Armoured Division from the south, had seventy-nine tanks. Only 4th Armoured Brigade, which followed the Africa Corps, still had 102 tanks. Including Mark IIs, the Germans still had 192 tanks.

The headquarters of the British XXX Corps and Eighth Army were still satisfied with the results of the fighting; precise figures on British losses were available only later, and the move of the Africa Corps from Qabr Salih to Sidi Rizq was mistakenly interpreted as a retreat. At the suggestion of Major-General Norrie, General Cunningham ordered XIII Corps to begin its advance westward. The break-out from Tobruk and the attacks near Sidi Rizq were to be continued the next day using 5th South African Brigade. On the German side, Lieutenant-General Crüwell was worried and wanted to transfer the Africa Corps to a point closer to its supply-base south of Kambut during the night. After Rommel had intervened, however, 21st Armoured Division was transferred to the area south of Belhamid to relieve 155th Infantry Regiment and 361st African Regiment, which were defending their positions on the edge of the heights west and east of the airfield at Sidi Rizq.[26]

The 155th Infantry Regiment was attacked by 5th South African Brigade on the afternoon of 22 November but was able to repel the attack. After nightfall the South Africans withdrew to the area south of Point 178. In the meantime 5th Armoured Regiment of 21st Division had begun an attack from the west to encircle the airfield at Sidi Rizq, while 104th Infantry Regiment launched a direct attack from the north. Against determined resistance of the British support group and 7th and 22nd Armoured Brigades, the airfield was captured. The intervention of the British 4th Armoured Brigade, which had followed stragglers of 15th Armoured Division eastward, could not change the situation. Finally the British withdrew to the position of 5th South African Brigade.

The 15th Armoured Division had replenished its supplies and began an encirclement movement to the south because it had received a request for

[26] Playfair, *Mediterranean*, iii. 45–7; Taysen, *Tobruk*, 236–41; *Seconda offensiva*, 52–3.

MAP V.VI.2. Operation Crusader, 19 November 1941
Sources: BA-MA RH 24-200/9; Playfair, *Mediterranean*, iii; *Seconda offensiva*.

MAP V.VI.3. Operation Crusader, 20 November 1941
Sources: BA-MA RH 24-200/9; Playfair, *Mediterranean*, iii; *Seconda offensiva*.

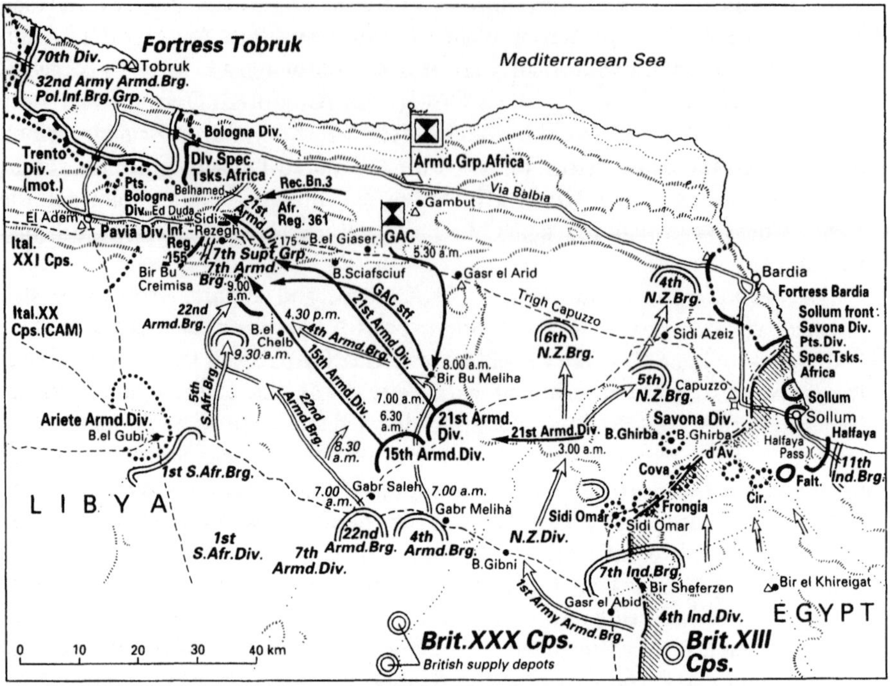

Fortress Tobruk
Mediterranean Sea
70th Div.
Tobruk
32nd Army Armd.Brg.
Pol.Inf.Brg.Grp.
Bologna Div.
Trento Div. (mot.)
Pts. Bologna Div.
Div.Spec. Tsks.Africa
Armd.Grp.Africa
Rec.Bn.3
Afr. Reg. 361
Via Balbia
Gambut
GAC
El Adem
Ed Duda
Sidi Rezegh
Pavia Div.
Inf. Reg. 155
Ital. XXI Cps.
7th Supt.Grp.
7th Armd. Brg.
B.el Giaser
B.Sciafsciuf
Gasr el Arid
Bir Bu Creimisa
Bardia
Fortress Bardia
Sollum front: Savona Div. Pts.Div. Spec.Tsks. Africa
Trigh Capuzzo
4th N.Z.Brg.
6th N.Z.Brg.
Ital.XX Cps.(CAM)
22nd Armd.Brg.
B.el Chelb
4th Armd.Brg.
21st Armd.Div.
GAC stf.
15th Armd.Div.
Bir Bu Meliha
Sidi Azeiz
5th N.Z.Brg.
Capuzzo
Sollum
Halfaya
Halfaya Pass
11th Ind.Brg.
Ariete Armd.Div.
B.el Gubi
5th S.Afr.Brg.
1st S.Afr.Brg.
21st Armd. Div.
15th Armd.Div.
Savona Div.
B.Ghirba
d'Av.
Cova
Falt.
Cir.
Frongia
Sidi Omar
LIBYA
Gabr Saleh
Gabr Meliha
22nd Armd.Brg.
4th Armd.Brg.
1st S.Afr.Div.
7th Armd.Div.
B.Gibni
N.Z.Div.
7th Ind.Brg.
Bir Sheferzen
Bir el Khireigat
Gasr el Abid
4th Ind.Div.
EGYPT
1st Army Armd.Brg.
Brit.XXX Cps.
Brit.XIII Cps.
British supply depots
0 10 20 30 40 km

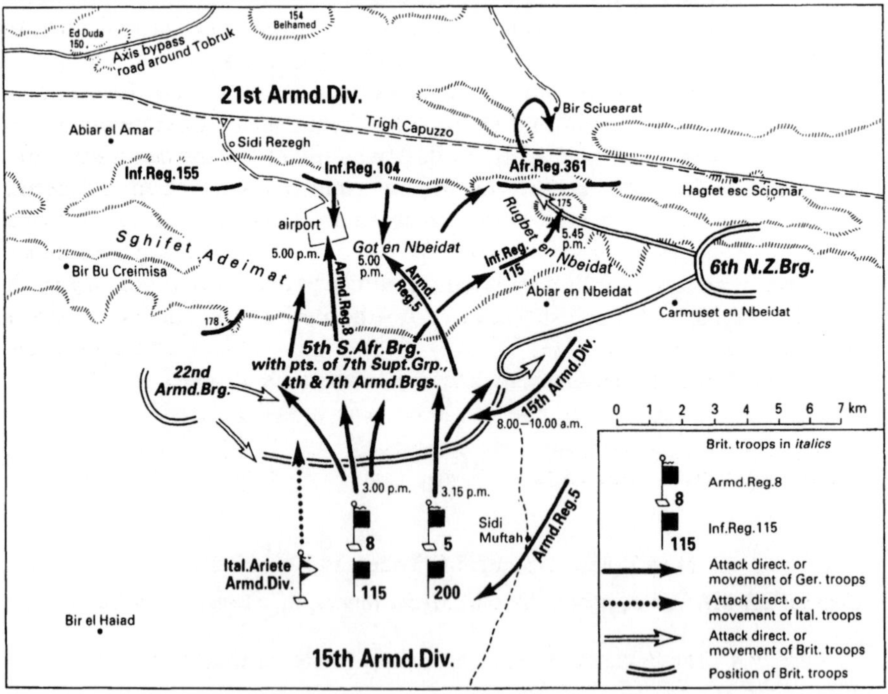

Ed Duda 150
154 Belhamed
Axis bypass road around Tobruk
21st Armd.Div.
Bir Sciuearat
Abiar el Amar
Trigh Capuzzo
Sidi Rezegh
Inf.Reg.155
Inf.Reg.104
Afr.Reg.361
Hagfet esc Sciomar
Rugbet en Nbeidat
airport
Sghifet Adeimat
Got en Nbeidat
Bir Bu Creimisa
Armd.Reg.8
Armd. Reg.5
Inf.Reg. 115
6th N.Z.Brg.
Abiar en Nbeidat
Carmuset en Nbeidat
5th S.Afr.Brg. with pts. of 7th Supt.Grp., 4th & 7th Armd.Brgs.
22nd Armd.Brg.
15th Armd.Div.
Sidi Muftah
Armd.Reg.5
Ital.Ariete Armd.Div.
Bir el Haiad
15th Armd.Div.
0 1 2 3 4 5 6 7 km
Brit. troops in italics
Armd.Reg.8
Inf.Reg.115
Attack direct. or movement of Ger. troops
Attack direct. or movement of Ital. troops
Attack direct. or movement of Brit. troops
Position of Brit. troops

assistance from 21st Armoured Division and the erroneous report that 180 enemy tanks were approaching the battlefield from that direction. When it again turned northward, in the darkness it unexpectedly overran the command post of the British 4th Armoured Brigade and one of its armoured battalions. The brigade lost 35 tanks and was temporarily leaderless. By evening 22nd Armoured Brigade had only 34 tanks, 7th Armoured Brigade 10; the Africa Corps on the other hand still had 173 tanks ready for action.

In Tobruk 70th Division improved its position at the break-out point during the day, but the actual break-out was postponed. On the Sollum front the New Zealanders and the Indians were able to penetrate the German and Italian strong-point system and cut the rear communication lines to the armoured group. Cunningham ordered the New Zealanders to advance on Tobruk with the greater part of their division; he wanted to start an infantry attack on the besiegers of the fortress on 24 November. XXX Corps was to continue to provide flank protection and to attack remnants of the German armoured units. The Germans, on the other hand, planned to complete the destruction of the remnants of the British forces south of Sidi Rizq. For this purpose Rommel intended to have the Africa Corps attack in the direction of Bir al Ghabi to push the enemy towards Ariete Armoured Division, which was to advance from Bir al Ghabi towards Kambut. However, Crüwell thought Ariete too weak for this task and therefore ordered 15th Armoured Division and 5th Armoured Regiment to join it near Bir al Ghabi and push the enemy northward towards the edge of the precipice, which was now held by the infantry units of 21st Armoured Division.

Rommel asked General Gambara to send his motorized corps to assist the Germans in the annihilation of the enemy near Sidi Rizq, but Gambara was only prepared to send parts of Ariete Division. Thereupon Rommel sent a telegram to Rome the next morning asking General von Rintelen to persuade Mussolini to place Gambara under his (Rommel's) command. He also complained about Army General Bastico, who had not appeared at his command post since the start of the fighting and had not participated personally in the conduct of the battle, which, however, Rommel himself no doubt hardly desired. The same day Mussolini placed the Corps Gambara under Rommel's command, but Rommel himself remained subordinate to Bastico.[27]

---

[27] Playfair, *Mediterranean*, iii. 47–9; Taysen, *Tobruk*, 240–7; *Seconda offensiva*, 53–4. For the subsequent fighting cf. Map V.VI.5.

MAP V.VI.4. Operation Crusader, 21 November 1941

Sources: BA-MA RH 24-200/9; Playfair, *Mediterranean*, iii; *Seconda offensiva*.

MAP V.VI.5. The Battle of Commemoration Sunday: Afternoon, 23 November 1941

Sources: BA-MA RH 24-200/9; Playfair, *Mediterranean*, iii; *Seconda offensiva*.

On the morning of 23 November Crüwell began his advance southward with 15th Armoured Division, without waiting for 5th Armoured Regiment, which had been delayed. He immediately encountered gun-positions and concentrations of vehicles of 7th Support Group, which had formed a front facing northwest and was completely surprised. Crüwell then turned westward and found numerous vehicles of 5th South African Brigade. The commander of 15th Armoured Division, Major-General Neumann-Silkow, wanted to continue the attack westward to exploit the surprise of the enemy, but Crüwell held to his battle plan. Presumably he considered joining Ariete Armoured Division and 5th Armoured Regiment to be more important for the attack than the loss of the element of surprise. During his continued advance southward he also came upon the points of 1st South African Brigade, which was supposed to reinforce 5th Brigade near Sidi Rizq but now had to change direction to avoid the German tanks.

At 3.00 p.m. Crüwell's attack marked the beginning of the battle of Memorial Sunday (*Totensonntag*, in German Protestant churches the Sunday before Advent and the day for remembering the dead). The 5th South African Brigade had thoroughly prepared its defences. According to German reports its position was approximately ten kilometres deep and seven to eight kilometres wide with over 100 artillery pieces and numerous anti-tank guns. The Africa Corps attacked with 5th Armoured Regiment on the right wing and 8th Armoured Regiment in the centre. Ariete Division was supposed to advance on the left wing with infantry riding their vehicles close behind the tanks as the relatively late hour did not permit a more methodical attack. One hour later the infantry units of 21st Armoured Division attacked from the north. On the left wing Ariete was unable to advance because the British 22nd Armoured Brigade attacked on the flank and 5th Armoured Regiment was temporarily drawn away to the north-east by newly arrived New Zealand units. But by 5.00 p.m. 8th Armoured Regiment had broken through to the airfield.

5th South African Brigade was annihilated, and 22nd Armoured Brigade lost a third of its remaining 34 tanks, but the losses of the Africa Corps were also high: 72 of 162 tanks. Personnel losses were equally high, especially of non-commissioned and commissioned officers. In 8th Armoured Regiment both unit commanders and five of six company commanders had been wounded. Historians therefore generally agree that the battle of Memorial Sunday was a Pyrrhic victory for the Germans: the tactical success did not justify the high losses. The losses of tanks in particular, which could not be replaced, played a major role in the further course of the operations. Certainly the German victory would have been less costly if Crüwell had exploited the surprise of the enemy on the morning of 23 November instead of waiting to begin the attack in the afternoon after joining forces with the Italians.[28]

---

[28] Cf. Jackson, *Campaign*, 169; Pitt, *Crucible*, 415; Playfair, *Mediterranean*, iii. 49–50; Taysen, *Tobruk*, 247–51.

Other developments of 23 November were more favourable for the British. On the morning of that day 6th New Zealand Brigade was by chance able to capture a large part of the Africa Corps staff and almost all its radio units on the Tariq Capuzzo. In the afternoon, against the stubborn resistance of 361st African Regiment, the brigade was able to occupy part of the ridge at Point 175. In the meantime 4th New Zealand Brigade had captured Kambut and 5th Brigade had taken Upper Sollum, while 7th Indian Brigade captured more Italian defensive positions near Sidi Umar. Lieutenant-General Cunningham had, however, been very concerned since 22 November about the high British tank losses. The reports he had received indicated that XXX Corps now had only 44 tanks, while the enemy had 120. On 23 November, before 5th South African Brigade was annihilated, Cunningham therefore sent Auchinleck in Cairo an urgent request to come to his headquarters and decide on the spot whether Operation Crusader should be continued or broken off. Auchinleck arrived in the evening and explained forcefully that there could be no question of a retreat. In a written order the next day he instructed Cunningham to continue the operation to the last tank if necessary. His immediate objective was the destruction of the enemy's armoured forces, and his long-range objective remained the reconquest of Cyrenaica with a subsequent advance to Tripoli.[29]

The outcome of the battle of Commemoration Sunday strengthened Rommel's expectations of victory and caused him to develop fantastic plans quite beyond the bounds of feasibility. As late as the evening of 23 November he decided to complete the annihilation of 7th Armoured Division and to advance with parts of his forces in the direction of Sidi Umar to attack the enemy at the frontier. On the morning of 24 November he informed the staff of the armoured group that he wanted to command personally the Africa Corps and the subordinate Ariete Division in order to annihilate the remnants of the enemy's forces and cut off his retreat to Egypt. He intended to be back by evening or the next morning at the latest. His operations officer, Lieutenant-Colonel (General Staff) Siegfried Westphal, was to take over command of the armoured group and prevent a break-out from Tobruk. Rommel also said that he wanted to use the Africa Corps to attack the supply-lines of Eighth Army and capture its supply-depots. Lieutenant-General Crüwell, who had learnt by accident that Rommel would arrive at the headquarters of 21st Armoured Division for a conference at 6.00 a.m., made a counter-proposal: to pursue the defeated enemy, mop up his forces in the area between the Tariq Capuzzo and the Tariq al Abd, and collect the captured equipment. But Rommel declined to depart from his plan to pursue the enemy to the frontier and then re-establish the situation on the Sollum front.[30]

[29] Cf. Playfair, *Mediterranean*, iii. 50, 52; Pitt, *Crucible*, 424–38; *Seconda offensiva*, 55–8.
[30] Cf. Taysen, *Tobruk*, 252–5. According to Irving (*Rommel*, 127), Rommel told Maj.-Gen. von Ravenstein: 'You have the chance of ending this campaign tonight.' Cf. Map V.VI.6.

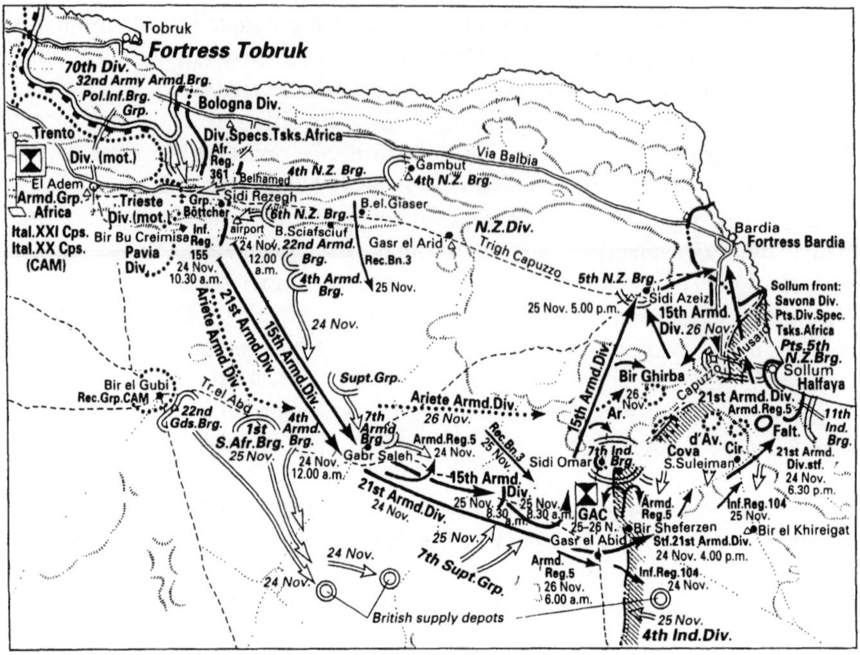

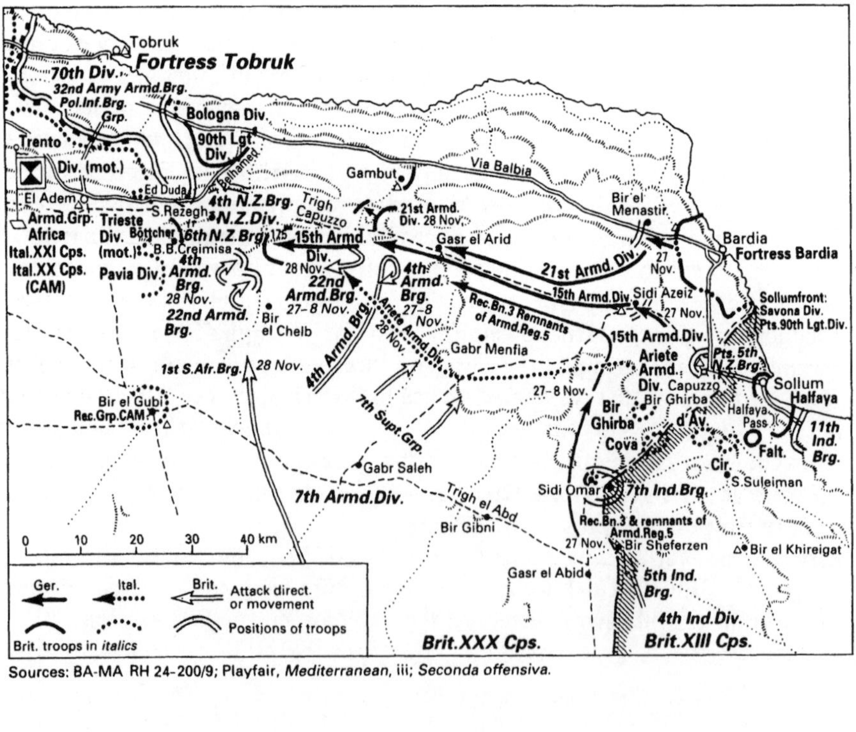

Sources: BA-MA RH 24-200/9; Playfair, *Mediterranean*, iii; *Seconda offensiva*.

V.VI. Operation Crusader

As Rommel did not write the part of his memoirs dealing with Operation Crusader himself, his ideas in this regard can only be surmised. He can hardly have seriously expected that a thrust to the frontier, from which he supposedly wanted to return in less than twenty-four hours, would be sufficient to cut Eighth Army off from its supplies and block its retreat to Egypt. The supposition is therefore quite possibly correct that Rommel hoped to force the British to retreat by achieving the desired psychological effect on their command and troops through a threat to their flanks, as he had done earlier at Zawiyat al Mukhayla and Sidi Sulayman.[31]

What followed bore little resemblance to a carefully planned military operation. Rommel had ordered the Africa Corps to advance in the direction of Sidi Umar along the Tariq al Abd before 10.00 a.m., without knowing the location of the remaining enemy forces defeated on Commemoration Sunday. As 15th Division was not able to finish its preparations in time, Rommel began the advance alone with 21st Armoured Division at 10.30 a.m. While he was driving the British baggage-train and staff before him, the 7th Support Group and 7th Armoured Brigade attacked his northern flank, and he came under fire from the south from 1st South African Brigade. When 5th Armoured Regiment had to defend the northern flank, Rommel continued the attack with the wheeled vehicles of the division. At 4.00 p.m. he reached the frontier fence at Qabr al Abid; by evening 21st Armoured Division was extended over a distance of seventy kilometres. The 15th Armoured Division followed in close formation up to twenty-five kilometres south-west of Sidi Umar.[32] A first fiasco in the command of the operation was reached in the night of 24–5 November, when Rommel's command vehicle broke down on the Egyptian side of the frontier. Together with his chief of staff, Major-General Gause, he was found by Crüwell, who, also without any protection, happened to pass by in his command car. As they did not find any opening in the frontier fence, the commanders of the armoured group and the Africa Corps spent the night on the Egyptian side of the frontier surrounded by British troops.[33] During the next two days the German operation disintegrated into a series of uncoordinated actions determined more by Rommel's presence at a given place than by a common plan. Conditions became chaotic, for the German units

---

[31] Taysen, *Tobruk*, 255–6. On Rommel's other possible motives cf. Jackson, *Campaign*, 175.
[32] Playfair, *Mediterranean*, iii. 54; Taysen, *Tobruk*, 257.
[33] Irving, *Rommel*, 129.

MAP V.VI.6. Operation Crusader, 24–6 November 1941

Sources: BA-MA RH 24-200/9; Playfair, *Mediterranean*, iii; *Seconda offensiva*.

MAP V.VI.7. Operation Crusader, 27–8 November 1941

Sources: BA-MA RH 24-200/9; Playfair, *Mediterranean*, iii; *Seconda offensiva*.

received orders from three different sources: Rommel, the Africa Corps, and Westphal, who was far away in the headquarters of the armoured group at Al Adam.[34] This is the account of the British historian Jackson and is very probably accurate, as Rommel had lost his radio units on the evening of 25 November; Crüwell had only one such unit, and 21st Armoured Division had only a single, mixed communications company, which, moreover, had to maintain contact with the armoured group in Al Adam.[35]

Rommel's radio messages to the staff of the armoured group were unintelligible, as he gave his location and described the tactical situation according to lines of attack not known there. Messages from the armoured group did not reach him, and aircraft which were supposed to inform him about the situation around Tobruk were shot down. Only on 26 November at 10.00 a.m. did a message from the armoured group reach him through the Africa Corps[36] with the news that on 25 November the New Zealanders, with the help of 86 close-support tanks of 1st Army Armoured Brigade, had captured the airfield at Sidi Rizq on the way to Tobruk. In the night of 25–6 November they had also captured most of Belhamid but had not been able to break through to Al Dudah. When Al Dudah still had not been taken at noon on 26 November, Major-General Scobie in Tobruk ordered a break-out attempt, which was successful. By 3.00 p.m. Al Dudah was in the hands of his troops and contact had been made with the New Zealanders.[37]

On 26 November Rommel was still determined to continue his operations with the Africa Corps on the Sollum front. The following night he evidently changed his mind and ordered the return to the Tobruk front for 27 November.[38] This decision marked the end of an adventure which was to contribute decisively to his defeat at Tobruk. His thrust did not even relieve the pressure on his own troops on the Sollum front, but it did lead to senseless losses of irreplaceable troops and equipment, especially as a result of the efforts of the Royal Air Force, which was able to attack the Africa Corps with impunity after the New Zealanders captured the airfield used by German fighters at Kambut. The Africa Corps was so exhausted after returning from its unsuccessful raid that it was not able to change the situation in Germany's favour.[39] But the enemy not only received an opportunity to break the siege of

---

[34] Cf. Jackson, *Campaign*, 172.

[35] Taysen, *Tobruk*, 267 n. 521. In contrast, Gause later stated: 'During the days when Rommel was absent from the command post he kept himself informed on the development of the situation as a whole and was in control of his forces. He remained in contact with the commanders of 15th and 21st Armoured Divisions and with the commanding general of the Africa Corps as well as with the Italian units' (Lt.-Gen. Gause (ret.) to MGFA, 27 Nov. 1962). For a different account cf. Irving, *Rommel*, 130 ff.

[36] Kriebel, 'Nordafrika', MGFA T 3, ii. 142, 157–8.

[37] Playfair, *Mediterranean*, iii. 61. On developments 24–6 Nov. cf. also *Seconda offensiva*, 58–63.

[38] Cf. Taysen, *Tobruk*, 276; *Seconda offensiva*, 63–7.

[39] Westphal, *Heer*, 168.

Tobruk; he now had enough time to reorganize his forces and replace the losses suffered by his armoured brigades.[40]

Another development in the North African theatre at this time was not caused by Rommel's thrust to the frontier. Auchinleck, who had returned to Cairo on 25 November, decided that evening to relieve Lieutenant-General Cunningham as commander-in-chief of Eighth Army. Cunningham had not made any tactical errors or wrong decisions, but Auchinleck felt that he had a defensive attitude and that he doubted the wisdom of the orders he (Auchinleck) issued. As Major-General Neil M. Ritchie, Cunningham's deputy chief of staff, was already familiar with the planning for Operation Crusader, Auchinleck appointed him commander-in-chief of Eighth Army, although he was actually too young for this command.[41]

How well the British armoured units had already recovered from their previous losses became evident on 27 November, when the 15th Armoured Division advanced westward with their 50 tanks still fit for combat. With its 42 Cruiser tanks 22nd Armoured Brigade blocked the Tariq Capuzzo, while 4th Armoured Brigade then attacked the left flank of the German 15th Armoured Division with its 77 Stuart tanks. The division was able to escape from this dangerous situation only because the British, as was their custom, broke off the fighting at nightfall, withdrew to their night encampment in the desert, and left the way westward open for the Germans. Major-General Neumann-Silkow took advantage of this opportunity and occupied the plateau around Bir Shurshuf during the night. Without the artillery of 7th Support Group, the British were unable to attack the Germans in their new position. The support group had formed mixed columns with 22nd Guards Brigade to search the desert for stragglers and attack the flanks of Ariete Armoured Division, which further south was attempting to maintain contact with 15th Armoured Division, while 21st Armoured Division caught up on the Tariq Capuzzo. Thus the tanks of XXX Corps had again been unable to carry out their orders, and the German and Italian armoured units now threatened the New Zealand Division from the rear.[42]

The New Zealanders spent 28 November mopping up enemy forces on the north slope of the Belhamid and captured the last two German strong points between Belhamid and Sidi Rizq and east of Sidi Rizq on the edge of the plateau, while 15th Armoured division was able to advance only to Point 175. Rommel and Crüwell disagreed about what to do the next day: Rommel at first wanted to have the Africa Corps attack from the north-east to cut the New Zealanders off from Tobruk, but Crüwell thought it would be better to attack along the Tariq Capuzzo to force them into the fortress.[43] Crüwell finally

---

[40] Playfair, *Mediterranean*, iii. 59–60.
[41] Ibid. 60–1; Pitt, *Crucible*, 434–5.
[42] Playfair, *Mediterranean*, iii. 62–3; Taysen, *Tobruk*, 278–81; Map V.VI.7.
[43] Kriebel, 'Nordafrika', MGFA T 3, ii. 185.

ordered an attack in accordance with his views: 21st Armoured Division, with support from the artillery of 90th Light African Division (previously Division for Special Tasks Africa), was instructed to capture Belhamid, while 15th Armoured Division was given Al Dudah as its objective. Ariete Division was to provide protection in the rear and on the flanks. Crüwell disregarded an order from Rommel that arrived later to cut the New Zealanders off from Tobruk and to carry out an attack from the south-west.[44]

The fortunes of the German forces in Africa did not improve on 29 November. Major-General von Ravenstein was captured by the New Zealanders when he tried to return to 21st Armoured Division after attending a briefing with the Africa Corps. In accordance with Rommel's orders, 15th Armoured Division then swung to the west and captured Al Dudah from the south-west, but it was retaken in a night attack by the last Australian battalion still in Tobruk. The 21st Armoured Division was hardly able to advance westward, but the Italians took Point 175. The New Zealanders had mistaken them for the South Africans of 1st Brigade, which was supposed to reach them from the south. The South Africans in turn were still much shaken by the destruction of the 5th Brigade of their division, which they had witnessed on Commemoration Sunday. In the afternoon of the following day 15th Armoured Division succeeded in forcing 6th New Zealand Brigade out of its positions near Sidi Rizq. Major-General Freyberg then requested permission from XIII Corps for the rest of the brigade to withdraw to Tobruk, but Lieutenant-General Godwin-Austin expected 1st South African Brigade to arrive as reinforcements and therefore refused the request. On the morning of 1 December 15th Armoured Division resumed its attack against 4th New Zealand Brigade at the Belhamid and finally forced Freyberg to withdraw to the east in the direction of Zafaran. Tobruk was again cut off; Rommel had achieved his aim. But he had not been able to destroy the New Zealanders.[45]

In this fighting the British had not been able to concentrate their armoured forces against the Africa Corps. On the morning of 1 December only 4th Armoured Brigade, coming from the south, appeared on the battlefield and reached the New Zealanders north of Sidi Rizq. But this did not result in a joint operation. While the New Zealanders withdrew to the east, the tanks finally pulled back to the south. Nevertheless, in spite of their superior tactics and their successes on the battlefield, the defeat of the armoured group and the Africa Corps was inevitable. On the evening of 30 November their original armoured strength had been reduced as follows: from 73 to 17 Mark II tanks, from 144 to 31 Mark IIIs, and from 38 to 9 Mark IVs.[46] Rommel again had

---

[44] Cf. Playfair, *Mediterranean*, iii. 64; Taysen, *Tobruk*, 284–5.

[45] Playfair, *Mediterranean*, iii. 65–9; Taysen, *Tobruk*, 285–95; *Seconda Offensiva*, 67–70; Map V.vi.8.

[46] Taysen, *Tobruk*, 303. The battle report of 4 Dec. 1941 contained lower loss figures (ibid. 314). Obviously they did not take account of the 35 tanks which had been left with the repair-shop company east of Tobruk and were destroyed at the approach of the enemy on 9 Dec.: ibid. 317.

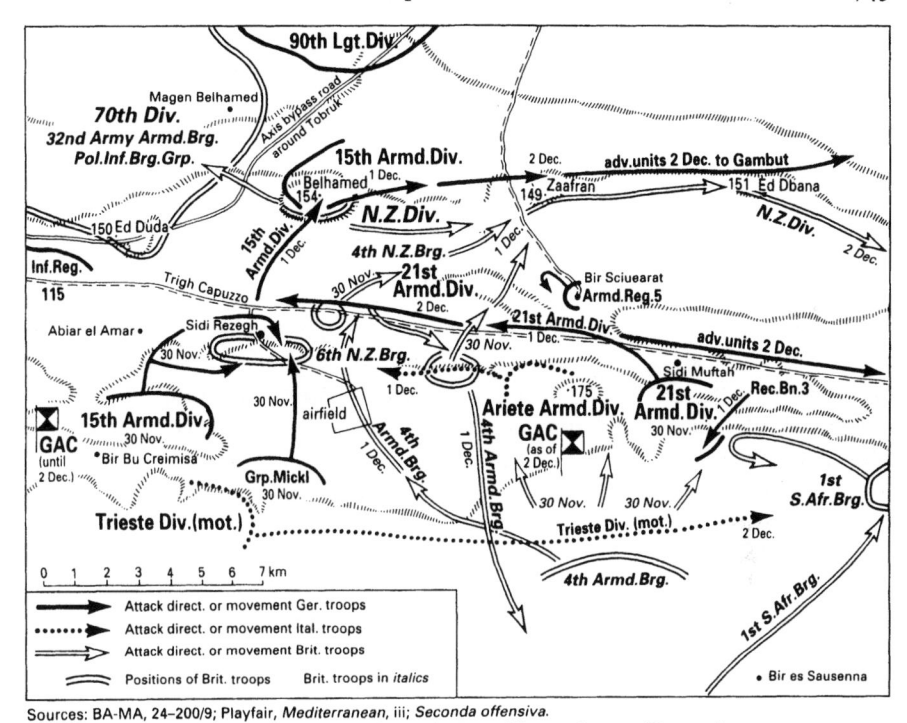

MAP V.VI.8. Operation Crusader, 30 November–2 December 1941

trouble accepting reality—the fact that he had lost the battle of Tobruk and, with his weakened forces, would not even be able to hold Cyrenaica much longer. After the end of the fighting with the New Zealanders he still believed that he would be able to re-establish the former line of the Tobruk front and contact with the Sollum front.[47]

But Lieutenant-General Ritchie was determined to give Rommel no respite and to continue the offensive. And he had the means to do so. On 1 December he ordered XXX Corps to capture Al Adam. For this purpose 7th Armoured Division, 22nd Guards Brigade, and 1st South African Brigade were assigned to the corps. The 4th Indian Division was to be added as soon as it could be relieved by 2nd South African Division on the Sollum front. The 5th New Zealand Brigade was left under its command there. In Maatar Baggush most units of the New Zealand Division were refreshed and received reinforcements from Cyprus and Palestine. Additional reinforcements from Syria and Egypt were sent west. Undoubtedly most important, however, was the fact that units of the British 1st Armoured Division began to arrive from Britain in the

[47] Ibid. 296.

second half of November. Moreover, from Tobruk Lieutenant-General Godwin-Austin reported that XIII Corps was quite capable not only of defence, but also of carrying out an attack.[48]

The next German operation, a thrust by two advance units along the Via Balbia and the Tariq Capuzzo towards Bardia and the Sollum front, began on 2 December with no armoured support available and was repulsed with heavy losses the next day. The following day, 4 December, an attack by 21st Armoured Division on Al Dudah was repelled; the division was able to reach only the bypass road. The 15th Armoured Division, which attempted to straighten out the situation west of Bardiyah after the complete failure of its two advance units, was more successful. Around noon, however, it was ordered back to the west; in the meantime Armoured Group Africa had perceived the aim of the British movements towards Bir al Ghabi, which were intended to establish a line of departure for the advance on Al Adam.[49] Although in the morning Rommel was still determined to capture Al Dudah in spite of the changed situation, during the day he realized that he could not maintain the encirclement of Tobruk from the east and south-east without the Africa Corps and the motorized Gambara Corps, which was to support the attack in the direction of Bir al Ghabi. Rommel's late decision resulted in the loss of much of his baggage-train and maintenance units; hundreds of German sick and wounded were taken prisoner.[50]

The thrust by the Africa Corps to Bir al Ghabi could not change the situation. It was originally planned that the corps should wait there for the arrival of the Gambara Corps before beginning the attack, but only Ariete Division was able to disengage from the enemy. When it finally arrived at Bir al Ghabi on 7 December, Lieutenant-General Norrie had assembled an armoured brigade and four infantry brigades with strong artillery support there. The British overestimated the strength of the enemy and hesitated to attack, but Lieutenant-General Crüwell concluded correctly that he could not defeat such a concentration of enemy forces.[51] This forced Rommel to order a retreat, initially only to the Ghazala position. The situation at Bir al Ghabi was not the only reason for his decision. On 5 December Lieutenant-Colonel Montezemolo had arrived from Rome to inform Rommel about the Italian high command's assessment of the situation. Rommel was told that until January he could expect only deliveries of foodstuffs and ammunition sufficient to cover basic requirements. For the time being there could be no question of larger shipments, let alone reinforcements. Rommel observed that under those circumstances Armoured Group Africa would be forced to disengage from the enemy and withdraw westward.[52] But he continued to

---

[48] Playfair, *Mediterranean*, iii. 73–4.
[49] Taysen, *Tobruk*, 296–314; *Seconda offensiva*, 72–5.
[50] Taysen, *Tobruk*, 315–18.
[51] Ibid. 329–31; Playfair, *Mediterranean*, iii. 76–7.
[52] Taysen, *Tobruk*, 324–5. On Montezemolo's mission cf. *Seconda offensiva*, 78 ff.

hope for two days that a favourable development at Bir al Ghabi would spare him such an unpleasant decision. Even the bad news he received the following day could not force him to take a final decision. On 6 December he received negative answers from the Wehrmacht and the army high commands to his demands for replacements and reinforcements. He was promised only 9,000 men and weapons, primarily anti-tank guns, in the near future.[53]

The Commander-in-Chief South, Field Marshal Kesselring, visited Rommel on 7 December but was unable to promise him more than increased fighter protection for the time being. Rommel indignantly rejected the order he received the same day from Bastico, his superior, to report to him at his headquarters. Bastico therefore came to Rommel the next morning, and Rommel used the opportunity to give vent to his anger and disappointment about the defeat. He even went so far as to state that he had decided to take his divisions to Tripoli and have himself interned in Tunisia.[54] With his outburst Rommel was able to persuade Bastico to place all Italian army troops in Cyrenaica under his command and to approve his retreat to the Ghazala position. But, unlike the Italian high command, which was prepared to accept such measures if the worst came to the worst, Bastico rejected categorically a further retreat or even the idea of abandoning Cyrenaica.[55]

On 8 December, after receiving an enquiry from Rommel the day before, the Italian high command, in agreement with the German army high command, decided not to withdraw the German and Italian troops from the Sollum front. However, Savona Division abandoned its strong point and withdrew to the nearer Halfaya pass, instead of to Bardiyah as planned, which led to supply problems. On 19 December Rommel again requested the evacuation of the garrisons on Italian warships, but the Italian high command refused to change its decision, as a result of which the coastal road remained blocked and more than one British division was tied down. After an attack by a brigade had been repulsed, the entire 2nd South African Division, supported by 1st Army Armoured Brigade, Western Desert Air Force, and coastal bombardments of the Royal Navy, attacked Bardiyah on 31 December. Two days later Major-General Schmitt had to surrender: 6,600 Italians and 2,200 Germans were taken prisoner. On 17 January 1942 the defenders of the Halfaya pass surrendered; there 3,800 Italians and 2,100 Germans laid down their arms.[56]

On 9 December Lieutenant-General Ritchie had ordered a change in the command structure of the British forces. The 7th Armoured Division and 4th Indian Division were assigned to XIII Corps, which now consisted only of the British forces in Cyrenaica. The staff of XXX Corps was withdrawn to take

---

[53] Taysen, *Tobruk*, 314–15.
[54] Cf. ibid. 332–4; *Seconda offensiva* 82–5, here 84.
[55] Playfair, *Mediterranean*, iii. 79–80.
[56] Playfair, *Mediterranean*, iii. 94–6; Taysen, *Tobruk*, 333, 336–7; *Seconda offensiva*, 85–6, 141 ff., 153–6.

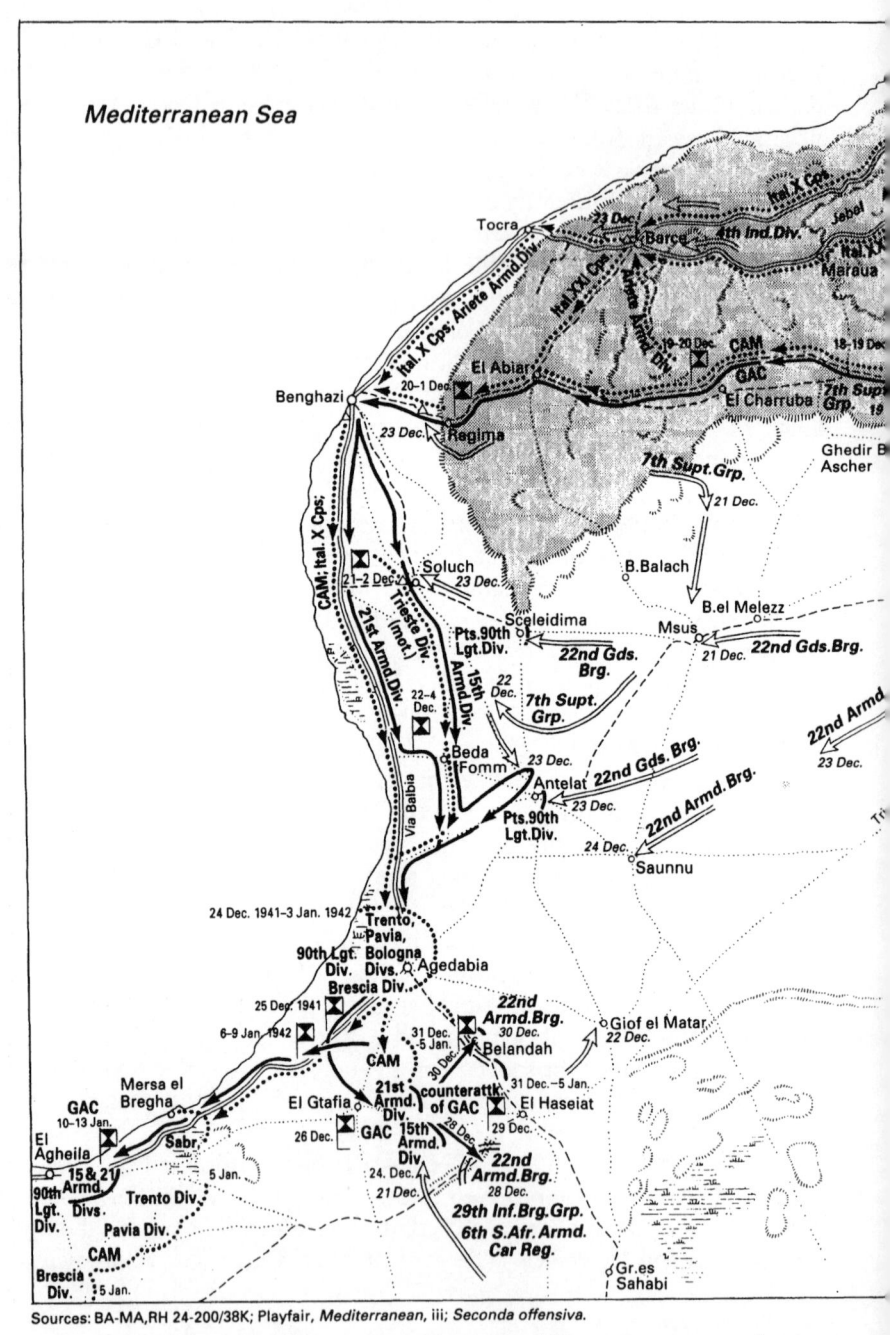

MAP V.vi.9. The Italo-German Retreat from Cyrenaica, 8 December 1941–10 January 1942

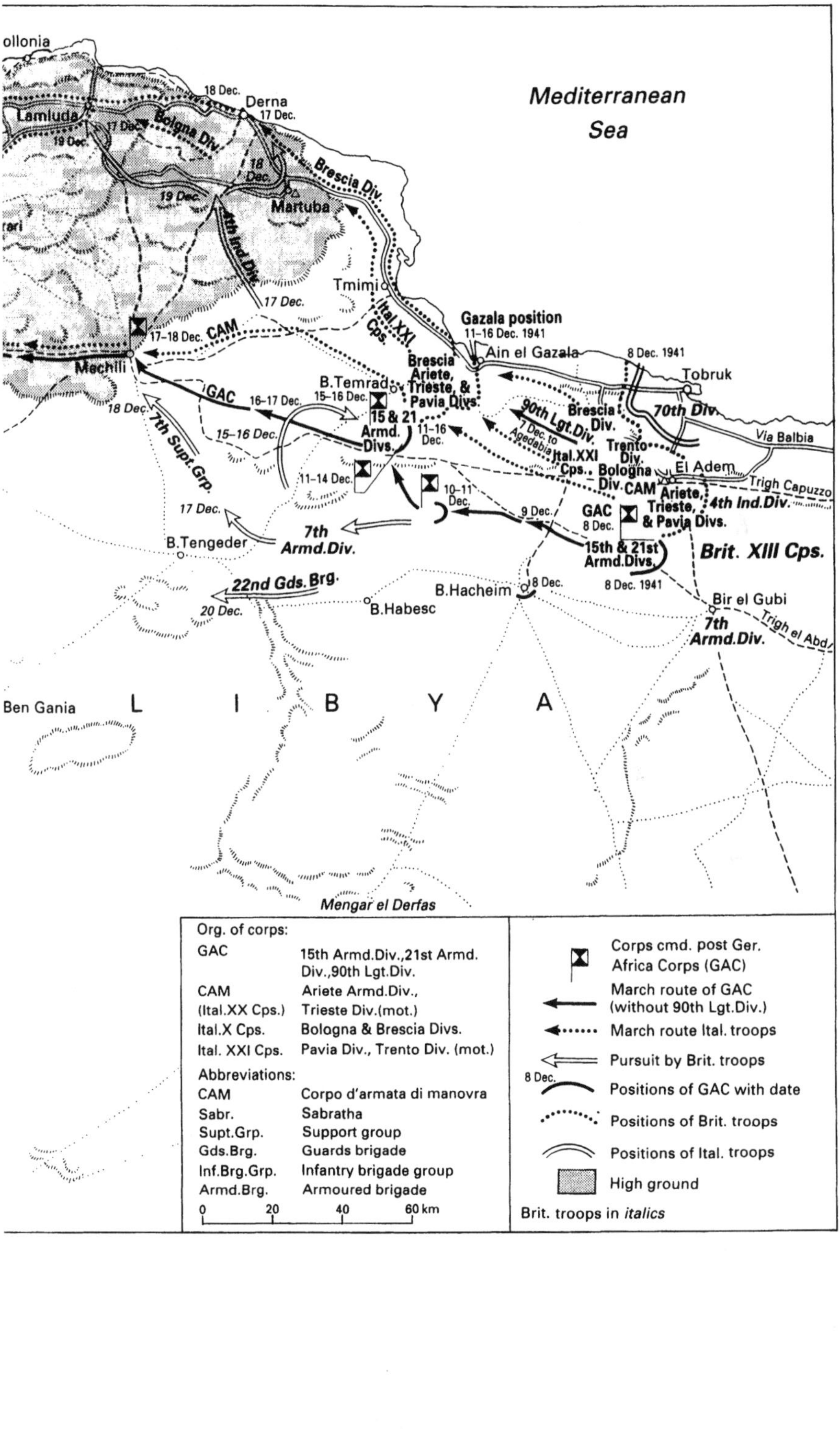

ollonia
Mediterranean Sea
Derna
18 Dec.
17 Dec.
Lamluda
19 Dec.
Bologna Div.
Brescia Div.
18 Dec.
19 Dec.
Martuba
4th Ind.Div.
Tmimi
17 Dec.
Ital.XXI Cps.
Gazala position
11–16 Dec. 1941
Ain el Gazala
8 Dec. 1941
Tobruk
17–18 Dec.
CAM
Mechili
GAC
16–17 Dec.
B.Temrad
15–16 Dec.
Brescia Ariete, Trieste, & Pavia Divs.
15 & 21 Armd. Divs.
11–16 Dec.
90th Lgt.Div.
7 Dec. to Agedabia
Brescia Div.
Trento Div.
70th Div.
Via Balbia
18 Dec.
7th Supt.Grp.
15–16 Dec.
11–14 Dec.
10–11 Dec.
Ital.XXI Cps.
Bologna Div.
CAM
El Adem
Trigh Capuzzo
Ariete, Trieste, & Pavia Divs.
4th Ind.Div.
9 Dec.
GAC
8 Dec.
17 Dec.
7th Armd.Div.
B.Tengeder
15th & 21st Armd.Divs.
Brit. XIII Cps.
22nd Gds.Brg.
20 Dec.
B.Habesc
B.Hacheim
8 Dec.
8 Dec. 1941
Bir el Gubi
Trigh el Abd
7th Armd.Div.
Ben Gania
L I B Y A
Mengar el Derfas
Org. of corps:
GAC 15th Armd.Div.,21st Armd. Div.,90th Lgt.Div.
CAM (Ital.XX Cps.) Ariete Armd.Div., Trieste Div.(mot.)
Ital.X Cps. Bologna & Brescia Divs.
Ital. XXI Cps. Pavia Div., Trento Div. (mot.)
Abbreviations:
CAM Corpo d'armata di manovra
Sabr. Sabratha
Supt.Grp. Support group
Gds.Brg. Guards brigade
Inf.Brg.Grp. Infantry brigade group
Armd.Brg. Armoured brigade
0 20 40 60 km
Corps cmd. post Ger. Africa Corps (GAC)
March route of GAC (without 90th Lgt.Div.)
March route Ital. troops
Pursuit by Brit. troops
8 Dec.
Positions of GAC with date
Positions of Brit. troops
Positions of Ital. troops
High ground
Brit. troops in italics

over command of the Sollum front; Auchinleck then wanted to keep it available to deal with possible threats on the northern front (in Syria and Iraq). Ritchie intended to keep 22nd Guards Brigade under his direct command in order to have it advance on Benghazi via the desert route as soon as possible and block the enemy retreat to Tripolitania.[57]

On 15 December the British began their attack on the Ghazala position, but Rommel decided to continue the retreat in time. He ordered XXI Corps to withdraw to Darnah via Al Tamimi in the night of 16–17 December. XX Motorized Corps and the Africa Corps were to withdraw to Zawiyat al Mukhayla. Bastico had alerted Cavallero, who appeared with Kesselring in order to clarify the situation. Rommel was to be permitted to withdraw from Cyrenaica as slowly as possible and in an orderly manner, but Tripolitania was to be defended at all events. Rommel, on the other hand, intended to reach Ajdabiya and Al Uqaylah as soon as possible after abandoning the Ghazala position, to avoid having his line of retreat cut. In this he was successful, as XIII Corps was encountering increasing difficulties bringing up supplies. Rommel's position was improved by the arrival of two ships with a total of 45 tanks in Tripoli and Benghazi. Crüwell immediately took advantage of the opportunity and attacked 22nd Armoured Brigade near Ajdabiya on 28 and 30 December. The brigade lost a total of 60 tanks and had to be taken out of the fighting. This victory cost the Germans 14 tanks, but Rommel held to his decision to continue his retreat to Al Uqaylah. The retreat began on 1 January 1942 and on 6 January the last rearguard units left Ajdabiya without being hindered by the British, who had been aware of the German intentions since the day before.[58]

For an overview of casualties on both sides in Operation Crusader see Table V.VI.1. German tank losses were 220, those of the Italians 120. On the British side by 1 January 1942 7th Armoured Division had lost about 600 tanks (including breakdowns); in addition over 200 close-support tanks were lost.[59] British aircraft losses were 300, those of the Germans 232, and of the Italians 100, but the figures for the Axis probably do not include aircraft left behind unable to fly.[60]

At first glance the British seemed to have achieved a victory in Operation Crusader, as they reconquered Cyrenaica and forced Rommel to retreat. Even before the Soviet counter-offensive around Moscow began on 5 December they had started the first successful offensive to be conducted against the Wehrmacht in the Second World War. But they had not been able to destroy the German and Italian armoured forces, nor had they been able to repeat their

---

[57] Playfair, *Mediterranean*, iii. 81; *PWT*, Middle East II, Hist (B) 8, No. 163, pp. 70–2 (9 Dec. 1941). Cf. also Map V.VI.9.
[58] Cf. *PWT* (n. 57 above), Nos. 202–22, pp. 84–92 (19–27 Dec. 1941); Jackson, *Campaign*, 180–1; Pitt, *Crucible*, 460–1; Map V.VI.9.
[59] Playfair, *Mediterranean*, iii. 100; Hinsley, *British Intelligence*, ii. 336.
[60] Playfair, *Mediterranean*, iii. 99.

V. VI. Operation Crusader

TABLE V.VI.1. *Losses in Operation Crusader*

	Total strength	Killed	Wounded	Missing[a]
British	118,000	2,900	7,300	7,500
German	65,000	1,100	3,400	10,100
Italian	54,000	1,200	2,700	19,800

[a] The figures include 13,800 German and Italian taken prisoner at Bandia or at Halfaya pass.
Sources: Playfair, *Mediterranean*, iii. 97; Hinsley, *British Intelligence*, ii. 334.

success at Bayda Fumm and cut the enemy's line of retreat from Cyrenaica. Their tactical and operational conduct of the operation was still far inferior to that of the Germans, and only their material superiority had enabled them to achieve final victory.

In reality the British victory in Operation Crusader prepared the way for a new defeat. The fighting had lasted too long and drained material reserves; after the conquest of Cyrenaica the British forces were no longer strong enough to reach their final objectives, Tripoli and the frontier between Libya and Tunisia. The results of the last tank battles clearly showed that the situation had begun to shift in favour of the Germans, for now the British had the problems of long supply-lines, while Rommel's retreat had greatly shortened his rear communication lines.

The question presents itself again as to whether Rommel's conquest of Cyrenaica in April 1941 was not a serious mistake. Supplying the Africa Corps would undoubtedly have been considerably easier if he had limited his operations to the defence of Tripolitania. In April 1941 the forces at his disposal were still far too weak to achieve a decisive victory; the resulting problem of Tobruk dominated all other considerations in North Africa. Rommel's chances of success would probably have been better if he had waited until all units of 15th Armoured Division had arrived and had then launched a surprise offensive at the same time as the German attack on Crete, without drawing the enemy's attention to the danger to his flank beforehand.

The geographical position of Cyrenaica seemed in itself to be a sufficient reason to occupy that part of the Libyan coast. Aircraft based there could protect Axis supply-routes from Italy and attack enemy convoys to Malta and Egypt. But geographical position alone was not decisive. Remarkably enough, it was possible to transfer the German 5th Light Division to Africa almost without losses, although Cyrenaica was still in British hands. After Rommel conquered the area, Axis convoy losses began to rise until convoy traffic to Tripoli had to be stopped altogether. When German and Italian forces retreated from Cyrenaica, the Italians were able to resume convoy traffic to Tripoli in spite of the unfavourable situation. Occupation of Cyrenaica alone was obviously not decisive in the matter of domination of the central Mediterranean.

It is therefore difficult to find any positive result which would justify the high-handedness with which Rommel disregarded his orders. Hitler's favour enabled Rommel to satisfy his personal ambitions and give the North African theatre an importance which neither Hitler nor the Wehrmacht and army high commands had originally intended it to have. This was evident in the transfer of additional army units and II Air Corps, and especially in the sending of U-boats to the Mediterranean, which almost amounted to stopping the U-boat war in the Atlantic.

It is hardly possible to say with certainty whether the defeat of the German and Italian forces in North Africa in the winter of 1941–2 could have been avoided. It is, however, clear that Rommel himself contributed significantly to the defeat by stubbornly basing his own assessment of the situation more on wishful thinking than on facts, e.g. in his insistence on attacking Tobruk or in his thrust to the Egyptian frontier. His behaviour revealed one of his weaknesses—his tendency to underestimate others, especially the enemy.

Rommel had led his weakened forces to the Egyptian frontier, but he was not able to take Tobruk behind the front, and an advance into Egypt was not possible as long as the siege of the fortress had to be maintained. This situation created the worst possible conditions for supplying Rommel's troops, as most supplies had to be transported by land from Tripoli around Tobruk to the Egyptian frontier.

The transports across the Mediterranean represented an even greater problem, which could not be solved by using Tunis, for the value of an additional supply-port would have been completely outweighed by the great extension of supply-lines it involved. Moreover, French co-operation would have provoked British retaliation, which would have required defensive forces the Axis did not have in Africa. The German troops in the North African theatre remained dependent on supplies unloaded at the quays in Tripoli.

Protecting the convoys to North Africa and conducting the naval war in the Mediterranean in general involved problems whose dimensions in some respects were not understood at all. The Italians quickly realized the disadvantage of not having any aircraft-carriers: if their fleet had to remain within the range of land-based fighter protection, they were deprived of any possibility of carrying out strategic operations. The earlier decision, for financial reasons, not to develop radar or a similar system also proved to be a serious mistake, for it meant that the Italian fleet was blind at night and had to avoid night battles, which restricted its operational possibilities even more. In addition, in the summer of 1941 the British broke the code the Italians used in radio traffic with their convoys in the Mediterranean. They had introduced this code at the urging of the Germans, who considered the previous one to be insecure.

When information gained from the deciphering of Italian radio traffic in London reached Malta in time, it was possible as a rule to locate the convoy concerned with the help of radar and attack it at night with torpedo-bombers or to direct submarines to waiting-positions along the known convoy-routes; the Italian air force and the Luftwaffe were unable to prevent such attacks. With light surface ships stationed in Malta, under the existing conditions an ably commanded force was often able to destroy an entire convoy in a single night.[61]

It is clear that the Italians suffered from serious disadvantages, both known and unknown, in their war with the Royal Navy. It is, however, equally clear that they made mistakes in planning and carrying out their operations which had nothing to do with these disadvantages. What gave the German navy the right to assume the role of teacher to the Italians is, of course, another question, as the Germans had also made numerous tactical and operational mistakes: in the battle of the River Plate, the occupation of Norway, and the ill-fated cruise of the *Bismarck*. The naval war staff pressed the Italians to pursue the same kind of hyperactive, unrealistic tactics that it demanded of the German fleet. In the first year of the war the staff had worn down two commanders-in-chief of the German fleet by insisting that the two German battleships should be in constant use regardless of obstacles and dangers, even if the navy itself could find no appropriate operational objectives for them.

The relationship between the two navies was also very one-sided, for the German naval war staff was not prepared to inform the Italian navy in detail about its conduct of the war at sea and certainly not to accept advice from the Italians.

Relations between German and Italian forces in the North African theatre were also not free from tension, which with Rommel's personality was no doubt inevitable. Unlike the war at sea, however, German 'suggestions' for the land war carried more weight; because of their equipment and training the presence of the Germans made the difference between victory and defeat. In the desert war a remarkable change had taken place. The Italians had marched into Egypt in 1940 as if on parade; the British had then used their Cruiser tanks to attack the enemy from the flanks and the rear, while the Matildas penetrated the Italian defensive positions with the British infantry. The battle for the desert flank was necessitated by geographical conditions. For this reason the Germans attempted to block a British withdrawal from Cyrenaica in a similar manner. In Operation Crusader the fighting in the desert assumed forms reminiscent of naval warfare. While the infantry defended or attacked strong points and important topographical features, the armoured forces moved between them like naval formations at sea. The Germans undoubtedly displayed greater skill in such mixed-arms combat, while the British still were not able to use their armoured forces in concentrated attacks.

[61] The resulting problems are presented in Somerville, 'Britische Strategie', and Santoni, 'Planungen der Achsenmächte'.

While Hitler at first wanted to limit German involvement in North Africa to what was absolutely necessary, he permitted his ambitious general a freedom of action and decision which required increasing numbers of troops and quantities of supplies. On the other hand, Hitler firmly rejected the more ambitious wishes of the naval war staff. In autumn his assessment of the situation clearly changed. By the end of 1941 he believed that the campaign in the Soviet Union had come to a temporary conclusion and that the time had come to shift the main German war effort to other fronts. This judgement proved to be a serious mistake, for the war against the Soviet Union did not end till more than three years later in Berlin. But doubtless Hitler's mistaken assessment in the autumn of 1941 made little or no difference to that result.

Conclusion

IN attempting to summarize the central events, theses, and statements of this volume, one may draw the following lines of interpretation.

Since 1937 Germany had assigned to Italy the role of threatening British and French interests in the Mediterranean in the event of an armed conflict in continental Europe. In this way Italian pressure would, without additional military burdens for Berlin, prevent France and Britain from attacking Germany directly.

Although the expectation, based on economic and military arguments, that Italy would provide a strategic diversion in this way was not fulfilled in September 1939, developments soon began which caused Mussolini to end his policy of non-belligerence and, in June 1940, to become Hitler's coalition partner, even though at first he was still intent on preserving his independence of action.

By entering the war on Germany's side, the Italian government had taken a step already agreed upon in the 'Pact of Steel'. Italy hesitated for a long time, but, notwithstanding the occasional difficulties in the Italo-German alliance after September 1939, Mussolini always planned to enter the war on Germany's side when the struggle between Germany and the Anglo-French alliance had in his view taken a course favourable to Hitler.

The decision to enter the war was in accord with the logic of the policies and methods practised by the Fascist regime since the 1920s. Of course no deterministic necessities were at work. But the present study affords no support for interpretations which, for example, suggest that right until the end of 1939 or the beginning of 1940 there were serious indications that Mussolini might turn away from Hitler. Such interpretations assume not only a tactically motivated reorientation of Italian foreign policy, but, in view of the imperialistic aims of the Fascist regime, also a fundamental change in its nature. In fact the political aims of the Fascists, which were by no means mere propaganda, limited Mussolini's room for manœuvre in regard to the alliance and in the end even bound him more closely to Hitler, in so far as he was determined to achieve his aims.

An analysis of Mussolini's political intentions and actions in the 1920s and 1930s shows that he was motivated by imperial ambitions. In the context of Fascist domestic and foreign policy his decision in the summer of 1940 can hardly be considered planless opportunism, even though some of his particular actions may seem opportunistic. In fact he attempted, while entering the war on the basis of a short-term calculation, to move closer to realizing at least some of his long-term aims.

Nevertheless, Mussolini's calculations and planning were directed not only against Britain and France, or Greece and Yugoslavia, but also indirectly against Germany. His constant aims were to achieve Italian domination of the Mediterranean, to strengthen and improve Italy's position in the international power-system, and to prevent unrestricted German hegemony in Europe.

All these ambitions, which basically remained within the sphere of traditional great-power politics, proved to be Utopian by the summer of 1940, when, contrary to Mussolini's expectations, the war failed to come to an end. For the developments that now began not only exposed Italy's military weakness, which had been predicted by various observers and resulted from economic, industrial, and financial causes. They also made Italy, cut off from all overseas supplies and without adequate reserves for a long war, completely dependent on Germany.

German intervention in North Africa and the Balkans put a definitive end to Italian visions of great-power status. This engagement of German troops, in the guise of assistance, had been a German aim since the signing of the armistice with France, but it became unavoidable only as a consequence of Italian military reverses and the resulting threat to the southern flank of Europe. Mussolini's 'parallel war'—which, in view of the weakness of the Italian economy and armament industry, had in reality never been more than an empty phrase intended to assert Italy's independence of Hitler—came to a clear and inglorious end in December 1940.

The Mediterranean became a theatre of the Wehrmacht in 1940–1, at a time when Operation Barbarossa (the attack on the Soviet Union) had already long dominated German strategic planning. Operations Marita and Merkur (Greece and Crete, 1941) as well as the actions in North Africa following Operation Sunflower (Tripoli, 1941) were overshadowed by the preparation and conduct of the war for 'living-space in the east'. After May 1941 North African operations remained dependent on developments on the eastern front, either in a direct material sense or in terms of the setting of priorities within Hitler's conduct of the war.

When Italy entered the fray on 10 June 1940 most contemporary observers, including Mussolini, considered the war to be still a normal conflict among the major European powers, but this assessment was inaccurate. As a result of Hitler's programme-orientated strategy the Second World War developed in German eyes as an ideological war against the Soviet Union, planned as such from the very beginning, and in a very concrete sense since July 1940.

In a historical sense, the conflict with the Soviet Union forms the perspective from which developments from June 1940 to December 1941 are described. The present volume thus constitutes a prelude to Volume IV of the series, *The Attack on the Soviet Union*. For this reason, considerable attention is devoted to German political and military deliberations and actions in the second half of 1940, all of which were ultimately intended to give Germany a completely or at least relatively secure rear area for the war against the Soviet Union.

Conclusion

It is generally agreed that in the first phase of the developing strategic dilemma Hitler was mainly concerned with inducing Britain to come to terms with Germany. All measures he considered or carried out at that time were not in themselves intended to achieve a complete victory, but were aimed instead at convincing Britain of the advantages and necessity of reaching an understanding with Germany. On the other hand, the second phase was determined by the realization that British resistance could be eliminated neither by attacks on the British homeland nor by a war on the periphery.

An invasion of Britain had soon proved to be unfeasible; the failure of the air war against the island became obvious in the third quarter of 1940; the war in the Atlantic against British supply-routes threatened but did not sever a vital artery of the British war effort; and, in view of the military capacity of the Wehrmacht, a war on the periphery would only have been feasible in the Mediterranean, and only then with Spanish or Italian consent. The stalemate in the struggle with Britain on the one hand, and the decision to realize German military intentions in the east on the other, led to a change in German thinking as regards inclusion of the Mediterranean, and thus the Atlantic approaches, in the operational tasks of the Wehrmacht. The North African coast opposite Europe, especially French North and North-West Africa, as well as the Middle East, south-east Europe, the Iberian peninsula, and the Atlantic islands, were increasingly judged in terms of defence for the strategic southern flank during Operation Barbarossa, which now had to be carried out without a completely secure rear area in the west. This factor assumed an increasingly important role in German assessments after the failure of Hitler's attempt to form an anti-British bloc consisting of several states.

In the weeks after the victory in the west Hitler's ideological final aim determined German strategy. The efforts of several high military officers, such as Warlimont, to place operational plans in Spain or the eastern Mediterranean at the centre of German strategy were not incompatible with Hitler's plan for a war in the east. On the contrary, from a military point of view they were intended to improve the conditions for such a war. It would be a serious mistake to consider such plans as proof that Hitler did not determine the guidelines of German strategy, including military-operational strategy, in 1940–1.

The analysis of German policy and planning in the second half of 1940 also shows that the importance of Britain's determination to continue the war after the defeat of France can hardly be overestimated. In terms of the situation as a whole—and this is especially true because of the effect of Britain's stubborn resistance on the policy of President Roosevelt—Britain's refusal during these months to accept German domination of Europe was an important, if not the most important, factor in determining the ultimate fate of the aggressors. In any case Britain's intransigence in the summer of 1940 indirectly influenced the extension of the European war into a world war, the American entry into the war, and the development of the anti-Hitler coalition, which united the Western democracies and the totalitarian Soviet Union.

The fact that the months between July and December 1940 did not produce any favourable results for Hitler in the war on the periphery was primarily due to the refusal of Mussolini and Franco, for different reasons but with equal firmness, to open the way south for the Wehrmacht. In the present volume this phase of the war is described as a battle lost from Germany's point of view, since it involved a halt in the conduct of the war and a marking time in the pursuit of German objectives. Gibraltar remained British, the French possessions in North Africa continued to be a source of uncertainty, and British successes against Italy affected Germany's prestige, although at first only to a limited extent. Nevertheless, both the Vichy government and Spain adopted a reserved attitude in their relations with Germany. In this regard Britain's ability to apply economic pressure made them even more aware of signs of weakness within the Italo-German alliance.

In view of the Spanish refusal to enter the war on the side of Germany and Mussolini's opposition to the use of German troops in Africa, it cannot be said that the Axis failed to take advantage of any real opportunities in the Mediterranean before the end of 1940. Because of the conflicting German and Italian interests in the area, such opportunities did not exist at the time. Suggestions to the contrary can only be considered unrealistic speculation and would require Hitler and Mussolini to have completely changed their character and personalities.

Mussolini's ill-timed and amateurish attack on Greece, begun under the worst conceivable conditions, together with the critical situation in Libya, endangered German oil supplies from Romania and the survival of his regime, to which Hitler attached great importance. To this extent the situation presented opportunities for a joint Italo-German conduct of the war against Britain. But these opportunities did not include the possibility of ending the conflict with that country, for the British government was prepared, if necessary, to continue the struggle even after the loss of British positions in the Mediterranean.

Admiral Raeder's proposal to defeat Britain by shifting the main German war effort to the Mediterranean merely showed that, in this case, he made precisely the same mistake for which his staff reproached political figures and leading army officers: he failed to understand the essential conditions and elements of British strategy. In the summer of 1940 it became clear that the decisive basis of Britain's strength was not in the Mediterranean, although that area was certainly important, but beyond the reach of German arms, not least in the United States.

Moreover, to consider Raeder's plan, within the framework of Hitler's strategy, as a realistic alternative to the war against the Soviet Union is to commit the same error to which the admiral himself obviously succumbed. Raeder evidently assumed that Hitler's argument that the Soviet Union must be attacked because it represented Britain's 'sword on the Continent' was the real reason for the dictator's decision to turn east. That, however, was clearly not the case.

It is also important to remember that by the end of 1940, when German intervention in south-east Europe had become unavoidable, Hitler had already decided to postpone a definitive resolution of the political and military problems in the Mediterranean area until after the conclusion of Operation Barbarossa.

The firm intention to attack the Soviet Union in the early summer of 1941, and especially the resulting pressure of time, also determined the attitude of the German leadership towards the countries of south-east Europe after the Italian attack on Greece. Hitler's decision at the end of 1940 to resort to brute force was in itself characteristic of National Socialist foreign policy. The possibility of a bloodless occupation of Greece was considered only for a short time, and then only because of the need to concentrate forces in the east for the attack on the Soviet Union.

But German impatience, nervousness, and aggressiveness in the negotiations with representatives of the states of south-east Europe increased as the date for the attack on the Soviet Union approached. This was evident in Hitler's use of massive intimidation to force the Yugoslav government to join the Tripartite Pact. When this policy led to a coup in Belgrade, Hitler, typically, was immediately prepared to use force, without even attempting to seek a non-military solution in the new situation.

The examination of German and Italian relations with the states of south-east Europe has revealed or clarified important characteristics of the Berlin–Rome Axis. The counter-productive effects of conflicting German and Italian political interests and aims in this region were already felt before 1939. In general the Axis was no more than a temporary pragmatic compromise. In almost all areas it suffered from considerable tension between the two partners. In the period of decline, which in the view of some Italians began for their country the moment Germany seemed to achieve hegemony in Europe, the underlying conflicts became increasingly obvious.

The political decision-making examined in this context confirms the thesis that the foreign relations of the National Socialist government were conducted in accordance with a consistent programme. The fact, already evident in *Mein Kampf*, that Hitler concentrated on relations and conflicts between great powers and considered the rest of the world to be dependent on them determined his attitude towards south-east Europe and the Middle East. Representatives of the foreign ministry negotiated there with states below the level of great powers, whose governments in Hitler's eyes were nothing more than pawns in the political chess-game of the more powerful, to be used as political opportunities and tactics dictated.

In the present volume the attempt has been made to interpret German diplomacy in relations with states of the Mediterranean area on the basis of the two primary features of National Socialist policy—the initially unsuccessful, programme-orientated exploitation of local possibilities, and the all-important role of confrontations with major powers in Hitler's strategic calculations.

The conclusions of this study can be summarized somewhat briefly but pointedly in two theses. In the first place, the relative historical importance of the war in the Mediterranean, from a Germany perspective, can be understood only against the background of Hitler's political programme. This requires that developments there be seen within the context of the Second World War as a whole. The second thesis is that the Axis itself, and not only the military coalition formed in May 1939, must be considered a *mésalliance*. This is especially clear in regard to the co-operation made necessary by Mussolini's failed attack on Greece and the defeats which he suffered at the same time in Africa. It is therefore necessary to summarize briefly these military developments.

The war in the Mediterranean must be considered primarily from two points of view: the Italo-German coalition and the military strength of Italy. Apart from non-binding and in any case very general agreements, Rome and Berlin made no preparations for a coalition war. Political and military resentments obviously prevented an attempt to solve the related problems, although the urgent need for discussion had been recognized since the crisis of September 1938. Paradoxically, the coalition was based on calculations of national policy hostile to any alliance in the long run. Formally it was an alliance—this had been spelt out in May 1939—but it lacked the common aims and co-ordination necessary to give it real content. This is borne out by the fact that Axis military co-operation in the Second World War was first occasioned by the defeat of Italian arms. Against this background it is understandable that in daily practice the coalition war was burdened with numerous difficulties resulting from pressure of time and improvisation.

Germany and Italy did march side by side in the Mediterranean area after 1940, and were often quite successful, but a closer look soon reveals that the quality of a war alliance cannot be measured solely by its ability to act militarily. It must be judged according to such criteria as the political organization of the coalition and its psychological basis, the extent to which military planning can be co-ordinated, economic co-operation, total economic capability, the co-ordination of arms production, and especially agreement on strategic aims. This last-mentioned factor is indispensable for the joint conduct of a war. The fact that Mussolini, Hitler's closest ally, hindered German efforts to force the British to come to terms by means of a peripheral strategy in the second half of 1940 shows that the agreements of the Axis powers did not even begin to fulfil the essential requirement of effective strategic planning.

Mussolini's behaviour was not only important for the climate of relations in the alliance between Berlin and Rome in the summer and autumn of 1940; it also reflected a basic attitude on the Duce's part. However, neither the German nor the Italian leaders had analysed and thought out, within the framework of their respective political ambitions, the implications of the joint conduct of a war, the need for which had been under discussion since 1937–8. Both sides considered their coalition to be primarily an operational and not a strategic matter. Significantly, they had distinct operational areas, but co-ordinated plans and precise war aims agreed upon by both sides were lacking. Italy requested assistance but was not prepared to enter into a realistic stock-taking of material resources. Relations between Germany and Italy were marked by mistrust, not confidence. Exceptions only confirm this rule; the alliance existed only on paper and in the propaganda of its political leaders.

This situation led to numerous problems and friction in the conduct of the war by the Axis powers. Admittedly, similar inadequacies and problems can be found in other alliances. They were not limited to the Axis powers, but represent a general characteristic of coalitions, including the Axis.

The second criterion for understanding the war in the Mediterranean is the analysis of the military material and performance of the Italian armed forces until the end of 1940. In terms of the level of armaments, Italy's armed forces were not prepared for a long conflict with other great powers, and, before June 1940, the Italian military staffs had made no plans for such a conflict. Like the military leaders of other states, Italian officers had studied the course and results of the First World War, and their analyses and conclusions were as perceptive as those produced by the military staffs of other countries. But carrying out a military policy that would satisfy Mussolini's desire for political power and prestige proved to be impossible. The inefficiency of the political and military system, organizational inadequacies, and the weak Italian economic and industrial base were key factors in the decisive discrepancy between political claims and available instruments of power, between theory and practice.

Italy had not achieved a degree of industrialization sufficient to meet the needs of modern, mechanized armed forces. Moreover, the country had to import almost all raw materials necessary for arms production, and the chronic shortage of foreign exchange placed narrow limits on such imports. Since the beginning of the international arms race in the second half of the 1930s economic and military realities made the claim of the Fascist regime to be a great power seem absurd. Italy was simply not able to maintain the same pace of rearmament as the European great powers, unless the Italian military preferred quantity to quality. In various areas this seems indeed to have been the case. Because of this development, Italy had actually lost any claim to great-power status even before entering the war. At first this remained unnoticed, but it quickly became evident after 10 June 1940. Clearly the material losses in the wars in Ethiopia, Spain, and Albania, which could not be made good by the time Italy entered the Second World War, were an especially serious handicap in view of the lack of an adequate infrastructure.

In practice the first phase of the 'parallel war', until about the end of October 1940, consisted primarily of small, isolated operations, which in most cases only demonstrated Italy's inability to wage a modern war. Almost everything necessary to force a decision against Britain, and in the beginning against France, was lacking. The fact that most of the Italian military did not provide especially dynamic leadership was, however, not only a reaction to the depressing material situation of the armed forces, but was also due to specific inadequacies of many sections of the Italian military apparatus. In addition, many high officers were basically opposed to entering the war.

The Italian military leaders committed serious tactical and operational mistakes in almost all theatres of the war. Graziani's offensive in North Africa also suffered not only from a delayed and then improvised start, but also from the half-heartedness with which it was carried out. Of course geographical and climatic conditions in Africa caused special problems, but these had to be mastered by the troops of all countries fighting there. The ability to solve them better and faster than the enemy was decisive. And in this respect, at least for a long time, the performance of the Italian armed forces was inferior to that of the other troops in Africa. This failure can be explained, though not exclusively, as due to Italy's material situation and structural weaknesses, and the lack of a consensus between the Italian public and the Fascist leadership with regard to the war.

In East Africa, where the personality of the Italian commander-in-chief strongly influenced the course of the war, Italy achieved a victory, which, however, was only Pyrrhic. Because of the geo-strategic location of this theatre, a long war there was bound to take a heavy toll of the Italian troops. Even after successes against the British, the Italians there could not be adequately supplied from Italy or North Africa.

It was typical of Mussolini's way of conducting a war, accepted without strong opposition by most of the Italian military, that he decided to begin a new, poorly prepared campaign—the attack on Greece—which should have been precluded by military developments in Africa, the foreign-policy interests of the Axis, and the domestic political and economic situation in Italy. This was at a time when the campaign in North Africa was going badly and every tank, artillery piece, vehicle, and rifle was needed for operations there. The results of the attack on Greece demonstrated clearly that Italy was unable to defeat even a relatively weak enemy. The reason was not that the Italian soldiers lacked courage or fighting spirit. In this respect they were in no way inferior to their enemy.

At the turn of the year 1940–1 the fighting in Albania reached a stalemate. The Greeks were too exhausted to continue their counter-attack, but Mussolini was already fighting with his back to the wall. Still threatened with defeat in the Balkans, in serious danger in North Africa, and increasingly unpopular at home, he finally turned to Hitler for assistance. His military dilettantism and policy of *Sacro egoismo* had forced him to ask for German help. The German government met his request; under the circumstances it had no choice.

Having decided to intervene militarily in the Balkans and North Africa, the German military and political leaders wanted to defeat the Greeks and the British quickly and with only a relatively small commitment of troops and other resources, in order not to weaken the forces for the imminent attack on the Soviet Union more than absolutely necessary. The military potential of

Germany's allies hardly came into question. Only Italy was in a position to protect at least the right flank of the German advance. Hungary, Romania, and Bulgaria limited their efforts largely to logistical support.

Although Hitler's intervention in south-east Europe significantly increased the strength of the Axis, it also led to greatly increased risks, especially in the war against the Soviet Union. It was quite possible that Stalin would also intervene in the Balkans, which might have unforeseeable consequences for Hitler's war plans. Although the German forces did not encounter serious difficulties, the conquest of Greece and Yugoslavia marked the beginning of an overextension of German resources. In retrospect this is clear if one considers on the one hand the approaching war against the Soviet Union with its rapidly expanding fronts and, on the other, the fact that after May 1941 German troops were tied down in south-east Europe. In this regard it is especially important that the conquest of Greece and Yugoslavia led to the rise of resistance movements requiring the presence of large German forces.

With regard to the strength and composition of the divisions envisaged for the Balkan operation, the army high command assumed that it had to be in a position to repel a possible Turkish or Soviet intervention as well as to eliminate the Greek and British forces as rapidly as possible. Special geographical and infrastructure problems in south-east Europe also had to be taken into consideration. The high command therefore decided to provide Twelfth Army with mobile armoured units as well as mountain and infantry divisions and to ensure strong tactical air support by the Luftwaffe.

The slow advance of the German army units through Bulgaria in March 1941 showed that a mechanized army in particular, despite intensive preparations, inevitably encountered problems in deploying all its units for an attack in difficult terrain with an inadequate transport system. For this reason the army leaders had decided not to deploy their forces along the Greek frontier during the winter months.

For the British the decision to support Greece militarily raised the concern that a promising attack—against the Italians in North Africa—would have to be interrupted so as to send part of the forces involved to Greece in a risky and overhasty operation. The decision to send troops from Egypt was therefore a matter of considerable scepticism, which was strengthened when efforts began to develop a joint defence plan. For the Allies were not able to devise a plan which took into account all possibly important factors, especially the vacillating position of Yugoslavia. Even the new situation after the coup in Belgrade on 27 March 1941 did not lead to any change; the situation remained critical. The expectation that Yugoslav troops would protect the approaches to Greece was based more on wishful thinking than on a realistic assessment of the hesitant attitude of the Yugoslav government.

While German army and Luftwaffe units were able to reach their starting-positions along the Yugoslav–Bulgarian frontier quickly after the coup in Belgrade in spite of the poor communications, only parts of an army could be deployed along the northern frontier of Yugoslavia. That, in spite of this improvisation, the conquest of Yugoslavia was able to be carried out according to plan was in all probability due largely to the fact that the German troops were opposed by a divided, incompletely mobilized, and technically inferior army. German air supremacy in particular and the strength of the motorized formations contributed to the rapid collapse of the enemy's armed forces.

The advance into Greece proved to be more difficult; German military leaders had clearly underestimated the fighting ability and spirit of the Greek troops, which led to heavy losses especially in the attack on the skilfully defended Metaxas line. After these positions had been overcome, however, Greek military strength was almost exhausted. Months of fighting in Albania, inadequate supply and transport capacity, and especially German air supremacy prevented the continuation of organized resistance. The German units were thus able to turn their attention quickly to the main enemy, the British expeditionary corps. The numerically inferior but well-equipped Empire troops took advantage of every opportunity to inflict losses on the attackers and were able to extricate themselves repeatedly from threatening encirclements. Thereupon the Germans attempted to use their air supremacy to prevent the evacuation of the expeditionary corps from Greece, but in this they were also unsuccessful. The effective camouflage of the British units and British command of the sea enabled most of the troops of the expeditionary force to escape to Egypt and Crete.

The course of the fighting showed that highly mobile defenders with good morale in a mountainous country with a poorly developed transport system could be pushed back only step by step and with considerable forces. Moreover, the Germans were merely beginning to create mixed formations of motorized troops and infantry units that could attempt to pin the enemy down with a frontal attack and outflank his positions at the same time. But the British were flexible enough to prevent such envelopments.

During the Balkan campaign the German leaders planned the conquest of the last British base in Greece, the island of Crete. In this regard, Hitler's determination to eliminate any threat to the strategic southern flank of the attack on the Soviet Union was probably decisive. The fear that the British could use airfields on Crete for attacks on the Romanian oilfields played a particularly important role in his thinking. Preparations for the landing on the island were carried out under great pressure of time, as the start of the war in the east could not be postponed. Only with great effort could the special units be assembled and supplied before the start of the operation. In addition, German reconnaissance was not able to provide sufficient information on the preparations of the defenders. Even more dangerous, however, was the fact that completely incompatible proposals were submitted for the operation, based on differing ideas of the airborne and Luftwaffe staffs. A compromise was finally reached that envisaged the capture of four different areas on the island.

The execution of this plan almost ended in disaster, for when the German units landed in their planned target areas, they not only encountered vigorous resistance but were also quickly isolated in groups and suffered very heavy losses. Only the concentration on the capture of a single airfield, necessitated by operational developments, enabled them to avert a catastrophe. In this they were aided by certain British tactical mistakes.

In view of the difficulties of Operation Merkur, the question must remain open as to whether Hitler and his generals would have ordered the operation shortly before the attack on the Soviet Union if they had realized the risks involved. It is also uncertain whether the victory was worth the cost. Crete was conquered with very high losses of aircraft and officers, but this victory gave the Germans no immediate advantage in the conduct of the war in the eastern Mediterranean.

In the conquest of Yugoslavia and Greece as well as Crete, different views about the conduct of operations became evident among the German units and their staffs. The effect of these differences on the course of operations was not decisive—German superiority in most areas was too great—but they could have had very serious consequences against larger enemy forces. Disagreements among the German commanders were expressed primarily in open rivalries which often could be settled only with the help of higher and the highest headquarters. This was true not least of the co-operation between the army and the Luftwaffe. Friction developed which occasionally led to delays and even losses. The inclination of some commanders to concentrate on their own units or service branch and consider common objectives to be of secondary importance led to situations in which Wehrmacht services were given tasks which, because of their specific structure, they could perform only with difficulty.

In the situation in the spring of 1941, however, success in the Balkans and the stabilization of the Axis position in North Africa were extremely important for Germany, as they eliminated a potential threat to the campaign in the east.

For Britain the withdrawal from the Greek mainland and Crete represented a military defeat, but its negative consequences were more than made up for by the strengthening of the British position in the Middle East after the victories in Iraq and Syria. Britain was able not only to improve her operational position for the war in North Africa but also—something equally important in the long term—to stabilize the economic base of her war effort. It must also be noted that at this time Britain was already receiving arms shipments on very favourable terms from the United States, which had long been expanding its production of military equipment.

Especially after the end of 1941 and the failure of the blitzkrieg in the east, the war in the south, at first in North Africa, became a constant drain on German resources. It should be noted that developments in the desert war were dependent in every respect on the war in the east. Of course there was also a reciprocal effect, even for Italy, as Mussolini had insisted on sending an expeditionary corps to fight in the Soviet Union.

The longer the war continued, the more evident it became that even the relatively small number of German troops and the quantities of material sent to Africa had an adverse effect on supplies for the eastern front. On the whole, although the precise extent cannot be determined, the campaign in North Africa contributed to the acceleration of a strategic divergence in the Third Reich, i.e. the widening gap between what was required at the front and what could actually be delivered.

In the long term a not unimportant factor in the course of the war was that in future every British success meant a defeat for Germany as well as Italy, as German troops remained tied down in the Mediterranean, operationally only in North Africa at the start, but later also against partisan groups in the Balkans.

The war in North Africa, the primary subject of the present volume after the conclusion of Operations Marita and Merkur (Greece and Crete), cannot be understood in purely military terms. German intervention was certainly a direct reaction to Italian requests for help, but this was only the most visible of many factors. In the light of subsequent discussion and in a historical perspective, especially revealing are the hopes and expectations which caused German planning and deliberations to concentrate on the Mediterranean long before the Wehrmacht appeared in North Africa. In February 1941 the realization of these ideas and aims seemed to be within reach. For many members of the German political, economic, military, and intellectual élites the campaign in North Africa became a vehicle for the fulfilment of old dreams of power politics.

Some of them probably believed that the time had come for a repartition of the world. They wanted to establish a single large economic area, dominated by Germany and comprising Europe and part of Africa, but their interests also extended to Egypt and the rest of the Middle East, the Sudan, the Persian Gulf—another potential field of conflict between the Axis powers—and Germany's demands for a colonial empire in central Africa. Their aims included control of the sea routes from ports on the Black Sea and in Greece through the eastern Mediterranean, via the Suez Canal, to the Indian Ocean. The inclusion of this region in the area under German domination was demanded not only by the naval high command. The aims of the groups in question can be summarized in a few words: oil, bread, and strategic positions.

North Africa was and remains a synonym for a strategy whose true face is concealed behind the veil of carefully and selectively preserved memories. In retrospect the dying, suffering, and destruction recede into the background. But this does not mean that the fighting in Libya, Egypt, and finally Tunisia was less terrible than on the other battlefields of the Second World War. And the battles were by no means a fascinating game played by sovereign strategists. Pseudo-scholarly accounts, e.g. the story of the 'desert fox', have contributed much to the creation of legends but little to establishing the truth, and have largely prevented or even supplanted the development of a realistic picture of what actually took place in Africa. At best the desert war remains faceless. Of course the fighting there cannot be compared with the war of annihilation in the east. But in this regard it should be noted that German troops in the Mediterranean area were also recipients of criminal orders.

The desert war, moreover, was not, perhaps not even primarily, a mechanized, personalized war to be judged from a purely operational point of view. In daily practice as well as its aims it was far more.

Finally, it is necessary to consider the historical importance of the war in the Mediterranean. For it first became evident there how small the aggressors' room for manœuvre had become as the war continued its course after the late autumn of 1940. The events of 1941 provided the first concrete signs that the Axis no longer held the initiative; in the second half of 1942 this fact could no longer be denied, and by the first half of 1943 it had become obvious. In the words of contemporary observers, in the summer of that year Germany definitely ceased to be the 'hammer' and became the 'anvil'.

GERHARD SCHREIBER
DETLEF VOGEL

Bibliography

I. UNPUBLISHED SOURCES

1. Federal German military archives, Freiburg

(a) Oberkommando der Wehrmacht (OKW) [Wehrmacht high command]

OKW/Chef des Oberkommandos der Wehrmacht [Chief of Wehrmacht high command]

RW 2/v. 138   Berichte der Wehrmachtuntersuchungsstelle für Verletzungen des Völkerrechts, Kreta, 1941 [Reports of the Wehrmacht office for the investigation of violations of international law, Crete, 1941]

OKW/Chef Wehrmachtführungsstab [Chief, Operations staff]

RW 4/v. 35   Abschriftensammlung 1938–1945 (Gen. Oberst Jodl) [Collection of transcripts: Col.-Gen. Jodl]

OKW/WFSt/Abteilung Landesverteidigung (L) [Department of home defence]

RW 4/v. 42   Aufzeichnungen H. Greiner, 1940 [Notes by H. Greiner]
RW 4/v. 578 Chefsachen 'Barbarossa', 1941 [Secret papers concerning Operation Barbarossa]
RW 4/v. 588 Chefsachen Sammelmappe 'Marita', 1941 [Secret file concerning Operation Marita]
RW 4/v. 662 Vortrag OTL d.G. v. Loßberg vom 5.5.1941: Die Operationen im Südosten [Report by Lt.-Col. (GS) von Loßberg on operations in south-east Europe]

OKW/Amt Ausland/Abwehr [Foreign countries: counter-espionage]

RW 5/v. 7   Neues zur Lage (mil. u. pol.), Bruchstücke 1940 [New information (military and political): misc. papers]
RW 5/v. 350 Außenpolitische Übersichten, Mitteilungen, 1937–1940 [Foreign policy surveys, reports]
RW 5/v. 354 Abt. für Wehrmachtspropaganda: Außen- und militärpolitische Nachrichten, 25. Juni 1940–4. August 1941, Heft 3 [Dept. for Wehrmacht propaganda, foreign and military political reports, vol. 3]

OKW/Wehrwirtschafts- und Rüstungsamt (WiRüAmt) [War economy and armaments office]

OKW/WiRüAmt/Wehrwirtschaftliche Abteilung [Dept. of war economy]

Wi/I 339   Vortrag des Kapitäns zur See Dose gelegentlich der wehrwissenschaftlichen Übungsreise nach Schwalbach am 20.6.1939

	[Report by naval Captain Dose on visit to Schwalbach by the military science staff, 20 June 1939]
Wi/I B 1.64	Länderakte Finnland/Italien, 1937–1942 [Country files: Finland, Italy]
Wi/I C 5/36	Bulgarien, Wirtschaftsberichte 1939–1941 [Bulgaria, economic reports]

OKW/WiRüAmt/Geheimarchiv [Secret archives]

RW 19 Anhang I/648	Die Selbstversorgungsmöglichkeiten und die versorgungspolitischen Maßnahmen Italiens auf dem Gebiet der Mineralölwirtschaft, Mai 1940 [Italy's possibilities of self-sufficiency and supply-policy measures with regard to petroleum]
RW 19 Anhang I/650	Die wichtigsten Firmen der italienischen Rüstungsindustrie, Mai 1940 [The principal firms in the Italian armaments industry]
RW 19 Anhang I/655	Die Selbstversorgungsmöglichkeiten und die versorgungspolitischen Maßnahmen Italiens in der Kohlewirtschaft, April 1940 [Italy's possibilities of self-sufficiency with regard to coal and supply-policy measures in the coal industry]
RW 19 Anhang I/656	Die Selbstversorgungsmöglichkeiten und die versorgungspolitischen Maßnahmen Italiens auf dem Gebiet der NE-Metalle und sonst. Materialien, Mai 1940 [Italy's possibilities of self-sufficiency and supply-policy measures in respect of non-precious metals and other minerals]

(b) Oberkommando des Heeres (OKH) [Army high command]

OKH/GenStdH/Operations-Abteilung (Op.Abt.) [General staff, Operations dept.]

RH 2/v. 390	Chef sache-Hauptakte, Gruppe Landesbefestigung, 16. Okt. 1939–7. Juni 1940 [Principal secret documents, home defence group]
RH 2/v. 460	Chefsachen, 11.1.1941–11.9.1942 [Secret papers]
RH 6/v. 3	Chef Heeresnachrichtenwesen, Aufmarschanweisungen für 12. Armee ('Marita'), 26.11.1940–16.4.1941 [Head of army signal units, deployment orders for Twelfth Army]
M VII e 17	Lagenberichte des Balkanfeldzuges 1941 der Op.Abt. d. Gen.St.d.H., 6.4.1941–30.4.1941 [Situation reports of the Balkan campaign of 1941 by the operations dept. of the army general staff]

OKH/GenStdH/OQuIV/Abt. Fremde Heere West [Army general staff, assistant chief of staff (operations) IV, foreign armies west]

RH 2/v. 1497	(Fernschreib)-Lageberichte 1941 [(Teletype) situation reports]

OKH/GenStdH/OQuIV/Attaché-Abteilung [Army general staff, assistant chief of staff (operations) IV, attachés dept.]

H 27/43	Chefsachen 1941 [Secret papers]

I. Unpublished Sources

RH 2/v. 2954 — Entwürfe, Unterlagen, 'Bildung Militärmission Rumänien', 1941 [Drafts, documents, organization of military mission to Romania]

(c) Kommandobehörden und Divisionen des Heeres, sonstige Dienststellen [Commands and divisions of the army, other offices]

2. Armee [2nd Army]

RH 20-2/130 — KTB, Abt. Ia, 28 März–14 April 1941 [War diary, Dept. Ia]

RH 20-2/137 — Ia, Anl.Bd 8 zum KTB (Jugoslawien), 21.4.1941–24.4.1941 [Annex to vol. 8 of war diary (Yugoslavia)]

RH 20-2/140 — Ia, Handakte, OTL i.G. Feyerabend, 4 April 1941–11 Mai 1941, Balkan [Ia, reference file, Lt.-Col. (GS) Feyerabend; Balkans]

RH 20-2/149 — Anl. zum KTB Jugoslawien, Erfahrungsberichte aus dem Feldzug, 12.5.–3.6.1941 [Annex to war diary Yugoslavia, operation experience reports from campaign]

RH 20-2/1085 — Ic, AO, Waffenstillstandsverhandlungen Jugoslawien, 14.4.–16.4.1941 [Ic, counter-espionage officer, armistice negotiations (Yugoslavia)]

12. Armee [12th Army]

RH 20-12/60 — Ia, Organisation Balkan, Akte 01, 30.1.1941–11.5.1941 [Ia, Organization Balkans, file 01.]

RH 20-12/62 — Wehrmachtsbefehlhaber Südost, Abt. Ia, KTB, März–Nov. 1941 [Wehrmacht commander south-east, dept. Ia, war diary]

RH 20-12/93/D — Balkanfeldzug 12. Armee, 1941. Armeebefehle [Balkan campaign Twelfth Army, 1941. Army orders]

RH 20-12/105 — Wehrmachtsbefehlhaber Südost, Abt. Ia, Aktenbund II, Berichte über den Balkan-Feldzug 1941, März–Mai 1941 [Wehrmacht commander south-east, dept. Ia, file packet II, reports on Balkan campaign]

RH 20-12/129 — E. Wisshaupt, Der Balkan-Feldzug der 12. Armee, Generalfeldmarschall List [The Balkan campaign of the Twelfth Army]

RH 20-12/356 — Tätigkeitsberichte Abt IVb mit Anlagen über Einsatz im Südosten, 5.1.–4.5.1941 [Activity reports, dept. IVb, with annexes on operations in south-east Europe]

RH 20-12/397 — Ia, Kriegsgliederung der 12. Armee vom 5.4.1941 und verschiedene andere Akten vom Balkanfeldzug [Ia, war organization of Twelfth Army, 5 Apr. 1941, and miscellaneous files on Balkan campaign]

75090/1 — Balkanfeldzug der 12. Armee, Karten [Balkan campaign of the Twelfth Army: maps]

Panzerarmeeoberkommando 1 [Armoured army high command 1]

RH 21-1/40D — KTB der Panzergruppe v. Kleist, 7. Dez. 1940–28. April 1941 [War diary of armoured group von Kleist]

Deutsches Afrikakorps [German Africa Corps]

RH 24-200/1	Ia, KTB, 1941 [War diary]
RH 24-200/9	Ia, Anlagen zum KTB Nr. 3, insbes. Gefechtsberichte unterstellter Verbände und Einheiten, 31.10.1941-12.1.1942 [Annexes to war diary No. 3, esp. battle reports of subordinate formations and units]
RH 24/200/38K	Ia, KTB-Anlagen, Lagekarten, Gefechtsskizzen, Januar-März 1942 [War diary annexes, situation maps, battle maps]

15. Panzerdivision [15th Armoured Division]

RH 27-15/4	Ia, KTB Nr. 1, 1941 [War diary No. 1]

5. lei. Division (mot) [5th Light Division (mot.)]

RH 27-21/52	Ia, KTB, 1941 [War diary]
RH 37/6478	KTB, M.G.-Btl 2 (d. 5 lei. Div.) [War diary, MG Bn. 2 (of 5th Light Division)]

5. Gebirgsdivision [5th Mountain Division]

RH 28-5/1	KTB der Führungsabteilung, 1941 [War diary of operations dept.]
RH 28-5/3, 3b, 4	Anlagen zum KTB, 1941 [Annexes to war diary]

13. Panzerdivision [13th Armoured Division]

RH 27-13/2	Ia, Bd I, Chefsachen, Anlagen zum KTB 4, 24.9.1940-10.5.1941 [For div. commander, secret annexes to war diary]

Deutsche Heeresmission in Rumänien [German military mission in Romania]

RH 31-1/v. 23	Ia, Anlagen zum KTB 'Marita', 8.12.1940-5.4.1941 [Annexes to war diary 'Marita']

(d) Der Reichsminister der Luftfahrt und Oberbefehlshaber der Luftwaffe (R.d.L. u. Ob.d.L.) [The Reich minister of aviation and commander-in-chief of the Luftwaffe]

R.d.L. u. Ob.d.L./Generalstab der Lw/Luftwaffenführungsstab [General staff of the Luftwaffe and Luftwaffe operations staff]

RL 2 II/38	Akte 'Alex' II, 1941 ['Alex' file II]

R.d.L. u. Ob.d.L./Generalstab d. Lw/Generalquartiermeister [General staff of the Luftwaffe and deputy chief of staff]

RL 2 III/712	6. Abt. Pers. u. mat. Einsatzbereitschaft, flieg. Verbände, 5.4.1941-31.5.1941 [6th dept. personnel and material combat readiness, air units]
RL 2 III/957	versch. Vorgänge über Verluste der Luftwaffe 1941/1942 [Miscellaneous records of Luftwaffe losses]

Truppenführungsstäbe der Lw [Luftwaffe field operations staffs]

RL 7/463	Bericht 'Kreta' der Luftflotte 4 vom 21.11.1941 [Report on Crete by Air Fleet 4]

I. Unpublished Sources

RL 7/656   Auszug aus dem Tagebuch der Jugoslawischen Obersten Heeresleitung, 1941 [Extract from diary of the Yugoslav army high command]

RL 7/657   Befehl für die Luftkriegführung Jugoslawien (Unternehmen 25), 1941 [Order for air war against Yugoslavia (Operation 25)]

RL 7/668   KTB, Führungsabteilung, Ia op 2, 17.8.1940–27.3.1941 [War diary, operations dept.]

Truppenführungsstäbe der Fliegertruppe [Field operations staffs of air and maintenance personnel]

RL 8/46   H. W. Deichmann, 'Balkanfeldzug des VIII. Fliegerkorps' ['Balkan campaign of the VIIIth Air Corps']

RL 8/237   Sammlung Luftkrieg 1939/45. Balkan-Griechenland. R. Meister, 'Der Einsatz des VIII. Fliegerkorps bei der Besetzung Griechenlands und Kretas', Teil I [Collection on air war 1939–45, Balkans–Greece. 'Operations of the VIIIth Air Corps in the occupation of Greece and Crete', Part I]

RL 8/238   Sammlung Luftkrieg 1939/45. Balkan-Griechenland. H. W. Deichmann, 'Balkanfeldzug des VIII. Fliegerkorps' ['Balkan campaign of the VIIIth Air Corps']

RL 8/241   Generalkommando VIII. Fliegercorps. Abgestellte Akten und Schriftstücke, Abt. Ia, Erfahrungsberichte 'Griechenland-Kreta', 12.3.1941–28.11.1941 [Corps command VIIIth Air Corps, stored files and documents, dept. Ia, operation experience reports 'Greece–Crete']

RL 8/242   VIII. Fliegerkorps, verschiedene Erfahrungsberichte Südosten, Okt. 1940–Mai 1941 [VIIIth Air Corps, miscellaneous operation experience reports, south-east]

RL 8/243   Erfahrungsberichte 'Merkur', Mai/Juni 1941 [Experience reports Merkur]

RL 8/245   Gen.Kdo VIII. Fliegerkorps, Feldzug Griechenland-Jugoslawien 30.4.1941 [Corps command VIIIth Air Corps, campaign in Greece and Yugoslavia]

Komm. General der Luftwaffe in befreundeten und besetzten Gebieten [Commanding general of the Luftwaffe in friendly and occupied areas]

RL 9/85   Deutsche Luftwaffenmission in Rumänien, Unterrichtung der Kommandeure, 1940/41 [Luftwaffe mission in Romania, information for commanders]

Truppenführungsstäbe, Verbände und Einheiten Fallschirmtruppe [Field operations staffs, paratroop formations and units]

RL 33/31   XI. Fliegerkorps, Einsatz Kreta, Tagebuch Sturmregiment, 23.4.1941–13.7.1941 [XIth Air Corps, action Crete, diary of shock regiment]

RL 33/34   XI. Fliegerkorps, Taktische Einsatzbefehle [XIth Air Corps, tactical operation orders]

RL 33/36   XI. Fliegerkorps, Gefechtsbericht I. Sturm-Rgt., Aug. 1941 [XIth Air Corps, Combat report, I shock regiment]

RL 33/98	Gefechtsbericht des XI. Fliegerkorps—Einsatz Kreta–11.6.1941 [Combat report of XIth Air Corps, action Crete]
RL 33/99	Anlage zum Gefechtsbericht des XI. Fliegerkorps—Einsatz Kreta—11.6.1941 [Annex to combat report of XIth Air Corps, action Crete]
RL 33/116	Vorläufiger Erfahrungsbericht des XI. Fliegerkorps—Einsatz Kreta—vom 11.6.1941 [Preliminary operation experience report of XIth Air Corps, action Crete]

(e) Oberkommando der Kriegsmarine [Navy high command]

OKM/Oberbefehlshaber der Kriegsmarine (ObdM) [Commander-in-chief of the navy]

RM 6/73	Persönlich, Großadmiral Raeder, 1.8.1940–31.1.1941 [Personal file, Grand Admiral Raeder]
RM 6/83	Flotte–Neubauten, 29. April 1940–27. January 1943 [Fleet, new construction]

OKM/Seekriegsleitung (Skl) [Naval war staff]

CASE GE 439 (PG 32485)	Akte VII, I 'Attila', Weisung Nr. 19 und allg. Schriftwechsel, 10.13.1940–15.5.1942 [File VII, I 'Attila', directive No. 19 and general correspondence]
CASE GE 440 (PG 32488)	Akte VII, 4, Bd I, 'Felix', Weisungen OKW und allg. Schriftwechsel, 24.10.1940–27.8.1941 [File VII 4, vol. I. 'Felix', directives of Wehrmacht high command and general correspondence]
GASE GE 529 (PG 32604)	Handakte 'Felix'/'Gisela', Nov. 1940–Juni 1944 [Reference file 'Felix' and 'Gisela']
CASE GE 941 (PG 32937)	1./Skl. I La 6-1 (I L 16-1), Fremde Luftmächte und fremde Marinen, 22. Dezember 1934–18 Apr. 1939 [Foreign air forces and navies]
CASE GE 1076 (PG 33087)	1./Skl. I-m, Kriegsakte Bd 6: Allgemeines, Juni 1940–Dez. 1940 [War files, vol. 6, general file]
CASE GE 1080 (PG 33122)	1./Skl. I-m, Kriegsakte Bd 33. Deutsche Dampfer in Italien, Juni 1941–Jan. 1942 [War files, vol. 33, German steamships in Italy]
CASE GE 1084 (PG 33101)	1. Skl. I-m, Kriegsakte, Bd 20. 'Merkur' vom 7.5.–27.5.1941 [War files, vol. 20, Merkur]
CASE GE 1793 (PG 33092)	1. Skl. I-m, Kriegsakte, Bd 11. Deutsche Dampfer in Italien, Okt. 1940–April 1941 [German steamships in Italy]
CASE GE 1794 (PG 33097)	1. Skl. I-m, Kriegsakte, Bd 15. Deutsche Dampfer und Transporte in Italien, März–Juni 1941 [German steamships and transports in Italy]
RM 7/4	1. Skl. KTB, Teil A, Bd 1, 15.8–30.8.1939 [War diary, part A, vol. 1]
RM 7/12–30	1. Skl. KTB, Teil A, Bde 9–27, 1.5.1940–30.11.1941 [War diary, part A, vols. 9–27]
RM 7/233	1. Skl. KTB, Teil C, Heft XIII, Italienische Kriegführung,

I. Unpublished Sources

	Juli 1940–April 1944 [War diary, part C, book XIII, Italian strategy]
RM 7/234	1. Skl. KTB, Teil C, Heft XIV, Deutsche Kriegführung im Mittelmeer, Feb. 1941–Dez. 1941 [War diary, part C, book XIV, German strategy in the Mediterranean]
RM 7/255	1. Skl. KTB, Teil C, Heft XVI, Verhältnis zu Frankreich, Okt. 1940–März 1943 [War diary, part C, book XVI, relations with France]
RM 7/258	1. Skl. KTB, Teil Ca, Grundlegende Fragen der Kriegführung, Bd 2, Aug.–Dez. 1941 [War diary, part Ca, basic questions of war strategy, vol. 2]
RM 7/262	1. Skl. KTB, Teil Cb, Stützpunktabsichten, Kolonien, Juni 1940–Juli 1943 [War diary, part Cb, plans for bases, colonies]
RM 7/940	Unternehmen 'Merkur', 22. April–24. Mai 1941 [Operation Merkur]
RM 7/945	Handakte Malta, 15.4.1941–22.7.1942 [Reference file Malta]
MBox 57 (PG 32087b–d)	Mar. Verb. Offizier zum OKH (Gen.St.d.H.), Chefsachen, 1. Juli 1940–14.8.1942 [Naval liaison officer with army high command (army general staff), secret papers]

OKM/Seekriegsleitung/Kriegswissenschaftliche Abteilung der Marine [Navy high command/Naval war staff/military science dept. of the navy]

RM 8/1209	Study by Vice-Admiral Kurt Assmann, 'Die Bemühungen der Seekriegsleitung um einen Ausgleich mit Frankreich und um die Sicherstellung des franz. Kolonialreiches in Afrika' (Nov. 1944) ['The efforts of the naval war staff to reach a settlement with France and to safeguard the French empire in Africa']
RM 8/1257	Handakte Vizeadmiral Kurt Assmann, Betr. Material zur Kriegführung im Mittelmeer 1940–1943 (1944–1945) [Reference file of Vice-Admiral Kurt Assmann, material on conduct of the war in the Mediterranean, 1940–3]
MBox 1961 (PG 33967g)	Undated study, 'Betrachtung zur Frage: Japan im Dreimächtepakt' ['Observations on the question of Japanese membership of the Three-power Pact']

Admiral Südost [Admiral south-east]

RM 35 III/2–4	KTB Admiral Südost, 16.4.1941–31.5.1941 [War diary]
RM 35 III/120	Unternehmen 'Merkur' 1941 [Operation Merkur]
M 721 (PG 46229–46249)	KTB Marinebefehlshaber 'A' bzw. Marinebefehlshaber Griechenland, bzw. Admiral Ägäis, 8.2.–31.12.1941 [War diary, naval commander 'A', naval commander Greece, Admiral Aegean]

Deutsches Marinekommando Italien [German naval command Italy]

RM 36/1	KTB des Chefs des Verbindungsstabes beim Admiralstab der Kgl. ital. Marine, Konteradmiral Weichold, 28.6.–19.7.1940 [War diary of Rear-Adm. Weichold, head of the naval liaison staff, with the staff of the Royal Italian Navy]

RM 36/8	Id., 16–30.9.1940
RM 36/11	Id., 1.11.–15.11.1940
RM 36/16	Id., 1.1.1941–15.3.1941
RM 36/19	Id., 1.–31. März 1941
MBox 629 (PG 39972) NID	Unterlagen zum KTB, Bd 23, 1.12.–31.12.1941 [Documents to war diary, vol. 23]
MBox 646 (PG 45098)	Akte Chefsachen Bd 1: Operative Absichten—Allgemeines, 15.5.1940–23.7.1941 [File for head of command, vol. 1, operational plans, general matters]
III M 2001/1	Italienische Denkschrift aus den militärischen Akten Rom [Italian memorandum from military files, Rome]

(*f*) *Posthumous papers*

N 19/8, 9	Nachlaß v. Weichs, Erinnerungen, Bd 4, 5: Balkan-Feldzug 1941 [Weichs papers, vols. 4 and 5, Balkan campaign]
N 316/v. 36	Nachlaß Weichold, Eberhard, Teil 1, 1941 [Papers of Eberhard Weichold, part 1]
N 449/4	Nachlaß Clemm v. Hohenberg, 'Kurzer Überblick über den italienisch-griechischen Krieg 1940/41 und seine Vorgeschichte', 1941 [Papers of Klemm v. Hohenberg, 'Brief survey of the Italo-Greek war of 1940–1 and its origins']
N 449/7	Nachlaß Clemm v. Hohenberg, 'Der Krieg Griechenlands 1940–1941' [Papers of Klemm von Hohenberg, 'Greece's war']

(*g*) *Various*

ZA 3/19	Verschiedene Ausarbeitungen und Notizen über den Einsatz auf Kreta [Miscellaneous studies and notes on the operation in Crete]
ZA 3/21	Ludovico Domenico, 'Die Eroberung Kretas aus der Luft', 1953 ['The capture of Crete from the air']

2. Militärgeschichtliches Forschungsamt (Research Institute for Military History), Freiburg im Breisgau

Unpublished studies

A-914	'Strategy prior to 1944': Beantwortung allgemeiner Fragen an Generaloberst Jodl vom 28.7.45 [Answers to general questions by Col.-Gen. Jodl]
B-495	E. von Rintelen, 'Die deutsch-italienische Zusammenarbeit im Weltkrieg' ['German–Italian co-operation in the World War']
B-525	Greiffenberg, 'Die Invasion in Jugoslawien' ['The invasion of Jugoslavia']
C-065g	G. Greiner, 'Das Eingreifen auf dem Balkan 1941' ['The German intervention in the Balkans']

I. Unpublished Sources

C-065h	H. Greiner, 'Das Unternehmen "Felix"' ['Operation Felix']
C-100	B. Müller-Hillebrand, 'Der Kampf um Kreta "Merkur"' Teil II ['The battle for Crete, "Merkur"', part 2]
C-101	B. Müller-Hillebrand, 'Der Zusammenhang zwischen dem deutschen Balkanfeldzug und der Invasion in Rußland' ['The connection between the German campaign in the Balkans and the invasion of Russia']
D-087	H. von Holtzendorff, Gen.-Maj. [Maj.-Gen.], 'Der Angriff auf den Ras Mdaua (Tobruk) am 30. April/1. Mai 1941' ['The attack on Ras Mdaua (Tobruk)']
D-216	H. Heggenreiner, 'The Operations under the Command of Marshal Graziani prior to the Arrival of the German Troops' (orig. English)
D-350	H. G. Kirchheim, Gen.Lt. a.D. [Lt.-Gen., retired], 'Angriffsgruppe Kirchheim am 30.4. und 1.5.1941 beim Angriff auf Tobruk. Kritische Untersuchung der Ursachen für das Scheitern des Angriffes' ['The Kirchheim assault group in the attack on Tobruk. A critical examination of the reasons for the failure of the attack']
D-121	R. Kriebel, Oberst i.G. [Colonel (GS)], 'Die Schlacht bei Sollum vom 15.–17.6.1941 ['The battle of Sollum']
P-030	B. Müller-Hillebrand, 'Die Improvisierung einer Operation' ['The improvising of an operation']
P-216, I–III	W. Warlimont, 'Die Kriegführung der Achsenmächte im Mittelmeer. Ein strategischer Überblick' ['The conduct of the war in the Mediterranean by the Axis powers. A strategic survey']
T-3	R. Kriebel, 'Der Feldzug 1941 (bis 7.2.1942)' (Geschichte des Feldzuges in Nordafrika 1941/43) ['The campaign of 1941 (to 7 Feb. 1942)', from 'History of the North African campaign, 1941–3']

3. Political Archives of the Foreign Ministry, Bonn

Dienststelle Ribbentrop [Ribbentrop's private office]

35/1	Files concerning Italian material, [Brigadier] SS-Oberführer Likus, 1935–1941

State secretary's office

Files on	England, vol. 4, 1941
"	Greece, vol. 2, April, 1941–March 1942
"	Italy, vols. 1–3, 9.12.1938–31.12.1940 Yugoslavia, vols. 1–3, 1939–1941

Handelspolitische Abteilung IVa [Commercial policy dept.]

Files on	Handelsbezichungen zu Deutschland (Bulgarien) Eng. [Trade relations with Germany (Bulgaria)], 1936–1941, vol. 1

4. Public Record Office, London

Premier 3/374/13a   Various (1940–1945)
CAB 80/56   1940

5. War Archives, Vienna

B-521   Nachlaß Löhr, J. Diakow, 'Unternehmen "Kreta" im Mai 1941, Bemerkungen des Generalobersten Löhr aus einem Schreiben vom 8.12.1942' [Löhr papers: J. Diakow, 'Operation Crete in May 1941. Remarks by Col.-Gen. Löhr from a letter of 8 Dec. 1942']

B-521 Nr. 20   Nachlaß Löhr, Erfahrungsbericht KG 2, Ia Nr. 1206/41 vom 9. Mai 1941 [Löhr papers, operation experience report]

B-521 Nr. 25   Nachlaß Löhr, Erfahrungsbericht über Vorbereitung und Durchführung 'Merkur' (Admiral Schuster) [Report on preparation and execution of Operation Merkur]

B-521 Nr. 29   Nachlaß Löhr, J. Diakow, Der Luftkrieg im jugoslawisch-griechischen Feldzug 1941 [Löhr papers: J. Diakow, 'The air war in the Yugoslav–Greek campaign of 1941']

B-556 Nr. 47   Nachlaß Böhme, Aufzeichnungen 1941 [Böhme papers, memoranda 1941]

II. PRINTED SOURCES

Edited works which have no single author are listed under titles.

ABENDROTH, HANS-HENNING, 'Spanien: Das Ringen um die Gestaltung des Franco-Staates', in *Innen- und Außenpolitik* (q.v.), 110–29.

ABETZ, OTTO, *Das offene Problem: Ein Rückblick auf zwei Jahrzehnte deutscher Frankreichpolitik*, with intro. by Ernst Achenbach (Cologne, 1951).

ACKERMANN, JOSEF, 'Der begehrte Mann am Bosporus: Europäische Interessenkollisionen in der Türkei (1938–1941)', in *Hitler, Deutschland und die Mächte* (q.v.), 489–507.

ÁDÁM, MAGDA, 'Les pays danubiens et Hitler (1933–1936)', *Revue d'histoire de la deuxième guerre mondiale*, 25/98 (1975), 1–26.

ADAMEC, LUDWIG W., *Afghanistan's Foreign Affairs to the Mid-Twentieth Century; Relations with the USSR, Germany, and Britain* (Tucson, 1974).

ADAP: see *Akten zur deutschen auswärtigen Politik*.

ADÈS, LUCIEN, *L'Aventure algérienne 1940–1944: Pétain—Giraud—De Gaulle* (Paris, 1979).

Africa settentrionale: see *In Africa settentrionale*.

Akten zur deutschen auswärtigen Politik 1918–1945, Series C: *1933–1937, Das Dritte Reich*, 6 vols. (Göttingen, 1971–81); Series D: *1937–1945*, 13 vols. (Göttingen, Baden-Baden, and Frankfurt a.M., 1950–70). [For trans. see *Documents on German Foreign Policy*.]

II. Printed Sources

ALANBROOKE, VISCOUNT: see Bryant.

ALFIERI, DINO, *Due dittatori di fronte* (Milan, 1948). [Trans. David Moore, *Dictators Face to Face* (London and New York, 1954).]

ALLARD, SVEN, *Stalin und Hitler: Die sowjetrussische Außenpolitik 1930–1941* (Berne and Munich, 1974).

AL-QAZZAZ, AYAD, 'The Iraqi–British War of 1941: A Review Article', *International Journal of Middle East Studies*, 7 (1976), 591–6.

AMORETTI, GIAN NICOLA, *La vicenda italo-croata nei documenti di Aimone di Savoia (1914–1943)* (Collana di fonti e studi a cura della cattedra di storia contemporanea facoltà di magistero—Università di Salerno, 1; Rapallo (?), 1979).

AMOUROUX, HENRI, *La Grande Histoire des Français sous l'occupation*, i. *Le Peuple du désastre 1939–1940* (Paris, 1976); ii. *Quarante millions de pétainistes, Juin 1940–Juin 1941* (Paris, 1977).

Anatomie des Krieges: Neue Dokumente über die Rolle des deutschen Monopolkapitals bei der Vorbereitung und Durchführung des zweiten Weltkrieges, ed. with intro. by Dietrich Eichholtz and Wolfgang Schumann (East Berlin, 1969).

ANCHIERI, ETTORE, 'Das große Mißverständnis des deutsch-italienischen Bündnisses: Zur Aktenpublikation des römischen Außenministeriums', *Außenpolitik*, 5 (1954), 509–19.

—— 'Der deutsche "Bündnisverrat" an Italien', *Außenpolitik*, 5 (1954), 588–95.

—— 'Italiens Ausweichen vor dem Krieg', *Außenpolitik*, 5 (1954), 653–62.

—— 'Die deutsch-italienischen Beziehungen während des Zweiten Weltkrieges', in *Faschismus—Nationalsozialismus: Ergebnisse und Referate der 6. italienisch-deutschen Historiker-Tagung in Trier*, ed. Georg Eckert and Otto-Ernst Schüddekopf (Schriftenreihe des Internationalen Schulbuchinstituts, 8; Brunswick, 1964), 73–88.

ANDÒ, ELIO, and BAGNASCO, ERMINIO, *Navi e marinai italiani nella seconda guerra mondiale* (Parma, 1977).

—— and GAY, FRANCO, *Gli incrociatori pesanti nella seconda guerra mondiale* (Rome, 1978).

ANDRÉ, GIANLUCA, 'La politica estera del governo fascista durante la seconda guerra mondiale', in *L'Italia fra tedeschi e alleati* (q.v.), 115–26.

ANFUSO, FILIPPO, *Roma, Berlino, Salò (1936–1945)* (Milan, 1950).

Anschluß 1938: Protokoll des Symposiums in Wien am 14. und 15. März 1978, ed. Rudolf Neck and Adam Wandruszka (Veröffentlichungen/Wissenschaftliche Kommission des Theodor-Körner-Stiftungsfonds und des Leopold-Kunschak-Preises zur Erforschung der Österreichischen Geschichte der Jahre 1918 bis 1938, 7; Munich, 1981).

ANSEL, WALTER, *Hitler Confronts England* (Durham, NC, 1960).

—— *Hitler and the Middle Sea* (Durham, NC, 1972).

ANSPERGER, FRANZ, *Auflösung der Kolonialreiche* (dtv-Weltgeschichte des 20. Jahrhunderts, 13; Munich, 1966).

ARALDI, VINICIO, *Dalla non belligeranza all'intervento: Come e perchè l'Italia entrò in guerra* (Bologna, 1965).

ARMELLINI, QUIRINO, *Diario di guerra, nove mesi al comando supremo (1940/41)* (Milan, 1946).

ATTARD, JOSEPH, *The Battle of Malta* (London, 1980).

AUPHAN, PAUL, and MORDAL, JACQUES, *La Marine française pendant la seconde guerre mondiale* (Paris, 1958).

AUSTERMANN, HEINZ, *Von Eben Emael bis Edewechter Damm: Fallschirmjäger, Fallschirmpioniere: Berichte und Dokumente über den Einsatz der Fallschirmpioniere* (Holzminden, 1971).

AVAKUMOVIĆ, IVAN, 'Yugoslavia's Fascist Movements', in *Native Fascism* (q.v.), 135-43.

AVRAMOVSKI, ŽIVKO, 'The International Isolation of Yugoslavia: An Objective of German Foreign Policy in the Period from 1933-1939', in *The Third Reich and Yugoslavia* (q.v.), 259-77.

BAAR, STEFAN, *Die Jugoslawienpolitik des faschistischen deutschen Imperialismus in der Zeit von 1935 bis zum 6. April 1941* (Leipzig, 1968).

BADOGLIO, PIETRO, *L'Italia nella seconda guerra mondiale: Memorie e documenti* (Milan, 1946). [Trans. Muriel Currey, *Italy in the Second World War: Memories and Documents* (London, 1948).]

BAER, GEORGE W., *The Coming of the Italian-Ethiopian War* (Cambridge, Mass., 1967).

—— *Test Case: Italy, Ethiopia, and the League of Nations* (Stanford, Calif., 1976).

BAGNASCO, ERMINIO, *Le armi delle navi italiane nella seconda guerra mondiale* (Milan, 1978).

BAGNELL, PRISCA VON DOROTKA, 'The Influence of National Socialism on the German Minority in Yugoslavia: A Study of Relationships of Social, Economic and Political Organizations between the German Minority of the Vojvodina and the Third Reich, 1933-1941' (diss. Syracuse University, New York, 1977).

BAILEY, THOMAS A., and RYAN, PAUL B., *Hitler vs. Roosevelt: The Undeclared Naval War* (New York and London, 1979).

BALDWIN, HANSON W., *Battles Lost and Won: Great Campaigns of World War II* (London, 1967).

BALFOUR, MICHAEL, *Propaganda in War, 1939-1945: Organizations, Policies and Publics in Britain and Germany* (London, 1979).

BANDINI, FRANCO, *Tecnica della sconfitta: Storia dei quaranta giorni che precedettero e seguirono l'entrata dell'Italia in guerra*[2] (Milan, 1964).

BARCLAY, GLEN ST J., *The Rise and Fall of the New Roman Empire: Italy's Bid for World Power, 1890-1943* (London, 1973).

—— *Their Finest Hour* (London, 1977).

BARGONI, FRANCI, GAY, FRANCO, and ANDÒ, ELIO, *Le corazzate italiane nella seconda guerra mondiale* (Rome, 1978).

BARKER, ELISABETH, *British Policy in South-east Europe in the Second World War* (Studies in Russian and East European History; London and Basingstoke, 1976).

BARTHEL, KONRAD, 'Die Kriegsziele der deutschen Imperialisten im zweiten Weltkrieg', *Militärwesen*, 5 (1961), 934-52.

BAUDINO, CARLO, *Una guerra assurda: La campagna di Grecia* (Milan, 1965).

BAUER, ERNEST, 'Italien und Kroatien 1938-1945', *Zeitschrift für Geopolitik*, 26 (1955), 112-22.

BAUM, WALTER, and WEICHOLD, EBERHARD, *Der Krieg der 'Achsenmächte' im Mittelmeer-Raum: Die 'Strategie' der Diktatoren* (Studien und Dokumente zur Geschichte des Zweiten Weltkrieges, 14; Göttingen, Zurich, and Frankfurt a.M., 1973).

BEHRENDT, HANS-OTTO, *Rommels Kenntnis vom Feind im Afrikafeldzug: Ein Bericht über die Feindnachrichtenarbeit, insbesondere die Funkaufklärung* (Einzelschriften zur militärischen Geschichte des Zweiten Weltkrieges, 25; Freiburg, 1980).

BELOT, RAYMOND DE, *La Guerre aéronavale en Méditerranée (1939–1945)* (Paris, 1949).

Berichte des Oberkommandos der Wehrmacht, 1. Januar 1941 bis 31. Dezember 1941, Die. Nur für den Dienstgebrauch (Berlin, 1942).

BERNOTTI, ROMEO, *La guerra sui mari nel conflitto mondiale*, 3 vols.: i. *1939–1941³*, revised and enlarged (Livorno, 1950).

—— *Storia della guerra nel Mediterraneo (1940–43)²* (I Libri del Tempo, 10; Rome, Milan, and Naples, 1960).

BESYMENSKI, LEW, *Sonderakte Barbarossa: Dokumentarbericht zur Vorgeschichte des deutschen Überfalls auf die Sowjetunion—aus sowjetischer Sicht* (Hamburg, 1973).

BETHELL, NICHOLAS, *The Palestine Triangle: The Struggle between the British, the Jews and the Arabs, 1935–48* (London, 1979).

BLASIUS, RAINER A., *Für Großdeutschland—gegen den großen Krieg: Staatssekretär Ernst Frhr. von Weizsäcker in den Krisen um die Tschechoslowakei und Polen 1938/39* (Cologne and Vienna, 1981).

BLOCH, JOHANN VON [Jan Bloch], *Der Krieg: Übersetzung des russischen Werkes des Autors. Der zukünftige Krieg in seiner technischen, volkswirtschaftlichen und politischen Bedeutung*, 6 vols. (Berlin, 1899).

BOCCA, GIORGIO, *Storia d'Italia nella guerra fascista 1940–1943* (Universale Laterza, 247, 248; Rome and Bari, 1973).

BOELCKE, WILLI A., *Die deutsche Wirtschaft 1930–1945: Interna des Reichswirtschaftsministeriums* (Düsseldorf, 1983).

BÖHME, HERMANN, *Der deutsch-französische Waffenstillstand im Zweiten Weltkrieg*, i. *Entstehung und Grundlagen des Waffenstillstandes von 1940* (Quellen und Darstellungen zur Zeitgeschichte, 12; Stuttgart, 1966).

—— 'Deutschland und Frankreich im Zweiten Weltkrieg 1940–1944: Die Geschichte des Waffenstillstandes', *Aus Politik und Zeitgeschichte*, B 31 (1966), 3–30; B 33 (1966), 3–22.

Bollettini di guerra del comando supremo, Ministerio della Difesa, Stato Maggiore dell'Esercito Ufficio Storico (Rome, 1970).

BOND, BRIAN, *Liddell Hart: A Study of his Military Thought* (London, 1977).

BONJOUR, EDGAR, 'Wirtschaftliche Beziehungen zwischen England und der Schweiz im Zweiten Weltkrieg', *Schweizerische Zeitschrift für Geschichte*, 22 (1972), 591–627.

—— *Geschichte der schweizerischen Neutralität: Vier Jahrhunderte eidgenössischer Außenpolitik*, vi. *1939–1945* (Basle and Stuttgart, 1970); ix. *Dokumente 1939–1946* (Basle and Stuttgart, 1976).

BONNET, GEORGES, *Défense de la paix*, 2 vols.: i. *De Washington au Quai d'Orsay* (Geneva, 1946); ii. *De Munich à la guerre* (Geneva, 1948).

BOREJSZA, JERZY W., 'Italiens Haltung zum deutsch-polnischen Krieg', in *Sommer 1939* (q.v.), 148–94.

—— 'Die Rivalität zwischen Faschismus und Nationalsozialismus in Ostmitteleuropa', *VfZG* 29 (1981), 579–614.

—— *Il fascismo e l'Europa orientale: Dalla propaganda all'aggressione* (Biblioteca di Cultura Moderna, 846; Bari, 1981).

BORGERT, HEINZ-LUDGER, 'Grundzüge der Landkriegführung von Schlieffen bis Guderian', in *Handbuch zur deutschen Militärgeschichte 1648–1939*, founded by Hans Meier-Welcker, ed. for Militärgeschichtliches Forschungsamt by Friedrich Forstmeier, Wolfgang von Grote, Othmar Hackl, Hans Meier-Welcker, and Manfred

Messerschmidt; general eds. Gerhard Papke and Wolfgang Petter (Munich, 1979), v. 427-584.
BORGHESE, J. VALERIO, *Decima Flottiglia MAS: Dalle orgini all'armistizio* (Milan, 1959).
BORGIOTTI, ALBERTO, and GORI, CESARE, *La guerra aerea in Africa settentrionale 1940-1941: Assalto dal cielo* (Collezione Storica del Risorgimento e dell'Unità d'Italia: Documenti e testimonianze, 1; Modena, 1973).
BORUS, JOSEF, 'Die militärgeographische und kriegswirtschaftliche Bedeutung Ungarns für das faschistische Deutschland', *Bulletin des Arbeitskreises 'Zweiter Weltkrieg'*, 3/4 (1971), 45-63.
BOSE, SUBHAS CHANDRA, *The Indian Struggle 1920-1942* (New York, 1964).
BOTTAI, GIUSEPPE, *Vent'anni e un giorno (24 luglio 1943)* (Milan, 1949).
—— *Diario 1935-1944*, ed. Giordano Bruno Guerri (Milan, 1982).
BOTTI, FERRUCCIO, and ILARI, VIRGILIO, *Il pensiero militare italiano dal primo al secondo dopoguerra (1919-1949)* (Rome, 1985).
BRACHER, KARL DIETRICH, *Zeitgeschichtliche Kontroversen: Um Faschismus, Totalitarismus, Demokratie* (Serie Piper, 142; Munich, 1976).
—— *Europa in der Krise: Innengeschichte und Weltpolitik seit 1917* (Frankfurt a.M., Berlin, and Vienna, 1979).
BRADLEY, DERMOT, *Generaloberst Heinz Guderian und die Entstehungsgeschichte des modernen Blitzkrieges*, with foreword by General der Panzerwaffe Walter K. Nehring (Studien zur Militärgeschichte, Militärwissenschaft und Konfliktforschung, 16; Osnabrück, 1978).
BRAGADIN, MARC'ANTONIO, *Che ha fatto la marina? 1940-1945*[5], rev. edn. (Milan, 1956). [Trans. *The Italian Navy in World War II* (Annapolis, Md., 1957).]
BRECCIA, ALFREDO, 'Le potenze dell'Asse e la neutralità della Jugoslavia alla vigilia della II[a] guerra mondiale (febbraio-settembre 1939)', in *The Third Reich and Yugoslavia* (q.v.), 107-31.
—— *Jugoslavia 1939-1941: Diplomazia della neutralità* (Università di Roma, Facoltà di Scienze Politiche, 25; Milan, 1978).
BRISSAUD, ANDRÉ, *Canaris 1877-1945*, spec. edn. (Stuttgart, Hamburg, and Munich, 1977).
BROTZU, EMILIO, and COSOLO, GHERARDO, *Aerei scuola e collegamento nella seconda guerra mondiale* (Rome, 1978).
—— CASO, MICHELE, and COSOLO, GHERARDO, *Aerotrasporti italiani nella seconda guerra mondiale* (Rome, 1978).
—— —— —— *Bombardieri italiani nella seconda guerra mondiale* (Rome, 1978).
—— —— —— *Caccia italiani nella seconda guerra mondiale* (Rome, 1978).
BROUÉ, PIERRE, and TÉMIME, ÉMILE, *La Révolution et la guerre d'Espagne* (Paris, 1961).
BROWNING, CHRISTOPHER R., *The Final Solution and the German Foreign Office: A Study of Referat D III of Abteilung Deutschland 1940-43* (New York and London, 1978).
—— 'Nazi Resettlement Policy and the Search for a Solution to the Jewish Question, 1939-1941', *German Studies Review*, 9 (1986), 497-519.
BRYANT, ARTHUR, *The Turn of the Tide, 1939-1943: A Study Based on the Diaries and Autobiographical Notes of Field Marshal the Viscount Alanbrooke* (London, 1957).
BUCHANAN, ALBERT RUSSELL, *The United States and World War II*, 2 vols. (New York, Evanston, and London, 1963).

BUCHNER, ALEXANDER, *Der deutsche Griechenland-Feldzug* (Die Wehrmacht im Kampf, 16; Heidelberg, 1957).
—— 'Kampf um die Metaxas-Linie', *Allgemeine Schweizerische Militärzeitschrift*, 10 (1957), 727–37.
BUCKLEY, CHRISTOPHER, *Five Ventures: Iraq–Syria–Persia–Madagascar–Dodecanese* (London, 1954).
BUFFOTOT, PATRICE, 'Le projet de bombardement des pétroles soviétiques du Caucase en 1940: Un exemple des projets alliés pendant la drôle de guerre', *Revue historique des armées*, 4 (1979), 79–101.
BURDICK, CHARLES B., ' "Operation Cyclamen": Germany and Albania, 1940–41', *Journal of Central European Affairs*, 19/1 (1959–60), 23–31.
—— *Germany's Military Strategy and Spain in World War II* (Syracuse, NY, 1968).
—— ' "Moro": The Resupply of German Submarines in Spain, 1939–1942', *Central European History*, 3 (1970), 256–84.
—— *Unternehmen Sonnenblume: Der Entschluß zum Afrika-Feldzug* (Die Wehrmacht im Kampf, 48; Neckargemünd, 1972).
BUTLER, JAMES RAMSAY MONTAGU, *Grand Strategy*, ii. *September 1939 to June 1941* (History of the Second World War, United Kingdom Military Series; London, 1957).
CADOGAN, Sir ALEXANDER, *The Diaries of Sir Alexander Cadogan, O.M., 1938–1945*, ed. David Dilks (London, 1971).
CALVINO, ITALO, *L'entrata in guerra* (Nuovi Coralli, 88; Turin, 1974).
CAMPUS, ELIZA, 'Der Balkanblock der Neutralen (September 1939–März 1940)', *Wissenschaftliche Zeitschrift der Karl-Marx-Universität Leipzig, Gesellschafts- und Sprachwissenschaftliche Reihe*, 6 (1956–7), 17–22.
CANEVARI, EMILIO, *La guerra italiana: Retroscena della disfatta*, 2 vols. (Rome, 1949).
CANZIO, STEFANO, *La dittatura debole: Storia dell'Italia fascista e dell'antifascismo militante dal 1926 al 1945* (Milan, 1980).
CAPPELLINI, ARNALDO, *Sfida nel Mediterraneo* (Turin, 1979).
CARL, JOACHIM, *Das amerikanische Leih- und Pacht-Gesetz (Lend-Lease Act): Entstehung und Bedeutung für der Ausgang des Zweiten Weltkrieges* (WWR suppl. 6; Berlin and Frankfurt a.M., 1957).
CAROCCI, GIAMPIERO, *La politica estera dell'Italia fascista (1925–1928)* (Bari, 1969).
—— 'Contributo alla discussione sull'imperialismo', *Il movimento di liberazione in Italia*, 23/102 (1971), 3–14.
CATALANO, FRANCO, 'Les ambitions mussoliniennes et la réalité économique de l'Italie', *Revue d'histoire de la deuxième guerre mondiale*, 19/76 (1969), 15–38.
—— *L'economia italiana di guerra: La politica economico-finanziaria del fascismo dalla guerra d'Etiopia alla caduta del regime, 1935–1943* (Milan, 1969).
—— 'L'économie de guerre italienne', in *La Guerre en Méditerrannée* (q.v.), 101–38.
—— *Dal trionfo dei fascismi alla resistenza europea* (Milan 1979).
CAVAGLION, ALBERTO, *Nella notte straniera: Gli ebrei di S. Martin Vésubie e il campo di Borgo S. Dalmazzo 8 settembre–21 novembre 1943* (Cuneo, 1981).
CAVALLERO, UGO, *Comando supremo: Diario 1940–43 del Capo di S.M.G. Premessa di Carlo Cavallero*, with a preface by Giuseppe Bucciante (Testimoni per la storia del 'nostro tempo', collana di memorie, diari e documenti, 2; Bologna, 1948).
CAVIGLIA, ENRICO, *Diario (aprile 1925–marzo 1945)*, with intro. by Mario Zino (Rome, 1952).

CEADEL, MARTIN, *Pacifism in Britain 1914–1945: The Defining of a Faith* (Oxford, 1980).
CECIL, ROBERT, *Hitler's Decision to Invade Russia, 1941* (London, 1975).
CERVI, MARIO, *Storia della guerra di Grecia* (Milan, 1965). [Trans. Eric Mosbacher, *The Hollow Legions: Mussolini's Blunder in Greece, 1940–1941* (London, 1972).]
CEVA, LUCIO, *La condotta italiana della guerra: Cavallero e il comando supremo 1941/42* (I fatti e le idee: Saggi e biografe, 294; Milan, 1975).
—— 'L'incontro Keitel-Badoglio del novembre 1940 nelle carte del Generale Marras', *Il 'Risorgimento'*, 29 (1977), 1–44.
—— 'Altre notizie sulle conversazioni militari italo-tedesche alla vigilia della seconda guerra mondiale (aprile–giugno 1939)', *Il 'Risorgimento'*, 30 (1978), 151–82.
—— 'La guerra italiana in Africa settentrionale (1940–1943): Saggio bibliografico', *Revue internationale d'histoire militaire*, 39 (1978), 126–208.
CHABOD, FEDERICO, *L'Italia contemporanea (1918–1948)* (Turin, 1961).
CHURCHILL, WINSTON S., *The Unrelenting Struggle: War Speeches (from November 12, 1940, to December 30, 1941)*, compiled by Charles Eade (London, 1942).
—— *The Second World War*, ii. *Their Finest Hour*: bk. 1, *The Fall of France*; bk. 2, *Alone*; iii. *The Grand Alliance*: bk. 1, *Germany Drives East* (London and Boston, Mass., 1949–50).
Churchill and Roosevelt: The Complete Correspondence, i. *Alliance Emerging, October 1933–November 1942*, ed. with commentary by Warren F. Kimball (Princeton, NJ, 1984).
CIANO, GALEAZZO, *L'Europa verso la catastrofe* (Milan, 1948). [Trans. Stuart Hood, *Ciano's Diplomatic Papers*, ed. Malcolm Muggeridge (London, 1948).]
—— *Diario 1937–1943*, ed. Renzo De Felice (Milan, 1980). [Trans. Andreas Mayor, *Ciano's Diary 1937–1938* (London, 1952); anon., *Ciano's Diary 1939–1943* (London, 1947); both with intro. by Malcolm Muggeridge.]
CIGLIANA, CARLO, 'La strategia tedesca nell'estate autunno 1940', *Rivista militare*, 23 (1967), 429–34.
—— 'I precedenti della campagna di Grecia', *Rivista militare*, 29 (1973), 1227–48.
CLIADAKIS, HARRY, 'Neutrality and War in Italian Policy 1939–1940', *Journal of Contemporary History*, 9/3 (1974), 171–90.
—— 'Le régime de Metaxás et la deuxième guerre mondiale', *Revue d'histoire de la deuxième guerre mondiale*, 27/107 (1977), 19–38.
CLOUGH, SHEPARD B., *The Economic History of Modern Italy* (New York, 1964).
COFFEY, THOMAS M., *Lion by the Tail: The Story of the Italian–Ethiopian War* (New York, 1974).
COHEN, DAVID B., 'Le pillage de l'économie bulgare par les Allemands', *Revue d'histoire de la deuxième guerre mondiale*, 18/72 (1968), 43–66.
COLLIER, RICHARD HUGHESON, *Duce: The Rise and Fall of Benito Mussolini* (London, 1971).
COLLOTTI, ENZO, 'La politica dell'Italia nel settore danubiano-balcanico dal patto di Monaco all'armistizio italiano', in id., Teodoro Sala, and Giorgio Vaccarino, *L'Italia nell'Europa danubiana durante la seconda guerra mondiale* (Florence, 1967), 5–71.
—— 'Il ruolo della Bulgaria nel conflitto tra Italia e Germania per il Nuovo Ordine Europeo', in *Il movimento di liberazione in Italia*, 24/108 (1972), 53–90.
—— 'Penetrazione economica e disgregazione statale: Premesse e conseguenze

dell'aggressione nazista alla Jugoslavia', in *The Third Reich and Yugoslavia* (q.v.), 278–312.

—— 'L'alleanza italo-tedesca 1941–1943', in *Gli italiani sul fronte russo* (q.v.), 3–61.

COLVIN, IAN, *Vansittart in Office: An Historical Survey of the Origins of the Second World War Based on the Papers of Sir Robert Vansittart* (London, 1965).

COMPTON, JAMES V., *The Swastika and the Eagle: Hitler, the United States and the Origins of the Second World War* (London, 1968).

CORBINO, EPICARMO, *Cinquant'anni di vita economica italiana 1915–1965*, ed. F. Assante and D. Demarco (Banco di Napoli, Biblioteca di Storia Economica, 1.1; Naples, 1966).

CORSELLI, RODOLFO, *Cinque anni di guerra italiana nella conflagrazione mondiale 1939–1945: Quadro storico-politico-militare 1919–1950* (Rome, 1951).

COVERDALE, JOHN F., 'The Battle of Guadalajara, 8–22 March 1937', *Journal of Contemporary History*, 9/1 (1974), 53–75.

—— *Italian Intervention in the Spanish Civil War* (Princeton, NJ, 1975).

Creation of Yugoslavia, 1914–1918, The, ed. Dimitrije Djordjević (Santa Barbara, Calif., 1980).

CREVELD, MARTIN L. VAN, *Hitler's Strategy 1940–1941: The Balkan Clue* (International Studies; London, 1973).

—— *Supplying War: Logistics from Wallenstein to Patton* (Cambridge, 1977).

CRUCCU, RINALDO, 'La presenza italiana nel 2° conflitto mondiale, Motivazioni e operazioni', *Rivista militare*, 99/1 (1976), 41–8.

—— 'L'Italia e la Corsica nella seconda guerra mondiale', in *Memorie storiche militari 1977*, ed. Stato Maggiore dell'Esercito, Ufficio Storico (Rome, 1977), 9–27.

CRUICKSHANK, CHARLES, *Greece 1940–1941* (The Politics and Strategy of the Second World War, 5; London, 1976).

CUNNINGHAM OF HYNDHOPE, VISCOUNT, 'The Battle of Crete', in *Supplement to the London Gazette*, 21 May 1948, pp. 3103–19.

—— *A Sailor's Odyssey: The Autobiography of Admiral of the Fleet Viscount Cunningham of Hyndhope* (London, 1956).

CVETKOVIĆ, DRAGISHA, 'Prince Paul, Hitler and Salonika', *International Affairs*, 27 (1951), 463–9.

CVIJETIĆ, LEPOSAVA, 'The Ambitions and Plans of the Third Reich with Regard to the Integration of Yugoslavia into its So-called Großwirtschaftsraum', in *The Third Reich and Yugoslavia* (q.v.), 184–96.

DAHLERUS, BIRGER, *Sista försöket: London–Berlin sommaren 1939* (Stockholm, 1948). [Trans. Alexandra Dick, *The Last Attempt* (London, 1948).]

DAHMS, HELLMUTH GÜNTHER, *Roosevelt und der Krieg: Die Vorgeschichte von Pearl Harbor* (Munich, 1958).

DALLEK, ROBERT, *Franklin D. Roosevelt and American Foreign Policy, 1932–1945* (New York, 1979).

DANKELMANN, OTFRIED, *Franco zwischen Hitler und den Westmächten* (East Berlin, 1970).

D'AURIA, ELIO, *L'Italia contemporanea: Dal primo al secondo dopoguerra* (Rome, 1979).

D'AVANZO, GIUSEPPE, *Ali e poltrone*, 2 vols. (Rome, 1976).

DAVIN, DANIEL MARCUS, *Crete* (Official History of New Zealand in the Second World War 1939–45, 3; London, 1953).

DAWIDOWICZ, LUCY S., *The War against the Jews 1933-1945* (London, 1975).
DEAKIN, FREDERICK WILLIAM, *The Brutal Friendship: Mussolini, Hitler and the Fall of Italian Fascism* (London, 1962).
DE CARO, GASPARO, *Gaetano Salvemini* (La vita sociale della nuova Italia, 16; Turin, 1970).
DEDIJER, VLADIMIR, 'Sur l'armistice germano-yougoslave', *Revue d'histoire de la deuxième guerre mondiale*, 16/23 (1956), 1-10.
DE FELICE, RENZO, *Mussolini il fascista*, ii. *L'organizzazione dello stato fascista 1925-1929*^{5} (Biblioteca di cultura storica, 92; Turin, 1968).
—— *Storia degli ebrei italiani sotto il fascismo*^{3}, with preface by Delio Cantimori, rev. and enlarged edn. (Turin, 1972).
—— 'Beobachtungen zu Mussolinis Außenpolitik', *Saeculum*, 24 (1973), 314-27.
—— *Der Faschismus: Ein Interview von Michael A. Ledeen*, with afterword by Jens Peterson (Stuttgart, 1977).
—— *Mussolini il duce*, i. *Gli anni del consenso 1929-1936*^{2} (Turin, 1974); ii. *Lo stato totalitario 1936-1940* (Biblioteca di cultura storica, 126; Turin, 1981).
DE GRAND, ALEXANDER, *Italian Fascism: Its Origins and Development* (London, 1982).
DEIGHTON, LEN, *Blitzkrieg: From the Rise of Hitler to the Fall of Dunkirk*, with a foreword by General W. K. Nehring (retd.), formerly Guderian's Chief of Staff (London, 1979).
DE LOVERDO, COSTA, *La Grèce au combat: De l'attaque italienne à la chute de la Crète (1940-1941)* (Paris, 1966).
DE LUNA, GIOVANNI, *Benito Mussolini: Soggettività e pratica di una dittatura* (Milan, 1978).
DESPOTOPOULOS, ALEXANDRE I., 'La guerre gréco-italienne et gréco-allemande (28 octobre 1940-31 mai 1941)', *Revue d'histoire de la deuxième guerre mondiale et des conflits contemporains*, 34/136 (1984), 3-47.
DETWILER, DONALD S., *Hitler, Franco und Gibraltar: Die Frage des spanischen Eintritts in den Zweiten Weltkrieg* (Veröffentlichungen des Instituts für Europäische Geschichte Mainz, 27; Wiesbaden, 1962).
Deutsche Reich und der Zweite Weltkrieg, Das:
  i. *Ursachen und Voraussetzungen der deutschen Kriegspolitik*, by Wilhelm Deist, Manfred Messerschmidt, Hans-Erich Volkmann, and Wolfram Wette (Stuttgart, 1979). [Trans. P. S. Falla, E. Osers, and Dean S. McMurry, *Germany and the Second World War*, i. *The Build-up of German Aggression* (Oxford, 1990).]
  ii. *Die Errichtung der Hegemonie auf dem europäischen Kontinent*, by Klaus A. Maier, Horst Rohde, Bernd Stegemann, and Hans Umbreit (Stuttgart, 1979). [Trans. P. S. Falla, E. Osers, and Dean S. McMurry, *Germany and the Second World War*, ii. *Germany's Initial Victories in Europe* (Oxford, 1992).]
  iv. *Der Angriff auf die Sowjetunion*, by Horst Boog, Jürgen Förster, Joachim Hoffmann, Ernst Klink, Rolf-Dieter Müller, and Gerd R. Ueberschär (Stuttgart, 1983).
Deutschland im zweiten Weltkrieg, i. *Vorbereitung, Entfesselung und Verlauf des Krieges bis zum 22. Juni 1941*, by a group of authors under the direction of Gerhard Hass (Cologne, 1974).
Deutschlands Rüstung im Zweiten Weltkrieg: Hitlers Konferenzen mit Albert Speer 1942-1945, ed. with intro. by Willi A. Boelcke (Athenaion-Bibliothek der Geschichte; Frankfurt a.M., 1969).
DIAKOW, J., *Generaloberst Alexander Löhr: Ein Lebensbild* (Freiburg i.Br., 1964).

Diario storico del comando supremo, i. *(11.6.1940–31.8.1940)*, vol. i (diary), vol. ii (annexes), ed. Antonello Biagini and Fernando Frattolillo (Raccolta di documenti della seconda guerra mondiale; Rome, 1986).
Dictionnaire de la seconde guerre mondiale, ed. Philippe Masson and Alain Melchior-Bonnet, 2 vols. (Paris, 1979–80).
DI GIAMBERARDINO, OSCAR, *La marina nella tragedia nazionale* (Rome, 1947).
DILKS, DAVID, 'The Unnecessary War? Military Advice and Foreign Policy in Great Britain, 1931–1939', in *General Staffs* (q.v.), 98–112.
DIVINE, ROBERT A., *The Reluctant Belligerent: America's Entry into World War II* (America in Crisis; New York, 1965).
—— *Roosevelt and World War II* (Baltimore, 1969).
DJORDJEVIĆ, DMITRIJE, 'Fascism in Yugoslavia: 1918–1941', in *Native Fascism* (q.v.), 125–34.
Documenti diplomatici italiani, I, ed. Ministero degli Affari Esteri, 8th series: *1935–1939*, xii (Rome, 1952); xiii (Rome, 1953); 9th series: *1939–1943*, i–v (Rome, 1954–65).
Documents of Distinction: Germany and Jewry 1933–1945, ed. Raul Hilberg (London, 1972), 89 ff.
Documents on German Foreign Policy, Series C and D (London, 1957–83; 1949–64). [Trans. of *Akten zur deutschen auswärtigen Politik* (q.v.).]
DOENECKE, JUSTUS D., 'Non-interventionism of the Left: The Keep America out of the War Congress, 1938–41', *Journal of Contemporary History*, 12 (1977), 221–36.
DOERR, HANS, 'Verbindungsoffiziere', *WWR* 3 (1953), 270–80.
Dokumente zum Konflikt mit Jugoslawien und Griechenland, ed. Auswärtiges Amt, Berlin (Berlin, 1941).
Dokumente zum Unternehmen 'Seelöwe': Die geplante deutsche Landung in England 1940, ed. Karl Klee (Studien und Dokumente zur Geschichte des Zweiten Weltkrieges, 4b; Göttingen, Zurich, and Frankfurt a.M., 1959).
DOMARUS, MAX, *Hitler: Reden und Proklamationen 1932–1945. Kommentiert von einem deutschen Zeitgenossen*, i. Triumph (i/1 1932–4, i/2 1935–8); ii. Untergang (ii/1 1939–40, ii/2 1941–5) (Wiesbaden, 1973).
—— *Mussolini und Hitler: Zwei Wege—gleiches Ende* (Würzburg, 1977).
DONLAGIĆ, AHMET, ATANAČKOVIĆ, ŽARKO, and DUŠAN, PLENČA, *Jugoslawien im Zweiten Weltkrieg* (Belgrade, 1967).
DOUGHERTY, JAMES J., *The Politics of Wartime Aid: American Economic Assistance to France and French Northwest Africa 1940–1946* (Contributions in American History, 71; Westport, Conn., and London, 1978).
DOUHET, GIULIO, *Il dominio dell'aria, e altri scritti* (Milan, 1932). [Trans. Dino Ferrari, *The Command of the Air* (London, 1942).]
—— *La guerra integrale*, with preface by Air Marshal Italo Balbo (Rome, 1936).
DRAKE, EDSON JAMES, 'Bulgaria at the Paris Peace Conference: A Diplomatic History of the Treaty of Neuilly-sur-Seine' (diss. Georgetown University, 1967).
Drang nach Afrika: Die koloniale Expansionspolitik und Herrschaft des deutschen Imperialismus in Afrika von den Anfängen bis zum Ende des zweiten Weltkrieges, ed. Helmuth Stoecker (East Berlin, 1977).
DRECHSLER, KARL, GROEHLER, OLAF, and HASS, GERHART, 'Politik und Strategie des faschistischen Deutschlands im zweiten Weltkrieg', *Zeitschrift für Geschichtswissenschaft*, 24 (1976), 5–23.

DÜLFFER, JOST, *Weimar, Hitler und die Marine: Reichspolitik und Flottenbau 1920–1939*, with appendix by Jürgen Rohwer (Düsseldorf, 1973).

DUPUIS, DOBRILLO, *Forzate il blocco! L'odissea delle navi italiane rimaste fuori degli stretti allo scoppio della guerra* (Biblioteca del mare, 130; La guerra sui mari, 17; Milan, 1975).

EDEN, ROBERT ANTHONY, *The Reckoning: The Memoirs of Anthony Eden, Earl of Avon* (London and Boston, Mass., 1965).

EL DESSOUKI, MOHAMED KAMAL, 'Hitler und der Nahe Osten' (diss. Berlin, 1963).

ENGEL, GERHARD, *Heeresadjutant bei Hitler 1938–1943: Aufzeichnungen des Majors Engel*, ed. with comm. by Hildegard v. Kotze (Schriftenreihe der Vierteljahrshefte für Zeitgeschichte, 29; Stuttgart, 1975).

ERICKSON, JOHN, *The Soviet High Command: A Military-political History 1918–1941* (London and New York, 1962).

Esercito italiano dal I° tricolore al I° centenario, L', Stato Maggiore dell'Esercito, Ufficio Storico (Rome, 1978).

Esercito italiano nella 2ª guerra mondiale, L': Immagini, Stato Maggiore dell'Esercito, Ufficio Storico (Rome, 1978).

Esercito italiano tra la 1ª e la 2ª guerra mondiale, L': Novembre 1918–giugno 1940, Ministero della Difesa, Stato Maggiore dell'Esercito, Ufficio Storico (Rome, 1954).

FABRY, PHILIPP WALTER, *Balkan-Wirren 1940–41: Diplomatische und militärische Vorbereitungen des deutschen Donauüberganges* (Beiträge zur Wehrforschung, 9–10; Darmstadt, 1966).

FALDELLA, EMILIO, *Revisione di giudizi: L'Italia e la seconda guerra mondiale*[2] (Testimoni per la storia del 'nostro tempo', collana di memorie, diari e documenti, 23; Forlì, 1960).

FAVAGROSSA, CARLO, *Perchè perdemmo la guerra: Mussolini e la produzione bellica*[2] (Milan, 1947).

FECHTER, HELMUT, and HÜMMELCHEN, GERHARD, *Seekriegsatlas Mittelmeer—Schwarzes Meer 1940–1943*, with 42 principal and 34 secondary maps, two of these in three colours; foreword by Vice-Admiral (retd.) Professor Friedrich Ruge (Munich, 1972).

FEHRENBACH, THEODORE REED, *F.D.R.'s Undeclared War, 1939 to 1941* (New York, 1967).

FERRETTI, VALDO, 'La politica estera giapponese e i rapporti con l'Italia e la Germania (1935–1939)', *Storia contemporanea*, 7 (1976), 783–824.

FEST, JOACHIM, *Hitler: Eine Biographie*[7] (Frankfurt a.M., 1974). [Trans. Richard and Clare Winston, *Hitler* (New York, 1974).]

FINK, JÜRG, *Die Schweiz aus der Sicht des Dritten Reiches 1933–1945: Einschätzung und Beurteilung der Schweiz durch die oberste deutsche Führung seit der Machtergreifung Hitlers. Stellenwert des Kleinstaates Schweiz im Kalkül der nationalsozialistischen Exponenten in Staat, Diplomatie, Wehrmacht, SS, Nachrichtendiensten und Presse* (Zurich, 1985).

FIORAVANZO, GIUSEPPE, 'Die Kriegführung der Achse im Mittelmeer', *MR* 55 (1958), 17–24.

—— 'Italian Strategy in the Mediterranean 1940–1943', *United States Naval Institute Proceedings*, 84/9 (1958), 65–72.

FISCHER, FRITZ, *Griff nach der Weltmacht: Die Kriegszielpolitik des kaiserlichen Deutschland 1914/1918*[3], rev. edn. (Düsseldorf, 1964). [Trans. *Germany's Aims in the First World War* (London, 1967).]

FLEISCHER, HAGEN, *Im Kreuzschatten der Mächte: Griechenland 1941–1944*, 2 vols. (Studien zur Geschichte Südosteuropas, 2; Frankfurt a.M., Berne, and New York, 1986).

FORBES, DENIS LUTHER, 'The Battle of Crete from the German View: Pyrrhic Victory or Unexploited Success?' (diss. Mississippi State University, 1975).

Foreign Relations of the United States: Diplomatic Papers 1940, i. *General*; ii. *General and Europe*; iii. *The British Commonwealth, The Soviet Union, The Near East and Africa* (New York, 1972).

FÖRSTER, GERHARD, HELMERT, HEINZ, and SCHNITTER, HELMUT, 'Der Überfall Hitlerdeutschlands auf Jugoslawien und Griechenland im Frühjahr 1941', *Militärwesen*, 5 (1961), 358–76.

FÖRSTER, JÜRGEN, 'Rumäniens Weg in die deutsche Abhängigkeit: Zur Rolle der deutschen Militärmission 1940/41', *MGM* 25 (1979), 47–77.

FRICKE, GERT, *Kroatien 1941–1944: Der 'Unabhängige Staat' in der Sicht des deutschen bevollmächtigten Generals in Agram, Glaise v. Horstenau* (Einzelschriften zur militärischen Geschichte des Zweiten Weltkrieges, 8; Freiburg i.Br., 1972).

FRIEDLÄNDER, SAUL, *Auftakt zum Untergang: Hitler und die Vereinigten Staaten von Amerika 1939–1941* (Stuttgart, Berlin, Cologne, and Mainz, 1965). [Trans. Aline B. and Alexander Werth, *Prelude to Downfall: Hitler and the United States 1939–1941* (London, 1967).]

Fronte terra: L'armamento italiano nella 2a guerra mondiale. Carri armati in servizio fra le due guerre, i (Rome, 1972).

FRUS: see *Foreign Relations of the United States*.

FRYE, ALTON, *Nazi Germany and the American Hemisphere, 1933–1941* (New Haven, NJ, 1967).

FUDULI, FRANCO, 'La fanteria italiana: Regina delle battaglie', *Rivista militare*, 103/2 (1980), 33–56.

'Führer Conferences on Naval Affairs': see *Lagevorträge*.

FUNK, ARTHUR L., 'Negotiating the "Deal with Darlan"', *Journal of Contemporary History*, 8/2 (1973), 81–117.

FUNKE, MANFRED, *Sanktionen und Kanonen: Hitler, Mussolini und der internationale Abessinienkonflikt 1934–1936*[2] (Bonner Schriften zur Politik und Zeitgeschichte, 2; Düsseldorf, 1971).

—— 'Die deutsch-italienischen Beziehungen: Antibolschewismus und außenpolitische Interessenkonkurrenz als Strukturprinzip der "Achse"', in *Hitler, Deutschland und die Mächte* (q.v.), 823–46.

—— 'Italien: Zur Großmachtpolitik eines deutschen Juniorpartners', in *Innen- und Außenpolitik* (q.v.), 77–86.

—— 'Hitler, Mussolini und die Substanz der "Achse"', in *Nationalsozialistische Diktatur 1933–1945: Eine Bilanz*, ed. Karl Dietrich Bracher, Manfred Funke, and Hans-Adolf Jacobsen (Schriftenreihe der Bundeszentrale für politische Bildung, 192; Bonn, 1983), 345–69.

GABLE, DAVID LEE, 'Italy, Germany and the Alto Adige Question 1938–1945' (diss. Memphis State University, Tennessee, 1977).

GABRIELE, MARIANO, *Operazione C 3: Malta* (Rome, 1965).

—— 'La guerre des convois entre l'Italie et l'Afrique du Nord', in *La Guerre en Méditerranée* (q.v.), 281–301.

GAFENCU, GRIGORE, *Préliminaires de la guerre à l'Est*. [Trans. Fletcher-Allen, *Prelude to* the *Russian Campaign: From the Moscow Pact . . . to the Opening of Hostilities in Russia* (London, 1945).]

GALLINARI, VINCENZO, *Le operazioni del giugno 1940 sulle Alpi occidentali* (Rome, 1981).

GARELLO, GIANCARLO, *Regia aeronautica e armée de l'air 1940–1943* (Rome, 1975).

GAYDA, VIRGINIO, *Was will Italien?* (Leipzig, 1941).

GEHRKE, ULRICH, *Persien in der deutschen Orientpolitik während des Ersten Weltkrieges*, 2 vols. (Darstellungen zur auswärtigen Politik, 1; Stuttgart, 1960).

General Staffs and Diplomacy before the Second World War, ed. Adrian Preston (London and Totowa, NJ, 1978).

GENTILE, RODOLFO, *Storia delle operazioni aeree nella seconda guerra mondiale (1939–1945)*^{2} (Rome, 1956).

—— *Storia dell'aeronautica dalle origini ai giorni nostri*^{2} (Rome, 1958).

Geschichte des zweiten Weltkrieges 1939–1945, in 12 vols., by an editorial committee, iii. *Der Beginn des Krieges: Die Vorbereitung der Aggression gegen die UdSSR* (East Berlin, 1977).

GESCHKE, GÜNTER, *Die deutsche Frankreichpolitik 1940 von Compiègne bis Montoire: Das Problem einer deutsch-französischen Annäherung nach dem Frankreichfeldzug* (*WWR*, suppl. 12–13; Berlin and Frankfurt a.M., 1960).

GIANNINI, AMEDEO, 'Il convegno italo-francese di San Remo (1939)', *Rivista di studi politici internazionali*, 20 (1953), 91–9.

—— 'L'accordo italo-germanico per il carbone (1940)', *Rivista di studi politici internazionali*, 21 (1954), 462–8.

GILBERT, MARTIN, *Finest Hour: Winston S. Churchill 1939–1941* (London, 1983).

GIURATI, GIOVANNI, *La parabola di Mussolini nei ricordi di un gerarca* (Bari, 1981).

GLASNECK, JOHANNES, and KIRCHEISEN, INGE, *Türkei und Afghanistan: Brennpunkte der Orientpolitik im zweiten Weltkrieg* (Schriftenreihe des Instituts für Allgemeine Geschichte an der Martin-Luther-Universität Halle-Wittenberg, 3; East Berlin, 1968).

GOEBBELS, JOSEPH, *Die Tagebücher von Joseph Goebbels: Sämtliche Fragmente*, ed. Elke Fröhlich for the Institut für Zeitgeschichte and in collaboration with the Bundesarchiv. pt. 1: *Aufzeichnungen 1924–1941*, vol. iv. *1 Jan. 1940–8 July 1941* (Munich, New York, London, and Paris, 1987).

GORDON, BERTRAM M., *Collaborationism in France during the Second World War* (Ithaca, NY, and London, 1980).

GORNENSKI, NIKIFOR, 'Hitleristkata politika na razedinjavane i protivopostovjane na dăržavite v Jugoiztočna Europa prez Vtorata svetovna vojna' (Hitlerite policy of disuniting and confronting the states of south-east Europe during the Second World War), *Mitteilungen der militärgeschichtlichen wissenschaftlichen Gesellschaft* [Sofia], 6 (1968), 108–47.

—— and KAMENOV, E., 'La politique intérieure', *Revue d'histoire de la deuxième guerre mondiale*, 18/72 (1968), 23–41.

GÖTZEL, HERMANN, 'Die Luftlandung bei Korinth am 26.4.1941: Ihre Vorgeschichte, Vorbereitung und Durchführung', *Wehrkunde*, 10 (1961), 199–205.

—— *Generaloberst Kurt Student und seine Fallschirmjäger: Die Erinnerungen des Generaloberst Kurt Student* (Friedberg, 1980).

GRAZIANI, RODOLFO, *Ho difeso la patria: Otto documenti fuori testo* (Milan, 1949).

GRAZZI, EMANUELE, *Il principio della fine: L'impresa di Grecia* (Rome, 1945).

II. Printed Sources

Great Britain, Cabinet Office: Principal War Telegrams and Memoranda 1940–1943. Middle East, vols. i–iii (Cabinet History Series; Nendeln, 1976).

GREENFIELD, KENT ROBERTS, 'Die acht Hauptentscheidungen der amerikanischen Strategie im zweiten Weltkrieg', in *Probleme des Zweiten Weltkrieges* (q.v.), 271–6.

GREINER, HELMUTH, *Die oberste Wehrmachtführung 1939–1943* (Wiesbaden, 1951).

GREISELIS, WALDIS, *Das Ringen um den Brückenkopf Tunesien 1942/43: Strategie der 'Achse' und Innenpolitik im Protektorat* (Europäische Hochschulschriften, Ser. 3, vol. 67; Frankfurt a.M. and Berne, 1976).

GRENZEBACH, WILLIAM SOUTHWARD, jun., 'Germany's Informal Empire in East-Central Europe: German Economic Policy towards Yugoslavia and Rumania, 1933–1939' (diss. Brandeis University, Mass., 1978).

Griff nach Südosteuropa: Neue Dokumente über die Politik des deutschen Imperialismus und Militarismus gegenüber Südosteuropa im zweiten Weltkrieg, ed. with intro. by W. Schumann (East Berlin, 1973).

GRIMALDI, UGOBERTO ALFASSIO, and BOZZETTI, GHERARDO, *Dieci giugno 1940: Il giorno della follia* (Rome and Bari, 1974).

GROBBA, FRITZ, *Männer und Mächte im Orient: 25 Jahre diplomatischer Tätigkeit im Orient* (Göttingen, Zurich, Berlin, and Frankfurt a.M., 1967).

GROEHLER, OLAF, 'Die Rolle Nordafrikas in der Kriegführung des deutschen Imperialismus während des zweiten Weltkrieges', *Militärwesen*, 7 (1963), 412–28.

—— 'Kolonialforderungen als Teil der faschistischen Kriegszielplanung'. *Zeitschrift für Militärgeschichte*, 4 (1965), 547–62.

GROSCURTH, HELMUTH, *Tagebücher eines Abwehroffiziers 1938–1940*, ed. Helmut Krausnick and Harald C. Deutsch in collaboration with Hildegard von Kotze (Quellen und Darstellungen zur Zeitgeschichte, 19; Stuttgart, 1970).

GRUCHMANN, LOTHAR, 'Völkerrecht und Moral: Ein Beitrag zur Problematik der amerikanischen Neutralitätspolitik 1939–1941', *VfZG* 8 (1960), 384–418.

—— *Nationalsozialistische Großraumordnung: Die Konstruktion einer 'deutschen Monroe-Doktrin'* (Schriftenreihe der Vierteljahrshefte für Zeitgeschichte, 4; Stuttgart, 1962).

—— *Der Zweite Weltkrieg: Kriegführung und Politik* (dtv-Weltgeschichte des 20. Jahrhunderts, 10; Munich, 1967).

—— 'Die "verpaßten strategischen Chancen" der Achsenmächte im Mittelmeerraum 1940/41', *VfZG* 18 (1970), 456–75.

GUARNERI, FELICE, *Autarkie und Außenhandel* (Kieler Vorträge, 65; Jena, 1941).

—— *Battaglie economiche tra le due grandi guerre*, ii. 1936–1950 (Milan, 1953).

GUEDALLA, PHILIP, *Middle East 1940–1942; A Study in Air Power* (London, 1944).

Guerra in Africa orientale, giugno 1940–novembre 1941, La, Ministero della Difesa, Stato Maggiore Esercito, Ufficio Storico (Rome, 1952).

Guerre en Méditerranée 1939–1945, La: Actes du Colloque International tenu à Paris du 8 au 11 avril 1969, ed. Comité d'histoire de la deuxième guerre mondiale (Paris, 1971).

GUNDELACH, KARL, 'Der Kampf um Kreta 1941', in *Entscheidungsschlachten des zweiten Weltkrieges*, commissioned by Arbeitskreis für Wehrforschung, Stuttgart, ed. Hans-Adolf Jacobsen and Jürgen Rohwer (Frankfurt a.M., 1960), 95–134.

—— *Die deutsche Luftwaffe im Mittelmeer 1940–1945*, in 2 parts (Europäische Hochschulschriften, Ser. 3, Vol. 136; Frankfurt a.M., Berne, and Cirencester, 1981).

GÜNZEL, KARL, 'Die wirtschaftliche Entwicklung zwischen den Kriegen', in *Osteuropa-Handbuch* (q.v.), i. 215–27.

GUNZENHÄUSER, MAX, *Die Pariser Friedenskonferenz 1919 und die Friedensverträge 1919–1920; Literaturbericht und Bibliographie* (Schriften der Bibliothek für Zeitgeschichte, Weltkriegsbücherei Stuttgart, NF der Bibliographien der Weltkriegsbücherei, 9; Frankfurt a.M., 1970).

HABEDANK, HEINZ, 'Zur Eingliederung des deutsch-bulgarischen Waren- und Zahlungsverkehrs in die wirtschaftlichen Kriegsvorbereitungen und in die Kriegswirtschaft des deutschen Imperialismus (1931–1941)', *Bulletin des Arbeitskreises 'Zweiter Weltkrieg'*, 3–4 (1978), 88–116.

HALDER, FRANZ, *Hitler als Feldherr* (Munich, 1949).

—— *Generaloberst Halder: Kriegstagebuch. Tägliche Aufzeichnungen des Chefs des Generalstabes des Heeres 1939–1942*, pub, by Arbeitskreis für Wehrforschung, Stuttgart, ed. Hans-Adolf Jacobsen and Alfred Philippi: i. *Vom Polenfeldzug bis zum Ende der Westoffensive (14.8.1939–30.6.1940)*; ii. *Von der geplanten Landung in England bis zum Beginn des Ostfeldzuges (1.7.1940–21.6.1941)*; iii. *Der Rußlandfeldzug bis zum Marsch auf Stalingrad (22.6.1941–24.9.1942)* (Stuttgart, 1962–4). [Trans. and ed. Trevor N. Dupuy, *The Halder Diaries, 1939–1942*, 2 vols. (Boulder, Colo., 1975). German edn. cited as Halder, *KTB*.]

Handbuch der europäischen Geschichte, vii. *Europa im Zeitalter der Weltmächte*, ed. Theodor Schieder (Stuttgart, 1979).

HANDEL-MAZZETTI, PETER Frhr, VON, 'Der britische Flugzeugangriff auf die italienische Flotte im Hafen von Tarent in der Nacht 11./12. November 1940', *MR* 50 (1953), 115–20.

HARDIE, FRANK, *The Abyssinian Crisis* (London, 1974).

HARRIMAN, HELGA H., 'The German Minority in Yugoslavia, 1941–1945' (diss. Oklahoma State University, 1973).

HARRIMAN, W. AVERELL, and ABEL, ELIE, *Special Envoy to Churchill and Stalin, 1941–1946* (New York, 1975).

HARRIS, RUTH ROY, 'The Shifting Winds: American Soviet Rapprochement from the Fall of France to the Attack on Pearl Harbor, June 1940–December 1941' (diss. The George Washington University, Washington, DC, 1975).

HART, B. H. LIDDELL, *History of the Second World War* (London, 1970).

HARTMANN, PETER CLAUS, 'Frankreich im Jahr 1941: Seine militärische, politische und wirtschaftliche Situation', in *Das Jahr 1941* (q.v.), 39–55.

HASS, GERHART, *Von München bis Pearl Harbor: Zur Geschichte der deutsch-amerikanischen Beziehungen 1938–1941* (East Berlin, 1965).

—— 'Kriegsziele und militärische Entschlußfassung im faschistischen Deutschland', *Revue internationale d'histoire militaire*, 43 (1979), 89–104.

HASSELL, ULRICH VON, 'Deutschland und der Südosten im Rahmen der zukünftigen europäischen Wirtschaft', *Der Vierjahresplan*, 5 (1941), 322–4.

—— 'Deutschlands wirtschaftliche Interessen und Aufgaben in Südosteuropa', *Zeitschrift für Politik*, 31 (1941), 481–8.

—— *Vom anderen Deutschland: Aus den nachgelassenen Tagebüchern 1938–1944* (Zurich and Freiburg i.Br., 1946). [Trans. Hugh Gibson, *The von Hassell Diaries. 1938–1944* (London, 1948).]

HAUNER, MILAN, 'Das nationalsozialistische Deutschland und Indien', in *Hitler, Deutschland und die Mächte* (q.v.), 430–53.

—— 'Did Hitler Want a World Dominion?', *Journal of Contemporary History*, 13 (1978), 15–32.

—— *India in Axis Strategy: Germany, Japan, and Indian Nationalists in the Second World War* (Veröffentlichungen des Deutschen Historischen Instituts London, 7; Stuttgart, 1981).

HECKMANN, WOLF, *Rommels Krieg in Afrika: 'Wüstenfüchse gegen Wüstenratten'* (Bergisch Gladbach, 1976).

HELBICH, WOLFGANG J., *Franklin D. Roosevelt* (Berlin, 1971).

Hellēnikos stratos kata ton deuteron pagkosmion polemon, Ho [The Greek Army in the Second World War], i–vi, ed. Genikon Epiteleion Stratou [general staff of the army] (Athens, 1956–9).

HENKE, JOSEF, *England in Hitlers politischem Kalkül 1935–1939* (Schriften des Bundesarchivs, 20; Boppard, 1973).

HENRICI, SIGFRID, 'Sarajevo 1941: Der raidartige Vorstoß einer mot. Division', *WWR* 10 (1960), 197–208.

HEPP, LEO, 'Die 12, Armee im Balkanfeldzug 1941', *WWR* 5 (1955), 199–216.

HERDE, PETER, *Pearl Harbor. 7. Dezember 1941: Der Ausbruch des Krieges zwischen Japan und den Vereinigten Staaten und die Ausweitung des europäischen Krieges zum Zweiten Weltkrieg* (Impulse der Forschung, 33; Darmstadt, 1980).

—— *Italien, Deutschland und der Weg in den Krieg im Pazifik 1941* (Sitzungsberichte der Wissenschaftlichen Gesellschaft an der Johann Wolfgang Goethe-Universität Frankfurt am Main, 20.1; Wiesbaden, 1983).

HERING, GUNNAR, 'Griechenland vom Lausanner Frieden bis zum Ende der Obersten-Diktatur 1923–1974', in *Handbuch der europäischen Geschichte*, vii (q.v.), 1313–38.

HERINGTON, JOHN, *Air War against Germany and Italy 1939–1943* (Australia in the War of 1931–1945, Series 3: Air, vol. 3; Canberra, 1962).

HIGHAM, ROBIN, 'Generals and Guarantees: Some Aspects of Aid to Greece in 1940–1941' (lecture).

HILDEBRAND, KLAUS, *Vom Reich zum Weltreich: Hitler. NSDAP und koloniale Frage 1919–1945* (Veröffentlichungen des Historischen Instituts der Universität Mannheim, 1; Munich, 1969).

—— 'Deutsch-Mittelafrika: Ein Kriegsziel Hitlers in den Jahren 1940–1942?', in *Hitler, Deutschland und die Mächte* (q.v.), 383–406.

—— 'Hitlers "Programm" und seine Realisierung 1939–1942', in *Hitler, Deutschland und die Mächte* (q.v.) 63–93.

—— 'Deutschland, die Westmächte und das Kolonialproblem: Ein Beitrag über Hitlers Außenpolitik vom Ende der Münchener Konferenz bis zum "Griff nach Prag"', in *Nationalsozialistische Außenpolitik* (q.v.), 377–413.

—— *Das Dritte Reich* (Oldenbourg Grundriß der Geschichte, 17; Munich and Vienna, 1979). [Trans. P. S. Falla, *The Third Reich* (London, 1984).]

—— *Deutsche Außenpolitik 1933–1945; Kalkül oder Dogma?*[4], with afterword: 'Die Geschichte der deutschen Außenpolitik (1933–1945) im Urteil der neueren Forschung' (Stuttgart, Berlin, Cologne, and Mainz, 1980). [Orig. edn. trans. Anthony Fothergill, *The Foreign Policy of the Third Reich* (London, 1973).]

—— 'Der Hitler-Stalin-Pakt als ideologisches Problem', in Hillgruber and Hildebrand, *Kalkül* (q.v.), 35–61.

HILLGRUBER, ANDREAS, 'Deutschland und Ungarn 1933–1944: Ein Überblick über die politischen und militärischen Beziehungen im Rahmen der europäischen Politik', *WWR* 9 (1959), 651–76.

—— *Südost-Europa im Zweiten Weltkrieg: Literaturbericht und Bibliographie* (Schriften der Bibliothek für Zeitgeschichte, Weltkriegsbücherei Stuttgart, NF der Bibliographien der Weltkriegsbücherei, 1; Frankfurt a.M., 1962).

—— 'England in Hitlers außenpolitischer Konzeption', *Historische Zeitschrift*, 218 (1974), 65–84.

—— *Der Zenit des Zweiten Weltkrieges Juli 1941* (Institut für Europäische Geschichte Mainz, Vorträge, 65; Wiesbaden, 1977).

—— 'Politik und Strategie Hitlers im Mittelmeerraum', in id., *Deutsche Großmacht- und Weltpolitik im 19. und 20. Jahrhundert* (Düsseldorf, 1977), 276–95.

—— 'Der Faktor Amerika in Hitlers Strategie 1938–1941', in *Nationalsozialistische Außenpolitik* (q.v.), 493–525.

—— 'Die "Hitler-Koalition": Eine Skizze zur Geschichte und Struktur des "Weltpolitischen Dreiecks" Berlin-Rom-Tokio 1933–1945', in *Vom Staat des Ancien Regime zum modernen Parteienstaat: Festschrift für Theodor Schieder zu seinem 70. Geburtstag*, ed. Helmut Berding et al. (Munich and Vienna, 1978), 467–83.

—— *Sowjetische Außenpolitik im Zweiten Weltkrieg* (Königstein im Taunus and Düsseldorf, 1979).

—— *Zur Entstehung des Zweiten Weltkrieges: Forschungsstand und Literatur. Mit einer Chronik der Ereignisse September–Dezember 1939* (Düsseldorf, 1980).

—— 'Der Hitler-Stalin-Pakt und die Entfesselung des Zweiten Weltkrieges', in Hillgruber and Hildebrand, *Kalkül* (q.v.), 7–34.

—— *Hitlers Strategie: Politik und Kriegführung 1940–1941*[2] (Munich, 1982).

—— 'Noch einmal: Hitlers Wendung gegen die Sowjetunion 1940. Nicht (Militär-) "Strategie oder Ideologie", sondern "Programm" und "Weltkriegsstrategie"', *GWU* 33 (1982), 214–26.

—— *Der Zweite Weltkrieg 1939–1945: Kriegsziele und Strategie der großen Mächte* (Stuttgart, Berlin, Cologne, and Mainz, 1982).

—— and HILDEBRAND, KLAUS, *Kalkül zwischen Macht und Ideologie: Der Hitler-Stalin-Pakt. Parallelen bis heute?* (Texte und Thesen, 125, Sachgebiet Politik; Zurich and Osnabrück, 1980).

—— and HÜMMELCHEN, GERHARD, *Chronik des Zweiten Weltkrieges: Kalendarium militärischer und politischer Ereignisse 1939–1945*, rev. and enlarged edn. (Düsseldorf, 1978).

HINSLEY, FRANCIS HARRY, *British Intelligence in the Second World War: Its Influence on Strategy and Operations*, 2 vols. (History of the Second World War; London, 1979, 1981).

HIRSCHFELD, YAIR P., *Deutschland und Iran im Spielfeld der Mächte: Internationale Beziehungen unter Reza Schah 1921–1941* (Schriftenreihe des Instituts für Deutsche Geschichte, Universität Tel Aviv, 5; Düsseldorf, 1980).

HIRSZOWICZ, LUKASZ, *The Third Reich and the Arab East* (London et al., 1966).

Hitler, Deutschland und die Mächte: Materialien zur Außenpolitik des Dritten Reiches, ed. Manfred Funke (Bonner Schriften zur Zeitgeschichte, 12; Düsseldorf, 1976).

Hitler e Mussolini: Lettere e documenti, with intro. and notes by Vittorio Zincone (Milan, 1946).

Hitler's Testament: see *Testament of Adolf Hitler*.

Hitler's Secret Book: see *Hitlers zweites Buch*.

Hitler's War Directives: see next entry.

II. Printed Sources

Hitlers Weisungen für die Kriegführung 1939–1945: Dokumente des Oberkommandos der Wehrmacht, ed. Walther Hubatsch (Frankfurt a.M., 1962 for pt. III; Munich, 1965 (= dtv-documente, 278–9) for pts. I, II, IV, V). [Trans. with comment by H. R. Trevor-Roper, *Hitler's War Directives 1939–1945* (London, 1964).]

Hitlers zweites Buch: Ein Dokument aus dem Jahre 1928, with intro. and commentary by Gerhard L. Weinberg (Quellen und Darstellungen zur Zeitgeschichte, 7; Stuttgart, 1961). [Trans. Salvator Attanasio, *Hitler's Secret Book* (New York, 1962).]

HNILICKA, KARL, *Das Ende auf dem Balkan 1944/45: Die militärische Räumung Jugoslawiens durch die deutsche Wehrmacht* (Studien und Dokumente zur Geschichte des Zweiten Weltkrieges, 13; Göttingen, Zurich, and Frankfurt a.M., 1970).

HÖHNE, HEINZ, *Canaris: Patriot im Zwielicht* (Munich, 1976). [Trans. J. Maxwell Brownjohn, *Canaris* (London, 1979).]

HOPPE, HANS-JOACHIM. 'Deutschland und Bulgarien 1918–1945', in *Hitler, Deutschland und die Mächte* (q.v.), 604–11.

—— 'Die Balkanstaaten Rumänien, Jugoslawien, Bulgarien: Nationale Gegensätze und NS-Großraumpolitik', in *Innen- und Außenpolitik* (q.v.), 161–75.

—— *Bulgarien: Hitlers eigenwilliger Verbündeter. Eine Fallstudie zur nationalsozialistischen Südosteuropapolitik* (Studien zur Zeitgeschichte, 15; Stuttgart, 1979).

HOPTNER, JACOB B., *Yugoslavia in Crisis 1934–1941* (East Central European Studies of Columbia University; New York and London, 1962).

HORY, LADISLAUS, and BROSZAT, MARTIN, *Der kroatische Ustascha-Staat 1941–1945* (Schriftenreihe der Vierteljahrshefte für Zeitgeschichte, 8; Stuttgart, 1964).

HOWARD, CONSTANCE, 'Switzerland 1939–1946', in *Survey of International Affairs*, ed. Arnold and Veronica Toynbee, vii. *The War and the Neutrals* (London, New York, and Toronto, 1956), 199–230.

HOWARD, MICHAEL, *The Mediterranean Strategy in the Second World War* (New York and Washington, 1968).

HUGHES, SERGE, *The Fall and Rise of Modern Italy* (New York and London, 1967).

HÜMMELCHEN, GERHARD, and ROHWER, JÜRGEN, 'Vor zwanzig Jahren', *MR* 58 (1961), 116–23.

IACHINO, ANGELO, *La sorpresa di Matapan* (Verona, 1957).

—— *Tramonto di una grande marina*[2] (Milan and Verona, 1960).

Imperialismo italiano e la Jugoslavia, L': Atti del convegno italo-jugoslavo. Ancona 14–16 ottobre 1977 (Studi sulla Resistenza, 15; Urbino, 1981).

IMT: see *Trial*.

In Africa settentrionale: La preparazione al conflitto. L'avanzata su Sidi el Barrani (ottobre 1935–settembre 1940), Ministero della Difesa Stato Maggiore Esercito, Ufficio storico (Rome, 1955).

Innen- und Außenpolitik unter nationalsozialistischer Bedrohung: Determinanten internationaler Beziehungen in historischen Fallstudien, ed. Erhard Forndran, Frank Golczewski, and Dieter Riesenberger (Opladen, 1977).

IRVING, DAVID, *The Trail of the Fox: The Life of Field-Marshal Erwin Rommel* (London, 1977).

—— *The War Path: Hitler's Germany 1933–9* (London, 1978).

Italia fra tedeschi e alleati, L': La politica estera fascista e la seconda guerra mondiale, ed. Renzo De Felice (Bologna, 1973).

Italiani sul fronte russo, Gli, ed. Istituto Storico della Resistenza in Cuneo e Provincia (Bari, 1982).

JÄCKEL, EBERHARD, *Frankreich in Hitlers Europa: Die deutsche Frankreichpolitik im Zweiten Weltkrieg* (Quellen und Darstellungen zur Zeitgeschichte, 14; Stuttgart, 1966).

JACKSON, WILLIAM G. F., *The North African Campaign, 1940-43*, with maps by Caroline Metcalfe-Gibson (London and Sydney, 1975).

JACOBSEN, HANS-ADOLF, *Fall Gelb: Der Kampf um den deutschen Operationsplan zur Westoffensive 1940* (Veröffentlichungen des Instituts für Europäische Geschichte Mainz, 16 Abt. Universalgeschichte; Wiesbaden, 1957).

—— *1939-1945: Der Zweite Weltkrieg in Chronik und Dokumenten*[5] (Darmstadt, 1961).

—— *Deutsche Kriegführung 1939-1945: Ein Überblick* (Schriftenreihe der Niedersächsischen Landeszentrale für Politische Bildung: Zeitgeschichte 12; Hanover, 1961).

—— *Der Zweite Weltkrieg: Grundzüge der Politik und Strategie in Dokumenten* (Fischer Bücherei, 645-6; Frankfurt a.M. and Hamburg, 1965).

—— *Der Weg zur Teilung der Welt: Politik und Strategie 1939-1945*[2] (Koblenz and Bonn, 1979).

JACOMONI DI SAN SAVINO, FRANCESCO, *La politica dell'Italia in Albania nelle testimonianze del Luogotenete del Re Francesco Jacomoni di San Savino* (Rocca San Casciano, 1965).

Jahr 1941 in der europäischen Politik, Das, ed. Karl Bosl (Munich and Vienna, 1972).

JAKOBSEN, MAX, *Diplomatie im Finnischen Winterkrieg 1939/40* (Düsseldorf and Vienna, 1970).

JÄSCHKE, GOTTHARD, 'Das Osmanische Reich vom Berliner Kongreß bis zu seinem Ende (1878-1920/22)', in *Handbuch der europäischen Geschichte*, vi. *Europa im Zeitalter der Nationalstaaten und europäische Weltpolitik bis zum Ersten Weltkrieg*, ed. Theodor Schieder (Stuttgart, 1968), 539-46.

—— 'Die Türkei als Nationalstaat seit der Revolution Mustafa Kemal (Atatürk)s 1920-1974', in *Handbuch der europäischen Geschichte*, vii (q.v.), 1339-51.

JUKIĆ, ILIJA, *The Fall of Yugoslavia* (New York and London, 1974).

JUNKER, DETLEF, 'Zur Struktur und Organisation der amerikanischen Rüstungswirtschaft 1939-1945', in *Kriegswirtschaft und Rüstung* (q.v.), 314-32.

—— *Franklin D. Roosevelt: Macht und Vision, Präsident in Krisenzeiten* (Persönlichkeit und Geschichte, 105-6; Göttingen, 1979).

KAHLE, GÜNTER, *Das Kaukasusprojekt der Alliierten vom Jahre 1940* (Rheinisch-Westfälische Akademie der Wissenschaften: Geisteswissenschaftliche Vorträge, G 186; Opladen, 1973).

KEHRIG, MANFRED, 'Der Balkan als Kriegsschauplatz im Zweiten Weltkrieg: Literaturbericht und Bibliographie' (typescript; Freiburg i.Br., 1970).

KENNEDY, PAUL M., *The Rise and Fall of British Naval Mastery* (London, 1976).

KESKIN, HAKKI, *Die Türkei: Vom Osmanischen Reich zum Nationalstaat. Werdegang einer Unterentwicklung* (Berlin, 1981).

KESSELRING, ALBERT, 'Der Krieg im Mittelmeerraum', in *Bilanz des Zweiten Weltkrieges: Erkenntnisse und Verpflichtungen für die Zukunft* (Oldenburg and Hamburg, 1953), 65-80.

Keyes Papers, The: Selections from the Private and Official Correspondence of Admiral of the Fleet Baron Keyes of Zeebrugge, iii. *1939-1945*, ed. Paul G. Halpern (Navy Records Society, 122; London, 1981).

KIMBALL, WARREN F., *The Most Unsordid Act: Lend-lease. 1939-1941* (Baltimore, 1969).

KIMCHE, JON, *Spying for Peace: General Guisan and Swiss Neutrality* (London, 1961).
KIRKPATRICK, Sir IVONE A., *Mussolini: Study of a Demagogue* (London, 1964).
KISZLING, RUDOLF, *Die Kroaten: Der Schicksalsweg eines Südslawenvolkes* (Graz and Cologne, 1956).
KITSIKIS, DIMITRI, 'Informations et décision: La Grèce face à l'invasion allemande dans les Balkans (13 décembre 1940–6 avril 1941)', in *La Guerre en Méditerranée* (q.v.), 181–209.
KLEE, KARL, 'Der Entwurf zur Führer-Weisung Nr. 32 vom 11. Juni 1941; Eine quellenkritische Untersuchung', *WWR* 6 (1956), 127–41.
KLJAKOVIĆ, VOJMIR, 'The German–Italian Agreement on Spheres of Influence in the Balkans: With Particular Reference to Yugoslavia. A Survey of the Evolution of German Policy towards Italian Interests', in *The Third Reich and Yugoslavia* (q.v.), 132–44.
KNÉJÉVITSCH, RADOJE (Knežević, R.), 'Prince Paul, Hitler and Salonika', *International Affairs*, 27 (1951), 34–44.
KNIPPING, FRANZ, *Die amerikanische Rußland-Politik in der Zeit des Hitler-Stalin-Pakts 1939–1941* (Tübinger Studien zur Geschichte und Politik, 30; Tübingen, 1974).
KNOLL, HANS, *Jugoslawien in Strategie und Politik der Alliierten 1940–1943* (Südosteuropäische Arbeiten, 82; Munich, 1986).
KNOX, MACGREGOR, *Mussolini Unleashed, 1939–1941: Politics and Strategy in Fascist Italy's Last War* (Cambridge et al., 1982).
—— 'Fascist Italy Assesses its Enemies, 1935–1940', in *Knowing One's Enemies: Intelligence Assessment before the Two World Wars*, ed. Ernest R. May (Princeton, NJ, 1984), 347–72.
KOGAN, NORMAN, *The Politics of Italian Foreign Policy* (New York, 1963).
KOLIOPOULOS, JOHN S., *Greece and the British Connection 1935–1941* (Oxford, 1977).
Konzept für die 'Neuordnung' der Welt: Die Kriegsziele des faschistischen deutschen Imperialismus im zweiten Weltkrieg, by a group of authors under the direction of Wolfgang Schumann (East Berlin, 1977).
KOSIER, LJUBOMIR ST, *Großdeutschland und Jugoslawien (Aus der südslawischen Perspektive)*[2] (Berlin and Vienna, 1939).
KRAMER, HANS, *Geschichte Italiens*, ii. *Von 1494 bis zur Gegenwart* (Urban Bücher: Die wissenschaftliche Taschenbuchreihe, 109; Stuttgart, Berlin, Cologne and Mainz, 1968).
—— 'Über den Seekrieg Italiens 1940–1943', *Zeitgeschichte*, 2 (1974–5), 257–65.
—— 'Die italienische Luftwaffe vor dem Zweiten Weltkrieg und der italienische Luftkrieg 1940/41', in *Beiträge zur Zeitgeschichte: Festschrift für Ludwig Jedlicka zum 60. Geburtstag*, ed. Rudolf Neck and Adam Wandruszka (St Pölten, 1976), 263–80.
KRAUTKRÄMER, ELMAR, 'Die Entmachtung Lavals im Dezember 1940: Ein außenpolitisches Kalkül Vichys', *VfZG* 27 (1979), 79–112.
KREBS, GERHARD, *Japans Deutschlandpolitik 1935–1941: Eine Studie zur Vorgeschichte des pazifischen Krieges*, 2 vols. (Mitteilungen der Gesellschaft für Natur- und Völkerkunde Ostasiens, 91; Hamburg, 1984).
KRECKER, LOTHAR, *Deutschland und die Türkei im zweiten Weltkrieg* (Frankfurter wissenschaftliche Beiträge: Kulturwissenschaftliche Reihe, 12; Frankfurt a.M., 1964).
KREIDLER, EUGEN, *Die Eisenbahnen im Machtbereich der Achsenmächte während des Zweiten Weltkrieges: Einsatz und Leistung für die Wehrmacht und Kriegswirtschaft*

(Studien und Dokumente zur Geschichte des Zweiten Weltkrieges, 15; Frankfurt a.M. and Zurich, 1975).

Kriegspropaganda 1939-1941: Geheime Ministerkonferenzen im Reichspropagandaministerium, ed. with intro. by Willi A. Boelcke (Stuttgart, 1966).

Kriegstagebuch des Oberkommandos der Wehrmacht (Wehrmachtführungsstab) 1940-1945 [War diary of the OKW (Wehrmacht operational staff)], compiled by H. Greiner and P. E. Schramm; ed. P. E. Schramm for the Arbeitskreis für Wehrforschung, i. *1. August 1940-31. Dezember 1941*, with comments by Hans-Adolf Jacobsen (Frankfurt a.M., 1965).

Kriegswende Dezember 1941: Referate und Diskussionsbeiträge des internationalen historischen Symposiums in Stuttgart vom 17.-19. Sept. 1981, ed. Jürgen Rohwer and Eberhard Jäckel (Koblenz, 1984).

Kriegswirtschaft und Rüstung 1939-1945, ed. Friedrich Forstmeier and Hans-Erich Volkmann for the Militärgeschichtliches Forschungsamt (Düsseldorf, 1977).

KRIZMAN, BOGDAN, 'Yugoslavia's Accession to the Tripartite Pact', in *The Third Reich and Yugoslavia* (q.v.), 399-422.

KRÜGER, PETER, 'Das Jahr 1941 in der deutschen Kriegs- und Außenpolitik', in *Das Jahr 1941* (q.v.), 7-38.

KRUMPELT, IHNO, *Das Material und die Kriegführung* (Frankfurt a.M., 1968).

KUBY, ERICH, *Verrat auf deutsch: Wie das Dritte Reich Italien ruinierte* (Hamburg, 1982).

KÜHNE, HORST, 'Zur Kolonialpolitik des faschistischen deutschen Imperialismus, 1933-1939', *Zeitschrift für Geschichtswissenschaft*, 9 (1961), 514-37.

—— *Faschistische Kolonialideologie und zweiter Weltkrieg*, ed. Institut für Gesellschaftswissenschaften beim ZK der SED, Lehrstuhl für Geschichte und Arbeiterbewegung (East Berlin, 1962).

Kum'a N'dumbe III, Alexandre, *Hitler voulait l'Afrique: Le Projet du 3ᵉ Reich sur le continent africain* (Paris, 1980).

Lagevorträge des Oberbefehlshabers der Kriegsmarine vor Hitler 1939-1945, ed. Gerhard Wagner (Munich, 1972). [Trans. 'Führer Conferences on Naval Affairs, 1939-1945', in *Brassey's Naval Annual* (Portsmouth, 1948), 25-496.]

LANGER, JOHN DANIEL, 'The Formulation of American Aid Policy toward the Soviet Union, 1940-1943: The Hopkins Shop and the Department of State' (diss. Yale University, Conn., 1975).

LASH, JOSEPH P., *Roosevelt and Churchill, 1939-1941: The Partnership that Saved the West* (New York, 1976).

LATOUR, CONRAD F., *Südtirol und die Achse Berlin-Rom 1938-1945* (Schriftenreihe der Vierteljahrshefte für Zeitgeschichte, 5; Stuttgart, 1962).

LAWLOR, SHEILA, 'Greece, March 1941: The Politics of British Military Intervention', *Historical Journal*, 25 (1982), 933-46.

LEACH, BARRY A., *German Strategy against Russia 1939-1941* (Oxford, 1973).

LEE, JOHN M., *The Churchill Coalition* (London, 1980).

LEHMANN, HANS GEORG, 'Leitmotive nationalsozialistischer und großjapanischer Wirtschaftspolitik: Funks Unterredung mit Matsuoka am 28. März 1941 in Berlin', *Zeitschrift für Politik*, 21 (1974), 158-63.

LEIGHTON, RICHARD M., 'Les armes ou les armées: Origines de la politique d' "arsenal de la démocratie"', *Revue d'histoire de la deuxième guerre mondiale*, 17/65 (1967), 7-23.

LEUTZE, JAMES R., *Bargaining for Supremacy: Anglo-American Naval Collaboration 1937-1941* (Chapel Hill, 1977).
LEWIN, RONALD, *Rommel as Military Commander* (London, 1968).
—— *Churchill as Warlord* (London, 1973).
—— *The Chief: Field Marshal Lord Wavell, Commander-in-chief and Viceroy 1939-1947* (London et al., 1980).
LIBAL, MICHAEL, *Japans Weg in den Krieg: Die Außenpolitik der Kabinette Konoye 1940/1941* (Düsseldorf, 1971).
LICHERI, SEBASTIANO, *L'arma aerea italiana nella seconda guerra mondiale, 10 giugno 1940-8 settembre 1943* (Milan, 1976).
—— 'Sul potere aereo nella seconda guerra mondiale: Comparazione fra le principali aviazioni partecipanti al conflitto', *Revue internationale d'histoire militaire*, 39 (1978), 251-75.
LILL, RUDOLF, 'Italiens Außenpolitik 1935-1939', in *Weltpolitik 1933-1939: 13 Vorträge*, ed. Oswald Hauser for the Ranke-Gesellschaft (Göttingen, Frankfurt a.M., and Zurich, 1973), 78-109.
LINK, WERNER, 'Das nationalsozialistische Deutschland und die USA 1933-1941', *NPL* 18 (1973), 225-33.
LOI, EDOARDO, *Le operazioni delle unità italiane in Jugoslavia (1941-1943): Narrazione, documenti* (Rome, 1978).
LONG, GAVIN, *Greece, Crete and Syria* (Australia in the War of 1939-1945, Series 1, vol. ii; Canberra, 1953).
LORBEER, HANS-JOACHIM, *Westmächte gegen die Sowjetunion 1939-1941* (Einzelschriften zur militärischen Geschichte des Zweiten Weltkrieges, 18; Freiburg i.Br., 1975).
LOSSBERG, BERNHARD VON, *Im Wehrmachtführungsstab: Bericht eines Generalstabsoffiziers*[2] (Hamburg, 1950).
LUKACS, JOHN, *The Last European War: September 1939-December 1941* (London, 1977).
LURAGHI, RAIMONDO, *Storia della guerra civile americana*[4] (Biblioteca di cultura storica, 87; Turin, 1976).
—— 'L'ideologia della "guerra industriale", 1861-1945', in *Memorie storiche militari 1980*, ed. Stato Maggiore dell'Esercito, Ufficio Storico (Rome, 1980), 169-90.
LUTTON, WAYNE CHARLES, 'Malta and the Mediterranean: A Study in Allied and Axis Strategy. Planning and Intelligence during the Second World War' (diss. Carbondale, Ill., 1983).
MAČEK, VLADKO, *In the Struggle for Freedom* (New York, 1957).
MACINTYRE, DONALD, *The Battle for the Mediterranean* (London, 1964).
MACMILLAN, NORMAN, *The Royal Air Force in the World War*, iii (London, 1949).
MCNEILL, WILLIAM H., *America, Britain and Russia: Their Cooperation and Conflict 1941-1946* (Survey of International Affairs 1939-1946; London, New York, and Toronto, 1953).
MACVEAGH, LINCOLN, *Ambassador MacVeagh Reports: Greece 1933-1947*, ed. John O. Iatrides (Princeton, NJ, 1980).
MAHRAD, AHMAD, *Die Wirtschafts- und Handelsbeziehungen zwischen Iran und dem nationalsozialistischen Deutschen Reich* (Enzeli, 1979).
MAIONE, GIUSEPPE, *L'imperialismo straccione: Classi sociali e finanza di guerra dall'impresa etiopica al conflitto mondiale (1935-1943)* (Universale Paperbacks Il Mulino, 93; Bologna, 1979).

MANOUSAKIS, GREGOR, *Hellas—wohin? Das Verhältnis von Militär und Politik in Griechenland seit 1900* (Godesberg, 1967).
MARAVIGNA, PIETRO, *Come abbiamo perduto la guerra in Africa* (Rome, 1949).
MARDER, ARTHUR J., *From the Dardanelles to Oran: Studies of the Royal Navy in War and Peace 1915–1940* (London, 1974).
—— *Operation 'Menace': The Dakar Expedition and the Dudley North Affair* (London, New York, and Toronto, 1976).
MARGUERAT, PHILIPPE, *Le IIIe Reich et le pétrole roumain 1938–1940: Contribution à l'étude de la pénétration économique allemande dans les Balkans à la veille et au début de la Seconde Guerre mondiale* (Institut Universitaire de Hautes Études Internationales, Collection de Relations Internationales, 6; Geneva and Leiden, 1977).
Marina italiana, il 10 giugno 1940, La, suppl. to *Rivista Marittima*, 6 (June 1980).
Marina italiana nella seconda guerra mondiale, La, ed. Ufficio Storico della Marina Militare:

  i. *Dati statistici*[2], compiled by Giuseppe Fioravanzo (Rome, 1972).
  ii. *Navi perdute*, pt. 1: *Navi militari*[2] (Rome, 1959).
  iii. *Navi perdute*, pt. 2: *Navi mercantili* (Rome, 1952).
  iv. *Le azioni navali in Mediterraneo: Dal 10 giugno 1940 al 31 marzo 1941*[2], compiled by Giuseppe Fioravanzo (Rome, 1970).
  v. *Le azioni navali in Mediterraneo: Dal 1 aprile 1941 all'8 settembre 1943*[2], compiled by Giuseppe Fioravanzo (Rome, 1970).
  vi. *a guerra nel Mediterraneo: La difesa del traffico coll'Africa settentrionale*, pt. 1: *Dal 10 giugno 1940 al 30 settembre 1941*, compiled by Aldo Cocchia (Rome, 1958).
  vii. *La difesa del traffico con l'Africa gettentrionale: Dal 1 ottobre 1941 al 30 settembre 1942*, compiled by Aldo Cocchia (Rome, 1962).
  xii. *I sommergibili negli oceani*[2], compiled by Ubaldino Mori Ubaldini (Rome, 1966).
  xiii. *I sommergibili in Mediterraneo*, pt. 1: *Dal 10 giugno 1940 al 31 dicembre 1941*[2], compiled by Marcello Bertini (Rome, 1972).
  xiv. *I mezzi d'assalto*, compiled by Carlo De Risio (Rome, 1964).
  xxi. *L'organizzazione della marina durante il conflitto*, pt. 1: *Efficienza all'apertura delle ostilità*, compiled by Giuseppe Fioravanzo (Rome, 1972).

MARSHALL, GEORGE C., ARNOLD, HENRY H., and KING, ERNEST J., *The War Reports of General of the Army George C. Marshall. . . . General of the Army Henry H. Arnold . . . and Fleet Admiral Ernest J. King . . .* (New York, 1947).
MARTIN, BERND, *Deutschland und Japan im Zweiten Weltkrieg: Vom Angriff auf Pearl Harbor bis zur deutschen Kapitulation* (Studien und Dokumente zur Geschichte des Zweiten Weltkrieges, 11; Göttingen and Zurich, 1969).
—— *Friedensinitiativen und Machtpolitik im Zweiten Weltkrieg 1939–1942* (Geschichtliche Studien zur Politik und Gesellschaft, 6; Düsseldorf, 1974).
—— 'Japans Weltmachtstreben 1939–1941', in *Weltpolitik II* (q.v.), 98–130.
—— 'Die deutsch-japanischen Beziehungen während des Dritten Reiches', in *Hitler, Deutschland und die Mächte* (q.v.), 454–70.
—— 'Das "Dritte Reich" und die "Friedens"-Frage im Zweiten Weltkrieg', in *Nationalsozialistische Außenpolitik* (q.v.), 526–49.
—— 'Amerikas Durchbruch zur politischen Weltmacht: Die interventionistische Globalstrategie der Regierung Roosevelt 1933–1941', *MGM* 30 (1981), 57–98.

MARZARI, FRANK, 'Projects for an Italian-led Balkan Bloc of Neutrals, September–December 1939', *Historical Journal*, 13/4 (1970), 767–88.
MATL, JOSEF, 'Jugoslawien im Zweiten Weltkrieg', in *Osteuropa-Handbuch* (q.v.), i. 99–121.
MATLOFF, MAURICE, and SNELL, EDWIN M., *Strategic Planning for Coalition Warfare 1941–1942* (United States Army in World War II: The War Department, 3; Washington, 1953).
—— 'Strategische Planungen der USA 1940/1', in *Probleme des Zweiten Weltkrieges* (q.v.), 52–74.
MAUGERI, FRANCO, *From the Ashes of Disgrace*, ed. Victor Rosen (New York, 1948).
—— *Ricordi di un marinaio: La marina italiana dai primi del Novecento al secondo dopoguerra nelle memorie di un dei suoi capi* (Milan, 1980).
MAYDELL, UWE, 'Der Aufmarsh zum Balkanfeldzug 1941 mit besonderer Berücksichtigung des österreichischen Raumes' (typescript; Innsbruck, 1972).
MAZZETTI, MASSIMO, *La politica militare italiana fra le due guerre mondiali (1918–1940)* (Salerno, 1974).
Mediterranean Fascism 1919–1925, ed, Charles F. Delzell (Documentary History of Western Civilization; New York, Evanston, Ill., and London, 1970).
MEDLICOTT, WILLIAM NORTON, 'Economic Warfare', in *The War and the Neutrals*, ed. Arnold and Veronica M. Toynbee (Survey of International Affairs 1939–1946; London et al., 1956).
MEJCHER, HELMUT, 'Palästina in der Nahostpolitik europäischer Mächte und der Vereinigten Staaten von Amerika 1918–1948', in *Die Palästina-Frage* (q.v.), 182–92.
MELKA, ROBERT L., 'Darlan between Britain and Germany 1940–41', *Journal of Contemporary History*, 8/2 (1973), 57–80.
MENEGHELLO-DINČIĆ, KRUNO, 'La politique étrangère de la Yougoslavie (1934–1941)', *Revue d'histoire de la deuxième guerre mondiale*, 15/58 (1965), 57–66.
MERGLEN, ALBERT, 'Subversiver Kampf und konventioneller Krieg: Der Feldzug in Äthiopien 1940–1941', *WWR* 10 (1960), 132–8.
—— *Geschichte und Zukunft der Luftlandetruppen* (Einzelschriften zur militärischen Geschichte des Zweiten Weltkrieges, 5; Freiburg i.Br., 1970).
MESKILL, JOHANNA MENZEL, *Hitler and Japan: The Hollow Alliance* (New York, 1966).
MESSENGER, CHARLES, *The Art of Blitzkrieg* (London, 1976).
MEYER-SACH, MICHAEL, 'Politische Gedanken und Bemühungen der deutschen Seekriegsleitung gegenüber Frankreich in der Zeit vom Waffenstillstand bis zur alliierten Landung in Nordafrika 1940–1942', in *Geschichte der französischen Marine*, ed. Wilhelm Treue (Schriftenreihe der Deutschen Marine-Akademie und des Deutschen Marine Instituts, 3; Herford, 1982), 127–91.
MICHAELIS, HERBERT, *Der Zweite Weltkrieg, 1939–1945* (Frankfurt a.M., 1972).
MICHAELIS, MEIR, 'World Power Status or World Dominion? A Survey of Literature on Hitler's Plan of World Dominion (1937–1970)', *Historical Journal*, 15 (1972), 331–60.
—— *Mussolini and the Jews: German–Italian Relations and the Jewish Question in Italy 1922–1945* (Oxford, 1978).
MICHALKA, WOLFGANG, 'Vom Antikominternpakt zum euro-asiatischen Kontinentalblock: Ribbentrops Alternativkonzeption zu Hitlers außenpolitischem "Programm"', in *Nationalsozialistische Außenpolitik* (q.v.), 471–92.

—— *Ribbentrop und die deutsche Weltpolitik 1933–1940: Außenpolitische Konzeptionen und Entscheidungsprozesse im Dritten Reich* (Veröffentlichungen des Historischen Instituts der Universität Mannheim, 5; Munich, 1980).

MICHEL, HENRI, *Pétain et le régime de Vichy* (Paris, 1978).

MIELI, PAOLO, 'Voleva la pace, fece la guerra: Mussolini alla vigilia del secondo conflitto mondiale, Nuove ipotesi (Intervista con Renzo De Felice)', in *Espresso* (8 June 1980), 170–2.

Militär und Militarismus in der Weimarer Republik: Beiträge eines internationalen Symposiums an der Hochschule der Bundeswehr Hamburg am 5. und 6. Mai 1977, ed. Klaus-Jürgen Müller and Eckardt Opitz (Düsseldorf, 1978).

MILLER, MARSHALL LEE, *Bulgaria during the Second World War* (Stanford, Calif., 1975).

MILWARD, ALAN S., *War, Economy and Society, 1939–1945* (History of the World Economy in the Twentieth Century, 5; London, 1977).

—— 'The Reichsmark Bloc and the International Economy', in *Der 'Führerstaat': Mythos und Realität. Studien zur Struktur und Politik des Dritten Reiches*, ed. Gerhard Hirschfeld and Lothar Kettenacker, with intro. by Wolfgang J. Mommsen (Veröffentlichungen des Deutschen Historischen Instituts London, 8; Stuttgart, 1981), 377–413.

MINNITI, FORTUNATO, 'Aspetti della politica fascista degli armamenti dal 1935 al 1943', in *L'Italia fra tedeschi e alleati* (q.v.), 127–36.

—— 'Il problema degli armamenti nella preparazione militare italiana dal 1935 al 1943', *Storia contemporanea*, 9/1 (1978), 5–61.

MITROVIĆ, ANDREJ, 'Ergänzungswirtschaft: The Theory of an Integrated Economic Area of the Third Reich and Southeast Europe (1933–1941)', in *The Third Reich and Yugoslavia* (q.v.), 7–45.

MIYAKE, MASAKI, 'Japans Beweggrund für den Abschluß des Dreimächtepaktes Berlin-Rom-Tokio: Zum Forschungsstand in Japan', *GWU* 29 (1978), 681–92.

MOCKLER, ANTHONY, *Our Enemies the French: Being an Account of the War Fought between the French and the British, Syria 1941* (London, 1976).

Moderne Imperialismus, Der, ed. with intro. by Wolfgang J. Mommsen (Stuttgart, Berlin, Cologne, and Mainz, 1971).

MOELLHAUSEN, EITEL FRIEDRICH, *Il giuoco è fatto!* (Florence, 1951).

MOLTMANN, GÜNTER, *Amerikas Deutschlandpolitik im Zweiten Weltkrieg: Kriegs- und Friedensziele 1941–1945* (Beihefte zum Jahrbuch für Amerikastudien, 3: Heidelberg, 1958).

—— 'Weltherrschaftsideen Hitlers', in *Europa und Übersee: Festschrift für Egmont Zechlin*, ed. Otto Brunner and Dietrich Gerhard (Hamburg, 1961), 197–240.

MONTANARI, MARIO, *Le truppe italiane in Albania (anni 1914–20 e 1939)* (Rome, 1978).

—— *La campagna di Grecia*, 3 vols. (Rome, 1980).

—— *L'esercito italiano alla vigilia della 2ª guerra mondiale* (Rome, 1982).

—— *Le operazioni in Africa settentrionale*, 2 vols. (Rome, 1985).

MONTANELLI, INDRO, and CERVI, MARIO, *L'Italia dell'Asse (1936–10 giugno 1940)* (Milan, 1980).

MORISON, SAMUEL ELIOT, *The Battle of the Atlantic: September 1939–May 1943* (History of the United States Naval Operations in World War II, 1; Boston, 1957).

MORITZ, ERHARD, 'Planungen für die Kriegführung des deutschen Heeres in Afrika und Vorderasien', *Militärgeschichte*, 16 (1977), 323–33.

MOURIN, MAXIME, *Ciano contre Mussolini* (Paris, 1960).

II. Printed Sources

MÜHLEISEN, HANS-OTTO, *Kreta 1941: Das Unternehmen 'Merkur' 20. Mai bis 1. Juni 1941* (Einzelschriften zur militärischen Geschichte des Zweiten Weltkrieges, 3; Freiburg i.Br., 1968).

MUHR, JOSEF, *Die deutsch-italienischen Beziehungen in der Ära des Ersten Weltkrieges (1914-1922)* (Göttingen, Frankfurt a.M., and Zurich, 1977).

MÜLLER-HILLEBRAND, BURKHART, *Das Heer 1933-1945: Entwicklung des organisatorischen Aufbaues*, ii. *Die Blitzfeldzüge 1939-1941: Das Heer im Kriege bis zum Beginn des Feldzuges gegen die Sowjetunion im Juni 1941* (Frankfurt a.M., 1956).

MURDOCK, EUGENE C., 'Zum Eintritt der Vereinigten Staaten in den Zweiten Weltkrieg', *VfZG* 4 (1956), 93-114.

MURRAY, WILLIAMSON, 'The Role of Italy in British Strategy 1938-1939', *Journal of the Royal United Services Institute* (Sept. 1979), 43-9.

—— *Strategy for Defeat: The Luftwaffe 1933-1945* (Washington, DC, 1983).

Nationalsozialistische Außenpolitik, ed. Wolfgang Michalka (Wege der Forschung, 297; Darmstadt, 1978).

Native Fascism in the Successor States 1918-1945, ed. Peter F. Sugar (Santa Barbara, Calif., 1971).

NENNI, PIETRO, *Vent'anni di fascismo*[2], ed. Gioietta Dallo (Milan, 1965).

NEUGEBAUER, KARL-VOLKER, *Die deutsche Militärkontrolle im unbesetzten Frankreich und in Französisch-Nordafrika 1940-1942: Zum Problem der Sicherung der Südwestflanke von Hitlers Kontinentalimperium* (Wehrwissenschaftliche Forschungen: Abteilung Militärgeschichtliche Studien, 27; Boppard am Rhein, 1980).

NOLTE, ERNST, *Die faschistischen Bewegungen: Die Krise des liberalen Systems und die Entwicklung der Faschismen*[5] (dtv Weltgeschichte des 20. Jahrhunderts, 4; Munich, 1975).

—— *Der Faschismus in seiner Epoche: Die Action française. Der italienische Faschismus. Der Nationalsozialismus*[5] (Munich and Zurich, 1979). [Trans. Leila Vennewitz, *Three Faces of Fascism* (London, 1965).]

—— 'Italien vom Ende des 1. Weltkrieges bis zum ersten Jahrzehnt der Republik 1918-1960', in *Handbuch der europäischen Geschichte*, vii (q.v.), 619-50.

OLSHAUSEN, KLAUS, *Zwischenspiel auf dem Balkan: Die deutsche Politik gegenüber Jugoslawien und Griechenland von März bis Juli 1941* (Beiträge zur Militär- und Kriegsgeschichte, 14; Stuttgart, 1973).

—— 'Die deutsche Balkanpolitik 1940-1941', in *Hitler, Deutschland und die Mächte* (q.v.), 707-27.

OMRČANIN, IVO, *Diplomatische und politische Geschichte Kroatiens* (Neckargemünd, 1968).

ONDER, ZEHRA, *Die türkische Außenpolitik im Zweiten Weltkrieg* (Südeuropäische Arbeiten, 73; Munich, 1977).

ORLOW, DIETRICH, *The Nazis in the Balkans: A Case Study in Totalitarian Politics* (Pittsburgh, 1968).

Osteuropa-Handbuch, i. *Jugoslawien*, ed. Werner Markert with the collaboration of numerous scholars (Cologne and Graz, 1954).

Ostmitteleuropa im zweiten Weltkrieg: Historiographische Fragen über die Geschichte des 2. Weltkrieges in Ostmittel- und Südosteuropa. Internationale Konferenz, Budapest, September 1973, ed. Ferenc Glatz for the Ungarisches Nationalkomitee für die Erforschung der Geschichte des 2. Weltkrieges (Budapest, 1978).

OVELMEN, ROBERT CHARLES, 'The British Decision to Send Troops to Greece, January-April 1941' (diss. Univ. of Notre Dame, Ind., 1979).

OVERY, RICHARD JAMES, 'Die Mobilisierung der britischen Wirtschaft während des Zweiten Weltkrieges', in *Kriegswirtschaft und Rüstung* (q.v.), 287–313.
—— *The Air War 1939–1945* (London, 1980).
PACK, STANLEY WALTER CROUCHER, *Sea Power in the Mediterranean: A Study of the Struggle for Sea Power in the Mediterranean from the Seventeenth Century to the Present Day* (London, 1971).
PACOR, MARIO, 'Die italienische Geschichtsschreibung über die Geschichte des Donaubeckens und des Balkans im Zweiten Weltkrieg', in *Ostmitteleuropa im zweiten Weltkrieg* (q.v.), 163–82.
PAGLIANO, FRANCO, *Storia di 10 mila aeroplani* (Serie storico-militare, 3; Milan, 1947).
PAIKERT, GEZA CHARLES, *The Danube Swabians: German Populations in Hungary, Rumania and Yugoslavia and Hitler's Impact on their Patterns* (The Hague, 1967).
Palästina-Frage 1917–1948, Die: Historische Ursprünge und internationale Dimensionen eines Nationenkonflikts, ed. Helmut Mejcher and Alexander Schölch (Sammlung Schöningh zur Geschichte und Gegenwart; Paderborn, 1981).
PALLA, MARCO, 'La fortuna di un documento: il diario di Ciano', *Italia contemporanea*, 33/142 (1981), 31–54.
PALLOTTA, PIETRO, *L'esercito italiano nella seconda guerra mondiale attraverso i giudizi dei comandanti avversari e alleati* (Rome, 1955).
PALUMBO, MICHAEL VINCENT, 'The Uncertain Friendship: Hitler–Mussolini 1922–1939' (diss. New York, 1979).
PAPAGOS, ALEXANDROS, *Ho polemos tēs Hellados, 1940–1941* (Athens, 1949). [Trans. P. Eliascos, *The Battle of Greece, 1940–1941* (Athens, 1949); German trans. *Griechenland im Kriege, 1940–1941* (Bonn, 1954).]
PAPEN, FRANZ VON, *Der Wahrheit eine Gasse* (Munich, 1952). [Trans. (abr.) Brian Connell, *Memoirs* (London, 1952).]
PARKER, ROBERT ALEXANDER CLARKE, *Europe 1919–1945* (London, 1969).
PASTORELLI, PIETRO, *Italia e Albania 1924–1927: Origini diplomatiche del Trattato di Tirana del 22 novembre 1927* (Florence, 1967).
—— 'La politica estera fascista dalla fine del conflitto etiopico alla seconda guerra mondiale', in *L'Italia fra tedeschi e alleati* (q.v.), 103–14.
PAUL-BONCOUR, JOSEPH, *Entre deux guerres: Souvenirs sur la IIIe République*, iii. *Sur les chemins de la défaite 1935–1940* (Paris, 1946).
PERNACK, HANS-JOACHIM, *Probleme der wirtschaftlichen Entwicklung Albaniens: Untersuchung des ökonomischen und sozioökonomischen Wandlungsprozesses von 1912/13 bis in die Gegenwart* (Südosteuropa-Studien, 18; Munich, 1972).
PERTICONE, GIACOMO, *La politica italiana dal primo al secondo dopoguerra: Saggio storico-politico* (Milan, 1965).
PETERSEN, JENS, *Hitler—Mussolini: Die Entstehung der Achse Berlin-Rom 1933–1936* (Bibliothek des Deutschen Historischen Instituts in Rom, 43; Tübingen, 1973).
—— 'Die Außenpolitik des faschistischen Italien als historisches Problem', *VfZG* 22 (1974), 417–57.
—— 'Gesellschaftssystem, Ideologie und Interesse in der Außenpolitik des faschistischen Italien', *Quellen und Forschungen aus italienischen Archiven und Bibliotheken*, 54 (1974), 428–70.
PETZOLD, JOACHIM, 'Der deutsche Imperialismus und Bulgarien vom Ersten bis zum Zweiten Weltkrieg', *Bulletin des Arbeitskreises 'Zweiter Weltkrieg'*, 3–4 (1978), 65–87.
PICKER, HENRY, *Hitlers Tischgespräche im Führerhauptquartier: Vollständig überarbeitete*

und erweiterte Neuausgabe mit bisher unbekannten Selbstzeugnissen Adolf Hitlers. Abbildungen, Augenzeugenberichten und Erläuterungen des Autors. Hitler wie er wirklich war (Stuttgart, 1976).

PIERI, PIERO, 'La stratégie italienne sur l'échiquier méditerranéen', in *La Guerre en Méditerranée* (q.v.), 61–78.

—— and ROCHAT, GIORGIO, *Pietro Badoglio* (La vita sociale della nuova Italia, 22; Turin, 1974).

PIRRONE, GIORGIO, 'La brigata corazzata speciale in Africa settentrionale', *Rivista militare*, 102/3 (1979), 105–12.

PITT, BARRIE, *The Crucible of War: Western Desert, 1941* (London, 1980).

PITZ, ARTHUR HUGE, 'United States Diplomatic Relations with Vichy France from 1940 to 1942' (diss. Northern Illinois University, 1975).

PLAYFAIR, IAN STANLEY ORD, *The Mediterranean and Middle East*, i. *The Early Successes against Italy (to May 1941)*[3], enlarged edn. (London, 1974); ii. *The Germans Come to the Help of their Ally (1941)*[3], enlarged edn. (History of the Second World War: United Kingdom Military Series; London, 1974).

POLASTRO, WALTER, 'La marina italiana nella seconda guerra mondiale nell' interpretazione della nostra memorialistica', *Il movimento di liberazione in Italia*, 24/109 (1972), 107–13.

POTTER, ELMER B., and NIMITZ, CHESTER W., *Sea Power: A Naval History* (London, 1960; 2nd, rev. edn., Annapolis, 1981). [German trans. *Seemacht: Eine Seekriegsgeschichte von der Antike bis zur Gegenwart*, ed. Jürgen Rohwer for Arbeitskreis für Wehrforschung (Munich, 1974).]

POULAIN, MARC, 'Deutschlands Drang nach Südosten contra Mussolinis Hinterlandpolitik 1931–1934', *Donauraum*, 22 (1977), 129–53.

PRANGE, GORDON W., *At Dawn We Slept: The Untold Story of Pearl Harbor*, in collaboration with Donald M. Goldstein and Katherine V. Dillon (New York et al., 1981).

PRASCA, SEBASTIANO VISCONTI, *Io ho aggredito la Grecia* (La seconda guerra mondiale: Collezione di memorie, diari e studi, 5; Milan, 1946).

PRESSEISEN, ERNST L., *Germany and Japan: A Study in Totalitarian Diplomacy 1933–1941* (The Hague, 1958).

—— 'Prelude to "Barbarossa": Germany and the Balkans, 1940–1941', *Journal of Modern History*, 32 (1960), 359–70.

PRETI, LUIGI, *Impero fascista: Africani ed ebrei* (Testimonianze fra cronaca e storia, 28; Milan, 1968).

PRICE, ALFRED, *The Bomber in World War II* (London, 1976).

Prima controffensiva italo-tedesca in Africa settentrionale (15 febbraio–18 novembre 1941), La, ed. Ministry of Defence, Stato Maggiore dell'Esercito, Ufficio Storico (Rome, 1974).

Prima offensiva britannica in Africa settentrionale (ottobre 1940–febbraio 1941), La, i. *Narrazione e allegati*, ed. Ministry of Defence, Stato Maggiore dell'Esercito, Ufficio Storico (Rome, 1964).

Probleme des Zweiten Weltkrieges, ed. Andreas Hillgruber (Neue Wissenschaftliche Bibliothek, Geschichte, 20; Cologne and Berlin, 1967).

PUZZO, DANTE A., *Spain and the Great Powers 1936–1941* (New York and London, 1962).

PWT: see *Great Britain, Cabinet Office: Principal War Telegrams*.

QUARTARARO, ROSARIA, *Roma tra Londra e Berlino: La politica estera fascista dal 1930 al 1940* (I fatti della storia: Saggi, 6; Rome, 1980).
RAHN, RUDOLF, *Ruheloses Leben: Aufzeichnungen und Erinnerungen* (Düsseldorf, 1949).
RAINERO, ROMAIN, *La rivendicazione fascista sulla Tunisia* (Clio, collana storica; Milan, 1978).
RÁNKI, GYÖRGY, 'Geschichtsliterarische Fragen Ostmitteleuropas im zweiten Weltkrieg', in *Ostmitteleuropa im zweiten Weltkrieg* (q.v.), 17–44.
RASPIN, ANGELA, 'Wirtschaftliche und politische Aspekte der italienischen Aufrüstung Anfang der dreißiger Jahre bis 1940', in *Wirtschaft und Rüstung* (q.v.), 202–21.
RAY, DEBORAH W., 'The Takoradi Route: Roosevelt's Prewar Venture Beyond the Western Hemisphere', *Journal of American History*, 62/2 (1975), 340–58.
REINHARDT, KLAUS, 'Das Scheitern der Strategie Hitlers vor Moskau im Winter 1941/42', in *Das Jahr 1941* (q.v.), 95–119.
REISWITZ, JOHANN ALBRECHT VON, 'Die politische Entwicklung Jugoslawiens zwischen den Weltkriegen', in *Osteuropa-Handbuch* i. 67–98.
REITLINGER, GERALD, *The Final Solution: The Attempt to Exterminate the Jews of Europe 1939–45* (London, rev. edn. 1987).
REUTH, RALF GEORG, *Entscheidung im Mittelmeer: Die südliche Peripherie Europas in der deutschen Strategie des Zweiten Weltkrieges 1940–1942* (Koblenz, 1985).
—— *Erwin Rommel: Des Führers General* (Munich and Zurich, 1987).
RHODE, GOTTHOLD, 'Die südosteuropäischen Staaten von der Neuordnung nach dem 1. Weltkrieg bis zur Ära der Volksdemokratien', in *Handbuch der europäischen Geschichte*, vii (q.v.), 1134–312.
RHODES, ANTHONY, *The Vatican in the Age of the Dictators 1922–1945* (London, 1973).
RICH, NORMAN, *Hitler's War Aims*, i. *Ideology: The Nazi State and the Course of Expansion* (London, 1973); ii. *The Establishment of the New Order* (London, 1974).
RICHARDSON, CHARLES, 'French Plans for Allied Attacks on the Caucasus Oil Field, Jan.–Apr. 1940', *French Historical Studies*, 8/1 (1974), 130–56.
RICHTER, HEINZ, *Griechenland zwischen Revolution und Konterrevolution (1936–1946)*, with foreword by Komninos Pyromaglou (Frankfurt a.M., 1973).
RINGS, WERNER, *Schweiz im Krieg 1933–1945: Ein Bericht* (Düsseldorf and Vienna, 1974).
—— *Leben mit dem Feind: Anpassung und Widerstand in Hitlers Europa 1939–1945* (Munich, 1979). [Trans. J. Maxwell Brownjohn, *Life with the Enemy: Collaboration and Resistance in Hitler's Europe, 1939–1945* (London, 1982).]
RINTELEN, ENNO VON, *Mussolini als Bundesgenosse: Erinnerungen des deutschen Militärattachés in Rom 1936–1943* (Tübingen and Stuttgart, 1951).
—— 'Mussolinis Parallelkrieg im Jahre 1940', *WWR* 12 (1962), 16–38.
ROATTA, MARIO, *Otto milioni di baionette: L'esercito italiano in guerra dal 1940 al 1944* (Milan and Verona, 1946).
ROBERTSON, ESMONDE M., *Mussolini as Empire Builder: Europe and Africa, 1932–36* (London, 1977).
ROCHAT, GIORGIO, *L'esercito italiano da Vittorio Veneto a Mussolini (1919–25)*, with intro. by Piero Pieri (Bari, 1967).
—— *Militari e politici nella preparazione della campagna d'Etiopia (1932–1936)* (Milan, 1971).
—— 'Mussolini et les forces armées', in *La Guerre en Méditerranée* (q.v.), 39–59.

—— 'Il ruolo delle forze armate nel regime fascista: conclusioni provvisorie e ipotesi di lavoro', *Rivista di storia contemporanea*, 1 (1972), 188–99.

—— 'Mussolini, chef de guerre (1940–1943)', *Revue d'histoire de la deuxième guerre mondiale*, 25/100 (1975), 43–66.

—— *Italo Balbo: Aviatore e ministro dell'aeronautica 1926–1933* (Ferrara, 1979).

—— and MASSOBRIO, GIULIO, *Breve storia dell'esercito italiano dal 1861 al 1943* (Piccola Biblioteca Einaudi, 348; Turin, 1978).

RÖHRICHT, EDGAR, 'Der Balkanfeldzug 1941', *WWR* 12 (1962), 214–26.

ROHWER, JÜRGEN, 'Der Nachschubverkehr zwischen Italien und Libyen vom Juni 1940 bis Januar 1943', *MR* 56 (1959), 105–7.

—— and HÜMMELCHEN, GERHARD, *Chronik des Seekrieges 1939–1945*, ed. Arbeitskreis für Wehrforschung und Bibliothek für Zeitgeschichte (Oldenburg and Hamburg, 1968).

ROMMEL, ERWIN, *Krieg ohne Haß*², ed. Lucie-Maria Rommel and Generalleutnant Fritz Bayerlein (Heidenheim an der Brenz, 1950). [Trans. Paul Findlay, *The Rommel Papers*, ed. B. H. Liddell Hart (London, 1953).]

RONDOT, PIERRE, 'Les mouvements nationalistes au Levant durant la deuxième guerre mondiale (1939–1945)', in *La Guerre en Méditerranée* (q.v.), 643–65.

Roosevelt and Churchill: Their Secret Wartime Correspondence, ed. Francis L. Loewenheim, Harold D. Langley, and Manfred Jonas (London, 1975).

ROSENBERG, ALFRED, *Das politische Tagebuch Alfred Rosenbergs 1934/5 und 1939/40*, ed. Hans-Günther Seraphim (dtv-dokumente, 219; Munich, 1964).

ROSKILL, STEPHEN W., *The War at Sea 1939–1945*, i. *The Defensive* (History of the Second World War: United Kingdom Military Series; London, 1954).

—— *Churchill and the Admirals* (London, 1977).

ROSSI, FRANCESCO, *Mussolini e lo stato maggiore: Avvenimenti del 1940* (Rome, 1951).

RUGE, FRIEDRICH, *Der Seekrieg 1939–1945*² (Stuttgart, 1956).

RUHL, KLAUS-JÖRG, *Spanien im Zweiten Weltkrieg: Franco, die Falange und das 'Dritte Reich'* (Historische Perspektiven, 2; Hamburg, 1975).

RUIZ HOLST, MATTHIAS, *Neutralität oder Kriegsbeteiligung? Die deutsch-spanischen Verhandlungen im Jahre 1940* (Reihe Geschichtswissenschaft, 4; Pfaffenweiler, 1986).

RUSINOW, DENNISON L., *Italy's Austrian Heritage 1919–1946* (Oxford, 1969).

RUTHERFORD, WARD, *Blitzkrieg* (New York, 1980).

SALA, TEODORO, '1939–1943: Jugoslavia "neutrale", Jugoslavia occupata', *Italia contemporanea*, 32/138 (1980), 85–105.

SALEWSKI, MICHAEL, *Die deutsche Seekriegsleitung 1935–1945*, i. *1935–1941* (Frankfurt a.M., 1970); iii. *Denkschriften und Lagebetrachtungen 1938–1944* (Frankfurt a.M., 1973).

SALVADORI, MASSIMO L., *Gaetano Salvemini*² (Turin, 1963).

SALVATORELLI, LUIGI, and MIRA, GIOVANNI, *Storia d'Italia nel periodo fascista* (Biblioteca di cultura storica, 53; Turin, 1974).

SANTARELLI, ENZO, 'Mussolini e l'imperialismo', in id., *Ricerche sul fascismo* (Urbino, 1971), 17–72.

SANTONI, ALBERTO, 'Il servizio informativo inglese nel Mediterraneo alla vigilia delle ostilità secondo documenti britannici inediti', *Rivista marittima*, 113/10 (1980), 77–82.

—— 'The British Knowledge of the German Movements into the Balkans before the Operations "Marita" and "Barbarossa", through the ULTRA Intelligence' (typescript, 1980).

SANTONI, ALBERTO, 'Der Einfluß von "Ultra" auf den Krieg im Mittelmeer', *MR* 78 (1981), 503–12.
—— *Il vero traditore: Il ruolo documentato di ULTRA nella guerra del Mediterraneo*[2] (Milan, 1981).
—— 'Die Planungen der Achsenmächte im Mittelmeer 1941 und der Einfluß von "Ultra" auf die Operationen', in *Kriegswende* (q.v.), 149–66.
—— and MATTESINI, FRANCESCO, *La partecipazione tedesca alla guerra aeronavale nel Mediterraneo (1940–1945)* (Protagonisti, 5; Rome, 1980).
SANTORO, GIUSEPPE, *L'aeronautica italiana nella seconda guerra mondiale*[2], i (Milan and Rome, 1966); ii (Milan and Rome, 1957).
SCALA, EDOARDO, *Storia delle fanterie italiane* (Le fanterie nella 2ª guerra mondiale, 10; Rome, 1956).
SCHACHT, HJALMAR, *Abrechnung mit Hitler* (Hamburg, 1948). [Trans. Edward Fitzgerald, *Account Settled* (London, 1949).]
SCHECHTMAN, JOSEPH BORIS, *The Mufti and the Führer: The Rise and Fall of Haj Amin el-Husseini* (New York and London, 1965).
SCHIEDER, THEODOR, 'Italien vom Ersten zum Zweiten Weltkrieg (1915–1945)', in Michael Seidlmayer, *Geschichte Italiens: Vom Zusammenbruch des Römischen Reiches bis zum Ersten Weltkrieg* (Kröners Taschenbuchausgabe, 341; Stuttgart, 1962), 447–98.
—— 'Die Neuordnung Europas auf der Pariser Friedenskonferenz', in *Handbuch der europäischen Geschichte*, vii (q.v.), 113–38.
SCHINNER, WALTER, *Der österreichisch-italienische Gegensatz auf dem Balkan und an der Adria von seinen Anfängen bis zur Dreibundkrise 1875–1896* (Beiträge zur Geschichte der nachbismarckschen Zeit und des Weltkrieges, 31; Stuttgart, 1936).
SCHINZINGER, FRANCESCA, 'Kriegsökonomische Aspekte der deutsch-italienischen Wirtschaftsbeziehungen 1939–1941', in *Kriegswirtschaft und Rüstung* (q.v.), 164–81.
SCHLAUCH, WOLFGANG, *Rüstungshilfe der USA an die Verbündeten im Zweiten Weltkrieg* (Beiträge zur Wehrforschung, 13; Darmstadt, 1967).
SCHMIDT, HEINZ WERNER, *Mit Rommel in Afrika* (Munich, 1951).
SCHMITT, BERNADOTTE E., 'Italian Diplomacy, 1939–1941', *Journal of Modern History*, 27 (1955), 159–68.
SCHMOKEL, WOLFE W., *Der Traum vom Reich: Der deutsche Kolonialismus zwischen 1919 und 1945* (Gütersloh, 1967).
SCHÖNFELD, ROLAND, 'Deutsche Rohstoffsicherungspolitik in Jugoslawien 1934–1944', *VfZG* 24 (1976), 215–58.
SCHOT, BASTIAAN, 'Selbstbestimmungsrecht—Nationalismus—Machtpolitik: Die territoriale Neuordnung Ostmitteleuropas auf der Pariser Friedenskonferenz 1919', *NPL* 10 (1965), 23–33.
SCHRAMM-VON THADDEN, EHRENGARD, *Griechenland und die Großmächte im Zweiten Weltkrieg* (Veröffentlichungen des Instituts für Europäische Geschichte Mainz, 9; Wiesbaden, 1955).
SCHREIBER, GERHARD, 'Die Seeschlacht von Matapan', *Marineforum*, 50 (1975), 332–3.
—— *Revisionismus und Weltmachtstreben: Marineführung und deutsch-italienische Beziehungen 1919 bis 1944* (Beiträge zur Militär- und Kriegsgeschichte, 20; Stuttgart, 1978).
—— 'Reichsmarine, Revisionismus und Weltmachtstreben', in *Militär und Militarismus* (q.v.), 149–76.

—— 'Zur Kontinuität des Groß- und Weltmachtstrebens der deutschen Marineführung', *MGM* 26 (1979), 101–71.

—— 'Der Mittelmeerraum in Hitlers Strategie 1940: "Programm" und militärische Planung', *MGM* 28 (1980), 69–99.

—— 'Les structures stratégiques de la conduite de la guerre italo-allemande au cours de la deuxième guerre mondiale', *Revue d'histoire de la deuxième guerre mondiale*, 30/120 (1980), 1–32.

—— 'Die Rolle Frankreichs im strategischen und operativen Denken der deutschen Marine', in *Deutschland und Frankreich 1936–1939*, ed. Klaus Hildebrand and Karl Ferdinand Werner (Beihefte zur Francia, 10; Munich, 1981), 167–213.

—— 'Thesen zur ideologischen Kontinuität in den machtpolitischen Zielsetzungen der deutschen Marineführung 1897 bis 1945', in *Militärgeschichte: Probleme—Thesen—Wege. Im Auftrag des Militärgeschichtlichen Forschungsamtes aus Anlaß des 25jährigen Bestehens*, selected and edited by Manfred Messerschmidt, Klaus A. Maier, Werner Rahn, and Bruno Thoß (Beiträge zur Militär- und Kriegsgeschichte, 25; Stuttgart, 1982), 260–80.

—— 'Problemi generali dell'alleanza italo-tedesca 1933–1941', in *Gli italiani sul fronte russo* (q.v.), 63–117.

—— 'Italien im machtpolitischen Kalkül der deutschen Marineführung', *Quellen und Forschungen aus italienischen Archiven und Bibliotheken*, 62 (1982), 222–69.

SCHRÖDER, BERND PHILIPP, *Deutschland und der Mittlere Osten im Zweiten Weltkrieg* (Studien und Dokumente zur Geschichte des Zweiten Weltkrieges, 16; Göttingen, 1975).

—— *Irak 1941* (Einzelschriften zur militärischen Geschichte des Zweiten Weltkrieges, 24; Freiburg i.Br., 1980).

SCHRÖDER, HANS-JÜRGEN, *Deutschland und die Vereinigten Staaten 1933–1939; Wirtschaft und Politik in der Entwicklung des deutsch-amerikanischen Gegensatzes* (Veröffentlichungen des Instituts für europäische Geschichte Mainz, 59; Wiesbaden, 1970).

—— 'Der Aufbau der deutschen Hegemonialstellung in Südosteuropa 1933–1936', in *Hitler, Deutschland und die Mächte* (q.v.), 757–73.

—— 'Südosteuropa als "Informal Empire" NS-Deutschlands; Das Beispiel Jugoslawien 1933–1939', in *The Third Reich and Yugoslavia* (q.v.), 240–58.

—— 'Das Dritte Reich und die USA', in Manfred Knapp, Werner Link, Hans-Jürgen Schröder, and Klaus Schwabe, *Die USA und Deutschland 1918–1975: Deutsch-amerikanische Beziehungen zwischen Rivalität und Partnerschaft* (Beck'sche Schwarze Reihe, 177; Munich, 1978), 107–52.

SCHROEDER, PAUL W., *The Axis Alliance and Japanese–American Relations 1941* (Ithaca, NY, 1963).

SCHULZ, GERHARD, *Revolutionen und Friedensschlüsse 1917–1920* (dtv-Weltgeschichte des 20. Jahrhunderts, 2; Munich, 1967).

SCHUMANN, WOLFGANG, 'Aspekte und Hintergründe der Handels- und Wirtschaftspolitik Hitlerdeutschlands gegenüber Jugoslawien', in *The Third Reich and Yugoslavia* (q.v.), 221–39.

—— and WAPPLER, ANKE, 'Literatur in der DDR über die Länder Südosteuropas während des zweiten Weltkrieges', in *Ostmitteleuropa im zweiten Weltkrieg* (q.v.), 109–24.

SCHÜTT, WERNER, 'Der Stahlpakt und Italiens Nonbelligeranza 1938–1940', *WWR* 8 (1958), 498–521.

SCHWABE, KLAUS, *Deutsche Revolution und Wilson-Frieden: Die amerikanische und deutsche Friedensstrategie zwischen Ideologie und Machtpolitik 1918/19* (Düsseldorf, 1971).

SCHWARZ, URS, *The Eye of the Hurricane: Switzerland in World War Two* (Boulder, Colo., 1980).

SECHI, SERGIO, 'Imperialismo e politica fascista (1882–1939)', *Problemi del socialismo*, 14 (1972), 766–96.

Seconda offensiva britannica in Africa settentrionale e ripiegamento italo-tedesco nella Sirtica orientale (18 novembre 1941–17 gennaio 1942), ed. Ministero della Difesa, Stato Maggiore Esercito, Ufficio Storico (Rome, 1949).

Second World War, The, i. *Europe and the Mediterranean*, ed. United States Military Academy (West Point, NY, 1981).

SEGRÈ, CLAUDIO G., 'Douhet in Italy: Prophet without Honour?', *Aerospace Historian*, 26/2 (1979), 69–80.

SERAPHIM, HANS-GÜNTHER, '"Felix" und "Isabella": Dokumente zu Hitlers Planungen betr, Spanien und Portugal aus den Jahren 1940/41', *Die Welt als Geschichte*, 15 (1955), 45–86.

SERRANO SUÑER, RAMÓN, *Zwischen Hendaye und Gibraltar: Feststellungen und Betrachtungen, angesichts einer Legende, über unsere Politik während zweier Kriege* (Zurich, 1948).

SFORZA, CARLO, *L'Italia dal 1914 al 1944 quale io la vidi* (Rome, 1944).

SHERWOOD, ROBERT E., *The White House Papers of Harry L. Hopkins: An Intimate History*, i. *September 1939–January 1942* (London, 1948).

—— *Roosevelt and Hopkins: An Intimate History*[2] (New York, 1950).

SHIRER, WILLIAM L., *The Rise and Fall of the Third Reich* (London and New York, 1960).

SIEBERT, FERDINAND, 'Der deutsch-italienische Stahlpakt: Entstehung und Bedeutung des Vertrages vom 22. Mai 1939', *VfZG* 7 (1959), 372–95.

—— *Italiens Weg in den Zweiten Weltkrieg* (Frankfurt a.M., and Bonn, 1962).

SIEDENTOPF, MONIKA, *Die britischen Pläne zur Besetzung der spanischen und portugiesischen Atlantikinseln während des Zweiten Weltkrieges* (Spanische Forschungen der Görresgesellschaft, 2nd ser., 21; Münster, 1982).

ŠIMONČIĆ, ZDENKA, 'The Influence of German Trade Policy on Economic Development in Croatia in the Period from the Great Depression to the Second World War', in *The Third Reich and Yugoslavia* (q.v.), 363–82.

[SIMOVIĆ], 'Memoari Generala Simovića i Dokumenti 1939–1942', ed. with commentary by V. Kljaković, in *Politika* (Belgrade, 1970).

SIMPSAS, MARCOS-MARIOS, 'Die griechische Marine im Zweiten Weltkrieg: Der Kampf einer kleinen Marine', *MR* 74 (1977), 627–34.

SKENDI, STAVRO, *Albania* (East-central Europe under the Communists, Praeger Publications in Russian History and World Communism, 46; New York, 1956).

SMALL, MELVIN, *Was War Necessary? National Security and US Entry into War* (SAGE Library of Social Research, 105; London, 1980).

SMITH, DENIS MACK, *Mussolini's Roman Empire* (London and New York, 1976).

—— *Mussolini* (London, 1981).

SMITH, ELBERTON R., 'La mobilisation économique', *Revue d'histoire de la deuxième guerre mondiale*, 17/65, *Sur l'économie de guerre américaine* (1967), 37–74.

SNELL, JOHN L., *Illusion and Necessity: The Diplomacy of Total War. 1939-1945* (Boston, 1963).
SNIEGOSKI, STEPHEN J., 'Die amerikanische Reaktion auf den Ausbruch des Zweiten Weltkrieges in Europa', in *Sommer 1939* (q.v.), 314-36.
SOMERVILLE, JOHN, 'Die britische Strategie im Mittelmeer von Mitte 1941 bis Februar 1942', in *Kriegswende* (q.v.), 123-47.
SOMMER, THEO, *Deutschland und Japan zwischen den Mächten 1935-1940: Vom Antikominternpakt zum Dreimächtepakt: Eine Studie zur diplomatischen Vorgeschichte des Zweiten Weltkriegs* (Tübinger Studien zur Geschichte und Politik, 15; Tübingen, 1962).
Sommer 1939; Die Großmächte und der europäische Krieg, ed. Wolfgang Benz and Hermann Graml (Schriftenreihe der Vierteljahrshefte für Zeitgeschichte, spec. No.; Stuttgart, 1979).
SPAETER, HELMUT, *Die Brandenburger: Eine deutsche Kommandotruppe zbV 800* (Munich, 1978).
SPEER, ALBERT, *Erinnerungen* (Frankfurt a.M., and Berlin, 1969). [Trans. Richard and Clara Winston, *Inside the Third Reich* (London, 1970).]
—— *Der Sklavenstaat: Meine Auseinandersetzungen mit der SS* (Stuttgart, 1981). [Trans. Joachim Neugroschel, *The Slave State: Heinrich Himmler's Masterplan for SS Supremacy* (London, 1981).]
Staatsmänner und Diplomaten bei Hitler: Vertrauliche Aufzeichnungen über Unterredungen mit Vertretern des Auslandes 1939-1941, ed. Andreas Hillgruber (Frankfurt a.M., 1967).
STADTMÜLLER, GEORG, *Geschichte Südosteuropas* (Geschichte der Völker und Staaten; Munich, 1950).
Statistisches Jahrbuch für das Deutsche Reich, ed. Statistisches Reichsamt, 59 (1941-2) (Berlin, 1942).
STEFANOV, GUÉORGUI, 'La politique extérieure', *Revue d'histoire de la deuxième guerre mondiale*, 18/72, *Sur la Bulgarie en guerre* (1968), 1-21.
STEGEMANN, BERND, 'Der Entschluß zum Unternehmen Barbarossa: Strategie oder Ideologie?', *GWU* 33 (1982), 205-13.
STEINERT, MARLIS G., *Hitlers Krieg und die Deutschen: Stimmung und Haltung der deutschen Bevölkerung im Zweiten Weltkrieg* (Institut Universitaire de Hautes Études Internationales, Geneva; Düsseldorf and Vienna, 1970).
STETTINIUS, EDWARD R., jun., *Lend-lease: Weapon for Victory* (New York, 1944). [German trans. *Welt in Abwehr: Leih-Pacht* (Leipzig and Munich, 1946).]
STEURER, LEOPOLD, *Südtirol zwischen Rom und Berlin 1919-1939* (Vienna, Munich, and Zurich, 1980).
STEWART, IAN MCDOUGALL GUTHRIE, *The Struggle for Crete, 20 May-1 June; A Story of Lost Opportunity* (London, New York, and Toronto, 1966).
STEWART, NORMAN, 'German Relations with the Arab East, 1937-1941' (diss. St Louis University, Missouri, 1975).
STOLER, MARK A., *The Politics of the Second Front: American Military Planning and Diplomacy in Coalition Warfare, 1941-1943* (Contributions in Military History, 12; Westport, Conn., and London, 1977).
STOYADINOVITCH, MILAN, *La Yougoslavie entre les deux guerres: Ni le pacte, ni la guerre* (Paris, 1979).
Südosteuropa-Handbuch, iii. *Griechenland*, ed. Klaus-Detlev Grothusen in association

with Südosteuropa-Arbeitskreis der Deutschen Forschungsgemeinschaft (Göttingen, 1980).
SUNDHAUSSEN, HOLM, *Geschichte Jugoslawiens 1918–1980* (Stuttgart, Berlin, Cologne, and Mainz, 1982).
SUÑER: see Serrano Suñer.
Survey of International Affairs 1939–1946, ed. Arnold J. and Veronica M. Toynbee:
 i. *The World in March 1939* (London, New York, and Toronto, 1952).
 ii. *The Eve of War, 1939* (London, New York, and Toronto, 1958).
 iii. *The Initial Triumph of the Axis* (London, New York, and Toronto, 1958).
 vii. *The War and the Neutrals* (London, New York, and Toronto, 1956).
SWEET, JOHN JOSEPH TIMOTHY, *Iron Arm: The Mechanization of Mussolini's Army 1920–1940* (Contributions in Military History, 23; Westport, Conn., and London, 1980).
TASSO, ANTONIO, *Italia e Croazia*, i. $1918-1940^2$, rev. edn. (Macerata, 1967); ii. *La tormentata estate del 1940* (Macerata, 1972).
TAYLOR, ALAN J. P., *The Origins of the Second World War* (London, 1961).
—— *The War Lords* (Harmondsworth, 1978).
TAYSEN, ADALBERT VON, *Tobruk 1941: Der Kampf in Nordafrika* (Einzelschriften zur militärischen Geschichte des Zweiten Weltkrieges, 21; Freiburg i.Br., 1976).
TEICHOVA, ALICE, 'Die deutsch-britischen Wirtschaftsinteressen in Mittelost- und Südosteuropa am Vorabend des Zweiten Weltkrieges', in *Wirtschaft und Rüstung* (q.v.), 275–95.
Testament of Adolf Hitler, The: The Hitler–Bormann Documents, February–April 1945, ed. François Genoud, trans. Col. R. H. Stevens, with an introduction by H. R. Trevor-Roper (London, 1961).
THACKRAH, J. R., 'The Italian Invasion of Greece and its Effect on Allied and Axis Policy 1940–41', *Army Quarterly and Defence Journal*, 109 (1979), 337–49.
THALMANN, RITA, 'Das Protokoll der Wannsee-Konferenz: Vom Antisemitismus zur "Endlösung der Judenfrage"', in *Wie war es möglich? Die Wirklichkeit des Nationalsozialismus. Neun Studien*, ed. Alfred Grosser (Munich and Vienna, 1977), 147–67.
THAMER, HANS-ULRICH, and WIPPERMANN, WOLFGANG, *Faschistische und neofaschistische Bewegungen: Probleme empirischer Faschismusforschung* (Erträge der Forschung, 72; Darmstadt, 1977).
THIERFELDER, FRANZ, 'Deutsch-indische Begegnungen 1926–1936', in *Indien und Deutschland: Ein Sammelband*, ed. H. O. Günther, with foreword by Eugen Gerstenmaier (Frankfurt a.M., 1956), 146–57.
THIES, JOCHEN, *Architekt der Weltherrschaft: Die 'Endziele' Hitlers*^{2} (Düsseldorf, 1976).
—— 'Hitlers "Endziele": Zielloser Aktionismus, Kontinentalimperium oder Weltherrschaft?', in *Nationalsozialistische Außenpolitik* (q.v.), 70–91.
Third Reich and Yugoslavia 1933–1945, The, ed. Inst. for Contemporary History (Belgrade, 1977).
THOMAS, DAVID A., *Crete 1941: The Battle at Sea* (London, 1972).
THOMAS, GEORG, *Geschichte der deutschen Wehr- und Rüstungswirtschaft (1918–1943/45)*, ed. Wolfgang Birkenfeld (Schriften des Bundesarchivs, 14; Boppard am Rhein, 1966).
THOMAS, ROWAN T., *Britain and Vichy: The Dilemma of Anglo-French Relations 1940–42* (London and Basingstoke, 1979).

TILLMANN, HEINZ, *Deutschlands Araberpolitik im zweiten Weltkrieg* (Schriftenreihe des Instituts für Allgemeine Geschichte an der Martin-Luther-Universität Halle-Wittenburg, 2; East Berlin, 1965).

TIPPELSKIRCH, KURT VON, 'Hitlers Kriegführung nach dem Frankreichfeldzug im Hinblick auf "Barbarossa"', *WWR* 4 (1954), 145–56.

—— 'Der Deutsche Balkanfeldzug 1941', *WWR* 5 (1955), 49–65.

TOMASEVICH, JOZO, *War and Revolution in Yugoslavia, 1941–1945: The Chetniks* (Stanford, 1975).

TOSCANO, MARIO, 'Le conversazioni militari italo-tedesche alla vigilia della seconda guerra mondiale', *Rivista storica italiana*, 64 (1952), 336–82.

—— *Una mancata intesa italo-sovietica nel 1940–1941* (Florence, 1952).

—— *The Origins of the Pact of Steel* (Baltimore, 1967).

TOYE, HUGH, *The Springing Tiger: A Study of Subhas Chandra Bose* (London, 1959).

TREUE, WILHELM, 'Das Dritte Reich und die Westmächte auf dem Balkan: Zur Struktur der Außenhandelspolitik Deutschlands, Großbritanniens und Frankreichs 1933–1939', *VfZG* 1 (1953), 45–64.

TREVOR-ROPER, HUGH REDWALD, 'Hitler und Franco: Warum nahm Spanien nicht am Krieg teil?', *Der Monat*, 5 (1952–3), 625–34.

Trial of Major War Criminals by the International Military Tribunal Sitting at Nuremberg, Germany (42 vols.; London, 1947–9). (Vols. i–xxii are cited according to the English version; the remaining vols. according to the German text, which was not translated.)

TRYTHALL, ANTHONY JOHN, *'Boney' Fuller: The Intellectual General 1878–1966* (London, 1977).

'Ein Überblick über die Operationen des griechischen Heeres und des britischen Expeditionskorps im April 1941', *Militärwissenschaftliche Rundschau*, 8 (1943), 67–87, 167–88.

'Ein Überblick über die Operationen des jugoslawischen Heeres im April 1941 (dargestellt nach jugoslawischen Quellen)', i. 'Die Mobilmachung und die Kämpfe vom 6.–8. April 1941', *Militärwissenschaftliche Rundschau*, 7 (1942), 276–88; ii. 'Die Kämpfe vom 9. April bis zum Abschluß des Waffenstillstandes am 17. April', ibid. 387–99.

UEBERSCHÄR, GERD R., *Hitler und Finnland 1939–1941; Die deutsch-finnischen Beziehungen während des Hitler-Stalin-Paktes* (Frankfurter Historische Abhandlungen, 16; Wiesbaden, 1978).

—— 'Hitlers Entschluß zum "Lebensraum"-Krieg im Osten: Programmatisches Ziel oder militärstrategisches Kalkül?', in *'Unternehmen Barbarossa': Der deutsche Überfall auf die Sowjetunion 1941. Berichte, Analysen, Dokumente*, ed. G. R. Ueberschär and W. Wette (Sammlung Schöningh zur Geschichte der Gegenwart; Paderborn, 1984), 83–110.

ULMAN, A. H., 'La neutralité turque et les États-Unis', in *La Guerre en Méditerranée* (q.v.), 553–71.

UMBREIT, HANS, *Der Militärbefehlshaber in Frankreich 1940–1944* (Wehrwissenschaftliche Forschungen, Abteilung Militärgeschichtliche Studien, 7; Boppard am Rhein, 1968).

Ursachen und Folgen: Vom deutschen Zusammenbruch 1918 und 1945 bis zur staatlichen Neuordnung Deutschlands in der Gegenwart. Eine Urkunden- und Dokumentensammlung zur Zeitgeschichte, ed. Herbert Michaelis and Ernst Schraepler, with the assistance of Günther Scheel, xvi. *Das Dritte Reich: Versuche einer festländischen Koalitionsbildung gegen England. Der Dreimächtepakt. Die Vorgänge in Südosteuropa und auf dem Balkan. Der Kriegsschauplatz in Nordafrika* (Berlin, 1971); xix. *Das Dritte Reich: Auf dem Weg in die Niederlage. Wirtschaft und Rüstung*, pt. 2: *Die Radikalisierung der inneren Kriegsführung: Rückzug im Osten* (Berlin, 1973).

VALENTIN, ROLF, '*Ärzte im Wüstenkrieg*': *Der deutsche Santitätsdienst im Afrikafeldzug 1941–1943* (Koblenz, 1984).

VAUHNIK, VLADIMIR, *Memoiren eines Militärattachés* (Buenos Aires, 1967).

VEDOVATO, GIUSEPPE, *Gli accordi italo-etiopici dell'agosto 1928* (Biblioteca della 'Rivista di studi politici internazionali', ser. 2.7; Florence, 1956).

Verbali delle riunioni dal Capo di S M Generale, i. *(26 Gennaio 1939–29 Dicembre 1940)*, ed. Carlo Mazzaccara and Antonello Biagini (Raccolta di documenti della seconda guerra mondiale; Rome, 1982).

VERNIER, BERNARD, 'La guerre italo-grecque (28 octobre 1940–20 avril 1941)', *Revue d'histoire de la deuxième guerre mondiale*, 10/38 (1960), 15–36.

VETSCH, CHRISTIAN, *Aufmarsch gegen die Schweiz: Der deutsche 'Fall Gelb'. Irreführung der Schweizer Armee 1939/40* (Olten and Freiburg i.Br., 1973).

VIAULT, BIRDSALL S., 'Mussolini et la recherche d'une paix négociée (1939–1940)', *Revue d'histoire de la deuxième guerre mondiale*, 27/107 (1977), 1–18.

VIEFHAUS, ERWIN, *Die Minderheitenfrage und die Entstehung der Minderheitenschutzverträge auf der Pariser Friedenskonferenz 1919: Eine Studie zur Geschichte des Nationalitätenproblems im 19. und 20. Jahrhundert* (Marburger Ostforschungen, 11; Würzburg 1960).

VILLARI, LUIGI, *Italian Foreign Policy under Mussolini* (New York, 1956).

VOGEL, GEORG, 'Mussolinis Überfall auf Griechenland im Oktober 1940', *Europa-Archiv*, 5 (1950), 3389–98.

VOGEL, ROLF, *Ein Stempel hat gefehlt: Dokumente zur Emigration deutscher Juden* (Munich and Zurich, 1977).

VOIGT, JOHANNES H., 'Hitler und Indien', *VfZG* 19 (1971), 33–63.

—— *Indien im Zweiten Weltkrieg* (Studien zur Zeitgeschichte, 11; Stuttgart, 1978).

WARLIMONT, WALTER, 'Die Insel Malta in der Mittelmeer-Strategie des Zweiten Weltkrieges', *WWR* 8 (1958), 421–36; ibid. 9 (1959), 173–6 (Entgegnung zu der Stellungnahme des Admirals Weichold).

—— *Im Hauptquartier der deutschen Wehrmacht 1939–1945: Grundlagen, Formen, Gestalten* (Frankfurt a.M. and Bonn, 1964). [Trans. R. H. Barry, *Inside Hitler's Headquarters, 1939–45* (London, 1964).]

WARNER, GEOFFREY, 'Politique de l'Italie à l'égard de la Grèce et de la Yougoslavie (mars 1939–octobre 1940)', in *La Guerre en Méditerranée* (q.v.), 513–34.

WATSON, MARK SKINNER, *The War Department: Chief of Staff. Prewar Plans and Preparations* (United States Army in World War II; Washington, 1950).

WATT, DONALD CAMERON, 'The Rome–Berlin Axis, 1936–1940: Myth and Reality', *The Review of Politics*, 22 (1960), 519–43.

—— 'Document: The Secret Laval–Mussolini Agreement of 1935 on Ethiopia', in *The Origins of the Second World War: Historical Interpretations*, ed. Esmonde M. Robertson (London, 1971), 225–42.

WEBER, FRANK G., *The Evasive Neutral: Germany, Britain and the Quest for a Turkish Alliance in the Second World War* (Columbia University and London, 1979).

WEBER, HERMANN, *Die Bukowina im Zweiten Weltkrieg: Völkerrechtliche Aspekte der Lage der Bukowina im Spannungsfeld zwischen Rumänien, der Sowjetunion und*

Deutschland, with the assistance of Hellmuth Hecker (Darstellungen zur Auswärtigen Politik, 11; Hamburg, 1972).

WEHLER, HANS-ULRICH, *Nationalitätenpolitik in Jugoslawien: Die deutsche Minderheit 1918-1978* (Göttingen, 1980).

WEICHOLD, EBERHARD, 'Die deutsche Führung und das Mittelmeer unter dem Blickwinkel der Seestrategie', *WWR* 9 (1959), 164-73.

WEINBERG, GERHARD L., 'German Colonial Plans and Policies 1938-1942', in *Geschichte und Gegenswartsbewußtsein: Historische Betrachtungen und Untersuchungen. Festschrift für Hans Rothfels zum 70. Geburtstag*, with contributions from colleagues, friends, and students, ed. Waldemar Besson and Friedrich Frhr. Hiller von Gaertringen (Göttingen, 1963), 462-91.

—— *World in the Balance: Behind the Scenes of World War II* (London, 1981).

—— 'Hitler and England, 1933-1945; Pretence and Reality', *German Studies Review*, 8 (1985), 299-309.

Weizsäcker-Papiere 1933-1950, Die, ed. Leonidas E. Hill (Frankfurt a.M., Berlin, and Vienna, 1974).

Weltherrschaft im Visier: Dokumente zu den Europa- und Weltherrschaftsplänen des deutschen Imperialismus von der Jahrhundertwende bis Mai 1945, ed. with intro. by Wolfgang Schumann and Ludwig Nestler, with the assistance of Willibald Gutsche and Wolfgang Ruge (East Berlin, 1975).

Weltpolitik II, 1939-1945: 14 Vorträge, ed. Oswald Hauser for the Ranke-Gesellschaft—Vereinigung für Geschichte im öffentlichen Leben (Göttingen, Frankfurt a.M. and Zurich, 1975).

WENDT, BERND JÜRGEN, 'England und der deutsche "Drang nach Osten": Kapitalbeziehungen und Warenverkehr in Südosteuropa zwischen den Weltkriegen', in *Deutschland in der Weltpolitik des 19. und 20. Jahrhunderts: Fritz Fischer zum 65. Geburtstag*, ed. Imanuel Geiss and Bernd Jürgen Wendt with the assistance of Peter-Christian Witt (Düsseldorf, 1973), 483-512.

—— 'Strukturbedingungen der britischen Südosteuropapolitik am Vorabend des Zweiten Weltkrieges', in *Wirtschaft und Rüstung* (q.v.), 296-307.

WERNICKE, ANNELIESE, *Theodor Anton Ippen: Ein österreichischer Diplomat und Albanienforscher* (Albanische Forschungen, 7; Wiesbaden, 1967).

WERTH, ALEXANDER, *Der Tiger Indiens: Subhas Chandra Bose. Ein Leben für die Freiheit des Subkontinents* (Munich and Esslingen, 1971).

WESTPHAL, SIEGFRIED, *Heer in Fesseln* (Bonn, 1950).

Weyers Taschenbuch der Kriegsflotten: Mit Benutzung amtlicher Quellen, ed. Alexander Bredt, 33, 34 (Munich and Berlin, 1939, 1940).

WHEELER, MARK C., *Britain and the War for Yugoslavia, 1940-1943* (East European Monographs, 64; New York, 1980).

WHITTAM, JOHN, 'The Italian General Staff and the Coming of the Second World War', in *General Staffs* (q.v.), 77-97.

WIESENTHAL, SIMON, *Großmufti: Großagent der Achse. Tatsachenbericht mit 24 Photographien* (Salzburg and Vienna, 1947).

WINKEL, HARALD, 'Die "Ausbeutung" des besetzten Frankreich', in *Kriegswirtschaft und Rüstung* (q.v.), 333-74.

WINTERBOTHAM, FREDERICK WILLIAM, *The Ultra Secret* (London, 1974).

WIPPERMANN, WOLFGANG, *Faschismustheorien: Zum Stand der gegenwärtigen Diskussion*[2] (Erträge der Forschung, 17; Darmstadt, 1975).

Wirtschaft und Rüstung am Vorabend des Zweiten Weltkrieges, ed. for the Militärgeschichtliches Forschungsamt by Friedrich Forstmeier and Hans-Erich Volkmann (Düsseldorf, 1975).
WISKEMANN, ELIZABETH, *The Rome–Berlin Axis: A History of the Relations between Hitler and Mussolini*, rev. edn. (London, 1966).
WOODALL, ROBERT L., 'The Albanian Problem during the Peacemaking 1919–1920' (diss. Memphis State University, Tennessee, 1978).
WOODWARD, Sir LLEWELLYN, *British Foreign Policy in the Second World War*, i (History of the Second World War, United Kingdom Civil Series; London, 1970).
WUESCHT, JOHANN, *Jugoslawien und das Dritte Reich: Eine dokumentierte Geschichte der deutsch-jugoslawischen Beziehungen von 1933 bis 1945* (Stuttgart, 1969).
ZAMAGNI, VERA, *La distribuzione commerciale in Italia fra le due guerre* (CESCOM-Centro di Studi sul Commercio dell'Università L. Bocconi di Milano, ser. 1: Economica e politica commerciale; Milan, 1981).
ZAMBONI, GIOVANNI, *Mussolinis Expansionspolitik auf dem Balkan: Italiens Albanienpolitik vom I. zum II. Tiranapakt im Rahmen des italienisch-jugoslawischen Interessenkonflikts und der italienischen 'imperialen' Bestrebungen in Südosteuropa* (Hamburger Historische Studien, 2; Hamburg, 1970).
ZANUSSI, GIACOMO, *Guerra e catastrofe d'Italia*, i. *Giugno 1940–giugno 1943* (Documenti della seconda guerra mondiale, 2; Rome, 1945).
ZAPANTIS, ANDREW L., *Greek–Soviet Relations, 1917–1941* (East European Monographs, 11; New York, 1982).
ZAYAS, ALFRED MAURICE DE, *Die Wehrmacht-Untersuchungsstelle: Deutsche Ermittlungen über alliierte Völkerrechtsverletzungen im Zweiten Weltkrieg*, with the assistance of Walter Rabus (Heyne, No. 5929(01); Berlin, 1981).
ZIMMERMANN, HORST, 'Die "Nebenfrage Schweiz" in der Außenpolitik des Dritten Reiches', in *Hitler, Deutschland und die Mächte* (q.v.), 811–22.
—— *Die Schweiz und Großdeutschland: Der Verhältnis zwischen der Eidgenossenschaft, Österreich und Deutschland 1933–1945* (Munich, 1980).
ZOGRAFSKI, DANCO, 'Macedonia and the Third Reich's Balkan Policy', in *The Third Reich and Yugoslavia* (q.v.), 383–98.
Zweite Weltkrieg in Bildern und Dokumenten, Der, ed. Hans-Adolf Jacobsen and Hans Dollinger, i. *Der europäische Krieg 1939–1941* (Wiesbaden, 1963).

Index of Persons

(Hitler and Mussolini are not listed)

Abetz, Otto 575–83, 591, 600
Agnelli, Giovanni 10
Alexander, King of Greece 333
Alexander I, King of Yugoslavia 318, 321, 322, 323, 324, 358
Alfieri, Dino 120, 185, 200, 241, 269, 391, 398, 399
Amanullah, King of Afghanistan 163
Ambrosio, Vittorio 520
Amedeo di Savoia-Aosta, Duke of Aosta 58, 94, 259, 261–3, 266, 613, 643, 651, 653
Amery, Leo 456
Anfuso, Filippo 10, 13, 14, 23, 60, 122
Antonescu, Ion 408, 461, 462, 521
Aosta, Duke of, *see* Amedeo di Savoia-Aosta
Armellini, Quirino 391, 394, 404, 406–8, 422
Asmis, Rudolf 294
Assmann, Kurt 201, 211, 213, 217, 585, 612, 616, 628
Atatürk, *see* Kemal
Attolico, Bernardo 14, 24, 34, 157, 382–4
Auchinleck, Sir Claude 703, 724, 727, 739, 743, 750

Babini, Valentino 272, 652
Badoglio, Pietro 45–7, 52–62, 92–5, 124, 202, 217, 224–7, 235, 246, 247, 250, 252, 253, 261, 264, 266–9, 271, 276, 277, 387, 396, 400, 404, 406–10, 412, 413, 418, 419, 422, 423, 438–41, 443, 447, 448
Baistrocchi, Federico 64
Bakopoulos, Nokos 502, 503
Balbo, Italo 51, 55, 59, 75, 78–82, 94, 247, 252, 253, 267
Balfour, Arthur James, 1st Earl of 166
Bárdossy, László de 460
Bastico, Ettore 705, 726, 737, 747, 750
Beck, Ludwig 42, 301
Beigbeder y Atienza, Juan 191
Benini, Zenone 435
Beresford-Peirse, Sir Noel 680, 701, 703
Bergonzoli, Annibale 271, 272, 650
Bertello 264
Berti, Mario 269
Bertoldi, Giuseppe 264
Bethmann-Hollweg, Theobald von 283
Bielfeld, Ernst 296, 297
Blamey, Sir Thomas Albert 511

Bloch, Johann von 80
Boetticher, Friedrich von 566, 567
Bonnet, Georges 12, 36
Boris III, King of Bulgaria 329–32, 357–61, 422, 464
Bormann, Martin 186
Borne, Klaus Kreuzwendedich von dem 706
Bose, Subhas Chandra 606–11
Bottai, Giuseppe 98, 99, 120, 246, 270, 377, 378, 394
Bouthillier, Yves 579
Brandenstein, Rudolf Frhr von 342
Brauchitsch, Walther von 40, 41, 203, 204, 208, 219, 237, 290
Brinckmann, Fritz 598
Buffarini-Guidi, Guido 21
Bullitt, William Christian 106
Bülow, Bernhard W. von 347
Burckhardt, Carl J. 137

Cadogan, Sir Alexander 38, 133, 183
Campioni, Inigo 255, 663
Campos, Martinez 147
Canaris, Wilhelm 46, 163, 170, 201, 202, 206, 207, 227, 236, 238, 239, 590
Carls, Rolf 285, 286, 294
Carol II, King of Romania 461
Catroux, Georges 591
Cavagnari, Domenico 11, 45, 57, 58, 60, 62, 94, 258, 418, 419, 422, 441, 443
Cavallero, Ugo 95, 242, 447, 485, 512, 705, 750
Caviglia, Enrico 51
Chamberlain, Neville 12, 96, 127, 379
Chatfield, Alfred Ernle Montacute, 1st Baron 454
Churchill, Sir Winston Leonard Spencer 87, 96, 104–5, 111, 120, 127, 128, 130, 132–7, 152, 195, 402, 451, 454, 455, 462, 469–71, 480, 493, 495, 503, 505, 510, 511, 524, 531–3, 540, 550, 555, 560, 562, 563, 568, 596, 614, 615, 621, 644, 645, 651, 653, 671, 677, 678, 680, 694, 696, 697, 699–701, 704, 727
Ciano di Cortellazzo, Galeazzo, Count 8, 10, 14–25, 33, 36–9, 42, 61, 65, 102, 105–7, 111, 122, 151, 154, 157, 178, 179, 185, 191, 196, 199, 200, 209, 217, 241, 246, 252–4,

Ciano di Cortellazzo (*cont.*)
  256, 268–70, 276, 277, 307, 350–6, 367, 377, 378, 380–8, 390–400, 401, 407–11, 414, 417–19, 422, 424, 438, 441–3, 447, 456, 473, 475, 484, 528, 529, 580, 600, 609, 610
Cinca-Marković, Aleksandar 370, 380, 473, 474, 476, 479, 481, 522
Clemm von Hohenberg, Christian 436, 469, 471, 509
Clodius, Karl 282, 285
Colonna, Ascanio, Prince 102, 103
Constantine I, King of Greece 332–5, 339
Cordero Lanza di Montezemolo, Giuseppe 746
Cornwallis, Sir Kinahan 596
Crüwell, Ludwig 705, 726, 730, 731, 735, 737–9, 741–4, 746, 750
Cunningham, Sir Alan 653, 727, 730, 735, 739, 743
Cunningham of Hyndhope, Andrew Browne, 1st Viscount 87, 130, 136, 255–8, 443, 470, 533, 539, 541, 542, 548, 550, 551, 643, 660, 665, 668, 670, 672, 680, 696, 720, 722–4
Curri, Bajram 311
Cvetković, Dragiša 325, 370, 475, 477, 479, 481, 483

Darlan, Jean-François 574, 578–84, 600, 611, 612, 628
De Gaulle, Charles 195, 218, 219, 221, 230, 239, 574, 575, 581, 585, 591, 592, 617
Demertzis, Konstantinos 336
Dentz, Henri 580, 611, 612, 615–17
De Simone, Carlo 264
De Vecchi di Val Cismon, Cesare Maria 51, 94, 422
Dieckhoff, Hans Heinrich 566, 572
Dill, Sir John Greer 470, 484, 493, 494, 618, 680
Dimitrov, Georgi 329
Döhle, W. 168
Dollfuss, Engelbert 347
Dönitz, Karl 214, 638
Donovan, William Joseph 461, 464, 470, 474
Dose, Walter 25
Douhet, Giulio 79–81, 632
Draganov, Parvan 463, 485, 486
Drews 468
Dučić, Jovan 353, 354

Eden, Sir Anthony 126, 470, 474, 480, 484, 494, 618, 645, 680
El Husseini, Mohammed Amin, Grand Mufti of Jerusalem 167, 168, 177–9, 590, 593, 597, 605
Engel, Gerhard 414
Engels, Friedrich 338
Epp, Ritter von, Franz 294

Erbach-Schönberg, Prince Viktor 374, 497
Espinosa de los Monteros, Eugenio 587
Ettel, Erwin 589
Etzdorf, Hasso von 42, 294

Faiz, Mohammed Khan 164
Farinacci, Roberto 10, 51
Favagrossa, Carlo 30, 35, 59, 64–9, 72–4, 76, 81, 82
Feine, Gerhard 475, 477, 485, 494, 497, 522
Felmy, Helmuth 601, 612, 630
Ferdinand, King of Bulgaria 326
Fichte, Johann Gottlieb 338
Filoff, Bogdan 464
Franco y Bahamonde, Francisco 92, 130, 132, 145, 146, 148–52, 183, 184, 187, 190–6, 200–2, 208, 209, 217, 226, 229, 236–40, 243–5, 295, 413, 417, 586–8, 630, 634, 635, 758
François-Poncet, André 36, 106
Freud, Sigmund 338
Freyberg, Bernard Cyril, 1st Baron 540–2, 547–51, 744
Fricke, Kurt 204, 206, 214, 226, 229, 231, 283, 284, 285, 294, 575, 634, 663, 713
Fröhlich, Stefan 673, 686–8, 701, 702, 726
Fromm, Friedrich 455
Fuad Bey Hamza 170
Fuller, John Frederick Charles 80
Funck, Hans von 655

Gabbrielli, Luigi 177
Gafencu, Grigore 380, 385
Gailani, Rashid Ali al- 176, 177, 589, 590, 593–9, 605, 609, 611, 622, 680
Gallina, Sebastiano 271, 272
Gambara, Gastone 726, 737, 746
Gambier-Parry, Major-General 678, 679
Gandhi, Mahatma Mohandas Karamchand 608
Gariboldi, Italo 646, 656, 673, 675, 676, 688, 704, 705
Gause, Alfred 704, 705, 741, 742
Geisler, Hans 654, 688, 692
Geist, Raymond H. 387
Geloso, Carlo 391, 440
George II, King of Greece 334, 336, 337, 511, 516, 533
Georgiev, Kimon 331
Gerede, Husrev R. 157, 499, 620
Germain, Maxime 262
Ghigi, Pellegrino 407
Godwin-Austen, Sir A. Reade 264, 727, 744, 746
Goebbels, Hermann 24, 34, 40, 43, 137, 150, 157, 351, 360, 378, 382, 460, 492, 514, 529, 530, 534, 535, 548, 670, 684, 712, 714
Goethe, Johann Wolfgang von 338
Göring, Hermann 24, 34, 40, 43, 137, 150,

157, 351, 360, 378, 382, 460, 492, 514, 529, 530, 534, 535, 548, 670, 684, 712, 714
Gott, Brigadier 697, 699
Grand Mufti of Jerusalem, see El Husseini
Grandi, Dino 10, 113, 114
Graziani, Rodolfo 45, 46, 59–62, 93, 94, 252–4, 261, 266–71, 273, 276, 277, 399, 408–10, 412, 417, 419, 422, 424, 643, 650, 652, 655, 656, 762
Grazzi, Emanuele 388, 410, 423, 435
Greiffenberg, Hans von 510
Grobba, Fritz 169–73, 598–600, 604, 612
Groscurth, Helmut 17, 42
Grote, Otto von 481, 483
Guariglia, Raffaele 101
Guzzoni, Alfredo 95, 377, 378, 410, 412, 695, 696

Haddad, Osman Kemal 177, 178
Haile Selassie 261, 653
Halder, Franz 41, 44, 46–8, 61, 147, 187, 201–6, 208–12, 216, 217, 219, 222–4, 226–31, 233, 235–40, 244, 290, 294, 300, 387, 392, 393, 395, 396, 418, 451, 456, 457, 459, 460, 462, 466, 469, 472, 484, 486–8, 490, 498, 502–6, 522, 525, 528, 530, 534, 535, 539, 553, 578, 579, 587, 588, 598, 620, 625–7, 629–34, 636, 639, 654–6, 674, 675, 684, 685, 692, 693, 695, 704–5, 724
Halifax, Edward Frederick Lindley Wood, 1st Earl of 38, 127, 138, 156, 195
Hansen, Erik 458
Harriman, W. Averell 134
Hassell, Ulrich von 341, 344–9, 354, 473, 481
Heeren, Viktor von 353, 354, 366, 367, 474, 477, 479–85, 526
Heggenreiner, Heinz 250
Heine, Heinrich 338
Hemmen, Johannes 579
Hentig, Otto-Werner von 169
Herff, Max von 683, 699, 700
Heske, Franz 298
Hess, Rudolf 580
Hewel, Walter 600
Heydrich, Reinhard 290
Hikmet, Suleiman 168
Himmler, Heinrich 14, 15, 21, 22, 139, 289
Hoare, Sir Samuel 148
Hoffmann von Waldau, Otto 686
Hohenberg, see Clemm von Hohenberg
Hohenlohe-Langenburg, Max Egon, Prince of 137
Holtzendorff, Henning von 283
Horthy, de Nagybánya, Miklós 460, 461, 486
Hoyningen-Huene, Oswald, Baron von 467
Hull, Cordell 133
Huntziger, Charles Leon Clement 126, 246, 574, 575

Iachino, Angelo 662, 664, 665, 669, 697, 710, 723
Ibn Saud, Abd al-Aziz III 168–73, 590, 600
İnönü, İsmet 154, 159, 161, 162, 618–20

Jacomini di San Savino, Francesco 376, 391, 396, 409–11, 441
Jamil al-Mifai 605
Janković, Momčilo 493, 522
Jeschonnek, Hans 529
Jevtić, Boguljub 324
Jodl, Alfred 44, 45, 175, 198–200, 202, 204, 206–8, 216, 217, 220, 221, 226–9, 231, 237, 247, 300, 456, 469, 481, 512, 568, 574, 576, 586, 612
Junck, Werner 601
Junge, Wolf 206, 210, 216

Keitel, Wilhelm 46, 48, 93, 150, 174, 185, 204, 206, 218, 225, 227, 235, 237, 244, 269, 270, 554, 578, 588, 598
Kelly, Sir David 137
Kemal Atatürk (Mustafa Kemal Pasha) 155, 310, 333, 334
Kennedy, Joseph 134
Kesselring, Albert 713, 714, 747, 750
Keyes, Roger John Brownlow, 1st Baron 136, 442
Khalid al Hud 172
Kioseivanov, Georgi 362
Kirchheim, Heinrich Georg 689, 693
Kleist, Ewald von 488, 490, 506, 516–19, 521
Kluge, Gunther von 457
Knudsen, William S. 564
Köpke, Gerhard 344
Korten, Gunther 529, 537
Koryzis, Alexandros 469, 479, 503, 512, 590, 601
Kramarz, Hans 472, 479, 503, 512, 590, 601
Kvaternik, Slavko 520

Lammers, Hans-Heinrich 287
Lane, Arthur 474
Laval, Pierre 191, 192, 194, 196, 225, 226, 413, 417, 575–8, 585
Legentilhomme, Paul 262
Ley, Robert 20–2, 41
Liddell Hart, Sir Basil 80
Linlithgow, Victor Alexander John, Marquess of 596
List, Wilhelm 457, 487, 488, 499, 506, 508, 509, 511, 512, 514, 518
Ljotić, Dimitrije 322
Löhr, Alexander 492, 497, 498, 529, 534, 535, 537, 539, 542, 546, 548–50, 552
Longmore, Sir Arthur 84, 85, 455, 470, 513, 531, 533, 643, 646, 680, 704
Loraine, Sir Percy 38, 107

Lossberg, Bernhard von 519, 526
Ludendorff, Erich 80
Lyttelton, Oliver 704

Maček, Vladimir 325, 474, 476, 482, 483
Machiavelli, Niccolo 113
Mackensen, Hans Georg von 41, 59, 241, 354, 390, 408
MacVeagh, Lincoln 375, 376
Magistrati, Massimo, Count 382
Majid Khan, Abdul 163, 164, 605
Maletti, Pietro 271-3, 646
Mandel, Georges 101, 102
Marinković, Vojislav 324
Marras, Efisio 39, 243
Marx, Karl 338
Matsuoka 573
Mecozzi, Amedeo 81
Melchers, Wilhelm 589
Menemencioğlu, Numan Rifaat 621
Messervy, Sir Frank W. 703
Metaxas, Ioannis 336-7, 373-6, 425, 435, 442, 446, 447, 454, 455, 469
Meyer-Ricks, Hermann 224
Milch, Erhard 241
Mitchell, Sir William 84
Mohammed Zahir Shah 164
Molotov, Vyacheslav Mikhailovich 157, 161, 165, 197, 230, 234, 296, 452, 458, 459, 464, 467, 498, 589, 629
Monnet, Jean 564
Montezemolo, *see* Cordero Lanza di Montezemolo
Montgomery, Sir Bernard L. 693
Montigny, Karl von 225, 658
Morshead, Leslie 680, 683
Moscardo, Ituarte Jose 635

Nasci, Gabriele 430, 437
Nasi, Guglielmo 264
Navarini, Enea 724
Neame, Sir Philip 676, 678, 679
Nehru, Jawaharlal 608
Nenni, Pietro 110
Neumann-Silkow, Walther 700, 703, 738, 743
Neurath, Constantin Alexander Frhr von 167, 343, 344, 348, 364
Niedermayer, Oskar Ritter von 173, 174
Ninčić, Momčilo 483, 485
Noguès, Auguste Paul 77, 226
Noli, Fan 313
Norrie, C. W. M. 727, 730, 735, 746
Nuri as-Said, Pasha 176, 590, 605

O'Connor, Sir Richard N. 645, 646, 648, 650-3, 676, 678, 679
O'Conor, R. C. 723
Oshima, Hiroshi 573, 632

Pacelli, Eugenius (Pope Pius XII) 138
Palairet, Sir Michael 471
Pangalos, Theodoros 335, 338
Papagos, Alexandros 372, 425, 432-4, 437, 444, 446, 455, 469-71, 476, 493-5, 501, 502, 506-8, 510, 511
Papen, Franz von 155, 159, 161, 164, 176, 177, 348, 363, 455, 474, 590, 613, 618-22
Pariani, Alberto 66, 410, 412
Paul, Prince of Greece 333
Paul, Prince of Yugoslavia 321, 324, 338, 359, 370, 392, 474-7, 479
Paulus, Friedrich 631, 685, 688, 689, 692, 696, 704, 705
Pavelić, Ante 321-3, 520
Peel, William Robert Wellesley, Earl 167, 168
Peresić, Miloslav 476
Pešić, Petar 476
Pétain, Henri Philippe 3, 138, 141, 145, 186, 187, 191, 192, 194, 195, 196, 226, 237, 239, 262, 295, 413-17, 574-6, 579, 584
Peter I, King of Yugoslavia 318
Peter II, King of Yugoslavia 324, 479, 522
Pfitzner, Joseph 22
Phillips, William 102, 105, 106
Pilger, Hans 163
Pirelli, Alberto 10
Pitsikas, J. 511
Pius XII, *see* Pacelli
Platt, Sir William 653
Plesman, Albert 137, 138
Pohl, Maximilian Ritter von 225, 251
Pricolo, Francesco 45, 60, 94, 251, 419, 422, 435, 441, 686-8
Pridham-Wippell, Sir Henry 513, 515, 665, 668
Prittwitz und Gaffon, Heinrich von 679, 680
Puttkamer, Karl-Jesko von 222, 713

Rademacher, Franz 288
Radić, Stjepan 321
Raeder, Erich 49, 198, 204, 206, 211-24, 227, 229, 231-6, 241-4, 283, 286, 288, 291, 294, 300, 529, 554, 568, 569, 585, 628, 634, 635, 638, 662, 663, 671, 687, 711, 712, 714, 758
Rahn, Rudolf 579, 600, 612, 617, 618
Revenstein, Johannes von 703, 739, 744
Reichenau, Walter von 387
Renzetti, Giuseppe 185
Reynaud, Paul 101, 104-6
Ribbentrop, Joachim von 10, 20, 24, 33, 34, 37, 39, 100, 149, 150, 155, 159, 161, 163, 165, 172, 174, 183, 184, 188, 189, 192, 193, 200, 211, 220, 223, 225, 235, 241, 244, 282, 288, 298, 355, 356, 361, 385, 386, 387, 394, 397-9, 401-4, 407, 408, 414, 453, 458, 465, 472, 475-7, 481, 482, 484, 498, 499, 569, 573, 578, 580, 581, 583, 584, 590, 593, 594,

597–600, 607–12, 619, 621, 629
Riccardi, Arturo 663, 664, 669, 711
Riccardi, Raffaelo 10
Richthofen, Wolfram Frhr von 466, 492, 504, 507, 510, 511, 513–15, 534–6, 540, 546, 548, 552
Ringel, Julius 501, 549–51
Rintelen, Emil von 569
Rintelen, Enno von 18, 41–3, 46, 47, 61, 100, 123, 202, 250, 251, 253, 276, 381, 395, 396, 414, 512, 537, 656, 657, 696, 737
Ritchie, Neil M. 743, 745, 747
Ritter, Karl 282, 285, 472, 569, 574, 575, 577, 586, 600, 612
Roatta, Mario 42, 43, 46–8, 94, 253, 395, 386, 405, 406, 409, 410, 412, 419, 422, 439, 441, 447, 528, 656, 673
Rohde, Hans 631
Rommel, Erwin 496, 533, 537, 567, 578, 593, 595, 617, 656–8, 671, 673–81, 683–6, 688, 689, 692–4, 699, 700, 702, 707, 724, 725, 727, 729, 731, 735, 737, 739, 741–7, 750–3
Roosevelt, Franklin Delano 100, 102–6, 131, 133, 135, 138, 152, 221, 379, 464, 470, 499, 560–9, 571, 588, 757
Rosenberg, Alfred 163–4, 169, 213
Rossi, Francesco 424
Rougeron, Camillo 81
Rümelin, Eugen 360

Salvemini, Gaetano 111
Santoro, Giuseppe 422
Saracoğlu, Şükrü 161, 619
Schacht, Hjalmar 342, 373, 374
Schlemm, Alfred 529
Schmidt, Rudolf 229
Schmitt, Artur 747
Schniewind, Otto 291, 575
Schulenburg, Friedrich Werner, Count von 462, 467, 498
Schuster, Karlgeorg 537–9, 547, 548
Scobie, R. M. 727, 731, 742
Senger und Etterlin, Fridolin von 250
Serrano Suñer, Ramón 148, 150, 151, 187, 188, 191, 193, 211, 222, 235, 629
Shaw, George Bernard 338
Shawkat, Naji 176
Sillitti, Luigi 171
Simović, Dušan 325, 370, 451, 475, 479–85, 493, 494, 498, 522
Soddu, Ubaldo 47, 58–62, 94, 95, 268, 396, 409, 410, 419, 422, 435, 440, 441, 447
Somerville, Sir James F. 709, 710, 724
Somigli, Edoardo 422, 435
Sophocles 338
Speer, Albert 139
Speidel, Hans 575
Srškić, Milan 324

Stalin (Dzugashvili), Josif Vissarionovic 10, 11, 24, 128, 174–5, 189, 245, 397, 402, 453, 458, 459, 498, 620, 763
Stambolüski, Alexandŭr 326, 328
Starace, Achille 10
Stark, Harold R. 560–2
Stohrer, Eberhard von 149, 150, 245, 587, 588, 629
Stoiadinovič, Milan 323, 324–5, 352, 361, 366, 367, 369, 370, 479
Streich, Johannes 657, 675, 678, 693
Student, Kurt 529, 535, 536, 540, 546, 552
Sussmann, Wilhelm 529, 535

Taha al-Hashimi 590
Tardieu, André 350
Tedder, Arthur 704
Téleki, Pál, Count 187, 486
Tellera, Giuseppe 652
Teodorov, Todor 327
Thoma, Wilhelm Ritter von 224, 227, 228
Thomas, Georg 142, 143, 205
Thomsen, Hans 565
Thucydides 338
Tirpitz, Alfred von 283
Todt, Fritz 162
Toscano, Antonino 722
Toussaint, Rudolf 483, 494, 497
Trezzani, Claudio 261
Tsolakoglou, Georgios 512, 524
Tsouderos, Emanuel 512–16

Uzonović, Nikola 324

Vansittart, Sir Robert 126
Vargas, Getulio 106
Vauhnik, Vladimir 473, 479, 496
Venizelos, Eleftherios 333–5
Vercellino, Mario 440
Vian, Sir Philip L. 722
Victor Emmanuel III, King of Italy 45, 61, 94, 109, 371
Vigón, Juan 183, 184
Visconti Prasca, Sebastiano 391, 396, 405, 410–12, 420, 423, 424, 430, 436, 437–41
Vogl, Oskar 579
Volpi di Misurata, Giuseppe, Count 10
Vrioni, Elin Bey 311

Wagner, Eduard 706
Wagner, Gerhard 292
Warlimont, Walter 44, 46, 206, 207, 217, 219, 221, 225, 227, 230, 238, 243, 512, 524, 528, 553, 574–7, 581–4, 587, 600, 601, 612–13, 625, 628, 630, 638–40, 671, 674, 757
Wavell, Sir Archibald 77, 264, 273, 276, 469, 470, 511, 512, 528, 532, 533, 540, 541, 548, 550, 551, 643–6, 648, 651, 653, 671, 676–8,

Wavell (*cont.*)
  680, 696, 697, 699–701, 703, 704, 727
Weddell, Alexander W. 152
Weichold, Eberhard 225, 251, 255, 527, 659, 663, 668, 669, 671
Weichs, Maximilian, Frhr von 481, 486, 490, 519, 520, 522
Weizsäcker, Ernst, Frhr von 48, 107, 109, 137, 161, 164, 177, 188, 189, 191, 195–7, 234, 240, 241, 244–6, 354, 379, 382, 383, 389, 407, 408, 414, 415, 418, 458, 463, 468–70, 473, 474, 481, 482, 484, 498, 499, 580, 585, 592, 593, 605, 610, 624, 628, 629, 633, 640
Welles, Sumner 100, 102
Westphal, Siegfried 739
Wever, Paul 230
Weygand, Maxime 57, 77, 78, 104, 239, 577, 598

Wiehd, Wilhem, Prince of 310
Wiehl, Emil Karl Josef 360, 587
Willkie, Wendell 560, 565
Wilson, Henry Maitland, 1st Baron 264, 493, 495, 506–8, 510–13, 515, 645, 648
Windsor, Duke of, Edward 137
Winterbotham, Frederick William 129, 133, 387
Woermann, Ernst 177, 178, 298, 299, 481, 590–4, 597, 600, 607, 609, 610

Yasin, Yusuf 169, 170

Zamboni, Guelfi 177
Zeitzler, Kurt 457
Živković, Petar 324
Zogu, Ahmed, King of Albania 312–15, 378

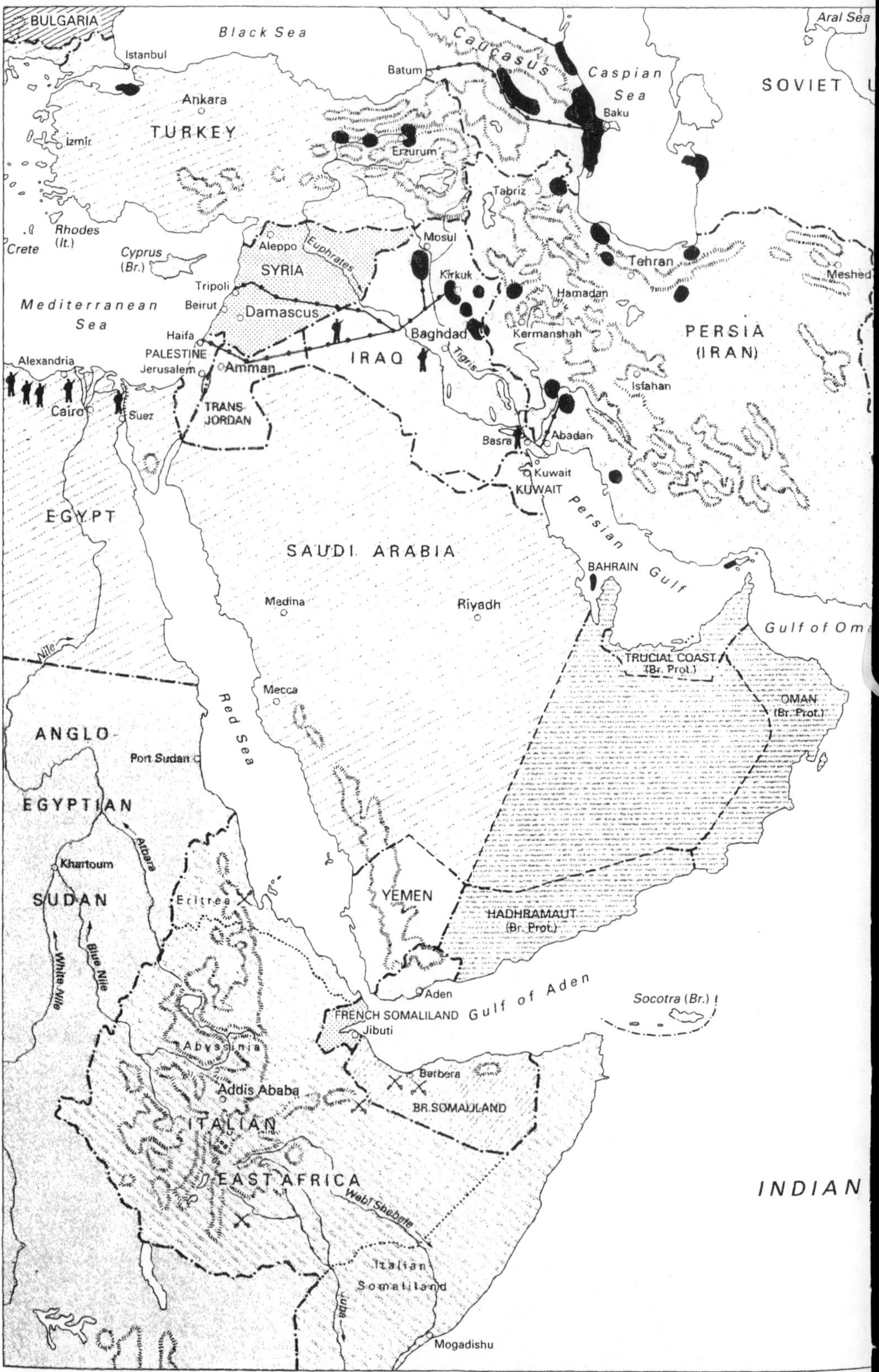

BULGARIA
Black Sea
Caucasus
Aral Sea
Istanbul
Batum
Caspian Sea
SOVIET U
Ankara
Baku
TURKEY
Izmir
Erzurum
Tabriz
Rhodes (It.)
Crete
Cyprus (Br.)
Aleppo
Mosul
Euphrates
SYRIA
Tehran
Meshed
Tripoli
Kirkuk
Hamadan
Mediterranean Sea
Beirut
Damascus
Haifa
Baghdad
Kermanshah
PERSIA (IRAN)
PALESTINE
Jerusalem
Amman
IRAQ
Tigris
Alexandria
Isfahan
Cairo
Suez
TRANS JORDAN
Basra
Abadan
Kuwait
KUWAIT
EGYPT
Persian Gulf
SAUDI ARABIA
BAHRAIN
Medina
Riyadh
Gulf of Om
Nile
TRUCIAL COAST (Br. Prot.)
Mecca
OMAN (Br. Prot.)
Red Sea
ANGLO
Port Sudan
EGYPTIAN
Atbara
Khartoum
SUDAN
Eritrea
YEMEN
HADHRAMAUT (Br. Prot.)
Blue Nile
White Nile
Aden
Gulf of Aden
Socotra (Br.)
FRENCH SOMALILAND
Jibuti
Abyssinia
Berbera
Addis Ababa
BR.SOMALILAND
ITALIAN
EAST AFRICA
INDIAN
Webi Shebele
Italian Somaliland
Juba
Mogadishu

Legend

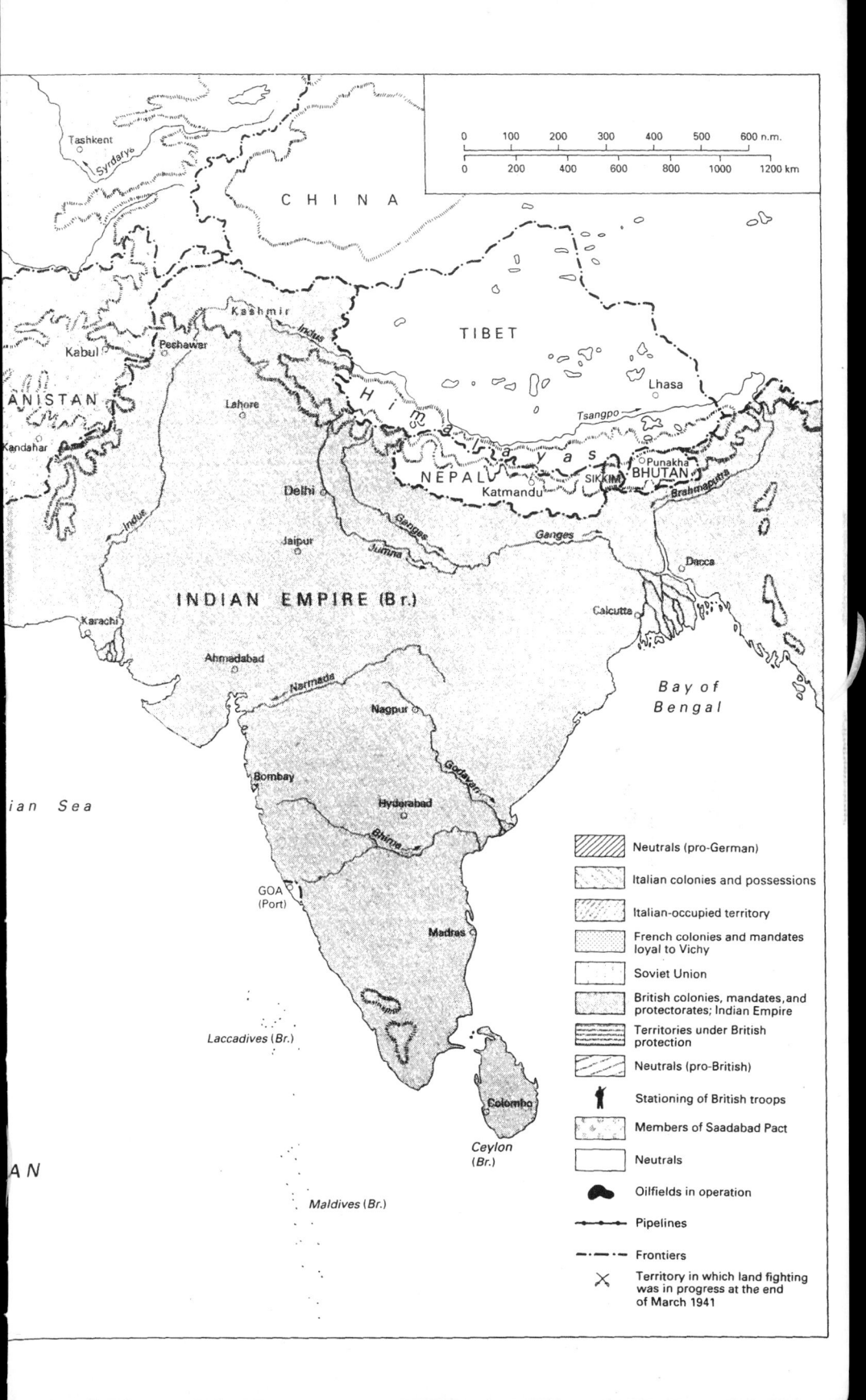

▨	Neutrals (pro-German)
▦	Italian colonies and possessions
▧	Italian-occupied territory
▩	French colonies and mandates loyal to Vichy
▢	Soviet Union
▤	British colonies, mandates, and protectorates; Indian Empire
▥	Territories under British protection
▨	Neutrals (pro-British)
⚑	Stationing of British troops
▦	Members of Saadabad Pact
▢	Neutrals
●	Oilfields in operation
—●—	Pipelines
—·—·—	Frontiers
×	Territory in which land fighting was in progress at the end of March 1941